Social Psychology

An Applied Approach

Ronald J. Fisher

Social Psychology

An Applied Approach

St. Martin's Press • New York

cover design: Mies Hora
typography: Bernard Klein
photo editor: Flavia Rando

ISBN: 0-312-73473-5

ACKNOWLEDGMENTS

Figure 2.3 adapted from *Contemporary Topics in Social Psychology* by John W. Thibaut, Janet T. Spence, and Robert C. Carson. Copyright © Scott, Foresman and Company. Reprinted by permission. **Figure 2.4** after Figures 11 and 43 in *Field Theory in Social Science* by K. Lewin, copyright 1951 by Harper & Row Publishers. Reprinted by permission. **Cartoon, p. 70,** by Ben Wicks. Reprinted by permission of Canada Wide Features Services Limited (Toronto). **Figure 3.3** adapted from Chart 1, The system of categories used in observation and their relation to major frames of reference, R. F. Bales, A Set of Categories for the Analysis of Small Group Interaction, *American Sociological Review*, 1950, 15, 257–263. Copyright 1950 by the American Sociological Association. Reprinted by permission of the publisher and author. **Box 3.5** adapted from R. J. Fisher and J. J. Andrews, The Impact of Self-Selection and Reference Group Identification in a University Living-Learning Center. *Social Behavior and Personality*, 1976, 4(2), 209–218. **Figure 3.5** adapted from Connecticut traffic fatalities, D. T. Campbell, Reforms as Experiments, *American Psychologist*, 1969, 24, 409–429. Copyright 1969 by the American Psychological Association. Adapted by permission of the publisher and author. **Figure 4.1** reproduced by permission from *Organizational Behavior in Action* by William C. Morris and Marshall Sashkin, Copyright © 1976 by West Publishing Company. All rights reserved. **Box 4.4** adapted from G. Lippitt and R. Lippitt, *The Consulting Process in Action*, San Diego, CA: University Associates, 1978. **Figure 4.2** reprinted from G. Lippitt and R. Lippitt, *The Consulting Process in Action*. San Diego, CA: University Associates, 1978. Used with permission. **Figure 4.3** adapted from

Acknowledgments and copyrights continue at the back of the book on pages 710–712, which constitute an extension of the copyright page.

To Carol, Cindy, and Sheri
with great appreciation
and
to Daniel Katz
with great admiration

Contents

16   Emerging Areas of Application and the Future   667

Glossary   G-1

References   R-1

Author Index   I-1

Subject Index   I-13

16   Emerging Areas of Application and the Future   667

Glossary   G-1

References   R-1

Author Index   I-1

Subject Index   I-13

Preface

Traditionally, social psychologists have explained real-world social behavior almost exclusively on the basis of theories developed from research in the laboratory. Such research is important, but there are several problems inherent in a reliance on laboratory experiments. Because laboratory research is undertaken in an artificial, contrived environment, away from real-world settings, it can be difficult to generalize the results. Although social behaviors are exceedingly complex, involving many factors, laboratory experiments necessarily focus on causal relationships among only a few variables. Further, such research tends to mirror the ways in which people typically behave toward each other, rather than offer insight into new forms of social behavior that may occur.

Applied social psychology undertakes research in real-world settings in order to develop and test theories, instead of extrapolating from laboratory studies alone. It is concerned with all levels of human social behavior, from individual to international. And it is concerned with facilitating productive change in social systems, seeking ways for people to share their feelings openly and respectfully, to make decisions democratically, and to work together toward common goals. The rationale for applied social psychology is simple: almost all human problems are social problems—for example, the threat of nuclear war, the population explosion, world poverty, mass starvation, bigotry, intergroup conflict, the distribution of wealth, the effects of crime and urban decay. It is the goal of applied social psychology to integrate theory, research, and practice to point the way to solutions of these problems.

Social Psychology: An Applied Approach includes coverage of both classic and contemporary topics; it integrates the traditional and applied streams of the discipline and seeks to show how the efforts of social psychologists may be directed into areas of utility for the solving of social problems. Traditional texts in social psychology generally approach the subject by taking up, in turn, the various social behaviors—e.g., aggression, attitudes, altruism, prejudice, moral judgment, sexual behavior—as separate entities. In contrast, this book explores most of these subjects within the framework of the social system, progressing from the simplest of interpersonal relations, the self, to the most complex, international relations.

The book is divided into three parts. Part I lays a foundation by introducing the applied approach (Chapter 1) and then explaining the essential elements of theory (Chapter 2), research methods (Chapter 3), and practice skills (Chapter 4) in social psychology. Part II blends traditional and applied topics at each major level of human social functioning, beginning with the individual person (Chapter 5) and going on to examine interpersonal relations (Chapter 6), small-group processes (Chapter 7), intergroup relations (Chapter 8), organizations (Chapter 9), communities (Chapter 10), social issues and social change (Chapter 11), and international relations (Chapter 12). Part III investigates special areas of application including program development and evaluation

(Chapter 13), the resolution of social conflict (Chapter 14), contemporary work in education, environmental psychology, and the law (Chapter 15), and health care, consumer behavior, and public policy (Chapter 16).

In writing this book, I have tried to make the presentation both scholarly and readable. Although the material is interesting in its own right, I have highlighted its applications to everyday life by the use of examples, vignettes, and personal anecdotes. Boxed inserts complement the text, presenting especially significant theoretical issues, research studies, and problem-solving techniques. At the end of each chapter, I have suggested some selected further readings which students will find particularly illuminating and interesting. The reference list is one of the most comprehensive to be found in a text on social psychology. A glossary is included to assist students in studying and in reviewing for examinations.

I want to thank three friends and teachers who significantly affected my approach to the discipline. Dan Sydiaha presented me with an initial view of social psychology that accepted all methods for learning about social behavior and supported the role of social psychologists as social practitioners rather than simply theoreticians and researchers. Rafe Ezekiel gave me the support and the freedom to further my vision of a social psychology dedicated to constructive social change. Dan Katz broadened my awareness of the power of conceptual models for understanding social behavior at all levels of functioning, thus affirming my commitment to a truly comprehensive social psychology.

To write any textbook is to travel a long road, and many people have helped me on the journey. A number of friends and colleagues reviewed one or more chapters and provided candid comments and useful suggestions. For this, I wish to thank Leonard Bickman, Marvin Brown, Dorwin Cartwright, John Conway, Thomas D. Cook, Leonard Doob, Raphael Ezekiel, Donald Fischer, Michelle Gillard, Benjamin Gottlieb, Peter Grant, Daniel Katz, Robert Kidd, Dennis Martin, Helen Maupin, Larry Peters, Stan Sadava, Eric Smith, Gary Wells, and James White. The critical comments of several reviewers commissioned by the publisher added significantly to the quality of the book. For these contributions, I thank Reuben Baron, University of Connecticut; Valerian J. Derlega, Old Dominion University; Robert Folger, Southern Methodist University; Eugenia P. Gerdes, Bucknell University; Martin S. Greenberg, University of Pittsburgh; Richard Lippa, California State University–Fullerton; Robert Pellegrini, San Jose State University; Daniel Perlman, University of Manitoba; and David J. Senn, Clemson University. Any shortcomings in the text are, of course, my own responsibility.

The people at St. Martin's Press are particularly deserving of praise. Ron Herder judiciously performed the first phase of developmental editing, and Paula Gower provided further editing. Patricia Mansfield, the book's project editor, skillfully guided the manuscript through its final editorial, photo research, and production stages. And from beginning to end, Walter Kossmann, senior editor at St. Martin's, patiently and effectively orchestrated the total endeavor, never losing sight of the concepts on which the work is based.

At the University of Saskatchewan, several individuals assisted in the production of the manuscript. Karlyn Bland and Michelle Gillard provided library research assistance in a diligent and conscientious manner. Helene Christensen, Rosemarie Hazelwanter, and Dorothy Milburn contributed to the typing of the first draft. Eve Behr mastered a sophisticated word-processing system and successfully met numerous deadlines for the revised manuscript. Part of the financial assistance for these activities was provided by the department of psychology and by the President's Publication Fund at the University of Saskatchewan. I am deeply grateful for all these contributions, as I am for the encouragement and patience shown by department staff, my colleagues, and my students over the duration of this project. Most importantly, I want to thank my wife Carol and our two children, Cindy and Sheri, for their understanding, their support, and their faith that all those stolen hours would indeed be worthwhile.

RONALD J. FISHER

Social
Psychology
An Applied Approach

PART ONE

Foundations of Applied Social Psychology

CHAPTER OUTLINE

ONE

Introduction to Social Psychology

WHAT IS SOCIAL PSYCHOLOGY?

The summer of 1956 is etched in my memory. I was twelve years old and spent the school vacation with my sister and brother-in-law on the family farm in north-western Saskatchewan. The world situation—already heavy with tension—grew even more so following the nationalization of the Suez Canal by Egypt in July. By late October, Israel and Egypt were at war. Britain and France entered the armed conflict, while an even more frightening confrontation loomed in the background between the United States and the Soviet Union. For some weeks, as threats and counterthreats were exchanged, the world crouched in the shadow of a possible nuclear holocaust. As I looked up at the clear prairie sky, I came to the shocking realization that if the United States and the Soviet Union began hurling nuclear bombs back and forth, some might fall on my doorstep! The Suez Crisis was one of the crucial experiences of my life that sowed the seeds for my becoming an applied social psychologist.

Of course many other life experiences led me to wonder why people treat others the way they do and how we can improve relations among people. As a child I experienced an intense sibling rivalry with one of my older brothers. We were ingenious at devising ways to get at each other, to gain the upper hand, to inflict the most hurt. Years later, I realized that as children we had become locked into a destructive interpersonal conflict that cost us both far more than anything we gained. Little did I know that my brother and I *might* have behaved differently toward each other if the adults around us had applied some appropriate interpersonal skills. (I say "might" because I am now facing the specter of sibling rivalry between my own two children.) I now realize that interpersonal relationships, like all social interactions, are potentially good or bad. All of us can actively seek to improve the situation we are in.

I've always had questions about social groups. Some of the best and worst experiences of my life have been associated with groups. I find myself waging a constant battle to maintain my individuality in the face of pressures to conform to group norms. I remember being persuaded by a childhood friend to join the boy scouts. I lived in British Columbia at the time, and I was attracted to hiking, camping, and "mountain" climbing (they were very small mountains, but not to a 10-year-old). At the first scout meeting I attended, it was clear that the group intended to initiate me properly: the scout leader endeavored to have me repeat an oath of loyalty, while the troop delighted in spanking me with a large wooden paddle. I fought like hell, much to my friend's astonishment and disappointment: he wanted me to go along without a fuss. Nobody said a thing about hiking or camping or mountain climbing—which would have acknowledged my personal needs for wanting to join the group. I left angry and disillusioned and never returned.

Since then I have joined a large variety of groups, and that encounter with the boy scouts has clearly helped me to crystallize a number of crucial questions about groups. These include: Do I belong here? Will I be respected here? What is expected of me as a group member? What happens if I don't meet the group's expectations? What can we accomplish together? As an applied social psychologist, I have given high priority to the individual's ability to be sensitive to group processes and to behave in ways that maximize group satisfaction and accomplishment.

The ethnic and racial variety of North America yields both delight and disaster. The delight derives from appreciating the unique strengths of different groups and seeing these differences combine to produce a stronger and more humane mosaic of people. The disaster is the result of prejudice and discrimination wherein stereotypes in people's minds distort reality and perpetuate inequality. I value the variety of people I have met, and I shudder at the irrational prejudice I have repeatedly encountered. As I reflect on my childhood and adolescence, I am pleasantly surprised that I was able to remain relatively "color-blind." (I say "relatively" because awareness of one's prejudices is a lifelong process that I am still learning.) I have been fortunate that over the years, my friends have included métis (*métis* is a French term for a person of mixed blood, especially one of Indian and French heritage), recent immigrants from Italy and elsewhere, Chinese, blacks, and others—none of whom were part of the white Anglo-Saxon majority. Yet in referring to each of these groups, many adults and children bombarded me with a constant stream of such hurtful and prejudicial statements as: "You can't trust a half-breed" (métis), "We don't have anything to do with those people" (blacks), "Look, I can make my eyes like theirs" (Chinese), "The Indians were savages before the white man came." As an applied social psychologist, I continue to seek ways for different groups of people to discard their stereotypes, to see each other as they really are, and to live in harmony and cooperation rather than in hostility and conflict. We have some solutions; we need a lot more.

These experiences and questions existed in my mind in varying degrees of consciousness and clarity. They did not suddenly crystallize in my eighteenth year with the realization that I wanted to become an applied social psychologist. I didn't even know that such an occupation existed! When a person left my little town in northern Saskatchewan to go to a university, it was to become a physician, a lawyer, or an engineer. That was it. Because a university education opened career possibilities that I had never dreamed of, I soon came to a profound realization: if I chose to, I could actually spend my professional life working on questions that I had always deeply cared about. I could pursue my commitment to find better ways of resolving conflicts among individuals, among groups, among nations. I eventually discovered that social psychology was the discipline concerned with the questions I had about human social behavior. I learned that social psychology is the scientific study of how the behavior of people is influenced by the actions of others. I was hooked.

After completing my undergraduate and master's degrees, I was accepted into the doctoral program in social psychology at the University of Michigan. The strength and depth of that program expanded my vision of social psychology. I realized that my questions about organizations, communities, and societies could be approached profitably from a social-psychological perspective. As I began my professional career, I realized that social psychology must not only develop useful theories based on sound research, but must put those theories into practice. This was the way to realize the potential usefulness of the discipline. The knowledge and expertise of social psychologists could then be freely shared for the improvement of human welfare. I began a personal and professional journey to integrate theory, research, and practice within the field of social psychology. I am still on my journey, looking for ways to help people resolve conflicts effectively and developing programs to train others in the knowledge and skills of applied social psychology.

It is that journey that I will share with you in this book. I will present ideas that will help you understand your own social life. I will describe rigorous research methodology so that we don't kid ourselves about the validity of our ideas. I will present principles of social practice that you can use to improve situations in your own life. I also will give you a picture of social psychology that realistically acknowledges assumptions and limitations. Most of all, I will share my excitement and enthusiasm about a social psychology that promises potential benefits for the future of all people.

To begin this learning process, we will look at the history of social psychology and examine some of the current controversies relating to its creative potential. We will also explore the potential roles that social psychologists can play in society. We will then be in a position to examine the challenge for applied social psychology: Can it answer our questions about people? Can it help us live together in peace?

History of Social Psychology

Psychology is the scientific study of the principles of individual behavior. *Sociology* is the study of social systems—families, organizations, and societies—and of complex social processes, such as social change and the socialization of

Social psychology is concerned with human interaction and human relationships in the social world—including the relationship of labor and management. *(Hazel Hankin)*

children. *Social psychology*—a subdisipline of both psychology and sociology—is thus defined as *the scientific study of how the behavior of an individual is influenced by and in turn influences the actions of others in the social environment.*

Social psychology is concerned with human interaction and human relationships in the social world. It is concerned with how an individual's thoughts, feelings, and actions are intertwined with the beliefs, motives, and behavior of others as these are expressed in complex social structures and processes. The scope of social psychology can be immense, overlapping such social sciences as anthropology and political science. At the same time, social psychology has evolved as a unique discipline with its own theories and methods for studying human social behavior. We can gain a sense of both this potential and uniqueness by briefly tracing the history of social psychology.

It is difficult to call any one individual the "founder of social psychology." Philosophers from the time of Plato have speculated on sociopsychological questions, especially on matters concerning relations between the individual and the political state. Nevertheless, Gordon Allport's (1968) illuminating review of the history of social psychology credits the French philosopher Auguste Comte (1798–1857) with initiating sociology and with proposing "a true final science" that clearly parallels modern psychology and social psychology. Comte suggested that the behavior of the individual could be studied scientifically in relation to its biological and social influences. Many decades would pass, however, before psychologists and sociologists would join to create the empirical study of individual behavior in society. The first textbook of social psychology was written by the sociologist E. A. Ross (1908), the second by the psychologist W. McDougall (1908). Like many philosophers before him, Ross focused on a single principle as the major explanation of social behavior. For Ross, that principle was "imitation" or "suggestion." He also examined areas that have become aspects of classic and contemporary social psychology: conformity, mob or crowd influence, conflict resolution, and public opinion. McDougall, on the other hand, claimed that human social behavior was caused by any one of a number of individual "social instincts"—that is, innate tendencies—common to all people. The social instincts, according to McDougall, were the sources of social interaction, and each social instinct induced a related emotion. For example, among the social instincts were flight (the inborn tendency to flee from danger), which led to the emotion of fear, and curiosity, which led to the emotion of wonder.

For some time, McDougall's attempt to explain so much in this simple manner was well received in social psychology. However, as the popularity of the idea of innate tendencies declined, McDougall's theory was increasingly called into question. According to critics, the theory explained very little: one observed relatively common behavior and emotional reactions, and then inferred an instinct. When similar behavior occurred, the instinct was used as the explanation of the behavior. This circular reasoning went nowhere except to support the notion that human behavior is relatively unchangeable. But McDougall's ideas were typical of theories proposed in the early days of a science: a few concepts attempt to explain a wide range of phenomena.

Since the appearance of the first two social psychology textbooks, both sociologists and psychologists have developed the field substantially. This has led to so much independence and separation that it is now accurate to speak of two schools of social psychology: "psychological social psychologists" emphasize the functioning of the individual; "sociological social psychologists" emphasize the functioning of the social system in which the individual is embedded.

From the start, the new science of social psychology emphasized its methods for studying human social behavior:

- The first laboratory experiment in social psychology is attributed to Triplett (1897). He investigated the hypothesis that individuals perform at higher levels when they are competing with one another than when they are acting alone.
- According to Krech, Crutchfield, and Bellachey (1961), one of the early "milestones in social psychology" was Starbuck's (1901) attempt to take the young science into the field to study the psychology of religion.

During the 1920s and 1930s, the measurement of social attitudes was very prominent:

- Katz and Braly (1933) assessed the racial stereotypes of college students.
- Thurstone (Thurstone & Chave, 1929) and Likert (1932) developed methods for measuring attitudes that are still widely used today.
- Gallup began the systematic polling of public opinion.
- Social psychologists explored the use of questionnaires, interviews, and observations for collecting information (Allport, 1968).
- The development of *sociometry*—the measurement of interpersonal preferences—by Moreno (1934) gave researchers a method for assessing personal attractions within a group.

By the 1930s, the scientific ideals of objectivity and precision dominated the fledgling field of social psychology (Allport, 1968).

Interest in *group dynamics* began in the 1930s. This area of study focused on the social forces or pressures that affect the behavior of the individual in a small group. Social psychologists began looking for objective ways to study the influences that groups have on their members:

- Muzafer Sherif (1935) used a laboratory setting to demonstrate the development of *group norms* (standards of behavior that are enforced by the group) and their effect on the perceptual judgment of individuals.
- Theodore Newcomb (1943) documented the powerful effects of *reference groups* (groups we use as a source of information and standard of comparison) on the social attitudes of individuals in a real world setting, that of a small residential college.
- William Whyte (1941) became an active participant in groups of "corner boys" (a form of street gangs), so that he could observe and describe their social functioning.
- Kurt Lewin, Ronald Lippitt, and Ralph White (1939) initiated the era of experimental group dynamics by studying the effect of different leadership styles on the productivity and morale of boys' play groups.

In its formative years, social psychology was called upon to alleviate many of the world's social problems. The great depression, racial prejudice and discrimination, labor-management conflicts, and the rise of fascism in Germany all contributed to this demand for applied knowledge and expertise. One early textbook of social psychology attempted to relate the discipline to the problems of society at large (Brown, 1936).

In 1936, a small group of psychologists founded the Society for the Psychological Study of Social Issues (SPSSI), an organization committed to the use of social science to promote human welfare (Finison, 1976; Krech & Cartwright, 1956). The society (now a division of the American Psychological Association) continues to flourish with a membership of over 3,000 psychologists and allied social scientists—all sharing a common interest in conducting research on the psychological aspects of important social issues.

It was also during the 1930s and 1940s that the profound influence of Kurt Lewin shaped the course of the discipline. His creativity, dedication, and vision clearly mark him as the founder of applied social psychology. Lewin was one of many Jews who fled the institutionalized tyranny and genocide of Nazi Germany. This experience had much to do with his humanitarian commitment to the resolution of social problems. Yet, above all, he was a dedicated scientist who fervently believed that the integration of theory, research, and practice was the essential ingredient of a useful and valid social psychology. The wide variety of original concepts that he developed includes action research (see Chapter 3), field theory (see Chapter 2), and sensitivity training (see Chapter 7) (Marrow, 1969). Lewin's ability to engender enthusiasm in his colleagues led to the formation of three influential organizations: the Commission on Community Interrelations, the Research Center for Group Dynamics, and the National Training Laboratories (see Box 1.1).

During World War II, other psychologists also responded to the demand for applied theory and research. Social psychologists took action quickly, partly

Box 1.1   FOCUS ON PRACTICE
National Training Laboratories

In 1946 the Connecticut Advisory Committee on Intergroup Relations asked for assistance from two organizations founded by Kurt Lewin: the Research Center for Group Dynamics and the Commission on Community Relations. The result was a two-week workshop designed to help volunteers, teachers, and social workers improve race relations in their communities.

The leadership team for this workshop consisted of active, pioneering researchers and practitioners—reflecting Lewin's high priority for the integration of both aspects of social psychology. Lewin and the principal trainers—Leland Bradford, Kenneth Benne, and Ronald Lippitt—represented the forefront of applied social psychology in the 1940s.

Each trainer led a work group devoted to discussions of problems, role playing of specific situations and the strategies used in dealing with them, and practice in obtaining the skills needed to handle particular difficulties. Each evening a research staff reported to the trainers, sharing their observations about that day's group activities.

When some of the workshop participants asked to attend these evening feedback sessions, a major breakthrough in the development of human relations training resulted. The participants' preception of and reaction to feedback about their behavior in the group triggered more involvement, learning, and change than did any other aspect of the workshop. Individuals increased their self-awareness and their sensitivity toward others by discussing their feelings and perceptions as they occurred in the group.

The experience gained during the workshop led to the first National Training Laboratory (NTL) in Group Development (1947), a continuing series of summer workshops, an association between the NTL program and the National Education Association, new laboratory learning techniques (see Chapter 7), and increasing involvement by NTL members in initiating social change within organizations and communities (see Chapters 9 and 10).

In the 1960s the program was reorganized as the NTL Institute for Applied Behavioral Science, and training and consultation sevices were provided to an increasingly wide variety of individuals and organizations.

Kurt Lewin died in 1947, having helped to plant the seeds for the NTL Institute. He was a major developer and provider of applied social-psychological services in North America and throughout the world.

Source: Bradford, L. P. Biography of an institution. *Journal of Applied Behavioral Science*, 1967, 2, 127–143.

because the growth of fascism in Germany clashed with their predominantly humanistic and democratic values. They established and developed several important research areas including attitude measurement and change, morale and leadership, propaganda and mass communication, organizational administration, economic behavior, and international relations (Cartwright, 1948; Hovland, Lumsdaine & Sheffield, 1949; Stouffer et al., 1949a, 1949b, 1950). The profound and numerous contributions of wartime research, in turn, led to new aspects of research after the war (Katz, 1951). Postwar researchers emphasized the combination of sound methodology and useful theory to understand practical problems. The early postwar period was thus one of rapid development and enthusiasm in the field.

In the 1950s, social psychology continued to expand and develop in a variety of established and new directions. Carl Hovland and his colleagues completed numerous studies on the effect of persuasive communication on social attitudes. Leon Festinger developed theories of social comparison and of cognitive dissonance which were highly influential in the field of social psychology. Festinger (1957) described *cognitive dissonance* as the unpleasant tension a person experiences as a result of cognitive elements (such as ideas, attitudes, beliefs) that are discrepant or contradictory.

The emergence of cognitive dissonance theory marked a shift away from the study of social interaction of groups and toward a concentration on processes within the individual. Concurrently, the laboratory experiment became the methodological standard of the social psychologist rather than fieldwork. Complex social processes were increasingly reduced to particular elements that could be studied at the level of individuals rather than society at large. This trend, permitting easier, more precise studies in the lab, continued through the 1970s, thus establishing experimental social psychology as the mainstream of the discipline.

In the 1960s, social psychologists studied many individual processes having potential relevance for real-world behavior—aggression, altruism and helping behavior, obedience to authority, and conformity to group norms. At the same time, the group as an interacting social system was virtually simplified out of existence in order to study "social interaction" more precisely (Steiner, 1974). The results were that a huge number of research papers dealing with the small group seemed to lack a shared frame of reference or mutual purpose (McGrath & Altman, 1966).

If we contrast this absence of significant problems and clear directions with the demands in the late 1960s for social relevance—especially those voiced by the student protest movement—we can easily imagine the confrontation that was to come. If these factors were not enough to create a crisis in social psychology in the 1970s, we need only add two more ingredients: the challenge of feminists and minority groups for more relevant and respectful treatment, and a shift in government funding from pure laboratory research to applied field research (Elms, 1975; Nelson & Kannenberg, 1976; Sherif, 1977). Thus, the concerns of social psychology were expanding.

Current areas of interest in social psychology range from topics involving individuals or small groups (such as attitude change, affiliation, and leadership) to topics involving a broader scope in society (such as intergroup conflict and the evaluation of social programs).

Modern social psychology is predominantly an American enterprise. Some European social psychologists (for example, Moscovici, 1972) as well as some American social psychologists (for example, Triandis, 1975) contend that the questions studied are determined by and limited to the predominant values, norms, and problems of American society. Some of the major influences on research topics and methods have been the demands of World War II, the political ideology and social problems of American society, and the predominant white, male, middle-class identity of social psychologists (Cartwright, 1979). For exam-

The challenge of feminists and minority groups for more relevant and respectful treatment has added to the current unrest in social psychology. *(Esais Baitel/Rapho/Photo Researchers, Inc.)*

ple, studies on achievement motivation reflect the value Americans place on accomplishment, while studies of the prejudiced personality relate to Americans' concerns about racism and fascism. But the generalizability of results to other cultures is limited, and the search for universal laws of social behavior may be illusory and misleading (Jahoda, 1979). As a result—fortunately—there has been a growing interest in cross-cultural research, which would study the same behaviors in different cultures. Triandis (1977) presents a framework for linking cultural influences to social behavior, and this in turn suggests numerous studies that might increase the generalizability of social psychology.

Thus we view social psychology in the 1980s: there is unrest in social psychology that has been clearly expressed by challenges from minority groups and by changes in research funding; there is an increasing interest in studying different cultures; there are challenges to current methods. How these issues and demands are resolved in the 1980s will probably determine the shape of social psychology for the rest of this century.

Current Controversies

You may have heard the story about the minister who was walking home late one evening when he came upon a fellow who had clearly had too much to drink. The poor man was frantically searching for something under a lamppost. Being a Good Samaritan, the minister stopped to ask if the fellow needed assistance. "I lost the key to my house—right over there by the bushes," the man mumbled, pointing to the dark shadows beyond the glow of the streetlight. "Well, what on earth are you doing looking here?" exclaimed the minister. "Because," came the reply, *this is where the light is!*"

In social psychology, as in many other disciplines, there is always the danger of "looking under the lamppost"—that is, "doing science the easy way" by using simple, and at times inadequate, methods; studying questions that yield quick results; and shying away from the dark corners that hide complex and difficult problems. Social psychology must be concerned with the most complex aspects of human social interaction, however. But how do researchers determine which problems are worthy of study and which methods are appropriate? To help answer these questions, let us now discuss a number of issues.

The Issue of Relevance. A discipline concerned with the study of human social interaction should be relevant, that is, concerned with problems that pertain to society. Thus, social psychology should be specifically concerned with producing the knowledge and expertise needed to help solve social problems. In social psychology the question of relevance has been a particularly thorny one. On one side of the issue, Sherif (1970) castigated the field for neglecting the persistent problems of social change. Smith (1972, 1973) raised two questions: Is experimental social psychology advancing? Is psychology relevant to the new priorities forced on us by rapid social change? He pessimistically concluded that experimental social psychology has generated little that is useful in helping us understand people as social beings, and that psychology is in such disarray that psychology itself is part of the problem!

There is another viewpoint, of course—one that is not so pessimistic. It holds that although social psychologists of the 1960s and early 1970s failed to focus on the solution of pressing social problems, their work was not irrelevant. Persons holding this view maintain that the scientific study of general social processes will eventually yield theories that are applicable to social problems (for example, Deutsch, 1969), and that social psychology is relevant by the sheer fact of its subject matter (Weick, 1969). Moreover, in the late 1970s, the amount of work devoted to such social problem areas as crime, poverty, and urban decay actually increased. The trend continues today.

Social psychologists have been criticized not only for the lack of relevance in their areas of study, but also for the lack of relevance in their methods. A chief criticism is that since the 1950s, they have used the laboratory experiment rather than work in the field as the primary method for testing theories of human social behavior. The social environments of laboratory experiments tend to be artificial and unique, created and controlled by the researcher to test a hypothesis that most likely will be verified (McGuire, 1973). Some charge that the simplicity of the laboratory experiment—it usually involves only two or three variables and only one direction of causation—fails to represent the complexity of a real social system with its numerous, mutually interacting variables (Smith, 1972). To remedy this difficulty there have been calls for more theoretical research in field settings (for example, McGuire, 1969). However, while the 1970s showed a gradual increase in field studies (Mark, Cook & Diamond, 1976), we must keep this in mind: A brief, weak field study will develop no more substance or direction than an artificial experiment in the laboratory (Silverman, 1977).

During these times of change, Kurt Lewin's vision should become an attainable goal: the effective integration of laboratory studies and field research to create a coherent whole.

The Issue of Validity. Do our measures or representations of variables really measure or represent what they are supposed to? This is the question of validity. Valid studies represent social reality, and we can therefore apply the results.

Let us examine this issue by looking at some actual research. Dorwin Cartwright (1973) reviewed 196 studies on the *risky-shift phenomenon*, that is, the tendency for individuals in groups to make riskier decisions than they would make acting alone. Cartwright noted that almost all the studies used the same questionnaire—based on hypothetical risk situations—to measure the risky shift. Most studies duplicated the original results: the mean score of the group's responses on the questionnaire showed greater risk taking than did the average individual scores (which were recorded before a group discussion and decision took place). At the time of the initial research, this was an exciting finding because it contradicted the conventional belief that groups tend to be environments that cause conformity and stifle creativity and riskiness.

As a result, it was soon generalized that "groups make riskier decisions than individuals," and a variety of explanations were offered for this new "fact." As data on the subject accumulated, however, there was reason to doubt the validity of the risky-shift phenomenon *as represented in the standard laboratory procedure:* The risky shift only occurred when those tested used the original questionnaire. Other testing measures produced mixed results: some groups become more cautious; some became riskier; some showed no change. In other words, the risky shift was the product of a particular measuring instrument used in a particular laboratory procedure. The entire line of investigation thus lacked validity in relation to the real world of group decision making. Researchers had neglected to use other measures or to see if the risky shift occurred in natural settings. Partly as a result of Cartwright's (1973) analysis, researchers improved their methods and have since documented the specific conditions under which groups intensify the opinions of their members, sometimes in a riskier direction and sometimes toward greater caution (see Chapter 7). This outcome demonstrates the self-correcting nature of scientific inquiry.

This episode illustrates the issue of validity. If a study does not represent a larger social reality, then it creates only a distant reflection, if not a false picture, of that reality.

Unfortunately, invalidity is not a rarity in our field. Too often, researchers use a simplistic measure without questioning whether it really measures what it is supposed to measure. Too often, they follow a standard procedure that may not represent social reality. Social psychologists must develop research models that accurately reflect behavior in the real world. Otherwise they are in danger of developing pseudoknowledge—knowledge that is irrelevant because it is invalid from the start (Silverman, 1971).

The Issue of Triviality. Kenneth Ring shocked the field of social psychology when he accused researchers of a "fun-and-games" approach that perverted Kurt Lewin's vision of a scientific social psychology:

Experimental social psychology today seems dominated by values that suggest the following slogan: "Social psychology ought to be and is a lot of fun." The fun comes not from the learning, but from the doing. Clever experimentation on exotic topics with a zany manipulation seems to be the guaranteed formula of success which, in turn, appears to be defined as being able to effect a *tour de force*. One sometimes gets the impression that an ever-growing coterie of social psychologists is playing (largely for one another's benefit) a game of "can you top this?" Whoever can conduct the most contrived, flamboyant, and mirth-producing experiment receives the highest score on the Kudometer. (1967, p. 117)

While Ring does not identify particular experiments, examples abound of studies which have instructed subjects to solve repetitive arithmetic problems, sort garbage, suck on pacifiers, and so on. Ring was concerned that such frivolous values would lead to rejection of the field by cynical undergraduates, disenchantment and corruption of graduate students, and a flood of exciting, then abandoned, research fads. The picture Ring painted was certainly not that of a cumulative, coherent discipline closely related to significant social problems.

The main response to Ring came from William McGuire (1967). He agreed that the pendulum had swung too far in the direction of basic research with an overemphasis on laboratory experiments. About the fun-and-games approach, McGuire proposed a compromise for the advancement of social psychology: Theories tested in the laboratory would also be tested in natural environments, both to judge their relevance to social problems and to provide directions for social action. According to McGuire (1969), theory-oriented research that occurs in natural settings and uses a variety of methods yields the most valid theories and, in the long run, the best solutions to social problems.

The issue of triviality does not concern laboratory experimentation alone. Any research method can be used to examine insignificant questions. It does not even matter if the work is valid in some minute, inconsequential way. If it is trivial, it wastes precious time and resources—which brings us to our next controversy.

What Does Society Expect from Social Psychology? As an applied social psychologist, I have worked in a variety of field settings for over ten years—yet I constantly have to explain who I am and what I do. Most people, including some who work in social agencies, do not know what the field of social psychology involves (for example, see Edwards, 1975). The consequences of this situation are not surprising: It has been increasingly difficult to acquire financial support for research and to find jobs for new graduates.

A contributing factor in the financial crisis in research, for both psychology in general and social psychology in particular, has been a simple lack of dollars (McKeachie, 1972). It is difficult to justify public expenditures on areas of social psychology that seem trivial or irrelevant (Smith, 1972). With the growing social conscience of the 1970s followed by the economic problems of the 1980s, government agencies increasingly want *usable* research. As a result, funding has shifted to applied research (Atkinson, 1977; Kiesler, 1977). The point is clear enough: Society now demands utility in the research products of social psychology.

However, applied social psychologists need not despair. To the question, "Who will hire us?" the answer is "a lot of people"—*if we can increase the usefulness of our work and make people aware that we have done so* (Edwards, 1975; Levy, 1976). Nonacademic career opportunities exist in many expanding and emerging areas of government, business, and private agencies, if we capitalize on them (Woods, 1976). To do so will require a commitment to utility in social psychology seldom seen since the days of Kurt Lewin. This book emphasizes such a commitment.

Social Psychology as Contemporary North American History. In a highly provocative article, Kenneth Gergen (1973) proposed that social psychology is primarily a historical rather than a scientific inquiry. That is, our theories are not general principles based on *cumulative* knowledge, but rather are reflections of behavior at a particular point in our history. Since there are no enduring social facts, we cannot develop a science of social behavior. Gergen further contends that social behavior is unstable because of psychological knowledge given to the public. If, for example, the eight million students who annually take psychology courses hear that superstitious behavior is symptomatic of an authoritarian personality (see Chapter 5), they might conceal or change such behavior, thus invalidating the theory. To overcome limitations of time and culture, Gergen suggests that social psychology focus intensively on contemporary social problems, using scientific methods and general concepts.

Many social psychologists rejected Gergen's position. In a systematic defense, Schlenker (1974) affirmed the utility of the scientific approach for accumulating knowledge of social behavior. Theories can be developed which are broad enough to allow for the effects of public knowledge or cultural change. Applied research can work on immediate solutions to contemporary problems. Pure research can search for general explanations of social behavior which may help solve future problems. In this way, the basic and applied approaches are complementary.

Later statements by Gergen (1976) and Schlenker (1976) continued the debate on whether social psychology is history or science. Numerous others entered the debate, and some proposed compromise solutions (e.g., Gottlieb, 1977) including one based on Kurt Lewin's vision of social psychology (M. A. Lewin, 1977). A recent statement of the issues by Gergen is described in Box 1.2 (Gergen, 1978).

The Social Psychology of Social Psychology. Only recently have social psychologists seriously considered the social forces that have shaped the destiny of their own discipline. We now see emerging a "psychology of psychology" (Coan, 1973) and a "sociology of psychological knowledge" (Buss, 1975). To increase our understanding and to improve our efforts we also need a "social psychology of social psychology" (for example, see Strickland, Aboud & Gergen, 1976). This would permit us to examine the pressure that influences what and how we study and the conclusions we draw: our personal inclinations, social norms, communication networks, cultural values, and so on. Cartwright (1979) has provided a historical analysis of contemporary psychology which indicates how a variety of social, cultural, and political influences have significantly shaped the discipline. The demands of World War II, the political ideology and social problems of American society, and the predominant white, male, middle-class identity of social psychologists have all worked to determine research topics and methods.

Box 1.2 FOCUS ON THEORY
Is Social Psychology Science or History?

Kenneth Gergen, a social psychologist at Swarthmore College, has questioned whether social psychology is or can be an empirical science such as physics or chemistry. In a highly provocative article, Gergen (1973) proposed that social psychology is primarily a historical rather than a scientific inquiry—that is, social psychology's theories are not general principles based on cumulative knowledge, but rather reflections of behavior at a particular point in history. Since there are no enduring facts, stated Gergen, we cannot develop a science of social behavior.

Social psychologists' emphasis on science, in Gergen's view, has had an ironic effect: the scientific emphasis has hampered imaginative thinking and has yielded theories that lack generative potency—that is, the ability to challenge existing assumptions and patterns of social behavior and to offer alternatives for social life.

Since contemporary social-psychological theory merely describes existing social reality, it has had little success in predicting what *will* happen and has shied away from the value-laden question of what *should* happen in social affairs. Gergen attributes these limitations to several factors:

1. an overemphasis on objective facts rather than imaginative thinking

2. a tendency for theories to perpetuate themselves through the biases of the scientist

3. the verification of theories based on consensus among scientists rather than on any ultimate truth

4. the testing of hypotheses that are obviously correct or self-fulfilling

5. the assumption that theories and research results hold over time rather than being a glimpse of history

6. a neutral scientific stance that implicitly supports the status quo in society

In short, Gergen charges that contemporary social psychology is merely a reflection—a rubber stamp—of existing social reality. It offers no new insights and few alternatives for positive social change. The overemphasis on being scientific has in fact curtailed the discipline's capacity to be useful to society.

Source: Gergen, K. J. Toward generative theory. *Journal of Personality and Social Psychology*, 1978, *36*, 1344-1360.

As the field moves more deeply into social issues, we will have to change our ways of thinking and valuing, particularly in research involving causes of social problems, as suggested by Caplan and Nelson (1973). These critics point out that there appears to be a *person-blame causal attribution bias* in psychological research. This bias blames the individual or the victim—rather than the social environment—for existing problems (Ryan, 1971). If, for example, fewer blacks attend college than whites, researchers often study the motives and abilities of black individuals, rather than look for the causes of inequity in the educational

Box 1.3   FOCUS ON RESEARCH
The Person-Blame Causal Attribution Bias

Nathan Caplan and Stephen Nelson, social psychologists at the University of Michigan's Institute for Social Research, have examined psychological research on social problems. In what they term the *person-blame causal attribution bias*, they see too much focus on individual characteristics, rather than on environmental qualities, as the causes of social problems. Research that tends toward the person-blame interpretation thus plays a part in blaming the victims of difficult situations for their own predicaments.

Caplan and Nelson point out that potential solutions depend on how a problem is defined. If, for example, we identify delinquency with individual traits, we will try to change the person, perhaps through counseling. If we identify delinquency with environmental factors, we will try to change the social system, perhaps through increased job opportunities.

To support their argument, the authors examined all research studies on black Americans reported in *Psychological Abstracts* for the first half of 1970. Of the 69 studies, 82 percent interpreted social problems as being somehow related to traits of the individual—in other words, a clear person-blame evaluation. By contrast, only 16 percent blamed environmental factors, and *none* looked at interactions of personal and environmental factors as possible roots of a problem.

Caplan and Nelson made several observations and conclusions: Psychologists find it more rewarding to conduct acceptable theoretical research than to help disadvantaged groups through applied work. Person-blame interpretations reinforce stereotypes, supporting the public's view that social problems are caused by the individuals who suffer from them. For example, funding institutions often prefer treatment programs that center on the individual as the cause of social problems; this does not threaten the traditional distribution of resources in society. But as Caplan and Nelson point out, the spread of social scientific information is not necessarily good, moral, or wise. Divorced from social reality, knowledge is not truth. The validity of research must be based on this realization.

Source: Caplan, N. & Nelson, S. D. On being useful: The nature and consequences of psychological research on social problems. *American Psychologist*, 1973, *28*, 199–212.

system or society at large. Thus, the challenge is to combine scientific research and humanistic values in order to search for solutions to problems at the societal level, rather than to attribute blame at the individual level (see Box 1.3).

With the integrity of their profession at stake, social psychologists have freely commented on potentially negative influences. Smith criticized social norms producing faddish research that "serves a self-perpetuating priestcraft rather than the advancement of science" (1972, p. 92). Cartwright (1973) spoke against the restricted communication network surrounding the risky-shift research, insulating the work from outside criticism. Lowe (1976) pointed out pressures to publish articles acceptable to the field and restraints against new topics and techniques. Sherif (1977) spoke against competing factions that increased production of trivia to support their positions at the expense of attention to fundamental questions.

Social psychology, like all disciplines, will continue to be shaped by positive and negative forces. To fulfill its promises, however, the discipline must overcome current issues and redirect its energy toward making effective contributions to human welfare through a number of challenging roles.

Potential Roles for Social Psychologists

Social psychologists are often asked, Just what do social psychologists do? We can restate this, given the demands of contemporary life: What existing and potential roles can social psychologists play in relation to society? The social psychologist can function in either applied research or pure research. Pure research can involve a search for general explanations of social behavior—explanations that may help solve future problems. Applied research can involve work on immediate solutions to contemporary problems. In this way, the pure and applied approaches are complementary.

The Pure Scientist. The emphasis on experimentation during the 1960s showed that many social psychologists saw themselves as pure scientists—that is, as theoreticians and researchers. The job of the pure scientist is to develop general theories of human social behavior, and to test deductions from these theories in the clearest way possible. Simple theories that explain a great deal are most appealing to the pure scientist. For example, the theory of cognitive dissonance (see Chapter 2) is a small set of straightforward principles that has a large range of potential applications. The goal of the pure scientist is thus to develop basic principles of human behavior that have demonstrated validity. Using these principles as a base, the pure scientist may then be able to apply his or her knowledge to the understanding and resolution of social problems. In Chapter 3, we will discuss methods used by the pure scientist.

The Applied Scientist. The applied scientist is concerned with developing general theories through social research in field settings. The research is thus relevant to both theory and the actual problems, although one aspect is often emphasized at the expense of the other (see Deutsch, 1969). The work of the applied scientist is directed more toward the short-term solution of social problems.

One basic type of applied research, created by Kurt Lewin, is *action research.* In this the applied scientist collaborates with a group or organization that is experiencing difficulty. He or she collects data relevant to the problem, which are then interpreted and transformed into appropriate action. For example, an applied scientist might interview selected residents of a neighborhood experiencing racial strife, and report the results and make recommendations for action to city officials, community groups, and so on.

Another form of applied research is *evaluation research*, which involves the use of social-science research methods to evaluate the process and results of a social policy or program. The social psychologist thus takes the role of "program evaluator" and helps to assess, for example, the effects of an educational program to improve nutritional habits. These types of applied research will be discussed more fully in Chapter 3. Whereas most pure scientists work in academic settings, applied social psychologists are more likely to be found in government departments, community agencies, or private corporations.

The Professional Practitioner. As a professional practitioner, the social psychologist may take on a variety of roles: trainer, consultant, community developer, program developer, or social advocate. All of these roles involve the application of professional knowledge and skills to the development of effective social relations (see Chapter 4).

A *human relations trainer* designs and facilitates experiential learning situations in which participants learn to deal with social problems in personal and organizational environments. This complex and demanding role can be traced back to the early days of the National Training Laboratories (see Box 1.1). A common function of a human relations trainer is to lead workshops designed to help participants improve their interpersonal communications skills, group leadership skills, and the like.

In the role of *consultant*, the social psychologist serves as an expert on social process and social theory, helping groups, organizations, or communities that are experiencing difficulties. This role may take the form of *organizational consultant* or *community developer.* For example, an organizational consultant might help a management team clarify its roles and responsibilities, while a community developer might help a group of social service agencies better coordinate their services.

A newly emerging role is that of *program developer,* concerned with the most effective methods of developing or improving social programs. This and other roles often combine theory, research, and practice, creating the desirable joint role of scientist/practitioner.

A final practitioner role, that of *advocate,* moves the applied social psychologist into the political arena. The advocate uses his or her expertise to press for social change, usually in collaboration with a specific group, lobby, or institution that is working to change some aspect of the sociopolitical system. For example, in the role of advocate, a social psychologist might assist a poor people's organization in its struggle to gain better public housing programs, or testify at government hearings that segregated education is detrimental to the educational development of children. Few social psychologists would hesitate to make knowledge available to the public or to interpret it in relation to policy questions. However, there is some fear among social psychologists that strong advocacy based on limited knowledge will tarnish their public image (see Atkinson, 1977). The advocate role points out the necessity for social psychologists to increase their awareness of the values underlying their work, and to decide clearly when to advocate and when not to, depending on their sense of values and the scientific strength of their position.

THE CHALLENGE FOR APPLIED SOCIAL PSYCHOLOGY

Social psychology must recommit itself to the development of valid and relevant theories of human interaction through a variety of research and practice activities in real-world settings. Allport (1968) effectively stated this required shift in emphasis:

Here surely lies the current challenge to social psychology. Can the improved objectivity in method be brought to serve broad theory and practical application. . . . [we] noted how the burning issues of war and peace, education for life in a world community, population control, effective democracy, all urgently call for assistance from social psychology. Such assistance is unlikely to come from small gemlike researches [sic], however exquisite their perfection. The question at issue is whether the present preoccupation with method, with miniature models, will in the near future lead to a new emphasis on theory and application. (p. 69)

Allport's call is more than a decade old, yet it is only recently that we have begun to see the changes he proposed. There is renewed interest in theories that are useful for understanding and changing human social behavior. There is increasing support for the development and use of a greater variety of research methods. There is a growing realization that effective practice skills for working with people must become a more integral part of the discipline.

The required revitalization of the field can best be accomplished and organized through the continuing development of applied social psychology: *social-psychological research and practice in real-world settings, directed toward the understanding of human social behavior and the solution of social problems.* We must reaffirm the creative integration of theory, research, and practice that Kurt Lewin envisaged and exemplified. We must make a renewed commitment to the joint goals of understanding *and* action for human welfare. Only then can we reduce the gaps between theoretical knowledge and the reality of social behavior, and between humanistic values and social injustices.

Applied vs. Applying Social Psychology

It is essential to distinguish between *applied* social psychology and *applying* social psychology. *Applying social psychology* attempts to explain real-world social behavior by using theories developed mainly from laboratory research. There are several problems inherent in this approach. First, the research is carried out in an artificial, contrived environment, away from real-world settings, and it is often difficult to generalize the results. Second, it attempts to explain complex social behavior caused by many factors through experiments that study the causal relationship between only two or three variables. Third, it tends to mirror the ways that people typically behave toward each other rather than offer new forms of social behavior (Argyris, 1969, 1975). Some theories in social psychology represent controlling and potentially destructive forms of social behavior that can be applied to influence people without their knowledge and against their best interests. For example, in Chapter 4 we will look at an application of cognitive dissonance theory used to sell merchandise at a time when consumers had little money to spend.

Nevertheless, applying existing theories of social psychology *can* be useful in understanding human social behavior; in fact, this is an important part of an applied approach to social psychology. Moreover, for our efforts to be considered applied social psychology, it is essential that we conduct the major part of our research in real-world settings to develop and test our theories and to practice interventions directly, rather than extrapolate from laboratory studies alone. In addition to increasing our awareness of social reality, we must also look for alternative strategies and behaviors to improve human interaction. In the ideal setting, applied social psychology seeks ways for people to share their feelings openly and respectfully, to make decisions democratically, and to work toward common goals in a collaborative fashion. It therefore requires a unique rationale and set of objectives, and should be based squarely on humanistic values.

Rationale and Objectives of Applied Social Psychology

The rationale for applied social psychology is simple: All human problems have social components, and the most serious human problems are primarily social. The threat of nuclear holocaust, the population explosion, world poverty, mass starvation, hatred and bigotry, intergroup conflict, the inequitable distribution of wealth, the debilitating effects of crime and urban decay—all these are human social problems that involve the complexities of human social interaction. Furthermore, we are becoming a "human-service society"—a society with an emphasis on social relationships and social processes. This will create more concern about attitudes and behavior required for survival and for promoting human welfare. Communication and negotiation will continue to enter into all decisions. Cooperation and conflict resolution will become increasingly important as we deal with threats to world survival.

The debilitating effects of crime and urban decay are among the most serious human social problems today. (George W. Gardner/Stock, Boston)

A viable applied social psychology, in conjunction with allied social sciences, should have much to offer this world. To be of use to humanity, applied social psychologists must have clear objectives: We must increase our understanding of how human beings interact with and influence each other. We must increase our capacity to improve the quality of social interaction in such areas as communication, negotiation, conflict resolution, decision making, and social change. We must learn how to work together to improve human welfare. We must commit ourselves to the well-being of *all* people. It is not enough to know, or even to know how to act; we must also care and we must also hope, or we will never choose to act. In her presidential address to the American Psychological Association in 1973, Leona Tyler summed up this call:

> The activities in which we as psychologists engage—research, teaching, writing, service to individuals and to organizations—can be a source of hope for mankind. My special hope for the American Psychological Association is that we may transcend our differences of background and orientation and concentrate our energies on our central tasks: to increase our individual and collective understanding of our own nature, and to join with others in building a structure of human relations richer than any the world has heretofore known. (p. 1029)

Humanistic Value Base of Applied Social Psychology

The strongest base for applied social psychology is in the philosophy of humanism (Kurtz, 1968, 1971). *Humanism* contends that the basis for moral values, of what is right and wrong, should be found in human experience and human needs. Humanists contend that people have the capacities of critical reason and scientific intelligence that can aid them in solving social problems and constructing moral values. In the same way, the common values expressed in the world's major religious codes are a potential basis for resolving humanity's problems.

Humanism is also humanitarian and democratic. It recognizes that each individual needs dignity, respect, equality, and compassion. It calls for the involvement of people in decisions that directly affect them. It calls for individuals to have the freedom and responsibility to develop their full potential, and to exercise their competence and excellence in the pursuit of human welfare.

In psychology, the philosophy of humanism finds expression in *humanistic psychology* (see Bugental, 1967, 1971), which is concerned with the full development of human potential. It has more recently found expression in what we might call "humanistic social psychology" (Johnson, 1973), which emphasizes how we use our understanding and experience of interpersonal relationships to help us achieve a full individual potential. Applied social psychology follows this line of development by asking how human well-being can be increased in all social environments through the power of scientific inquiry and the practice of professional skills. As Kelman (1969) has emphasized, it is "essential to view social science within the context of humanistic values and societal needs" (p. 7). We need to "humanize" social psychology so that it can contribute to the amelioration of unprecedented problems that beset humanity (Smith, 1974).

Uniting Humanism and Science. Applied social psychology certainly does not ask that our endeavors be any less scientific. On the contrary, we require a social psychology *that is both humanistic and scientific* in which the social psychologist, using the most effective methods of rationality available, collaborates respectfully with other people. Thus, social psychologists must be sensitive to their own individual values for these values affect the questions they ask and the conclusions they draw. They should realize that social research is not value-free and that their findings are not scientifically validated facts about nature (Kelman, 1969). Rather, their findings can be valuable input into humanity's thinking about social behavior and can contribute to the improvement of human welfare. A broad approach to *ways of knowing* is required rather than a restrictive commitment to any particular methodology, such as only the laboratory experiment or only one type of field research. The social psychologist, as scientist or practitioner, is essentially a problem solver who follows a rational sequence of steps in order to answer a question or resolve a problem (see Chapters 3 and 4).

Theory, Research, and Practice and the Utilization of Knowledge

Do you remember how much fun it was to ride a tricycle? And do you remember how hard it was to ride your first bicycle, having to balance yourself on two wheels instead of having the stability of three? That stability is mirrored in the three "wheels" that stabilize and advance applied social psychology: *theory, research, and practice.*

Research is the front driving wheel; it is the power of the discipline through which most advancement will come. Theory is one of the back wheels; it provides guidance and continuity to research. And practice is the third wheel, the final component of a balanced social psychology; it applies the theory to actual social situations. Unless we like to go around in circles, we need two back wheels that *work.* Without adequate theory and without practice in natural settings, working on real problems with people behaving as they usually do, social psychology will go in circles.

Only through the integration of all three components can we work toward our objectives: theory guiding research and practice . . . research and practice relating back to theory to validate, refine, and extend our concepts and principles . . . research pointing to important areas for practice . . . practice uncovering more research questions . . . research being used to assess the effects of practice, to evaluate the appropriateness of strategies and the effectiveness of skills. In the words of Lewin, "No action without research, no research without action."

Unfortunately, a schism has developed in social psychology between scientists and practitioners, between the pure and applied areas (Helmreich, 1975; Ring, 1967). Lewin strongly urged the pure and applied orientations to work together, as shown by his statement that "there is nothing so practical as a good theory." Some pure scientists have taken this dictum so seriously that the testing of important theories has become an end in itself, divorced from the wider social reality of application. Lewin had no such intention. As the full quotation indicates, he was very concerned with continuous integration of the two approaches (Lewin, 1951):

> It would be most unfortunate if the trend toward theoretical psychology were weakened by the necessity of dealing with natural groups when studying certain problems of social psychology. One should not be blind, however, to the fact that this

development offers great opportunities as well as threats to theoretical psychology. The greatest handicap of applied psychology has been the fact that, without proper theoretical help, it had to follow the costly, inefficient, and limited method of trial and error. Many psychologists working today in an applied field are keenly aware of the need for close cooperation between theoretical and applied psychology. This can be accomplished in psychology, as it has been accomplished in physics, if the theorist does not look toward applied problems with high-brow aversion or with a fear of social problems, and if the applied psychologist realizes that there is nothing so practical as a good theory. (p. 169)

The Lewinian tradition has not been lost to social psychology. Here is a recent sampling of suggested orientations:

- development of valid, nontrivial, socially relevant theories (Deutsch & Hornstein, 1975)
- shift from theories about individuals to theories of social systems (Smith, 1973; Tajfel, 1979).
- use of a variety of research methods, and the cross-checking of their results (Sherif, 1977)
- theory-relevant research in natural settings, which investigates the multiple, reciprocal causation of human behavior (McGuire, 1969)
- emphasis on the creation of research hypotheses, not just methods alone (McGuire, 1973)
- renewed commitment to applied research, such as action research and evaluation research (Smith, 1973)
- revitalized expansion of practice to move us beyond "what is" to "what should be" (Fisher, 1977)

As we develop valid and relevant knowledge, we must become concerned with the dissemination and utilization of that knowledge. A combination of theory, research, and practice is essential for this. We need theories of utilization, and we must carry out research on utilization itself (see Havelock, 1969). We must make difficult value judgments about how far our responsibility goes as professionals for the utilization of our findings. At times we may enter into practice interventions to bring about the implementation of our results (for example, Fairweather, 1967, 1977). These difficult decisions will be resolved not by ignoring their existence, but by our active and sustained participation as social psychologists. We need a clear sense of our individual values and a strong commitment to our collective responsibility to humanity.

Interaction Approach to Understanding and Action

Social psychology studies such individual characteristics as attitudes, motives, and values, and such environmental properties as group norms and organizational communication patterns. Both the person and the environment include a wide array of important variables—that is, properties that can vary or take on different values. Social scientists have worked to identify the most important individual and environmental variables that lead people to behave the way they do. But even more important is the idea that *behavior is determined by these two sets of variables working together.*

For example, suppose that you are a black person with a positive attitude toward whites in general. Among your liberal friends you do not hesitate to express your respect for white people and your hope that interracial hostility can be reduced. If, during your first week at college, however, you find yourself among blacks who talk about whites in a derogatory fashion, you may not express your attitudes directly. The social norms of the environment (the group's negative sentiments) will combine with the individual variable (your positive attitude) to produce new behavior—possibly silence—in this situation.

Kurt Lewin was one of the earliest and strongest proponents of the idea that *person variables (P)* interact with *environmental variables (E)* to determine behavior *(B)*. He expressed this interaction principle in the equation: $B=f(P,E)$ (Lewin, 1951). In other words, behavior is a function of both the person and the environment, with f representing this functional relationship, and the entire equation representing a law of social behavior.

Lewin also emphasized that P and E are not independent of each other, but may influence each other in a reciprocal fashion. The way you perceive an environmental situation may be determined by your emotions, affecting how you behave in that situation: $E=f(P)$. In other words, the perceived environment is a function of the person.

The reciprocal is also true: the state of the person is a function of the environment, or $P=f(E)$. For example, your motivations in a democratic group atmosphere may differ from your motivations in an autocratic atmosphere. In the former, you might work hard to achieve the group goals; in the latter, you might be more motivated to maintain your independence and autonomy.

Psychology has recently taken a renewed interest in this interaction of variables (Buss, 1977). This is because interaction explains more about behavior than about the single effects of person or environmental variables acting alone (for example, see Bowers, 1973; Endler & Magnusson, 1976). Furthermore, the simple experimental approach excludes the study of how P and E reciprocally influence each other. This relationship can be better handled by a Lewinian holistic, field approach. Strong interest in the interaction perspective is evident in personality psychology (for example, Endler, 1975, 1976; Magnusson & Endler, 1976; Mischel, 1973) and in educational psychology (Hunt, 1975; Hunt & Sullivan, 1974; McKeachie, 1974).

Social psychology has also called for a new approach to its work. For example, Secord (1977) supports most elements of the interaction perspective. He contends that we must focus more on person variables since these interact with environmental variables imposed by either the real world or by experimental conditons. We must also recognize that people are active agents who direct their own behavior and reciprocally affect their environment. In addition, we must classify social situations because social behavior varies greatly from one situation to another. The Lewinian notion of interaction remains alive and well in the social psychology of today.

Levels of Analysis in Human Social Functioning

When we study how humans function in society, we look at two basic systems of forces: the person and the environment. However, the social environment actually consists of several subsystems, each with its own characteristic variables that influence behavior. The social world has "wheels within wheels," all turning simultaneously to affect the actions of people. Since each subsystem has its own unique properties, we must develop theories, research methods, and practice skills to understand and affect each level of interaction. In this book, we will discuss principles of applied social psychology in the context of each level of analysis.

The *individual level* includes such variables as personality traits, motives, and attitudes—all strong determinants of social behavior. Individual-level variables are also useful for comparing persons or groups of persons. The concept of *role* enters at this level—a pattern of behavior appropriate to a person's position in life (for example, manager, student, homemaker). Role can serve as a linking concept between the individual level and other levels because each social system can be seen as an interlocking set of roles, each governed by certain expectations.

The *interpersonal level* is concerned with interaction between two people. This is the first, most basic social situation, yet it is one that can become unusually complex. Many questions in social psychology revolve around interpersonal perception, attraction, communication, and influence. Interrole behavior is also an important aspect of most social systems.

At the *group level* we see the development of "emergent properties" that do not exist at simpler levels. For example, the study of group atmosphere, group norms, and communication networks focuses on the way group forces impinge upon individual behavior.

Just as individuals behave in relation to each other, so also do groups. The *intergroup level* includes many of the classic concerns of social psychology, such as the study of prejudice and discrimination. In addition, each succeeding level can be influenced by "wheels" turning in the systems below: for example, group factors such as morale and cohesion can affect and, in turn, be affected by intergroup relations.

The *organizational level* includes both structured organizations (businesses, schools) as well as less structured ones (self-help associations, social movements). Many studies have focused on groups in organizations, as well as on intergroup relations between such subsystems as labor and management.

The *community level* can be exceedingly complex because of the countless factors that affect both geographical and cultural communities. Community psychologists have rekindled interest in the community as a social system. When their work is combined with the traditional theoretical interest of sociologists and the practice skills of community developers, the result is an exciting area of interdisciplinary activity. The unique contributions that social psychologists can make to this effort will require a revitalized social psychology following the Lewinian tradition.

The *societal level* takes as its unit of analysis the *nation*—that is, a politically intact collection of geographical regions sharing a common cultural and national identity. At this level, social psychologists are concerned with social issues that are affected by national policies and laws, cultural norms, and social change. The issues of racism, sexism, and poverty have been prime objects of study at the societal level.

Interaction among nation-states brings us to the *international or global level* of analysis. International relations partly parallel intergroup relations, but also involve their own unique structures and processes. Political scientists have contributed most to our understanding of this level, and the insights of the social psychologist have also been very useful.

A few final points are important to remember. Many social-psychological processes, such as communication, operate at all levels; others, such as group norms, emerge only at their respective level and do not operate below it. In addition there is both upward and downward influence among the various levels. Groups, for example, clearly affect their individual members, but an individual can also exert considerable influence on a group. Adjacent levels of functioning merge into one another.

To develop an adequate understanding of human social behavior, we must study the interaction of variables from all levels of analysis. By being attuned to this "big picture" of social functioning, we can contribute understanding to that complexity that is humanity, and take action on the problems that plague our existence.

PLAN OF THE BOOK

The organization of *Social Psychology: An Applied Approach* is based both on the integration of theory, research, and practice, and on the levels of analysis. Part One includes chapters on theories in social psychology, research methods, and practice skills and lays the foundation for the remainder of the book.

Part Two devotes one chapter to each level of analysis, from the individual to the international. Each of these chapters focuses on additional theories and research results relevant to that level and will describe practice interventions that can be used for improving social functioning.

Part Three of the text focuses on special areas in applied social psychology. In addition to chapters on program evaluation and conflict resolution, a number of contemporary and emerging areas of study, such as environmental psychology, consumer behavior, and public policy, are examined. Finally, the current development and the future challenge of applied social psychology are considered.

Summary

Social psychology, a subdiscipline of both psychology and sociology, is the scientific study of how the behavior of an individual is influenced by and in turn influences the actions of others in the social environment.

Social psychology has a short but rich history, based on the assertion of Auguste Comte in the nineteenth century that social processes are amenable to scientific study. Following the publication in 1908 of the first two social psychology textbooks, by Ross and by McDougall, the field rapidly developed a variety of research methods and study areas.

Stimulated by the work of Kurt Lewin and other socially concerned scientists, the field developed a strong applied emphasis during the 1930s and 1940s. The applied emphasis declined during the 1950s and 1960s as the rise of the experimental method and the development of individual-level theories precluded the study of more complex phenomena in the natural environment. In the 1970s, feminists and minority groups challenged social psychologists to expand their research concerns. The state of the economy and a shift toward funding applied research are key factors in the 1980s.

Current controversies within social psychology include the issues of relevance, validity, and triviality. The relevance issue calls for theories and methods that relate to social reality and that are useful in resolving social problems. The issue of validity is concerned with the use of accurate, valid measures and procedures, while the issue of triviality expresses the need for significant areas of study.

The expectations of society and the limitations of time and culture must be understood in conjunction with the development of a "social psychology of social psychology." This would articulate the social forces that continuously determine the identity of the discipline.

Social psychologists have the opportunity to carry out a variety of challenging roles: pure scientist, applied scientist, and professional practitioner. Each role has its particular emphasis and its particular contributions to make to the field and to society. The possibility of combining roles, as a means of advancing social psychology and contributing to human welfare, is particularly attractive.

Clearly, the present crisis challenges social psychology to recommit itself to the development of relevant theories of human interaction through a variety of research and practice activities in natural environments. Accordingly, applied social psychology is concerned with social-psychological research and practice in real-world settings directed toward the understanding of human social behavior and the solution of social problems.

Applied social psychology differs from "applying social psychology"—that is, attempting to explain real-world social behavior by using theories developed solely through laboratory research. In contrast, applied social psychology is concerned with understanding real-world behavior and with facilitating productive change in social systems based on a clear set of humanistic values. These values affirm the dignity and freedom of all peoples, and their responsibility to enrich the quality of life in accordance with rational human experience.

The rationale for applied social psychology is, first, that all human problems involve a social component, and second, that there is an increasing concern with human relationships in society.

Our objective, therefore, is to increase our understanding and our capacity for action to improve the quality of social life. To do this, social psychology must unite a humanistic value base with its scientific methods.

The development of applied social psychology requires a recommitment to the creative blending of theory, research, and practice. The practice component, while relatively underdeveloped, is essential to maintain contact with social reality. Each element of the theory-research-practice "tricycle" reinforces the other elements.

Social psychology must involve basic questions of human interaction in social systems, the deployment of a wide variety of research methods, and the increasing use of a demanding range of practice skills. All of these endeavors should be tied to the utilization of social scientific knowledge for the public good.

The principle of interaction is finding renewed support within social psychology. The classic formulation by Lewis—$B = f(P,E)$—concisely states that social behavior is both a function of the person and the environment, and that P and E mutually influence each other.

The levels-of-analysis approach subdivides the social environment into eight systems: individual, interpersonal, group, intergroup, organization, community, society, and international. Each of these systems has a unique set of variables that influence behavior and, in turn, are influenced by it.

Further Readings

Allport, G. W. The historical background of modern social psychology. In G. Lindzay and E. Aronson (Eds.), *The handbook of social psychology* (Vol. 1) (2nd ed.). Reading, Mass.: Addison-Wesley, 1968.

Deutsch, M. & Hornstein, H. *Applying social psychology.* Hillside, N.J.: Lawrence Erlbaum, 1975.

Kelman, H. C. *A time to speak.* San Francisco: Jossey-Bass, 1969.

Lewin, K. *Field theory in social science.* New York: Harper, 1951.

Smith, M. B. *Humanizing social psychology.* San Francisco: Jossey-Bass, 1974.

Strickland, L. H., Aboud, F. E., & Gergen, K. J. *Social psychology in transition.* New York: Plenum Press, 1976.

Woods, P. J. (Ed.). *Career opportunities for psychologists: Expanding and emerging areas.* Washington, D.C.: American Psychological Association, 1976.

CHAPTER OUTLINE

Useful Theories from Social Psychology

When I was in my early teens, I had a favorite place to go on warm, sunny afternoons. It was a piece of high ground, a hill on the northern edge of the farm. From up there I could see the rolling prairie stretch away for miles. The "big sky," with bits of puffy white cloud, appeared to be endless. I could see every rise of land, every grove of trees, and the checkered pattern of crops and cultivated land. I could watch the interaction of the wind and the clouds, and of the clouds and the rain showers that often came in the late afternoon. It was both comforting and exciting to be able to see the world on this grand scale, to have an illuminating overview of what is, to better understand some of the connections among the separate elements, and at times to wonder about what could be.

This is essentially the appeal that theories have for me and for many other social scientists. Theories are our attempts to construct a wider view of social reality, to describe relationships among different aspects of social behavior, and to speculate on the missing links in social interaction. This broader understanding of social reality satisfies our curiosity, strengthens our sense of security, and provides stimulation and guidance for answering questions and resolving problems.

For example, you probably enjoy talking with someone who is attentive and responsive. You may tend to say more and to converse longer with a person who smiles, maintains eye contact, and responds affirmatively to what you are saying. This phenomenon can be explained by the principles of social learning theory. When your speaking behavior is followed by rewards—the signs of the other person's acceptance—the predictable outcome is greater participation in the conversation. You can use this understanding to affect the behavior of other people. Responding positively to others can influence not only how much they say, but also what they say—as will be shown in this chapter. Thus, social learning theory can help us to understand, predict, and change our own behavior and that of others.

This chapter presents some basic ideas about social behavior that have been developed and tested by social psychologists. My list is intentionally selective, and my discussion limited in order to give a brief overview of useful theories and basic principles. This will help you understand some of the processes and problems that are outlined in later chapters, each of which will add more theories applicable to its particular level of analysis.

Before we talk about the *content* (the *what*) of theories, we should look at the *process* (the *how*) of theory construction. How do we develop theoretical concepts and relate them? A theory is an abstract or symbolic representation of reality; it exists in our minds, our words, and our writings as an attempt to describe or explain what exists in the world. A theory can be both a goal and a tool. As a goal, theory gives us an efficient way to summarize and organize large amounts of information. As a tool, it allows us to go beyond existing information to see implications and gain insight, and to make predictions that guide further research (Marx, 1963; Shaw & Costanzo, 1970).

As social scientists, social psychologists are committed to the development of *empirical theories*—that is, theories, based on observation, that describe relation-

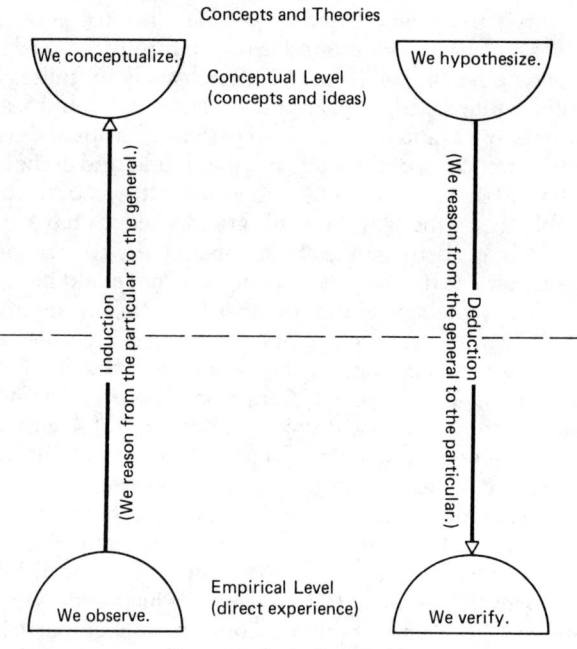

Figure 2.1   Process of Theory Construction.

ships that can be verified by the scientific method (Lewin, 1951). In developing empirical theories we begin by observing social behavior (see Figure 2.1). (For example, we might observe that when our friend Milton fails an exam, he blames the teacher and complains that the textbook was unreadable, whereas others suggest that Milton did not study hard enough.) Based on what we see and hear, we *induce* concepts and theories. *Induction* is reasoning that moves from the particular to the general. In this act of conceptualizing we describe the interrelationships of what we have seen and heard in general terms and in laws of social behavior. This permits us to understand what we have observed. (In our example, we conceptualize a tendency for the individual actor in a situation—Milton—to attribute causation to external factors—the teachers, the textbooks—whereas observers of the situation tend to see personal characteristics as the cause— Milton's failure to study hard enough.)

To use theory as a tool, we must follow the process of deduction. *Deduction* is reasoning that moves from the general to the particular. We observe certain phenomena and note how they interact; we use logical reasoning to make further predictions about their relationships, and we end up with a deduction in the form of hypothesis. Then, using experimentation or observation, we test the hypothesis. (For example, from our general principle we might hypothesize that when our Uncle Hiram's Hula-Hoop franchise goes bankrupt, he will attribute this to factors beyond his control rather than to his misperception of the demand for Hula-Hoops. Sure enough, when disaster strikes, Uncle Hiram writes nasty letters to his advertising agency, his banker, and the various government officials whose ineptness and unrealistic demands he believes have cost him his fortune.)

BASIC PROCESSES OF SOCIAL INTERACTION

Social-psychological theories vary considerably. Some consist of a small number of principles pertaining to a particular segment of social behavior. The theory of *psychological reactance*, for example, states only that if an individual's freedom of choice is eliminated, he or she will attempt to restore it. Other theories are broader in their coverage and implications and can be used to interpret a wide range of social interaction. Social learning theory, for instance, states that we develop our social behavior by observing others and by being rewarded for certain acts. These broader theories are more like orientations to studies of the social world than simply summary descriptions of observations.

In the effort to generalize an idea from particulars, however, we sometimes stretch a theory beyond its scope, thus distorting or leaving out part of reality. For example, if we attempt to explain all social behavior through social learning theory, we will ignore other equally valid explanations. With our limited knowledge, we can avoid blind spots by examining *all* valid and useful theories.

In the following sections, we will introduce some of the more important processes in social interaction. These processes are the focus of a number of social-psychological theories.

Social Perception

Perception is the process of experiencing the world through the senses: we see, we hear, we feel, we smell, and we taste. *Social perception* exists when other people are involved, directly or indirectly, in the process of experiencing the world. It covers a wide range of social behavior, including how we form impressions of others and how we attribute causes to people's behavior. This includes the process of social cognition, or how we think about others. Social perception is a critical process in many areas of application including the formation of stereotypes (see Chapter 8), distortion in international communication (Chapter 12) and the escalation of social conflict (Chapter 14).

Selectivity and Distortion. A basic principle of social perception is its *selectivity.* We must be selective because it is impossible to attend to all the stimuli that occur in our social and physical world. To bring order to it, we create a filtering process so that we can focus on certain elements.

It is a part of the work of social psychologists to study the factors that affect the selectivity process: How do we perceive what we want to perceive? How do expectations and cultural background affect our perception?

Let us examine a study in order to begin answering these questions. Participants in a management training program—themselves managers in sales, production, and accounting—read a case study that described how a steel company was organized and run. The participants then were asked what they considered to be the most important problem facing the steel company. Right down the line, each manager reflected the interests of his or her department: sales managers saw sales as the most important problem areas; production managers focused on organizational procedures; and so on for several subjects in a row. It was evident that the managers' departmental identification was the major factor in determining the selectivity of their perception (Dearborn & Simon, 1958).

A second principle of social perception relates to *distortion.* We tend to see what we *want* to see, and we will distort whatever comes into the senses for this to happen. A series of classic experiments in social psychology illustrates the distortion principle. Allport and Postman (1945) were interested in the process of rumors that occur during wartime. They noted that fear rumors and hostility rumors were common in the United States during World War II; such rumors helped explain and relieve emotional tensions. To study this process, the investigators set up an experiment in which a subject viewed a slide of a social situation and then told another subject, who did not see the slide, what was in it. The second subject then described the slide to a third subject; the third told a fourth; and so on for several subjects in a row.

If you have ever played the rumor game that is based on this procedure, you know that a number of types of distortion can occur. These include the process of *leveling*—the rumor grows shorter until only a small number of details are retained; the process of *sharpening*—selected details are retained and emphasized; and the process of *assimilation*—the rumor is modified in line with interests, major themes, linguistic habits, and so on. Allport and Postman found that some amazing assimilations were based on expectations and prejudices. For example, one slide showed a white man and a black man standing and talking to each other in a subway car. The white man held a straight razor in his hand. In over half the experimental trials, as the scene was described by successive white participants, the straight razor somehow magically moved from the white man's hand to the black man's hand.

Mann and Taylor (1969) investigated the effect of motives on perceptual distortion. They interviewed people waiting in line for tickets to an Australian football match, for Batman T-shirts, and for free chocolate bars. They asked each individual in line to estimate the number of people ahead of him or her. In all cases, those in the front part of the line overestimated the number of people ahead. However, when the supply of the commodity was likely to run out, people tended to *underestimate* the number ahead of them. This suggested that latecomers are motivated to underestimate numbers *to justify being in the line and to reassure themselves*—an example of the powerful effect of motivation on perceptual distortion.

Many of the selective and distorting effects of perception have been summed up in the "Pollyanna principle," which states that pleasantness predominates in the processing of information (Matlin & Stang, 1978). (Pollyanna was that optimistic, irrepressibly happy little girl who, as the heroine of a 1913 novel, always found a silver lining in the darkest of clouds.) Based on their research results, Matlin and Stang (1978) contend that we are all Pollyannas, at least to a greater extent than we are incorrigible pessimists. For example, pleasant words occur much more frequently in our language than do unpleasant ones. People tend to seek out pleasant events and avoid the unpleasant; we tend to overestimate the occurrence of pleasant events in recalling the past as well as in predicting the future. Our perceptions are often distorted in favor of pleasantness. For example, most college students who were asked to draw a chocolate bar and a piece of wood drew the candy bar larger than the wood. Similarly, coins were perceived to be larger than cardboard disks of the same size. Why do these distortions occur? It may be that we find pleasant stimuli more rewarding or that we defend ourselves against unpleasantness. We are not really sure.

Impression Formation. A basic area of interest in research on social perception is *impression formation.* One of the earliest studies of impression formation was performed by Asch (1946). He read a list of adjectives describing a hypothetical person to two different groups of subjects. Each group heard the same list except that in one list the word *warm* was substituted for the word *cold.* This simple difference affected the overall impression formed by each group. The group that heard *warm* described the individual more positively, rating him as generous, happy, good-natured, and sociable. Descriptive words such as *warm* and *cold* were seen as central traits that had an above-average effect in the determination of an overall impression.

Further studies have supported Asch's work while raising some questions and qualifications. For example, Wishner (1960) found that central traits such as warm and cold helped to determine the ratings given to other traits, but that a total impression actually comes from not one but a number of central traits.

The primary implication of Asch's research—that central impressions influence our total picture of others—has long been observed in interviewing. This phenomenon, in which our general impression of a person leads us to evaluate most of his or her other qualities in a similar manner, is referred to as the *halo effect*. For example, in a job selection interview, a positive halo effect might lead the interviewer to see the youthful age of a candidate as a plus factor ("She is highly energetic and willing to learn"), whereas a negative halo effect might produce the opposite outcome ("She is so inexperienced and not as motivated as an older worker").

An experiment by Nisbett and Wilson (1977) provides a clear demonstration of the halo effect. Two different videotapes of a college instructor were shown to students. In one tape, the instructor behaved in a warm and friendly way; in the other, he was cold and unfriendly. Students who saw the "warm" tape were more likely to provide favorable ratings of the instructor's appearance, mannerisms, and voice than were students who received the "cold" impression. The halo effect sensitizes us to be wary of the powerful and sometimes unwarranted effects that global impressions can have on our evaluations of other people.

In interviewing and other social interactions, first impressions have a strong influence—this is generally known as the *primacy effect* (Luchins, 1957). In a job interview, the first five minutes are often the most important in determining the interviewer's impression of the applicant *and* the subsequent decision to hire or reject. Sometimes, however, a *recency effect* occurs if new information becomes available after a period of intervening activity since the first impression was formed. Again, the admonition is to be sensitive to the biases we construct.

Forming an overall impression, how do we combine our favorability ratings of various traits? Two basic models have been proposed: the averaging model and additive model (Anderson, 1965). In the averaging model we calculate the mean rating of likability over all the traits we use to describe a person, which determines our general impression. For example, using a five-point rating scale (-2 to $+2$), let us suppose you see a new acquaintance, Pamela, as sociable ($+2$) and intelligent ($+2$), but also as conforming (-1) and overly sensitive (-2). Your global impression would be expressed as $(2+2-1-2)/4=1/4=+.25$). You have an almost neutral impression of Pamela. Using the additive model, your impression would be somewhat more positive ($2+2-1-2=+1$). The averaging model appears to yield better predictions of actual impressions, but its accuracy is limited because some traits seem to carry more weight than others in determining the overall impression. To overcome this deficiency, Anderson (1968) has proposed a weighted averaging model which takes into account the relative importance of the component traits. By being sensitive to both the favorability and the significance of the characteristics we attribute to others, we can thus come to understand how our impressions of them are formed.

Attribution Theory. In the past several years the study of *attribution theory* has become prominent in social psychology. Attribution theory was initially concerned with how we infer stable characteristics (motives, attitudes, abilities) of others by observing their behavior (Heider, 1958; Jones & Davis, 1965). The big question is, do we attribute behavior to internal factors within the person or to external characteristics of the environment? If a person is quiet and withdrawn, is that characteristic of the person, or is it due to his or her social situation? If people espouse certain opinions, are they being sincere or are they swayed by social presence?

Kelley (1967,1973) has developed a theory of causal attribution that focuses on how we explain the behavior of others by inferring causation. He contends that we usually attribute behavior to one of three causes: (1) dispositions or stable characteristics of the person, (2) the particular circumstances of a specific situation at a given time, or (3) enduring properties of the environment in which the behavior occurs. For example, if you are walking down the street and you see a man walk into a parking meter, you would probably wonder about the cause of his behavior. You might attribute it almost entirely to a personal characteristic and add a derogatory comment ("He's got to be pretty stupid to walk into a parking meter!"). Or you might attribute his behavior to specific circumstances (for example, it is windy and you believe that some dust blew into the man's eyes). Suppose, on the other hand, that while contemplating this situation you also walk into a parking meter. You observe that the meters are placed three feet into the sidewalk from the curb rather than the usual one foot. You would probably then attribute the man's behavior to this enduring characteristic of the environment.

Kelley maintains that in making attributions, people examine three crucial factors about the situation: *consensus* (the degree to which others act in the same way in the same situation as the person being observed); *consistency* (whether the person being observed always behaves this way in this particular situation); and *distinctiveness* (whether the person behaves this particular way only in this particular situation). When the degree of occurrence of all these factors is high, we tend to make external attributions. That is, if other people would act the same way in the situation (high consensus); and the person consistently acts this way in the same situation at different times (high consistency), and the person acts only this way in this situation and not in others (high distinctiveness), then we tend to see the behavior as caused by environmental forces. For example, suppose your cousin Arnold, who seldoms resorts to physical violence, got into a fight in a bar. Now you know this is very rare behavior for Arnold (high distinctiveness). In addition, others in the bar were also involved in the altercation, which was an attempt to stop a gang from stealing the chains from the hanging chandeliers (high consensus). Furthermore, you know that Arnold has at other times come to the aid of victims of criminal acts (high consistency). The conclusion: Arnold's behavior was largely in response to the demands of the situation rather than to aggressive or sadistic tendencies.

Another important idea in attribution theory, contributed by Jones and Nisbett (1972), is that our role in a situation (as actor or observer) determines the kinds of attribution we make. Actors tend to attribute their own behavior to the environment that is the focus of their perception, rather than to themselves. In addition, they know how they've acted in similar and different situations. (When *you* walked into that hypothetical parking meter, you were more likely to attribute your behavior to some characteristic of the situation or to the particular circumstances.) Observers, on the other hand, usually attribute the behavior of actors to the actors; they focus on the actor even though they have little information about the actor's disposition ("He's got to be pretty stupid . . ."). The tendency to make individual attributions regarding the behavior of others is a fundamental attribution error which exacerbates many social problems such as racial prejudice (see Chapter 8).

When do we make dispositional attributions—that is, see the cause of some behavior in a person's characteristics or disposition? When consensus and distinctiveness are low and consistency is high, according to Kelley. Back to your cousin Arnold. He gets into a fight in a bar with a man who is pounding a malfunctioning cigarette machine. Arnold seems to get into a fight every time he walks into a bar (high consistency), as well as in almost any other social situation (low distinctiveness). No one else is involved except Arnold's victim (low consensus). In this case, you would likely conclude that your aggressive, impulsive cousin had lost control and gotten into trouble again. As you can see, Kelley's notions make good sense— and it is not surprising that they, along with other principles of attribution theory, have received much attention in both research and application in social psychology (Freize, Bar-Tal & Carroll, 1979; Kelley & Michela, 1980). In Chapter 16, we will consider the role of attribution in consumer choice and in the maintenance of unhealthy life-styles.

Social Motivation

Social psychologists are not content simply to observe and describe human social behavior. They want to know *why* the behavior occurs. Although their questioning begins in the realm of attribution theory, it soon moves to the area of *social motivation.*

Motives are the consistent internal conditions that produce behavior or a behavioral direction (Berkowitz, 1969). *Social motives* are related more to other people than to aspects of the physical environment. Hunger, for example, is considered to be a *psychological* motive: it is a function of the environment. Affiliation, on the other hand, is a *social* motive: its expression requires either the direct or indirect involvement of other people. Among the social motives studied by social psychologists are aggression, competition, cooperation, affiliation, achievement, power, and altruism.

Early motivational theorists stated a *classic drive theory* to account for the vigor and direction of human behavior. They postulated a limited number of primary drives, including hunger, thirst, sex, and pain avoidance. These drives supposedly lead to states of internal excitation that, in turn, supposedly lead to behavior designed to satisfy the drive and reduce the associated tension. But since this theory could not account for all human behavior, especially in the social arena, social psychologists explored still further (Berkowitz, 1969).

Maslow's Hierarchy of Needs. Abraham Maslow (1943, 1970) examined the *positive* motives that people exhibit rather than destructive needs such as aggression. Maslow's motives were directly related to basic human needs. He stated a comprehensive set of these basic human needs, organizing them into a hierarchy: needs at the lower end of the hierarchy must be satisfied before a person can move up to the next level of needs. Although Maslow considered the hierarchy of needs to hold true for all persons, he recognized individual exceptions in the order in which needs were satisfied.

Maslow's hierarchy of needs includes:

- *Self-actualization needs:* the ultimate motivation, involving the need to fulfill one's unique individual potential
- *Esteem needs:* the need for achievement, competence, and mastery, as well as motives for recognition, prestige, and status
- *Belongingness and love needs:* needs that are satisfied by social relationships
- *Safety needs:* needs that must be met to protect the individual from danger
- *Physiological needs:* basic internal deficit conditions that must be satisfied to maintain bodily processes

Maslow also recognized *cognitive needs* (a desire to know, to understand, and to satisfy one's curiosity) and *aesthetic needs* (the craving for beauty, symmetry, and order). Although these were not included in the hierarchy, they would likely be placed at the level of the esteem needs.

Maslow's model of motivation has been useful in counseling psychology and in organizational psychology, particularly in understanding what motivates people to work in organizations (see Chapter 9). His concept of self-actualization is further explained in Chapter 5. Alderfer (1969) developed and tested an extension of Maslow's model that identified three major types of human needs: those related to existence, to relatedness, and to growth. Contrary to Maslow, Alderfer's model does not assume that lower order needs must be satisfied before higher level needs emerge. However, Mathes and Edwards (1978) found that safety needs were a prerequisite to self-actualization, whereas belongingness and esteem needs were not. Thus, the hierarchical aspect of Maslow's theory requires further investigation before it can be accepted or rejected.

Need for Achievement. A second area of motivational theory and research was developed by McClelland, Atkinson, Clark, and Lowell (1953). They examined three of the personality needs first postulated by Murray (1938): the need for achievement (nACH), the need for affiliation (nAFF), and the need for power (nPOW). The achievement need involves our desire to accomplish, to manipulate, to do well at our tasks. The affiliative need includes a desire to interact with others in ways that please them and maintain their affection. The power need involves our desire to control other people and influence social situations.

In their research, McClelland et al. found that

- The socialization process, especially as it is exercised in the family, is central in determining one's level of motivation (McClelland, 1961).
- The degree of independence training that a child receives will be important in determining his or her future level of need achievement (McClelland, 1961).
- People engaged in occupations involving initiation, responsibility, and risk-taking had scored high on need-achievement tests while in college many years earlier (McClelland, 1965b).
- Measures of need achievement scored from children's storybooks were found to correlate with measures of economic production in a number of different countries (McClelland, 1961).

McClelland has also been involved in achievement-motivation training (1965a,

Box 2.1   FOCUS ON RESEARCH
Motives of American Presidents, 1905–1969

Richard Donley and David Winter followed in the creative footsteps of David McClelland by studying the motives of American presidents. Since high-level decision makers are seldom available for personality assessment through direct testing, Donley and Winter scored inaugural speeches for need achievement (nACH) and need power (nPOW). Inaugural addresses generally express the concerns, hopes, fears and aspirations of presidents, and are seen as a good source of information about social motives.

Presidents from 1905 to 1969 were first grouped into high and low categories of achievement and power, based on their political behavior, record of accomplishments, and innovations during their period in office. Thus the presidents were separated into two main groups: those high on both power and achievement (such as Lyndon Johnson), and those low on both power and achievement (such as Dwight Eisenhower).

The inaugural speeches were then scored sentence by sentence for nACH and nPOW themes. For example, when Herbert Hoover said, "To consider these evils, to find a remedy, is the most soaring necessity of our times," he was expressing a need for achievement. When Franklin Roosevelt said, "These are the lines of attack. I shall presently urge upon a new Congress in special session detailed letters for their fulfillment," the investigators scored a need for power.

When Donley and Winter looked at motive scores in relation to their prior categorization of political behavior, they found a high degree of relationship. Presidents whose behavior was categorized as high on power and achievement did in fact receive higher scores on nPOW and nACH themes in their inaugural address. Donley and Winter conclude that the analysis of political speeches can assess underlying motives that play an important role in determining the political behavior of decision makers.

Source: Donley, R. E. & Winter, D. G. Measuring the motives of public officials at a distance: An exploratory study of American presidents. *Behavioral Science*, 1970, *15*, 227–236.

1978) (see Chapter 4) and has investigated the power motive (1975). A study of the power motive as a means of understanding political behavior appears in Box 2.1. The importance of the achievement and affiliation motives in organizational settings will be considered in Chapter 9.

Social Learning

Learning is any change in behavior that occurs as a result of experience. Consequently, *social learning* is learning that involves other people in this process of change.

The learning process includes the central elements of motivation, association, stimulus, response, and reinforcement. Learning requires both a minimal level of motivation (that is, people must want to learn) and an association between elements in the learning situation. This association is often between the stimulus that impinges upon the person and the person's behavioral responses in the environment. Reinforcement helps to determine what changes in behavior will occur, or what behavior will be performed, or both.

Social psychologists have adapted the principles of general learning theory from psychology, especially in the area of social reinforcement. As early as 1911, Thorndike's *law of effect* expressed the commonsense notion that behavior that has a satisfying effect on an organism will tend to be repeated, whereas behavior that has an unpleasant effect will tend not to be repeated. The effect, then, can become a cause of later behavior.

Positive reinforcement refers to condition or event whose presence increases the probability that a preceding behavior will be repeated. For example, you say "hi" to a woman and she smiles and says, "How ya doin'." Her nonverbal and verbal behavior are positive reinforcers—they increase the chance that you will say hello to her again.

Negative reinforcement refers to a condition or event whose *withdrawal* increases the probability that the preceding behavior will be repeated. For example, when you say "hi" to your classics professor, she frowns at you and says, "Good morning, Miss Smith." You reply, "Good morning, Professor Uptight," and her frown disappears. Your more formal greeting has been reinforced by the withdrawal of the negative reinforcer (the frown) and will likely be repeated in the future.

Punishment refers to an aversive condition or event that decreases the frequency or strength of a preceding behavior. Professor Uptight's frown is a form of punishment: unpleasant, it serves as a negative reinforcer when it is withdrawn. The implication is that behavior might be changed as much by removing an aversive condition as by actively applying the same condition as punishment. For example, when I send my daughter to her room for calling her sister names, her confinement is active punishment. However, when I say she can come out when she decides not to call names anymore, the withdrawal of the punishment becomes a negative reinforcer. She decides to change her behavior, and the end of the unpleasant confinement reinforces this change.

Following in the footsteps of Thorndike and other classic learning theorists, Skinner (1938, 1953) applied basic principles of learning to social behavior in a procedure known as *operant conditioning*. In this procedure, an organism's response is immediately reinforced. As a result, the response is learned, and the effect of reinforcement is seen as the later cause of the behavior, rather than any internal motive or need. Suppose that when a pigeon in a cage lifts its head, the action is reinforced with a food pellet. This happens every time the behavior occurs. Soon, the pigeon is walking around with its head held high—the schedule of positive reinforcement is the cause of the behavior.

Skinner's work in learning theory has been especially useful in programmed instruction in the field of education, and in behavior modification, an area of clinical pscyhology that employs the technology of behavior change based on principles of learning.

The classic study of *verbal reinforcement* was carried out by Greenspoon (1955). He asked each experimental subject to say "all the words that you can think of individually for fifty minutes." For some subjects, the experimenter said "mmm-hmm" every time the subjects named a plural noun. As predicted by the law of effect and the principle of positive reinforcement, these subjects gave more plural nouns than those who had received no such reinforcement. When this verbal reinforcement was withdrawn, plural nouns decreased, eliminating any difference between the conditions. This decrease in the expression of a behavior when a positive reinforcement is withdrawn is known in learning theory as the process of *extinction.*

Greenspoon's experiment has led to the active investigation of other behaviors and other situations. In one study, verbal reinforcement affected opinions about a variety of issues and groups including opinions about clinical and experimental psychologists (Cialdini & Insko, 1969). For example, if a positive statement about clinical psychologists was made, approval by the experimenter (e.g., "good") increased the frequency of such statements. In another study, the frequency of participation in a seminar class increased substantially when the instructor gave approval to every comment that was made.

A controversial aspect of verbal reinforcement studies is the issue of whether subjects are aware of the learning process that is going on. Opinion now holds that subjects who are at least minimally aware of the associations in the learning situation are the ones who learn through verbal reinforcement.

The concept of reinforcement carries considerable importance in explaining a wide range of social behavior from interpersonal attraction (see Chapter 6), to employee motivation in organizations (see Chapter 9), to criminal activities (see Chapter 16).

Observational Learning. The strongest challenge to the idea that the principles of general learning theory can explain social learning comes from the work of Albert Bandura (1965, 1977) and that of other social psychologists who have studied *observational learning.* Bandura believes that much social learning is vicarious—that is, it occurs through our observation of other people. We acquire responses by observing the actions of others and the reinforcement that follows. Learning can occur without overt responding or direct reinforcement to the observer.

Bandura outlines three different effects of exposure to models. The first is *acquisition:* An observer who sees a model engage in novel responses can repeat these responses at a later time, indicating that learning has occurred. For example, a preschool boy watches his mother draw the letter O. Soon he is drawing O's.

The second effect is *inhibition or disinhibition:* An observer who sees a model being punished for certain behaviors shows fewer imitative responses (inhibition) than would be shown if the model were not punished. A child who sees another child punished for fighting on the school playground is less likely to fight. Disinhibition occurs when previously learned, presently inhibited responses are released by observing a model engaging in similar behaviors. (A girl might observe fighting on the playground and then go home and yell at her little brother.)

The third effect is the elicitation of existing responses, or *response facilitation.* This involves responses that have not been previously punished (as occurred in inhibition and disinhibition). When a model exhibits these responses, the observer is more likely to imitate them—a matter of simple facilitation. For example, one might volunteer services or donate money to some cause after observing a model doing so. These types of effects have led the observational learning theorist to conclude that reinforcement appears to affect the performance (overt enactment) of responses more than it does the acquisition of responses.

Observational learning has been central in understanding the acquisition of prejudice (see Chapter 8), the learning and expression of aggression (see Chapter 14), and the effect of television on violence in society (see Chapter 16).

Experiential Learning. Remember the old saying, "Experience is the best teacher"? We do acquire much of our knowledge and skills by doing something and learning from it. This approach is known as *experiential learning*—that is, learning through direct participation. Although this type of learning has been long stressed in human relations and adult education (Bradford, 1958; Dow, 1976), it has only recently been applied to such areas as the acquisition of language and reading skills (Braun & Froese, 1977). Experiential learning requires an awareness of the entire process and context of human learning: this includes the relationship between learner and teacher, and between learner and other learners. Experiential learning also requires a clear diagnosis of expectations and learning goals, as well as the matching of these needs to available resources through the establishment of a learning contact between the teacher and the learners. Other key elements include the blending of conceptual information with experience or practice; feedback to learners, permitting them to learn as much as possible from their experience; active learner participation; a supportive learning climate; and a flexible approach to the learning process (see Chapter 4).

Socialization

Why do people turn out to be the way they are? How do people develop in order to establish their identity within society? These questions relate to *socialization*, the complex process by which we acquire the knowledge, skills, and attitudes necessary for successful participation in our society. Socialization settings can be small, closely knit units, such as the family, or institutional settings, such as the schools. Furthermore, within such places as prisons and psychiatric hospitals, another level of socialization takes place. (See Box 2.2 for a discussion of socialization within a psychiatric institution.)

A complete study of socialization clearly requires the contributions of several disciplines (Goslin, 1969). Psychology focuses on individual characteristics related to social behavior in such basic areas as learning and motivation. Sociology focuses on the characteristics of groups and institutions in which socialization occurs and on the social skills acquired through the socialization process. Anthropology helps our understanding of how the broader culture of a society sets the overall boundaries within which socialization occurs.

Socialization is a concept that will be used in other chapters. Socialization helps explain the existence of sexism in society (see Chapter 11), the adaptation of employees to organizations (see Chapter 9), and the phenomenon of nationalism in international relations (see Chapter 12). For now, let us explore the socialization of sex roles as an example of how the socialization process occurs.

Why do people turn out to be the way they are? This question is related to *socialization*, the complex process by which they acquire the knowledge, skills, and attitudes necessary for successful participation in society. Socialization settings can be small, closely knit units, such as the family, or institutional settings, such as the schools. *(Leonard Freed, Magnum Photos, Inc.)*

Socialization of Sex Roles. How do individuals acquire behavior that is appropriate to their sex? The acquisition of sex differences has received much attention in social psychology (Maccoby, 1966; Maccoby & Jacklin, 1974; Mussen, 1969). A social-learning explanation stresses the process of *sex-typing*—how children acquire sex role behaviors appropriate to their gender. The first step is discriminating what behavior is appropriate through *observational learning:* children learn by watching a powerful model who is performing appropriate sex-typed behavior and has the power to reward their correct behavior. At the same time, children learn the appropriate emotional and attitudinal responses to certain stimuli. They learn the appropriate behavior of *both* sexes; the differences in their overt behavior, however, are a result of different kinds of reinforcement (Mischel, 1966). We then learn to generalize sex-typed behavior to other situations. In this way, society comes to elicit different sex-role behaviors among children of different sexes.

These differences have been well documented by a variety of approaches both within and across societies. For example, the classical anthropoligical approach of documenting sex differences in behavior is provided by Barry, Bacon, and Child (1957), who looked at anthropological reports on socialization practices in 110 nonliterate cultures. A clear majority of these societies encouraged nurturance (helping, caring) in girls and achievement in boys. The persistence of these clearly differentiated tendencies is one of the important elements in the analysis of sexism as a social issue (see Chapter 11).

Box 2.2   FOCUS ON THEORY
The Socialization Setting of the Psychiatric Hospital

What is the institutional world of the psychiatric patient like? Sociologist Erving Goffman carried out a classic study of this question by spending an entire year working in a large psychiatric hospital. Goffman posed as an assistant to the institution's athletic director and, when pressed to explain his role, described himself as a student of recreation and community life. He spent all his time with patients and avoided social contact with hospital staff. He was thus able to gain an in-depth view of the socialization of psychiatric patients in a total institution—one in which all aspects of life are controlled by a central authority and activities are tightly scheduled.

The first socialization experience of the newly admitted patient is a stripping away of the self and the complete loss of personal identity. The standardized process of admission removes the patient's individuality—he or she becomes one case of many, dressed the same, treated the same. Contact with the outside world is restricted; previous roles—father, mother, worker, and so on—become meaningless. The patient is immediately socialized into acceptable patterns of behavior. Obedience and deference to staff are rewarded; defiance is punished. The patient has little privacy, and all behavior is regularized and controlled by staff. The institution thus provides a framework for the complete reorganization of the person's world.

Often the socialization process is not completely successful. Patients enter into a common-fate association that rejects the system. They engage in forbidden activities such as drinking and gambling. However, concerted and organized action against the institution is rare, and most inmates adopt individual ways of adjusting—such as withdrawal, intransigence, or "keeping cool." The inmate culture is dominated by the themes of low status, self-pity, and increasing anxiety about returning to the outside world. In a word, the patient has become "institutionalized."

Source: Goffman, E. *Asylums: Essays on the social situation of mental patients and other inmates.* Garden City, N.Y.: Anchor Books, 1961.

THEORIES OF SOCIAL INTERACTION

Attitudes and Social Behavior

If you or I took the time to think about our own social behavior, we would be surprised at how often the idea of *attitude* comes to mind. We would find ourselves continually voicing beliefs about this or that group or institution or person, expressing our feelings about them, and commenting about our tendency to behave in certain ways toward them.

It is not surprising, then, that social psychology has also focused on attitude as one of its key concepts. We have long been involved in defining attitudes, developing techniques for measuring them, constructing theories about attitude formation and change, and considering the relationship between attitudes and overt behavior.

Social psychologists have come up with a number of definitions of the concept of attitude; the following one catches the flavor of most: *An attitude is an individual's tendency to evaluate and respond to social objects in a consistently favorable or unfavorable way.* Given this definition, you might ask why the study of attitudes is so appealing to the social psychologist. Attitude is an important concept that holds a great deal of potential for generalizing and predicting social behavior. If we know an individual's attitude or the modal attitudes of a group or nation, then we can better understand and predict aspects of social perception, social motivation, and social behavior. If, for example, your Uncle George has an unfavorable attitude toward men with long hair, you can predict that he will probably give a cool reception to your friend Joe, who avoids barbers.

While the concept of attitude appears simple on the surface, it is quite complex. Therefore, it is useful to break down the concept into components—a process that came early and stayed late in the development of the discipline (McGuire, 1969). Katz and Stotland (1959) (among others) conceived attitude to be composed of three separate components: the *cognitive*, which is the set of beliefs about the object; the *affective*, which includes the feelings connected with the object; and the *behavioral*, which includes the action tendencies toward the object.

An *attitude* is an individual's tendency to evaluate and respond to social objects in a consistently favorable or unfavorable way. People who have an unfavorable attitude toward men with long hair, for example, may give them a cool reception. *(Richard Kalvar/ Magnum Photos, Inc.)*

One component may come to dominate the entire attitude. Your attitude about a political issue, for example, may be highly intellectualized (strongly *cognitive*), with little expression of feelings (lightly *affective*), and with no strong predispositions of action toward the social object (minimally *behavioral*). In studies of consistency among the attitude components, there seems to be a positive relationship when the overall attitude is favorable (McGuire, 1969). However, there is a continuing question about the degree of relationship among the attitudinal components, just as there is about the wider correspondence among thoughts, feelings, and behavior (e.g., Bagozzi & Burnkrant, 1979; Zajonc, 1980). Nonetheless, breaking attitudes into components has helped social psychologists understand phenomena such as racial prejudice (see Chapter 8), international images (see Chapter 12), and the issue of environmental conservation (see Chapter 15).

Functional Theory of Attitudes. Attitudes are complex because they serve many functions. Therefore, any attempt to influence attitudes must take these functions into account. Katz's (1960) comprehensive functional theory of attitude formation and change attempted to grapple with the complexity and dynamic nature of these processes. He described four functions that attitudes may serve:

- The *adjustive function* is based on the principle that we hold attitudes that maximize the rewards and minimize the punishments we receive. (There is a strong parallel between this and the effect of social reinforcement on behavior and attitudes.)

   The factor that determines how we form an attitude based on the adjustive function is *utility:* How useful is the social object of the attitude in satisfying our needs? Obviously the positive or negative usefulness of the object will be linked to our favorable or negative attitude about it. For example, a long-time male resident of a country may have a negative attitude toward recent immigrants—especially in the frustrating times of unemployment and job insecurity. Thus adjustive attitudes are aroused when the related need is active, assuming that the expression of the attitude is socially appropriate. If the long-time resident is supported by his family and peer groups in his derogatory remarks about immigrants, we would expect the expression of his attitude to be quite frequent.

   To change adjustive attitudes there must be changes in a person's needs and levels of aspiration, or a shift in available rewards and punishments. To continue with our example, if the job market brightens considerably and the long-time resident has no fear of losing his job and its rewards, then his attitude toward immigrants might become more favorable.

- The *ego-defensive function* underlies attitudes that protect the ego or self from unpleasant realities within the person or in the world. This idea, which parallels the psychodynamic theory of personality (see Chapter 5), maintains that attitudes are formed more through the psychological functioning of the person than through objective reality. For example, a person who is afraid of and is in conflict over his or her own sexuality may form negative attitudes toward sex education; the ego is thus protected from internal conflict and external dangers.

   Ego-defensive attitudes are aroused by the posing of threats to the self, through authoritarian suggestion, through rising frustrations, and through moral justification or repressed hostility.

   To change ego-defensive attitudes it is necessary to remove threats to the self, to bring about a catharsis (purging) of hostility or other negative feelings, and to work toward the development of self-insight. If, for example, a person comes to understand his or her own anxiety and defensiveness toward sex education, then a more positive attitude may result.

• The *value-expressive function* serves to express or enhance the individual's identity or self-image and personal values. A person who holds strong humanistic values, for example, may express negative attitudes toward large bureaucratic institutions that are perceived as limiting people's ability to participate in decision making that directly affects them.

The environmental conditions that arouse value-experience attitudes relate to both the person's values and to the person's desire to assert his or her self-image.

To change our value-expressive attitudes, either we must be dissatisfied with our self-image and values or recognize that existing values are being undermined by changes in the social environment. Attitudes toward religion, for example, seem to be ebb and flow with the prevailing cultural norms of the time.

• The *knowledge function* underlies attitudes that help us to explain social reality. These attitudes help us to understand the world and to develop and maintain meaning and consistency among our various beliefs and behaviors.

The arousal conditions for these attitudes include direct contact with the object along with the acquisition of relevant information about it. When we come in contact with a member of another social or racial group, we are often sensitive to that person's presence, and we acquire information that may support or disconfirm an existing attitude.

A change in an attitude serving this function can occur if new information about the object contributes significantly different data or results in unpleasant uncertainty. For example, I am convinced that one way of reducing racial prejudice is to bring members of different groups together in respectful and cooperative interaction (see Chapters 8 and 14). When we see each other as people rather than as stereotypes, our existing attitudes are challenged and the chances for positive change are increased.

As we review these functions of attitude, we must keep in mind that individuals have many predispositions to act and many influences impinging upon them. Thus we can only speak of the *general* conditions under which this or that function will be aroused. When the attitude no longer serves its function, the results are frustration of needs and a potential for change.

Congruence Between Attitudes and Behavior. If we know someone's attitudes, can we predict his or her behavior? Social psychologists have long been interested in this question and the key to its answer: the behavioral, or action, component of attitudes. This component is the classic link between how we intend to act and how we actually behave in the social world. For example, a model of attitudes developed by Fishbein and Azjen (1975) will be used in Chapter 16 to help explain consumer behavior in choosing among different brands of products.

Studies in this area, however, have yielded inconsistent results (Calder & Ross, 1976; Ehrlich, 1969). To accurately predict behavior, we must combine attitude measurements with a number of other variables that affect behavior. Behavior is a function of many personal factors—motives, habits, attitudes, and so on—and of many environmental factors, such as social norms, laws, rewards, and punishments. An example of research on the question of attitudes and

Box 2.3   FOCUS ON RESEARCH
Attitudes or Behavior: Which Comes First?

The question of whether attitudes cause behavior or vice versa has a long and controversial history in social psychology. Laboratory studies on cognitive dissonance and self-perception theory clearly suggest that we develop or infer our attitudes after enacting our behavior. Two social psychologists, Lynn Kahle and John Berman, examined this question by using a new statistical technique known as cross-lagged panel correlation to measure the relationships between variables.

Correlation analysis is used for estimating the degree of relationship between variables. In *cross-lagged panel correlation*, two variables are measured at more than one time, and the cross-lagged correlations between the variables are computed. That is, variables A and B are measured at times 1 and 2, the scores on variable A at time 1 are correlated with scores on variable B at time 2, and B1 scores are correlated with A2 scores. From the size of the correlation, it is possible to see which variable causes the other. If the correlation between A1 and B2 is greater than that between B1 and A2, then we conclude that changes in A cause changes in B rather than vice versa, since A scores measured first permit prediction of later B scores better than the prediction of A2 by B1.

During the summer of 1976, Kahle and Berman (1979) had a large number of college students rate their attitudes and report their behavior on four issues: Jimmy Carter's presidential candidacy, Gerald Ford's presidential candidacy, drinking, and religion. For example, respondents rated how strongly they supported Carter for president and reported how many times in the previous two weeks they have commented favorably on him.

The results were very clear. On all issues, the correlations between initial attitudes (A1) and later behaviors (B2) were greater than between initial behavior (B1) and later attitudes (A2). Kahle and Berman concluded that attitude was more likely to cause behavior (rather than vice versa) on all four issues. This implies that knowledge of attitude helps us predict people's behavior, and that successful attempts to change attitudes will indeed result in changed behavior.

Source: Kahle, L. R. & Berman, J. J. Attitudes cause behavior: A cross-lagged panel analysis. *Journal of Personality and Social Psychology*, 1979, 37, 315-321.

behavior is provided in Box 2.3. We must realize that attitudes are only one important element in the complex interaction of behavior and attitudes and that behavior, in turn, influences attitudes in a relationship of reciprocal cause and effect (Eagly & Himmelford, 1978).

Sometimes we may not have a clearly formed attitude toward a social object until we encounter it and see how we behave toward it. This idea partly motivated the development of cognitive consistency theories.

Theories of *cognitive consistency* state that each of us has a tendency to look for consistency among our beliefs, and that we are motivated to maintain consistency in our thoughts, feelings, and behavior. We may seek this consistency among the different components of attitude or between the components and new information we acquire from our environment.

Theory of Cognitive Dissonance. The best known and most widely researched theory of cognitive consistency is the theory of *cognitive dissonance* (Festinger, 1957; Wicklund & Brehm, 1976). Festinger states that a person experiences unpleasant "dissonance" whenever any two cognitive elements are incongruent with (that is, discrepant from) each other. This discomfort pressures us to make the elements consistent or "consonant," so that one follows from the other. Cognitive elements include beliefs, attitudes, values, knowledge, and perceptions of our own behavior or that of others.

The discomfort or tension created by dissonant elements is assumed to be an unpleasant state that we are motivated to reduce in one way or another. We may change one of the elements, add new elements to explain the inconsistency, change our behavior to reduce dissonance, or simply avoid dissonance-producing situations.

One type of dissonance research concerns *the effect of insufficient rewards for counterattitudinal behavior.* The classic study in this area was carried out by Festinger & Carlsmith (1959). Subjects in an experiment were asked to perform a boring task for one hour. At the end of that time, some subjects were paid $1.00 to tell a new subject that the task was very interesting and "lots of fun"; other subejcts were paid $20.00 to tell the same lie; still others were given no such assignment. All subjects then rated how interesting and enjoyable the task was and indicated whether they thought the results had any scientific value.

Subjects who were paid $1.00 produced higher and more positive evaluations of the task than those who were paid $20.00. This finding was congruent with the dissonnace theory prediction: The $1.00 subjects had little external justification for voicing an opinion that was inconsistent with their true feelings of boredom. As a result, they experienced greater dissonance. One way these subjects could reduce their dissonance was to change their attitudes about the task—to actually perceive it and rate it as more interesting and enjoyable. In this way, their attitude would become more consistent with their statement that the task was "lots of fun."

Subjects who were paid $20.00 to lie would have more justification for the lies in that the large incentive was compatible with their behavior. There would be less dissonance and therefore less pressure to overevaluate the task.

This seemingly backward result ("small incentive = large change") became an exciting element of dissonance research that led to numerous studies on the effect of insufficient incentives on a variety of tasks. For example, subjects who were paid less to write essays that were contrary to their expressed attitudes consequently showed more change in their attitudes (e.g., Cohen, 1962).

Decision making in a free-choice situation is another kind of behavior that may trigger dissonance. In a classic study, Jack Brehm (1956) accurately predicted that the effects of making a choice between two attractive alternatives would lead to attitude change that could be attributed to the creation of dissonance. Since one attractive alternative would have to be rejected, its favorable aspects would be dissonant with the decision of having rejected it. Brehm further hypothesized that the reduction of dissonance would occur after the decision was made. By changing their attitudes, the subjects would make the chosen alternative seem more desirable and the rejected alternative seem less desirable. As we will see, this is precisely what happened.

Brehm asked female undergraduate subjects to rate eight different products (a coffee maker, a stopwatch, and so on) on an eight-point scale of desirability. Different subjects were then given a choice between two products. Brehm had preselected products according to their relative desirability in order to arouse varying degrees of dissonance among the subjects. The subjects then rated all eight products again.

In the evaluations made *after* the choice, the ratings were higher for the chosen product and lower for the rejected alternative—a clear case of dissonance reduction. Brehm also found that the more equal the two alternatives were in the ratings before the choice, the greater was the degree of dissonance and the amount of change of attitudes.

These results have been duplicated in a variety of situations, including the $2.00 betting window at a racetrack. It was demonstrated that bettors have more confidence in their chosen horse's performance *after* they've put their money down than when they are waiting in line with their choice in mind (Knox & Inkster, 1968).

Self-Perception Theory. A challenge to dissonance theory comes from *self-perception theory* (Bem, 1967, 1970, 1972). Bem maintains that we do not need to infer an internal state of cognitive dissonance to explain the kinds of behaviors and other results that have been documented in the various studies. He contends that people simply observe behavior and the conditions in which it occurs, then infer their attitudes from it.

In Bem's simulations of the classic cognitive dissonance experiments, observers were given descriptions of the experimental procedures, then asked to judge the attitude of the various groups of subjects. The observers had no trouble predicting the actual outcome of the experiments. (In the Festinger and Carlsmith experiment, for example, observers accurately predicted the greater attitude change in the $1.00 condition.) Bem provided an alternative to these findings by stating that in actual situations we are simply our own observer, and we form an attitude in accordance with our self-perceptions: a subject in the Festinger and Carlsmith experiment might have said to himself, "If I said this for only one dollar, I must really believe it!"

In the controversy between dissonance theory and self-perception theory, there is also the question of whether the subject is aware of his or her own initial attitude. Dissonance supporters say that the subject *is* aware and that therefore the behavior creates dissonance. Supporters of self-perception theory maintain that the subject is not aware until she or he behaves. These controversies have led to attempts at experiments testing the competing explanations, but the results are inconsistent. The important point, however, is that these propositions regarding the relationships between attitudes and behavior can help increase our awareness of possible influences and potential strategies for changing attitudes in the real world. An important contemporary instance of this is the use of cognitive dissonance theory to understand the issues surrounding school desegregation (e.g., Brehm & Cohen, 1962) (see Chapter 11).

Balance Theory. One last consistency theory that deserves mention is *balance theory,* developed by Fritz Heider (1958) and extended by Theodore Newcomb (1961). Heider assumes that we are motivated to maintain a "balanced" state of consistent relationships in our perceptions and knowledge of other people and social objects. The perceived connections or bonds among people may be positive or negative, and balance exists when the bonds are in agreement. An illustration of this is a triadic relationship involving you, another person (your roommate, for instance), and an attitudinal object such as rock music. A balanced state exists if you both love the object or both hate it. However, if you hate rock music and your roommate loves it, a state of imbalance would exist in your cognitions (not to mention a state of conflict when the music is played).

Newcomb's adaptation of Heider's theory focuses on interpersonal attraction or rejection between two people (*A* and *B*) in relation to a third person or some other object (*X*) that can be liked or disliked (see Figure 2.2). When all perceived bonds, or orientations, are positive, a balanced state of *symmetry* exists. For example, John and Cathy like each other and they both enjoy surfing. But symmetry also exists when two bonds are negative and one is positive: Cathy dislikes surfing *and* John—the beach bum of the century. Imbalance, however, can occur through a number of combinations. *A* and *B* may both like *X*, but not each other; or *A* and *B* may like each other, but not *X*. The important principle is this: when inconsistency is present, there will usually be attempts to somehow reduce the accompanying state of tension, through such mechanisms as changing your attitude toward *X*, or stopping interaction with *B*. The application of balance theory to interpersonal attraction will be noted again in Chapter 6.

Overview of Attitudes and Behavior. The flowchart in Figure 2.3, adapted from a model developed by Calder and Ross (1976), summarizes our information about attitudes, behavior, and cognitive consistency. It illustrates the following points:

1. A person's attitudes develop from the interaction between the person and past and present environmental conditions.
2. Through cognitive processes of integration and consistency, attitudes are formed into the components of beliefs, feelings, and predispositions to behave.
3. Once an attitude is formed, it may directly affect overt behavior.
4. There are, however, many other person and environmental variables that enter simultaneously to determine how a person behaves.

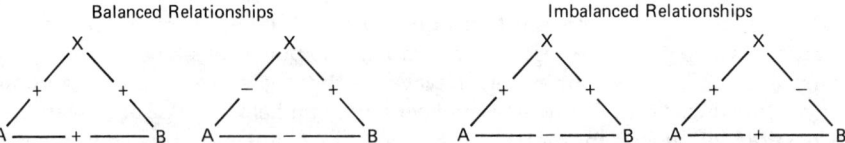

Figure 2.2   Examples of Balanced and Imbalanced Relationships According to Balance Theory.

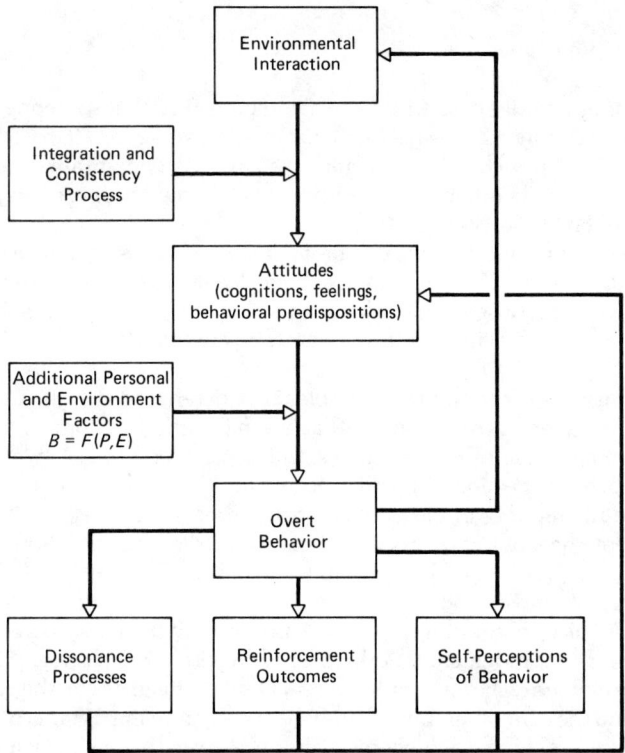

Figure 2.3   Overview of Attitudinal Processes.
Source: Calder & Ross (1976).

5. Once a behavior is expressed, a number of outcomes are possible.
6. Dissonance processes may be stimulated, with outcomes fed back into existing attitudes; this results in attitude change.
7. The reinforcement outcomes of overt behavior are similarly fed back into the attitudinal system in ways that may support or detract from existing attitudes.
8. Self-perception of our behavior may feed back into our cognitive awareness in such a way that we then infer out attitude from our behavior.
9. Our behavior produces effects on the existing environment; these effects then recycle into the attitude-change process. In this way, a self-fulfilling prophecy may be established. (For example, if the hostility we feel toward another person shows in our behavior—a facial expression, perhaps—this may trigger antagonistic behavior on the part of the other person. In turn, we will then perceive this effect on our environment as supporting our initial attitude—which may then become even more negative.)

This overview of attitudinal processes clearly points out their complexity. We must take this complexity into account when we think of applications of attitude theories in real-world settings. And the complexity plainly shows how much work remains to be done.

Psychological Reactance

There have undoubtedly been times when you perceived that someone was telling you what to do and thereby restricting your freedom of action. If you experienced negative emotions in such a situation and acted in way to maintain or restore your freedom, you were behaving in accordance with the theory of *psychological reactance* (Brehm, 1966, 1976).

This theory assumes that we can best satisfy our needs when we can behave freely and can maintain this freedom of action. When our freedom is threatened or eliminated, we are aroused to do whatever we can to restore it. It is this motivational arousal, this driving force to maintain our freedom, that Brehm calls *reactance.*

The theory also specifies the variables that determine the magnitude of the reactance. If we confidently believe that we have the freedom to choose and behave, the magnitude of our reactance will depend on at least two things: the *importance* of that freedom (the significance of the motives that the freedom satisfies) and the *number* of freedoms that are threatened.

What are the consequences of reactance? Its effects are both subjective (internal, unobservable) and behavioral (external, visible). Since reactance is an internal state, we must infer its existence from a person's attempts to exercise freedom, from physiological tension, or from the way the person modifies his or her perceptions and judgments. A threatened freedom or behavior will often be evaluated more highly. For example, parents tell a little girl that she can't have a candy bar, and the candy bar immediately becomes more important to her. But if a person is forced to behave against his or her will, negative feelings and unfavorable evaluations will result. Behavioral effects of reactance include the actual exercising of the threatened freedom and attempts to attack the threatening agent directly. The child who is denied the candy bar might sneak it from the cupboard or engage in verbal aggression (crying and screaming) toward the parents.

One of the studies demonstrating the effects of reactance did in fact involve children and candy bars. Hammock and Brehm (1966) had children rank the desirability of nine different candy bars. Some were then told that they could choose between two candy bars, thus inducing a sense of freedom. Others were simply told that would receive one of the bars, which the experimenter would choose. However, *all* of the children were then shown their third- and fourth-ranked bars and given the one that was third-ranked. The subjects whose freedom of choice had been eliminated subsequently gave lower rankings of desirability to the bar that was forced upon them and higher rankings to the bar that was denied them. These findings were precisely predicted by reactance theory.

The effects of reactance in a number of different situations have been demonstrated by Brehm and his coworkers. Sensenig and Brehm (1968) demonstrated that telling a person to support a particular side of a social issue led to less positive attitudes on the issue, even when the person initially supported that side. Both laboratory and field studies have shown that attempts to usurp a person's choice lead to the negative effects predicted by reactance. Regan and Brehm (1972), for example, tried to direct and bribe customers in a supermarket to buy a certain brand of bread thus reducing reactance. As a result, these customers bought less of the bread than did shoppers who were simply asked to try it and given just enough money to purchase it.

Theories of Social Exchange

In my social psychology classes, I often tell the students that *reciprocity* is the first law of social behavior: that is, in social interactions we usually get about as much as we give. This simple statement points to the principle of *social exchange* as a major explanation of human interaction. George Homans (1958, 1974) has made a strong case for social exchange as the basic explanation of all *elementary* social behavior—that is, any situation in which two or three individuals influence one another. According to Homans, looking at social behavior as exchange clarifies the relations among at least four areas of theory about human behavior, including behavioral psychology, economics, the dynamics of influence, and the structures of small groups. This suggests that we can see all social systems as fundamentally composed of elementary social behavior—a concept that has generated a number of related theories by Homans and other social psychologists (e.g., Blau, 1964; Thibaut & Kelly, 1959).

Social exchange theories hold that people engage in behavior that is rewarding or reinforcing, as predicted by social learning theory. Since social interaction involves both rewards and costs, we behave in order to maximize our rewards and minimize our costs—a process that produces the most profitable outcome.

Homans's work has produced a list of fundamental propositions:

- His first general proposition (similar to Thorndike's law of effect) states that the more often an action is rewarded, the more likely we are to perform that action again.
- His *stimulus proposition* (reminiscent of the principle of association in learning theory) states that if we are in the presence of stimuli that are similar to stimuli associated with rewarded behavior, we are more likely to repeat that behavior.
- The principle of *satiation* states that the more often a person has received a particular reward, the less valuable the reward becomes.
- The rule of *distributive justice* (an important principle about our perceptions of the rewards and costs involved in social relationships) states that our rewards should be proportional to the costs incurred; the profits that we receive from relationships should be proportional to the investments that we put into them.
- *Rewards* may be any kind of positive reinforcement, but social approval and disapproval are the most basic reinforcers in social relations. *Costs* include not only punishments incurred, but also the cost of lost alternatives—that is, behavior we *could* have engaged in but did not. *Profits are the differences between rewards and costs. Investments* are the characteristics we bring to the situation, as well as our past activities that can be evaluated positively. Taking all of these elements into account, we compare ourselves with others in order to judge whether the rule of distributive justice is being followed in our social relationships.

Thibaut and Kelly (1959) add two important concepts to the theory of social exchange: the *comparison level (CL)* and the *comparison level for alternatives (CLalt)*. CL is a simple standard of evaluation: outcomes above it are pleasing;

outcomes below it are unpleasant. CLalt is the least favorable level of outcome available from alternative relationships.

CLalt is the most important concept: we compare our present profits to it if we are considering leaving a relationship. If our outcomes from a relationship (our profits) drop below our CLalt, either we will be motivated to leave the relationship for one that provides superior outcomes, or we will attempt to change the behavior in the relationship in order to increase our profits. We may, however, stay in an unpleasant relationship (where the outcomes are below CL) if there are no better outcomes available in other relationships. CLalt is therefore a major determinant of whether we continue in a social relationship.

This theory explains that we can become trapped in a relationship if the alternatives are even less desirable or are nonexistent. For example, as difficult as your relations may get with your parents, they are still your *only* parents, and there is no alternative that involves the same natural relationship. The theory also helps explain power imbalance in interpersonal relationships: the person closer to his or her CLalt in a relationship is less dependent and more powerful because he or she could more easily choose to terminate that relationship. Dating relationships, for example, often exhibit this type of inequality, where one partner is more vulnerable to the ending of the relationship than the other.

These basic ideas explain a variety of behaviors in interpersonal and small group situations: why we remain; why and at what point we may leave; why and at what point we attempt to change a relationship (see Chapter 6).

Another phenomenon of interpersonal relationships is status: The individual with the higher status—the one who has more investments to bring to the relationship—will exchange his or her expertise or other investments for deference and dependence on the part of the other person. As long as individuals see that what they are gaining from a relationship is proportional to what they are putting into it, the relationship will continue—that is, the rule of distributive justice will hold. If, for example, you are receiving advice from someone, you will continue the relationship as long as you believe that the degree of deference and dependence you are giving is proportional to the rewards you are receiving.

The basic principles of exchange theory also help us to understand a variety of small group processes. We join groups and conform to group norms to receive social rewards. If we choose to deviate from group norms, we do so either because a deviant behavior is more profitable, or because we can join a different group if our profit drops below our CLalt. Thus, the degree of cohesiveness or togetherness in a group is related to both the value of available rewards and the frequency of reward exchanges in the group and the alternative groups available (see Chapter 7).

In the study of more complex social systems, exchange theorists usually categorize people into groups (labor and management, for example) and then look at exchanges between them. Although this simplification is practical, it reduces the precision and validity of the principles for understanding complex social relations. Exchange theory, therefore, can not stand alone in such studies. Like many areas of social psychology, that of complex social structures requires the integration of a number of concepts from various levels of analysis.

A line of theorizing that bears some resemblance to exchange theory is that of *equity theory* (Adams, 1965; Walster, Walster, & Berscheid, 1978). The questions of "what is fair?" and "what is just?" in social relations lie at the heart of equity theory. Thus we are concerned with whether the rewards we gain are congruent with what we contribute (note the similarity to distributive justice). More importantly, we make this assessment by *comparing* our outcomes with those of other people. If we are doing about the same as others, equity prevails; if not, inequity exists. Inequity is unacceptable for us and for others, regardless of whether we are undercompensated or overcompensated. Inequity is a distressing state (in the same manner as dissonance) and motivates individual and groups to restore and maintain equity. Walster et al. (1978) suggest that equity theory has the potential to become a general theory of social psychology which is applicable to numerous social relationships. It has been successfully used to understand aspects of interpersonal attraction (see Chapter 6) and employee satisfaction in work organizations (see Chapter 9).

Role Theory

The basic idea of *role theory* is a direct contribution from the world of the theater, where actors and actresses perform their roles in ways that meet the expectations of the audience and their fellow players. A *role* can be thought of as the pattern of behavior that we perform when we occupy a particular position in the social system. Right now you are in the role of student. You are expected to attend classes, write papers, take exams, wear certain types of clothes, and have fun in certain ways on the weekend. If you play your role right—in line with others' expectations—there will be compatibility in your social relations. However, if you violate these role expectations—cut all your classes, refuse to write papers, ignore all exams, wear a tuxedo or evening gown all the time, and have fun reading your textbooks at parties—then you will run into conflict in your relations with others and with social institutions.

The concept of role is an extremely useful bridge between the individual and the group and between the levels of personaity and culture, because it is an *integrating* concept (Sarbin & Allen, 1968; Secord & Backman, 1974); it links the individual to more complex levels of social functioning (interpersonal relationships, roles in groups, in organizations, and so on). Work on role theory, therefore, is a highly interdisciplinary effort within social science, with contributions by psychologists, sociologists, and anthropologists.

Role concepts are applicable to a wide range of study areas, including interpersonal attraction, leadership, child development, family dynamics, group decision making, and socialization. Because of the unusual flexibility and generalized use of role concepts, there is a considerable amount of confusion in role theory, which is largely due to the use of the same words for different phenomena (Shaw & Costanzo, 1970). We should therefore look at role theory in its most basic principles.

The linkage between the concept of role and the social system is the idea of *role position*—the category or grouping of people who exhibit common attributes and behavior and who are subject to similar reactions from others. Each role position is associated with certain *role expectations*—that is, beliefs about appropriate behaviors, obligations, rights, and privileges that are assigned to the role position. Secord and Backman (1974) point out that we expect a person in a given role to behave in a prescribed manner and that we believe that the person *should* behave that way. In this way, role expectations become a conceptual bridge between role behavior and social structure: they link the person to his or her position in the social system (Sarbin & Allen, 1968).

Role expectations may be held by a very large or a very limited number of people within a society. If, for example, I told you that my main occupational role was that of professor, you would understand the appropriate behavior and expectations related to that position in the social system of the university. On the other hand, if I told you that during summer holidays I worked on an engineering project and once performed the role of gravel-checker, you would probably wonder what I was talking about. However, if you were among the limited number of people in the construction industry, particularly those working with sand and gravel, you would know all about the role of gravel-checker and the appropriate expectations related to it. You would know that it was my responsibility to observe and record all gravel-unloading operations and to have the truck driver initial a notation that the gravel had been delivered. Obviously this role must be performed satisfactorily for the particular system to function effectively. Thus my role behavior consisted of actions relevant to my role expectations.

Sarbin and Allen (1968) use the term *role enactment*, rather than role playing, in order to avoid any connotation of sham or phoniness in role behavior. Role behavior must occur within certain limits; however, there is flexibility in role enactment since each individual brings unique attributes to a situation, thus resulting in somewhat different behavior (the interaction equation holds). Role enactment is of course influenced by many factors: the clarity of the expectations, the degree of consensus on the expectations, the skills that the person brings to the role, and the degree of compatibility between self and role (Sarbin & Allen, 1968).

To add a final complement to role theory, Biddle and Thomas (1966) provide two additional terms that expand the normative quality of role expectations. *Role evaluation* refers to the expression of approval or disapproval of role behavior; *role sanction* is behavior on the part of others designed to influence role behavior.

All of these contributions to role theory bring us closer to understanding the dynamic complexity of ongoing social systems.

As you are aware from your own experience, each of us has *multiple roles* that we enact in our social system. This can be demonstrated through an exercise, often used in human relations workshops, called the "Who am I?" technique. As a participant in such workshops, you would be asked to list on separate cards your answers to the question "Who am I?" For example, you might write down terms such as *student, daughter or son, friend, musician,* and *community volunteer.* You would then be asked to begin deleting cards, and to note the order in which you do so. The purpose of this process is to make you aware of the multiple roles you enact and of the priorities that you give them. You would also note that all of your roles exist only *in relation to other roles.* For example, your family role is linked to other positions within the family (the role of parent only has meaning in relation to the role of child). Your occupational or institutional role only has meaning in relation to other roles in that social setting (a supervisor must have subordinates in order to supervise).

The idea of role is truly a social concept. The people who play complementary roles within your social system are your *role partners;* together, your role and theirs constitute a *role set.* Their expectations about appropriate role behavior, both for your role and theirs, are extremely important determinants of how you and they interrelate. (See Chapter 9.)

The complexity induced by having multiple roles and a variety of complementary roles sometimes induces *role strain* or *role conflict.* Role conflict is usually experienced by the individual through negative feelings—guilt, embarrassment, shame, and so on—and is observed within the social system as interpersonal conflict and an inability of the system to meet its goals (Secord & Backman, 1974).

There are different types of role conflict. *Person-role conflict* is strain or inconsistency between individual characteristics, such as values and beliefs, and the role behavior expected of the individual. For example, many young men who chose the role of conscientious objector during the Vietnam War were in considerable person-role conflict. That conflict was between their individual values of pacifism and the expectations relating to the role of a good citizen.

Interrole conflict occurs when a person holds two or more positions that require contradictory role enactment. For example, many parents of conscientious objectors may have found themselves experiencing incompatibility between the role expectations of parent and the role expectations of United States citizen.

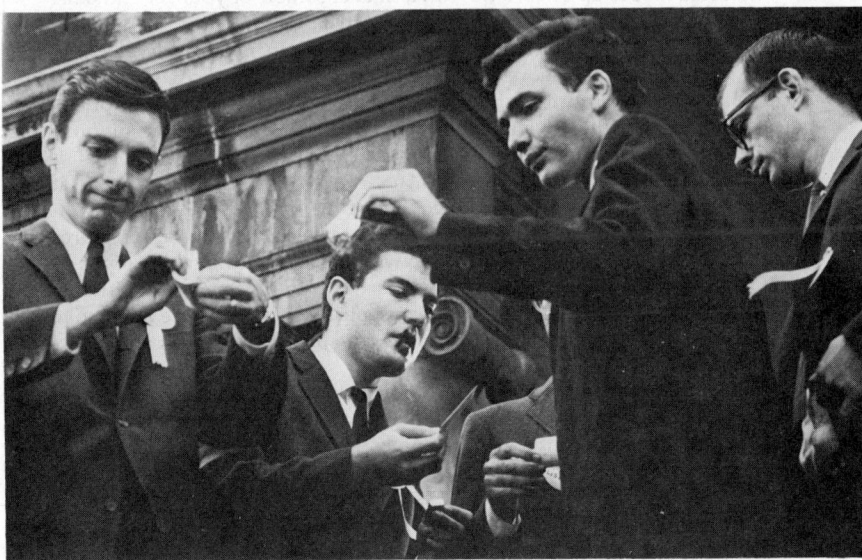

Many young men who chose the role of conscientious objector during the Vietnam War were in considerable person-role conflict. The conflict was between their individual values of pacifism and the expectations relating to the role of a good citizen. *(Hiroji Kubota)*

Their obligation toward their country was in conflict with their obligation toward their sons.

In *intrarole conflict*, different role expectations are held by two or more partners or groups. The role actor is faced with conflicting role expectations about how one should behave in that role. For example, your friends might expect you to study hard for two weeks before final exams, but to goof off the rest of the time. Your professors might expect you to study ten hours a day, except on Sunday. Your parents might expect you to spend every weekend with them. How to respond to such conflicting role expectations is one of the greatest challenges of social life. An interesting case study of role conflict among Roman Catholic priests is presented in Box 2.4.

Box 2.4   FOCUS ON RESEARCH
Role Conflict in the Priesthood

As society changes, social institutions and the roles within them are subject to differing expectations that are often a source of conflict and tension. Mary Ellen Reilley, a sociologist at the University of Rhode Island, became interested in sources of role conflict among Roman Catholic priests. Increasing resignations from the priesthood, withdrawals from seminaries, and internal disagreements within the clergy all seemed to indicate a difficult time for priests in American society.

To study this issue, Reilley mailed questionnaires to a large number of priests and conducted follow-up interviews with a smaller sample of younger and older clergy. She found clear differences between the two age groupings, the younger priests consistently experiencing greater role conflict than older clergy. First, younger priests were much more concerned about both a lack of communication and problems with authority within the church. Second, the younger priests indicated less agreement with church policy on such important issues as divorce, birth control, and celibacy of the priesthood. These findings documented significant sources of person-role conflict in which the views of the individual were at variance with the institutional policies governing the role.

Intrarole conflict resulting from differing role expectations was also a source of tension for the priests. Most noticeable were the conflicting expectations of young people and old people, including parishioners, priests, and bishops. Younger members of the church tended to support a socially aware and active clergy, whereas older members wanted priests who provided comfort and spiritual guidance.

While most priests acknowledged role conflict, it did not seem to interfere seriously with their role performance. They used a variety of coping strategies to reduce the impact of the conflict. For example, many priests adjusted their role behavior according to the demands of the particular group with which they were interacting. Reilley concluded that if priests are given the freedom to practice their roles as they interpret them, role conflicts are not likely to significantly impede their role performance.

Source: Reilley, M. E. A case study of role conflict: Roman Catholic priests. *Human Relations*, 1978, 31, 77–90.

To reduce role conflict, society has developed mechanisms for *role socialization* and for *role negotiation* between the actor and the actor's partners. Role socialization—learning what is appropriate behavior in any given case—produces common role expectations, thereby preventing incompatibility. As a student, for example, you learn to sit quietly, write neatly, and not to openly criticize what the teacher does. Role negotiation maintains compatibility among expectations through the process of bargaining. Role partners negotiate over which behaviors are or are not appropriate. This often takes place subtly, rather than through direct negotiation. For example, one spouse forgets to take out the garbage one day, so the other does it. This activity then becomes mutually shared rather than being solely the domain of one role partner.

Even a brief review of role theory clearly demonstrates its usefulness in understanding a great part of social behavior. Because of its implicit compatibility with the basic interaction approach, and its function as a link between a variety of levels, role theory is a fundamental part of social psychology. It is especially useful in understanding individual behavior in social organizations (see Chapter 9), including educational institutions (see Chapter 15).

Field Theory

Field theory was developed by Kurt Lewin as a *means of representing the psychological and social forces that interact to determine individual behavior* (Lewin, 1951; Shaw & Costanzo, 1970). The central concept of field theory is the *life space* (*LS*)—the constellation of determining factors in both the individual and the environment. The behavior of an individual (*B*) could then be seen as a function (*f*) of the life space, which included both person (*P*) and environmental forces (*E*). Or, in terms of the interaction equation: $B = f(LS)$. For example, your life space is composed of all the motives, habits, attitudes, and so on, that are part of your unique personality, plus all of the social pressures (norms, role expectations, laws) to which you are subject.

The life space is divided into different regions or life spheres, such as family and occupation (see Figure 2.4a). The life space is viewed as one *field*—a totality of coexisting and mutually interdependent facts; it is from this concept that field theory draws its name. *Behavior* is regarded as movement within the life space that results from *forces*—that is, anything that can cause change.

Particularly important are *driving forces* and *restraining forces*, which push for and against movement toward a goal, respectively. Opposition between forces leads to a state of tension in the affected goal region. For example, Figure 2.4b depicts some of the forces that might have affected your decision (i.e., behavior) to attend college, for instance, a positive goal represented in the field of forces by G+. Your personal aspirations, family preferences, and the norms of your friendship group might have all been pushing toward the goals as driving forces. However, a major restraining force might have been the rewards (financial and otherwise) of taking a job right after finishing high school. These positive and negative forces combine to determine the ultimate behavior. Lewin developed a technique known as *force-field analysis* to define and assess these forces as an aid in practical decision making and problem solving (see Chapter 4).

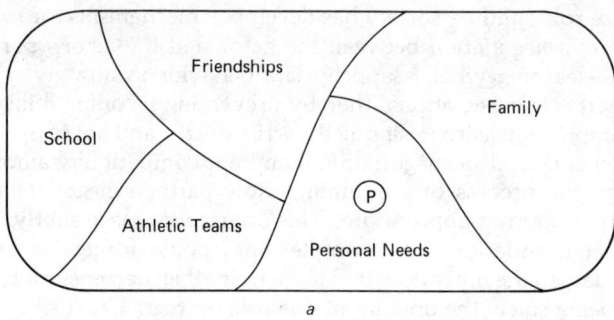

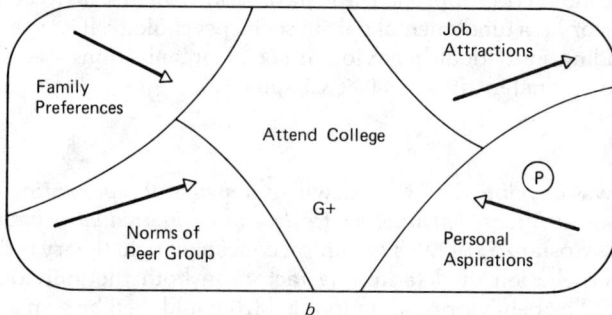

Figure 2.4   Lewin's Field Theory, *a*, Sample Space; *b*, Sample Force Field.
Source: Lewin (1951).

Field theory is important in social psychology because it is a basic approach to social science and has had considerable impact on it (Cartwright, 1951; Deutsch, 1968). The important qualities of field theory include:

- It is an empirical theory that uses a small number of constructs to develop general laws of behavior.
- It stresses the interaction of the person and the environment.
- It is dynamic through its study of forces and the process of change.
- It is phenomenological in that the field is defined from the point of view of the actor.
- It follows the systems approach by describing the whole field and then analyzing it into parts.
- It stresses present, here-and-now forces in determining behavior, rather than past experiences.

Lewin applied field theory to a variety of situations including interpersonal conflict (e.g., making decisions) and aggressive behavior in groups (see Box 2.5). Even though the basic concepts of field theory are not being directly studied in contemporary research, *the underlying qualities have significantly altered the history and character of social psychology.*

Box 2.5 FOCUS ON THEORY
Conflict in the Life Space

Kurt Lewin was especially interested in explaining real-life behavior through the application of field theory. Personal conflict was one phenomenon that could be better understood by seeing behavior as a function of the total psychological field of the individual. Lewin defined conflict as a situation in which forces acting on a person are opposite in direction and about equal in strength.

Driving forces can result in three different types of conflict. First, the person may be located between two positive valences or goals—we usually call this a choice between mutually exclusive positive alternatives. (A girl cannot go on a picnic with her family and play basketball with her friends at the same time.) This is known as approach-approach conflict. Second, conflict can result from being caught between two negative valences—again a choice situation. (You can decide to study for that midterm exam or bear the consequences of failing). This is avoidance-avoidance conflict. Third, a person may be in conflict between a positive and negative valence, both of which lie in the same direction in the life space. (A reward may be offered to a boy for doing a disagreeable task such as cleaning up his room.) This is approach-avoidance conflict.

Lewin also discussed conflict between driving and restraining forces. The most common situation occurs when barriers in the life space prevent a person from reaching a goal. (The child wants a cookie, but cannot reach the jar on the top shelf of the cupboard.) In another situation, the person is in the region of a negative valence, but barriers prevent him or her from leaving. (The child may have had enough of school for one day, but the rules and the teacher do not allow the child to leave until the bell rings.)

Conflict involves tension. In all of these situations the person searches for a solution that resolves in the tension. Lewin theorized about what the most likely reactions would be in the different types of conflict situations. For example, in the case of two negative valences (avoidance-avoidance conflict), there is a tendency to avoid both negative goals by withdrawing from the situation altogether. (You decide you neither want to study nor fail the exam. You subsequently drop the class or quit school.) Lewin's theroretical analysis has stimulated a considerable amount of research on the topic of personal conflict.

Source: Lewin, K. *Field theory in social sciences.* New York: Harper & Row, 1951.

Summary

Theories in social psychology are abstract representations of social reality describing the relationships among phenomena. Empirical theories are based on observation and can be verified by the scientific method. Theories serve as both a goal and a tool: they are a means of summarizing and organizing information, and they go beyond existing information to provide insights and predictions.

Theories are developed through either induction or deduction. Induction conceptualizes our observations of phenomena into theoretical concepts. Through deduction, or logical reasoning based on theory, we can make further predictions about relationships among phenomena that can be tested by observation or experiment.

Social perception is the process of experiencing the world through the senses in situations where other people are either directly or indirectly involved. Social perception is selective: it involves a filtering process wherein we sometimes perceive what we both expect to and want to perceive. Social perception can involve distortion: our expectations and motives modify what we perceive. Impression formation is based on a number of component traits, and is influenced more by central traits than by peripheral ones. Attribution theory studies how individuals make causal explanations regarding the behavior of other people.

Social motives are consistent internal conditions that produce behavior. Maslow has postulated a hierarchy of human needs, ranging from the physiological through the esteem needs to the final need for self-actualization. McClelland has studied the needs for achievement, affiliation, and power, and has related these motives to other variables of social behavior.

Social learning is any change in behavior that comes about as a result of an experience in which other people are involved. Positive reinforcement is any condition whose presence increases the probability that a preceding behavior will be repeated. Negative reinforcement is the withdrawal of an aversive stimulus. Social reinforcement has clear effects on behaviors such as verbal expression. Observational learning or modeling may have a number of different effects, including response acquisition, disinhibition or inhibition, and response facilitation.

Socialization is the process through which the individual acquires the knowledge, skills, and attitudes necessary for successful participation in society. Socialization continues beyond the family setting throughout life in a variety of contexts. The socialization of sex differences can be explained through a social learning approach that emphasizes the process of sex-typing.

An attitude is a predisposition to respond to and evaluate a social object in a consistently favorable or unfavorable way. Attitudes are usually seen as having three components: the cognitive, the affective, and the behavioral.

The relationship between attitude and behavior is not one of direct correspondence since there are many other factors involved in determining behavior. The realtionship is one of mutual influence.

Theories of cognitive consistency assume that people are motivated to maintain congruence in their thinking, feeling, and behaving. The theory of cognitive dissonance postulates that a person experiences dissonance when any two cognitive elements are discrepant with each other. This motivates the person to reduce the dissonance by changing an attitude, changing behavior, or some other mechanism. Cognitive dissonance theory has been challenged by the theory of self-perception.

The theory of psychological reactance assumes that a person is motivated to restore a freedom that has been eliminated or threatened. The consequences of reactance involve both subjective effects such as a more positive attitude toward a restricted object and behavioral effects such as increased attempts to exercise the freedom.

Theories of social exchange built on the postulate of reciprocity in interpersonal relations and state that individuals will behave to obtain the most profitable outcome from their relationships with others. The rule of distributive justice holds that our profits from social relationships should be proportional to our investments. The concepts of comparison level and comparison level for alternatives help us understand the continuation and termination of social relationships. Equity theory suggests that, through comparisons with other people, we judge whether the rewards we receive are worth the input we contribute.

Role theory is a direct transfer from the stage, where actors and actresses perform roles. A role is the pattern of behavior that a person performs when occupying a particular position in the social system. Thus, the concept provides integration between the individual and other levels of analysis.

Field theory is a means of representing the psychological and social forces that interact to determine individual behavior. The life space is the psychological field in which driving and restraining forces act to cause movement toward and away from goals. The approach of field theory is empirical, interactive, dynamic, phenomenological, systemic, and contemporary and has significantly affected the character of social psychology.

Further Readings

Bandura, A. *Social learning theory.* Englewood Cliffs, N.J.: Prentice-Hall, 1977.

Calder, B. J. & Ross, M. Attitudes: Theories and issues. In J. W. Thibaut, J. T. Spence & R. C. Carson (Eds.), *Contemporary topics in social psychology.* Morristown, N.J.: General Learning Press, 1976.

Goffman, E. *Asylums: Essays on the social situation of mental patients and other inmates.* Garden City, N.J.: Anchor Books, 1961.

Homans, G. C. *Social behavior: Its elementary forms* (rev. ed.). New York: Harcourt Brace Jovanovich, 1974.

Maslow, A. H. *Motivation and personality* (2nd ed.). New York: Harper & Row, 1970.

Matlin, M. W. & Stang, D. J. *The Pollyanna principle: Selectivity in language, memory and thought.* New York: Schenkman, 1978.

Shaw, M. E. & Costanzo, P. R. *Theories of social psychology.* New York: McGraw-Hill, 1970.

CHAPTER OUTLINE

TYPES OF SOCIAL RESEARCH
Scientific Method
Descriptive Research
Correlational Research
Experimental Research
Correlational vs. Experimental Research
Action Research
Evaluation Research
Values and Ethics in Social Research
Obligations to Participants
Costs vs. Benefits

METHODS OF SOCIAL RESEARCH
Observational Methods
Content Analysis
Interviewing
Self-Report Measures
Questionnaires
Rating Scale
Sociometric Techniques
Attitude Scale
Psychological Tests
Response Sets
Survey Methods
Laboratory Experimentation
Validity
Games and Simulation
Field Experimentation and Quasi-Experimental Design
Field Experiment
Natural Experiment
Quasi-Experimental Design

SUMMARY

FURTHER READINGS

Research Methods in Social Psychology

TYPES OF SOCIAL RESEARCH

My father was a farmer by choice and a jack-of-all-trades by necessity. When I was a boy I would sit in his woodworking shop and watch as he turned out a variety of items ranging from cabinets and cupboards to lawn chairs and picture frames. First, he would design what he wanted to produce, choose quality materials appropriate to the overall design, and select the appropriate tools and methods. Then he would follow a careful sequence of steps to produce a useful product.

Years later as I took courses in personality assessment, measurement theory, and research methods, it became clear to me how important it is to select the proper tool or method for a particular task. This seems to be true whether you are building a lawn chair, constructing a psychological test, or designing a research project to answer an important question.

The ability and the systematic approach usually associated with craftspersons are to me the most important tools that social scientists have for learning about the world. To be able to create or synthesize new ideas, and to be able to follow through in testing and applying those ideas skillfully—this is the essence of the research process. It is important to study social reality in a rigorous manner so that our findings accurately represent the world as it is.

Scientific Method

The term *scientific method* refers to the sequence of steps that scientists follow to learn more about the world. This process for learning is particularly applicable to social psychology: our discipline is characterized as much by its scientific approach and methods of gaining knowledge as it is by the areas of content that it studies. The areas of human experience that we study are not, after all, anything new. Rather, they have been the cause of human concern and reflection for a long time. Therefore, social psychology is defined as a contemporary social science not simply by *what* we study but *how* we study it.

The basis of the scientific method lies in *empiricism*. This philosophical approach maintains that knowledge is generated through observation and experience—that is, by way of the senses. It is the opposite of such nonempirical methods of acquiring information as intuition, revelation, and simple reasoning.

Subjective empiricism involves relying upon our raw experience of sensing the world. The information obtained is then combined with reasoning, permitting us to draw conclusions about the world. For example, Sigmund Freud, the founder of psychoanalysis, combined logical reasoning with his observations of patients in psychotherapy to develop some very influential ideas about the functioning of human personality.

Objective empiricism, on the other hand, uses refined experience to generate knowledge about the world. This is done by using a variety of sensing and measuring devices and by looking for consensus among observers who are following the same rules of acquiring information. For example, suppose that you have a hunch that the male psychology majors in your psychology class wear their hair longer than their cohorts in your chemistry class. You also suspect that shorter hair is related to the more conservative political attitudes of natural science majors, who predominate in the chemistry class. Your first step is simply to document your hunch about hair length. Accordingly, you enlist the aid of two friends and train them to categorize hair length as long, medium, and short. Then, you station one friend at the entrance to each class (the classes are equal in size and have the same number of male students) and ask them both to record the hair length of every male student who walks in. (You must not tell them of your hunch since doing so could bias their ratings.) You then check the reliability of the ratings by determining whether they agree almost all the time on which student is placed in which category. Finally, for both classes, you count the number of students in each category. You find that there is little difference between the hair length of male students in the psychology class and that of those in the chemistry class. Having followed a systematic procedure, you can now see that your raw experience, and possibly the reasoning on which it was based, was indeed incorrect. In this way, objective empiricism helps us to gain a more accurate picture of social reality.

The combination of objective empiricism with logical reasoning is called *logical positivism*— which stipulates that meaningful knowledge is developed and verified through observation and experiment. For example, let us suppose that your hypothesis about hair length and college major had proven correct. You might then examine the relationship between male hair length and political attitude. As a fair experiment, you might circulate a petition on a controversial issue, such as gun control, and compare the rates of support for gun control among groups that differed in hair length. The results would help confirm or disconfirm your initial reasoning about the relationship among the different variables. Logical positivism calls for clear and direct connections between the empirical world of phenomena and the conceptual world of theories. Social psychology has for the most part assumed the approach of logical positivism in its study of social behavior. At the same time, the discipline has assumed a stance of *determinism*. This view holds that social behavior is determined or caused by a variety of factors that are open to empirical investigation. For example, that you are enrolled in a social psychology course is not simply a chance occurrence, but is due to a host of variables that affected your choice of courses. Your attitudes, career aspirations, the norms of your friendship group, a counselor's suggestions, the cost of the textbook—all of these factors might have helped determine your social behavior in this instance. The methods outlined in this chapter are based on both empiricism and determinism.

A great deal of social-psychological research and practice springs from intuition and is parented by common sense—that is, from the distilled wisdom of experience. But whereas common sense offers simple solutions to complex problems, social psychology attempts to specify the conditions under which general principles hold true. A useful process is to get our hunches from experience and common sense, and then to test these hunches systematically and rigorously using the methodology of science.

The sequence of steps of the scientific method used in social psychology is relatively straightforward. First, we must define a question or pose a problem in a way that is answerable or solvable. At this stage, our personal interests, values, and creativity come into play. We formulate the question of interest in the form of a *hypothesis*, which is a statement describing the relationship between two or more variables. For example, we could adapt a hypothesis from the work of Triplett (1897): a person runs faster in the presence of another than when alone.

The second step is to design a research procedure to collect information relevant to the hypothesis. Being able to design a study that will *clearly* answer the question or solve the problem is a skill that is a hallmark of the social scientist. For example, we could set up an experiment in which several persons are tested in repeated trials in several situations: running alone, pacing but not competing with another person, and running a race with others.

The third step is to collect the information following the established rules of science. Thus, in our example, we measure each person's running speed using the same timer and under identical conditions (amount of rest, time of day, wind, location) in each trial. The results we obtain should be verifiable by anyone who follows the same procedures under the same conditions. Taken to the extreme, this principle leads to the approach of *operationism:* only propositions based on operations that are public and repeatable are admissible as scientific evidence (Stevens, 1963). In any event, it is the wise social scientist who follows the adage "Do not fool thyself too much" (Agnew & Pike, 1978).

The final step of the scientific method is to interpret the information, drawing conclusions in order to answer the original question. Thus, if our data indicate that in 88 percent of the trials the fastest running speeds occurred when the individual ran in a race, we conclude that competition increases a person's speed.

The scientific process has its limitations. It is certainly not an endeavor of perfection in which scientists never disagree and never resist new findings. In recent years, there has been increasing concern that the logical-positivist approach has been pushed too far in psychology and social psychology. Some believe that this denies the inherent subjectivity of science, separates scientists from their own experience and humanity, and treats individuals as objects rather than as persons. The emerging view is that science is a very complex and at the same time a very human process (Agnew & Pike, 1978). Out of this complexity and a variety of approaches, we hope to develop a discipline that is adequate to human behavior rather than to any one restricted view of science (Koch, 1959).

Descriptive Research

Descriptive research, the most basic type of social research, documents social reality by looking at "what is." It may describe the characteristics of events in the social world, or count the frequency of those events. It studies such events as the utilization of health services, the major types of criminal offenses, or the rate of family breakdown. In this process, social psychologists might observe a situation and then record their reactions or ask other people for their observations and reactions. For example, a social psychologist might observe that persons of a particular age group tend not to use a particular type of health care facility. This involves a straightforward description of social reality without looking for relationships among variables or intervening in a social situation.

To achieve its goals, descriptive research uses such methods as observation, interviews, survey research, and self-reports. In our example, the social psychologist might consult a health care facility's patient records, conduct interviews with users and nonusers of the facility, and so forth. Descriptive research also uses the case study—an intensive description of a particular person, group, or organization—with the ultimate intention of generalizing the findings to other, similar cases.

The principal tools of descriptive research are measuring instruments that are

"What do you mean you're undecided?"

both reliable and valid. A *reliable* measuring instrument gives us a consistent measure of the characteristic being assessed. The consistency may be analyzed within the same instrument, across measurements taken at different times, or across measurements taken by different observers or raters. A *valid* measuring instrument measures what it is supposed to measure. Although validity is difficult

Box 3.1   FOCUS ON RESEARCH
The Reliability and Validity of Measurement

Measurement in the natural sciences often seems simple because so many physical characteristics are obvious. Take length, for example. It's easy to see. We use a rule or some other measuring instrument to quantify length into some meaningful units—such as feet and inches or meters and centimeters. Psychological and social qualities, however, are not so easily quantified. How do we measure the need for achievement, or sociability or perceptions of organizational climate? We need to be just as concerned about certain properties of our measuring instruments as are the natural sciences. Two of these properties are reliability and validity.

Reliability refers to the consistency and stability of measurement. A reliable measure will be consistent within itself (the inch from "2" to "3" on the rules is the same as the inch from "9" to "10"). It will produce the same measurement at different times (your waist is 27 inches on Friday and also the following Monday—unless, of course, you overeat on Saturday and Sunday.

In the social sciences, reliability is more complex. Different methods have been developed to gauge consistency and stability. One method, for example, is to rate persons on some variable using a rating scale—to assure reliability, two different raters would perform ratings using the same scale. Another method is to assess the stability of a measurement over time. Thus, the same group of people is tested at different times using the same testing instrument, and the degree of relationship between their scores is computed. The average degree of relationship is expressed in a reliability coefficient between 0 and 1.00. The closer the reliability coefficient to 1.00, the greater the stability of the instrument. Reliability coefficients above 0.80 are usually required for research work in social psychology.

A valid instrument is one that measures what it is intended to measure. A ruler obviously measures length. Again, in the social sciences validity is more complex. It is assessed in three different ways: content, predictive, and construct validity.

Content validity is the adequacy or representativeness with which the items sample a domain of content. A valid exam in social psychology, for example, would provide a representative selection of the topics that were covered in the course. *Predictive validity* is the ability of a measure to estimate some important form of behavior. For example, a scholastic aptitude test used to select students for college should accurately predict successful performance in college. *Construct validity* is the degree to which an instrument adequately measures a theoretically important variable or construct. Relationships among many different variables, as specified by theories, must be studied to assess this more complex type of validity. Validity is not an all-or-none quality, but is slowly assessed through a cumulating series of studies.

Source: Nunally, J. C. *Psychometric theory* (2nd ed.). New York: McGraw-Hill, 1978.

to establish, it can be assessed through such methods as agreement with other reliable measuring instruments designed to assess the same characteristic. The goal of descriptive research is to provide a reliable and valid picture of social reality. However, sometimes it is used in an exploratory fashion to paint an initial picture. Such exploratory research can then be followed up by more detailed documentation, or by the formation of specific hypotheses for further research. The characteristics of the reliability and the validity of measurement are described in Box 3.1.

An example of descriptive research is provided by Cox (1970) in his study of the stereotyping of blacks and whites. Using a method developed by Shuey, King & Griffith (1953), Cox assessed the occupational role of black and white adults portrayed in advertisements in a number of popular American magazines published in 1949–1950 and in 1967–1968. He used two categories to describe the occupational roles: (1) "above-skilled labor," which included such occupations as businessman, professional athlete, and clerical worker, and (2) "below-skilled labor," which included such occupations as maid, servant, and farmer.

The results of the study were striking, as shown in Figure 3.1. In 1949–1950, only 6.1 percent of blacks in the advertisements were coded as above-skilled labor, contrasted with 93.4 percent of whites in the advertisements. In 1967–1968, however, 71 percent of blacks in the advertisements were in the higher occupational category, whereas the rate for whites remained about the same. The below-skilled labor category showed similar results: the proportion of blacks coded as below-skilled shifted from 93.9 percent in 1949–1950 to 28.7 percent in 1967–1968. By comparison, the percentage of whites portrayed in the lower occupational category was less than 10 percent in both samples.

As a result of his research, Cox provided some support for the general

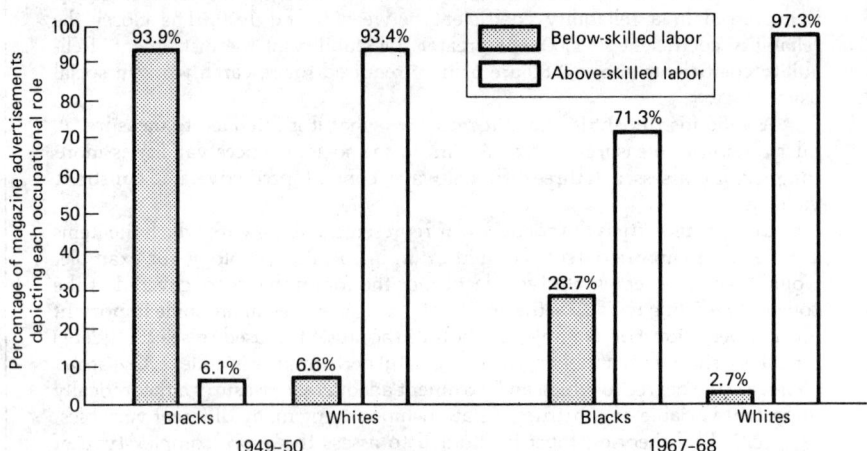

Figure 3.1   Occupational Roles of Blacks and Whites in Magazine Advertisements: 1949 versus 1967.
Source: Cox (1968).

impression that blacks are being more readily accepted into higher occupational categories. As his study illustrates, descriptive research allows us to check out our impressions of what exists in the social world—"what is"—in a rigorous and detailed fashion.

Correlational Research

Correlational research goes beyond descriptive research to describe "what goes with what." It is concerned with studying whether or not certain factors or variables are related to one another. If the variables are related, the next step is to determine how. For example, if increases in one variable are shown to be associated with increases in another, then there is a *positive correlation* between the two variables. On the other hand, if increases in one variable are shown to be associated with decreases in another, then there is a *negative correlation* between the two variables. (See Box 3.2 for a discussion of methods of correlation.)

A classic example of correlational research in social psychology is the study of the authoritarian personality by Adorno, Frenkel-Brunswick, Levinson, and Sanford (1950). (An authoritarian personality is one which demands of others unquestioning submission to authority.) The investigators were interested in the degree to which the authoritarian personality is related to ethnic prejudice and to political and economic conservatism. Attitude scales that measured all these elements were administered to a large sample of people with varying backgrounds. Then all the scores were correlated to see if the variables were related. As predicted, all correlations were positive. The researchers concluded that individuals with authoritarian personalities tend to exhibit greater ethnic prejudice and political-economic conservatism. (see Chapter 5).

The relationship established between any two variables may be due to the influence of a third, underlying variable (Crano & Brewer, 1973). In the study of authoritarian personality, for example, an anti-Semitism scale showed a high correlation with the scale of general ethnic prejudice. At the same time, both of these attitude scales were moderately related to the authoritarianism scale. The investigators concluded that authoritarianism was the underlying factor that explained the relationship between anti-Semitism and general ethnic prejudice.

We have to be extremely cautious about inferring causality from correlation. *Simply because two conditions vary together does not mean that one causes the other!* For example, the height and weight of individuals are moderately related, but no one suggests that a person's weight *causes* his or her height. To infer causation we also have to know the proper time sequence—with the supposed cause *preceding* the effect.

In addition, we have to eliminate alternate explanations for the relationship between the variables we are studying (Selltiz, Wrightsman & Cook, 1976). Furthermore, we must take great care to interpret our conclusions correctly. Let us use two hypothetical investigations to illustrate this point: first, let us say that in some parts of the world there seems to be a high positive correlation between ice cream consumption and infant mortality—in other words, the number of babies dying rises with the amount of ice cream consumed; second, let us say there appears to be a high positive correlation between cigarette smoking and lung

Box 3.2   FOCUS ON RESEARCH
Methods of Correlation

Correlation refers to the degree of relationship between two variables. The *correlation coefficient* is a statistic that describes the direction and degree to which two measures are related. This coefficient can vary from -1.00 through 0 to $+1.00$. When two measures are positively correlated, say $+0.63$, it means that higher scores on one tend to be associated with higher scores on the other. When two measures are negatively correlated, say -0.47, then higher scores on one are associated with lower scores on the other. The absolute size of the coefficient indicates the strength of the relationship between the two variables, while the sign indicates the direction. If the coefficient is near 0, there is little or no correlation between the variables.

Often, we wish to study simultaneously the relationships among more than two variables. Advanced techniques of correlation will help us do this. First, we can calculate coefficients of correlation between all pairs of variables. For example, in a study of job performance of maintenance personnel, we find that both job satisfaction and mechanical aptitude relate to the performance measure—that is, there are positive correlations among all three. However, we might want to know the relationship between job satisfaction and job performance when medhanical aptitude remains constant. To do this, we would use a technique called *partial correlation*, which estimates the degree of relationship between two variables while a third related variable is held constant. Partial correlation helps us discover which are the strongest correlations among a larger number of variables.

Multiple correlation, or multiple regression, is a method for correlating a number of predictor variables with one outcome variable. For example, to predict attitudes toward a minority group, we might want to take into account several variables shown to be important by past research—education, geographic location, age, income, personal contact, and so on. Using multiple regression, we could estimate the degree of relationship between two elements: all these variables in combination, and scores on a measure of attitude toward the minority group. We could also estimate how much each predictor variable contributes to the overall contribution.

Factor analysis is an advanced statistical procedure based on the methods of correlation. It is used to study the relationships among a large number of variables. By analyzing the correlation coefficients among all the variables, factor analysis identifies a smaller number of underlying variables (factors) that account for most of the scores on the variables and the relationships between them. For example, suppose we had scores for a group of people on a large number of personality tests, measuring traits such as sociability, dependence, affiliation, dominance, achievement, and self-esteem. A factor analysis might show that the group's scores can be accounted for by two underlying factors—extraversion and independence. Factor analysis thus helps us "boil down" complex relationships into simpler explanations of social reality.

Source: Nunnally, J. C. *Psychometric theory* (2nd ed.). New York: McGraw-Hill, 1978.

cancer. We could very quickly assume a direct cause-and-effect connection between the two variables in each example. However, let us take a closer look.

In the first example, careful study would point out that there is also a third variable present—hot weather. This factor influences both the high consumption of ice cream and the high infant mortality rate. Ice cream itself has nothing to do with infant deaths. Thus, the relationship between ice cream consumption and infant mortality is *spurious*, that is, it has the outward appearance of being legitimate, but on careful analysis it is false.

In the second example, smoking may indeed cause cancer. Or, our investigation might point to a third variable that links cigarette smoking with lung cancer. For example, there might be some genetic factor that predisposes a person to cancer and at the same time produces a craving for nicotine. Only experiments on humans would prove the existence of this third variable; but since it is neither possible nor ethical to conduct such research, the existence of the third variable cannot be proven. Thus, the relationship between cigarette smoking and lung cancer *might* be spurious—as many of the tobacco companies claim. Even though the existence of this mysterious third variable seems implausible, we at least have to consider the possibility of a spurious relationship between cigarette smoking and cancer. Thus, in interpreting data on correlations, it is important to analyze all the factors involved and to find evidence for all claims.

A recent development in correlational methods—one that *does* indicate causation—is *cross-lagged panel correlation* (Campbell, 1973; Kenney, 1975, 1979). In Chapter 2 we saw an example of how this method is used to study causation between attitudes and behavior. The simplest variation of this approach requires the measurement of two variables—X and Y—at two points in time—1 and 2. This yields four different sets of measures: X1, X2, Y1, and Y2. The two correlations between the two variables at the two different times (X1 with Y2 and X2 with Y1) are termed the *cross-lagged correlations: cross* because they are across the two variables, and *lagged* because there is a lag between the two times.

The difference between these two correlations is the most important element of the method. If X causes Y, then the X1Y2 correlation should be greater than the X2Y1 correlation. In other words, the stronger relationship between variable X at time 1 with variable Y at time 2 indicates that X causes Y rather than vice versa. In our previous example, attitudes at time 1 showed a stronger relationship with behavior at time 2, than behavior at time 1 did with attitudes at time 2. The conclusion: attitudes cause behavior rather than the reverse.

The detailed application of the method is, however, quite complex, and a number of important assumptions must be met before causation can be inferred with confidence. Nonetheless, the method does enable us to infer causation between two correlated variables and to rule out the causal effects of some other third variable. More complex correlations methods have also been developed to study causation in data that are collected on a longitudinal basis (e.g., Goodman, 1973; Markus, 1980).

In social behavior there is also a strong possibility of *multiple* causation among variables (Crano & Brewer, 1973). Since most of the important social behaviors are determined by more than one other variable, we must never take a restricted view of "what goes with what." Behavior associated with juvenile delinquency, for example, may be caused by a number of factors: amount of education, socioeconomic status, parental discipline, and so on. If, in your investigations, you were to focus on any one of these relationships and restrict your awareness and analysis of other important factors, you would produce a simple and incorrect picture of social reality.

The question of relationships among variables becomes more and more complex as our studies uncover the possibility of multiple causes. Perhaps the idea of a single, "real" cause, leading directly to a given effect, is nothing more than an illusion. Correlational research can help give us a more valid picture of social behavior that is multiply determined.

Experimental Research

Experimental research answers the question, What would happen if . . . ? With this approach, the social psychologist intervenes in either a natural or contrived situation, and manipulates one or more variables to see if this leads to changes in another variable. The "other" variable or condition is called the *dependent variable*—it is the factor that may be shown to be dependent on the condition that is manipulated. The variable or condition that is manipulated is called the *independent variable*. The experimenter attempts to hold constant all other conditions that might affect the dependent variable, and then assesses the change observed in the dependent variable when the independent variable changes. The experimenter uses a statistical test to determine whether the effect of the independent variable on the dependent variable is large enough to be considered a real difference (see Box 3.3).

The experimental approach involves all the requirements needed to infer causality in a relationship between variables. The experimental manipulation creates the opportunity for the variables to vary together—if indeed they *are* related. The proper time sequence of causation is implicit in the experimental design—that is, the independent variable is manipulated and the dependent variable is then observed for possible changes. The elimination of alternate reasons for the effect is achieved through the control of extraneous variables (Kidder, 1981). *Extraneous variables* are other existing factors that are not being studied; since changes in these factors could affect the dependent variable, the extraneous variables are held constant. This is called experimental *control*. The strong appeal of the experimental method in social psychology is its power to enable us to infer causality through our ability to control the events of the situation.

An example of experimental research is provided by Miller and Bugelski (1948), who intervened in a natural situation—young white men working in a camp—in order to study a relationship between variables. They were interested in this question: Does induced frustration lead to displaced aggression toward outgroups? *Outgroups* are ethnic, racial, or religious groups that we see as different from our own.

When members of a group are frustrated by interference, aggressive responses may be aroused. However, it may be inappropriate or unwise for them to

Box 3.3   FOCUS ON RESEARCH
Statistical Significance: When Is a Difference Really a Difference?

How do researchers conclude that the changes in the dependent variable are real changes—changes that would be likely to occur again if the study were repeated? After all, an experiment might show only slight changes in the dependent measure. Because of the random fluctuation of scores on any measure, researchers expect some change simply due to chance. How do they conclude that the effect is due to their manipulation of the independent variable and is not simply a chance occurrence? They do so by applying a *statistical test* to the results of their studies. The scores of subjects on the dependent variable are analyzed to produce a *statistic*—a single number whose size represents the strength of the effect that has occurred. Associated with each possible value of a statistic is a probability estimate indicating how likely it is that a value of that magnitude could occur by chance alone—that is, by random fluctuations in the scores. When the results of a study have a very low probability of occurring by chance alone, then researchers conclude that they are in fact due to the manipulation of the independent variable. These low probabilities are called *levels of significance.* Two commonly used levels are 0.05 and 0.01. These levels mean that an effect this large in the dependent variable would only occur five times in one hundred or once in one hundred, respectively, if chance alone were operating. Conversely, the probability is high that experimental manipulation caused the effect, and we assume that if the study were carried out again it would yield the same results. We refer to such results as *statistically significant,* since a level of significance has been reached.

For example, we wish to study the effects of a movie concerning racial prejudice on the attitudes of white college students toward blacks. We first ask the subjects to complete an initial attitude measure; then we show the movie; and then we assess attitudes a second time. Based on the pretest and posttest scores, we calculate a statistic called *t,* which summarizes the magnitude of the change in scores. By examining the probability level associated with the value of *t,* we conclude whether or not the movie actually affected racial attitudes.

A variety of tests are available for estimating the statistical significance of various research results. Tests of difference between pretest and posttest scores, and between means of different groups, are commonly used in experimental research. Measures of the degree of relationship among variables are also expressed as statistics. For example, the correlation coefficient (see Box 3.2) is a statistic whose value relates to different probability levels and whose statistical significance can therefore be estimated. Almost all of the results reported in social psychology have been analyzed using a statistical test, and we therefore have confidence that they represent true findings.

Source: Guilford, J. P. & Fruchter, B. *Fundamental statistics in psychology and education* (6th ed.). New York: McGraw-Hill, 1978.

directly express this aggression toward the frustrating agent; for example, if that agent is a powerful member of the same group, the cost of expressing the aggression might be considerable. Therefore, a safer route is to express the aggression toward an outgroup identified as different—and relatively powerless to combat the aggression.

Using a checklist of adjectives, Miller and Bugelski measured the racial attitudes of their subjects. The men could place a check next to any number of positive ("friendly," "honest") and negative ("selfish," "cruel") adjectives that they believed described Japanese and Mexicans. This measurement assessed the *dependent* variable: racial attitudes.

The independent variable was put into operation through a frustrating experience: the men were required to complete boring, lengthy, and difficult tests, which interfered with their opportunity to go to an event in town where they could win money. Obligated to spend more than two hours on the tests, they missed the truck that was to take them. Judging by their hostile comments, it was clear that frustration had indeed been induced.

The investigators were now ready to assess the dependent variable. They asked the men to complete a second checklist of adjectives about Japanese and Mexicans. The results indicated that the manipulation of frustration was followed by a definite decrease in the number of positive adjectives checked, and a slight increase in the number of negative adjectives. To rule out alternative explanations, the investigators administered the same tests to another group of young men who did *not* have to complete a frustrating task. This group—called the *control group* in experimental design—showed no change in attitude. The investigators then concluded that the instigation of frustration (the independent variable) caused an increase in aggressive or prejudicial responses (the dependent variable).

Despite countless experiments that have successfully documented realtionships among variables, there are clear disadvantages to this approach. For example, does the way the variables are put into operation in an experiment adequately represent the conceptualization of the theory being tested? Let us suppose we are studying the effect of failure on a person's self-esteem. In the experiment, suppose we tell subjects that they did not do well on a simple puzzle. Does this adequately induce the experience of failure, and, therefore, does the situation to do justice to our concept of failure?

Another very serious issue in experimental research is the problem of generalizing results from contrived experimental situations—especially in laboratory settings—to real-life behavior in natural environments. This concern can be partly offset by incorporating *simulations* that represent more aspects of reality. A *simulation* is an artificial situation that is set up to represent a natural situation. An example of a simulation would be a mock disaster designed to test medical personnel. In a controlled situation, some persons would role-play as patients with faked injuries, and hospital personnel would demonstrate their responses. As we will see later, simulations tend to add reality to the experimental situation, and yet maintain much of the power for sorting out cause and effect.

Correlational vs. Experimental Research. Cronbach (1957) has provided an insightful commentary on the existence of two separate disciplines of scientific psychology: correlational psychology and experimental psychology. Correlational psychology is concerned with the study of relationships that already exist in the real world. It focuses on individual differences in relatively enduring personality characteristics such as intelligence. In contrast, experimental psychology studies variations created by manipulations of the experimenter. It is interested in establishing general laws and tends to ignore individual differences.

Cronbach maintains that a schism exists between these two branches of psychology that results in either no answers to important questions or wrong answers. Each type of study has its particular strengths. Correlational research allows us to study variables that are difficult or inappropriate to manipulate and control, such as intelligence or self-esteem. Experimental research allows us to study causation among variables in a precise fashion.

Rather than using only one method or the other, however, the mutual, reciprocal contribution of both correlational and experimental approaches to the discipline of psychology could be more productive. Cronbach suggests that experiments could be used to help assess the validity of measures used in correlational psychology. The experimental approach could profitably use the more sophisticated measurement of variables available from the correlational approach. To understand and predict behavior, psychology should study both the variations among individuals and the variations provided by experimental treatments, as well as the interactions between these two kinds of variations.

Action Research

In the 1940s, Kurt Lewin was in touch with many people who were concerned about relations among different racial and religious groups: whites, blacks, Jews, Christians. Although they seemed to have a great amount of goodwill with which to face the problem, Lewin saw that it would be difficult to transform their positive attitudes into organized, efficient action. Most concerned persons were unclear about three aspects of the problem: What is the present situation? What are the dangers? What can we do?

Lewin saw that social science could perform a valuable service by collaborating with professionals involved in intergroup relations and other social problems. He defined this as *action research:* "a comparative research on the conditions and effects of various forms of social action, and research leading to social action." Lewin added, "Research that produces nothing but books will not suffice" (1948, p. 203). According to Lewin, very rigorous social scientific research was essential. Action research would deal with the general laws of group life as well as the diagnosis of specific situations to see how the laws applied. Lewin also believed that the essential element of diagnosis "has to be complemented by experimental comparative studies of the effectiveness of various techniques of change" (1948, p. 205).

The use of research to support collaborative social action was also pioneered by John Collier, who served as commissioner of Indian affairs in the United States from 1933 to 1945. Collier (1945) involved administrators, professionals, and lay people in research projects and action programs designed to improve the living conditions of American Indian tribes.

In the process of action research, activity begins with a *planning phase.* This involves analysis and conceptualization in order to understand the initial situation. The planning phase is followed immediately by a phase of *fact-finding* or *data collection*, which provides better understanding of the situation. Based on planning and fact-finding, decisions are then made about actions that should be taken. This leads to the phase of *action* or *execution*. Following execution, the action must be evaluated through additional *fact-finding*. The results then provide *feedback* that is incorporated into subsequent planning and action phases.

In short, action research consists of a sequence of cumulative steps, producing a spiral of activity that maximizes both the depth of understanding and the effectiveness of action. Implicit in Lewin's conception of action research are the processes of diagnosing a social situation and of providing feedback to actors in the situation. The cycle of phases of action research are represented in Figure 3.2.

Lewin and other early proponents of action research realized that it was more difficult than laboratory-based research. This was due to both the increased complexity of the situation to be studied, and the difficulty and challenging requirement of collaboration with other citizens. The complexity of action research is partly illustrated by examining the varieties of action research outlined by Chein, Cook and Harding (1948):

- *Diagnostic action research* is concerned with the analysis of the problem situation in a way that yields recommendations that can lead to social action.
- *Participant action research* is more collaborative; people who are to take action are directly involved in the research process from the beginning. Collaboration then leads to motivation for change rather than resistance to change.
- *Empirical action research* involves taking an action, such as setting up a social program, and then keeping a day-to-day record of the type and effects of activities that are carried out. This is a participant-observation and case-study approach that can be made more effective through the involvement of an external, objective researcher.
- *Experimental action research* involves the performance of controlled research on the relative effectiveness of different action strategies. While this type may have the greatest potential because it provides definitive test of hypothesis, it is also the most difficult since it requires predicting and controlling the course of social action.

Each type of action research is full of potential pitfalls and frustrations, as we can see in the examples given by Chein et al. (1948). One illustration of diagnostic

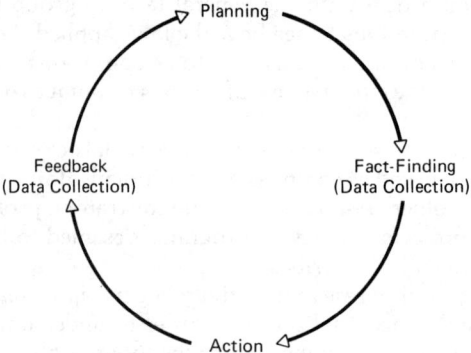

Figure 3.2   Cycle of Action Research.

action research came in response to escalating racial and religious tension in a city neighborhood that climaxed in a minor riot in front of a synagogue. The action researchers interviewed persons from each major ethnic group as well as institutional leaders to assess intergroup attitudes and participation in community affairs. Based on the results, a series of recommendations were made. Some, like the construction of a public housing project, were simply unfeasible. Others, such as the formation of an intergroup community council to coordinate civic improvement, fell on deaf ears. Other recommendations, however, were successful in reinforcing existing proposals for positive change. For example, one recommendation led to the acquisition of a neighborhood recreation center.

Action researchers must not expect instant or complete success. Many of the social problems they confront are intractable—they have to be solved again and again (Sarason, 1978). Action researchers must therefore be content with making limited contributions to the slow progress of society toward greater justice and equality.

In 1970, Nevitt Sanford asked, "Whatever happened to action research?" He noted that while the approach was rather inactive within mainstream social psychology, it was very much alive in other areas, such as social welfare and criminology. Furthermore, the fields of education and organizational psychology quickly had incorporated the use of action research (see Corey, 1953; Shepard, 1960; Whyte & Hamilton, 1964), and we now see its usage growing in community psychology (see Price & Cherniss, 1977). Sanford maintained that action research never really got off the ground in social psychology because of the unfortunate separation of pure science from applied science. As applied social psychology develops, it may bring renewed interest in action research, thus elevating it once again within our discipline to the level of prestige that it deserves.

Evaluation Research

Evaluation research is the use of social research methods in assessing the effects of a social program or policy (Suchman, 1967; Rutman, 1977; Weiss, 1972; Wortman, 1975). It is an extension of action research in that it provides evaluative feedback on the effects of a social action.

Evaluation research grew out of a humanitarian concern to improve the lot of all people, and the viewpoint that consumers of social programs should have a say in those programs (Perloff & Perloff, 1977). Furthermore, the effectiveness of social programs today must be assessed in order to provide accountability to the society that supports them—often through government agencies. Given the need to provide the best service for the least cost, it is not surprising that the business of evaluation research has become a growth industry in social science in the 1980s. One reason is that all segments of society can see merit in increasing the effectiveness of costly social programs. Evaluation research contributes to this effectiveness by increasing the rationality that goes into decision making regarding social policies. It does this by providing reliable and valid data to complement the wide array of information, impressions, and values that also go into the process.

Evaluation research involves more than the simple application of existing research methodology. In the first place, it poses more difficult technical problems than pure research conducted in settings controlled by the social scientists (Rossi & Wright, 1977; Weiss, 1972). Moreover, it is carried out in sociopolitical systems that not only pose constraints on the research but are often inhospitable to it (Rutman, 1977; Weiss, 1972). The research, therefore, is not merely a technical activity; rather, it becomes part of the social and political decision-making processes of the setting in which it occurs. In this sense, we can look upon the field of evaluation research as a *social movement* that is lobbying to maximize the rationality of program planning (Freeman, 1977).

Evaluation research is similar to basic research in many ways (Weiss, 1972). The basic researcher describes social reality and studies relationships among variables, especially causal linkages between program activities and program outcomes. Evaluation researchers use the full range of research methods for studying programs. However, they generally see the experimental approach as the most powerful way of sorting fact from fancy. For example, Donald Campbell (1969, 1973) suggests that social reforms present unique opportunities for experimental evaluation. He proposes that the social scientist has a unique role to play as the "methodological servant of the experimenting society." The social scientist must use his or her research skills to help society decide whether its humanitarian goals are being reached without damaging side effects.

Because it is necessary to adapt the research process to the realities of the social and political world, the role of evaluator is difficult to play. Administrators and staff tend to resist evaluation (Rutman, 1977). Policymakers control many important elements of the research: definition of the problem, significant variables, and sample of respondents. The evaluator is often faced with vague program goals, deep-rooted social problems, the programmers' high expectations about program outcomes—and yet frequently weak program effects (Rossi & Wright, 1977). Evaluation researchers must struggle to maintain both their competence and their autonomy. They must do the best possible job under difficult circumstances, using the most powerful research tools available. They must work to understand, and to document in a comprehensive way, both the process and the outcomes of the program. And through all this, they must maintain the role of social scientist, rather than simple technician, by critically investigating *all* side effects, by studying theoretical questions, and by providing significant information to decision makers (Rutman, 1977).

An example of evaluation research involved the assessment of the television program "Sesame Street," which was developed to stimulate conceptual learning among disadvantaged children (Ball & Bogatz, 1971). The researchers randomly selected children (ages 2–5) in four different locations and tested their cognitive abilities. Then, also at random, some children from the four locations were encouraged to watch the show. Home visits and discussions with parents and children were used to increase their awareness of the program and the children's motivation to watch it. These children were then compared to nonencouraged children (who watched the program less) on measures of cognitive learning such as number and letter recognition. The encouraged children showed dramatic improvement on most measures. Unfortunately, the design of the study combined the effects of encouragement with the effects of actually watching the program.

This overemphasized the positive benefits of "Sesame Street" (Cook, Appelton, Conner, Shaffer, Tomkin & Weber, 1975). Nonetheless, evaluation research provided useful information on the effects of the program itself.

Evaluation research is both fascinating and complex, and has become a major area of interest in applied social psychology. We must recognize it as an interdisciplinary activity to which social psychologists can make unique contributions based on their specialized skills and training (Wortman, 1975).

Values and Ethics in Social Research

Researchers who work with human subjects are caught in a dilemma of values. On one hand, they value their contributions to knowledge and to the common good; on the other hand, they must value the welfare of participants in their research. Upholding both values, however, is not simple in the reality of complex research processes. Our values can influence all stages of the research process from the selection of the problem to the interpretation of results. Ethical issues related to treatment of participants can arise at any point in the research process: the way subjects are chosen, how they are treated, and the use to which the results are put (Cook, 1981). *This, it is essential that the researcher constantly weigh the potential benefits of research against the possible costs to participants who may be exposed to questionable research practices.*

Ethical issues arise in all methods of social research. The experimental approach tends to involve more questionable practices than either descriptive or correlational research since it involves more intervention in the lives of the subjects. Action research and evaluation research tend to move the relationship between researcher and subject toward a greater degree of collaboration. This minimizes the number of ethical issues, because the subjects are involved more as persons and less as objects. Professional associations of psychologists and other social scientists have developed codes of ethics governing the treatment of research subjects. Stuart Cook, who helped develop the American Psychological Association's Code of Ethics, has outlined a number of concerns and questionable practices regarding the ethics of research (Cook, 1981).

A major ethical concern revolves around the principle of *informed consent.* Based on humanitarian and democratic values, the principle specifies that people have a right to know about their participation in any activity and have a right to have free choice regarding participation. Potential subjects must be told of any possible unpleasant or harmful effects of the research. Nevertheless, researchers often carry out their work without the full knowledge or consent of the people involved. It may be impractical or impossible to do otherwise. Or the researcher may fear that informed participants will react to the research situation in an unnatural manner, and therefore distort the results.

In descriptive research, for example, participants are often observed without their knowledge. The researcher is somewhat like an undercover agent whose presence might lead to resentment or even hostility on the part of those being observed. Field experiments are also often designed to study and influence people's behavior without their awareness. For example, in studies of "helping behavior" in natural settings, confederates of the experimenter have dropped papers and books, feigned sickness or injury, or created other situations in which they apparently needed assistance. The subjects were people who happened to come by. Such a practice, obviously, is in conflict with the basic principle of informed consent; however, is it unethical?

Another major area of ethical concern is *invasion of privacy*. Since research pries into its subjects' lives to some degree, social researchers have long recognized the principles of confidentiality and anonymity for their subjects. The right to privacy may be violated in a number of ways; how we judge the severity of the violation varies according to individual opinion. Methods of covert observation—such as videotaping without informed consent, or covert techniques for collecting information—generally would be regarded as questionable. The use of interviews or other methods to elicit personal and sensitive information is another serious issue. Many people regard information about their intimate relationships, their political and religious beliefs, or their sexual behavior as nobody's business but their own. Thus, the researcher's need to know, and the social benefits this "knowledge" might provide, must be weighed against the individual's right to privacy.

The issue of *deception* in research has probably received more attention in social psychology than any other ethical concern. Even though subjects may be aware that they are participating in research, and even though they may give a degree of informed consent, the true nature of the research may be withheld. In fact, the subjects may be actively misled about the nature of the experience. These situations represent an act of deception by the researcher. Deception is most often associated with the experimental approach since the experimenter wishes to keep the subject unaware of the causal relationships being studied and to maximize the social reality of the experimental situation.

The use of deception can have serious consequences (Eisner, 1977; Kelman, 1967; Warwick, 1975). It can cause a subject embarrassment and lowered self-esteem. In addition, deception can damage a trusting relationship between the experimenter and the subject. Finally, deception negatively affects the way that society as a whole perceives social research.

Building social-psychological knowledge on a foundation of deceit may carry a stronger message than the content of that knowledge. Yet, to fully inform subjects might lead to different results from those obtained when deception is used. For example, Resnick and Schwartz (1973) found that subjects who were fully informed of the purposes and procedures of a verbal conditioning experiment showed negative rather than positive conditioning (see Chapter 2). It had been shown that when an experimenter said "good" or "okay" each time a subject used the words "I" or "we," the subject would increase the use of those words. In Resnick and Schwartz's study, however, the fully informed subjects *decreased* such usage. For such reasons, researchers continue to use deception in some studies, but it is carefully regulated by professional codes of ethics and by peer review committees who judge the ethical aspects of the research.

A lack of informed consent, an invasion of privacy, and deception are obviously *disrespectful behaviors* that violate the human rights of research participants. However, there are other questionable practices that are more actively disrespectful, and some that are potentially harmful to the subject.

One example is a form of *coercion* that occurs when an employer or an institution uses varying degrees of influence to promote participation in research. Sometimes, such involvement is considered to be part of the organizational role of the individual; in other situations, the researcher may use rewards to attract and persuade potential participants. Potential subjects may often be a relatively powerless group—such as prisoners, psychiatric patients, or university students—that responds to the social approval of the powerful members of the organization or to small financial incentives. The ethical position is that the recruitment procedure should protect the participant from coercion and should preserve a substantial amount of free choice.

Another type of disrespectful treatment is that which involves participants in actions that reduce their self-respect. Subjects have participated in studies where they were strongly encouraged to cheat or steal, fail to help people in emergency situations, or ostensibly harm other people. For example, in some experiments, participants were led to believe that they were administering electrical shocks to other people.

Sometimes research has the potential of violating an individual's right to self-determination because it attempts to produce changes in his or her behavior or personality characteristics. Such attempts may involve negative behavior (inflicting pain) or positive changes (increasing academic achievement or decreasing racial prejudice). In either case, the individual is often being affected without his or her full awareness.

Other questionable practices are simply thoughtless and may result in a general lack of fair and respectful treatment of the subjects. Examples of such practices are failure to provide reports to participants at the end of the experiment, or failure to bring about personal benefits (such as increased self-understanding) that participants expect. Such practices not only sour the researcher-subject relationship, but damage the broader relationship between social science and society.

Finally, we must avoid practices that subject participants to physical or mental stress. Many important aspects of social behavior involve stressful situations, which often result in such negative emotional reactions as fear, shock, or a sense of inadequacy. Researchers have subjected participants to unpleasant stimuli (such as pictures of emaciated victims of Nazi concentration camps), demeaning and false information (such as incorrect failing grades on a college examination), and simulated emergencies (such as smoke seeping into a locked room). The fact that such manipulations also involve deception and an absence of informed consent makes them even more questionable. Cook (1981) concludes that investigators should attempt to achieve their research objectives with less stressful experiences.

Obligations to Participants. After the collection and analysis of data, the researcher continues to have ethical obligations to the participants and to society. At a minimum, the researcher must inform the participants about the nature and the results of the study. If questionable practices were used, the researcher must clarify these aspects fully—including the reasons for them—and work to reestablish a relationship of trust with the subjects. If there were any potentially harmful consequences, the researcher should do everything possible to alleviate these. These activities, along with a consideration of the subjects' emotional reactions, are typically included in the *debriefing*—an ethical requirement in which the researcher fully explains the research to the subjects at the conclusion of the study. Furthermore, if potentially harmful effects are more serious, then follow-up studies are highly recommended.

Finally, researchers must consider their obligations to the many constituencies—including society at large, the institutional setting, and the participants—that may compete for the dissemination and utilization of their results. They must maintain confidentiality and anonymity, often in the face of apparently legitimate demands from institutions, other researchers, or data banks.

Greater understanding usually involves the potential of greater control. However, because research subjects tend to be the more disadvantaged, less powerful members of society, they are least able to use the knowledge gained from social scientific study to better their position. It is more likely that government decision makers, organizational leaders, and administrators will use such knowledge to make decisions for them. This conflicts with the humanistic value base of applied social psychology. Moreover, this problem is growing because more and more research is done under contract for specific agencies or institutions that pay for the research and therefore control the use of the results. Thus, it is increasingly difficult for social researchers to exercise their social responsibility to disseminate results in an easy-to-understand form to society at large.

Costs vs. Benefits. The procedure of weighing the benefits of research against the costs to participants in resolving ethical questions has some disadvantages (Eisner, 1977). First, it is difficult to estimate costs and benefits. Second, some researchers may believe that they are being ethical as long as they weigh the pros and cons of their research, when in fact their decision on procedure may be quite unethical. Furthermore, it is the researcher's benefits that are weighed against the participants' losses—and researchers may show some bias in their own favor.

Baumrind (1971, 1972) proposes the unequivocal protection of the fundamental human rights of research participants as an alternative to the cost-benefit approach. All questionable practices should be resolved in favor of the well-being of the subject rather than in favor of the maintenance of social scientific rigor or realism. Baumrind further maintains that each researcher is responsible for the effects of his or her actions on the participants, and that scientific ends do not justify means that would be deemed reprehensible in everyday interaction.

The consideration of ethnical issues will certainly continue to play an important role in social research.

METHODS OF SOCIAL RESEARCH

How do we go about translating the major types of research into concrete activities for gathering information? A wide variety of methods of social research are designed to help us do this (Kidder, 1981). These methods can be grouped into three basic ways of gaining knowledge about the social world:

1. observing people and then recording and analyzing what they do or what they produce
2. asking people for information in either written or verbal form
3. intervening to varying degrees in the lives of people and recording the effects

Each of the methods described in this section can be grouped into this rough categorization. All of these methods can be used with any of the major types of resarch, with one exception: laboratory experimentation is applicable only to experimental research.

Observational Methods

Observation is the selecting, recording, and encoding of both the behaviors and the characteristics of settings for the empirical aims of description or theory development (Weick, 1968). (Something is *empirical* if it is based in experience.) Observation usually occurs in natural settings, although it can also be used in such contrived settings as laboratory experiments and simulations. In situations where interviewing or experimental manipulation are not possible, observation is often the only feasible method of obtaining information (Bickman, 1976).

Observational methods can be used for descriptive or correlational purposes; they can be a component of experimental research; and they are often involved in action research and evaluation research. Observational methods are widespread since they are fundamental to empiricism: observers attempt to report what they see and hear rather than what they think or believe. According to Bickman (1976), observation is scientific when it is planned and recorded systematically, when checks are made on its reliability and validity, and when the results are related to general propositions (rather than simply presented as a set of interesting curiosities). Therefore, there is an important distinction between naive or informal observation and the rigorous, systematic observation that is acceptable to social scientific inquiry (La France, 1981).

Bickman (1976) noted that all types of observation are characterized by three important dimensions:

1. *Degree of concealment.* The researcher must first decide to what extent the identity of the observer will be concealed from the participants in the research. Sometimes observers are outside the process of interaction and are identified as such. At other times, they are participants in the interaction, with the understanding that they are also observers of the behavior. In other situations, the identity of the observer is completely concealed from the subjects.
2. *Extent of observer intervention.* In cases of intervention, the observer may be entirely passive and not affect the social situation at all. Or the observer may actively affect the interaction through his or her own behavior.
3. *Degree of structure in the observational process.* Some observations are comparatively unstructured, consisting solely of the observer's most important impressions. Other observations are highly structured, with the researcher checking off certain predetermined behaviors of the subject as they are observed.

Participant observation is an observational method in which the observer describes a social situation in which he or she is actively involved (Kidder, 1981). Participant observation is relatively unstructured—the observer has some flex-

In *participant observation*, the observer describes a social situation in which he or she is actively involved. The observer keeps field notes, a record of the important elements observed: participants, social setting, purpose of the interaction, specific social behaviors that occur, and frequency and duration of various interactions. Anthropologist Margaret Mead acted as a participant observer, living among the people she studied. *(Ken Heyman)*

ibility in deciding what to observe and how to record it. Usually the observer keeps field notes, a narrative account of the observations. These notes record the important elements observed: particpants, social setting, purpose of the interaction, specific social behaviors that occur, and frequency and duration of various interactions. Participant observation is often used to provide descriptions that otherwise would be unavailable. For example, in a provocative study by Rosenhan (1973), participant observers in a psychiatric hospital posed as patients and later provided an account of the experience (see Box 3.4).

Roger Barker and his colleagues in ecological psychology pioneered a second type of observational method in which specimen records are constructed through continuous detailed behavior description. This approach has provided descriptions of such complete behavior episodes as all of the activities in a single day of one boy's life (Barker & Wright, 1951, 1954). Behavior description has also been used to develop a complete inventory of the *behavior settings* in both a small American town and an English town (Barker, 1963, 1968; Barker & Schoggen, 1973). The investigators provided a comprehensive behavioral description of social environments that invoked typical patterns of behavior in the towns, thus documenting the importance of environmental influences in determining social

Box 3.4   FOCUS ON RESEARCH
Participant Observers in Insane Places

Participant observation can provide an inside view of social situations that would otherwise not be available. To study the world of the hospitalized psychiatric patient, David Rosenhan, a professor of psychology and law at Stanford University, instructed eight normal individuals in how to gain admission to psychiatric hospitals as "pseudopatients." At different times, these individuals (including Rosenhan) gained admittance to twelve different institutions. After calling for an appointment, they arrived at the admissions office complaining of hearing voices saying "empty," "hollow," and "thud." These symptoms indicate "existential psychosis"—a disorder supposedly arising from perceived meaninglessness in one's life. The pseudopatients gave false names and occupations, but otherwise presented their past histories exactly as they had occurred.

All pseudopatients were admitted; all but one was diagnosed as schizophrenic. Once on the psychiatric ward, they stopped simulating or reporting any symptoms of abnormality. Nonetheless, the average length of hospitalization was 19 days, and the typical diagnosis at discharge was "schizophrenia in remission." Having labeled the patient as psychotic, the hospital staff seemed reluctant to admit that the patient was normal at discharge, or had ever been normal. On the ward itself, the pseudopatients were friendly and cooperative. Their only distinctive behavior was their taking notes based on their observations. Many of the other patients questioned their true identity, saying, for example, "You're not crazy. You're a journalist or a professor." In contrast, the hospital staff never once questioned the note-taking; they recorded it on patient records and apparently interpreted it as a symptom of abnormal behavior. The pseudopatients noted that many patient behaviors were similarly misinterpreted. A patient who became upset because of mistreatment was seen to be acting out his pathology rather than reacting to the mistreatment. On a regular basis, pseudopatients asked staff members questions about their disposition. Psychiatrists, nurses, and attendants commonly gave brief answers with their heads averted, avoiding eye contact as they moved on past the pseudopatient. The staff members spent very little time on the wards with the patients, but remained for the most part in their glassed-in offices. The results were segregation of staff and patients and an overwhelming depersonalization and powerlessness on the part of the patients.

Source: Rosenhan, D. On being sane in insane places. *Science*, 1973, *197*, 250–258.

interaction. (For example, the behavior setting of a basketball game involves certain patterns of behavior for players, officials, and spectators. Generally, everyone knows how he or she should behave in that social environment, and everyone acts accordingly.) Barker and his colleagues also compared types of behavior settings, major social activities, and prominent individual behaviors in the American and English towns. They found that the Americans spent more time in religious activities; the English, in artistic activities. This systematic observational work has helped to foster an ecological approach to community psychology (see Chapter 10).

The *behavior setting* of a basketball game involves certain patterns of behavior for players, officials, and spectators. Generally, everyone knows how he or she should behave in that social environment, and everyone acts accordingly. *(Eric A. Roth/The Picture Cube)*

The most structured observational method involves behavioral checklists, or categorizing systems, that describe certain behaviors. Using this method, the observer records the frequency of occurrence of a given behavior during a social interaction. One of the best-known categorizing systems, *Interaction Process Analysis*, was developed by Bales (1950) for the systematic observation and coding of behavior in small groups. In this system, the observer, set apart from the group, has the job of observing and recording behavior. Figure 3.3 illustrates Bales's twelve categories of observation, grouped within the major areas of social-emotional behaviors and task activities.

Using this system, Bales and other investigators have documented the typical behavioral interactions and developmental processes that occur in a variety of small groups. Their subjects have ranged from nursery school children to university faculty members. Flanders (1970) adapted Interaction Process Analysis to observe and encode the classroom behavior of teachers and students (see Chapter 15). Category systems are thus useful for providing systematic and reliable descriptions of behavior in natural settings. These descriptions can be fed back to the people being observed and can serve as a stimulus and guide for social change. For example, methods for changing small-group behavior often begin with observations of present functioning (see Chapter 7).

Regardless of which observational method we use, we must consider two

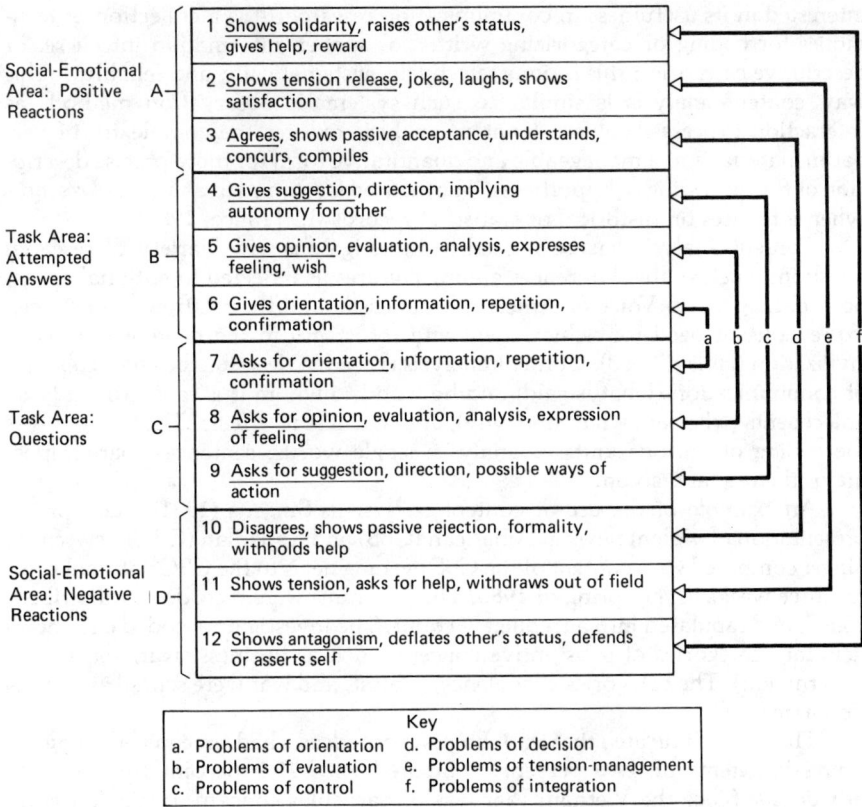

Figure 3.3   The System of Categories Used in Observation and Their Relation to Major Frames of Reference.
Source: Bales (1950).

factors: (1) the manner in which the mass of available information is reduced to a manageable form, and (2) the reliability of our methods. Bakeman and Dabbs (1976) present examples of simple conceptual and analytical tools that facilitate the handling of observational data. As for assessing reliability, a number of approaches have developed (for example, Weick, 1968; Wicker, 1975).

Content Analysis

A great deal of human social behavior is represented in the form of communications: letters, historical records, transcripts of speeches, diplomatic notes, propaganda messages, books, radio or television programs, newspapers, statistical records, and so on. To use this naturally occurring information, we must analyze its contents.

The method of *content analysis* was first defined by Berelson (1952), who was interested in its usefulness in communication research. It is a collection of techniques for coding or categorizing written or spoken information into a set of descriptive categories; this is done selectively, systematically, and reliably. In this way, content analysis is similar to such systematic observation methods as Interaction Process Analysis. Content analysis reduces the complexity of verbatim material into a manageable and quantitative form for more precise description or for the testing of hypotheses. The method is referred to as *archival research* when it focuses on historical or statistical records (La France, 1981).

Content analysis has been used to investigate a wide variety of research questions, such as the differences among cultures as reflected in national songs, Soviet reactions to Voice of America broadcasts, and the relationship between expressions of need for achievement and the stages in the development of a civilization (Holsti, 1968). Content analysis is used to describe the characteristics of communication (what is said, and how and to whom it is said), to study its antecedents (who said what, and why), and to assess its effects. Thus, it involves the coding of various units of analysis: single words, sentences, paragraphs, major themes, and so on.

An example of the use of content analysis is Singer's (1971) study of the presentation of violent news in American (CBS) and Canadian (CBC) newscasts. Singer compared with content of the CBS evening news to the CBC national news for three weeks in the spring of 1980. The programs were recorded, transcribed, coded, and tabulated into a frequency count. The investigators coded each news item into categories of substantive concern (such as business, war, space, and government). The categories of violence, protest, and war were scored as aggression items.

The results indicated that the CBS news broadcasts had a mean percentage of aggression items of 49.3 percent, compared with 25.9 percent for the CBC broadcasts. Since the Vietnam War was of particular concern to the American news media at the time, investigators removed all items referring to the war. This resulted in a comparative drop of aggression items for both newscasts—to 40 percent and 19 percent, respectively—indicating that the differences were not related solely to Vietnam.

There are various interpretations of *why* the difference occurred. Content analysis itself cannot tell us this. American culture may have more aggressive events; the United States population may be more interested in violent events; or American news media may choose to emphasize violence. Regardless of the interpretation of results, content analysis provides a useful way for documenting social reality.

Content analysis and observational methods do not require social interaction between the researcher and the subject. Therefore they are referred to as *unobtrusive methods:* the subject is not aware of being studied and will not react in an unnatural fashion. Researchers have constructed some very creative unobstrusive measures, such as counting whiskey bottles in garbage cans to measure drinking in a "dry" town, and gauging the popularity of museum exhibits by assessing the wear of floor tiles (Webb, Campbell, Schwarts & Sechrest, 1966). These methods represent our first way of gaining knowledge of the social world: simply observing, recording, and analyzing.

Interviewing

In contrast to unobtrusive measures, *interviewing* is intrinsically a social interaction: all parties are aware that the process is occurring, and communication between the interviewer and the interviewee is of paramount importance. The interview is therefore our first method of directly asking for the information we desire. There are several types of interviews, including job interviews, counseling interviews, persuasive interviews, and research interviews. The latter, of course is our concern here.

The interview *as a research method* is defined by Cannell and Kahn (1968, p. 527) as "a two-person conversation, initiated by the interviewer for the specific purpose of obtaining research-relevant information, and focused by him on contents specified by research objectives of systematic description, prediction, or explanation." Thus, the research interview is a directive, information-gathering process in which the interviewer maintains control over the situation, sets the purpose of the interview, and controls the pacing (Stewart & Cash, 1978). Research interviews are used to investigate as wide range of topics in the area of attitudes, values, future plans, past behavior, knowledge, and other information about the respondent. Given this flexibility, interviews are commonly used in conjunction with other research methods, particularly survey research, as a useful

Research interviews are used to investigate a wide range of topics in the area of attitudes, values, future plans, past behavior, knowledge, and other information about the respondent. *(Esais Baitel/Rapho/Photo Researchers, Inc.)*

technique for all of the major types of research, including evaluation research (Kidder, 1981; Weiss, 1975).

A research interview consists of a standard list of questions, the *interview schedule*. It may be unstructured, allowing the interviewer flexibility in the question asked, or it may be highly structured, specifying a carefully worded sequence of questions that are to be asked of all interviewees in the same manner. The interviewer may ask *open-ended questions*, which allow the respondent to answer as he or she wishes, or *closed questions*, which provide fixed alternatives from which to choose an answer. The responses are usually recorded by hand or on tape, and are later coded and tabulated. If the interview has generated a large amount of detailed material that must be simplified, content analysis is sometimes used.

To be successful, an interview must have certain basic requirements. The interviewer must be properly selected, trained, and supervised. The interviewees must have access to the required information. The interviewees must understand their role and the information required, and they must be adequately motivated to fulfill the role requirements (Cannell & Kahn, 1968). These procedures will help ensure that the interview provides a reliable, valid, and precise measure.

The interview has a number of important advantages as a research method (Kidder, 1981; Steward & Cash, 1978). Since the interview requires people to talk instead of write (or do something demanding), it can be used with almost all segments of the population. Also, it usually elicits a better completion rate than such methods as mail-out questionnaires; interviews motivate respondents to provide larger amounts of accurate information. In addition, the interviewer can work to maximize understanding and can institute flexibility in how information is obtained. However, to do so, the interviewer must have knowledge of both the inhibitors and facilitators of communication in the interviewing process (Gorden, 1980). (*Inhibitors* of communication are statements or actions that cause communication to decrease. *Facilitators* are statements or actions that enhance communication.)

Interviews are especially useful for obtaining threatening or anxiety-producing information. However, studies that compare interview responses to actual behavior have shown that respondents tend to distort their responses to threatening questions. For example, more people will report having voted in an election than actually did, and not everyone who has been arrested for drunken driving will admit it in an interview. Bradburn and Sudman (1979) studied different ways of conducting interviews so that inaccurate responses to threatening questions could be minimized. They found, for example, that using a longer introduction to threatening questions, and using open questions rather than closed ones, increased the amount of accurate responding.

The successful interviewer fulfills his or her role in a manner that increases interviewee participation in the interview (Richardson, Dohrenwend & Klein, 1965). If the interviewer can create a rapport with the interviewee, establishing an atmosphere of trust and openness, the interview will be useful for obtaining information on personal or emotional topics (such as attitudes toward racial minorities, or information on sexual practices). Interviewing, however, is costly and time-consuming, and the problems of bias and inaccuracy in measurement are greater than with simpler techniques of self-report.

Self-Report Measures

If you have ever partipated in a research study, you have probably responded to a questionnaire, an attitude scale, or another form of self-report measure. These commonly used methods are based on the assumption that the subject is in the best position to report on his or her own internal state. In a *self-report measure*, the respondent gives written replies to questions provided by the researcher. Like all verbal reports, the written approach raises the question of validity: Is the person motivated and able to provide a true report (Selltiz et al., 1976)? What biases does the person have? Social scientists have developed several different self-report methods, all of which require the respondent to indicate his or her position on some dimension of interest to the researcher. The following sections present five common techniques of self-report measurement, ranging from the least structured to the most structured. The greater the structure, the more precise, reliable, and valid a measurement usually is—and the more work it takes to develop.

Questionnaire. The *questionnaire* is essentially a written interview. Since the questionnaire method requires less expertise to carry out than interviewing, it can be easily administered to a large number of respondents. The questionnaire method usually guarantees anonymity and allows respondents the freedom to work at their own pace. The instructions and the questions are standardized; however, researchers do not have the opportunity to check whether each respondent is interpreting the question correctly. Questionnaires can be designed for almost any area of study, but their reliability and validity are often not well assessed: researchers tend to take the results at face value.

Rating Scale. Using the self-report measure known as a *rating scale*, the respondent directly rates the amount of a variable, basing the rating on personal judgment. For example, using a 7-point scale ranging from "very dissatisfied" to "very satisfied," you might be asked to rate one of your courses; or, in a study of interpersonal attraction, you might be asked to indicate how much you like another person.

The rating scale is simple and straightforward; its results are usually taken at face value by the researcher. However, the rating-scale process is complicated by the decisions that must be made about what type of rating scale to use and how to counteract measurement errors that creep into the process (Guilford, 1954; Selltiz et al., 1976). Rating scales are often incorporated into questionnaires and form the basis for more complex methods of attitude scaling.

Sociometric Techniques. Sociometry is the application of quantitative methods (measuring methods) to social relations. *Sociometric techniques* are self-report methods for describing interpersonal relations (Moreno, 1934, 1951, 1960). The most common sociometric technique is the sociometric test, which asks the respondents to choose other individuals with whom they would like to be associated. Respondents usually base their choices on interpersonal attraction or liking. However, they can also use other dimensions, such as status and competence; for example, you might be asked to choose the one person in your social psychology class with whom you would want to carry out a research project. It is important that the sociometric test be clear and concise rather than general or vague. It is easier to respond to a criterion such as "a person with whom you would like to play cards," than to a statement such as "a person you like a lot." Finally, sociometric tests are usually stated in positive rather than negative terms so that the choice is a movement toward rather than away from another person.

The results of a sociometric test are plotted on a graph known as a *sociogram.* Each person is represented by a circle, and choices are indicated by arrows that connect the circles. Several different methods are used to construct sociograms. Reciprocal choices are often grouped closer together so that the distance indicates the degree of attraction between the persons who made those choices. Sociograms may also be constructed to highlight subgroupings within the social unit under study. Numerical analyses may be applied to sociometric data in order to calculate indices relating to individual variables such as status or to group characteristics such as cohesion. For example, status—an individual variable—would be calculated using the number of choices a person receives. Cohesion—a group characteristic—would be calculated based on the number of choices within the group. An example of the use of sociometric techniques as well as other self-report measures to describe social reality is given in Box 3.5.

Sociometric methods have been used to study many different social processes—friendship patterns, leadership, intergroup relations—in a diversity of settings (Moreno, 1960; Selltiz et al., 1976). A surprising application of sociometry in the field is provided by Milgram (1970) through his documentation of the "small-world phenomenon." In this study, two individuals who did not know each other were selected; one was designated as the starting person and the other as the target person. To select starting persons, letters of solicitation were sent to residents of Wichita, Kansas. Those who volunteered were sent instructions. The target person was selected at random. A starting person was instructed to get a message to a target person through a chain of friends or acquaintances. Messages could move only through persons who knew each other on a first-name basis.

Starting persons in Wichita, Kansas, were asked to get the message to a target person living in Cambridge, Massachusetts. To trace the process, persons who were links in the chain were asked to mail in tracer cards. The first message took only four days and two intermediate persons. In general, the average number of links required was six—it's a small world, indeed! Milgram's findings, which have been replicated in a variety of environments, have helped stimulate interest in the study of social networks—one's collection of relatives, friends, and acquaintances (for example, Burt, 1978).

Attitude Scale. Social psychologists have long been concerned with the measurement of social attitudes. The approach they use most often is to ask respondents to indicate their level of agreement with statements about the social object of an attitude. For example, to assess a person's attitude toward capital punishment, he

Box 3.5   FOCUS ON RESEARCH
Sociogram of a University Living-Learning Center

Within their student residences, many universities have established living-learning centers that focus on a particular area of academic and vocational interest. At the University of Guelph, John Andrews and this author used a number of research methods to study the activities of a living-learning center for the arts during its first year of operation.

The arts center was designed to appeal to students interested in painting, sculpture, music, drama, and creative writing—whether or not they were enrolled in an academic art program. The center, housed in one wing of a high-rise student residence, had its own lounge-studio area and rooms for forty to fifty students. During registration, only nineteen students expressed an interest in living in the center; the remaining rooms were assigned to twenty-two students who had expressed no such interest. Nonetheless, the program staff invited all students living in the wing to participate in center activities. This created a natural experiment in which the independent variable was self-selection into the center versus non–self-selection.

One way to study social relationships within the center was to administer sociometric choice questions and construct a sociogram. Students were asked to

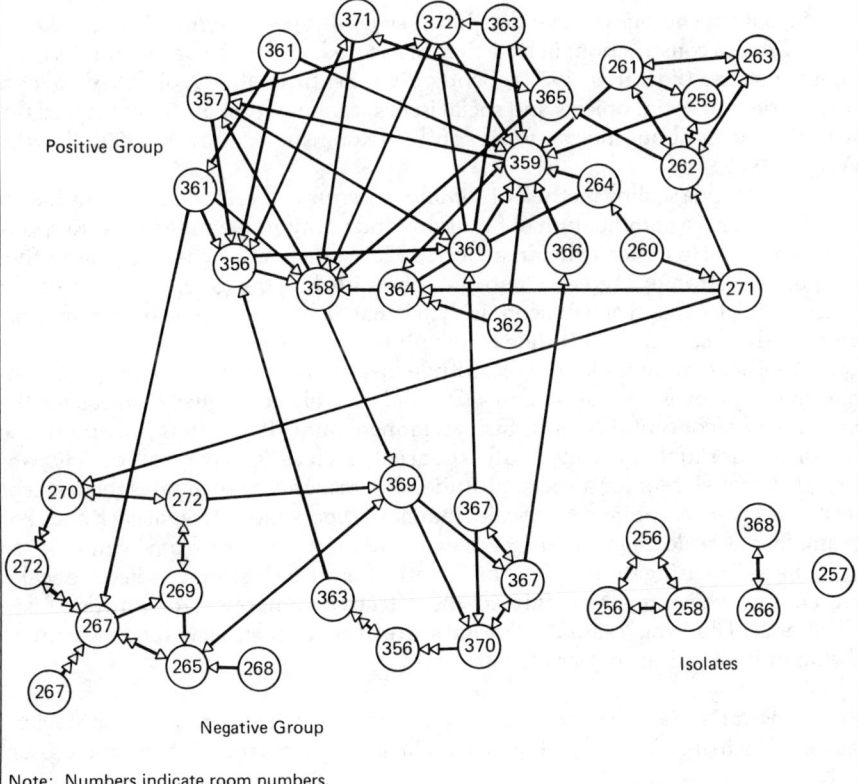

Note: Numbers indicate room numbers.

choose three other members of the center with whom they would prefer to engage in specified activites (for example, play bridge or work on a project). A sociogram was constructed to provide a picture of the total membership group.

The sociogram highlighted the observation that the total membership group had split into a positive group, with interest in the center's activities, and a negative group, uninterested in the center's activities. In addition, a few isolates were not socially connected to either the positive or negative group. As expected, the positive group included significantly more members who had selected to live in the center. Moreover, a number of non–self-selected individuals became positive about the center. Additional differences in interests, attitudes, and activities were also evident between the subgroups identified by the sociogram.

Source: Fisher, R. J. & Andrews, J. J. The impact of self-selection and reference group identification in a university living-learning center. *Social Behavior and Personality,* 1976, 4, 209–218.

or she might be asked to indicate agreement or disagreement with such statements as "capital punishment is a necessary form of justice" and "an eye for an eye, a tooth for a tooth." Thus, respondents do not rate their attitude directly; rather, their responses are scored in order to indicate the degree of favorableness of the attitude being studied.

Social psychologists have developed several types of *attitude scales.* These scales differ in construction, in how they are scored, and in the bases for interpreting their scores (Edwards, 1957a; Scott, 1968; Selltiz et al., 1976). They cover a wide variety of social objects and social issues, ranging from attitudes toward the self to attitudes about international conflict (Robinson & Shaver, 1969; Shaw & Wright, 1967).

The attitude scaling method of *summated ratings,* developed by Rensis Likert (1932), presents a combination of favorable and unfavorable statements. Respondents are asked to indicate their reaction to each statement by checking one of five categories: "strongly agree," "agree," "undecided," "disagree," and "strongly disagree." A total agreement score is then calculated which indicates the favorability of the respondents' attitude to the object in question.

Another common method of attitude measurement is the *semantic differential,* initially developed by Charles Osgood and his colleagues to measure the meaning of a concept (Osgood, Suci & Tannenbaum, 1957). In this method, the respondent is simply presented with a concept, such as "gun control" or "Hispanics," that is a referent for a social attitude. The respondent then rates the concept on a series of seven-point rating scales that have bipolar adjectives at each end. For example, one scale might run from "clean" to "dirty," another from "valuable" to "worthless." In using the semantic differential for attitude scaling, adjective scales are chosen which relate mainly to the affective component of attitudes (see Chapter 2). Thus, the respondent's total score over all scales serves as a measure of the favorability of his or her attitude.

Psychological Tests. The most refined method of self-report is psychological testing which has been developed by clinical and personality psychologists.

Psychological tests measure a wide range of individual abilities, aptitudes, and personality characteristics. Respondents signify their response to a series of questions or items that relate to the underlying concept being measured. More care goes into the construction of psychological tests than into any other self-report measure, and more study of measurement reliability and validity is required before the test is acceptable for use. Tests must be administered under standardized conditions, including the same instructions, time limits, and so on, for all respondents. Also, a large set of scores, or norms, must be available for comparing an individual score to scores of a larger population.

In social psychology, psychological tests are most often used for personality measurement of such characteristics as an individual's values, interests, or personality traits. These factors may then be related to social behavior. For example, Howard & Williams (1970) capitalized on a unique opportunity to relate scores on a personality measure of personal control to attitudes expressed about the 1967 Detroit riot—the subjects were black high-school students living in the riot area. Students who had scored high on personal control a year earlier were more positive in their attitudes toward the riot, that is, they said it was justifiable—an important message to the larger community. Students who scored low on personal control tended to be negative in their attitudes; they said the riots were wrongly hurting people and damaging the cause of civil rights. These results supported the researchers' interpretation that ghetto militants tend to be those who have confidence in their ability to control the events of their lives if they are given the opportunity to do so. Such individuals are in contrast to defeated and isolated fatalists, with little internal control, who resort to violence.

Response Sets. One of the major problems of self-report measures concerns *response sets*—that is, the tendency of people to respond in a certain way *regardless of the content of the item* (Cronbach, 1946; Rorer, 1965). An *acquiescence response set*, for example, is a tendency to agree or acquiesce to items regardless of what they say. Because these tendencies can affect testing validity, social psychologists have studied their potential seriousness. As a result, it has become accepted practice to balance attitude scales by stating half of the items in a favorable direction and the other half in an unfavorable direction. Thus, the effects of an acquiescence response set, or similar response sets, tend to cancel out in the summation of total scores.

Another major response set is *social desirability* responding. First identified by Edwards (1957b), it is defined as the tendency for respondents to agree with statements that they believe will present them in a socially desirable light, and to reject statements that will not. This tendency is of particular concern in personality assessment, where respondents might want to present themselves in the best possible light (a distortion that interviewers must also guard against). Edwards (1953, 1957b) and other investigators typically found high correlations between the judged social desirability of common personality test items and the freqeuncy with which these items were endorsed by respondents. For example, an item such as "I generally help people in need" would be rated as high on social desirability and would be endorsed by a large proportion of respondents, not necessarily because it was true of them, but because it is a good statement to make about oneself.

Edwards suggested the use of *forced-choice techniques* in scale construction to control social desirability. In this technique, the respondent must choose between two items of different content that are equivalent in judged social desirability, thus eliminating social desirability responding as a factor in the choice. For example, one might have to choose between "I generally tend to help people in need" and "I like to complete jobs that I start." These statements are equal in social desirability, but the first indicates caring for other people, whereas the second relates to achievement motivation. Unfortunately, the forced-choice method is only a rough means of control: a respondent may not judge the two items as equal in social desirability, and personal judgment still helps to determine item choice (see Bernhardson & Fisher, 1971). Nonetheless, researchers are now more sensitive to the possible contaminating effects that social desirability responding may have on all types of self-report measures.

Survey Methods

At some time or other, you may have wondered who will win the next election, or what type of motorcycle is most appealing, or what the relationship between economic difficulties and marital breakdown is. Such questions are amenable to one of the oldest and best-developed approaches in applied social research—the *survey method* (Babbie, 1973; Campbell & Katona, 1953; Hyman, 1955; Glock, 1967).

We are all familiar with opinion polls that provide efficient and reliable answers to many of the issues of the day. Opinion polls on political preference are one example. Surveys have been used over a wide range of populations, varying from nations as a whole, to particular regions, to cities and towns, to a specific organization or group. Surveys often cover a cross section of the general population, but they also can be used to research the opinions of any group: homemakers, Vietnam War veterans, high-school seniors, and so on. What topic will be investigated and who will be asked to respond depend on the objectives of the research. These objectives might be simply descriptive or might involve the correlational study of the relationship between variables. Surveys usually use either personal interviews, telephone interviews, or mail questionnaires as the specific method of data collection.

Regardless of objectives and specific data-gathering techniques, the process of *sampling* is the key consideration in survey research. It is essential to obtain a *representative sample* of the population under study so that, with a low degree of error, the investigators can generalize the results obtained to the entire population. Using sophisticated techniques of sampling, the expected degree of error in the survey results can be predicted (see Lazerwitz, 1968). Thus, we can estimate, for instance, how close our predictions of election results are likely to be in comparison to the actual vote.

A simple *random sample* (one in which each individual in a population has an equal chance of being included) is the best example of a representative sample.

However, social researchers have developed a number of more sophisticated methods of drawing samples in order to gain representativeness from a relatively small number of respondents. One method is *stratified random sampling.* In this method, respondents are selected from certain categories (age, occupation, and so on) in numbers proportionate to the size of those categories in the total population. Thus, the main goal of survey research is fulfilled: the quick and economical collection of reliable information that applies to a large number of people.

Survey research has certain limitations. Much of the information that is gathered in surveys is relatively superficial; it seldom provides in-depth knowledge of the respondents and their attitudes and opinions. Each method of gathering survey data—personal interviews, telephone interviews and questionnaires—has its particular biases and weaknesses. Various factors can affect survey results. For example, predicting elections can be affected by biased sampling of respondents, last-minute changes in voter preferences, and the enigma of the undecided voter. All make accurate prediction difficult. Nonetheless, on most topics, well-conducted surveys can usually provide valuable and accurate information.

You may wonder whether people are bored with being surveyed. Let's take a look at a survey of survey respondents designed to study their reactions to the

Predicting elections can be affected by biased sampling of respondents, last-minute changes in voter preferences, and the enigma of the undecided voter. Above, President Harry S Truman holds up an early edition of the *Chicago Tribune* for November 4, 1948. *(United Press International Photo)*

survey process. The United States Bureau of the Census, in conjunction with the Survey Research Center of the Institute for Social Research (University of Michigan), interviewed a nationwide sample on this topic (*ISR Newsletter,* 1978). The findings indicated that about half the respondents had taken part in at least one survey in the past five years; almost 40 percent had been requested to take part in more than one survey. The majority of respondents were not "turned off" by the survey research process; rather, most indicated they would be interested in taking *more* surveys if asked. In fact, the more surveys the respondents had participated in, the more willing they were to participate in another. Apparently, social researchers are correct in assuming that people enjoy taking part in surveys that show interest in their personal opinions; it is a reinforcing process. There was, however, a small percentage of respondents who indicated that they had refused *all* survey requests that they had received. In conclusion, we can expect that survey methodology will continue to play a very important role in applied social research.

Laboratory Experimentation

In discussing experimental research, we outlined the essence of the *experiment:* to study the effect on the dependent variable, an experimenter manipulates the independent variable, while holding extraneous variables constant. This basic approach is employed in a number of different experimental designs.

In the simplest of these, the *before-and-after design* or the *pretest–posttest design,* a group of experimental subjects receives the treatment of an independent variable and is assessed on a dependent variable measure both before and after treatment. For example, an investigator might want to study the effect of personal contact on the attitudes of college students toward college administrators. Following a pretest of their attitudes, students subjects might engage in a group discussion of college life with a university president (or a confederate posing as one), and their attitudes would be measured again. If a difference occurs between the two measurements, the investigator could theorize that it is due to the intervention of the independent variable. To prove this, however, the skillful elimination of all other extraneous variables that might intervene and affect the dependent variable would be necessary. For example, it's possible that the changes in attitude might have resulted from the opportunity to discuss issues of college life rather than from personal contact with the university president. The difficulty of eliminating all extraneous variables weakens the before-and-after design. To overcome this problem, the strength of the design can be expanded by taking repeated measurements of the dependent variable over a period of time.

The power of laboratory experimentation was greatly enhanced with the advent of the *control group method.* In this method, two equivalent groups participate in the experiment, but only one group has any association with the independent variable. In all other respects, the groups are treated in exactly the same manner. If, at the end of the experiment, the treatment group (also called the experimental group) differs from the control group, then the experimenter can infer that the difference is due to the effect of the independent variable (see Figure

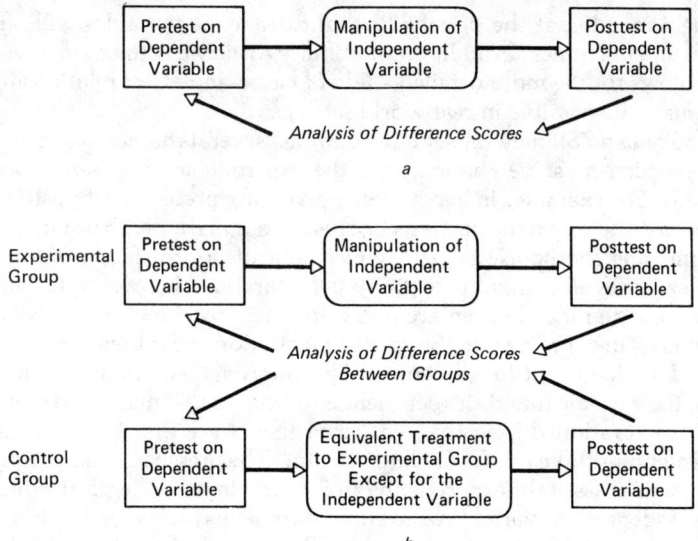

Figure 3.4   Two Common Experimental Designs.

3.4). For example, in the experiment on the effects of personal contact, both a control group and an experimental group would be tested regarding their attitudes about college administrators. Then, a control group of students would engage in a discussion of college life without the university president being involved. The experimental group would engage in the discussion with the president. Then, changes in attitude would be compared. The key to the success of this method is to be sure that the groups are truly equivalent and that they are given equivalent treatment throughout the experiment (with the exception, of course, of the independent variable).

The most effective method for obtaining equivalent groups is random assignment. If subjects are randomly assigned to the two groups, there should be no systematic differences between them.

Validity. Regardless of the particular design employed, the researcher who uses the laboratory experiment must be concerned with two questions of validity. First, has the experiment adequately tested the relationship that it was intended to test? Campbell and Stanley (1966) translated this concern into the concept of *internal validity.* If an experiment has internal validity, then the results in the dependent variable are indeed attributable to the manipulation of the independent variable, rather than to the effects of extraneous variables.

The prime advantage of the experimental method is its ability to effectively study cause-and-effect relationships with high internal validity. The random assignment of subjects and the control of random variations in the experimental setting help to rule out the possibility that extraneous variables will affect the treatment and outcomes. In addition, the ability to vary treatment in a systematic manner allows for the more detailed study of cause-and-effect relationships than would usually be possible in real-world settings.

Campbell and Stanley (1966) have outlined several threats to internal validity, all of which must be eliminated if the experimenter hopes to draw valid conclusions. For example, in experiments involving pretests and posttests, subjects may score better on the posttests because of familiarity with test items. Thus, the experimenter should use a design which controls for the factor of familiarity. Another example of a threat to validity is maturation. For example, suppose a group of second-grade children are tested for their coordination skills and then given exercises in coordination. Suppose that after one year they are tested again and found to have improved scores. The improvement may be due to the exercises, the variable that the experiment is testing—but it may also be due to the children's maturation during the year since they were first tested. Again, the experimenter must take this factor into account. The presence of a control group, of course, would assist the experimenter in determining whether the findings were due to the independent variable or to some extraneous factor(s). The importance of controlling for the various threats to validity in applied work will be discussed in greater detail in Chapter 13.

The most common criticism of laboratory experimentation is that it is far removed from the real-life phenomena that it purports to study. This leads us to the next question of validity: To what degree can the results of an experiment be generalized to the real world? This concern is expressed by Campbell and Stanley (1966) in the concept of *external validity:* Even when internal validity is very high, there is no guarantee that findings are applicable to any situation *other than the experiment itself.*

As control of the situation increases, realism decreases (Aronson & Carlsmith, 1968). The experimenter faces the difficulty of having *low-impact* treatments, applied in a *limited* time frame, in a *contrived* situation that may or may not mirror social reality. Can we say, for example, that asking subjects to rate how much they like photographs or descriptions of other people is a study of interpersonal attraction?

There is another important point researchers must consider. Do subjects in laboratory experiments behave the way they do in real life? This is an empirical question, open to investigation (e.g., Bem & Lord, 1979).

The problem of external validity is compounded by the fact that experiments can study only limited numbers of independent variables at the same time. Since behavior in the real world is determined by a large number of variables, it is altogether possible that relationships demonstrated in a restricted laboratory environment may not be the same relationships that exist in natural settings.

Researchers engaged in laboratory experimentation must also be concerned with the issues of deception, subject bias (behaving according to expectations), experimenter bias (unintentional influence), and the possibility that volunteer subjects differ from the population at large (a matter of reduced external validity). These factors can lead to spurious results and invalid conclusions.

The concern with subject bias comes through most strongly in the concept of *demand characteristics*—the implicit and explicit perceptual cues that communicate what is expected in the experimental setting (Orne, 1962; Adair, 1973). When you walk into the laboratory, you are in a unique and arousal-producing situation. You are especially sensitive to signs that tell you what behavior is appropriate. Orne suggests that most research participants want to be "good" subjects, to behave in ways that are expected, to give the right answers. Unfortunately, this may lead them to behave in ways that confirm the experimenter's hypothesis, whether or not it is true! For example, in a study of consumer preferences, subjects rated the quality of three samples of beer in the expected direction—according to brand names provided by the experimenters. However, all samples were actually the same beer. The experimental situation apparently had communicated certain demands, (i.e., expectations about the quality of the different brands) and the subjects willingly obliged (Adair, 1973).

The problem of *experimenter bias* may be even greater than that of subject bias. Rosenthal and his colleagues (Rosenthal, 1963, 1966; Rosenthal & Rosnow, 1969) have documented how the expectations and characteristics of the experimenter can unintentionally influence the results. The experimenter's sex, race, status, warmth, anxiety level, and so on have been shown to affect the responses of subjects. For example, a high-status experimenter—a professor—tends to elicit more conforming responses than does a low-status experimenter—a student assistant. More importantly, the expectations of the experimenter seem to be communicated to subjects through facial expression, tone of voice, and so on.

In one classic example, ten different research assistants had subjects rate photographs of people's faces on the degree of success or failure they exhibited. The rating was made on a scale from -10 (extreme failure) to $+10$ (extreme success). All ten researchers were given identical instructions for conducting the experiment—with one exception: half were told that the well-established finding for this type of research was that people generally rated the photos as successful (about $+5$); the other half were told that people generally rated the photos as unsuccessful (about -5). The result? They experimenters who were given a "successful expectation" obtained a higher mean rating from their subjects than did those whose who expected failure ratings.

Rosenthal makes a number of suggestions for controlling the effects of experimenter bias. One solution is to use "blind" experimenters, that is, experimenters who do not know the hypothesis under study or who are not aware of all the conditions of the experiment including the particular variable being studied. For example, in an experiment on how well ex-convicts adapt to stress, the "blind" experimenter will not be told which subjects are ex-convicts and which are members of the control group. Another solution to the problem of experimenter bias is to develop better training procedures so that experimenters can learn to be more objective and more neutral.

Selection of participants is another concern in experiments. College sophomores may not be real people! Results that are based on *volunteer* subjects who were drawn mainly from university classes may not generalize to the public at large. Rosenthal and Rosnow (1975) have demonstrated that people who volunteer to participate in research generally are different in some important ways from people who do not volunteer. Higher sociability, higher intelligence, and higher need for approval are just three examples of characteristics that distinguish volunteers from nonvolunteers. How well results based on this select group can be generalized to the public is an open question. It is also a limiting factor in the external validity of laboratory experiments.

The study of factors that limit internal and external validity has led to a veritable "social psychology of the psychological experiment" (Adair, 1973; Gergen, 1978; Silverman, 1977). This line of investigation is concerned with all the processes and conditions that enter into the complex interaction of subject, experimenter, and laboratory. According to Adair (1973), many findings of experimental research may be artifacts of social interaction in the laboratory setting, rather than valid principles of human behavior at large. The need to understand these contaminating effects and to establish controls for them where possible is therefore the greatest current challenge to laboratory experimentation.

Games and Simulations. In an attempt to inject more social reality into the contrived laboratory situation, social scientists have turned to the more complex methods of gaming and simulation. *Simulation,* an intentional imitation of the essential processes and outcomes of a real social situation, is carried out in order to better understand the underlying mechanisms of that situation (Abelson, 1968). A simulation is an operating model of a social system that continues over time (Streufert & Suedfeld, 1977). The investigator attempts to represent more of social reality without sacrificing experimental control (Crano & Brewer, 1973). However, simulation does not provide as much isolation and control of variables as does laboratory experimentation.

As a theory-testing device, simulation is used when the relationships among variables must be studied in a more realistic manner than is possible in the laboratory. As a closer reflection of the real world, simulation permits the study of a larger number of variables in more complex interaction than does the laboratory experiment. In simulation, the research participants must be able and willing collaborators with the experimenter, helping to develop the reality of the social situation through their role-playing behavior.

Laboratory games include business games, war games, and bargaining games (Abelson, 1968). In this method, the participant is given a role in a situation designed and controlled by the experimenter. The participant behaves in accordance with his or her role perception, making choices that seem to be appropriate. Usually, the participant is given instructions that will enable task success (maximizing the outcomes), and the range of responses is more restricted than in simulations.

The *mixed-motive game,* a commonly used design, studies the mixture of cooperation and competitive behavior in negotiation and conflict resolution. Most mixed-motive games involve two players, each of whom has two choices— to cooperate with the other or to compete. If both players cooperate, joint outcomes are maximized; if both compete, then minimum outcomes are obtained. If one competes and the other cooperates, then the competitor wins big—but possibly only on that trial. (The game is commonly run through a large number of trails.) The mixed-motive game permits the investigator to study the effect of such independent variables as personality characteristics or amount of communication on the amount of competitive-versus-cooperative behavior shown by the players. Mixed-motive games have been used a great deal to study conflict (see Chapter 14). However, there are questions about the advantages and disadvantages of games for the study of real-world conflict (e.g., Schlenker & Bonoma, 1978).

The simulation of social systems in the laboratory is more complex than gaming. Usually, a larger number and variety of roles are involved, and there is more flexibility in the range of behaviors available to role players. While the investigator can study a larger number of variables in more complex interaction, control over the situation and the outcomes is sacrificed. Simulations have been used to represent such real-life social situations as a ward in a psychiatric hospital, a police communications center, a mock prison, and decision making in international relations.

Field Experimentation and Quasi-Experimental Design

Field Experiment. Many social situations are difficult or impossible to create in the laboratory; nevertheless, they must be studied if social psychology is to create a valid knowledge base. At times, it is possible to increase external validity significantly by moving the experimental methodology out of the laboratory and into the field. In the *field experiment*, the researcher intervenes in a real-world setting by introducing or manipulating the independent variable and assessing the resulting effects on the dependent variable. Often this will involve a before-and-after design, but it is sometimes possible to create control groups as well.

With field experimentation it is far more difficult to control extraneous variables and create effective manipulations. But at the same time, internal validity may be increased since the method is *nonreactive*—subjects do not know they are in a study, and will not react in ways that may invalidate the results. Therefore, the behavior in question—say, for example, interpersonal attraction—will be more realistic than in the laboratory.

Field experimentation raises some very difficult ethical issues: invasion of privacy, deception, and a lack of informed consent. In the early 1970s, criticism of laboratory experimentation led many social psychologists to move their experiments into the real world. As a result, the use of nonreactive methods increased, which led to a concern regarding the ethical and legal aspects of such research (Silverman, 1975; Wilson & Donnerstein, 1976). Consider the following situations:

1. An experimenter knocks on someone's door, says that he has misplaced the address of a friend who lives nearby, and asks to use the phone. If the subject lets him in, he pretends to make the call.
2. A male experimenter pretends to collapse in a subway car; "stage blood" trickles from his mouth. If someone offers to assist him, he allows the subject to help him to his feet. If no one does, a second experimenter provides assistance, and they get off at the next stop.

3. A subject sitting alone on a park bench is asked to participate in interviews ostensibly being carried out by a research organization. At the same time a confederate of the researcher sitting nearby is asked to participate. The confederate responds with answers that are directly opposite to those of the subject, and makes demeaning remarks about the subject's answers.

Silverman (1975) wondered whether intrusions such as these involved fraud, trespass, harassment, and the like. In short, were they legal? Accordingly, he asked two lawyers to determine whether ten such nonreactive methods violated the law. One saw little violation; the second thought the prosecution for criminal action was justifiable in several cases. Wilson and Donnerstein (1976) took a different tack. Assessing the public's reaction to the same ten examples, they found in general that the majority of subjects did not react negatively on ethical or legal grounds. However, since a substantial minority—and in some cases a majority—did object to certain of the methods, they echoed Silverman's caution that social psychologists should be more sensitive to the ethical issues in field experimentation.

An example of a field experiment is provided by Lupfer, Kay, and Burnette (1969). These researchers studied the influence of picketing on the purchase of toy guns. The investigators placed two pickets in front of a large Memphis department store. Their signs said, "Toy Guns Today Mean Real Guns Tomorrow." Picketing occurred in three mornings in late December, capitalizing on the usual Christmas toy-buying rush. On three other mornings, the investigators observed toy-buying behavior to provide a control measure. Observers were placed inside the store near the cash registers to tally the number of persons who bought toys and the number of purchases that included toy guns. There was a significantly smaller number of toy-gun buyers on the mornings that picketing occurred than on the control mornings, thus supporting the hypothesis that picketing depressed the sale of toy guns. The short time between the intervention of the independent variable (the picketing) and the observation of the dependent variable (toy-buying behavior) is one of the strong points of this study. Picketing, however, probably served more as a temporary inhibitor of the actions of potential gun buyers rather than as a factor effecting long-term attitude and behavioral change.

Natural Experiment. In the *natural experiment,* a change occurs in a real-world independent variable. The investigator capitalizes on this natural intervention by studying its effects on some appropriate dependent measures. The natural experiment involves less planning and control on the part of the investigator and requires him or her to react to a natural occurrence. As a result, some disadvantages exist: subjects are not chosen in a representative fashion, but either are self-selected or just happen to be available. Thus, generalizability of results may be limited. Of course, it is difficult or impossible to anticipate such natural disasters as tidal waves or earthquakes, or such human actions as labor strikes or the outbreak of war. Nonetheless, the social researcher who can capitalize on such situations will obviously have a study that encompasses a much greater degree of reality than is possible in laboratory experimentation.

A classic example of a natural experiment is provided by Lieberman (1956), who studied the effects of role position on the attitudes of role occupants. Lieberman was involved in a continuing study of an industrial organization that included an assessment of attitudes toward management and the union. During the first phase of the study, two groups of rank-and-file workers underwent role changes: some were promoted to supervisors; others were elected as union stewards. Before-and-after measurements of attitudes indicated that workers who were made supervisors became more favorable in their attitude toward management; workers who were elected stewards tended to become more favorable toward the union.

The impact of even further changes was assessed due to a period of economic recession. At that time, some of the supervisors were demoted to worker positions; some union stewards did not run again or were not reelected to their union positions. Once more, Lieberman capitalized on these occurrences by assessing attitudes. As he predicted, he found that supervisors who were demoted reverted to the attitudes they had previously held; on the other hand, supervisors who remained in their role maintained their positive attitudes toward management. The results for union stewards were less clear-cut. In general, however, the results strongly supported the proposition that an individual's role has a definite impact on the attitudes relevant to carrying out that role.

Quasi-Experimental Design. Quasi-experimental designs are studies in which the experimenter has partial rather than full experimental control over the variables and the setting (Campbell & Stanley, 1966; Cook & Campbell, 1976, 1979). In other words, the experimenter has little or no control over the independent variable, and is unable to adequately control all of the extraneous variables; however, he or she does have the ability to measure the dependent variable. The usefulness of each quasi-experimental design has to be judged in relation to threats to its internal and external validity. Each design will rule out some threats but not others; the researcher must be aware of these strengths and weaknesses before deciding what design to apply in a given situation. To illustrate, let's take a look at two common quasi-experimental designs.

The *interrupted-time-series design* is an extension of the simple before-and-after method. It can be used to gauge the effects of a legislative or policy change (or some other independent variable) when relevant records (dependent variable measures) are available. The design involves measuring the dependent variable at a number of points over time in order to gauge the effect of the change or intervention.

An example is the analysis of the Connecticut speed crackdown instituted by Governor Abraham Ribicoff in the mid-1950s (Campbell & Ross, 1968; Ross & Campbell, 1968). In 1955, automobile accidents caused 324 deaths in Connecticut—a record high for the decade. As the most hazardous time of the year, the Christmas holidays, approached, Governor Ribicoff initiated a severe crackdown on speeders. Speed limits were more strictly enforced and licenses of drivers convicted of speeding were suspended. As 1956 unfolded, there was an increase in license suspensions and a decrease in fatalities and arrests. Although late summer

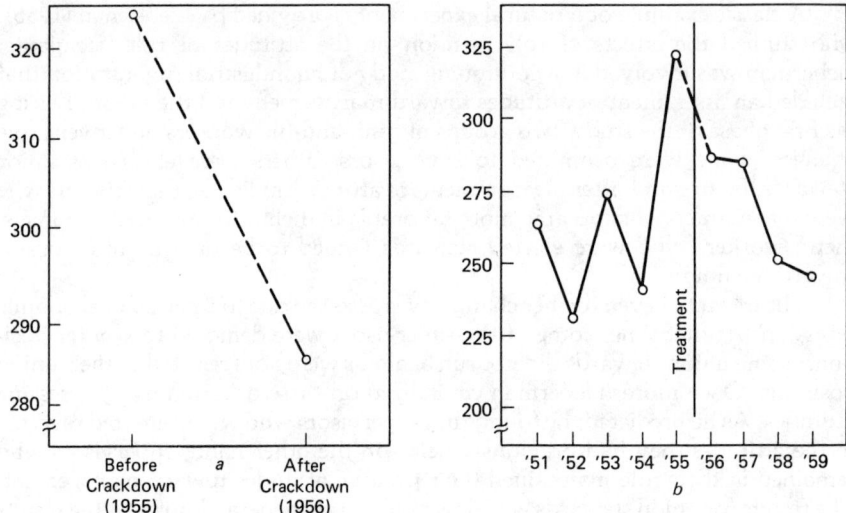

Figure 3.5   Time Series Analysis and the Connecticut Speed Crackdown.
Source: Campbell (1969).

brought a large number of traffic fatalities, the total for the year was 284. Since this was considerably less than the 1955 total, the governor concluded that the crackdown was definitely worthwhile.

On the basis of the figures for 1955 and 1956, the governor's conclusion seemed warranted. Campbell and Ross, however, believed that a more detailed look should be taken. Using an interrupted-time-series design, they examined the data for several years before and after the intervention in order to gauge trends over a longer period of time (see Figure 3.5). Considering the related threats to validity, their analysis made it seem doubtful that the crackdown actually had the effects attributed to it. For example, over the longer time period there was considerable instability in the figures of traffic fatalities; some years showed very large increases, whereas others showed large decreases. Therefore, the decline in 1956 could simply be evidence of further instability. In addition, the year 1955 was a high point in the series. Through the process of *regression* (where high random variations tend to regress back toward the average), we would expect a decrease in 1956. The time series analysis thus did not support the efficacy of the crackdown.

A second type of quasi-experimental design is the *control-series design*. For example, in the study of speeding crackdowns, the researchers compared the traffic fatalities of the experimental state (the state initiating the crackdowns) with the fatalities of several control states (that is, states with no crackdowns). This analysis showed a more rapid decline in fatalities in Connecticut following the crackdown, but the difference was not large enough to conclude that the crackdown was the main reason.

We can see how useful it is to employ the most sophisticated designs possible to assess the effects of social policies or programs (see Chapter 13). This is more effective than relying on initial impressions or superficial appearances. Through the use of quasi-experimental designs, the social scientist is in a much better position to do valuable research in field settings.

Summary

The scientist is a craftsperson who selects the best tools available to work on a topic of interest to produce a scientific product. The scientist carefully follows the steps of the scientific method—steps that have their foundation in empiricism—a philosophical approach that maintains that knowledge is generated through experience by way of the human senses. Objective empiricism specifies that meaningful knowledge is developed and verified through observation and experiment, with clear connections between the empirical and the conceptual levels.

There are five major types of research in social psychology:

1. *Descriptive research* documents the existing social reality by describing characteristics and their frequency of occurrence. It requires reliable and valid measuring instruments.
2. *Correlational research* studies how variables correlate (vary together). Extreme caution must be used in inferring causality from correlational research. At the same time, correlational research sensitizes us to the reality of multiple causation in social behavior.
3. *Experimental research* tests causal linkages among variables. The experimenter manipulates the independent variable, controls extraneous conditions, and assesses the effect on the dependent variable.
4. *Action research* blends the activities of social research and social action. The researcher collaborates with citizens to analyze a problem, engages in fact-finding or data collection about the situation, executes an action designed to alleviate the difficulty, and then evaluates the effects of the action.
5. *Evaluation research* involves the application of research methods to assess the effects of a social program or policy. This activity is strongly affected by the sociopolitical context in which it occurs. Evaluation research is similar to pure research, but it is usually more technically difficult and politically demanding.

Professional codes of ethics require researchers to weigh the benefits of a study to science and society against the costs to the welfare of the participants. Major ethical concerns include informed consent, invasion of privacy, the use of deception, disrespectful and harmful treatment, and the social responsibility of the researchers for dissemination of results.

Observational methods are the most straightforward empirical approach to understanding the world. The various types of observation vary on the dimensions of concealment, intervention, and structure. Participant observation involves the observer as a participant in the social event that is being documented. The continuous observational approach results in the construction of detailed specimen records of individual behavior in behavior settings. A number of categorizing systems such as Interaction Process Analysis permit resarchers to observe various social situations.

Content analysis is the study of what people have done. It includes the study of transcripts of speeches, books, statistical records, and so on. Its purpose is to categorize written or spoken information into a small number of descriptive categories in a selective, systematic, and reliable manner.

The research interview is a structured two-person conversation designed to elicit the information desired by the researcher. The interviewer contorls the situation by asking a carefully worded sequence of questions. The interview situation tends to engender positive motivation on the part of respondents and allows the interviewer to maximize understanding.

There are a number of self-report techniques for gaining written information directly from respondents, including questionnaires, sociometric methods, rating scales, attitude scales, and psychological testing. Self-report measures are usually more economical than interviewing methods and can attain a high degree of measurement precision.

Survey methodology involves sampling a segment of the population by asking questions through interviews or self-report methods. The key process in survey research is the selection of a representative sample. Although surveys are useful for collecting information economically, they tend to do so in a relatively superficial manner.

Laboratory experimentation, games, simulation, and field experimentation all require the intervention of the researcher in the lives of the research participants. Experimental designs include the before-and-after method and the control-group method.

Internal validity exists when an experiment has adequately tested the relationship it was designed to test. External validity exists when the results of an experiment can be generalized to the real world.

Games and simulations represent an attempt to capture more of social reality without sacrificing experimental control. Games provide the participants with a well-specified role that requires them to make choices to maximize task success. Simulations in the laboratory are considerably more complex than games; they usually involve a larger number and variety of roles and put fewer constraints upon the behavior of the participants.

Field experimentation includes the field experiment, in which the researcher controls the variables and the situation, and the natural experiment, in which the effects of a naturally occurring independent variable on dependent measures are assessed. Field experiments raise the ethical issues of deception, invasion of privacy, and informed consent. In quasi-experimental designs, the experimenter has no control over the independent variable and some control over extraneous variables. The interrupted-time-series design and the control-series design are two examples.

Each method of social research has its particular advantages and disadvantages. Researchers must consider which method is most appropriate to the particular problem under study.

Further Readings

Adair, J. G. *The human subject: The social psychology of the psychological experiment.* Boston: Little, Brown, 1973.

Agnew, N. & Pyke, S. *The science game: An introduction to research in behavioral sciences* (2nd ed.). Englewood Cliffs, N.J.: Prentice-Hall, 1978.

Crano, W. D. & Brewer, M. B. *Principles of research in social psychology.* New York: McGraw-Hill, 1973.

Kidder, L. H. *Selltiz, Wrightsman and Cook's research methods in social relations (4th ed.). New York: Holt, Rinehart & Winston, 1981.*

Lewin, K. *Resolving social conflicts.* New York: Harper, 1948.

CHAPTER OUTLINE

CHANGE AGENT: TRAINER, CONSULTANT, TECHNOLOGIST, OR ADVOCATE?
Human Relations Training
Process Consultation
Social Technology
Social Advocacy
The Problem-Solving Process
Values and Ethics of the Change Agent

AREAS OF SKILL TRAINING
Personal Motivation Training
Interpersonal Communication Skills
Small-Group Skills

METHODS OF CONSULTATION
General Models of Consultation
Lippitt and Lippitt's Multiple Role Model
Blake and Mouton's Consulcube
Forms of Process Consultation

SUMMARY

FURTHER READINGS

Practice Skills for the Applied Social Psychologist

I remember the first time I saw Detroit. It was 1969. Driving into the city from the suburbs, I noticed that with each passing mile the houses deteriorated, the air changed to smog, and the freeway became more littered. On my right was the deserted hulk of a multimillion-dollar public housing complex, the victim of social isolation, vandalism, and crime. On my left were burned-out stores, the ruins of the summer riot of 1967. All around me was the pall of the belching smokestacks of the steel factories where jobs were too often gained by patronage, favoritism, and family ties. All around me was the ghetto decay of broken families, vast unemployment, schools that graduated illiterates, and crime that left the night streets deserted.

During the years I lived near Detroit, watching it lose its strength and vitality, observing the urban decay as a social psychologist, I asked myself: Is it enough to simply *know*? Research studies help us to understand; theories explain the decay, the riots, the racism, the everything! *And yet little has changed.* Is it enough to document injustice and the maltreatment of people? Or do we need to care, and then based on our knowledge and our caring, to act? I am now certain that we must translate our knowledge into action in every social system from interpersonal relationships to human service organizations to society at large.

This fundamental truth of applied social psychology was clear to Kurt Lewin (1948) as he reflected upon his community work in intergroup relations, and particularly as he reflected upon the usefulness of training workshops for practitioners:

This and similar experiences have convinced me that we should consider action, research, and training as a triangle that should be kept together for the sake of any of its corners. It is seldom possible to improve the action pattern without training personnel. In fact today the lack of competent training personnel is one of the greatest hindrances to progress in setting up more experimentation. The training of large numbers of social scientists who can handle scientific problems but are also equipped for the delicate task of building productive, hard-hitting teams with practitioners is a prerequisite for progress in social science as well as in social management for intergroup relations. (p. 211)

Today I live in a small, pleasant prairie city—a beautiful place to live, to work, and to raise a family. But looming on the horizon is the plague that debilitated Detroit—the plague of racism, hostility, discrimination, and social decay. The people of full Indian ancestry and the people of mixed ancestry, the métis, are a group apart in my society. Their racial background is physically apparent; most live on reserves, or on their own side of town; they have their own value system and way of living. They belong to a people who once owned this continent, yet most of them have meager incomes that contrast pitifully with their former land wealth.

The signs of racism and intercultural conflict are unmistakable and diverse. Life on most Indian reserves is a personal and social tragedy of immense proportion by any yardstick of physical or social well-being. The stark reality of an oppressed people destroying themselves is expressed in alcoholism and crime rates that shock even the most insensitive observer. Many Indians and métis are migrating to the cities—and, sadly, with this migration comes the rise of intergroup conflict and the development of ghettos. In ten or twenty years, my city may be another Detroit. And it may be too late to reverse the powerful social and economic forces that are pushing us in these destructive directions.

With potential social destruction hanging in the air, we have formed a city hall committee charged with facilitating the urban adjustment of Indians and métis, of increasing the social awareness of white people, and of improving intergroup relations among all people in the city. The committee is composed of Indian and métis community leaders, local politicians, and a representative of the city police force. I serve on this committee as a human relations consultant. It is my job to carry out applied research projects to document social needs and the barriers to meeting those needs; to organize and evaluate intercultural workshops to reduce racism; and to help develop human service programs to address our social problems.

As an applied social psychologist and as a citizen, I can contribute to the process of productive social change. But while I am hopeful and committed to our goals, I am pessimistic about our chances of preventing another Detroit. The powerful forces that produce racism and poverty are pervasive and relentless. And yet I know that useful change can occur at all levels of functioning and that our skills can facilitate change at those levels.

That is why this chapter is important to me. It deals with the humanistic qualities and the approaches we social psychologists need to work with people to increase our mutual well-being. The chapter looks at a variety of ways we can actively confront social problems. It explores the promise that practice holds for a vital social psychology and a just society. It examines the variety and depth of the possibilities that practice skills hold for applied social psychology.

CHANGE AGENT: TRAINER, CONSULTANT, TECHNOLOGIST, OR ADVOCATE?

The applied social psychologist is essentially a *change agent*. Taking a variety of roles, the change agent focuses on human interaction and how that interaction can be facilitated, developed, and made more effective. The change agent is thus concerned with the basic elements of social relationships—and how they can be improved to create open, competent, and productive social systems that meet our human needs (Bennis, 1973).

A change agent may take the role of researcher, human relations trainer, consultant, counselor, or teacher (Bennis, 1973). These roles fall into three general categories: research, orientation, and social technology (Hornstein, 1975). In the first category the change agent may deal with applied research, action research, or evaluation research. All are forms of social intervention that should result in social change. In an orientation role the change agent disseminates research results in the form of recommendations for action and statements on social policy. This activity bridges the gap between knowledge and its direct utilization—that is, application for social change. In the category of social technology, the applied social psychologist is a catalytic agent with the knowledge and expertise needed to improve the functioning of a given social system. In this category, the typical roles are those of human relations trainer, process consultant, social technologist, and social advocate.

It is not easy to shift from academic discipline to social practice, from theoretical research to applied work (Maslach, 1975). The shift means movement from passive reflection and freedom of action to active involvement as a participant open to outside influences. The abstract must be translated into the concrete, and the temptation to behave as an expert (who may turn out to be woefully wrong) is often great. As a result, the social psychologist who moves from theory to practice may face difficult issues of changed professional identity, reduced status, and shifting personal power, values, and ethics. Applied work, however, is increasingly appreciated by society for the extent of its personal and professional demands, and for its usefulness for both people and science. The role of change agent, already difficult to enact well, also carries the added responsibility of clearly articulating one's values and competencies in relation to the work carried out with other people. The payoff, however, is great: The effective change agent will have significantly increased the probability that society will change for the better through rational design, rather than change for the worse by default or decay (Blake & Mouton, 1973).

Human Relations Training

As a change agent, the social psychologist may take on the role of human relations trainer, a role linked with social psychology since the early workshops that led to the formation of the National Training Laboratories (NTL). The goals of these workshops included self-awareness as well as understanding and skills in group relations and social change (Benne, Bradford, Gibb & Lippitt, 1975). These objectives were approached through lectures, skill practice groups, and general sessions involving the entire laboratory community. The heart of the experience, however, turned out to be within the basic skill training groups: participants interacted, provided each other with feedback, then analyzed and discussed their own behavior in the group. These basic skill training groups served as the forerunner of sensitivity training groups.

There are a number of characteristics that are unique to the laboratory method of learning and human relations training (Benne et al., 1975). Human relations training helps people learn how to learn *from* themselves—a process called *experiential* or *experience-based learning.* To do this the trainer creates a temporary social system in which participants feel free to behave in ways that may not be possible in real-life situations. The human relations laboratory thus becomes a supportive, nonthreatening environment for experiencing the consequences of one's behavior in the "here-and-now" of ongoing social interaction.

Even though the participants may function relatively well in the real world, they may have blind spots about the effect of their behavior on others. They may have been socialized to keep their thoughts and feelings to themselves, thereby reducing effective communication with other individuals and with groups. Although they are group members in the real world, participants may also be unaware of how groups function, and of how this functioning can be improved. The participants may understand some of the principles of communication and group dynamics, yet may be unable to act upon this understanding (Lubin & Eddy, 1970).

The laboratory environment, carefully structured and controlled by the trainer, permits individuals to look at the impact of their typical behavior on other people. The environment helps them to be aware (perhaps for the first time in their lives) of the effect of their behavior and of possibilities for change to alternative, more productive behaviors. This awareness grows out of several forces at work in the laboratory: the trainer as a model of behavior; the emphasis on open communication among participants; the encouragement of feedback among participants; the active collaboration between the trainer and the group; and the trainer's interventions, aimed at improving communication, feedback, and interaction among participants (Dyer, 1972).

For example, in one human relations workshop in which I was a trainer, one participant was unaware of how her behavior was affecting other people. She was skilled in understanding other participants' feelings, but rarely expressed any of her own feelings. She also spoke in a smooth and polished fashion, and her facial expression was composed and pleasant. In short, her behavior detracted from her genuineness as a person, leading other participants to feel distant from her. When she requested and received feedback on her behavior, she was astounded. For years she had been working to increase her self-confidence and her communication skills, and she did not realize she had gone too far. In wanting to understand others and convey an impression of composure and control, she had become plastic and distant. The feedback greatly affected her behavior. Her facial expression and tone of voice became softer and more varied. She expressed more of her own feelings. The other participants felt closer to her, and she was able to relate to them in a more authentic fashion.

As a part of the laboratory process, the role of the human relations trainer goes still further. Coupled with his or her interventions, the trainer translates items of interaction, communication, and conflict resolution into appropriate theoretical concepts, sharing these with the participants to help illuminate the nature of their behavior. Participants, for example, are often unaware that the intentions of their behavior and the actual effects of their behavior can be two very different things. I remember one participant who finished most of her sentences to others by looking away and injecting a tone of finality into her voice. She intended to mean that she was finished speaking, but the effect on others was the impression that she did not want a response from them. In the role of trainer, I explained the discrepancy between intentions and effects in interpersonal communication, a useful concept for her and for other participants.

The trainer, as an active participant, also invites feedback about his or her own behavior, and may engage in conflict with the group. This of course triggers still greater self-awareness on everyone's part, trainer included.

The effectiveness of human relations training has been evaluated by a large number of research studies (see Chapter 7). I have been impressed that most of the trainers I have worked with, regardless of experience, are continuing to learn about themselves and how they affect others. As Gordon Lippitt (1979) points out, it is essential that human-resource professionals follow a number of strategies for continuing growth of their awareness, knowledge, and expertise. Receiving feedback, co-training with others, enrolling as participants in advanced workshops, and being involved in a professional association are all activities that foster ongoing professional development.

In the years since the pioneering workshops, human relations training has expanded both its direction and approaches (Benne et al., 1975; Bradford, 1976). Different types of laboratories focus on personal growth and interpersonal relations (often called *encounter groups*), on interpersonal communication and group processes (for example, NTL's human interaction laboratory), on group development, intergroup relations, and conflict management. The development of occupational laboratories for such specialized groups as managers, church workers, educators, and community workers has expanded the laboratory method into the practice fields of organization and community development. At the same time, human relations training has expanded geographically, moving into Europe, South America, and Africa.

In addition, the basic laboratory method of learning has been supplemented by the training of more specific skills, such as those of interpersonal communication and group leadership. These have added to the structure of the learning environment and have more closely linked conceptual input with the practice experiences of the participants.

Human relations training workshops are offered to the general public through the major training organizations—the NTL Institute in Arlington, Virginia, and University Associates of San Diego, California and Burlington, Ontario. In addition, many universities and colleges have extension departments, counseling centers, and/or institutes for human development that offer workshops to the

An *encounter group* is a type of human relations training that focuses on personal growth and interpersonal relations. *(Bohdan Hrynewych/Stock, Boston)*

community at large. Finally, many professional consultants conduct training laboratories for particular organizations—businesses, government departments, hospitals, schools. Many organizations now employ trainers within their personnel or human resources departments to offer services to employees on a full-time basis. Goldstein (1980) provides a review of the various training activities that are carried out in work organizations.

Human relations training is a significant area of professional practice; it provides participants with increased understanding of the roles they have undertaken in the social system and the opportunities for effective change; it provides a new perspective on the complex forces at work in social relations.

Process Consultation

There are many areas in which an applied social psychologist may provide consultation services. To give a clearer picture of what the consultation role involves, we will focus on only one classic type: process consultation.

Process consultation expands the role of human relations trainer from the context of the individual and the small group to the larger context of the organization. Schein (1969) provided the initial definition of process consultation as "a set of activities of the consultant which help the client to perceive, understand and act upon process events which occur in the client's environment" (p. 9). Schein's definition of this role was based on his own experience as an organizational consultant. He states that process consultation is designed to help the client organization diagnose human problems within its social system and to seek a solution through active collaboration with the client. In diagnosing the problems of the client's system, the process consultant focuses on the effectiveness of interpersonal communication patterns, decision making, leadership, group functioning, and intergroup relations. Then, combining his or her expertise in human relations with acquired knowledge about typical processes within the organization, the process consultant examines the critical areas of that human system and interprets those elements for the client. The consultant's goal is not to provide specific solutions for the client, but rather to help the client system use its human resources more effectively by increasing awareness of crucial processes and by acquiring new values and skills (see Box 4.1).

To provide a useful service for the client system, the process consultant works through a series of stages (Schein, 1969; Lippitt & Lippitt, 1978): (1) contact, contract, establish client relationship; (2) select work setting and appropriate methods; (3) gather information for problem identification and diagnosis; (4) with client, set goals and plan actions; (5) collaborate through active intervention in the system; and (6) evaluate effects of the intervention and terminate contract as appropriate.

While this sequence is fairly straightforward, each stage involves the consultant in key issues or dilemmas. The complexity of these issues increases with the range of multiple roles that the consultant is willing to enact. For example, a consultation contract that involves the gathering of information through surveys and the implementation of training interventions is more complex than an intervention based on simple observation and feedback. These are typical issues in each stage of consulting:

- *Stage 1: Contact.* The expectations in the psychological contract with the client must be made clear. The process consultant is not the expert who will terminate the intervention with a list of recommendations for action. The client who is seeking a doctor-patient relationship or technical advice on finances or production should be referred elsewhere.
- *Stage 2: Select settings.* The method used to select the work settings to be analyzed should also serve to build an effective helping relationship. Personal interviews, for example, create more trust and openness between the consultant and the members of the client system than do questionnaires.

Box 4.1 FOCUS ON PRACTICE
An Example of Process Consultation

Edgar Schein, one of the pioneers of process consultation in organizational settings, provides several examples of this form of practice. One example involves helping company managers improve the effectiveness of their meetings.

At the weekly executive meeting, Schein served as a process observer. It became quickly apparent that the group was very loose in its manner of operating: members contributed freely, topics were explored fully, and conflict was openly confronted. While this approach resulted in constructive communication, the committee was never able to complete its agenda. The backlog of items to be discussed grew longer, members became frustrated, more meetings were scheduled, the members worked harder—all to no avail.

Schein suggested to the group that it was overloaded—the agenda was too large and was usually a mixture of operational or production items and policy items. The group discussed how to develop the agenda for their meetings, and with Schein's help they sorted the agenda into different categories. They decided to devote some meetings entirely to the simpler operational items and to discuss these in a tighter and more efficient manner. They would use other meetings to discuss in depth the more complex policy issues. This led to a more efficient use of the group's time and greater satisfaction on the part of the members.

The executive committee then decided to hold policy meetings once a month for an entire day in a less hectic environment away from the office. The president asked Schein to attend these meetings and to provide process observations and theoretical analyses of the committee's functioning. After building a greater climate of trust in this setting, the group asked Schein to help members provide direct feedback to each other on their strengths and weaknesses.

Based on his experience in human relations training and his observations of the group, Schein was able to provide some useful guidelines. For example, he had observed that whenever one person commented on someone else, there was a strong tendency for the person being discussed to answer back and stay locked in on that comment. Thus, additional feedback from other members was cut off. Schein therefore suggested that the group discuss one person at a time, and that the person being described was not to respond until all group members had given their feedback.

For several hours, the group discussed each member's managerial and interpersonal style. Schein encouraged the discussion of both positives and negatives, asked members to make concrete and specific comments, aided clarification, and added his own feedback. This exercise deepened relationships within the group and exposed some chronic problems that could now be worked on effectively. The role of the process consultant was essential in bringing this about.

Source: Schein, E. H. *Process consultation: Its role in organization development.* Reading, Mass.: Addison-Wesley, 1969.

- *Stage 3: Gather information.* The consultant should involve the client in the collection of data. The client system will then take the data more seriously and will be more motivated to collaborate in the next steps. For example, if clients contribute ideas to a questionnaire to measure worker satisfaction, they will accept the findings more readily.

- *Stage 4: Set goals, plan actions.* The consultant must make the client aware of the importance of skill training and action practice in achieving the goals that have been set. If a work group is diagnosed to have inadequate listening skills, then training interventions must be planned to help them learn paraphrasing, how to reflect feelings, and so on.
- *Stage 5: Intervention.* Within the vast range of possible interventions, the consultant must choose the most appropriate ones—and the most appropriate times to initiate them. Schein's (1969) concise set of potential interventions includes agenda-setting interventions (suggest a meeting to discuss interpersonal relationships); feedback (provide process comments to a group on how effectively it is working); coaching or counseling (work with an individual to change unproductive behavior); and structural interventions (suggest a change in the communication patterns of the organization). Such choices are crucial to the success of consultation.
- *Stage 6: Evaluation and termination.* Beyond the consultation period, the consultant will provide follow-up support. His or her values and skills, however, must be transmitted to the client to avoid the client's dependence on the consultant. The goal of consultation is increased resourcefulness and competence, not increased reliance on the consultant.

The pioneering work in process consultation has now expanded into the practice field of *organization development*, which provides consultation to a wide range of business and human service organizations (see Chapter 10).

Social Technology

In a general sense, social technology refers to a wide range of social interventions including human relations training, process consultation, and other approaches in which a catalytic agent helps groups and organizations improve their functioning (Hornstein, 1975). In a more specific sense, *social technology* is the application of social-psychological knowledge to the solution of social problems (Varela, 1971). This bears some similarity to what George Miller (1969) had in mind when, as president of the American Psychological Association, he spoke about "giving psychology away" to improve human welfare. If we can use our knowledge to increase people's understanding of the social processes that are affecting their lives, we perform a valuable service.

Unfortunately, the picture is not so simple. Social technology, like any technology, can be abused. It can be used in a deceptive and manipulative manner to covertly influence people to behave different from the way they might behave if given a free and informed choice. People can be influenced to buy products they don't need and to make decisions that are not in their best interests (as defined by a full weighing of the costs and benefits to them). It is these abuses of social technology that Vance Packard has identified in *The Hidden Persuaders* (1957) and *The People Shapers* (1978)—his provocative analyses of deceptive advertising and the manipulation of behavior.

The crucial question is whether or not our use of social technology flows from the humanistic value base (see Chapter 1). Interventions that value each person's right to dignity, respect, and free choice are ethically and morally right. Interventions that deceive and manipulate people are unacceptable and merit our censure. Let's take a look at two examples of social technology: one, a positive use of knowledge to potentially increase people's freedom and dignity; the other, an illustration of the abuse of social-psychological knowledge.

In the field of medicine, the procedure of transplanting organs has created numerous legal and ethical issues. Michael Saks (1978), serving as a social psychologist on a legislative subcommittee concerned with the issue of organ transplants, made a number of social-psychological contributions to the deliberations of the committee. When a person needs an organ transplant, it is important to find a donor whose physical characteristics are compatible with those of the recipient, so that the recipient's immune system is less likely to reject the transplant. The most likely donors are therefore close relatives, particularly siblings. This places the donor in a difficult choice situation: Donating the organ (a kidney, for example) will enhance the recipient's chances of survival, but may also place the donor's health at greater risk. Thus, the law specifies that consent of the donor must be arrived at through a free and informed decision.

It was on the process of selecting the prospective donor and requesting a decision that Saks was able to make an important contribution. The usual procedure followed by physicians was to delay asking a donor for a decision until the end of the selection process. Following the usual procedure, prospective donors would undergo a series of examinations and briefings. Only after they understood the procedures and risks and were found to be compatible with the recipient and in good health, would a request for a donation be made. The moral rationale for this approach was that only compatible donors should have the burden of making a decision placed on them.

However, Saks pointed out that—through a process of subtle influence—the usual procedure would probably increase the proportion of persons who would consent to donate. First, social-psychological research on the "foot-in-the-door technique" has demonstrated that inducing compliance with a small favor increases the chances that a later and larger request will also be acceded to (Freedman & Fraser, 1966). In particular, the small acts of compliance such as submitting to an examination make it more likely that a donor will eventually agree to the large request of donating an organ. Second, the principles of social learning theory also predict that the more preliminary behaviors induced the greater the probability of donation. A series of successive approximations to the target behavior are rewarded. Coming to the hospital, giving a blood sample, and so on, are all met with positive reinforcement, and therefore the likelihood of eventual donation is enhanced. In effect, the common medical practices might be operating in such a way as to reduce free and informed consent unintentionally. Thus, in these and other ways Saks's analysis was valuable in illuminating the meaning of free choice in a complex and difficult situation.

Our negative example of social technology comes from the work of Varela (1971, 1975, 1977), who maintains that the social technologist can bring about change through the combined application of existing principles. Thus, each application of social psychology does not require its own research studies, but simply a strategy of influence based on available knowledge.

Varela's social technology (reported in Zimbardo & Ebbesen, 1969) was used to help a Uruguayan wholesaler sell ready-made curtains to retailers in the face of almost insurmountable difficulties: (1) Since most windows in Uruguay are not a standard size, curtains are usually custom made; (2) the curtains had to be sold in April due to the wholesaler's high inventory—in spite of the fact that retailers traditionally buy in September; and (3) in the course of the sales program, the government took action to combat spiralling inflation by freezing all prices and wages and devaluing the currency by 50 percent, thus virtually ending all buying of nonessentials by retailers.

Varela responded to the challenge by mounting two programs of persuasion. In the first intervention, retailers were subtly influenced to come to the wholesaler's showroom through the use of the "foot-in-the-door technique." The technique worked as follows: each retailer first was asked to do a small favor—displaying a small sign in his shop window advertising an unknown product, thus further inducing the retailer's curiosity. The larger favor was asked a week later when the salesperson returned and asked the retailer if he would come to the showroom. The result? Most of the shopkeepers agreed.

The showroom was essentially an experimental laboratory in which a sales presentation was made while at the same time the retailers' behavior was observed without their knowledge or consent. Whenever a retailer would respond positively, his commitment would be increased by a salesperson asking his opinion about the product and encouraging him to give the reasons for his opinion. A final commitment was obtained by salespeople immediately asking the retailer to place an order, and with few exceptions this procedure was successful.

To sell uncut fabric as well as curtains, the salespersons were trained by Varela in the technique of "distraction from persuasive intent." The new fabric used in the curtains was very unusual, and a retailer would be influenced to compare the new designs with older ones, but never would be asked directly about his opinion of the fabric. When a retailer would inquire about the fabric, the salesperson *very hesitatingly* would agree to show him samples of the fabric—thus inducing the retailer to make a strong verbal commitment to see the material. Hence, after the material had been shown, the retailer was in a dissonant position. Given his strong demand to see the material, *not* to buy it would create cognitive dissonance (see Chapter 2). Thus, many retailers justified their behavior by placing an order for the fabric! The inducing of cognitive dissonance by the salespersons was an essential component of the persuasion program.

The sales of curtains were far beyond expectations, and the retailers were then trained in similar techniques to persuade unsuspecting housewives to purchase the ready-made curtains. However, it was at this point in the sales campaign that the government economic sanctions came into effect, and it was necessary to design a second and even stronger program of persuasion. This sales strategy was based on reactance theory and principles of social conformity and was very successful in continuing to sell the wholesaler's merchandise.

Varela (1971) delineates how his techniques of persuasion follow from principles derived from theories of attitude change, cognitive dissonance, reactance theory, and social conformity. For maximum impact, his techniques require a series of influence strategies making use of a number of principles in succession. In teaching classes in social technology, Varela (1975, 1977) has instructed students how to create combined influence attempts to deal with "social problems" in their own environment. This involves strategies of interpersonal manipulation designed to bring about change in other people's behavior "for their own good." Thus, for example, a friend is persuaded to stop smoking marijuana and continue her career training, a friend is manipulated into going to a doctor for professional help, and a mother is influenced into accepting a medical operation (see Box 4.2 for one of these examples of social technology).

Varela's work clearly raises fundamental questions of values and ethics. Even though we might regard some of the outcomes as desirable, strong reservations must be raised about the manner in which these ends are accomplished. The elements of deception and manipulation conflict most strongly with a humanistic value base. Furthermore, the ethical principles of informed consent and invasion of privacy are being violated. Suedfeld (1973) raises ethical concerns in a review of Varela's book, and adds that these applications of social psychology work very effectively so we had better start deciding who uses them and for whose benefit. Varela (1977) believes that his social technology creates its own ethical safeguards since the principles can be made freely available to all people, whether well intentioned or not. In addition, if the principles are used to "over influence," Varela predicts that a backfire effect will result and the manipulator will suffer long-term effects. These arguments raise even greater concerns regarding values and ethics since they seem to prescribe a spiralling continuation of secretive,

Box 4.2   FOCUS ON PRACTICE
Social Technology or Interpersonal Manipulation?

In his approach to social technology, Jacobo Varela maintains that a vast depository of social-psychological theories exists, just waiting to be applied to social problems. As a visiting professor at a number of North American universities, Varela has taught courses on social technology in which students are asked to design and implement a solution to a real-life problem. The following case involved a student, identified only as Beatrice, and her younger friend Rosa.

Rosa is a lively and carefree 19-year-old who has loved artwork since she was a child. Her wealthy and conservative parents have never accepted her liberated ways or her interest in art. Rosa recently received a rejection note on her application to an art school and since then has indulged in heavy drinking and marijuana smoking.

Beatrice diagnoses the cause of Rosa's drug abuse as the shock of rejection from art school. Rosa sees the rejection as an invalidation of her artistic values and abilities. Beatrice uses the approach-avoidance model of personal conflict to understand that Rosa is caught between a strong desire to pursue artistic work and an even stronger fear of further rejection. In collaboration with Varela, Beatrice plans a strategy of influence based on the theories of psychological reactance and cognitive dissonance.

First, Beatrice constructs a series of attitude statements that vary in their unacceptability to Rosa. Beatrice plans to get Rosa to agree with the statements, beginning with the least rejected statement, by inducing psychological reactance. This procedure will pressure Rosa to agree with each statement, thus inducing cognitive dissonance between her public assertion and her private belief. The prediction is that she will change her private belief and act accordingly, thus resolving the conflict.

The interchange goes something like this. Beatrice asks Rosa about a long-overdue painting that was to be a birthday present for Beatrice. Rosa replies she just doesn't have the will to do it.

Beatrice replies, "Well, I guess the whole art thing was just a phase with you. You never were that dedicated." Rosa reacts strongly, asserting that she has always loved art.

Beatrice now introduces the first unacceptable statement: "Maybe you should have listened to your mother when she disapproved of your art." Reactance leads Rosa to disagree strongly: "How can you say that? You know I don't care what she likes." Rosa is now in a dissonant state, and has to reconvince herself that she did in fact make the right choice in not following her mother's advice.

Following the same strategy, Beatrice convinces Rosa that the art school's judgment is not infallible and that she should reapply next term. Rosa then voices what was initially the most unacceptable statement. "Do you still have those sketch pads around? I'm starting right now." Rosa's behavior follows the changed attitude: Rosa worked all afternoon, returned to her art classes, and eventually reapplied to art school. She began to limit her use of alcohol and marijuana to social occasions.

Varela maintains that the attitude-change design worked because Rosa really wanted to get back to art but couldn't do so on her own. The ethical question is whether there might have been other ways to influence her without the use of deception and manipulation.

Source: Varela, J. Social technology. *American Psychologist*, 1977, *32*, 914–923.

manipulative relationships among all segments of society, each trying to "out-influence" the other (Argyris, 1975). A society of persuasion based on deceit is not compatible with the view of applied social psychology expressed in this book.

Social Advocacy

In *social advocacy* the social psychologist takes the role of participant activist, joining forces with disadvantaged people to increase their power and improve their standard of living. This role, developed in social work and sociology, is an important model of community organization (Perlman & Gurin, 1972; Rothman, 1978) (see Chapter 10).

The advocate motivates people by pointing out the discrepancies between what is and what should be, and by initiating tactics to achieve the desired goal. The goal is defined by the needs of the disadvantaged people with whom the advocate works, but the tactics or strategies are designed by the advocate in collaboration with the client system. Social advocates differ in their choice of tactics, with the majority subscribing to nonviolent means. Many, however, take the position that the ends justify the means within some reasonable limits and that quibbling over questionable tactics is counterproductive.

In *social advocacy*, the social psychologist takes the role of participant activist, joining forces with disadvantaged people to increase their power and improve their standard of living. The advocate role is closely associated with Saul Alinsky, who successfully organized labor unions and have-not community groups. Alinsky often developed novel and disruptive tactics that successfully increased the disadvantaged group's power to make demands and have those demands met. *(United Press International Photo)*

The advocate role is closely associated with Saul Alinsky (1946, 1971), who successfully organized labor unions and have-not community groups. Alinsky often developed novel and disruptive tactics that successfully increased the disadvantaged group's power to make demands and have these demands met. For example, to force a Chicago department store to increase the number of jobs for blacks, Alinsky organized 3,000 black persons to order small COD packages and then refuse them on delivery. The resulting tie-up of delivery trucks, plus the presence of a large number of blacks in the store (which scared away many white customers), forced management to capitulate and negotiate the provision of 100 jobs for blacks (Ecklein & Lauffer, 1972). As with social technology, ethical questions must be raised about the use of deception (ordering packages with no intent of paying for them) and manipulation (tying up delivery trucks). While we might applaud the goals of equality and freedom in Alinsky's work, we should not ignore the conflict between the humanistic value base and many of his tactics.

The advocate's approach is to crystallize and polarize the issue at hand and to use various strategies of confrontation and persuasion, including the mobilization of public opinion. In this way such groups as civil rights organizations, labor unions, tenant organizations, and women's liberation groups have gained a measure of social justice and equality that they may not have obtained otherwise.

The knowledge on which social advocacy is based has developed more from the advocates' direct experience than from social-psychological theories. This is partly due to social psychology's past neglect of the processes of power confrontation. (Another example of social advocacy appears in Box 4.3.)

The Problem-Solving Process

Each of the change agent roles—trainer, consultant, technologist, advocate—can be subsumed under a more general role—that of the problem solver. *Problem solving* is a systematic sequence of steps through which solutions to difficulties are developed, implemented, and evaluated. Each of us becomes a problem solver in our everyday life whenever we attempt to resolve some difficulty that besets us. This is true whether the difficulty is a physical problem—how to arrange the furniture in a new apartment—or a social problem—how to rescue a relationship that is deteriorating. *Decision making* is similar to problem solving, but usually refers to a simpler situation in which we must make a choice among specified alternatives. It can therefore be seen as a component of problem solving.

Problem solving can be regarded as the extension of the scientific method into the arena of human affairs (Morris & Sashkin, 1976). *The problem-solving process underlies practice in much the same way that the steps of the scientific method underlie research.* In research, we define a question, develop a hypothesis, test the hypothesis, and draw our conclusions. The problem-solving sequence follows a similar series of steps. However, in the area of practice we must be concerned with much more than ideas and information. We must be concerned about the people involved in the problem-solving process—their attitudes, feelings, concerns, needs, and typical behavior. The challenge for the change agent is

Box 4.3   FOCUS ON PRACTICE
Social Advocacy, or Alinsky Starts a FIGHT

Rochester, New York, 1964. A small manufacturing city of 350,000 people, of whom 35,000 are black and recent arrivals to the city. The summer of 1964 brings riots in the black ghetto, an air of tension, and a strong concern for preventing further racial strife. The local churches turn to Saul Alinsky, a well-known social advocate, to help them organize for social change.

Alinsky plays hard to get. He knows that the local people must be initially organized, committed, and have adequate resources to see them through a long struggle for power and equality. Black leaders must feel comfortable in turning to a "white Moses" to help take them out of the wilderness. Financial arrangements must be secure to support the salaries and other costs of two years of organizing. After a number of meetings with black and white leaders of the movement, Alinsky agrees to come. He stresses there must be no rioting in the summer of 1965 or it will mean the end of the organization.

An Alinsky-trained organizer is assigned to take the lead role in Rochester to organize the black community. Local organizers are hired—they must be angry, intelligent, and willing to learn. A steering committee is formed, and a public meeting is held in which local groups pledge their commitment to FIGHT (Freedom, Integration, God, Honor, Today). A constitution is prepared and presented to a convention six weeks later. There are over seven hundred delegates representing 130 organizations. An executive is elected, and FIGHT is on its way. Issues are identified—slum housing, youth problems, school segregation, police activities, a lack of jobs. Action is taken—slum landlords are picketed to bring attention to unenforced housing codes; the major employer in Rochester (Eastman Kodak) is pressured to improve its employment program for blacks. The organization is successful.

However, FIGHT is not without its problems. The "I" for integration becomes largely ignored as whites are firmly pushed out of the organization. They regroup as the "Friends of FIGHT." Several churches refuse to contribute to a third year of operation. Some middle-class blacks shift their support to the Urban League. More militant black organizations spring up in the ghetto. But throughout all this furor and confusion, FIGHT is able to maintain its Alinsky approach and bring greater justice and equality to the people of Rochester.

Source: Ecklein, J. L. & Lauffer, A. Alinsky starts a FIGHT. In *Community organizers and social planners.* New York: Wiley, 1972.

to be sensitive to and skilled in working with both the task—the job, the problem—and the social elements of the problem—the people and their relationships.

The study and practice of problem solving in applied social psychology have been pioneered by Norman Maier (1963, 1970), who has identified the principles of effective problem solving in both groups and organizations. These principles have been extended by Morris and Sashkin (1976) into their model of integrated problem solving (see Figure 4.1). This model identifies the major steps of the process and integrates the task (or rational "acts") and the social "interacts"

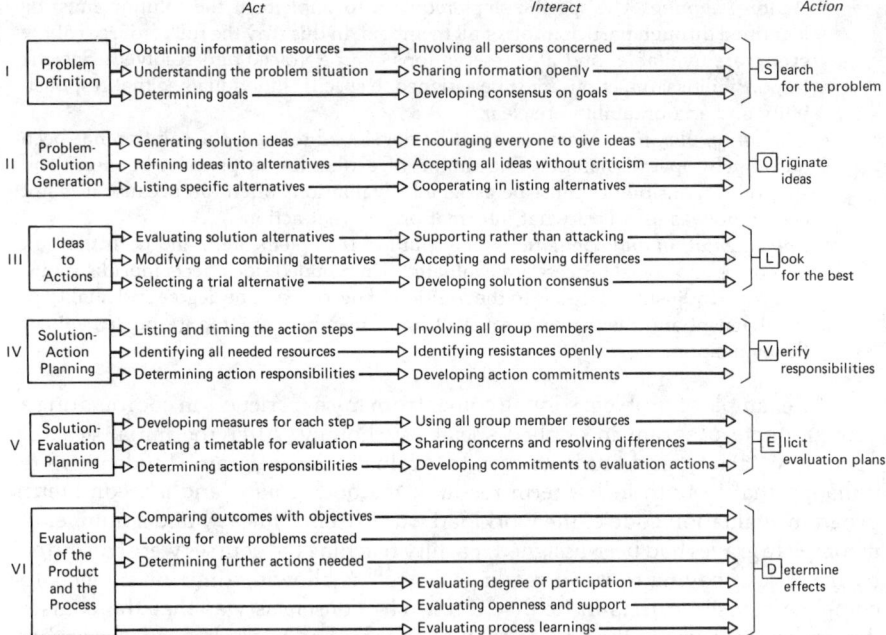

Figure 4.1   **The Process of Integrated Problem Solving.**
Source: Morris & Sashkin (1976).

required for successful problem solving. Each step has its crucial task and social demands that must be met for the achievement of a viable solution. The sequence includes:

- *Problem definition.* The problem must be accurately identified and understood. All persons concerned with the problem must be involved so that all important information is shared and the existence of the problem is affirmed. Involvement also increases "ownership" of the problem rather than evasion of responsibility. Consensus must be reached on the goals of problem solving—that is, the conditions to be changed—or the sequence will ultimately be unsuccessful.
- *Generation of alternative solutions.* To overcome the common pitfall of jumping to a quick but inadequate solution, everyone must be encouraged to share ideas on solutions. Brainstorming—generating a large number of ideas *without* criticism or discussion—can yield possible solutions that can be refined down into a list of workable alternatives.
- *Selection of a solution.* Ideas are transformed into actions by evaluating the alternatives, modifying or combining them, and choosing the best solution to implement on a trial basis. Participants must be respectful of differences and must resolve conflicts in productive ways to achieve consensus on the chosen alternative. Consensus means that the solution is acceptable to every member of the group, even though it may not be their first choice. Without consensus there will not be full support for the chosen solution, and the process may ultimately fail.

- *Action planning.* The specific steps required to implement the solution must be identified through participation of all members. In this way the full resources of the group are available, and any reservations can be voiced and resolved. Specific responsibilities for actions must be assigned to specific individuals so that responsibility and accountability are clear.
- *Evaluation planning.* Measures must be developed to see if the solution has been adequately operationalized. The timing of evaluation steps must be clear, and specific responsibilities must be assigned. Evaluations often fail because it is not clear who was to collect what information on what actions.
- *Implementation and evaluation.* The solution is implemented, and both the task outcomes and social process are evaluated. Unintended side effects must be monitored, and adjustments made to the solution, if necessary. The degree and quality of involvement and the personal satisfaction of members are important elements of the evaluation.

An example of problem solving comes from my experiences in coordinating a new graduate program in applied social psychology. After the initial year of operation, faculty and students met to evaluate the program. Students were unhappy that in both a first-term research methods course and a second-term program evaluation course, the workload was extremely heavy and a number of incomplete grades had been assigned. Faculty teaching the courses were frustrated by the task of having to cover readings as well as allowing time for students to complete course projects in field settings. The consensus was that the courses demanded too much in the time available, and this had to be changed. A number of alternative solutions were generated and discussed. The best alternative appeared to be to spread the two courses over two terms while keeping the course demands similar. In this way, conceptual material could be covered in both courses during the first term, and the course projects could be completed in the second term. This would allow for more contact with field settings to develop mutually acceptable projects. Action was taken. The courses were redesigned accordingly. A year later, the results were evaluated through faculty-student meetings. No incompletes were assigned, and both students and faculty were pleased with the new arrangement. The shared commitment to problem solving had paid excellent dividends.

Effective problem solving doesn't just happen. The organization and integration provided by the change agent or group leader can make the difference (Maier, 1967). The trainer, consultant, technologist, and advocate can all play a key role in facilitating the successful resolution of important human social problems. In terms of ethics, problem solving is very compatible with the humanistic value base, since it involves open communication, informed consent, and shared decision making among the parties involved.

Values and Ethics of the Change Agent

Working with people in ways that influence their lives carries very important professional and ethical responsibilities. Applied social psychologists working as change agents have given considerable attention to the guidelines for ethical practice (Feinberg, 1977; Lakin, 1969; Luke & Benne, 1975). These issues are clearly described by Lippitt & Lippitt (1978):

> In any area of helping, the consultant occupies a position of trust and, therefore, the ethical aspects of his or her work and relationships occupy a significant place in the discussion of the consulting process. The work of all professional helpers requires the constant exercise of discretion in judgment. Their clients may not be qualified to appraise the quality of service being offered or the risks involved and, therefore, they have to rely for support and protection on the helper's standards of conduct and on the network of professional peers. The client is justified in expecting certain standards of conduct, and can derive confidence from knowing that a code of professional behavior will help to protect him.
>
> In all the standard definitions of the professions there are elements of dedication, of giving one's ethical position a place of extreme importance, of taking pride in applying one's knowledge and skills, and of functioning with integrity. In a field as complex and varied as consulting, ethical practice implies far more than simply profiting from the past mistakes of the profession. It demands a willingness to be alert to novel situations and to respond to them as they develop. (pp. 57–58)

In the search for a value base for a code of ethics, change agents are confronted with two opposing ethical positions: that of the individual's right to freedom and self-determination, and that of the individual's responsibility to the social system. Since neither extreme is acceptable to the change agent, a sensible combination of the two—responsibility to oneself and to one's fellow human beings—serves as workable base of values. One important type of ethical dilemma involves conflict between the consultant's personal values and the goals of the organization that is a potential client. For example, should a consultant who is a conscientious objector provide service to a national defense project? Should a consultant who favors gun control consult with the National Rifle Association? Unless the relationship with the client can be completely divorced from the consultant's personal values and the client is made fully aware of these values, the consultant would be jusitifed in declining such assignments (Lippitt & Lippitt, 1978).

Given this value base, the professional change agent can turn to various sources for ethical guidelines. These include the NTL Institute, the International Association of Applied Social Scientists (now Certified Consultants International), the American Society for Training and Development, and the Academy of Management. These are summarized by Lippitt & Lippitt (1978) in their concise code of ethical principles for the professional consultant. This set of ethical principles, covering such important areas as competence, confidentiality, and client welfare, is reproduced in Box 4.4.

Even with codes of conduct, ethical decisions are very difficult to make. Change agents are advised to consult with peers who have the experience and the wisdom to understand the situation and to advise on appropriate behavior. Codes of ethics are designed to protect the profession as well as the clients and the public. Establishing these standards of behavior and providing regulatory mechanisms to empower them help to insure the survival and the autonomy of the professional organization. Professionals thus serve their own and the public's interests in considering these fundamental issues (Luke & Benne, 1975).

Box 4.4   FOCUS ON PRACTICE
Principles of Ethical Conduct for Change Agents

Ronald and Gordon Lippitt have both contributed a great deal to the practice of consultation in the areas of human relations training, organizational effectiveness, and community development. Drawing on their combined experience and on a number of codes of ethics for professional associations, they have produced a set of principles of ethical conduct for change agents:

1. *Responsibility.* The consultant:
   - places high value on objectivity and integrity and maintains the highest standards of service
   - plans work in a way that minimizes the possibility that findings will be misleading
2. *Competence.* The consultant:
   - maintains high standards of professional competence as a responsibility to the public and to the profession
   - recognizes the boundaries of his or her competence and does not offer services that fail to meet professional standards
   - assists clients in obtaining professional help for aspects of the project that fall outside the boundaries of his or her own competence
   - refrains from undertaking any activity in which his or her personal problems are likely to result in inferior professional service or harm to the client
3. *Moral and Legal Standards.* The consultant shows sensible regard for the social codes and moral expectations of the community in which he or she works.
4. *Misrepresentation.* The consultant avoids misrepresentation of his or her own professional qualifications, affiliations, and purposes, and those of the organization with which he or she is associated.
5. *Confidentiality.* The consultant:
   - reveals information received in confidence only to the appropriate authorities
   - maintains confidentiality of professional communications about individuals
   - informs client of the limits of confidentiality
   - maintains confidentiality in preservation and disposition of records
6. *Client Welfare.* The consultant:
   - defines the nature of his or her loyalties and responsibilities in possible conflicts of interest—such as between the client and the employer of the consultant—and keeps all concerned parties informed of these commitments
   - attempts to terminate a consulting relationship when it is reasonably clear that it is no longer beneficial to the client
   - continues responsibility for the welfare of the client, in cases involving referral, until the responsibility is assumed by the professional to whom the client is referred or until the relationship with the client has been terminated by mutual agreement
7. *Announcement of Services.* The consultant adheres to professional standards rather than solely economic rewards in making known his or her availability for professional services.

8. *Interprofessional Relations.* The consultant acts with integrity toward all professional colleagues.
9. *Remuneration.* The consultant ensures that the financial arrangements for his or her professional services are in accordance with professional standards that safeguard the best interests of the client and the profession.
10. *Responsibility Toward Organization.* The consultant respects the rights and reputation of the organization with which he or she is associated.
11. *Promotional Activities.* The consultant, when associated with the development or promotion of products offered for commercial sale, ensures that the products are presented in a factual way.

Lippitt and Lippitt point out that simply establishing a code of ethics does not guarantee that it will be followed. There needs to be a practical system of enforcement that is accepted by professionals. One example is the Committee on Scientific and Professional Ethics of the American Psychological Association, which investigates potentially unethical practices and confronts the alleged offender when the code has been violated. In this way the public as well as the profession is protected against ethically questionable behavior.

Source: Lippitt, G. & Lippitt, R. *The consulting process in action.* La Jolla, Calif.: University Associates, 1978.

AREAS OF SKILL TRAINING

Skill training in applied social psychology follows the principles and procedures of experience-based or experiential learning (see Chapter 2). We learn by doing, from our experience, and by active involvement in the learning process. Participants in skill training use their own interaction as the core of the training process. Beyond these principles, the systematic process of experience-based learning usually involves the following steps:

- conceptual background and definition of skills through readings, lectures, and discussions
- demonstration of skill usage by trainers or in recorded interactions
- practice in skill usage through structured exercises
- feedback on skill usage from trainers and other participants
- further discussion and analysis of practice exercises
- discussion of application of skills to real-world situations

Several variations of this structured approach to experience-based learning have been provided at the interpersonal level (Carkhuff, 1969; Egan, 1975; Gazda, 1973; Johnson, 1972) and at the small-group level (Napier & Gershenfeld, 1981; Pfeiffer & Jones, 1977). In each case, the training attempts to teach the core behaviors of effective interpersonal and group functioning; these behaviors can then be applied to specific situations such as interviewing or conflict resolution. In addition, skill training has been applied to the individual level of functioning, particularly in the acquisition of personal motives. This section will consider each of these valuable areas of training.

Personal Motivation Training

Is it possible to change deep-seated and enduring characteristics of an individual's personality? Not easily. Personality traits, motives, and attitudes become part of our personality over a lengthy, complex process of development and socialization from birth to adulthood. Our motivation to achieve, for example, appears to depend on certain continuing qualities of our childhood experience, particularly the degree of independence and responsibility we are given. Training programs have generally shied away from changing attributes of personality for both practical and ethical reasons. David McClelland and his associates provide an interesting exception. After years of research on the need for achievement (nACH) and the need for power (nPOW) (see Chapter 2), McClelland developed training programs to increase the level of these crucial motives.

McClelland (1965) assumes that human motives are arranged in a hierarchy of importance for each person. For you, need achievement may be high on the list; for someone else, it may be low. The question is whether individuals can increase the level of a motive through training. Can a person low on need achievement develop a greater desire to do things well? Can individuals low on need power find ways to gain more control over themselves and their environment? To answer these challenging questions, McClelland drew on principles of changing behavior from four major areas of psychology: animal learning, human learning, psychotherapy, and attitude change. He translated propositions about effective training into the design of a short-term (one to three weeks) voluntary training program. Let's take a look at a typical program for increasing need achievement in small-business operations.

The training program begins with a description of the research results on need achievement, including the use of the nACH scoring system. This sensitizes trainees to the meaning and importance of the achievement motive and encourages them to increase their own level of entrepreneurial functioning. Participants then engage in a business game that allows them to practice achievement behavior. Analysis of case studies of actual business situations further demonstrates appropriate and effective achievement behavior. This improved understanding is then linked directly to the life of the participants through individual feedback and consultation. Finally, the compatibility of nACH to other characteristics of personality is considered so that potential changes will not be resisted by the individual. Discussions and role play exercises are used to determine if the individual's self-concept and cultural values are supportive of need achievement. Trainees develop concrete goals and are encouraged to monitor their progress when they return to their home setting.

How successful have these training programs been? The results are encouraging. For example, a number of nACH programs have been conducted in India. Businessmen who have participated show subsequently higher rates of unusual entrepreneurial activity (for example, winning a major promotion, starting a new business) than those who have not (McClelland, 1965). They also invest more money, employ more people, and show greater participation in community affairs (McClelland & Winter, 1971). The results may even affect the wider social system. McClelland (1978) compared two Indian cities, one of which included trained businessmen and one which did not, and found differences in economic well-being that were congruent with the effects of different levels of need achievement.

What about the need for power (nPOW)? Can it be affected by training programs? Rehabilitation counselors who work with alcoholics certainly hope so. Why? Research indicates that nPOW is a definite factor in alcohol abuse. The alcoholic often drinks to gain a feeling of strength and potency. If alcoholics could find less destructive alternatives to gain a sense of power and competence, both they and society would be better off. Consequently, McClelland (1977) and others have developed and evaluated programs for power motivation training with alcoholics (see Box 4.5).

Despite its success, McClelland's program has its limitations. Many factors influence achievement and power, and it is difficult to attribute positive changes directly to the training programs. It is especially difficult to attribute changes in social systems, such as organizations or cities, to interventions focusing solely on the individual level. Important ethical questions also arise. Programs must be truly voluntary, so that trainees are making a free and fully informed choice to participate in an experience that may affect fundamental aspects of their personality. However, when the ethical and practical demands are met, training programs such as McClelland's offer an exciting possibility for individual change that is relevant to society at large. Helping people become what they want to become, based on humanistic values, can help create a better world.

Interpersonal Communication Skills

Both applied social psychologists and clinical psychologists have designed training programs to increase people's ability to develop more trusting and satisfying relationships. These programs identify skills for open, accurate, and effective communication between individuals and provide the ideas and practice needed to implement those skills. See Chapter 6 for a detailed discussion of interpersonal communication.

John Wallen (1973), a pioneer of this work, has been concerned with finding ways for people to bridge the *interpersonal gap*—"the degree of congruence between one person's intentions and the effect produced in the other." To do this, Wallen (1973) defines four basic communication skills:

- *Paraphrasing.* State in your own words what the other person's message means to you. (Example: "You mean the report is too long and unclear in places," rather than "What do you know about writing reports, anyway?")
- *Perception checking.* Describe tentatively and without evaluating what you perceive the other person feels. (Example: "You seem upset by what I said. Is that accurate?" rather than "Boy, some people sure are touchy!")
- *Behavior description.* Describe the other person's specific observable actions rather than make inferences, accusations, or generalizations. (Example: "You interrupted me several times during the interview," rather than "You sure are a dominating person.")

- *Description of feelings.* Identify your feelings by name, simile, or the actions they suggest. (Example: "I'm too angry to talk with you now," rather than "Will you shut up and get lost!")

Each of these skills can be used in the transmission and reception of information to increase the likelihood that the effect intended by a message is consonant with the effect produced. Paraphrasing and perception checking improve the accuracy of communication by checking out the other person's intentions (feelings, desires, motives) and the meaning of his or her message. Description of feelings helps describe intentions. Description of behavior helps describe other people's actions clearly and in a nonthreatening fashion.

The training process begins with a simple model of interpersonal communication, a description of the interpersonal gap, and an outline of basic communication skills to close that gap. The skills are then illustrated and practiced, with feedback, in interactions between two or three participants. For example, one person might practice description of feelings by talking about how he or she feels when entering a new social situation for the first time. A second person uses paraphrasing and perception checking to understand the first person, while a third person observes the interaction and then provides behavior description on how well the first two implemented the skills. To complete the process the participants analyze and discuss the applicability of the skills to each participant's real-life role. In this way individuals can enhance their ability to deal effectively with a variety of interpersonal situations.

Associated with Wallen's basic communication skills are four qualities that are important to the development of interpersonal relationships. These are drawn from clinical psychologists Carl Rogers's (1961) and Robert Carkhuff's (1969) work on helping relationships:

- *Empathy* is sensitivity to the other person's feelings, and the ability to communicate this understanding. (Example: "You are very pleased with your mark.")
- *Respect* is the ability to feel and express acceptance, nonpossessive warmth, and active delight in the other person's unique personal qualities. (Example: "I can understand how you would be disappointed with that low grade.")
- *Genuineness* is the ability to be open, spontaneous, and congruent, and to use such responses constructively. (Example: "I'm very unhappy about this. What can we do about it?")
- *Concreteness* is the ability to focus the other persons's expressions on specific feelings and behavior related to personally significant experiences by using such questions as who, what, where, when, and how. (Example: "What is it you are unhappy about? Could you be more specific?")

Skill training for the understanding and use of these qualities is similar to that used for interpersonal communication skills: the skills are outlined, defined, and demonstrated. They are then practiced, and subjected to observation, feedback, and an analysis of their effectiveness. (We will discuss additional interpersonal skills in Chapter 6.)

Interpersonal skill training has also been used to solve problems and resolve conflict between individuals. An example is Thomas Gordon's (1970) approach to parent-child relations—*parent effectiveness training.* This program uses such basic

Box 4.5   FOCUS ON PRACTICE
Power Motivation Training with Alcoholics

Excessive drinking stems in part from a sense of powerlessness and in part from impulsive ways of expressing power motivation. It therefore seems plausible that training in power motivation might help alcoholics control their drinking behavior. In conjunction with psychologist David McClelland, staff members at a Veterans Administration hospital added a special program in power motivation training (PMT) to their standard treatment. This included medication, individual and group therapy, and encouragement to join Alcoholics Anonymous.

The PMT program is an intensive 35-hour group course held over a two-week period. It is designed to help participants learn other ways of feeling powerful and of controlling themselves and their environment. First, participants learn to identify the links between power concerns and excessive drinking. Next, they learn methods of self-diagnosis to identify when they are feeling powerless and are likely to want to drink heavily. Finally, they practice alternative ways of feeling powerful through techniques of interpersonal conflict resolution, giving and receiving help, yoga and meditation, and reality-based planning. The session ends by setting goals and planning actions for the future.

Participants in the PMT program had long histories of alcoholism; most reported physical symptoms such as blackouts, seizures, delirium tremens, and liver problems. Detoxicated patients in residence at the hospital were asked to join in a study of a new form of treatment. Of the 100 patients who volunteered over a ten-month period, half were randomly assigned to PMT while the other half continued with the standard treatment. Following discharge from the hospital, participants were assessed at a six-month and twelve-month follow-up on the dependent variables of number of days they were intoxicated and number of weeks they had worked.

Cutter, Boyatzis, and Clancy did not find any positive effects of PMT on these two dependent variables. However, when they examined the attitude and personality test scores of patients, they found that authoritarian patients (with a high need and respect for authority) showed less intoxication following the standard treatment. On the other hand, nonauthoritarian patients (more rebellious and nonconventional) did better following the PMT program. McClelland suggests that both dependent measures of rehabilitation should be used together to give a more realistic picture of the outcomes of the different programs. Using this combined criterion, McClelland found that 46 percent of the patients receiving PMT were improved after a year, whereas only 24 percent of those receiving the standard treatment had improved.

We can therefore conclude that PMT is effective in rehabilitating alcoholics and that it may be more effective with nonauthoritarian individuals.

Sources: Cutter, H. S. G., Boyatzis, R. E. & Clancy, D. D. The effectiveness of power motivation training in rehabilitating alcoholics. *Journal of Studies on Alcohol*, 1977, *38*, 131–141. McClelland, D. C. The impact of power motivation training on alcoholics. *Journal of Studies on Alcohol*, 1977, *38*, 142–144.

skills as active listening (a combination of paraphrasing and perception checking), and the presentation of "I" messages (very similar to description of feelings). Other training programs also prescribe effective communication and collaborative problem solving as the best method of interpersonal conflict resolution (for example, Filley, 1975).

Small-Group Skills

One of the primary goals of the early human relations training laboratories was to increase the participants' ability to function effectively as both members and leaders in the small-group setting (see Lippitt & Bradford, 1945). In their expansion of these skills, applied social psychologists have developed an array of systematic methods beyond the initial, unstructured approach of sensitivity training. Interpersonal communication skills are an implicit part of small-group training, and some approaches systematically blend interpersonal skills into group process (for example, Egan, 1976). Thus the depth and sophistication of this area of skill training continue to grow.

Leadership functions are an excellent example of the usefulness of small-group training. These are the crucial behaviors that enable a group to get its job done—through the acquisition and elaboration of information—while still meeting the personal and social needs of its members through encouragement, reconciliation, and compromise (Benne & Sheats, 1948). For example, someone needs to initiate the activity of the group and suggest procedures for getting the task accomplished; someone needs to check for consensus on decisions; someone needs to encourage the participation of all members; and someone needs to help resolve conflict between members. The leader and members must provide these types of behaviors if the group is going to function effectively.

The training of leadership functions begins with a conceptual definition of these functions, followed by an illustration of behaviors. This uses a role play or actual small-group discussion in what is known as a "fishbowl design." In this format an inner group sits in the middle of an outer ring of observers. During the inner-group discussion the observers note the use of leadership functions within the group. Observers then provide feedback to each individual and to the group in general on the effectiveness of their leadership functions. This type of training leads to immediate gains in the participants' sensitivity to key behaviors and their ability to work well with others in the small-group setting. This and other forms of small-group training are discussed in Chapter 7.

METHODS OF CONSULTATION

Consultation is a help-giving process in which the consultant uses his or her expertise to facilitate the problem solving of the consultee. Consultation is usually associated with professional work: for example, a physician engaged in general practice consults a medical specialist on a particular case, or a businesswoman consults a management specialist on how to increase her profit margin. Consultation thus occurs in all manners of professional relationships and settings and focuses on all types of human problems.

While there exist many methods of consultation, the core activity is similar. The consultant aids the consultee to better understand his or her problem situation, to develop and evaluate different courses of action, and to generate actions to put the chosen solution into practice.

General Models of Consultation

General models of consultation are an attempt to describe the wide range of consultant activities in a concise and systematic manner. These models are primarily inductive, descriptive attempts to gain an initial understanding of consultation.

Lippitt and Lippitt's Multiple Role Model. Drawing on their consulting experience, Gordon and Ronald Lippitt (Lippitt & Lippitt, 1978) have presented a model based on the multiple roles that consultants may enact (see Figure 4.2). The roles are arranged on a nondirective–directive continuum, since this dimension of the consulting relationship is seen as a general factor that runs through all approaches. Essentially, the continuum reflects the degree of activity and responsibility that the consultant exhibits in the problem-solving process. For example, as an advocate, the consultant is very directive over the problem-solving process; as a process counselor, the consultant merely provides nondirective feedback and raises issues to be considered by the client.

The scope of activities covered is comprehensive enough to be considered as

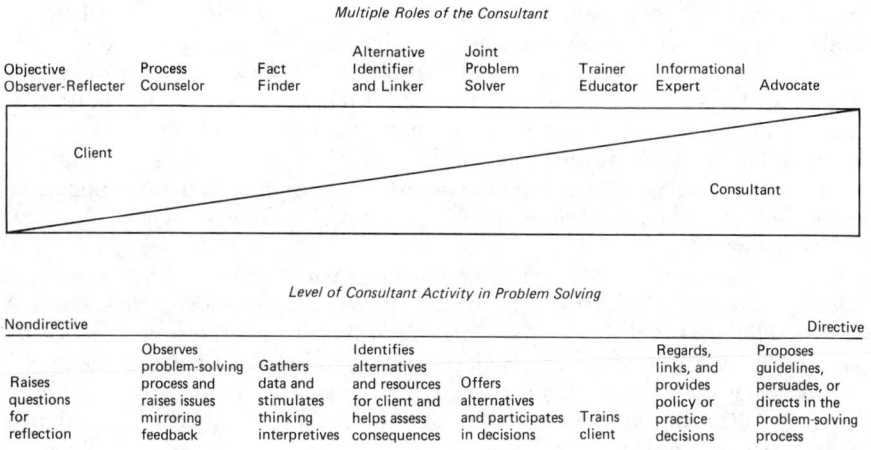

Figure 4.2   Multiple Role of the Consultant on a Nondirective–Directive Continuum.
Source: Lippitt & Lippitt (1978).

a general model of consultation—in fact, the role descriptions include all the change agent activities we have discussed. More importantly, Lippitt and Lippitt do not see these roles as fixed and exclusive alternatives of which the consultant chooses one, enacting it in all situations with all client systems. Rather, they propose that consultants may vary their role from moment to moment to maximize their effectiveness.

Lippitt and Lippitt identify a number of factors that help determine role choice at any given time in any given situation. The mutual understanding or contract between the consultant and the client sets the initial hierarchy of consultant roles, indicating which role or roles are to be given priority. However, roles may shift to meet the goals of the intervention. For example, the role of joint problem solver might shift to that of group trainer if the group appears to be deficient in the human relations skills required to solve its problem. Other role-determining factors include the consultant's personal style and set, whether the consultant is a member of the client system or external to it, and the norms of the client system and the consultant. In conjunction with other important elements such as the phases of consultation and typical interventions, as well as the researchers' earlier work (R. Lippitt, Watson, & Westley, 1958; G. Lippitt, 1969), this description of multiple roles provides a valuable model for understanding consultation activities.

Blake and Mouton's Consulcube. The most systematic general model of consultation comes from the work of Robert Blake and Jane Mouton, applied social psychologists who have pioneered major accomplishments in the field of organization development. Blake and Mouton (1976) have developed a concise, comprehensive model that applies to the entire field of helping, including such diverse disciplines as psychiatry, religion, social work, and applied social psychology.

Blake and Mouton first note that all human behavior tends to be cyclical in nature—that is, certain patterns of behavior tend to be repeated over and over—and is therefore very resistant to change. Individuals, groups, and organizations appear to be stuck in the same ruts, day after day and year after year. The alcoholic starts each day the same way, with the same predictable result. The family initiates the same fight pattern it engaged in last week, even though the focus of the argument may have changed. The organization persists in attempting to solve its operating difficulties in the same manner, such as firing "incompetent" managers, often without full awareness of what it is doing or what alternative behaviors might be available.

Consultation is any attempt to intervene in a way that might break a cycle. A social worker helps a ghetto resident fill out a form for housing assistance. A human relations trainer provides an interpretation of an interpersonal conflict in a group. An organization development consultant confronts top management with the idea that their over-reliance on past practices hampers innovative problem solving. According to Blake and Mouton, all of these cycle-breaking activities constitute consultation.

To capture the range and richness of consultation activities, Blake and Mouton developed the *consulcube,* which categorizes consultation on three separate dimensions (see Figure 4.3). The first dimension is the *kind of intervention*

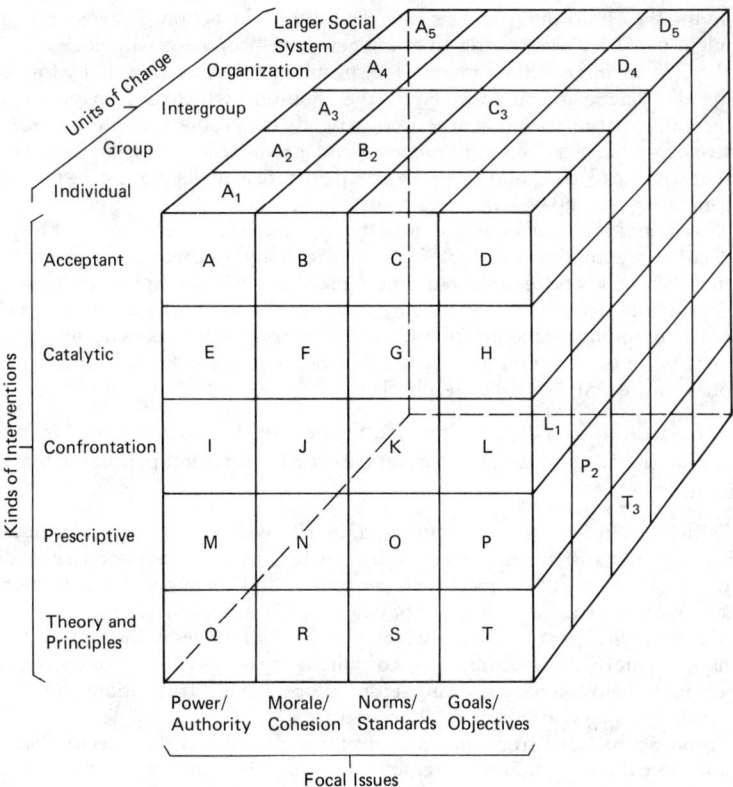

Figure 4.3   The Consulcube.
Source: Blake & Mouton (1976).

that the consultant undertakes as a cycle-breaking attempt. The authors list five main types of intervention on the *vertical axis* of the consulcube:

- *Acceptant interventions* are designed to give the client a sense of personal security, so that through expressing thoughts and feelings the client will come to gain a more detailed and objective view of the situation. (Example: Consultants facilitate collective bargaining by holding "off-the-record" meetings in which they encourage union and management groups to express and discuss their hostile feelings toward each other.)
- *Catalytic interventions* assist the client in collecting additional information to use in reinterpreting his or her perceptions so that the client may gain a better awareness of the problem and how to deal with it. (Example: Consultants conduct a survey in a school district on the quality of communication and problem solving. The results are fed back in conjunction with process observations, and the organization develops more effective ways of operating.)
- *Confrontation interventions* challenge the clients to examine their assumptions about the situation which may be restricting alternative actions that are potentially effective. (Example: Consultants confront the members of an organization on

myths they hold that paralyze their ability to take action. For instance, a myth might be, "It's no use trying anything new here—someone will block it.")

- *Prescriptive interventions* involve the consultant taking responsibility for developing the diagnosis and formulating the solution—which is then provided as a recommendation to the client on how to rectify the problem situation. (Example: A work team has just had its funding cut and is in a crisis of despair. The consultant takes over leadership and keeps the group on its task of diagnosing the problem and generating new goals.)
- *Theory and principal interventions* offer systematic and tested ways of helping the client conceptualize the situation in a more analytic, cause-and-effect fashion so that the client is better able to diagnose problems and plan solutions. (Example: A consultant creates an understanding and appreciation of the importance of group norms or implicit standards of behavior. The group examines its norms, affirms the positive ones—for example, cooperativeness—and works at changing negative ones—for example, lack of feedback.)

The *horizontal axis* of the consulcube specifies the *focal issues for intervention*—that is, the content areas or social categories in which problems may arise. These include:

- Difficulties in the exercise of *power/authority* wherein conflicts arise in decision making and assignment of responsibility between superiors and subordinates. (Example: A consultant meets with a manager and her subordinates to discuss the subordinates' frustrations at not having a say in important decisions.)
- *Morale/cohesion* problems, in which there are difficulties in the sense of togetherness and motivation. (Example: A consultant organizes workshops for community groups to help combat a growing sense of hopelessness, frustration, and interracial conflict in a deteriorating neighborhood.)
- Problems that arise from *standards or norms* of conduct that specify appropriate and acceptable behavior. (Example: Consultants work with youth discussion groups in an attempt to establish norms of interaction that society regards as positive—for example, listening rather than ridiculing.)
- Difficulties in *goals/objectives,* wherein there may be lack of clarity or agreement on what the desirable end states of the system are. (Example: A consultant conducts a goal-setting workshop with a human service organization to establish objectives and determine priorities for action.)

The third key dimension of the consulcube is composed of the *units of change* or the level of analysis at which the consultant intervenes: the individual, group, intergroup, organization, and larger social system (the community, society, or world). Consultant interventions on focal issues *need to be tailored to the particular level of analysis* that is represented by the client system. The consultant must determine who the *real* client is in order to solve the problem. If, for example, it is the group that needs to make changes in its manner of functioning, it is inappropriate to use interventions at the individual level. Personal counseling for the boss will not help a management team that lacks clear goals.

Blake and Mouton's consulcube provides a clear way of describing up to one hundred different combinations of how a consultant intervenes in a given unit of change on a given focal issue. The consulcube has been successfully applied to understanding more than six hundred published examples of interventions. Blake & Mouton (1978) maintain that their model results in a systematic and coherent basis for a theory and practice of consultation, wherein the similarities and differences among approaches can be clearly identified.

Forms of Process Consultation

With the growth of social science, people have stopped taking the existing social order for granted. We now question what is happening in interpersonal relationships, families, organizations, and society at large. Process consultation is highly compatible with this general emphasis on understanding social relations. However, process consultation goes beyond casual analysis and impression formation. It begins with an existing knowledge base regarding social behavior and proceeds in a systematic manner, often supplemented by additional methods of research or practice.

The last twenty years have seen an increasing proliferation of different forms of process consultation: Some are clear extensions of the basic method articulated by Schein (1969); others are forms developed before or concurrently with process consultation. Using the levels of analysis approach, let's examine the various forms of process consultation and the major fields of practice in which they find expression. In conjunction with change agent roles and areas of skill training, this analysis shows how the problem-solving process is implemented in the practice domain of applied social psychology (see Figure 4.4).

Before proceeding we should first distinguish process consultation from the related approach of mental health consultation. Process consultation is concerned with the general social functioning of the client system (which can be an interpersonal relationship, or a group, or an organization). It helps the members of the client system understand and act upon the process events that occur in their environment (Schein, 1969, 1978). In contrast, mental health consultation is specifically concerned with the prevention and treatment of mental illness and the promotion of mental health (Bindman, 1959; Caplan, 1970; Mannino, MacLennan & Shore, 1975). The mental health consultant aids the consultee—a mental health worker such as a psychiatric nurse or social worker—to work more effectively with his or her patients (see Chapter 10).

The first two types of consultation are therefore different in several ways (Fisher, 1977; Goodstein, 1978). For example, mental health consultation focuses on individual emotional problems, and works mainly through interpersonal relationships. In contrast, process consultation is concerned with overall social functioning at all levels of analysis. However, at the program and organizational levels, there can be some overlap between the two approaches.

The early work on human relations training centered primarily on the facilitation of group processes. This led to the major field of practice known as laboratory eduction (see Chapter 7). Trainers not only became adept at improving human relations in laboratory groups, but also developed the consulting skill of helping real-world groups increase their ability to function effectively. Thus, many present-day consultants work with committees, boards, or management teams to increase their sensitivity to group processes and to improve communication and decision making. Consultants can help transform meetings from boring and frustrating failures to well-planned, enthusiastic successes (see Doyle &

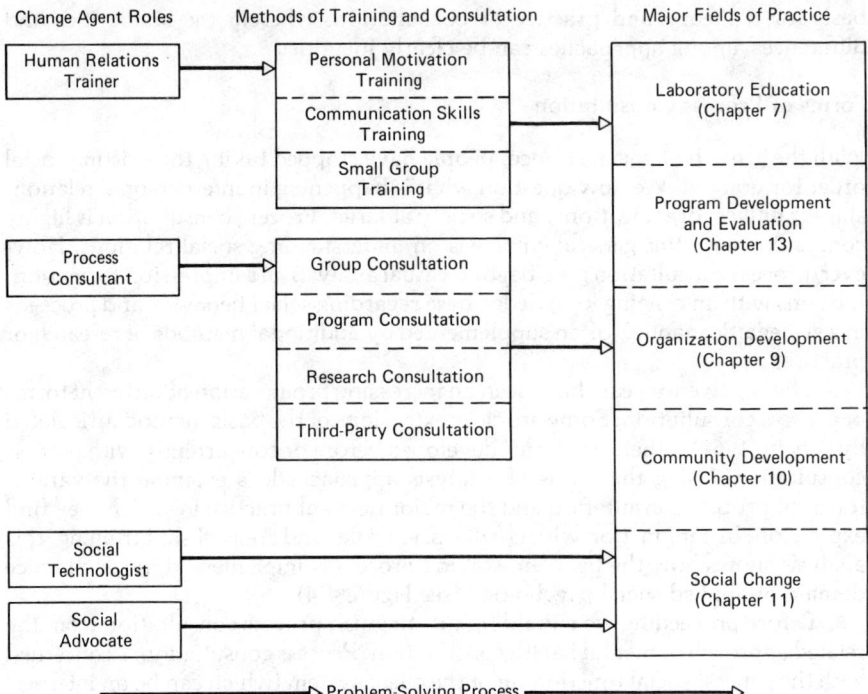

Figure 4.4   The Practice Domain of Applied Social Psychology.

Straus, 1976; Schindler-Rainman & Lippitt, 1975). Similarly, major conferences can be designed and executed in ways that maximize satisfaction and utility (see Nadler & Nadler, 1977). In these ways, *group consultation* has become a major form of process consultation (see Lippitt & Lippitt, 1978; Russ, 1978).

Program consultation builds on the knowledge and skills of group consultation. The consultant provides diagnosis, information, and guidance relative to the planning, implementation, administration, and evaluation of a human service program. When the program is directed toward improving the mental health of the participants, then program consultation becomes a form of mental health consultation (Caplan, 1970). Even when program consultation is practiced in mental health settings, it involves the fundamental characteristics of process consultation (see Blanton & Alley, 1978). For example, I once helped a mental health clinic develop a training program for parents to improve their child-rearing skills. The program group had to design the training sessions, the resource materials, the evaluation instruments, as well as maintaining its own functioning at an effective level.

Important areas to focus on during program consultation involve goal-setting, staff selection and training, group functioning, communication, decision making, and so on. This form of consultation leads directly into the major practice field of program development and evaluation (see Chapter 13).

Consulting on the evaluation of programs has coincided with the development of a new and exciting consultation role for applied social psychologists. *Research consultation* involves the provision of knowledge and guidance relevant to the execution of a social research project. Applied social research is difficult to do well, and numerous factors that determine its failure or success have been identified (see Glaser & Taylor, 1973; Rossi, Wright & Wright, 1978). The research consultant draws on his or her expertise in the scientific method and the major types of social research to assist a project team in planning and implementation.

A number of important content areas must be considered: the design of the research project, the methods of measurement, the collection and statistical analysis of the data, the drawing of conclusions, and the making of recommendations. In addition, process expertise can help the research team identify the best roles for each of its members, improve communication and decision making, and generally facilitate the problem-solving sequence. When the consultant's expertise is combined with the organization members' understanding and skill in the delivery of service, collaborative projects of considerable benefit are the outcome. For example, a counseling program may wish to evaluate its services by surveying past clients, but the staff may know little about interview design, survey research, or statistical analysis. An applied social psychologist could assist in all of these activities even though he or she might not have in-depth knowledge of personal counseling.

Problems in interpersonal and intergroup relationships often stop us from maximizing productivity and satisfaction in social settings. The basic ideas of process consultation can be applied here. For example, Walton (1969) has developed a model of *third-party consultation*, directed toward improving interpersonal relationships among business executives working in the same organization. Concurrently, Blake and Mouton (1964) have developed consulting strategies for resolving intergroup conflicts within organizational settings, particularly between labor and management. My own contribution in this area has been the development of a general model of third-party consultation and its application to different intergroup conflicts in community settings (Fisher, 1972, 1976). This method involves the facilitative and diagnostic actions of an impartial consultant who helps the antagonists move toward a collaborative, problem-solving mode of resolving their conflict rather than remaining locked into a competitive, destructive orientation. Third-party consultation is an important contribution to practice in intergroup relations (see Chapter 8), international relations (see Chapter 12), and the general resolution of social conflict (see Chapter 14).

Schein (1969) developed his description of process consultation from his experience as an organizational consultant. Ways of working with organizations have expanded a great deal, and it is now appropriate to speak of the practice field of *organization development*, of which process consultation is a major part. Organization development can be defined in various ways—it is a diverse and rapidly developing area (see French & Bell, 1978). At the base of organization development, however, is the involvement of a professional consultant who uses her or his social-science knowledge and skill to collaboratively initiate a systematic process of diagnosis and change in the organization, so that the organization's human resources are used more effectively (see Chapter 9).

The practice field of *community development* has been fostered primarily in the disciplines of sociology and social work—and in some cases within schools of extension or community development. Applied social psychologists have also made important contributions. The essential characteristics of community development strongly parallel process consultation. The community developer serves as a catalyst who collaborates with community groups in diagnosing and improving social relations among people in ways that lead to productive community change. There are different approaches to community development (Perlman & Gurin, 1972; Rothman, 1974), and in Chapter 10 we will consider the relationship between these approaches and applied social psychology.

Finally, the change agent roles of the social technologist and social advocate institute the problem-solving sequence toward social change (see Chapter 11). Social technology has focused more on interpersonal relations while social advocacy has concentrated on community and societal issues. Each has the potential to make an important contribution to the practice domain of applied social psychology.

Summary

Besides knowing and caring about social problems, we as applied social psychologists must be involved in the development and the use of productive methods of social change.

The change agent is a professional practitioner who works with others to facilitate personal and social development. The change agent focuses his or her efforts on the processes of human interaction and facilitates the development of interpersonal and group relations. This process improves the ability of social systems to meet the needs of their members. Change agent roles include those of applied researcher, trainer, consultant, social technologist, and advocate.

Human relations training follows the laboratory method of learning; the participants are involved in diagnosing learning needs and in changing behavior to meet those needs. With the guidance of a trained facilitator, individuals can increase their awareness of themselves and others and find more effective ways of functioning in the small-group setting.

Process consultation helps the client system diagnose problems by focusing on interpersonal and group relations and then collaborating with the client system in the active solution of the problems.

Social technology involves the application of existing social-psychological knowledge to the solution of social problems. Social technology can be used in accordance with the humanistic value base—or it can be abused.

The social advocate is a participant activist who joins forces with disadvantaged groups to increase their share of resources and power. The advocate crystallizes and polarizes issues, uses various tactics of confrontation and persuasion, and attempts to mobilize public opinion in support of the cause.

The activities of change agents are designed to influence people's lives. Therefore, we must be very aware of the ethical implications of this work. As professionals, change agents have developed a number of codes of ethics that cover such crucial areas as competence, confidentiality, and client welfare.

The practice area of skill training follows the systematic format of experience-based learning: conceptual preparation, demonstration and practice of the skills, feedback, analysis, and discussion of applications. Areas of skill training include: personal motivation, interpersonal communication, and small group.

Consultation is a help-giving process in which the consultant aids the consultee to better understand the problem situation, develop alternate solutions, and generate actions to implement the solution. General models of consultation are useful for gaining a concise and comprehensive view of the field. Lippitt and Lippitt provide a description of the multiple roles that consultants may enact while Blake and Mouton offer a systematic model in the form of the consulcube.

There are a number of forms of process consultation. These include: group consultation, program consultation, research consultation, and third-party consultation. All these forms involve the consultant serving as a catalyst who collaborates in the diagnosis and remediation of social problems in the client system.

Further Readings

Alinsky, S. *Rules for radicals.* New York: Random House, 1971.

Benne, K. D., Bradford, L. D., Gibb, J. R. & Lippitt, R. D. *The laboratory method of changing and learning: Theory and application.* Palo Alto, Calif.: Science and Behavior Books, 1975.

Goodstein, L. D. *Consulting with human service systems.* Reading, Mass.: Addison-Wesley, 1978.

Lippitt, G. & Lippitt, R. *The consulting process in action.* La Jolla, Calif.: University Associates, 1978.

Morris, W. C. & Sashkin, M. *Organization behavior in action: Skill building experiences.* St. Paul, Minn.: West Publishing, 1976.

Varela, J. A. *Psychological solutions to social problems: An introduction to social technology.* New York: Academic Press, 1971.

PART TWO

Levels of Analysis for Understanding and Action

CHAPTER OUTLINE

FIVE

The Person and the Situation

All of us tend to rely on our *implicit theory of personality* in the way we understand and deal with the people around us (Bruner & Taguiri, 1954; Wagner & Vallacher, 1977). We see others as having *personalities*, sets of enduring dispositions that determine many of their behaviors. Out of our personal experiences, we form impressions of people and attach dominant traits to them. We usually look for one piece of information and infer other characteristics or behaviors on that basis (for example, "People who are friendly are usually helpful too"). Once we form an impression of a person's disposition, we behave accordingly ("Jennifer is aggressive; watch what you say to her," "Bob is submissive; feel free to say what you like to him").

But individuals are complex and not so easily pinned down. They live not in a vacuum, but in the context of a real world of overlapping social situations. They have multiple roles and intricate relationships that affect their behavior and modify the way their personality traits are expressed.

In short we need to depend on far more than our implicit personality theory *to make sense of people's behaviors so that we can more effectively relate to and work with the individuals around us.* All social systems involve individuals, and to understand and change social behavior and institutions, it is essential to "know people." To increase the depth, reliability, and validity of this perception, personality and social psychologists have developed a number of theories of personality. These theories will be examined in the first part of this chapter.

Personality theories have focused on the individual as an integral part of society, on the connections between people and their position in the social environment. Conversely, most theories of society make assumptions about the nature of the individuals. For example, the hedonistic assumption that people are motivated by pleasure and pain underlies much theorizing about large-scale social and economic behavior. Consequently, theories of human behavior are usually social-psychological theories, that is, they integrate the individual level of analysis with more complex levels of social functioning. Some theories of social psychology, such as dissonance theory or attribution theory, place more emphasis on processes occurring within the individual than on the social environment. In this way, they can be seen as "minitheories" of personality as much as theories of social behavior. It is therefore understandable that the fields of personality and social psychology are intermixed to a great extent and are often difficult to separate. Thus, once more we see the necessity of dealing with the individual level if we wish to develop valid theories of human social behavior.

Most of the theories in this chapter are *"individual theories"*: they look for the causes of behavior within the dynamics of the individual—his or her characteristics, motives, and stage of development. Others are *"social theories"* of personality: assuming that the major influences on behavior come from the environment, these theories focus on differences among situations rather than individuals (Bavelas, 1978).

In addition to these differences of approach, however, there appears to be a crisis in personality psychology (Helson & Mitchell, 1978; Phares & Lamiell, 1977). Disagreement stems from a schism that apparently has developed between theory and research on one hand, and clinical exposure and practice on the other. In other words, personality psychologists may have increasingly separated themselves from sustained contact with the very people they are trying to understand! Some personality psychologists attempt to develop theories based on the limited contact of laboratory experiments or psychological tests. Carlson (1971) voiced this with his question "Where is the person in personality research?" Some critics have observed that the situation in personality psychology is parallel to the crisis within social psychology: personality psychology may be compromising its relevance, validity, and utility by its denial of the importance of collaborative research and practice, and by its lack of integration among theory, research, and practice.

However, the more hotly debated issues are how we can understand human behavior by examining the *interaction* between person and environment; how we can explore the factors of both personality and situation that determine behavior; and how we can develop systems of classification for these components (Helson & Mitchell, 1978). These are crucial questions that will be the focus of the second part of this chapter.

THEORIES OF PERSONALITY

Trait Approach

Some theorists study personality by describing people in terms of their *traits*. Traits are enduring characteristics, qualities, or predispositions to respond in a consistent manner. Samples of behavior—usually responses to items on a personality test—indicate a measurable underlying predisposition in the individual's personality. While this information is meant to help the theorist predict the person's behavior in other situations, there are differences of opinion about the nature and number of the most influential traits.

Allport's Trait Theory. In Gordon Allport's (1961) theory of personality, traits are enduring and pervasive personal dispositions to respond, leading to unique patterns of consistent behavior. Allport points out that common speech and common sense presupposes traits: we speak of a friend who is ambitious, talkative, and enthusiastic; we describe a professor as hard-working, distant, and inscrutable. As a social scientist, Allport has stressed the importance of critically examining and refining the concept of trait as the fundamental unit of personality. A trait is seen as a broad system of similar action tendencies existing in the person. Allport even speculates that traits may have a neurophysiological basis.

Like other trait theorists, Allport makes distinctions among kinds of traits. *Cardinal traits* are general predispositions that pervade all aspects of a person's life; almost every behavior seems traceable to the influence of a cardinal trait. Our terms for describing such individuals are often drawn from historical figures who possessed a particular striking characteristic—we say someone is sadistic (after the Marquis de Sade), quixotic (after Don Quixote), or that someone is Christlike or a Don Juan. However, very few people can be sufficiently described in this way. Usually, individuals are better described by a handful of *central traits* that strongly influence consistent behavior in a variety of situations. For example, if we say the Joanne is sociable, we mean that she will be friendly and outgoing in almost all interactions with others. Allport has also defined *secondary traits,* likened to attitudes, which consist of predispositions to respond in particular ways to specific social situations. These tendencies are less conspicuous and consistent, but nonetheless important. An example would be feeling anxious in seminar classes, but not in most other social situations.

Allport believes that the uniqueness of each personality is due to the particular combination of traits that each of us possesses and expresses in our own way. This is consistent with a further distinction between common and individual traits. *Common traits* exist in all people within the same culture to some degree, and through collecting the same information from many people we can make comparisons among individuals on these common dimensions. The basis for common traits lies in our shared culture and typical modes of adjustment to social reality. However, the use of common traits forces individuals into categories and can only be seen as an approximation. To truly understand a person, we must also consider his or her unique *individual traits,* and we must use long-term and in-depth case studies to adequately assess these unique predispositions.

Although Allport stresses that behavior is determined by traits rather than situations, he recognizes that traits are only one determinant of behavior, and that trait theory must allow for the influences of a situation or behavior. However he fears that a denial of internal predispositions is equivalent to a denial of the existence and validity of a self-directed human being and the acceptance of a social robot who simply responds to external stimuli (Allport, 1966).

Cattell: Source and Surface Traits. Using psychological tests and statistical techniques, Raymond B. Cattell (Cattell, 1950, 1966; Cattell & Kline, 1977) has searched for fundamental traits as the basic units that make up the organized structure of personality. To provide a scheme by which persons can be categorized, Cattell emphasizes common traits and examines *surface traits*—that is, clusters of consistent behavior that correlate positively on personality tests. He then identifies *source traits*—the underlying tendencies that account for the patterns of surface traits. Source traits can best be identified through factor analysis (see Chapter 3). That is, the major factors that consistently emerge from analyzing the responses of many individuals to many tests become the major building blocks—the source traits—of Cattell's theory of personality. Through studying responses to psychological tests, observations of everyday behavior and self-ratings, Cattell has identified approximately fifteen source traits (see Table 5.1). For example, a person weak in the source trait of ego strength is at the mercy of his or her feelings and is easily upset; a person rated high in ego strength is emotionally stable and faces reality calmly.

Cattell also identifies *dynamic traits* (expressed in our interests and motives), *ability traits* (reflected by our capacity to reach goals effectively), and *temperament traits* (related to our emotional responses). In the context of person-versus-environment, Cattell further divides source traits into *constitutional traits* (reflecting influences of each person's physiology), and *environmental traits* (reflecting the influences of our environment, acquired and absorbed early in life). Taken together, these various traits constitute Cattell's theory of personality.

Eysenck: Extraversion-Introversion and Emotional Stability. In contrast to the numerous traits outlined in the personality theories of both Allport and Cattell, Hans Eysenck's work emphasizes only two preeminent traits: *extraversion-introversion* and *emotional stability* or neuroticism. Eysenck maintains that these two dimensions account for a large amount of the variability among individual personalities.

An extraverted person tends to be outgoing, sociable, carefree, and impulsive; an introverted person tends to be reserved, quiet, introspective, and controlled. Emotional stability is considered to be unrelated to extraversion-introversion. The unstable or neurotic person tends to be anxious, restless, touchy, and moody; the stable person tends to be calm, carefree, even-tempered, and reliable.

Table 5.1   THE MAJOR SOURCE TRAITS OF PERSONALITY

Technical title	*Popular label*
Affectia-Sizia	Outgoing-reserved
Intelligence	More intelligent–less intelligent
Ego strength	Stable-emotional
Dominance-Submissiveness	Assertive-humble
Surgency-Desurgency	Happy-go-lucky–sober
Super ego strength	Conscientious-expedient
Parmia-Threctia	Venturesome-shy
Premsia-Harria	Tender-minded–tough-minded
Protension-Alaxia	Suspicious-trusting
Autia-Praxernia	Imaginative-practical
Shrewdness-Artlessness	Shrewd-forthright
Guilt proneness–Assurance	Apprehensive-placid

Source: Cattell (1966).

To study the significance of these major dimensions of personality, Eysenck and his colleagues (Eysenck, 1952, 1957; Eysenck & Eysenck, 1969) have constructed personality tests measuring extraversion and neuroticism, correlating and factor-analyzing these scores with a variety of other personality measures. This has produced a broad-ranging theory that postulates relationships among physiological tendencies, personality traits, the socialization process, social attitudes, and political preferences. (For example the extraverted person does not condition (learn) well, tends to be impulsive and aggressive, and consequently develops more tough-minded social attitudes and more conservative political beliefs.) While Eysenck's theory involves considerable stretching to link these diverse areas, it illustrates how dominant personality patterns may affect complex social behavior.

Rotter: Locus of Control. Rotter's *locus* ("location," "placement") *of control,* developed within his theory of social learning, can be considered a single-trait theory of personality (Bavelas, 1978). It accounts for differences in our expectations regarding the control of reinforcement which follows our behavior. Rotter (1966, 1975) proposes that individuals who believe in an *external* locus of control perceive that their actions and consequent reinforcement is determined by such powerful outside influences as luck, fate, or complex life forces. Individuals who believe in an *internal* locus of control attribute outcomes of events to their own personal characteristics or behavior. How we perceive locus of control thus determines our perception of the degree of control or power we have over the events in our lives.

This dimension of personality is measured by Rotter's *I-E (Internal-External) Scale.* A person scoring high on internal control is more likely to be a high achiever, influential, and more active in mastering his or her environment (Rotter, 1966). The importance of locus of control for social behavior rests on the sense of personal agency and power which people believe they possess. For example, Seeman (1963) found that reformatory inmates with an internal locus of control were more likely to learn about factors influencing parole decisions than were prisoners with an external locus of control. Presumably the latter inmates saw themselves as more powerless and were more alienated in the situation and did not see the usefulness of learning about parole decisions. This sense of power or lack of it may have a direct bearing on the degree to which people are willing to participate in activities that benefit the welfare of themselves or others.

A more dramatic example of the importance of a sense of control in one's life comes from the work of Rodin and Langer (Langer & Rodin, 1976; Rodin & Langer, 1977). Elderly residents of a nursing home were given one of two messages depending on which floor they lived. One message emphasized the staff's responsibility for decision making on such matters as seeing a movie and caring for a plant given to each of the residents. The second message emphasized the residents' responsibility: they would decide when to see a movie, they could rearrange their own furniture, they would care for their plants. Three weeks later, the residents who were given greater personnel control expressed greater happiness, were seen as more improved and active by the nurses, and showed greater attendance at the movie. Eighteen months later, these residents were rated as more active and in better health and had a lower rate of mortality (15% versus 30%) than the residents in the low-control floor. Sense of control is a personal variable with important real-life application.

Questioning Trait Theory. The preceding examples of trait approaches to personality theory show a great deal of variety with regard to the number and identity of traits proposed. At the same time, there are a number of commonalities in most trait theories, including an attempt to describe the fundamental and general characteristics of human personality and the reliance on psychometric and statistical methods.

Trait theory, however, has been beset by a number of difficulties; some critics, for example, charge that trait theory is based on circular reasoning, a charge that also applies to our implicit theories of personality. For example, labeling some behaviors assertive and then inferring a trait of assertiveness to explain the behaviors actually explains little of a causative nature. Similarly, trait theory explains little of a dynamic nature: it does not address the ongoing flow of a person's behavior in interaction with the environment (Mischel, 1979). In addition, it is not clear to what degree traits actually exist in the consistent behavior of others and to what degree they are merely a result of our own stereotyped thinking (see Box 5.1). Nonetheless, Mischel (1979) maintains that the trait approach is one of the oldest and most influential positions in the field of personality psychology.

Box 5.1   FOCUS ON RESEARCH
Basic Personality Traits: How Many, Which Ones, and in Whose Head?

Warren Norman and his associates at the University of Michigan have studied personality traits as revealed in the way individuals rate others. By drawing on the work of earlier researchers such as Cattell, Norman selected a set of rating scales that seemed to capture the major elements of personality. These scales were administered to different samples of respondents and their ratings were subjected to factor analysis (see Chapter 3) to see if a set of basic dimensions could account for the ratings. The results showed that five main personality factors could account for the ratings on the twenty different scales, as follows:

Basic Factor	*Rating Sale*
1. Extraversion	talkative-silent open-secretive adventurous-cautious sociable-reclusive
2. Agreeableness	good-natured–irritable not jealous–jealous gentle-headstrong cooperative-negativistic
3. Conscientiousness	tidy-careless responsible-undependable scrupulous-unscrupulous persevering-fickle

4. Emotional Stability   poised-nervous
calm-anxious
composed-excitable
not hypochondriacal–hypochondriacal

5. Culture   artistically sensitive–insensitive
intellectual-unreflective
refined-crude
imaginative-simple

However, the validity of these peer ratings became suspect when a group of people who had just met (a university class) rated each other using the scales and the analysis yielded the same results! Since the individuals did not know each other, it seemed doubtful that their ratings of each other could be based on accurate perceptions. The interpretation? As a rater, each person was relying on his or her implicit theory of personality, and there seemed to be a shared consensus of that implicit theory, thus producing general agreement among raters as to what scales went together. If, for example, you rated someone high on cooperative, you would probably also rate them high on good-natured, thus producing a general factor of agreeableness.

Further analysis showed that self-ratings in unacquainted groups (such as the university class) did not correlate with ratings by peers, whereas self-rating and ratings by peers did show agreement in groups of people who had known each other for some time. One way of checking if the peer ratings truly represent the characteristics of the person rated (rather than the rater's implicit personality theory) is to have two or more raters rate the same person and look for agreement among their ratings. Norman also found that *predicted* or expected peer ratings had a lower correlation to *actual* peer ratings in unacquainted groups than in acquainted groups. It is therefore a complicated matter to ascertain what the basic traits of human personality are and in whose head they exist.

Source: Norman, W. T. "To see oursels as ithers see us!": Relations among self-perceptions, peer-perceptions, and expected peer perceptions of personality attributes. *Multivariate Behavioral Research*, 1969, 4, 417–443.

Psychodynamic Contribution

Freud: The First Psychoanalyst. Psychodynamics is an approach to studying personality that emphasizes underlying forces or motives, often of an unconscious nature. *Psychoanalysis*, the original psychodynamic approach to personality pioneered by the Austrian physician Sigmund Freud, has profoundly affected not only psychiatry and psychology but society's image of itself. Freud's psychoanalytic theory developed out of his experience in treating individuals suffering from neurotic disorders largely characterized by inappropriate ways of dealing with internal conflict and anxiety. Although its goal was *psychotherapy*— the psychological treatment of mental, emotional, and nervous disorders— Freud's approach was also concerned with the way the normal individual functions alone and in society.

Freud (1923, 1940) emphasized the role of unconscious processes in determining people's thoughts and actions. He maintained that what we do is determined by powerful innate instincts—unlearned impulses that motivate our behavior by operating through the unconscious part of our mind. Freud postulated two basic instincts: the *libido*, or sexual drive, and the *ego*, or drive for self-preservation. Later he added the *death or aggression instinct*.

These powerful motives conflict with other considerations that influence behavior: the constraints of reality and society. Thus, in attempting to express these unconscious motives, the person experiences conflict and anxiety and attempts to find alternate and often indirect or pathological means of expression. Since these strong sexual and aggressive impulses are often threatening to the individual, the conscious mind resists their expression. When the individual attempts to repress or resist such impulses, the extreme result is indirect expression in the form of neurotic symptoms (such as physical complaints with no physiological basis).

Freud's later work described three separate parts of the structure of the personality:

- the *id*—the unconscious mind's storehouse of powerful innate instincts, which seek immediate gratification in accordance with the pleasure principle of tension reduction
- the *ego*—the conscious, rational mediator that attempts to satisfy id impulses within the constraints of the environment and social reality
- the *super-ego*—the element that internalizes society's moral standards and includes the individual's conscience, representing judgments of "good" and "bad"

These three basic elements of personality are in constant conflict as the id strives for expression of its irrational instincts, and the ego attempts to accommodate these expressions in line with the limitations imposed by reality and the super-ego. To reduce the anxiety and fear associated with these internal conflicts, the ego may engage in a number of *defense mechanisms*:

- In *repression* the ego attempts to force instinctual impulses to remain in the unconscious mind. Since it is usually unable to do so, the impulses are expressed in disguised form, and the person experiences continuing anxiety with no understanding of its cause. The individual may then engage in other defense mechanisms. For example, a female child may find that her expression of aggression is met with consistent punishment by her parents. Her super-ego incorporates strong admonitions against aggressive behavior by "nice little girls." In an attempt to resolve the resulting conflict between the id and the super-ego, the ego represses all aggressive impulses, and the girl often experiences anxiety, especially in the presence of others who are potential targets for her aggression.
- *Denial* is a refusal to accept external signs as indications that an unconscious impulse is seeking expression. In our example, the girl grows to be a young woman who has difficulty establishing relationships with others. She often "turns people off" by ignoring them, frowning at them, and so forth, but she does not see her behavior as related to repressed aggression.
- *Projection* involves attributing unacceptable impulses, motives, or characteristics to other people rather than accepting their existence in oneself. The young woman comes to be very suspicious of other people, seeing them as hostile, manipulative, and untrustworthy. She sees most others as basically aggressive, whereas she is a "good person."

- *Displacement* is the shifting of an emotion, such as anger, from the original and appropriate target to an inappropriate object. The young woman's anger toward her parents for frustrating her aggressive impulses is expressed toward "women's libbers" for trying to make females into something they are not. Being assertive is perceived by the young woman as being aggressive and destructive and she consciously rejects such behavior quite strongly.
- *Sublimation* substitutes socially acceptable activities for unacceptable ones, while still allowing expression of the sexual or aggressive impulses. In our example, the young woman participates a great deal in organized sports. She sees this competitive behavior as socially appropriate and emphasizes enjoyment rather than the competitive and aggressive elements.
- *Rationalization* attributes behavior to socially acceptable causes rather than the true instinctual impulse. Sports are seen by the woman as a means of developing character and meeting social needs. The suggestion that participation serves aggressive impulses is strongly denied.
- *Reaction formation* in the conscious expression of a motive opposite to the true motive that has been repressed. In our example, the woman whose expression of aggressive impulses has been strongly inhibited may campaign against women's liberation as a disguised form of motive expression. This campaign meets aggressive needs while still maintaining a conscious denial of aggressive behavior on her part.

Freud's theories expanded beyond individuals to relate parent-child concepts to the formation and functioning of groups and the larger society. He suggested that the individual's identification with the parents serves as the basis for the moral and religious codes of society, and that group leaders within the society are perceived and reacted to as parental substitutes, thus serving a strong super-ego function. Jealousy and rivalry among group members are thus transformed into a common loyalty to the leader, leaving the group vulnerable to directives toward even irrational behavior. Thus Freud reiterated his theme that much human behavior is motivated by irrational instinctual determinants that seek expression at every level of human functioning.

The prime difficulty with psychodynamic theory is the lack of research support. Numerous studies have not only questioned the importance but even the *existence* of such basic processes as repression (Mischel, 1979).

Freud's unique contributions to personality theory and psychotherapy, while rejected by many psychologists, have been accepted and extended by others. Some have developed theories that give more emphasis to the rational and aggressive gratification. Although Freud's strong emphasis on sexuality is often regarded as the result of the sexually repressive Victorian era, his theorizing has provided useful concepts that help illuminate some important dynamics of the human personality.

Erikson: Psychosocial Development. A neo-Freudian psychoanalyst, Erik Erikson (1963, 1968), maintained Freud's interest in unconscious processes and the role of conflict and anxiety, but postulated a different developmental sequence of personality. Whereas Freud's sequence focuses on *psychosexual stages,* Erikson's focuses on *psychosocial stages.*

In Freud's view of the psychosexual stages during childhood, the id seeks pleasure through activities involving the erogenous zones of the body—the mouth and lips, the anus, and the genitals. If the child is overindulged or frustrated during any one of these stages, the adult character will be pathological in some fashion. For example, an infant who is frustrated during the oral stage in the first years of life may develop personality characteristics of greediness, passivity, and dependence on others.

While not ignoring this aspect of human development, Erikson has postulated a series of *psychosocial* developmental stages that proceeds in a predetermined order and involves crucial crises at each step. Each of these eight stages involve a major personal and social issue that must be resolved satisfactorily if the individual is to mature positively. Each is a period of both increased vulnerability and potential; each is a turning point toward either maladjustment or greater strength. Erikson stresses the importance of the ego in navigating this development and of society in encouraging and supporting the proper rate and sequence of its unfolding.

Each stage, spanning a period of the individual's life, has its attendant crises and outcomes:

- The *oral-sensory* stage: the first year. The infant, in relation to its mother, develops basic attitudes of getting, giving, trust, mistrust. If needs are met consistently and dependably, the infant gains a sense of familiarity and comfort, leading to outcomes of trust, confidence, and optimism in relation to the social environment.

Erikson's *oral-sensory* stage encompasses the first year of life. The infant, in relation to the mother, develops basic attitudes of getting, giving, trust, and mistrust. If the infant's needs are met consistently, he or she gains a sense of familiarity and comfort, leading to trust, confidence, and optimism in relation to the social environment. *(Martin Weaver/Woodfin Camp & Associates)*

Erikson's *latency* period (the sixth year to the start of puberty) is critical for a child's feeling of competence. The early school years provide the child with an opportunity for recognition through production and performance in a variety of skills. Success gives the child a sense of industry, rather than a feeling of inferiority, and adds competence to his or her growing identity. *(Constantine Manos/Magnum Photos, Inc.)*

- The *muscular-anal* stage: the second year. The young child develops attitudes about holding on and letting go—of bowel movements, of objects, of people. Support of the child's sense of independence helps develop a sense of autonomy, rather than the shame, guilt, and doubt that result from failure and frustration. The ideal outcome is the development of a sense of control over oneself and the environment without a loss of self-esteem.
- The *locomotor-genital* stage: the third to fifth years. This stage emphasizes the importance of initiative in the child's development and the pleasure to be derived from attack and conquest. Depending on the child's success in the more active engagement with the environment, the crisis of initiative or guilt is resolved positively or pathologically. The positive outcome is a sense of purpose and direction in the child's developing identity.
- The *latency* period: the sixth year to the start of puberty. This stage is critical for the child's feeling of competence. The early school years provide an opportunity for recognition through production and performance in a variety of skills. Success gives the child a sense of industry, rather than a feeling of inferiority, and adds competence to his or her growing identity.
- The stage of *puberty and adolescence* takes Erikson's theory beyond the childhood period covered by Freud and points to the importance of looking at a continuing

series of crises over the *entire* life cycle. Identity, rather than role confusion, is the most crucial issue of this stage. The adolescent struggles to put together past identifications with present motives and aptitudes. This growing sense of identity must then be linked to future goals as represented in the opportunities offered by social roles. If these combinations are successful, the person develops a feeling of inner continuity and confidence in the form of an integrated *ego identity*. The development of identity is a strong determinant of how the individual then relates to society.

- The *young adult* stage is characterized by the issue of intimacy versus isolation. Given the development of a strong personal identity, the individual is now ready to fuse his or her identity with those of other people, to commit to others, and to develop the ethical strength to abide by these commitments. The negative outcome of the crisis is alienation and prejudiced and destructive relations with other people.

- The stage of *adulthood*, the middle years, can yield positive outcomes only if all earlier crises have been satisfactorily resolved. The mature person needs to be needed and needs to develop a sense of *generativity*—that is, productivity in the formation and guidance of the next generation. Failure at this stage results in stagnation and self-destruction fed by a childish overemphasis on the satisfaction of one's own personal needs.

- In the last stages of *maturity* the individual faces the final crisis of ego integrity versus despair. The successful resolution of all earlier crises allows the individual to develop a sense of order and perspective, a love of humanity, a feeling of satisfaction with one's life, and the possession of dignity and wisdom. By contrast the elements of despair are a lack of acceptance, a sense of failure, disgust with life, and a fear of death.

According to Erikson each culture supports the development of a particular style of integrity. At the same time each individual must sufficiently develop the ego qualities associated with each stage. Thus "a wise Indian, a true gentleman, and a mature peasant share and recognize in one another the final stage of integrity" (Erikson, 1963, p. 269).

To complete his outline of the life-cycle stages, Erikson notes the circular relation between trust and integrity, the first and last ego qualities. Trust is essentially a reliance on another's integrity: "Healthy children will not fear life if their elders have integrity enough not to fear death" (1963, p. 269).

The psychological development of individuals thus has important consequences for the *quality of social relationships*. The positive characteristics of trust, identity, intimacy, and so forth, enable individuals to enter into open, authentic, and collaborative interpersonal and group relations. The qualities of generativity and integrity of the mature adult enable him or her to contribute meaningfully to the welfare of the community and society. The applied social psychologist understands that these personal qualities of individuals help to determine their willingness and ability to contribute to valuable social goals.

Adorno: The Authoritarian Personality. The far-ranging theories of Freud and Erikson relate to the development and functioning of the individual to his or her social world. A more specific attempt to use psychodynamic personality theory to explain social attitudes and behavior was made by T. W. Adorno and his colleagues in their study of the *authoritarian personality* (Adorno, Frenkel-Brunswik, Levinson & Sanford, 1950).

First focusing on prejudice toward Jews, the investigators then followed the "widening circle of covariation" (Brown, 1965)—the discovery that anti-Semitism was only one expression of *ethnocentrism*, a much wider form of generalized prejudice that also related to conservative political and economic attitudes. To explain this consistency of social attitude, the authors turned to the level of personality functioning, using psychoanalytic theory to interpret the development and expression of the authoritarian personality. Relationships among the id, ego, and super-ego, as well as the use of defense mechanisms, provided a link between the dynamics of the person and his or her social attitudes and behavior. See Box 5.2 for a description of this classic illustration of personality theory applied to the field of social relations.

Self Theories: Mead, Rogers, and Maslow

Mead: Symbolic Interactionism. George Mead, a founder of social psychology, was influenced by Charles Cooley's concept of the "looking-glass self" (Schellenberg, 1978)—the idea that each of us, imagining how others perceive us, reflects these appraisals in our own self-image.

Building upon Cooley's idea, Mead (1934) strongly emphasized the role of the social world as the influential shaper of the mind and the self. This powerful link between the individual's self-concept and social settings and processes grows out of several elements: We gain self-awareness by observing how other people respond to us. For example, if your parents treat you as a "bad little child," you come to see yourself partly in that way. Our behavior can be understood only in terms of the social group of which we are a member; we adopt our group's attitudes through our symbolic conception of our group as the "generalized other." A member of a sorority, for example, tends to think and behave in ways that meet the generalized expectations of other members. We perceive the world around us in symbolic terms, using the symbolic representations of thought and language based on common experience to think about others, to communicate with others, and to interact with others. We develop meanings for environmental events through our interaction with them: a chair is an object to sit on, a police officer is a person to be afraid of, a university is an institution for learning. Each of us uses symbols to develop our subjective meanings—some of these will be shared by others, some will not, and this will affect our interaction with others.

It is through this "symbolic interaction" with others that we develop our own distinctive concept of ourselves. This strong emphasis on the social world as the shaper of the mind and the self is known as *symbolic interactionism* and has been the most influential single force in sociological social psychology (Schellenberg, 1978). The self, however, is not simply a reflected agent of society; through awareness it develops an innovative and creative side, which in turn affects society. Thus our behavior is determined through the combination of past influences with our present intentions and perceptions.

Mead's contribution, in its own way stressing the interaction between the individual and the social environment in determining human behavior, stimulated and influenced a number of other important areas in social psychology, including

Box 5.2   FOCUS ON THEORY AND RESEARCH
The Authoritarian Personality: An Application of Psychoanalytic Theory

In the mid-1940s a research team of social and clinical psychologists led by T. W. Adorno completed a massive study of personality and prejudice which has become a classic in the field. The study combined the methods of attitude scaling, personal interviews, and personality assessment to yield a portrait of the highly prejudiced individual—the authoritarian personality.

The study began by developing a series of attitude scales, first on anti-Semitism, next on generalized prejudice or ethnocentrism, and finally on political and economic conservatism. Ethnocentrism also contains elements of ingroup loyalty and glorification (for example, "Patriotism and loyalty are the first and most important requirements of a good citizen"); conservatism values financial success and maintenance of the status quo. Over many different samples, these various attitude scales showed moderate to high correlations. A person who was anti-Semitic tended to be ethnocentric and politically conservative.

How could this totality of social attitudes be explained? According to the authors, the explanation was in the underlying dynamics of the individual's personality. To measure implicit, anti-democratic trends they constructed the Authoritarianism or Fascism Scale, popularly known as the F scale. Items were constructed from anti-Semitic speeches, writings of fascists, and interviews with highly ethnocentric individuals. The scale assessed nine characteristics of the authoritarian personality syndrome including conventionalism, submission to authority, destructiveness and cynicism, and superstition and stereotypy. Scores on the F scale were moderately related to scores on the previous scales, thus showing a relationship between personality and social attitudes.

Through the use of clinical interviews with subjects scoring very high or very low on ethnocentrism, a picture was formed of the development and dynamics of the authoritarian personality. This analysis drew on psychodynamic personality theory, using the concepts of id, ego, and super-ego and the defense mechanisms.

According to Adorno and associates, the development of the authoritarian personality begins early in childhood, when parents who are overconcerned about social status and proper behavior use harsh autocratic discipline to produce socially acceptable children. This leads to the *repression* of both the child's shortcomings as well as the aggression that is felt toward the parents. Through *projection* the unacceptable faults are projected onto powerless minority groups, thus fueling prejudiced attitudes. Through *displacement*, the aggression toward parents is redirected toward minority groups in the form of antagonism and hostility. The id thus gains expression of aggressive impulses, while a strong but not well internalized super-ego holds sway over a weak ego that continues to submit to authority figures and to defend the status quo.

Further research has both supported and criticized this intriguing picture of the prejudiced personality. The work stands as a rare integration of clinical and social psychology.

Source: Adorno, T. W., Frenkel-Brunswick, E., Levinson, D. J. & Sanford, R. N. *The authoritarian personality.* New York: Harper & Row, 1950.

role theory (see Chapter 2), reference group theory (see Chapter 7), and the dramaturgical approach to social interaction as exemplified by the work of Erving Goffman (see Chapter 6). Mead's ideas serve as a continuing foundation for symbolic interactionism (Lauer & Handel, 1977).

Rogers: Self-Concept. Carl Rogers is a humanistic clinical psychologist whose ideas about personality evolved from his experience in psychotherapy. His theory (1959) views the *perceived experience* of the individual as the basis of his or her behavior and personality. That experience is the individual's reality, and it is the individual who has greater potential awareness of that reality than anyone else. Only you or I really know how we see the world—others can understand our view, but only we can experience it.

Rogers makes two assumptions about human motivation: first, we are motivated to actualize ourselves to our fullest potential; second, we have a strong need for positive regard from others. Out of our need for self-actualization, we interact with our environment, valuing our experiences to the degree that they help us satisfy our needs for growth. If we perceive that going to college will aid our personal development, we go; if not, we look for positive experiences elsewhere. Through our experience we become aware of our own functioning; through interaction with others we develop a *self-concept* that is central to our further development. We gain a sense of our actual self as it is reflected in the appraisals of significant others, especially our parents.

Once our self-concept develops, our need to be evaluated positively and valued by others becomes a powerful motive. In this search for self-regard, we become sensitive to the demands put upon us by those who would give us positive regard. These demands—the criteria we must live up to—are the *conditions of worth* that we incorporate as guides to our behavior. For example, our parents want a child who can eat without making a mess, who can keep his or her room tidy, and so on. Unless we meet the condition of worth—being neat and tidy—we will not gain positive regard from our parents.

Now motivated to meet such conditions of worth (rather than to actualize our potential), we face conflict and anxiety. We create incongruities between our self and our experience whenever our experience runs contrary to our conditions of worth. As a young adult, we notice how our apartment is usually messy. This conflicts strongly with our ideal self-concept of a "tidy person" and creates anxiety for us—especially if our parents are about to visit!

To cope with such threatening discrepancies between self-concept and some aspect of experience or behavior, we engage in the process of *defense* protecting our self-concept, which may be expressed through different mechanisms such as denial or distortion of reality. For example, we may maintain that our apartment really isn't as messy as it looks, or we may project our untidiness onto our roommate and blame him or her for the mess.

Now if in the early stages of our development we were given *unconditional positive regard*, we would not become controlled by conditions of worth nor would we experience destructive discrepancies. We would develop congruence between our self-concept and our experience. We would see ourselves as others see us. For example, if our parents communicated that we were a "good person" regardless of the state of our room, we would come to see that being messy does not make one a bad person. We would also learn that in some situations being messy has negative consequences—for example, not being able to find an overdue library book. We would be free to experience the degree of untidiness that we choose and develop our self-concept accordingly, that is, "I can be tidy or untidy depending on the circumstances and consequences." This would allow us to move toward a more important goal—the actualization of our full potential to become a *fully functioning person.* Such a person is open to his or her experience, has no conditions of worth, guides and values personal behavior through a complete awareness of self, and creates relationships of reciprocal positive regard with others. The challenge for the social environment is to provide the conditions that allow this growth to take place.

Maslow: Self-Actualization. Carl Rogers and other humanistic psychologists have given attention to the human being's drive to fulfill all of his or her potential—that is, to actualize the self. Abraham Maslow, however, accords the process of *self-actualization* a central place in his theorizing about personality (Maslow, 1968, 1970).

Maslow's theory of human motivation (see Chapter 2) places the need for self-actualization at the top of a need hierarchy in which lower-order needs for survival, safety, love, and esteem must be adequately satisfied before the individual is free to move toward self-actualization. This focuses on "man's desire for self-fulfillment . . . the tendency for him to become actualized in what he is potentially . . . the desire to become more and more what he idiosyncratically is, to become everything that one is capable of becoming" (1970, p. 46).

Maslow based his theory on impressions gained through interviews and observations and on analyses of such historical figures as Thomas Jefferson, William James, and Eleanor Roosevelt. The picture of the self-actualizing person that emerged clearly set off such individuals from the general population and suggested that very few people become self-actualized. The fact that these few tend to be older members of society follows Maslow's theory that all lower-order needs must be satisfied before the process of self-actualization can begin.

What are the qualities of self-actualizing persons? They have a more efficient perception of reality and more comfortable relations with reality. They are less apt to distort or defend against what is, but are able to accept it—including parts of reality that are ambiguous or unknown. They tend to accept and respect themselves, their strengths, and their weaknesses, as they are.

They have little or no guilt, shame, and anxiety related to the typical objects of neurosis (such as sexual behavior), but may feel guilty about discrepancies between what exists and what is ideal.

They value spontaneity, simplicity, and naturalness. They lack artificiality, but will behave conventionally to avoid hurting others.

They tend to be problem-centered rather than self-centered individuals. They often commit themselves to a task or mission that has broad philosophical or ethical roots, and strongly invest their energies in working to achieve their goals.

They exhibit a quality of detachment, an above-average need and liking for

Eleanor Roosevelt was one of the very few people who have become self-actualized, according to Abraham Maslow. *(Inge Morath/Magnum Photos, Inc.)*

privacy, and a sense of reserve and calm in difficult or chaotic situations that may be viewed as coldness or snobbishness.

They are independent, have a continually fresh appreciation for life, have mystical "peak" experiences when they feel fully alive, show a deep identification with and concern for all people as equals, experience deep interpersonal relations, have strong, often unconventional ethical codes, possess an unhostile sense of humor, are especially creative in a fresh, uninhibited manner, and are able to resist and transcend the homogenizing influence of their culture.

Obviously very few among us embrace most or all of these demanding qualities. Maslow's subjects, in fact, not only lacked one or more of these qualities, but also shared in many of our common failings: they could be silly, irritating, vain, extraordinarily ruthless, and experience nonneurotic conflict and anxiety.

Thus (Maslow concluded), while there are no perfect human beings, there are a few great ones whose adjustment to life and integration of personality illuminate the healthier aspects of human processes and qualities. (See Box 5.3 for a way to measure self-actualization.)

Box 5.3   FOCUS ON RESEARCH
Personal Orientation Inventory: A Measure of Self-Actualization

Everett Shostrom, a clinical psychologist in the field of psychotherapy, became interested in developing a personality test to measure the quality of self-actualization. Shostrom noted that many personality instruments give estimates of a client's maladjustment or pathology whereas he wanted to measure a person's level of mental *health* and directions for personality *growth*.

Shostrom developed test items from observations of both healthy and troubled patients and from the writings of a variety of therapists. Items were grouped to provide scores on the following dimensions:

- *Time incompetence/time competence:* the efficient use of time
- *Other/inner directedness:* the degree of reactivity toward others versus oneself
- *Self-actualizing values:* the affirmation of values which support self-actualization
- *Existentiality:* the ability to react to situations without rigidity
- *Feeling reactivity:* sensitivity to one's own feelings and needs
- *Spontaneity:* freedom to be oneself
- *Self-regard:* affirmation of one's worth or strength
- *Self-acceptance:* acceptance of self in spite of deficiencies
- *Nature of man:* degree of constructive view of people
- *Synergy:* ability to transcend dichotomies (self-others, work-play) and integrate them successfully
- *Acceptance of aggression:* ability to accept one's aggressiveness rather than denial, repression, and defensiveness
- *Capacity for intimate contact:* ability to develop intimate relationships unencumbered by expectations and obligations

From these test dimensions Shostrom developed the Personal Orientation Inventory (POI). The POI was shown to have good test-retest reliability (see Chapter 3). In addition, the test was administered to a wide variety of groups to determine its validity. Patients in therapy, psychologists in training, and participants in sensitivity training (see Chapters 4 and 8) all demonstrated changes in scores over time that indicated the POI was measuring self-actualization and increased mental health. For example, as patients progressed through psychotherapy, they showed increasing inner-directedness as opposed to a strong reliance on others.

In addition to normal individuals, Shostrom administered the POI to groups of self-actualized and non–self-actualized persons as identified by clinical psychologists. The self-actualized group showed freedom from social pressure and a sense of self-support—a healthy balance of inner and outer directedness. They were also time competent—living more fully in the present, unburdened by past guilt and resentment, and able to tie present activities to future aspirations. In short, the POI was able to differentiate the self-actualized group from both normal and non–self-actualized individuals.

The POI has enjoyed wide usage in personality and social psychology and a number of reviews (including some criticisms) have been completed. It serves as a good illustration of measuring the positive side of the human personality.

Source: Shostrum, E. L. An inventory for the measurement of self-actualization. *Educational and Psychological Measurement,* 1964, *24,* 207–218. *Manual for the personal orientation inventory.* San Diego, Calif.: Educational and Industrial Testing Service, 1974.

Significance and Limitations of Self Theories. Self theories emphasize the approach of phenomenology, which is a cornerstone of much contemporary social-psychological theory (see Chapter 2). How the individual perceives the social world is seen as crucial in determining how he or she then behaves in interaction with others. In addition, self theories see the concept of self as central to understanding social relations. Our self-concept constantly guides and affects how we interrelate with others, providing an organized quality to our social being. Thus, to help understand how individuals behave in social settings, a sensitivity to the concept of self is very important.

However, we must realize that a focus on an individual's subjective perceptions does not necessarily illuminate the *causes* of his or her behavior (Mischel, 1976). For example, knowing that a friend has a "Pollyanna" attitude toward life doesn't explain why she is motivated to see things as brighter than they are. For this we need to understand her motives or other deeper elements of personality. In the same way, the self-concept is only one factor that influences social behavior. We must take into account numerous other forces, such as group norms, to understand and predict a person's relations with others.

Interpersonal Theories

Sullivan: Interpersonal Theory of Psychiatry. Neo-Freudian psychoanalyst Harry Stack Sullivan went beyond Freud in conceptualizing psychiatry as the study of *interpersonal* relations. Defining personality as "the relatively enduring pattern of recurrent interpersonal situations which characterize a human life" (1953, p. 111), Sullivan, like Mead, saw the development of the person as inextricably linked to the social environment in which it occurs.

In this social-psychological approach, the human personality cannot be isolated from the interpersonal situations in which it develops and expresses itself; it exists only in relation to other people. The individual's needs are met by others. Through interaction with others the individual comes to develop attitudes toward the self. The organization of personality—and such processes as perceiving and thinking—relate to interpersonal events involving real or imagined others.

An illustration of how individual personalities are intertwined with interpersonal relationships is provided by Sullivan's example of a conversation between a married couple (Conway, 1980). The wife makes a derogatory remark such as: "We never seem to go out anymore. What's wrong with you anyway?" The husband's face tenses for an instant—he glances sharply at his wife and then turns away. His verbal response is that he is very tired. The husband's immediate reaction of anger is repressed into the unconscious—he is not aware of his initial hostility toward his wife, nor is he aware of the resentment in her remark. Each individual's "self-system" works to alleviate anxiety over potential conflict and to provide illusions that mask real behavior. The husband sees his wife as affectionate and caring and himself as a gentleman who could never be hurt by such a devoted partner. The wife sees herself as a caring and tolerant mother substitute for a somewhat incompetent but loving husband. Thus, neither becomes consciously aware of the anger and the underlying anxiety in their interactions, and the inauthentic relationship continues to provide an illusion of security.

Sullivan's theory integrates concepts of personality structure (the self-system), stages of development, and dynamics (defenses against anxiety) with the ongoing flow of interpersonal processes. In this way, his work anticipated much later theorizing on such topics as interpersonal communication and transactional analysis (see Chapter 6) (Swensen, 1973).

Carson: Interaction Concepts of Personality. Robert Carson (1969), stressing person-situation interaction as a way to understand and predict behavior, saw the necessity of a classification system of interpersonal behavior. Consistency, or lack of it, in human behavior needs to be seen as the combination of tendencies within the person and the demands of the interpersonal situation. Using the framework developed by Leary (1957), Carson organizes types of interpersonal behavior around two fundamental dimensions: dominance versus submission, and hate versus love. Eight major styles of interpersonal behavior are then defined n relation to these basic dimensions. Carson uses social-psychological concepts including balance theory, exchange theory, social norms, and social roles to understand interpersonal transactions.

These interpersonal styles—competitive, self-effacing–masochistic, narcissistic, cooperative-overconventional, and so on—help define the relationships between two people, and resultant rewards (satisfactions) and costs (frustrations). For example, people with a competitive style will usually get what they want when they interact with someone who exhibits a self-effacing style. The high-pressure car salesman may succeed in selling a less-than-desirable vehicle to a shy and anxious young man. But persons with a competitive style will be frustrated in transactions with a managerial-autocratic type of person. The same salesman may run into trouble when he tries to pressure a confident school principal. The concept of norms and the process of interpersonal contracting (being clear on mutual expectations) are used to explain the general rules of social behavior as well as the specific agreements that individuals reach within a particular interpersonal relationship.

Carson's analysis provides a fine example of the use of higher-level concepts to understand personality functioning. By contrast, most personality theorists try to explain behavior by going in the opposite direction, that is, using personality theory to explain social interaction. In actuality, Carson represents a powerful middle-of-the-road position by considering how individual predispositions, especially personal style, interact with crucial elements of the social situation, such as norms, to co-determine the person's behavior.

Power of Interpersonal Theories. The basic premise of the interpersonal theories is that individuals can only be understood in terms of their relations with others. The individual characteristics and behavior identified by interpersonal theories only make sense in relation to their effects on others.

A simplified extension of Leary and Carson's framework is presented in Figure 5.1 (Conway, 1980). The two basic dimensions of dominant-submissive and hostile-loving have meaning only when other people are considered: Are we typically dominant or submissive toward others? Are we usually loving or hostile? The circle breaks down into the four major quadrants of friendly-

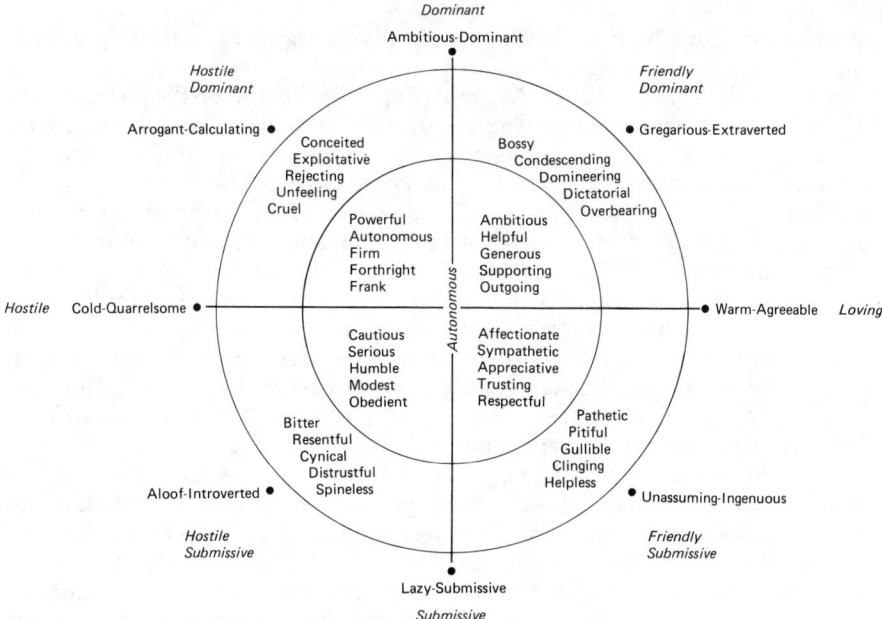

Figure 5.1   An Interpersonal Model of Personality.
Source: Conway (1980).

dominant, friendly-submissive, hostile-dominant, and hostile-submissive. The eight interpersonal styles identified in the model—ambitious-dominant, gregarious-extraverted, warm-agreeable, and so forth—are inextricably related to interpersonal relationships, not just to the individual. The adjectives in the inner circle are the typical trait names that we use to describe a person who exhibits a mild form of that particular style. The adjectives in the outer circle describe an exaggerated and undesirable style—one that can disrupt and destroy relationships.

The power of interpersonal theories is in their direct linkage of the individual and interpersonal levels of analysis. For individuals, these theories can help us understand our own interpersonal styles and our relationships and can help us question whether our behavior is leading to the social rewards we desire. *For applied social psychologists, interpersonal theories could serve as one of the main bridges between personality psychology and social psychology.* The limitation is that much more research needs to be done on the propositions that Carson and others have brought forward.

Recent Social-Psychological Contributions

Within personality and social psychology, social psychologists have recently shown interest in individual characteristics which affect how a person relates to others. This interest is represented in the study of shyness, loneliness, and learned helplessness.

Shyness. One day Philip Zimbardo, a social psychologist at Stanford University, was lecturing to a large class about the power social situations have to affect the way people think, feel, and act. As one example, he touched on the phenomenon of shyness, in which the person wants to interact with others, but is held back by his or her fears about the reactions of others. After class, some students approached Zimbardo to ask about their own problem of shyness. Soon Zimbardo was holding a seminar on shyness and had embarked on a research program to understand shyness and to suggest ways of alleviating this common barrier to social interaction (Zimbardo, 1977).

What is shyness? Zimbardo found few answers to this question. Dictionaries use phrases like "sensitively timid, shrinking from self-assertion, uncomfortable in the presence of others." However, very little research had been done on shyness, especially on understanding the dynamics of shyness. Consequently, the *Stanford Shyness Survey* was constructed, revised, and administered to over 5,000 people in several different countries.

The Stanford Shyness Survey asks respondents to decide for themselves whether they are shy and to describe the thoughts, feelings, actions, and situations that they associate with shyness. *A startling finding is that shyness is a common if not universal experience.* Over 80 percent of respondents indicate that they are or were shy at some point in their lives. Of these, 40 percent presently see themselves as shy—that is, 4 out of 10 people! Even respondents who don't see themselves as shy report physical symptoms of shyness, such as butterflies in the stomach, in some social situations. However, only 4 percent saw themselves as shy *all* of the time in *all* situations. These findings may be higher than the actual rate of shyness in the general population since the survey has been answered predominantly by young adults—college students—who might be experiencing more social anxiety at that stage in their lives than older people would. Nonetheless, the results indicate that in all groups and cultures sampled, shyness is a significant personal and social reality.

What situations lead people to be shy? Most respondents indicated that interactions with strangers, persons of the opposite sex, or authority figures led to feelings of shyness. Social situations in which the person was the focus of attention (for example, making a speech), was in a large group, or was in a lower status position elicited high responses of shyness.

Why are people shy? Trait theorists suggest shyness is an inherited or acquired predisposition; social learning theorists say that shy people simple did not learn the social skills for effective relating; social psychologists, according to Zimbardo, suggest that shyness starts with a simple label of "shy"—"I am shy because that's what myself and others call me." Unfortunately, there is no simple answer to the question, "Why shy?"

For many people who experience shyness, what can be done to improve their lives? Zimbardo offers several possibilities, based on his experience in developing a shyness clinic at Stanford University.

- First, you have to come to understand yourself better. Exercises such as looking in a mirror and describing yourself, and listing the labels that describe yourself, are useful ways to increase self-understanding.

- Understanding your shyness is essential. Writing a letter on how your shyness developed is one interesting avenue.
- Building your self-esteem can stop you from being your own worst enemy. Zimbardo offers fifteen steps to self-confidence (such as, recognize your strengths and weaknesses and set your goals accordingly) along with several other strategies for increasing a sense of self-worth.
- Developing social skills to initiate interaction and to keep it going. Zimbardo suggests ways for learning and using assertiveness skills and conversational skills in a variety of social situations, as well as some ideas on handling interpersonal conflict.

Many of Zimbardo's suggestions for reducing shyness are more appropriately placed in the fields of counseling and clinical psychology rather than social psychology. They are aimed at individual behavior change, and it must be emphasized that such changes are best accomplished in consultation with a professional helper in a recognized agency such as a university counseling center. At the same time, shyness is a social as well as a personal phenomenon, and social psychologists can appropriately contribute to both its understanding and its alleviation. Many human relations training workshops have as one of their goals helping people find more effective ways of relating to others (see Chapter 7).

Loneliness. In a national survey of Americans, over 25 percent indicated that they had recently felt lonely or remote from others (Bradburn, 1969). Surveys in other Western industrialized countries show similar results. Loneliness, like shyness, appears to be a common experience, and many clinical studies have documented the individual pain and anxiety of loneliness. However, it is only recently that loneliness has become a subject of social scientific inquiry. An important element of this development has been the attempt to articulate a social-psychological theory of loneliness (Peplau & Perlman, 1979; Perlman & Peplau, 1980; Russell, Peplau & Cutroni, 1980). These efforts cover the definition and measurement of loneliness, its manifestations and antecedents, the role of attribution and other social-psychological processes, and ways of coping with loneliness.

Is being alone or socially isolated the same as loneliness? Not necessarily: only if the person desires more social contact will they experience loneliness. Peplau and Perlman (1979) define *loneliness* as a social deficiency that exists to the extent that one's network of relationships is smaller or less satisfying than one desires. Loneliness is therefore a *discrepancy* between achieved and desired levels of social contact. The high school student with only two friends is not lonely unless he or she wants more than two friends.

Loneliness has been linked with many negative manifestations including unhappiness, depression, anxiety, and emptiness. In some cases, loneliness seems to motivate the individual toward increased social contact while in other cases the individual becomes less motivated toward any kind of activity. In either case, the person may become more sensitive to social relationships, constantly assessing their potential for reducing his or her loneliness.

Loneliness appears to be caused by two sets of factors: those that *predispose* individuals to become or stay lonely and those that *precipitate* the onset of loneliness. Any personal characteristics that increase the difficulty of establishing

Loneliness is not the same as being alone or being socially isolated. Rather, loneliness exists when there is a discrepancy between a person's actual and desired levels of social contact. *(Bruce Davidson/Magnum Photos, Inc.)*

or maintaining satisfactory relationships can lead to loneliness. Shyness as defined by Zimbardo (1977) may be a cause of loneliness. Similarly, physical attractiveness and social skills may be associated with loneliness: individuals who are attractive and competent are less likely to be lonely. Precipitating factors affect either the achieved or the desired levels of social contact. The ending of a relationship or changes in status or role, such as a promotion, can immediately reduce the actual level of contact and induce loneliness. Alternately, a person may increase his or her expected or desired level of interaction, and thereby precipitate loneliness. The college student who looks forward to increased socializing following graduation and employment may be sadly disappointed. New social networks may not open up easily and the higher expectations may not be met. The same absolute level of social interaction that was accepted during the years of study may now be inadequate to meet the new desired level and loneliness and dissatisfaction may result.

How can theories of social psychology help us understand loneliness? An extension of attribution theory by Weiner (1974) demonstrates how people give causal explanations for success and failure on two underlying dimensions of *stability over time* and *internal versus external locus of control*. This extends the work of Kelley and others which helps us predict when individuals will make personal versus environmental attributions (see Chapter 2). Loneliness is a failure experience in North American culture. If one attributes loneliness to stable factors, one will likely expect to be lonely in the future and may be less motivated to combat one's loneliness. If one attributes loneliness to stable personal factors such as ability or personality traits, one will likely experience depression and hopelessness. If one attributes loneliness to stable environmental causes such as other people, one may feel hostility and aggression toward others. The causal attributions one makes about loneliness can have important effects on feelings and behavior (Peplau, Russell & Heim, 1979). Peplau and Perlman (1979) also use theories of social comparison and personal control to explain experienced levels of loneliness.

Coping with loneliness involves some of the same mechanisms as overcoming shyness. First, one can increase one's achieved level of social contact by forming new relationships or increasing the quality of existing relationships. Second, one can reduce one's desired level of contact, for example, by engaging in more enjoyable activities that are completed alone. Finally, one can alter one's perception of the importance or magnitude of the discrepancy between desired and achieved levels. It's like saying, "So I don't have a lot of friends—so what?" Losses due to loneliness could be reduced by other means. For example, reduced self-esteem due to loneliness might be bolstered by high achievement in artistic or scholarly pursuits. Peplau and Perlman are hopeful that continuing social-psychological research on loneliness will be translated into practices that prevent and reduce the negative impact of loneliness.

Helplessness. A middle-aged women seeks psychotherapy from a clinical psychologist. She is extremely depressed; she cries a great deal; small chores such as shopping seem very difficult; on bad days she cannot even get out of bed. A few months ago she was active in all aspects of life—socializing, sports, community affairs. Then her husband was promoted to a position that took him away from home more often, and her twin boys went away to college. She now asks whether life is worth living.

Victor is a lively, quick, and outgoing 9-year-old who is a leader among his playmates. However, his grade three teacher finds him slow and a problem in the classroom. When he started school, Victor was eager but had trouble connecting words on paper to speech and therefore found it hard to learn to read. He tried hard but he consistently failed. The more he failed the less he said. Soon he became sullen or aggressive when he encountered anything related to reading. This attitude spread to affect his entire school day. Victor vacillated between being despondent and being a troublemaker.

What do these two examples have in common? According to Martin Seligman (1975), they all involve aspects of *learned helplessness*—a state that results when events are uncontrollable, when the outcome of events is independent of the voluntary responses the person makes. (Voluntary responses are those that the person initiates and that are controlled by reward and punishment, that is, reinforcement.) But when a person can make no voluntary response that controls an outcome, the situation is uncontrollable. In this situation, the person is helpless.

The underlying premise of Seligman's theory is that we learn when outcomes are uncontrollable, and we are then helpless. In such situations, a common response is to become exceedingly passive. Seligman first discovered learned helplessness when studying laboratory learning in dogs who were subjected to uncontrollable shocks. These animals were then placed in a shuttle box—a two-sided chamber in which the dog must jump over a barrier from one side to the other to avoid shock. In this situation, the animal has control. Dogs typically run around until they accidentally jump over the barrier and thus escape the shock. On succeeding trails they become quicker and quicker to escape the shock. However, the dogs that had previously experienced uncontrollable shocks did not learn in the typical fashion. These animals ran around for a moment, but then laid down and whined. On each succeeding trial, these animals became more and more passive and simple endured the shock without trying to escape. The earlier experience in helplessness had sapped their motivation to learn. Experiments with humans produced similar results. Subjects who first experienced an uncontrollable loud noise on a number of trails showed less learning to escape in a subsequent experiment. Seligman concludes that helplessness reduces the motivation to learn; it disrupts the ability to learn through the expectation that one's responses do not affect success or failure; and over the longer term it produces emotional disturbance.

Learned helplessness has been used to explain emotional problems, especially depression such as that experienced by the middle-aged woman described above. The expectation that traumatic outcomes are independent of one's responses initially produces fear about the uncontrollability of the outcome and then produces depression. In the example above, the woman could not control her sons' and husband's absence from home or the outcomes of such absence, and this uncontrollability led to severe depression. Seligman's theory has enjoyed considerable popularity in clinical psychology, and has stimulated much research and some criticism (for example, Costello, 1978: Depue & Monroe, 1978). A recent reformulation uses attribution theory to make more specific predictions about when helplessness leads to depression and when it does not (Abramson, Seligman & Teasdale, 1978).

Seligman speculates on the connection between learned helplessness and the social problem of poverty. Helplessness is not equated with poverty, but a low income does expose the poor person to an independence between effort and outcome. Extreme poverty may produce helplessness through exposure to a vast amount of uncontrollability. Small misfortunes are calamities; social assistance often depends on conditions beyond one's control; and helplessness culminates in a sense of powerlessness, defeatism, and passivity. Only when people believe that their actions can actually lead to changed conditions will effective social action occur to overcome poverty and other social problems.

An Integrated Image of the Human Personality

What can we make of all these ideas about human personality? Are we basically good or evil? Are we motivated by powerful sexual and aggressive urges? Can be actualize our full potential? Are we basically competitive or cooperative? Can we control experiences like shyness and loneliness?

We are complex organisms. Our behavior is caused by a multitude of factors.

Human motivation is complex; the development of personality is complex; and the interaction of the person with the environment is complex. Each theory of personality makes its contribution to our understanding of these complexities. Each has something valuable to say about human personality and social interactions. To develop a sufficiently comprehensive view of human behavior, we must somehow blend these contributions with additional social-psychological theories (see Chapter 2). The resultant eclectic approach may be the best present means to greater understanding. Personality theorist Walter Mischel (1976) expressed the same viewpoint in this way:

> This image is one of the human being as an active, aware problem solver, capable of profiting from an enormous range of experiences and cognitive capacities, possessed of great potential for good or ill, actively constructing his or her psychological world, interpreting and processing information in potentially creative ways, influencing the world but also being influenced by it lawfully—even if the laws are difficult to discover and hard to generalize. It views the person as so complex and multifaceted as to defy easy classifications and comparisons on any single or simple common dimensions, as multiply influenced by a host of determinants, as uniquely organized on the basis of prior experiences and future expectations, and yet as studyable [sic] by the methods of science, and continuously responsive to stimulus conditions in meaningful ways. It is an image that has moved a long way from the instinctual drive-reduction models, the static global traits, and the automatic stimulus-response bonds of earlier times. It is an image that highlights the shortcomings of all simplistic theories that view behavior as the exclusive result of any narrow set of determinants, whether these are habits, traits, drives, constructs, instincts, genes, or reinforcers. And yet it is an image that is sure to shift in still unpredictable directions as our understanding and knowledge increase. (p. 506)

A complex view of personality is essential to a viable applied social psychology. To work with people effectively, whether in the execution and utilization of social research or in the practice of social intervention, we need ways to understand people at the individual level. To create comprehensive theories of social systems, we need valid theories of personality.

INTERACTION PERSPECTIVE: JOINT DETERMINATION OF BEHAVIOR

Failure of the Individual Approach and the Power of the Environment

Many personality theories look for the causes of behavior by analyzing the individual. Trait theories, for example, attempt to classify the basic tendencies of the human personality. In recent years, however, there has been increasing criticism that the study of individual predispositions is not a comprehensive or valid base for the study of personality.

At present, trait analysis neither explains nor predicts people's behavior across different situations. Behavior, often inconsistent from one setting to the next, seems more a result of the characteristics of the specific situation than the characteristics of the person. Evidence reviewed by Mischel (1968)—concerning such traits as aggression, conformity, and dependency (see Box 5.4)—and by

Box 5.4   FOCUS ON RESEARCH
Personality Versus Environment in Generating Consistent Human Behavior

The work of Walter Mischel, a clinical psychologist at Stanford University, has had a profound impact on the field of personality psychology. Mischel has been a central figure in developing the cognitive social learning approach to personality and in questioning the power of individual traits to generate consistency in social behavior.

Mischel has reviewed extensive evidence on the consistency and specificity of behavior across different situations. Intellectual and cognitive variables tend to show greater consistency than personality variables. Intellectual ability and related variables such as achievement strivings show consistent expression through childhood and adolescence. However, if the situation changes markedly, performance can be strongly affected—for example, striving on a mechanical task is not related to striving at athletics. Cognitive variables such as reaction time tend to generalize across situations—the person who is able to judge weight quickly is also able to recognize a figure in record speed.

Personality traits, attitudes, and values do not evidence consistency over different situations. Attitudes toward authority, for example, are assumed to be rooted in one's relationship with his or her parents. However, studies show little relation between attitudes toward father and attitudes toward boss—especially when the attitudes are measured by different methods. Studies on moral behavior, dependency, and aggression have likewise demonstrated inconsistencies in behavior. For example, observations of a number of dependency behaviors among preschool children (such as attention seeking, touching, seeking reassurance) showed almost no relation to each other. When consistency is found, it could be a result of using similar measuring instruments—that is, similar situations—and to the operation of similar response sets (see Chapter 3).

Mischel concludes that behaviors that are often construed as indicators of stable personality traits are actually very specific and dependent upon the environment and the particular measuring instrument. This is not to say that individual differences are unimportant. We can readily observe that different people will behave differently in the same situation. The real question focuses on the true nature and the causes and consequences of these differences for social behavior. The final implication is that the power of the environment has much to say about how and why people behave the way they do.

Source: Mischel, W. *Personality and assessment.* New York: Wiley, 1968.

Endler (1976)—citing studies of honesty, anxiety, and hostility—show only moderate consistency over different situations and tasks.

Testing methods need to be reevaluated. A change in the testing situation may result in a change in performance. There may be deficiencies, including built-in limitations and a lack of objectivity, in the self-respect and observational rating methods that assess personality characteristics (Fiske, 1974). Despite limited measurements or too specific procedures, researchers may be tempted to make a large inductive leap from a few specific test items to a generalized trait that supposedly determines behavior in many situations.

Traits, like attitudes, are only one element of behavior. A number of traits along with other factors may work together to multiply determine behavior. We must also consider "moderator variables" such as age, intelligence, and attitude that help to determine whether or not a given trait is expressed in behavior. We must look at the effect of environmental factors such as social norms and roles. We must understand the dimensions and psychological nature of the situation: How is it perceived by the individual? What meaning does it have? (Endler, 1975).

Our exploration is *not* about the psuedo-issue of how much of behavior is due to the environment and how much is due to personal attributes (Endler, 1973; Mischel, 1976). Rather we are concerned with how individual characteristics and situational factors *interact* to jointly determine behavior.

Argyle and Little (1972) stress the importance of assessing personality to understand and predict social behavior such as leadership, persuasibility, conformity, and so on. But the crucial question is: How do we apply personality traits to social behavior? Argyle and Little see four different approaches, or ways in which social-psychological theories can attribute variability in behavior to persons versus situations. (Figure 5.2 illustrates how the social behavior of assertiveness would be expressed for different persons (P_1, P_2, P_3) across different situations according to the various approaches.) The four different approaches are:

- Type A, the trait approach, sees variability in behavior as due totally to person characteristics. A person high on assertiveness (P_3) expresses the same amount of that behavior across different situations in relation to others (P_1 and P_2).
- Type B, the situational approach, sees the environment determining behavior to the point where there are *no* individual differences. P_1, P_2, and P_3 express the *same* amount of assertiveness in each situation.
- Type C, the dispositional approach, sees personality traits as major determinants of behavior, with the situation having some effect. Assertiveness therefore varies across situations, but P_3, having a stronger disposition, is always more assertive than P_1 and P_2.
- Type D, the interaction approach, gives equal opportunity to the person and the situation to affect behavior. In some cases, the situation will have strong effects (situation 2); in others, person and situation factors will interact to determine the level of assertiveness. P_1 is highly assertive in situation 1 but not in situation 3.

As with Mischel (1968) and Endler (1976), Argyle and Little (1972) review several areas of research, all of which indicate the most support for Type D: the interaction approach.

Important Elements of the Person

We have already looked at such personal elements as achievement motivation, the processes of perception and attribution, the innate instincts of the id, extraversion-introversion, and the concept of the self. An additional frame of reference, organizing important variables at the individual level of analysis, is based on Mischel's (1973, 1976) cognitive social learning approach—an attempt to blend cognitive variables with social learning principles for understanding human behavior. The integration of other concepts into his scheme may help provide new

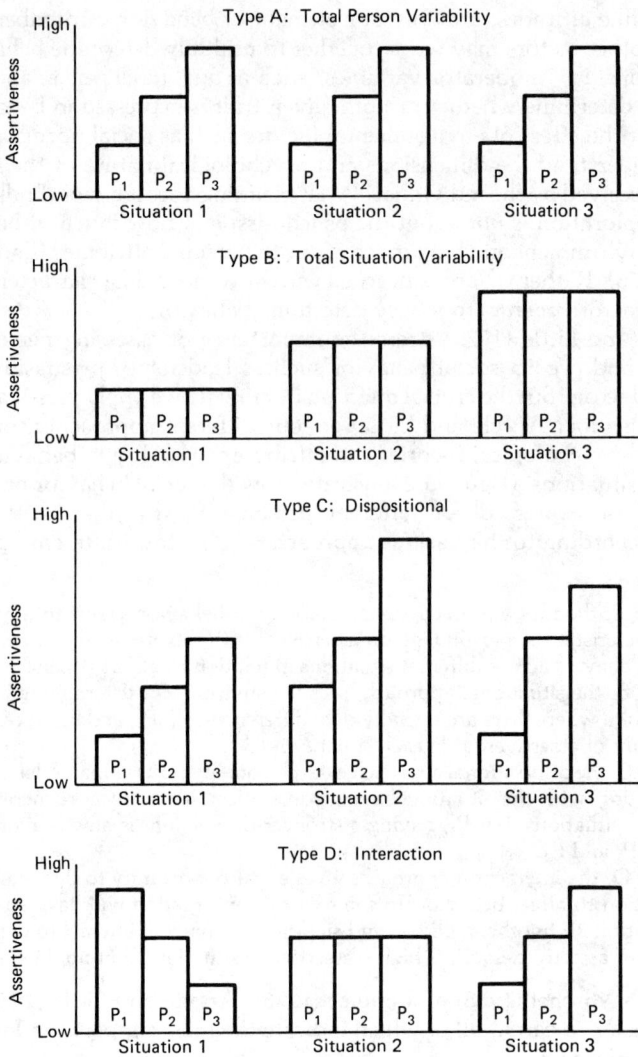

Figure 5.2   Approaches to the Study of Personality.
Source: Argyle & Little (1972).

insights into the way interaction between personal characteristics and the situation determines behavior. Mischel includes the following as important elements of the person:

- *Competencies* are what each of us can do based on what we know. Each person is capable of enacting many behaviors based on his or her knowledge and skills. The chemist, the opera star, the basketball player, all have their unique capacity to construct behaviors appropriate to their role. Competencies are related to our intelligence, maturity, ego development, and social-intellectual achievements and abilities.

- *Encoding strategies and personal constructs* is the system of categories each of us develops, based on our perception, to represent the world around us. What one person perceives as "dangerous" another may see as "thrilling." Related concepts include the selectivity and distortion of perception, the processes of attribution, and our own implicit theory of personality.

- *Expectancies* are our predictions about the consequences and appropriateness of different behaviors in a given situation. Expectancies guide our selection of behavior based on our memory of what reinforcement we have received in the past. On a first date, for example, we tend to behave in ways that will create a good impression—that will lead to a second date as predicted by our past experience. The principles of social learning are thus related to our development of expectancies. Strong expectancies, however, can lead to rigid behavior similar to that generated by psychoanalytic defense mechanisms.

- *Subjective value* is the importance we place on objects, behaviors, and situations that determines how we will behave toward them. Praise from a teacher, for example, may have much value and a strong effect on an ambitious scholar, but may have no value and no effect on a rebellious delinquent. Values and their related preferences and aversions for different stimulus situations bear similarity to the concept of attitude as an evaluative tendency to respond positively or negatively toward social objects. Personal motives are also related to values since different individuals show different preferences for the same outcome or incentive.

- *Self-regulatory systems and plans* are the self-imposed standards and self-produced consequences that affect our behavior even in the absence of external constraints and monitors. We adopt rules and plans that specify appropriate behavior, the levels of performance to be achieved, and the consequences of failure or success. Internal praise, self-instructions, and self-appraisals are all elements of self-regulation that help us choose how to create the most desirable environment for ourselves. The college student, for example, sets high standards for academic achievement and must regulate his or her behavior accordingly—attend classes, study for exams, party only one night a week, and so on. Success—the diploma—leads to self-praise and a positive appraisal of one's abilities and accomplishments. Even though Mischel does not conceptualize the "self" as an entity, these self-regulation processes resemble activities related to the self-concept as defined by other theorists.

Important Dimensions of the Situation

The incredible variety and complexity of human environments—the situations in which people behave—seems to defy conceptualizing and categorizing. And yet there are theorists and researchers who are attempting to do just that. Rudolf Moos (Moos, 1973, 1976; Moos & Insel, 1974), an ecological psychologist, identifies six major methods by which characteristics of human environments can be conceptualized, assessed, and related to ways in which we function within them.

- The characteristics of the inhabitants help define the environment: age, ability level, major activities, socioeconomic background, educational attainment, and so on make important contributions to the overall character of the environment. For example, Astin (1968) proposes that college environments can be assessed on factors such as type and extent of individual behaviors (such as attending classes, watching television) and organizational memberships (such as, fraternities, sororities, athletic teams). The character of the institution determined by the cumulation of these individual characteristics can have considerble impact on the entering student. Yale is not like Auburn, and San Francisco State is not like Northwestern.

- The reinforcement consequences for particular behaviors in a situation tell us much about why people act as they do. In accordance with social learning theory, environments can be analyzed in terms of the functions that behaviors serve in giving reinforcement. "Token economies" are a good illustration of the power of reinforcement in determining social behavior. In juvenile detention centers, for example, residents have been given the opportunity to earn tokens for good behavior such as taking part in craft activities, or doing schoolwork. The tokens— which serve as money—can then be exchanged for more tangible rewards such as candy or a field trip.

- The behavior settings making up the environment consist of the physical components and the usual pattern of behavior appropriate to the situation (Barker, 1968). Put simple, each behavior setting (such as classroom, basketball game, drugstore) elicits particular behaviors from the participants (such as, sitting, yelling, buying) through the operation of social norms.

- The organizational climate as perceived by organizational members is a useful way of describing environments. Moos and his colleagues (Moos, 1974, 1976; Moos & Insel, 1974) have developed a number of Social Climate Scales to study environments. Nine types of environments (such as families, high school classrooms, correctional institutions, hospital progams) are grouped into four major categories which include community settings, educational environments, total institutions and treatment environments. Moos sees three basic dimensions of environments: (1) relationship dimensions including involvement, support, and expressiveness; (2) personal development dimensions such as autonomy, competition, and task orientation; and (3) system maintenance and change dimensions including order and organization, clarity and innovation. These dimensions have effects on individual behavior in the setting, and can therefore help us understand how person X behaves in situation Y.

- The dimensions of organizational structure including size, average salaries, control mechanisms, and so on have been suggested as a means of assessing environments. Structural characteristics are related to individual attitudes and behavior such as morale, satisfaction and turnover (see Chapter 9). The larger the size of an organization, for example, the more difficult it is to have satisfactory communication and coordination among the various parts and members.

- The physical characteristics of the environment such as weather, geography, architecture, design of internal space, lighting, noise level, and so on have long been postulated as important determinants of human behavior. The range of variables included here is immense and no clear typologies have developed for organizing them. Nonetheless, numerous endeavors in environmental psychology show significant linkages between physical characteristics and individual and group behavior (see Chapter 16).

Each of these major approaches involves its own set of "blinders" which lead us to see some characteristics and not others. The integration of the diverse findings which flow from these and other approaches is the greatest challenge facing the developing field of environmental psychology.

Person × Situation Interaction

Neither the trait approach to personality nor an exclusive reliance on the characteristics of the situation will yield valid general laws of human social behavior (Cronbach, 1975). We need to consider both the person and the situation to develop useful concepts and theories.

The limitations of the trait approach have been shown by a lack of consistent behavior across different situations. However, trait theorists are not about to abandon ship to a simplistic approach of "situationism" (Allport, 1966; Bowers, 1973). Allport sees pure behaviorists like Skinner as overemphasizing observable behavior and denying the existence of any internal variables such as traits or motives. The result? An empty organism without *any* aspect of personality—an eventuality that Allport says is absurd.

While reaffirming the trait concept, Allport does concede that different situations elicit different tendencies. While not directly supporting an interaction approach, he does call for theories that more accurately relate the inside of the organism to the outside world. He thus joins a growing movement in personality psychology that is seeking ways of blending the important elements of the person with the significant influences of the environment. This is the challenge for the interaction perspective.

To understand the interaction approach, we must distinguish three different conceptions of interaction (Bavelas, 1978; Buss, 1977).

- *Theoretical interaction* involves combining both person variables and situational variables in the same theory. This will allow us to understand and predict the general behavior of people better. The theories of Lewin, Carson, and Mischel provide examples of theoretical interaction.
- *Reciprocal interaction* involves the mutual influences that people have on each other in the ongoing stream of behavior. We constantly influence other people and situations, and they in turn influence us. Often the strongest determinant of what we do is the preceding behavior of another person. Reciprocal interaction challenges us to study *ongoing systems* of interrelating, not just individuals and not just situations.
- *Statistical interaction* involves testing the combined effect of person and situation variables that have been manipulated in the same study. Typically, subjects are selected who are either high or low on a person variable and these groups are then studied under two different situational conditions. Through statistical analysis, we can determine how much of the variability in the dependent measure is due to the person variable alone and to the situation variable alone. More importantly, we can estimate the effect that the two variables have in combination, that is, in interaction with each other.

    As an example of studying statistical interaction, a researcher interested in advice-seeking behavior might select subjects who scored either high or low on a trait measure of dependency. Then one half of each of these high and low groups would be subjected to a different situation. One half would be asked to seek the advice of a high status person (such as a college dean), while the other half would be requested to seek the advice of a low status person (such as a janitor). By analyzing the degree of advice-seeking behavior in these four different conditions (low dependency–low status, high dependency–high status, low dependency–high status, and high dependency–low status), the strength of the two variables operating together can be compared to the single effect of either. We might find, for example, that dependency or status by themselves had little effect, but that high dependency with high status produced the greatest amount of advice-seeking behavior.

Research designs that allow estimates of statistical interaction are becoming increasingly common in the study of personality. The consistent findings are that interaction effects are stronger than the single effects of either person or situation variables (see Argyle & Little, 1972; Bowers, 1973). Although these studies have been criticized (for example, Golding, 1975), the argument for the power of interaction has been given a strong boost.

The interaction perspective is not without its limitations. Mischel (1973) qualifies the power of the environment by stating there are times when individual differences are highly important. Weak situations in which expectancies are unclear or incentives are inadequate will allow person variables to predominant in determining behavior. Price (1974) points out how important it is for researchers to determine appropriate or inappropriate behavior in a given situation before we draw any conclusions regarding behavioral consistency. What seems inconsistent to us *may be appropriate for the people involved.* Bem and Allen (1974) caution that our usual research designs may not be adequate to document the behavioral consistency that we observe in our everyday experience. They suggest that if we could identify individuals who show consistency versus those who do not, we might accurately predict the behavior of some of the people some of the time based primarily on person variables (see Box 5.5).

Regardless of the above qualifications, it appears that the interaction approach will predominate in the field of personality psychology for the foreseeable future. Theoretical interaction will be favored in conceptualizing human behavior, reciprocal interaction will be studied in increasing detail, and statistical interaction will predominate in research design and analysis. The individual and situational approaches will experience continuing difficulty in having their strongly one-sided arguments accepted. Already, we are witnessing the development of a new field termed *interactional psychology* (Endler, 1976; Endler & Magnusson, 1976; Magnusson & Endler, 1977). Interactional psychology is directed toward the complex interplay of persons and situations in determining behavior and is based on four fundamental propositions:

1. Behavior is a function of a continuous process of multidirectional interaction between the person and the situations, including other persons, that he or she encounters.
2. The person is both an active and intentional agent in the interaction process.
3. With respect to person variables, cognitive factors are the essential determinants of behavior in the interaction process, although emotional factors do have a role.
4. With respect to situation variables, the psychological meaning of situations, as defined by the person, is the important determining factor (Endler, 1976, p. 175).

While the basic features of interactional psychology are appealing, it will be no easy task to build a new approach to the study of personality. However, the

Box 5.5   FOCUS ON RESEARCH
Consistency for Some of the People Some of the Time

Why does personality research not back up our intuitive belief that people behave consistently across different situations? Social psychologists Daryl Bem and Andrea Allen came up with a way to explain this apparent contradiction. They argued, as did Gordon Allport, that persons are unique individuals who are consistent *within themselves.* However, most personality researchers study traits that they believe are *universally applicable to all people,* and they further decide what test items or behaviors should be indicators of a given trait for all people. Now if a particular individual does not define a trait in the same way as the researcher or see the same behaviors as related to it, then he or she should not be expected to show such consistency of behavior. The key is for the research to study only those people who identify themselves as consistent performers on the trait in question.

To test their ideas, Bem and Allen ask college students to assess the variability in their behavior on the traits of friendliness and conscientiousness. Respondents also rated their overall level on the trait and responded to questions about specific situations (for example, "When in a store, how likely are you to strike up a conversation with a sales clerk?") To gain independent measures of friendliness across different situations, ratings by the respondents' parents and a close friend were obtained, and the person's behavior was observed in a group discussion and in an experimental waiting room. Similar measure were obtained for conscientiousness.

Individuals who reported themselves as showing low variability on friendliness indeed showed less variation across the different situations than those who reported less variability for themselves. Furthermore, as a group these low variability individuals exhibited much higher relationships among the various measures of friendliness. For example, for the low variability group, the self-report measure of friendliness correlated $+0.61$ with the observation of friendliness in the waiting room; for the high variability group the correlation was -0.06. Conscientiousness exhibited more complex but similar results.

Bem and Allen thus argue that the best we can do is predict the behavior of some of the people some of the time on the basis of personality traits. Also, we should be able to predict the behavior of some of the people some of the time from situational variables. Thus, personality researchers must attend seriously to situations, but they must also attend seriously to persons as unique individuals.

Source: Bem, D. J. & Allen, A. On predicting some of the people some of the time: The search for cross-situational consistencies in behavior. *Psychological Review,* 1974, *81,* 506–520.

challenge for a new perspective in personality psychology bears some strong similarities to the challenge facing social psychology. We must find ways of getting closer to the specific variables of importance in a detailed and longitudinal manner. We must find ways of respecting the complexity of persons and situations and of collaborating with people in research and practice to approach the complexities of human social behavior. We need the continuing development of a variety of methods for studying and classifying what seem to be the important determinants of behavior. And we need to place our work in a humanistic value context that frees people to contribute more fully to human welfare.

Summary

Beyond our own implicit theories of personality, scientific theories are useful to sensitize us to the wide range of determinants of behavior.

The trait theorists have isolated the fundamental predispositions that are generally expressed in the human personality.

The psychodynamic contributions of Freud and others have drawn attention to the potential importance of unconscious processes. For example, Erikson has described a series of psychosocial stages from birth to death, which emphasize the major social crises that must be satisfactorily resolved for effective personality development and functioning. Adorno provides a classic example of using psychodynamic theory to explain social attitudes.

The self theories of Mead, Rogers, and Maslow give central importance to the self-concept and the process of self-actualization.

The interpersonal theories of Sullivan and Carson shift the level of analysis from the individual to two-person relationships. Sullivan could not conceive of personality independent of the interpersonal situations in which it is expressed. Carson's theory is one of interaction: personal tendencies must be combined with situational demands to adequately conceptualize personality.

Recent studies of shyness, loneliness, and learned helplessness further illuminate how individual characteristics are linked to social behavior. Learned helplessness is a state that results when events are uncontrollable. This typically leads to passivity, reduced motivation and ability to learn, and ultimately to emotional disturbance.

Personality theories in conjunction with social-psychological theories lead to an integrated image of the human personality. People are seen as complex and purposive organisms whose behavior is the result of a multitude of factors.

The individual approach to understanding personality has been severely questioned. Individual characteristics such as traits tend not to result in consistent behavior across situations, due to the effect of environmental factors. The appropriate question is how crucial person variables interact with significant elements of the environment to jointly determine behavior.

Mischel proposes a cognitive social learning approach to delineating the important person variables in the interaction equation. Moos provides a scheme that identifies six major methods of conceptualizing and assessing environments.

Trait theorists have reacted against an extreme "situationism" which almost totally denies individual characteristics. Nonetheless the field of personality psychology appears to be accepting the utility of the person × situation interaction as expressed in theoretical interaction, reciprocal interaction, and statistical interaction.

It is important to realize that consistency in behavior continues to occur for "some of the people some of the time" and that situations that are weak, ambiguous, or trivial will not contribute appreciably to the interaction equation. The study of interaction is expressed in the new field of interactional psychology, which takes account of both persons and situations.

Further Readings

Bavelas, J. B. *Personality: Current theory and research.* Monterey, Calif.: Brooks-Cole, 1978.

Carson, R. C. *Interaction concepts of personality.* Chicago: Aldine, 1969.

Hall, C. S. & Lindzey, G. *Theories of personality* (3rd ed.). New York: Wiley, 1978.

Mischel, W. *Introduction to personality* (2nd ed.). New York: Holt, Rinehart & Winston, 1976.

Moos, R. H. & Insel, P. M. (Eds.). *Issues in social ecology.* Palo Alto, Calif.: National Press Books, 1974.

CHAPTER OUTLINE

BASIC PROCESSES IN INTERPERSONAL RELATIONS
  Social Affiliation and Social Comparison
  Interpersonal Attraction: The Major Determinants
    Newcomb's Classic Study
    Explanations of Attraction
    Extending the Major Determinants
  Self-Disclosure, Social Penetration, and Love
    Love
  Presentation, Ingratiation, and Manipulation
    Ingratiation

INTERPERSONAL COMMUNICATION
  A Model of Interpersonal Communication
  Verbal Skills
  Nonverbal Communication
  Training in Communication Skills

THE HELPING RELATIONSHIP
  Basic Qualities of Helping
  Developmental Model and Core Skills
  Training in Core Interpersonal Skills
  Effectiveness and Applicability of the Helping Relationship

SUMMARY

FURTHER READINGS

SIX

Interpersonal Relations

Every day of our lives we interact with people. We talk, we argue, we plan, we joke, we fight, and we love. Some of these interactions are superficial, some important, some crucial. Our friendships, work partnerships, and intimate relationships affect the degree of satisfaction and happiness we experience. We wonder why we are liked or disliked, how we really get to know other people, and how we can build truly satisfying relationships.

Social psychologists, asking similar questions, have completed many studies of interpersonal relations. They have defined interpersonal attraction, measured it, and sometimes manipulated it to gain insight into its determinants. They have looked at the ways we form relationships and the strategies we use to influence other people, sometimes in hidden and manipulative ways. They have even tried to define and measure that elusive form of attraction we call love.

The applied social psychologist, however, must go beyond simple descriptions of social reality. We want to know how poor relationships can be improved, and how good relationships can be made even more meaningful and satisfying. We are concerned not only with what *is*, but with what *could be*. We are concerned with the skills necessary to enhance interpersonal communication, with the constructive resolution of conflict between people, and with the processes that create mutual trust and openness. We must also ask how the values and skills of effective helping as developed by clinical psychologists can be applied to the everyday interaction of friends, families, and fellow workers.

Interpersonal relations are the first and simplest form of social interaction. They are the *building blocks* for more complex social interactions. The functioning of the small group—a family or a work team, for example—is in part only as good as the one-to-one relationships embedded in it. If, for example, there are a number of hostile, suspicious interpersonal relationships, then the group as a whole will not function effectively. The functioning of highly structured groups—social organizations, corporations, and governments—also depends in part on the effectiveness or deficiencies of interpersonal relations among individuals.

In sum, the importance of interpersonal relations in applied social psychology cannot be overemphasized. This chapter will first provide an overview of the major findings that the descriptive and experimental study of interpersonal relations has produced. Then we will consider interpersonal communication (verbal and nonverbal) and basic communication skills that we can use to increase the accuracy and the openness of communication. Last, we will look at the learnings gleaned from experiences of effective interpersonal helping which can be applied to one-to-one relationships in general. My hope is that you will acquire some additional ideas and ways for understanding and improving how you get along with other people.

BASIC PROCESSES IN INTERPERSONAL RELATIONS

Social Affiliation and Social Comparison

The need to affiliate with other people is a fundamental part of human motivation (McClelland et al., 1953; Murray, 1938). We are social animals. We seek friends to satisfy our physical and social needs. As infants we depend on others for survival. As we mature we may associate the act of human affiliation with the satisfaction of our needs, transforming affiliation into a functionally autonomous driving force behind social behavior. From infancy to adulthood we seek others to help us survive, meet our goals, achieve recognition and power, and to arouse and stimulate us.

We need others to give meaning to our existence. Through affiliation, we learn about ourselves, acquire a sense of who we are, and better understand our social situations. Those around us create a meaningful framework for living. When we move into a new class, a new school, a new job or neighborhood, we use our affiliations with others to better survive the situation: to sense its history or background, learn about its norms, learn the limits of our responsibilities, and to understand what is and is not appropriate behavior in that situation. We do not like the discomfort of uncertainty. We need information, insights, stability, and the tools for evaluating ourselves, those around us, and our environment.

The idea that we approach others to gain self-evaluation is explored in *social comparison theory*. Leon Festinger (1954) assumes that we have a basic need to evaluate ourselves—particularly our abilities, attitudes, and opinions. We look to others for information about where we stand comparatively. We seek the most precise estimate of ourselves by comparing ourselves with others who have similar abilities; it follows that we are attracted to situations involving others like us.

In *The Psychology of Affiliation* (1959), Stanley Schachter extended social comparison theory to the study of emotions, including the effects of fear on affiliation. In one study, fear was induced in subjects through causing them to expect an electrical shock. Following the arousal of fear, the subject was given the choice of waiting either alone or with others for the experiment to begin. When subjects were told to expect only a mildly tingling shock, a third of them chose to wait with their fellow subjects. However, when they were told to expect a painfully intense shock, almost two-thirds chose to wait with others. There was an obviously strong relationship between the degree of fear arousal and affiliation.

Bringing in a new independent variable, that of similarity, Schachter then allowed subjects to wait either with the other subjects (high similarity) or with *non*subjects—students waiting to see a professor (low similarity). When their fear was greatest (waiting for the intense shock), 60 percent of the subjects chose to wait with other subjects, but *no* subjects chose to wait with nonsubjects. (This led Schachter to revise the notion that "misery loves company" to the statement that "misery doesn't love just *any* kind of company, it loves only *miserable* company!") These results supported social comparison theory: People sought human affiliation with similar others as a way to evaluate themselves—in this instance, to compare their own fear to the emotions of those around them.

An interesting side effect of Schachter's work was the finding that subjects who were firstborn children showed the strongest tendency to affiliate with others. This has led to studies of the relationship between birth order and affiliative behavior. It appears that firstborn children are generally more oriented toward and dependent on others. This is likely due to the greater amount of attention and interaction that firstborns experience within the family.

Extending and supporting Schachter's work, Mills and Mintz (1972) found that the emotional uncertainty associated with fear and anxiety increases the desire for affiliation: people do want to compare their emotional state with others in a similar condition. These investigators manipulated the independent variable by giving caffeine to two groups, and by then providing two sets of information. In one group, subjects were told incorrectly that they had been given a painkiller; in the second group, subjects were told correctly that they had received a stimulant. A control group was given a placebo and told it was a painkiller. Subjects who had received caffeine and were given the incorrect (painkiller) information were more likely to affiliate with other subjects than the group who had received correct information or the control group. In other words the subjects who could not explain the arousal effects of caffeine, and thus were in *a condition of uncertainty*, showed a greater need for social comparison.

Similar studies have kept the area of social comparison theory an active one in social psychology. A recent compilation of major developments is provided by Suls and Miller (1977).

Interpersonal Attraction: Major Determinants

The processes of social affiliation and social comparison help us understand in general terms why individuals are attracted to each other. However, we must also ask about attraction between *particular* individuals, and whether or not there are general principles that specify the major determinants of interpersonal attraction.

Newcomb's Classic Study. The major classic contribution to the study of interpersonal attraction has been made by Theodore Newcomb (1956, 1961) in his study of *The Acquaintance Process.* Newcomb reviews and summarizes the major explanations of interpersonal attraction that are most prominent in social-psychological theorizing. These major determinants include:

- *Propinquity* or *proximity.* We are attracted to people with whom we are in close contact. (The "boy or girl next door" may not be more desirable than someone else who lives two miles away—they just happen to be more available to interact with!)
- *Reciprocity.* We like people who like us. (Have you ever tried to like someone who doesn't like you? It's not easy!)
- *Similarity.* We are attracted to people with similar interests, abilities, and attitudes. (Consider most of your friends. My hunch is that you have a lot in common.)
- *Complementarity.* We are attracted to people whose characteristics complement our strengths and weaknesses. (The best examples come from mate relationships where a powerful and dominant partner is complemented by a weak and dependent spouse—each needs the other!)

Newcomb points out the importance of specifying the particular characteristics of these broad hypotheses. He also notes the need to study attraction in a longitudinal, comprehensive manner since these four basic factors may be in a continuous interaction with attraction itself. Unfortunately most studies of interpersonal attraction consist of one-time experiments where the relationship between one factor and attraction is studied in isolation from the effects of other factors. Newcomb, however, took his own advice seriously and arranged to produce his classic study on the longitudinal development of interpersonal attraction. He rented a house at the University of Michigan and made accommodations available to first-year transfer students from other universities. His control for past acquaintanceship was so careful that he selected only one student from even such large cities as New York and Detroit. In return for their accommodations, students were asked to participate in interviews and to complete questionnaires; both involved response measures on attraction, subgroup associations, social and political attitudes, and values.

Newcomb found that most of the results could be interpreted in terms of the major explanations of interpersonal attraction. Concerning proximity, most of the subjects became more attracted to their roommates than to other individuals living in the house. Newcomb interpreted this as an indication that the interpersonal communication brought about by close interaction *led* to the development of perceived similarity of attitudes.

With regard to reciprocity the house developed into a "mutual admiration society": individuals who expressed a liking for particular people were in turn liked more by those people. This reciprocity, noticeable after only four days, held throughout the four months of the study.

Similarity of social attitudes was one of the strongest predictors of attractions. Newcomb used balance theory (see Chapter 2) to explain the impact that similarity had on attraction: if the bonds between two people and their attitudes on the same topics are all positive, then a balanced and comfortable relationship results.

Newcomb's longitudinal explanation of attraction used all major determinants: Proximity increased the frequency of interaction, allowing for the development of reciprocity; this in turn allowed for the exploration of similarity in attitudes.

Newcomb's work helps us see anew that it is often useful to go beyond proximity in our search for personal interaction. If we develop relationships only with those near us, we deprive ourselves of other potential relationships.

Explanations of Attraction. The basic determinants of attraction that Newcomb identified have received considerable attention in social-psychological research, increasing our knowledge of their importance and how they operate. It is now common to explain most aspects of interpersonal attraction in terms of social learning theory, especially the principle of reinforcement. According to Berscheid and Walster (1978): "The general psychological principle which threads through virtually all theories of interpersonal attraction is the principle of reinforcement: we like those who reward us: we dislike those who punish us" (p. 22).

Attraction theorists also use attitude theory and measurement to understand and assess interpersonal attraction (or hostility), defining it, for example, as "an individual's tendency or predisposition to evaluate another person or the symbol of the person in a positive (or negative) way" (Berscheid & Walster, 1978, p. 4).

Furthermore, the major reinforcement models of interpersonal attraction (such as that of Byrne & Clore, 1970) resemble the adjustive function of attitudes proposed by Katz's functional theory of attitudes (see Chapter 2): We come to identify interaction with some people as rewarding. For example, your new roommate Steve supports most of your political opinions on the state of the nation. He also has a car (which you don't) and this allows you to more easily satisfy other important needs. This type of interaction leads to positive feelings, and we develop positive attitudes (we are attracted) to such individuals. Other stimuli (such as criticism) punish us, thus arousing negative feelings (such as frustration) that lead to negative attitudes and interpersonal hostility. For example, your new history professor greets every comment you make in class with sarcasm and disdain—you attempt to avoid her whenever possible. In general, we behave (develop attitudes and interact) in ways that will maximize our rewards and minimize our punishments.

Also our decisions to continue or terminate relationships are in line with theories of *social exchange* (see Chapter 2): When the outcomes of a relationship drop below our comparison level for alternative relationships, we are motivated to leave that relationship (Thibaut & Kelley, 1959). Your roommate Steve is all right, but he can't compete with your new friend Sheila who not only supports your political opinions and has a car but also wants to date you! With these general explanations in mind, let's take a more detailed look at how the major determinants of attraction operate to affect our choices of both friends and enemies.

Extending the Major Determinants. Newcomb saw proximity as more of a factor creating the *potential* for attraction (or rejection) than as a dynamic cause in its own right. Proximity creates the potential for contact, which then leads to attraction through the effect of familiarity and the operation of dissonance reduction: that is, "I'm with this person, therefore I must like him or her." Dislike for the person creates a discrepancy and the uncomfortable cognitive dissonance associated with it.

The relationship between proximity and attraction has been repeatedly demonstrated in a wide variety of field settings and real-life relationships from student friendships to marriage partners, and through experimental studies (for example, Insko & Wilson, 1977). Although Berscheid & Walster (1978) point out the role of proximity in *hostile* interactions—for example, crime statistics indicate that robbery, assault, and murder are more often perpetrated by those close to the victim than by distant strangers—most theorists contend that proximity tends to lead to attraction rather than rejection. Because we are more often rewarded than punished in social interaction, the probability of developing positive attitudes is generally greater (Newcomb, 1956). We must also acknowledge the effect of mere exposure on familiarity. Zajonc (1968) and others have demonstrated that repeated exposure to a stimulus (even meaningless objects such as nonsense syllables) leads to a more favorable attitude toward that stimulus. Thus, we may develop more positive attitudes simply through repeated exposure to a person; thus proximity (frequency of interaction) usually leads to interpersonal liking.

Just as reciprocity is the first law of social behavior in general, so it is with interpersonal attraction: we tend to like those who like us. Common wisdom, as well as popular courses in social effectiveness, tell us to show a positive attitude toward others if we wish to be liked by them. It is rewarding for us in terms of social approval (a powerful reinforcer) to be liked by others. Thus our attitude is positively affected by such rewards and we experience attraction. This does not mean that the reciprocity hypothesis will be confirmed under all conditions, but mainly when group members are free to make choices, including leaving the group (Newcomb, 1979).

Another important qualification of the reciprocity principle is *the degree to which we like ourselves.* According to cognitive consistency theories, if someone likes us but we don't like ourselves, then it follows that we will dislike the other person in order to maintain balance or consonance. For example, an experiment by Deutsch and Solomon (1959) indicated that although people like positive social approval, they also like those who provide accurate criticism rather than false praise. It appears that *both* reinforcement theory and cognitive consistency are useful in explaining reciprocity (Berscheid & Walster, 1978).

Similarity is probably the most closely observed determinant of attraction. Newcomb's interpretation of the power of similarity was that we are most likely to be rewarded by those who have interests, attitudes, and abilities similar to our own. This learning theory explanation has subsequently received support from work in experimental social psychology (for example, Byrne, 1971). It has been consistently demonstrated that subjects show liking toward a hypothetical stranger in direct relation to the proportion of similar attitudes they have in common. In the typical laboratory study, subjects' attitudes on a range of social issues are measured, and at a later session each subject is shown the attitude responses of another subject and asked to rate his or her liking toward that person. Without the subject's knowledge, these attitude scores have been assigned by the experimenter to agree or disagree in varying proportions with the subject's own attitudes. Over a number of subjects, the degree of attitude similarity and the degree of attraction have consistently been found to be positively related (Byrne, 1971).

It is hypothesized that support for our attitudes evokes positive feelings and is thus reinforcing. In addition, we would probably develop the expectation that it would be rewarding to interact with that person. Assuming further similarities become apparent, we would develop greater and greater attraction toward each other. The support for these contentions found in Newcomb's work has been further clarified and extended by a number of interesting field studies (for example, Kandel, 1978). One of the most interesting is a creative simulation by Griffitt and Veitch (1974) of ten days in a fallout shelter (see Box 6.1).

A less obvious aspect of the similarity-attraction relationship is the flip side of the coin: *attraction also leads to perceived similarity.* That is, we tend to overestimate the degree of attitudinal similarity between ourselves and those we like, as well as the amount of difference between ourselves and those we dislike. These attributions that we make about others have been demonstrated in a number of studies including Newcomb's classic work: residents who were immediately attracted to each other *perceived* a greater degree of attitude similarity between themselves than actually existed. As the weeks passed, more realistic attributions of others' attitudes developed (as shown by greater correspondence between perceived attitudes and the other's measured attitudes), and attraction level changed accordingly. Thus, a balanced state was maintained, both in each person's head *and* in the actual interpersonal relationship itself—a duality that has been ignored by most later research that looks only at balance in the perceiver's mind (Newcomb, 1978).

The appealing hypothesis that complementarity of attributes, especially personal needs such as power, leads to attraction has not fared well in actual research. The results of early studies showing limited-need complementarity in married couples (Winch, 1958) have not been reproduced successfully in later studies. Even though we might assume that a dominant person is more compatible with a submissive person, there appears to be more overall support for mate selection on the basis of similarity rather than of complementarity (Berscheid & Walster, 1978).

A number of physical and social characteristics have been investigated as possible determinants of interpersonal attraction. For instance, marriage partners tend to be similar in physical stature, intelligence, educational attainment, and socioeconomic background—probably the result of both proximity and preference. There is also some similarity in physical attractiveness in male-female relationships—possibly through preference, possibly as a consequence of settling for a partner who is no more or no less attractive than oneself (Berscheid & Walster, 1978). It is also not clear to what degree physical beauty is appreciated simply for aesthetic reasons, to what degree we infer additional positive qualities from it, and to what degree we enhance our social standing by associating with attractive individuals. There is some support for all these interpretations (Berscheid & Walster, 1974; Huston & Levinger, 1978). Finally, as you might expect from your own experience with sex-role stereotypes, physical attractiveness is more important to the interpersonal evaluations that males make of females than vice versa.

Box 6.1   FOCUS ON RESEARCH
Similarity and Attraction in a Fallout Shelter

Laboratory studies on interpersonal attraction and attitude similarity have been criticized since they involve brief impressions formed by strangers based on similarity that is arranged and explicitly communicated by the experimenter rather than on actual similarity. To test laboratory results in a more natural setting, social psychologists William Griffith and Russell Veitch of Kansas State University arranged for sixteen male paid volunteers to spend ten days in a simulated fallout shelter.

Following a pretest of attitudes, subjects were confined in a room measuring 12 by 24 feet and furnished with bunk beds, tables, chairs, a television set, and toilet facilities. Subjects were free to interact in any way they desired. On the first, fifth, and ninth days of confinement, each subject completed a sociometric choice instrument that asked him to select three people whom he would most like to have remain (keep) in the shelter (ranked as K1, K2, and K3), and three people he would least like to have remain (reject) (ranked as R1, R2, and R3).

The similarity of attitudes between all the keep and reject choices was then assessed by calculating the proportion of times that each subject and his choices' responses were both positive or both negative to the attitude items. Also, a discrepancy score was calculated by summing the difference in attitude scores between each subject's responses and those of his keep and reject choices. As shown below, the proportion of similar attitudes was generally higher for keep choices than reject choices, while the attitudinal discrepancy score was lower for keep choices than reject choices.

	Sociometric Choice Category					
	Keep			Reject		
Measure	K1	K2	K3	R1	R2	R3
Proportion of:						
Similar Attitudes	0.70	0.68	0.61	0.69	0.61	0.59
	(Mean=0.67)			(Mean=0.63)		
Attitudinal Discrepancy	54.3	56.5	61.7	60.1	64.5	64.5
	(Mean=57.5)			(Mean=63.2)		

Griffith and Veitch also studied the relationship between reciprocity and similarity. Subjects who reciprocated keep choices were found to be more similar in attitudes than those who did not. Also, subjects who reciprocated reject choices were more dissimilar on attitudes.

The results thus indicated that the relationship between attitude similarity and interpersonal attraction held when previously unacquainted subjects were allowed to interact intensively over time and when impressions were based on actual rather than arranged attitudes.

Source: Griffith, W. & Veitch, R. Preacquaintance attitude similarity and attraction revisited: Ten days in a fall-out shelter. *Sociometry*, 1974, *37*(2), 163–173.

Huston & Levinger (1978) also point out the limitations in contemporary research on interpersonal attraction. The predominant use of the laboratory experiment to study attraction has emphasized the first impressions and brief encounters of *strangers* rather than the long-term development of interpersonal relationships in natural settings. Only a few studies have looked at real-life relationships over time, for example, those of dating couples (Peplau, Rubin & Hill, 1977). This brings up issues of relevance, validity, and utility. Also most studies focus on college students in same-sex friendships, on cross-sex romantic relationships, and on marriage relationships. Thus, many other important relationships such as cross-sex friendships, kinships, or homosexual relationships have been studied very little by attraction researchers. There is now an increasing interest in studying long-term affective relationships to help us understand how people develop, maintain, and dissolve the linkages on which a good deal of their happiness depends (see Kelley, 1979; Levinger, 1978; Levinger & Moles, 1979).

Self-Disclosure, Social Penetration, and Love

Allowing others to come to know us is one of the most essential and pervasive processes in forming and sustaining interpersonal relationships. This involves *self-disclosure:* communicating information about oneself to someone else. The term was introduced by Sidney Jourard (1964, 1968, 1971) to focus attention on what he believed to be the most important behavior in developing satisfying interpersonal relationships to foster personal growth: "A truly personal relationship between two people involves disclosure of self, one to the other in full and spontaneous honesty" (1964, p. 28).

Many facets of self-disclosure have been examined since Jourard (Chaikin & Derlega, 1976; Chelune, 1979; Cozby, 1973; Goodstein & Reinecker, 1974). Among these the relationship of self-disclosure to interpersonal attraction raises three questions (Huston & Levinger, 1978). First, does attraction lead to self-disclosure? That is, are you likely to reveal more about yourself to someone to whom you are attracted? Research appears to answer "yes" to this question.

Consider yourself in the following situation. You have been selected (ostensibly at random) to participate in an experiment on interpersonal communication. You arrive at the lab and are instructed that your role in the experiment is to describe yourself to a person of the opposite sex to give him or her "a complete picture of yourself." The other person isn't allowed to ask questions or respond but just to listen to you. You are led to another room where you and the listener are seated at a comfortable distance, and you are told to keep talking for ten minutes until the experimenter returns. The listener responds to your disclosures in a relaxed, interesting manner by smiling, making eye contact, and nodding the head. However, you notice that in terms of physical appearance, the listener is *very unattractive.* What is likely to happen to the intimacy of your self-disclosure? If on the other hand the listener is *very attractive,* what would likely happen?

This experiment, conducted by Pellegrini, Hicks, Meyers-Winter, and Antol (1978), found that intimacy of self-disclosure was significantly greater with an attractive listener than with an unattractive one. It appears that the social attraction value of a good-looking person of the opposite sex elicits a greater openness in the expression of personally intimate information. Furthermore, subjects who were selected from previous observation as unattractive themselves expressed more intimate self-disclosure than did attractive subjects. Is it possible that attractive individuals "let their looks speak for themselves" while less attractive persons rely more on verbal means of generating interpersonal attraction?

The second question is: Does disclosure lead to attraction? This time the answer is not so simple. Whether revealing yourself to others leads them to like you depends on several factors including the timing, the level of intimacy, and the social desirability of the disclosure. If the important characteristics of the disclosure are appropriate to the existing relationship, then the disclosure usually increases attraction (Chaikin & Derlega, 1976).

In a study by Murphy and Strong (1972), interviewers talked with male undergraduates for twenty minutes about the effect of college on their friendships, attitudes, values, and goals. The interviewers made from two to eight self-disclosures; each self-disclosure was similar to the interviewee's preceding statement. Following the interview, subjects completed questionnaires about their perception of the interviewer. Interviewers who gave a higher number of self-disclosures were perceived as warmer and more friendly, indicating that increased self-disclosure led to increased attraction. However, there is an important qualification to these results. Inappropriate disclosure, such as revealing highly intimate information early in a relationship, will likely be harmful to the further development of the relationship. This qualification has some parallel to the typical relationship between social desirablity and mental health, wherein either very low or very high disclosure is usually regarded as indicative of maladjustment (Cozby, 1973; Jourard, 1959).

The third question is whether self-disclosure leads to reciprocity. Do we tend to return the frequency and depth of disclosure that we receive from someone else? The answer is a resounding "yes": we tend to reveal ourselves to those who reveal themselves to us. Social exchange theory (see Chapter 2) explains why this is so: If we are rewarded by receiving a self-disclosure, then we are obligated to exchange another reward for the one received. We reciprocate the frequency and the intimacy of self-disclosure, creating a balanced outcome. Giving a self-disclosure may also be a rewarding and pleasurable process in itself.

An extension of exchange theory, known as *equity theory*, makes this point even clearer (Adams, 1965; Walster, Berscheid & Walster, 1973; Walster, Walster, & Berscheid, 1978). Equity exists in an interpersonal relationship when each person's ratio of rewards to costs is approximately equal. If not, both persons develop a sense of inequity and are motivated to restore equity. Thus a person who has been disclosing less is motivated to reciprocate more disclosures while the higher discloser may work to reduce the frequency of his or her disclosure.

Self-disclosure, reciprocity, and exchange theory underly ideas about how we develop satisfying, long-term interpersonal relationships. Altman and Taylor's (1973) model of *social penetration* sees mutual self-disclosure as the basic process that determines how interpersonal relationships develop and decay over time. As relationships develop, the exchange of both explicit and implicit (or nonverbal) disclosure of thoughts, feelings, and behaviors becomes increasingly broad and intimate.

We can conceive of these stages of relationship development as a series of wedges penetrating the life-space of each individual. If we represent the individual's personality as a series of concentric circles—in the Lewinian tradition—each penetration of the wedge indicates a new level of breadth and intimacy in the relationship. Figure 6.1 represents this penetration process by modifying ideas and diagrams found in Altman and Taylor (1973) and Altman and Haythorn (1965).

The sequential development of the relationship is governed by social exchange. If initial interactions—especially those involving self-disclosure—are rewarding, then the relationship will become more intimate. More important, the reward-to-cost ratio is directly related to the rapidity of the growth of the relationship—that is, the relationship will develop more rapidly if the partners feel they are gaining a large proportion of rewards relative to costs. If costs begin to outweigh rewards, however, there will be a pulling back in the breadth and depth of disclosures. Most of us have had the experience of holding back information from another person in a relationship that is going sour, when only a short time before we would have unhesitatingly revealed that same information. This reversal process tends to be reciprocated to the point where each person is again satisfied with the rewards-to-cost ratio, such as when dating partners move back to being "just good friends."

Incremental exchange theory (Huesmann & Levinger, 1976; Levinger &

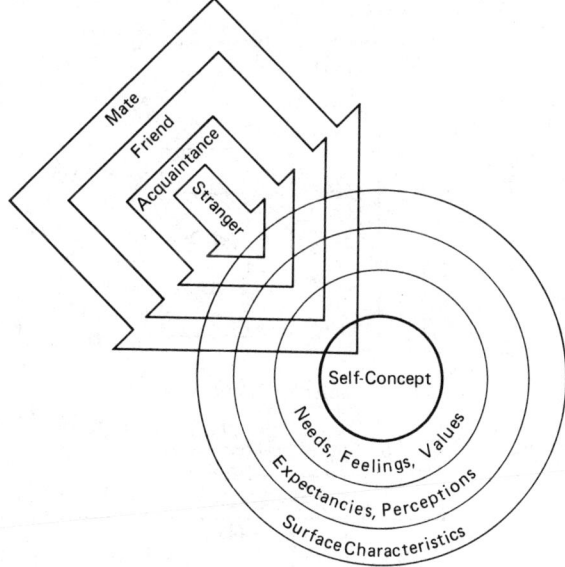

Figure 6.1 Process of Social Penetration.

Snoek, 1972) presents another approach to the step-by-step development of interpersonal relationships through the process of mutual self-disclosure. Relationships advance along the dimension of relatedness moving through the stages of *awareness, surface contact,* and *mutual relationship.* Figure 6.2 places this developmental sequence within the social, cultural, and temporal environment (Huston & Levinger, 1978). This representation sensitizes us to the fact that relationships develop over time and are affected by a variety of environmental factors in addition to the behavior of the two individuals.

In the first stage of awareness, each person sizes up the other in terms of how rewarding interaction might be. If each one forms positive impressions, the individuals move to surface contact.

Surface contact involves superficial, stereotyped interaction in accordance with social norms. But it also generates enough information—in indirect ways such as role behavior—to enable the parties to either terminate the relationship at this point or to move to the next stage. During surface contact the operation and effect of the social stereotypes we accept play an important role. Recent studies (Snyder, Berscheid & Tanke, 1977) indicate that the holder of the stereotype treats the other person in ways that lead the other person to conform to this stereotype—a confirmation of the power of self-fulfilling prophecy. (See Box 6.2.)

If surface contact results in exchanges with favorable outcomes to both partners, the pair moves to the stage of mutual relationship. In this stage social norms are less relevant, and the parties experience honest and spontaneous reciprocal disclosures. An increasingly positive exchange leads to greater affec-

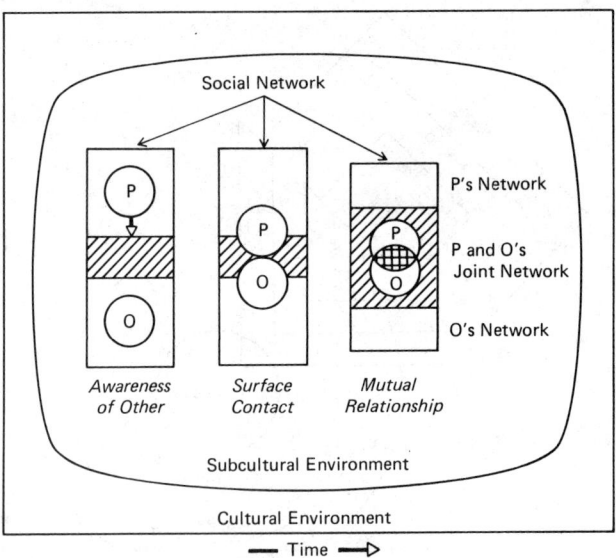

Figure 6.2   Development of a Dyadic Relationship in Its Social Context.
Source: Huston & Levinger (1978).

Box 6.2   FOCUS ON RESEARCH
The Self-Fulfilling Prophecy in Interpersonal Relations

In developing interpersonal relationships do our perceptions of others influence our behavior toward them? More importantly, does our behavior subtly influence the other person's behavior in ways that confirm our initial expectations? Mark Snyder, a social psychologist at the University of Minnesota, and two of his colleagues, Elizabeth Tanke and Ellen Berscheid, designed an intriguing laboratory study to address these questions.

Social stereotypes—simple, overgeneralized and widely accepted beliefs about a group of people—are an ideal testing ground for the effects of perception on interpersonal interaction. Stereotypes may guide how we behave toward another and may thus generate reactions in the other person that confirm our expectations. The investigators chose the stereotype of the physically attractive person—who is typically perceived to be more interesting, kind, poised, sociable, sexually responsive, and so on.

Pairs of previously unacquainted individuals were asked to engage in a getting-acquainted conversation using a telephone device that separately recorded their voices. One member of the pair (a male "perceiver") was given information about the physical attractiveness (a photograph) of the other member (a female "target"). Half the male perceivers received a photograph of an attractive woman while the other half received an "unattractive" photograph. This manipulation was designed to activate the male perceiver's stereotype of physical attractiveness.

Before beginning the ten-minute conversation over the telephone, the male perceiver rated his initial impressions of the target person on numerous dimensions including friendliness, social adaptness, enthusiasm, and so forth. Tape recordings of *only the female target's contributions to the conversation* were then rated on the same dimensions by judges who knew nothing about the experimental hypothesis or manipulation.

The results? First, the typical stereotype was successfully activated. Male perceivers who were expecting to interact with a physically attractive target rated that person as more sociable, poised, humorous, and so on. Second, the women who were designated as attractive (without their awareness) were rated by the judges as *behaving in ways that confirmed the stereotypes on the same dimensions.*

What was mediating this process of behavioral confirmation? Apparently the male perceiver's behavior. Judges' ratings showed that males who believed they were interacting with attractive females were more sociable, interesting, humorous, and so forth. Both they and their targets were rated as showing greater animation, confidence, and enjoyment in the conversation. The males' stereotypes had led to a higher level of sociability, which elicited and nurtured reciprocal behavior by the females. The social stereotype had channeled interpersonal interaction in ways that created its own social reality.

Source: Snyder, M., Tanke, E. & Berscheid, E. Social perception and interpersonal behavior: On the self-fulfilling nature of social stereotypes. *Journal of Personality and Social Psychology*, 1977, 35, 656–666.

tion and intimacy—although highly inappropriate or undesirable disclosure may reverse the reward-to-cost ratio. At the stage of mutual relationship each person's social network shrinks and a joint social network grows up around the partners.

The sophisticated work of Levinger and his colleagues demonstrates the importance of studying relationships over the long-term rather than through one-time questionnaire or laboratory studies. However, much more work needs to be done on the effects of social networks and societal and cultural influences on interpersonal attraction and the development of interpersonal relationships (Huston & Levinger, 1978).

Love. The ultimate development of a cross-sex interpersonal relationship involving intimacy and affection is captured by the term "love." Although we do love individuals other than our mate, most studies have focused on two types of love as expressed in sexually intimate male-female relationships: romantic love and companionate love (Berscheid & Walster, 1978).

Romantic or passionate love involves a state of intense physiological arousal and intense absorption with another person, leading to a sense of complete fulfillment (Walster & Walster, 1978). The intense feelings of attraction in romantic love may be qualitatively different from simple liking and the attraction feelings are often associated with wish-fulfilling fantasies. Berscheid and Walster (1978) use Schacter's two-component theory of emotion to explain the experience of romantic love. That is, we experience emotional arousal and we look for situational cues that will help us identify and understand this arousal. Thus, the ideas that we learn about love from our culture, our family, and our own experience influence how we make sense of and label our emotions in situations of intense physiological arousal. When we experience arousal, including sexual arousal, *and* find situational cues that we associate with being in love, then we attribute our arousal to the loving relationship, and our feelings of passionate love are enhanced.

Social psychologists are giving increased attention to the scientific study of romantic love, partly as a result of Rubin's (1970, 1973) successful attempt to define love as an attitude and to develop a scale for its measurement.

Companionate love is "the affection we feel for those with whom our lives are deeply intertwined" (Berscheid & Walster, 1978, p. 177). This interdependent affectionate state is seen as the final stage of relationship development, like Levinger's stage of mutuality. A truly happy marriage is a good example of this type of relationship—assuming it also involves romantic love. Encompassing continuing high levels of self-disclosure, a great deal of trust and affection, and a stable level of exchange and reciprocity, a relationship involving companionate love is probably the most satisfying that we are able to experience as human beings.

Social psychologists are becoming increasingly interested in understanding the processes of mate selection that will increase the chances of securing satisfying companionate love. In addition, practitioners in a number of disciplines have developed methods such as couples counseling to help partners improve existing relationships so that they may achieve the full joy of companionate love.

A couple with a truly happy marriage are a good example of *companionate love*, which encompasses high levels of self-disclosure, a great deal of trust and affection, and a stable level of exchange and reciprocity. A relationship involving companionate love is probably the most satisfying that human beings can experience. *(Ellen Pines Sheffield/Woodfin Camp & Associates)*

Presentation, Ingratiation, and Manipulation

Almost all of what we've discussed so far presents a very positive view of interpersonal relations. That is, we affiliate with others to increase our mutual goal attainment, we are attracted to some individuals more than others, we disclose ourselves in open and honest ways in the hope that we will develop lasting and satisfying relationships. However, there is also a negative side to human interaction. Often people operate on the basis of hidden and destructive intentions to control other people. The principles of reciprocity and equity are replaced by the goals of maximizing one's own rewards and "to hell with the other guy."

Since much social interaction is a mixture of both constructive and destructive processes, the job of sorting out this complexity is a tough one. What follows will highlight some of the covert and controlling mechanisms studied by social psychologists. We must understand how they work in order to see them in contrast to the open, collaborative approach to interpersonal relations recommended by the humanistic value base of applied social psychology.

Erving Goffman is a sensitive sociological observer who has taken seriously Shakespeare's statement that "all the world's a stage." Working from a strong base of symbolic interactionism, Goffman (1955, 1959, 1967) has developed a drama-turgical analysis of the symbolic rituals that take place in social interaction.

He believes that each of us acts out a "line," expressing our views and evaluations of the situation we are in by presenting and maintaining our "face"— the positive image that we claim for ourselves. When the image we present is internally consistent and compatible with the situation, we are "in face" and we feel confident. If we lack the line that participants in the given situation are expected to take, then we are "out of face." An example is the sports-loving jock in the company of music-loving acquaintances at a symphony concert—and stuck for conversation at intermission.

Being "in the wrong face," that is, having to deal with information that is inconsistent with our line, is even more embarrassing and shame-inducing. How-ever, others will usually come to our rescue and help us to save face because of a mutual commitment we all have to continue social interactions. In this way each of us engages in the art of *impression management*, including our own *"face work"* and the support of other people's *self-presentation*. This allows us to comfortably continue the interaction and benefit from the social rewards that interaction brings.

At times individuals may engage in the aggressive use of face work: they threaten other people's images to "make points" for themselves. This is a risky business because if the other wins, for example, by introducing more inconsistent facts about the aggressor, the loss of face is greater than the potential gains would have been.

Suppose for example that two male college friends are out on a double date and trying to impress their companions by kidding around with each other. One remarks that the other really shouldn't be in college because he once flunked high school algebra. The second retorts that the first guy is the one who has failed three midterms this year. The first has been "put down" and may feel stupid and shameful. Their companions may figure he got what he deserved.

Much of the time, however, people engage in appropriate and cooperative face work that supports self-images and reduces the effects of offending moves. For example, an aggressor who has threatened and offended someone may seek forgiveness by punishing himself or herself through self-abasement or "self-put-downs." In our example, the college guy who came out "one down" may start playing the role of the "fun-loving jerk" to regain acceptance. People will endure both psychological and economic costs to maintain face (for example, Brown, 1970). Unless such threats and put-downs are so offensive that someone withdraws from the interactions, all the parties will support the ongoing face work. In essence, then, most of us enter into a passive agreement to play by the social rules and thereby establish a *ritual order* that presents our most comfortable and appealing image to others and allows others to maintain their face as well.

Goffman's ideas should not be exaggerated to the point of portraying us all as hypocrites and chameleons who engage in any form of impression management. For Goffman and other symbolic interactionists, the ritual order is very real and very important in affecting our behavior. Impression management portrays us partly as we are and partly as we would like others to see us. Without a set of supportive game rules, people would not know what to do! However, the alternative proposed by the humanistic base of applied social psychology is that we should look for ways of being more open and trusting with other people, so that the time and energy taken up by face work can be devoted to establishing more authentic and fulfilling interpersonal relationships.

Ingratiation. Face work is usually mutually supportive and beneficial. But other approaches to self-presentation and social interaction are designed to gain advantages for one person over the other. One such strategy is *ingratiation*—covert behaviors that are designed to illicitly influence another person concerning our personality qualities (Jones, 1964). Although much of our social behavior is designed to create favorable impressions (increase our attractiveness to others), the techniques of ingratiation stretch the limits of acceptable impression management in subtle ways. Ingratiation is designed to gain favorable treatment and protection from others (especially powerful others) and to create a positive image in their eyes.

In terms of exchange theory, the ingratiator (usually a lower-status person) attempts to change the inputs and outcomes of a relationship to achieve more balanced power. Ingratiators attempt to increase the reward value that they have for the other person. This is done through biased self-presentation, conformity to the other's opinions, flattery or enhancing the other's image, and doing favors for others.

In using biased self-presentation, the ingratiator subtly emphasizes his or her positive qualities and plays down the negative ones. This behavior, however, is dependent on other variables, such as the relative status of the participants. For instance, Jones's experiments with United States Naval Academy cadets involved freshmen (low status) and upperclassmen (high status). When they were instructed to create a good impression—that is, told to be as compatible as possible—high-status cadets were openly positive about their important qualities, but modest about unimportant ones. Low-status cadets showed the opposite behavior: they were ingratiatingly modest about important qualities, but played up unimportant ones. Everyone, regardless of status, worked to create the best impression—but they did so in ways that reflected their status and power in the relationship.

Similarly conformity was used differently under different conditions, but given ingratiation instructions, *all* cadets became more conforming to the other person's statements. This strategy reflects the relationship between similarity and attraction: our apparent similarity to someone improves the chances that they will like us.

As for flattery, everyday experience tells us that its judicious use creates favorable impressions. If the compliments seem sincere and spontaneous and relate to an area where the other person wants assurance, the strategy will probably be successful. Blatant flattery, however, will probably be rejected, creating a poor impression. Similarly, favors done for others must appear to be based on real liking and must be appropriately valuable to the relationship; otherwise, this covert strategy will not work.

Why do we go to so much trouble to subtly and covertly influence what people think of us? Ingratiation is one of the few alternatives that low-status, dependent people have to improve their position, protect themselves, and gain some self-recognition. If you have limited investments (power, money, status, physical attractiveness) to put into an exchange, then you must look for ways of *increasing* your contribution so that you will receive adequate rewards from the other person. If your self-presentation leads your boss to like you, or flattery reduces the probability that the school principal wil punish you, or conformity to your supervisor's attitudes leads to acceptance, then you have gained in outcomes in all of these relationships through the use of ingratiation. Is there a simpler, more honest way to relate to other people? Undoubtedly so, but to build open and trusting relationships is neither easy nor without risk, especially from a low-power position. Before we look at how to work toward authentic relationships, let's examine one more deceitful approach to interpersonal relations—that of outright manipulation.

Some of the work of Varela (see Chapter 4) has involved deception and manipulation. His approach of *social technology* uses social-psychological theories (such as cognitive dissonance and reactance) to get people to do what the manipulator "knows is best for them." This disrespect for the individual's right to make a free and fully informed choice is echoed by other manipulative approaches to interpersonal relations. It is especially characteristic of the approach called *Machiavellianism.*

This strategy of control and manipulation for self-gain is named after Niccolo Michiavelli, a sixteenth-century Italian nobleman who wrote *The Prince,* a guidebook to practical politics for aristocratic rulers, which was intended for the Prince of Florence. In this book he contended that people are basically evil and corrupt and should be manipulated for personal and political gain, much like one moves the pieces on a chessboard. Although this sounds callous, we must remember that this attitude was typical and perhaps necessary for survival in the political turmoil of Machiavelli's time.

Social psychologists Richard Christie and Florence Geis (1970), aiming at a description and understanding of Machiavellian behavior, have developed a self-report scale to reliably assess Machiavellian tendencies. High "Mach" scorers tend to agree with statements such as "Anyone who completely trusts anyone else is asking for trouble," and "It is wise to flatter important people." Low "Mach" scorers endorse statements such as "Honesty is the best policy in all cases," and "Most people are basically good and kind."

In con games and bargaining games, high Machs use all available tactics to manipulate and exploit low Machs, so that highs consistently win and lows lose. For example, in a bargaining game that involved splitting ten dollars, high Machs averaged a return of over five dollars, middle Machs about three dollars, and low Machs barely one dollar. Machiavellians are unconcerned about ethics, defending unethical tactics with the viewpoint that "the end justifies the means," and by their own negative view of human nature. When confronted about deceitful behavior—for example, cheating on tests—high Machs were able to maintain eye contact unflinchingly and deny any wrongdoing. In general, high Machs divorce themselves emotionally from other people *and* from themselves—the "cool" syndrome—to avoid manipulation and to insulate themselves from their own uncomfortable emotions.

Unfortunately, Christie and Geis (1970) see an increase in Machiavellian tendencies in recent times in North American society. The Watergate affair in which the nation's highest decision makers engaged in illegal and immoral behavior to reach their goals (all of which was initially denied) serves as a powerful example of Machiavellianism. Also distressing is the possibility that non-Machiavellians tend to shift toward deceitful, manipulative behavior to defend against Machiavellians! They do this even though the effects of manipulation on them are typically anger, mistrust, and more superficial relationships.

On the positive side, social psychologists are continuing to unravel the process of deception as it occurs in interpersonal interaction. For example, Harrison, Hwalek, Raney, and Fritz (1979) had undergraduates assume interviewer and respondent roles in an experimental interview consisting of questions such as "Tell me about one of your activities last weekend" and "If someone were to give you a twenty-dollar bill later today, what would you do with it?" The catch was that half the time the respondent was instructed to answer the question deceptively rather than honestly. Each answer was judged by the interviewer as true or false. Results indicated that deceptive answers were both more hesitant and lengthier than truthful ones. This reduced the believability of the deceptive messages—and helps explain why interviewers were able to discriminate truth from falsehood. It may be that deceiving others is not as easy as high Machs and con artists believe it to be!

Another approach to understanding covert and manipulative interpersonal behavior is the theory of *Transactional Analysis,* developed by Eric Berne (1964). Transactional Analysis has been applied primarily in psychiatry and clinical psychology to help maladjusted individuals discontinue destructive and dissatisfying interpersonal behavior and develop more satisfying and authentic relationships. In general, however, the concepts of this theory help us to understand communication and influence in many interpersonal relationships. While strategies of ingratiation and manipulation are probably closer to our conscious level of understanding, Berne maintains that people are unaware of the "games" they play while interacting with others (see Box 6.3).

INTERPERSONAL COMMUNICATION

Communication is a basic, pervasive process in human interaction. It is a fundamental part of the more complex processes of social interaction—of social influence, cooperation, conflict, and decision making—and of such aspects of interpersonal relations as social affiliation, attraction, and manipulation. It is, in fact, impossible *not* to communicate when we interact with others; even silence is a form of communication. Just as interpersonal relations are the building blocks of higher levels of interaction, interpersonal communication is a basic process in almost all social processes. It therefore makes good sense to look at what interpersonal communication is and how we can increase our sensitivity and our ability to communicate.

Box 6.3 FOCUS ON THEORY
Transactional Analysis and the Games People Play

Eric Berne, a well-known psychiatrist, developed a theory of personality and social interaction out of his experience in psychotherapy. *Structural analysis* refers to the analysis of individual personality while *transactional analysis* refers to the analysis of interaction between individuals.

Structural analysis followed the Freudian approach and divided personality into three different *ego states* or coherent systems of feelings and behaviors:

1. *The child*—the aspect of personality which is spontaneous, fun-loving, and innocent, and which fosters intuition, creativity, and enjoyment.
2. *The parent*—the surviving image of one's own parents which guides and evaluates behavior and provides nurturance and support.
3. *The adult*—the objective, rational aspect of personality which orientates toward reality and helps the person deal effectively with the outside world. The adult also regulates the activities of the parent and child and mediates objectively between them.

The ego states alternate in their control of feelings and behavior, and individuals vary in their readiness to shift from one state to another. Each has its value and contributes to productive living.

Transactional analysis reduces social interaction to four basic categories of transactions:

1. *Procedure*—a series of adult transactions designed to manipulate reality, for example, buying a new coat.
2. *Ritual*—a parental social interaction prescribed by culture, such as exchanging greetings in the morning.
3. *Pastimes*—a simple, semi-ritualistic conversation dealing with a particular topic such as "the kids" or automobiles.
4. *Games*—a series of transactions with ulterior motives, which leads to a predictable outcome with an emotional payoff.

Games are the most interesting and serious form of transactions because they are basically dishonest and have dramatic outcomes. Here is one example, which was actually the first game to be articulated by Berne:

Why Don't You—Yes But. The initiator of this game complains to others about a problem that he or she would like to resolve. However, every suggestion (Why don't you . . .) is met with an objection (Yes, but . . .). The initiator stands off suggestions until the others give up (as signified by crestfallen silence). Why? The game is played not for the ostensible purpose of achieving an adult solution but to reassure and gratify the initiator's child. The others are transformed into wise parents who are then shown to be inadequate much to the delight of the initiator's child.

Berne provides a detailed analysis of transactions between the different ego states at both the social (observable) level and the psychological (ulterior) level. He has articulated many games in a number of different social situations including party games, marital games, and consulting room games. His analysis provides an intriguing and sometimes illuminating way of looking at interpersonal relations.

Source: Berne, E. *Games people play: The psychology of human relationships.* New York: Grove Press, 1964.

A Model of Interpersonal Communication

Although communication may be unintentional, let us first look at it as an intentional or purposive act. In this light *interpersonal communication* refers to the transmission of a message from one person to another with the intention of having an effect. Figure 6.3 simplifies a generalized model of purposive interpersonal communication (Carroll, 1955; McCroskey, Larson & Knapp, 1971). It involves four basic elements of communication: the source of the message or the *sender,* the *message,* the *channel* through which the message is transmitted, and the *receiver* of the message (Berlo, 1960). The model also indicates that the disruptive factor of "noise" may enter the communication process at any point (Shannon & Weaver, 1949).

In this model the sender has an *intention* (the reason for the communication) that is some type of motive—a desire to transmit information, a need to control the other person, or some other reason. The sender activates this intention by *encoding* a message in appropriate terminology and behavior. The sender then *transmits* this message to the other person.

The receiver must first *decode* the message into a meaningful form. At this point *noise* may enter the process. Noise is any element that disrupts the clarity of communication: For example, a frame of reference or language background not shared by both sender and receiver; the sender's prejudices or expectations; disruptive acoustical noise; external distractions; the receiver's attitudes and emotional state; and so on.

Noise, for example, may take the form of a teacher who speaks with a condescending tone, transmitting strong impressions of status and power. Whether this part of the message is intentional or unintentional, it creates difficulties in the communication process, primarily through the resistance of lower-status students. Or the sender may engage in disruptive behavior, such as rapid hand movements, thereby contributing to the total amount of noise in the communication: for example, a frame of reference or language background not shared by both sender and receiver; the sender's prejudices or expectations;

In any case the interpretation that the receiver puts on the message will have its *effect.* The effect may be simply cognitive (you now know something you didn't know before), or it may be emotional (you are now angry; before you were not). The effect in turn leads to a response or feedback (McCroskey, 1968),

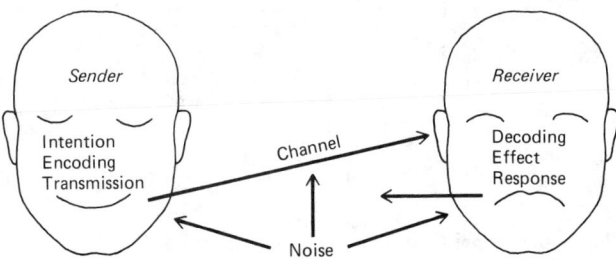

Figure 6.3   A Model of Interpersonal Communication.

beginning the reciprocal-exchange process of interpersonal communication (the above diagram repeated in the opposite direction).

The model is thus a *dynamic* interaction model (Osgood, 1954): The effect on the receiver triggers an intention to communicate, an encoding process takes place, and a message is transmitted back to the sender—with or without noise.

The goal in interpersonal communication is to reduce the amount of noise in all parts of the system—the elements that distort and disrupt the transmission and reception of messages. Effective communication can only occur when the receiver decodes, interprets, and is affected by the message *in the manner intended by the sender.* But why is effective interpersonal communication so difficult to achieve? And what are the skills that we might use to work toward it?

Verbal Skills

John Wallen (1973) is one of a number of social psychologists concerned with finding ways of improving both the accuracy and the openness of interpersonal communication. He notes that while our best intentions sometimes end in disaster, on other occasions we are credited for desirable effects that we did not intend. In other words our intentions are not *always* transformed into actions that produce a hoped-for effect. Wallen uses the term *interpersonal gap* to describe the degree of congruence between intention and effect.

From time to time we all experience this interpersonal gap, thinking things such as "That isn't what I meant!" or "Now why did she do that?" These thoughts indicate that somewhere along the line something has gone wrong in interpersonal communication. The points at which misunderstandings may occur in interpersonal communication are shown in Figure 6.4.

Intentions are private and known only to the sender. (Although the term intention does not refer here to *unconscious* motives, such motives can clearly affect the communication process.) Intentions cover a wide range of hopes, desires, fears, and so on, from very simple intentions ("I don't want to talk with him") to mixed or more complex intentions ("I don't want to talk with him, but I don't want him to feel rejected and resent me").

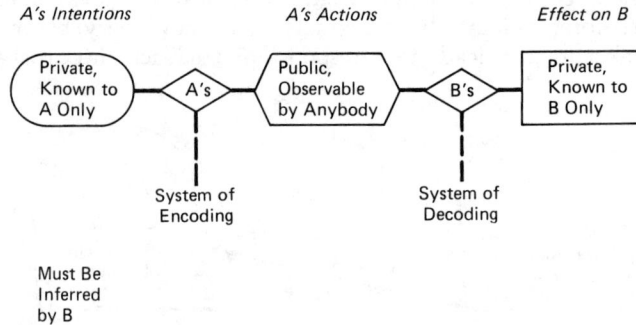

Figure 6.4   The Interpersonal Gap.
Source: Wallen (1973).

The sender then translates intentions into the *actions* that comprise the message. In contrast to private intentions, actions are public and observable. They may consist of spoken words, or such nonverbal behavior as facial expression or body posture. Actions include attempts by the sender to transmit a message that may or may not be received, as well as actions that are interpreted in ways unintended by the sender. For example, you happen to meet an old friend while shopping. You want to talk for a few minutes, but you also have a bus to catch to get to a job interview. You fidget a bit due to your anxiety, and your friend interprets this as not wanting to be with her, though that is not your intention.

All actions are part of the message and result in an *effect* in the receiver. The effect, like intentions, is private and known only to the receiver. Thus the interpersonal gap or degree of congruence is affected both by the encoding of intentions into actions and by the decoding of actions into effects.

The communication process may be complicated by other possibilities:

- The same intention may be expressed by different actions.
- Different intentions may be expressed by the same actions.
- The same action may lead to different effects.
- Different actions may lead to the same effect.

It is not surprising that communication breakdown can occur even in what seems to be a very simple situation of information exchange.

A broader approach to the breakdown of communication focuses on such barriers as distrust, suspicion, and alienation (Giffin & Patton, 1976). Distrust and suspicion are heightened by a number of factors that result in an atmosphere of defensive communication rather than openness and trust (Gibb, 1961). Defensive behavior of attack, avoidance, or self-enhancement occurs when an individual perceives or anticipates a threat in any of the following areas:

- If the receiver perceives that the sender is expressing an evaluation or judgments of the receiver's behavior, rather than providing a straightforward description, the receiver will tend to react defensively.
- When communication is used to control and manipulate rather than to define and solve a problem, the receiver hears the hidden message that he or she is inadequate and needs to change in some manner.
- When the sender is perceived as engaging in hidden strategies to influence the receiver, rather than behaving in an open and spontaneous manner, the receiver will tend to react negatively to these deceptions.
- If the sender appears to be so neutral that he or she has a clear lack of concern for the receiver's welfare, rather than an emphathic understanding of the receiver's situation and feelings, the receiver will sense a lack of acceptance.
- When the sender implicitly or explicitly communicates that he or she feels superior to the receiver, this lack of equality in the relationship will reduce the receiver's motivation to enter into shared problem solving.
- If the sender appears to be so certain in his or her opinions to the point of being perceived as rigid and dogmatic, then the receiver will tend to stop listening. However the receiver's defensiveness can be reduced if the sender communicates a willingness to experiment with his or her behavior and attitudes; this contributes to the provisional nature of the communication and to the development of a supportive climate.

Since all these barriers to communication are noise in the system, they must be understood and reduced if interpersonal communication is to be effective.

The rationale for the use of communications skills is clear: Berlo (1960) includes the communication skills of the sender and the receiver as important variables that affect the accuracy of communication; Wallen (1973) suggests that the interpersonal gap can be bridged through the use of basic communication skills. Such skills increase shared understanding so that each person has accurate information about the other person's ideas, feelings, intentions, and the effects of the communication.

Wallen proposes four basic communication skills that encourage a spirit of joint inquiry rather than of competition or blaming, that increase the amount of information held in common, that reduce the amount of depreciation and hostility that is transmitted, and that lessen the possibility of hurtful feelings and damage to the interpersonal relationship.

These four skills, which were defined in Chapter 4, fall into two categories of *reception skills* (important in the behavior of the receiver) and *transmission skills* (important in the behavior of the sender). Reception skills include *paraphrasing*, which is especially useful in checking out the intended meaning of a communication before you respond, and *perception checking of feelings*, which helps you find out the other person's private intentions and assumptions about your relationship. Transmission skills include *behavior description*, which describes the specific observable actions of the other person, and *description of feelings*, which is especially useful for describing intentions.

It is also useful to combine skills. Thomas Gordon's (1970) model of *Parent Effectiveness Training* incorporates *active listening*—a combination of paraphrasing and perception checking. This skill helps parents understand their children's mental and emotional state *before* the parents start communicating their ideas and feelings. *Feedback*, a complex skill used in human relations training, combines behavior description and description of feelings (Mill, 1976). Feedback tells the other person how you perceive his or her behavior and how it affects you. Self-disclosure, another complex communication skill, combines description of feelings with descriptions of other information that the sender wishes to communicate.

The importance of self-disclosure and feedback in building interpersonal relationships is illustrated in Figure 6.5: the Johari Window, named after developers Joseph Luft and Harry Ingram and used to represent the degree of self-awareness and awareness that others have of you in interpersonal relationships (Luft, 1970).

The window consists of four panes that vary in how much information is available to you and others. The upper-left pane is free information known to you and to others. The upper-right pane is information that you are blind to, but that is available to others. The lower-left pane is information that is known to you but that you hide from others. The lower-right pane is information that is unknown to you and to others.

Self-disclosure increases the amount of information that is known to other people and thus moves the horizontal slat of the window downward as a relationship grows in intimacy. At the same time, the use of feedback from other people

Areas of the Self at the Beginning of a Relationship

	Known to Self	Unknown to Self
Known to Others	Free to Self and Others	Blind to Self, Seen by Others
Unknown to Others	Hidden Area: Self Hidden from Others	Unknown Self

Areas of the Self after the Development of a Close Relationship

	Known to Self	Unknown to Self
Known to Others	Free to Self and Others	Blind to Self, Seen by Others
Unknown to Others	Hidden Area: Self Hidden from Others	Unknown Self

Figure 6.5 The Johari Window.
Source: Luft (1970).

can help you to reduce the blind and the unknown areas. At the beginning of a relationship the free area is small in comparison to the other panes of the window (top of Figure 6.5), whereas in an intimate and trusting relationship the free area has expanded and the hidden, blind and unknown are reduced in size (bottom of Figure 6.5). The Johari Window thus represents the degree of awareness in different interpersonal relationships.

Nonverbal Communication

We do not communicate with words alone. We use a variety of other behaviors to get the full meaning of our message across to other people. These behaviors include such elements as tone of voice, body posture, and facial expression. Sometimes there are parts of the full meaning that we do not intend or do not wish to communicate, but nonetheless our nonverbal behavior may make these elements of the message apparent to other people. Our concern must then be with the *total* communication process, both verbal and nonverbal, and its impact in determining the effect on the other person. Social psychologists have identified several important elements of nonverbal communication (Danziger, 1976; Harper, Weins & Matarazzo, 1978; Mehrebian, 1972).

One aspect of nonverbal communication is *proxemics*—that is, our physical distance from and relative position to the person receiving our message. In addition to cultural and subcultural differences in physical distance during communication, distance relates strongly to the variables of intimacy and status. We tend to come closer to friends and acquaintances, and stay farther away from those we regard as different in status or power. (I find it interesting that students will usually stand closer to me in discussion after class at the end of the term than

In nonverbal communication, individuals tend to come closer to friends and acquaintances and to stay farther away from those they regard as different in status or power. *(Richard Kalvar/Magnum Photos, Inc.)*

at the beginning. As they come to see me as a person, and not simply in the role of professor, they apparently feel more equality and closeness in our interpersonal relationship.)

Equally important is the element of *body posture* as well as the relationship between posture and interpersonal attraction. Usually a communicator who leans toward the receiver and takes a direct orientation is perceived as having a more positive attitude toward the receiver. For example, Mehrebian (1968) had subjects view pictures of a seated communicator, and then rate how much they thought the communicator liked them (the subjects). The pictures varied in their degree of leaning (forward or backward), the openness of the posture, and the amount of relaxation. The subjects perceived greater liking when the communicator leaned slightly forward, adopted an open posture, and appeared to be relaxed. Similar experiments have shown the importance of a direct versus side orientation, and close versus distant position between sender and receiver.

The amount of *body movement*—expressed by such behaviors as hand gestures, head nods, eye contact, and facial expressions—contributes to the total flow of communication. We often use such behaviors to underline our verbal expressions and to help regulate interaction. For example in everyday conversation we often gesture with our hands to show our desire to speak next. Our facial expressions usually indicate the degree of affiliation and warmth in the relationship. Eye movement and eye contact may reflect the closeness of the relationships (positive eye contact expresses attraction and respect). Eye contact and head nods are powerful social reinforcers. If you want to keep someone talking, maintain eye contact, nod your head a lot, maintain a pleasant expression and say "uh-huh" at regular intervals. All these "encouragers" will reinforce the talking behavior of the other person. Eye contact and hand gestures may also be used to regulate the interaction. (We tend to look at another person when we begin a long statement, then tend to look away until the end of the statement. The implicit message of looking back says "Now it's your turn" and expresses interest in the reaction of the other person.) In these subtle ways nonverbal elements of communication complement and guide the interaction.

Eye contact may interact with other elements of nonverbal communication as suggested by Argyle and Dean's (1965) *affiliative conflict theory.* This theory stipulates that eye contact is related to our need to affiliate with others, and that approach and avoidance forces produce an equilibrium between proximity, eye contact, and other elements of intimacy. We maintain a level of eye contact with others that in conjunction with our interpersonal distance produces the degree of intimacy we desire. If our distance becomes closer, we tend to reduce the frequency and duration of eye contact to maintain that same degree of intimacy. If we are further away, we increase eye contact. Experiments by Argyle and others have found both support and disconfirmation of various aspects of this equilibrium theory (Harper et al., 1978).

Paralanguage refers to the process of verbal communication in terms of *how* something is said rather than *what* is said. This includes voice qualities of loudness, pitch, and stress, and usually expresses the emotional side of communication. Our perception of these elements is important in understanding the feelings and intentions of the speaker. Discrepancies between *what* is said and *how* it is said can create an interpersonal gap. If, for example, you react to someone's statement with the comment "That certainly is interesting," but say it with a bored tone of voice, you can be sure that the other person will question the sincerity of your message.

What is the significance of the nonverbal channels of communication for interpersonal relations? Nonverbal aspects of communication tend to indicate the *basic qualities* of the relationship—closeness, trust, power, attraction, and status. Verbal communication often will not focus directly on these critical dimensions. We need merely look to the nonverbal behaviors to see where the relationship stands on these qualities. Watch a typical student talk to a typical professor after class. They both will likely behave differently than when they are interacting with their own peer groups. The student may stand a little farther away, have a vocal tone of deference or respect, and may gesture less. The professor may have a vocal tone of certainty or even condescension and may gesture dramatically. Furthermore, nonverbal elements do a better job of expressing the internal states of sender and receiver. They provide feedback on people's emotional reactions to the ongoing interaction, and they help sensitize us to inconsistencies in the total communication package. For example, a woman who looks and sounds angry, but is saying she is not, is deceiving herself, or others, or both.

Nonverbal behavior may also be useful in detecting deception on the part of the sender. Although various studies have yielded inconsistent results on how well observers can detect deception, Zuckerman, DeFrank, Hall, Laurence, and Rosenthal (1979) found generally better-than-chance detection based on both facial and vocal cues. Subjects responded to four questions on controversial issues (such

A student and teacher talking together are likely to behave differently with each other than when interacting with their own peer groups. The student may stand back, speak in a tone of deference or respect, and gesture less. The teacher may speak in a tone of certainty or condescension and may gesture dramatically. *(Richard Wood/The Picture Cube)*

as, should abortion continue to be legal?), and were asked to answer two questions honestly and two deceptively. They were then asked to role play or pose honest and deceptive answers to all four questions. Videotape segments were categorized by subjects serving as judges as either deceptive or honest and various ratings were completed. Facial expressions associated with honesty were rated as more pleasant and vocal expression was rated as more assertive and dominant. It thus appears that observers are able to distinguish deception from honesty and that this distinction is related to attributes of nonverbal communication. However, much more research is required in this complex area before conclusions can be drawn.

Mehrebian (1972) completed numerous studies looking at the relative contributions that verbal, vocal, and facial channels make to the overall impression of attitude formed by the receiver. The effect of the communication on the sender was assessed by a 6-point scale of liking varying from +3 to −3. The variable of verbal content was operationalized by having three different categories of words: positive (thanks, dear), negative (terrible, don't), and neutral (maybe, oh). Vocal expression was varied by training speakers to say all types of words with a voice quality of liking, neutrality, or disliking. Facial expression was operationalized by using photographs of models expressing liking, neutrality, or dislike. These three independent variables (verbal content, vocal expression, facial expression) were then combined in all possible ways and subjects were asked to judge the overall degree of liking conveyed by each message. For example, some messages involved negative verbal content expressed with a neutral voice quality and a positive facial expression whereas other messages involved negative words expressed with a voice quality of disliking and a facial expression of disliking.

Mehrebian's analysis indicated the relative contributions that each of the three variables made to the overall assessment of liking and has commonly been expressed in the following formula:

$$\text{Total liking} = 55\% \text{ facial} + 38\% \text{ vocal} + 7\% \text{ verbal}$$

This formula is often cited as indicating that nonverbal components (facial and vocal elements) carry much more weight in communication than the verbal content and this may be true. However, we must not *overgeneralize* from these results. We must realize that the particular contributions obtained are limited to the particular operationalizations of the variables used in Mehrebian's experiment. For example, the use of single words by themselves without any connected conceptual meaning in the verbal message would clearly reduce the contribution that verbal content could make to the total effect. Nonetheless, nonverbal aspects of communication are definitely important, and when there are inconsistencies between nonverbal and verbal elements, the nonverbal may be given more weight. What is required is more integrated study of how verbal and nonverbal elements combine to determine the overall effect of communication (Firestone, 1977).

Training in Communication Skills

After reading about basic communication skills, you might wonder why social psychologists spend time to define such simple and straightforward behaviors. You might assume that simple skills such as paraphrasing or perception checking are used by people most of the time to understand others. Unfortunately this assumption does not mirror what *really* goes on around us. People simply do not use these basic skills in everyday interaction. In North American society at least, children are not trained in the socialization process to describe their feelings clearly and to understand actively what other people are saying and feeling.

In his work on Parent Effectiveness Training, Gordon (1970) describes twelve ways (known as "the typical twelve") in which parents usually respond to children. Instead of clearly describing their own feelings and using active listening skills to understand the child, parents engage in behavior such as criticizing, commanding, name-calling, interpreting, and moralizing. As we well know, these behaviors do not result in increased accuracy or openness of communication.

In a similar vein, Carl Rogers, the humanistic clinical psychologist, kept a record of the types of communicative messages overheard in different social situations. The most common message that people used offered evaluations rather than direct expressions of feelings or active listening to understand other people.

D'Augelli, Danish, and Brock (1976) also support the notion that we tend not to listen well to other people even in situations where that is the clear expectation. In this study, college students enrolled in a course in helping skills were asked to take part in a brief two-person interaction at the beginning of the course. One student, designated as the helpee, was to talk about a matter of personal concern; the second student, the receiver, was asked to "be as effective and helpful as you know how." The interactions were taped, and the responses of the helpers were coded.

The most common type of response (almost 60 percent) consisted of *leading responses*—that is, behavior *not* in response to what the sender said but rather in the form of injected questions or advice. Only one-third of the receivers' responses were coded as *continuing responses*—that is, responses that followed the direction set by the sender, using paraphrasing or perception checking of feelings. The obvious conclusions was that untrained receivers of communication tend to ignore or not perceive feelings (of the continuing responses only 6 percent were perception checking of feelings), and tend to be directive rather than truly responsive.

Our own experience confirms these observations. People usually do not listen well to others; they either *assume* that they understand the intended meaning or simply ignore it altogether. On the sending side, people often describe their own feelings in disguised ways so that the message is sometimes confusing, sometimes contradictory. For these reasons, the systematic training of basic communication skills makes a lot of sense.

There are various models and approaches for training communication skills; however, most involve basic skills such as paraphrasing or description of feelings. A brief introduction to this area was given in Chapter 4.

Written exercises are one approach for increasing awareness of behavior in the communication process and for practicing new skills. Wallen (1973) provides a series of written questions for the description of feeling. In one type of question, the respondent is presented with different statements and asked to choose the one that actually describes the speaker's emotional state. For example:

1. Can't you see I'm busy? (This is a question.)
2. I'm beginning to resent your interruptions. (This describes a feeling: resentment.)
3. You have no consideration for anyone else's feelings. (This is an accusation.)

Other questions ask the respondents to describe how they would express their feelings in various situations such as being bored in a group or annoyed with another person.

Johnson (1972) provides self-report questionnaires that increase awareness of typical behavior. The *Friendship Relations Survey* presents a number of communication situations and respondents are asked to choose the alternative that they would most likely respond with. For example, in one situation, a friend begins to avoid you—the alternate responses are to tell the friend about her behavior or to reciprocate her aloofness. Each item in the survey can then be scored on receptivity to feedback and willingness to self-disclose. If you choose to tell your friend about her aloofness, you would score higher on self-disclosure. The scores are used to construct a Johari Window indicating your general approach to others in terms of self-disclosure and feedback.

The *Questionnaire on Listening and Response Styles* (Johnson, 1972; Porter, 1950) presents a statement of a personal problem by another person and the respondent is asked to choose one of five responses. Responses are scored in terms of five underlying intentions: evaluative, interpretive, supportive, probing, and understanding. Here's a sample question and the five possible responses with the underlying intentions in brackets (Johnson, 1972):

> *Statement:* "I'm determined to get good grades. I am not afraid of hard work. I am not afraid to take a few hard knocks, if I can see my goal out there in front. And I'm not averse to climbing over a few people who get in my way because this means a lot to me. I can't be satisfied with just mediocre grades. No, I want to *be* somebody."

> *Responses:*
> 1. You see yourself as a really ambitious person, is that it? (understanding)
> 2. You just have to be out on top, no matter what you may do to others. (interpretive)
> 3. Why do you feel that it's so important to get good grades? (probing)
> 4. Why don't you take some tests to determine what courses you'd do best in? It might be a big help to you, although I bet that with your drive you could do well in most fields. (supportive)
> 5. Determination can be a real asset to anyone. Are you really sure, though, that you mean it when you say you're not against climbing over those who get in your way? Couldn't that be a problem? (evaluative)

Thus, you can gain awareness in a relatively nonthreatening manner about your typical ways of responding to others. These written exercises can be very useful; however, they do not allow for the individual to receive feedback on actual behavior or to practice new ways of communicating.

Behavioral exercises in an experienced-based learning format (see Chapter 4) do provide the opportunity for practice and feedback. Applied social psychologists have developed a wide variety of exercises for the practice of communications skills (see Johnson, 1972; Pfeiffer & Jones, 1979). One typical exercise which I use in training communications skills involves the following activities. First, there is a description of a simple model of interpersonal communication, the interpersonal gap, and the basic communications skills. Next, the group is divided into small groups of three, each of whom will take one turn in each of three roles:

- The *sender* practices the skill of description of feelings by describing some relevant experience. For example, the sender might talk about how he or she is reacting to the training workshop or how he or she feels about communication barriers in his or her work situation.
- The *receiver* actively responds to the sender using the skills of paraphrasing and perception checking.
- The *observer* provides feedback, in the form of behavior description, to both the sender and the receiver with regard to how they used the skills.

Following three interactions in which each person has a chance to enact each role, there is general discussion of the difficulties encountered and the utility of the basic communications skills in everyday situations.

This exercise may seem straightforward, but I am consistently amazed at how difficult it is for many people to break out of old communication patterns and implement new skills. For example, how often in a discussion (let alone an argument) do you see one person actively listening to another before responding? Usually we press on with our points and misunderstanding abounds. Evaluations of the effectiveness of communication-skills training therefore show mixed results in terms of both skill acquisition and personal change (Altmann & Black, 1978; Genthner & Falkenberg, 1977; Pyke & Neely, 1975). (See Box 6.4.)

THE HELPING RELATIONSHIPS

Although the topic of helping is in the domain of clinical psychology, social work, and similar professions, the theory, research, and practice that has developed within the field of human service has clear implications of interpersonal relationships in general. In other words the basic qualities of effective helping relationships, and the skills required to develop such relationships, aim to both improve the accuracy and openness of interpersonal communication and to develop productive and satisfying interpersonal relationships.

In this section, therefore, we turn to clinical and consulting psychologists who have helped dissatisfied persons and organizations search for more effective ways of functioning. In doing so, we are asking: What are the important implications of this work for social interaction in all manner of settings?

Basic Qualities of Helping

Carl Rogers, one of the greatest contributors to the practice of interpersonal helping, began his professional career as a clinical psychologist working with children. Even at that time he sensed that many of the directive, controlling ways thought to be effective in working with children contrasted strongly with his inner sense of what was useful and acceptable. Later, during the development of his practice approach of client-centered therapy, Rogers (1951) not only prescribed a more respectful and humanistic orientation to clients in counseling, but pioneered the development of scientific research on psychotherapy itself (Rogers & Dymond, 1954). Social psychologists have recently shown an increased interest in interpersonal helping, primarily between strangers in emergency situations (see Chapter 14).

From his experience in helping troubled individuals, Rogers developed his own theory of personality (see Chapter 5), and became a proponent of experiental groups for fostering personal growth (see Chapter 7). In addition to producing important works on such diverse areas as teaching and learning (Rogers, 1969) and marriage (1972), Rogers has recently integrated much of his thinking into a treatment of the importance of personal power and inner strength (Rogers, 1977).

Rogers (1961) saw himself as moving from asking the directive question of "How can I treat or cure this person?" to the more general humanistic question of *"How can I provide a relationship that this person can use for personal growth?"* Based on his clinical experience, Rogers illuminated the *basic qualities* of an effective helping relationship.

First, the helper must develop an *empathic understanding* of the other person's feelings. This demonstrates acceptance of the person and induces a sense of *freedom* within the relationship. In this way the other person may come to better understand himself or herself and experience personal growth.

Box 6.4   FOCUS ON RESEARCH
Improving Self-Concept Through Communication Skill Training: Wishful Thinking or Reality?

Interpersonal communication plays a key role in the development of our self-concept—that central perception that guides and organizes much of our experience. It could thus be expected that training in communication skills might have beneficial effects on self-concept. Hal Altmann and Donald Black, two educational psychologists at the University of Calgary, designed a field study to address this possibility.

University students taking a one-semester course in communications were randomly assigned to six different sections, taught with varying degrees of structure. For example, one section used a group discussion approach with low structure, while two others used a systematic and structured approach to communication skill training. The two classes with systematic skill training were specifically designed to enhance students' self-concept, whereas the other classes were not. A self-concept scale was completed by the students in the first and last class sessions. This scale measures overall positive self-concept (high scorers see themselves as persons of value and worth), the capacity for useful self-criticism, and the degree of certainty the person has regarding his or her self-concept.

The outcomes of communication training showed mixed effects on self-concept. Three of six sections showed overall gains in positive self-concept. Only one of the sections was a systematic skill training session. Two sections showed increases in the capacity for self-criticism, while three sections showed increased certainty scores. One of the groups—using systematic skill training—experienced increases in overall self-concept and certainty, while the other showed improvements in self-criticism and certainty.

The systematic skill training groups were specifically designed and conducted to improve communications skills and to enhance self-concept. However, even in this case, the improvements in self-concept, while encouraging, were not consistent and compelling. Sections which did not use systematic skill training also showed gains in self-concept. Thus, direct training in communication skills appeared to have no more influence on self-concept than did lectures or group discussions. The authors suggest that enhancing self-concept might better be approached by direct teaching to increase self-awareness, rather than through possible spin-off effects from communication skill training.

Source: Altmann, H. A. & Black, D. G. Enhancing student self-concept with communication skill training. *Small Group Behavior,* 1978, *9,* 80–91.

Helpee: I don't know what's going to happen! I've got three essays due next week and two midterms on top of that. It's just impossible.

Helper: You're quite anxious about all these pressures—the essays and exams—and you're afraid of not completing them all successfully.

Second, the helper must show *acceptance and liking* of the other person as a separate and unique human being who has unconditional self-worth. (This is in contrast to our tendency to put conditions of worth on the behavior of other people and to accept them only if they meet our conditions.) Acceptance of the other person and their feelings induces *safety* in the relationship so that the other person will not feel threatened.

> *Helpee:* I really wanted to take her out, but I didn't want to call because she might say no.
> *Helper:* I can understand that you would be afraid she would reject you. I see that as being sensitive to what might happen.

Third, Rogers stresses the importance of the *genuineness* of the helper. The helper must be sensitive to his or her own feelings in the relationships and be willing to express these in ways appropriate to the helping process. This brings a degree of *reality* to the relationship, a quality that is absent if participants withhold their feelings and behave in a cold or aloof manner.

> *Helpee:* And so when I called her and she said yes, I really jumped for joy.
> *Helper:* Hey, I'm very pleased that it worked out for you.

This client-centered approach proved to have positive benefits for the person being helped. The client developed a more positive self-concept in which the actual self became closer to the ideal self. Clients valued themselves more, developed more self-confidence, and became more adaptive and resistant to stress (Rogers & Dymond, 1954). Further research demonstrated how the basic qualities of empathy, acceptance, and genuineness were translated into helper skills that related to successful outcomes in therapy (Halkides, 1958). These findings have been replicated with many different helpers and many different groups of clients (Truax & Carkhuff, 1967).

Carl Rogers became convinced that psychotherapy was only one type of helping relationship and that the same general principles were valid for many other relationships: between parent and child, teacher and student, physician and patient, and so on. In short any relationship that intends to promote the development and improved functioning of the other person through the use of his or her own inner resources can be made more effective by incorporating empathy, acceptance, and genuiness. The implication for interpersonal relationships in general is that the more we can be empathic, respectful, and genuine, the more likely we are to develop safe and authentic relationships in which mutual personal growth can occur.

Jack Gibb, a consulting psychologist with a humanistic orientation, has provided training and consultation services to a wide range of groups and organizations. From this experience he has provided a description of the basic qualities of helping in a paper entitled "Is Help Helpful?" (Gibb, 1964). Gibb first notes the range of roles that involve helping others: the counselor, consultant, teacher, lawyer, and so on. Although helping is a central social process, Gibb also notes a basic problem: help that is offered is not always helpful to the recipient. Recipients of help may feel resentment, increased helplessness, dependency, or hostility in reaction to the behaviors of the helper. But under certain conditions both the giver and receiver of help feel satisfied and experience personal growth and development as a result of the helping process.

Table 6.1 outlines both the helping and hindering orientations of helping relationships. Gibb came to the following conclusions about help:

- Recipients accept help from those they trust, rather than those they fear or are suspicious of. When there is acceptance and warmth in the relationship, offers of help are appreciated, listened to, and often acted upon. The child who fears a teacher will have more difficulty learning than the child who feels safe.

Table 6.1 HELPFUL AND HINDERING ORIENTATIONS

Helpful Orientations	Hindering Orientations
1. Reciprocal trust (confidence, warmth, acceptance)	1. Distrust (fear, punitiveness, defensiveness)
2. Cooperative learning (inquiry, exploration, quest)	2. Teaching (training, advice giving, indoctrinating)
3. Mutual growth (becoming, actualizing, fulfilling)	3. Evaluation (fixing, correcting, providing a remedy)
4. Reciprocal openness (spontaneity, candor, honesty)	4. Strategy (planning for, maneuvering, gamesmanship)
5. Shared problem solving (defining, producing alternatives, testing)	5. Modeling (demonstrating, information, giving, guiding)
6. Autonomy (freedom, interdependence, equality)	6. Coaching (molding, steering, controlling)
7. Experimentation (play, innovation, provisional try)	7. Patterning (standard, static, fixed)

Source: Gibb (1964).

- Helping occurs in a relationship of joint inquiry rather than a "one-up, one-down" relationship where the helper tries to teach, persuade, or indoctrinate. The counselor who attempts to tell a child how to live will be sorely disappointed in the child's behavior.
- Effective helping occurs when both parties are growing together in a supportive climate. In contrast, a sense of evaluation elicits resistance and hostility. The parent who constantly criticizes and scolds the child will engender alienation rather than love and admiration.
- Help is based on a reciprocal openness between the partners, rather than on covert strategies of influence. The football coach who attempts to subtly induce shame in his charges rather than being open about his disappointments and joys will soon find his players respect neither themselves nor him.
- The helping relationship involves mutual problem solving where the focus is on the problem to be solved. If the helper acts as an expert who defines the problem and offers a solution, it will only increase the dependency of the helpee on the helper. The professor who describes in great detail how students should complete their research projects may find little initiative, creativity, and involvement in the process.
- The helping relationship involves interdependence in which each person exercises freedom and responsibility for learning. The alternate approach of coaching involves controlling the behavior of the recipient in a directive fashion. The manager who gives his or her subordinates the power to make appropriate decisions will engender a greater degree of motivation and satisfaction.
- Helping requires experimentation in which there is tentativeness, innovativeness and an expectation that errors will occur. Contrasted to this is a patterning orientation in which the helper has a prescribed goal set out in advance and expects the recipient to conform. The boy scout leader who plans all activities by the book and demands uniformity will soon see his troup's enthusiasm drain away.

Gibb concludes that help is not always helpful, but that it *can* be. When helping relationships are developed based on an atmosphere of trust, joint inquiry, openness, and interdependence, personal growth will occur and groups and organizations will function in a healthier manner.

Developmental Model and Core Skills

The work of Carl Rogers laid the basis for both a general model of helping and the interpersonal skills that put the model into practice. Rogers's approach placed emphasis not on theories of personality but on the social process of helping. Building on the humanistic values of Rogers's approach, other psychologists have extended his work through systematic training of the core interpersonal skills.

Robert Carkhuff and his associates (Carkhuff, 1969; Carkhuff & Berenson, 1977) have contributed specifics to Rogers's general approach. They proposed a model of helping that involved two principal phases over time: (1) the *downward or inward phase*, in which the helpee's problem is explored and understood; and (2) the *upward or outward phase*, in which the participants begin to develop a direction toward action and problem solving.

Carkhuff also defined the three basic qualities as the facilitative skills of empathy, respect, and genuineness, added the skill of concreteness to improve the accuracy of communication, and articulated the action-oriented skills of self-disclosure, immediacy, and confrontation to facilitate problem solving in the second stage (see Table 6.2). Together, these seven core interpersonal skills form the essence of effective helping and are useful in improving all types of interpersonal relationships.

Gerard Egan (1975a) has extended the work of Rogers and Carkhuff by specifying his three-stage, *developmental model* of helping. In a developmental model such as Carkhuff's or Egan's, one stage proceeds to the next with each stage building on the previous one. The effectiveness of each stage is thus dependent on the success of the previous stages. Egan's model encompasses a pre-helping phase followed by three successive stages:

- *The pre-helping or attending phase.* The helper makes use of nonverbal behavior (eye contact, head nods, and so forth) as well as active verbal listening to develop rapport with the helpee.

Table 6.2 THE CORE INTERPERSONAL SKILLS

Empathy: sensitivity to the helpee's current feelings and the ability to communicate this understanding.

Respect: the ability to feel and express acceptance, nonpossessive warmth, and active delight in the helpee's unique personhood.

Genuineness: the ability to be open, spontaneous, and congruent and to use such responses constructively.

Concreteness: the ability to focus helpee exploration on specific and definite feelings and behavior relating to personally meaningful experiences.

Self-Disclosure: the ability to fully share personal information, ideas, values, and feelings in ways that are relevant and helpful to the helpee.

Immediacy: the ability to relate relevant helpee expressions directly to the helper-helpee relationships in the here-and-now.

Confrontation: sensitivity to discrepancies in the helpee's behavior, feelings, and perceptions, and the ability to present and discuss these in ways that constructively further helpee self-understanding.

Source: Carkhuff (1969).

- *Stage 1: Exploration.* The helper responds to helpee expressions with the skills of empathy, respect, genuineness, and concreteness, thus freeing the helpee to openly explore his or her feelings in specific terms.
- *Stage 2: Understanding.* The helper puts together central themes in the helpee's behavior and uses the skills of self-disclosure, immediacy, and confrontation to move the helpee to the verge of action.
- *Stage 3: Action.* Based on new understandings of unproductive ways of living, the helper facilitates the development of action plans and uses the skills to encourage the helpee to risk and to act in a more productive manner.

Egan emphasizes that the same principles and skills apply to interpersonal relations in general—to families, to friendships, to work relationships. Each of us experiences difficulties in such relationships, and the understanding and collaborative approach of the developmental model can be used to resolve such difficulties to our mutual satisfaction. Skills such as empathy, concreteness, and confrontation can be used to increase understanding and effective problem solving in many social situations from a parent-teacher interview to a committee meeting. The values, attitudes, and skills developed by Rogers and others have a general utility for improving human relations.

Training in Core Interpersonal Skills

Largely through the efforts of Robert Carkhuff and his associates, training in the core interpersonal skills has become a widely acknowledged method for improving people's ability to develop and sustain effective interpersonal relationships. Much of the training has focused on professional and paraprofessional helpers (Carkhuff, 1969; Egan, 1975a), but has also expanded to a number of additional areas including education (see Gazda, 1973), parent-child relations (Carkhuff & Bierman, 1970), and race relations (Carkhuff & Banks, 1970).

Regardless of the roles of the two individuals in the interpersonal relationship, the basic training format remains the same. However the conceptual foundation, the ethical considerations, and the extent of usage of the interpersonal skills must all be tailored to the nature of the specific relationship. For example the training of professional counseling psychologists involves much more consideration in all these areas than does the training of community volunteers, say, as companions to disadvantaged children. What is important in all relationships is that each participant recognizes the limitations of his or her ability and responsibility to influence the other person.

Training in core interpersonal skills involves two distinct but related elements (Carkhuff, 1969). The first is *discrimination training:* the trainee must acquire the ability to pick out which skills are being used and at what level of effectiveness. Discrimination training moves from gross discrimination of effective helping behavior to the more specific discrimination of particular interpersonal skills.

Written exercises in the form of questionnaires are useful for discrimination training purposes. For example, Carkhuff's (1969) *Index of Discrimination* (similar to the Questionnaire on Listening and Response Styles described earlier) presents typical helpee statements in written form and asks the trainee or potential helper to pick out one of a number of alternative responses that they would give in that situation. The responses vary in the degree to which they combine the various interpersonal skills into a helpful response. Potential helpers thus come to understand what constitutes helpful and unhelpful responses.

In addition, Carkhuff (1969) and others have developed *rating scales* for assessing helper behavior on each of the core skills. Table 6.3 presents a five-point scale for the discrimination of empathy. For more advanced discrimination training, it is common practice for trainees to listen to tape-recorded excerpts of helpee statements followed by helper responses and then to rate the responses. In these ways, trainees understand and gain an ability to discriminate helpful levels of interpersonal skills from unhelpful or even destructive levels of responding.

The second element in the acquisition of interpersonal skills involves *communication training:* the active acquisition of behavior that put the skills into practice (Carkhuff, 1969). Here an attempt is made to combine conceptual learning with experiential learning—a necessity if the trainee is expected to improve his or her ability to respond effectively to other people.

Communication training can be initiated with written exercises that present a helpee statement and ask the trainee for an answer that uses one of the interpersonal skills (see Egan, 1975b). Verbal communication training can use taped excerpts, can move to role-played interactions, and finally may involve helping interactions based on real issues. In the first step trainees respond to tape-recorded expressions of a personal concern, attempting to verbalize the skill in question. For example, a trainee might listen to a father who is angry because his son took the family car without his knowledge or permission. If the trainee is practicing the skills of empathy, he or she attempts to form an expression that would reflect the anger that the father was expressing. Carkhuff points out that the advantage of this approach is that it does not expect naive trainees to be able to respond productively in real interactions.

Role-play interactions, wherein one partner talks about a made-up problem or concern, is a step closer to reality. It is likely more common, however, to use actual helping interactions. In this case potential helpers or trainees are expected to perform in the role of helpee and to discuss a meaningful but minor personal problem. In doing so they engage in a two-way interaction with a partner who takes the role of helper. For example, one person might speak about the frustration of finding a suitable career; the helping partner attempts to respond with empathy, or with another interpersonal skill, or with a combination of skills, depending upon the instructions of the exercise.

This approach, commonly called "Carkhuff training," is carried out with a small group of approximately ten participants. The trainer, serving as the leader of the group, must be a highly competent helper who is expert in interpersonal skills. Otherwise it is not possible for the trainees to receive accurate feedback on their behavior, or to see an adequate model of the effective use of the interpersonal skills. Following the helping interaction, other members of the group provide feedback to the helper on the use of the particular skill in question. Thus the Carkhuff training format is a highly systematic form of human relations training, integrated at all times with the conceptual background of the developmental model and the core interpersonal skills.

There has been a growing realization that the development and effective use of interpersonal relationships is the most important part of both effective helping and effective living. For example, Patterson (1974) presents a model of relation-

Table 6.3   EMPATHY SCALE

Level 1

The verbal and behavioral expressions of the helper either *do not attend to* or *detract significantly from* the verbal and behavioral expressions of the helpee in that they communicate significantly less of the helpee's feelings and experiences than the helpee has communicated himself. The helper does everything but express that he is listening, understanding, or being sensitive to even the most obvious feelings of the helpee in such a way as to detract significantly from the communications of the helpee.

Level 2

While the helper responds to the expressed feelings of the helpee, he does so in such a way that he *subtracts noticeable affect* from the communications of the helpee. The helper may communicate some awareness of obvious, surface feelings of the helpee, but his communications drain off a level of the affect and distort the level of meaning. The helper tends to respond to other than what the helpee is expressing or indicating.

Level 3

The expressions of the helper in response to the expressions of the helpee are essentially *interchangeable* with those of the helpee in that they express essentially the same affect and meaning. The helper is responding so as to neither subtract from nor add to the expressions of the helpee. He does not respond accurately to how that person really feels beneath the surface feelings—but he indicates a willingness and openness to do so.

Level 4

The responses of the helper *add noticeably* to the expressions of the helpee in such a way as to express feelings at a level deeper than the helpee was able to express himself. The helper's responses add deeper feeling and meaning to the expressions of the helper.

Level 5

The helper's responses *add significantly* to the feeling and meaning of the expressions of the helpee in such a way as to accurately express feelings at levels below what the helpee himself was able to express or, in the event of ongoing, deep self-exploration on the helpee's part, to be fully with him in his deepest moments. The helper is responding with a full awareness of who the other person is and with a comprehensive and accurate empathic understanding of that individual's deepest feelings.

Source: Carkhuff (1969).

ship counseling and psychotherapy; Guerney (1977) sees relationship enhancement as the crucial process in therapy, problem prevention, and human enrichment; and Carkhuff and Berenson (1977) reaffirm their position that helping and training is a *way of life*, rather than something confined to the therapy hour.

Effectiveness and Applicability of Helping Relationship

Core interpersonal skills can be useful for improving a variety of social situations. For example, Kenneth Clark, a distinguished applied social psychologist, has recently commented on the central importance of empathy in human affairs (Clark, 1980). This capacity to feel others' experiences, needs, and feelings as if they are our own can be learned as a technique to counterbalance more destructive tendencies. The blocking of empathy, mainly by a need for power, can be seen as one of the primary causes of many social problems including social conflict, violence, and war. According to Clark, empathy is an essential but neglected topic in social psychology.

If we consider the extent of overlap between core interpersonal skills and basic communication skills, we can see the value of using these skills to improve both the accuracy and the openness of communication. Empathy overlaps both paraphrasing and perception checking of feelings. Genuineness is similar to the description of feelings. Self-disclosure is included as a core interpersonal skill. Behavior description comes into the use of immediacy and confrontation. In all these areas the effective use of the skills can help us better understand other people and develop more open, trusting, and authentic relationships with them. An example of such positive outcomes is given in Box 6.5.

The effectiveness of the core interpersonal skills has been demonstrated in psychotherapy research (see Rogers, 1967; Truax & Carkhuff, 1967; Truax & Mitchell, 1971), in child development as affected by both parents and teachers (Bierman, 1969), by human relations specialists working in integrated high schools (Carkhuff & Griffin, 1970), and in teacher behavior as it affects the student's intellectual gains and self-attitudes (Aspy, 1975). Similarly in the field of social work, Shulman (1978) found that the most effective helpers are those who understood their clients' feelings (empathy) and who share their own thoughts and feelings (self-disclosure and genuineness).

Based on such positive results, Carkhuff suggests that training in his model of *human resource development* is effective for acquiring the core interpersonal skills and that these skills are useful in a wide variety of situations (Carkhuff, 1972a, 1972b). Evaluations of numerous training programs indicate that these skills can be trained and used effectively. However, the picture is not so rosy. Lambert and his colleagues (Lambert & DeJulio, 1977; Lambert, DeJulio & Stein, 1978) raise some serious questions about the quality and breadth of research that supports Carkhuff training. They point out that the components of the training program are not clearly specified, that they vary from one study to the next, that control groups are seldom used, and that the same scales are used to assess final outcomes as are used during the training itself.

Lambert et al. (1978) also question the effectivenes of the core skills in therapy and other helping situations, noting that accumulating research shows that while these skills are important, they are not the "be all and end all" of successful helping. Many other factors, such as helper's experience and seriousness of the problem, also have a strong bearing on the outcomes. Similarly, Gladstein (1970, 1977) finds that the use of empathy in counseling yields mixed results; its usefulness seems to depend, for example, on whether the client clearly perceives the counselor's empathy. These qualifying results show how important it is not to accept any *one* model of interpersonal relating as the absolute truth, and to realize that social interaction is a complex process whose outcomes are determined by many factors.

The work on the helping relationships has important implications for social interaction in general, because it can help sensitize us to a wider range of possibilities in interpersonal functioning. In looking toward the future, in a statement entitled "Interpersonal Relationships: U.S.A. 2000," Carl Rogers (1973)

Box 6.5   FOCUS ON RESEARCH
Training in Interpersonal Skills and General Social Comfort

Proponents of interpersonal skill training suggest that such experience increases general social functioning. A number of training approaches attempt to increase the core interpersonal skills of empathy, warmth or respect, and genuineness. Arthur Bohart and his colleagues at the University of California, Riverside, asked the question of whether such training was relevant only to helping roles or whether it had positive effects on the trainee's general ability to establish a socially comfortable climate.

Undergraduate students from a number of fields participated in a ten-week class in interpersonal effectiveness training. Students were assigned to two different types of training groups or to a no-training control group. The *response training format* involved lectures, tapes, and skill practice while the *concept training approach* avoided practice but involved discussion of the usefulness of the interpersonal skills in everyday life and encouraged participants to be empathic, warm, and genuine.

At the end of training, all participants were interviewed for five minutes concerning their happiness in interpersonal relations, their best friend, and their opinions on capital punishment. The interview was specifically designed so that trainees had no opportunity to use any of the skills they had learned. At the end of the interview, the interviewer rated each subject on the item "I feel comfortable talking to him/her." The rating could be from completely disagree (-4) to completely agree ($+4$).

Students in both types of training group were rated higher on social comfort that students in the control group as shown below.

Group	Mean Social Comfort Rating
Control	1.76
Response Training	3.00
Concept Training	2.95

The results thus suggested that interpersonal skill training increased the ability of trainees to place another individual at ease in a social situation. It therefore appears that such training may have beneficial effects on general interpersonal effectiveness.

Source: Bohart, A. C., Hewitt, B., Heilmann, A. & Threlkeld, D. Effects of paraprofessional training on one aspect of generalized interpersonal effectiveness. *American Journal of Community Psychology*, 1976, 4, 309–312.

speaks of these possibilities. We can retain the traditional view of people as creatures who play various appropriate roles in constrained ways, or we can choose to move towards a new reality in relationships—one that involves open communication and "a love for one another which grows not out of a romantic blindness but out of the profound respect which is nearly always engendered by reality in relationships" (p. 124). By moving toward a new authenticity in interpersonal relationships, we can find better ways to teach and learn, better ways to resolve conflicts. We can move toward male-female relationships that are more enriching, family relations that are more real, and a sense of community that enables us to face the unknown in a clearer and stronger fashion.

The challenge for applied social psychologists is clear. We need to use our research expertise to help differentiate between what is effective and what is ineffective in establishing and maintaining viable interpersonal relationships. We need to broaden the study of processes such as the core interpersonal skills to move beyond helping relationships to encompass friendship, marriage, and all manner of everyday interactions. In this way we can come to see whether or not the choices that face us can in fact to realized in ways that further the humanistic value base of applied social psychology.

Summary

Social psychologists have long-standing interest in interpersonal relations—social affiliation, social attraction, and the development and improvement of relationships. Interpersonal relations are the building blocks for higher levels of social interaction. If there are difficulties in interpersonal functioning, we would not expect adequate functioning at higher levels of analysis.

The need to affiliate is a basic human motive. Affiliation helps us meet our individual needs and acquire a moderate amount of stimulation. Social comparison suggests that we associate with others, especially when we are uncertain, to compare our abilities, attitudes or emotions.

The major determinants of interpersonal attraction include proximity, reciprocity, similarity, and complementarity. The principle of reinforcement helps explain how these factors determine interpersonal attraction.

Self-disclosure is the communication of information about oneself to another person. Social penetration theory sees mutual self-disclosure governed by the principles of social exchange as the basic process in the development and decay of interpersonal relationships. Incremental exchange theory sees relationships as developing through the stages of awareness, surface contact, and mutuality. The study of love includes both romantic love and companionate love.

Individuals can exhibit a number of deceptive and manipulative strategies in interpersonal relations. Goffman explains the interaction rituals through which we present our face or self-image to others. Jones's study of ingratiation—behaviors which are designed to illicitly influence another person with regard to the attractiveness of our personal qualities—indicates that ingratiators use the techniques of biased self-presentation, conformity, flattery, and doing favors to shift the outcomes of the interaction to their advantage. Machiavellianism involves active attempts to control and manipulate others in order to maximize one's personal gains.

Interpersonal communication is a basic and pervasive process in social interaction and underlies more complex processes. A simple purposive model of interpersonal communication includes the main elements of the sender, the message, noise, the channel, and the receiver. Important elements include the intention of the sender, the encoding and decoding processes, the effect on the receiver, and the response of the receiver.

The interpersonal gap is the degree of congruence between the intended effect of the sender and the actual effect produced in the receiver. To prevent gaps in communication, we may use the basic communication skills of paraphrasing, perception checking, behavior description, and description of feelings. Combinations of these skills into active listening and feedback also increase our ability to communicate more effectively (having the effect on the receiver that we intended).

Nonverbal communication may carry a large amount of the meaning, especially the emotional meaning, of messages. The major nonverbal channels include proxemics, body posture, body movements, eye contact and paralanguage.

Training communication skills can be approached through written questionnaires showing our typical responses to others and behavioral exercises following the experience-based learning format.

Carl Rogers provides a humanistic view which sees all relationships as having the potential for personal growth. The basic qualities of helping and of all interpersonal relationships include empathic understanding, acceptance and liking, and genuineness.

Gibb has spelled out orientations that result in help actually being helpful rather than in being hindering or destructive. Carkhuff has defined seven core interpersonal skills: empathy, respect, genuineness, concreteness, self-disclosure, immediacy, and confrontation. Egan provides a developmental model that includes a pre-helping phase of attending, and the stages of exploration, understanding, and action.

Carkhuff training or human resource development involves both discrimination training (the trainee discriminates different skills and different levels of skills as they are expressed in written exercises or taped excerpts) and communication training (the trainee actually practices the skills in response to expressions of another person).

The effectiveness of the core interpersonal skills has been demonstrated in a number of areas from psychotherapy to child development, from teaching and learning to social work practice. However, the strength of these demonstrations varies considerably and the research that supports the effectiveness of the Carkhuff training model has been criticized. Nonetheless, the work on the helping relationship is useful to develop more authentic and satisfying interpersonal relationships in ways that further the humanistic value base of applied social psychology.

Further Readings

Altman, I. & Taylor, D. *Social penetration: The development of interpersonal relationships.* New York: Holt, Rinehart & Winston, 1973.

Berscheid, E. & Walster, E. *Interpersonal attraction* (2nd ed.). Reading, Mass.: Addison-Wesley, 1978.

Egan, G. *The skilled helper: A model for systematic helping and interpersonal relating.* Monterey, Calif.: Brooks-Cole, 1975.

Giffin, K. & Patton, B. *Fundamentals of interpersonal communication* (2nd ed.). New York: Harper & Row, 1976.

Goffman, E. *Interaction ritual: Essays on face-to-face behavior.* Garden City, N.Y.: Doubleday, 1967.

Jourard, S. M. *The transparent self.* Princeton, N.J.: Van Nostrand, 1964.

Rogers, C. R. (Ed.). *On becoming a person: A therapist's view of psychotherapy.* Boston: Houghton Mifflin, 1961.

CHAPTER OUTLINE

Small Group Processes

BASIC CONCEPTS OF GROUP DYNAMICS

This weekend I'll be co-leading a 24-hour workshop in sensitivity training. This original form of experiential group learning is designed to help participants increase their self-awareness, learn interpersonal communication skills, and come to understand more about group processes. The participants are expected to learn from their own interaction.

In my role as co-trainer, I will facilitate the interaction of the group in ways that will help individuals reach their particular learning goals. To fulfill this role, I have had to participate in a variety of human relations training workshops, take on the junior co-leader role, acquire trainer skills in professional development workshops, and finally take on the role of trainer in a number of different workshop designs. Such a lengthy journey of personal and professional development is essential to working as a small-group practitioner.

A knowledge of human personality (as covered in Chapter 5) will help me understand the participants' behavior. Given the relatively ambiguous and unstructured environment of sensitivity training, participants will tend to inject their own personal needs, characteristics, and styles into the situation. Some people will behave in an extraverted manner, taking social initiative and actively attempting to establish relationships with other members of the group. Others will behave in an introverted way, saying little, waiting to see what happens.

People will begin participating with their characteristic interpersonal styles: some passive and dependent, others controlling and competitive, others aggressive and rebellious. Some participants may be motivated to exhibit a strong need for power, to control and to have impact on the rest of the group; others will want to affiliate, nurture, and support. The high achievers may push so hard to find meaning and utility, and to "get something done," that they will endanger their opportunity to learn in a different way. Individuals will vary in their openness to learn about their behavior from the reactions of other group members. Thus, the group will bring a variety of interacting abilities, expectancies, motives, and defenses to the situation.

In this amazing complexity, I will work to understand the behavior of individuals in order to move the group toward self-awareness, self-realization, and self-actualization. Theories of social interaction will give me useful insights into what is happening: participants' initial behavior will be partly guided by the search for social comparison; individuals will be attracted by similarities, repelled by differences; self-disclosure will be essential to the growth of satisfying interpersonal relationships and the mutuality and cohesion of the group. A productive group climate will at times be hampered by destructive strategies of ingratiation and manipulation. Some of these deceitful behaviors will be confronted, and we, the trainers, will work toward a productive resolution of interpersonal conflicts. The possibility that either of us may at times be directly involved in interpersonal conflict is one of the main reasons for co-training: when one trainer is involved, the other facilitates the resolution of the conflict. Co-training also helps us grasp the complexity of the behavioral processes found in this unstructured learning environment.

Personal and interpersonal processes, however, are only two parts of a three-part picture; we must add the level of *group functioning*. As a trainer, I must also be sensitive to and intervene with processes occurring at the level of the total group. I must be sensitive to how the group develops cohesion, how decisions are made and to what effect, how norms are developed and enforced; I must be sensitive to the communication pattern of the group as well as to how the group deals with conflict. As a trainer, I will work to increase the participants' sensitivity and understanding of these crucial elements of group dynamics. That is the same goal that I have in writing this chapter—to share with you the major ideas about small-group processes so that you may better understand groups.

Our Life in Groups

We spend a good deal of our time in groups. Our immediate family is a type of small group referred to as a *primary group*—one in which there is frequent face-to-face contact on an intimate basis. In the same way, many of our friendship and peer groups, composed of people like us, and many of our work groups, organized to achieve a given goal, are considered primary groups.

Secondary groups, on the other hand, consist of larger, more impersonal collections of individuals in which there is a lower level of interaction and intimacy—such as professional organizations and community service clubs.

Both primary and secondary groups serve as *membership groups*—those in which we are active participants—and may also serve as *reference groups*—those which we may use, whether we are members or not, as a source of information and a standard of comparison for our own attitudes and behavior. In other words, we understand and evaluate ourselves by making reference to groups that appear relevant to us for these purposes. For example, when we are in high school, our group of friends is an important reference group for us: we share common attitudes and behavior and define ourselves as one of the group. At the same time,

The family *(top)* and high-school friends *(bottom)* are examples of *primary groups*—groups in which there is frequent face-to-face contact on an intimate basis. *(Jean Gaumy/ Magnum Photo, Inc.)*

we might identify with a reference group to which we don't belong—students at the college we wish to attend—and we may compare our attitudes and behavior to that group as well. We can also make other distinctions among groups: ingroups versus outgroups, structured versus unstructured groups, and so on.

There are numerous dimensions that cut across all types of small groups, that is, those having between two and twenty members. This makes a definition of "group" difficult. Not only are there numerous definitions of the term group, but there are several different approaches to defining groups—for example, in terms of member perceptions, motivations, or goals, or in terms of interdependence or interaction among members (Shaw, 1981). However, the key elements identified by Shaw are *interaction* and *influence*; *group* is thus defined as "two or more persons who are interacting with one another in such a manner that each person influences and is influenced by each other person" (1981, p. 8).

By considering the basic characteristics of small groups, we can understand the groups that we participate in on a day-to-day basis. We also gain a better understanding of the influences that operate in groups, influences that affect the behavior of the individual members. This study of the powerful, interrelated forces in groups, which Kurt Lewin called *group dynamics*, now spans four decades of research in social psychology (Cartwright & Zander, 1968; Zander, 1979). Such studies allow us a closer look at our social behavior, and how changes in behavior can make our life in groups more effective and satisfying.

Attraction and Membership: Do I Belong Here?

Why are people attracted to groups? Much like our desire to affiliate with others, we join groups to meet our physical, psychological, and social needs. We are attracted to *particular* groups because of the major determinants of interpersonal attraction: proximity, similarity, reciprocity, and complementarity. Thus, we can identify four major factors that influence our decision to join and remain in a wide variety of groups: attraction to members of the group; the activities, goals, or the task of the group; affiliating with the people in the group; and meeting needs or goals lying outside the group (Quey, 1971; Shaw, 1981).

Attraction to members of the group grows out of *proximity* and *frequency of interaction.* (Consider your own experience of friendship groups that are largely determined by who is available for interaction: your neighbors, school chums, roommates, and so on.)

In a classic demonstration of the effect of proximity on group formation (Festinger, Schachter & Back, 1950), couples living in a married-student housing complex were found to be likely to form a friendship group with the couples living next door to them. Couples who lived in end or corner units tended to be isolated from other people in the complex.

However, we must remember that proximity creates only the potential for attraction; other factors usually come into play when actually establishing a relationship. The power of similarity, especially attitudinal similarity, appears to be as strong in group formation as in interpersonal attraction. However, the competing explanation of complementarity may have some merit, especially when complementarity of abilities or needs is conducive to effective group functioning. For example, Rychlak (1965) found that after participating in group problem-solving exercises, subjects selected co-workers for the roles of boss, employee, and neighbor more on the basis of need complementarity (such as dominance with submission, order with change) than need similarity. In general, however, similarity of attitudes, economic background, race, sex, and other variables tell us more about group formation (Shaw, 1981).

The task of a group, as expressed in its activities and goals, is often an important reason for joining: the group helps its members meet their individual needs. You join a photography club because you enjoy taking pictures and discussing that activity with others. You join a baseball team because it's pretty hard to play by yourself. You join a protest group against higher tuition fees because you can't afford to pay more. In all these examples, you are gaining rewards directly through group membership. The application of social exchange theory to group formation predicts that we join and remain in groups when the rewards for doing so outweigh the costs, thus yielding profits (see Chapter 12). We expect our profits to be proportional to the investments we put into the group; when outcomes drop below the comparison level for alternative group associations, we are motivated to leave the group.

The third general reason we join a group is because we like to affiliate with the people in that group. We satisfy our need for affiliation through interacting with people, just as we meet our need for achievement through the activities and goals of the group. Whether we see affiliation as an innate need or a learned motive, we must acknowledge the power of attention and companionship as a social reinforcer. Whether we affiliate for social comparison, or to reduce anxiety, or to satisfy an innate craving, it is clear that the group is a powerful forum for meeting our basic social needs and a strong influence on our behavior.

Group membership may help us meet needs that lie outside the group—thus, group membership may be a stepping-stone to achieve an external goal, rather than a source of direct satisfaction. College students may join fraternities or sororities to increase their prestige in the college community (Willerman & Swanson, 1953). A college professor may regularly attend meetings of a professional association to enhance the probability of promotion. A candidate for political office may join a host of community organizations to enhance his or her chances for election. And so it goes; the reasons for joining a group cannot always be found within the group itself.

When we consider attraction to a group, we must also consider the characteristics of the group itself. Several attributes of groups generally make them more attractive to prospective members (Napier & Gershenfeld, 1981):

- The more *prestige* a group can offer a member, the more attractive the group. Members who have positions of higher authority and prestige are usually most attracted to remain in the group.
- *Cooperative relationships* and joint rewards heighten the attractiveness of a group, whereas individual striving and competition detract from it.
- The degree of *positive interaction* among members directly affects attractiveness since it increases the range of personal and social needs being met.
- The *size* of the group affects its attraction. Smaller groups generally offer more possibility for interaction, for sharing similarities, and for meeting individual needs, and therefore tend to be more attractive.

- *Positive relations with other groups* may add to the prestige, etc., of the group and make it more attractive.
- Nothing succeeds like *success*. Groups that are perceived as meeting their goals effectively usually appear to be more attractive.

Finally, we must relate attractiveness to the process by which a person becomes a member. Most of the above findings refer to groups in which membership was largely voluntary, rather than nonvoluntary or coerced. In addition, we have been concerned more with actual membership than with aspiring membership; the factor of attractiveness, however, should help us predict whether an aspiring member will in fact become an actual member. Also, most of us hold multiple memberships in a variety of groups and this affects our attraction to any one group (as predicted by social exchange theory). Then, we should consider the actual manner of joining a group to see whether the characteristics of this process might affect the ultimate attraction to the group. In a classic example, Aronson and Mills (1959) found that the unpleasantness of the initiation procedure into a group affected the evaluations of the attractiveness of the group—and not necessarily in the direction that common sense would predict. More severe initiation actually increased the attractiveness of membership, probably through the operation of cognitive dissonance: to put forward great effort to get into a group and then not to be attracted to it would be quite discrepant. Thus, to reduce dissonance, the evaluation of the group becomes more positive. The questions of why we join groups and why we are attracted to particular groups do not always lead to simple, straightforward answers.

Group Cohesiveness. Each level of analysis involves the existence of *emergent characteristics* that have not been expressed at any lower level of analysis. At the group level, the interpersonal variable of attractiveness contributes to the emergent property of *cohesiveness*.

Although cohesiveness has been defined in at least three general ways—to refer to attraction, morale, and coordination—it usually refers to the extent to which members are motivated to remain in the group (Shaw, 1981), or to "the resultant of all the forces acting on the members to remain in the group" (Festinger, 1950, p. 274). Thus, cohesiveness emphasizes not simply interpersonal attraction, but the overall pattern and strength of attractions within and toward the group. Cohesiveness is usually measured by the number of sociometric choices for various activities that are made within the group as compared to the number of choices made outside the group.

Cohesiveness is a key variable in group development and relates to other important properties, most notably degree of interaction, social influence, productivity, and satisfaction (Shaw, 1981). More cohesive groups show greater quantity and quality of interaction in terms of friendliness, cooperativeness, and relevance to the group task. Thus, members accept the responsibilities of membership and make positive contributions through steady attendance and participation. I can recall serving on several committees that lacked cohesion. Members usually attended every other meeting, a lot of discussion was irrelevant to the committee's purpose, and so on. Needless to say, little was accomplished.

One interesting effect of cohesion is the degree to which members take credit for group accomplishments (Schlenker & Miller, 1977). In one study, members of small problem-solving groups were first told that their group was cohesive or not cohesive on the basis of previously completed attitude and personality scales. The groups then solved a real-life problem, such as the case of Tom, a college student who had stolen money from his employer. Groups were then told that they had been successful, unsuccessful, or average on the problem. Members of low cohesive groups tended to take personal responsibility for success, but attributed failure to other group members. In cohesive groups, assignment of responsibility was unrelated to outcome. In other words, members shared the responsibility for success with other group members, and did not dissociate themselves from unsuccessful outcomes. In cohesive groups, it appears that members will stick together for better or worse.

Members of cohesive groups are more receptive to social influence within the group—they adhere more to group norms or standards of behavior. Festinger et al. (1950) found that residents in more cohesive friendship groups in student housing showed greater conformity to group norms related to both opinions and behavior. For example, they showed a more favorable attitude toward, and active participation in, a tenants' organization. Similarly, laboratory studies that manipulate the level of cohesiveness—such as the Schlenker and Miller (1977) experiment—indicate that higher cohesiveness opens members up to greater social influence (Shaw, 1981). This does not mean that cohesiveness and conformity are necessarily good—at times they will clash with the principles of individual freedom and democracy. Extreme cohesiveness and conformity in groups, such as in religious cults, is a form of tyranny that actually subverts humanistic values.

Sometimes the cohesiveness and conformity demanded by a religious cult are so extreme that they clash with the principles of individual freedom and democracy and subvert humanistic values. *(Hiroji Kubota/Magnum Photo, Inc.)*

Cohesiveness aids productivity and satisfaction whether in the classroom, the military, or the industrial organization. Studies in these and other settings indicate that cohesiveness increases motivation and performance. However, this assumes that the group accepts the goals the organization prescribes for it. In some cases, work groups do not fully accept organizational goals for production, and more cohesive groups in the factory may be *less* productive (see Chapter 9). They hold productivity down by ostracizing members who produce more and may even engage in sabotage. In general, however, cohesive groups produce more and experience greater satisfaction. Therefore, practice in applied social psychology which helps groups develop greater cohesiveness can have clear benefits for members and their organization.

Norms and Conformity: How Should I Behave Here?

Consider your own behavior in groups. Once you have joined a group and have developed some initial answers to the question, "Do I belong here?" you become more concerned with the question, "How should I behave here?" You start to look for appropriate and accepted ways of expressing yourself, of reacting to others, and of interacting to work toward the group goals. In other words, you start to develop a sense of the *group norms* or standards of behavior that are prescribed and enforced by the group through the use of rewards and sanctions. You are well aware of the usual costs of deviance, such as social rejection and condemnation, and are careful to weigh the consequences of any behavior that does not conform to the group norms.

This brings us to the powerful issue of how conformity limits individual freedom, and of the consequences of pressures toward uniformity in groups.

Muzafer Sherif (1936) initiated the study of group norms in experimental social psychology with a clear demonstration of the effect of group influence on individual judgments. Sherif asked his subjects to judge the degree of movement of a stationary light in a dark room. This phenomenon, known as the autokinetic effect, is a perceptual illusion of movement where none exists. It is an ambiguous situation since individuals vary a great deal in the amount of movement they perceive. In the experiment, subjects estimated the movement of the light in inches under two different conditions: when they were alone and when they shared their judgments in a group. In the group situation, the judgments became dramatically more uniform. In addition, the effect of the group norms that developed carried over to later individual judgments.

The power of conformity was even more strongly demonstrated in classic experiments by Solomon Asch (1956) using a nonambiguous situation. Asch asked his subjects to judge the length of lines, a straightforward task in which individuals almost always agree. Lines of different lengths were drawn on cards and the task was to match the length of the test line to one of three comparison lines on another card. However, in the experiment, most members of the group were actually *confederates* of the experimenter who gave bogus judgments to place conformity pressure on the one or two true subjects. In this situation, a surprising degree of conformity to the erroneous judgments occurred. Approximately 75 percent of the subjects yielded to group pressure once or more on twelve trials, and approximately 25 percent yielded most of the time. Through the use of different experimental situations and interviews with the subjects, Asch concluded that the main reason for conformity was conscious social acceptance in which the subjects decided to give conforming responses. Subsequently, Asch studied a number of other factors affecting conformity. He found, for example, that the group effect tends to level off after there are three or four judgments in opposition to the subject.

Asch's results were surprising because they involved objective physical stimuli. What about the effects of group conformity with more subjective and complex social variables such as attitudes, opinions, and values? Is there even more of a conformity effect? The answer seems to be yes. Research by Crutchfield (1955) and others has demonstrated a clear conformity effect on statements of individual attitudes and opinions. People often say what they think others want to hear.

Laboratory experiments on conformity have been paralleled by field studies of social influence in groups, especially reference groups. A *reference group* is a group of similar others to which an individual refers his or her behavior, attitudes, or other characteristics for purposes of social comparison (Hyman, 1942, 1960; Merton & Kitt, 1950). Kelley (1952) indicates the reference group may serve two functions: (1) a comparison function in which group characteristics serve as a point of comparison for the individual, and (2) a normative function in which the group evaluates the individual in relation to its standards of behavior or attitudes and rewards or punishes the member accordingly.

A classic illustration of the power of reference groups over individual attitudes and behavior is provided by Theodore Newcomb's Bennington College study (1943). Newcomb studied the attitudes of female college students over four years using a variety of measures including attitude scales on political and economic progressivism and interviews with the most conservative and most liberal students. On important social and political issues, the students became more liberal over their 4 years at college. Why? The interpretation was that this was due to the influence of the college reference group—in the college reference group, influential faculty members who held relatively liberal opinions tended to inspire similar group norms. Newcomb also found that the most liberal students tended to be the most popular, that is, were being most rewarded for their conforming behavior. Thus, the results of field studies combine with those of laboratory experiments to demonstrate the pervasive effects that group norms can have on us an individuals.

Obedience to Authority. Obedience to authority is another instance of conformity—one in which the group leader is the prime definer and enforcer of group norms. A dramatic illustration of the power of authority figures is provided by the work of Milgram (1963). Three people were involved in this situation: the experimenter (the authority figure), a confederate who is designated a "learner," and a true subject who is designated by a bogus coin flip to be a "teacher." The teacher was instructed to aid the learner in associating pairs of words and to administer electric shock as negative reinforcement.

The learner, a 50-year-old man, is strapped to a chair with an electrode on his wrist. The teacher is seated in the next room before a shock generator which has thirty switches ranging from 15 to 450 volts, the latter being labeled "Danger— severe shock." The experimenter instructs the teacher to begin with the 15-volt switch and to increase the punishment for each mistake that is made. The learner makes many mistakes. Hence, the instructions dictate that the level of shock should go up very rapidly. As increasing levels of shock are administered, the learner engages in standardized behaviors: at 100 volts he complains; at 150 he demands to be released; at 285 he screams and shouts that he is unable to continue the experiment; after that there is silence. The experimenter says that silence is the same as errors. If the teacher hesitates to administer shock, the experimenter says, "You have no other choice; you must go on!"

In this manufactured yet very real situation, 62 percent of the male subjects between 20 and 50 years of age from various occupational backgrounds went all the way to using the 450-volt switch. They did so with a great deal of tension, but at the same time they exhibited obedience to the authority figure. Milgram subsequently ran a series of experiments under a variety of different conditions to investigate the effect of additional variables. For example, when the teacher had to sit right next to the learner, only 40 percent used the highest level of shock.

This very dramatic illustration raised serious ethical questions about treatment of experimental subjects, and there was an ensuing debate between Milgram and other psychologists as to whether the benefits of demonstrating conformity outweighed the potential costs to the subjects who experienced considerable tension. Milgram maintained that the message to society was more important than the short-term anxiety experienced by the subjects as assessed by follow-up interviews.

Milgram (1965) saw the main factor behind obedience as a denial of personal responsibility which had been transferred to the authority figure:

> With numbing regularity, good people were seen to knuckle under the demands of authority and perform actions that were callous and severe. Men who are in everyday life responsible and decent were seduced by the trappings of authority, by the control of their perceptions, and by the uncritical acceptance of the experimenter's definition of the situation into performing harsh acts. . . .
>
> A substantial proportion of people do what they are told to do, irrespective of the content of the act and without limitations of conscience, so long as they perceive that the command comes from a legitimate authority. If, in this study, an anonymous experimenter could successfully command adults to subdue a 50-year-old man and force on him painful electric shocks against his protests, one can only wonder what government, with its vastly greater authority and prestige, can command of its citizenry. (pp. 261–262)

The answer to Milgram's question has occurred many times, in the Nazi death camps of World War II, in the My Lai massacre of the Vietnam War, and in the slayings of students at Kent State University by the U.S. National Guard. When acting under the auspices of authority, whether real or perceived, there are few limits to humankind's inhumanity.

Diffusion of Responsibility, Deindividuation, and Polarization. The denial of personal responsibility in the Milgram study is an example of a general group phenomenon known as *diffusion of responsibility*—a decrease in the sense of individual responsibility for decisions or actions that are taken in a group setting. Diffusion of responsibility may relate to increases in antisocial behavior and to a lack of prosocial behavior in a wide range of situations from refusing to help in an emergency to the unrestrained violence of an angry mob. A related phenomenon sometimes experienced in groups is *deindividuation*—a state of affairs in which individuals in a group are not seen as individual persons but become submerged and experience a loss of personal identity (Festinger, Pepitone & Newcomb, 1952). Again, this process—especially when combined with anonymity—has been linked to a releasing of negative social behavior such as aggression, theft, and rowdyism. The original Festinger et al. (1952) experiment demonstrated that college males in a deindividuated condition (wearing large grey coats and taking part in a group discussion in a dimly lit room) made significantly more hostile and critical statements about their parents than did subjects in a control condition (wearing usual dress and taking part in a discussion group in a regular classroom).

The work on deindividuation has been extended by Zimbardo (1970) through the combined use of laboratory and field studies. In the lab, Zimbardo created a situation similar to the Milgram experiment in which college females were given the opportunity to administer electric shocks to a young woman in order to empathically judge her reactions. Zimbardo manipulated deindividuation and anonymity by having subjects put on large hoods (similar to those of the Ku Klux Klan), by not using their names, and by carrying out their procedures in the dark. In contrast, the control subjects, who wore their regular clothes, were greeted by name, and given name tags. In a depressing parallel to the Milgram results, all subjects administered shocks on the vast majority of trials even though the victim groaned in misery each time. However, the deindividuated subjects administered shocks of longer duration and were not influenced to reduce their amount of shocking when the victim was identified as a "nice girl" as opposed to an "obnoxious creep." These results clearly indicate the releasing influence of deindividuation and anonymity on hostile and destructive social behavior.

Zimbardo attempted to create a demonstration of deindividuation in the real world by abandoning two cars in radically different urban environments: one in New York City (assumed to be a highly deindividuated and anonymous environment) and the other in Palo Alto, California (assumed to be a relatively responsible and socially viable setting). In New York, the car was almost completely stripped in little more than 24 hours—hubcaps, battery, radiator, the one good tire, a gas can—and all by middle-class whites, often working as a family team. The Palo Alto car was left untouched for a week—except for one passerby who lowered the hood to protect the engine when it started to rain.

Diffusion of responsibility is also one explanation of faulty group decision making. The *risky shift* phenomenon (discussed briefly in Chapter 1) came as a surprise to many social psychologists who had assumed that strong conformity pressures moved groups toward making more conservative decisions than individuals did when acting alone. Even though the early risky shift research has some clear limitations in methodology and external validity, it does raise the distinct possibility that under certain conditions, groups may take riskier and potentially costlier decisions than individuals working alone (for example, Wallach, Kogan &

Bem, 1962, 1964). However, inconsistent results in the risky shift research (see Pruitt, 1971) led to the general interpretation that groups engage in *extremity shifts* which may involve polarization toward risk *or* cautiousness (Cartwright, 1971).

Results now indicate that group discussion may lead to polarization in a number of areas including attitudes (for example, Moscovici & Zavalloni, 1969; Myers & Lamm, 1975), perceptions of others (see Myers, 1976), and simulated jury decisions (see Myers & Kaplan, 1976). Myers (1976) had college students individually read descriptions of three "good" and three "bad" professors, and then rate their attitudes toward the professors and distribute pay raises among them. Then groups of students discussed their allocation of pay increases and repeated the ratings. The result? Following group discussion, there was a polarization of individual opinions in which "good" faculty were rated even more positively and given higher raises, whereas the opinions of "bad" faculty shifted even more in the negative direction.

Groupthink. How might these processes of conformity, deindividuation, and polarization affect national decision making that carries grave consequences for all of us. After analyzing a number of major decisions made by United States presidents and their closest advisors, Irving Janis (1972) coined the term *groupthink*—the process by which a cohesive and insulated group fosters concurrence-seeking to the point where it overrides the realistic appraisal of alternate courses of action. The invasion of Cuba's Bay of Pigs, the escalation of the Vietnam War, the intensification of conflict between the United States and China in the Korean War—all these decisions were partly based on faulty group problem solving!

In groupthink, critical individual judgment and the expression of alternate opinions are stifled by a number of subtle conformity pressures. An illusion of invulnerability reduces caution and enhances risk taking; a fear of disapproval for having divergent views plus group pressure of deviants squashes alternate opinions and minority viewpoints and creates an illusion of unanimity; evidence contrary to the developing decision is denied or rationalized; and the opinions of the leader are protected from criticism. The outcome? Decisions emerge that are neither rational nor moral and are based on the biased consideration of a limited number of alternatives. Some of the simplistic thinking that supports groupthink is documented in Box 7.1.

It may be possible to safeguard ourselves from the specter of groupthink. For example, some members can be assigned a "devil's advocate" role to raise criticism and objections. Outsiders can be brought in to share alternate opinions. Such procedures would work against the destructive processes that stifle both individual creativity and democratic functioning.

A Note on Application. What can applied social psychologists do to improve the effective functioning of groups? We could suggest with tongue in cheek that because of conformity, diffusion of responsibility, groupthink, and so forth, *human beings would do better without groups* (Buys, 1978). Realistically, we can first help document the reality of destructive group processes and increase so-

Box 7.1   FOCUS ON RESEARCH
Policy Statements by Victims of Groupthink

The dangerous phenomenon of groupthink was initially identified by analyzing case studies of national policymaking that appeared to involve poor decision making. However, the evidence on which these analyses were based—memoirs of participants and observer accounts of private conversations—is quite subjective and open to biased interpretation. Social psychologist Philip Tetlock decided to take a different approach to studying the groupthink phenomenon. He applied standardized content analysis procedures to public statements (speeches, congressional records, collected papers) made by key decision makers involved in crises identified as either groupthink or non-groupthink situations:

Groupthink		Non-Groupthink	
Crisis	Decision Makers	Crisis	Decision Makers
Korean War	Harry Truman Dean Acheson	Marshall Plan	Harry Truman George Marshall Dean Acheson
Bay of Pigs	John Kennedy Dean Rusk	Cuban missile crisis	John Kennedy Dean Rusk
Vietnam War	Lyndon Johnson Dean Rusk		

The content analysis focused on two major aspects of groupthink: the processing of information in simplistic and biased ways and the tendency to positively evaluate one's own group while negatively evaluating the opposition. In particular, Tetlock coded the *integrative complexity* of policy statements and used *evaluative assertion analysis* to measure the favorability of attitudes toward ingroups and outgroups.

As predicted, the relevant statements made by key decision makers during groupthink crises were significantly less complex than statements made by decision makers involved in non-groupthink crises. They showed less differentiation of ideas and less integration of thinking relevant to the crisis situation. Secondly, decision makers in groupthink crises evaluated the political group with which they identified (American government, American people, South Korea, South Vietnam) more positively than did decision makers in non-groupthink crises. There was no difference in the evaluations of opposing groups.

Tetlock concludes that the results strongly support the groupthink analysis. This convergence of findings is especially impressive since Tetlock's analysis was based on very different types of data than the original groupthink studies. The need still remains, however, for the content analysis of verbatim records of actual policy deliberations.

Source: Tetlock, P. E. Identifying victims of groupthink from public statements of decision makers. *Journal of Personality and Social Psychology*, 1979, *37*, 1314-1324.

ciety's awareness of them. We can demonstrate how a moderate amount of conformity is necessary to bring about shared understanding, coordination of effort, and commitment to common goals. Then through methods of training (such as sensitivity training described later in this chapter) and consultation (such as organization development described in Chapter 9), we can provide alternate models of group process that arrest destructive elements and enhance cooperative effort toward common goals. By demonstrating that groups, like all social relations, can have good *or* bad effects, we can collaborate with others in developing the exciting potential of democratic group functioning.

Communication in Small Groups: Who Talks to Whom?

Who talks to whom in a group setting involves the study of *communication networks*—the pattern of communication channels available to group members. Investigators have created different communication networks in laboratory groups and have studied the effects of these structures on dependent variables such as satisfaction, efficiency, and perceptions of leadership. Some examples of commonly used networks of five-person groups, adapted from the work of Shaw (1964), are shown in Figure 7.1.

In the *wheel pattern*, only the central person is allowed to communicate with the other members of the group; in the *chain pattern*, members may only communicate with the person adjacent to them, and so on. Only the *comcon* (short for *completely connected*) *pattern* allows totally open communication among all members of the group. Hence, patterns may be constructed to vary in their degree of restrictiveness and centralization of communication. The wheel pattern, for example, is more restricted than the *circle*, and the *Y* is more centralized than the comcon.

Following the methodological lead of Bavelas (1950), researchers have imposed these networks on the group, isolating members in separate cubicles and allowing only certain communication channels to be open. (Channels are created by such mechanisms as slots in the walls or intercoms between given cubicles.) The group members are then assigned a task to perform that requires communication for its completion; upon completion, the dependent variables are assessed.

Some results have been fairly consistent (Shaw, 1981). The person placed in a central position (as at the center of wheel) tends to emerge as the perceived leader of the group: he or she has the most information to complete the task and is in a position to coordinate the activities of the other group members. Satisfaction and

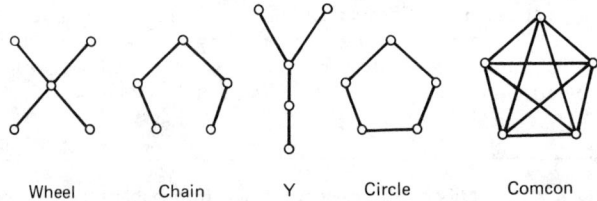

Wheel   Chain   Y   Circle   Comcon

Figure 7.1   Examples of Communication Networks in Five-Person Groups.
Source: Shaw (1964).

morale are greater in decentralized networks than in centralized ones (Leavitt, 1951). Although centralized networks appeared to work better for simple tasks, more complex tasks—such as the solution of mathematical problems (see Shaw, 1954)—are completed more efficiently with decentralized, unrestricted networks.

One interesting aspect of these results is that they run *counter* to the usual assumptions about communication and task efficiency. Real-world groups and organization usually restrict and centralize communication to get the job done (see Chapter 9). In the case of complex tasks, however, this arrangement may be self-defeating. Communication structures such as networks directly affect the process of communication in terms of accuracy and openness, which in turn affects the efficiency of group performance (O'Reilly & Roberts, 1977). The practical implication is for groups to build communication networks that are decentralized and less restricted so that a communication climate of openness and accuracy can lead to effectiveness and satisfaction, especially when the task demands are complex.

Communication networks are not artificial fabrications of the experimental laboratory. Their different forms exist in real-world organizations and have significant effects on morale and performance. Mears (1974) reports on a case study in a business corporation where management tried out a series of different communication networks. Initially, a top management group, consisting of the chief executive and the heads of several divisions (engineering, manufacturing), were organized in a *circle network* with virtually free communication among all members. Although morale was very high, almost no work was accomplished since needless time was spent in discussion and useless debate. The group was therefore reorganized in a *wheel network* with the chief executive at the center. This restriction of communication reduced motivation and produced errors in relaying information, thus damaging both morale *and* performance. Finally, a *modified circle network* was introduced that allowed each member to communicate only with others who were directly involved in the decision at hand. This took pressure off the central person and yet did not waste the time of members who did not need to be consulted. The result? Increased satisfaction and productivity—and a clear message that communication networks are important in real-life situations.

Communication in groups is also affected by members' *spatial position* (where they sit) and *role position* (the position they hold). For example, the chair at the head of the table tends to bring out higher participation from the person sitting there than does a seat at a corner (Hare & Bales, 1963). More reciprocal communication tends to flow between people sitting across from each other. In addition, the status and role positions in groups clearly affects who talks to whom: persons of equal status tend to communicate more with each other; when communication is directed across status differences, at least in experimental groups, it tends to go *upward* (e.g., from subordinate to boss) (see Cohen, 1958); in natural (rather than laboratory) environments, especially within large organizations, communication tends to flow *downward:* bosses tell subordinates what to do and that's that.

An interesting study by Bradley (1978) examined the effects of power and status on upward communication in small decision-making groups. Previous research has shown that messages directed toward high-power, high-status members tend to be cautious, supportive, longer, and more frequent—apparently designed to create a favorable impression with the person who has power—that is, the person who controls the satisfaction of individual needs in the group. Unfortunately, most studies confuse power with status—the amount of desirability and prestige in a given position.

Bradley (1978) sought to separate the effects of power and status on communication. Groups of undergraduates who were very interested in university policy were brought together to discuss grading practices. In the high-power condition, a confederate was introduced as the person who would evaluate members' suitability to serve on a universitywide policy committee. In the low-power condition, the confederate had no control over the selection of committee members. Status was manipulated by identifying the confederate as either a professor (high status) or an undergraduate (low status).

Ratings based on transcripts of the ensuing group discussions showed that messages directed toward high-power figures were longer, more frequent, more reasonable, more intense, and friendlier. Status had almost no effect on communication. Group members communicated with the high-power person in ways designed to present a good impression and maximize beneficial relations—apparently hoping they would be chosen for the committee. Power appears to be a strong influence on upward communication in groups.

The role position of leadership also has a strong effect on communication in groups. More communication is directed toward and received from leaders than among the other group members. This is true for both formal leaders and for leaders who emerge in groups that are initially leaderless. Schultz (1978) found that an analysis of communication functions based on the first session of university student discussion groups was adequate for predicting the emergence of leaders with a high degree of accuracy. Students in an undergraduate class were divided into small groups and asked to choose a topic of common interest, develop a solution, and design a presentation to the class. After the first session, group members rated everyone in the group on nineteen variables relating to personal qualities and contribution to the group (such as, cooperative/uncooperative, gives directions/does not give directions). Five sessions later, the students who were initially seen as most involved in the communication functions of formulating goals and summarizing the discussions emerged as the designated leaders of their group.

In addition to structural and process variables in small-group communication, we must also consider so-called *climate* variables. These refer to Gibb's (1964) distinctions between supportive and defensive climates in interpersonal and group communication (see Chapter 6). Defensive climates are characterized by behaviors such as evaluation, control, and strategizing; supportive climates, by attributes of description, problem orientation, and spontaneity. In short, many of the same barriers (such as suspicion or hostility) that impede interpersonal communication may operate within the group to constrain the openness and accuracy of communication.

Napier and Gershenfeld (1973, 1981) identify a number of these inhibiting factors. Each member of the group has personal needs and goals for survival and integrity that may or may not coincide with the needs and the goals of the group. Strong discrepancies between one's personal objectives and group objectives often result in psychological withdrawal from the group and a lack of communication with other members. For example, the student in a seminar class who is there "just for the credit" will likely contribute little to the discussion. Often group members take a strategizing approach to their participation to project the best possible image. As in interpersonal relations, covert strategies of self-presentation, ingratiation, or manipulation can build barriers to effective communication. Where there is a lack of openness and honesty, there will also be a lack of accurate communication.

The issues of power and control in the group can cloud communication processes. The distribution and use of power in the group partly determine who talks to whom and with what effect. A group dominated by one or two members is not a group engaged in productive communication. Closeness or intimacy also affects the communication climate: if members feel free to risk themselves and to engage in appropriate self-disclosure, then the group will be more likely to develop a supportive climate, in the same way that interpersonal relationships develop through mutual self-disclosure. Unfortunately, past experience leads many members to be pessimistic about the effectiveness of groups, which further inhibits communication. Family conflict, useless meetings, and frustrating class projects lead many to conclude that groups are a waste of time.

Observing Group Communication. The improvement of group communication is as much a challenge to the applied social psychologist as it is to anyone who works every day in a group setting. In human relations training, we are concerned with the ability of the trainer to facilitate communication; we are concerned with the teaching and use of interpersonal communication skills to create effective group communication; and we are concerned with leadership functions for the development of supportive climates in which participants feel free and are helped to communicate openly, accurately, and clearly.

To prepare for our later look at the work of the human relations trainer at the group level, we must first describe and understand group communication patterns and processes through the use of *observational skills* (Dimock, 1970; Morris & Sashkin, 1976). Among a number of well-developed observational techniques, *Interaction Process Analysis* (see Figure 3.3) produces a set of behavioral categories for coding the communication behavior of group members. Observations are coded into twelve different categories in four different areas: (1) positive reactions (shows tension release, jokes, laughs), (2) negative reactions (shows antagonism), (3) task answers (gives opinion), and (4) task questions (asks for suggestion). Using these categories, trained observers are able to code the ongoing behavior of a group interaction and provide a description of the dominant behaviors over time.

A simpler technique uses a communication chart on which is noted who talks to whom during a group session; this is useful for identifying rates of participation and patterns of communication in the group (see Figure 7.2 for an example communication chart). What can we learn from this chart? Since it shows that most communication in a group of five people was directed to Kim, we might

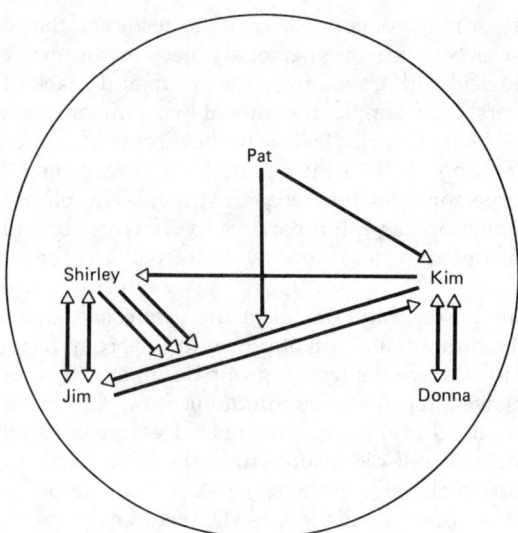

Figure 7.2   Communication Chart for a Five-Person Group.

suspect that Kim is emerging as a leader. The largest amount of interpersonal communication is between Shirley and Jim, whereas no messages were directed toward Pat, who seems to be isolated. In addition, Shirley addressed the group as a whole on three occasions, while Pat did so once.

The utility of such observations is this: once we have a picture of the communication process occurring in a group, *we are in an informed position to intervene* as a leader or a member in order to improve both the quantity and the quality of communication. Just when and how we do this depends on many considerations and requires a great deal of skill; however, without a fundamental understanding of communication processes in general as well as an understanding of the pattern emerging in a particular group, we would have little chance of success. When we can improve communication, the group will more effectively integrate the individual resource of its members, will make better decisions, and will more adequately reach its goals. Communication, after all, lies at the very heart of group process and effective group functioning (Shaw, 1964, 1981).

Group Structure and Leadership

Communication networks are one form of *group structure* that lends stability to group interaction in the same way that beams and girders give physical structure and stability to a skyscraper. Without a minimal degree of structure, groups fall apart just like an old building whose superstructure is blasted away by dynamite. But *social* structure takes on many different forms that affect the behavior of group members in a variety of ways, varying in their degree of formality.

Group norms, or standards of behavior, bring continuity to the ways members relate to each other and to the outside world. (Inmates in a prison develop their own ways of interacting, including language—*square John, fink,* and so forth—and behave with standardized suspicion and derision toward guards and other authority figures.)

Positions and roles—visible aspects of group structure—may be assigned to or spontaneously taken by different members. (The captain of an airplane is expected to behave in certain ways, to fulfill certain obligations, and to exercise power in ways that meet the crew members' expectations.)

Status hierarchies develop within the group, either formally assigned through role definitions (professor, teaching assistant, student) or developed informally as a result of continuing interaction. (Friendship groups almost always develop a "pecking order" in which one person is seen as the leader, other members as central to the group, and others as hangers-on.)

The *distribution of power* or the ability to influence can become stabilized into a relatively constant pattern, thus adding another element to the social structure of the group. (Power in friendship groups usually relates to status, the leader or leaders having most of the influence on the group and the fringe members having the least.) To understand and improve group functioning, we must be aware of all these aspects of structure.

Why do groups develop structure?

- Structure reduces individual uncertainty and anxiety by providing rules and standardized ways of doing things.
- Effective group performance usually requires the specialization of roles that are then clearly coordinated for purposes of communication, responsibility, and authority.
- The group members' differing abilities and motivations lead to the enactment of different roles in a stable and secure fashion.
- The group environment—such as the amount of space available or the size of the group—helps determine the amount and form of necessary structure (Cartwright & Zander, 1968).

Leadership. Among all aspects of group structure, however, the element of *leadership* is central to its development and to the continuing effectiveness of the group. In a wide range of definitions, leadership has been seen as an expression of individual personality, as the exercise of influence, as an instrument of goal achievement, and as linked to the initiation of structure (Stogdill, 1974). A similarly wide variety of theories of leadership seek to explain both its emergence and nature. These theories fall into one of three general approaches: the individual, the environmental, and the interactional.

The *individual approach,* often referred to as the "great man" theory, links leadership to superior personal traits—the "typical" personality attributes of leaders. This approach, however, has had little success: No particular pattern of personality traits consistently identifies leaders, and although all leaders require certain minimal abilities, these appear to be well distributed among *non*leaders as well (Cartwright & Zander, 1968).

The *environmental approach* suggests that the time, place, and circumstances of particular events present opportunities for a leader to emerge. However, the appeal of this idea—that the forces of history sweep along certain individuals who happened to be in the right place at the right time—falls short of the current strength of the *interactional approach*. According to this approach, the qualities and skills of the individual *combine* with the demands of the situation to determine the emergence and the effectiveness of leadership.

The importance of *leadership style* was illustrated four decades ago when Kurt Lewin and his associates studied the effects of three different styles of leadership on the behavior of boys' play groups (Lewin, Lippitt & White, 1939). The "autocratic" leader directed and scrutinized the work of the boys and remained socially distant; the "democratic" leader facilitated interaction and decision making among the boys; and the "laissez-faire" leader allowed the boys to carry out the task, offering assistance only when it was requested.

The results were dramatic. Boys under the laissez-faire leader produced little and exhibited low group responsibility and morale. Boys under the autocratic and democratic leaders demonstrated effective task performance (the autocratic being somewhat superior), but the democratic condition produced a greater degree of involvement, responsibility, and friendly cooperation. By contrast, the autocratic group was dependent upon the leader, less cooperative, and exhibited hostility by behaving aggressively toward lower status members of the group. Following this classic demonstration, theory and research on leadership has tended to concentrate on the autocratic-versus-democratic styles of leadership, labeling them in a variety of ways: task-oriented versus social-emotional, structured versus considerate, controlling versus participative, and so on.

The search for the effective elements of leadership has increasingly focused on the actual behavior of the group leader. Based on his pioneering work on Interaction Process Analysis, Bales (1950) and his associates (Bales & Slater, 1955; Bales, 1970) identified the common emergence of two kinds of leaders within a group: a *task leader* and a *social-emotional leader*. The task leader tends to give opinions and ask for suggestions; the social-emotional leader stresses activities such as showing tension release (laughs, jokes) and agreeing with other opinions and suggestions. The task leader pushes to get the job done, sometimes offending other members; the social-emotional leader works to keep the group together by supporting members and by smoothing over conflict, thus usually becoming the best-liked member of the group.

Bales's observation that these two basic functions are rarely carried out by the same person may be due in part to his experimental model: an initially leaderless discussion group in which the emergence of a hard task master needs to be countered by someone concerned with the group's personal and social needs. Other leadership studies, by contrast, have relied on examining the behavior of a single leader designated by the organization as supervisor, manager, and so on.

A long series of studies initiated at Ohio State University in the 1940s focused on leadership behavior. This was measured by questionnaires completed by subordinates and superiors of leaders in education, industry, and the military. Two basic factors of leadership behavior emerged: initiation of structure and consideration for others (Stogdill & Coons, 1957). Leaders high in both factors tend to be more effective in the group situation, both in areas of task efficiency and achievement and in such social process variables as cohesiveness and morale (Stogdill, 1974). To understand and implement successful group leadership, however, we must break down these two factors into more specific functions.

Among a number of detailed systems for categorizing leadership functions is the classic description of *functional roles* (Benne & Sheats, 1948) developed in conjunction with the first National Training Laboratory in Group Development. Underwood's (1977) detailed version appears in Table 7.1.

Leadership functions are behaviors that are essential if the group is to perform in an effective and satisfying manner. The *task functions* are required to facilitate and coordinate group effort in the selection, definition, and solution of the problem confronting the group. However, this can be accomplished only if people work together effectively. Therefore, the *maintenance functions* are designed to build a supportive climate of communication and to productively resolve conflicts. Individual needs for recognition, acceptance, and security must be taken into account; but when their strong expression interferes with group functioning, the behavior is categorized as *hindering functions*. Task and maintenance functions are not necessarily mutually exclusive; in actual practice, many of the functions blend together.

One crucial and enlightening element of the functional approach is that these leadership behaviors can be carried out by *any* member of the group. In this sense, we would regard them more broadly as group rather than leadership functions. Of course, certain factors influence how widely the functions are distributed in the group—the skill level of the designated leader, for example, and the attitudes of the members towards sharing the functions (Cartwright & Zander, 1968). Nonetheless, the functional approach to leadership has been successfully generalized to provide useful techniques for both leaders and members to increase group participation and productivity (Bertcher, 1979).

The idea of leadership functions is implicitly an interaction theory in that the required functions depend upon the specific group situation. However, a much more explicit interaction theory of leadership has been developed by Fred Fiedler and his associates (Fiedler, 1967).

Fiedler's *contingency model of leadership* emphasizes that the success of a particular leadership style is contingent upon characteristics of the group situation. Leadership style is assessed by the leader's favorableness of attitude toward his or her "least preferred co-worker" (LPC), taking into account all the people that the leader has worked with past and present. The resulting LPC score differentiates participative, democratic leaders from controlling, task-oriented ones: a leader high on LPC (who sees the least preferred co-worker as more pleasant, cooperative, efficient) tends to show greater consideration toward group members; a low LPC leader (who sees the least preferred co-worker as unfriendly, hostile, unenthusiastic) is more concerned with successful performance of the group task.

The effectiveness of leaders who differ on the LPC measure depends on at least three important characteristics of the situation: (1) leader-member relations, the degree to which the leader is liked and respected by the group members; (2) task structure, the degree to which the group's activities are structured on the dimensions of goal clarity, decision verifiability, goal path multiplicity, and solution specificity; and (3) the leader's position power, the degree of authority the leader has to reward and punish group members. Each of these situational variables can be present in positive or negative ways and different combinations of the three thus yield situations that vary from favorable to unfavorable for the

Table 7.1   LEADERSHIP FUNCTIONS IN THE SMALL GROUP

Inhibitive	Task Functions	Inhibitive
	Facilitative	
	Initiating New Ideas	
Not initiating ideas when needed.	Suggesting or proposing new things to do or changes in doing something.	Initiating ideas or changes when not needed.
	Seeking Information	
Allowing issue to bog down when new information is needed.	Asking for clarification of additional facts.	Seeking information when enough is already present.
	Seeking Opinions	
Not asking others for opinions when they might be helpful.	Asking not for facts but for the opinions or values pertinent to issues.	Seeking opinions when facts are relevant.
	Giving Information	
Withholding information when it is needed.	Offering facts or generalizations about issues or relating own pertinent experience.	Clouding the issue by supplying more information than is needed.
	Elaborating	
Withholding sufficient elaboration.	Developing clearer or additional meaning or providing reasons or deductions.	Providing elaboration when issue is already clear.
	Coordinating	
Not providing coordination when needed.	Showing relationships between ideas and events. Pulling ideas, suggestions and activities together.	Forcing relationships between ideas or events.
	Orienting	
Failing to supply needed orientation.	Defining the position of a goal with respect to its start and goal. Showing deviation from appropriate direction.	Orienting that is overdeterminative and restrictive.
	Evaluating	
Too little or no evaluating.	Supplying standards of accomplishment and subjecting group progress to measure.	Too much or unrealistic evaluating.
	Stimulating	
Accepting lethargy or apathy.	Prodding the group to greater on-target action. Arousing greater or higher quality activity.	Overstimulation resulting in nonproductive activity.

Table 7.1   (Continued)

Maintenance Functions

Inhibitive	Facilitative	Inhibitive
	Encouraging	
Failing to encourage others, or deflating them.	Commending, complimenting, supporting the contributions of others. Indicating understanding, interests, and acceptance of others.	Shallow encouraging.
	Harmonizing	
Not acting to reduce stifling conflict.	Mediating differences between *others*. Endeavoring to reconcile disagreements.	Preventing needed conflict from occurring or surfacing.
	Compromising	
Refusing to yield or give in.	Yielding own position, admitting error, or "coming half way" when involved in disagreement or conflict.	Yielding too soon or too far.
	Opening Communication	
Undertalking or not trying to encourage or control others.	Keeping channels open. Assuring that those who want to contribute feel comfortable to do so. Limiting overtalkative members, soliciting information from nontalkative members.	Overtalking or overcontrolling others.
	Evaluating Process	
Inattentiveness to or ignoring process problems.	Calling attention to group needs. Offering observation about group functioning problems. Encourages members to work on process needs.	Overfocusing on process, or creating pseudo issues.
	Accepting	
Too little accepting and interested listening.	Going along with group movement. Serving as interested audience.	Being too passive and not contributing.

Table 7.1   (Continued)

Facilitative	Hindering Functions	
	Inhibitive	*Facilitative*
	Aggressing	
Withholding aggressive behavior.	Deflating others. Expressing disapproval of ideas, opinions, feelings of others. Degrading members or group.	Expressing aggression in a constructive way.
	Blocking	
Withholding blocking behavior.	Being negativistic, stubbornly resistant. Maintaining or returning issues which the group has rejected. Disagreeing or opposing beyond reason. Being caustic, cynical.	Admitting blocking tendencies and asking to help deal with these tendencies.
	Dominating	
Withholding dominating behavior.	Trying to exert authority in manipulating the group or certain members. Using flattery, directing, demanding.	Channeling dominating tendencies into constructive help for the group.
	Seeking Recognition	
Shifting recognition to others.	Maintaining a central position or the center of attention. Over-talking, being boastful, or seemingly humble.	Entering central position for specific purpose; then leaving it.
	Playing	
Inhibiting low involvement behavior cues.	Maintaining and displaying lack of involvement. Using nonchalance, joking, raising off-target or mundane issues.	Using levity to relieve tension for constructive purposes.
	Pleading Special Interests	
Resisting pleading special interests when not constructive to the group.	Using the group to satisfy personal interests only. Standing on stereotypic principles to detriment of group.	Expressing only those personal interests which are helpful to the group.
	Sympathizing	
Withholding expression of self-pity.	Endeavoring to elicit sympathy responses from whole group or certain members. Depreciating self beyond reason. Self-pitying.	Honestly expressing feelings when useful to the group.

Source: Underwood (1977).

leader. For example, good leader-member relations, a structured task, and strong leader power yields a very favorable situation, whereas poor relations, an unstructured task, and weak power results in very unfavorable conditions.

Fieldler's analysis of hundreds of studies of leadership (including the past work of others plus his own research directly using the measures described here) indicates that *low LPC leaders tend to be more effective in either very unfavorable or very favorable situations, whereas high LPC leaders produce better outcomes under mixed conditions.* Consider, for example, John, the highly talented captain of his high school basketball team, but who has little concern for social relations and regards many of his team members as lacking enthusiasm (low LPC). However, the team situation is a very favorable one: the team members admire John because of his superior athletic ability; the task is straightforward, and the coach handles all the technical instruction; and John's approval is actively sought since he chooses the player of the week. Thus, John is a successful leader under these conditions: the team plays well and members meet their social-emotional needs through interaction with each other. In contrast, consider the situation that Brenda is in as chairperson of a chapter of the League of Women Voters: there are good leader-member relations, but the task of organizing people for political involvement is complex and difficult and Brenda has little power to reward members for their voluntary contributions. However, Brenda shows much consideration for members and works very well with them, thus overcoming the difficult characteristics of the situation to lead a very successful group.

Although Fiedler's results do not consistently show strong support for his theory and it has been criticized on a variety of grounds, the contingency model is an appealing attempt to develop a truly interactive approach to leadership effectiveness (Saha, 1979). Productive leadership style depends on the characteristics of the situation, and no one style is the ultimate answer to good leadership.

What are the practical implications of all this?

- How we behave in a group, as a member or leader, can significantly affect group satisfaction and productivity.
- The use of leadership models can increase our sensitivity to what is required in a group at a given time.
- Leaders can often be distinguished by the communication functions they perform (see Shultz, 1974), and studies of actual task groups continue to show the existence and the importance of both instrumental and social-emotional leadership behavior for group productivity and satisfaction (see Simmons, 1972).
- Leadership skills can be improved through human relations and small-group training programs, using various models of effective leadership.

The functional approach to leadership has been used extensively in training programs. The contingency model initially emphasized improving leadership effectiveness through organizational engineering—by changing the leader's position power, the degree of task structure, or the leader-member relations through assigning particular members and leaders to certain tasks. Fiedler and his colleagues (Fiedler, Chemers & Mahar, 1976) have now moved toward developing a training program for leaders based on the contingency model (see Box 7.2). The successful training of leadership behavior augurs well for the continued successful application of group dynamics to real-world problems (Fiedler & Mahar, 1979).

Box 7.2   FOCUS ON PRACTICE

The Contingency Model and Leader Match Training

Using the contingency model of leadership as a base, social psychologists Fred Fiedler, Martin Chemers, and Linda Mahar have developed a self-instructional program for improving leadership effectiveness. The "leader match" approach is designed to match the individual's leadership style with the degree of situational control—the influence the leader has over the group, the task, and the outcome.

Participants in leader match training follow a systematic procedure of learning basic concepts and using them to analyze their own leadership situation. The first step is for the participant to identify his or her own leadership style. This is done by completing the Least Preferred Co-worker (LPC) Scale, which distinguishes task-motivated (low-LPC) leaders from relationship-motivated (high-LPC) leaders. It is immediately pointed out that neither type of leader is effective in all situations. Questions and answers are then provided to be sure that the trainee accurately understands the key concepts.

The second step is to identify the participant's leadership situation. Separate self-report rating scales are used to assess the three elements of situational control: (1) leader-member relations, (2) task structure, and (3) position power. At each point, conceptual background is presented and quizzes help assess the participant's level of understanding before proceeding. Scores from the three scales are then combined to yield an overall situational control score that is categorized as low, moderate, or high. In the low-control situation, the group does not support the leader, and both the task and position limit the leader's influence. In the moderate situation, a mixed set of conditions exists, for example, poor relations but a structured task and high position power. The high-control situation is characterized by good relations, a structured task, and high position power.

The final step of the program is for participants to match their leadership style to their situation. In essence, task-motivated (low-LPC) leaders perform best in situations of either low or high control, whereas relationship-motivated (high-LPC) leaders perform most effectively in situations of moderate control. Following this analysis, trainees are presented with a variety of strategies for modifying their leadership situation in order to develop a more effective match. For example, leader-member relations can be improved by increased communication and socializing with subordinates; more task structure is added by preparing a detailed plan for the job; position power can be raised by making sure that information to your group is channeled through you. If used for continuous monitoring and adjustment of one's situation, leader match training provides an opportunity for improved leader effectiveness and satisfaction. It also points to areas where further training or new behaviors might be more productive.

Source: Fiedler, F. E., Chemers, M. M. & Mahar, L. *Improving leadership effectiveness: The leader match concept.* (Rev. ed.). New York: Wiley, 1977.

Group Decision Making and Problem Solving

In November 1978, over nine hundred members of the People's Temple sect led by Reverend Jim Jones committed mass suicide in a remote settlement in Guyana. The members killed themselves by drinking a mixture of potassium cyanide and a flavored drink. The sect, comprised mainly of Americans, had moved from San Francisco with the goal of establishing an independent agricultural colony in the jungles of South America. The mass suicide was apparently related to the murder by sect members of a United States congressman and other members of his party who had visited the settlement to determine whether any of the members were being mistreated and held against their will. The majority of sect members went willingly to their deaths, apparently confident that their leader and the group were doing the right thing. Reports indicated that at least one woman balked, but was shouted into compliance by other members.

One haunting question raised by this horrendous tragedy is: How many members would have freely made the decision to kill themselves if they had been allowed to decide alone instead of in the face of the powerful group forces of deindividuation, diffusion of responsibility, obedience, and conformity?

Beneath the horror of this extreme example, however, is a fundamental question that relates to our daily lives and everyday situations: Is it the group or the solitary individual who can make the better decision and solve problems more effectively? The answer, which favors neither one side nor the other, depends on a number of factors; the demands and constraints of each situation must be weighed in order to make a judgment.

Individual versus Group Problem Solving. The question of whether individuals or groups are more task-effective has been studied with various activities including judgment tasks, learning situations, and problem solving (Shaw, 1981). Decision making, which involves the process of choosing between two or more alternatives, is an important component of problem solving. On experimental tasks involving simple judgments—the temperature in a room, the rank order of weights, the number of beans in a bottle—group estimates are often superior to the average individual estimate. However, group performance is usually less accurate than the *best* individual judgment. Learning in groups has been found to be faster and more effective on a number of tasks such as algebra solutions, maze learning, the acquisition of nonsense syllables, and the recall of stories. Similarly, problem solving by groups often demonstrates superiority over individual performance, although this depends on a number of factors including the past experience of the members, the kind of task, and the measure of effectiveness.

Kelley and Thibaut (1969) conclude that: (1) groups perform below the level of the most competent member when the task is quite complex and the group cannot agree on which tact to take; (2) groups are about the same as the best individual when confronted with an insight problem where the "aha" solution discovered by one member is obviously correct; and (3) groups perform better than individuals when success requires a combination of complementary abilities and solutions. These results are mainly based on time of solution and numbers of solutions and do not take into account the *larger total investment* of "person-time" in the group. If the measure of effectiveness is "person-hours" required for solution, then individual problem solving is usually better than group problem solving (Shaw, 1981).

Most studies of group problem solving involve groups of strangers who are thrown together in a laboratory setting and asked to solve a problem. According to Napier and Gershenfeld (1981), virtually no research exists that compares the effectiveness of *trained and practiced groups* with the performance of individuals or in which individuals work independently and then pool their contributions. When individuals are trained in group skills, their increased effectiveness is evident in group problem-solving situations (for example, Hall & Williams, 1970).

Effective Group Problem Solving. Since a great deal of problem solving behavior takes place in group settings—the family, the work group, the sports team—the important question is not whether individuals or groups are more effective, but how can we maximize the potential of group problem solving?

The practical study of group decision making in social psychology was initiated by Kurt Lewin (1947) in studies that compared the lecture method, group discussion, and individual instruction in terms of their effect on changing food habits. Results indicated that when housewives participated in a group discussion and made an individual decision in the group, they were much more likely to change their food habits than if they heard a lecture on the subject or received individual instruction or advice. The effects underlying these results were studied in later replications by Pelz (1958) who found that the *process* of making a decision and the degree of group *consensus* were more important than group discussion by itself or the public commitment. The implication is to find ways of improving the decision-making process in groups in line with humanistic values.

Based on a wide range of theory, research, and practice, Maier (1967) maintains that when the potential for group problem solving is exploited and the deficiencies are avoided, groups can attain a level of proficiency much greater than individuals. Groups usually have a number of *assets*—greater knowledge, greater number of approaches to the problem, greater acceptance of the solution through participation and support, better comprehension of the decision. However, several deficiencies of group interaction may become *liabilities:* social pressure may silence important disagreements, premature acceptance of the first adequate solution may limit discussion of alternative solutions, domination of the solution by one individual may inhibit others, arguing strongly for one solution may induce win-lose dynamics, which lower the quality of the overall outcome.

The crucial factor in maximizing the assets and minimizing the liabilities is the implementation of a leadership style that provides organization and integration (Maier, 1967). Disagreements must be handled in ways that foster innovation and acceptance rather than negative feelings and "digging in." Discussion must be organized to allow adequate problem exploration and to follow a systematic problem-solving procedure (see Chapter 4). Time must be used wisely so that the group neither moves too fast toward inadequate solutions nor moves so slow that boredom and "fatigue solutions" result. Minority positions must be understood and respected so that they may contribute to the overall quality rather than being lost in a wave of conformity. The role of the well-trained leader (as well as all members of the group) should be to facilitate the process of problem solving rather than engaging in competitive and aggressive behaviors designed to "sell" a particular solution. When the problem-solving approach can be implemented, it will likely prove superior in effectiveness in comparison to other methods of group decision making (for example, Miner, 1979).

Improving problem solving is no easy task as pointed out by Napier and Gershenfeld (1981):

> The fact is that a democratic group in the real sense of the word requires enormous patience, understanding, and cooperation. It also is very time-consuming. Few groups are willing to face these realities and thus reduce the process to one of convenience rather than effectiveness. (p. 407)

The use of group discussion methods is a difficult and delicate matter. However, under appropriate conditions, with good use of process skills, and with an eye to humanistic values and ethical conduct, groups can be highly effective and satisfying forums for problem solving. This requires a set of ideal conditions for putting the problem-solving sequence into action which include the following:

- The goals of the group are clearly understood by the participants. . . .
- Member roles are differentiated according to group needs and specific skills.
- Problems are stated as conditions and explored in terms of the factors causing the particular condition to exist.
- Communication channels are kept open by using process observers and making efforts to look at both the task and emotional dimensions of the group's work together. . . .
- The group is held accountable for its own decisions. (Napier & Gershenfeld, 1973, pp. 217-218)

These general prescriptions can improve the productivity of groups. However, we should not allow them to oversimplify our thinking about how individual characteristics *interact* with group variables in subtle and complex ways to determine effectiveness. Box 7.3 provides an example of how member variables interact with group structure to co-determine ultimate productivity.

Group Development: How Far Have We Come?

Running like a lifeline through the murky waters of group dynamics is the theme of *group development*. All the important processes and questions of group functioning revolve around the process of group development and, by extension, around this question: how far have we come in developing an effective and satisfying social unit?

Most of the numerous theories of group development—covering all types of groups from the work group to the therapy group to the experiential learning group (for example, Bennis & Shepard, 1956; Bion, 1961; Bradford, 1978; Tuckman, 1965)—can be grouped into one or three major types (Shambaugh, 1978):

1. A *sequential phase model*, in which group development proceeds through a series of developmental phases, each of which involves central concerns that require resolution before the group can move to the next phase (for example, a group of new sorority members must get to know one another's interests before they can decide how to spend their leisure time).
2. A *recurring phase model*, in which the group moves through a series of stages and then recycles through these stages dealing with many of the same concerns

but in a more intense fashion each time (each time the sorority members experience conflict over how to spend their leisure time, the disagreement may be more severe).

3. *A changing leadership model*, in which initial dependence and hostility toward the leader is replaced by the growing individuality of members and the centrality of the group's culture as the main point of reference (the new sorority members initially look mainly to their executive for direction, and after experiencing some frustration, will develop some shared initiative).

Shambaugh (1978) produces a synthesis of the major approaches by focusing on the crucial dimensions of closeness and culture as expressed in a series of group structures and phases.

A recurring phase model, developed by Napier and Gershenfeld (1981), draws on a collection of theories. By supplementing this work with ideas drawn from other sources, we can develop a composite picture of the process of group development.

Phase One: The Beginning. People who enter a new group situation are typically anxious and tentative. They ask themselves, "Will I be accepted here? What are the norms here?" They are searching for what is expected of them and what is appropriate. To dispel confusion and anxiety, they need to make sense of the

Box 7.3   FOCUS ON RESEARCH
Interaction between Member Motivation and Group Structure in Determining Productivity

To predict group performance, it is important to know something about the characteristics of the members as well as the group. John Wilson of Cleveland State University and Joel Aronoff and Lawrence Messé of Michigan State University were particularly interested in exploring the relationship between member motivation and social structure in determining group productivity. Their approach contrasts with many studies of group performance that assume equal motivation on the part of all members.

Specifically, the investigators were interested in the safety needs and the esteem needs described by Abraham Maslow. They hypothesized that members with a high need for safety would be most congruent with a hierarchical group structure that reduced uncertainty, risk, and responsibility, and increased direction. Conversely, members with a high need for esteem would be most compatible with an egalitarian group structure that offered the opportunity for creative input and displays of competence. The greater the congruence between dominant need and group structure, the greater the productivity should be.

Through an assessment of needs, thirty-six college students high on safety (and low on esteem) and thirty-six subjects high on esteem (and low on safety) were selected. Three-person homogenous groups of high-safety or high-esteem individuals were then asked to construct a model building out of toy blocks. Half the groups had a hierarchical structure (one member was designated as the leader), while the other half had an egalitarian structure (all members were asked to share the leader role equally). Group productivity was measured by the total number of blocks actually used within the one-hour time limit.

The dramatic results are shown below. Neither motive nor structure alone generally affected productivity—only the interaction did. Esteem-oriented groups performed well under egalitarian structure, but poorly with a hierarchical structure. Conversely, safety-oriented groups performed poorly with an egalitarian structure, but well under hierarchical structure.

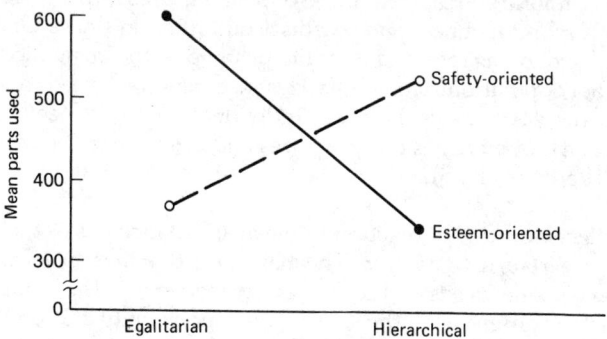

Imposed Social Structure

The findings clearly indicated that group productivity is enhanced in situations where individual motives are congruent with the social structure. This suggests that a comprehensive interactive approach may be necessary to develop adequate theories of group functioning.

Source: Wilson, J. P., Aronoff, J. & Messé, L. A. Social structure, member motivation, and group productivity. *Journal of Personality and Social Psychology*, 1975, *32*, 1094–1098.

situation and develop meaning out of uncertainty. Most important, however, each person needs assurance of acceptance and recognition (Bradford, 1978). Thus, the overriding interpersonal need and the crucial issue facing the group in the first phase is that of *inclusion* (Shutz, 1958, 1967). At this point, members are highly motivated to gain a sense of belonging and recognition within the group. Once these assurances are forthcoming, the group is ready to move to the next phase.

Phase Two: Movement toward Confrontation. In the second phase of group development, there is movement from "being nice" to asking for what you want, both for oneself and for the group. Thus, questions of social influence become paramount, and members ask questions such as "How do I get what I want? How do we make decisions here?" Leadership, power, and conformity now become crucial issues to the functioning of the group. Each group member is asserting his or her need for *control*—the major issue that must be worked out in the group at this stage (Shutz, 1967).

At this point, members attempt to make the group safer: some do this by attempting to take over the group; others try to block problem solving, thinking that it is safer to do nothing than something. As a result, confrontation among members or withdrawal of members become common behaviors. Having confronted the issue of power and control for the first time, the group is now likely to back off from these issues.

Phase Three: Compromise and Harmony. Assuming that the power and conformity issues are temporarily resolved, the group now moves into a period of relative calm. There is more openness and self-disclosure than in Phase One, but at the same time the group has returned to polite behavior—to "being nice." There is a high degree of cooperation that emphasizes meeting group needs and goals, and consequently there is some denial of the individual's personal needs, particularly for control. The group creates the structures and procedures necessary to get the work done (Bradford, 1978).

Phase Four: Reassessment. In reaction to the artificial niceness of the third phase, Phase Four is a return to reality. The harmony that has been established is confronted as personal needs and control issues reemerge in the group. The group works to reach a consensus on the sharing of responsibility and on the degree of intimacy. In Shutz's terms, the individuals and the group are grappling with the issue of *affection:* Members are asking, "How interdependent and close are we going to be here?" The important development step for the group to take is to reach a balance between the personal needs of the members and the task and social maintenance needs of the group.

Phase Five: Resolution and Recycling. The final phase of group development is that of *mature functioning.* The group can collaborate well, yet does not suppress important conflict among group members or between personal needs and group needs. At this point, the group recycles through the earlier phases whenever it confronts a crisis. The processes of inclusion, control, and affection also recycle, but they do so in a spiral fashion so that with each resolution of a major issue the group moves to a higher level of belongingness, collaboration, and intimacy. Maturity in group development is characterized not by a lack of problems but by the open and skillful fashion in which problems are handled. Again, the carrying out of leadership functions is one hallmark of a well-functioning group.

This composite model is applicable to a wide variety of groups, most passing through a similar recurring sequence of development. Of course, the expression and duration of the phases will vary. For example, Shaw (1981) compares the phases of problem solving in discussion groups as developed by Bales and Strodtbeck (1951) with the phase theory of Bennis and Shepard (1956), based primarily on sensitivity training groups. In both situations, the members must first orient themselves and organize the available information so that they can deal affectively with the problem at hand. In a problem-solving group with a clearer task, orientation happens much faster, and the processes of evaluation and control have a much different content than in the ambiguous environment of the sensitivity training group, which struggles toward interpersonal and group clarity. For example, in a student committee set up to plan social events, each member understands his or her role and the chairperson provides the obvious leadership functions of setting the agenda, calling the meeting to order, and so forth. The issue of control will likely come up in arguments about what events—concerts, dances, socials—should be given priority. In a sensitivity group, the trainer refuses to play the role of task leader and members struggle to make sense of the situation. Control issues are likely to arise as members in conflict share negative feelings and feedback directly with each other.

Group development is affected by factors other than the nature of the task: the type of membership, the degree of initial structure, the behavior and style of the leader, and the constraints of the external environment. Regardless of setting, however, the members of the group have the potential to determine the level of group development through increased knowledge and improved skills. Avoiding the inhibiting and limiting factors of group functioning described earlier, the effectively functioning group makes clear and direct attempts to limit the effect of destructive processes such as diffusion of responsibility, conformity, anonymity, and blind obedience to authority.

Such a group would exhibit most of the following characteristics (Napier & Gershenfeld, 1973):

- a shared sense of purpose and a strong feeling of involvement among the members
- open and accurate communication, using basic communication skills and leadership functions
- roles and tasks appropriate to the members' interests and the skills
- an acceptance and respect for individual differences, made possible through core interpersonal skills with an understanding of individual accountability and responsibility
- effective leadership, appropriately shared
- effective decision making and problem solving
- the ability to diagnose problems that minimize group effectiveness, and the skills both to learn from the diagnosis and to productively handle conflict and change

How realistic is this picture of a mature, functioning group? It is realistic, yet difficult to attain in practice—so rare, in fact, that we might think of such groups as a constantly "endangered species." One of the goals of human relations training and its applications is to see that such effectively functioning groups become the rule rather than the exception in everyday life.

EXPERIENTIAL LEARNING IN GROUPS

Almost all human relations training takes place in small groups. Such settings enhance and support experiential learning, permitting members to learn about human relations in a climate of unparalleled openness and support. Thus, the individual learner has the opportunity to experiment with new behaviors, to practice new skills, and to receive accurate and respectful feedback on the effects of his or her behavior. A successful learning group, like a mature working group, is a rare and exciting experience that unfolds out of the mutual caring and shared competence of the individual participants and the leader.

However, human relations training is only one form of experiential learning in groups. What follows is an overview of these various forms, followed by a focus on the approach perhaps most compatible with the general rationale and goals of applied social psychology—that of sensitivity training. By examining sensitivity training in detail, including the role of the trainer, the research on benefits and risks, and the areas of application, we will gain a general sense of the major aspects of experiential learning in groups.

Types of Experiential Learning in Groups

Mary is a very capable and ambitious woman in her early thirties. She has recently been promoted to a responsible supervisory position in a human service organization. However, Mary is experiencing increasing frustration in her work with her team of subordinates. She is unable to understand why she seems to "turn off" the people who work for her; they do not take the initiative that she would like to see. Mary is therefore looking for more effective ways of working with other people.

Helen, a graduate student in her mid-twenties, spends considerable time puzzling over her identity and her relationship to society. She has a sense of alienation from society, finding much of it trivial and artificial. She finds most relationships too superficial to be worthwhile. Although she has few close friends, those friendships are very satisfying. Helen appears to be searching for meaningful contact with other people and for the meaning of her existence.

Mark is a university student in his early twenties. He exhibits highly anxious behavior in most social situations and appears to have very low self-esteem. Over the past few years, he has entered into psychotherapy on more than one occasion, but he has not experienced the understanding and changes that he is searching for within himself. From time to time, he has taken medication to moderate his level of anxiety. The most central question in Mark's life is why he behaves the way he does. His existence is characterized by a continual struggle to understand himself and cope with the demands of living.

The descriptions of Mary, Helen, and Mark direct us to these questions: Should all people who are struggling with some difficulty in their lives enter into an experiential learning group? If so, what type of group should they enter? Would it make sense for Mary, Helen, and Mark to seek out the same type of experiential learning in a group setting?

Even from the brief description of each potential group participant, it is clear that each is in a different psychological state and different social-psychological situation, that each has different competencies and learning goals. Thus, it would be inappropriate and even dangerous for them to enter into a learning situation that is incompatible with their abilities and motives. Each requires a unique and appropriate type of group experience.

The experiential learning group most appropriate for Mary is the *training or educational group*. It is designed for participants who are moderately well-adjusted and who function in generally effective ways in their living and working situations. The goal of training groups is to increase the awareness that participants have of themselves and other people, to allow people to observe and practice interpersonal skills that improve communication and enhance conflict resolution, and to gain sensitivity into the functioning of the group as a whole. Thus, training or educational groups typically take an interpersonal and a group focus, using a variety of methods that vary a great deal in the amount of structure imposed upon participants. The group may follow a series of written and behavioral exercises, or simply engage in free interaction with appropriate interventions by the leader. The role of the leader or trainer is that of a facilitator who improves communication, helps resolve interpersonal conflicts, and focuses on the important group forces that affect behavior.

In this setting, Mary would be able to engage in typical behavior, receive feedback on how her behavior affects other people, and experiment with new more effective behaviors. For example, feedback to Mary might indicate that she expresses herself with a tone of certainty and condescension, and often shakes her finger in making a point to another person. As a result, the receiver of the communication feels intimidated and is not motivated to respond in ways that develop the relationship. While such feedback would be threatening for Mary to hear, a supportive group atmosphere would give her the option to consider the feedback and attempt to implement new behaviors. Given that her basic adjustment and competence would not be threatened, Mary would be in a good position to apply what she has learned to her job situation.

An experiential learning group best suited to Helen's needs is one designed primarily to enhance the *personal growth* of the participants. It is most useful for people who are searching for wider and more creative ways of understanding and expressing their identity as human beings. The goal of personal growth groups is to foster the development of the individual through a freer expression of personal desires and aspirations in relation to other people. Through the development of a highly supportive and intimate group climate, individuals will be able to form interpersonal relationships involving much more honesty and closeness than exists in most everyday relationships. Thus, the focus in personal growth groups is on the individual and on the development of authentic interpersonal relationships within the group context. To achieve this freer and deeper expression of self, leaders of personal growth groups have developed verbal and nonverbal exercises designed to heighten awareness and expressivity. The role of the leader is to deepen and highlight the emotional experiencing of the participants, giving them the opportunity to find new meaning for themselves in relation to other people and even to society at large. The personal growth group provides an oasis in which the combined supportiveness and challenge of the group is meant to facilitate self-awareness, self-realization, and self-actualization.

In light of Mark's difficulties with anxiety and low self-esteem, he most needs an experiential learning group designed for psychotherapy or counseling. (Although one might at first question whether this is a learning group, we must remember that the personal change inherent in the learning process is fundamental to the success of psychotherapy.) The goals of psychotherapy are to bring about major changes in the personality functioning of dissatisfied and disturbed individuals. Thus, the focus of psychotherapy groups is predominantly at the individual level. The leader, a clinical psychologist or professional psychotherapist who specializes in helping troubled individuals, attempts to assist each individual in the group to come to grips with the major issues that are inhibiting effective living, and to search for ways that might improve motivation and the capability to live effectively. The leader uses a variety of therapeutic techniques usually derived from the theoretical orientation of the leader. In other words, group psychotherapy parallels many of the same processes of individual psychotherapy; these are modified to varying degrees to fit the group situation. A psychotherapy group would make available the appropriate setting and the necessary expertise to help Mark in his struggle to understand his personal issues in living. (An excellent overview of the variety of experiential learning groups is provided by Shaffer and Galinsky [1974] and by Lieberman [1976].)

A study that supports the existence of three types of experiential groups is provided by Lomranz, Lakin, and Schiffman (1972), who examined the variants of sensitivity training and encounter groups. A questionnaire was completed by a large sample of group trainers covering their goals, techniques, values, and professional background. Analysis of the results yielded three distinct types of trainers:

- The first type was most concerned with *learning* in the group and highlighted group and interpersonal conflicts with the aim of increasing the social effectiveness of the participants.
- The second type of trainer was concerned with *expanded experiencing* and expressiveness and used exercises and techniques to highlight these processes.

The leader of a psychotherapy group helps a participant come to grips with issues that inhibit effective living. *(Jim Anderson/Woodfin Camp & Associates)*

- The third type was concerned with *remediation* or therapy and took as their aim the personality integration of the individual participants.

Overall, these results correspond to the separation of experiential learning groups into those that take a training approach stressing cognitive learning, those that use interpersonal encounter to heighten emotional expression, and those that use techniques derived from individual therapy in order to aid the personality functioning of the participants.

History of Experiential Groups

As we've discussed earlier, the forerunner of experiential groups used for training purposes was the basic skill training group pioneered by the National Training Laboratories following the historic 1946 workshops on community relations organized by Kurt Lewin and his associates (see Chapters 1 and 4). Out of these early efforts grew both the sensitivity training and the encounter group movements. *Sensitivity training* emphasizes a here-and-now focus for understanding the ongoing interaction of the participants. *Encounter groups* shift the emphasis toward emotional expressivity and personal growth, with less concern about skill acquisition and cognitive learning.

Another form of unstructured training group has been developed by Bion and his associates at the Tavistock Institute in Great Britain. According to Shaffer and Galinsky (1974), the Tavistock leaders were influenced by Kurt Lewin's field theory and made an attempt to combine it with psychoanalytic principles into their own unique understanding of group processes. The *Tavistock group* focuses on the processes of group behavior and group development, and interprets all individual behavior as an expression of group forces. As in psychoanalytic therapy, the leader takes a detached and inactive role especially in the early stages of the group. Special emphasis is given to the manner in which the participants deal with the lack of involvement by the authority figure (the trainer) in the group.

Encounter groups are an outgrowth of early sensitivity training groups, which focused more on the personal growth of individual participants. During the late sixties, the turning away from conventional life-styles and the search for a more meaningful existence contributed to the proliferation of encounter groups. The encounter group movement has been furthered by personal growth institutes (such as Esalen in California), which offer group experiences directed toward self-actualization. The encounter group movement has been supported by many humanistic psychologists including Will Shutz (1967, 1971) and Carl Rogers (1970). Rogers has developed a group format in which individuals search for open and authentic ways of relating to other people based on the facilitative conditions of empathy, respect, and genuineness (see Chater 6). A systematic model for integrating interpersonal skills into the experiential group is offered by Gerard Egan (1976). This "skills/contract" approach begins with a clear statement of participant learning goals (the contract), followed by structured skill training, and culminates with use of the skills in the group setting.

Sensitivity Training: The Classic Model

The classic model of sensitivity training, which typified the early National Training Laboratories in Group Development, has served as the basis for a wide variety of experiential learning groups. At the same time, the classic model has maintained a surprisingly clear identity in theory, research, and practice over the past thirty years (Benne, Bradford, Gibb & Lippitt, 1975; Golembiewski & Blumberg, 1977; Lakin, 1972). It is estimated that well over ten million people have participated in sensitivity training (Benne, 1975). Training groups (T-groups) continue to be offered in a variety of settings (educational, organizational, community) for various durations (usually 15 to 50 hours spread over a weekend, a few days, or even several weeks) and in combination with a variety of other components of laboratory learning. This section will describe the distinguishing characteristics, the norms, the learning goals, the personal needs of members that give rise to the major group issues, the phases of development, and the role of the trainer.

Gibb (1975) identifies eight *criteria* that distinguish sensitivity training:

- The T-group focuses on the existential experience of the members in the *here and now*, rather than discussing past experiences or future expectations. Thus, for example, members are encouraged to share their feelings and perceptions about the present situation and about other members rather than sharing their "life stories."
- The emphasis in the group is on understanding the *process* of the ongoing interaction, that is, *how* people are behaving, rather than on the content or information that is being discussed. For example, identifying the process of how the group made a decision and identifying the emotional effects of this is more important than what the decision was about.
- The T-group has *low structure* since it does not have a planned agenda or a set of clearly described roles for members. There is minimal direction by the trainer except for illuminating the group process.
- The focus is on the *group level* of analysis rather than the individual and interpersonal levels. An attempt is made to understand the emergent properties of group functioning. For example, the trainer might point out that a group norm has developed that supports the sharing of personal feelings.
- Interaction is largely *verbal* with only a minimal emphasis upon the processes of nonverbal communication. The T-group is characterized by a blend of cognitive and affective learning rather than an emphasis on emotional expression through nonverbal exercises.
- The purpose is clearly centered on *interpersonal and group competence* rather than on therapeutic or personal growth outcomes. Changes in behavior (such as skill at paraphrasing) are emphasized over changes in personality (such as reduced achievement motivation).
- The *internal dynamics* of the group are stressed as opposed to an external task. The meaningfulness of the experience is judged with regard to internal understanding rather than external productivity.
- Group members are usually in *cultural and geographical* isolation from their external environment of work, home, or play and are therefore better able to disengage themselves from these other life concerns and put their energy into participating in the group.

These characteristics are appropriate for a group of people who have come together to better understand themselves, how they relate to others, and how they function in a group.

Group *norms* provide a strong element of group structure, in sensitivity training. Members come to realize that it is appropriate to describe their present feelings, to give and to ask for interpersonal feedback, to confront other members on behaviors that affect them negatively, and to make decisions by consensus. T-groups do not lack social structure; they simply have less than most other group experiences.

A number of authors (Campbell & Dunnette, 1968; Egan, 1970; Seashore, 1976) have addressed the questions of appropriate *learning goals* in sensitivity training:

- At the *individual* level, participants increase their self-awareness by seeing how other people perceive their behavior and what impact their behavior has on others. Also, participants develop increased sensitivity to others through the processes of feedback and confrontation.
- At the *interpersonal* level, participants learn to communicate more effectively with others and experience ways of resolving interpersonal conflicts more productively.
- At the *group* level, one goal is to understand and diagnose group processes (communication, decision making) and the effects of emergent properties (cohesion, conformity). Members have an opportunity to practice their skills in intervening to improve group functioning.
- Goals at the *intergroup* and *organizational* level may also be approached since the T-group is a social microcosm of organizational functioning. Intergroup conflict among subgroups that may develop shows clear parallels to other settings, such as conflict between departments in an organization. Leadership style, division of labor, and values of working with others can all be illuminated through the T-group experience.

Thus, the efforts of each member and the group can be directed toward a multitude of potential learning goals, and each participant is expected to focus on his or her own unique combination. It is this flexibility of learning goals that underlies the broad utility of sensitivity training.

The flexible and unstructured nature of the T-group allows members to inject in their own personal needs for inclusion, control, and affection. This results in a number of typical group issues (Blumberg & Golembiewski, 1976; Shutz, 1976). Members are usually concerned about acceptance and identity—how they are perceived in the group and how they will be included. The issue of control is expressed in how members influence each other and how the group makes decisions. The issue of goals often arises from a concern regarding productivity—participants question whether their needs will be met by the group. Finally, members have concerns about affection and intimacy—members struggle with the degree of closeness that the group will experience.

The major issues give rise to an amazing complexity of behavior that can be better understood by looking at the process of group development in sensitivity training.

Lundgren and Knight (1978) provides a five-stage model: (1) the initial encounter, (2) intermember conflict and confrontation of the trainer, (3) group solidarity, (4) exchange of interpersonal feedback, and (5) termination.

The initial encounter results from the low structure of the T-group. The trainer briefly states that the group will learn from its own experience and that the trainer's role is to facilitate this. Group norms and goals have not been specified, and twelve or so strangers react with confusion and anxiety—some withdraw, others make suggestions, and other attempt to play an autocratic leader role. Discussion focuses on safe self-disclosures and members often attempt to influence the trainer into taking a more direct role.

The second stage of conflict among members and the trainer can be seen as a reaction to the initial lack of structure. Issues of power and authority are confronted in the relationships between the trainer and the group. Often, subgroup conflict develops—dependent members push for more directive leadership while independent and rebellious members want the trainer to remain nondirective. The trainer refuses to play a dominant role, and this heightens the frustration and hostility that members express.

Group solidarity and cohesiveness grows out of the successful resolution of conflict among members and the trainer. The group comes to see that shared responsibility for decision making is an effective resolution of the control dilemma. Members experience a sense of belonging and togetherness in the group.

The fourth stage emphasizes the exchange of interpersonal feedback among members. As unresolved interpersonal conflicts and problems of group functioning reemerge, members become more effective in using communication skills to resolve such difficulties. Concurrently, participants achieve insights into their own personal functioning and the manner in which they relate to others. The amount of openness, support, and trust will determine the degree of affection and intimacy that is achieved.

The final stage of termination attempts to deal with concerns about separation. Affection is expressed through positive feelings among members and indications of group solidarity as conflict and confrontation decline. T-groups often end on an emotional high based in part on the resolution of earlier issues.

The integrated model of T-group development by Lundgren and Knight (1978) has been used to study the actual processes of development in sensitivity training. Results suggest that the second stage of confronting the trainer may not be as important as the theory suggests.

The role of the trainer is central to the development of productive learning in the T-group. The trainer is more influential and more likely to create tension than other members in the group (Smith, 1980). The trainer's role is best understood as a combination of several functions (Lippitt & This, 1967; Tannenbaum, Weschler & Massarik, 1961). The trainer:

- models the values and behavior of sensitivity training
- helps set group norms
- facilitates communication and conflict resolution
- creates learning experiences for participants
- diagnoses group functioning using theories and research results
- serves as a group member with his or her own needs for inclusion, control, and affection

In enacting this role, the trainer must be sensitive to a number of pitfalls such as becoming too directive over the group or becoming too clinical in analyzing the personality dynamics of individual members (Lippitt & This, 1967). Such pitfalls can be avoided by following guidelines for trainer interventions which maximize learning and decrease personal threat. The most common trainer interventions involve behaviors such as summarizing and reflecting issues back to the group, eliciting the feelings of participants, and raising issues about group functioning (Biberman, 1979).

The trainer role is based on competence developed through professional training and experience in group work (Blumberg & Golembiewski, 1976). In addition, the professional trainer follows a strict code of ethics and is usually a member of a recognized professional association (see Chapter 4).

The values and functioning of T-groups are in direct contrast to a number of the destructive processes of interpersonal and group functioning discussed earlier. Sensitivity training provides a format in which undemocratic and manipulative behavior can be diagnosed and confronted. The assumption that each member will take responsibility for his or her learning is directly counter to diffusion of responsibility and obedience to an autocratic leader. Attempts to bring about conformity through any form of coercion are exposed for what they are. Conformity pressures on deviant members are highlighted as they occur. For example, the trainer may be supportive of group members who are reluctant to engage in self-disclosure and confrontation: The humanistic norm of respect for each individual takes precedence. Destructive strategies of interpersonal influence such as ingratiation or manipulation can be described through the use of communication skills. In sum, *sensitivity training is a resocialization setting in which participants can acquire more productive and respectful ways of relating to other people.*

Risks and Benefits of Experiential Groups: Research Evidence

Marty, a woman in her thirties, holds a supervisory position in a large manufacturing organization. One summer she attends a week-long human relations workshop, consisting mainly of sensitivity training, sponsored by a major training association. On her return, her friends and co-workers notice some definite changes in Marty's behavior. She is more aware of her feelings and intentions and is more confident and assertive. She shows greater sensitivity and understanding toward others and is able to communicate more effectively. She says her "new me" is more the way she has always wanted to be.

Rob is a high school dropout in his early twenties who has wanted to change his life for as long as he can remember. He has low self-esteem and is often sullen and hostile around others. He has sought professional counseling on a couple of occasions. One weekend, he decides to participate in an encounter group offered by the local personal growth institute. The leader is very charismatic and aggressive. She confronts most members of the group, including Rob, on behavior that inhibit their ability to share themselves fully with others. Rob experiences considerable stress and following the group is more withdrawn than before. Rob decides to reenter personal counseling.

Clint is a young mechanic who is generally disappointed with his life. He has few friends and sees each day as one more boring piece of drudgery. One night he reads in a newspaper advertisement about a new organization that offers personal development seminars. The ad claims that the seminars result in increased self-insight, greater personal responsibility, and maximum effectiveness in living. Although the tuition is very high, Clint arranges a personal interview with the seminar leaders (who turn out to be the entire organization). Both leaders are very personable and persuasive. Although they have no professional training in human relations, Clint is sold on their approach. In the seminar, the leaders' demand for obedience is very strong; all members are to divulge intimate and embarrassing events from their lives in order to benefit from the training. Clint resists and experiences strong conformity pressures from other members and is confronted and ostracized by the leaders and the group. Following the seminar, Clint is depressed and more socially isolated than before.

Each of these persons has gone through very different group experiences with very different outcomes. As professionals concerned about competent and ethical conduct, applied social psychologists must ask some hard questions about the potential benefits and risks that experiential groups hold for individuals. In the past 20 years, researchers have done just that and have completed literally hundreds of studies and numerous reviews (Bednar & Kaul, 1978; Gibb, 1971; Hare, 1976; Lieberman, 1976; Stockton, 1978). Let's take a look at some of the benefits (such as experienced by Marty), some of the negative outcomes (such as illustrated by Rob's case), and some of the questions that should be asked by individuals (such as Clint) before they participate in an experiential group.

The personal and interpersonal benefits of sensitivity training have been well documented. Campbell and Dunnette (1968) reviewed early studies on T-groups with participants drawn mainly from management positions in business and industry. Results generally showed positive changes in self-perception (such as more congruence between actual and ideal self) and in interpersonal sensitivity (such as describing relationships in more interpersonal terms). Ratings provided by co-workers back in the job situation indicated that group participants were seen as more open, tolerant, understanding, and skillful in interpersonal relations. However, results were mixed over different studies and many studies had methodological limitations such as a lack of control groups.

The encounter group explosion of the late 1960s and early 1970s was paralleled by a profusion of research studies that typically lumped different types of groups and leaders together, thus making it difficult to know what was actually being studied. Nonetheless, some positive trends emerge. Bebout and Gordon (1972) analyzed self-reports and peer and leader ratings for over one thousand participants in personal growth groups. Before-and-after comparisons showed increased self-esteem, a more positive self-concept, reduced alienation from others, and improved interpersonal relations. These results were strongest in groups with helpful but not intrusive leaders and active self-initiating members. Participants in groups with inactive and insensitive leaders gained little. The conclusion? Encounter groups with a supportive and group-centered (rather than leader-centered) climate have a positive impact on participants.

A very extensive review of studies on sensitivity training is provided by Smith (1975a). Unlike earlier reviews, Smith was able to include only studies that met high research standards, for example, repeated measures from *both* control groups and training groups. Outcomes were assessed in five different areas:

1. Global measures of self-concept as provided by self-ratings and personality tests showed positive changes in 61 percent of the studies.
2. Specific measures of self-concept (particularly inner directness and locus of control) yielded positive changes in 59 percent of the studies. Measures of prejudiced and open-mindedness showed positive gains in 50 percent of the cases.
3. Perceptions of others such as increased sensitivity showed positive shifts in 38 percent of the reports.
4. Perceptions of participants' behavior by others in such areas as communication skills and job performance showed successful changes in 81 percent of the studies.
5. Organizational behavior such as more effective teamwork was successfully affected in 77 percent of the cases.

Smith also compared immediate changes with effects over the longer term (usually several months) and found that on follow-up the positive benefits of training were markedly reduced. In the shorter term, however, sensitivity training does have beneficial effects for participants in a number of intended directions.

The case of Rob illustrates an encounter group *casualty*—a person who becomes more distressed or pathological following the group experience. Continuing concern over such negative concerns was heightened by a study by Lieberman, Yalom, and Miles (1973) in which some two hundred university students were randomly assigned to eighteen different encounter groups. Participants completed numerous self-report measures and took part in follow-up interviews.

Although many positive results occurred, the investigators took pains to identify casualties through questionnaires, peer evaluations, leader ratings, and later requests for psychiatric help. Of one hundred participants who were identified as suspected casualties, sixteen were classed through the interviews as bona fide casualties who had experienced persistent psychological deterioration as a result of the group experience. This number—representing 7.5 percent of the original sample—was several times higher than the usual rate of casualties reported in other studies.

Lieberman et al. (1973) were also particularly interested in identifying leadership styles that related to positive and negative outcomes for participants. Aggressive, stimulating, and charismatic leaders produced a disproportionate number of casualties in their groups. While these leaders showed high caring for participants, they were very active and confronting and tended to use structured exercises that demanded participation. In contrast, leaders in groups with a low rate of casualties were characterized as "love leaders" who provided high caring and an emphasis on understanding the group process with little stimulation and structuring.

The Lieberman et al. (1973) study initially led to higher concern regarding negative group outcomes, but was subsequently criticized for exaggerating the degree of adverse effects (Rowan, 1975; Shutz, 1975). The study involved a number of group experiences generally regarded as more therapeutic than personal growth and dealt with a population—university students—who typically were experiencing a changing and stressful period in their lives. Since these participants received course credit for their involvement, their motivation might differ considerably from that of the typical group participant. Also, the students were given strong warnings that the experience might be emotionally upsetting— this could raise the expectation and the probability of negative outcomes. For these and other reasons, the results on group casualties should be viewed with caution.

A review of studies of deterioration effects in encounter groups by Hartley, Roback, and Abramowitz (1976) places the typical rate of casualties at less than 1 percent. Individuals who have experienced previous psychological disturbance are most likely to experience negative effects. By screening participants, by setting realistic expectations for the group, and by encouraging professional certification of trainers, even these risks could substantially be reduced. Cooper (1975) concludes that the cries that encounter groups are psychologically dangerous have simply not been proven and that some evidence indicates that other experiences such as university examinations are actually more stressful. Nonetheless, continuing research involving cooperation between researchers and trainers is required to further understand the experiential group and how it affects participants (Bedner & Kaul, 1979). For example, Cooper (1977) has found that both positive and negative outcomes are more related to trainer qualities than to participant characteristics or group factors (see Box 7.4).

Guidelines for Selecting a Group Experience. Clint's unfortunate experience in a "personal growth seminar" illustrates how well-meaning but unsuspecting individuals can be deceived, exploited, and abused by unscrupulous and incompetent charlatans. In North America, there is no one professional or legal mechanism for assuring that group experiences offered to the public will be conducted in a competent manner. Usually, the abused individual's only recourse is to pursue civil or criminal charges through the courts.

As a potential group participant, there are questions you can ask and guidelines you can follow in selecting a group experience that is appropriate for you (Shostrum, 1969; Siroka, Siroka & Schloss, 1971):

1. *Carefully consider your learning goals.* Match these goals to the methods and the objectives of the group experience. If you are primarily interested in remedial work on major personal issues, look for a counseling or psychotherapy group. If you wish to expand your sense of personal awareness and intimacy with other people, then a personal growth group may be appropriate. If you are interested in developing your interpersonal and group competence, choose sensitivity training. Be cautious about joining a group on impulse, or of entering an unknown experience. Be suspicious of the quality and ethical conduct of programs that either say little about their objectives, or that promise amazing changes.
2. *Enter only groups led by a reputable professional* affiliated with a human service agency or a professional association. You can check out the trainer's credentials by phone or by contacting human service professionals in your

Box 7.4   FOCUS ON RESEARCH
The Effects of T-Groups: What Helps and What Hurts?

Research on the adverse effects of experiential learning groups gave rise to considerable concern among professional psychologists and other group leaders. Cary Cooper of the University of Manchester in England pointed out that all the research on group casualties had some methodological problems; for example, not one study examined the rate of casualties in a comparable control group. However, Cooper realized that the important question is to identify the conditions and processes that lead to adverse outcomes so that these may be minimized. Conversely, conditions that lead to positive outcomes might be maximized.

Cooper addressed this question by studying 227 members and thirty-two trainers in twelve experiential groups representing a cross section of training experiences available in the United Kingdom. As potentially important conditions of the group experience, Cooper assessed trainer personality and style, member personality, and group characteristics. Trainers completed a personality questionnaire and their style was rated by participants on numerous dimensions such as influential vs. uninfluential and relaxed vs. tense. Participants also completed the personality questionnaire. To assess group characteristics, two independent observers rated each session on scales such as degree of confrontation in the group and degree of trust between trainer and participants.

Each participant nominated those in the group who he thought were *helped* by the experience or *hurt* by the experience (made worse, became overly upset). In addition, follow-up reports on positive or negative changes were obtained from work colleagues at six weeks and again at seven months following the training.

The findings were extremely illuminating in relation to the original question. Both positive and negative effects related most strongly to trainer behavior and personality and were related to participant characteristics in the short run (6-week follow-up) but not in the long run. Characteristics of the group process and structure showed little relation to outcomes.

Specifically, participants who were seen as being hurt tended to be self-assured and opinionated, independent, and unaffected by feelings. Persons such as these are likely to appear as more confident than they really are and may attract more negative feedback. Adverse effects were strongly related to trainer behavior that was withdrawn, closed, and incongruent. On the positive side, participants who were helped were seen as self-sufficient and affected by feelings; they had trainers who were relaxed, open, and congruent. Improved work relationships tended to result from a trainer style that was enthusiastic, supportive, and competent.

Cooper concludes that the success or failure of the group experience seems strongly related to the personality and style of the trainer.

Source: Cooper, C. L. Adverse and growthful effects of experiential learning groups: The role of the trainer, participant, and group characteristics. *Human Relations*, 1977, *30*, 1103–1129.

area. Leaders with no professional training may have the skills to enhance emotional expressivity and to precipitate a crisis for participants, but may be ill-equipped to then deal productively with the situation.

3. *Look for indications of competence and responsibility* in the operation of a program. Reputable programs usually involve some degree of screening of participants, a clear articulation of the methods and goals, and an indication of follow-up support for participants, as required.

4. *Avoid groups that have an evangelical bent* to reshape society, including you. Such groups resemble cults more than legitimate learning experiences and may often use inhumane methods of persuasion, manipulation, and confrontation in an attempt to reach supposedly humane ends.

By actively following such guidelines, you can minimize the risks and potentially maximize the benefits of experiential learning groups.

Areas of Application: Where Can Group Dynamics Be Used?

Kurt Lewin's driving vision was that a scientific approach to group dynamics would help ameliorate social problems (Cartwright, 1951). Along with Lewin, the other founders of the group training movement, Ken Benne, Lee Bradford, and Ron Lippitt, considered the major problems of civilization to be problems in human relations. Bradford (1961) maintains that the complexity of the modern world makes cooperation mandatory among people who are interdependent. The need for cooperation, and therefore for understanding group behavior, is evident in many areas. In industry, management decisions are increasingly being made by teams, that is, groups, rather than individuals. In communities, the predominant way of resolving problems is through committees and meetings, that is, through group process. In schools and universities, the teacher or administrator who facilitates the development of mature groups will release powerful forces for learning and effective decision making. In international relations, the success of many agencies and conferences rests on the ability of individuals to understand and work well with groups.

Experiential groups, especially sensitivity training, help participants learn about crucial *group* processes—norms, conformity pressures, decision making—and therefore continue to be at the core of many human relations workshops. Although the direct transfer of learnings to back-home groups is limited by a number of barriers (see Blumberg & Golembiewski, 1976), many of the basic ideas can be applied to other group situations such as family interaction (for example, Anderson, 1974; Golembiewski, 1973) and meetings (for example, Bradford, 1976; Schindler-Rainman, Lippitt & Cole, 1975). In addition, many other forms of groups—consciousness-raising, self-help, and assertiveness training—have been partly developed with knowledge derived from sensitivity training. Further applications of group methods will be presented throughout the remainder of the book.

The destructiveness of *intergroup* conflict was one of the social problems that concerned Lewin, and he saw group dynamics as one avenue for developing effective methods of conflict resolution. This hope has been carried forward by the development of intergroup confrontation workshops at both the societal and international levels of analysis (see Chapters 8 and 12). In addition, a general method for resolving conflict—third-party consultation—has its roots firmly placed in the approaches of human relations training (see Chapter 14).

A great deal of work with experiential groups has been designed to help members of *organizations* fulfill their roles more effectively. However, the early T-groups which brought people together from different organizations had little impact on the organizations themselves. Participants might behave somewhat differently when they returned to their jobs, but this had little effect on overall organizational climate and performance. Therefore, trainers and consultants began to hold experiential groups with members of the same work group within the organization. This approach has now developed into "team-building"— training interventions designed to improve the effectiveness of work teams— which is a central part of the practice of organization development (see Chapter 9). In fact, the whole field of organization development can be seen as based on the approach of laboratory learning (Beckhard, 1975).

Experiential groups call for active participation, taking responsibility for oneself, and being sensitive to the needs of others. These same requirements underlie the practice field of *community* development which seeks the cooperative participation of community members toward common goals (see Chapter 10). An experiential learning approach to community development has a lot in common with sensitivity training and laboratory methods (Klein, 1965; Schindler-Rainman, 1975).

How do you get students involved in their own *education?* One way is to adapt human relations training to the classroom (see Stanford, 1970). A whole range of experiential approaches requiring student *interaction* with the teacher and with other students have been developed out of the pioneering efforts of laboratory learning (see Chapter 15). These approaches can aid the teaching and learning process to be more involving, challenging, and rewarding for both teacher and students.

The small group has the power to change human relationships in all manner of settings. The group may be a *medium* of change wherein individuals experience personal growth; it may be a *target* of change wherein norms or climate are altered; or it may be an *agent* of change that influences organizations, communities, or societies toward more effective functioning (Cartwright, 1951). As such, the small group is a central element in the theory, research, and practice of applied social psychology.

Summary

Each of us spends a great deal of our lives in groups—primary groups (with frequent face-to-face, intimate contact), secondary groups (larger more impersonal collections), and reference groups (a source of information and standard of comparison for our attitudes and behavior).

People are attracted to groups much like they are attracted to individuals— through proximity, similarity, reciprocity, and complementarity. In addition, the characteristics of the group, including prestige, size, degree of positive interaction, and success, affect the degree of attraction to the group. Cohesiveness—an emergent group property—refers to the extent to which members are motivated to remain in the group.

Group norms affect member behavior in situations involving ambiguous judgments, objective estimates, expressions of attitudes, the influence of an authority figure, and the power of reference groups. Conformity pressures, diffusion of responsibility, deindividuation, anonymity, and polarization all operate to influence the individual's behavior, usually in negative ways. The concept of "groupthink" illustrates how conformity and other insidious processes may negatively affect decision making.

Communication networks are the pattern of communication channels available to group members. Less restrictive and less centralized patterns result in greater member satisfaction and also effectiveness when the task is complex.

Group structure is represented by communication networks, position and roles, norms, leadership, status, and power. Popular theories of leadership take an interaction approach in which the characteristics of effective leadership are seen to depend partly on the demands of the social situation. Leadership functions include both task behaviors and social maintenance behaviors which must be blended together in order to improve both satisfaction and effectiveness. Fiedler's contingency model relates leadership style to three characteristics of the situation—leader-member relations, task structure, and the leader's position power.

Various theories of group development specify the major stages that groups go through from beginning to end. A composite model (following a recurring phase approach) include five phases: the beginning, movement toward confrontation, compromise and harmony, reassessment, and resolution and recycling. Each phase involves a major issue revolving around inclusion, control, and affection that must be resolved before the group can move to the next part of the sequence.

Experiential groups can be categorized into three basic types. Training groups help relatively well-adjusted individuals acquire greater competence in interpersonal and group skills. Personal growth groups (encounter groups) emphasize individual emotional expression and the development of authentic interpersonal realtionships. Psychotherapy groups try to bring about fundamental personality changes in participants who are experiencing psychological distress.

The classic model of sensitivity training focuses on the here-and-now interaction of participants in order to increase their self-awareness, interpersonal competence, and understanding of group processes. A skilled trainer serves as a model, helps set group norms, facilitates communication and conflict resolution, and diagnoses group functioning to create useful learning experiences for the participants.

Research on sensitivity training has shown important benefits for participants at the individual, interpersonal, group, and organizational levels of functioning. Research has also raised some concerns about potential risks that can be reduced by using reasonable guidelines for selecting a group experience.

Applications of group dynamics as expressed by experiential groups can be found in a wide variety of fields including intergroup conflict resolution, organization development, community development, and education.

Further Readings

Benne, K. D., Bradford, L. P., Gibb, J. R. & Lippitt, R. O. *The laboratory method of changing and learning: Theory and application.* Palo Alto, Calif.: Science & Behavior Books, 1975.

Blumberg, A. & Golembiewski, R. T. *Learning and change in groups.* Markham, Ontario: Penguin, 1976.

Cartwright, D. & Zander, A. (Eds.). *Group dynamics. Research and theory* (3rd ed.). New York: Harper & Row, 1968.

Janis, I. L. *Victims of groupthink.* Boston: Houghton Mifflin, 1972.

Napier, R. W. & Gershenfeld, M. K. *Groups: Theory and experience* (2nd ed.). Boston: Houghton Mifflin, 1981.

Shaw, M. E. *Group dynamics: The psychology of small group behavior,* (3rd. ed.). New York: McGraw-Hill, 1981.

Shutz, W. C. *Here comes everybody.* New York: Harper & Row, 1971.

CHAPTER OUTLINE

PREJUDICE AND DISCRIMINATION
  Some Definitions
  Origins of Prejudice
    Historical Approach
    Sociocultural Approach
    Situational Approach
    Psychodynamic Approach
    Phenomenological Approach
    Earned Reputation
    Multiple Causation
    The Ultimate Attribution Error
  Ethnic Stereotypes: The Pigeonholes of Perception
  Ethnocentrism: Generalized Prejudice and Ingroup Glorification
  Discrimination: The Behavior of Injustice

STUDYING AND REDUCING INTERGROUP CONFLICT
  Process and Symptoms of Intergroup Conflict
  Positive Potential of Intergroup Contact: Facilitating Conditions
  Reducing Prejudice and Conflict through Intergroup Contact: The Challenge for Practice

SUMMARY

FURTHER READINGS

Intergroup Relations

PREJUDICE AND DISCRIMINATION

On December 7, 1941, two hours after the Japanese attack on Pearl Harbor, Canadian government authorities began the roundup and detention of all Japanese-Canadians living on the west coast of British Columbia. Under the legal provisions of wartime, individual human rights were violated, property confiscated, families broken up, and 22,000 people sent to ghost towns, sugar-beet farms, and concentration camps spread across western Canada. The majority of these people were Canadian citizens, and yet they were branded "enemy aliens" whose allegiance and trustworthiness were highly suspect. No legal charges of spying or sabotage had been brought to bear on these citizens before that fateful day, nor after. To those Japanese-Canadians, the treatment they received was not inconsistent with other forms of prejudice and discrimination that they had encountered in their daily lives (Broadfoot, 1977). The situation in Canada was paralleled by a similar response by United States authorities to Japanese-Americans living in California.

In a less extreme fashion, we encounter prejudice and discrimination every day of our lives. The media constantly bring us reports of individual mistreatment, intergroup hostility, and community strife. The battle for equality and dignity is fought in many subtle and pervasive ways. At supper one evening, my seven-year-old daughter commented, "I'd like to be a nurse or a teacher when I grow up." I countered, "Wouldn't you like to be a doctor or a principal?" She was incredulous, "You mean a woman can be a principal?" It is not yet in her experience, nor is it in the sex-role expectations that society communicates to her, that she can actually be a school principal if she wants. Even at her young age, the insidious processes of prejudice have begun to influence her perceptions of what is appropriate for women and what is not.

But what is prejudice? And what is discrimination? How can these phenomena be understood and how can they be influenced? In this chapter, we will look at the definitions, origins, and characteristics of prejudice and discrimination and the processes of intergroup conflict and cooperation. The issues of racism and sexism—two specific areas of prejudice and discrimination—are covered in Chapter 11.

Some Definitions

Prejudice has been defined in a variety of ways, and there is no clear consensus on a generally accepted meaning of the term (Ehrlich, 1973). For some authors, prejudice is a preconceived judgment, for others a pattern of hostility, and for others a collection of normative precepts regarding appropriate behavior. However, most social psychologists (for example, Krech, Crutchfield & Ballachey, 1962; Simpson & Yinger, 1972) regard *prejudice* as an attitude—more specifically, as a simplistic, hostile attitude toward a group of people and the individuals in that group. Thus, prejudice involves more than prejudgment in which one makes a judgment or decision before all the relevant information is available. A prejudgment becomes a prejudice only when it is not open to revision in the light of new information (Allport, 1954). Thus, for example, the Arab who is prejudiced toward Israelis not only holds a simplistic, hostile attitude, but ignores or distorts information that challenges that attitude. The most common objects of prejudice are ethnic groups and minority groups. An *ethnic group* is a collection of people having a common racial or national background, a common culture and language, or a combination of these characteristics (Harding, Proshansky, Kutner & Chein, 1969). A *minority group* is usually, but not necessarily, an ethnic group; its distinguishing characteristic is not necessarily that it is a minority in numbers but that it is in a minority position in terms of power, status, and wealth (Simpson & Yinger, 1972). For example, minority groups such as the blacks of South Africa may far outnumber the dominant white ruling group; yet they remain the victims of prejudice, discrimination, and subservience. Usually, however, minority groups are smaller in number—such as American blacks or French Canadians—and must struggle against a lack of power in all its dimensions.

But let us be clear about what prejudice is and what it is not. There will always be differences among groups in a variety of characteristics, and in a pluralistic and democratic society these differences should be acknowledged and respected with fair treatment available to all regardless of group identity. Prejudice and discrimination, on the other hand, involve stereotyping and discriminating against an individual solely or primarily on the basis of his or her group membership, rather than on the unique personal qualities he or she possesses. It is the processes of irrational judgment and unfair treatment that are unacceptable to the humanistic value base of applied social psychology.

A person need not be a member of an ethnic group or a minority group to be a target of rigid, antagonistic attitudes. We find prejudice toward police officers, college professors, and sellers of vacuum clearners, as well as toward blacks, Chicanos, and women. But negative attitudes toward various occupations will not be as pervasively ingrained into the social fabric of a society as the prejudices toward minority and ethnic groups. In either case, defining prejudice as an attitude is useful because we can apply our earlier ideas about the structure of attitudes to help us more fully understand prejudice and discrimination.

Attitudes are made up of three components: the *cognitive* component, including all the ideas and beliefs about the social object of the attitude; the *affective* component, involving the feelings toward the object; and the *action* component, comprising the behavioral tendencies toward the object (see Chapter 2). In the case of prejudice, the cognitive component is simplistic and inaccurate. For example, white Southerners may be seen as ignorant, superstitious, and racist, when in fact most may be knowledgeable, rational, and egalitarian. This irrational aspect of prejudice is expressed in the concept of *stereotype:* an oversimplified and rigid set of beliefs about a group of people. Stereotypes involve gross generalizations—acquired through misinformation—that ignore individual differences and are resistant to change even in the light of new information.

The affective component of prejudice involves strongly negative evaluations of the attitude object, accompanied by feelings of hostility, fear, and hatred. The highly emotional quality of prejudice and discrimination makes these evaluations particularly resistant to change. Since these negative feelings serve as the motivational base of prejudice, strong defenses arise when bigoted opinions or practices are challenged. Civil rights workers have been subjected to every form of verbal abuse and physical violence because they dare to confront the discrepancy between the norms of equality and freedom and the irrational beliefs and hostility of bigots.

The action component of prejudice is comprised of behavioral orientations seen as appropriate responses to the group and individuals in question. Thus, the prejudiced person adopts strong prescriptions for harsh treatment, segregation, and discrimination against the targets of his or her hostility: "American Indians should be restricted to reservations." "We don't hire women with young children." "The immigration of East Indians must be stopped."

Such action tendencies expressed in actual behavior become *discrimination:* overt behavior that restricts the human rights of an individual, or denies access to opportunities or resources on the basis of group membership.

Origins of Prejudice

Prejudice and discrimination can stem from any one, or a combination, of a number of roots. A social-psychological analysis of the origins of prejudice is particularly powerful because it enables us to look at this broad spectrum: at both its social factors (in the society, community, or group) and its individual causes (in the person's personality and perception of the situation). At the same time, we must draw on the knowledge and approaches of other disciplines, such as history and anthropology, to fully understand the origins of prejudice. In his classic work, *The Nature of Prejudice* (1954), Gordon Allport has done precisely that (see Figure 8.1). His comprehensive discussion of major theories or approaches is the basis of the following discussion.

Historical Approach. Racial and ethnic conflict is usually embedded in a long history of deteriorating relations, economic conflict, and memories of past injustices and atrocities. Theorists taking a historical approach to understanding prejudice often emphasize the economic gains that accrue to the dominant majority group through the exploitation of minority groups.

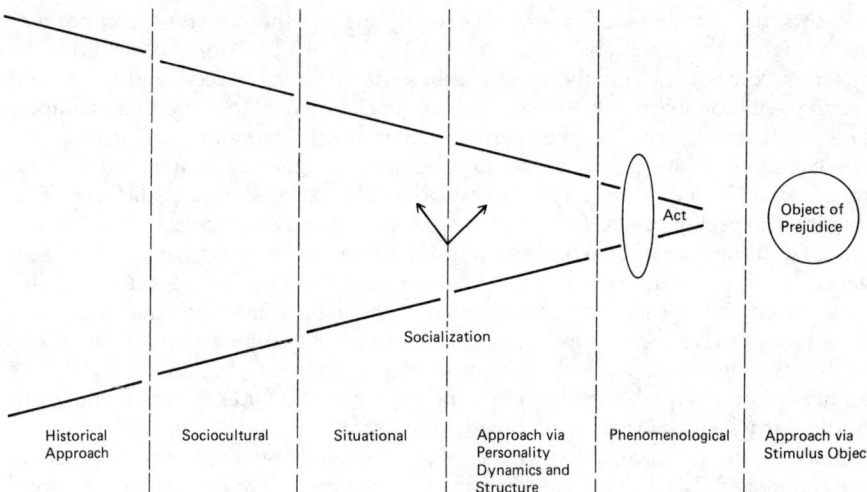

Figure 8.1   Theoretical and Methodological Approaches to the Study of the Causes of Prejudice.
Source: G. W. Allport, Prejudice: a problem in psychological and social causation. *Journal of Social Issues,* Supplement Series, No. 4, 1950. Reprinted with permission of the publisher. Copyright 1950, Society for the Psychological Study of Social Issues.

One of the most compelling cases is the development of prejudice toward black Americans: its history of slavery, social and educational segregation, and employment discrimination can be seen as sources of considerable economic benefits to white Americans (Elkins, 1968).

The historical-economic approach also helps explain the congruence between stereotypical beliefs and economic gains, evident in prejudicial rationalizations such as, "Why give the Indians more money for their land? They'll only spend it on booze" or "The black worker who is promoted will only feel singled out and embarrassed in his new position." However, the historical emphasis fails to explain other phenomena: why some individuals in the dominant group become prejudiced and practice discrimination while others do not; why some minorities become the exploited victims of prejudice while others prosper and are accepted as equals; why there is prejudice and discrimination that has no economic ramifications for the groups involved.

Sociocultural Approach. Sociologists and anthropologists, like historians, often emphasize the total social context in which prejudice has developed. They point to broad sociocultural forces as the causes of prejudice: the relative upward mobility of dominant and minority groups, population density, urbanization, and so on. City life, for example, may destroy our sense of human affiliation and personal power, creating frustration, uncertainty, and insecurity.

We have come to set our standards through advertising media and the materialistic trappings of status, and we behave in a condescending and condemning manner toward those who cannot "make it": the poor, the blacks, those on welfare. At the same time, we resent the selfishness, the cleverness, and the deceit that our competitive materialistic milieu demands of us, and we channel our resentment into stereotypes of groups, such as the Jews, who appear to symbolize city life (Rose, 1948). Now that is quite a leap—from the broad issue of urbanization to the individual expression of prejudice—but the sociocultural approach is appealing partly because it attempts to make such challenging connections. We will see, however, that there are other connections that must be made to gain a full picture of the causes of prejudice.

Situational Approach. These theories emphasize present environmental factors as causes of prejudice. If our social environment has an atmosphere of prejudice, then we may come to adopt and express prejudice and discrimination.

Two social-psychological processes (described in Chapter 2) are especially relevant here: social learning and conformity. Through the processes of reinforcement and modeling, the child (or newcomer) soon learns the appropriate beliefs and behaviors attached to relations with other groups. The prejudices of the father and mother are soon visited upon the sons and daughters. Think of your own experience. What stereotypes and emotional reactions have you picked up

Through reinforcement and modeling, children learn the appropriate beliefs and behaviors attached to relations with other groups. Parents' prejudices are soon visited upon their sons and daughters. *(Telegraph Sunday Magazine by John Marmaras/Woodfin Camp & Associates)*

from your family toward groups of people that you may have had little or no contact with?

The social norms of prejudice and discrimination are further supported by the influences of the family, peer group, and ingroup through the subtle but powerful processes of conformity. In many situations, in fact, we might better ask the more amazing question of why some individuals remain unprejudiced, rather than what causes prejudice. The situational approach also examines such current conditions as competition for scarce jobs and the relative size of group populations.

Psychodynamic Approach. The psychodynamic approach focuses almost entirely on individual factors: on the functioning (or, better, the malfunctioning) of the prejudiced person's personality.

We have already seen (in Chapter 5) how Freud's psychoanalytic theory served as the basis for understanding the authoritarian personality syndrome (Adorno et al., 1950): a highly authoritarian man, for example, has repressed both his unacceptable faults and his anger against the harsh parental discipline of his upbringing. At the same time, he tends to be insecure and threatened; in psychoanalytic terms, he possesses a weak ego. To protect himself from the resulting anxiety, he projects his faults and shortcomings and displaces his repressed anger onto a convenient and relatively powerless target—a minority group.

The process of displacing anger onto the outgroup is also found in the frustration or *scapegoat theory of prejudice:* here, frustration arises from environmental factors such as high unemployment and job competition. The blocking of goals leads to anger that again is displaced onto minority groups—the scapegoats, such as blacks or immigrants, who are blamed for the poor employment market.

While these explanations of prejudice are intriguing, it is clear that not all prejudiced individuals have weak egos and use defense mechanisms to protect themselves from anxiety. As with the other approaches, the psychodynamic emphasis gives us only part of the picture.

Phenomenological Approach. Phenomenology maintains that we develop a picture of the world through our senses, and that our subjective experience is the reality out of which we operate. In other words, the way we respond to an objective stimulus depends on our own personal perception of that stimulus rather than on its objective characteristics. If the prejudiced person perceives Jews as conniving, threatening, and repulsive, he or she will respond to them with suspicion, fear, and anger. Moreover, that person will tend to select and interpret objective events or innocuous behavior in ways that support the prejudice. This process of maintaining congruence among perceptions, thoughts, and behavior is one of the basic tenets of cognitive dissonance theory (see Chapter 2).

Now the question of how the individual acquires a particular definition of the world and the groups in it requires a consideration of *all* the approaches we have looked at. History, culture, current economic and social situations, and the internal dynamics of personality all work to determine the phenomenology of the individual. How these forces will be expressed depends on what the individual believes and perceives right here and now. One crucial implication of the phenomenological approach is this: if we wish to reduce prejudice, we must first work hard to understand and accept the subjective reality of the prejudiced person. Only then will we be in a position to confront the discrepancies and challenge the injustices that prejudice and discrimination involve.

Earned Reputation. Is it possible that minority groups actually have some of the negative characteristics included in the stereotypes that others hold of them? Of course it is. There are cultural and economic differences among groups, and there are differences in how outsiders value these characteristics. Thus, we can expect there to be a kernel of truth in ethnic stereotypes (Triandis & Vassiliou, 1967). However, we can also expect there to be a ton of chaff produced by all of the causal factors we've talked about. Unfortunately, the kernel of truth can lead to the self-fulfilling prophecy in which social stereotypes create their own reality. In Chapter 6, we saw how the stereotype of the physically attractive female led males to behave in a more friendly and outgoing manner. This led the female targets to respond in like fashion, that is, to behave in ways that confirmed the stereotype. How often in all manner of intergroup relations might a kernel of truth be exaggerated in similar ways, thus justifying the original prejudice?

To fully understand prejudice, we must realize that the characteristics of the target group interact with the personal and environmental dynamics of the intolerant individual to produce the final outcome. It is not the fact that differences can be perceived, but the manner in which we respond to and deal with these differences that determines our sense of equal rights and our humanity.

Multiple Causation. There are multiple causes for prejudice as an attitude and for discrimination as a behavior. In different situations and with different individuals, different causes are more or less important: for some it may be the individual's inadequate personality; for others, the social learning environment.

The implications should be clear. If we wish to reduce prejudice, we must be aware of the major determinants operating in any particular situation. Prejudice interacts with other social forces to determine important societal decisions. For example, Miyamoto (1973) provides a multiple causation analysis of the forced evacuation of Japanese-Americans during World War II (see Box 8.1).

The Ultimate Attribution Error. Thomas Pettigrew, a well-known social psychologist who was a student of Allport, has recently reaffirmed the continuing utility of Allport's analysis and has extended it further by drawing on attribution theory (see Chapter 2). Pettigrew (1979) notes that Allport gave much emphasis to cognitive factors in prejudice and saw these as extensions of normal processes rather than as the aberrant distortions of prejudiced personalities. Stereotyping, for example, begins with the normal process of categorization, which by itself is neither irrational nor unjust.

Allport also anticipated the role of causal attribution in prejudice by noting the human tendency to see causation as something that people are responsible for, thus predisposing us all toward prejudiced thinking. Pettigrew notes the tendency of observers to attribute the behavior of others to personal or dispositional factors

Evacuees of Japanese ancestry being registered at the Santa Anita reception center, Arcadia, California, in April 1942. The evacuees were later transferred to war relocation authority centers for the duration of World War II. *(Library of Congress)*

rather than situational factors. He extends this to the *ultimate attribution error:* When a prejudiced observer (who is a member of an ingroup) sees a member of an outgroup engage in antisocial or undesirable behavior, the observer will attribute it to personal causes often believed to be innate in members of the outgroup. If the behavior happens to be positive (prosocial or desirable), the prejudiced observer will explain it away through a variety of mechanisms depending on the characteristics of the situation. The outgroup member may be seen as the "exceptional case" who is then contrasted with the majority of the outgroup ("She's really bright and competent—not like the rest of those Indians"). The behavior may be attributed to luck or to some special advantage given to the outgroup member ("If it wasn't for the affirmative action program, *she* never would have gotten that job"). Sometimes, the positive behavior will be perceived as due to uncommonly high motivation ("He's really a credit to his race") or as due to situational factors that led the outgroup member to behave atypically ("What could that cheap Scot do but pay the check with everyone watching him!"). In sum, prejudiced individuals will hold outgroup members responsible for negative behaviors but not for positive behaviors. *If you are a target of prejudice, you cannot win.* Pettigrew also points out that the ultimate attribution error will be greatest when there is a history of intense conflict and highly negative stereotypes between the groups.

There is only a small amount of direct evidence in support of the ultimate attribution error, although general research on attribution theory provides much

Box 8.1   FOCUS ON THEORY
A Causal Analysis of the World War II Evacuation of Japanese-Americans

Discrimination on a wide scale is often due to the interplay of a complex set of forces. S. Frank Miyamoto of the University of Washington has provided an analysis of the causes of the World War II evacuation of Japanese-Americans that shows some parallels to Allport's coverage of the origins of prejudice.

At the time of the Japanese attack on Pearl Harbor on December 7, 1941, 127,000 persons of Japanese ancestry were living in the United States—94,000 of them in California. The majority of these people were native-born Americans. Over a thousand Japanese aliens (immigrants who were ineligible for citizenship) were suspected of subversive activity; they were immediately arrested and held for the duration of the war. No espionage was ever uncovered. Nevertheless, the public mood irrevocably swung in a negative direction, with a number of groups calling for mass evacuation amid growing support from the press, the military, and the government.

In March 1942, a proclamation designated most of the West Coast as a military area from which all persons of Japanese ancestry were excluded. By June, more than one hundred thousand of these people had been relocated in detention centers that were spread over several states and typically located in undeveloped and inhospitable areas. Families had to dispose of or store virtually all their belongings, and farmers and businesspeople had to liquidate their investments in a matter of weeks. Within a year, many were released after signing an oath of loyalty and were permitted to resettle in nonmilitary areas. Many chose to sit out the entire war, so that they could return to their homes on the West Coast.

Miyamoto points out that the evacuation was not a simple error in policy that could have been prevented or corrected by any individual or group. Rather, it was the result of multiple causation by historical, economic, sociocultural, and situational factors.

Anti-Japanese prejudice in California had a long history based on racial differences and cultural disparities. In a continuing conflict between organized labor and the owning class, the Japanese were held up as a threat to jobs and fair pay, even though Japanese rarely engaged in unionized trades. In farming, the Japanese were resented as more-than-able competitors, and the Pacific Coast states all passed laws barring immigrants from owning land. Partly by choice and partly by exclusion, the Japanese tended to live in closely knit communities, thus accentuating racial stereotyping and reducing interracial contact.

In terms of situational factors, the surprise attack on Pearl Harbor left a strong impression of the treacherous character of the Japanese. Rumors of sabotage were given much publicity, while disconfirmations were ignored. Fear of Japanese attacks on the West Coast accelerated the hysteria, and with the news media fanning the flames of outcry, the government acted quickly and under pressure. At base, however, Miyamoto sees the historical prejudice as the most important influence leading to the evacuation.

Source: Miyamoto, S. F. The forced evacuation of the Japanese minority during World War II. *Journal of Social Issues*, 1973, *29*(2), 11–31.

indirect evidence. One directly relevant study is provided by Duncan (1976), who showed white college students a videotape of one person (either black or white) ambiguously shoving another person (either black or white). The white observers tended to attribute the shoving to personal factors when the harm-doer was black, but to situational factors when the harm-doer was white. A more complete test is offered by Taylor and Jaggi (1974) who had Hindu office clerks in India provide attributions of positive or negative behaviors involving either Hindus or Muslims—two cultural groups with a long history of intense conflict. The behaviors involved such situations as a shopkeeper either being generous or cheating, and a person helping or ignoring a slightly injured individual. The results showed dramatically that negative behavior by an outgroup member (a Muslim) was attributed more to internal factors than was positive behavior. In contrast, negative behavior by an ingroup member (a Hindu) was hardly ever attributed to personal dispositions but was seen as caused by external factors. It appears that the ultimate attribution error allows prejudiced individuals to explain away behavior that is inconsistent with their prevailing stereotypes.

Ethnic Stereotypes: The Pigeonholes of Perception

Each of us has friends or relatives who hold simplistic and inaccurate images of different groups of people. You may have an aunt who considers anyone of Irish descent to be fun-loving and irresponsible, or a cousin who attributes criminal intent to every Italian-American he meets. Such stereotypes—these sets of over-simplified, rigid beliefs regarding an ethnic group—largely correspond to the cognitive component of prejudice. We usually regard stereotypes as negative— that is, involving derogatory beliefs about the target group. But we can recall *positive* stereotypes that are equally simplistic, erroneous, and resistant to change. For example, I have often found Americans to have an overly positive view of Canadians, perceiving them as decent, reasonable, and trustworthy people who have dealt more effectively with social problems in their society. The negative side of the picture—Canadians as overly cautious, timid people, some of whom endure great hardship without asserting their rights—is simply given less attention.

In a classic study on stereotypes, Katz and Braly (1933) selected eighty-four characteristics commonly used to describe different racial and ethnic groups. One hundred Princeton University undergraduates then selected the five trait names judged to be most characteristic of ten different ethnic groups.

Approximately 50 percent agreed on the most typical trait of every group, indicating the existence of commonly held stereotypes. For example, 79 percent of the respondents described Jews as shrewd, 49 percent as mercenary, and 48 percent as ambitious. Blacks were described as superstitious (84 percent), lazy (75 percent), and ignorant (38 percent). The English were seen as sportsmanlike (53 percent), intelligent (46 percent), and conventional (34 percent).

The students then evaluated the groups, ranking them by preference. Demonstrating a clear agreement between rank and desirable assigned traits, they ranked Americans and the English in the most positive position, and Turks and blacks in the most negative. Katz and Braly (1933) conclude, "Racial prejudice is thus a generalized set of stereotypes of a high degree of consistency which includes emotional responses to race names, a belief in typical characteristics associated with race names, and an evaluation of such typical traits" (p. 290).

One appealing and unique aspect of this study is that it has been replicated on two later occasions with similar samples of Princeton undergraduates—that is, white, mostly Protestant, American-born students—allowing us to make comparisons among *three* succeeding generations of young Americans (Gilbert, 1951; Karlins, Coffman & Walters, 1969). Using the original measurement procedure, Gilbert (1951) found evidence for both the persistence and the fading-out of racial and ethnic stereotypes. The characteristics most frequently ascribed in 1932 were by and large the ones most frequently checked in 1950. However, almost all attributes checked exhibited a lower percentage of agreement, never exceeding 60 percent. Blacks were still viewed as superstitious, lazy, and ignorant, but by much lower percentages of agreement than in the earlier study: 41 percent, 31 percent, and 24 percent, respectively. This fading-out of stereotypes was especially pronounced for target groups, such as Turks, with which the students had very little contact.

Gilbert also encountered considerable resistance to the stereotyping task. Many respondents resented what they regarded as the unreasonable task of making simplistic generalizations about groups of people. Gilbert attributed this apparent liberalization of attitudes to the effects of increased intergroup contact, the influence of egalitarian social science courses, and the disappearance of stereotypes from the mass media.

Karlins, Coffman, and Walters (1969), repeating the original experiment 20 years after Gilbert, also encountered resistance to the task. However, they found less evidence for the fading-out phenomenon in that there was more uniformity in stereotypes than with the Gilbert sample. But what did occur were *changes in the content* of the images; that is, there were different assignments of attributes to most target groups. Blacks were no longer seen as superstitious (13 percent agreement), lazy (36 percent), or ignorant (11 percent), but were more commonly assigned the characteristics of musical (47 percent), pleasure-loving (26 percent), and ostentatious (25 percent). Jews were seen as ambitious (48 percent), materialistic (46 percent), and intelligent (37 percent). These new assignments appeared to be based on present-day cultural differences and current events. As might be expected during the student protest and civil rights movements of the late 1960s, all stereotypes had become more positive except for the target group of Americans. However, these variations might also be partly due to socioeconomic differences among the three samples. In each successive sample, the proportion of students who came to Princeton from private, upper-class schools declined while the proportion from public, middle-class schools increased. Thus, changes in stereotypes might be due to a combination of changes in time, culture, and socioeconomic status of the respondents.

Although we might conclude that negative ethnic stereotypes are on the decline in the United States, Bettleheim and Janowitz pointed out in 1964 that there really was not adequate systematic evidence to reach that conclusion. The situation is still the same. We simply do not have representative samples of opinions from similar samples over an extended time period. On particular attitudes toward specific groups, however, there is some evidence of change over time. For example, a number of studies have indicated that white attitudes toward blacks in America have become more positive throughout the 1960s and early 1970s. A recent review is provided by Condron (1979) who studied over the 1963–1977 period responses to five questions that had been used in a series of national opinion surveys (see Table 8.1). These items essentially tap the respondents' attitude toward racial integration in five different areas: schools, socializing (dinner), marriage, housing, and intrusion. Condron found that in the first four areas, white attitudes had become substantially more positive from 1963–1972. However, in the 1972–1977 period, positive gains were quite limited, and in the areas of housing and intrusion, negative changes in attitude occurred. This apparent backlash may be a white response to the difficulties encountered in residential and school desegregation (see Chapter 11).

Another factor that makes it difficult to know if prejudice is increasing or decreasing is social desirability (see Chapter 3). It is simply not as socially acceptable to make prejudiced statements as it once was, and people may therefore keep their stereotypes to themselves. For example, Carver, Glass, and Katz (1978) found that white college students tend to hold a positive bias toward blacks due to the social desirability of this attitude. In contrast, handicapped individuals were also viewed with a positive bias, but this effect was not due to social desirability.

The investigators used an impression formation task in which subjects read a transcript of an interview which portrayed the interviewee in a negative light (few friends, no particular interests, no plans for the future). When the transcript was identified as that of a black or handicapped person, subjects gave a more positive evaluation than when no group identification was present. Why? Carver et al. (1978) raise three possibilities:

1. White college students may hold a genuine positive bias toward these outgroups.
2. Subjects might unconsciously distort their true feelings in a more positive direction.
3. Subjects may consciously distort their true feelings in order to give socially desirable responses.

In order to test the third possibility, the researchers used the "bogus pipeline" technique developed by Jones and Sigall (1971). With this method, the subject is attached with electrodes to a set of electronic equipment purported to measure the subjects' true emotional response to any stimulus. To see if subjects are really in touch with their true feelings, they are asked to estimate the reading that the machine will give. The subjects are therefore under less social pressure to react favorably and are motivated to express their true opinions. Using this technique, Carver et al. (1978) found that the white students rated the black interviewee significantly more negatively while attitudes toward the handicapped persons remained positive. The initial high rating of the black interviewee therefore appears to be due to social desirability responding.

**Table 8.1   ATTITUDE ITEMS FROM NATIONAL SURVEYS OF OPINION REGARD-
ING INTEGRATION, 1963 TO 1977**

Schools— Do you think white students and Negro students should go to the same schools or
to separate schools? (same, separate)

Dinner— How strongly would you object if a member of your family wanted to bring a
Negro friend home to dinner? (not object, object)

Marriage—Do you think there should be laws against marriages between Negroes and
whites? (no, yes)

Housing— White people have a right to keep Negroes out of their neighborhoods if they want
to, and Negroes should respect that right. (disagree, agree)

Intrusion—Negroes shouldn't push themselves where they're not wanted. (disagree, agree)

Source: Condron (1979).

Finally, it is useful to draw on some of the principles proposed by Ehrlich
(1973) to account for prejudice, discrimination, and stereotyping:

> Stereotypes about ethnic groups appear as a part of the social heritage of society. They
> are transmitted across generations as a component of the accumulated knowledge of
> society. They are as true as tradition, and as pervasive as folklore. No person can
> grow up in a society without having learned the stereotypes assigned to the major
> ethnic groups. But while ethnic stereotyping has been a constant in folklore, in
> literature, and in history, we should not overlook the fact that within societies the
> primary targets of stereotype assignments have changed over time. Even where
> targets remained stable, the content of assigned stereotypes stand in a reciprocating
> relation: as intergroup relations change, intergroup imagery changes. In cycle,
> changes in intergroup imagery affect changes in intergroup behavior. These recipro-
> cated effects may be stable or they may spiral in an increasingly negative or positive
> direction. (p. 35)

The contention that attitude changes follow changes in ethnic group relations
underscores the importance of studying and intervening at the level of intergroup
relations if we wish to reduce prejudice and discrimination. At the same time, a
broader definition of stereotypes might include a socially desirable side in support
of cultural distinctiveness and intergroup harmony (see Box 8.2).

Recently, social psychologists have shown more interest in cognitive processes in stereotyping as opposed to psychodynamic or sociocultural factors.
Hamilton (1979) reviews these major aspects of the cognitive approach. First,
cognitive biases have been found to result in stereotyping. Categorization of
similar objects into classes reduces complexity and brings order to our world.
Unfortunately, when we group persons into ingroups and outgroups, we automatically develop a positive bias toward our own group and a simplistic perception of other groups. This process is enhanced when real-world groups have clear
distinguishing characteristics such as skin color or manner of dress. Second, once
stereotypes are formed, they result in further cognitive biases. The ultimate
attribution error is a good example. In general, we tend to process information
about social groups in ways that are congruent with out existing stereotypes.
Third, stereotypes have important consequences on our behavior. Essentially,
stereotypes are maintained through the self-fulfilling effect they have on social

Box 8.2   FOCUS ON THEORY
Socially Desirable Consequences of Ethnic Stereotypes

Ethnic stereotypes are usually seen as unfair caricatures of entire groups and as such are equated with prejudice. Social scientists are almost unanimous in their condemnation of stereotyping as an inaccurate, unjustified, and immoral process. In contrast, social psychologists Donald Taylor of McGill University and Lise Simard of the Université de Montréal suggest that stereotypes may have a more positive role to play in intergroup relations.

It is possible that the negative view of stereotype arises from a North American ideology that emphasizes ethnic and cultural homogeneity—the "melting pot" approach, which attempts to eliminate cultural differences and the stereotypes that represent them. However, recent events are challenging the "melting pot" philosophy, as many ethnic groups are revitalizing their cultural distinctiveness—the blacks in the United States, the French-Canadians in Canada, the native Indians in both countries. Stereotypes that reflect cultural differences of which groups are proud may help these groups relate effectively with one another while still retaining their cultural distinctiveness. The cognitive process underlying positive stereotypes is the same as with negative stereotypes—but the underlying motivation and social consequences are very different.

Taylor and Simard define *stereotype* as a consensus among members of one group regarding the attributes of another group. Socially desirable stereotypes reflect mutual attraction between groups while at the same time each group maintains its cultural distinctiveness. Each group stereotypes the other in the same way that the group stereotypes itself. Members of each group value their own attributes as well as those of the other group.

The relationship between English and French-Canadians in Quebec is illustrative. While intergroup tensions definitely exist, mutually positive attitudes generally prevail. French-Canadians stereotype themselves and are stereotyped by English Canadians as sensitive, proud, and emotional. English Canadians are stereotyped by both groups as conservative, formal, and reserved. Both groups maintain their cultural distinctiveness and value or at least tolerate each other at the same time.

The social reality of a multiethnic society is that different groups will seek constructive relations with each other, while still maintaining their cultural distinctiveness. A broader concept of stereotyping that includes socially desirable consequences would help social psychology better understand this social reality.

Source: Taylor, D. M. & Simard, L. M. *Socially desirable and undesirable consequences of ethnic stereotyping in intergroup relations.* Paper presented at the Annual Meeting of the Canadian Psychological Association, Ottawa, Canada, June 1978.

interaction. The prejudiced white may hold a stereotype of blacks as distant, untrustworthy, and less intelligent. In interaction, the white person may be unfriendly, maintain greater interpersonal distance, and end a conversation as soon as possible. The black person will likely reciprocate this unfriendly behavior, thus "confirming" the white person's stereotype. A variety of studies have demonstrated such negative behavioral effects of stereotypes. The cognitive approach thus helps us understand why stereotypes are so persistent over time. As Hamilton suggests, the next question is how stereotypes can be altered in ways that increase our social effectiveness.

Ethnocentrism: Generalized Prejudice and Ingroup Glorification

In 1906, Sumner coined the term *ethnocentrism* to describe a provincialism or cultural narrowness wherein the individual was "ethnically centered"—that is, rigidly accepting those who are culturally alike, and just as rigidly rejecting those who are different. Sumner's description of ethnocentrism has been elaborated by Levine and Campbell (1972) by specifying the major orientations toward the ingroup and toward the outgroup that comprise the ethnocentric individual's view of the social world (see Table 8.2).

In *The Authoritarian Personality*, Adorno et al. (1950) provide one of the most explicit definitions of ethnocentrism:

> Ethnocentrism is based on a pervasive and rigid ingroup-outgroup distinction; it involves stereotyped negative imagery and hostile attitudes regarding outgroups, stereotyped positive imagery and submissive attitudes regarding ingroups, and a hierarchical, authoritarian view of group interaction in which ingroups are rightly dominant, outgroups subordinate. (p. 150)

The study of authoritarianism and ethnocentrism actually began as a study of anti-Semitism motivated by the horrendous atrocities of Nazi Germany against Jewish people. Many were concerned that fascism fueled anti-Semitism and that

Table 8.2   INGROUP AND OUTGROUP ORIENTATIONS OF ETHNOCENTRISM.

Orientations toward Ingroup	Orientations toward Outgroup
See selves as virtuous, and superior	See outgroup as contemptible, immoral, and inferior
See own standard of value as universal, intrinsically true	Rejection of outgroup values
See selves as strong	See outgroup as weak
Sanctions against theft	Sanctions for theft
Sanctions against murder	Sanctions for murder
Cooperative relations with other group members	Absence of cooperation
Obedience to authorities	Absence of obedience
Willingness to retain membership in group	Rejection of membership
Willingness to fight and die for group	Virtue in killing outgroup members in warfare
	Maintenance of social distance
	Negative affect, hate
	Use as bad examples in training children
	Blame for ingroup troubles
	Distrust and fear

Source: Levine & Campbell (1972).

this social aberration could just as easily rear its ugly head in America. Accordingly, Adorno and his colleagues first constructed an attitude scale to measure prejudice toward Jews on a number of stereotypical attitudes, including such things as the threatening character of Jews ("There are too many Jews in the various federal agencies and bureaus in Washington, and they have too much control over our national policies"), their seclusiveness ("The Jews keep too much to themselves, instead of taking the proper interest in community problems and good government"), and the offensive nature of Jews ("I can hardly imagine myself marrying a Jew"). These various dimensions showed strong relationships with each other: a respondent who saw Jews as threatening also saw them as seclusive, offensive, and so on.

What about generality of prejudice toward a variety of outgroups? The investigators constructed the Ethnocentrism Scale, measuring attitudes toward blacks ("Manual labor and menial jobs seem to fit the Negro mentality and ability better than more skilled or responsible work"), Japanese-Americans ("It is a mistake to allow any Japanese to leave internment camps and enter the army where they would be free to commit sabotage"), Filipinos ("Filipinos are all right in their place, but they carry it too far when they dress lavishly, buy good cars, and go around with white girls"), and the "Okies"—people from Oklahoma and other parts of the Dust Bowl who moved to California to seek work during the droughts of the Depression ("The many faults and the general inability to get along of the Okies who have recently flooded California prove that we ought to send them back where they came from as soon as conditions permit"). Other items measured the ingroup side of ethnocentrism—blind patriotism to the "American way" ("The main threat to basic American institutions during this century has come from the infiltration of foreign ideas, doctrines, and agitators").

The findings supported the concept of ethnocentrism. Respondents who rejected blacks tended to reject Okies and other outgroups. Furthermore, respondents who were prejudiced toward outgroups tended to glorify and be loyal toward the white Protestant American ingroup. For some people to love themselves, it seems that they must hate others.

The items of the Anti-Semitism and Ethnocentrism Scales may seem trite and uncouth by today's standards, but they were part of the vernacular of prejudiced Americans in the 1940s. Unfortunately, the scales contain many items with more than one idea, thus making responses ambiguous. More seriously, the items were all worded in one direction, and this led to a controversy about how much the various scales, especially the authoritarianism or F scale, were eliciting an acquiescence response set. After numerous studies, it appears that the scales were basically measuring what they intended to, and that they certainly could be improved.

The generalized prejudice of ethnocentrism has been documented by other studies before and after *The Authoritarian Personality.* In 1946, Hartley had found that respondents who rejected a wide variety of racial, ethnic, and religious groups also rejected the Wallonians, Pireneans, and Danireans. *The fact that none of these groups existed did not deter prejudiced respondents.* They wanted to keep these groups socially distant along with all other minority groups. By contrast, egalitarian respondents who accepted most groups were also willing to accept the fictitious groups, even though they had no prior knowledge of them. In 1951,

Campbell and McCandless used the Xenophobia Scale to measure fear and hatred toward blacks, Japanese, Jews, Mexicans, and English. They found generalized prejudice (and for some respondents, generalized acceptance) toward these outgroups on five different social dimensions—blaming, capability, morality, affection, and social distance.

The wide net of ethnocentrism is not restricted to racial, ethnic, and religious groups, but may include any groups who are different in some way—the physically handicapped, the mentally ill, single parents on welfare, homosexuals. For example, Chesler (1965) found that attitudes toward the physically disabled were related to attitudes toward a variety of racial, religious, national, and socioeconomic groups. Even though the physically disabled are often targets of prejudice, they constitute a minority outgroup rarely studied by social scientists. Chesler's results indicate that the handicapped may bear the brunt of ethnocentrism along with minority ethnic and racial groups. Individuals who were highly ethnocentric rejected the physically disabled along with other outgroups. Finally, a generalized suspicion and hostility toward people in general—termed *misanthropy*—may underlie ethnocentrism (Sullivan & Adelson, 1954).

The weight of research evidence gives strong support for the existence of ethnocentrism. For some people, the joke, "I hate everybody regardless of race, creed, or color," is close to being true. However, certain aspects of the typical research procedures might exaggerate the degree of generalized prejudice that has been found. Most studies have used the same type of attitude scale to measure prejudice toward different groups, usually a scale which allows only fixed responses. Some of the generality of attitudes might be due to subjects responding similarly on similar scales regardless of the group. If different types of scales were used for different groups, we might see less consistency in responses. For example, Ehrlich (1964) found that the correlation between attitudes toward the same two groups (Negroes and Jews) was reduced from 0.54 to 0.37 when changes were made in the response format such that respondents were able to qualify their answers. Ehrlich (1973) also contends that the degree of generality found by Hartley (1946) has been exaggerated since a large proportion of the respondents (as estimated by Ehrlich's examination of Hartley's tables) refused to give a social distance judgment for the three nonexistent groups.

Further research has also added to our understanding of the ingroup side of ethnocentrism. It is well established that perceptions of positive ingroup qualities are exaggerated by the ethnocentric individual. Moreover, there appears to be a positive bias in evaluating the performance of the products of ingroup members. Hinkle and Schopler (1979) introduce their review of research in this area with an interesting anecdote. Psychology faculty at two leading universities were asked to rank a number of graduate programs including their own. In almost every case where there was a disagreement in ranking, it was resolved in favor of the faculty members' own program. Thus, there was a strong tendency for faculty to rank the quality of their performance higher than it was ranked by faculty from other universities. The classic studies of intergroup conflict, discussed in the next section, also show this bias for overestimating group performance.

Hinkle and Schopler (1979) present evidence from experimental studies covering a number of different tasks (for example, creating titles for abstract designs) that generally show more positive evaluation of ingroup products. Why?

A number of competing explanations have been studied. One hypothesis follows balance theory (see Chapter 2). If the ingroup member likes the group, and the group produced the product, it is then congruent for the ingroup member to like the product. At present, there is no comprehensive theory to account for such evaluation biases, although some conditions governing their expression have been established. For example, when evaluations are to be made in public rather than in private, the ingroup bias appears to be enhanced. Further studies will provide additional insight on this important aspect of ethnocentrism and intergroup relations.

Finally, knowing that ethnocentrism exists does not tell us how it is formed in the minds of individuals. There are a number of ideas on this:

- Adorno et al. (1950) contend that ethnocentrism is an outgrowth of the authoritarian personality syndrome, which involves psychodynamic processes and structures at a deep level of functioning (see Chapter 5).
- Rokeach (1960) sees ethnocentrism as related to the way a person thinks in general, whether the person is *closed-minded*—thinking in rigid stereotypical ways—or *open-minded*—perceiving the world in a flexible and more realistic manner. Rokeach (1960) sums up his approach in the concept of *dogmatism*, which involves a closed cognitive system organized around a core set of beliefs about absolute authority that provides a framework for intolerance toward others.
- Prothro (1952) emphasizes historical and situational factors. He found a lower correlation between attitudes toward Jews and toward blacks in a sample of white Southerners than did Adorno et al. (1950) in their studies of white Westerners (0.49 as compared to 0.74). The effect of social conformity in producing prejudice should not be underestimated (Pettigrew, 1971). Southerners who were anti-black, were not necessarily anti-Semitic or ethnocentric.

Prothro's conclusion is reminiscent of Allport's (1954) stand for multiple causation: "It would seem from these results that the problem of 'the American dilemma' cannot be solved by approaching it from the level of personality dynamics alone. Situational, historical, and cultural factors appear to be of considerable, perhaps major, import (Prothro, 1952, p. 108)." Similarly, the complex concept of ethnocentrism requires more research for us to reach a better understanding. As Brewer (1979) points out, the elaboration of ethnocentrism involves numerous orientations, some of which seem logically incompatible (for example, the outgroup is perceived as weak and inferior and yet is feared). Different perspectives on ethnocentrism yield discrepant predictions about intergroup relations, and these can only be tested by further research.

Discrimination: The Behavior of Injustice

Prejudice, as we have seen, is an attitude; discrimination, a behavior. Discrimination consists of overt reactions that restrict an individual's opportunities based on his or her group membership rather than on individual abilities or characteristics. When a recovered psychiatric patient is denied a job in a factory, or an East Indian is told a vacant apartment is rented—solely on the basis of his visible racial or ethnic characteristics—we are faced with a violation of human rights and an instance of discrimination. Prejudice may or may not be expressed in overt discrimination, depending on the given situation. But we do look for congruence between prejudice and discrimination if there are no constraining forces, and for a relationship of mutual cause-and-effect between the two (Simpson & Yinger, 1972).

The relationship between prejudice and discrimination is made more insidious by the *self-fulfilling prophecy*. If the prejudices of the dominant group subtly influence how the dominant group behaves toward minority group members, this in turn may influence the behavior of the minority in precisely the direction that is expected. The resulting congruence between expectations and behavior is then seen as justification for further prejudice and discrimination. For instance, if a male teacher expects female students to be poor in math, the teacher may make few demands and give little encouragement; this in turn will negatively affect the female students' academic performance. The teacher is then justified in not recommending them for advanced math classes or awards or scholarships—and the self-fulfilling prophecy strikes again.

Another factor that fuels discrimination is the process of deindividuation wherein outgroup members are not seen as individual persons but only as members of a category (see Chapter 7). An experimental evaluation of the role of deindividuation in discrimination is provided by Wilder (1978). While some explanations of discrimination emphasize tangible factors such as intergroup competition or dissimilar values, it is possible that bias and discrimination may be induced by the simple categorization of groups on even the most trivial pretext (see Tajfel, 1970). In Wilder's study, college students were divided into two groups allegedly on the basis of their preferences toward a series of paintings. The groups were then asked to render a jury judgment in a civil trial case and were provided with the decision made by the other group. In one condition, the other group's decision was presented as unanimous, that is, deindividuated. In a second condition, that of individuation, one member of the group dissented from the majority recommendation. Questionnaire measures showed that in the latter condition, subjects perceived the other group to be a collection of individuals rather than a single entity. Discrimination was then assessed by having subjects divide rewards (small amounts of money) between members of the two groups. In the deindividuated (unanimous) condition, subjects awarded more money to their own group and less to outgroup members, that is, they discriminated against the other group. However, when individuation was present, no discrimination occurred—rewards were divided equally.

The problem of discrimination is made even more complex because of clear and valid differences among ethnic groups in terms of customs, values, religion, and philosophies of life. These differences may become the basis for conflicting value judgments that underlie intergroup conflict (Simpson & Yinger, 1972). For example, when Europeans first came to the continent of North America, many value judgments were made that were critical of Indian customs, language, and religion. A concerted effort was made to strip the Indian people of their culture and to either segregate them from mainstream society or to completely assimilate them into it. Schools punished Indian children for speaking their native tongue, and European religion was touted as a superior alternative to the Indians' pagan beliefs. Little effort was made to respect cultural differences, and generations of prejudice, discrimination, and conflict have followed. If these differences had been respected, they might have served as the basis for meaningful accommodation and integration between the contrasting cultures. To disagree with someone who holds a contrasting opinion or value, and to debate and negotiate for what you think is right, is far different from discriminating against someone on the basis of a superficial physical characteristic.

Acknowledgement of valid distinctions among groups of people is not discrimination. In fact, to take these distinctions into account in societal decision making, by allowing the full participation and acceptance of all groups, is the democratic and humanistic ideal. For example, if American Indians have a more conserving and respectful approach to the physical environment, this should be acknowledged and accepted; white people should be open to the influence of this value on social planning and economic decision making. On the other hand, if white society values achievement and productivity, then this should be accepted by Indian people. Both sides should understand and acknowledge the benefits of their differing approach to life.

There will be many times in decision making when such difference in values will be in clear conflict, and it will not be possible to satisfy all groups. However, resolutions will be easier to find if prejudice and discrimination are not allowed to cloud the picture. Unfortunately, what happens in practice is another story: conflict is confounded and aggravated by hostility, misperception, and discrimination, and potential resolutions are lost in the indifference and hatred of intergroup conflict.

We must, also understand that prejudice and discrimination often serve very functional purposes for the dominant groups in a society. Their attitudes and behaviors serve ingroup interests in terms of power, status, and all the resources that contribute to a "better" life. At the same time, discrimination denies outgroup interests for better education, more job opportunities, or equal pay for equal work. When such discrimination is widespread and becomes a focus for conflict, a social issue is created and forces for social change come into play in the form of educational programs, protest movements, and legal sanctions.

In Chapter 11, we will examine the social issues of racism, sexism, and poverty in an attempt to further understand widespread discrimination and the ways of combating it.

STUDYING AND REDUCING INTERGROUP CONFLICT

Prejudice and discrimination are an integral part of the broader phenomenon of *intergroup conflict*—a situation in which groups perceive themselves as having incompatible goals and engage in antagonistic actions to control each other. To more fully understand intergroup conflict, we must look into theory and research on the actual behaviors of groups as they interact with each other in conflict situations. As we shall see, social psychologists have been very adept at designing real-life field experiments wherein they could study the common processes and symptoms of intergroup conflicts as they unfolded before their eyes. These detailed documentations of how groups interact destructively and constructively add valuable insights to our awareness and our ability to plan action strategies for the reduction of prejudice, discrimination, and intergroup conflict.

Numerous strategies have been proposed and implemented to improve relations among groups (Bettleheim & Janowitz, 1964; Simpson & Yinger, 1972). Some strategies attempt to change the prejudiced individual through propaganda, intergroup contact, education, or personal therapy. Others direct their efforts to changing the broader social context. These approaches, exemplified by organizations opposing discrimination (such as the National Association for the Advancement of Colored People or the National Organization of Women), also may include such strategies of change as civil disobedience and nonviolent resistance (Simpson & Yinger, 1972).

Most theorists agree that change attempts must strengthen both the personal controls (motives, values) as well as the social controls (norms, laws) that work to reduce prejudice, discrimination, and conflict (Bettleheim & Janowitz, 1964). We will look at innovative projects designed to facilitate productive dialogue among members of antagonistic groups and observe what happens when guided intergroup contact brings together members or representatives of conflicting groups.

Process and Symptoms of Intergroup Conflict

In a series of three classic field experiments in intergroup conflict and cooperation, young boys were brought into camp groups in order to manipulate and study the intergroup relations that developed among them (Sherif, 1966; Sherif, Harvey, White, Hood & Sherif, 1961; Sherif & Sherif, 1953). The last of these studies, known as the "Robbers Cave Experiment" (it took place near the Oklahoma caves where the Jesse James gang once hid), involved a group of 11- to 12-year-old, white, middle-class, Protestant boys, who were of average intelligence and had no psychological problems. In other words, they were "good kids" who could be expected to behave in a typical fashion. The camp staff members were participant observers; the boys did not know that they were research subjects. The informed consent of their parents was obtained before they took part in the study.

In the first phase of the experiment, the boys, all strangers to one another, were formed into two separate camps and kept unaware of each other's existence. Through the usual camp activities, the boys developed a strong sense of ingroup cooperation, identity, and loyalty. Leadership patterns, status hierarchies, and normative expectations and sanctions developed in each group, and the degree of cohesiveness and morale was shown by the selection of group names: the Eagles and the Rattlers.

In the second phase of the experiment, the groups were brought together in a series of competitive win-lose interactions that included tug-of-war, target practice with bows and arrows, and baseball. This led to the development of hostile attitudes and destructive behavior between the groups. Each group overestimated its abilities and outcomes in the competitions and underestimated those of the other group. Highly evaluative negative and positive stereotypes developed, and name-calling and belittling became common behaviors. In addition to scuffles and raids on each other's territory, neutral contacts deteriorated into conflict situations. For example, a meal together became a garbage-throwing war.

Fortunately, Sherif had a third phase in his back pocket. The experimenters imposed a series of *superordinate goals* on the group—that is, common goals that could only be achieved by intergroup cooperation. In one case, the camp water supply stopped, requiring the cooperation of both groups in order to quickly locate a leak in a mile-long pipe. In another situation, the truck used to get food for an outing would not start; the boys had to all pull together, using a tug-of-war rope, to get the truck running. These cooperative interactions did not bring immediate results, but a series of superordinate goal attainments gradually led to a decrease in hostility and antagonism and a development of favorable attitudes and respectful behavior between the groups.

Sherif (1966) maintains that superordinate goals exist in all intergroup relationships and can be brought to the surface through effective communication and productive confrontation between group representatives.

The second illustration of how we can study intergroup conflict comes from the work of Robert Blake and Shirley Mouton, two applied social psychologists who have made significant contributions to organizational psychology and organization development (Blake & Mouton, 1961a, 1961b). Their thirty separate studies involved over a thousand adults drawn from various business and industrial organizations in training programs in intergroup relations. Each study lasted two weeks and followed the same phases of intergroup development, intergroup competition, win-lose outcome, conflict reduction, and intergroup collaboration.

In the first phase, participants engaged in 10 to 18 hours of ingroup interaction, leading to the development of group goals, norms, power structure, and cohesion. Then two different groups in the same laboratory were presented with a common problem of organizational functioning, such as how to evalute different styles of supervision, and were asked to develop a solution. The win-lose element was imposed by indicating that the "best" solution would be selected either by the groups or by an arbitrator.

During this phase, Blake & Mouton (1961b) observed and documented a number of classic symptoms of intergroup conflict. As competition increased, there was greater intergroup cohesion, with members putting aside personal differences and pulling together for "victory." Unfortunately, this also meant that disagreement was not to be tolerated. In fact, deviant ideas often triggered insidious pressures to conform and even expulsion from the group. These observations are similar to the negative elements of groupthink (see Chapter 7). The power relations in the groups shifted, with the more articulate and aggressive members taking the lead. This created resentment among those less influential members who were denied a voice, sowing the seeds of dissension which arose if the group was defeated.

Once the groups had developed their separate solutions to the problem, some definite distortions in perception and judgment became evident. Individuals typically judged their own group's solution as superior, with little or no regard for important differences among the solutions (see Figure 8.2). Objective tests of how well group members really understood the competing solutions showed that similarities were overlooked ("We have this, but they don't"), but distinctive elements were clearly recognized—more so if they belonged to one's own group.

In the phase of selecting the best solution, the groups studied the proposals, discussed clarifications, and then interacted through elected representatives to make the final choice. The supposed clarification process typically deteriorated into belittlement and denigration of the other group's proposal. At the same time, hostile attitudes, including negative stereotypes, developed between the groups

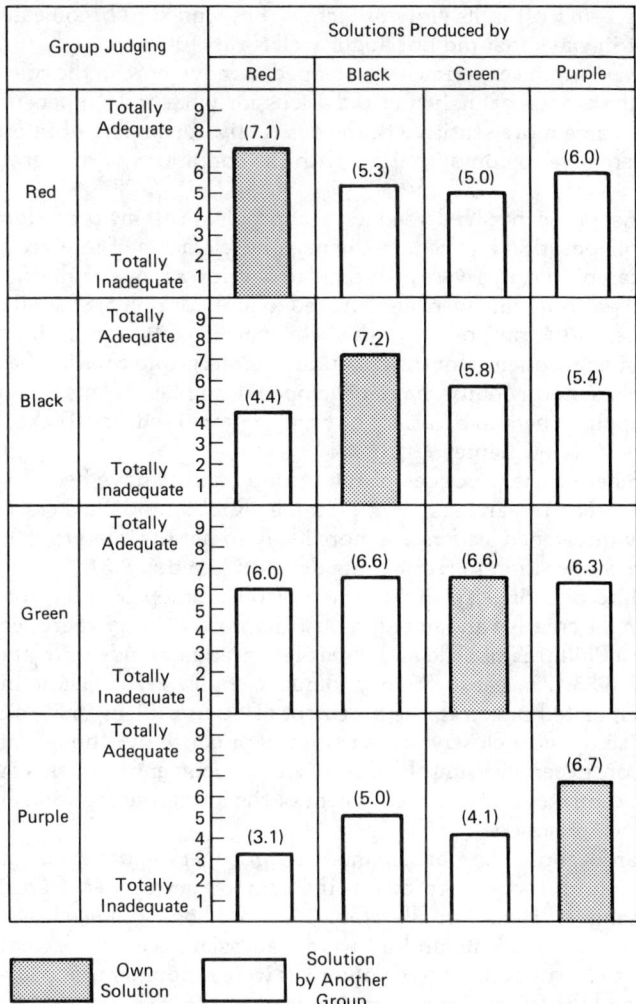

Figure 8.2   **Judgments of Adequacy of the Solutions of One's Own Group and of Another Group.**
Source: Blake & Mouton (1961).

and provocative statements were traded back and forth, escalating as they went. When the representatives met to choose the winner, the most common outcome was a deadlock. Representatives put loyalty to their group's position before objectivity, due to their fear of being ostracized as traitors.

If an impartial judge was called in, he was initially perceived as "fair" and "honest" by both groups—until he made his decision. Once the verdict was in, the losers perceived him as "incompetent," "biased," and "tactless."

The losing group often deteriorated into ingroup fighting, splintered into factions, and rejected the leaders who lost the day. The winning group was temporarily better off in its glow of victory, but tended to become arrogant and complacent in ways that did not augur well for its future.

At this point, the experimenters stepped in, now more in the role of trainers, and began the process of analyzing and discussing what had happened. The group members became more sensitive to the destructive behaviors of intergroup conflict and were able to compare these with the conditions of intergroup collaboration.

The final phase involved a sequence of problem-solving procedures designed to create collaboration and reduce the negative elements of intergroup competition. For example, groups were instructed to develop a range of alternatives rather than a fixed position, and were encouraged to look for points of similarity as well as differences in the proposals. In this way, participants were trained to use the problem-solving sequence for the resolution of intergroup conflict. Based on their research, Blake and Mouton have developed a number of intergroup interventions and applied them in a variety of organizational settings (Blake, Shepard & Mouton, 1964) (see Chapter 9).

A number of the processes of intergroup conflict have been further documented by other researchers. For example, Rabbie and Bekkers (1978) have shown how threatened leaders are more likely to opt for intergroup competition rather than cooperation to resist being deposed (see Box 8.3).

The third and final example of a controlled study of intergroup relations comes from the creative and now famous "Stanford Prison Experiment" of social psychologist Phillip Zimbardo and three of his graduate students (Haney, Banks & Zimbardo, 1973; Zimbardo, Haney, Banks & Jaffe, 1973). These investigators created a simulated prison in the basement of Stanford University's psychology building to study more closely the dynamics of prison life. Although many aspects of the prison experience unfolded and were documented in this work, what follows concentrates on the development of the intergroup relationship between "guards" and "prisoners."

Zimbardo chose the participants (ten prisoners and eleven guards) from volunteers who responded to ads in the campus newspaper. Careful selection yielded a sample of emotionally stable, law-abiding, middle-class, college-age males. Most were students and all were Caucasian, with the exception of one Oriental. By a flip of a coin, these volunteers were randomly grouped as guards or prisoners, and the two-week experiment began.

One Sunday afternoon, without warning and without expecting it, the prisoners were "arrested" by police, read their rights, searched, handcuffed, and taken to the police station for booking and detention. Later, the blindfolded prisoners were transported to the "Stanford County Prison" where they were stripped, skin-searched, deloused, given a smock and cap, and read a list of harsh rules covering the most basic and mundane behaviors. The guards wore khaki uniforms and silver reflector sunglasses, and carried a whistle, handcuffs, keys, and a billy club.

The two-week experiment lasted six days before it had to be terminated. At first, the prisoners revolted. The guards, who had considerable latitude in running the prison, squashed the rebellion viciously, punished the ringleaders with solitary confinement, and generally began to harass and intimidate the prisoners (Zimbardo et al., 1973).

Box 8.3   FOCUS ON RESEARCH
Threatened Leaders Opt for Intergroup Competition

The idea that leaders may enter into intergroup conflict in order to unify their group behind them is popular among journalists and some social scientists. However, there is very little empirical evidence to support this notion. Jacob Rabbie and Frits Bekkers of the Institute of Social Psychology at the University of Utrecht in the Netherlands designed an experimental situation to this hypothesis.

University students were recruited as subjects for a simulation of labor-management negotiations. Each subject was told that, on the basis of a personality questionnaire, he or she had been selected as the leader of a four-person union group that was now meeting in another room. As in real negotiations, the leader would negotiate with management and could not communicate with the union group during negotiations. However, the leader would be allowed to listen to the union group's discussion at appropriate points. The leader's position was not assured—he or she was told that the union group would hold an election every hour of the three-hour experiment.

Over a series of simulations, Rabbie and Bekkers investigated a number of factors in relation to the competitive or cooperative choices made by the leaders. In response to the leader's position on the matters under negotiation (such as the division of profits between management and labor), the management group (in reality the experimenters) offered either "all or none" negotiations (the competitive choice) or a sharing of profits or whatever (the cooperative choice).

First, it was found that leaders in an unstable condition (who were told that any two union members could depose them) made more competitive choices than leaders in a stable condition (all four members of the union group were required to depose them). Second, competitive choices were further increased by group divisiveness, that is, higher disagreement over the negotiation proposals. Third, when leaders had a strong negotiating position, they were more likely to choose a competitive response. Finally, when instability was further increased by saying that only one member opposed to the leader meant downfall, almost all leaders chose competition over cooperation.

These results suggest that stability of leadership may be important in the development of intergroup conflict. Stable leaders appear to choose cooperation rather than endangering their position through competition. Unstable leaders, on the other hand, may choose competition in order to prove themselves and strengthen their position. Especially when the group is divided internally, and the leader has a strong negotiating position, there is a clear tendency to opt for intergroup competition.

Source: Rabbie, J. M. & Bekkers, F. Threatened leadership and intergroup competition. *European Journal of Social Psychology*, 1978, 8, 9–20.

It was clear after this episode that the guards really began to demonstrate their inventiveness in the application of arbitrary power. They made the prisoners obey petty, meaningless and often inconsistent rules, forced them to engage in tedious, useless work, such as moving cartons back and forth between closets and picking thorns out of blankets for hours on end. (The guards had previously dragged the blankets through thorny bushes to create this disagreeable task.) Not only did the prisoners have to sing songs or laugh or refrain from smiling on command, they were also encouraged to curse and vilify each other publicly during some of the counts.

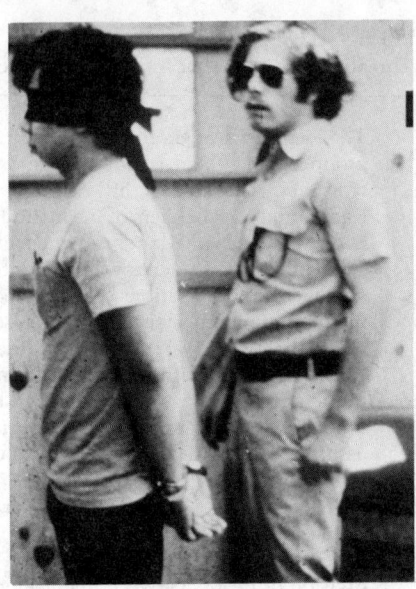

A new "prisoner" is ushered to his cell in the "Stanford County Prison." *(Philip G. Zimbardo/New York Times)*

They sounded off their number endlessly and were repeatedly made to do push-ups, on occasion with a guard stepping on them or a prisoner sitting on them. (p. 42)

The relationship between guards and prisoners became a complementary one in a perverted, symbiotic fashion. As the guards became increasingly aggressive, assertive, and self-aggrandizing, the prisoners became more and more passive, dependent, and self-deprecating. Hostility, antagonism, suspicion, and stereotyping became the hallmarks of the intergroup relationship. The personal stress of the situation began to show. Within 36 hours, the first prisoner had to be released because of "extreme depression, disorganized thinking, uncontrollable crying, and fits of rage" (Zimbardo et al., 1973, p. 44). On each of the next three days, another prisoner showed similar symptoms and had to be released, a fifth was released after developing a psychosomatic rash following the rejection of his parole appeal.

At the end of the experiment, a series of debriefing sessions as well as year-long follow-ups indicated that the mental anguish was temporary and situational, but that personal learnings gained by the participants were permanent. The shocking implication of this dramatic story is that well-adjusted, mature young men slip very easily into roles and intergroup behavior that is myopic, sadistic, and inhuman, thus clearly demonstrating the power of institutional structures and the dynamics of intergroup conflict to shape such attitudes and behaviors. It can be argued that the demand characteristics of the experiment (see Chapter 3) led the subjects to behave in the ways they did. Zimbardo et al.'s position is that the subjects took on the well-known roles of guards and inmates very well indeed, and that the intergroup horror they created is similar to that which unfolds in real prisons every day of the year.

The work of Sherif, Zimbardo et al., and Blake and Mouton clearly demonstrates how competitive interaction between groups creates intergroup conflict.

This approach to understanding intergroup relations is referred to as *realistic group conflict theory*, which basically states that real or objective conflicts of interests between groups causes conflict (Campbell, 1965). In the camp studies, only one group could win the games; in the training workshops, only one group could have the superior product; and in the simulated prison, only one group had ultimate power and control over all the resources. These real conflicts of interest lead to intergroup hostility as well as the ingroup loyalty and glorification of ethnocentrism.

A complementary view of intergroup conflict is offered by Tajfel and Turner (1979), who maintain that real differences in interests are not necessary to produce conflict, even though they are often sufficient to do so. Their experimental work has shown that the mere presence of an outgroup is sufficient to produce an ingroup bias and discrimination toward an outgroup. Subjects who have been assigned to groups on some minor pretext or even by an explicit random process tend to show ingroup favoritism and outgroup discrimination in distributing monetary rewards. There is no conflict of interest or antagonism between the groups, and no social interaction has taken place. What then is happening? It appears that individuals desire a positive social identity, which is obtained by first distinguishing one's group from others and by then evaluating one's group more positively. This need for positive social comparison thus motivates intergroup competition and conflict where no real differences exist. In real life, it is most likely that the objective and subjective sources of intergroup conflict are mutually integrated and reinforcing, thus making the problem even more difficult to deal with.

Positive Potential of Intergroup Contact: Facilitating Conditions

Many people believe that simply bringing members of different ethnic groups together in face-to-face interaction will reduce prejudice and conflict, and there is some research evidence for such a simple frequency effect in community settings (Williams, 1964). However, as the preceding studies indicate, interaction among groups can in fact induce and increase hostile attitudes and destructive behavior.

The crucial factors are the *conditions* under which intergroup contact occurs. When the contact conditions involve intense competition, tension, frustration, and inequality, we can expect the interaction to foster antagonism and escalation of conflict. If, on the other hand, the opposite conditions prevail, we can expect positive outcomes.

Reviews of theory and research on intergroup contact have led to descriptions of the facilitative conditions for productive interaction and positive attitude change (Amir, 1969, 1976; Allport, 1954; Cook, 1957, 1970; Simpson & Yinger, 1972). These conclusions are based on a wide variety of studies from laboratory experiments to social surveys, and cover a wide range of intergroup relationships (the emphasis being on race relations in the United States). The distilled wisdom of these reviews represents our best hypotheses on the conditions necessary to develop the positive potential of intergroup contact:

- The *acquaintance potential* refers to the extent to which the contact situation offers the opportunity for the participants to get to know one another. This includes not only the opportunity for contact but also the extent to which the interaction is personal and intimate versus casual and impersonal. Research findings clearly indicate that the more individuals can get to know each other as *persons*, the more the stereotypes and barriers between them are broken down.

- The *relative status* of the individuals from the different groups is a key factor in determining the results of contact: interaction on an equal status basis is essential. Higher status on the part of minority group participants is also facilitative. The intergroup interaction must therefore maintain or increase the status of minority group members. Consider how often this is not the case. Consider how often the *black* person from the ghetto interacts with the *white* teacher, the *white* social worker, the *white* police officer, the *white* store owner—all the powerful individuals who hold the keys to the good life (or the poor life) in their hands. A refreshing contrast is provided by Clore, Bray, Itkin, and Murphy (1978) in their description of positive intergroup contact in a summer camp for black and white children where power and status were relatively equal (see Box 8.4).

- The *social norms* of the contact situation further affect its positiveness: friendliness, trust, respect, and openness support productive interaction through influencing both expectations and behavior. Contact that is sanctioned by institutional supports (laws, customs, local atmosphere) and authority figures will more likely result in positive outcomes.

- A *cooperative task and reward structure* involves participants in functionally important activities directed toward common goals. Such a cooperative atmosphere is emotionally pleasant and rewarding and thus adds to the power of the situation to affect attitudes and behavior. Worschel (1979) stresses the centrality of cooperation in reducing intergroup conflict and discusses a number of strategies for inducing cooperation including communication and superordinate goals.

- The *characteristics of the individuals* involved affect the outcomes of intergroup contact. The competence of the minority group members is an important force in contradicting the stereotypes of dominant group members. At the same time, some prejudiced individuals may be so insecure that the contact situation will have little positive impact on their attitudes. The direction and intensity of the initial attitude must also be considered, in that initially favorable attitudes tend to become more favorable while initially negative attitudes tend to become more hostile—and from the same contact experience. The self-fulfilling prophecy is at work once more. Highly prejudiced persons may manipulate contact situations for their personal advantage, whereas less prejudiced individuals are most likely to develop close associations leading to a reduction in stereotyping and hostility. Thus, individual characteristics must be considered in planning and evaluting programs of intergroup contact.

A classic study of the facilitative conditions of intergroup contact was carried out during the 1960s in the southern United States by social psychologist Stuart Cook (1970). This project brought together highly prejudiced white female college students, one at a time, with two confederates (one white and one black) under the guise of studying how a small group of strangers would work together on a cooperative task—a railroad game requiring the operation of a small railway system. The game required two hours a day for a one-month period, with a half-hour lunch break at the middle of each session.

To heighten the acquaintance potential, the black confederate self-disclosed a variety of information about herself, including accounts of racial discrimination to which she had been subjected. The black confederate was of equal status to the white subject in the task and also fulfilled her role in a competent fashion—an individual characteristic that would likely contradict the white subject's stereo-

Box 8.4   FOCUS ON RESEARCH
Equal Status and Positive Change in Interracial Attitudes

Class differences between whites and blacks is one of the greatest obstacles of positive changes in interracial attitudes. Economic inequality ensures inequality in almost every area of human interaction, and this lack of equal-status contact means that prejudiced attitudes are not likely to change through intergroup contact. In contrast, Gerald Clore, Stuart Itkin, and Pamela Murphy of the University of Illinois and Robert Bray of the University of Kentucky were able to study interracial attitudes in a situation of equal-status contact.

An interracial summer camp was designed to satisfy all the criteria of positive contact. Equal numbers of black and white children attended the camp. They all came from similar socioeconomic backgrounds and had equal privileges and duties at the camp. The social structure of the camp was also equalized in power and status—half the administrators and counselors were black, and half were white. Living together in a camping situation for one week provided high acquaintance potential and numerous cooperative tasks toward superordinate goals. Approximately two hundred children attended the camp at the rate of approximately forty children per week for five weeks.

Interracial attitudes were measured at the beginning and end of the camp by a semantic differential consisting of bipolar adjectives (for example, good-bad, valuable-worthless). Sociometric measures were obtained through games that required interpersonal choices in the racially mixed camp groups. For example, in the "name game" at the end of the camp, children wrote down the names of three others whose addresses and phone numbers they would most like to have.

Positive attitude changes occurred for girls, but not for boys. Boys began the camp with neutral cross-race attitudes and did not have much room to change. Girls, however, began with negative attitudes that became more positive by the end of the experience. The sociometric measures showed similar results—a significant increase in cross-race choices that were due mainly to changes for girls. These positive changes were evident for both black and white children.

The authors conclude that intimate, prolonged, cooperative, rewarding, equal-status contact produced positive changes in attitudes and behavior. The crucial question is how to change the social structure of society so that this type of contact between racial groups occurs on a regular basis.

Source: Clore, G. L., Bray, R. M., Itkin, S. M. & Murphy, P. Interracial attitudes and behavior at a summer camp. *Journal of Personality and Social Psychology,* 1978, *36,* 107–116.

type. Furthermore, the norms of the situation supported integration—one of the experimenters was black—and all crew members received equal treatment. In addition to a cooperative task, the reward structure was also cooperative—a good group effort resulted in a bonus to all members.

Prior to and following the railroad game, white subjects were tested on a number of attitude measures. (It is important to note that the pre- and post-assessments were not known by the subjects to be related to their participation in the game.) Subjects were also observed during the running of the game itself. What happened? In many cases, the white subjects, who had been selected on the basis of highly prejudiced attitudes toward blacks, became more friendly and open in their interaction with the black confederate. As information replaced ignorance and stereotyping, the whites came to see a more complex picture of black experience. Observations during the game showed that subjects shifted from giving almost total attention to the white confederate to an almost equal division of communication between the white and black confederate. On the attitude measures, a significant number of subjects showed positive changes as compared to a control group of highly prejudiced subjects who chose not to participate in the game but did complete the pre- and post-attitude measures. Although the attitude changes in the experimental group were quite large in magnitude, they were experienced by only about a third of the subjects. Most of the participants showed no change. However, given the extreme negative initial attitudes, these results are encouraging. If the time of contact had been greater than forty hours, it is possible that the facilitative conditions might have had an even greater effect.

Reducing Prejudice and Conflict through Intergroup Contact: The Challenge for Practice

The facilitative conditions for positive intergroup contact serve as guideposts for the development and execution of action programs to reduce prejudice and discrimination. Based on this knowledge, social psychologists and other practitioners have brought together members of different groups in a variety of social and recreational programs with generally positive results (Bettleheim & Janowitz, 1964; Dean & Rosen, 1955; Simpson & Yinger, 1972).

Applied social psychologists have taken different approaches in developing a variety of guided intergroup discussion projects. The earliest projects took the form of workshops on intergroup or community relations (Levinson, 1954; Lippitt, 1949). Later approaches have adapted interpersonal skill training (Carkhuff & Banks, 1970) and sensitivity training (Cobbs, 1972). Out of these efforts, a new social technology is developing for applying interpersonal and small-group skills to programs of intergroup contact. (Chapter 15 presents my own model, called *third-party consultation*. This builds upon the work presented here and shifts the emphasis to the crucial role of an impartial facilitator in resolving intergroup conflict.)

The major pioneering effort in the application of human relations skills to the problem of interracial conflict was a two-week workshop designed by the founders of the National Training Laboratories (Lippitt, 1949). This workshop, described in Chapter 4, was the forerunner of the human relations training movement. The workshop came from a request by the Connecticut Advisory Committee on Intergroup Relations to the Research Center for Group Dynamics and the Commission on Community Relations of the American Jewish Congress, both of which were the brainchilds of Kurt Lewin. The request was for information on research developments and training programs that would enable community leaders to work more effectively at improving intergroup relations.

Subsequently, a planning team of social practitioners and social scientists designed a two-week workshop for teachers, social workers, and community volunteers who were directly involved in a variety of interracial activities. In terms of racial and ethnic composition, the participants were 29 percent black-American, 25 percent Jewish-American, 23 percent English-American, and 23 percent Irish-, Canadian- or Italian-American. The forty participants were divided into three racially mixed work groups, which spent most of their time diagnosing typical interracial problems and used role playing, psychodrama, and reality practice to learn new strategies of handling these problems. For example, a teacher who was uncertain and reluctant about requesting the school principal to implement an interracial curriculum program could role play the actual situation using another participant briefed in the role of the principal. Following analysis and evaluation of the role play, the teacher could try again, taking into account suggestions made by other participants and the group leaders.

Lippitt (1949) presents an excellent documentation of the activities and the effects of the workshop. All workshop interaction was observed. The effects of the workshop were assessed by pre- and post-interviews with participants and co-workers, and by later observations by consultants from the state committee. Most trainees experienced higher motivation, increased optimism, and more social support for their work. The trainees developed a broader view of the overall problem and of their own role in terms of strategies and goals. Trainees showed increased participation in intergroup relations work and made use of the skills and methods acquired in the workshop. All in all, Lippitt (1949) gives an impressive picture of this classic attempt to blend theory and research toward the solution of social problems.

A second example of early intergroup work comes from Levinson (1954) and Levinson and Shermerhorn (1951) who report on three workshops that brought together groups of well-motivated individuals for a program of lectures, discussions, and extracurricular activities lasting several weeks. Although the participants came from a variety of ethnic and religious backgrounds, the majority were white, middle-class professionals. The main functions of these programs were: (1) to provide knowledge and skills on intergroup relations; (2) to induce emotional-ideological change through clarification of concepts, such as prejudice, and to further self-insight and democratic thinking; and (3) to provide an intense supportive living experience.

To what extent did the participants become more democratic and understanding in their approach to self, others, and social problems? To answer this question, the researchers administered a battery of personality and attitude scales (including the Authoritarianism and Ethnocentrism Scales) to participants before and after the workshops (one workshop also used a control group). In general, workshop participants showed more democratic and egalitarian attitudes and less prejudice as a result of the training experience. While it is unclear what the long-term effects on intergroup behavior might be, the changes in individual attitudes is encouraging.

The work of Carkhuff and Banks (1970) and Carkhuff and Griffin (1970) moves us to the direct application of human relations skill training to the intergroup behavior of trainees. This concerns the improvement of communication between representatives of a majority-dominated system and members of a minority group within the system.

In the Carkhuff and Banks (1970) study, fourteen white teachers and ten black parents were brought together in two racially mixed training groups that met for 20 hours spread over three weeks. Black and white children were also included in the workshop for later interactions. These sessions followed the standard Carkhuff training format described in Chapter 6: skill definition, discrimination training, and communication training through helping interactions and feedback. The training covered the core interpersonal skills of empathy, respect, genuineness, concreteness, immediacy, and confrontation.

The helping interactions began with similar helper-helpee pairs (black adult with black adult), moved to racially mixed pairs (black adult with white adult), and ended with the most dissimilar pairs (white adult with black child).

The participants were assessed before and after the workshop on their abilities to discriminate different skill levels and to communicate using the skills effectively. These assessments included written responses to standard helping problems and race relations situations as well as ratings on tape-recorded excerpts from helping interviews with four different helpers: white adult, black adult, white child, black child. Here are two examples of the kind of race relations situations used in the training (Carkhuff & Griffin, 1970). The task of the trainee was to respond to these statements in as helpful a manner as possible.

> *Black adult:* Every time we start anything and become involved in it, it seems like the power structure in some manner arranges to take it away from us or make it inadequate—they do something to make it a bad thing or completely stop it in some manner.
>
> *Black child:* When I was in school, I was going to my class, this kid called me a dirty name. I just wanted to beat his face in. There's this kid in school—he called me a nigger and I wanted to just beat his face in. I knew if I had to fight him I would get kicked out of school or something or even get the paddle. I don't want to fight the guy. But he kept on tempting me. I went to my next class all upset and everything. And I went home—I was upset and nervous and just scared and didn't know what to do. (pp. 444–445)

The results were very clear. Participants showed significant gains on all measures and with all helpees: after the workshop, the trainees were able to communicate more effectively with other people *regardless of race or age.* There was a slight tendency for whites to communicate at a higher skill level with other whites than with blacks. The same held true for black helpers, but these trends were not statistically significant.

In the Carkhuff and Griffin (1970) study, fourteen adult black human relations specialists were trained to met the needs of young black students in integrated junior high schools. The specialists were assessed as functioning at a facilitative level of helping and were rated as effective by students and staff in the schools.

The investigators concluded that problems in race relations may be part of a larger human relations problem, wherein most people communicate at low levels of functioning with their own group as well as with others. The implication is that wider training in human relations skills will work to alleviate misunderstanding and prejudice among groups within our society. This makes sense, but is only part of the picture. We must also consider ways of bringing members of different groups into direct contact, focusing specifically on their intergroup perceptions and behavior.

Robert Bell and his colleagues (Bell, Cleveland, Hanson & O'Connell, 1969; Cleveland, 1971) present a fine example of the application of sensitivity training to intergroup relations. (These practitioners also used some of the intergroup development techniques created by Blake and Mouton [Blake, Mouton & Sloma, 1965; Blake, Shepard & Mouton, 1964].)

The setting is Houston, Texas, in the late 1960s. The city had enjoyed relative calm in race relations and was hopeful that the racial crises of Watts and Detroit could be avoided in Houston. However, tensions appeared to be rising. In May 1967, the first outbreak of violence occurred when four hours of gunfire erupted between police and students at Texas Southern University, a predominantly black institution in Houston. One officer was killed by a bullet of undetermined origin, and students' rooms and belongings were ransacked.

Attitude surveys conducted by a research psychologist in the mayor's office before and after the incident showed a dramatic increase in hostility on the part of the black community members toward police. The city approached a group of professional psychologists at the Houston Veteran's Administration Hospital to see if they could provide a small-group interaction program involving police and hostile community members. Its goal was to bring about mutual respect, harmony, and cooperation. The psychologists drew on their experience in human relations training to design a series of intergroup laboratories, each meeting three hours a week for six weeks, and involving approximately twenty officers and community members divided into three small groups. By leading a separate laboratory every morning and afternoon, the trainers were able to involve 200 police and 200 citizens over a six-week period. The work continued until all 1400 police had been involved with an equal number of community members.

The phases of the laboratory were structured to discuss: (1) the damaging stereotypes each group had of the other; (2) the effect of these stereotypes on attitudes, perceptions, and behavior toward each other; (3) the ways each group reinforced these stereotypes in the eyes of the other; and (4) the development of a cooperative problem-solving attitude so that the groups could work together constructively. A very useful technique in examining stereotypes was to have each group develop both its self-image and its image of the other group, and then to exchange these images through dialogue.

The program encountered many difficulties including inconsistent and destructive participation as well as a high rate of attrition of group trainers due to the taxing demands of the role. Nonetheless, evaluation of the program through questionnaires and attitude scales showed positive gains, more so for community members than for police. Participants generally rated the program as good to excellent, expressed more positive feelings about the other group, and developed a more complex appreciation of the other group's role and situation.

On the community level, the city reported a 70 percent drop in citizen complaints about police behavior in the seven months following the beginning of the program. Informal intergroup contacts in the city appeared to increase, and the summer of 1968 did not bring Watts or Detroit to Houston. However, as the investigators point out, "No claim is made that eighteen hours of discussion will sweep away years of rancor and distrust. But it is a necessary beginning" (Bell et al., 1969, p. 246).

The Houston program is an enlightening demonstration of the potential that structured human relations training holds for intergroup realtions. Other practitioners have made similar attempts to improve police-community relations, especially as they represent friction between whites and blacks (Allen, Pilnick & Silversweig, 1969; Diamond & Lobitz, 1973; Klein, Thomas & Bellis, 1971; Lipsett & Steinbruner, 1969). In addition, a variety of workshop designs and structured exercises have been developed to increase interracial awareness and to foster collaborative action among blacks and whites (see Fromkin & Sherwood, 1976).

Two final examples illustrate the application of small-group techniques to intergroup relations. The first, the work of Martin Lakin, adapted the sensitivity training approach to the relationship between Jewish and Arab people living in Israel. The second is the challenging work of Leonard Doob in arranging a problem-solving workshop involving Protestants and Catholics from Northern Ireland.

Lakin and his colleagues brought together Jews and Arabs living in Israel in two mixed sensitivity groups (Lakin, Lomranz & Lieberman, 1969). Their goals were to improve intergroup communication and reduce intergroup suspicion. In addition to group dialogue and analysis, the program included exercises for communication skill development and ethnically mixed team projects for developing proposals to improve Arab-Jewish relations in Israel. Assessment of the program included pretraining questionnaires, tallies of key behaviors and main topics, observation of group activities, sociometric ratings, projective tests, and posttraining interviews.

While there was a certain degree of resistance to the intervention, participants and trainers were moderately positive about the outcomes and felt that they had gained new insights into their mutual problems of living together. Although the trainers concluded that the actual achievements in conflict reduction were small, this work is a laudable example of the systematic application and assessment of human relations training to the difficult arena of intergroup relations.

Leonard Doob has been instrumental in organizing a number of problem-solving workshops in conflict resolution. In Chapter 12, which deals with international relations, we will look at his work on conflict in the Horn of Africa. Our focus here, however, is on his initiatives in organizing a workshop centering on the interreligious conflict in Northern Ireland (Doob & Foltz, 1973).

Based on initial contacts in the summer of 1971, Doob and his colleagues developed the objectives of, first, bringing together influential leaders from the grass-roots level in Belfast to establish some degree of mutual trust and, second, developing plans for improving intergroup relations. Encouraged by the willingness of potential participants, Doob obtained funds, recruited a training staff, and developed an intervention design. With the help of two co-workers who were residents of Belfast, fifty-six participants were recruited for a ten-day workshop held at Stirling University, in Scotland, in August of 1972.

The first phase of the workshop followed the Tavistock model of training (see Chapter 7), with participants meeting in small mixed groups, with no expressed purpose other than to study the group's behavior. Unstructured total-group meetings were also held and, as a transition to the second phase of the workshop, application groups were formed; these consisted of both Protestants and Catholics from the same neighborhood.

The second half of the workshop included an experience in NTL style

Box 8.5   FOCUS ON PRACTICE
Promoting Intergroup Cooperation Between "Haves" and "Have-nots"

Can social scientist/practitioners facilitate cooperation between conflicting groups that are very different in background and very unequal in power? L. Dave Brown of the Department of Organizational Behavior at Case Western Reserve University served as a consultant in a project designed to improve communication and promote cooperation between "haves" and "have-nots" in a large metropolitan area.

Under the sponsorship of a philanthropic foundation, chief executive officers of large corporations (the "haves") were brought together with community activists (the "have-nots") in a two-day residential workshop to plan community projects. These two groups differed on every dimension related to power and status in American society. The "haves" were predominantly white, older, wealthy males who were members of the city's social elite. The "have-nots" were young, minority-group males and females; all of them worked in community organizations, and most were part-time students.

After introductory activities, the workshop moved to a stilted discussion of city problems. Definitions of problems by the "have-nots" (such as the steel companies pollute our neighborhoods) were met with sophisticated economic analysis by the "haves" beyond the expertise of the "have-nots." Frustration turned to passivity. Two mixed groups attempted to generate proposals for community projects, but all attempts failed. The workshop produced neither effective communication nor long-term cooperation.

An analysis of the workshop led to the planning of a second dialogue designed to overcome the difficulties that had been experienced. A more diverse group of "haves" was created so that a more varied approach to community problems might emerge. The consultant held orientation meetings with each "have" before the workshop to set expectations and develop better rapport. Similarly, premeetings were held with the diverse group of "have-nots" to clarify expectations and build group cohesion that was lacking in the first workshop. Finally, there was an emphasis on generating a range of alternate proposals rather than locking in on a single project.

The second dialogue was a resounding success. The consultant-participant rapport from the premeetings transferred to the sessions, and consultant interventions were accepted more readily and with more positive effects. Conflict and cooperation was not defined by group boundaries. Coalitions of "haves" and "have-nots" developed a number of proposals. Following the workshop, participants continued to work together, and two projects received funding. In addition, participants helped launch a series of locally sponsored workshops to bring together other "haves" and "have-nots." The positive interaction between the groups had forged a long-term cooperative effort.

Source: Brown, L. D. Can "haves" and "have-nots" cooperate? Two efforts to bridge a social gap. *Journal of Applied Behavioral Science*, 1977, *13*, 211–224.

sensitivity-training (see Chapter 7), followed by an opportunity to plan back-home activities and to practice the skills required to implement the plans.

Participants learned about group process, especially around issues of authority and power in the Tavistock phase, and about group identities and the difficulties of intergroup communication. There was significant learning about others, especially across religious lines, and a number of plans for community development projects were discussed. There was considerable personal stress on the participants as they examined their own behavior in conflict situations. This put additional pressure on the two Belfast co-workers, who were caught between the participants and the organizers; they, in fact, resigned from the project some time after the workshop.

Given these mixed reactions, Doob and Foltz (1974) returned to Belfast ten months later and interviewed forty participants. Most maintained that the workshop had been a profitable, rewarding experience. Many felt they had been helped as persons and were more effective in their organizational work. Some reported that the workshop had helped them to develop and carry out their own plans for community activities.

In contrast to this relatively positive picture, the two Belfast co-workers and others presented a searing criticism of the project's conception and execution (Boehringer, Zeruolis, Bayley & Boehringer, 1974). They maintained that the workshop's goals were ill-defined and contradictory, that the research methodology was inadequate, and that the workshop was generally ineffective and harmful to many of the participants. It appears that considerable misunderstanding and differences in expectations occurred between the organizers and their Belfast co-workers around such issues as the intent of the training design and informed consent of participants. Some of the confusion was cleared up in a rejoinder by the organizers and trainers (Alevy, Bunker, Doob, Foltz, French, Klein & Miller, 1974), but an unfortunate air of acrimony remains.

The potential pitfalls for applied social psychologists who wish to intervene in real-world intergroup conflicts are made abundantly clear by this episode. By learning from our experience, we can improve our ability to design and execute workshops for improving intergroup relations (see Box 8.5). There are also a number of strategies by which the would-be third-party consultant can increase the probability of success. We will look at these in Chapter 15.

Summary

Prejudice is a simplistic hostile attitude toward a group of people. The cognitive component of prejudice is a stereotype: a rigid oversimplified set of beliefs about a group of people. Stereotypes have been found to be pervasive, generally accepted images that persist over time but also show the effect of current events and changes in intergroup relations.

The origins of prejudice include historical relations among groups, broad sociocultural and situational factors, internal personality dynamics, the phenomenology of the prejudiced individual, and the characteristics of the target groups, which may give a kernel of truth to the prevailing stereotypes. The ultimate attribution error involves the prejudiced person attributing negative behavior by an outgroup member to personal causes rather than social or environmental influences.

The influence of personality on prejudice is supported by research on ethnocentrism. Individuals who are prejudiced toward one outgroup tend to hold negative attitudes toward other outgroups and show exaggerated loyalty and glorification toward their ingroup. In addition, ethnocentrism includes a bias for ingroup members to overestimate the quality of their group's performance or products.

Discrimination is overt behavior that restricts an individual's opportunity or access to resources solely on the basis of his or her group membership rather than individual abilities. Discrimination involves an unfair prejudgment and categorization that violates the human rights and the dignity of the individual. Prejudice and discrimination can operate through a self-fulfilling prophecy wherein they become mutually supportive and highly resistant to change. Discrimination also appears to be accentuated by the deindividuation of the outgroup. In contrast to prejudice and discrimination, valid differences among groups should be respected within the context of a democratic society.

Through controlled studies of intergroup relations, social psychologists have come to understand the basic determinants and the common symptoms of intergroup conflict. Competitive win-lose situations, gross inequalities in power and status, and stereotyping and rigidity in approaching problems lead intergroup relationships to deteriorate into hostility, antagonism, and brutality. These effects have been demonstrated in studies of boys' camps, training workshops for managers involving intergroup competition, and in a simulation of a prison. Realistic group conflict theory stresses objective differences of interest as the cause of conflict. However, subjective factors, in conjunction with the simple separation of people into groups, appear sufficient to produce discrimination.

Social psychologists as practitioners have brought together members of conflicting groups in settings that maximize the facilitative conditions of intergroup contact: equal status, a high acquaintance potential, supportive norms, cooperation in functionally important tasks toward common goals, and participants who are emotionally stable, competent, and not highly prejudiced.

Given the facilitative conditions, a variety of workshop approaches (lecture, discussion, interpersonal skill training, sensitivity training) have resulted in positive changes in attitudes and behavior as assessed by a variety of methods. Nonetheless, there continues to be a need for increased sensitivity to all the crucial considerations that arise when we bring members of antagonistic groups together. Practitioners must continue to learn from their experience in order to improve their work.

Further Readings

Allport, G. W. *The nature of prejudice.* Cambridge, Mass.: Addison-Wesley, 1954.

Austin, W. G. & Worschel, S. (Eds.). *The social psychology of intergroup relations.* Monterey, Calif.: Brooks-Cole, 1979.

Blake, R. R. & Mouton, J. S. *Group dynamics: Key to decision making.* Houston, Texas: Gulf, 1961.

Sherif, M. *In common predicament: Social psychology of intergroup conflict and cooperation.* Boston: Houghton Mifflin, 1966.

Simpson, G. E. & Yinger, M. J. *Racial and cultural minorities: An analysis of prejudice and discrimination* (4th ed.). New York: Harper & Row, 1972.

CHAPTER OUTLINE

UNDERSTANDING ORGANIZATIONS: THE THEORY AND RESEARCH BASE
  Complex Organizations
    Characteristics
    Types
  Approaches to Understanding Organizations
    Machine Approach
    Human-Relations Approach
    Open Systems Theory Approach
  The Individual in the Organization: Selection, Socialization, Motivation, and Satisfaction
    Selection and Socialization
    Motivation and Satisfaction
  Organizational Roles: Positions of Partial Inclusion
  The Group in the Organization: Leadership and Participative Decision Making
    Supervision and Leadership
    Worker Participation: Democracy on the Shop Floor
  Communication, Control, and Conflict in Organizations

IMPROVING ORGANIZATIONAL EFFECTIVENESS: THE PRACTICE OF
ORGANIZATION DEVELOPMENT
  Organization Development: Definition and History
  Contrasting Approaches to Organization Development
    Process Consultation and Intervention Approach
    Survey Feedback Approach
    Human Relations Training Approach
    Sociotechnical/Structural Approach
    Systems Approach
  Process Interventions in Organization Development
    The Individual Level
    The Interpersonal and Interrole Level
    Group Interventions
    Intergroup Interventions
    The Organizational Level
  Comprehensive Programs of Organization Development
    Likert's System 4 Management
    Blake and Mouton's Grid Organization Development
    Dimock's Systems-Improvement Research
    New Factories of Sweden
  Research on the Effectiveness of Organization Development

SUMMARY

FURTHER READINGS

NINE

Organizational Psychology and Organization Development

Anders Hansson works in an auto plant in Sweden. He is one member of a fifteen-person team that assembles the electrical system of each car that passes through the team's work area on a moving platform. The speed of the platform can be adjusted by the workers, and there are buffer areas at the start and finish of the team's miniature assembly line so that variability in assembly speed is possible without disrupting the work of other teams in the factory. Anders and his co-workers decide how specific tasks will be assigned and rotated, help socialize and train new workers, determine the team's work speed and length of rest periods, and monitor the quality of their production. The team also has a say in the designation of a team leader who serves as a vital communication link with management. Studies indicate that production in Anders's factory is as efficient as with traditional assembly-line methods, that worker absenteeism and turnover are lower, and that worker satisfaction is higher. These changes in production methods have come about through the growth of industrial democracy in Sweden, as evidenced by cooperation between union and management and by the presence of worker representatives with voting rights on company boards of directors and work councils.

Linda Mitchell is a nurse in a large metropolitan hospital in the United States. Her duties are clearly defined and monitored by her supervisor. As with any large human service organization, there are a variety of specialties organized into different departments. Linda has little contact with nonmedical personnel such as

social workers and clinical psychologists—even though they work with many of her patients. Within the organization, Linda's power and status position is made apparent through her interpersonal interactions with other personnel. In a world of life-and-death decisions, it is important that all personnel have a clear picture of who is responsible and accountable in each specific situation. Even though Linda has little decision-making power in her role, she works hard to remain involved and to keep her medical care from becoming solely an objective, technical interchange with her patients.

John Sanders is a farmer in one of the northern states of the Great Plains region. He is also a member of a cooperative store. John buys most of the products he needs to live and work through his co-op. At the end of the year he receives a percentage dividend based on the total purchases he has made; the greater the profits, the greater the dividends returned to members. John has also been elected to the board of directors, a mechanism through which the consumers control the operating policies and procedures of the enterprise. Thus the business is owned by and accountable to the people that it serves. John has trouble seeing why businesses should be organized any other way.

Each of these individuals—Anders, Linda, and John—are members of social organizations: a factory, a hospital, a cooperative business. Their behavior in these settings will be affected by their particular personality characteristics, their interpersonal styles and interactions, and their group memberships. However their behavior will be even more strongly affected by the emergent qualities of social structure and process that exist at the organizational level. Organizational roles, the organizational climate, the communication networks, and the decision-making structure—all help determine the degree of satisfaction and productivity that Anders, Linda, and John will experience as members of organizations.

One goal of applied social psychology is to describe in theory and research our possible choices of social organizations, and to encourage through social practice those most compatible with humanistic values. Despite their variety, most organizations share fundamental elements of structure and process that serve as the basis for the social-psychological study of organizational functioning. In the past, however, social psychologists restricted their levels of analysis to the individual, the dyad (an interacting pair), and the group, without direct examination of higher levels of social interaction. Katz and Kahn (1966), in their pioneering work on the social psychology of organizations, point out that we must move beyond these lower levels. We must examine our behavior *as it is embedded in the social structure of organizations in which we spend most of our waking life.* We must develop conceptual tools and research methods to understand the internal dynamics of organizations and how organizations relate to the larger environment.

In the past twenty years, social psychologists have turned increasing attention to organizational structure and functioning. In doing so they have joined other social scientists in an interdisciplinary effort to develop theories of organizational behavior and strategies of organizational change (Vroom, 1969). Industrial psychologists have developed the technology of personnel selection; experimental psychologists, the design of efficient man-machine systems. Sociologists have produced classic theories of organizational structure; and economists and political scientists have studied decision-making processes that lie at the heart of organizational functioning.

To this activity, the applied social psychologist brings a particular perspective and a unique potential. It is a perspective aware of lower levels of analysis—a perspective that attempts to see how individual, interpersonal, group, and intergroup phenomena are integrated into the organization. It is a potential that portends how large formal organizations may be humanized to better meet their members' personal and social needs, while maintaining the advantages of organized efficiency. Based on the related initiatives of action research, group dynamics, and human relations training, applied social psychologists have moved strongly into organizational psychology and the practice of organization development.

UNDERSTANDING ORGANIZATIONS: THE THEORY AND RESEARCH BASE

Complex Organizations

The *formal organization* is a social system designed to coordinate the specialized activities of a large number of people toward the efficient achievement of some stated objective. Although different theories stress different elements of organizations, there are a number of common characteristics that run through most approaches to understanding organizations (Tannenbaum, 1966; Katz & Kahn, 1978).

Characteristics. First, organizations are *purposive:* they have a purpose, a stated objective to produce a product or provide a service. The product may be TV sets, chocolate layer cakes, or hand grenades; the service may be vocational counseling, medical care, or production of a Broadway play.

Organizations are expected to be *efficient*—to produce or perform with a minimum of waste and a maximization of profit. Whether the organization is a private business or a government department, efficiency is survival for the organization, at least in its present form: a loss of sales or an unused service usually results in organizational changes. Organizational outcomes, however, include much more and much less than the stated purposes. The process that

Assembly-line worker performs a specialized task, sorting merchandise. While *specialization* is a key to efficiency, it can also cause worker frustration and boredom since it often involves the assignment of simple, repetitive jobs. *(John Blaustein/Woodfin Camp & Associates)*

makes chocolate layer cakes may be polluting the river; the vocational counseling may be discriminating against minority groups by using culturally biased tests (Katz & Kahn, 1978).

Organizations involve *specialization* of tasks, or division of labor: subgoals of the overall purpose require specialized tasks performed by different members. While specialization is a key to efficiency, it is also a cause of member frustration and boredom since it frequently involves the assignment of simple, repetitive jobs. The growth of technology has not only contributed to the rise of specialization (especially in production organizations), but has also affected the physical placement of workers and opportunities for social interaction. This situation underscores the importance of viewing the modern formal organization as a *sociotechnical system*, rather than simply as a social system or as a technical system (Tannenbaum, 1966). For example, the technical and physical arrangements of the modern university are geared to communicating information (lecture theaters, textbooks, audiovisual aids), but this requires a host of social arrangements (specialized departments, faculty committees, student clubs).

Once the work of the organization has been broken down into specialized tasks, these must then be *coordinated* toward the overall goal. The behavior of members must be patterned in a complementary and integrated fashion. (The professor teaches, the student learns.)

This patterning of behavior results in the *enduring* quality of organizations as social systems. The structuring of events provides continuity over time regardless of the addition of new members and the loss of old ones. (Green recruits may replace combat veterans, but the army marches on.) Thus an organization is characterized by the replaceability of its members and is not dependent upon the continuity of individuals for its survival. Similarly, an organization is not dependent on its physical structure for its continuation. Its social structure provides that stability.

The existence of social structure sensitizes us to the *contrived* nature of organizations as social systems. Patterns of behavior are invented and enacted by people. Choices are made about what and how something should be done to reach the overall goal. We may forget that the same end can be accomplished in different ways. (Professors may lecture every hour of class time, or they may use class discussions and student exercises to accomplish some of the same teaching-learning goals.) Organizations are arbitrary systems whose present state is determined by a large number of variables rather than by a few givens of some social reality.

Specialization and coordination of tasks and maintaining the replaceability of members require that organizations induce *uniformity* in the behavior of their members. Organizations need to constrain the usual range of human variability to more uniform and dependable patterns. Members must come at regulated times to coordinate their activities. Tasks must be carried out in a standardized fashion, in the interests of coordination and efficiency. Members who behave in predictable and acceptable ways are compensated with pay, promotion, job security, and other rewards. Members who deviate from prescribed patterns experience sanctions and, ultimately, loss of membership.

Finally, we must understand that a formal organization is an *integrated* social system. Katz and Kahn (1978) single out three important bases for integration: (1) the functionally interdependent roles of individual members (for example, the worker turns to the supervisor when guidance is required); (2) the norms that govern acceptable behavior, defined by the authority structure and enforced by rewards and sanctions (for example, every schoolchild knows that consistent lateness means a trip to the principal); and (3) the values or ideological justifications that support the roles and norms and provide for the individual's commitment to the organization (for example, most professors believe that the creative search for knowledge is a good thing). Thus, the organization functions as an integrated whole, moving more or less effectively toward its common objective.

Types. We can distinguish at least three types of organizations: *private, profit-making organizations; public, human service organizations;* and other human service organizations, termed *third-sector organizations.* Private, profit-making organizations exist to produce and successfully market a tangible product or a commercial service (for example, a furniture factory, a real estate firm, a dry cleaning company). Public human service organizations are generally under the administration of some sector of government—city, county, state, federal—and are funded by public monies; they deliver a personal service such as health care or family counseling (for example, a county hospital, a city welfare department). Third sector organizations are neither completely private nor public and provide services not adequately available through either business or government (for example, a family planning agency, a recreation association). Their primary function is to alter a person's attributes and behavior to increase his or her well-being (Goodstein, 1978; Hasenfeld & English, 1974; Levitt, 1973).

Most of our knowledge of the differences between profit-making organizations and human service organizations comes from the observations of organizational consultants (see Golembiewski, 1969; Goodstein, 1978):

- For example, all organizations are purposive, but business and industry have a clear criterion of success: *profit.* Without profit the organization does not survive. Public institutions, however, are more enduring. They rarely go out of business and usually have no competitors.
- Profit-making organizations are ultimately accountable to a smaller number of owners: perhaps a group of shareholders, a family unit, or one person. The manager of a public organization, however, must be attuned to all branches of government, to consumers, and to special-interest groups.

Third-sector human service organizations contrast with profit-making organizations in many of the same ways that public agencies do. However this type also has its unique characteristics.

- These organizations tend to fill missing service gaps, and often bend toward social reform by influencing existing public or private organizations. For example consumer advocates do not provide a direct service, but attempt to improve the quality of available services.
- Role taking and decision making tend to be more flexible and less centralized, thus enhancing innovation but increasing turmoil and conflict.
- In summary, third-sector agencies tend to show less uniformity of behavior and are less integrated and enduring than public sector agencies or private organizations.

Approaches to Understanding Organizations

Given the complexity of organizations, it is not surprising that a number of approaches to understanding these social systems have evolved. Each approach emphasizes certain of the common organizational characteristics and adds others. Each approach has been translated into practical applications. And each approach is compatible with a particular view of human nature, underlining the inherent social-psychological quality of the study of organizations.

The *machine approach* likens organizations to machines, emphasizing their impersonal rationality and legalistic procedures. The *human relations approach* stresses the individuality and emotionality of organization members and the importance of social interaction. *Open systems theory* provides a wide-angle lens for describing the basic structures and processes of all types of organizations (March & Simon, 1958; Katz & Kahn, 1978).

Machine Approach. One of the classic examples of the machine approach is Max Weber's (1947) *bureaucratic model*, inspired by the rise of large, impersonal bureaucracies in the early era of industrial capitalism. Weber, a German sociologist, wanted to specify the ideal type of production organization that would accomplish its goal in the most efficient and just manner.

In this model, tasks and roles are highly specialized so that they can be expertly executed and so that responsibility for their completion can be easily determined. Definite rules and procedures are followed for the division of labor and the coordination of activities, ensuring smooth, continuous functioning without duplication of effort. Control and decision making are centralized, with a clear and detailed chain of command. Offices or positions are depersonalized so that interaction is based on specified roles and responsibilities rather than on personal characteristics. Uniformity of practices means fair and equal treatment of all members based on qualifications and performance rather than on friendship, nepotism, or group membership. Thus members are selected and rewarded on the basis of merit, and the organization is accountable to the individual. The military is a good example of a bureaucratic organization.

Weber's ideal bureaucratic model replaced many of the inequities and injustices of traditional approaches to organizations. According to Perrow (1972), bureaucracy based on rational and legal considerations took centuries to develop and now functions effectively on a widespread basis, although never in its ideal state. That is because not all tasks are the stable, routine activities that bureaucracies are most adapted to, and not all (in fact very few) organizational members fit the rational, impersonal, and average molds required by the ideal bureaucracy. Nonetheless, this form of organization continues to be of great interest to applied social psychologists because it is through bureaucracies, especially government departments, that most proposals for resolving social problems are developed and implemented (Bush & Gordon, 1978; Littrell, 1980).

Another contribution to the machine approach from the early twentieth century is Frederick Taylor's (1923) theory and practice of *scientific management*. Its goal was to find the most effective ways of integrating people with machines for maximum production. By observing the most efficient movements required to complete routine tasks, activities were standardized to bring about uniformity and replaceability. The approach was based on the assumption of "economic man"—that a worker is motivated by money and little else. Therefore scientific management instituted the piecework system of pay: workers were paid not on a time rate but on the basis of how many items they produced.

At the broader level of organizational functioning, scientific management espoused many ideas that were similar to the bureaucratic model (Katz & Kahn, 1978; Tannenbaum, 1966). For example, Taylor believed in a hierarchical chain of authority and a uniformity of practices for dealing with members on the basis of performance. Scientific management practices—such as time-and-motion studies, machine and workplace design, and piecework incentive systems—have been widely adopted throughout the industrialized world.

Although the machine approach may highlight important organizational characteristics, there is much that it misses from a social-psychological perspective (Katz & Kahn, 1978; March & Simon, 1958; Tannenbaum, 1966). It does not consider the complex relationship between the organization and its wider environment. And it can also produce unintended dysfunctions: the heavy reliance on rules leads to a rigidity in dealing with clients of the organization; this tends to protect the bureaucrat rather than help the client (Merton, 1957). Also, the creation of minimum performance standards results in mediocrity that leads to conflict as supervisors press for more production (Gouldner, 1954). The machine approach thus becomes self-defeating.

The greatest deficiency of these classic models of the machine approach, however, is that they ignore the human element: the characteristics of individuals, the dynamics of the small group, the importance of relationships among persons and among groups—all of the personal needs and social interactions that make up the informal organization and help determine the ability of the organization to effectively accomplish its purpose.

Human Relations Approach. In the mid-1920s a series of experiments aimed at increasing productivity was initiated at the Hawthorne Plant of the Western Electric Company in Chicago. Although this research was initially designed within the framework of scientific management, the unexpected results sparked the human relations approach to organizational functioning (Tannenbaum, 1966).

Several sets of different experiments were conducted over a number of years, the later ones in collaboration with Elton Mayo and his colleagues from the Harvard Business School (Roethlisberger & Dickson, 1939). One set of experiments studied the effect of illumination on the productivity of women workers engaged in the assembly of small electrical parts. The results showed either no effects or erratic effects seemingly unrelated to illumination. For example, in one experiment a group of workers continued to increase productivity in a level of illumination equivalent to moonlight! Some additional variables were clearly at work.

In a subsequent series of experiments, workers were isolated in a test room where researchers could study the relationship of worker behavior and productivity to variations in rest periods and the work week. Again the results did not appear to be fully explained by the manipulations of the physical variables. For example, productivity generally increased over the experimental period regardless of the number and length of rest periods!

The investigators realized that four significant changes in human relations had indirectly come about as an unintended consequence of the experimental manipulations (Tannenbaum, 1966):

- The supervisory style of the test room was more friendly, attentive, considerate, and less restrictive, coercive, and punitive than regular supervision in the factory. (This was done to make the experiment more acceptable to the workers.)
- Decision making was shared more with the workers. They participated in deciding whether or not changes should take place.
- The test workers formed a small cohesive group, helping one another for the common good. Group norms supported productivity.
- The workers achieved a higher sense of satisfaction and morale. They not only experienced greater fulfillment of personal and social needs, but increased their pay through higher productivity.

The phenomenon of increased attention of researchers leading to behavioral changes is now called the *Hawthorne effect*. However, this interpretation of the results downplays the power that considerate supervision, increased autonomy, and group cohesion may have on people (Kahn, 1975). According to Tannenbaum, "The Hawthorne test room revealed a social psychology of the work organization which, to those concerned with problems of organizational performance, seemed to hold within it a force of revolutionary power" (1966, p.25). However, the Hawthorne results, based mainly on observation and later interview projects, may have actually overestimated the power of human relations factors in improving productivity. For the first detailed statistical analysis of the Hawthorne data, see Box 9.1.

The human relations approach stresses three elements: the importance of the individual—his or her perceptions, motivations, aspirations; the interpersonal relationship between the worker and the supervisor; and the importance of the small group—the effectiveness of communication and decision making and the crucial role of cohesion and morale.

One of the earliest examples of the human relations approach is provided by Douglas McGregor's (1960) work, *The Human Side of Enterprise*, which makes a distinction between managers who follow Theory X and those who ascribe to Theory Y. Theory X supervisors typify the traditional, autocratic approach to management. They assume that workers are inherently lazy, have a dislike of work, and prefer direction and security rather than responsibility and accomplishment. Therefore, workers must be controlled, directed, and threatened with punishment to achieve organizational objectives.

Theory Y managers, on the other hand, assume that human beings like to expend energy, can exercise self-direction towards rewarding objectives, have the capacity to be creative problem solvers, and will not only accept but will also seek responsibility. Theory Y managers also assume that under typical conditions of modern industrial life the potential of the average person is only partly utilized. Thus, the Theory Y supervisor works to develop this potential by being supportive, understanding, and trusting of his or her subordinates.

According to Katz and Kahn (1978), McGregor and most other theorists of

Box 9.1   FOCUS ON RESEARCH
Questioning the Hawthorne Conclusions

For decades, the insights gleaned from the Hawthorne studies have provided the rationale for the human relations approach to organizations. The results indicated that a participative, considerate style of supervision increased the satisfaction and productivity of workers. However, these conclusions were based on a visual inspection of productivity measures and on anecdotal accounts of the importance of human relations.

Richard Franke and James Kaul were able to obtain the original Hawthorne data and subject it to statistical procedures using time-series analyses (see Chapter 3) which had not been developed at the time of the original experiments. In particular, they analyzed the data from the main experiment, which followed the productivity of five female workers in a special test room over a 5-year period. They were able to relate the original independent variables, such as number of rest periods and length of work week, to measures of the quantity and quality of production. Also included by Franke and Kaul as independent variables were the onset of the great Depression and an instance of "managerial discipline" in which two somewhat insubordinate and mediocre workers were replaced by two more productive employees, one of whom took the role of "straw boss." (In line with the original Hawthorne interpretations, this move might have improved supervisory relations.)

Quantity of production over the 5-year period was most strongly affected by the managerial replacement of the two workers, due both to their greater productivity and the apparent effect of this disciplinary action on the other workers. The occurrence of the Depression also increased production, possibly through the increased importance of jobs and the fear of losing them. The length of rest periods and the introduction of a group incentive system also had positive— although smaller—effects on productivity. These variables accounted for almost all of the variation in productivity during the experimental period. Therefore, even if the human relations variables of supervisory relations and social interaction had been measured, which they were not, there was very little variation in productivity left to be accounted for. Only the small effect of rest periods supports the human relations interpretation of the findings.

In contrast, the scientific management variables of the exercise of discipline and the use of incentives show a greater effect on worker performance. Social science may have been too ready to embrace the original Hawthorne interpretations since it was looking for theories of work motivation that were more humane and democratic. Franke and Kaul encourage further analyses of the original Hawthorne data.

Source: Franke, R. H. & Kaul, J. D. The Hawthorne experiments: First statistical interpretation. *American Sociological Review*, 1978, *43*, 623–643.

the human relations school limit their thinking to the levels of the individual and the small group and do not consider how higher-level structures of the organization may need to be changed to develop the potential that the theorists envisage. An exception to this is the work of Rensis Likert. He has gone beyond a consideration of interpersonal relations to develop a theory of organizational functioning in which small working groups are linked together through all levels of the organization. Likert's contributions to organization development will be considered in the second half of this chapter. However, even Likert's broader human relations approach misses some important aspects of organizational behavior—particularly the complexity of relations between the organization and its wider environment.

All these models focus primarily on the internal dynamics of the organization, seeing it as a *closed system* that has limited interchange with external forces. A fundamental shift in emphasis, however, was initiated by the pioneering work of Daniel Katz and Robert Kahn (1966, 1978): the development and application of *open systems theory* to the understanding of organizations.

Open Systems Theory Approach. Katz and Kahn (1978) drew on the formulation of *general systems theory,* which seeks laws and concepts that apply at all levels of scientific analysis from a single cell to an entire society (von Bertalanffy, 1956; Miller, 1955, 1978). The basic characteristics of all organisms provide a starting point for an approach that has unique relevance to human organizations and that emphasizes two central aspects: (1) their character as interdependent systems, in which movement in one part leads to predictable movement in other parts; and (2) their openness to inputs from the environment, resulting in a continuous state of flux. Open systems theory is a social-psychological approach that includes the interrelationships among different levels of analysis and that begins *at the level of the social system rather than of the individual.*

What are the common characteristics of open systems as expressed at the level of the social organization? Katz and Kahn (1978) outline ten fundamental qualities. These, combined with the common organizational characteristics alone, yield a very comprehensive picture of organizations.

1. *Importation of energy.* Open systems must import energy from their environment to survive. Organizations require raw material, human resources, and other types of energy to accomplish their functions and meet their objectives. Those objectives may be the production of goods or the provision of services.

2. *Throughput.* Open systems transform energy into new forms in the process of production or servicing. The input is reorganized through the expenditure of effort within the organization. Factories produce automobiles, sewing machines, cassette tape recorders, and so on; human service organizations process and change people through teaching and counseling as well as other activities.

3. *Output.* Open systems export some identifiable product into the external environment. The production organization sells or provides its output to consumers; in so doing it may export other side effects such as pollution or dependency. The university graduates people with degrees, the prison attempts to release rehabilitated offenders.

4. *Cycles of events.* Open systems repeat the pattern of energy exchange in a cyclical manner. The energy cycle is self-renewing; the profit-making organization uses money from sales to buy more raw materials; the third-sector voluntary organization revitalizes its members through the personal satisfaction they derive from their work.

5. *Negative entropy.* All living systems follow the general entropic process that moves towards disorganization and death. Therefore, to survive, open

systems must reverse this process and acquire negative entropy by importing more energy than they expend. This provides a buffer or organizational slack that can aid survival in time of crisis—that is, of high energy loss. Most organizations attempt to build up assets and cash reserves that can be drawn on during lean times.

6. *Information input and feedback.* Open systems receive additional input from the environment in the form of signals about the state of the environment and about the organization's functioning. Feedback about its performance allows the organization to correct any deficiencies: faulty brake lines are replaced by the auto manufacturer; ineffective programming is improved by the social service agency.

7. *Homeostasis and maximization.* Open systems work to maintain adequate importation of energy to offset energy loss and to maintain a steady state. However, human organizations add to this homeostatic process of preserving the system by their tendency to grow and expand, thereby maximizing the basic character of the system. Thus schools get bigger, but stay the same; industries amalgamate, but their basic identity is unchanged.

8. *Differentiation.* Open systems move to replace global patterns of behavior with more differentiated functions. Through the division of labor, specialized roles develop and the need for generalists declines. Some teachers teach only mathematics, others only chemistry, and so on.

9. *Integration and coordination.* Specialized roles must be coordinated so that an integrated output is produced. Coordination is provided in complex organizations by devices such as setting priorities, regularizing routines, synchronizing functions, and sequencing events. The automobile assembly line coordinates a variety of tasks so that an integrated unit is produced in the proper sequence.

10. *Equifinality.* An open system can reach the same end or final state from different beginnings and through different paths. Thus, organizations can produce the same product or offer the same service in many different ways, depending on the differentiation and coordination strategies they employ. The Swedish car factory of Anders Hansson operates differently than most of its North American counterparts, and yet the final product is equivalent.

What are the advantages of seeing organizations as open systems rather than as closed systems? The open system approach recognizes fully the dependence of the organization on its external environment. Environmental inputs are seldom constant, and their variation must be taken into account to understand the functioning of the organization. The school must be sensitive to changing community needs or dissatisfaction and conflict will result. At the same time, the openness of the system is selective; *boundaries* do exist between the organization and the environment, and important transactions occur at these boundaries. The concept of boundary role—a person who mediates between the organization and the environment—is thus a crucial element in the systems approach. The crucial process of feedback is also highlighted by open systems theory. The corrective interchange between the organization and its environment is central to survival. The production organization that ignores declining sales is headed for bankruptcy. Finally open systems theory stresses the contrived nature of organizations through the principle of equifinality. There is no one best way, or any one best model of organizational functioning. On the contrary, there is an exceedingly complex pattern of interrelated behaviors that must be studied in its entirety if we are to understand human organizations.

Open systems theory also helps our thinking about organizations by defining five general types of subsystems that exist in organizations or other social systems (Katz & Kahn, 1978).

- *The production or technical subsystem* is concerned with throughput—the cycles of activity that transform input into output. In a production organization, the assembly line is the prototypical throughput subsystem.
- *The supportive subsystem* interacts with the environment to procure input, dispose of output, and carry on the necessary institutional relations with other systems. The materials department must acquire the raw resources necessary for production; the sales department must market the products.
- *The maintenance subsystem* ties organizational members to their roles—that is, by recruiting, selecting, socializing, and motivating the people who work in the organization. The personnel department interviews, selects, and trains new employees.
- *The adaptive subsystem* senses important changes in the environment and engages in research, planning, and development activities that help the organization adjust to these changes. The research and development unit designs and tests new products before a commitment to production is made.
- *The managerial subsystem* provides overall direction, coordination, and control of all the subsystems and activities of the organization. The board of directors and senior management make major decisions about new products and new markets.

These five subsystems define the basic functions or major strategies and activities that are central to organizational life. They also help us understand the parts of other social systems, such as the major institutions of a community or society (see Chapter 10). Other system approaches that break down the organization into subsystems along different lines—for example, in terms of major departments such as sales, engineering, and so forth—do not yield the same depth of insight into organizational functioning as does the Katz and Kahn typology. Thus, in a number of ways, open systems theory provides us with a very powerful looking glass for examining the operation of a variety of real-world organizations.

The Individual in the Organization: Selection, Socialization, Motivation, and Satisfaction

Organizations consist of individuals. Regardless of the approach we take to understand organizations, or the strategies that managers develop to run organizations, the individual element cannot be ignored. In fact, each approach makes assumptions about individual motivation and behavior based on its particular conception of human nature (Schein, 1980).

The machine approach of bureaucracy and scientific management assumes a *rational-economic* view of people. That is, they are motivated only by material gain, and they must be controlled and directed so that irrational feelings do not get in the way of the worker's rational self-interest and the organization's goals. The human relations approach is based on a *self-actualizing and social view* of humankind. McGregor's Theory Y manager assumes that people will freely expend effort to release their creativity and develop their full potential. The Hawthorne studies clearly demonstrate that the individual is motivated by social needs such as affiliation and that the peer group exerts powerful social forces on the behavior of the individual. Finally open systems theory is compatible with the assumption that human beings are exceedingly *complex* and are motivated by a variety of needs that interact with other elements of the organizational setting to determine overall satisfaction.

All organizations must therefore address a number of fundamental questions regarding the involvement of individuals in organizational activities. Each organization must consider the most effective methods of selecting appropriate individuals to enact organizational roles, or alternatively to design organizational roles and tasks to make best use of the available individuals. Each organization must determine how to best socialize and train the individual to become an integral part of the organization's social system.

A central and complex question is how to best motivate organization members to work toward organizational goals—that is, how to create working conditions, how to reward and sanction, how to meet important individual needs, and how to foster the informal organization in ways that support formal objectives. At the heart of this question is the inherent incompatibility of individual needs with organizational goals. According to Katz and Kahn (1978):

> The inevitable conflict between collective task demands and individual needs is sometimes erroneously attributed to the fact that human beings are inherently lazy and have to be bludgeoned into productive performance. The real reason is that the technical systems for getting work done are set up to ensure predictability, efficiency, and coordination of the efforts of a great many individuals. The uniformity, the routinization, and the fragmentation of behavior run counter not only to the factor of individual differences but to the needs of people for self-determination, spontaneity, accomplishment, and the expression of individual skills and talents. (p.73)

The human relations approach has been most vocal about the dehumanizing effects of control, conformity, and alienation which bureaucratic organizations have on individuals (see Argyris, 1964; Bennis, 1966). Factory workers who repeat the same task endlessly may have economic security and good physical working conditions, but experience little satisfaction of psychological and social needs. High school students required to memorize fact after endless fact with little justification other than to get their diploma will find little room to express individual creativity and responsibility for learning.

What is the answer to this dilemma? Surely not to abolish organizations that hold the promise of collaborative effort toward the common good. On the contrary, we must come to understand the complex interplay of individuals and organizations, and we must develop strategies that enable organizations to be both humane and effective. We must find ways for individuals to meet important personal and social needs at the same time they work toward organizational goals. At the level of the individual, this means inquiring into the bases of good match between personal needs and organizational goals and the maintenance of motivation and satisfaction. At the level of the organization, it means developing strategies of organizational change that serve both the humanistic and cost-effective goals of persons and organizations.

Selection and Socialization. The selection of individuals to fill organizational roles is a major task of industrial psychology, specifically personnel psychology, which has developed strategies of recruitment, selection, training, and allocation of human resources to meet the needs of organizations (Schein, 1980). Advertising and contact procedures are followed by selection methods—interviewing and psychological testing of abilities, aptitudes, and interests. Selection, a two-way process, is successful when both the job applicant and the organization sees a satisfactory fit between the person and the social setting. For example, recruiters from many organizations regularly visit college campuses to interview graduating students as prospective new employees. Each person asks the same question: "Is this for me?"

Organizational socialization is the social learning process by which organizational members acquire the knowledge, attitudes, and behaviors necessary for successful participation in the social system of the organization. While skill training is the responsibility of the formal organization, the process of organizational socialization takes place through the efforts of both the formal and the informal organization (Graen, 1976; Van Maanen, 1976, 1978). Through interpersonal relationships and group interaction, the newcomer to the organization must come to understand the social norms of the setting. Very subtle cues and reinforcements, as well as outright direction, impart the knowledge and the incentives required to discriminate appropriate behavior from inappropriate. I remember a friend telling me of his socialization experience in a small manufacturing plant where union membership was not a compulsory element of employment. After three polite but increasingly firm requests by co-workers that he join the union, my friend was simply told to join or he would have both his legs broken. He joined; the socialization process had made the norm and the sanction for noncompliance very clear.

Through selection, training, and socialization, the individual and the organization form a *psychological contract* that covers the understandings and expectations about contributions that the individual and the organization will make to each other (Kolb, Rubin & McIntyre, 1974; Schein, 1980). These expectations cover not only the obvious points (such as how much pay for how much work—a detail usually specified in a legal, written contract), but also the full range of rights, privileges, and obligations between worker and employer. The psychological contract entails many expectations regarding appropriate behavior that are implicitly understood; their power surfaces only when they are violated. For example, the employee who is not promoted when he or she is clearly "in line," or the executive whose trade secrets are sold to a competitor by a subordinate, are equally outraged by these flagrant violations of the psychological contract.

Motivation and Satisfaction. To understand what motivates employees to perform at satisfactory levels, organizational psychologists have drawn on the full range of ideas developed about human motivation (for example, Lawler, 1973; Tannenbaum, 1966), particularly the *personal needs* described by McClelland and by Maslow. (See Chapter 2.)

Each of McClelland's three primary needs of *affiliation* (nAFF), *achievement* (nACH), and *power* (nPOW) has important implications for the integration of the individual into the organization. (The first two have received somewhat more attention; studies of need power in organizational settings, now increasing, should yield further insights. See McClelland, 1975; McClelland & Burnham, 1976.)

The need for affiliation is especially crucial in the development of the informal organization that satisfies a member's wants for contact and interaction with others on a personal basis: "Many organizations have discovered—to their sorrow—that jobs that do not provide opportunities for social contact have higher turnover and absenteeism rates because employees simply cannot stand the isolation. Frequently, unnecessary social isolation results from mechanical and architectural designs that do not consider employees' needs for social relationships" (Lawler, 1973, p.17).

Similarly need achievement (nACH) is an important motivator of performance in organizations. Good job performance is very attractive to individuals who are high in nACH. However the job must be challenging and involving, creating the potential to excel; when the task is routine and repetitive, nACH will not be relevant. Furthermore greater nACH comes out of competitive situations that require a valued skill and provide feedback (Lawler, 1973). Clearly the

Jobs that do not provide opportunities for social contact have higher turnover and absenteeism rates because employees cannot stand the isolation. Frequently, mechanical and architectural designs do not consider employees' needs for social relationships. *(Charles Harbutt/Archive Pictures, Inc.)*

demanding, creative, or managerial position will be particularly attractive to high nACH individuals.

Organizational psychologists have also paid close attention to the concepts of *self-actualization* and the *hierarchy of needs.* Maslow has described how individuals must satisfy their lower-order needs for hunger, safety, and belongingness before they are motivated by the higher-order needs for self-esteem and self-actualization. According to Lawler (1973), Maslow's theory and extensions of it (for example, Alderfer, 1969) can provide useful clues for understanding what outcomes will be important to employees in what situations. For example, if a person's job security is threatened, self-actualization will be irrelevant at that point; if needs for physical comfort, safety, belongingness, and self-esteem are satisfied, the person is then in a position to be motivated toward self-actualization. One disturbing implication (as many managers have discovered) is that employees may never be satisfied! Once the lower-order needs have been satiated, they become less important; however, the need for self-actualization is insatiable because it is a process of experiencing intrinsic satisfaction and is not an end state of final fulfillment.

A theory of job satisfaction somewhat similar to Maslow's need hierarchy is the *two-factor model* developed by Herzberg (1966). Interviews were held with professional and nonprofessional workers, asking them about the times they felt exceptionally good or exceptionally bad about their jobs. Good times were associated with such factors as achievement, recognition, responsibility, and the intrinsic value of the job; bad times, with supervision, policies, working conditions, and relations with fellow workers. From these results it was concluded that the characteristics that produced dissatisfaction (and that can be used to prevent dissatisfaction) are different from those aspects that lead to job satisfaction. The former are primarily extrinsic to the job (such as policies and salary), whereas the latter are mainly intrinsic (such as opportunity for achievement and degree of recognition). Thus two-factor theory holds that job dissatisfaction and satisfaction are separate dimensions and that a person may indeed be satisfied and dissatisfied at the same time! However, for overall satisfaction, both extrinsic and intrinsic factors must be at acceptable levels. (As yet, further research has neither confirmed nor rejected the basic tenets of two-factor theory. Katz & Kahn, 1978; Lawler, 1973.) The relationship between the motivation theories of Maslow, McClelland, and Herzberg is shown in Table 9.1.

Other useful approaches to understanding job satisfaction include the use of *equity theory* (see Chapter 2) and *discrepancy theory.* Both stress the importance of a person's perceived outcomes, but in different ways. In equity theory, the perceived outcome is compared with the outcomes of similar others. If there is inequity between one's rewards and those of similar others, the person will be distressed and will attempt to restore equity. For example, Charlie the construction worker looks in his pay envelope and compares what he sees to what he knows his co-workers are receiving. If his pay is less, he will be dissatisfied. In discrepancy theory, the outcome is compared with the outcomes the person wants or believes he or she should receive. The comparison is between that which is received and an internal standard, and discrepancy here leads to dissatisfaction. In this case, Charlie compares his pay with his expectation of what a construction

Table 9.1   BASIC CATEGORIES OF MOTIVATION BY MASLOW, McCLELLAND, AND HERZBERG

Maslow Categories Hierarchy	McClelland Needs	Herzberg Factors (Implied Hierarchy)
1. Physiological needs		Working conditions
2. Safety needs (material)		Salary and benefits
Safety needs (interpersonal)	Power	Supervision
3. Affiliation love, social needs	Affiliation	Fellow workers
4. Self-esteem needs (feedback from others)		Recognition
		Advancement
Self-esteem (self-confirming activities)	Achievement	Responsibility
5. Self-actualization		Job challenge

Source: Schein (1980).

worker at his level should be paid. Lawler (1973) draws on both approaches to develop a comprehensive *model of facet satisfaction*, which considers all facets or aspects of the job that lead to satisfaction. This requires a consideration of other people's outcomes, one's actual outcomes, and one's desired outcomes. Overall satisfaction is determined by the difference between all the things that a person feels that he or she *should* receive and all that is *actually* received.

The complexity of individual motivation and satisfaction in organizations is summarized by Katz and Kahn (1978) through their delineation of three basic types of motivational patterns. These patterns support behaviors necessary for one to join and stay in the organization, to perform roles in a dependable fashion, and to engage in innovative and supportive actions beyond the role requirements.

The first motivational pattern is *rule enforcement*. Members accept role prescriptions and organizational directives because these come from legitimate sources of authority and carry legal sanctions. This, the motivational basis of machine theory, is effective for gaining minimum performance of roles, but no more. It is also a poor basis for attracting or holding people to the system—unless, as in compulsory military service, the enforcement is clearly legislated. However there is some evidence that the clarity of rules emphasized by this pattern helps hold people in the system, and that punishment as a means of rule enforcement does motivate better performance.

The second pattern, *external rewards*, includes pay, promotion, fringe benefits, and social approval. As learning theory suggests and as scientific management proposes, these are powerful motivators and reinforcers. Individual rewards (as opposed to system rewards for simply being a member) can attract people to the organization and help keep them there. These rewards elicit adequate role performance and can motivate members to perform above minimum standards and engage in innovative behavior *if* doing so does not threaten other workers. However, individual rewards—especially pay incentives based on a piece-rate system—are often seen by workers as not worth the effort and as inequitable. The person who produces at a high level shows up fellow workers and breaks the norms of average production and worker solidarity. On the other hand, system rewards (such as a pension plan) are seen as legitimate results of simple membership and seniority rather than individual performance. Although they are most effective for holding members in the system, system rewards usually lead to no more than minimum performance.

Internalized motivation is the third basic pattern. This refers to the intrinsic job satisfaction experienced by the worker and to the internalization of the organization's goals as part of the individual's value system. Some jobs offer opportunities for self-expression and self-determination: the worker derives intrinsic satisfaction from creating and accomplishing interesting and challenging tasks—a powerful way to hold that person in the system. College professors, for example, often comment that the opportunity to pursue their individual scholarly interests is a strong motivator in their job. Studies of job enrichment show that increased autonomy and responsibility lead to greater satisfaction, improved quality of work, and increased productivity. The opportunity to express one's values through one's work—the case, for example, of a dedicated political party worker—supports all three types of organizational behavior, but it is particularly important in eliciting innovative and spontaneous activities beyond the call of duty. We can readily see the powerful effect of successful organizational socialization that leads to this level of individual commitment. We can also see that drawing on all three types of motivation would resolve the apparent dilemma between individual needs and organizational goals.

Organizational Roles: Positions of Partial Inclusion

Mary Johnson is the executive director of a small, third-sector human service organization that provides social and recreational programs to the community at large. Her role involves the overall coordination and administration of the organization's service activities. To enact her role, Mary relates primarily to the president of the board of directors, the business manager and the office staff, the programming staff, and a variety of volunteers.

The concept of role helps us understand a great deal about Mary's behavior and the functioning of her organization. Her role involves a specific pattern of behavior associated with the position of executive director. As such, Mary's role links Mary as an individual—with her own unique needs, atttitudes, and abilities—to the social system of the organization—with its values, norms, and goals. The interrelationship of Mary's role to other roles forms a network of standardized behaviors that constitute the social structure of the organization. In other words, human organizations are basically role systems (Katz & Kahn, 1978).

Roles help us understand the contrived nature and yet the durability of organizations. Roles can be set up, changed, or abolished quite easily; thus, any arrangement is somewhat arbitrary. However, roles are usually defined in relation to the specialized tasks required to produce organizational output and therefore have a basis in reality. In addition, roles contribute to the continuation and stability of the organization. Particular individuals may come and go, but the system continues to function in much the same way. If Mary Johnson is replaced as executive director, the organization will still operate much as it has in the past, with some adjustments required to take the new individual into account.

A very important characteristic of organizational roles, as compared to roles in a primary group such as the family, is their quality of *partial inclusion* (Allport, 1933). Partial inclusion means that the organization, in filling functional roles, wants to include only a *segment* or part of the person rather than the whole person. The manufacturing plant only wants the skilled physical labor of the worker; it is not interested in his or her sense of humor or need for affiliation. The advertising agency wants an executive who can influence clients; it couldn't care less if she skydives on the weekend or eats black olives at lunch (assuming that neither behavior results in premature death!). North American organizations show a strong emphasis on partial inclusion, compared with European and Japanese organizations, which attempt to create a more encompassing sense of community or family within the organization.

Partial inclusion solves some problems and creates others. It reduces the effect of seemingly irrelevant personal factors on role behavior. For example, the professional helper in a human service organization must often put aside personal problems or wants to provide unbiased service to the client. However, partial inclusion also helps us understand many of the problems of social organizations (Katz & Kahn, 1978). Even though the organization only wants part of the person, it is the entire individual who walks in. The demand that the person deny many aspects of the self is a very depersonalizing process; as a result, individuals often react in negative ways, including minimal performance, absenteeism, or withdrawal. It is not surprising that the individual turns to the informal organization of peer relationships to meet personal needs and to literally fight for his or her identity as a human being. In a few types of organizations, such as the Israeli *kibbutz*—a cooperative farm community—there is total inclusion of members and this tends to reduce alienation and apathy.

Role behavior in organizations is affected by many factors. Each role is interrelated with a variety of other roles, but each person is usually directly associated with only a small number of people who work closely together at the same organizational level. This grouping of role partners constitutes the *role set* of the individual. Their role expectations are strong determinants of behavior within the group.

Figure 9.1 is a model of organizational role taking, developed by Katz and Kahn (1978). It includes these expectations and other important variables.

The members of the role set constitute the *role senders*. (In the case of Mary Johnson, the role set would include the president, business manager, and others she interacted with on a continuous basis.) The role senders communicate their expectations to the *focal person* in the form of the *sent role*. (Members of Mary's role set communicate how they define the role of executive director.) The information that is communicated in role sending includes instructions on role behavior, messages about rewards and punishments, and evaluations of role performance. Since the *received role* is the picture that the focal person perceives, what we know of interpersonal communication immediately raises the possibility of gaps be-

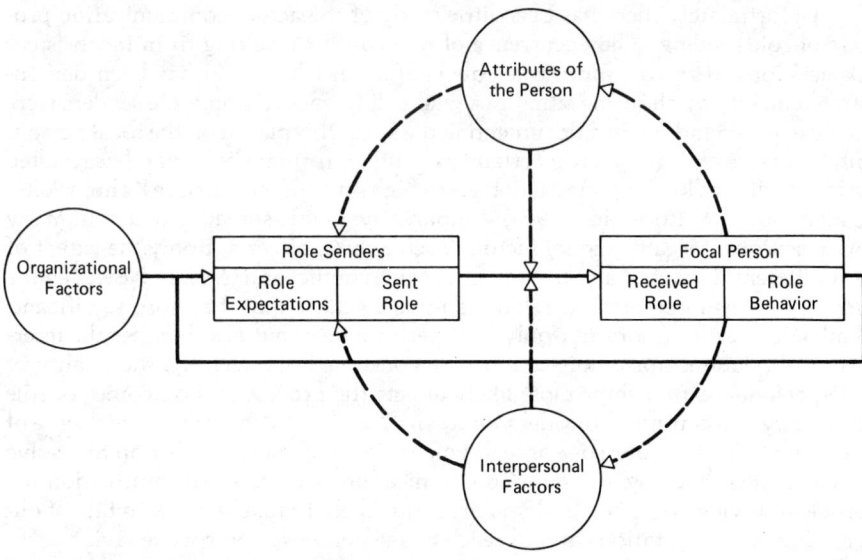

Figure 9.1   Model of Organizational Role Taking
Source: Katz & Kahn (1978).

tween this perception and the intended picture of the role senders. (Mary's definition of the executive director role may differ from that which is sent.) The person responds to role sending by engaging in role behavior which—when influenced by interpersonal factors—will in turn affect future expectations.

This interchange of sending and reacting to role expectations is a cyclical process that allows the members of the role set to move through *role socialization* to ongoing *role negotiation* to minimize the discrepancies and maximize effective interdependence. (If Mary perceives differences between her perception of the role of executive director and the perception held by the president, both Mary and the president would be well advised to sit down and iron out such differences.)

The process of role taking does not occur in isolation, but is strongly affected by other individual, interpersonal, and organizational factors related to the role set. *Attributes of the person* will affect how the sent role is perceived and will help determine the role evaluations that occur. (If Mary has a high need for power, she may ignore or counter aspects of the sent role with which she disagrees; negative evaluations and conflict will ensue.) *Interpersonal factors*, mainly the quality of interpersonal relationships—whether supportive or suspicious, for example—will affect the communication and influence that occurs around role behavior. Finally, the role expectations of the role set are largely determined by *organizational factors*, particularly the job definition of the position. Also, policies, structures, technology, the reward system, and other system factors will bear heavily on role behavior. (If the president is able to demonstrate that Mary has not fulfilled one of the prescribed functions of executive director, for example, orientating new volunteers, then Mary is in a vulnerable position.)

Unfortunately there has been little study of the actual communication process of role sending. The occurrence of *role conflict* resulting from inconsistent expectations (defined as intrarole role conflict in Chapter 2) has been demonstrated mainly by choosing situations where differences among role senders were likely to occur and by then documenting the stress this placed on the focal person. Similarly *role ambiguity*, or uncertainty about appropriate behavior, has resulted in effects such as low job satisfaction and a high sense of tension (see Kahn, Wolfe, Quinn, Snoek & Rosenthal, 1964)—apparently a wide-spread problem in many organizations. Organizational factors, such as size, affect not only the extent of role differentiation, but also the amount of role conflict and tension. However, the importance of interpersonal relations in role taking may be more significant. Ambiguous expectations not only hurt performance, but also hamper the interpersonal relationships among the people concerned. Conversely, the quality of interpersonal relationships most likely affects the process and outcomes of role ambiguity and conflict. Consider your own experience. When you have a sense of trust and liking for your co-workers, you are in a much better position to resolve role conflicts that might occur. Communication is more open, motivation for problem solving is greater, and you are more likely to take the risk to talk about differing role expectations and to reach a new consensus on role behavior.

The Group in the Organization: Leadership and Participative Decision Making

We have already seen the power of the small group to affect the behavior of its members. The organizational setting is no exception. The small group of related workers and their supervisor, defined as the *organizational family*, is the heartbeat of social influence processes in the organization. The organizational family is the primary socialization agent in the organization; it plays an important part in motivation by rewarding and punishing behavior and by providing social affiliation, and it constitutes the role set that directly influences member performance.

The early Hawthorne studies showed the importance of group support and group conformity in affecting productivity. The atmosphere in the relay assembly test room was supportive, and the norms of the group were in favor of high productivity. However, other experiments in the series showed the opposite effect: that is, of group norms that restrained performance. For example, a group of male workers engaged in wiring telephone equipment were isolated with a friendly observer, but were supervised and rewarded in the standard manner. Both the behavioral and productivity norms of the group became apparent: when the supervisor was present, the atmosphere was task-oriented and serious; when he walked out, the men relaxed and enjoyed themselves. The level of productivity was limited to the group's low production goals.

The majority of studies on group norms and productivity indicate that restrictive norms are more common than norms that are in line with organizational goals (Vroom, 1969). In either case, the influence of group cohesiveness is important: the greater the cohesiveness, the stronger the effect of the norms on members' behavior. The person who attempts to violate group norms, especially restrictive ones, in a highly cohesive group is in for a lot of heavy social influence, all the way from mild suggestions ("take it easy, we got all day") to verbal abuse ("you 'bleeping' rate-buster"), to physical violence ("this'll teach ya").

Thus we are faced with the paradox of the informal group in organizations (Tannenbaum, 1966). Groups are highly effective in directing and determining their members' attitudes and actions, but this power can just as easily be in opposition to organizational goals as in support of them, especially where productivity is concerned. The crucial question, from the organization's point of view, is how the power of the cohesive group might be harnessed. Fortunately for the individual, this turns out to be closely related to another question: how can the organization be made more responsive to the personal and social needs of its members?

Supervision and Leadership. In the Ohio State leadership studies (see Chapter 7), we saw the importance of the supervisor's role in initiating structure and showing consideration as means of achieving effective group functioning. Another series of studies on effective supervision was carried out at the University of Michigan's Institute for Social Research (see Katz & Kahn, 1953). By comparing what workers had to say (in questionnaires) to how supervisors reacted (in interviews), investigators picked up a pattern of supervision that differentiated high-productivity groups from low-productivity groups (Tannenbaum, 1966). Supervisors of productive groups took a human relations approach to their subordinates, treated them with respect, and regarded deficiencies as problems to be solved rather than as faults to be blamed. In contrast, supervisors of unproductive groups regarded their subordinates as cogs in a machine, supervised them closely, and criticized them for poor performance. The effective supervisor also clearly differentiated his role from that of his subordinates by engaging in planning, coordinating, and regulating activities, rather than by taking a direct part in production activities. This resulted not only in a highly cohesive group, but in one in which the group members and the leader had mutually favorable attitudes toward each other. All these factors positively affected job satisfaction and personal adjustment (Tannenbaum, 1966).

Organizational leadership concerns far more than the activities of a supervisor in a work group. Leadership is required to give direction in all the uncertain areas not covered by policies or regulations, to respond to changing environmental conditions, to coordinate and mediate among the various subsystems, and to adapt to the many human elements such as partial inclusion that interact with organizational structure.

Katz and Kahn (1978) propose three basic patterns of organizational leadership that meet these needs. The first is the *introduction of structural change* or new policy formulations required for continued successful functioning. Usually the organizational leadership will resort to such changes only when environmental pressures make them necessary for survival. For example, the Ford Motor Company initiated the costly and massive retooling from the Model T to the Model A only when it faced a disastrous decline in sales. The second essential leadership behavior is the filling out and *improvisation of organizational policy* in supervisory situations. This ability to get the job done, sometimes in spite of policy and structure, often prevents system failure. The third pattern of leadership is that of *routine administration*—the use of existing policies and procedures to keep the organization functioning smoothly and prevent potential disasters. From a systems point of view, these three demands of leadership are both considerable and crucial to organizational survival.

Worker Participation: Democracy on the Shop Floor. The increased autonomy of the workers in the more productive Hawthorne test room raised the possibility that participation in organizational decision making might have beneficial effects on satisfaction and productivity. In addition, Lewin's work on leadership styles and group decision making (see Chapter 7) provided a strong impetus for the efforts of social psychologists who had a strong commitment to democracy on the shop floor.

The classic experiment on participative decision making in work groups, conducted by Coch and French (1948), took place in a pajama factory that experienced difficulties whenever a change in job methods was instituted. Coch, the personnel manager, and French, a colleague of Lewin, instituted different methods of job change with four different groups of workers. The control group experienced the usual procedure: management retimed the jobs, set new piece rates, and explained the reasons for the change to the workers. A second group was given an explanation of the economic necessity for the changes and then elected representatives to help design the new jobs. These representatives then provided explanation and training to the other workers in the group. The remaining two groups were *fully* participative: all members took part in discussions, gave suggestions, and helped design the new jobs. Before-and-after analyses of a case study nature indicated superior productivity in direct relation to the degree of democratic decision making in the groups. The control group fell in productivity and stayed there; the two full participation groups dropped slightly but recovered rapidly and rose to new highs of performance; the representation group showed intermediate results.

Although the Coch and French experiment stimulated a great deal of subsequent research, it has methodological flaws that are often overlooked. Vitales (1954) and Gardner (1977) have pointed out a number of these, including group differences in the nature of the job and the job changes, differences in the nature of the job and the job changes, differences in group size, method of presentation and quality of training, and an element of competition between the two participative groups that may have raised their production. In fact, Gardner identifies almost twenty extraneous variables that could have accounted for part or all of the differences in productivity that Coch and French attributed to differences in degree of participative decision making.

Fortunately for the humanistic approach, further research and practice have shown the importance of group decision making (for example, Morse & Reimer, 1956). At the same time, our understanding of group processes in organizations has been modified and extended (see Box 9.2).

Participation appears to have a positive impact on job satisfaction; however, its effects on productivity are not as clearcut (Tannenbaum, 1966; Vroom, 1969). Research on group problem solving suggests that allocating decision making to

Box 9.2 FOCUS ON RESEARCH
Worker Participation and Satisfaction

The human relations approach to organizations has long maintained that worker participation in decision-making is a good thing—based on humanistic and democratic values—and that it leads to increased satisfaction and productivity. Toby Wall and Joe Lischeron of the Social and Applied Psychology Unit at the University of Sheffield, England, set out to re-examine these basic propositions. They focused on three main questions: What is the demand for participation? How does it affect individual well-being? How do workers respond to a participative system?

A review of past research indicated that most workers desire involvement in decision making, but that the relationship between participation and satisfaction is not clear cut. Many studies only look at correlations between the two variables, thus not showing that participation causes increased satisfaction. Experimental studies have yielded inconclusive results.

To overcome ambiguities in past research, Wall and Lischeron defined participation as *influence* in decision-making exerted through *interaction* between workers and managers based on *information sharing*. They also distinguished three levels of participation: *local*, involving concerns of immediate relevance to the worker's job (such as how tasks are scheduled), *medium*, covering decisions usually made by managers that affect large numbers of workers (such as purchase of new equipment), and *distant*, involving decisions usually made by top management affecting the entire organization (such as expansion of the organization).

Three extensive surveys of attitudes toward participation were completed in two hospitals, a steel plant, and a recreation department of a local government. The results were unambiguous. Nurses, factory workers, and groundskeepers all expressed moderate to strong interest in increased influence, interaction, and information sharing. Furthermore, perceived levels of existing participation were related to job satisfaction.

Wall and Lischeron then designed an experimental field study to see if participation would work in practice. Results of the attitude survey became the basis for developing a participative system in the recreation department. With management and union approval, 150 workers were randomly selected to take part in *Action Planning Groups* (APGs)—small discussion groups of workers and relevant managers designed to influence medium and distant decision making. The APGs had no formal authority and were designed to complement existing decision-making structures. The APGs had access to all relevant information and sent suggestions to appropriate decision-making bodies.

The APGs were an overwhelming success. Involvement was high and many suggestions were implemented. Workers in the APGs perceived that they had greater influence in decision making than control subjects who did not participate in the groups. However, most indicators of job satisfaction did not increase—only the immediate relationship between workers and managers showed improvement. Wall and Lischeron conclude that to fully understand worker participation, psychologists must become more actively involved with participative practices in organizations.

Source: Wall, T. D. & Lischeron, J. A. *Worker participation: A critique of the literature and some fresh evidence.* London: McGraw-Hill, 1977.

the group rather than to the supervisor requires more person-hours but produces higher acceptance and more efficient execution of decisions. The quality of the decisions and the effect on productivity seem to depend on a number of factors such as the complexity of the task. However, it is clear that participation has its distinct advantages, including increased satisfaction, personal adjustment, and motivation of organizational members.

The importance of participative decision making remains a vital issue in applied social psychology. A model of collaborative leadership in work settings, developed by Finch (1977), involves work groups that provide their own leadership functions (task, social, and decisional) as a means of improving the quality of work life and the degree of industrial democracy. As workers take responsibility for how work is accomplished, the role of the manager will need to shift from worker supervision to broader questions of organizational functioning, both internal and external. Interdependencies among subsystems and the relationship between the organization and its environment will require planning, goal setting, coordination, representation, and consultation of a very crucial and challenging nature. The manager of production in a factory, for example, would spend less time overseeing supervisors and workers, and more time meeting with the manager of sales to resolve interdepartmental conflicts, or more time with community groups concerned about environmental pollution. When work-group activities are restructured to give greater participation in decision making, the supervisor essentially loses part of his or her job, and new activities must be found to utilize this surplus capacity (Walton & Schlesinger, 1979). This new model of management is similar to Katz and Kahn's (1978) most recent description of organizational leadership—and may indeed represent the wave of the future.

There is a very important question of values underlying worker participation: *Meaningful control in decisions that directly affect oneself is a direct tenet of humanism and democracy.* Unfortunately the predominant North American approach has been for both workers and managers to exert power through the adversary system of union-management relations rather than through collaborative decision making at any level. A humanistic approach, however, assumes a commonality of interest between workers and management and believes that the doctrines of humanism and materialism—and of democracy and capitalism—are compatible. Whether these assumptions are true is an open question of immense social, political, and economic importance. Thus, social psychologists may find themselves increasingly called upon to assist in the planned democratization of work organizations through both applied research and practice interventions.

Communication, Control, and Conflict in Organizations

Beyond the level of the individual, the role, and the work group we come to the level of the organization as a system of interdependent parts. Viewing the organization as a totality sensitizes us to important social processes operating on a system-wide basis. In particular, the processes of communication, control, and conflict cut across all levels and subsystems of the organization and contribute substantially to member satisfaction and organizational effectiveness.

Communication processes are omnipresent in organizations. Supervisors talk with subordinates. The work group discusses its performance goals. Union sits down with management at the bargaining table. The president speaks to a community club or a government committee. The exchange of information and the transmission of meaning—that is, *communication*—is the very essence of an organization and has the broadest relevance for its functioning (Katz & Kahn, 1978). The centrality of communication is emphasized by Sanford, Hunt, and Bracey (1976), who place the communication system at the center of organizational functioning. In this way, communication serves a *mediating function* between environmental influences and internal organizational elements, and organizational effectiveness.

The quality of communication among elements of the organization and the accuracy of feedback on effectiveness help determine organizational success or failure. To this end, Sanford et al. (1976) provide suggestions for improving communication within organizations, many of which parallel ideas presented earlier in this book for increasing effective communication at the interpersonal, group, and intergroup levels. It is assumed that many organizational problems are the result of ineffective communication, and this is undoubtedly true. However, the prescription that totally free and full communication eliminates organizational difficulties is a gross oversimplification (Katz & Kahn, 1978).

Social systems are essentially restricted communication networks (Katz & Kahn, 1978). In the organization, communication is deliberately restricted to channels that are appropriate to the accomplishment of organizational objectives. The worker speaks to the supervisor, not to the president or the personnel manager. But effective two-way communication with feedback is much easier at the interpersonal level than at the organizational level, with its complexities and barriers. Often, the chief executive officer never really finds out how his or her directions are interpreted and reacted to on the shop floor. Often, the president of the university has little exposure to the attitudes and concerns of first-year students. A great deal of communication in organizations is one-way (memos, directives) and flows downward—the first form of *vertical communication*—job instructions, procedural information, performance feedback, and so on.

Communication *up* the line—a second form of vertical communication—can be useful to identify and solve problems. But upward communication decreases as the steepness and height of the organizational hierarchy increases (see Hage, 1974), and information communicated upward is often used to control subordinates (Katz & Kahn, 1978).

Along with this vertical flow, a certain amount of *horizontal communication* must occur among peers to coordinate their tasks. For example, the production and sales managers must stay in touch to match production level with market demands. Horizontal communication also supports the informal organization—possibly posing a threat to the power of organizational authority if group norms of resistance develop. However, when work groups are given the autonomy and responsibility to do their job, horizontal communication often supports the task, and everyone, including the organization, benefits.

Organizational control is the ability to influence organizational decisions—a universal feature of social organizations. While the process of communication is essential to the rule enforcement and legal compliance of the hierarchical organization, it is this concept of control that is really at the heart of organizational authority.

Arnold Tannenbaum and his co-workers have studied control in a variety of organizations in different countries (Tannenbaum, 1966, 1968, 1974). These include profit-making, public human service, and third-sector organizations. In this research, members at different levels of the organization are asked their opinion about the amount of influence held by different persons and groups. The results show a similar pattern: persons and groups at the top of the organization are seen as having more control than those in the middle or at the bottom. While this general finding may appear obvious, the degree to which it holds for different types of organizations in different social and policital systems is surprising (see Box 9.3).

Box 9.3   FOCUS ON RESEARCH
Control in Organizations

Arnold Tannenbaum and his colleagues at the Institute for Social Research at the University of Michigan have carried out numerous studies on the concept of organizational control. Members of the organization are asked to rate the amount of influence that they feel various groups—managers, supervisors, workers— have. The average ratings of different groups of respondents or different organizations are then plotted on the control graph, such as that shown in the following graph.

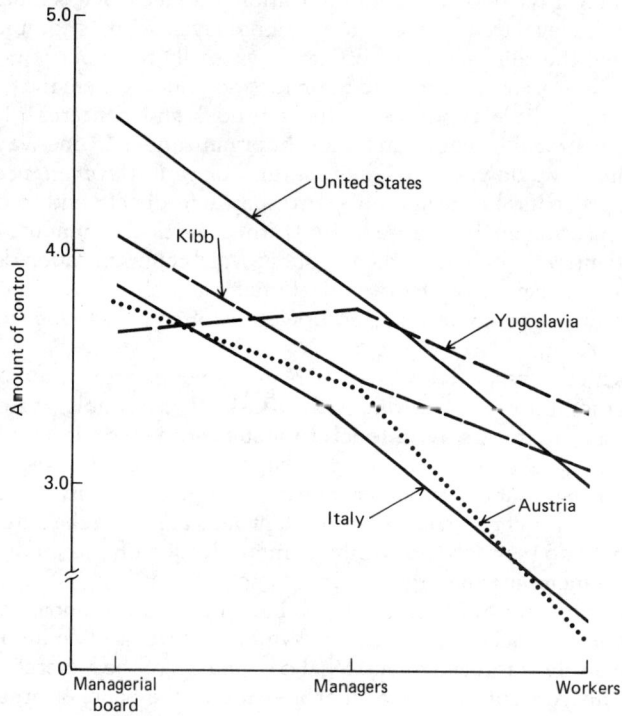

The vertical axis of the control graph represents the amount of control while the various groups in the organization are placed on the horizontal axis. Thus, the slope or steepness of the graph indicates how hierarchical the organization is, that is, how much control is vested in the top echelons as compared to the rank and file. In general, Tannenbaum has found that most organizations, from the military to business to voluntary associations, produce similar control graphs.

The control graph shown is based on a cross-national study that looked at perceptions of control in Israeli kibbutzim and manufacturing plants in the United States, Austria, Italy, and Yugoslavia. The control curve for Yugoslavia is the flattest, indicating that the involvement of workers in decision making as instituted by the socialist government has dispersed influence more equally among workers, managers, and the board. The Israeli kibbutzim are essentially agricultural cooperatives in which managers and board managers are elected, thus constituting a democratic organization. However, in terms of everyday functioning, the control graph indicates a traditional hierarchical distribution of power. Organizations in the three capitalist countries have similar control graphs, with Austrian organizations showing more influence on the part of managers. The absolute amount of control appears to be greatest in the U.S. plants—employees may have more day to day influence on an informal basis than in capitalist European organizations.

The control group thus represents a useful way of illustrating the distribution of influence in organizations and provides some interesting comparisons among various types of organizations.

Source: Tannenbaum, A. S. *Hierarchy in organizations.* San Francisco: Jossey-Bass, 1974.

One controversial aspect of Tannenbaum's work that challenges traditional thinking is that the *total amount of control in organizations is not fixed.* Moreover the total amount of control can be increased by developing the mutual influence that different parts of the organization have on each other. This possibility creates the intriguing paradox that management, by developing participation, *actually increases its control by giving up some of its authority.* For example, workers who gain more influence by participating in work councils also become more open to influence by management. In other words, participative decision making decreases resistance to organizational goals, increases worker satisfaction and motivation, and, in so doing, enhances the supervisor's control while simultaneously increasing the workers' influence. The advocates of the human relations approach to organizations firmly believe that effective democratic leadership increases the size of the "control pie" so that there is a bigger slice of influence for all. However, many other theorists and practitioners, particularly managers and union representatives, take a less optimistic win-lose approach to control. They believe just as firmly that whatever one party gains, the other loses.

Conflict in organizations is a process of interaction between systems in which the actions of one tend to obstruct the goal activities of the other, thereby triggering resistance (Katz & Kahn, 1978). The barriers to communication and the struggles for control underlie the potential for conflict in organizations. Conflict can occur at all levels within the system—interpersonal, group, intergroup—as well as between the organization and other organizations or elements of the wider environment. Conflict at each of these levels shows the same processes and symptoms we've described in earlier chapters. For example, union-management conflict exhibits the same kind of stereotyping, hostility, and ineffective communication that is apparent in racial or religious conflict (Blake, Shepard & Mouton, 1964; Stagner, 1967).

Organizations as open systems create potential for conflict simply by working to maintain themselves in the face of limited resources. Furthermore, this potential is heightened by the principle of maximization and the structure of bureaucracy. This means that subsystems will fight for their share of organizational resources, and that the organization will be in an ongoing competition with similar systems. Within most colleges and universities, for example, there is a constant question as to which departments will get new faculty positions and which may lose some. The college as a whole competes with other institutions—and recent times have seen the use of increased advertising designed to attract more students. Within the system, individual needs will be in conflict with organizational demands; in addition, the authority hierarchy designed to prevent and adjudicate conflicts will create conflict by attempting to control individual members. For example, the college that attempts to place many restrictions on students living in residences will not only encounter resistance from individuals, but may find fewer students wanting residence accommodation. Katz and Kahn (1978) sum up this situation:

> [E]very aspect of organizational life that creates order and coordination of effort must overcome other tendencies to action, and in that fact lies the potentiality for conflict. Organizational roles prescribe one set of behaviors out of a very large repertoire, and in prescribing necessarily proscribe as well. Rewards and incentives are necessary inducements to membership and performance, but consensus about their allocation is almost unattainable, and conflict about it increases with their attractiveness. Authority is a conflict-reducing invention, but its exercise implies submission to influence, which is almost never perfect. Organizational change is necessary for survival, but an organization with no internal resistance to change would be no organization at all; it would move in any direction and in response to any suggestion. Change and the resistance to change, however, mean conflict. (p.617)

Complex models of organizational conflict are presented by Thomas (1976) and Katz and Kahn (1978). These models help sensitize us to the wide variety of factors that affect the process and outcomes of conflict. Organizational properties, conflicts of interest, role expectations, personalities, laws and procedures, and the quality of interaction between the parties all intertwine to determine the nature and the extent of organizational conflict.

As a result of these studies, conflict has become an issue of central concern. Organizational psychologists have become increasingly attuned to its importance as a central process in organizational functioning. Consultants who practice in organizational settings have developed techniques to assess and manage the variety of conflicts that occur. This growing attention, finally, is highlighted by the latest contribution from the human relations approach of Rensis Likert, *New Ways of Managing Conflict* (Likert & Likert, 1976).

In the balance of this chapter, we will explore the potential for developing productive methods of resolving organizational conflict.

IMPROVING ORGANIZATIONAL EFFECTIVENESS: THE PRACTICE OF ORGANIZATION DEVELOPMENT

Organization Development: Definition and History

The impressive body of theory and research on organizations lays a strong foundation for practice. As social psychologists and other professionals came to understand the functioning of organizations, the driving forces of pragmatism and humanism pushed practitioners toward change efforts designed to increase organizational effectiveness. These efforts have aimed at meeting the personal and social needs of members and of reaching organizational goals for production or service. Here are three examples of organization development offered by French and Bell (1978):

- The president of a business firm senses trouble—morale is sagging and customer complaints and costs are rising. He calls in an organizational consultant. A meeting is held with the top management group and a decision is made to hold a three-day workshop to focus on the organization's difficulties. The consultant interviews each executive and at the start of the workshop presents the major problems (such as poor meetings, lack of cooperation between departments). The group prioritizes the problems, and in turn analyzes the dynamics of each one and develops solutions. The consultant injects theory where useful—for example, on effective group decision making—and provides feedback to the group on its own behavior. As a final step, the group develops concrete action steps to be implemented back on the job. Follow-up meetings show progress on some problems, while others require more work. Company morale increases, customer complaints and costs decrease. The organization decides to hold similar workshops for each department and institutes an annual problem-solving workshop for the total organization.
- A division of a large corporation wants to improve its effectiveness and requests the aid of consultants to develop an attitude survey of employees. The consultants advise a fully participative approach in which organizational members would help design the questionnaire and in which feedback workshops would be used to report the results back to all respondents. The attitude questionnaire is subsequently designed to cover several key areas of organizational functioning: organizational climate, relations between units, opportunities for personal growth and advancement. In the feedback workshops, participants discuss the reasons for questionnaire results, develop ideas on possible improvements, and make specific recommendations to higher mangement. Everyone agrees the workshops are highly successful and that the procedure should be repeated in the future.
- A new junior high school is about to open. The principal, two vice-principals, thirty teachers, the librarian, cooks, and custodians have never worked together before. The principal calls in an organizational consultant to help form the staff into an interdependent team. A week-long workshop is held to help staff get acquainted, to improve interpersonal communication skills, to prescribe methods of leadership and decision making, and to develop the psychological contract between individual staff and the organization. At the end of the workshop, members feel much closer together and have a clear sense of how to approach organizational problems in a collaborative manner. Further meetings and workshops are held. Staff report working well together and enjoying the climate of the organization. The new school experiences very low turnover of staff and is seen as a model in the district.

As these vignettes indicate, organization development, expanding at an amazing rate over the past twenty years, is an exciting and varied field of endeavor. To capture its essence, French and Bell (1978) define it this way:

[O]rganization development is a long-range effort to improve an organization's problem-solving and renewal processes, particularly through a more effective and collaborative management of organization culture—with special emphasis on the culture of formal work teams—with the assistance of a change agent, or catalyst, and the use of the theory and technology of applied behavioral science, including action research. (p. 14)

Organization Development (or OD) traces its roots back to laboratory training and survey feedback. The first grew out of the interest of Kurt Lewin and others in the practical application of group dynamics to human relations training. The Connecticut Workshop in Community Relations and the birth of the National Training Laboratories lie at the base of both human relations training and OD. Many of the early trainers in laboratory education wanted to apply group methods toward organizational change, but were frustrated when the skills required in the T-group did not transfer back to the organizational roles of participants. This led to an interest in training family groups or work teams from the same organization. Consequently a number of practitioners began holding different types of training labs specifically designed for particular organizations. Some of these trainers were employed by business and industry; others served as external consultants. In either case, the consultant role—developing beyond that of human relations trainer—became one that provided consultation to managers and supervisors from a human relations perspective. This was the birth of the concept of "organization development," growing out of the idea of a "development group" in conjunction with a broad organizational focus.

The second crucial ingredient in the creation of OD was a special type of action research known as survey research and feedback. During the late 1940s and early 1950s, social psychologists at the University of Michigan's Institute for Social Research began adapting the methodology of survey research to the measurement of employee attitudes in the organizational setting (Mann, 1957). The question was how to best use this data to improve organizational performance. Feedback of results to managers alone resulted in little change, but feedback to work groups of managers and subordinates, followed by group discussion and action planning, had significant impact. This combination of action research with human relations training and group dynamics provided the underlying expression of scientific humanism that supports the field of OD.

The great growth of organization development has been accompanied by an increase in theory and the proliferation of practice methods (Adams, 1974; Alderfer, 1977a; Beer, 1976; Burke, 1972, 1977, 1978; Friedlander, 1980; Friedlander & Brown, 1974). While research on OD has not been neglected, it has lagged behind the development of theory and practice, only recently showing signs of increasing quality (Alderfer, 1977a).

The field of OD is in its adolescence. Applications of OD continue to spread to all types of organizations and to most countries of the industrialized Western world (French & Bell, 1978). In its current stage of growth and achievement, OD has also shown important adaptations that speak well for its future (Alderfer, 1977a; Burke, 1977). From a field limited almost exclusively to settings in business and industry (with some early work in education), OD has moved into organizations in both the public and third sectors. Practice technology has become more sophisticated, and the consultant's function has expanded. The number of professionals in applied social psychology and related disciplines who identify themselves as OD practitioners has mushroomed from a handful of individuals in the 1950s to thousands in the late 1970s. We have yet to see how long this differentiation phase will continue before core models and strategies clearly emerge.

What follows is an overview of the major OD approaches—and some examples of process interventions and comprehensive programs. In addition, we must explore the crucial issue of effectiveness by examining research on the OD process and its outcomes.

Contrasting Approaches to Organization Development

When you consider the social complexity of organizations, the range of research methods available to study organizations (see Chapter 3), and the variety of practice skills available to change organizations (see Chapter 4), it should come as no surprise that there are a number of contrasting approaches to OD rather than just one commonly accepted strategy.

Several authors have tried to clarify this diverse field by developing a description of the different major approaches (for example, Bowers, 1973; Friedlander & Brown, 1974; Sashkin, Morris & Horst, 1973). The various forms of OD are identified mainly by their primary emphasis and focus: What are their core strategies and methods of change in terms of how they impinge upon the system? At what place in the organization do they center their change efforts? However, the major approaches are not mutually exclusive; they are often blended in various combinations to produce an overall change effort. Similarly, all approaches follow the general problem-solving process of planned change described in Chapter 4. For example, French and Bell (1978) see OD as composed of the following major operational components: diagnosis of the state of the organization, action to correct problems (including evaluation of actions and the planning of new actions), and the ongoing process maintenance required to support OD activities. Within this framework each major approach performs its diagnosis in different ways, stresses certain actions over others, and manages the overall process somewhat differently.

By synthesizing different typologies, we can identify five major approaches to OD: the process consultation and intervention model, the survey feedback approach, the human relations approach, the sociotechnical/structural model, and the systems approach.

Process Consultation and Intervention Approach. The vignette describing a consultant's work with a business firm typifies the *process consultation and intervention approach* to OD. This approach began with the work of McGregor, Schein, Argyris, and other organizational theorists who used their expertise to help organizations solve problems and improve their functioning. (See Chapter 4 for

Schein's basic statement of process consultation, 1969.) The process consultant, entering into interactions within the client system, promotes members' sensitivity and constructive response to the ongoing processes that occur in their environment. The consultant collaborates with the client system in diagnosing, planning, intervening, and evaluating. The consultant must establish an effective helping relationship, must be expert in social processes, and must move the consulting relationship through a series of necessary stages to help the client system increase the satisfaction and productivity of its members. Thus the focus of this model is on the human-process aspects of the organization rather than on its physical technology or social structure.

Argyris (1970) has added to our understanding of process consultation by developing a general model of intervention. In this model, the consultant enters an ongoing system of persons or groups with the purpose of helping them. He or she helps generate valid information, helps the client system maintain its autonomy and capacity for free, informed choice, and helps develop internal commitment to the choices made.

Three major types of interventions include improving communication using a variety of tested methods (surveys, T-groups); developing new methods that creatively rearrange existing knowledge; and collaborating with the client in the creation of a unique intervention that solves the problem and adds to theoretical knowledge. The last type of activity is rare, but is typified by the work of Kurt Lewin who "was able to relate such practical problems as inducing people to drink orange juice, eat liver, buy bonds, and produce higher quality pajamas to basic conceptual issues" (Argyris, 1970, p.32).

The process consultation approach continues its strong emphasis on improving communication, building trust, and improving decision making. This is done by diagnosing problem areas through individual interviews and group discussions, and by implementing such process interventions as interpersonal conflict resolution, group consultation, and intergroup dialogue. Process consultation often serves as the core of an OD enterprise with other strategies and interventions being blended into it as required.

Survey Feedback Approach. The second vignette at the beginning of this section exemplifies the *survey feedback approach,* which has its roots in both survey methodology and action research (see Chapter 3). Following the classic work by Mann (1957) and his associates, this approach begins with a questionnaire and/or interview survey. Employees and management are asked their opinions on topics such as supervision, morale, and interpersonal relations. The results are then fed back to the organizational units or families through a series of interlocking conferences that proceed downward from the top of the organization. That is, presentation and discussion of results begins with the top executive group, proceeds to a meeting with each executive and his or her subordinates, then moves on down the line. The reported results are tailored for unique relevance to each organizational unit, permitting in-depth analysis of that unit as well as comparisons with other units. Through group discussions and decision making, plans are then developed for constructive administrative action. These outcomes are then fed back up the line. The researcher/consultant collaborates with organizational members on the design of questions, the analysis and interpretation of results, and on feedback and planning activities.

Mann's basic approach, extended and elaborated by other researchers, is now an integral part of data-based methods of organization development (see Bowers & Franklin, 1976; Nadler, 1977). The survey feedback method is also useful for an initial diagnosis of organizational change—assuming that the perceptions and attitudes that are measured by the survey method are relevant to the change process. The effectiveness of this approach is increased when there is collaborative involvement of employees, participation of managers, and when specific decisions are made about follow-up actions. However, while survey methods can provide a useful bridge between diagnosis and intervention, it is not guaranteed that survey feedback by itself leads to personal or organizational change (Friedlander & Brown, 1974).

Human Relations Training Approach. The example of consultation with the new junior high school comes under the *human relations training approach* to OD. The aim of this approach is to improve the effectiveness of group functioning in ways that enhance personal growth and organizational productivity. The primary method of change for many years was the sensitivity training group, the early hope being that individual changes in interpersonal and group skills would transfer to the organizational role behavior of participants. (Schein and Bennis [1965], provide a representative statement of this application of laboratory methods to persons in organizational settings.) While there were some indications of positive transfer effects at the individual level (for example, Campbell & Dunnette, 1968), it soon became apparent that it was futile to try to change organizational procedures and structures through group training alone (Katz & Kahn, 1978). Shifting its procedures, the human relations approach used sensitivity training in conjunction with other OD methods, and focused the training on intact work groups in the organizational setting itself.

This approach is now represented by a variety of group development methods, particularly that of team building designed to improve the task behavior and social maintenance skills of an organizational family. At the same time the human relations training model has continued to stress the importance of interpersonal competence (see Argyris, 1962), whether gained through unstructured group methods or through more systematic training programs. Also, organizations are still strongly interested in leadership training within their own settings, whether for managers and supervisors in bureaucratic organizations (see Suessmuth, 1978) or for leaders of third-sector voluntary organizations (see O'Connell, 1976; YMCA, 1974).

However, the human relations training approach has its problems. One is the immense difficulty of changing interpersonal behavior that is the product of many years of socialization and is supported by many forces in the organizational and cultural environment (see Box 9.4). Another is that research results on group development and team-building interventions leave a number of important processes and outcomes unclear (Friedlander & Brown, 1974). And a third is continuing criticism, on certain practical grounds, of the human relations approach to management (see Nord & Durand, 1978). Nonetheless interventions based on the human relations model play a large part in the present practice of OD (Dyer, 1976; French & Bell, 1978).

Sociotechnical/Structural Approach. The *sociotechnical/structural approach* to OD seeks to change either the social structure of the organization or its physical technology and arrangements of work activities. This invovles a wide-ranging and rapidly developing mix of strategies: sociotechnical alterations, job enlarge: ment and job enrichment, changes in the reward system, and the creation of different organizational structures. All these strategies simultaneously stress the importance of considering both the sociopsychological aspects (personal motivation, group dynamics) and the technical and structural aspects (job design, division of labor).

The classic sociotechnical approach was introduced by the work of the Tavistock Institute in England, through studies of British coal mining at the time of major technological changes. The introduction of new and much larger equipment had spread the miners over a wide area, had created specialized tasks with individual rewards, and had broken down the close interpersonal and small-group relations that had existed under the older team method. Productivity took a nose dive, and absenteeism and accidents skyrocketed. To correct these severe problems, the consultants helped to develop a composite method that used the new technology in conjunction with smaller work groups that shared and rotated tasks and received rewards on a group basis. The clear superiority of this approach showed the importance of combining the social and technical aspects into an integrated sociotechnical system (Emery & Trist, 1960).

Similar adaptations were successful in other settings—in Indian weaving mills for one—partially laying the basis for the development of studies of industrial democracy in Europe (Emery & Thorsrud, 1969, 1976). However, as Katz and Kahn (1978) point out, the early sociotechnical studies mainly involved adapting the social system to new technology rather than changing the technical system to meet the personal and social needs of the workers. More recent developments in Norway and Sweden have produced more of a proper fit between social and technical systems by instituting organization-wide changes in technology and structure to improve the quality of work life. (We will look at Sweden's new factories later in this chapter.)

A more limited sociotechnical strategy is represented by *job enlargement* and *job enrichment.* Job enlargement is designed to increase worker satisfaction by adding activities that increase the sense of variety and wholeness of the job. For example, rather than having a worker tighten five bolts on an automobile steering assembly, she might work with a partner to put together the entire assembly. In this way job enlargement increases the scope of *horizontal* activities of the role—that is, activities at the same level of production and decision making. Job enrichment, on the other hand, adds work functions in a *vertical* direction—that is, to higher levels of decision making to make the role more interesting, challenging, and intrinsically motivating (Friedlander & Brown, 1974; Katz & Kahn, 1978). In this instance a worker on an assembly line might be given responsibility for quality control, or a secretary might be made responsible for some administrative decisions. Since these strategies are limited to single jobs, they are not expected to result in organization-wide change.

Box 9.4 FOCUS ON THEORY AND PRACTICE
The Challenge of Changing Leaders' Behavior

Chris Argyris, a professor of education and organizational behavior at Harvard University, has demonstrated how difficult it is to change leadership behavior in organizational settings. Argyris maintains that, in American society, individuals are programmed with *theories of action* that are counterproductive for both individual growth and organizational effectiveness. There are two types of theories of action: *theories of action*, which individuals report as guiding their behavior, and *theories-in-use*, which are determined by actually observing the individuals' behavior. There is often a large discrepancy between these two types of theories.

Most theories of action of organizational leaders follow what Argyris terms Model I, based on the values of achieving one's purpose, winning not losing, suppressing negative feelings, and emphasizing rationality. Model I behaviors include controlling the task and the environment and protecting oneself and others from being hurt. This is essentially a controlling, autocratic, paternalistic style of leadership. The consequences of Model I include increased individual and group defensiveness; reduced freedom, risk taking, and commitment; a lack of learning based on feedback; and ultimately, reduced organizational effectiveness.

Argyris's alternative theory of action is Model II, which values the sharing of valid information, free and informed choice, and internal commitment. Model II behaviors include the sharing of power to jointly control the task with relevant others who are competent. Protection of both self and others replaces defensiveness. The consequences include high freedom of choice, risk taking, and commitment; learning from experience; public testing of theories; and increased organizational effectiveness. Model II is essentially the enactment of the problem-solving process using human relations skills.

Sounds good, but as Argyris points out, moving to Model II as a theory-in-use is a tall order. It requires much time, pain, and self-doubt, as well as considerable assistance. Simply learning Model II as an espoused theory is not enough. One group of 100 managers, all of whom had learned Model II, produced written solutions for a case study involving a subordinate whose performance was unsatisfactory. Almost all their solutions involved Model I behavior. Futhermore, even when the managers were able with assistance to design Model II interventions, they were not able to implement these in a role play based on the case study problem.

Learning to change leadership behavior requires awareness of the typical discrepancy between espoused theories and theories-in-use. It requires a sequence similar to that of experience-based learning wherein participants openly discuss their problems and receive feedback on their attempted solutions. In these ways, change toward Model II can occur.

Source: Argyris, C. Leadership, learning and changing the status quo. *Organizational Dynamics*, 1976, 4, 29–43.

Studies in the United States, Great Britain, Sweden, and other countries clearly demonstrate that job enlargement and job enrichment lead to increased satisfaction and motivation and to improvements in both the quality and quantity of performance (Friedlander & Brown, 1974; Katz & Kahn, 1978). However these studies relate almost exclusively to profit-making business and industrial organizations; the applicablity of these strategies to nonprofit human service organizations is still unclear. In human service organizations, rules for the equal treatment of clients may hamper job enrichment—the worker is to provide basic service, and that's all! In third-sector organizations, jobs are often *too* enlarged or too enriched with workers having to be a Jack or June of all trades. A worker may have such a number and variety of responsibilities that it is difficult to cope with the job. Some initial evidence does indicate that certain elements of job design are related to employee satisfaction in human service organizations. Sarata and Jeppesen (1977) interviewed psychologists, nurses, social workers, teachers, and nonprofessional staff in a variety of agencies providing services to children— mental health centers, adoption agencies, residential care settings. Variety in a person's job and opportunities to learn new skills were positively related to employee satisfaction, but other elements such as degree of autonomy showed no relationship. To what degree sociotechnical applications are useful in human service organizations remains an open question.

Pay and other rewards are clearly a part of employee motivation and job satisfaction. Although structural variables such as reward mechanisms are changed all the time by owners and managers, it is only recently that this sociotechnical approach—the manipulation of reward mechanism and of the entire reward structure of an organization—has become a legitimate and important part of OD.

As Katz and Kahn (1978) point out, organizational leaders have been reluctant to experiment with such tangible and significant variables, and social scientists have lacked the power and assertiveness to intervene on the reward structure of organizations. Fortunately a few pioneering efforts have occurred where changes in reward mechanisms served as an important part of broader OD programs (see Beer & Huse, 1972; Patten & Fraser, 1975). Profit-sharing plans appear to be successful in certain cases, mostly with executives, but there has been little study of these. A noteworthy exception, the *Scanlon Plan*, making a broad attempt to change both the reward and the authority structures of the organization, has been documented and evaluated over a long period of time (Katz & Kahn, 1978). It works like this: All members of the organization have a say in decision making and a share in the profits. A collection of elected departmental and organization-wide committees, headed by appointed supervisors, elicit suggestions and make decisions about work methods. Both union and management are committed to a formula for profit sharing that returns a large part of the gains in productivity to the workers. Thus changes in reward structure motivate workers to improve performance, and the participative decision making of the communications structure provides the arrangements for bringing it about. Studies indicate that the Scanlon Plan is effective (Frost, Wakely & Ruh, 1974; Lesieur & Puckett, 1969; White, 1979). In fact, hundreds of companies—mostly smaller organizations—have adopted the plan in whole or in part, and wages are typically 25 percent above union rates. To date, the Scanlon Plan stands as the clearest example of organizational change brought about by manipulating the allocation of extrinsic rewards.

The Scanlon Plan and later sociotechnical experiments in Europe, as organization-wide attempts at change, come close to producing *new forms of work organizations* (Klein, 1976). These new forms are attempts to improve both the quality of work life in terms of satisfaction, and the depth of industrial democracy in terms of employee responsibility and power in decision making. In their aspects of reward structure and authority structure, these approaches to organizational change are beginning to approximate alternative forms of organizations that have been around for some time, particularly the cooperatives found in different parts of Europe and North America and the agricultural *kibbutzim* of Israel. These types of organizations provide alternatives to the predominantly bureaucratic structure of most profit-making and public service organizations.

Most cooperative organizations, whether production or service oriented, are based on the principles of consumer control and profit sharing (Spaull, 1965). Users of the organization's products or services enter into decision making through voting power at meetings and through election to a board of directors that controls policy and planning. Users receive dividends based on their quantity of consumption of goods or services, rather than on their amount of investment (the case with shareholders of private corporations). The employee work structure, however, often parallels a bureaucratic pattern without a sharing of decision making or profits.

The *kibbutz* model, on the other hand, involves the election of workers to the major decision-making positions and committees of the organization and is based on the communal sharing of property and profits. In this way, the *kibbutzim* provide a strong mechanism for the effective integration of the individual into the social system (Katz & Golomb, 1974).

Harvesting apples on an Israeli *kibbutz*. *(197 Stephen Shames)*

The cooperative and the *kibbutz* are organizational forms that are compatible with the democratic alternative outlined by Katz and Kahn (1978)—which is also expressed in democratic government structures and voluntary organizations. The basic difference between the democratic alternative and the typical autocratic hierarchical organization is the managerial subsystem—specifically the authority structure that holds decision-making power. The democratic model separates the several forms of organizational power by vesting legislative or policy-making power in the hands of members and/or workers. Thus, elected members determine policy, hire and fire executive officers, and have the power of the veto in decision making. At the same time, executive power remains with management for the day-to-day operation of the organization.

Each form has its advantages and disadvantages with respect to effectiveness in different situations. Katz and Kahn (1978) contend that democratic organizations operate more effectively when there is a necessity for openness and adaptation to a rapidly changing environment, and when individual roles require the exercise of creativity and an understanding of and commitment to the total organization. Thus, it is likely that the democratic alternative might be more appropriate to both public and third-sector human service organizations. Certainly these alternate forms of organization are more compatible with the humanistic value base of applied social psychology than is the hierarchical bureaucracy.

Systems Approach. The *systems approach* is an eclectic strategy for viewing the organization as a whole in relation to its environment. It therefore adopts a variety of interventions to facilitate organizational change. These are multifaceted programs of OD that work with some combination of survey feedback, training workshops, sociotechnical changes, and overall process consultation (Friedlander & Brown, 1974). This approach is based on an open-systems framework that encompasses all levels of analysis, all subsystems, and the interaction with the wider environment. It is therefore possible to match interventions to problems that cross the full range of human relations, and technical and structural concerns (Bowers, Franklin & Pecorella, 1975).

An early example of a systems approach to OD is the work of Michael Beer and Edger Huse with plants of the Corning Glass Works (Beer & Huse, 1972). These practitioners developed a systems model of organizations that specified the major input, throughput, and output variables (see Figure 9.2). They then adopted an eclectic approach to change within a background of ongoing process consultation. Sociotechnical interventions played a major part in the program. For example, the redesign of a hotplate assembly line gave each worker total responsibility for the assembly of the product; lower-level worker and secretarial jobs were enlarged, increasing both satisfaction and productivity; autonomous work groups were organized with total responsibility for scheduling, assembly, training, and quality control. Mutual goal-setting and a redesigned reward system based on merit gave workers some control of both the authority and the reward structure.

These interventions required mutually consistent changes in all the subsystems of the organization, with structural and process changes reinforcing and

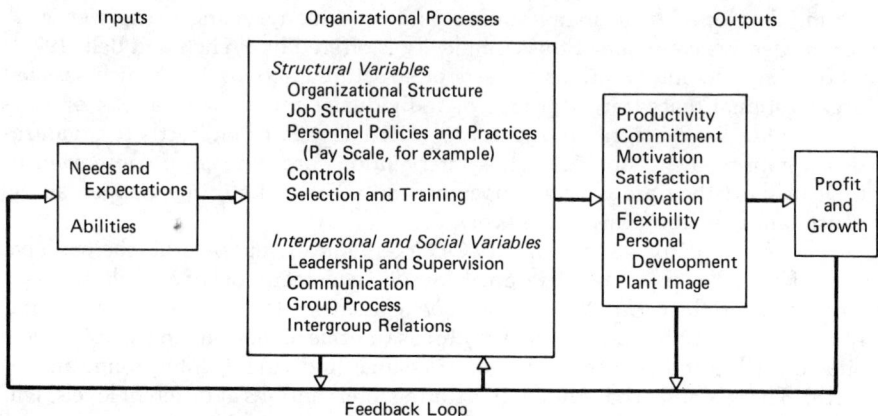

Figure 9.2   **A Systems Approach to Organization and Development.**
Source: Beer & Huse (1972).

legitimizing each other. But some problems developed: for instance, the usual job evaluation procedures did not cover all aspects of the enriched jobs and a number of supervisory positions were eliminated—hardly a positive outcome for supervisors! Despite such shortcomings, the overall results indicate open communication, interesting and challenging jobs, mutual goal-setting, a considerable reduction in turnover, and productivity increases of up to 50 percent.

Apparently the multifaceted systems approach is becoming the OD strategy of choice, when conditions permit, because of its greater probability of success within existing forms of organizations. (We will look at other examples of comprehensive OD programs later in this chapter.)

Process Interventions in Organization Development

Organizational problems are often human and social problems: ineffective communication, faulty group interaction, dysfunctional decision making, and so on. The first step of the consultant is of course to diagnose organizational functioning—to establish a shared understanding of how well the system is functioning and to determine if change is desirable (Alderfer, 1980). Interventions are then designed to match the diagnosis, to address the problems that have been identified. Because applied social psychology is particularly suited to the diagnosis and alleviation of human social problems, its practitioners, working in organizational settings, have been at the forefront of the development of interventions designed to improve organizational functioning. In contrast, the development of sociotechnical interventions (such as job enrichment and work flow) has been of a more interdisciplinary nature, involving professionals in business administration and industrial engineering, and nonprofessionals from labor and management. Similarly, structural changes are often initiated through executive or legislative authority at the organizational or societal level.

The full range of process interventions in OD is complex and sophisticated, having developed from many sources and over many years of experience. A comprehensive coverage of this complexity is offered by French and Bell (1978), who define OD interventions as "sets of structured activities in which selected organizational units (target groups or individuals) engage with a task or a sequence of tasks where the task goals are related directly or indirectly to organizational improvement" (p.102). Thus interventions are the *action component* of OD. In short they are what's happening and what make things happen as the consultant goes about his or her work.

There are many ways to classify OD interventions and several schemes have been offered. For example, Blake and Mouton's general model of consultation (see Chapter 4), in the form of the *consulcube*, classifies interventions by type (catalytic, confrontation, and so forth), by focus (morale/cohesion, goals/objectives, and so forth), and by unit or target of change (individual, intergroup, and so forth). The examples that follow, illustrating interventions at different levels, will give us further insight into the role of an applied social psychologist as a process intervenor in organization settings.

The Individual Level. Working with individual people is an important part of OD. Interventions at this level include information giving, training, counseling, and behavior modification (Katz & Kahn, 1978). It is also at the individual level that methods are used to diagnose organizational problems—usually through personal interviews or survey questionnaires. This is why the OD consultant should have a degree of clinical sensitivity: personality dynamics and, in some cases, individual pathology can easily affect organizational functioning and the success or failure of OD efforts.

Goodstein (1978) provides examples of the importance of clinical sensitivity and the ability to deal with the individual behavior. In one case an administrator with paranoid tendencies (suspicion and fear of persecution by others) was creating a log jam in communication because of his desire to ascertain the hidden meaning of all the messages that came through his office! In another situation, a young president (who took over the company after his father's death) behaved recklessly just to prove himself, ignored the confronting diagnoses of the consultants, and promptly drove the business into bankruptcy. Such instances of individual pathology are crucial when the person is seriously ill and/or in a position of power in the organization. In most cases, however, a limited degree of individual dysfunction does not seriously affect the broader organization, and we would not expect individual counseling to bring about change in the total system (Katz & Kahn, 1978).

If the consultant is trained in clinical psychology, he or she may provide personal counseling to troubled individuals or may make referrals to other clinicians. Most of the interventions at the individual level, however, will come about through process consultation. The consultant will work to develop effective helping relationships with many individuals in the organization to facilitate the problem-solving process. In so doing, a certain amount of personal consultation helps the individual to understand his or her behavior in relation to organizational problems. Failing adequate intervention at the individual level, the OD process cannot work effectively at any higher level.

The Interpersonal and Interrole Level. An important element of OD is the variety of techniques designed to improve relations between persons who occupy related roles. Problems may develop in a number of areas—ineffective communication in role sending or receiving, role conflict due to differing expectations, or a lack of feedback in reaction to role sending. Process interventions help clarify who is supposed to do what, who wants to do what, and who is prepared to do what.

French and Bell (1978) present a description and illustration of one method for clarifying roles: Dayal and Thomas's (1968) *role analysis technique.* This approach clarifies roles in new organizations or in situations where role ambiguity exists.

- The first step calls for the individual in the focal role to analyze his or her role in terms of its duties and behaviors, its rationale, its place in the organization, and its relation to organizational goals. The other members of the role set inject their ideas, and discussion continues until everyone is satisfied with the role definition.
- The second step requires the focal person to describe his or her role expectations of every other member of the role set. Discussion and modification go on until everything is clear. In the third step the role partners describe their expectations of the focal role, and discussion again moves to consensus.
- In the last step the focal person writes a summary of his or her role; this is reviewed by the members of the role set. Then the analysis moves on to the next role, continuing until each person knows what everyone else is supposed to be doing, and why.

This simple technique produces a fresh clarity about and renewed commitment to role demands and organizational objectives. For example, French and Bell (1978) have successfully used this approach to clarify the organizational roles of board members (to determine policy) and of executive officers (to implement policy)—a simple way to avoid a common mixup.

In some cases role clarification is inadequate, necessitating more systematic and impersonal bargaining techniques to resolve problems. Harrison's (1972) *role negotiation* is an intervention in which role partners explicitly state what behaviors they want from each other and what behaviors they are prepared to change to get what they want. A written contract seals the agreement. Another technique is Sherwood and Glidewell's (1972) systematic model for the *planned renegotiation* of roles, providing for ongoing changes in role expectations. By these means role conflict can be handled in an acceptable, uniform manner that productively resolves issues and prevents the escalation of conflict. Of course the successful implementation of interpersonal and group skills is essential to these types of intervention.

Group Interventions. The power of the work group in organizational functioning leads to this question: How can the OD consultant intervene to maximize the task and social effectiveness of work teams? Many interventions at the group level come under the concept of *team building.* This consists of activities designed to enhance the effective operation of work teams by analyzing concerns, developing group skills, improving coordination, setting goals, and building stronger relationships.

French and Bell (1978) and Dyer (1977) present a variety of interventions for facilitating the development of cohesive and collaborative work teams. One of French and Bell's team interventions is the family group team-building meeting. The organizational family, consisting of a manager and his or her immediate subordinates, collaborates with the OD consultant in a two- to three-day session that focuses on task effectiveness, relationship demands, and group processes. The consultant usually interviews all team members prior to the session and develops major themes around problems and obstacles that are inhibiting group performance. These themes are presented at the first meeting and are clarified and placed in order of priority by the group. With the aid of the consultant (in a role similar to that of T-group trainer), the team examines underlying dynamics—such as poor communication or power conflict—and develops alternative solutions and action steps to alleviate the difficulties. For example, two subordinates might be constantly competing for recognition within the work group with negative side effects on group morale. Analyzing this situation and developing additional ways of recognizing group members might alleviate the problem.

Within this general problem-solving framework, a great deal of variety is possible with respect to the specific purpose of the meeting, the method for generating information, the inclusion of skill-training exercises, the use of conflict-resolution techniques, and the time devoted to goal setting. Because of this flexibility, and its capacity to tailor an intervention to specific problems, team building is fast becoming one of the most popular forms of process intervention.

Intergroup Interventions. The classic symptoms of intergroup conflict such as stereotyping and hostility occur as much in organizational settings as elsewhere (see Chapter 8). Following their studies of intergroup conflict in training workshops, Robert Blake, Jane Mouton, and their colleagues took the lead in developing process interventions specifically directed to improving intergroup relations in organizational settings (Blake, Shepard & Mouton, 1964).

These practitioners have worked with various dysfunctional intergroup relationships, including union versus management, headquarters versus field offices, and new versus old companies in a merger situation. In each case the goal of the intervention is to change a hostile win-lose orientation to one of collaborative problem solving. This requires the help of a skilled third-party consultant for the parties to focus on the nature of the conflict and explore possible resolutions.

One way to approach this is through an intergroup intervention involving the development and exchange of images—that is, the views that each group has of itself and of the other group. In one case of union-management relations, for example, the union felt that management was opposed to organized labor, was concerned only with production, and used underhanded methods to reach company goals. On the other hand, management felt that it showed equal concern for production and people, wanted to establish a problem-solving relationship with the union, and was honest and aboveboard in its methods. As for its view of the union, management thought that it was controlled by a scheming professional leader, was rigid in interpreting the contract, and pushed every grievance to arbitration. But the union's image of itself was far different. It considered that it was governed by its total membership, approached problems with an open mind, and wanted to work out grievances. Through a controlled sequence of procedures, the sharing and discussion of these black and white images led to increased understanding and the development of a number of crucial issues. These were stated in neutral and rational ways (for instance, a lack of mutual trust and respect), making the issues approachable through constructive problem solving.

Such interventions create the potential for improving intergroup relations, opening the way for techniques that move the situation to action steps and their evaluation by both parties. Given the centrality of intergroup relations between departments, between subsystems, and between management and labor, there is no question that we must continue the development and application of intergroup interventions (see Alderfer, 1977b; Burke, 1974).

The Organizational Level. Single interventions that attempt to deal with the total organization are rare. In fact there appears to be only one such design in the OD field, *the confrontation meeting* developed by Richard Beckhard. Other designs that approach the organization as a complete system are either combinations of interventions—following a general approach such as survey feedback—or are even more comprehensive programs of OD.

Beckhard's (1967) *confrontation meeting* is designed as a one-day intensive assessment of the "state of the organization." It is essentially a problem solving session involving all management personnel or, in the case of a small organization, possibly all of its members. To accomplish this in one day, the conditions must be appropriate. For example, there must be a clear and general commitment to resolving the issues that are confronting the organization.

After a climate-setting session in which the top manager and the consultants stress open communication and the need for problem solving, heterogeneous small groups discuss and report whatever problems they believe the organization is experiencing. This information is categorized into a few major problem areas. Work teams then meet to discuss which problems are relevant to their area, set priorities, and develop action plans. These groups also indicate what they see as the most pressing issues for top management to work on and develop ways of communicating the outcomes of the meeting to their own subordinates. These later two activities facilitate the vertical flow of communication within the organization. At this point the confrontation meeting ends for everyone except top management, which plans action steps based on the information generated. These actions are made known to the rest of the organization, and a follow-up meeting with the consultant reviews the implementation of action steps.

When conditions are appropriate and time is short, the confrontation meeting is a quick way to expose organizational difficulties and to generate action and commitment toward their resolution.

Comprehensive Programs of Organization Development

Likert's System 4 Management. The work of Rensis Likert is central to the human relations approach to organizations. The research on leadership in organizational settings, initiated at the University of Michigan, led Likert to formulate his principle of supportive relationships: "The leadership and other processes of the organization must be such as to ensure a maximum probability that in all interactions and all relationships with the organization each member will, in the light of his background, values, and expectations, view the experience as supportive and one which builds and maintains his sense of personal worth and importance" (1961, p.103).

A further derivation of the principle showed the central importance of the work group in effective organizational functioning: " . . . management will make full use of the potential capacities of its human resources only when each person in an organization is a member of one or more effectively functioning work groups that have a high degree of group loyalty, effective skills of interaction, and high performance goals" (Likert, 1961, p.104).

Likert then expanded his theory beyond principles of interpersonal and group relations to include structural changes in the organization through his model of overlapping work groups (see Figure 9-3). In this model, each organizational family is linked to the next higher level by virtue of the supervisor's membership in the work group above. Supervisors thus serve as linking pins that tie together succeeding organizational families and provide vital channels for communication, feedback, and decision making. The model further specifies that each work group take responsibility for making decisions and monitoring the performance of its own work.

By comparing organizations, Likert (1961, 1967) has identified four types of management systems, moving from autocratic and controlling to participative and democratic: (1) exploitative-authoritative, (2) benevolent-authoritative, (3) consultative, and (4) participative-group. The fourth type of system, labelled *System 4* by Likert, combines supportive leadership with democratic team functioning, creating an interlocking hierarchy of organizational families. Likert saw this as the best way to maximize the motivation of individuals, harness the power of the work group, enhance effective communication and democratic decision making and prevent and resolve conflict most productively (Likert & Likert, 1976).

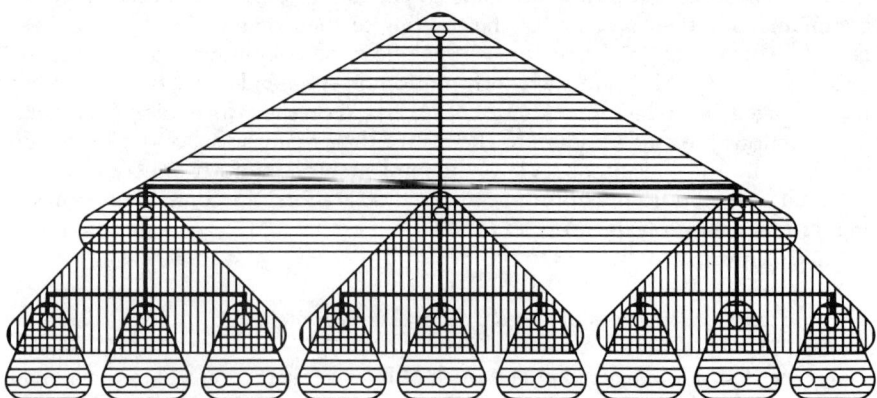

Figure 9.3   Likert's Mode of Overlapping Work Groups.
Source: Likert (1961).

Likert and his colleagues have put System 4 into practice by initiating comprehensive OD programs in a large number of organizations—usually with positive results. These programs combine survey feedback to assess the management system with various process and sociotechnical/structural interventions designed to move the organization toward the System 4 style of operation.

One of the best examples is the Weldon project. A manufacturing firm, following a traditional, authoritative management style, was taken over by the Harwood Company, a participative, System 4 organization. (Harwood was where the original Coch and French study had taken place.) To improve sagging productivity, low worker motivation, and poor labor relations, the managers and consultants initiated a wide-ranging change program. This involved human relations training for managers, sociotechnical modifications in work flow, and a new reward system that included incentive payments. Assessment of these changes showed a measurable move toward System 4 management, more positive worker attitudes toward the company, and impressive gains in productivity (Likert, 1967; Marrow, Bowers & Seashore, 1967). In short, Weldon came to resemble the parent Harwood Company on every major dimension of organizational functioning. Furthermore, follow-up data obtained 5 years after the end of the initial project showed that these changes not only persisted over time but that there was further movement toward the System 4 style (Seashore & Bowers, 1970). We can only conclude that Likert's approach, a valuable contribution to OD, works both in theory and in practice.

Blake and Mouton's Grid® Organization Development. Robert Blake's and Jane Mouton's many years of innovative work at all levels of organizational functioning have culminated in a comprehensive program of intervention known as *Grid Organization Development* (Blake & Mouton, 1969). According to French and Bell (1978), this approach is probably the most thorough-going and systematic OD package available. It consists of several phases of development over a 3- to 5-year period, using several research and practice methods, that focus on increasingly complex levels of analysis.

At the heart of this complex process is the Managerial Grid, defined by two dimensions: concern for production and concern for people (see Figure 9.4). Each dimension in the Managerial Grid runs from a low point of 1 to a high point of 9. A questionnaire assesses the position of individual managers on each dimension. The most effective managers are those who score high on both dimensions: the ultimate is the "9,9" manager—one who builds open and trusting relationships with others, and engenders a shared commitment and strong performance toward organizational goals.

The consulting process begins with groups of key managers attending Grid Seminars, where basic concepts and human relations skills are taught in an experience-based format. Some managers then proceed to advanced seminars that equip them to be the change agents who will initiate the Grid OD program in their own organization. This begins with Phase 1: all the organization's managers are trained in Grid concepts, and start working toward the goal of enacting the "9,9" style. Phase 2 moves to the level of group development; this is designed to increase both sensitivity to group processes and the ability to institute effective group

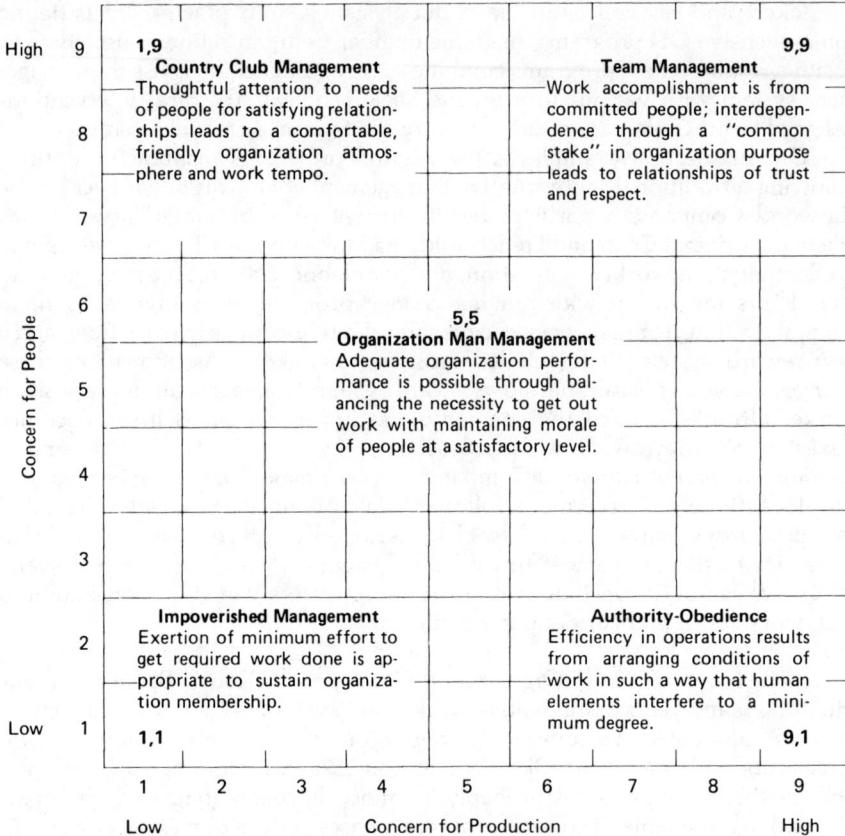

Figure 9.4   The Managerial Grid.
Source: Blake & Mouton (1969, 1978).

problem solving in the context of ongoing work teams. Intergroup development is carried out in Phase 3, moving interrelated teams toward more cooperative and productive relationships. Phase 4 focuses on the development of an ideal corporate model by involving the top management team in strategy and action planning directed toward organizational excellence. The implementation of this model takes place in Phase 5. It is here that sociotechnical and structural changes may be introduced so that each component of the organization is redesigned in line with the total reorganization of the system. Phase 6, the final step, is a systematic critique at every level: What has the program accomplished in both human and economic terms? What remains to be accomplished on the way to corporate excellence?

The scope and potential impact of Grid Organization Development are truly exciting. The method is almost all-inclusive, integrating the basic human relations approach into an explicit hard-hitting system that has its own unique terminology and strategy.

But there is always that final question: *Does it work?* A number of case studies by Blake and Mouton and their colleagues look very promising. One such successful program is described by Blake, Mouton, Barnes and Greiner (1964). However Keller (1978) presents a longitudinal assessment of a Grid Organization Development program that was not successful (see Box 9.5).

Dimock's Systems-Improvement Research. Most of the examples of OD we've discussed so far have occurred in production organizations. That is reality. There has simply been much less work done on multifaceted approaches to change in human service organizations. One recent exception is the model of *Systems-Improvement Research* (SIR), developed by Hedley Dimock (1978) and his colleagues at the Centre for Human Relations and Community Studies, Concordia University, Montreal.

After more than fifteen years of consultancy practice with over one hundred human service organizations, Dimock and his associates were dissatisfied with their degree of impact. Training interventions had little organizational effect, and research interventions often produced results that were lost in the turbulent organizational climate of staff and program changes. Even when useful data was produced in a short time, organizational resistance interfered with its effect on decision making.

In reaction to these unsatisfactory outcomes, SIR was designed as a data-based collaborative intervention strategy for planning and implementing organizational change, for training participants in OD skills, and for evaluating organizational effectiveness. Based on a combination of the survey feedback, human relations training, and process consultation approaches, SIR consists of five major components: (1) data feedback to stabilize and improve the system, (2) collaborating work pairs (one organizational member plus one consultant) to jointly diagnose problem areas and collect data, (3) an emphasis on process-oriented data within a systems-theory perspective, (4) member participation in analyzing the data and introducing changes, and (5) a focus on the organization's culture.

The model has five phases that are similar to those of action research and process consultation (see Chapters 3 and 4): entry, data collection, data analysis and goal setting, taking action and stabilizing change, and evaluation. The role of the SIR consultant is multifaceted: it includes being a model for effective helping relationships, a developer of structures, a technical trainer and resource on research methods, an information giver, and a trainer of human-relations and problem-solving skills.

Initial experiences with the SIR model have demonstrated both its potential usefulness and its limitations. Its humanistic value base, with a strong emphasis on equalitarianism and participation, appears to give SIR the potential for affecting significant changes in human service organizations. Therefore, we can only hope that the next decade will see increasing application of such comprehensive models to the field of human service, both in public-sector and third-sector organizations.

Box 9.5 FOCUS ON PRACTICE AND RESEARCH
Grid OD: Examples of Success and Failure

The Grid OD program developed by Robert Blake and Jane Mouton represents one of the most comprehensive approaches to organizational change. An early application of the program that had beneficial effects is reported by Blake, Mouton, Barnes and Greiner (1964). These interventions took place during 1962 and 1963 in a manufacturing plant of a major American oil company and consisted of the first four phases of Grid OD. Over 800 managers and technical staff participated in Phase 1 seminars based on the Managerial Grid. These concepts were applied to work teams (Phase 2); some intergroup interventions occurred (Phase 3); and some task forces were established to improve organizational functioning (Phase 4).

The research evaluation of the program indicated that productivity and profits increased substantially in 1963. There was also an increase in regular meetings and team problem-solving meetings. Finally, questionnaire responses showed positive increases in perceptions and attitudes. For example, 55 percent of respondents reported an improvement in the way their team worked together.

In 1974 and 1975, the same company instituted another Grid OD program in the same plant. Phase I consisting of Grid Seminars was provided to 131 employees who had not participated in the earlier program. The seminars were instructed by managers trained by Scientific Methods, Inc. (Blake and Mouton's consulting firm) and the program was independently evaluated by Robert Keller from the University of Houston. A battery of questionnaires administered before and after Phase 1 assessed four different variables: (1) organizational climate—the degree of warmth and trust, the use of groups for decision making, and the emphasis on a hierarchy of authority; (2) job satisfaction including the work, supervision, co-workers, promotion, and pay; (3) power relationships—the amount of control perceived at each organization level; and (4) leadership style in terms of initiating structure and consideration for others.

The results were predominantly negative. Leadership style and power relationships remained unchanged while job satisfaction and organizational climate became worse. Why? Keller's interpretation is that factors external to the Grid program produced these results and also led to the cancellation of the program following Phase 1. First, there was a lack of commitment and support by top management—they did not expect the program to accomplish much. Second, only Phase 1 was implemented and little attempt was made to use Grid concepts in other activities such as performance appraisal. Third, the seminars were attended by only a small portion of newer employees who were not able to influence the total organization.

Keller points out that there is little scientifically sound research on Grid OD and that many applications never get past Phase 1. Management commitment, implementation of concepts, and a system-wide effort are the likely ingredients of success.

Source: Blake, R., Mouton, J., Barnes, J. & Greiner, L. Breakthrough in organization development. *Harvard Business Review*, 1964, November-December, 133–155. Keller, R. T. A longitudinal assessment of a managerial grid seminar training program. *Group and Organization Studies*, 1978, *3*, 343–355.

The New Factories of Sweden. Since World War II, a number of European countries have experimented with system-wide organizational change. This is a result of both political developments at the national level (Tannenbaum, 1966) and a general shift to new forms of organizations (Klein, 1976). The election of worker representatives to boards of directors and the formation of workers' councils have given a variety of advisory and decision-making powers to employees. The goal of these efforts at industrial democracy is to improve worker morale and motivation through active participation in areas of direct concern.

In Norway and Sweden, this background of joint consultation has led to the design and testing of new organizational structures and sociotechnical arrangements. These are very different from the traditional ones still largely practiced in North America. Another interesting aspect is that most of these experiments have been instituted *without* the help of social scientists or organizational consultants; they have been planned by joint committees of managers and workers. Nonetheless these initiatives clearly qualify as comprehensive programs of OD, and many have been systematically evaluated with the help of social scientists.

Katz and Kahn (1978) provide an overview and synthesis of the developments taking place in Norway and Sweden. The Volvo Plant at Kalmar, Sweden (where the fictitious Anders Hansson works), is one example of the drive to change technological design to achieve social goals related to the quality of work life. These directions arose in reaction to the increasing mechanization of work and its disastrous effects on worker morale. That situation peaked in the mid-1960s to the point where it was difficult to recruit new workers for the assembly lines.

Collaborative planning groups of workers (with strong union support), managers, and staff tackled the tough question of how to produce automobiles efficiently by using small work groups rather than the conventional assembly line method. The new factory was designed so that each group of fifteen to twenty workers has its own work area, each with its own entrances and services (such as a coffee lounge). The factory as a whole runs on a central assembly line: each auto chassis is mounted on a platform powered by electrical tracks in the floor and propelled at a pace negotiated by union and management. Each work area then becomes a miniature assembly line with buffer areas at the start and finish. The chassis and platform leave the central assembly line and enter the work area. When the work is completed, the platform and chassis return to the central assembly line.

Each work group decides how it will accomplish its task of assembling some major subassembly of the car. Teams work in pairs or in subgroups each of which completes the entire task assigned to the work group. Thus, the work cycle—the time each worker has to complete his task—is anywhere from 16–40 minutes, as compared to the repetitive 1–2 minutes on a conventional line. Teams receive verbal feedback on quality and can adjust their work accordingly.

Work teams have a considerable amount of decision-making power and responsibility. They assign work within the team, train new members, monitor quality and quantity, and generally "run their own show" to get the job done. A team representative is elected to factory councils, and a team spokesperson is designated to communicate with management; therefore, the need for supervisors is considerably reduced.

A comprehensive evaluation of this new factory indicates that production and efficiency are equal to comparable plants with conventional assembly lines. However, some production costs such as absenteeism and turnover are lower and worker satisfaction as assessed by interviews is higher (Agurén, Karlsson & Hansson, 1976). This positive move to industrial democracy in Sweden is only one of many successful initiatives taken in the last decade (Lindholm, 1975). As Katz and Kahn (1978) point out, "For the 1970s . . . Sweden provides a unique example of significant and spreading work reform, and of sociotechnical change" (p.738).

Research on the Effectiveness of Organization Development

The pragmatic and rational values underlying OD force the questions: *Does it work? How does it work?* The research skills of the applied social psychologist hold the potential answers to these questions, but research and theory have lagged behind practice. In their 1974 review, Friedlander and Brown believed that research might either come to play a more crucial role in the advancement of OD or become an "increasingly irrelevant appendage" to it. Happily, the quantity and quality of evaluative research on OD appear to be on the rise, and there are positive signs of research designed to build comprehensive theories of OD practice.

These gains in research have been made in the face of considerable difficulties. OD, like all applied endeavors, is a tough field in which to do good research. French and Bell (1978) point out a number of specific problems that confront the OD researcher. Given the complexity of many OD programs, it is hard to identify specific independent variables and to understand their change effect on dependent variables. Furthermore, there is often a lack of precision in defining both treatments and outcomes in operational terms. For example, what does team building involve, and how do you measure increased organizational effectiveness?

These questions are related to the problem of *internal validity* in OD research. Given the complexity of real-world organizations and their environments, many extraneous variables can enter in. For example, the resignation of a key administrator during an OD program might affect the outcomes. Such threats to internal validity are not ruled out by weak experimental designs in OD. Even in cases where performance does improve, it is difficult to attribute this effect to the consultation process itself (Kaplan, 1979).

Yet another problem centers around *external validity.* Since OD is applied in markedly different settings—from large factories to small third-sector voluntary agencies—we are faced with a very real issue: How validly can results be generalized from one setting to another? It will probably be many years before OD practitioners have a moderate degree of certainty about "what works where, and when."

Finally OD research struggles along without a comprehensive theory of how systematic change occurs in organizations; the need for valid theory to guide practice and research is glaringly apparent. Such theory needs to be developed out of OD practice experience in an inductive manner, rather than being brought in from other areas or disciplines (Friedlander & Brown, 1974; Dunn & Swierczek, 1977).

In contrast to research difficulties, there were a number of positive trends occurring in OD research in the late 1970s (Alderfer, 1977a; French & Bell, 1978). There was an increasing use of more rigorous experimental and quasi-experimental designs, such as time-series analysis, to better evaluate the impact of OD interventions. Further a number of longitudinal programs of research are collecting data from a variety of organizational change efforts over many years. This kind of analysis is necessary to accurately evaluate the impact of OD on a broad scale. Improved methods of measuring variables—especially dependent ones such as job satisfaction and organizational climate—are coming about through the development of new techniques, and through a better understanding of how old techniques tap or fail to tap the important changes induced by OD (see Golembiewski, Billingsley & Yeager, 1976). Finally improved theories of social change are beginning to flow from OD practice and research. These theories, which are mainly inductive models, augur well for the power of OD research to shift more from straight evaluation of efforts to sophisticated theory-building in the 1980s and beyond.

Beyond the difficulties and potential of OD research, the predominant message from the work of the 1970s is that OD works. The present picture looks like this:

- Both the evaluation of specific interventions and comprehensive programs are yielding generally positive outcomes.
- The use of survey feedback, alone or in combination with other techniques, continues to produce improvements in both process and performance variables (see Frye, Seifert & Yancy, 1977).
- The human-process approaches appear to influence the attitudes of organizational members in constructive ways. There is, however, less support for their impact on organizational-level variables or overall effectiveness (Friedlander & Brown, 1974).
- Team building appears to be increasingly adopted as an intervention of choice; and research has documented some beneficial effects on interpersonal and group functioning (for example, Patten & Dorey, 1977).
- Sociotechnical interventions, such as job enlargement, show good potential for increasing job satisfaction; their effect on performance is not yet clear-cut (Friedlander & Brown, 1974).
- The most powerful effects of OD stem from comprehensive, multifaceted programs that use methods of systematic diagnosis, a combination of process and sociotechnical interventions—and that embed all of these activities in an effective, authoritative consulting relationship.

The sky is not all blue in OD land. There have been failures (see Mirvis & Berg, 1977)—possibly more than ever see the light of publication. But when these failures are made public, it is important that we learn from them. Bowers (1976) presents a searing critique of OD, assessing much of it as superficial, commercial, and based on inappropriate and wasted consultant effort. But he also acknowledges a limited number of well-documented accounts of systematic and impactful OD programs that returned their investment many times over in terms of both human satisfaction and organizational productivity.

A further problem in assessing OD is that, given the complexity of OD programs, it is hard to be sure whether positive results are due to the actual interventions or to some intangible artifact. For example, King (1974) presents an intriguing and disturbing study showing that *expectations* of greater productivity had more effect than the sociotechnical interventions of job enlargement and job rotation! It is clear that the accolade "OD works" requires a great deal of further specification over the next decade.

One way to increase our understanding of how OD works is through comparative studies of different approaches. Bowers (1973) analyzed the results from twenty-three different OD efforts using the *Survey of Organizations* which measures organizational climate, managerial leadership, peer leadership, group process, and employee satisfaction (Taylor & Bowers, 1972). Survey feedback interventions showed the strongest positive effects on perceptions of organizational effectiveness in almost all of these areas. Interpersonal process consultation resulted in improved managerial and peer leadership, but had no effect on the other measures. Task process consultation and laboratory training showed mixed, mostly negative effects. It is possible that changes induced by these more limited interventions might not be picked up by an attitude questionnaire administered to the whole organization. In any event, continuing research on the effects of different OD approaches—alone and in combination—is essential in the years ahead (e.g., Nadler & Pecorella, 1975).

A second way of specifying how OD works is to ascertain what characteristics of programs are related to success versus failure. Early studies by Greiner (1967) and Buchanan (1967) indicated that success requires a developmental change process that redistributes power and a new model of organizational functioning with a clear sequence of action steps. A more comprehensive study by Franklin (1976) classified 25 organizations as having experienced successful or unsuccessful OD programs. The results showed that three broad characteristics were generally related to success: (1) the organization is open to and involved in change rather than taking a status-quo orientation, (2) there is higher interest and greater commitment to the OD program, and (3) the program uses internal change agents who are carefully selected and possess good diagnostic and prescriptive skills. These findings have practical implications for increasing the probability of successful OD programs: consultants and involved managers should work to elicit and maintain the support of top management and should select internal change agents with care.

A second attempt to develop an inductive theory of the characteristics of success and failure in OD is provided by Dunn and Swierczek (1977). These researchers applied retrospective case analysis (a form of content analysis) to sixty-seven successful and unsuccessful change efforts. Of eleven hypotheses that represent the present wisdom of effective OD, only three were confirmed. Similarly disappointing results are reported by Porras (1979). However, according to

Dunn and Swierczek (1977), successful programs involved collaborative modes of intervention, participative change agent orientations, and strategies that employed high levels of participation. It appears that the humanistic value base is coming through strongly in successful OD.

Where then does the research on the effectiveness of OD leave the field as a whole? OD continues to be an area of great promise. It is one of the few areas of applied social psychology that has made broad-ranging attempts to integrate Lewin's essential trinity of theory, research, and practice. The strengths of OD lie in the action research mode, which will keep it relevant to personal and organizational needs; in the scientific method, which will give it a self-correcting research mechanism; and in its focus on organizational culture, which holds the promise of control by participating individuals, rather than subjugation of individuals to social forces (French & Bell, 1978).

Summary

Organizations have the general characteristics of being purposive, involving specialization of tasks or division of labor, exhibiting patterned and coordinated behavior, being enduring and yet contrived, and inducing considerable uniformity within an integrated social system. Profit-making production organizations can be differentiated from public and third-sector human service organizations.

The machine approach to understanding organizations includes the bureaucratic model and scientific management and sees organizations as similar to physical systems, thus placing a strong emphasis on impersonal rationality and legalistic procedures. The human relations approach stresses the individuality and emotionality of organization members and the importance of social interaction. The open systems approach applies general systems theory to organizations and generates a number of basic attributes of organizations such as input, throughput, and output. In addition, open systems theory identifies five major subsystems of organizations: production, supportive, maintenance, adaptive, and managerial.

All organizations must select and socialize new members. The psychological contract and the process of organizational socialization are crucial in determining the relationship between the individual and the organization. General theories of motivation (McClelland, Maslow), the two-factor model of job satisfaction (Herzberg), and a model of facet satisfaction (Lawler) are all useful for understanding the motivational basis of individual behavior in organizations. Three basic types of motivational patterns include rule enforcement, external rewards, and internalized motivation.

The concept of role best describes how individuals are integrated into the social system of the organization. Partial inclusion specifies that the individual is only segmentally involved in his or her organizational role. The role set or group of role partners sends role expectations which are received by the focal person and thereby influence role behavior. Role conflict and role ambiguity can lead to stress for the individual which may partly be alleviated by supportive interpersonal relations.

The power of the small group is demonstrated by norms on productivity which are often in opposition to organizational goals. A human relations approach to supervision increases both worker satisfaction and organizational productivity. Worker participation in decision making is one avenue for increasing individual motivation, satisfaction, and control. Concurrently, the concept of organizational leadership can be broadened to include the introduction of structural change, the improvisation of organizational policy, and routine administration.

Communication is at the center of organizational functioning. Organizations are restricted communication networks in which most communication is one-way, vertical communication from the top down. Organizational control, the ability to influence decisions, increases as one goes up the organization hierarchy, and studies suggest that the total amount of control is not fixed but can be increased by developing participation and mutual influence. Organizational conflict involves the obstruction of goal activities and resulting resistance between parties.

Organization development is a field of practice directed toward organizational improvement with a joint commitment to personal satisfaction and organizational effectiveness. The history of OD has two important precursors: laboratory training and survey feedback. Action research combined with human relations training has provided the underlying base of scientific humanism. From a handful of consultants who focused on social processes, OD has grown to a multifaceted endeavor involving thousands of professional practitioners.

The five major approaches to OD are: (1) process consultation and intervention, (2) survey feedback, (3) human relations training, (4) the sociotechnical/ structural model, and (5) the systems approach. The sociotechnical/structural approach covers a mix of strategies including job enlargement, job enrichment, changes in the reward structure, and new forms of work organizations. The systems approach attempts to combine both human process and technostructural interventions.

The process approaches assume that organizational problems are often human social problems, and have developed a variety of OD interventions or structured activities to improve organizational functioning. Individual level interventions typically involve process consultation; interpersonal and interrole level interventions often use role clarification and negotiation techniques; the group level largely involves team building interventions; the intergroup level is exemplified by interventions to reduce intergroup conflict; finally, interventions at the level of the total organization such as the confrontation meeting are rare.

The total organization is most effectively approached by comprehensive programs of OD. Likert's System 4 management links the human relations approach with structural changes based on interlocking work groups. Blake and Mouton's Grid Organization Development involves a systematic sequence of interventions at each level of organizational functioning. Dimock's Systems Improvement Research is a multifaceted strategy directed toward increased effectiveness for human service organizations. The new factories of Sweden represent innovative forms of production organizations that change technological and structural properties in order to attain quality of working life and industrial democracy.

There are numerous difficulties in carrying out research on the effectiveness of OD. Nevertheless, the quality of OD research is on the rise. In general, results indiate that OD works when there is an adequate investment of time, effort, and expertise. Comparative studies of different approaches help specify how OD work and studies of the characteristics of successful versus unsuccessful programs are helping to build an inductive model of effective OD. OD is an essential component of a relevant applied social psychology.

Further Readings

French, W. L. & Bell, C. H. *Organization development: Behavioral science interventions for organization improvement* (2nd ed.). Englewood Cliffs, N.J.: Prentice-Hall, 1978.

Goodstein, K. D. *Consulting with human service systems.* Reading, Mass.: Addison-Wesley, 1978.

Katz, D. & Kahn, R. L. *The social psychology of organizations* (2nd ed.). New York: Wiley, 1978.

Likert, R. & Likert, J. G. *New ways of managing conflict.* New York: McGraw-Hill, 1976.

Schein, E. H. *Organizational psychology* (3rd ed.). Englewood Cliffs, N.J.: Prentice-Hall, 1980.

CHAPTER OUTLINE

TEN

Community Psychology and Community Development

A community health center sits in a poverty-ridden ghetto area of the Bronx in New York City. It was the first health delivery system in the United States to be controlled by the people of the community that it serves. This situation was in part due to the involvement of social psychologist Hannah Levine, who served as a consultant and advocate for the people of the community. Rather than work in the traditional professional role of helping individuals or groups adjust to society, Levine chose the role of the radical professional—a professional who uses his or her skills to work for social change and to help the disadvantaged gain power over their lives.

Levine had first been asked to write a proposal for a comprehensive health center to better distribute health care to the poor. Instead she helped organize a small committee of persons who wanted better services, *but also wanted to run the center.* A series of confrontation meetings with city health officials and professionals produced predictable results: the officials maintained that professionals must control the center with the community having input only through an advisory board. They asked innocently, "What's the difference between participation and control?" And the committee replied, "If you don't see any real difference between participation and control, then you can participate and the community will control" (Levine, 1970, p. 123).

Mental health professionals also had very different priorities than community members: they were concerned about services for suicidal and acutely disturbed individuals. The community, on the other hand, wanted consultation and educational programs to help their children and youth, so that the limited funds could serve the widest needs by preventing future problems. In the role of advocate, Levine helped the people gain power over the services provided to the community. She clearly defined her role as taking a strong value position—as a social scientist and practitioner committed to improving the quality of life.

I chose this example of social advocacy to begin the chapter because it highlights many of the issues and objectives of community psychology and community development—two relatively independent fields of theory, research, and practice that appear to be moving in similar directions. *Community psychology* has developed out of clinical psychology, a subfield of psychology concerned with the diagnosis and treatment of mental illness. Community psychology is particularly concerned with the contribution of social and environmental factors to mental illness and mental health and with the prevention of mental illness and the promotion of mental health through social and environmental interventions. *Community development* is primarily a subfield of social work, although sociology, agricultural extension, and organized religion have contributed to its growth. Community development is concerned with organizing community members to work toward the solution of common problems that restrict the quality of their lives.

Unfortunately, Hannah Levine's involvement in community affairs is a rare exception. In general, social psychologists have either ignored concerns at the community level (Lehmann, 1971; Sarason, 1974) or have become involved in one-sided social advocacy. Similarly, few social-psychological concepts have been applied to community functioning. Nevertheless, a few professionals have engaged in useful community practice, and workable theories of community functioning have been developed. Thus the field remains wide open—an opportunity for the development of theory, research, and practice toward an understanding of community-level problems and our ability to deal with them. In this arena, applied social psychologists would work hand in hand with community psychologists and community developers.

WHAT IS THE COMMUNITY?

It would be helpful if we could nail down one clear definition for the concept of "community," but this is impossible. There are literally scores of definitions offered by sociologists, social workers, political scientists, and anthropologists (Greenberg, 1974). These focus on central characteristics—for example, a community is a body of people who are geographically, ethnically and/or subculturally related, or who have an organized set of social activities that provide basic services; or who are part of a social structure with communication and control mechanisms; or who have some degree of awareness and identity as a social group.

Greenberg (1974) points out some clear distinctions between "community" and "municipality" (a legal-geographical concept). A community:

- does not exist in a legal sense
- may be based on characteristics such as race, religion, or ethnicity, in addition to geographic proximity
- does not have an organizational chart with clear lines of responsibility
- does not have one official spokesperson, and its responsibilities are so wide as to be vague

Thus, there is great variety in what may be defined as a community. For example, although the Italian-American community of New York City lives within a fairly defined geographical area known as "Little Italy," it is more distinguished by its ethnic and subcultural ties. While there are different groups within that community, each with its opinion leaders and spokespersons, the community as a whole is integrated by its sense of similar identity and experience. In contrast, the small city of Guelph, Ontario, is both a legally constituted municipality and a community. As a municipality it has a geographic definition, official decision makers, and clear lines of responsibility within its local government. As a community it has different constituencies—such as business, industry, the arts, and education—with a variety of spokespersons. These various constituencies (as well as the city's ethnic groupings) may also be considered as communities. Each is a body of people organized in some fashion to provide services for an area of basic needs.

The concept of community becomes more complex when we realize that we can approach it through entirely different theories: in particular, *systems theory* and *conflict theory* are based on different assumptions and values and have different implications for how a community practitioner would approach his or her work (Holland, 1974). (These theories are also useful as models of society in general—a point we will examine in Chapter 11). By looking at both, we will be in a better position to understand some of the issues in contemporary community psychology and community development.

Systems theory (see Chapter 9) stresses the integrated wholeness of the social system through the coordination of interdependent, specialized subsystems. The system works to maintain internal equilibrium and to adapt to changes in the external environment. Thus, when applied to community and society, systems theory sees social problems as tensions that threaten to upset equilibrium and stability. The homeostatic (balancing) mechanisms react to tension by initiating appropriate changes to control the situation and restore order. Decision making on a national scale by political elites and experts is seen as best serving the collective interests of the whole system.

The assumptions and implications of *conflict theory*, on the other hand, strongly contrast with those of systems theory. The conflict approach views community and society as an arena in which various groups compete to attain maximum gain for themselves. Social problems arise when the more powerful groups restrict the lesser constituencies, denying them the resources and decision-making power that they want. In this case, social planning is seen as a means for extending the control of the powerful who are unwilling to act in the best interests of either the disadvantaged or of society as a whole. In the same light, change is thought to be brought about by partisan efforts designed to maximize power, engage in conflict, and obtain the desired resources or decisions.

The contrasting approaches of conflict theory and systems theory are represented in different strategies of community development. Although their use is at the root of some of the present confusion and contradiction in community psychology, it is possible that the two models might be partially blended to handle both integration and conflict at the community level—where, obviously, there are no easy, simple answers (see, for example, Bates & Bacon, 1972).

COMMUNITY PSYCHOLOGY

Clinical Psychology, Community Mental Health, and Community Psychology

The treatment of disturbed individuals has long been the concern of psychiatry and, more recently, of clinical psychology. In addition to its use of individual and group psychotherapy, clinical psychology has also advanced the development of psychological testing for the assessment of mental and emotional problems. But traditional clinical psychology concentrated almost exclusively on the individual—one of the issues that led to the birth of the field of community mental health and community psychology. Other issues were of equal concern in the search to alleviate mental illness at the community level: environmental variables that contributed to this human misery, too few mental health professionals, overtaxed treatment facilities, and the questionable effectiveness of traditional psychotherapy (Heller & Monahan, 1977).

The concerns of mental health professionals were intertwined with government policies and funding patterns in the United States and Canada—policies that have had a profound impact on the provision of services from the late 1950s to the present time. In 1955, the United States Congress appointed a Joint Commission of Mental Health and Illness whose final report directly stimulated the growth of community mental health programs and community psychology (Rappaport, 1977). The resulting legislation, strongly supported by President Kennedy, provided the mandate and funds for the establishment of hundreds of Community Mental Health Centers during the 1960s. These centers were mandated to provide services at the local level and to engage in activities designed to prevent and reduce the incidence and severity of mental illness. Similar shifts to community-based treatment took place in Canada. In my home province of Saskatchewan, the 1950s and 1960s were marked by a dramatic reduction in the number of institutionalized mental patients and the concurrent development of regional centers to provide comprehensive mental health care in community settings. In fact, one recent article (Herbert, 1978) mentioned Saskatchewan as the only place in the Western Hemisphere that has completely closed down a large mental hospital, favoring community centers instead.

The birth of community psychology within the community mental health movement is usually attributed to a conference held in Boston in 1965 at which several clinical psychologists considered the education of psychologists who would work in community settings. The report of the conference (Bennet, Anderson, Cooper, Hassel, Klein & Rosenblum, 1966) called for community psychologists to become involved in social problems as consultants, as participant/conceptualizers of programs, as social change agents, and as political activitists. Quite a far cry from the individual assessment and therapy of the traditional clinician!

The shift toward community mental health and, within it, the christening of community psychology, represents a number of radical departures from traditional clinical psychology. First and foremost, there is a move from an individual to an environmental or system focus, stressing the importance of the group, organization, community, and society in understanding the existence of mental dysfunction and/or mental well-being. The second element that is stressed is the connection between the individual and the environment—looking at the goodness of fit between the person and the setting; it is this interaction that determines outcomes. A further implication of this environmental or ecological approach is its emphasis on social action that creates alternatives by developing people's resources and strengths, based on a value system of cultural diversity and equality (Rappaport, 1977). In other words, every racial and ethnic group in society has unique aspects of their culture to contribute to the making of a better whole, and this cultural uniqueness should be respected as a strength rather than as a justification for discrimination. Third, there is a concern with mental health—that is, with helping people develop their competencies and optimize their potential in living—rather than a restricted focus on mental illness alone. Fourth, these new emphases are put into practice through the development and use of a wider range of research and practice skills. Such skills include training, consultation, program development, organization and community development, action research, and evaluation research. Finally, these efforts are directed at the *prevention* of mental problems, not the treatment and rehabilitation of existing problems. To reach the goal of prevention, what is needed is both a long-term emphasis and the use of paraprofessional mental health workers to reach larger numbers of people.

Community mental health can thus be regarded as a broad, interdisciplinary movement, encompassing activities to study and utilize all community forces that affect the psychological well-being of most members of the community (Zax & Specter, 1974). As part of this movement, community psychology can be defined as "an approach to human behavior problems that emphasizes contributions made to their development by environmental forces as well as the potential contributions to be made toward their alleviation by the use of these forces" (Zax & Specter, 1974, p. 3).

Despite the clarity of this definition, we must still acknowledge the confusion about what community psychology *really* is. It is still in search of its identity—a fact that is clear from the many articles and texts that attempt to define crucial issues and determine central directions:

- Bloom (1973) welcomed the advent of innovative community mental health services to better deal with individual troubles, but maintained that community psychology should be directed instead toward the resolution of social issues. This typifies the attitude of the community psychologist who, interested in whatever limits the quality of life, intervenes in a social system to improve the relationships between individuals and the social context.

- Iscoe (1974) presented the concept of the "competent community"—a community that knows how to get the resources it needs— and saw the community psychologist as one who should facilitate growth toward power and independence.
- Zax and Specter (1974) stressed training and consultation, the development of preventive programs, and the creation of growth-enhancing settings.
- Murrell (1973) put more emphasis on social systems, including organizations, and discussed interventions that change social systems.
- Rappaport (1977) provided a strong example of a social-action approach to community psychology, stressing respect for differences among all groups, and the fully equitable distribution of psychological and material resources to all groups in society.

Within this diversity, community psychology, with its emphasis on social change and the quality of life, appears to be growing apart from community mental health, with its relatively status quo position of providing traditional services in community settings. In fact, Seymour Sarason, one of the founders of community psychology, has recently called for the divorce of community psychology from both clinical psychology and community mental health. Sarason (1976) maintains that the latter two fields, based on theories and practices largely at the individual level, simply cannot provide an understanding of the complexity of community-level structures and processes. Furthermore, clinical psychology and community mental health arose largely as quick responses to social needs and government funding, and as such have not developed the conceptual base necessary for a sophisticated understanding of communities (Sarason, 1974). Rappaport (1977), in his articulation of community psychology based on humanistic values, has also rejected the status quo position that characterizes much of community mental health. In doing so, he has adopted a conflict theory approach to communities, viewing conflict among diverse subgroups as inevitable—especially conflict between the powerful and the powerless. From this point of view, social scientists and practitioners cannot take a value-free position: they are either on the side of social progress toward greater equality or with the status quo. To do nothing is the equivalent of supporting the status quo.

The developing schism between community psychology and community mental health is shown in practice. Even though community psychology has called for community-level activities such as the development of preventive programs and social advocacy, studies have repeatedly indicated that psychologists working in community mental health centers spend most of their time in traditional clinical activities such as individual assessment and therapy (see Bloom & Parad, 1978).

Not all community psychologists see the inevitability of a split between community mental health and community psychology and some remain optimistic about integration (for example, Bloom, 1978). A positive step toward integration is offered by Dohrenwend (1978) in her model of how psychosocial stress leads to individual psychopathology (see Figure 10.1). This approach relates the diverse activities of clinical and community psychologists to a common framework. Stressful life events are determined both by the psychological characteris-

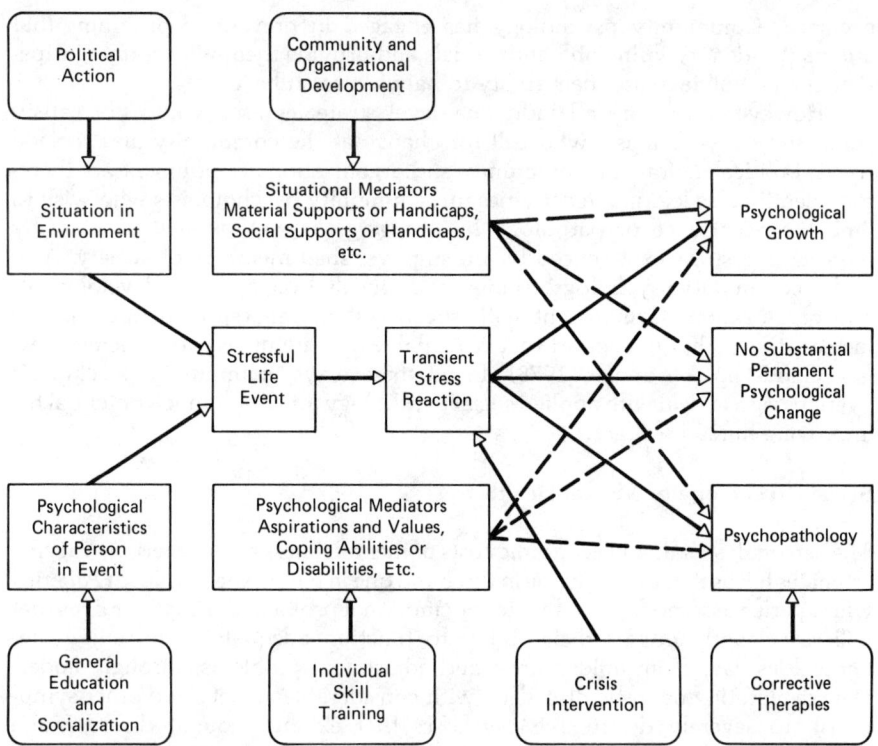

Figure 10.1   A Model of the Stress Process and Methods of Clinical and Community Psychology
Source: Dohrenwend (1978).

tics of the person and the situation in the environment. For example, a person may be fired from a job because he or she is incompetent or because of poor economic conditions, or some combination of both. The resulting crisis is expressed in a stress reaction that may lead to psychological growth, no change, or to psychopathology. Which outcome ensures will be determined by psychological mediators within the individual in interaction with situation mediators in the wider environment. For example, the individual with better coping or problem-solving abilities will more likely move to psychological growth rather than to mental illness. Similarly, a person with good economic and social support is less likely to move to long-term dysfunction.

In relation to the model, the activities of clinical and community psychologists are uniformly directed at undermining the stress process and reducing the occurrence of psychopathology. However, different strategies attack this sequence at different locations and at different times. Clinical psychology has emphasized the use of corrective therapies that attempt to deal with established problems. Community mental health recommends crisis intervention, wherein therapy is provided during the stress reaction before more permanent damage has occurred. Community psychology has engaged in preventive programs that attempt to identify vulnerable individuals and provide them with training experiences that will increase their ability to handle stressful events.

However, these are all individual-level strategies and would not satisfy community psychologists who call for change at the community and societal levels. Political action and community and organization development are therefore identified as legitimate activities for community psychologists who wish to limit the occurrence of pathology *by changing the environment*, that is, by reducing the stress experienced by the impoverished members of society. Also within community psychology, training and consultation, program development, and organization development with social systems all represent attempts to increase the quality of support that is available to individuals experiencing stress (see Goodstein & Sandler, 1978). In all these ways, community psychology overlaps a great deal with applied social psychology and holds much potential for improving human welfare.

Social Psychology of Mental Health

The personal, social, and economic costs of mental illness are staggering. Varying estimates tell us that between one in three and one in ten persons in North America will experience some form of mental or emotional problem during their lives that will significantly impair their ability to function adequately and enjoy life. Difficulties vary from milder stress and adjustment problems, through moderately debilitating neurotic disorders (with considerable anxiety and other symptoms), to severely destructive psychoses that exhibit thought disorder and extreme emotional reactions. In 1978, the President's Commission on Mental Health estimated that one in seven Americans will require treatment from mental health services at some point in their lives. In any given year, an estimated 2 million people will suffer from severe depression, 6 million children and teenagers will be emotionally disturbed, 20 million people will suffer from neuroses, and 1 million college students will withdraw from their studies due to emotional problems.

Along with a deemphasis of the traditional classifications of neurosis and psychosis, the current view is that mental illness is a *social* problem. It is characterized by deviant interpersonal behavior—socially inappropriate and disturbing to others—and as a breakdown in the performance of social roles. Conversely, good mental health is characterized by interpersonal behavior that adequately meets social norms and the requirements of the individual's role in society. Furthermore, the widespread occurrence of mental illness can be regarded as a *social issue*, that is, a significant problem that demands societal action (see Chapter 11).

The fundamentally social nature of mental illness and mental health becomes still clearer when we look at the probable origins of mental conditions and at how they are treated. They appear to stem from such social variables as family interaction, organizational stress, socioeconomic status, social crises, and social change. And the mental health practices designed to alleviate dysfunction or promote competence include such social elements as the helping relationship, the self-help group, the human organization, and the therapeutic community. It is understandable, then, that social psychologists are contributing to the study of mental illness and mental health in a number of crucial areas, including public attitudes toward mental illness and the interdisciplinary cooperation required to promote mental health (Wechsler, Solomon & Kramer, 1970).

To be viable, community psychology must be based clearly and strongly in a social-psychological concept of mental illness and mental health. Our purpose, then, is to look very selectively at changing conceptions in mental illness and at some illustrations of how a social-psychological analysis aids our understanding.

During the growth of Western civilization, conceptions of mental illness have changed in relation to the rationale of community mental health and community psychology (Golann & Eisdorfer, 1972; Zax & Specter, 1974): explanations of supernatural forces and demon possession gave way to moral-humanistic and scientific-physiological explanations; in turn, these were supplanted by psychodynamic and interpersonal approaches. In brief:

- Burning at the stake in the Middle Ages gave way to moral treatment in the nineteenth century: the mentally disabled were understood to be sick, not guilty, and deserving of humane care.
- Freud's theories and psychoanalytic practice refocused attention on a competing explanation—that psychological factors, especially internal conflict, are at the root of mental illness.
- The work of later psychoanalysts, particularly Erikson, moved the emphasis from intrapsychic forces to the development of the person's ego identity in the social context through the successful resolution of personal crises.
- The interpersonal theories of Sullivan and Carson explicitly emphasized social factors in dyadic relationships as being crucial in understanding and alleviating dysfunctional behavior.

It is now commonly accepted that biological, psychological, and social factors may all contribute to the many different forms of mental illness. Two recent reviews (Dohrenwend & Dohrenwend, 1974; King, 1978) have documented the large amount of research that is now being done on social and cultural influences on psychopathology—it is apparent that factors such as poor socioeconomic conditions and minority group membership are related to mental illness.

The important point is that *the way we conceptualize mental illness and mental health determines the strategies we adopt to combat mental illness and enhance mental health.* Conceptualizing in terms of social factors and the resolution of crises implies strategies that provide support to persons in their natural environments and that advocate community change and political action. The emphasis shifts to understanding the social forces such as life crises and the degree of social support that affect the adaptation of the individual to the environment— the ecological approach in community psychology that has been developed by James Kelly (1966, 1968) and others.

A provocative statement on the importance of social factors in mental illness is presented by psychiatrist Thomas Szasz in *The Myth of Mental Illness* (1974) and *The Manufacture of Madness* (1970). Szasz contends that mental illness is a social invention that society uses to categorize, stigmatize, and control deviants— people who behave in ways that seem inappropriate or upset others. The helping professions participate in creating this since it serves their vested interests—it

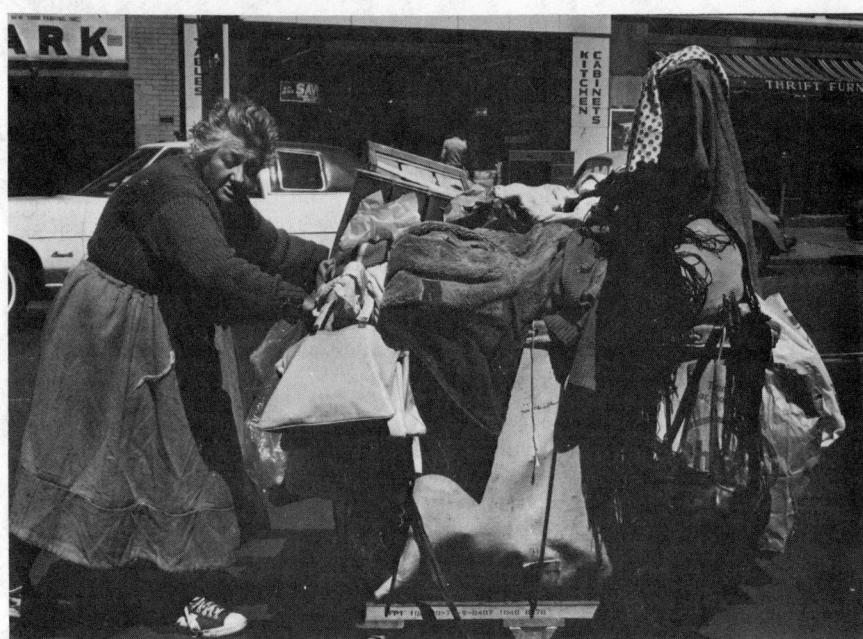

A homeless woman transports her possessions along a Manhattan street. Is she mentally ill? Thomas Szasz contends that mental illness is an invention that society uses to categorize, stigmatize, and control people who behave in ways that seem inappropriate or that upset others. *(Ann Marie Rousseau)*

gives them somebody to help. Society is thus provided with scapegoats who are stigmatized and rejected in order to protect the status quo. In short, society's inability to accept people who are different means that those who are in distress and unable to cope are perceived as a threat and therefore victimized.

Szasz's analysis makes clear that the real challenge to society is to accept differences among individuals and groups and to live together in harmony (Rappaport, 1977). However, Szasz's solution of simply leaving disturbed people alone is inadequate. Rappaport calls for a community psychology that supports cultural diversity and works toward the equitable distribution of resources among all people. In these ways, mental illness and the myth of mental illness will both be reduced.

An adequate social psychology of mental health needs to examine forces at *all* levels of analysis that interact to affect individual well-being. Glidewell (1972) draws on his combined expertise in both social psychology and community psychology to provide a systematic social-psychological analysis of factors contributing to mental health.

- At the level of society, both social order and social change can affect mental health. Some highly organized systems such as a bureaucratic organization may demand conformity and suppress individual needs to the point of inducing stress and dysfunction. Although rapid social change by itself may not induce mental illness, social mobility involving role and norm changes does appear to induce considerable distress. As the size and complexity of social systems increase, individual participation and power decrease. *Problems are generated when the system creates inequity between the individual's investments and his or her returns.*

- The group level of functioning provides an opportunity for meeting the person's needs in ways that support his or her well-being. Groups can provide emotional and material aid that will help the individual weather a crisis induced by social change.
- Interpersonal relations affect mental health. Repeated experiences of positive interpersonal attraction lead to increased self-esteem and enhanced interpersonal skills; repeated rejection leads to a sense of unworthiness and distress. The constant rejection of minorities by majorities may severely disrupt the minority person's motivation, intellectual efficiency, and interpersonal skills.
- At the individual level, a sense of personal competence is the basis for attractiveness, power, self-esteem, and social status. The most important dimension in determining mental health is that of social power—the ability to control valued resources. Power is determined by a combination of "competence, capital, courage, and charisma" and is exercised over others in exchange for valued resources—psychological, social, and material. People in low power positions are particularly likely to not have their needs met and to experience distressing levels of perceived inequity. The low power person will repeatedly be confronted with crises requiring the input of more resources than his or her power base can supply, and will respond by seeking resources by further giving up power or by seeking relief through a break with reality. The long-term outcomes will vary from apathy and denial to psychosis.

Glidewell (1972) maintains that one consistent theme runs through his entire social-psychological analysis of mental health: *the equity of resource exchange.* When the universal law of reciprocity is made unworkable by a lack of power or interpersonal attractiveness (which are based on the predominant values of the society), then the social system is unstable. Furthermore, the vulnerable individual is deprived of the social support and control required for effective functioning, and mental illness ensues. We thus see the potential importance of exchange theory and equity theory for understanding mental health.

Social power and its effects are useful in understanding the relationship between societal level variables—socioeconomic status, race, and sex—and mental illness. Classic studies have shown differences among social classes with regard to the incidence, diagnosis, and treatment of mental illness. For example, Hollingshead and Redlich (1958) found a higher incidence of schizophrenia among lower class individuals—who were also more likely to be hospitalized. Conversely, neurotic disorders were more common in the middle class, and psychotherapy was the more likely helping strategy.

According to King (1978), studies from a variety of cultures indicate that *members of minority groups as defined by class, race, and sex continue to be overrepresented in the general mental illness category.* What this means is much less clear. The findings could be partly due to methodological problems in the definition and diagnosis of mental illness (Dohrenwend & Dohrenwend, 1974). If the results are valid, there is then a continuing debate about the causal relationship between social variables and psychopathology. For example, with respect to social class, does the low power and high stress of low socioeconomic status induce mental illness, or does a history of biologically caused mental illness produce a "downward drift" of vulnerable and/or disturbed individuals to the lower strata of society? King (1978) points out that this fundamental question is still unresolved by research, even though there have been some excellent follow-up studies that have improved upon classic investigations (see Box 10.1).

However, King (1978) contends that the debate on causation is a false one since both social class and the definition of psychopathology are determined by society's predominant values. Values influence the poverty level, the definition of psychopathology, and the relationship between the two. The consistent finding is that race or sex alone do not relate strongly to mental illness, but must be

Box 10.1   FOCUS ON RESEARCH
Mental Health in the Metropolis Revisited

In 1952 a classic study of the incidence of mental dysfunction was initiated by an interdisciplinary team of medical and social scientists. Using a 2-hour structured interview, researchers gathered information from 1,660 white residents, aged 20–59, living in a residential section of Manhattan.

Interviewers asked a variety of questions regarding mental and emotional functioning: Are you bothered by nervousness? Do you ever have any trouble in getting to sleep or staying asleep? Do you feel somewhat apart, even among friends? Do you sometimes feel that people are against you without any good reason? From the responses to many questions like these, two psychiatrists provided a rating of overall mental health on a six-point scale ranging from well to incapacitated. In between were various levels of symptom formation indicating increasing levels of mental dysfunction ranging from mild to severe. Marked and severe symptom formation ratings were combined with the incapacitated rating to yield an overall category labeled "impaired."

In relation to major demographic variables, there was a higher proportion of impaired functioning among persons in the lowest socioeconomic stratum and among persons of both sexes who had been divorced. In relation to age, there was a higher proportion of well individuals in the 20–29 age range as compared to the above 30 range.

Twenty years later, the researchers were able to relocate and reinterview 695 of the original respondents. Mental health status was again estimated on the six-point scale derived from the same items used in the original study. Based on the original results which showed more impairment in older persons, the researchers expected to find a greater incidence of mental difficulties in their sample which was now 20 years older. This did not occur. Most of the respondents (46 percent) showed no change in mental health status, while some improved (32 percent) and some (27 percent) deteriorated.

It thus appears that the relationship between mental health and demographic variables is highly complex. However, the general relationship between low socioeconomic status and mental illness appears to have stood the test of time.

Sources: Srole, L., Langner, T. S., Michael, S. T., Opler, M. K. & Rennie, T. A. C. *Mental health in the metropolis: The Midtown Manhattan study* (Vol. 1). New York: McGraw-Hill, 1962. Srole, L. Measurement and classification in socio-psychiatric epidemiology: Midtown Manhattan study (1954) and Midtown Manhattan Restudy (1974). *Journal of Health and Social Behavior*, 1976, 17, 347–364.

combined with socioeconomic status to show a disproportionate trend toward mental illness. This indicates that social class as defined by society's values—and as exemplified by lower power and high vulnerability—is the crucial social variable. Thus, a community psychology that seeks to redress the inequitable distribution of resources through community development and political action appears to make considerable sense.

Training and Consultation in Community Psychology

The social-psychological approach to mental health indicates many points at which interventions could reduce the prevalence and severity of mental illness or could enhance the individual's capacity and the system's capability for maintaining or increasing mental health. Dohrenwend's (1978) model provides an integration of a number of activities at the individual and system levels that can be used to limit the impact of the stress process on the development of psychopathology. Clinical psychologists provide individual therapy to deal with clearly developed dysfunction and crisis intervention to help individuals cope and resolve the crises toward psychological growth.

Community and applied social psychologists can provide skill training to individuals for increasing their capacity to deal with stressful events. Furthermore, the practice skills of training and consultation can aid other people in the environment increase their ability to help persons under stress. These interventions, while individual or interpersonal in scope, are designed to increase the system's capability to provide better mental health services.

Individual Skill Training. Dohrenwend (1978) suggests that skill training can help us develop a "high level of ability to face and solve complex social and emotional problems" (p. 8). Unfortunately theory and research describing productive and nonproductive reactions to stressful events have not been translated directly into training programs. More commonly, community psychologists have developed special training programs to increase the coping capacity of individuals, especially school children, who have been identified as vulnerable to stress.

One example of an elementary school program is the Primary Mental Health Project in Rochester, New York, organized by Emery Cowen and his associates (Cowen et al., 1963, 1975). These investigators used classroom observation, parent interviews, teacher reports, and psychological testing to identify children who exhibited early difficulties in school adjustment and social/emotional functioning. In addition to mental health consultation with the school staff, the vulnerable children participated in a small group program, led by selected teachers, that provided interpersonal understanding and support in an informal environment. Teachers were selected as group leaders on the basis of their interest in children and their effectiveness in working with the socioeconomically disadvantaged. The groups took part in a variety of activities (such as baking cookies) designed to encourage social participation. Comparisons between an experimental school which had the small group program and a control school which did not showed that the program led to increased scholastic aptitude and achievement and better socioemotional adjustment (for example, lower anxiety). However, these gains did not hold up over the longer term so the program was modified to provide greater involvement with the children. This was accomplished by including nonprofessionals—teacher aides, university students, and homemaker child aides—who developed an interpersonal helping relationship with the children; this was combined with some use of small peer-support groups to help the children develop better social relationships.

The long-term results of the program have been encouraging, essentially showing that the interventions have positive effects on school achievement and socioemotional functioning (Cowen, Gesten & Wilson, 1979). This has led to an expansion of the program to several schools, and more recently to a nationwide dissemination of the program's procedures (Cowen, Davidson & Gesten, 1980). In 1976–1977, the program was operating in over 200 schools across the United States and brought helping services to over 3,000 selected children. Unfortunately, from a skill training point of view, it is not entirely clear what interpersonal or small group skills the children might be acquiring from their program experiences, and of course the program involves much more than a skill training component.

More explicit and limited ideas about individual skill training have grown out of work on interpersonal helping (see Chapter 6). Both Wallen's basic communication skills and Carkhuff's core interpersonal skills can potentially increase an individual's capacity to relate well to others and to deal more effectively with stressful situations. Egan (1975a) believes that clients in counseling can be trained in interpersonal skills—particularly those of empathy and concreteness—better equipping them to explore and understand their own problems and to develop more effective social relationships. This approach sees "training as treatment" as a way to increase the individual's capacity to deal with stressful situations through increased self-awareness and improved social support.

In a more practical vein, training courses in "life skills"—a combination of skills for basic communication and problem solving—have been developed to help potentially vulnerable individuals (especially those of low socioeconomic status) cope with the difficulties of living (for example, Conger, 1973; Himsl, 1972). As a final example of skill training, British social psychologist Michael Argyle has recently turned his attention to the important relationship between social skills and mental health (see Box 10.2).

Training Nonprofessionals. Zax and Specter (1974) define a *nonprofessional* as "any individual who is recruited to provide mental health services without having completed customary training in one of the traditional mental health disciplines" (p. 369). The Primary Mental Health Project, described above, was in fact one of the first community psychology programs to use nonprofessional or paraprofessionals as mental health workers. And since the early 1960s, it has become increasingly popular to engage a variety of nonprofessionals, including university students, housewives, hospital attendants, ghetto residents, parents, and patients to provide direct mental health services to clients.

Skill training may be offered to such nonprofessionals who work with persons experiencing stress and dysfunction. In Dohrenwend's 1978 model, this approach comes under the development of social supports that are situational

Box 10.2   FOCUS ON PRACTICE
Social Skills Training to Improve Mental Health

Many forms of mental illness involve a lack of social competence. In some cases, social inadequacy may lead to frustration, rejection, and stress which creates the disturbed mental state. In other cases, mental disturbance may disrupt social behavior and thereby induce even greater stress on the individual. In either situation, training in basic social skills should help patients overcome social inadequacy and improve their mental health.

Based on these premises, British social psychologist Michael Argyle and his colleagues have spent several years developing a social skills training program for psychiatric patients. The first step was to clearly document social inadequacy, since numerous definitions abound. Psychiatric patients were observed during conversation, and the behavior of those who were rated as socially unskilled was studied in detail. Socially inadequate patients showed a continuously blank and unsmiling facial expression, had a closed posture, avoided eye contact, spoke in a monotonous and flat tone, and initiated very little in the conversation. These patients were rated as cold, unassertive, anxious, and unrewarding, and reported themselves as having more difficulty in social situations.

A training program was designed to help socially inadequate patients overcome their skill deficits. Principles of training were derived mainly from social psychology and followed the experience-based learning format of demonstration, practice, and feedback. After a description and modeling of the skill by the trainer, the patients take part in role play conversations where they attempt to use the skill. Feedback from the trainer and other trainees and the playback of videotape complete the sequence. The actual skills of the training program cover all areas required for effective social interaction: observation skills such as reading social signals from others, performance skills such as good nonverbal expression, and cognitive skills such as problem solving.

Evaluations of this and other social skill training programs generally show positive results. Patients suffering from various disorders not only increase in skill level, but also experience increased comfort and and satisfaction in social interaction.

Source: Trower, P., Bryant, B., Argyle, M. & Marzillier, J. *Social skills and mental health.* Pittsburgh: University of Pittsburgh Press, 1978.

mediators in the stress process. Such training activities can potentially help arrest the development of psychopathology and enhance the possibility of psychological growth.

Part of the impetus for using nonprofessionals stems from the work of Carkhuff and others indicating that persons with little or no training were as effective as highly trained professionals in individual and group therapy (see Carkhuff, 1968; Poser, 1966; Truax & Lister, 1970). Although these early studies have been criticized on methodological grounds (see McArthur, 1970; Rosenbaum, 1966), it has become generally accepted that nonprofessionals can play a very useful role in the delivery of mental health services. A recent and extensive review of forty-two studies comparing professionals and nonprofessionals indicated that in most cases nonprofessionals were as effective or *more* effective than professionals (Durlak, 1979). Why this is so is unclear; it may be due to the nonprofessional's higher enthusiasm as volunteers, or to their greater similarity with their clients. University students often help other students, ghetto residents serve as peer helpers, and so on. In short, the nonprofessional may be able to establish a more trusting and unique helping relationship. The nonprofessional also benefits from the meaningful and demanding involvement of the helper role. (One of the reasons that I provide opportunities to university students to serve as mental health volunteers is that they receive clear benefits in terms of personal awareness, enhanced learning about helping relationships, and important realizations about career alternatives.)

Paraprofessionals have played an important role in the community revolution of mental health and are helping to meet the manpower needs that professional training alone will never satisfy (Karlsruher, 1974; Lamb & Lafave, 1977; Siegel, 1973; Sobey, 1970). Most often the paraprofessional enters into a supportive, understanding, helping relationship with patients or clients, either in an interpersonal or a small group setting. Their effectiveness appears to be greatest when they fulfill a complementary role with professionals. Psychologists, social workers, and other professionals can provide for the careful selection and training of paraprofessionals and can develop clear and systematic mental health programs in which the paraprofessional's limited knowledge is not a handicap. Furthermore, professionals can provide supervision and consultation to paraprofessionals to increase their effectiveness (for example, Karlsruher, 1976).

One of the most common forms of training for nonprofessionals is Carkhuff's core interpersonal skills training or some variant of it. Usually the training is restricted to the facilitative conditions of empathy, respect, genuineness, and concreteness, and does not include the more challenging skills of confrontation and immediacy. Sophisticated clinical judgment, too, based on years of experience, is not easily trained; that is why selection and consultation are important to increase the nonprofessional's capacity.

Clearly nonprofessionals will be involved in community psychology for a long time to come with professionals providing the necessary training (see Guerney, 1977; Kelley, Kelley, Gauron & Rawlings, 1977).

Training for Community Care-Givers. The label "mental health professional" usually conjures up images of psychiatrists, psychologists, social workers, and counselors. But this is only one part of the real-world picture: mental health services are also provided by professional helpers from other disciplines. These community care-givers come from such fields as medicine, nursing, education, religion, and criminal justice. By providing training and consultation to these helpers, either on an individual or agency-wide basis, their effectiveness is enhanced and the value of their social support to vulnerable individuals is increased.

The skills training models described in Chapters 6 and 7—particularly basic communication skills, core interpersonal skills, and small group skills—help these care-givers increase their abilities to meet clients' needs (Fisher, 1977). These skills can be learned through experience-based learning (see Chapter 4), with the training process tailored to the trainee's specific learning goals. While nurses, for example, are not trained to be psychotherapists, they can learn to provide better understanding and support to a patient who is experiencing emotional stress and, if necessary, to make referrals for more intensive help.

Many community care-givers are involved in leading support groups or helping clients organize self-help groups. For example, a church minister might organize a teen discussion group focusing on dating problems or career aspirations; an employment officer might bring together a group of unemployed women to discuss barriers to employment in traditionally male jobs. Thus, training in group processes—through unstructured sensitivity training or structured exercises, such as leadership functions—can provide valuable ideas and behaviors to increase the care-giver's capacity as a group leader or consultant. (See Chapter 7.)

In a different arena of training, McClelland, Rhinesmith, and Kristensen (1975) provide an example of how power motivation training can be useful for increasing the effectiveness of community action agencies (CAA). Most CAA staff members were themselves from disadvantaged groups, and many of them lacked the knowledge and skill needed to acquire political power in their communities. CAA staff in ten Kentucky communities participated in workshops to help them understand their own power needs and how to use power effectively for community development. Evaluation interviews indicated that the majority of CAA workers were more active and effective in the communities following the training.

A dramatic example of training community care-givers involved the pioneering work of Bard in training police officers to intervene in family crises (Bard, 1970; Bard & Berkowitz, 1967). Intervening in family conflict is one of the most dangerous aspects of police work—many injuries and deaths of police officers, not to mention family members, occur in this way. Furthermore, the police are often the first service providers called in to deal with family crises, especially in lower socioeconomic areas where mental health professionals are either unavailable or ignored. Nevertheless, police typically receive little training in crisis intervention.

Bard implemented a demonstration project in which a small number of officers from one New York City precinct were trained through lectures, discussions, role plays, and human relations training to deal with family crises. These trained officers were then called in whenever a family conflict occurred in the precinct during the 21-month duration of the project. In comparison to a neighboring precinct, there were no injuries to the trained officers and there were no homicides within families that were dealt with by the trained unit. Consequently, more rigorous evaluations of crisis intervention training for police have been completed and such programs have been disseminated to a large number of other cities in North America.

Mental Health Consultation. A definition of mental health consultation was provided in Chapter 4, based largely on the seminal work of psychiatrist Gerald Caplan (1964, 1970). This definition has been further expanded by Altrocchi (1972) and others who see mental health consultation as any interaction in which a mental health specialist (or specialists) provides help to a mental health worker (or workers) on a current problem in their work situation. Consultation is thus extended beyond one-on-one relationships to include consultation in small groups of specialists and workers. Nonprofessionals are also included in Altrocchi's definition since they have become such an integral part of mental health services. This includes not only volunteer mental health workers, but also service providers such as bartenders, taxi drivers, beauticians, and so on, who often provide informal social support to their customers in times of stress. For example, in one recent study, interviews with ninety hairdressers indicated that one-third of the talking time with clients was devoted to discussing personal problems—marriage, physical health, depression. Hairdressers saw listening to customers' problems as an important part of their job and expressed a need for consultation with mental health professionals (Cowen, Gesten, Boike, Norton, Wilson & DeStefano, 1979).

Caplan (1970) distinguishes four types of mental health consultation. Each one involves three roles: the *consultant* who provides assistance and direction; the *consultee* who requests consultation; and the *client* or client system with which the consultee is working. The purpose of each type is for the consultant to help the consultee work more effectively with his or her client:

- *Client-centered case consultation* is designed to help the consultee deal more productively with a specific client or case. For example, Mrs. Hayworth, a generally competent high school teacher is having trouble with Randy Martin, a student who behaves aggressively in the classroom and is underachieving as a result. Dr. Peterson, an educational psychologist, is called in to help Mrs. Hayworth better understand and deal with this situation. As a consultant, he provides information, assists in the diagnosis of the problem, and suggests alternative solutions. For example, he might help Mrs. Hayworth develop alternate strategies for meeting Randy's need for attention and coach him in ways of directly confronting his aggressive behavior using communication and conflict resolution skills. In addition to resolving the immediate problem, an important secondary goal is that the consultee should be better able to handle similar problems in the future.

- *Consultee-centered case consultation* has the objective of helping the consultee resolve difficulties in *his or her own functioning* which hamper effectiveness. Thus, the main focus is on the consultee rather than the client. For example, Mrs. Hayworth may experience a great deal of frustration and anxiety in dealing with aggressive students and may be afraid of overreacting with harsh discipline that will only escalate the conflict. The educational psychologist can serve as a counselor to the teacher—understanding her feelings, exploring the pros and cons of different actions, and generally providing relief and support. Mrs. Hayworth may be able to make changes in her attitudes and behavior that will help her "keep her cool" and be appropriately assertive with students who behave aggressively.

- *Program-centered administrative consultation* helps the consultee(s) develop, improve, or evaluate mental health programs for which they are responsible. The consultant works to assess the goals of the program, the means of reaching the goals, and the overall functioning of the agency. For example, a volunteer mental health agency asks a clinical psychologist for assistance in improving their program service to discharged mental patients. The consultant helps define which patients would benefit most from the service, suggests way that volunteers can build good helping relationships with clients, and recommends measures for evaluating the effects of the program.

- *Consultee-centered administrative consultation* attempts to improve the consultee's administrative skills and to resolve difficulties in administrative functioning. Unfortunately, few mental health consultants know as much about administrative problems as they do about mental health problems (Altrocchi, 1972). Administrative consultation is more comprehensively seen as organization development with human service agencies, and the full range of theory, research, and practice known to applied social psychologists could be brought to bear on the task of improved functioning (see Chapter 9). The inclusion of organization development focusing on human relations can improve the day-to-day functioning of agencies and further advance the mental health movement (MacLennan, Quinn & Schroeder, 1975; Rand, 1978).

Finally, we must ask of mental health consultation: *Does it work?* Mannino and Shore (1975) reviewed consultation efforts from 1958–1972. Looking at the full range of consultation types, these authors found that 69 percent of overall efforts resulted in positive effects. Of consultation studies that focused on the client, 58 percent yielded useful outcomes, whereas 74 percent of the consultee-centered efforts produced positive results. Program or administrative consultation at the system level was rare (only 4 studies), but 50 percent of these efforts were judged successful. Despite the diversity in consultation methods and situations, and the need for improvements and refinements in their practice and research, the review concluded that mental health consultation appears to have beneficial effects.

Prevention of Mental Illness

The personal and social costs of mental illness must inevitably force this fundamental question: How can such dysfunction be *prevented?* For the concerned practitioner the goal is to make an impact at the very origin of the stress process described in Dohrenwend's (1978) model. Such impact could be at the *individual* level, through programs of general education and socialization, or at the *system* level, through political action designed to change environmental conditions that appear to cause emotional stress and mental illness. The former strategy would attempt to improve the coping abilities of children, or of people in high-risk groups (usually the socioeconomically disadvantaged). The latter approach would aim at helping the socioeconomic underdogs of society gain access to the material and social resources that can prevent stressful events.

The concept of prevention is very much a part of community psychology, again due to the definitive work of Gerald Caplan. In an attempt to move away from the medical model, with its emphasis on the treatment of disease, Caplan (1964) defined three types of prevention: (1) *primary prevention,* aimed at reducing the overall incidence of mental illness; (2) *secondary prevention,* designed to limit the duration and severity of problems that have become visible and could lead to serious disorders; and (3) *tertiary prevention,* aimed at reducing the degree of impairment once a disorder has occurred, and at improving the person's capacity to cope with future problems.

Primary prevention is an appealing "ultimate" solution for the elimination of mental disorders. How to go about such a task, however, is not a simple matter, either technologically or ideologically. Primary prevention is based on a social-psychological approach to mental health. This means that every individual requires adequate physical, psychosocial, and sociocultural resources to create optimal living conditions and cope with stressful events or crises. Caplan described two general approaches to primary prevention: *social action* to improve living conditions, and *interpersonal action* designed to educate community caregivers to increase their effectiveness in helping the population at large.

Secondary prevention is aimed at specific individuals who have already been identified as being in some form of difficulty. This is a strategy of early detection and remedial treatment designed to arrest the development of the problem and prepare the individual to function more effectively. The Primary Mental Health Project in Rochester described earlier is one of a number of examples of secondary prevention directed toward vulnerable children in elementary schools. Zax and Specter (1974), describing several programs of secondary prevention, make this important distinction: to be considered prevention rather than treatment, such activities must attempt to deal with disorders *on a large scale* and have some impact on *overall* rates of dysfunction in the system.

Tertiary prevention differs little from traditional treatment procedures such as psychotherapy, but stresses effective rehabilitation. In this way the problem is not only resolved, but the person is better equipped to improve the quality of his or her life. In other words the goal of tertiary prevention is *psychological growth* rather than a return to the condition that existed before the stress occurred. Typical examples of tertiary prevention are public education programs to encourage receptivity and support for the discharged mental patient, and the development of transitional settings such as group homes to ease the patient's integration back into the community.

The rationale for the prevention of mental illness is appealing yet elusive. In their review on primary prevention, Kessler and Albee (1975) point out that preventive efforts assume two things: that social and environmental conditions affect social-psychological variables—that is, interpersonal conditions and events; and that our childhood experiences affect our emotional adjustments as adults. It follows that we must make a positive impact on the preliminary factors to prevent negative effects on child rearing or family interaction or early social experience. The evidence supporting these assumptions is so voluminous and varied as to defy summarization. When we consider such large social variables as poverty and racism, the results supporting social causes of mental illness become complex and difficult to interpret. Some writers see no rationale for primary prevention in these findings (for example, Wagenfeld, 1972), while others maintain that poverty is at the root of disability (for example, Vance, 1963).

Nonetheless many community psychologists cite evidence that early emotional and social experiences profoundly affect mental health. Following this belief, they support preventive efforts to increase the quality of the child's early environments such as compensatory education programs. Sanford (1972), however, questions the necessity and usefulness of the concept of prevention. Does it make sense to believe that we can prevent particular problems such as schizophrenia or anxiety reactions? He suggests instead that we concentrate on activities designed to facilitate the development of healthy personalities and the promotion of mental health in general. Such nonspecific primary prevention to improve the quality of life can be justified on the basis of humanistic values—not simply for its preventive potential. In line with these sentiments, many community psychologists have come to see that activities designed to increase people's competence for effective functioning are equivalent to primary prevention (Kessler & Albee, 1975). Furthermore, it might make more sense to identify generally stressful life events—marriage break-up, loss of a job—which might precipitate different disorders in different people, and attempt to intervene with groups of people who have recently experienced such stressful events (Bloom, 1979).

If primary prevention can be accomplished by *any* activity that improves the human condition, imagine what a range of strategies are available! We can explore improved child-rearing, effective communication, the building of self-esteem, the reduction of stress, and the elimination of poverty; systematic changes in organizations to increase their ability to deal with crises, and the role of community organization designed to mobilize resources for action (Kelly, 1970); mental health consultation, crisis intervention, and anticipatory guidance to help potentially vulnerable individuals deal with the stress of such situations as marriage and raising children (Bloom, 1971). The list goes on: there are programs directed toward the family (training parents in communication skills), toward the preschool period (compensatory education programs, such as Head Start), and toward the primary school settings (training children in problem-solving skills).

Given the complexity of primary prevention, it is no surprise that results are mixed and that most authors conclude that its efficacy has not been well established (for example, Zax & Specter, 1974; Rappaport, 1977). Emory Cowen

Children and teacher participating in Head Start, a compensatory education program. *(Charles Harbutt/Archive Pictures, Inc.)*

(1977a) even criticizes community psychologists for advocating primary prevention as a potential major breakthrough in mental health, when in fact the concept is often misunderstood and rarely translated into concrete activities. The discrepancy between the abstract definition and rallying cry of primary prevention and what actually gets done appears to be attributable to two factors. First, there is slippage between the theory and the practice of primary prevention; many programs cited as primary prevention are actually secondary prevention, tertiary prevention, or therapy. For example, when Cowen (1977b) asked a group of community psychologists to name the most important contribution to primary prevention, the most frequent response was his own project in Rochester schools—a program in *secondary* prevention.

The second factor accounting for the discrepancy between definition and action is the failure of community psychologists to sufficiently consider what they are and are not qualified to do. While it may be true that almost any activity that improves the human condition can be considered primary prevention, mental health professionals do not have the knowledge or expertise to be urban planners, recreation specialists, nutritionists, or politicians. Therefore Cowen (1977a) suggests that community psychologists concentrate on areas where they have demonstrated competence—specifically, the qualities of social environments and their consequences for mental health, and the training of competence. For instance, one promising direction for primary prevention is an integration of Moos's work of social environments and Kelly's ecological emphasis on the interaction the individual and the environment (see Chapter 5). This means that once we identify the crucial environmental elements that foster psychological growth for particular types of individuals, it may be possible to alter environments and match persons to settings in ways that maximize mental well-being. As for competence training, there already exist a number of successful demonstrations of how training in core social skills has positive effects on children's scholastic adjustment and achievement. A well-documented example is the work of Spivak and Shure (1974), presented in Box 10.3.

Cowen (1977b) suggests that it is time for community psychologists to give real substance to the concept of primary prevention. In his 1973 review of social and community interventions, he found that no more than 3 percent of the efforts were directed toward primary prevention. At best, according to Vayda and Perlmutter's (1977) survey of community mental health centers, only half of the current activities in consultation and education could be classified as primary prevention. (Most of these activities were at the institutional or agency level, specifically training care-givers and providing program consultation.) Obviously, then, it will only be through the serious, concerted action of mental health professionals that we can hope to span the gap between the ideal of primary prevention and its effective application in the real world.

Natural Support Systems. Mental health professionals are not alone in society's efforts to reduce the incidence and severity of mental illness. All around us are individuals, groups, and social networks with the motivation and ability to intervene at various points in the stress process to reduce psychopathology and encourage psychological growth. In times of stress, we often turn to those we know and trust for some understanding and guidance. For example, a high school

Box 10.3 FOCUS ON PRACTICE
Training Children in the Skills of Interpersonal Problem Solving

When young children experience problems in living, adults often tell them what to do or give them explanations that go beyond their level of understanding. Psychologists George Spivak and Myrna Shure wanted to find ways to get children to think on their own. Specifically, they were interested in helping children develop problem-solving skills for generating and evaluating solutions to common interpersonal problems such as fighting over a toy or getting a parent to listen to a request.

Research has illuminated a number of thought processes that are directly related to social adjustment and mental health. These include a sensitivity to human problems, the ability to imagine alternate courses of action and to conceptualize the means and the obstacles to solving a problem, and an understanding of the consequences of various actions. Children who lack these abilities tend to be poorly adjusted, impulsive, overemotional, or inhibited in social relations.

Over a 3-year period, Spivak and Shure developed a training program for 4-year-olds who were deficient in interpersonal problem-solving skills and social adjustment. The program follows a detailed script of daily lessons in game form and is presented to small groups of children for a 10-week period. The games use pictures, storybooks, puppets, and trinkets and the teachers are provided with techniques for maintaining interest and eliciting responses from the children. The initial games deal with prerequisite skills for problem solving, such as how to tell when someone is hurt or sad or happy. The problem-solving games guide the children in the steps of developing alternative solutions, generating alternative consequences, and in pairing solutions to consequences. For example, children are presented with a picture in which one child cannot see a storybook because another child is standing. The teacher asks what the child can do or say to get the other child to sit down. As ideas are offered, the teacher says, "That's one idea. Now the idea of this game is to think of lots of different ideas, lots of ways the boy can get the other boy to sit down." To generate alternative consequences, the teacher asks what different things might happen if a suggested solution is attempted. For pairing solutions and consequences, children are encouraged to immediately think of the possible effects of a suggested action. In these ways, the children's ability to resolve interpersonal problems is systematically enhanced.

Evaluation research studies indicate that the Spivak and Shure program is effective. Trained children show increased problem-solving ability and a tendency to use fewer solutions that involve force (hitting, grabbing, and so forth). Furthermore, ratings by teachers based on everyday behavior show increased initiative, autonomy, and social adjustment. Problem-solving skills do enhance real-life effectiveness.

Source: Spivak, G. & Shure, M. B. *Social adjustment of young children: A cognitive approach to solving real-life problems.* San Francisco: Jossey-Bass, 1974.

senior who is upset by the ending of a dating relationship talks to her English teacher. A father who has lost his job turns to his family for support. A recently widowed mother of three joins a single parent association to socialize with similar others and to share common problems. Each of these invididuals has drawn upon an informal or natural support system.

A *self-help group* for widows and widowers. (© *Frank Siteman MCMLXXX)*

Gottlieb and Shroter (1978) have identified three types of *natural support systems*, based on Caplan's (1974) definition of a *support system* as "an enduring pattern of continuous or intermittent ties that play a significant part in maintaining the psychological and physical integrity of the individual over time" (p. 7). There are *community care-givers* (teachers, nurses, ministers, police officers), who extend understanding and support to the troubled individual. There is our informal *social network* of family and friends, providing emotional and physical assistance to persons undergoing stress. And there is the *self-help group* (the most formal natural support system), composed of persons sharing a common problem—a helping community that accepts the individual's experience and offers mutual assistance (see Levy, 1976). Studies indicate that people under stress tend to look to these natural sources of support rather than seek help from mental health professionals. In addition these natural networks often serve as a referral mechanism to professionals for individuals who need further assistance (see Gottlieb, 1976).

But how can community psychology enhance the preventive role of natural support systems when, in fact, mental health consultation (and similar efforts) may actually *weaken* the natural help-giving processes in the community by undermining or supplanting informal helping behaviors (Gottlieb, 1974)? Obviously we must find avenues of collaboration between the two. Gottlieb and Shroter (1978) give us three possibilities. First, professionals can serve as resources to informal helping systems: professionals can provide detailed descriptions of services to aid the referral process; they can serve as research associates in areas such as need identification; and they can conduct evaluations of the outcomes of support-system interventions. Second, members of natural support systems can serve as resources to professionals: they can collaborate in providing services; they can teach professionals about effective informal helping behavior; and they can contribute their knowledge and expertise to the planning of new services and programs. Finally, mental health professionals can help identify and create natural support systems. For example they can advise community planners in the design of settings that not only maximize the opportunities for social interaction and support-system development, but at the same time protect the residents' need for privacy.

So we are faced with two crucial, related questions: Will mental health professionals rise to the challenge of increasing the preventive potential of natural support systems? This would mean applying our knowledge of interpersonal relations, small group processes, and organizational functioning to the development and improvement of natural helping systems in the community setting. And will professionals take the initiative in collaborating with informal helpers? Further studies are certainly required (see Lieberman & Glidewell, 1978). Levy (1978), for example, reports the results of a survey of mental health facilities that exchanged referrals with self-help groups. Although most of these agencies expressed a positive evaluation of the self-help groups, less than one-third thought there was a high probability of exploring further integration of activities. Thus the preventive potential of natural support systems may depend on the readiness of mental health professionals to seek and develop collaborative mechanisms.

Human Service Programs

Community psychology is an action-oriented field of direct practice, involving the development of human service programs to help individuals or groups in need. These programs include a wide variety of activities including training, consultation, new forms of service, mental health education, and the creation of new settings (Cowen, 1973; Kelly, Snowden & Munoz, 1977; Bloom, 1980). Applied social psychologists could make positive contributions in many of these areas.

Rappaport (1977) extends earlier frameworks by outlining four sources of social interventions that can be used in community psychology practice. His framework touches on three aspects of each intervention: its values and goals, its level of analysis, and its major underlying concepts.

The first source, coming from clinical psychology and community mental health, assumes that social problems are due to the inability of some people to fit into society's existing structure. The goal is to help these deviants adjust by either minimizing their differences or becoming comfortable with them. Working at this individual level of analysis, the community psychologist has available a variety of concepts—from social learning theory to psychoanalysis—to help in the understanding of individual functioning (see Chapters 2 and 5). This leads to person-centered strategies of intervention: crisis intervention, the training of paraprofessionals as psychotherapists, and the training of high-risk individuals in new areas of competence.

The second source of social intervention—interpersonal work in clinical psychology and mental health—sees social problems as created by interpersonal difficulties within primary groups such as the family. With this emphasis on defects in group functioning, the group level of analysis highlights how dysfunctional groups harm individuals and inhibit higher level structures (such as organizations) from accomplishing their goals. The underlying concepts for this approach are drawn from the study of group dynamics in social psychology. Thus strategies of intervention focus on the group as the unit of change and include such methods as communication skill training, family therapy, and sensitivity training.

The social psychology of organizations is the third source of intervention strategies proposed by Rappaport. Social problems are created by organizations that fail to satisfactorily implement the goals of our social institutions in education, health care, rehabilitation of criminals, and so on. Organizations are designed to help integrate individuals into society, but organizational dysfunction precludes this happening at an acceptable rate. In this instance concepts or theories are systems-centered, drawn from social and organizational psychology, public health, and other fields that focus on organizations. The strategies of intervention are those of organization development (see Chapter 9), and of community mental health. The latter involves programs of early identification and secondary prevention of mental problems in the same way that public health works to identify the prevalence of physical disease and prevent its widespread occurrence.

The fourth and final source of interventions—a broad analysis of society—assumes that social problems are created by society's major institutions rather than by individuals, groups, or organizations. Thus the key to social change is found in the culture and ideology of social institutions and the organizations that comprise them. At this institutional or community level of analysis, basic concepts are drawn from such systems-centered social sciences as sociology, political science, and economics. The distribution of power and resources among the diverse groups of a society is the crucial variable. The ecological approach looks for ways of maximizing the person-environment fit. Strategies of intervention include social action and the creation of new settings. The aim is to build new organizations whose values differ from those of the dominant institutions. For example, social advocacy to change school policies, or the creation of an alternative school, are essentially similar ways of changing the institution of education to further the aims of cultural relativity and person-setting fit.

Rappaport points out that moving to each higher level of analysis and action does not preclude lower levels, but may in fact integrate these into the higher level. The task for community psychology, however, is to know which interventions from which level are appropriate to one's goals: we must diagnose each problem, then choose suitable strategies and tactics. The full practice of community psychology requires interventions based on multiple levels of analysis with multiple concepts at each level. This point raises the clear and crucial necessity for the integration of applied social psychology and community psychology when change is sought at the group, organizational, and community levels of analysis.

The development of human service programs must also include a continuous assessment of values and goals. As we look at the social systems of education, criminal justice, and mental health, we must ask ourselves: Are we creating structures that perpetuate dependency and inequality, or are we helping to foster independence and respect for cultural diversity? Let us view the various human service systems:

- Human service programs developed within the *educational system* have concentrated on preschool experience or the primary grades. The principle of early intervention as a preventive measure has been foremost in the minds of the program developers. Although enrichment programs for preschool children have shown positive intellectual and emotional gains (Cowen, 1973; Kelly et al., 1977), these gains do not appear to hold up once the child enters the regular school system (Rappaport, 1977). A number of secondary prevention programs, such as Cowen's Primary Mental Health Project, have produced beneficial results through remedial training and support efforts directed toward vulnerable children; and similar efforts have been directed toward the prevention of mental health problems among college students (Zax & Specter, 1974). (Chapter 15 will consider some of the contributions of applied social psychology to the educational system.)

- In programs developed within the *criminal justice system*, the focus is on adolescents, particularly on active and potential delinquents. Many inner city projects promote the development of "problem youth," and provide viable training and employment alternatives to delinquent behavior. But Rappaport (1977) suggests that the focus of community psychology should be on how to mobilize environmental resources so as to reduce the involvement of persons in the criminal justice system in the first place. The developing diversity of programs in the criminal justice system clearly marks this as a growth area for community psychology. (In Chapter 15, we will look at the contributions of applied social psychology in this area.)

- The *mental health system* remains the area of major concern to most community psychologists. Most human service programs—including preventive programs and the creation of alternate settings—are developed in community settings. Their goal is to enhance the mental health and/or living conditions of the participants through training, consultation, and crisis intervention, usually in concert with programs developed in community mental health centers (Zax & Specter, 1974; Heller & Monahan, 1977).

One excellent example of the creation of alternate settings in the mental health system is the *community lodge* program for discharged mental patients developed by George Fairweather and his colleagues (Fairweather, Sanders, Cressler & Maynard, 1969; Fairweather, Sanders & Tornatzky, 1974). Fairweather was concerned about chronic hospitalization—many of the patients who are admitted to mental hospitals and who are not discharged within the first few months simply end up staying for years! They often become so *institutionalized*—socialized in and dependent upon the hospital system—that they become incapable of functioning in the community. Initial studies identified characteristics of patients most likely to become chronic (for example, diagnosed psychotic, considered legally incompetent) and demonstrated that existing treatment programs had almost no beneficial effects for these patients. A new alternative was required.

Fairweather wondered whether small groups of patients might be organized to function autonomously to provide a bridge between the hospital and the community. By first studying supervised and unsupervised work groups of patients in hospital, Fairweather demonstrated that unsupervised groups accomplish their tasks (with some reduction in efficiency), and more importantly, developed a sense of cohesion and morale that supervised groups did not. The next step was a 5-year experimental innovation in which one ward of the hospital was organized along small group lines with patients taking major responsibility for making decisions about life on the ward. The results were very positive—patients showed greater improvement and satisfaction than patients in a traditional ward. However, when the patients from the experimental ward were discharged they returned to the hospital as quickly as regular patients. They had lost their support group and unless they found support in the community they were rehospitalized!

The final innovation was to create a new social system located in the community—the lodge—to continue the small group support so needed by the discharged patient. The group of patients living in the lodge were trained to handle their own affairs—including their own business, a gardening and janitorial service—and developed a totally autonomous society with their own rules, status system, and reward structure. The results? A 5-year evaluation showed that lodge residents were more gainfully employed and were much less likely to return to the hospital. Furthermore, the cost of the lodge system was only one-third that of hospitalization. Fairweather concludes that it is the supportive and democratic environment of the lodge as an alternate social setting that results in the more adequate adjustment of patients to the community.

It certainly is a challenge to combine the many considerations and strategies relevant to the mental health system into viable preventive programs in the community setting. Fortunately, a few examples of successful programs do exist. When I was living in Guelph, Ontario, I was involved in a small demonstration project, the Human Service Community, that instituted a number of the strategies described in this section (see Box 10.4).

A final note on human service programs: We must stress the fundamental importance of research activity and graduate training in community psychology. We need survey research to assess service needs, action research to help plan programs, and evaluation research to assure successful program implementation and outcomes. We need effective graduate training for community psychologists, and training at all levels in core competencies. Only through this integration of theory, research, and practice will community psychology continue to advance in its search for solutions to crucial human problems.

COMMUNITY DEVELOPMENT: COORDINATION OF HUMAN RESOURCES

The political action component of Dohrenwend's (1978) model raises this controversial issue: Should mental health professionals (such as community psychologists) function as political activists? Should they act to help particular groups of people gain the power to share more of society's resources (Heller & Monahan, 1977)?

Box 10.4   FOCUS ON PRACTICE
The Human Service Community

Ralph Bierman had a dream. Trained as a clinical psychologist he wanted to find ways of releasing the human potential for helping that exists in any community. To follow his dream he left his position as a Professor of Counseling and Human Relations at the University of Waterloo and sought funding to establish a community-based, preventive mental health program. With a 3-year demonstration grant from the Canadian federal government, he and five co-workers established the Human Service Community (HSC) in Guelph, Ontario in 1973.

The goals of HSC were several in number: to demonstrate a model of a preventive social service system; to develop volunteer helping resources in the community; to develop meaningful social roles and paraprofessional career opportunities for individuals on social assistance; to give professional helpers an opportunity to upgrade their skills; and to develop an interdependent helping community among volunteers, welfare recipients, and professionals.

To reach the goals, HSC developed through two major phases: a skill training phase and a preventive service phase. In the training phase, participants were recruited through grass roots contact with individuals, followed by small group discussions and a mini-training workshop to demonstrate the training program. The first wave of twenty-four volunteers, twenty-four welfare recipients, and twenty-four professionals (social workers, psychologists, ministers) then participated in a series of training workshops built around the core interpersonal skills (see Chapter 6). Members were also trained as leaders to provide further workshops to new participants. A rigorous evaluation showed that the training phase resulted in improved skills and increased self-esteem and self-actualization. The workshops provided by trained volunteers and paraprofessionals were as successful as those provided by the professional staff.

In the preventive service phase, HSC formed task forces to provide helping interventions to vulnerable populations in the community. One task force trained hard-core unemployed who had been involved with the psychiatric, criminal justice, or social service systems. Interpersonal skill training was combined with career exploration and job search. Participants gained increased skills and over 80 percent went on to further training or gainful employment. Another task force (in which I participated) worked with emotionally vulnerable children in an elementary school. Creative play sessions based on the core skills provided the children with a safe and supportive adult relationship. As a result, the children showed a greater sense of social acceptance and self-esteem.

When the major funding for HSC ceased, the professional staff moved on, but the project has continued for several years on a volunteer basis. In 1981, a major provincial grant was received to provide preventive services for children in community settings. Ralph Bierman's dream lives on.

Sources: Bierman, R. & Lumley, C. Toward the humanizing community. *Ontario Psychologist*, 1973, 5(5), 10–19. Bierman, R., Davison, B., Finkelman, L., Leonidas, J., Lumley, C., & Simister, S. *Toward meeting fundamental human needs: Preventive effects of the Human Service Community.* Final report to Department of National Health and Welfare, March, 1976.

Traditionalists, seeking to help individuals deal with life's problems, hold that political organizing is an individual responsibility in which mental health professionals should play no special role. But political activists in community psychology, assuming that stressful environmental conditions contribute directly to mental dysfunction, believe that their role is to work with the disadvantaged to bring about social change. From this perspective, the traditional approach must be challenged: Can we, in fact, ask individuals to adjust to society's injustices? Solely on the basis of democratic, humanistic values, one can argue that social injustice and inequity are unacceptable and that the involvement of mental health professionals in political activity should be expected on that score alone.

The controversy over involvement in social action is relatively new for community psychology and applied social psychology, but not so for social work and community development. For decades these professional practices have worked to improve the living conditions of the disadvantaged in societies throughout the world. Assuming that improved social conditions are linked to healthier psychological functioning, both aspects can be approached by actively involving people in delivering the services and making the decisions that directly affect their lives.

To come to grips with these vital issues, we must look at some of the history of community practice, and at the major strategies, principles, and methods of community organization.

Brief History of Community Practice

The involvement of human service professionals in community work has a rich and varied history (Rothman, 1979; Garvin & Cox, 1979; Levine & Levine, 1970). Professionals have come from such related yet distinct disciplines as social work, adult education, urban planning, and agricultural extension to work together in community development, social action, community planning and intergroup relations. The aims of community work have been just as diverse: to develop programs, increase citizen participation, and to change community institutions. Running through this complexity has been a central issue: should community work concentrate on improving services to people in need? or attempt to change the social conditions in which people live? or should it seek both goals? According to Rothman (1979), these two aspects of treatment and reform are complementary: both are directed toward improving the well-being of the individual.

In their coverage of preventive programs in the wider community, Zax and Specter (1974) point out such historical precursors as the Salvation Army and the settlement house movement. The Salvation Army, formed in England in the 1800s, is primarily a community program directed toward the rehabilitation of the disadvantaged. The provision of services for basic needs—food, clothing, and shelter—was seen as the first step in helping individuals develop a sense of responsibility and competence to improve their lot. The Salvation Army subsequently expanded to North America, developing community-based programs through the creation of orphanages, halfway houses for prisoners, and residences for the transient poor. Similar and related services have been developed by other third-sector human service organizations, including religious and voluntary agencies.

A detailed description of the settlement house movement is provided by Levine and Levine's (1970) history of the helping services. The immense social changes associated with the Industrial Revolution and immigration to the New World led to visible social problems of unprecedented proportions (poverty, unemployment, crime). In England and North America, one response was the development of settlement houses to deal with the unmet needs of the disadvantaged. From diverse religious, political, and educational backgrounds and motives, numerous middle-class individuals, often young and fervently committed to social change, came to work in settlement houses located in the slums and neighborhoods populated by the poor, the immigrants, and the uneducated. Settlement houses engaged in an incredible variety of service and reform activities, from nursing care to establishing libraries, from pushing for legislative changes to lobbying for improved municipal services.

As social conditions improved for workers and immigrants, and as more social services were taken over by professionals and government agencies, the settlement house movement declined in the early 1900s. At about the same time, the discipline of social work swung away from social reform to gain professional respectability through an emphasis on psychiatric case work. Despite this historical shift, it is interesting to note that the activities of the settlement house movement reflect the needs of today's urban ghettos, and its objectives mirror the call of modern community psychologists for social change to meet these needs.

Cox and Garvin (1979) present a comprehensive picture of the history of community organization practice from the mid-1800s to the present with an emphasis on the condition of oppressed minorities. They describe four separate time periods following the Civil War in the United States, each characterized by its major social conditions, its main ideological trends, and its central institutions of community practice. These periods (1865 to 1914; 1915 to 1929; 1930 to 1954; 1955 to 1977) are separated by major events that are significant for community work: World War I and the end of progressivism; the stock market crash of 1929, followed by the Great Depression; and the United States Supreme Court decision of 1954 that ruled against school segregation.

The progressive era up to World War I, exemplified by the settlement house movement, was intertwined with the social conditions of industrialization, urbanization, immigration, and black emancipation—all creating both immense problems and significant opportunities for social progress. The ideological forces of liberalism, socialism, and pragmatism combined to support the major community institutions of settlement houses for treatment and reform. In addition, other major developments included charity organizations to help the poor, and black organizations to adjust to or fight the white-dominated system.

The period from World War I to the Depression saw the strong reemergence of capitalism and free enterprise, as well as the retreat of social work from efforts for social change. As blacks continued their fight for equality in the United States, their efforts were countered by symptomatic behaviors of interracial conflict: violence, race riots, and lynchings. The conditions of Native Americans continued to decline. In a mood of prevailing anti-intellectualism and social conservatism, social activists were frustrated and endangered. Vice President Calvin Coolidge attacked universities as "hot beds of sedition," and social workers looked to psychoanalytic case work as the epitome of respected practice. At the same time, the continuing proliferation of welfare agencies raised the need for coordination of funding and activities, leading to the creation of the Community Chest and the Welfare Council.

The Depression, with its conditions of massive unemployment and destitution, severely affected community practice. The union movement was strengthened. Federal government increased its involvement in all sectors of life, particularly in the planning, funding, and administration of social services. Civil rights began to find expression in government programs and policies, and black organizations in the United States continued their campaign for equality. World War II advanced many of the trends begun in the Depression years—particularly the involvement of federal government in human service programming. And finally, this period saw the beginnings of professional training programs, mostly within social work, to equip community practitioners with the concepts and skills required for program development and coordination and for the amelioration of social problems.

The period from 1955 to the present has included a range of quickly changing conditions and political issues that have had a strong impact on the practice of community organization. The growth of the Civil Rights movement was followed by the involvement of other minorities, including women and students, in an expression of massive discontent, culminating in the late 1960s and early 1970s, much of which was directed against American involvement in Vietnam. These developments challenged social institutions and community practitioners to be more sensitive to grass roots interests and to involve local citizens in the planning process. The trend toward federal government responsibility for the amelioration of social problems was expressed in the War on Poverty in the United States and, in Canada, in the goal of a "Just Society." This led to the rapid expansion of training programs for community practitioners, including the emergence of community psychology programs. Other disciplines began to devote more attention to the goal of defining community organization practice and enunciating the principles underlying successful interventions in community settings.

Strategies and Principles of Community Practice

Three Models. The quality of our theoretical understanding about community practice has been increased significantly by the work of Jack Rothman and his colleagues in the School of Social Work at the University of Michigan. Their approach captures the existing reality of community work better than past attempts that have tried, without success, to place all activities under one grand, all-embracing theory. Rothman (1978) proposes three models of community organization: *locality development, social planning,* and *social action.* As outlined in Table 10.1, each has its own goals, assumptions, strategy, and other dimensions.

Locality development—Rothman's term for *community development*—

Table 10.1   MODELS OF COMMUNITY ORGANIZATION PRACTICE

Dimension of Comparison	Locality Development	Social Planning	Social Action
Goals	Self help; increase community integration and capacity to solve problems (process goals)	Problem solving on substantive community problems (task goals)	Shifting of power and resources; basic institutional change (process or task goals)
Assumptions	Community lacks viable relationships and democratic problem-solving capacity; differences are reconcilable; common interests exist	Substantive social problems exist in housing, recreation, health, etc.; interests may be reconcilable or in conflict	Disadvantaged populations experience social injustice, inequity and deprivation; interests are not reconcilable
Basic Change Strategy	Broad cross-section of community involved in determining and solving problems	Fact-gathering and rational decision making on most effective course of action	Crystallize the issues and organize people to take action against enemy targets
Characteristic Methods	Improve communication among different groups; Build consensus	Build consensus or induce conflict	Induce conflict through confrontation, direct action, and negotiation
Medium of Change	Small task-oriented groups and intergroup relationships	Formal organizations and agencies	Mass organizations and political processes
Practitioner Role	Coordinator; catalyst; skill trainer	Fact-gatherer and analyst; program implementer	Advocate; agitator; negotiator
Orientation toward Power Structure	Power structure as collaborators in mutual problem solving	Power structure as employers and sponsors	Power structure as oppressors and target of action
Conception of Client Role	Citizens; participants in problem solving	Consumers; recipients of service	Victims; employers; constituents
Agency Types	Settlement house; Peace Corps; consumer associations	Welfare councils; planning bodies	Social movements; human rights groups

Source: Rothman (1978).

stresses direct citizen participation in bringing about community change. Community development emphasizes the processes of inducing initiative and motivation, improving communication among people around mutual problems, and facilitating the functioning of small task-oriented groups toward increased economic and social progress. For example, a worker from a settlement house might help organize a small group of ghetto residents into a food-buying club so they can stretch their dollars further. The process of democratic involvement in decision making is seen as an important goal in itself, since it will foster self-reliance and community control in the future. The food-buying club might follow success in the consumer area by becoming concerned about recreation opportunities for children in the neighborhood.

Community development takes a systems theory approach—it assumes that differences among groups can be ironed out and that common goals exist. For example, workers concerned about antagonism between police and citizens will look for ways of increasing understanding and cooperation. They will organize meetings for police to talk with neighborhood residents to increase awareness of joint concerns and they will try to get citizens involved in crime control. In these ways, the professional practitioner is the catalyst who gets the problem-solving process moving through collaboration. The community developer does not plan for people or fight battles on their behalf; rather he or she encourages local initiative in a supportive, respectful and yet challenging manner, and withdraws into the background as the process builds up steam.

Community development is a difficult process that often must overcome significant barriers. People experiencing severe problems in living may be too downtrodden and distrustful or may lack the skills to become involved in complex and sustained problem solving. Even when a group develops a good idea—such as a teen drop-in center to reduce delinquency—the funds may not be forthcoming from politicians and bureaucrats who have given priority to some other area of programming at that point in time. And so on. However, when such limitations can be overcome, the community development model is a powerful approach requiring expertise at lower levels of functioning—particularly interpersonal and group relations. We will take a more detailed look at some of the methods of community development in the next section.

The *social planning* model emphasizes the technical and rational approach to problem solving that is carried forward by expert planners employed directly or indirectly by the power structure, that is, government or elites with resources. This approach is task-oriented—directed toward the solution of specific problems in areas such as housing, delinquency, health care, and so forth. The degree of citizen participation and community control can vary from minimal to moderate. For example, a city recreation department may simply decide what programs it wants to offer and then do so, or it may approach various neighborhood groups and clubs and collaborate with interested citizens in developing desired programs. The social planning model assumes that programs will be run by experts, rather than the citizen-consumers who are simply seen as recipients of service. Therefore, social planners tend to work with existing organizations rather than grass roots people. Needs are often assessed through survey research or existing statistics, programs are planned to meet these needs for service, and proposals for funding are taken forward to the appropriate place in the power structure. For example, a city housing department may look at the substandard quality and general lack of low-cost housing, and decide to increase the availability of public housing for citizens.

The main limitation of the social planning approach is that it leaves out participative decision making and community control. Thus, decisions for others may be made that are later resisted or rejected and programs may be developed that are underutilized or create greater dependency and need than previously existed. For example, few people may attend recreation programs planned *for* them, and an increase in public housing may indirectly reduce the amount of low-cost housing available on the private market, thereby making low-income families more dependent on public housing.

The *social action* model is characterized by the social advocacy approach of Saul Alinsky and others which was described briefly in Chapter 4. This change strategy assumes that a disadvantaged segment of the community needs to be organized and mobilized to gain more power and resources in accord with the principles of democracy and social justice. Social action is clearly built on conflict theory—differences are irreconcilable and changes only come about through pressure, agitation, and negotiation if the enemy does not capitulate. Alinsky was a master at devising novel ways for oppressed groups to gain power by immobilizing or embarrassing their more powerful opponents. For example, tying up all a company's telephone lines or surreptitiously threatening to constantly occupy all the toilets at O'Hare International Airport in Chicago are tactics that had immediate and devastating effects on the opposition. Alinsky held that the ends justified the means, but did not advocate open violence, and advised his organizers to create the impression that they would stop at nothing, rather than actually doing so. His goals were humanistic ones, and many of the organizations that use advocacy, such as civil rights groups and other social movements, are dedicated to institutional and social changes supported by the value base of democratic humanism.

However, there are negative side effects and limitations to the advocacy model and the conflict theory on which it is based. Heller and Monahan (1977) point out that strong and persistent social action may lead to an attitudinal backlash in the majority community, and in a wider conflict, the minority will usually lose. A second limitation is that gaining power and resources is one thing—developing sophisticated programs that actually alleviate very complex and longstanding social problems, such as poor housing, unemployment and crime, is quite another. Thus, the minority organizations may find they are as ineffective and frustrated as the bureaucracies they have replaced. Finally, the advocacy approach assumes that resources are fixed and that what one party gains another loses. In actuality, it may be that a community can increase its total level of power and resources through developing wider forms of influence and collaboration toward greater effectiveness.

Rothman points out that the three models are ideal types that may overlap in actual practice. Depending on conditions, the different strategies can be mixed and blended (Cox, Erlich, Rothman & Tropman, 1979). For example, community developers may shift to social advocacy to force change on an issue that remains unresolved despite attempts at collaboration. Social planners may seek greater involvement of community members in planning and developing programs built on community control. The successful practitioner uses a variety of strategies to achieve humanistic goals in both the process and the task areas.

It should also be noted that quite a bit of community organizing goes on without a professional practitioner ever being involved. A variety of citizen groups are constantly coming together around common concerns and using different strategies to influence decision makers at City Hall and other levels of government. The need for a new traffic light, an increase in utility rates, the proposed construction of a freeway, the need for better housing—all these are issues around which citizens come together to express their concerns. Boyte (1981) calls this grass roots participation "the backyard revolution" and sees it as an ongoing attempt to preserve the tradition of institutions such as family, church, and school. Thus community organizing can be seen as a crucial element of the democratic process.

Principles. The most common approach to developing principles of successful community work has been to engage in practice, describe the work in case study form, and then draw out the important guidelines that increase the probability of success the next time around. There is, however, a more systematic approach to developing principles of practice. The work of Rothman and his colleagues (1974) made an important step toward linking the results of empirical social science research to the practice of community organization. Their 6-year research project began with a survey of the social science literature in psychology, sociology, social psychology, political science, public administration, adult education, and city planning. Research studies were reviewed, and the results synthesized into generalizations on social change. These were then translated into specific action guidelines that cut across various models and strategies of community practice.

Rothman and his associates field-tested the action guidelines in a variety of practical situations including a community mental health center, a family service agency, a juvenile court, an intermediate school district, and an urban planning council (Rothman, Erlich & Teresa, 1976). Professional community workers implemented the guidelines, described their experiences in written logs, and participated in seminars and consultation meetings. Results on quantifiable outcome measures—such as an increase in dollars or clients—were combined with subjective ratings to determine the degree of success in implementing the guidelines. The result is a planning manual describing four central guidelines for promoting innovations in community settings:

1. Practitioners wishing to promote an innovation in a general target system should develop it initially in a partial segment of that target system (p. 25). (For example, a practitioner who was organizing a welfare workers' union concentrated his efforts initially on the workers in one office building rather than the whole city.)
2. Practitioners wishing to change an organization's goals may approach this problem by altering the structure of influence within the organization by either: (a) increasing the power of those groups within the organization that hold goals compatible with the practitioner's, or (b) introducing new groups into the organization that hold goals compatible with the practitioner's (p. 61). (For example, in organizing the welfare workers' union, the practitioner had to influence more members with working-class backgrounds to seek leadership positions in the union.)
3. Practitioners wishing to foster participation in organizations, voluntary associations, or task groups should provide (or increase) appropriate benefits (p. 99). (For example, in developing a community mental health program in a

housing project, the practitioner made sure that each family gained benefits by having specific problems resolved such as toilet repairs and transportation to the dentist.)

4. Practitioners can increase their effectiveness by defining a relevant role (or role aspect) and clearly specifying this role or role aspect and fostering mutual agreement among relevant superordinates concerning it (p. 136). (For example, the planner in charge of housing for a regional planning council found that community agencies were not taking his general role seriously enough. He specialized his role by becoming an expert in the analysis of data about housing and as such had much more infuence in the planning process.)

Rothman's work indicates that when systematic research is combined with the common sense of practice, the resulting guidelines are more valid and more widely applicable. The planning manual is a unique example of a beneficial step toward developing a science of community practice that is both systematic and relevant.

Methods of Community Development

Community development calls for the active involvement of a wide spectrum of people in decision making to improve human welfare—influencing government planning, developing human service programs, created institutional change. How does a community developer facilitate these activities? Essentially by serving as a *process consultant* at the level of the community—interacting with people to increase their awareness and effectiveness in problem solving (see Chapter 4).

Methods of community development are focused and time-limited activities designed to reach specified goals. As such, they are analogous to the "interventions" of organization development (see Chapter 9). Underlying these methods is a complex base of assumptions, values, and models (Biddle & Biddle, 1965; Lippitt, Watson & Westley, 1958; Ross, 1967).

A number of community development methods are described by Littrell (1973). The basic role of the community developer is that of a professional helper and problem solver (see Chapters 4 and 6) who aids people to articulate their needs, facilitates participative decision making, resolves conflict among groups, and aids the search for consensus and effective action. To enact the role, a variety of methods are available—data feedback, the use of resource people, the creation of new organizations, the community survey, the group decision-making workshop.

The *community survey* encourages people to express their attitudes and opinions about community issues and needs and can provide directions for improvement. For example, a community group in a small town contacted a community developer for assistance in surveying citizen concerns. The developer immediately suggested that many other individuals be involved and that the idea of a survey be publicized to increase participation and support. Following this, the planning group was expanded and new topics were added to the survey. Task groups were formed to carry out particular parts of the problem-solving process, and the developer served as a consultant to each of these groups—facilitating the group process and providing research expertise for planning the survey. The survey questionnaire was distributed to every home in the community and the results were hand-tabulated to maximize citizen involvement. A public meeting to discuss the results led to the formation of several study-action groups to address particular concerns. In all, over 350 people out of a community of only 2,000 had participated directly in the planning and execution of the survey. The role of the community developer was crucial in generating this high level of involvement and the positive outcomes to which it led.

The *group discussion and decision-making workshop* brings together diverse individuals and groups to crystallize major concerns and plan actions. It is typical in communities that common concerns are not realized since diverse groups communicate very little with each other. Better to have people interact around solving common problems than engaging in intergroup conflict! Workshops can reduce social barriers to communication, and increased understanding can lead to shared decisions.

For example, in one community, a developer had heard many different groups separately express a concern about youth unemployment. On the developer's initiative, a steering committee was formed. Their first conclusion was that there was a general lack of communication and information about the problem. Hence, a one-day workshop was held to bring together a variety of citizens and agency personnel. Discussion groups defined the problem and generated possible solutions. A study group was formed to investigate the feasibility of a vocational school for the area. A second workshop brought together interested citizens and generated strong support for an action group to carry forward the proposal. The area now has a vocational school to help alleviate youth unemployment. The community developer was the "enabler" who brought people together for collaborative problem solving toward a common goal.

A number of community development methods show the importance of integrating the fields of human relations training (see Chapter 4) and small group processes (see Chapter 7) with the process of community development (see Fessler, 1976; Schindler-Rainman & Lippitt, 1972). The methods described by Fessler (1976) are especially strong in small group problem solving based on principles of group cohesion, norms, and leadership.

To effectively use small group processes in community development, Fessler (1976) recommends a training workshop for community leaders in the techniques of effective group problem solving. The workshop brings together a variety of individuals who want change, who may be well intentioned but see the community only as an extension of their *own* group or organization. The workshop goals are therefore to increase awareness of the community as a whole and to train small-group skills that can be used for collaborative problem solving. A steering committee of diverse individuals makes contact with various groups and agencies and invites them to send participants. This builds broad community support rather than identifying any one agency as the sponsor. The community developer—most often a paid employee of a public or voluntary human service organization—leads the workshop. The format follows the approach of experience-based learning in which small groups work on a case problem with each participant having a chance to be the group facilitator. Each stage of the workshop involves a presentation of one aspect of group problem solving (for example, identifying obstacles to be overcome) followed by discussion and reporting of experiences. The workshop is therefore a vehicle for increasing the competence of community leaders while simultaneously fostering the development of collaborative relationships among diverse and often conflicting groups.

The methods of community development are not directly concerned with mental health. However, *community development is human development*—the growth of people toward greater competence, involvement, and responsibility. Therefore, individual well-being is part of a fuller and richer community life. There are, in fact, several classic examples of the positive effects of community development on mental health (see Box 10.5).

Community Development, Community Mental Health, and Community Psychology

The coverage of community development brings us full circle to our initial example of Hannah Levine's efforts to assist the disadvantaged in gaining power over the services provided to them. We have seen a variety of methods that can be used for increasing community members involvement in decision making and for improving the quality of life in community settings. We have seen the importance of community development drawing upon other levels of practice—including the interpersonal, the small group, and the organizational—within the broader frameworks of human relations training and process consultation. We have seen indications that effective community development may have positive effects on mental health even though reducing mental illness is not an explitict goal of community development. To conclude our examination of these issues, we should explore the rationale for some of the linkages that have been suggested, and raise some questions about their possible limitations.

Donald Klein (1968) provides a rationale for the linkages between community development, community mental health, and community psychology. He defines the community as the patterned interactions of individuals designed to meet their needs for security, support during stress, and a sense of self and of significance throughout their life cycle. Here the focus is on the social-psychological processes—such as communication, decision making, and conflict—that are the essence of community life. Community development and related fields are designed to improve the functioning of these social-psychological processes and to make the community into a more meaningful environment for individual. The basic functions of the community in meeting personal and social needs are seen as having significant implications for psychological well-being. Thus the community mental health worker collaborates with community leadership to develop healthier environments that more adequately meet human needs. The workers must help people overcome their neglect of community life and develop an awareness of their community. The worker must ask basic questions about how needs are met, how deviances are handled, and how identities are developed. The worker thereby acts as an agent of social change who finds the middle ground between clinical service and social reform. The models of community development and social action are appropriate strategies, as are the skills of action research and human relations training.

Box 10.5   FOCUS ON PRACTICE AND RESEARCH
Community Development and Mental Health: The People of the Road

The Road is a small rural neighborhood in maritime Canada. In 1950, it consisted of 118 people, mostly children and adolescents, living in twenty-nine houses scattered along a country road. The houses, which were small, cramped, and sparsely furnished, had no electricity or indoor toilets. The people lived in poverty, with occasional work at menial tasks and social assistance making up the weak economic base. The average eduation level was about fifth grade, and outsiders regarded the Road's inhabitants as mentally retarded.

The Road was included in a series of investigations known as the *Stirling County Study* conducted by psychiatrist Alexander Leighton of Cornell University and his colleagues. The main concern of the study was the relationship between social conditions and the prevalence of mental illness. The Road in 1950 was clearly seen as a socially disintegrated community. Families showed a high prevalence of broken marriages, parental conflict, and child neglect. Families were isolated from each other, and there was an almost complete lack of social organization in the community. Not surprisingly, structured interviews showed a high prevalence of psychiatric disorders among the people of the Road.

In 1950, one of the researchers presented to county and provincial officials a report that called for improved educational and economic opportunities and the introduction of greater social organization through the development of local leadership. Officials responded positively. An adult educator was hired to improve the employment potential of the adults. A new schoolteacher cooperated with the educator by showing evening films for the community. The need for a permanent electrical system for the school led to a communitywide fund raising effort. The teacher organized more social activities such as bingo games to finance new desks for the school. On her initiative, children above sixth grade were bused to a consolidated school in a nearby town; they soon brought new habits and new social values back to the Road.

Employment opportunities increased through a nearby public works project and the physical environment changed markedly over the next 10 years. Houses were renovated and expanded with comfortable furnishings. Lawns, gardens, and shrubbery appeared where none had been.

More importantly, the social and mental well-being of the residents markedly improved. The education level of children rose considerably; formal organizations such as a home and school association sprang up. The interview survey was repeated in 1962, and the prevalence of psychiatric disorders was found to be much lower. Social integration and economic viability had significantly improved the mental health of the community.

Source: Leighton, A. H. Poverty and social change. *Scientific American*, 1965, *212*(5), 21-27.

In the area of citizen participation, there are signs that the principles and methods of community development could have a positive influence on community psychology. The issue of citizen involvement in planning and evaluating services is the same one raised by Hannah Levine's work with the community health center in the Bronx. With the establishment of community mental health centers, federal and state laws in the United States required the active participation of citizens through the establishment of community boards and advisory committees. Unfortunately citizen involvement is vaguely defined and has been both frustrating and ineffective. Davis and Specht (1978) reviewed fifty studies dealing with this issue and generally found that citizen board members and committees were typically uncertain of their roles and this had detrimental effects on the workability and usefulness of citizen involvement. Mental health center staff tend to pay "lip service" to citizen participation, but few believe it will help determine policies and some passively resist it. A lack of trust between staff and citizen as well as status differences further move the citizens into a passive and subordinate position. To better understand this conflict between staff and citizens, Davis and Specht (1978) conducted a state-wide survey of mental health centers focusing on the types of information and the role duties required for citizen participation. Numerous differences were apparent. Staff members thought citizens should know about sources of income for the center, citizens indicated this information was not available and not required. Staff members thought citizens should be involved in developing a plan to organize mental health services in the region. Citizens did not. It was clear that staff and citizens did not share the same definition of community involvement.

The methods of community development could clearly be used to increase the effective participation of citizens in community mental health services. One example is provided by Pargament, Habib, and Antibi (1978) who struggled to develop a community advisory board to work with the staff of a small outreach unit of a large mental health center. The center's administration soon changed the name of the advisory board to "community program committee" to indicate there was no decision-making power outside the center. A series of meetings with staff taking a community development role facilitated the committee's interest in assessing mental health needs in the area and led to the development of new programs, for example, a volunteer program to assist discharged patients. Further conflicts within the center led the committee to take on a role as advocate of effective mental health services and further demonstrated that a basic commitment by the outreach staff was essential for developing a successful collaborative relationship with the community.

But before we question the beneficial contributions of community development to community mental health and community psychology, we must ask this fundamental question: what about the basic effectiveness of community development itself? Most evidence for its effectiveness comes from case studies in which new programs were initiated or some form of social change was brought about. But there have been numerous failures as well (see Brill, 1971; Spergel, 1972). Rothman's work on community intervention was in fact partly stimulated by the need to develop directions along which community practice might be improved. In view of the reality that we need far more research in this crucial area, especially because of its complex and confusing demands (see Cowen, Lorion & Dorr, 1974), it may be some time before the community developer can assert to kindred professionals that community development is indeed effective. There is an especially strong need for integrative work that brings a combination of theory, research, and practice to illuminate the process and outcomes of community development (Blakely, 1979). In the meantime, practice will need to continue more on the basis of humanistic values and faith than on the basis of rigorous evaluation.

Assuming that community development leads to an improved quality of life, we must still ask if it reduces the rates of psychological dysfunction (Heller & Monahan, 1977). We do not yet know if increased political power—such as that generated by successful community development or social action—has any positive effect on mental health. Thus the claim that community control is justified as a cure for mental dysfunction should be held suspect until research untangles the complex nature of such problems. On the other hand, the combining of theory, research, and values may give us a strong enough base for advocating political action as a viable strategy for community psychology—precisely what such community psychologists as Rappaport (1977) have done. Where this issue will lead the fields of community development and community psychology is anyone's guess. The degree to which these fields continue to put the humanistic value base into practice will depend largely on the political atmosphere of the times as reflected in citizen attitudes and government funding. If we are to move toward social justice, community psychology has much to learn from applied social psychology, particularly at the group and organizational levels of functioning.

Summary

Community psychology, community mental health, and community development have been particularly directed toward increasing the well-being of people in community settings.

Definitions of community usually embody some degree of interaction and social structure among people in ways that meet their basic needs and provide a degree of identity. The systems theory approach stresses the integration of the community through the coordination of interdependent, specialized subsystems and emphasizes equilibrium and adaptation to change. In contrast, conflict theory sees the community as an arena in which various groups compete to gain the most power and resources; conflict theory views social problems as the result of inequity.

Mental illness is a social problem of immense proportion. A social-psychological understanding of the etiology and treatment of mental disorders is essential. Changing concepts of mental illness have put increasing stress on social and environmental causes and have led to community approaches for ameliorating such difficulties. A comprehensive social psychology of mental health is provided by Glidewell's work which emphasizes inequity in social power.

Training and consultation activities—involving individuals, nonprofessionals, or community care-givers—can increase the individual's and the system's capacity for maintaining or increasing mental health. Caplan's model of mental health consultation involves four types and points the way for more organization development in the mental health field.

The prevention of mental illness has great appeal since it is very difficult to eliminate fully developed psychopathology. Primary, secondary, and tertiary prevention are mechanisms for reducing and limiting the incidence and severity of mental illness. The study of natural support systems offers another avenue for the prevention of mental health problems.

Human service programs serve as the practice of community psychology. Interventions can be organized at different levels of analysis in terms of their sources, values, goals, and major conceptions. Human service programs have been developed within the educational system, the criminal justice system, and the mental health system.

Community practice has a long history that shows a number of phases each with its major social conditions, major ideological trends, and central institutions of community practice.

Community organizing can be divided into three models: locality or community development stresses direct citizen participation in working towards consensus and community change; social planning emphasizes the technical and rational activities of expert planners, supported by the existing power structure; social action works from the "grass roots" up, organizing the disadvantaged segments of the community to gain more power and resources in accord with the principles of democracy and social justice.

There are numerous specific methods of community development, for example, the community survey, the group decision-making workshop, and the small group training workshop for community leaders.

Community development, while involving human development, is not directly concerned with mental health. However, research results indicate the mental health benefits of community health development, and more linkage between community development and community psychology would certainly by beneficial. The greater involvement of applied social psychology would also help increase the capacity of communities for improving the welfare of their members.

Further Readings

Cox, F. M., Erlich, J. L., Rothman, J. & Tropman, J. E. (Eds.). *Strategies of community organizations* (3rd ed.). Itasca, Ill.: Peacock, 1979.

Fessler, D. R. *Facilitating community change: A basic guide.* La Jolla, Calif.: University Associates, 1976.

Heller, J. & Monahan, J. *Psychology and community change.* Homewood, Ill.: Dorsey, 1977.

Klein, D. C. *Community dynamics and mental health.* New York: Wiley, 1968.

Rappaport, J. *Community psychology: Values, research and action.* New York: Holt, Rinehart & Winston, 1977.

Wechsler, H., Solomon, L. & Kramer, B. M. (Eds.). *Social psychology and mental health.* New York: Holt, Rinehart & Winston, 1970.

CHAPTER OUTLINE

SOCIAL ISSUES: THE SORE SPOTS OF SOCIETY
  Racism: The Color of Your Skin Makes a Difference
    Symptoms of Racism
    Racial Segregation or Integration?
  Sexism: The Injustice of Gender
  Poverty: The Inequitable Distribution of Wealth

SOCIAL CHANGE AND PROGRESS OF HUMAN SOCIETY
  Social Psychology of Planned Change
    Social Change
    Planned Change
  The Role of Research in Social Change
  Changing Attitudes through Persuasive Communications
  Changing Behavior through Legal Compliance
  Social Change through Social Movements

SUMMARY

FURTHER READINGS

ELEVEN

Social Issues and Social Change

The province of Alberta, in western Canada, is endowed with vast and valuable reservoirs of petroleum and natural gas. Because Alberta is oil-rich, the Provincial Goverment established the Heritage Savings Trust Fund to aid future generations. By December 1978, the fund had an accumulated balance of over $4 billion. In that same month, in the bitter cold of an Alberta winter, a 5-week-old métis infant (of mixed Indian and white ancestry) died of pneumonia. He had been sleeping with his parents and their two other children on the cold bathroom floor of a house trailer provided by the provincial housing corporation. Due to a severe housing shortage, the trailer (the home of the infant's grandparents) was occupied by no less than eighteen adults and children. "I kept him wrapped up well, but it was still very cold there and he got sick," said the infant's mother.

Farther to the west, on the Pacific coast of British Columbia, there was another housing problem. The corporate head of a large mining company—and scion of a wealthy industrialist family—did not like his 4-year-old, $300,000 mansion overlooking the inlet and mountains of Vancouver harbor. He decided to have it demolished and replaced with a $600,000 mansion that better suited his needs. The original mansion was so well built that it literally had to be cut apart with chain saws. Although the demolition workers had trouble salvaging much of value, they did manage to save $35,000 worth of windows and other incidentals—about the equivalent of the cost of a new home in northern Alberta.

The enormous inequity in these two stories is apparent. Inequity is at the base of such crucial social issues as poverty, racism, and sexism. In North America, the contradictions between espoused democracy and unequal power, and between social justice and continuing inequity, have led many social scientists to search for the source of social problems, a major area of activity for professionals who share a humanistic value base.

There are other social issues that are not so much a product of inequity and discrimination—issues such as environmental pollution, the shock of technology, and population control. These issues, as well as others, are of major concern to social psychologists. In this chapter, we will examine racism, sexism, and poverty as a means of illustrating how social psychologists have dealt with social issues.

SOCIAL ISSUES: THE SORE SPOTS OF SOCIETY

For Adolf Hitler and his fellow Nazis, the presence of Jews in Germany, and eventually throughout Europe, was a social problem. They believed that the Jews were secretly manipulating the economic system, attempting to incite revolution among the workers, and generally subverting and harming the German people. But the real social problem lay in the fanatical anti-Semitism of Nazi Germany— the source of responsibility for the murder of 6 million Jewish people and the annihilation of 22 million other victims of racist nationalism.

Stark (1975) cites this example to illustrate that the creation and definition of a social problem may or may not correspond to objective reality. Usually there *are* harmful conditions in the real world that lie at the base of social issues—the existence of poverty, crime, and alcoholism, to name but three examples. However, there is not a one-to-one relationship between social conditions and our perceptions of those conditions. Destructive conditions can be ignored for a long time: for example, it is only recently that the oppression of women has become expressed in the social issue of sexism. In other words, a state of affairs becomes a social issue *only when enough people see it as a problem and begin action to gain redress.*

There is a further aspect of this increasingly accepted approach: social problems arise through the growth of *social movements*—that is, activities by a concerned group of citizens to effect social change by improving the harmful conditions. It is this element that leads me to use the terms "social issue" and "social problem" interchangeably. An issue is a point of contention: some of us push for change; others attempt to maintain the status quo. We can thus define a *social issue* as the existence of harmful conditions that affect a significant proportion of society and that are perceived by a significant number of people as requiring redress by society.

Etzioni's (1976) analysis of social problems emphasizes the subjectivity and variety that abound in the definition of social problems. There are different criteria for deciding what constitutes a social problem, different definitions of a social problem, and many different lists of the major problems in our world. This diversity—stemming in part from different approaches to understanding society, individuals, and the process of social change—creates strong differences of opinion. To what degree can or should social problems be overcome? How should this be accomplished? How should social scientists be involved in this process?

Etzioni (1976) identifies four main approaches to the study of social problems: the *consensus and structural-functional approach*, the *conflict or alienation approach*, the *symbolic interaction approach*, and the *neo-conservative approach*.

The *consensus and structural-functional approach* is usually associated with the American sociologist Talcott Parsons. It emphasizes how the social structures of a society function to meet people's needs. Institutions help people adapt to society (schools socialize children), reach their goals (factories produce material goods), and integrate and maintain the diverse elements of society (government legislates and rules on appropriate behavior). The basic idea is that society must function as an integrated system to meet people's needs. The mechanism for accomplishing this is consensus among the diverse individuals and groups that constitute the society.

A society's norms—its goals and aspirations—are established by its dominant culture. But perhaps a segment of the people are denied equal opportunity to reach these goals. Perhaps one or more of society's basic needs are not being met. Perhaps a sizable number of people do not have adequate food or clothing or shelter. When a significant number of people recognize that conditions depart from society's own norms, the basis exists for the generation of a social issue. Other than seeking consensus, however, the structural-functional approach does not have explicit mechanisms to ameliorate social problems. In general, the social system is thought to function adequately with the expectation of some imbalance in meeting people's needs. Thus, few theorists of this school see the need for radical change in society. On the contrary, they see social problems as failures in socialization due to individual, family, and subcultural difficulties. These problems can be corrected by controlling and resocializing the deviants to conform to society's norms—through prisons to rehabilitate criminals, settlement houses to educate the disadvantaged, and psychotherapy and self-help groups for persons such as drug abusers. The consensus approach looks for the continuing adjustment of society to meet most of the people's needs most of the time.

The *conflict or alienation approach* presents a much more pessimistic picture of contemporary Western society. It argues that fundamental tensions or built-in contradictions exist between classes of people—essentially between the powerful and the powerless—and that these problems can be resolved only through radical changes in society. The founder of modern socialism, Karl Marx, was a proponent of conflict theory; he stressed the conflict between the owners of production (the capitalists) and the servants of production—the workers who are exploited for their labor and alienated from the production process and from the dominant values of society. Thus, the concept of *class* is central to the conflict approach: the working class is controlled by the upper class; consensus around mutual norms is impossible. Social problems are the expected manifestations of the class or power struggle: the powerful few exploit and dehumanize the powerless masses and, in so doing, amass wealth and privileges for themselves.

Although the traditional Marxist view was most relevant to a period following the Industrial Revoltuion, contemporary conflict theorists have broadened this approach to include conflict among collectivities other than classes—racial and regional groups, for example. These theorists see a great deal of both open and suppressed conflict in society, and they see the mechanism of integration as coercion by the society's dominant groups and institutions. There is no place here for consensus. The proposed solution is a significant transformation of society in ways that will share power and reduce or remove inequality among groups. The means for such transformation are public ownership of production and the equitable distribution of wealth—mechanisms to eliminate basic alienation, to destroy the roots of such social problems as crime, unemployment, and family breakdown. Since attempts at change within the system (such as remedial programs) only serve to maintain the status quo, it is only the possibility of revolution someday that gives conflict theorists cause for optimism. One assessment of the effects of Marxist revolutions throughout the world is offered in Box 11.1.

Symbolic interactionism stresses the immediate context in which human behavior occurs (see Chapter 5) and sees social problems as arising from labeling and stigmatization of deviant individuals. Social problems result from difficulties in such elementary processes as interpersonal communication and social approval. If people cannot agree on what is appropriate interaction, or cannot communicate effectively "according to the rules," some will be labeled as deviant, thus creating a social problem. Deranged individuals or delinquents who do not play by the accepted rules of social interaction will find themselves labeled, held accountable, and controlled by appropriate institutions. People suffering from mental disorders who embarrass and offend others will be committed to psychiatric hospitals. People who abuse drugs such as heroin will be labeled as criminals and incarcerated in prisons. Since the difficulties of communication, the ambiguities of meaning, and the presence of social norms will always be with us, social problems may be redefined or reduced, but can never be ultimately resolved. They are part of the price we pay for being human—that is, fallible.

The *neo-conservative approach*, a recent revitalization of classic conservatism, maintains that in a world of scarce resources some of us are destined to be among the elite, others to remain poor. The elites serve the essential entrepreneurial functions of creating economic activity and maintaining society's dominant values. The masses are not exploited or alienated, but yield legitimate power to a variety of elites in return for effective leadership in economic, political, cultural, and intellectual affairs. Social problems only develop when one side or the other fails to maintain its end of the social contract. Social problems result from a breakdown in authority, and deviant behavior—primarily a product of inadequate personalities—requires control, restitution, and rehabilitation. The delinquent is not a product of an inequitable society, but is an immature, impulsive individual who needs discipline and education. The amelioration of these problems requires not change but "more of the same" in terms of greater economic productivity, increased scientific progress, and more effective administration to meet people's needs and manage deviants. If society would function effectively and all individuals were socialized properly, there would be no criminals, mental patients, or drug addicts. The conservative stance appeals to many of the traditional values in Western society, particularly those of individual freedom and economic materialism. Neo-conservatives are neither optimistic nor pessimistic about social change; they think it basically unnecessary.

These varying approaches differ decisively in their definition and resolution of social issues. In some cases, however, it may be possible to combine approaches to create a more powerful model. For example, conflict may be included as an important element of the structural-functional approach, thus blending conflict with consensus in societal decision making. On the other hand, some aspects of different approaches are definitely incompatible. The neo-conservative approach, for instance, opposes the humanistic values inherent in the conflict and

Box 11.1 FOCUS ON THEORY AND RESEARCH
The Conflict Approach to Social Problems

The conflict theory of society, exemplified by Marx, maintains that social problems are the result of class conflict between the powerful and the powerless, the owners and the workers. By removing private ownership of the means of production and vesting it in the workers and the government, the conflict approach aspires to the elimination of poverty, sexism, and other social issues. But what has happened to social problems in countries that have experienced Marxist revolution?

Gerhard Lenski, a sociologist at the University of North Carolina at Chapel Hill, has drawn upon a variety of sources to present a picture of both the successes and the failures of socialist governments throughout the world. Marxist revolutions in Russia, China, Cuba, and so on represent massive experiments in the reorganization of the entire society with the hope of eliminating inequality, exploitation, and social injustice. How well have they fared?

On the success side, Marxist revolutions have demonstrated that modern societies do not require private ownership of production and the free enterprise system to experience rapid economic growth. More significantly, Marxist societies have substantially reduced economic inequality in their countries. For example, the ratio of top salaries to the minimum wage in the Soviet Union is approximately 50 to 1; in Cuba it is about 7 to 1; in the United States it is 300 to 1. This has partly been accomplished by eliminating very large "unearned incomes," that is, incomes derived from capital gains or dividends rather than from salaries. In addition, economic inequality has been reduced by the "social wage," a range of goods and services that are provided free to everyone—health care, education, public transportation, housing, child care.

On the failure side, gains in economic equality appear to be linked to increases in political inequality. Power tends to be monopolized by the elite at the top of the Communist party, and a stratum of political prisoners is created at the bottom. Also, Marxist societies have not reduced the inequalities in the attractiveness of different kinds of work. Many workers remain alienated and dissatisfied, and there is little democracy in the low-pay, low-status occupations. In addition, gross inequalities in all areas exist between rural and urban regions. Finally, there has been little success in creating a new socialist form of human being who is more honest, devoted, committed, and so forth than his or her capitalist counterpart. Social problems such as crime, alcoholism, and family breakdown continue to exist in Marxist societies.

In sum, the amelioration of social problems does not appear to be as simple as the conflict theories maintain. The one exception is poverty, which appears to have been substantially reduced in Marxist societies.

Source: Lenski, G. Marxist experiments in destratification: An appraisal. *Social Forces*, 1978, *57*, 364–383.

structural-functional approaches; these stress the recognition of and respect for the positions of different interest groups. Our recognition of these links and disparities will serve as a way for each of us to better understand and develop our own approach to the social issues of contemporary North American society.

Racism: The Color of Your Skin Makes a Difference

Prejudice is a simplistic, hostile attitude toward a group of people; *discrimination* is overt behavior restricting an individual's rights or access on the basis of membership in a particuar group (see Chapter 8). Seldom are these phenomena of intergroup conflict more severe than between *races*—that is, groups of people with distinctive physical characteristics that are genetically transmitted. Thus, we arrive at a definition of *racism*—a combination of prejudice and discrimination based on the belief that race is the primary determinant of human capabilities and that racial differences produce an inherent superiority of one race over others. A belief in racial superiority justifies hostile prejudice and blatant discrimination against less powerful racial groups. Characteristic of racism is a minority status of the target group, and their oppression or subordination by society's dominant racial group. Racism is thus the strongest expression of ethnocentrism to be found in contemporary society (see Chapter 8).

According to Stark (1975), race is the primary basis for group subordination in contemporary United States society. Prejudice and discrimination toward religious groups—usually toward Catholics and Jews by the Protestant majority—has declined substantially in the last half-century. In Canada, race is also the basis for some of the most severe intergroup conflicts, although regional differences are also important sources of conflict. Cultural differences between English- and French-speaking Canadians have become aggravated to the point where the political separation of the predominantly French-speaking province of Quebec is a distinct possibility.

In the United States, the prime targets of racism are three nonwhite minorities: blacks, Hispanics (primarily Mexican-Americans or Chicanos and Puerto Ricans), and American Indians. Stark does not include Asian-Americans; because of their comparative economic equality with white Americans, hostility toward Asian-Americans has greatly subsided. In Canada, Canadian Indians are the most subordinated group. The small black population, largely concentrated in Nova Scotia, are the so-called Forgotten Canadians who experience a clear socioeconomic disadvantage (Henry, 1973). In both countries, other racial and cultural groups, particularly immigrant groups, are also targets of discrimination—but to a far less devastating extent.

Symptoms of Racism. What are the symptoms of prejudice and discrimination toward racial minorities? What conditions of their lives express this subjugation and oppression? It hardly matters where we begin. In the United States, there are the issues of discriminatory employment, education, income, housing, and the administration of justice (Stark, 1975). The depressing Canadian scene is no better when we look at the disadvantaged black minority (see Henry, 1973), and at the glaring discrepancies between Canadian Indians and the white majority on all measures of socioeconomic well-being (Statistics Canada, 1977).

Education has often been cited as the bootstraps by which disadvantaged individuals have pulled themselves up toward economic and social equality (assuming that you have a pair of boots to begin with). But the real picture is not promising. Blacks, Chicanos, Puerto Ricans, and Indians in the United States complete fewer years of schooling than their white counterparts. Of all racial minorities, Indians in Canada are victims of the greatest lack of formal education. The majority never reach high school, and only a tiny number attend universities or other postsecondary educational institutions. If education is the ladder to success, the rungs certainly seem farther apart for racial minorities in North America.

Since education underlies employment, it is not surprising that minority groups not only have the highest unemployment rates but also fill most of the menial and low-paying jobs. A higher proportion of blacks, Chicanos, and Puerto Ricans are in blue-collar occupations and service positions, compared to white-collar occupations and professional, administrative positions. In addition, discrimination may occur in trying to get a job, in wages and promotions, and in keeping a job (Stark, 1975). Unemployment and underemployment are prevalent among all racial minorities; but for Indians in both the United States and Canada, this problem reaches staggering proportions. Often, the majority of potential wage earners on Canadian Indian reservations are unemployed.

This lack of meaningful and gainful activity is represented in all related social indices. Education and employment, of course, correlate closely with income. Many members of racial minorities live in abject poverty. Most blacks and Hispanics are invariably poorer than the white majority in terms of average income. North American Indians endure the greatest hardship, with alarming proportions living below the poverty line. Consequently, minority groups are overrepresented as recipients of social welfare services, most of which are designed to provide basic necessities rather than to move the recipients out of the poverty cycle. The same cycle locks racial minorities into conditions of inadequate housing and poor health. On Canadian Indian reservations, for example, most homes still do not have indoor toilets. Most devastating is that the infant mortality rate among Canadian Indians is *more than double* that of the non-Native majority.

Members of minority groups are also overrepresented in the workings of the criminal justice system. They are more likely to be apprehended, convicted, and sentenced to longer terms with less likelihood of parole (Stark, 1975). This is a vicious cycle, since contact with criminal justice system compounds itself; for example, a person with a record often receives a lengthier sentence. In Canada, the high proportion of Indians in prison has become a national disgrace. (In my home province of Saskatchewan, most of the people in prisons are Natives—although this group constitutes *less than 15 percent* of the general population.) In sum, every economic and social indicator cries out against the subjugation and devastation of these racial minorities.

The pervasive and dramatic symptoms of racism alert us to the realization that prejudice and discrimination are not simply matters of individual attitudes and behaviors. The very institutions of society themselves—the educational system, the business sector, the criminal justice system—may be permeated with formal regulations and informal social norms which limit the opportunities of a person because of race. This is *institutional racism*, which combines with prejudice at the individual level to further restrict the choices available to minority group members (Oskamp, 1977). Examples of institutional racism include laws prohibiting interracial marriages, informal agreements by colleges to limit minority enrollment, and attempts by real estate firms to maintain segregated neighborhoods. In the area of employment, the relatively lower educational attainment of minority group members may place them at a disadvantage in obtaining jobs even when the jobs do not require the knowledge gained in formal education (see Squires, 1979). It is therefore difficult to see how equality of opportunity can become a reality in an unequal society. The privileged members of society will always be able to provide their children with better skills and contacts than will the disadvantaged.

Institutional racism is difficult to document, and various pieces of legislation in the United States and Canada are designed to limit its impact. Informal expectations, however, are both powerful and difficult to control. If, for example, a corporation has an unwritten rule against black managers, it may appoint "tokens" who have little power or respect within the organization. In these ways, institutional racism serves to support and justify individual prejudice and discrimination.

Racial Segregation or Integration? Social psychologists have been more concerned with strategies to reduce the effects of racism than with documenting its social correlates. Similarly, as racism has grown as a social issue, politicians and other persons with decision-making power have struggled with ways by which racial minorities and the white majority can better relate to one another. *Democratic pluralism* proposes that diverse racial and cultural groups can live together harmoniously and can share the fruits of their integrated labor. One way social psychologists can further this goal is by studying intergroup attitudes within the multi-ethnic contest (for example, Berry, 1975). However, in its extreme independent form, pluralism may lead to secession—a condition wherein groups live separate geographic and cultural lives. On the other hand, *assimilation*—the opposite of pluralism—supports the absorption of racial minorities, racially and/ or culturally, into the dominant majority. The crucial question facing North America's racial minorities is the degree to which they wish to be assimilated or integrated. For the white majority, the parallel question is how and to what extent this will happen. The controversy surrounding these questions has generated one of the most powerful social issues of our time.

In his analysis of the controversy surrounding racial integration, social psychologist Thomas Pettigrew (1971) poses this basic question: Should black and white Americans choose to live separately or together? His treatment of the issue also applies to the dominant North American stance about other racial minorities, particularly Hispanics and Indians: many members of these minorities already live in separation from whites—whether in a black urban ghetto, a Chicano *barrio*, or an isolated Indian reservation. The persistence of racial segregation in metropolitan areas is especially strong. Based on United States census data, Schnare (1978) found that only 12 percent of whites and 14 percent of blacks lived in what could be considered integrated neighborhoods (having 6–30 percent black residents).

Pettigrew points out that the long-standing attempts by white segregationists to keep races apart are now being paralleled by calls from black segregationsists and other minority leaders for separation and autonomy. These similar positions, however, are based on somewhat different assumptions. Segregationists on both sides subscribe to the comfortable assumption that members of either race are happiest when they are with members of their own group rather than with a racially mixed group. However, white segregationists also assume that minorities are racially inferior and that contact of any form between the races will not only reduce the quality of the "superior" white race but will inevitably lead to racial conflict. Minority segregationists, on the other hand, assume that it is the responsibility of white liberals rather than minority members to confront white racists and that racial minorities have to gain a sense of autonomy and power before contact can be equal and beneficial. Many minority segregationists have an additional goal: to preserve their identity and cultural heritage—rather than merely assimilate the values of white culture.

Pettigrew questions separatist assumptions on the basis of social-psychological theory and research. While it is true that racial contact may produce anxiety, separation prevents groups from learning more about the shared beliefs and values that underlie interpersonal and intergroup attraction. Furthermore, isolation over time may lead to the evolution of genuine differences that work against future interracial contact. Racial segregation is thus a cumulative process that feeds upon itself, resulting in a preference for continued isolation and a continuing sense of awkwardness about interracial contact.

The solution is not to continue separation, but to foster intergroup contact under conditions of equal status and cooperation. The white supremacist's assumption that minorities are racially inferior must be confronted directly through contact with members of these groups (see Chapter 8). White liberals can attack racist attitudes and support minority positions, but only minority members can confront institutionalized racism and engage in the direct contact that will slowly erode racist attitudes, behavior, and policies. Some white liberals, particularly those who have little interracial experience, may actually harm the process of integration by engaging in *reverse discrimination*—treating minority group members better than they treat majority group members (Dutton, 1976).

How can we best challenge the assumptions that support segregation and work toward integration? Pettigrew (1971) relates personal and group autonomy to the dichotomy of living racially separate or together. Figure 11.1 is an adaptation of his diagram relating to black and other racial minorities.

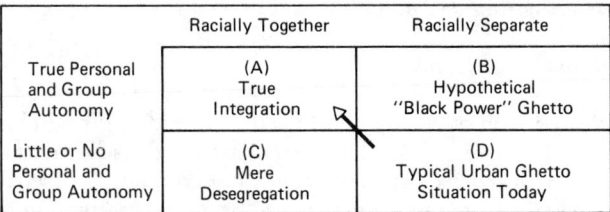

	Racially Together	Racially Separate
True Personal and Group Autonomy	(A) True Integration	(B) Hypothetical "Black Power" Ghetto
Little or No Personal and Group Autonomy	(C) Mere Desegregation	(D) Typical Urban Ghetto Situation Today

Figure 11.1 **Racial Contact or Separation in Relation to Personal and Group Autonomy.** Source: Pettigrew (1971).

The combination of dimensions results in four possible conditions. Position A—*true integration*—is the humanistic goal shared by white and minority group liberals: that all races can have a sense of autonomy and independence while living in a racially interdependent world of institutional integration and cross-racial friendship.

Position D—*typical racial isolation*—represents the reality of today: that minorities are segregated and have a limited sense of autonomy and power to interact with or confront the dominant group on an equal basis.

Position B—*racial isolation with power*—represents the stance of minority segregationists: that separation is required until the minority has developed its autonomy and power to the point where it can successfully challenge white dominance.

Position C—*mere desegregation*—represents the common situation of inter-racial contact: although institutions are biracial, there is little cross-racial accept-ance. The usual dominant, patronizing approach by whites fuels the self-fulfilling prophecy of minority inferiority and dependence.

The immense challenge facing integrationists is how to get from Position D (isolation) to Position A (integration) without passing through the less effective routes of mere desegregation or minority separation. The direct route, favored by social psychology, provides the sense of shared autonomy and power that only equal and cooperative contact can provide. In a democratic society, this route implies a policy not of total integration, but of providing a genuine choice between separation and integration, between the images of the ghetto as a racial prison or as an area of ethnic choice. Obviously, this requires a massive effort to enrich racial ghettos to the point where ghetto life becomes more viable and ghetto residents develop the necessary sense of racial autonomy and pride. Although the violence of the racial struggles of the late 1960s was not repeated in the 1970s, blacks and whites remain in a clear conflict situation (Ashmore, 1976). Without significant gains in racial equality, the prognosis for the 1980s is not good.

Pettigrew proposes a strategy of mixed integration and enrichment that would move racial groups together simultaneously on the two dimensions of Figure 11.1 Even though Pettigrew's analysis was made more than a decade ago, the conclusions drawn from social-psychological theory and research are just as valid today, evidenced by our numerous programs designed to achieve integra-tion. We will look at school desegregation and its effects in a later section of this chapter. But the vital question remains to be answered: Can we learn to live harmonious and productive lives together, or will we continue to exist as racial islands in a sea of ignorance, prejudice, and inequality?

Sexism: The Injustice of Gender

I have been blessed with two bright and beautiful children. If you have assumed that they are girls, you are correct. The asssociation of the adjective *beautiful* with the female gender illustrates the way our society commonly describes the sexes differently. If I had said that my children were "bright and active," you more likely would have assumed that they were boys. The fact is that they are bright, beautiful, *and* active. As a parent concerned about the social issue of sexism, I am working hard to keep them that way.

I refuse to devalue my children because they are female—something that many social forces try to get me to do. Even the female nurses at the hospital where my second daughter was born kidded my wife and me about "coming back for a boy." Little could they understand that as a parent I have no preference for one sex over the other. However, as a person concerned about social justice and equal treatment for both sexes, I do have a preference. It is a preference for helping to socialize my children as persons who reject sexism and work toward equality for all women and men.

Sexism is similar to racism: simply substitute "sex" for "race" and you have a definition. That is, *sexism* is a combination of prejudice and discrimination based on the belief that sexual differences produce an inherent superiority of one sex over the other—most typically, male superiority over females. Thus, women throughout the world are treated as a minority group, even though they outnumber males due to a marginally higher birth rate and a significantly longer life span.

Male dominance is an integral part of human history. However, technological and cultural changes have now made sexual equality a distinct possibility, thus casting sexual inequality and sexism as a social problem requiring redress (Stark, 1975). The growing demand for equality has become expressed as the social movement of women's liberation, dedicated to changing the basic conception of male and female and to eliminating the prejudice and discrimination of sexism. To understand this phenomenon, we must look at the symptoms of sexism and the conditions of inequality that underlie this potent social issue.

The prejudice of sexism is best expressed by sexist stereotypes—that is, oversimplified beliefs about the nature of men and women. Ask yourself these typical questions: What do you think most men are like? How would you describe the average woman? What are the major differences between the sexes? Social researchers, asking such questions, have come up with a considerable amount of agreement on sex-role stereotypes. For example, females are generally described as warm, expressive, and passive; males, as insensitive, independent, and aggressive. Women are generally regarded as person-oriented, with a sensitivity to feelings and an ability to be tactful; men are generally regarded as task-oriented, with a high degree of motivation and competence to take initiative and responsibility (see Broverman, Vogel, Broverman, Clarkson & Rosenkrantz, 1972).

As with other stereotypes, there is likely to be a kernel of truth to these widespread beliefs. Males and females *are* reared and socialized differently and do tend to exhibit different behaviors. The real problem lies in our *evaluation* of stereotypic characteristics—that different people make different judgments about these qualities. Qualities typically associated with men—activeness, competitiveness, and ambitiousness—tend to be more valued than qualities associated with women—submissiveness, quietness, and tact. These stereotypes and evaluations are held not only by males (who may benefit most from them) but by females as well—a clear symptom of the existence of sexism.

The discriminatory aspect of sexism flows from the traditional role expectations for women to serve as homemakers. The biological imperative—that it is the female who bears and nurses the child—lends a natural basis to this division of labor in which women take primary responsibility for the home. In addition, the larger stature and greater physical strength of the male provides a biological basis for his traditional involvement in occupational labor outside the home. For centuries these differences—determining the characteristic social roles of men and women and supporting sex-role stereotypes—have persisted, even into the modern age when the conditions of life are undergoing radical changes. Hence, women and men continue to be discriminated against in ways that no longer have a biological or a rational basis.

Job discrimination against women is the most obvious issue facing North American society. Women have consistently been restricted to traditional "feminine occupations": secretarial work, nursing, teaching, and the like (see O'Leary, 1974; Henshel, 1973). They have been discouraged or barred from traditional masculine occupations, such as machinist or physician, on the basis that they are neither physically nor psychologically suited for such work. Even those who have overcome prejudice and discrimination to enter the more lucrative and powerful masculine occupations usually face the discrimination of lower pay, fewer promotions, and restricted opportunities for advancement. Women generally earn only about 60 percent of what men earn—a discrepancy that persists despite equal education and similar occuaptions. The reasons? Perhaps a male employer cannot believe that a female employee will give as high a priority to her career as her male counterpart (see Rosen & Jerdee, 1974). Or perhaps the competent, successful woman becomes the target of competitive and hostile devaluations by her male peers (see Hagen & Kahn, 1975). Despite these and other reasons, the bottom line is this: male-dominated society exerts enormous pressure on women to remain in traditional roles and to meet the expectations of sexist stereotypes.

What about the causes of sexism? Where do the prejudice and discrimination against women stem from? Biological differences clearly affect child-rearing roles during the offspring's infant years, but beyond that there is little hard evidence that physiological differences affect the psychological or behavioral qualities of women versus men. Although the effect of *physiological* factors—such as the effect of sex hormones on male and female characteristics—is not yet conclusive, research on sex-related *psychological* differences supports certain distinctions and disproves others (Deaux, 1976; Maccoby & Jacklin, 1974; Wittig & Peterson, 1979). For example, Maccoby and Jacklin (1974), reviewing a large number of studies, conclude that only four sex-related differences appear to be true: that girls evidence greater verbal ability; boys evidence greater visual-spatial ability; boys evidence greater mathematical ability; and boys are more aggressive. Some commonly held differences that are either doubtful or possibly false include the notions that boys are more competitive, and that girls are more suggestible, lower in achievement motivation, and more sociable. Even on dimensions where males and females do seem to differ, there is a great deal of overlap between the sexes. For example, many boys are high in verbal ability, and many girls excel in mathematics. Thus, decisions based on group differences are highly discriminatory and unjust to the individual. There is simply no empirical support for exaggerations of sex-related differences or for decisions based on group membership alone; more important, there is no justification for such behavior in terms of the humanistic value of fair treatment.

Given the limited utility of biological explanations for sex-related differences, investigators have turned their attention to social-psychological processes that might account for sexist attitudes and behavior. Sex-role stereotypes, a starting point for sexism, are supported and advanced by other insidious mechanisms—most notably, the self-fulfilling prophecy, biased perception and evaluation, and inaccurate attribution.

The *self-fulfilling prophecy* means that women and men behave in ways that confirm their sex-role expectations (see Chapter 6). For example, if women are treated in ways that induce passivity and subordination, they are less likely to take initiative and seize responsibility and power. When they do take responsibility, their accomplishments (in the perspective of male-versus-female effort) may be devalued (see Mischel, 1974). Their success is more often attributed to luck or other situational factors rather than to true ability (Deaux, 1976). Unfortunately, these biased evaluations generally come from both males *and* females—reason enough for a wholesale reorientation of society's values, judgments, and attitudes.

In a review of studies on women in management positions, Terborg (1977) concludes that although women are being given increased opportunities, both overt and subtle discrimination continue to limit their achievement and advancement. Rosabeth Moss Kantor's *Men and Women of the Corporation* gives us an illuminating real-world account of the contrasting organizational constraints and processes under which men and women must operate (see Box 11.2).

Social psychologists have placed most responsibility for the cause of sexism on the process of socialization—more precisely, on the socialization of sex roles (see Chapter 2). The predominant view is that sex roles are learned and passed on from generation to generation, often in the face of changing conditions that make traditional conceptions obsolete. Through the social learning processes of reinforcement, modeling, and so on, children learn to display the behaviors appropriate to their sex. Their growing sense of sexual identity gradually forms an essential component of their self-concept. The power of the family as the main socialization force is augmented by the major institutions of society—schools, churches, businesses; these too show a clear preference for sex-role stereotyping.

Although change is occurring, the educational system has consistently shown a tendency to reflect and reinforce traditional sex-role stereotypes: most preschool and schoolbooks for children still tend to glorify the boy's pursuits as active, adventurous, and varied; the fictional girl's behavior, as typically passive, supportive, and restricted (see Oliver, 1974; Weitzman, Eifler, Hokada & Ross, 1972). In junior high school, different curricula, especially in vocational education, have girls taking traditional female courses such as home economics while boys study metalwork and graphic arts. Furthermore, vocational counseling in high schools and colleges often influences women toward traditional female careers (Wirtenburg & Nakamura, 1976).

The mass media, particularly commercial television, strongly supports the unbalanced picture of sex-related behavior. For example, content analysis of television commercials found that men were predominantly portrayed as the

Box 11.2   FOCUS ON RESEARCH
Sex Differences in Organizational Power and Opportunity

Karl Marx, the founder of socialism, and Adam Smith, the famous advocate of capitalism, held one key assumption in common about the world of work: the job makes the person. Social psychologist Rosabeth Moss Kanter suggests that the large modern corporation is the ultimate "people-producer." The organizational structure forms individuals' sense of themselves and their possibilities. This is especially true of the roles typically enacted by men versus women.

The large corporation is mainly composed of two groups of employees: the managerial, professional, and technical personnel; and the clerical and service personnel. Census data indicate a clear sex segregation between these two groupings: males constitute over 96 percent of all managers earning more than $15,000 per year; 98 percent of secretarial positions are filled by women.

Following several years of research and consultation with a large multinational industrial corporation, Kanter has provided a comprehensive description and analysis of how organizational structure shapes individual behavior and growth. Managers are subject to strong social conformity in order to advance. Organizational uncertainties lead senior managers to promote subordinates whom they can trust, that is, who are similar to them. This creates a closed circle among the managerial ranks into which only the rare woman gains entry. She is then often regarded as a token (a representative of the female sex rather than an individual) and can experience severe difficulties in peer acceptance and in being herself.

The predominantly female clerical staff members earn low pay and have little upward mobility. Their status is determined primarily by their bosses' status. This results in patriarchal relationships in which secretaries are wedded to a single boss and in which timid, emotional, and praise-addicted behavior is the norm.

The differences in opportunity and power between the managerial and clerical roles is phenomenal. The high opportunity of managers has its costs (anxiety, overwork), but the low opportunity of the clerical role saps any motivation to improve the situation. Managers wield power largely as a result of their role activities and alliances. Clericals experience powerlessness, and turn to rigid, rules-minded, possessive styles as a means of protection. The behavior of men and women is therefore determined by the traditional role structure of the organization.

The inequitable position of men and women in organizations needs to be addressed by policies and programs that enhance opportunity, distribute power, and balance numbers of males and females in the different groupings. Many people, especially women, are more capable than their organizational roles ever allow them to be.

Source: Kanter, R. M. *Men and women of the corporation*. New York: Basic Books, 1977.

expert; women were the willing buyers of products, largely motivated by a high need for social approval (MacArthur & Resko, 1975). Similarly, Manes and Melnyk's (1974) study of typical entertainment programs on Canadian television (which has a high proportion of American content) found that females who were portrayed as successful job holders were consistently depicted as having poor social relations with males, with a much higher rate of unsuccessful marriages than traditional female models—an obvious inhibition of achievement-oriented behavior in females.

The consistent picture in North American society is that every major social institution works to keep women in a subordinate and submissive position. Generally held values and beliefs create institutional norms and rules that create barriers to the full and equal participation of women (Zellman, 1976). For example, an emphasis on individual achievement has created rules in the workplace that demand a continuous work life and are compatible with men's rather than women's family responsibilities. The total effect of such barriers is that women tend to end up in segregated, low-paying, often part-time jobs for which they are overqualified. It is little wonder that a major social movement has evolved to combat sexist stereotypes and lobby for the equal treatment of women and men.

A major social force in reducing sexism over the past two decades has been the women's movement. Searching for the roots of the women's movement in the United States, Stark (1975) goes back to female abolitionists of the pre–Civil War period—women who successfully helped win the vote for black men only to find that same right denied to women of any race. Following a strong involvement in the settlement house movement (see Chapter 10), women activists turned their attention again to voting rights, securing that right in the early twentieth century in the United States, Canada, England, and other Western countries. From approximately 1920 to 1960, the women's movement was largely inactive, and the fight for equality lost ground. But growing inequities—between education and pay, for example—combined with other conditions to bring about the rebirth of the movement as a potent social force in the 1960s and 1970s. While technological advancements reduced the demands of the homemaking role, a decreasing birth rate signaled a greater freedom for women from the demands of child rearing. As more and more women joined the labor force, this change combined with a generally rising social conscience to bring to light the gross inequities experienced by women in almost all occupational roles. The publication of Betty Friedan's *The Feminist Mystique* (1963) seemed to capture the spirit of the movement and served as a signal for a social and political onslaught against the symptoms and causes of sexism.

The initial gains brought about by the women's movement—and, to a much lesser extent, the men's liberation movement—have been significant. Political pressure has resulted in the enactment and application of legislation that prohibits certain types of discrimination against women: the Civil Rights Act in the United States, and the Canadian Bill of Rights. Countless women have filed and won lawsuits against employers who practice discrimination. Affirmative action programs by government departments and employers have reduced discrimination in the hiring and promotion of female workers. The Equal Rights Amendment in the United States (not passed into law as of this writing) would guarantee equal rights to all persons in all aspects of life.

Despite these important gains, the fight for sexual equality will have to continue for some time to significantly reduce, reverse, or eliminate the effects of centuries of sexism. It is a complex and resistant social issue that will not easily fade away with the enactment of legal sanctions (see Hennig & Jardim, 1977).

Laws and policies are a leading edge in the process of social change, but the entire socialization process must slowly be rendered just and equal in its treatment of both sexes. In the same way that females need to be socialized to take initiative and responsibility, males need to learn to express feelings and communicate their compassion for others. In the family, the last bastion of sexism, the traditional roles of mother and father must change, with a more equal sharing of child rearing, homemaking, and employment activities between the sexes. But perhaps more important is the need for adult men and women to reassess their sex-role behavior and attempt to enact and accept behavior that is characteristic of both sexes rather than just one.

This intriguing possibility is well expressed in the social-psychological concept of *androgyny*, defined by Sandra Bem (1975) as the possession of approximately equal portions of feminine and masculine characteristics. Femininity and masculinity are seen not as two opposing characteristics, but as separate dimensions that may be complementary. Thus, a person may be high in one dimension and low in the other, or high in both, or low in both. The androgynous individual is high in both dimensions, exhibiting both "feminine" warmth and expression and "male" ambition and independence (see Table 11.1). Recently, however, Helmreich, Spence, and Holahan (1979) have questioned whether measures of androgyny are really measures of sex roles or more simply just measures of expressive and instrumental traits of personality that are only minimally related to sex-role behavior.

Through such practice techniques as consciousness-raising or assertiveness training in small groups, women and men can learn to understand and change their behavior in ways that increase their degree of androgyny, that is, both their expressiveness and independence. Ideally, such individuals will then serve as the role models for new generations of children who are free from the social chains of sexism, and are able to respond to their environment in a much freer, more adaptive, and rewarding fashion.

Table 11.1   THE CONCEPT OF PSYCHOLOGICAL ANDROGYNY

Do you consider yourself to be:

Self-reliant?	Helpful?
Independent?	Conscientious?
Assertive?	Affectionate?
Forceful?	Sympathetic?
Analytical?	Understanding?
Dominant?	Compassionate?
Aggressive?	Soft-spoken?
Individualistic?	Warm?
Ambitious?	Tender?
Competitive?	Gentle?

If you describe yourself more in terms like those on the left, you would tend to have a high masculinity score on measures of sex-role behavior. Conversely, the descriptors on the right usually represent femininity. If you describe yourself using terms from both columns, you are likely expressing androgynous behavior in your relations with others.

Source: Bem (1975).

However, we must realize that focusing on individual characteristics and socialization is a person-centered approach to understanding and reducing sexual discrimination against women. Situation-centered explanations that stress characteristics of the organizational environment—norms, attitudes, biased practices—must also be considered (partly in interaction with person characteristics) to understand reasons for the small number of women in positions of power and to correct this situation (Riger & Galligan, 1980). A truly social-psychological approach is required.

Poverty: The Inequitable Distribution of Wealth

The injustices of racism and sexism are linked to a wider inequality of North American society: the major social issue of poverty. To be female and black or Indian greatly increases the probability that you will also be poor. But poverty is not defined simply by its link with other injustices. It is an inherent part of the societal and economic structures and the individual attitudes and shared values on which North American society is built.

There are two common ways to define poverty. We can estimate the yearly income required for subsistence; then we can state that anything less amounts to poverty, that is, falls below the poverty line. But the apparent simplicity of this definition is deceptive (James, 1972): What really is subsistence? What is a necessity? A luxury? The cost of basic necessities—food, housing, clothing, health care, and the like—varies widely from region to region and situation to situation. A rural family living in poverty may find cheap housing and may be able to trade services for food; but a poor family in an urban ghetto is locked into a situation that demands hard cash for the same necessities. These considerations and further analyses led James (1972) to conclude that the subsistence definition has been adopted primarily because of its simplicity rather than because it is a true indication of poverty.

Poverty can also be defined as a disparity or deprivation relative to the total distribution of income in society—the gap between the "haves" and the "have-nots." This clearer approach emphasizes the inequity between the poor and the average or well-to-do—a definition with much wider ramifications for change in North American society (James, 1972). It does not rely on an absolute estimate that might indicate improvement when in fact the gap is widening (Stark, 1975). Reducing poverty (as defined this way) requires an extensive restructuring of the distribution of wealth. This entails major changes in the social, economic, and political order, as well as in the dominant values on which this order is based. In contrast, the subsistence definition implies less extensive change: Society would simply provide everyone with minimal purchasing power, either through full employment and/or guaranteed income.

By either definition the extent of poverty in affluent North America is as unbelievable as it is unacceptable. Based on subsistence level, approximately 20 percent of the population lives in poverty. Based on a scale of relative deprivation, the poorest 20 percent of the population receives approximately 5 percent of the total available income; the richest 5 percent receives close to 20 percent of that income. Even more disheartening is that, despite overall economic progress, this sizable gap is widening. The rich are indeed getting richer; the poor, still poorer.

Canadian census data, for example, indicate that in 1951 the poorest 20 percent of the population shared 4.4 percent of the total national income; by 1975, this share had dropped to 4.0 percent. Meanwhile, the richest 20 percent moved form sharing 41 percent in 1951 to 42 percent in 1975. On the surface, these appear to be small differences—but only because the situation could not get much more extreme. Such figures actually tend to underestimate the real pervasiveness of poverty. Due to alienation, transiency, and a resistance to surveys, many poor people are never counted in official estimates of poverty. Furthermore, many people living just above the official subsistence level can barely provide their children with the proper nutrition, shelter, and social environment necessary to improve their lives. People farther below the poverty line live in utter destitution, with almost no hope of change. To make this deplorable situation worse still, rising inflation further erodes the ability of the poor to better their condition.

Who are the poor people in North America? Can they be identified by age, sex, race, or location (James, 1972; Stark, 1975)? The poor—those living below the poverty line—tend to be the old (over 65) and the young (under 18). The aged poor include not only those who have been poor all their lives but people with inadequate retirement incomes. They cannot meet basic needs or major health crises, especially as dollars dwindle in the face of inflation. About 40 percent of the poor are children—a clear majority of people receiving welfare. The young are often members of larger, mother-led families—a point that leads us directly to the second correlate of poverty: being female. Families with a female head of the household (the family's wage earner or welfare recipient) make up more than half of the families in poverty. Since, at best, this female receives only 60 percent of the income of her male counterpart, her inability to earn an equitable wage directly contributes to poverty in North America.

The inequity of poverty is further compounded by racial and ethnic group status. As we have already noted, blacks, native Indians, and other minority groups tend to receive less income than the white majority. Most poor people in North American are white simply because whites are the largest group in the total population; but a much larger percentage of minority groups live below the poverty line. While only about one out of ten whites lives in poverty, about one of every *three* nonwhites is poor. On many Indian reservations, the majority of people subsist on incomes that pale in comparison to the national average. In general, a large proportion of nonwhites in rural settings, particularly farm families, are poor. Poverty is all around us, in all settings—but if you are nonwhite, the chances are far greater that you will live in destitution.

The overall picture characteristically portrays the poor as nonwhite, dependent children in mother-led families. But it is a mistake to equate the poor with welfare recipients, since less than half of those living in poverty receive assistance. The poor are varied and the causes of poverty are varied, pointing up the futility of simple solutions. The potential sources of inequality and poverty can be identified at all levels of analysis, from the societal to the individual (Stark, 1975). Where we place the cause has important implications for policies and programs of change that might be adopted to alleviate poverty.

At the societal level, we must consider the dominant economic system and how that society usually functions. In the capitalist economies of both the United

States and Canada, the means of production are privately owned and the distribution of wealth is governed by competition—by the processes of supply and demand. In this context, society gives greater rewards to roles that are more demanding and harder to fill, thus sanctioning an unbalanced reward system that is seen as unequal but justified. It is thus expected and accepted that ownership and wealth will not be evenly distributed, and that inequality will exist among people.

If capitalism is identified as the basic cause of poverty in North America, this implies that poverty can be eliminated only by changing the economic system itself. This is true if poverty is defined as relative deprivation, for the mechanics of private ownership and the competitive market will always produce inequality. But if we adopt a subsistence definition of poverty, the context shifts. Then capitalism can be seen as overcoming poverty by returning adequate resources to the poor—even though the returns to the rich will still be far greater.

The major alternative to capitalism is socialism, an economic system in which the means of production are publicly owned by government or cooperatives (see Chapter 9), and a planned economy or market system distributes wealth according to need rather than ability, birthright, or luck. Thus, socialism does not eliminate inequality. It only diminishes the range of inequality, reducing the numbers of both the poor and the rich. Within this smaller range, the greater rewards still go to roles that are more difficult to fill. However, there is less chance that these inequalities will be exploited for the personal gain that is fundamental to capitalism.

According to Stark (1975), most social scientists agree that capitalist societies could function with much less inequality than now exists, but the fundamental issue is the *basis* of social inequalities. When inequalities are based on race, sex, and other group characteristics, the society is seen as defective. When equality of opportunity and reward for merit are the principles of wealth distribution, then both capitalism and socialism are in some agreement. However only socialism—with its dictum "From each according to his or her ability; to each according to his or her need"—has the potential for significantly reducing inequity and relative disparity. Since the government decides what people's abilities and needs are, those actively involved in politics have considerable power, thus potentially causing greater political inequality to bring about economic equality (see Box 11.1).

Our model of society determines how we interpret poverty and how we believe it can be reduced or eliminated. Etzioni (1976) illustrates the major approaches to understanding society by analyzing the social problem of poverty. The structural-functional approach tends to see the behavior of the poor as dysfunction or maladaptive; poverty, therefore, is deviance that must be tolerated. The conflict approach disagrees, maintaining that poverty is functional to the operation of society: the poor yield a pool of cheap labor, provide work for certain middle-class professionals (such as social workers), and absorb the continuing costs of growth and expansion. This argument contends that if poverty were not functional it would have been eliminated a long time ago. Gans (1972), for instance, documents fifteen functions that poverty serves for American society. He notes that the strongest alternatives to poverty are dysfunctional to the affluent since they require some redistribution of wealth and power. His conclusions mirror those of the conflict and alienation approaches that call for major societal changes to reduce poverty (see Box 11.3).

Marxist thinkers—one wing of the alienation camp—see the basic cause of poverty in capitalism and its stratification of society into grossly unequal positions. Symbolic interactionists see poverty as a label placed on some members of society, stigmatizing and profoundly affecting them in degrading and demeaning ways in their interactions with others. Neo-conservatives, supporting the capitalist economic system, do not perceive inequality in the distribution of wealth as a problem. For them, subsistence poverty is a greatly exaggerated problem that will be eliminated by greater economic productivity that will raise everyone's standard of living. Thus, the implications for change generated by these different models run the full gamut—from a fundamental reorganization of economic power in society to a reaffirmation of the existing order.

We must also look at the dominant values of American and Canadian society that underlie poverty. Stark (1975) identifies the "ideology of individualism"—a support for freedom of the individual within a highly self-centered and competitive economic system in which the successful have no responsibility for the losers. The related strong belief in egalitarianism maintains that all should have equal opportunity regardless of birth, and therefore all ought to be successful. That some are poor is a result of personal inadequacy rather than defects in the system. As "proof" that individualism is best, this approach points to economic progress and social mobility, wherein people improve or worsen their position in society.

James (1972) also identifies materialistic individualism as one of the values underlying poverty. The liberal belief that individuals must be free to pursue private gain without government restrictions has strongly shaped attitudes and policies toward the poor. In addition, the pervasiveness of ethnocentrism (see Chapter 8), particularly as expressed in racism, has justified the discrimination that results in an inordinate proportion of minority group members living in poverty. James concludes that many minority members live in double jeopardy. Racism and discrimination plunge most of them into poverty; then, because they are poor, materialistic individualism further discriminates against them.

In an affluent society, the majority (being well-off) has no personal stake in changing the economic order; in fact, the well-to-do have a clear stake in maintaining the existing order. Salancik (1975) demonstrated how proposed social changes are related to the values we associate with groups living on different income levels. For example, the values promoted by shifting government spending from military purposes to urban assistance are more prevalent among poor people; but a social change that promotes professional and managerial jobs for women is related more to the values of higher income groups.

We can point to other factors, below the societal level, that appear to contribute to poverty (Stark, 1975; Etzioni, 1976), although the validity of these factors is not certain. The labeling of the poor, for instance, may lead to a stigma, of disrepute, placing them outside normal society and linking them to other forms of deviance—including crime, drug addiction, and mental illness—that are overrepresented in this group. Among the poor, typical norms and social roles may create learned responses, such as dependence, that perpetuate the "culture of

Box 11.3   FOCUS ON THEORY
The Functions of Poverty in American Society

According to sociologist Robert Merton, *functions* are consequences that aid the adaptation or adjustment of a social system or in economic terms have benefits for that system. *Dysfunctions* are consequences that lessen adaptation or result in costs. Events or items are seldom functional for an entire society, but are usually functional for some groups and dysfunctional for others. Herbert Gans of Columbia University has provided a functional analysis of the existence of poverty in American society.

Gans maintains that poverty is not generally dysfunctional for society, but indeed persists because it serves positive functions for many groups. Here is a sample of some of the fifteen positive functions he identifies:

- Poverty guarantees that society's "dirty work" is done—the menial, grubby, dead-end, underpaid jobs. The poor constitute a low-wage labor pool that is willing, that is, unable to be unwilling, to perform these tasks. Without this, many economic activities—restaurants, the garment industry, agriculture—could not exist in their present form.
- The poor subsidize many activities that benefit the affluent—by receiving low wages they enable those who are better off to consume and invest at higher rates. The domestic servant, for example, frees up many affluent women (and men) for a variety of professional, cultural, and civic activities. The poor also pay a higher proportion of their income in taxes than the affluent.
- Poverty creates many jobs for numerous occupations that serve the poor, or protect society from them. Criminology, penology, and the police serve the poor as a majority of their clientele. Social workers, public health specialists, social scientists, and journalists would all have less to do without the poor.
- The poor buy goods and services that others do not want, thus prolonging their economic usefulness. Day-old bread, secondhand clothes, used cars, old and/or incompetent lawyers, doctors, teachers, and others simply wouldn't get used if it was not for the poor.
- Poverty guarantees the status of the not-poor. The poor serve as a permanent measuring point for status comparison for those above, especially the working class, who must maintain their position in a class-conscious society.
- The poor serve as constituencies and opponents for several political groups. The revolutionary left could not exist without the poor as the beneficiaries and vanguard of the revolution. Conservatives need "welfare chiselers" to justify their demands for reductions in social assistance.

Poverty, of course, has a number of dysfunctions—mainly for the poor themselves. However, the functions it serves benefit the affluent, and possible alternatives would require a redistribution of income and power that would be dysfunctional for the affluent. Thus, Gans's functional analysis of poverty comes to many of the same conclusions as the more radical conflict theory analysis.

Source: Gans, H. J. The positive functions of poverty. *American Journal of Sociology,* 1972, 78, 275–289.

Migrant workers on an American farm. Without the low-wage labor pool that the poor constitute, many economic activities—including agriculture—could not exist in their present form. *(Paul Fusco/Magnum)*

poverty." And finally, to explain why some people move up the social ladder while others either remain in place or move to lower levels, we might look at personality characteristics—achievement motivation, the ability to defer gratification, and so on. Thus, there is utility in studying psychological factors in poverty (see Allen, 1970). In the long run, however, the true causes of poverty are far more likely to be found, not in the psychology of the individual, but in the way society functions.

Poverty is extensively linked to and intertwined with almost all other social issues. Racial inequality, a condition thought to benefit white workers, may in fact weaken the bargaining strength of the entire work force, thus strengthening the position of the owners (Reich, 1978). In the social problem of crime, both victims and perpetrators are disproportionately represented among the poor. Drug abuse and alcoholism flourish to a greater degree among the severely dispossessed, although this is exaggererated by the fact that similar behavior by the rest of society is less likely to come to the attention of the authorities. The physical health risks of being poor are significant; for example, the chance of infant mortality is 1.5 times greater among poor whites than among whites not living in poverty (Gortmaker, 1979). The prevalence and severity of mental illness relate to being poor—although we do not know which is cause and which is effect (a problem addressed in Chapter 10). The poor also have far fewer resources to cope with their difficulties and are treated in more severe ways (such as institutionalization) than their more affluent fellow citizens. There is more impersonal and family violence among the dispossessed, a tendency that is aggravated by their higher birthrates and by family breakdown. At every turn, the poverty-stricken are faced with major crises and continuing stress, and yet they are the least equipped in terms of knowledge, skill, money, or whatever source of power is required to cope. The challenge of ameliorating poverty and related social problems is as immense as it is complex.

SOCIAL CHANGE AND PROGRESS OF HUMAN SOCIETY

It is often said that the only thing that is constant is change itself. We have become so used to a changing world that some observers believe that we are numbed and disorientated by it all and, more significantly, may be incapable of acting in our own best interests. Many factors underlie the rapid pace of change today: the technological revolution and continuing progress, with their far-reaching effects on society and culture; the knowledge explosion that bombards us with more information than we could possibly incorporate in ten lifetimes; communications media that present a kaleidescope of change, inducing still further changes; the ongoing competition for scarce resources among society's different racial, ethnic, and class groupings, resulting in the continuation of contentious social issues; and broad societal and political transformations—such as urbanization and demo-cratization (and their opposites)—that reorder societies and create continuing conflicts among competing ideological systems. What is unique in our time is not that change is occurring, but that *it is occurring at a faster rate than ever before*. This in itself can be seen as a major social issue.

There is also a saying that the more things change, the more they stay the same. Even within change, there is a stability in human affairs, of social relations, of fundamental patterns of social behavior that meet the needs of individuals and society. The child needs a family, or some source of physical care and social learning, to survive and become socialized as an acceptable member of society. The individual and the organization continue to search for common ground in which the goals of each can be achieved.

These basic patterns or interrelations are also subject to modification and even transformation. Human beings and social systems are highly adaptable. Children may spend more time in day-care and educational facilities, thus reducing the influence of the family in socialization. The organization may change from a traditional bureaucracy to a cooperative in which consumer ownership is practiced. Thus, change and stability may coexist in varying amounts. This apparent contradiction between stability and change must be taken as a fact of social life if we wish to understand and improve human society.

The role of the applied social psychologist is to study, define, and document social change and its effects; to assess the need for change (for example, by studying social problems); to evaluate the effects of change (for example, by measuring attitudinal or behavioral outcomes); and to intervene as a practitioner in order to influence change in the direction of humanistic values. The study of attitude and behavior change illuminates the effects of the mass media and the influence that legal sanctions have in bringing about social change. Social psychologists have also been at the forefront in developing theories of practice in the arena of social change. These statements provide the change agent with a choice of strategies to encourage social progress. We will examine these functions as well as the role of social movements as a mechanism of social change. In later chapters, we will consider the developing role of social psychologists as program developers and evaluators and as contributors to public policy.

In all these areas, social psychology has unique contributions to make (Kelman & Warwick, 1973). As a connecting discipline, social psychology links psychological variables with sociological variables, both of which are essential to the study of social change. In addition, social psychology makes many methodological and theoretical contributions to the study of social change, especially in the areas of social influence, socialization, and attitude change.

Social Psychology of Planned Change

We all have a sense of what social change is. After all, we experience it every day. But how would we define it, and what would we list as the types and sources of social change? And how would we seek to understand it as a social-psychological process that can be brought about in different ways? These are questions that social psychologists have grappled with in trying to understand and facilitate social change.

Social Change. Social change is a modification or alteration in the social structure of a society—that is, in the basic arrangements of living as expressed in the society's shared values, norms, roles, and so on. An example of evolutionary, or slow-moving, social change is the liberation of women in industrial society, including alterations in attitudes, role expectations, and voting laws. In contrast, political revolutions are an abrupt and fundamental change in the social structure, especially the political structure, of a society. For example, the Cuba of today is not the Cuba of 30 years ago, if we were to look at its dimensions of social, economic, and political functioning.

To better understand the differing types of social change and the sources that give rise to them, Katz (1974) offers a social-psychological interpretation of social change that takes into account both the individual and the social system. In a similar vein to Caplan and Nelson (1973) (see Chapter 1), Katz chastizes social psychologists for being too occupied with the individual level of analysis, and for making "person-blame attributions" rather than examining forces in the social system that underlie change. Although it is individuals who feel, think, and act, social behavior is determined by much more than a simple cumulation of individual behaviors. For example, "wars are . . . more than the sum of the aggressive behavior of individuals acting in parallel" (Katz, 1974, p. 161).

Katz distinguishes four separate types of social change:

- *Individual change* in personal characteristics regardless of social settings. An example is changes in individual behavior brought about by psychotherapy or other types of individual learning or relearning experiences. This type of change may or may not persist in different social settings and is not a source of wider social change. Transcendental meditation for all will not guarantee a better world.
- *Incremental social change* that modifies existing social structure, but does not destroy the fundamental social, economic, or political arrangements of society. Such modification may elaborate on the existing structure or may shift it in new directions. An example of the former is the widening of suffrage in political democracies; an example of the latter is the growth of social welfare policies in societies that value free enterprise.
- *Radical social change* that involves a basic alteration in social structure, especially a restructuring of the political and economic systems so that power relations and reward mechanisms operate in a new fashion. Some elements of social structure are thereby destroyed, and new forms are made legitimate. Political revolutions, especially Marxist ones, are the best example of this type of social change.
- *Cultural change* that brings about modifications in individual attitudes, values, and behaviors across an entire society. Cultural change does not require alterations in social structure, although it may occur along with either incremental or radical social change. Thus, cultural change is a biased shift in ways of living, such as the Westernization of India and Japan.

Katz illustrates the differences among these types of social change by considering the social problem of prejudice and discrimination. An attempt to bring about individual change would simply make a personal appeal for people to change their ways. Incremental change would call for laws to make discrimination illegal. Radical social change would require a restructuring in the institution of private property so that wealth was equitably distributed to disadvantaged groups. Cultural change would use mass media and other forms of societal persuasion to bring about broad shifts in commonly held stereotypes. Each type of change has its own objectives and its characteristic way to reach those objectives.

What are the forces in societies that push for social change?

- Class differences in power and wealth that are related to the basic internal contradictions identified by the conflict theorists
- Competition among various groups that spurs technological progress and may lead to change in society's reward system
- Different growth rates in different sectors of society—such as technological and material progress that outstrips cultural advance
- Generational differences between parents and children who have been socialized in very different ways
- Clashes with other systems and the wider environment—such as the occurrence of wars or the problem of physical pollution

All of these sources bring pressures for change on a society. The degree to which the society sees change as legitimate will affect the type and degree of change that occurs. Katz maintains that in American society the internal contradictions underlying class differences have led to incremental rather than radical change, since there is not a broad support base for a revolutionary restructuring. Similarly, generational differences have produced cultural rather than structural change, since these cleavages have been contained within the present framework of society. However, on a wider scale, increasing competition and conflict between the American system and other systems may combine with internal differences and contradictions to yield more revolutionary change in the future. Thus, the questions of dealing with change, and planning for change, become more and more paramount.

Planned Change. Social psychologists make an important distinction between unplanned change and planned change (Bennis, Benne, Chin & Corey, 1976; Lippitt, Watson & Westley, 1958). *Unplanned change* operates by the "law of nonintervention," as supported by the economic doctrine of *laissez-faire*. This maintains that, in the long run, naturally occurring homeostatic forces (that is, the free market) will result in the good life for all or most of the world's citizens. Tampering with these natural forces will only upset the applecart.

One alternative to nonintervention is the "law of radical intervention." This approach (advocated by Marx and other conflict theorists) proposes to restructure the economic relationships of society by removing class distinctions and by sharing ownership and wealth through state control. However, for many social psychologists, the more appealing alternative is the middle road of *planned change* that "self-consciously and experimentally employs social knowledge to help solve the problems of men and societies" (Bennis et al., 1976, p. 2). Planned change, calling for a limited or moderate intervention into human affairs, involves the deliberate and collaborative use of valid knowledge to improve the functioning of human systems.

Benne, Bennis, and Chin (1976) provide a history of planned change in the United States, dating back only to the late nineteenth century—a time when social sciences began to develop knowledge that was potentially useful to government planners. An early controversy that continues to this day centers around both the acceptable degree of involvement of the social scientist and his or her knowledge in public planning. The increasing use of professional advisers in the first half of the twentieth century, particularly in the progressive era of the New Deal, established the union between social science advisers and policy makers.

The dream of finding solutions to social problems through advanced physical technology was shattered by the use of nuclear weapons and the holocaust in World War II. The human costs of the unfettered use of technology demonstrated the need for conscious and humane planning. The liberation movements of the 1960s questioned social science's alliance with the status quo, but at the same time affirmed the participative and collaborative values of planned change. The frustration and conflict in America that centered around the Vietnam War clearly demonstrated the failure of technology and power to solve social problems, as well as the crucial need for collaborative mechanisms to peacefully resolve social conflict. Thus, planned change has come through a turbulent history as one of social science's best hopes of making a contribution to the well-being and survival of humanity.

But how does planned change proceed? What are the major approaches available to the social scientist/practitioner who wishes to influence the process of social change? Chin and Benne (1976) outline three general strategies for effecting change in human systems: empirical-rational, normative-reeducative, and power-coercive. Table 11.2 depicts the major strategies of planned change and the specific intervention methods that can be grouped under each one.

The *empirical-rational strategy* assumes that people are rational and will act in their own best interests when they are given information that justifies change. The role of the change agent is thus to provide valid knowledge about social conditions and reasonable proposals for social change—with the belief that people will listen and act accordingly. This approach underlies the hope that science and education will expand our knowledge, reduce our ignorance, and resolve our social problems through general enlightenment.

The execution and diffusion of applied research is another example of the empirical-rational approach. The field of education in particular has made good use of applied research in developing and testing curriculum materials and in evaluating programs through student responses. At the societal level, the documentation of social problems follows the empirical-rational strategy, assuming that when citizens and government officials know the facts they will move to improve problematic conditions.

Unfortunately, neither people nor society are as simple as the empirical-rational strategy assumes. People are irrational as well as rational, and do not always act in their own best interests. How many people know that cigarette smoking is dangerous to their health and yet continue to puff away? Furthermore,

Table 11.2   THE MAJOR STRATEGIES OF PLANNED CHANGE

Empirical-Rational	Normative-Reeducative	Power-Coercive
Basic research	Action research	Law and government
Applied research	Human relations training	Nonviolent resistance
Evaluation research	Organization development	Social advocacy
Education and dissemination	Community development	

Source: Chin & Benne (1976).

society is composed of many competing group interests, and it is no simple matter to put knowledge into action. The shelves of government officials are filled with dust-covered research reports that have never been implemented due to competing interests, public resistance, economic restraints, and so on. The empirical-rational strategy may be appropriate for the general enlightenment of people—that is, it may promote individual and cultural change—but it has seldom been the vehicle for incremental or radical social change.

The *normative-reeducative* strategy also assumes that people are rational, but further assumes that social norms and the individual's commitment to them are very powerful determinants of behavior. Therefore, changes in social behavior will only occur if the people involved change their orientation to old norms and develop commitments to new ones. This requires changes in attitudes, values, and social relationships, as well as new knowledge and prescriptions for change.

In this approach, people are seen as more active and as interacting with their social environment in order to determine their behavior. Social change requires a process of active reeducation in which individuals examine their values and attitudes, and in which new group norms are allowed to emerge. Only with changes in normative expectations and sanctions will social change become a reality.

The role of the change agent involves collaboration with the client or target of change: a person, a group, an organization, or a community. The attitudes, values, and norms of the client system must be examined in a here-and-now fashion as part of the diagnosis of the problem and the need for change. The process of reeducation and resetting of norms must follow the participative and democratic values inherent in applied social psychology. The normative-reeducative strategy is best expressed by human relations training, the laboratory method of education, and the various types of consultation that have grown out of the early work of the National Training Laboratories. Action research is also a normative-reeducative approach. Underlying all these methods is an attempt to improve the problem-solving capabilities of the client system in ways that meet both social and technical needs. The person is seen as the basic unit of social organization, and a humanistic approach is seen as the best way to establish effective helping relationships that aid people to change and develop. In short, the normative-reeducative strategy lies at the very heart of applied social psychology as defined in this book.

The *power-coercive strategy* assumes that people change when they are forced to change through the application of social influence. The less powerful are obliged to comply with the demands of the more powerful, whether that be the legitimate authority of law or government or the coercive violence of an angry mob. Whereas the empirical-rational strategy uses knowledge as power, and the normative-reeducative strategy uses reciprocal influence as power, the power-coercive strategy applies economic, moral, or political power in one direction in order to force change. When we regard that power as legitimate—that is, as properly constituted authority—we tend to be more accepting and less aware of its influence. Thus, both the rule of law and the enforcement of government policies have brought about considerable social change—from the elimination of voting discrimination to the provision of social welfare.

Martin Luther King used nonviolent resistance as a form of moral power, demonstrating the injustice of racism to the American people—and evoking considerable guilt and moral indignation in doing so. *(Bob Fitch/Black Star)*

The power-coercive strategies of change agents are highly noticeable since these professionals must often use novel ways to amass and use power. The nonviolent resistance of Mahatma Gandhi and millions of followers to the British rule in India is one of the prime examples of a successful power-coercive approach. Like Gandhi, Martin Luther King used nonviolent resistance as a form of moral power, dramatically demonstrating the injustice of racism to the American people—and evoking considerable guilt and moral indignation in doing so. One master of the power-coercive strategy was Saul Alinsky (his advocacy approach was discussed in Chapters 4 and 10). Alinsky and his disciples, Cesar Chavez among them, have used a variety of creative tactics to harness economic and political power in the interest of helping disadvantaged groups gain their place in the sun. Violence has seldom been used as a power-coercive tactic, but the threat of violence has often been a source of secondary, or backup, power in many strikes, sit-ins, and boycotts. According to Alinsky, the enemy must believe you will stop at nothing, even if that is not the case.

The power-coercive strategy highlights the central role of power and influence in human affairs, but it also creates resistance and engenders a win-lose approach to solving problems, for example, one side wins and the other loses (see Chapter 14). Often it must be combined with the normative-reeducative strategy to bring lasting change based on attitudes, values, and social norms.

In actuality, change agents tend to mix their strategies as appropriate to the situation and the goals of change and may shift their emphasis from one approach to another as they see fit. However, this fusing of strategies should not hide the fact that most change agents usually have a strong preference for one approach.

We must also remember that different values are involved with different strategies. Freedom of choice is maximized by the empirical-rational approach; participative democracy is stressed by the normative-reeducative strategy; and the use of coercive means to achieve humanistic goals is the essence of the power-coercive approach. The change agent is thus faced with many difficult decisions in terms of both tactics and ethics in his or her quest for planned social change (see Chapter 4).

The Role of Research in Social Change

Social psychologists differ in their opinions about the usefulness of basic and applied research in helping to bring about social change (see Chapter 1). As we noted in discussing the empirical-rational strategy, there is no guarantee that knowledge produced by social scientists will be used for the improvement of society in humanistic directions. Many believe that for knowledge to lead to change, the social scientist must actively disseminate valid knowledge and bring it to bear on societal decision making. The research and dissemination activities of members of the Society for the Psychological Study of Social Issues (see Chapter 1) serve as a fine illustration of this approach. In addition to publishing the *Journal of Social Issues*, which for over 30 years has focused on a wide range of social problems, SPSSI provides grants-in-aid and awards for outstanding contributions to applied research. Each year at the Annual Convention of the American Psychological Association, SPSSI organizes a program of meetings that emphasizes the application of social scientific knowledge to social problems.

In contrast to the activities of SPSSI members, conflict theorists charge that social scientific knowledge is so biased by the class and power position of its creators that it simply affirms the status quo rather than argues for social change. Less radical social scientists contend that our chief role is the documentation of social problems such as racism, sexism, and poverty, and that, in fact, society does utilize our findings in useful ways over the longer term (see Box 11.4).

In his treatment of social problems, Etzioni (1976) discusses the role that knowledge plays in social change. It is assumed that all knowledge is biased to some degree by the interests and aims of the researcher, but that it can play an important role in societal decision making. For that to happen, the information must first represent a reliable reading of the social problem in question, and then it must be communicated in an effective way to policy makers.

This complex process of the dissemination and utilization of knowledge has been the main focus of a group of social scientists at the Center for Research on Utilization of Scientific Knowledge (CRUSK) at the University of Michigan.

Box 11.4   FOCUS ON RESEARCH
Social Research as a Force for Social Change

The mere enactment of law by itself does not appear to be adequate for social change in intergroup relations where ingrained prejudices die hard. A good example is federal open-housing legislation in the United States, embodied in the 1968 Civil Rights Act. Three years after the passage of the act, a volunteer open-housing group in Akron, Ohio, began a series of research audits to increase community awareness of racial discrimination in housing in order to effect social change. Juliet Saltman, a sociologist at Kent State University, served as the main organizer for the open-housing group and devised the research studies.

Audit I began with an interview survey of real estate executives. A large majority (76 percent) indicated specific knowledge of open-housing laws. In the second part of Audit I, six pairs of trained black and white volunteers, matched on family composition and income, contacted the same real estate companies and requested identical housing. Almost every company showed discrimination of one type or another. Blacks were consistently offered housing in black or integrated areas, whites in all-white areas. Blacks experienced various forms of discourtesy—having to call numerous times, not being offered a seat during an office visit.

The results of Audit I were presented at a public meeting in city council chambers sponsored by the mayor's human relations commission. Each company was notified of any discrimination by its employees and was invited to meet with the open-housing group to discuss the details. The results were sent to the Department of Justice for possible legal action. In response, the board of realtors established a human relations committee and issued a brochure on equal opportunities in housing.

Audit II assessed racial discrimination at apartment complexes. Audit teams of matched black and white volunteers arranged separate appointments at thirty complexes to view available apartments. The majority of complexes (63 percent) demonstrated discrimination—blacks were told no units were available and that credit checks were required. The results were used at a public meeting to show that adequate open housing was not available to relocate hundreds of black families about to be displaced by the construction of a new expressway.

Audit III was a combined study of real estate companies and apartment complexes. The results were similar to those of Audits I and II, thus indicating the persistence of racial discrimination in housing. Results were disseminated through a public meeting, letters to audited companies and apartments, and reports to government agencies. This time, the press called strongly for more effective action to reduce discrimination. The presidents of most of the audited companies met with the group to discuss specific findings so they could take corrective action. All government agencies responded and two began legal investigations. And the goal of the group for equal opportunity in housing was incorporated into three official documents concerned with metropolitan planning.

Source: Saltman, J. Implementing open housing laws through social action. *Journal of Applied Behavioral Science*, 1975, *11*, 39–61.

These investigators study the dissemination process and look for ways to maximize the utilization of valid social science knowledge. Havelock (1969) presents a broad analysis of the factors that affect utilization, including the internal characteristics of individuals, the organizational context, and the special linking role of consultants, trainers, and others that connects the researcher to the user of knowledge. In these and other ways, social science theory and research results can be incorporated into the formation of public policy (see Chapter 16).

One attempt to gain an accurate and useful measure of social conditions is the development of *social indicators*. These are standardized measures that can be used on a regular basis to yield a concrete picture of society's well-being (Bauer, 1966). Such indicators are being developed and used by governments in areas such as education, housing, and health to complement more traditional economic measures. The indicators provide a reservoir of valuable information on social conditions and problems and help monitor long-term social progress as well as the effects of technological and cultural change. However, it is questionable if such descriptive information on a mass scale will provide an impetus for incremental or radical social change.

Another difficulty with social indicators is that they describe "what is" in relatively objective terms—such as the percentage of children graduating from high school, or the incidence of tuberculosis. What such measures miss are the *subjective* perception that people have of such occurrences and the effect of this on their individual sense of well-being. To tap this aspect, social psychologists and others have developed measures of the perceived *quality of life*. Assessing the sense of satisfaction that people experience in their lives can have at least two useful purposes (Summers, 1978). First, since many potential policy changes are defended or attacked on the basis of how they may affect the quality of life, we need to understand this concept to judge the validity of such arguments. Second, reliable measures of general well-being could aid decision makers in monitoring the psychological state of the nation and spotting deficiencies as they arise.

Of course, it may be some time before such indicators reach the level of reliability required for national decision making. For example, Turner and Krauss (1978) found that two different measures of public confidence in national institutions (the congress, the supreme court, and so forth) differed significantly over a 4-year period. These discrepancies did not appear to be related to seasonal variations in the time of measurement or to differences in the samples of the two surveys. It is possible that the context in which the indicator is presented, that is, the other questions in the survey, may affect respondents' answers. Before subjective indicators are regularly used to assess the subjective state of the nation, such errors need to be reduced substantially.

One of the more ambitious research projects on perceived quality of life is the work of Andrews and Withey (1976). Their national surveys asked respondents how they felt about various aspects of their lives, from their income to how they spend their spare time. Satisfaction in most domains of life was found to relate rather well to how people feel about their life *as a whole*. Although most Americans have positive feelings about their lives, satisfaction relates substantially to socioeconomic status—that is, people of a lower status expressed less satisfaction with their lives.

Similar research by Campbell, Converse and Rodgers (1976) is also based on survey data. They assessed major domains of life (marriage, job, housing, and so on) in relation to a general sense of well-being, and examined the quality of life experienced by particular groups such as blacks and women. One interesting result, in apparent contradiction to other findings, is that the perceived sense of well-being does not necessarily relate to the more objective social indicators such as income and education. Obviously, the phenomenological experience of quality of life is a complex phenomenon that will take some time to understand. One example of a quality-of-life scale is given in Table 11.3.

There are other emerging areas of research that are relevant to the study of social change. *Program evaluation* assesses the impact of particular projects or policy changes (see Chapter 13). *Social impact assessment*, a newer research area, measures the effects of technological or physical changes on social life (Finster-busch, 1980; Finsterbusch & Wolf, 1977). Resource development projects, from new coal mines to hydroelectric dams, are increasingly being scrutinized for their impact on the quality of people's lives. This is occurring in the belief that the physical benefits of technology are there to be enjoyed without diminishing our psychological and social well-being.

Changing Attitudes through Persuasive Communication

Social issues reflect social attitudes. Racism, for example, is anchored in the prejudices of individuals as well as in the discriminatory practices of institutions. This means that constructive movement toward social change is intertwined with the question of individual attitude change, a form of the normative-reeducative strategy of planned change.

One major approach to attitude change is the effect of persuasive communication on the attitudes of the receiver. Beginning with an interest in the study of propaganda messages in World War II, social psychologists devoted a major share of their attention in the 1950s and 1960s to the classic question of "Who says what to whom, and with what effect?" Attempts to change our attitudes through persuasive communications abound in our everyday experience. Flip on the television and a popular football star is recommending a men's grooming product. Pick up a magazine and an article cautions against the spread of nuclear development. Turn on the radio and a religious broadcast implores you to change your ways before it is too late. Walk into your doctor's waiting room and a pamphlet warns of the health hazards of smoking. The people who create these messages are usually not social psychologists, but they have acquired the tricks of the trade in the art of persuasive communication.

"Who says what to whom, and with what effect?" Social psychologists have studied the components of this classic question in laboratory settings where the major variables can be manipulated and the effects of attitudes can be studied systematically. The *source* of the communication ("who") has been manipulated in terms of credibility, motives, and attractiveness. The *message* itself ("what") has been examined in a number of ways, including its potential for arousing fear. The *receiver* of the message ("whom") has been studied to see if certain personality characteristics are related to general susceptibility and openness to change. These

Table 11.3   A QUALITY OF LIFE SCALE

Variable	None	Lousy	Rating — OK				Great				
			20	30	40	50	60	70	80	90	100
My JOB is	No job (0)	10	20	30	40	50	60	70	80	90	100
My LEISURE TIME is	No leisure (0)	10	20	30	40	50	60	70	80	90	100
My ENVIRONMENT (where I live, home, neighborhood, weather) is		10	20	30	40	50	60	70	80	90	100
My EATING is		10	20	30	40	50	60	70	80	90	100
My SLEEP is		10	20	30	40	50	60	70	80	90	100
My INCOME/MONEY is	No income (0)	10	20	30	40	50	60	70	80	90	100
I get along with MY CHILDREN	No children (0)	10	20	30	40	50	60	70	80	90	100
I get along with the MAN/WOMAN I LOVE	No one (0)	10	20	30	40	50	60	70	80	90	100
I get along with OTHER PEOPLE		10	20	30	40	50	60	70	80	90	100
Do I like MYSELF?		No, I need a lot of change — 10	20	30	40	I'm OK — 50	60	70	80	90	Yes, I'm fine — 100

Note: It is suggested that an average score of 20%–50% represents considerable suffering, 50%–70% indicates painful but adequate coping, and above 70% represents doing well in terms of quality of one's life.
Source: Kedenburg (1980).

and other independent variables have been studied in relation to the *effect* of the message—that is, the dependent variable of attitude change (typically assessed by an attitude or rating scale on the topic). Attitude change itself is a complex variable, consisting of attention, comprehension, acceptance, retention, and action. Drawing upon key summaries of these extensively documented studies (see Hovland, Janis & Kelley, 1953; Insko, 1967; McGuire, 1969b; Oskamp, 1977; Triandis, 1971), we now need to focus on some of this work and the major conclusions that appear to be valid at the present time.

Imagine that Richard Nixon began a public campaign to convince the American people that the use of Vitamin C as a preventive health measure would drastically reduce the costs of medical care. His message, like most persuasive communications, might seem well-reasoned and be clearly understood. But as a *source* he would be in trouble on at least two counts. Memories of the Watergate scandal would generally discredit his message in the minds of many people, and questions would be raised about his expertise in the health field. In short, Richard Nixon would lack credibility, that combination of trustworthiness and competence essential to an effective communication.

While credibility is to a degree in the eye of the beholder, research results are consistent: highly credible sources tend to produce attitude change; those without credibility have little effect. Credibility is also linked to the perceived intentions or motives of the source. We have less faith in a communicator who may somehow benefit from the suggested changes than in one who has no ulterior motive. Television commercials of the "candid camera" type, which show a satisfied consumer discussing a production, will likely be higher in perceived trustworthiness than a message from a paid announcer. The attractiveness of the source also affects the degree of attitude change. As we already know from our study of interpersonal attraction, the communicator who is most like the recipient of the message generally includes greater attitude change. Politicians, for example, often go to great pain to demonstrate that they are not above their constituents, but just "a friend from down the road," or "one of the girls (or boys)."

Studies on the characteristics of the message have generally yielded complex results; that is, no simple guidelines emerge. The question of presenting a one-sided versus a two-sided argument was one of the first issues that attracted investigators, partly because of wartime propaganda messages that exhibited one or the other strategy. The most effective message appears to depend on the characteristics of the audience. If the audience is sympathetic or initially favorable to the position of the communicator, then a one-sided message is more effective. (Few politicians will give equal time to the opposition's viewpoint at partisan meetings.) On the other hand, if the audience is unfavorable to the communicator's position, and is knowledgeable about the issues, a two-sided presentation enhances credibility and induces greater attitude change.

The order of presentation for two-sided arguments is also no simple matter. Early studies first supported a *primacy effect* (that the first argument has the most impact) and then a *recency effect* (that the last part of the message is most influential). Later studies have shown that many other variables interact with the order of presentation to determine the eventual outcome. For example, if the issue is well known, the initial argument has more clout (the primacy effect); with an unfamiliar topic, the closing argument has the greater influence (the recency effect). There appears to be no universal law governing order effects.

Equally complex is the effect of fear-arousing communications. Such messages are especially common in preventive health care and accident prevention. Here the intent is to scare recipients into adopting recommended practices in order to avoid harmful consequences. The problem, however, is to know how to generate the *optimal* amount of fear. Some studies show that threatening stimuli (pictures of cancerous lungs to inhibit smoking behavior) are more effective than simple information ("The Surgeon General has determined that cigarette smoking is dangerous to you health"). But other studies have found that strong appeals to fear (emphasizing the pain and disfigurement of tooth decay) may be less effective than milder messages (describing the problem of cavities).

The current interpretation of these contradictory results is that a strong fear induction produces a high degree of anxiety and defensiveness, interfering with both the reception and adoption of the message. In addition, fear arousal must be followed up with a clear set of recommended behaviors for preventing the calamitous outcomes portrayed in the message. This reduces the recipient's anxiety, reinforcing the tendency to adopt changed attitudes and behaviors. Moderate fear appeals generally appear to be most effective.

The "whom" of the classic question on persuasive communications further complicates the picture. A recipient must first be motivated to attend to and comprehend the message; otherwise, we can't expect an attitude change. Beyond that initial reception, early studies looked for personality traits related to suggestibility. On a given issue in a given situation, some individuals are more likely to change their attitudes than others. However, many individual and situational factors influence the process. The degree of similarity between the persuasive message and the individual's initial attitudes may influence the degree of change. Communications which are outside the individuals' "latitude of acceptance" will be rejected. Personal characteristics may influence receptivity to the message and one's willingness to change. For these and other reasons, research results on receiver characteristics and attitude change through persuasive appeals have been difficult to interpret, and complex models have been required (see McGuire, 1969b). One example of equivocal results is the relationship between gender and receptivity to persuasive communication (see Box 11.5).

A perennial problem with research on attitude change due to communication is the conflicting results produced by laboratory experiments versus field surveys. A classic statement by Hovland (1955) drew attention to this discrepancy and suggested a means of integration. In the typical experiment, a group of subjects are exposed to a communication (such as a written statement or a film) and the change in attitude is compared to a control group not exposed to the communication. In the typical survey, interviews assess both the amount of communication received on a given topic and the respondents' attitudes on the topic. The two variables are then correlated to show the effect of exposure on attitudes. These studies generally find that very few individuals are influenced by mass communications. In contrast, experiments on persuasive communication generally show attitude change in one-third to one-half of the subjects.

Hovland suggests this discrepancy in results is not surprising when we consider the differences between the typical laboratory design and the field

Box 11.5 FOCUS ON RESEARCH
Are Women More Easily Influenced than Men?

Many current textbooks of social psychology and of attitude change conclude that there is a clear sex difference in influenceability—women generally show more attitude and opinion change as a result of a persuasive communication. This difference is then typically explained by differing sex roles: females are socialized to yield to social influence, to be submissive, while males are expected to remain relatively independent.

Alice Eagly, a social psychologist at the University of Massachusetts, took exception to this supposedly well-established conclusion by completing a comprehensive review of studies dealing with influenceability. She found that the empirical evidence was quite limited. In studies of persuasive communication, only 10 of 62 experiments (16 percent) showed females were more influenceable; 51 (82 percent) reported no differences. By common standards, this is not a large enough trend to conclude that a sex difference exists. However, Eagly did find a tendency for studies completed prior to 1970 to show greater influenceability among females than studies completed after 1970 (32 percent compared to 8 percent). It may be that textbook conclusions are based mainly on earlier results or that traditional sex roles are being eroded and women are becoming less persuasible.

Eagly contends it is more likely that aspects of the typical persuasion experiment account for what sex differences do exist. It is well-established that individuals are more readily influenced on topics on which they have little information or regard as unimportant. In persuasion research, the common topics are political, social, and economic issues—areas of opinion which research shows women are less knowledgeable about and less interested in than men. The one study that showed males as more influenceable was on the traditional female topic of nutrition. In addition, a limited amount of evidence shows that there is greater opinion change when the communicator and recipient are of a different sex. In persuasion research, the vast majority of communicators are males; thus, female recipients would show more influence than male recipients.

It is also possible that genuine differences between the sexes account for the findings. However, the popular interpretation involving the submissiveness of the female role does not stand up well on closer examination. Several studies have included measures of masculinity-feminity, but these have not shown a relation to persuasibility. Eagly also suggests that sex differences in interpersonal orientation may be important—females place somewhat greater emphasis on social harmony and may therefore display more agreement on opinions.

Why has social-psychological literature concluded a difference where one does not exist? Social psychologists may have selected studies for citation that supported their own everyday life beliefs that men and women differ on influenceability.

Source: Eagly, A. H. Sex differences in influenceability. *Psychological Bulletin*, 1978, *85*, 86–116.

survey. For example, in an experiment, the audience is composed of individuals exhibiting a wide range of initial attitudes all of whom are fully exposed to the persuasive message. In real life, however, individuals who expose themselves to a given communication are generally those who are favorable toward the material and are therefore least likely to show further changes. In addition, experiments involve concentrated messages rather than entire programs and the effects are measured immediately following communication. Such control in real-world studies is impossible. It is therefore to be expected that results will differ and that both laboratory and survey studies are required to fully understand the effects of persuasive communication.

Even with its ambiguities, 30 years of research has produced conclusions that have been adopted by advertisers and political campaigners. On more fundamental social issues, however, the application of these findings to induce change may be limited. Attempts at reducing racism and sexism, for example, have either been more subtle or in the form of more straightforward presentations of information. Over the past decade, television commercials and programs in North America have gradually increased the amount of interaction between minority group members and the white majority. (For example, the group of mothers who endorse a laundry detergent now includes a black woman.) Government media and advertising support affirmative action programs. In many ways, the blatant approach of World War II propaganda that stimulated much of the research has become passé, and a more sophisticated attempt is being made to influence attitudes and change behavior. Whether any type of persuasive communication will have significant effects on prejudice and discrimination, or any other social problem, remains an open question of considerable importance.

Changing Behavior through Legal Compliance

One of the most powerful forms of the power-coercive strategy for social change is the use of the law and its enforcement. Laws are relatively clear statements of what behaviors or standards are acceptable to society. To enforce these standards, the criminal justice system uses its considerable coercive power. Given this, you might believe that all we need do is legislate desirable social changes that are supported by most members of society and—presto!—we have established part of a new social order. Of course, the situation is much more complex and difficult, as we will see by examining the trials and tribulations of court-ordered desegregation in American public schools.

In 1954, the United States Supreme Court brought down a landmark decision that segregated schools were not only unconstitutional but also inherently unequal. In the field of public education, the doctrine of "separate but equal" facilities for blacks and whites was deemed to have no place. For the three decades that followed this declaration, the desegregation of American public schools became one of the hottest social controversies, particularly in the late 1960s and early 1970s when court-ordered desegregation plans were pursued as the necessary means to achieve racial integration.

The 1954 decision is often cited as the classic example of the involvement by social scientists in public policy making. A number of prominent social psychologists (including Kenneth Clark, David Krech, Otto Klineberg, Isidor Chein, and Brewster Smith) testified in support of desegregtion in the five separate cases that made up the court issue called *Brown* vs. *the Board of Education* (Stephan, 1978). Furthermore, Kenneth Clark, Isidor Chein, and Stuart Cook wrote a brief on the effects of segregation on prejudice and self-esteem. This was signed by thirty-two prominent social scientists.

The testimony and the brief provided a clear consensus of professional opinion on the harmful effects of segregated schools on both black and white children: that segregation was injurious to the self-esteem and learning motivation of black children, and that segregation contributed to racial prejudice and hostility. In contrast, the social scientists predicted directly or indirectly that desegregation would reduce prejudice in general and would improve the self-concept, educational aspirations, and scholastic achievement of black children.

After more than two decades of desegregation, Stephan (1978) and others (for example, Gerard & Miller, 1975; St. John, 1975) evaluated the predictions made in 1954. The results are not encouraging for those who believed that school integration was the solution to racism in America. Stephan's (1978) review of twenty-seven studies found that desegregation was as likely to increase prejudice as it was to decrease it. In fact, white prejudice toward blacks was typically more intense *following* desegregation. On the question of self-esteem, it is not clear that segregated schools create a more negative self-concept for black children. In elementary schools, their self-esteem appears to be lower, but in high schools it appears to be higher than in white segregated schools. These mixed findings extend to the issue of scholastic achievement. Some studies indicate that segregated black children achieve at lower levels than segregated white children (but the reasons for this are very controversial). Other studies found increased black achievement. Still others found that desegregation has no effect (Stephan, 1978).

What is going wrong? Why do the predictions of our best social science minds fall on barren ground? The answer lies in the following question: *Has desegregation been instituted in ways that should reduce racial prejudice?* The answer appears to be an outright "no." Stuart Cook, one of the authors of the 1954 social science brief, points out that desegregation has not been carried out in accord with the conditions originally specified as conducive to positive outcomes (Cook, 1979). Often, the events that actually take place in desegregated schools are simply unknown.

The general failure of desegregation in the short term has led social scientists to examine the conditions under which the predicted effects have actually occurred. Stephan and Rosenfield (1978) studied the individual and interpersonal factors that contributed to reduced prejudice on the part of white children during desegregation. They found that children who took part in greater interracial contact, and who were experiencing increases in self-esteem, tended to exhibit more positive racial attitudes. Children whose parents were less authoritarian and less given to meting out punishment also showed reduced prejudice during desegregation. But parental opposition to integration was an important "mediator variable." It determined the amount of interracial contact that was allowed, thus indirectly influencing changes on racial attitudes. These results are congruent with what we know about intergroup relations, including authoritarianism and the essential conditions for positive intergroup contact. In terms of Pettigrew's model presented earlier, legal compliance has mainly produced mere desegregation of the schools rather than true integration based on equality and respect.

Slavin and Madden (1978) analyzed school practices during desegregation that improve race relations. Previous studies indicated that the most important determinants of successful desegregation were the attitudes and teaching practices of school personnel and the actual amount of interracial contact. Using data from a national survey of 168 schools by the Educational Testing Service, Slavin and Madden found that for white students discussing race relations and working together with blacks on school projects had positive effects on race relations. The effects were not as strong with black students, but overall, activities involving interaction were the best predictors of more positive interracial attitudes and behaviors. Other suggested practices such as human relations training for teachers or textbooks written along multiethnic lines did not have such positive effects. Naturally, all of these practices need the general support of the school administrators and teachers to work.

Two applications of social-psychological theory will help us further understand the successes and failures of desegregation. First (as discussed in Chapter 8), we know that intergroup conflict will only reduce prejudice when certain conditions are met—that is, when individuals work cooperatively together as equals, come to know each other as persons, and have support from social norms. Mere desegregation does not induce these conditions. Simply placing black and white students together in the average classroom—with its focus on the competing individual—is going to affect racial attitudes negatively if at all. True integration, involving equal status and cooperative and friendly personal interaction, needs to be implemented by teachers and supported by principals and parents if positive individual change is to occur.

It is also instructive to apply some of the principles of cognitive dissonance theory (see Chapter 2) to the initial failures of school desegregation. In a work that appeared before the most active period of desegregation, Brehm and Cohen (1962) used the dissonance model to predict the elements of successful integration. Desegregation brings about a change in behavior (interracial contact), which may or may not lead to more positive attitudes (racial integration). Initially, there will be dissonance between the behavior of desegregation and existing negative attitudes. For desegregation to be successful, the choice to desegregate should be elicited more than forced—and yet the decision should be irrevocable. Therefore, the person who experiences dissonance in the new situation (1) cannot reduce it through the belief that forced compliance has produced the behavior, and (2) will not see changing the desegregation ruling as a possible way of reducing dissonance. This increases the probability of attitude change to reduce dissonance.

To make desegregation work, society must have clear public policy and social norms that support this change. If policy is vague and norms are anti-integration, even a change in behavior is unlikely to produce a change in attitude. Brehm and Cohen (1962) point out that the school setting is characterized by a relative absence of choice as compared to other areas such as housing. Desegregation orders usually cover entire districts and all children are required to attend desegregated schools. People who oppose desegregation will clearly see forced compliance as the reason for integration and will experience little change toward positive interracial attitudes and behavior. If we look at the grudging support of some school authorities and the anti-integration attitudes of many parents and students, it is easy to predict the furor, the resistance, and the violence that have attended cases of court-ordered desegregation and busing. In this type of situation, one predictable way to reduce dissonance is to "leave the field." The phenomenon of "white flight" to the suburbs is in part an avoidance, an attempt to do just that—leave the field. The increasing enrollment of white children in private schools follows the same strategy, but without the necessity of relocating the family home.

For the people who stay in the desegregated situation, we must ask how the conditions of contact can be maximized to create true integration. In the past few years, social and educational psychologists have been looking for ways to bring about more positive social contact in desegregated schools (Aronson, Blaney, Sikes, Stephan & Snapp, 1975; Aronson, Stephan, Sikes, Blaney & Snapp, 1978; Devries, Edwards & Slavin, 1978; Donleavy & Pugh, 1977; Weigel, Wiser & Cook, 1975).

Elliot Aronson and his colleagues looked for ways to turn the hostility and violence of busing and desegregation in Austin, Texas, into a productive atmosphere of racial peace and mutual learning. Beginning with an analysis of behavior in the typical elementary school classroom, they found that children were in fierce competition to give the teacher the right answer and to be rewarded. This not only created conflict and alienation between the "smart alecks" and the "dummies," but also fed into racial conflict, especially between groups who differed in scholastic achievement.

The solution was to stop the competition and engage the children in small cooperative learning teams in which they had to use each other as resources. This was accomplished by the "jigsaw-puzzle" method: each group of five or six students was given material to learn or a problem to solve, but the necessary information was divided among the students. In this way, no one individual could complete the task alone; the teams had to elicit the cooperation of each child, thus creating a working interaction.

This was not easy for children with years of competitive socialization. In one group, a withdrawn Chicano boy named Carlos had trouble communicating his information because he couldn't speak English well. The initial response of a "smart aleck" was to call him dumb and stupid. The psychologist supervising the group observed that the group could tease Carlos if they liked, but that this behavior wouldn't complete the task and help them pass the exam. The group, realizing that they needed Carlos, began to treat him with respect and ask him appropriate questions to draw him out. Carlos relaxed and began to communicate better; in a couple of weeks, the other children were amazed that he wasn't "dumb" anymore.

Compared with traditional classroom methods, the approach worked well. Children learned just as much and, more importantly, came to like their classmates regardless of race. A workshop was developed to train teachers to facilitate the learning groups, leading to a 6-week study involving ten teachers that confirmed the initial results. Children in the experimental groups came to like their classmates better, generally had more positive attitudes toward school, developed more positive self-concepts, and showed significant improvements in grades. Now that's integration! Although a liking for individuals in one's own group did not generalize to an overall reduction in racial prejudice, even that first step—friendship, with someone in an outgroup—is the beginning of positive attitude change.

Beyond the classroom, there are factors that may spell the defeat of desegregation. One of these is the continuing resistance of the white community, expressed in part by white flight. The segregation of residences—whereby blacks and other minorities inhabit the city core and whites live in the suburbs—is a fact of race relations in the United States and, to a lesser degree, in Canada. To overcome residential segregation, court-ordered plans for desegregation instituted the busing of students to gain an acceptable racial balance in the schools. Initial studies of the relationship between desegregation and the decline in white enrollment triggered a heated controversy within social science and the public at large (Rossell, 1978). One initial reaction was that busing would induce white flight to such a degree that no whites would be left in the city core, thus defeating the original purpose of desegregation. Proponents of integration criticized such results and conclusions on both scientific and humanitarian grounds.

It now appears that desegregation does accelerate white flight in the first year of implementation, but that white middle-class suburbanization and a declining birthrate are also important causes of declining white enrollment in city schools. Furthermore, the assignment of white students to formerly black schools with a moderate to high percentage of black students in the racial mixture appears to accelerate the decline of white enrollment. There is no agreement about the long-term impact of desegregation. Some studies show a lessening decline in white enrollment in later years following desegregation; others show a continuing negative impact on white enrollment. Desegregated schools may bring about racial interaction for only ten years or so, at which time the proportion of remaining whites will be insignificant.

The promise of the 1954 Supreme Court decision may never be realized. Equality in the schools may well become the victim of inequality in the larger society—an inequality that supports residential segregation. Members of different racial groups may continue to work together, to eat together, and to vote together, but it is doubtful whether they will come to live together in harmony and respect. The future prospects for race relations in North America are not very bright.

Social Change through Social Movements

I stood quietly on the "Diag"—a large open space at the center of the University of Michigan campus—listening to the leader of an antiwar demonstration address the crowd. He was highly agitated, flailing his arms about and screaming wildly into the microphone, "We're gonna march through this [expletive deleted] campus and tear it apart. Then we're gonna come back here and rip down that [expletive deleted] American flag and burn it to ashes." The crowd moved off on its march. Some of us drifted away, alienated by the venom and violence expressed by this fanatical, would-be agent of social change. But I willingly participated in the Black Action Movement at the same university, a civil-rights cause that organized a successful and peaceful strike by students and faculty that shut down that mighty institution until it met demands for increased opportunities for minority students.

These experiences represent two of my contacts with *social movements*—defined earlier as activities by a concerned group to effect social change that improves harmful conditions in society. It is an effort by a large number of individuals to solve together a social problem that they have in common (Toch, 1965). Social movements may also grow to resist rather than encourage social change. Witness the resistance to court-ordered busing as a means of school desegregation. As such, a social movement is one form of *collective behavior*— that is, large-group behavior that arises spontaneously and is relatively unorganized, unpredictable, and unplanned in its course of development (Milgram & Toch, 1969). In addition to social movements, there are other forms of collective behavior that have been studied by social psychologists: crowds, mobs, utopian communities, religious cults, and political revolutions. The study of social movements concentrated initially on institutions and the attitudes of their individual members, then shifted more attention to the organization and structure of the movement. Now this study has become concerned with the relationship of the movement to the wider environment or community (Perry, Gillespie & Parker, 1976).

But what is the role of social movements as indicators of social problems and as instruments of social change? While many harmful conditions exist in society, not all are seen as social issues at a given moment. One role of a social movement is to convince itself and the rest of society that a problem exists. Some would go so far as to say that social problems arise only when they are identified through social movements (Blumer, 1971). A more general approach says that social problems exist when some condition is selected, identified, and widely recognized by society as a problem (Stark, 1975). The contribution of social movements to this process is significant if not essential.

Another useful distinction is that social movements react against defining a problem as a misfortune; they rather conceive of it as a state of injustice in society (Turner, 1969). They do not appeal for change through petition, as victims of misfortune do, but rather demand redress of the injustice. The beggar on the street approaches the problem of poverty very differently than the Poor People's March on Washington. One wants charity; the other, justice.

Social movements are typically based in the power-coercive strategy of social change, although normative-reeducative processes occur within and outside the movement. Sit-ins, marches, strikes, demonstrations, boycotts—these are the tactics of social movements that demand and often get social change. Sometimes the change is more individual and cultural—such as that brought about by the youth movement of the 1960s. Sometimes the change is incremental—such as the continuing effects of the civil rights and women's liberation movements. And sometimes the change is radical—such as the social movement of the Sandinista rebels that led to the 1979 revolution in Nicaragua.

To complete our discussion, we must consider the general conditions that facilitate the emergence of social movements, the processes by which members are socialized, and the overall development and decline of this very important phenomenon of social change.

First, we must realize that social movements occur outside of society's regular, standardized channels of decision making, although as interest groups they may come to have considerable influence on government. These movements may represent a mixture of irrationality and rationality, and may remain trivial and noneventful. Or they may be harbingers of a new age if they capture the imagination of the people and gain popularity (Milgram & Toch, 1969). Consider that many people initially discounted the potential impact of Jesus Christ, and yet he initiated a religious movement that changed the shape of history.

Sometimes the popularity of a social movement is reduced by irrational elements: its extreme ideology, for instance, or its leader's inclination to oversimplify reality. For example, the John Birch Society in the United States has generally taken such an extreme right-wing position that its following is limited. On the other hand, even a perverse and illogical movement can gain support if it meets important needs of the people. Nazism in Germany, for example, was pathological in its twisted ethnocentrism of ingroup superiority and outgroup rejection, and yet it appealed to the people's pride in the German state. Social movements that are politically successful can thus come to influence or even dominate the government processes of rational decision making.

Social movements arise when there is a gap between human needs and society's response to these needs (Milgram & Toch, 1969). The needs may be tangible or material, such as the needs for food and shelter, or they may be intangible or psychological, such as the need for self-respect. But for a social movement to occur, the social problem related to these needs must be seen as both unacceptable *and* resolvable. Poverty has existed throughout human history, but it is only when some people expect society to reduce or eliminate poverty that social movements spring up to attack economic inequality. To set the stage for social movements, different interest groups must develop in society, and conflicts in values and norms must arise (Smelser, 1962). A generalized belief must develop within a segment of society that something is wrong and that something should be done about it. Then some precipitating events are required to mobilize the movement. A case in point is the early antiwar movement against United States involvement in Vietnam. Based on the belief that such intervention was wrong, it needed the impact of American casualties as precipitating events that began to coalesce the movement. The organizers of social movements operate on the assumption that the problem will not be resolved by the usual mechanisms—that only collective action will bring about social change (Toch, 1965).

A variety of people are attracted to social movements. Most are neither fanatics nor paranoid individuals who live on the fringe of society. Many are right in the middle of the problem, experiencing it directly through deprivation of some sort—such as the blacks, experiencing the injustice of racism, who spearheaded the civil rights movement. But many other people are also drawn to the cause on the basis of personal belief, and their supportive social and political philosophy—the case of whites and nondeprived blacks who act to further the cause of civil rights. However, people from oppressed minorities tend to join movements for immediate, tangible gain, not because of political commitment (Milgram & Toch, 1969). Communism has made more gains in the underdeveloped world because its leaders promised full stomachs—not the elimination of capitalism.

Once we join a social movement, a process of political socialization occurs in which we acquire the appropriate attitudes and behavior. You have probably had the experience of watching a friend or relative join a cause, then become increasingly committed, if not extreme, in his or her views. Sometimes recruitment into a movement occurs through conversion. Significant changes in beliefs occur relatively quickly. A sense of relief and even rapture is experienced as the person throws away old and apparently inadequate beliefs and embraces the new order. At times, the adoption of a new stance is not as new as it seems. For example, most members of the student antiwar movement had family backgrounds with parent values that were congruent with their membership (Haan, Smith & Block, 1968).

Social movements arise, gain prominence, and decline in various ways (Milgram & Toch, 1969). A process of disaffection may set in. Social movements often attract a wide range of individuals, and it is impossible to satisfy all their needs. It soon becomes clear to members that the movement's needs come first, not theirs.

Some movements—like religious cults or youth communes—attempt to break away from society and exist in almost complete independence. Others— such as today's labor unions—may become institutionalized, and relate to society in a regularized and accepted manner. Some maintain their vitality, continuing their impact on the making of laws and the enactment of policy by government bodies: the victories won against racism and sexism would not have occurred without social movements pressuring for them. The continuing injustices of prejudice and discrimination keep the civil rights movement and the women's liberation movement as necessary and viable forces in society.

Sometimes social movements become so institutionalized and successful that they become a powerful force for the status quo; they attempt to oppress new movements from occurring, even those based on similar values. This indicates that social movements are one aspect of a society in which different interest groups compete for available resources. For example, some of Saul Alinsky's earlier work in Chicago successfully organized poor white neighborhoods to improve their situation. Years later, these same organizations became adamantly opposed to the advances being made by black and other minority neighborhood organizations.

The world of social change is full of contradictions and controversy. There, in part, lie its vitality and richness for the social psychologist of today and tomorrow.

Summary

Social problems relate to objective and harmful conditions in society; they become social issues when they are perceived as requiring redress by society.

There are four major approaches to the study of social problems: the consensus and structural-functional approach, the conflict approach, symbolic interactionism, and neo-conservatism.

Racism is a combination of prejudice and discrimination based on the belief that race is the primary determinant of human capabilities and that racial differences produce an inherent superiority of one race over others. Blacks, Chicanos, Puerto Ricans, and people of native Indian ancestry are the foremost victims of racism as shown by their disadvantaged position on every indicator of socioeconomic well-being relating to education, employment, income, housing, and involvement with the criminal justice system.

Pettigrew emphasizes that true integration requires autonomy and self-respect for all groups in a situation of equal-status interaction. A mixed enrichment-integration strategy is thus required for reducing racism and injustice.

Sexism is a combination of prejudice and discrimination usually based on the belief of male superiority. Sex-role stereotypes show a common pattern: females are seen as warm, expressive, and passive; males are pictured as insensitive, independent, and aggressive. These stereotypes along with physical differences are linked to role expectations that limit the options available to both sexes. The family, the educational system, and the mass media all contribute to unequal sex-role socialization and therefore to sexism. The women's liberation movement and changes in child-rearing practices and role enactment are influencing both women and men toward androgyny—a relatively equal possession of both female and male characteristics.

Poverty—the inequitable distribution of wealth—has been defined in two ways: as living below the level of economic resources required for basic subsistence and as a state of relative deprivation assured by the economic gap between the "haves" and "have-nots." The poor tend to be the old, young, minority-group members, and females (particularly the heads of single-parent families).

Social change is proceeding at a rapid pace, and yet stability exists in fundamental social structures and processes. Social psychologists can help develop theories and strategies of social change and use their research and practice skills to document and facilitate social change.

Social change is a modification in the social structure of a society. Katz outlines four types of social change (individual, incremental, radical, and cultural) and identifies the sources in society that push for change—class differences, group competition, differential growth rates, generational differences, and clashes with the wider environment.

Planned change—the deliberate and experimental utilization of valid social knowledge to help solve social problems—has a brief history accelerated by the world's misuse of physical technology. The general strategies of planned change are: (1) the empirical-rational approach, which provides knowledge and assumes people will act rationally in their best interests; (2) the normative-reeducative strategy, which attempts to change social norms, attitudes, and relationships; and (3) the power-coercive approach, which uses social influence to force changes in people's behavior.

The role of social research in social change includes: the documentation of social problems, the development of social indicators, studies of the perceived quality of life, program evaluation, and social impact assessment.

Research on attitude change through persuasive communications asks the question, "Who says what to whom and with what effect?" Characteristics of the source, the message, and the receiver, alone and in combination, have been found to influence the degree of attitude change.

Behavior change through legal compliance is an effective power-coercive strategy, but is not a simple matter as school desegregation illustrates. The 1954 United States Supreme Court decision is the classic example of the involvement of social scientists in public decision making. Unfortunately, research indicates that in general desegregation has neither reduced racial prejudice nor aided black self-esteem and achievement. New teaching methods that stress cooperative interaction are promising, but increasing racial segregation due to "white flight" may spell the ultimate doom of integrated schools.

Social movements—a form of collective behavior—consist of activities by a concerned group to effect social change to ameliorate some harmful condition. Social movements perceive social problems as injustices and typically use power-coercive tactics. The socialization of members and the relationship of the movement to society are important, complex, and at times contradictory elements of social movements.

Further Readings

Aronson, E., Stephan, C., Sikes, J., Blaney, N. & Snapp, M. *The jigsaw classroom.* Beverly Hills, Calif.: Sage, 1978.

Bennis, W. G., Benne, K. D., Chin, R. & Corey, K. E. (Eds.). *The planning of change* (3rd ed.). New York: Holt, Rinehart & Winston, 1976.

Etzioni, A. *Social problems.* Englewood Cliffs, N.J.: Prentice-Hall, 1976.

Oskamp, S. *Attitudes and opinions.* Englewood Cliffs, N.J.: Prentice-Hall, 1977.

Stark, R. *Social problems.* New York: Random House, 1975.

CHAPTER OUTLINE

TWELVE

International Relations

In the next minute, the nations of the world will spend more than $1 million on weapons of human destruction. In the same minute, countless children will die of starvation in the underdeveloped countries of Africa, Asia, and South America. Over the course of a year, total world military expenditures now exceed $400 billion, over one-half of which is accounted for by the United States and the Soviet Union. This sum represents more than twenty times the aid that is provided to the developing countries in one year. It is also equivalent to the gross national productivity of all of Latin America, and more than double that of Africa. In less than four days, military expenditures will exceed the total yearly budget of the United Nations for development, food, health care, and other human needs. In addition, half a million of the world's best scientists are working for the arms industry rather than contributing to the improvement of human welfare (Stockholm International Peace Institute, 1978).

In the words of Robert McNamara, in his role as president of the World Bank, "We cannot build a secure world on a foundation of human misery." The resources used for military development must be re-allocated to human development (*New York Times*, June 1979). We must begin finding ways of discussing disarmament and world development at the same time—ways of transforming military expenditures into resources that support human life (Wallensteen, 1978).

If the costs of preparing for war seem exorbitant and unconscionable, we should not forget the enormous price of going to war—in dollars, in human agony, and in destruction. Twelve million soldiers died in World War I. Civilians in World War I were not affected in mass numbers since the battlefields were removed from centers of population and the weapons were limited in destructive capability. But World War II claimed 15 million civilians in air raids, 28 million people through the atrocities of Nazi Germany, and 21 million soldiers in battle. World War III, the nuclear holocaust that threatens us every minute of every day, will not simply kill us by the millions. It will probably result in the annihilation of all living things on this planet. According to a recent conference of scholars, scientists, and diplomats, the avoidance of nuclear war for the past 30 years has been more a result of luck than good management (Griffiths & Polanyi, 1979).

The first atomic bomb dropped on Hiroshima killed or maimed 160,000 people, about one-half of the population of the city. It devastated an area of 4½ square miles, demolishing about two-thirds of the 90,000 homes. If a modern 20-megaton bomb were dropped on San Francisco, 2 millon of the 3½ million people in the Bay Area would die within the first 10 minutes. Almost another million would be seriously injured, many suffering third-degree burns, deafness, and blindness. Persons as far as 35 miles away would be blinded if they made a reflex glance at the fireball. Medical facilities would be totally inadequate to deal with such a calamity; treatment of the wounded would be hopeless.

Such tremendous horrors of nuclear war led to the formation in 1980 of the Physicians for Social Responsibility—a group of medical doctors dedicated to increasing public awareness of the futility of the arms race. By holding seminars throughout the United States and Canada, the physicians are making clear that nuclear war would be a medical catastrophe that has no cure.

It does not make sense to most social psychologists that the preparation for and perpetration of international destruction have taken priority over the survival of starving children and floundering countries. It is anathema to the humanistic value base of applied social psychology. Social psychologists have sought to understand the processes of international relations that lead to competition and conflict rather than to global collaboration and problem solving. Most of our efforts have been directed to understanding the causes and mechanisms of war, and to developing alternate strategies that might reinforce peace or de-escalate conflict.

While less attention has been directed toward worldwide inequity and the related problems of population control and human rights, we must never forget that all international issues become connected when we view the world as the community of humanity. We must look at these problems that threaten as the ultimate sources of human annihilation.

Our discussion will illustrate the contributions that social psychologists have made to the social science of international relations. One contribution is the social-psychological approach itself. It seeks to link the individual to the structures and processes of world politics. It contributes theoretical components and research methods to the study of international relations. More specifically, the mechanisms of perception, communication, and decision making are social-psychological processes that, in conjunction with national images and attitudes of nationalism, can have considerable impact on relations among states.

Our discussion will also examine the contributions that social psychologists can make to improving international relations through cross-national contact, international negotiation, and the use of intermediaries and problem-solving workshops.

SOCIAL-PSYCHOLOGICAL APPROACHES

How can social psychology help us understand international relations? First, we can try to use the characteristics of individuals—that is, the nature of human beings—to explain interactions among nations. This *total individual approach* is best illustrated by the explanation of war as an expression of humanity's aggressive nature. Freud, for example, spoke of a very powerful aggressive instinct that might lead to the eventual destruction of the world through war and other aggressive acts. In Chapter 14, we will examine the need for aggression as a potential source of human conflict. For now, it serves as an example of an attempt to build a theory of war and peace based on a psychological concept. However, many serious questions must be raised about such attempts (Kelman, 1965).

To attempt to explain international relations through the use of individual characteristics (such as motives, or attitudes, or personality traits) is a gross oversimplification that ignores numerous intermediate levels of analysis and a multitude of other determinants. War is not the simple summation of the aggressive motives of a country's citizens, nor a reflection of the proportion of authoritarian personality types who live there. War, as any form of international interaction, is the outcome of a complex social process involving different individuals with different roles and different interests with differing degrees of influence on the final outcome (Kelman, 1965).

At the international level of analysis, war is the violent use of power by nations to protect or extend their self-interests and integrity. War is engaged in because no supreme world power or global government exists to guarantee such rights (Levi, 1960). Thus, while individual characteristics such as aggressive motives or hostile attitudes might be conditions that support conflict, the basic cause of war is to be found in an international system that has no acceptable mechanism for constructively resolving conflicts among nations. Any attempt to apply psychological principles must therefore begin with an analysis of the relations among nations, and must integrate theories and findings in that broader societal and political framework where they are most useful (Kelman, 1965).

The *partial individual approach* involves the selective application of psychological principles to increase our overall understanding of international relations. If we understand how individual minds operate, this can help illuminate how citizens and government leaders behave when they are relating on an international level. For example, the Freudian defense mechanisms (see Chapter 5) are useful not only for understanding individual pathology, but can also be applied in a milder form to potentially illuminate the reaction of leaders to each other's behavior. A hostile leader who tends to project his or her own impulses onto others may see aggressive intentions where none exist. A citizenry strongly socialized to use the mechanism of denial may not see that their interests are threatened by another state until it is too late.

In this way, the aggregation of individual characteristics and processes that underlie the cultural attributes of a society may influence perception, communication, and decision making, and so bring influence to bear on relations among countries (Singer, 1968). This is especially true when the individuals are the major decision makers in international politics. If, for instance, we accept as psychopathic the paranoid tendencies of Hitler and other Nazi leaders, we have a clear illustration of individual irrationality that had devastating effects on a world scale.

If we wish to fully understand phenomena such as war and peace, then we must consider the part played by the human dimension in international relations (Klineberg, 1964). This is most useful within a truly *social-psychological approach* that attempts to explain the processes of social interaction that make up international behavior. Here we are focusing on dynamic patterns of interaction rather than on fixed characteristics of individuals or social systems.

This approach to international relations begins at the level of interaction among states, applying social-psychological concepts to understand the processes and outcomes of international relations. Its emphasis is on understanding how international actors perceive, communicate, negotiate, and make policy decisions in concert with other individuals within the social and physical constraints of the national and international system in which they operate (Etzioni, 1969; Kelman, 1965). It views people neither as basically aggressive or peaceful, nor as irrational or rational, but as amazingly complex. It views outcomes such as war not as inevitable events determined simply, but as multiply determined events over which people have rational control, exercisable through awareness, understanding, and a reliance on humanistic values.

By studying such processes, social psychologists can help contribute to the understanding and the range of options that are available to humanity. This does not mean that we can develop an independent social psychology of international relations, but rather that we can contribute to the interdiscipliniary study of international behavior in which social-psychological concepts and methods play an integral part (Kelman, 1965).

Social Cognition and International Images

It now appears that World War I was a mistake. Can you believe it? A mistake! At the time, the powers of the Triple Entente—Britain, France, and Russia, later joined by the United States—believed that the Dual Alliance of Germany and Austria-Hungary was motivated by an insatiable thirst for power that would be satisfied by nothing less than a conquest of all of Europe, if not the world. Historical analyses, however, indicate that neither side wanted nor really expected war, but were sucked into an escalating spiral of misperception, threat, and miscalculation that eventually led to armed hostility and 4 years of agony and destruction on a massive scale.

Ralph White's (1966, 1970) social-psychological interpretation of World War I and other wars examines the perceptual processes and differing conceptions of reality that contribute to the outbreak of armed conflict. The enormous paradox of war is that people generally want peace, yet adopt policies and make decisions that lead to war. And they have done so consistently throughout history. White contends that part of the paradox is explained by misperceptions and faulty cognitions in the typically divergent views of reality that each side has of each other and of the situation.

The events leading to World War I were perceived very differently by the two sides. Austrian leaders, struggling to keep the Austro-Hungarian Empire from crumbling, believed that the Serbian agitation, including the assassination of the Austrian archduke, had to be forthrightly punished. The German government supported Austria's need to hold on to the empire, but at the same time tried unsuccessfully to stop Austria from attacking Serbia. Both Austria and Germany greatly feared the awesome military power of Russia and her allies, but Austria believed that the Russian leaders would understand the Empire's threatened position and would not attack in support of Serbia. As events escalated, Germany demanded that Russia cease the mobilization of its army. When this was rejected at the height of the crisis, Germany attacked the Triple Entente, triggering 4 years of massive destruction. From the viewpoint of the entente, Austria's declaration of war on Serbia was an act of cold-blooded aggression and was a clear attempt by Austria and Germany to launch a major European war. Looked at from this angle, the Serbian crisis was a pretext to initiate the conquest of Europe; it had little to do with the stability of the Austro-Hungarian Empire.

White maintains that these radically different views of reality were fueled by at least six forms of misperception and distortion. Each of these misperceptions were evident in the thinking and behavior of the Austrian leaders:

- *The diabolical-enemy image.* The imagined evil of the Serbian agitators convinced the Austrian leaders that everyone else shared this highly negative stereotype. To the German kaiser, Britain was the leader of the plot to isolate and destroy Germany; Britain in fact had desperately tried to stave off the war through negotiation. In a clear case of selective perception (see Chapter 2), the leaders, motivated by fear and frustration, tended to see only part of reality—the part that was congruent with their stereotype of the enemy.
- *The virile self-image.* To the Austrian leaders, preoccupied with their own prestige, the thought of humiliation was unbearable. Fear of humiliation led to an intransigence of positions: any form of retreat or conciliation amounted to an intolerable sign of weakness. (As we saw in Chapter 8, ethnocentrism glorifies the ingroup and denigrates the outgroup.)
- *The moral self-image.* The Austrian government wished to be seen as both strong and right. The ultimatum and mobilization against Serbia, thus maintaining the empire, were seen as justified, proper, orderly, and directed toward peace. So entrenched was this moral self-image that Austria saw no aggression in its move against Serbia—even though the rest of the world perceived it as such. A clear example of perceptual distortion.
- *Selective inattention.* A black-and-white picture of the world is hard to maintain unless one ignores a lot of gray. Austria was so concerned with preserving its empire that it failed to distinguish the important difference between punishing Serbian agitators within its borders and the more serious move of attacking Serbia itself. To Austria, both actions were legitimate. It failed to perceive that an attack on Serbia was much more likely to bring other powers into the conflict.
- *Absence of empathy.* The Austrian leaders failed to understand the positions of their enemies, to understand how the situation looked from their point of view. They did not comprehend that the Serbians saw their last vestiges of autonomy and

pride being threatened by Austrian demands. They did not realize that Russian honor was on the line. In the absence of negotiations, both ignorance and lack of empathy continued to fuel the crisis.

- *Military overconfidence.* Although the Austrians feared the breakup of their empire, they were confident that the combined strength of Austria and Germany would stop others, particularly Russia, from intervening. They did not believe that their enemies would risk a major war over a local issue that was rightfully within Austria's sphere of influence. They were wrong, and the world paid the price.

Historians and political scientists could take issue with this simplified social-psychological analysis. They could point out that broader social forces—such as rising nationalism, an intransigent imperialism, and a strong militarism—were the major causes of World War I—and they might be right. In that sense, the war was not a mistake, but an inevitable calamity of history. However, White's analysis blends the processes of misperception in with these causes, showing the importance of these interlocked sides of the issue. Broader social forces are translated through the perceptions and actions of individuals, and the mechanisms of selectivity, distortion, and misattribution play an important part in determining the outcomes.

Linked to almost every cause of destructive conflict are misperceptions on both sides of the issue. World War I is one of the best examples of how costly such misperceptions can be in world affairs. We have seen this demonstrated in the behavior of the Austrian leaders; but parallel misperceptions were evident on the other side as well. For example, the diabolical-enemy image of German leaders as cold-blooded, power-hungry aggressors, held by the leaders of the entente and the United States, is simply not corroborated by historical analysis.

White broadens his analysis by looking at World War II and the Vietnam War in the same light. The six mechanisms of misperception in World War II operated most clearly in the mind of Hitler, who may not have been psychotic but certainly had paranoid tendencies. In particular, Hitler's diabolical image of the Jews was part of an irrational delusion of persecution; his military overconfidence in attacking Russia was clearly linked to his delusion of grandeur. Of course, to provide a full explanation, these individual factors must be intertwined with causes at each higher level of analysis.

The case of Vietnam demonstrates the processes of misperception on the part of the Vietnamese communists (Vietcong) and militant Americans, both of whom fell victim to various distortions (White, 1966, 1970). Militant Americans held a strong black-and-white picture composed of a diabolical-enemy image and a moral self-image. They believed that the Vietcong fanatics committed outright aggression, coupled with hideous atrocities, to intimidate and conquer the Vietnamese peasantry. America joined the war in support of the clear majority of poor and downtrodden South Vietnamese to keep them free from oppression. According to White, this good-guy/bad-guy image simply does not hold up under closer scrutiny.

The virile self-image saw toughness as virtue, compromise as surrender, and negotiation as useful only if, backed by military superiority, it yielded the desired outcome. Military overconfidence on the part of the Americans and South Vietnamese grossly underestimated the tenacity and skill of the Vietcong. America's eventual withdrawal stands in stark contrast to its many prior statements of military superiority. Examples of the militants' selective inattention and absence of empathy complete the picture of misperceptions that permeated the debacle of Vietnam.

The Vietnamese communists, while eventually gaining their ends, were no less susceptible in general to similar distortions in their world view. The Americans were seen as cruel aggressors who were desolating South Vietnam, who had killed or wounded nearly a million Vietnamese, imprisoned 400,000 people, raped 40,000 women, and tortured and buried alive 5,000 more. In contrast, the Vietnamese communists saw themselves as peaceful and patriotic people, who believe in democracy and social justice for all, while ignoring the atrocities committed by their side.

Both sides in Vietnam also demonstrated a common tendency in conflict— the dehumanization of the enemy. Enemies are not people—they are animals or worse, and derogatory terms are used to refer to them (gooks, krauts, Japs). They therefore do not need to be treated with the fairness and respect that humans deserve. They can be mistreated, tortured, fire-bombed, exterminated. War *is* hell.

The Arab-Israeli conflict is another case of international hostility that is open to social-psychological analysis. Johnston (1977) points to mutual stereotypes, a

On March 26, 1979, Anwar el-Sadat, Menachem Begin, and Jimmy Carter signed an accord putting an end to the war between Israel and Egypt. *(William Karel/Sygma)*

shared disaster mentality, and the continuing inability of either side to comprehend the fears and aspirations of the other. Political factors in both camps work against peaceful resolution while the constant escalation of armaments moves the Middle East and the world closer to war. Although this view has been moderated by recent advances toward peace in the area, social-psychological factors remain as important and evident as ever. Box 12.1 presents a description of the Arab-Israeli conflict in terms of White's major forms of misperception.

Box 12.1   FOCUS ON RESEARCH
Misperception in the Middle East Conflict

A great deal is at stake in the Middle East conflict: the survival of Israel, justice for the Arabs, and, assuming the potential of the United States and the Soviet Union to clash in World War III, the lives of hundreds of millions of people. Some consensus exists regarding what is a fair and peaceful settlement. Why do both sides reject it? Social psychologist Ralph White of George Washington University draws on historical accounts and personal interviews to suggest that a number of nonrational processes are fueling the continuation of this dreadful and dangerous conflict.

According to White, a psychologically rational peace settlement must have two essentials: survival of Israel within pre-1967 borders and independence or autonomy for Palestinians in the West Bank and Gaza Strip. In addition, White offers a list of ten concessions on each side that would promote peace. For example, the Arabs could provide a clear commitment not to use war to challenge the existence of Israel and could participate in a Middle East arms control program. The Israelis could guarantee the return of all occupied territory and could withdraw most civilian settlements from Arab land.

How would each side react to this proposal? Each would declare that it makes no distinction between the aggressors (the other side) and the victims (their side). Each would cast the other side in the diabolical enemy image: Arabs seeing Israelis as a Zionist, racist, fascist cancer, and Israelis seeing Arabs as fanatical authoritarians who are unchangeably hostile to Israel. At the same time, each side maintains a righteous and virile self-image and shows a definite lack of empathy for the other.

However, the central misperception of both the Arabs and the Israelis is that they do not realize how much they could probably do to change the other's behavior. The Arabs do not see that Israeli fear of a second holocaust in the face of a hostile and much larger Arab enemy leads the Israelis to cling to the disputed land. The Israelis do not see that the majority of Arabs want peace, but are seeking assurances to maintain their honor and their rights. Arab anger fuels Israeli fear; Israeli cautiousness fuels Arab hostility.

To prevent war, the Arabs could clarify the "rights of the Palestinians" so that Israelis do not interpret this to mean the destruction of Israel. The Israelis could try to come to terms with the Arab nations—particularly Egypt. The United States could exert legitimate influence on both sides to reach a settlement. [The initiatives of President Carter and the resulting Camp David accords have since shown the way to peace in the Middle East.]

Source: White, R. K. Misperception in the Arab-Israeli conflict. *Journal of Science Issues*, 1977, *33*(1), 190–221.

International Images. We have seen, again and again, that social-psychological analyses of international relations rely heavily on the concept of *image*—the organized representation of a social object in a person's cognitive system (Kelman, 1965). Some of us may have an image of the Chinese as industrious and courteous, but also as mundane and ethnocentric. The concepts of image and of stereotype overlap. However, images of all nationalities or countries are not necessarily restricted or oversimplified sets of beliefs. Images may be very complex when we examine the social object on a multitude of descriptive and evaluative dimensions.

We can also define image in a broader way, making the concepts of image and attitude almost indistinguishable from one another. Scott (1965), for example, sees image as a composition of three different components: cognitive attributes about the object (You perceive Australians to be fun-loving, hard-working, and resourceful); an affective component, involving liking or disliking (You hold positive emotions of attraction and trust toward Australians); and an action component, consisting of a set of appropriate responses to the object (You hope to visit Australia someday and get to know some of the people). It might have been simpler if social psychologists had stayed with the concept of attitude rather than develop the idea of images. However, in the social psychology of international relations, the concept of image—representing all attitudinal variables—is particularly practical, useful, and legitimate. It gives us a means to study the views that different nationalities hold of themselves and others (Kelman, 1965).

Our images of nations and nationalities are affected by our psychological makeup, by the process of socialization, by contact and interaction with other nationalities, and by world events. These images, in turn, contribute to our behavior in international relations. Images affect the way we (or our leaders) define a situation, make decisions, formulate policy, negotiate our differences, and resolve conflict.

One of the most interesting aspects of the study of images is the concept of *mirror image.* This was popularized by Urie Bronfenbrenner (1961), an American social psychologist who also speaks Russian. During his 1961 trip through the Soviet Union (to visit universities and laboratories), Bronfenbrenner was able to wander alone through public places and strike up conversations with Russian citizens. Many people were eager to talk with a foreigner, but Bronfenbrenner also took the initiative to speak to those who remained silent. These conversations concentrated on Russia and America. Bronfenbrenner was at first troubled by the distorted image that the Russians tended to have of the United States. However, a much more disturbing awareness soon overtook him: the Russians' distorted view of America was very similar to the average American's view of Russia. In short, *a negative mirror image.* Such reciprocal distortion is a frightening realization, especially when it is probable that neither side is right. Sad to say, this specific form of the Cold War mirror image is 20 years old, and yet it is probably almost as accurate today as it was in 1960. The major components of the mirror image are presented in Table 12.1.

Part of the explanation for the mirror image is that each side hears what it wants to hear and discounts or ignores information that is discrepant with its existing image. This selectivity and distortion may ease the pain of cognitive dissonance, but it tends to cast the world in dangerous oversimplifications of

Table 12.1   MIRROR IMAGE OF THE COLD WAR

American View	*Russian View*
1. *They* are the aggressors.	
Russia is a warmonger bent on imposing its system on the rest of the world. Witness its intervention in Czechoslovakia, Berlin, Hungary, and Cuba.	America is a warmonger bent on imposing its power on the rest of the world and the Soviet Union itself. Witness its intervention in the Russian revolution, Korea, Taiwan, and Cuba.
2. *Their* government exploits and deludes the people.	
Convinced communists are a minority but control Russia. Elections with only one party are a travesty. The people are kept from the truth through government control of the mass media.	A capitalistic-militaristic clique controls America. Voting is a farce since all candidates are selected by the same powerful interests. A controlled news media keeps the truth from the American people.
3. The masses of the people are not sympathetic to the regime.	
Russians are not behind their government but praise is necessary for getting along. Most Russians would prefer to live under our system if they could.	The majority of Americans want peace but are under the control of the ruling clique. If Americans were allowed to become acquainted with communism they would choose it as their form of government.
4. *They* cannot be trusted.	
The Soviets do not keep promises. Their talk of peace is a propaganda maneuver. Everything they do is part of a scheme to further aggressive communist aims.	The Americans do not keep promises. They have no real intention of disarming. Everything they do is to be viewed with suspicion.
5. *Their* policy verges on madness.	
Soviet demands on crucial problems such as disarmament are completely unrealistic. In pursuit of their irresponsible policies, they do not hesitate to risk war itself.	The American position on crucial problems is completely unrealistic. In pursuit of their irresponsible policies, they run the risk of war itself.

Source: Bronfenbrenner (1961).

black and white, good and evil. Furthermore, the operation of the *self-fulfilling prophecy* (see Chapter 2) leads us to treat the object of our image in ways that lead to the confirmation of our image and to the continuing reciprocity of the mirror image. For example, Bronfenbrenner notes that the restrictions placed on the travel of Soviet scientists in the United States (in reaction to similar restrictions in the Soviet Union) only serve to reinforce the Russian view of a lack of American freedom.

The mirror image and the major forms of misperception have a great deal in common (White, 1970). The diabolical enemy image and the virile and moral self-image are the mainstays of the negative mirror image. Each has a kernel of truth in it, just as group stereotypes do, but each is fueled by the fears, aspirations, and policies of the image holder in ways that dangerously distort reality and negatively affect related behavior.

The American-Soviet mirror image, for instance, is developed and maintained by selective inattention, slanted interpretation, paranoid suspicion, and other perceptual and cognitive distortions of the human mind (White, 1965). Further studies of the mirror-image phenomenon have generally supported the occurrence and effect of such perceptions. For example, Oskamp (1965) asked American college students to evaluate fifty actions taken by both the United States and the Soviet Union in the recent past. The study showed that American actions were invariably rated more favorably than Soviet actions, even when they were quite similar.

But the phenomenon goes far beyond this obvious example. Mirror image is a widespread, powerful fact of global life and must be taken into account when we attempt to understand the social psychology of international behavior. Haque (1973), for example, has identified the mirror image shared by Indians and Pakistanis over more than two decades of international conflict. Salazar and Marin (1977) found support for the mirror-image hypothesis with Colombia and Venezuelan college students whose countries were engaged in a boundary dispute. Haque and Lawson (1980) demonstrated that the mirror-image phenomenon generalizes beyond the immediate antagonists to allies who may be involved in the conflict. Arabs and Israelis showed a black-white mirror image of the Russians and Americans just as they did for their own nationalities (see Figure 12.1). Because of the fundamental significance and implications of international images, we can expect a continuing interest in the processes of perception and misperception in the field of international relations (Jervis, 1976).

Communication and Decision Making in International Relations

Cognition blends almost imperceptibly into communication in the social-psychological study of international relations. The images one holds and the processes of misperception shape the style and content of communicative acts and, in turn, are revealed by those same acts. It is not easy to separate these two major processes. The actor's definition of the situation—composed of perceptions and images—helps determine the patterns of communication and interaction that develop between actors. The patterns of communications among nations help to shape events of international significance. Intertwined with this is the importance of the process of decision making as a crucial element of international relations, especially in crisis situations.

Pruitt (1965) presents a basic format for understanding how international actors define their situation. This involves their image of other people's intentions and capabilities and the actor's perception of how these elements relate to their own policies and goals. Within three broad classes of images, there are specific perceptions that influence behavior between nations:

- predictions about the future behavior of the other nation, particularly the degree of *threat* perception—that is, the belief that the other nation is likely to frustrate the attainment of desired goals

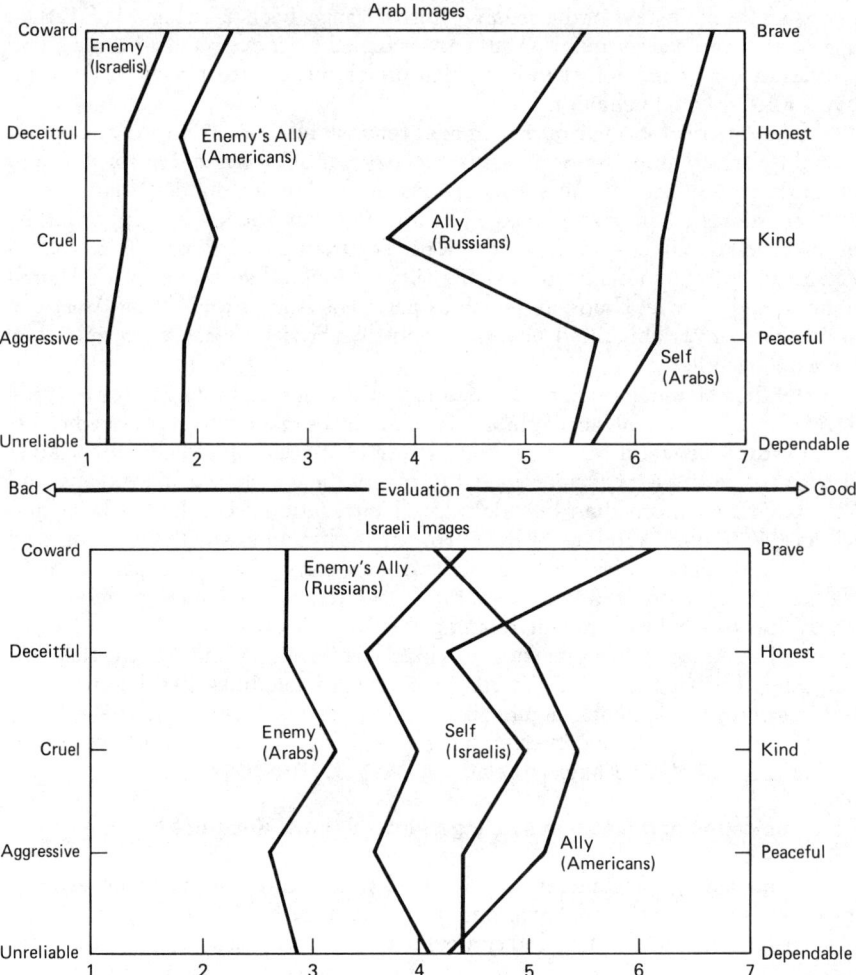

Figure 12.1   Mirror Images of the Arab/Israeli Conflict.
Source: Haque & Lawson (1980).

- perceptions of the basic characteristics of the other nation, related to degrees of *trust or distrust*—that is, the extent to which these characteristics may help or harm the relationship
- conceptions of appropriate ways to deal with the other nation, particularly the *responsiveness* or helpfulness that should be displayed

The shape of these major images and particular perceptions constitutes the main definition of the international situation. The degree of threat perception affects the actor's ability to solve problems effectively; a high level of threat is especially disruptive to this process. When national aspirations are threatened, actors become less aware of the complexity of the environment, consider fewer alternatives, and choose their course of action impulsively, without adequate review. Trust acts as a buffer or shock absorber against threatening information; it leads one to look twice or reinterpret threatening evidence rather than act impulsively. Distrust sets up a wall of suspicion; it sees subterfuge in every action, regardless of intention; it predisposes nations to blame their enemies for all misfortunes. Responsiveness or an orientation of helpfulness between nations leads to the seeking of middle ground in negotiations. A lack of responsiveness leads to harsh tactics in dealing with the other nation.

How these major perceptions of international actors are expressed in communicative acts has been studied systematically. In his content analysis of the "elite articulations" of American and Soviet policymakers, political scientist J. David Singer (1964) painted an accurate picture of Soviet and American policy goals during the Cold War (1957–1960)—a time of relatively stable but hostile relations. Singer randomly selected editorials and articles about foreign affairs from major newspapers and journals published in the United States (*New York Times, Department of State Bulletin,* and *Foreign Affairs*), and in the Soviet Union (*Pravda, Kommunist,* and *International Affairs*). For Singer's purposes, the articles had to be written by American or Soviet citizens, and had to deal with foreign affairs in an interpretive manner so that the writer's perceptions would be apparent.

Trained raters coded the material into four major areas, each composed of several categories:

1. the image of the international environment—for example, the relationship viewed as a struggle between ideologies, social systems, or power centers
2. an evaluation of the power balance—such as the question of the relative progress of American and Soviet military technology and production
3. an evaluation of the other's policies—for instance, their ultimate and dominant political goals
4. an evaluation of one's own policies—such as the prerequisites for successful negotiation

The results of the content analysis were intriguing in their comparisons of perceptions, and troubling in their implications for international relations. To cite but a few samples from this study: American policymakers tended to see conflict as a result of differing social systems or ideologies; the Russian opinion leaders perceived aggression by the "imperialist camp" led by the United States. The Soviets believed that their technology was developing faster; many Americans agreed, reflecting their shock at the then-recent success of the first Sputnik satellite. Americans believed that the Soviets were concerned with expanding their influence toward world domination; the Soviets reciprocated by accusing the United States of precisely the same goal. Neither saw the other side as interested in self-preservation, and yet each believed that the other side would give priority to security over ideology in making policy decisions. In its perceptions of its own policies, specifically the approach to negotiations, each side saw strength as the basis for successful negotiations. Parity or equality was not good enough; negotiating with a stronger adversary was hopeless.

Singer (1964) concludes that these articulations lead to pessimism about future American-Soviet relations. In fact, the policymakers themselves are aware that the two countries have many incompatible goals. Unfortunately, each country acts in a way that *aggravates* these differences. Each underestimates the extent to which its own behavior confirms the negative view held by the other. Each goes to excessive lengths to extol its own virtues and to exaggerate the aggressiveness of the other side. *Thus, the communications of the elite decision makers parallel the mirror images of the common people.* These maladaptive behaviors seem to result not from legitimate national interests or incompatible value systems, but from a mixture of these conflicts with inept and shortsighted policies.

The major powers have been slow to develop strategies for current and future survival. Singer's analysis and conclusions may be two decades old, yet his findings reflect what is still going on between the United States and the Soviet Union: threat perception, distrust, and a lack of responsiveness. Policies are articulated and negotiations are approached in the same competitive and cautious manner. The prospects of true detente and disarmament seem as remote as ever.

We can also study the processes of communication and decision making by examining the diplomatic notes and speeches of policymakers and political leaders, particularly during times of international crisis when there is a strong threat to fundamental values and time is short. These too indicate perceptions and positions and show certain common trends (North, Holsti, Zaninovich & Zinnes, 1963; Holsti, 1972). These documents reveal such dysfunctional patterns as a strong sense of time pressure, a concern with short-range solutions, and a decrease in novel information. Channels of communication become overloaded, freedom of action is perceived as increasingly restricted, and the adversary receives less attention than one's allies. Obviously, such limitations in communication and decision making may have dire consequences for the nations involved.

In their pioneering work, Holsti and his political science colleagues identify ways to differentiate between crises that escalate to armed conflict and crises that are resolved peacefully. Following up on these basic analyses, social psychologists have asked this question: Can communications made during a crisis be distinguished on the basis of their degree of complexity (Suedfeld & Tetlock, 1977; Suedfeld, Tetlock & Raminez, 1977)? The complexity of communication relates to the effectiveness of decision making and problem solving and a lack of complexity is one of the signs of the dangerous phenomenon of groupthink (see Chapter 7). Specifically, Suedfeld and his colleagues have developed the concept of integrative complexity based on earlier work measuring the degree of cognitive complexity in personality functioning. A communication that is high on complexity shows a larger number of choices that are being considered, a greater tendency to search for further information, and a view of social relationships as conditional rather than fixed or rigid. Written paragraphs are rated on a scale ranging from 1 (low complexity) to 7 (high complexity). An average rating for the entire document (speech, diplomatic note) thus indicates the overall level of integrative complexity.

Applying the concept of complexity of communication to international relations, Suedfeld and Tetlock (1977) compared speeches and diplomatic notes from the 1914 crisis (which led to World War I) with communications from the 1962 Cuban missile crisis (which was resolved without armed conflict). Random paragraphs were selected from statements of the leading decision makers at both the preliminary and climax phases of the crises. Communications during the 1914 crisis showed not only significantly lower complexity ratings, but also a *decreasing* complexity as the crisis moved toward its climax. That indicates that decision makers became more simplistic and rigid in their positions as they stumbled toward war.

By contrast, communications during the 1962 crisis showed not only higher complexity, but also an *increasing* complexity from the initial phase to the climatic resolution. American decision makers were aware of the dangers of oversimplification and took pains to consider all alternatives, to search for positive and negative information related to each alternative, and to maintain the flexibility of their options (Holsti, Brody & North, 1964; Suedfeld & Tetlock, 1977). The result was a high level of accurate communication between the United States and the Soviet Union, resulting in a detailed plan of mutually contingent steps rather than a series of unacceptable demands and ultimatums—such as occurred in 1914.

We might ask, however, if the differences in complexity were the result of other factors: the historical differences between 1914 and 1962, for instance, or the fact that different countries were involved in the two crises. To rule out these possibilities, Suedfeld and Tetlock examined two additional set of crises. Each set involved two crises that occurred in the same historical period between the same protagonists. One led to war; the other did not. The 1911 Moroccan crisis—a peacefully resolved conflict involving France, Germany, and England—was compared to the 1914 crisis. The Berlin crisis of 1948 and the Cuban missile crisis of 1962—both resolved peacefully—were compared to the 1950 crisis that led to the outbreak of the Korean War. As shown in Table 12.2, crises that led to war had lower levels of integrative complexity in their communications than crises that were resolved peacefully.

These results have very important implications for the study and improvement of international relations. Based on what we have already observed, suppose, for example, that crises leading to hostility may be signaled by a decrease in the complexity of diplomatic communications. To test this hypothesis still further, Suedfeld, Tetlock, and Raminez (1977) applied their technique of content analysis to the 30-year history of conflict between Israel and the Arab states. Speeches on the Middle East conflict, delivered at the United Nations by delegates from Israel, Egypt, Syria, and the United Arab Republic, were scored for their level of

Table 12.2   COMPLEXITY OF COMMUNICATION IN INTERNATIONAL CRISES

Country		Mean Complexity Score	
Early 20th-Century Crises		Moroccan Crisis (1911)	World War I (1914)
England		5.16	2.58
France		4.83	1.42
Germany		3.92	1.84
Mid-20th-Century Crises	Berlin (1948)	Korea (1950)	Cuba (1962)
United States	3.00	1.75	4.75
U.S.S.R.	2.50	1.67	4.67

Source: Suedfeld & Tetlock (1977).

integrative complexity. Four crisis points that led to war were identified beforehand: the Arab attack on Israel in 1948, the Anglo-French-Israeli invasion of Egypt during the Suez Canal crisis of 1956, the Six-Day War of 1967, and the October War of 1973. The Lebanese Civil War of 1976 was also included as a possible point of international hostility, although Israel was not directly involved. Speeches were selected from the years preceding a war, from the years in which wars occurred (in the months previous to the outbreak of hostility), and from the years immediately following the wars. In addition, speeches from other years were randomly selected to serve as an overall comparison.

The results, shown in Figure 12.2, clearly indicate that *complexity dropped dramatically during every one of the years in which war occurred.* One exception is the Arab scores in the Suez crisis of 1956—an unexpected invasion without mutual escalation of animosity and preparation for war. Even the questionable case of the 1976 Lebanese crisis shows a decline in complexity of communication. Thus, the study concludes that even in a continuing hostile confrontation, major outbreaks of violence are preceded by low levels of integrative complexity.

Is it possible to use results like this to predict and improve international relations? The answer is a cautious "yes." Communications of decision makers could be monitored for integrative complexity. Decision makers could attempt to maintain high levels of differentiation and integration during times of crisis. High-level policymakers could be selected partly on the strength of their capacity for cognitive complexity, then trained to think and communicate at a higher level of complexity. (This is a highly appropriate spot for the use of small-group training procedures to improve communication and problem-solving capacities. See Chapter 7.) In addition, decision makers could be made more aware of the pitfalls of simplicity and rigidity, and adjust their behavior accordingly (Suedfeld et al., 1977).

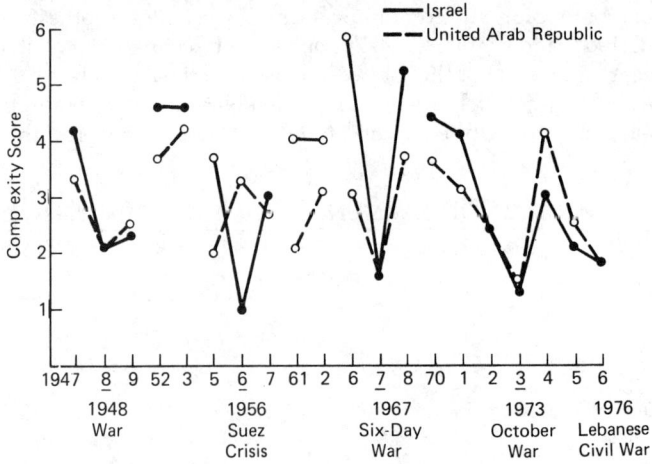

Figure 12.2   Integrative Complexity and the Arab/Israeli Conflict.
Source: Suedfeld, Tetlock & Raminez (1977).

These are then ways that social-psychological approaches can make a contribution to the wider study of international decision making (see Robinson & Snyder, 1965). Another way, following the partial individual approach, is to provide a psychological analysis of decision making. Kinder and Weiss (1978) review major advances in this area and suggest that human beings are incapable of carrying out the mental operations required by a fully rational model of decision making. We do not process information accurately and honestly all the time. We are not able to revise our judgments appropriately in the light of new information. Two major shortcomings in decision making are directly related to theories from social psychology. First, decision makers often cling to an irrational consistency as predicted by cognitive dissonance theory. New information is uncritically assimilated to established beliefs in order to reduce inconsistency. As discussed in Chapter 2, individuals often develop further justifications for decisions taken in order to reduce dissonance. Thus, postdecision dissonance leads to an emphasis on the benefits of the chosen alternative, while rejected options become less desirable. Second, attribution theory, particularly the fundamental attribution error (see Chapter 2), explains how decision makers overestimate the importance of personal characteristics of the enemy while neglecting situation forces. Add to these distortions the defensive effects of stress, and international decision making becomes a complex, multidetermined process that researchers have only begun to understand. The perceptions and images of decision makers, their definitions of the situation, and the manner in which they process information and communicate are fundamental parts of the policymaking process on which our lives depend.

Nationalism: The Ideology of the Nation State

So far we have focused on the thinking and behavior of the decision-making elites—the heads of governments, politicians, diplomats, and bureaucrats who are directly involved in international relations. But what of the attitudes of ordinary citizens? How do they think and feel about international policies? How do they relate to their country's involvement in international relations? Citizens at large have important beliefs and opinions about foreign policy. But what is the link between public opinion and official policy? Which one influences the other, and to what degree? Puzzling questions indeed, but ones we need to address. However, to do so, we will focus not on the functioning of public opinion in general (a slippery thing to grasp), but rather on the more accessible concept of nationalism.

Consider your friend down the street. John is, let's say, "a good American." This means that John is aware of being a citizen of the United States; that he is proud of being an American; that he is loyal to his country and tends to elevate its status above that of other countries. And it probably means that John sees the United States as having legitimate goals that it pursues in its interaction with other nations.

In an early definitive work, social psychologist Kenneth Terhune specified *national consciousness*, *national ethnocentrism*, and *national aspirations* as common dimensions of *nationalism*—a favorable attitude toward one's nation, involving national awareness, loyalty, pride, and a predisposition to support and assert the interests of one's nation.

Since nationalism involves support for advancing the separate interests of one nation, it is potentially a hindrance to international cooperation and a source of international conflict. For example, White's (1966) analysis of World War I saw nationalism as one of the strongest underlying causes of armed conflict. Strongly advancing the interests of one nation can lead to competition with opposing interests and, ultimately, to violent conflict. However, there is no fundamental reason why the pursuit of national interests should rule out cooperation among nations (Terhune, 1965). It is only when interests clash and national interests override the interests of other nations that conflict ensues.

Furthermore, Terhune found that attitudes of nationalism, defined mainly as national aspiration, did not relate to attitudes of internationalism as measured by a scale of international cooperation. A mixed sample of nationals from twelve countries were measured on scales of both nationalism and international cooperation, as well as for their loyalty to their family, their country, and the world. (A high nationalism score meant greater loyalty to one's country; a high internationalism score showed greater world loyalty.) Scores on nationalism related positively to scores on internationalism, indicating that a person can support both the aspirations of one's own country as well as the need for international cooperation. Thus, there seems to be no basic incompatibility between these two sets of attitudes of citizens. However, the development of internationalism may be prevented as long as nationalistic tendencies are subverted by pressures for countries to join one of several ideological camps that are in conflict with each other.

A truly social-psychological analysis must relate attitudes of nationalism to the functioning of the nation state, so that both the individual and societal levels are taken into account. Daniel Katz (1965) defines nationalism as the *ideology of the nation state*—that is, as an integrated set of values and attitudes that reflects and sustains the major functions of the state. What are the major functions of the nation state from a social-psychological point of view? Katz outlines three possibilities:

- *Internal integration.* The state has control over political decisions that affect the provision of services, the allocation of resources, and the resolution of conflicts among the society's competing interest groups.
- *Maximization of the input/output ratio.* The state uses many methods, including the forceful conquest of other states, to acquire as many resources (inputs) as possible. The resources are then distributed to its members.
- *Survival against external enemies.* The state is charged with protecting its people from outside aggression or, on a lesser scale, from competing interests. Therefore, the state must develop military power and join alliances to compete and survive.

Katz then identifies three components of nationalistic ideology:

- *statism,* which supports the state as having supreme authority, as protecting national sovereignty, and as being the legitimate source of political decisions
- *institutional nationalism,* which supports the political, economic, and educational institutions that serve the national purpose
- *cultural identity,* which reflects the unique heritage and way of life of the people as contrasted with the identity of other cultures

Thus, for example, a Canadian who is highly nationalistic supports Canada's claim of sovereignty over the continental shelf, favors school children singing "O Canada" to start the day, and sees the culture of Canada as having unique and superior qualities. These individual attitudes would be highly intertwined with institutional and national systems through the process of socialization and the enactment of national roles.

Socialization teaches the attitudes and behaviors that are appropriate to being a citizen of a given country. Most Americans, for example, come to see the Stars and Stripes as an important symbolic expression of national sovereignty and pride. They come to value the political institution of democracy, the economic system of free enterprise, and the use of technology to advance the national purpose. When they are called upon to enact national roles as citizens, they tend to comply. Most obey national laws and pay taxes; most vote on occasion; and almost all honor their national rituals, such as standing when the national anthem is played. During wartime, the national role becomes even more demanding, and may dominate other roles: the country calls its workers into defense production and its soldiers to the battlefield. In good times and bad, in times of peace and war, the attitudes of the citizenry are at the roots of nationalistic behavior.

One possible mechanism for counteracting the negative effects of nationalistic socialization which support international conflict is through *peace education* (Burns, 1980; Wulf, 1974). As a connecting link between peace research and social action, peace education would increase citizens' knowledge and concern about improved international cooperation. However, implementing peace education is no simple matter since there are a number of different definitions and a disagreement over whether it should take place within or outside of the formal education system. Some contend that integrating peace education within the existing system renders it incapable of challenging the injustices within and between societies that must be changed if true peace is to be obtained. Nonetheless, more attempts to implement and evaluate peace-education programs would be a useful step toward reducing the destructive elements of nationalism.

The socialization of nationalism and the enactment of national roles are related to the existence of the *military-industrial complex*—an element of any society that uses military power to protect and, at times, advance the national interest. In his 1961 farewell address to the nation, President Eisenhower spoke of the military-industrial complex, warning Americans about the possibility of unwarranted influence on national policy by the huge industrial and military sectors of society. Since Eisenhower was a military man before he became a politician, his warning had special significance; the issue, in fact, remains alive and unresolved to this day. However, an even more specific focus was presented in a review and analysis by Pilisuk and Hayden (1965), directed toward the question: *Is there a military-industrial complex that prevents peace?* Interpretations and conclusions are summarized in Box 12.2.

IMPROVING INTERNATIONAL RELATIONS

The powerful nations of the world hold in their hands the future of the human race and all life on this planet. All nations of the world, many of which are illogical confederations formed through historical accidents, cling ironically to two outda-

Box 12.2   FOCUS ON THEORY
Military-Industrial Complex: Myth or Reality?

Is there a military-industrial complex in the United States that prevents world peace? If such a conspiracy does exist in its most sinister form, then peace researchers are wasting their time; whatever steps they uncover that would lead to peace can just as easily be bypassed to prevent peace. In a classic analysis of this crucial issue, social psychologist Mark Pilisuk and economist (and later student activist) Thomas Hayden provide a disturbing conclusion about the military-industrial complex.

President Dwight Eisenhower cautioned about the unwarranted influence of the military-industrial complex. Other commentators before and after Eisenhower have drawn attention to the excessive profits of arms makers, to the tendency of the defense industry to lobby for greater military preparedness, and to the intermingling among military, industrial, and government leaders. The real question is whether this complex has the power to strongly influence foreign policy making, or whether it is simply one of many interest groups within a pluralistic society whose power is therefore held in check by other forces.

To help answer this question, Pilisuk and Hayden draw upon the theory of a power elite developed by sociologist C. Wright Mills. According to Mills, the United States since World War II has seen the rise of corporate and military elites to positions of institutional power, thus allowing control of the business cycle, foreign policy, and political decision making. The groups composing the power elite are not a conscious, coordinated conspiracy, but they do share a common ideology (capitalism) and many similar vested interests in military, political, and economic matters.

When the civilian component is added to the power elite, for example, through the involvement of university professors and institutes in military research and planning, Pilisuk and Hayden see no countervailing forces left to stand against the military-industrial complex. Furthermore, a number of core beliefs in American society justify the maintenance of the military, the corporate economy, and a partisan political system that offers limited democracy. One such belief is that efficacy is preferable to principle in foreign affairs and, therefore, that violence is preferable as a means of defense. These beliefs also clash with the necessary conditions for an enduring peace such as the acceptance of international authority.

The conclusion? American society does not simply contain a military-industrial complex. American society as a whole *is* a military-industrial complex with all of its institutions and mores geared to prevent the radical change necessary to produce an enduring world peace.

Source: Pilisuk, M. & Hayden, T. Is there a military industrial complex which prevents peace? Consensus and countervailing power in pluralistic systems. *Journal of Social Issues*, 1965, *21*(3), 67–117.

ted vines which they used to swing through the jungle of international relations. One is *national sovereignty*; the other, *national security*.

The concept and ideology of the nation state vests power in the weapons of destruction amassed to protect a country's sovereignty—its right to self-determination. The waging of war to maintain or maximize the interests of the state remains a destructive option of potentially catastrophic proportions. But the overriding goal of human survival is not strong enough to convince nations to yield power to some form of world government or world law. Thus, each day we warily walk along the precipice of potential annihilation.

As I look at this self-centered, irrational movement toward doomsday, I am concerned about the ability of the human race to overcome the ethnocentric forces that feed international conflict. I also worry about whether the world community will develop more equitable mechanisms for sharing the world's resources as a means of reducing this important source of conflict. Therefore, along with other social psychologists and social scientists, I look for ways of improving international relations. We search for, study, and sometimes implement what we see as constructive approaches to world affairs. We look for ways of changing attitudes, behavior, and social structures that will reduce the level of existing and potential destruction.

We must consider some of these approaches, including arms reduction, cross-national contact, international negotiation, and the use of problem-solving workshops. We must also speculate on the future of international relations, particularly in the areas of population control, human rights, and world order.

Deterrence versus Reciprocated Reduction

The development of military power is the common strategy followed by nations to protect their national security and interests, maintain internal control, and prevent or resist outside aggression. *Deterrence* involves the threat to use force as a response to prevent the use of force by an adversary (Morgan, 1977). Deterrence is a threat of punishment—a threat so costly, in the enemy's view, that the enemy does not dare initiate aggression. It is through this approach, this major world strategy, that strong and weak countries alike are able to stockpile weapons of human destruction and justify them as "defensive."

The essence of deterrence—manipulation via threat—is a primitive approach to social relationships (Morgan, 1977). It is most easily invoked when we see our opponents as unreasonable, or barbaric, or simple-minded, or as less than human. We resort to threat and punishment with children, animals, criminals, or other creatures who only appear to understand force and violence. In so doing we have admitted a failure to develop effective communication and problem solving as a means of settling our differences. At the same time, however, the expressed goals—peace, to take but one example—are perfectly laudable. The deterrence approach thus reflects the advice of Machiavelli or the interpersonal manipulation of Varela (see Chapters 4 and 6) wherein deceit and control are used to reach moral or humane objectives.

Although deterrence is the crudest attempt at behavioral control, it has been developed as an exceedingly complex field of study in military and political science (Dedring, 1976). It has been portrayed as a highly rational enterprise in which calculations are made regarding *what* weapons systems are necessary to back *what* threat with *what* punishment as a response to *what* attack. The technological details of modern warfare restrict such discussions to a select few, making it difficult (impossible, more likely) for most of the citizens of the world to know whether deterrence guarantees peace or even makes it more probable.

Deterrence has been practiced since the first caveman got a bigger club. Since

Nations commonly develop military power in order to protect their national security and interests, maintain internal control, and prevent or resist outside aggression. *(David Burnett)*

then each new development in the technology of violence has led to the same prediction: "War is now unthinkable." But gunpowder, the airplane, the tank, and the nuclear bomb have all been effectively used to maim and destroy human beings soon after each method was discovered. The buildup of arms itself communicates that war is not impossible, but is in fact acceptable under certain circumstances.

The claim that deterrence prevents war does not hold up even with a superficial historical analysis. In a sophisticated analysis, anthropologists Naroll, Bullough, and Naroll (1974) looked at the behavior of states over a 2000-year period. They found that military preparedness was typically practiced as a form of deterrence; but in the long run, the preparation for war through arms races made war *more* probable. This conclusion is supported by political scientist Michael Wallace (1979) whose quantitative analysis showed that international disputes preceded by an arms race were much more likely to lead to war than disputes with no prior arms race. As Morgan (1977) points out, the availability of military power makes force a plausible option in foreign policy. Forces developed to deter a major adversary can be used to coerce minor adversaries into acceptable policies and behavior. Thus, even in a time when "war is unthinkable," the threat of force goes on.

The viability of deterrence hinges on the use of threat, and the effectiveness of threat (which depends on some rather shaky assumptions) can lead to frightening outcomes. Obviously then, the use of threat in international relations is highly questionable (see Frank, 1960; Milburn, 1977; Singer, 1958). The simple point is that threats are typically invoked and responded to in ways that further aggravate the situation. Threats are used when one assumes that the adversary is untrustworthy and hostile. Not only does the threat communicate this, but it may easily invoke the self-fulling prophecy that leads the adversary to behave and be perceived in ways that are indeed hostile. The inevitable result is that the adversaries become locked into a vicious and self-generating conflict spiral of hostility and violence.

Threats are a form of stress that can reduce the effectiveness of communication and problem solving at a time when these processes are crucial to mutually acceptable and peaceful outcomes (Milburn, 1977). However, the use of threats is more complex than it first appears to be. The manner in which threats are perceived has a great deal to do with the response made to it. The side that makes a threat is most aware of the demands in the threat—that is, what the threat is supposed to accomplish. However, the receiver of the threat is likely to emphasize the dangers or costs that are threatened, including the loss of freedom that results from compliance. Threats that lack credibility tend to produce hostility, but not the desired changes in behavior. Very strong threats are often perceived as noncontingent statements of intent; in other words, the threatening party is seen as wanting to attack *regardless* of what the threatened party does. Consequently, noncontingent threats are most likely to lead to violent reactions. For threats to be effective, they require credibility and contingency. The receiver must believe that the demands and potential punishments are real and believe that his or her behavior will affect what the threatening party will do.

It follows that threats may vary in their effectiveness in preventing open hostility. Morgan (1977) notes that deterrence is justified as an attempt to induce "sensible" decision making on the part of the adversary, to get them to consider the seriousness of actions they may be planning. It may discourage a decision for war, *assuming that the decision makers remain sensible—predominantly rational—in a time of crisis.*

Lockhart (1973) takes the view that threats cannot be used indiscriminately *and* effectively, since they have limitations that are only partly understood. Threats are intertwined with misperception and miscommunication that may be the rule rather than the exception in international relations. Threats may have different effects than are intended since they involve additional costs such as loss of freedom, or of face, or of support within one's nation. Nonetheless, Lockhart analyzes the 1911 Moroccan crisis to illustrate that threats might be used effectively when their limitations are understood and counteracted. In this case, the various threats of armed intervention by French, British, and German diplomats forced all sides to realize the seriousness of the situation and to search for a mutually acceptable resolution. His rather sad conclusion is that threats will continue to be used as part of the common approach to resolving international conflict.

The use of threats and deterrence is particularly pointless and frightening because of its most common outcome: *that the stakes are continuously raised.* Mutual deterrence invariably leads to an arms race in which each side clamors for military superiority so that it will maintain effective deterrence through credible threats. To cite the most visible example, the arms race between the Soviet Union and the United States has consistently escalated from World War II to the present in ways that simply boggle the mind and chill the heart. The scope and sophistication of this mutually accepted technology of destruction have reached a point that is beyond the average person's comprehension. Both countries now have the capability to annihilate the opponent's entire population *many times over* (overkill). An all-out nuclear attack by one, countered by the retaliation of the other, would likely eliminate all life on this planet. To maintain this absurd level of deterrence, each country spends billions of dollars yearly—the lion's share of the national budget—on "defense." According to Barnaby (1976), innovation in new armaments is fully encouraged. For example, in the United States in 1976, $4 billion was allocated for the creation of options—that is, to create and explore technological innovations for possible military applications. The deterrence-armament spiral has cost this world more than we can imagine and it may cost us everything we have.

SALT versus GRIT. In response to the real and potential costs of deterrence and the arms race, the superpowers have attempted to institute arms control through the Strategic Arms Limitation Treaties (SALT I and II). These negotiations are attempts to limit the further development of nuclear weapons systems and as such are a laudable step. However, limiting the number of times each country can completely destroy the other is barely a beginning. While some control has been gained on the expansion of numbers of strategic (that is, nuclear) delivery systems, the search for and development of more sophisticated weapons systems has gone largely unconstrained (Steiner, 1978). Each superpower has apparently drafted plans to escalate the arms race if controls fail, and each continues to plan for the future on the basis of pessimistic predictions of the other side's intent and behavior.

It is most important to distinguish between arms control and disarmament (Dedring, 1976). Arms control means a reduction in or halt to the *rate* of weapons development and acquisition. Disarmament means an actual reduction of the stockpile of available armaments. Ironically, the weapons stockpile of the superpowers has been reduced by selling or giving older systems to less powerful states so that they may practice deterrence or aggression in their own self-interest (Barnaby, 1976; Dedring, 1976). Thus, the major East-West confrontation has measurably increased the entire world's capacity for destructive violence.

The conventional approach of negotiating arms controls must be seriously questioned. Sociologist Donald Granberg (1978), for example, sees two major deficiencies with SALT. First, the arsenals of the superpowers are complex and multidimensional and different in so many ways that it is impossible to define "who's ahead" and, therefore, where they should stop. Second, the lack of sustained political pressure in favor of peace and disarmament in both countries makes it unlikely that significant controls, no less cutbacks, will be forthcoming. The people of the United States and the Soviet Union appear to accept the arms race and, even worse, seem to expect war to continue. What's the answer?

Granberg suggests we take a second look at a systematic approach of graduated reductions that was proposed in the early 1960s—an approach that might be our last hope of making it through the final quarter of the twentieth century. In 1962, social psychologists Charles Osgood and Amitai Etzioni independently proposed a graduated reduction in armaments and hostility between the United States and the Soviet Union. Etzioni's (1962) plan was termed "gradualism"; Osgood's (1962) approach was entitled "Graduated Reciprocation in Tension Reduction" or GRIT. These plans were proposed as an alternative to unilateral disarmament by the United States, an action that American leaders found too threatening and politically unacceptable—in a word, unthinkable. Osgood believed that, since the hostile relationship and the arms race had grown bit by bit over many years, it should be possible to throw the process into reverse in a systematic, graduated manner. This would be done through actions that would require reciprocation from the other side to assure their continuation.

GRIT is simple and straightforward, and it does not create the vulnerability of complete or major unilateral disarmament. A series of unilateral reductions are planned and announced; these steps are then open to international verification. The steps are graduated, beginning with lower-risk moves; further moves become increasingly more significant. However, the initial moves must be reciprocated by some equivalent steps by the other side in order for the sequence to continue. At the same time, the initiator maintains an adequate deterrent and makes it clear that it will defend its national sovereignty and international interest. The initiatives are taken with clear communication and within a considerable time period so as to increase the probability of a positive response from the adversary.

An actual test of the gradualist approach occurred in the summer and fall of 1963, in what has been referred to as the Kennedy Experiment (Etzioni, 1967, 1969). In his "strategy for peace" speech on June 10, 1963, President John Kennedy called attention to the dangers of nuclear war and took a reconciliatory tone toward the Soviet Union. He called on the American people to reexamine their cold-war attitudes and to support American policies that encouraged Russia to agree to a genuine peace. As a unilateral reduction in tension, he announced a halt to all American nuclear tests in the atmosphere, saying that the tests would not be resumed unless another country did so first. The Soviet Union responded immediately by taking the rare step of publishing Kennedy's speech in the government newspaper *Izvestia* and by agreeing with an American request to send United Nations observors to war-torn Yemen. The next American move was to restore full recognition to the Hungarian delegation at the United Nations. Russia reciprocated by ordering a halt to the production of strategic bombers.

This thaw in the cold war, which was readily apparent in official and unofficial communications, was furthered by the ratification of the limited nuclear test ban treaty, the sale of American wheat to Russia, and the consideration of opening new consulates in both countries. The experiment was terminated by the assassination of John Kennedy in November 1963, and further initiatives were undermined by the escalation of the war in Vietnam. However, for a brief moment, a ray of hope shone through the cloud of American-Soviet hostility, and the gradualist approach received some validation.

Support for GRIT has also come from the social-psychological laboratory (for example, Lindskold & Collins, 1978; Pilisuk & Skolnick, 1968) and from simulations of international relations (for example, Crow, 1963). After reviewing both types of studies, Lindskold (1979) concludes that if all components are properly instituted, GRIT can reduce tension and increase trust to the point where further conflict-resolution strategies can be implemented. Recently, support for GRIT has also come from a content analysis of actual international disputes. Leng and Wheeler (1979) classified twenty serious disputes from 1905–1971 in terms of the major influence strategy employed by each of the antagonists: bullying, reciprocating, appeasing, or trial and error. For example, in the 1914 crisis that started World War I, Austria was seen as bullying while Serbia was judged to be appeasing; in the 1962 Cuban missile crisis, the United States was seen as reciprocating while the Soviet Union was appeasing. The analysis indicated that the reciprocating strategy (a key component of GRIT) was the most effective means of avoiding a diplomatic defeat without having to go to war. It builds on the universal norm of reciprocity as well as allowing for face-saving—an important element of diplomatic relations.

Even now, almost two decades since the Kennedy Experiment, the applicability of GRIT is as obvious as ever. In fact, Granberg (1978) maintains that GRIT is now even more crucial to human survival. In the 1960s, Osgood and Etzioni proposed their schemes as mechanisms for reducing distrust to the point where disarmament negotiations could be effective. In the 1980s, the SALT negotiations have only succeeded in producing inconsequential agreements while the arms race continues almost unabated. It is obvious that we need GRIT, not as a prerequisite to negotiations but as an alternative. In this direction, Granberg (1978) offers a detailed sequence of steps appropriate for initiating GRIT in the context of present American-Soviet relations (see Box 12.3). Whether America's leaders and people (and their allies) have the courage, patience, and foresight to implement such a strategy remains to be seen. The survival of humanity may well hinge on the answer.

International Negotiation

The SALT talks may seem snail-paced and inconsequential, but they do represent one of the most common and effective methods of resolving international conflict: direct negotiation between the parties. All manner of disputes are handled everyday through diplomatic negotiations—from fishing rights to nuclear proliferation, from airplane routes to boundary disputes, and from trading arrangements to treaties that end wars.

Negotiation, the common medium of dispute resolution in international relations, has been studied from a variety of perspectives. Diplomatic observers have produced descriptive accounts and analyses of negotiation (see Jackson, 1952; Ikle, 1964; Lall, 1966). Some social scientists have tried to reduce negotiation to simpler terms involving game theory and mathematics (see Fouraker & Siegel, 1963). Between these two approaches lies the social-psychological study of negotiation, relying on empirical data while developing models that capture the major conditions and outcomes essential to negotiation (see Druckman, 1973, 1977; Druckman & Mahoney, 1977; Rubin & Brown, 1975; Sawyer & Guetzkow, 1965).

Negotiation is a process through which two parties interact to develop agreements that guide and regulate their future behavior. Based on this definition, Sawyer and Guetzkow (1965) have developed a social-psychological model of international negotiation. Rather than make the simple-minded psychological assumption that all conflict is the result of misperception and misunderstanding, they acknowledge that international disputes typically result form objective

Box 12.3   FOCUS ON PRACTICE
GRIT for Survival Now

In the final quarter of the twentieth century, the arms race between East and West continues to escalate. Implementation of a plan of Graduated Reciprocation in Tension Reduction (GRIT) may be our last hope to avoid nuclear holocaust. Donald Granberg of the University of Missouri has offered a detailed scenario of how the United States could initiate such a strategy over a period of several months.

1. The president of the United States makes a conciliatory speech in which he describes GRIT and announces several unilateral initiatives to which he invites a Soviet response. These include:

   - the United States will not go into production of a new bomber
   - the United States will not produce and deploy the neutron bomb
   - American forces will gradually be withdrawn from Korea
   - the United States will dismantle 54 Titan missiles

2. The president works to sell the program to Congress and to the public. The military, defense department suppliers, and organized labor are strongly opposed. Nevertheless, the president presses on with a pledge to reverse the steady increase in United States weapon sales to other countries limiting the total to 90 percent of that of the previous year.

3. The secretary of the navy announces that freedom on the high seas should be guaranteed by an international navy organized under the United Nations to which the United States is ready to contribute eight ships. Contributions from other nations are invited.

4. The president recommends to Congress that the Defense Department budget for research and development be cut by 20 percent, the United States Arms Control and Disarmament Agency budget be increased by 20 percent, and that a National Peace Academy for peace research and education be established.

5. The president announces a phased withdrawal of American forward troops in Germany. Each withdrawal requires a corresponding withdrawal by the Soviets for the process to continue.

6. The American secretaries of defense and agriculture announce a plan to transfer land holdings from the Pentagon to agricultural cooperatives and homesteaders in the hope of increasing food production in order to meet world shortages.

7. The president announces that the United States will only use its nuclear weapons systems in retaliation for a nuclear attack and not in response to a nonnuclear attack.

   At this point, the president announces the end of the first stage of GRIT. New initiatives in de-escalation will come only in response to Soviet moves. The president expresses the willingness of the United States to develop mechanisms for the peaceful settlement of international disputes including the use of binding arbitration.

Source. Granberg, D. GRIT in the final quarter: Reversing the arms race through unilateral initiatives. *Bulletin of Peace Proposals*, 1978, *9*, 210–221.

incompatibility of goals among nations. However, social-psychological processes can aggravate existing conflicts and affect their resolution. Thus, to understand international negotiation, a comprehensive model must include these processes. The Sawyer and Guetzkow model (1965), given in Figure 12.3, specifies the five major aspects of negotiation: their *goals* motivate the parties to enter a *process* of negotiation. This involves communication and actions that lead to certain *outcomes* for each party. All of this is affected by preexisting *background* factors of culture and existing relations, as well as by the present *conditions* in which negotiation takes place. These major aspects are thus grouped into antecedent variables, concurrent conditions, and consequent factors along a time line that runs from before to after the negotiations.

This broad model of negotiations has helped stimulate, guide, organize, and integrate much of the theory, research, and practice in the social-psychological study of negotiation. Druckman (1975) uses the major categories of the model to organize and review a great deal of the experimental research on negotiations. He also summarizes the findings by developing useful, practical propositions about negotiation in each major area. Rubin and Brown (1975) take a similar approach in their review of experimental research on negotiation. Druckman and Mahoney (1977) present a concise review of the social psychology of negotiation by following a time line that flows from the formation of negotiating positions, then to the processes themselves, and finally to the consequences of negotiation. For our purposes, we can use the model to organize a selective overview of what goes on in international negotiation.

Parties enter into negotiations to achieve certain goals, to obtain the most favorable outcome that is agreeable to the other party. The more these goals do— or can be made to—agree, the greater will be the mutual satisfaction resulting from negotiations. The concept of superordinate goal introduced by Sherif (see Chapter 8) is therefore conducive to succcessful negotiations. Since countries engaged in war mutually experience the high cost of hostilities, a reduction in these costs is a strong inducement to negotiate. In peacetime, the reciprocal benefit of international trade is a complementary goal that motivates many agreements among nations. Unfortunately, parties to negotiations, being rivals, try to get more and give less. This tends to stir up competition rather than cooperation, further irritating the conflict and lengthening negotiations (Druckman, 1973).

Specificity of goals refers to the degree of concreteness and scope of the outcomes one hopes to achieve. Bargaining for vague or all-encompassing objectives is a difficult process; breaking goals into simpler, more measurable components aids negotiation. Discussions between the United States and the Soviet Union, introducing broad ideological positions, are bound to elicit defensive reactions that impede negotiation. However, a beginning that deals with smaller, more concrete issues such as the sale of wheat will not only have a greater chance for immediate success, but will also pave the way for a possible resolution of broader issues.

Because of the complexity of the negotiation process, adequate preparation is important and even matters of simple procedure are significant. (At the 1945 Potsdam Conference, for example, arrangements had to be made for the *simultaneous* entrance of Truman, Churchill, and Stalin from three separate doors leading into the conference room. In this way, no one would be given promi-

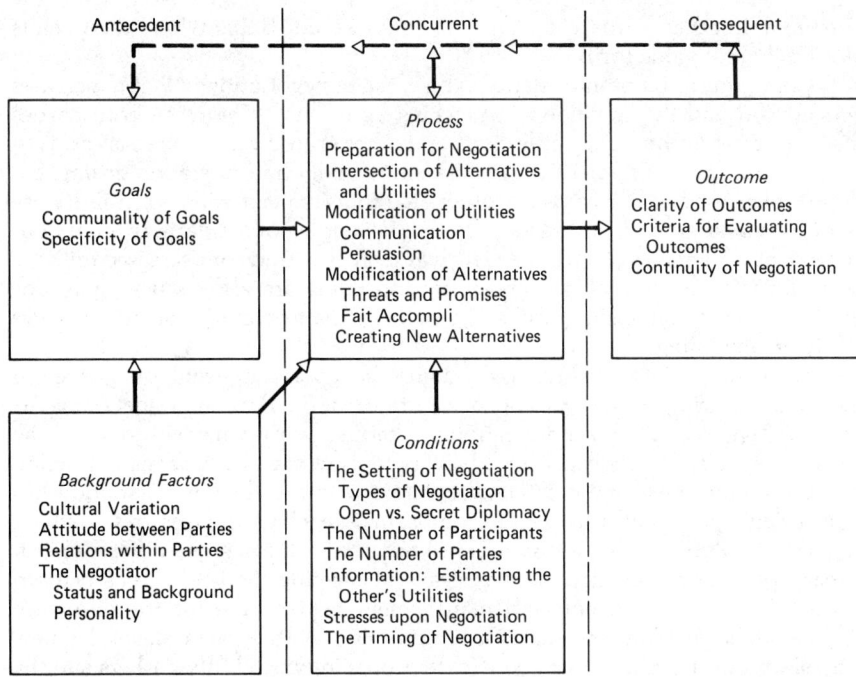

Antecedent | Concurrent | Consequent

Goals
Communality of Goals
Specificity of Goals

Process
Preparation for Negotiation
Intersection of Alternatives
and Utilities
Modification of Utilities
Communication
Persuasion
Modification of Alternatives
Threats and Promises
Fait Accompli
Creating New Alternatives

Outcome
Clarity of Outcomes
Criteria for Evaluating
Outcomes
Continuity of Negotiation

Background Factors
Cultural Variation
Attitude between Parties
Relations within Parties
The Negotiator
Status and Background
Personality

Conditions
The Setting of Negotiation
Types of Negotiation
Open vs. Secret Diplomacy
The Number of Participants
The Number of Parties
Information: Estimating the
Other's Utilities
Stresses upon Negotiation
The Timing of Negotiation

Figure 12.3   A Model of International Negotiation. Negotiation involves: (1) antecedent
or existing conditions including the negotiator's goals and background; (2)
concurrent or contemporary conditions which influence the process or ongoing behaviors of negotiation; and (3) consequent conditions which are the
outcomes produced by negotiation. All of these elements must be studied to
gain a social-psychological understanding of negotiation.
Source: Sawyer & Guetzkow (1965).

nence.) The development of the agenda is also no simple matter, since the choices
may very well influence the outcomes of the negotiation. Different emphasis on
different issues can lead to misunderstandings and hostilities that interfere with
the negotiation of issues of concern to both parties (Druckman & Mahoney, 1977).
In the early stages of SALT I, for instance, the Americans wanted to talk about
multiple warheads, but the Russians wanted to focus on forward deployments of
American missiles. This jockeying over agenda created antagonism and side-
tracked the negotiations from looking at the deployment of antiballistic missiles—
an issue on which agreement was more probable.

Once negotiations are under way, each party attempts to gain outcomes that
have payoffs for it. Each alternative that is put forth has a certain value or utility
for each party. Each side puts forward different alternatives that interact with one
another to produce different outcomes. The overall outcome is thus a combination of alternatives, and mutual satisfaction results if both parties gain more from
the negotiation than they would from remaining at the status quo. However,
during negotiation, each side engages in communication and persuasion in an
attempt to change the values or utilities that the other side ascribes to certain

outcomes. In other words, side A tries to convince side B that what side A wants also has higher value for B.

Communication of information is essential to negotiation in that it increases cooperation and the likelihood of reaching agreement. The more both parties make statements about fair settlements and other shared values, the easier it is to reach accord (Druckman, 1973). Persuasion, through interpretation or implication, is also used to convince the other side that its perceptions of utilities are erroneous and should be reassessed. (For example, one side may point out additional advantages of agreement such as increased trade or decreased military expenditure.) Tactics such as threats and promises are also used to press for modifications of the other party's alternatives, making them potentially more costly or rewarding.

The creation of new alternatives cannot be ignored in negotiation—even to the point of setting up the simultaneous entrance of the Potsdam leaders. It is the creative development and combination of alternatives that make negotiation the challenging and potentially constructive mechanism that it is. A classic distinction between compromise and creative integration or experience in negotiation has been articulated by Follett (1924). In compromise, each party gives up something to reach a solution. This is commonly known as "splitting the difference." In integration, the parties find creative ways of meeting the basic needs of both parties. For example, union and management might settle for the difference between their positions on wages (a compromise) or they might develop a new way of organizing production to increase profits in which both workers and the company would share (an integration). Druckman (1973) suggests that we might require different models of negotiation—one to deal with situations involving the division of resources where compromise is most appropriate and one to cover more complex issues requiring creative and integrative solutions. A third model might be required to combine both situations.

The outcomes of negotiation may vary in clarity or explicitness. One treaty might provide for precise limitations on troop numbers, or exact dollar amounts to be repatriated—all spelled out in highly explicit terms. Another might refer to general intentions to improve future relations. Each party must leave the negotiation table with a positive evaluation of fair outcomes if there is to be successful continuity of negotiation in the future. When this is not the case, when one party perceives the outcomes as humiliating and unfair, the prospect of future relations is invariably damaged. For example, we might view the outcomes of negotiation experienced by Germany at the end of World War I as foundations for the resentment and acrimony that increased the probability of World War II.

Negotiation is influenced by many conditions: the setting, including the diplomatic level and openness of the meetings; the number of parties involved, and the number of individual representatives; the information that is available, especially about the other side's utilities; and the effects of stress and timing. Druckman (1973) maintains that open negotiations—particularly with the audience in the role of evaluator—increase competitiveness, irrational face-saving, and cautiousness. Secrecy, on the other hand, facilitates agreement. "Closed-door" meetings are the order of the day in negotiations. Multiparty negotiations typically lead to coalitions among similar parties for the purpose of achieving a competitive advantage.

Stress enters negotiations in many forms: in extreme antagonism between the parties, in threatened actions in case of nonagreement, and in a lack of cohesion within a party. Stress and tension have motivating qualities; but beyond a certain point, increased tension is detrimental to negotiation—just as it is to any problem-solving activity. At that point, negotiators lose some of their ability to evaluate information and make the fine discriminations necessary for a satisfactory agreement (Druckman, 1973). Similarly, time pressures may hinder the search for the best, most effective outcomes (Druckman & Mahoney, 1977). Because stress level and other conditions change during negotiations, the skill of timing communications and actions becomes crucial. The skilled negotiator makes the right move at the right time to maximize his or her party's payoffs as well as the mutual satisfaction of both parties.

Background factors affect the process and outcomes of negotiations in subtle yet significant ways. Cultural differences in motives, styles, and norms of social behavior can interfere with the process of negotiation. For example, the Chinese approach to negotiation has been described as a tough offensive posture, a lack of reciprocal concession-making, and an unwillingness to begin with smaller issues and move to larger ones. American negotiators prefer to make small gains on the way to larger agreements and to a mixed competitive-cooperative strategy in which both parties make concessions. No surprise, then, that American-Chinese negotiations have often experienced difficulty and deadlock (Druckman & Mahoney, 1977).

In addition to cultural variations, the then-current attitudes and relations between the countries will influence how competitively or cooperatively they approach negotiations. (Imagine the difference in atmosphere between a meeting of Americans and Canadians, and one of Russians and Chinese.) Ethnocentrism and stereotyping influence the processes of perception and communication in negotiations the same as in other types of interaction.

Finally, we must look at the significance of the negotiator's background and personality. Status can affect negotiating behavior. For example, heads of state are probably more motivated by the fear of losing face than are lesser diplomats. The authoritarian personality syndrome (see Chapter 5) may be at work here, generating less cooperative, more rigid approaches to international relations. Many background and personality factors are summed up in the concept of personal style (Druckman & Mahoney, 1977)—a human element that can have considerable impact on negotiations, particularly on those that lack clearly defined purposes or structures, and are thus more susceptible to individual influence.

Social psychologists have provided a number of theoretical perspectives and considerable research data to help us understand the process of negotiation (Druckman, 1977; Mastenbroek, 1980; Zartman, 1977). They have also taken initiative in the area of practice (see Box 12.4).

Effects of Cross-National Contact

Most of the contact between people from different countries comes through international travel and exchanges. When this happens, especially when a visitor enters a foreign country for the first time, there is an effect of "culture shock"—the result of finding oneself in a different social and political environment. This effect of cross-national contact is a subject of considerable interest to social scientists, particularly as it influences the attitude or images of the participants.

A comprehensive review of earlier work on the effects of contact on international images is provided by de Sola Pool (1965), while Misler (1965) examines personal contact in scholarly exchanges. More recently, Brislin (1981) offers a comprehensive analysis of cross-cultural encounters of a face-to-face nature. Research on cross-national contact is now becoming part of the larger study of cross-cultural psychology as represented by the *Journal of Social Psychology,* the *International Journal of Intercultural Relations,* and the *Handbook of Cross-Cultural Psychology* (Triandis, 1979). In addition, the study of intercultural communication has expanded dramatically in the mid to late 1970s (see Asante, Newmark & Blake, 1979).

Box 12.4   FOCUS ON PRACTICE
Training in Negotiation Skills

Negotiation is a highly complex and difficult process for resolving disputes. Most negotiators learn the "tricks of the trade" by experience and discussions with other negotiators. However, it is possible to take a more direct approach to learning about the subtle strategies and tactics of negotiation. For several years, the NTL Institute of Applied Behavioral Science has offered a Negotiation Skills Workshop as one of its programs in personal and professional development. I was a participant in one of these workshops in 1977.

The main objectives of the Negotiation Skills Workshop are to increase understanding of the interpersonal processes of negotiation and to develop diagnostic frameworks for the analysis of one's own and others' bargaining behavior. Although there are important differences in negotiation procedures in different settings (industrial, educational, international), it is assumed that knowledge of basic processes can improve the effectiveness of negotiators regardless of setting. This is accomplished by following the experiential learning approach in the workshop itself. Theory sessions are integrated with exercises or simulations of negotiations and videotape feedback is used for analysis and evaluation.

For example, in the workshop I attended, led by social psychologist Bert Brown, one simulation involved negotiations between a striking teachers federation and a city board of education. Workshop participants were assigned to bargaining committees representing the two parties and were provided with a description of the major issues (such as salaries, credit for tenure) and the preferences of their groups. Representatives then participated in negotiations in an attempt to resolve the differences. Following the negotiation sessions, participant reactions, trainer observations, and videotape playback were used as a basis for analysis and discussion.

From such experiences, individuals are able to learn about how their strategies and tactics of negotiation affect the other party. They are able to improve their skills for assessing each party's needs, evaluating strengths and weaknesses, improving communication, and building the degree of cooperation and trust that is essential to successful negotiation.

Source: NTL Institute. *1981 programs.* Arlington, Virginia, 1981.

Most of the contact between people from different countries comes through international travel and exchange. Here, a 12-year-old French boy studying in Peking shares his skateboard with a group of Chinese children. *(James Andanson/Sygma)*

The complexity of studying cross-national contact can be seen when we realize that four different sets of images may be affected: the traveler's image of the host country, the host's image of the traveler, the traveler's self-image, and the host's self-image. Furthermore, we must ask whether these images become more or less favorable, more or less complex and accurate, and whether they lead to different behavioral predispositions. (All this, of course, leads us back to the three-part division of attitude into its affective, cognitive, and action components. See Chapter 2.)

In examining the effects of cross-national contact, de Sola Pool (1965) points to various, sometimes contradictory, outcomes. On the topic of response by the visitor to the host country and people, most studies show more positive images, but some indicate less favorable attitudes. Which way things go depends on several factors, including the traveler's initial psychological adjustment, the quality of interpersonal relations, and the extent of cultural differences. In general, individuals who develop deeper personal relations with people of the host country tend to develop more favorable attitudes, but this takes time. It is not surprising that two of the main components of operating effectively in another culture appear to be the ability to communicate effectively and the ability to establish good interpersonal relationships (Hammer, Gudykunst & Wiseman, 1978). That it takes time to develop positive attitudes is congruent with our knowledge of interpersonal attraction (see Chapter 6)—that favorableness toward others increases with frequency of interaction.

However, the international level of analysis adds a complexity that is not apparent if we restrict our thinking to interpersonal relations. For example, there appears to be a relationship between a visitor's favorable attitudes toward a country and his or her degree of support for that country's foreign policy. An American visiting Cuba who is critical of that country's socialist regime would likely maintain a negative attitude despite positive interpersonal interaction with individual Cubans. In addition, simplistic images or stereotypes are usually rendered more complex by cross-national contact, regardless of changes in favorability. To understand this process, we must study images longitudinally over a considerable period of contact. For example, Coelho (1958) looked at the attitudes of students from India studying in the United States. He found a growing differentiation and specificity of images over time, with an initial global attitude breaking into separate attitudes toward different aspects of America—such as American people, American foreign policy, and American institutions. This discovery and appreciation of complexity continued for at least two years. This suggests that visitors who make short trips abroad are not likely to develop complex images, but will tend to hold simplistic views, whether favorable or unfavorable.

The traveler's image of his or her own country is also dramatically affected by cross-national contact. In fact, these effects are often more profound than those on the images the visitor holds of the host (de Sola Pool, 1965). American students studying abroad, for example, typically return with a greater appreciation of and a stronger identification with the United States. And the same is true for foreign students in America: The different cultural contact enhances their understanding and appreciation of their own country, often with a firmer attachment to its values. This shift in perception—a new awareness of self through an experience of the differentness of others—is a clear illustration of the power of social comparison theory in social relations (see Chapter 2).

An example of the effects of cross-national contact comes from a recent study of Steinkalk and Taft (1979). These researchers examined the attitudinal and behavior changes experienced by a group of Australian college students and faculty during a 10-week tour of Israel. Before the trip started, the travel group and a matched control group completed a short questionnaire including bipolar adjective scales (for example, worthless–valuable, deep–shallow, kind–cruel) on a number of referents relating to both Australia and Israel (such as Israelis, Australian education system, Israeli kibbutz life). At the end of the visit, both groups again completed the scales, and the travel group completed a questionnaire about their reactions to the trip. The results showed increased favorableness toward certain aspects of Israel, some predictable changes in behavior (such as greater tolerance), and, more importantly, a greater understanding of *Australian* society. The travel group also developed a stronger opinion about foreign travel as a valuable broadening experience. The investigators point out, however, that the tour was planned to maximize participation in Israeli life, including 4 weeks of living in a kibbutz and a visit with an Israeli family. Obviously, this type of experience is much more involving than that of the average tourist, who relates mainly to hotel clerks, taxi drivers, and other service personnel, usually in a fairly superficial manner.

But what about the effect of cross-national exchange on that elusive attitude we might term "international mindedness"—that broad perspective of, and concern for, the world community? The East-West Center at the University of Hawaii in Honolulu was established in 1960 to foster understanding and respect among people from different cultures—Asia, the Pacific, and the United States—through cooperative study, training, and research. Hundreds of scholars and students from over forty countries and territories come together to work on various programs and are actively encouraged to attend a variety of intercultural events. Bochner, Lin, and McLeod (1979) devised a way to measure international minded-ness unobtrusively to see if participation at the center positively affected this perspective. They sent a questionnaire on foreign language acquisition to ninety American students who had attended the center, and to ninety other American students who had attended the University of Hawaii, but not the center. The measure of world mindedness was simply whether or not the person returned the questionnaire, since it dealt with an important element of intercultural relations. The findings? A much larger percentage of center participants than nonpartici-pants returned the questionnaire (45 percent versus 24 percent). A follow-up study indicated that a history of overseas residence (that is, intercultural expe-rience) is perhaps the underlying determinant of international mindedness. Insti-tutions such as the East-West Center can help foster the development of a world community.

Travel and exchanges are traditional forms of cross-national contact. More recently, we have seen the development of structured approaches for cross-cultural orientation and learning (see Brislin & Pederson, 1976). Richard Brislin, a social psychologist at the East-West Center, points out the importance of social-psychological processes in understanding tensions and hostilities between cultures and for designing contact programs to increase intercultural awareness (Brislin, 1978). For example, the functions that attitudes serve, as delinated by Katz (see Chapter 2), and the different forms of prejudice (see Chapter 8) are as applicable to relations among cultures as they are to intergroup relations within the same society. With such concepts in mind, it is possible to design a variety of programs to help people from different cultures interact effectively. These are usually short-term experiences designed to change the attitudes and behaviors of individuals about to enter another culture. For example, Peace Corps volunteers are trained to work in Papua New Guinea, or American teachers are provided an orientation for an exchange program in the Philippines. Some programs emphasize self-awareness—helping participants learn about the cultural bases of their *own* behavior so they may better understand their reactions to cultural differences. Other programs stress cognitive learning—providing information on food habits, male-female relations, decision-making styles, and other important aspects of the other culture. Some approaches involve experiential learning, where participants are immersed in realistic simulations of the host culture. In one example, teachers about to work in Micronesia were trained in rural Hawaii, providing their own food, rationing water, digging latrines, and performing all the day-to-day activi-ties that they would require to live effectively.

Numerous problems occur in cross-national contact (Stening, 1979). Dif-ferent views of social reality, gaps in communication, stereotyping, ethnocen-trism, and prejudice are all stumbling blocks to effective intercultural interaction. More research is needed to evaluate the effects of the various approaches to intercultural learning.

Our understanding of cross-national contact must be transformed into guidelines that will increase the chances for productive and satisfying interaction. Social psychologist Herbert Kelman and his colleagues have conducted research which has produced such recommendations. For example, Kelman and Ezekiel (1970) studied the experience of communication specialists from a number of countries who came to the United States for advanced technical training. The results indicated that these visitors were most satisfied when they were accorded an acceptable degree of status and respect by the American hosts. Based on these and other results, Brislin (1981) offers several recommendations for increasing the effectiveness of cross-national contact:

- The experience should be clearly relevant to the individual's specific professional concerns.
- Colleague relationships should be established with individual hosts who have cross-cultural experience.
- Participants should be able to make personal contributions and help organize the exchange program.
- Visitors should be able to make choices in activities that match their interests.
- Visitors should have opportunities for informal social contact with host nationals.
- The participants' personal and national status should be enhanced.

Through a combination of social-psychological theory and research, Brislin (1981) provides a variety of additional guidelines for practice in designing and implementing effective programs of cross-cultural interaction.

Cross-national contact clearly follows the same principles that underlie intergroup contact (see Chapter 8) and the desegregation of minority groups (see Chapter 11). An interaction of sufficient complexity, occurring under facilitative conditions, will usually produce greater favorability of attitudes. But a superficial, unequal, or uncooperative contact usually results in the reinforcement or generation of negative stereotypes. The implications are plain enough: those who organize and facilitate cross-national exchange and cross-cultural learning must make every effort to draw on the knowledge of social psychology, designing such experiences to maximize positive and realistic outcomes for the participants. This is one route to a smaller, fuller, and more peaceful world.

Problem-Solving Workshops in International Relations

Although their purposes differ, international negotiation and cross-national exchanges bring together the people of different countries. Now, for a third purpose, a relatively new type of international contact has been created by social scientists, bringing together the informal representatives of countries that are or have been engaged in international conflict. This method, referred to as the *problem-solving workshop*, involves the application of the methods of small-group, human relations training (see Chapter 7) and the sequence of problem solving (see Chapter 4) to the peaceful resolution of international conflict. It is similar to intergroup problem solving in community relations (see Chapter 8). In the same vein, international problem-solving workshops focus on the most helpful conditions of intergroup contact: equal status, a cooperative task, and norms that support positive interaction.

English political scientist John Burton and his colleagues at the Centre for the Analysis of Conflict, University College, London, were among the first social scientists to develop the problem-solving approach. Burton (1969) has referred to his method as *controlled communication*, emphasizing the importance of effective communication between the different representatives at the meetings. Using this approach, Burton has arranged small private discussions with representatives of countries that are engaged in conflict. In the mid-1960s, for example, meetings were arranged with delegates from Malaysia and Indonesia at a time when it was feared that relations between those countries had deteriorated to the point of armed conflict on a wide scale. Burton's approach is to use a panel of knowledgeable and skilled social scientists to control the discussions in a nondirective manner. This helps establish a nonthreatening, problem-solving atmosphere in which the participants are encouraged to examine their perceptions of each other, to analyze their methods of communicating, and to explore ways of resolving the conflict. Obviously, this is far more effective than the trading of accusations, threats, and ultimatums that often goes on in diplomatic interaction between conflicting states. The social scientists also play the role of experts in social relations, using their knowledge of conflict processes and international relations to help the representatives diagnose their mutual problem (the conflict) and search for alternative solutions. This helps the warring factions to look more objectively at their situation and their behavior, to better appreciate the other country's point of view, and to see the conflict not as a war to be won but as a problem to be solved together.

However, there is no guarantee or assurance that the generated solutions will actually be put into practice in the real world beyond the discussions. Although Burton maintains that controlled communication can improve international relationships, especially through fostering cooperation between countries in areas such as trade, it is difficult to judge if solutions carry over to the broader relationship among the countries.

Leonard Doob, a social psychologist well known for his classic contributions to learning theory, has recently turned his attention to international conflict. Along with several colleagues, he has brought the techniques of human relations training to bear on situations in which armed hostility has occurred or is threatening at any moment. In fact, one of Doob's (1974) intended workshops on the conflict between Turkish and Greek Cypriots was canceled at the last minute as a result of the Turkish invasion of Cyprus. Doob's work on the interreligious conflict in Northern Ireland was discussed in Chapter 8.

The foremost application of Doob's approach was a two-week workshop in the late 1960s that used sensitivity training and other techniques to produce innovative solutions to border disputes in the Horn of Africa (Doob, 1970; Doob, Foltz & Stevens, 1969). A lengthy recruiting process brought together eighteen informal representatives from Ethiopia, Somalia, and Kenya to discuss boundary and territory conflict that had been simmering for many years. In a resort hotel in the mountains of northern Italy, the representatives met under the guidance of American organizers and skilled human relations trainers. The participants were divided into two mixed sensitivity-training groups, taught about interpersonal and group processes, and then asked to work on possible solutions to the conflicts. This phase of the workshop was a success in that both groups produced solutions that were agreeable to members from all countries. Unfortunately, when all workshop participants gathered together, they could not reach a consensus on solutions and the meetings ended on a note of frustration. While it was clear that new ways of communicating had emerged and that favorable attitude changes came about, it was not possible to transfer the benefits to the relationships between the countries. Ethiopia and Somalia have since been engaged in a debilitating war that has brought terror and starvation to hundreds of thousands of people. Despite this eventual outcome, such pioneering efforts have demonstrated the potential of small-group problem solving for resolving international conflict.

Social psychologist Herbert Kelman has also contributed toward the use of problem-solving methods in international affairs. In a review of such workshops, Kelman (1972) compared and contrasted the approaches of Burton and Doob. Kelman and Cohen (1976, 1979), drawing on these earlier efforts to develop the rationale of their own interactional approach, assume that social interaction among antagonists is a *necessary condition* for the resolution of international conflict. In other words, if decision makers of countries engaged in conflict are not interacting in an authentic and detailed manner, it is unlikely that mutual problems can be solved other than through violent methods.

The central features of Kelman and Cohen's method are: first, to focus the interaction of workshop participants on a detailed analysis of the conflict; second, to promote a collaborative, problem-solving process; and third, to use social scientists in a special third-party role to facilitate the discussions. It is especially important that the social scientists intervene in ways that establish new norms of interaction. Rather than allow participants to engage in hostile accusations and legalistic debates, the discussions emphasize a respectful, task-oriented, analytic approach. The social scientists thus help improve communication and problem solving among the representatives, and contribute theories, observations on the context of the discussions, and process interventions that parallel those of the human relations trainer. In this way, the participants experience—often for the first time—an atmosphere of understanding and respect in which they can set aside their prejudices and hostility and look for mutually acceptable solutions to their conflict. Kelman and Cohen (1979) have demonstrated their approach by conducting pilot workshops on the India-Pakistan-Bangladesh conflict and on the Israeli-Pakistani dispute (Cohen, Kelman, Miller & Smith, 1977) (see Box 12.5). Kelman and Cohen are currently engaged in a long-term, action research approach to the Middle East conflict, in which further problem-solving workshops will play an important role.

Many questions have been raised about the nature of problem-solving workshops in relation to their effectiveness. Most of these center on issues of design, such as the numbers of representatives, the length of the sessions, the type of human-relations technique used, and so on (for example, Doob, 1975; Kelman & Cohen, 1979; Walton, 1970). The identity of participants is especially important since this aspect helps determine how much impact the results of the workshop might have on actual diplomatic relations between the countries. Some workshops involve appointed diplomatic representatives; some, informal members of decision-making elites, such as government officials or academics; and others, nationals of the respective countries, such as graduate students studying in the United States. Even though the workshop might create more favorable attitudes and produce creative solutions, these results will not be transferred to the relationship between the countries unless the participants are high-ranking decision makers. With the participation of official representatives at the same level as those involved in international negotiations, such workshops might indeed have significant positive effects on international relations—possibly as useful preparations or even adjuncts to official negotiations. In any event, the ultimate utility of

Box 12.5 FOCUS ON PRACTICE
An Israeli/Palestinian Problem-Solving Workshop

The problem-solving workshop is a potential alternative to formal negotiation or armed conflict as mechanisms of international conflict resolution. Social psychologists Herbert Kelman and Stephen Cohen applied the problem-solving approach to the Middle East conflict by organizing a pilot workshop that brought together Israelis and Palestinians (professionals and graduate students) living in the United States. The workshop was conducted in 1971 as part of a graduate seminar on social-psychological approaches to international relations.

Pre-workshop sessions were held separately with the four Israeli and four Palestinian participants. These sessions allowed each side to describe their positions and perceptions of the conflict and to develop some within-group cohesion. In addition, the neutral team of social scientists—Kelman, Cohen, and their colleagues—were able to gain information for planning the workshop and to establish their credibility and impartiality with the participants.

The weekend workshop began with a statement of purpose (to establish effective communication), the role of the third party (as facilitators of discussion rather than judges or adjudicators), and the ground rules (to analyze the conflict rather than advocate positions). However, the opening session on the theory of nationalism led to a Palestinian attack on Zionism as illegitimately merging nationalism with religion. Claims and counterclaims came to the fore and the analytic approach was lost. Nonetheless, there was a mutual acceptance of both Palestinian and Jewish nationalism.

At the next session, one of the Palestinians arrived with a typed statement of Palestinian rights, which he asserted the Israelis had agreed to sign. This document raised numerous complex issues and became the focus of the remainder of the workshop. Initial discussion became increasingly rigid and tense with the threat of either party withdrawing. The third party adjourned the sessions for within-group caucusing. This reduced tension and allowed each party to work on an acceptable formula for resolving the conflict over the document.

At the following session, the Israelis presented a version of the document that was acceptable to them. Different amendments were discussed until a mutually acceptable wording was found. The final document recognized Palestinian rights without denying any Israeli rights. The Palestininans were surprised and pleased with the Israeli recognition, but soon expressed doubt about the political utility of the document. The Israelis were disappointed that the signing coincided with the end of the workshop rather than beginning the discussion process. The third party emphasized and demonstrated that there was more to be learned from the process of the workshop in terms of participants' behavior than from the final outcome.

Source: Cohen, S. P., Kelman, H. C., Miller, F. D. & Smith, B. L. Evolving intergroup techniques for conflict resolution: An Israeli-Palestinian pilot workshop. *Journal of Social Issues*, 1977, *33*(1), 165–189.

problem-solving workshops in international relations will have to be judged by their eventual impact on the overall relationship between countries engaged in conflict. Until we see clearer results, the pilot demonstrations give us hope that the approaches of human relations and problem solving might someday contribute to a more peaceful and just world.

Future of International Relations and World Order

At this moment, our world's future looks grim. We are faced not only with the continuing threat of nuclear annihilation but with massive problems that beset much of the world's population every year, every week, every day. The world population continues to grow at an alarming rate. Although great masses live in abject poverty, the number of hungry mouths multiplies year by year. To meet this fundamental problem, birth control programs have been established, often on a national scale. This is particulary so in developing countries where severe over-population is an immense concern. But these programs must be sensitive to and aware of each level of analysis in their functioning. Individuals must be educated in decision making, yet be free from coercion. We must study the role of attitudes and the effect of intentions on family planning behavior (see Vinokur-Kaplan, 1978). We must understand how to work effectively with small groups and communities to ensure the successful utilization of family planning services (see Bhatt, Pachauri, Pathak & Chauhan, 1978). We must consider organizational factors that affect program operation and outcomes (see Simmons & Ashraf, 1978). We must understand the social-psychological processes that mediate family planning practices and act upon them through program development and dis-semination so that the world eventually gains control and a sense of choice over its ultimate fate.

The human costs of overpopulation are tragically evident. Each year, the United Nations Food and Agricultural Organization (FAO) estimates that hun-dreds of millions of people suffer from hunger and malnutrition. In 1979 alone, 500 *million* people suffered from severe malnutrition. Of these, many died from starvation and hunger-related diseases. Another 500 *million* suffered from less severe malnutrition that made normal life and activities impossible. As staggering as these estimates may be, they do not include the population of communist countries such as Vietnam; their governments refuse to supply the necessary information.

The problem of world starvation is not so much a problem of food produc-tion as it is one of food distribution. FAO estimates that it would require only three to five percent of world grain consumption to feed these starving millions. But many of the poor countries cannot afford what the food costs. Even more tragically, some of these same governments prefer to spend their money on armaments and the development of nuclear weapons while citizens starve in the streets. Nonetheless, the food distribution problem illustrates the glaring inequity between the rich and the poor countries of the world—an issue that will continue far into the future.

The fundamental inequity between the developed and developing countries has been identified by social scientists as a continuing and future source of world conflict. For example, Johan Galtung, a political scientist and leader in peace research, has identified status and power differences as being central to our understanding of peace and conflict (Galtung, 1971). International conflict can be seen as *symmetric*—that is, occurring between nations of similar power—or *asymmetric*, occurring between nations with very unequal resources at their disposal. In the latter case, open violence is usually avoided, but indirect or *structural violence* occurs in the control and oppression of the weaker party by the stronger one. Since conflict is due to incompatible goals in the relationship, asymmetric relations automatically involve conflict in which the poorer and weaker nations will aspire to the power and resources of the stronger nations—who, of course, will use their power to protect the inequitable status quo. Hence, the only way to reduce or eliminate conflict in the long run is to abolish asymmetric relations by redistributing resources on a more equal basis. However, as with the elimination of poverty within a society, we can expect more equitable sharing to be resisted since it would be dysfunctional, that is, more costly for the affluent and powerful (see Chapter 11). Thus, the challenge to the world in terms of survival does not relate only to symmetric conflict between the superpowers. It relates to the autonomy, dignity, equality, and justice that is available to all countries and all people of the world.

The importance of dignity and justice raises yet another crucial issue relevant to the world's future: the matter of *human rights.* Systematic and flagrant violations of basic rights and freedoms are continuing threats to world peace. Van Dyke (1971), for example, takes this approach in his analysis of the racist and colonialist policies pursued by South Africa—policies that are in clear contravention of the United Nations charter. Throughout the world, violations of individual and collective rights continue. Adolf Hitler may be physically dead, but his inhuman spirit can be seen in the unconscionable actions of Idi Amin's genocidal torture of Ugandans, in the Chilean junta's treatment of political dissidents, and in the Vietcong's devastation of Cambodia. The United Nations charter on human rights appears to be observed more in the breach than in its execution. The use of power to oppress and destroy will not prevent future violence, but only guarantee its future expression. The continuing issues of inequity and justice must be dealt with to some satisfactory degree before a lasting world order can emerge.

What are the prospects for a world order that includes peace and justice? We may not know the answer, but an increasing number of social scientists and other professionals are looking for viable paths into the future. Many have expressed the importance of a system of world law (for example, Anand, 1971; Clark & Sohn, 1965). For example, Clark and Sohn's (1965) systematic and detailed proposal for world peace through world law includes the arbitration of international conflicts coupled with disarmament and the development of an international police force. The United Nations would be considerably strengthened through increased revenues, and its general assembly would become an authentic lawmaking institution. Alternatively, it might be necessary to develop a new world organization for security and development, with the power to prevent war. Similarly, Eckhardt (1980) suggests that voting at the United Nations would be a much less costly and more humane alternative for deciding world issues that pit capitalist countries against socialist ones as compared to the predominant strategy of going to war.

Social scientists, including social psychologists, have contributed many perspectives to the search for world order (Lepawsky, Buehrig & Lasswell, 1971; Mendlowitz, 1975). They have developed specific models, complete with assumptions and mechanisms for putting them into practice. One impressive project involves the creation of an international team of scholars to develop different world-order models based on a common set of values yet responsive to the world's ideological, cultural, and socioeconomic differences (Beer, 1979; Mendlowitz, 1975). The five basic values include:

- *peace*—the absence of violent conflict to settle disputes
- *ecological stability*—the harmonious interacation between people and their natural environment
- *economic well-being*—the reorganization of the world's economic system to drastically reduce inequity
- *social justice*—the provision of basic rights and freedoms for all people
- *participation*—the condition that permits individuals to share decision-making power over their lives

Moving out from this fundamental core, social scientists from every major country and world region have developed concrete models for new and different futures. These are not simple-minded utopias based on single assumptions of human nature or encompassing only one or two basic values. These are potentially viable blueprints not just for human survival but for a world in which quality of life becomes a reality for all people. The question stands before us: Will the people and governments in power listen and act before it is too late?

Summary

Social psychologists seek to understand the processes of international conflict that could very well result in the annihilation of life on this planet. Social-psychological approaches to international relations include the total individual approach, the partial individual approach, and the true social-psychological approach. This analysis begins at the level of nations and applies social-psychological concepts to explain part of the behavior of decision makers.

Six major forms of misperception generally occur in international conflict: (1) the diabolical enemy image, (2) the virile self-image, (3) the moral self-image, (4) selective inattention, (5) absence of empathy, and (6) military overconfidence.

To understand the international behavior of high-level decision makers, we must know how they define their situation. The elements of threat perception, trust, and responsiveness may be particularly important in the actor's definition of the situation. Content analyses of the communicative acts of elite policymakers reveal difficulties and inconsistencies in their images which have serious implications for international relations.

Decision making during crises exhibits a number of deficiencies that limit the effectiveness of communication and problem solving. Crises that lead to war exhibit significantly lower complexity of communication than crises that were resolved peacefully.

Nationalism is a favorable attitude toward one's nation that involves national awareness, loyalty and pride, and a predisposition to support and assert the interests of one's nation. Nationalism supports the major functions of the nation through the processes of socialization and the enactment of national roles. The channeling of national roles toward military preparedness has led to concerns about the influence of the military-industrial complex in relation to national decision making in the United States and elsewhere.

Social psychologists study international relations in the hope of developing alternatives to armaments and war as a means of resolving disputes. Most nations protect their national sovereignty and security as a response in order to prevent the use of force by an adversary. Mutual deterrence inevitably leads to an arms race, which makes war more likely rather than less likely. In addition, the conventional approach to negotiating arms control as opposed to disarmament must be seriously questioned. As an alternative, social psychologists have developed plans for Graduated Reciprocation In Tension Reduction (GRIT), which have some experimental and real world support.

Negotiation, the common approach to dispute resolution in international relations, is a process through which two parties interact to develop agreements which guide and regulate their future behavior. A social-psychological model of negotiation involves the major components of goals, process, outcomes, background factors, and present conditions.

The effect of cross-national contact on international images is complex, but most experiences result in greater favorability and complexity of images as well as greater world mindedness. Usually, the deeper the contact, the greater the change in attitudes toward the host country.

Social psychologists have pioneered a number of problem-solving workshops in international relations. Representatives from countries engaged in conflict are brought together in small groups and are encouraged to create alternative solutions to the dispute which may be fed back into diplomatic relations between the countries. This approach is only in the pilot stage, but it is promising.

In addition to possible nuclear annihilation, the future of the world is plagued by a host of very serious problems: population growth, hunger and starvation, the gross inequity between rich and poor nations, and the flagrant violations of human rights in many countries. Social scientists are actively working on models for world order based on the values of peace, ecological stability, economic well-being, social justice, and participation.

Further Readings

Brislin, R. W. *Cross-cultural encounters: Face-to-face interaction.* Elmsford, N.Y.: Pergamon, 1981.

Druckman, D. (Ed.) *Negotiations: Social-psychological perspectives.* Beverly Hills, Calif.: Sage, 1977.

Griffiths, F. & Polanyi, J. C. (Eds.). *The dangers of nuclear war.* Toronto, Ont.: University of Toronto Press, 1979.

Kelman, H. C. (Ed.). *International behavior: A social-psychological analysis.* New York: Holt, Rinehart & Winston, 1965.

Osgood, C. E. *An alternative to war or surrender.* Urbana: University of Illinois Press, 1962.

White, R. K. *Nobody wanted war: Misperception in Vietnam and other wars.* Garden City, New York: Doubleday, 1970.

PART THREE

Special Areas of Application

CHAPTER OUTLINE

THIRTEEN

Program Development and Evaluation

In 1964, the United States government declared war on poverty. Its aim was to eradicate poverty from the face of America and to bring the nation's poor into the American dream; in the words of President Lyndon Johnson, the objective was "total victory." This dramatic announcement was followed by a concerted effort to develop a wide range of human service programs to combat the causes and consequences of poverty. Through the Office of Economic Opportunity (OEO), new programs were developed in several areas. The Community Action Program (CAP) was initiated to coordinate government services at the local level and to encourage the participation of poor Americans—blacks in particular—in the decision-making process. Medical and legal services were developed to increase the utilization rates of poor people. Employment training and education programs (Head Start was one of the most visible) were initiated to develop the capability and the skills required for educational and job success. All of these programs were designed to give the poor the access, the involvement, and the training that would help them climb the ladder to achievement in American society.

But according to evaluations, the War on Poverty fell far short of the original dream (see Clark & Hopkins, 1968; Marris & Rein, 1973). Seymour Sarason (1978b), a leading community psychologist with firsthand experience in a number of the programs, suggests that most people look back on the War on Poverty with a mixture of disillusionment, puzzlement, and despair. Some critics are even less charitable. Daniel Moynihan (1969), who was involved in the initial planning stages, contends that the War on Poverty was implemented so as to produce a *minimum* of the social change that was initially envisaged. According to Moynihan, rather than involving the "maximal feasible participation" of the poor, the programs were developed with "maximum feasible misunderstanding." Similarly, Sarason (1978b) suggests that one of the main motives for the war was a fear of the developing militancy among blacks and youth. As a result, programs were developed to give the disadvantaged certain opportunities and services rather than to give them greater power to change the status quo. Thus, the War on Poverty was never seriously fought; to do so would have required a redistribution of power and resources that would have been unacceptable to most Americans.

Detailed assessments of the War on Poverty provide a more balanced picture. In the decade from 1965–1975, the amount of real poverty in America was substantially reduced (Haveman, 1977); but, at the same time, poverty defined as relative inequity continued to increase, causing continuing concern (see Chapter 11). However, little of the absolute reduction can be directly attributed to the programs launched by the War on Poverty, which, in fact, yielded varied results. The training and education programs generally did not lead to increased income. The medical, legal, and community programs did seem to enhance the utilization and participation of poor people in service delivery. More importantly, the traditional income-maintenance programs external to the War on Poverty increased dramatically during the decade, and these efforts had the greatest effect on reducing poverty (Plotnick & Skidmore, 1975). Direct welfare payments as well as provision of food and housing increased in ways that were neither planned nor anticipated in 1965. Haveman (1977) suggests that the War on Poverty may have indirectly affected the provision and utilization of many government programs in ways that benefited the poor. Thus, any final evaluation of the War on Poverty requires more than a simple cost-benefit analysis of specific programs.

For social scientists, the War on Poverty raised the important questions of how social programs are to be evaluated, and how resources can be allocated and services developed so that program goals are actually attained. As we saw in Chapter 3, *evaluation research* is the application of social research methods in order to assess the effects of a social program or policy. It thus requires the skillful use of research techniques in the highly charged and value-laden arena of political decision making. In the 1960s, evaluation research emerged as a legitimate and appealing activity for applied social psychologists and other researchers. By the 1970s, their involvement was even greater, extending to roles as research consultants who helped program staff conduct their own evaluations.

The frustration associated with the War on Poverty also points up the importance of the planning and development aspects of social programming. A poorly conceived or poorly implemented program cannot be expected to reach its objectives and produce a positive evaluation. The process of program development is thus intertwined with program evaluation—two mutually supportive activities that require our closest attention. We must understand how they interrelate if we are to grasp the roles of applied social psychologists who are called upon to help plan programs, and to monitor program development and implementation in ways that maximize their chances for success.

Applied social psychologists have often put the cart before the horse by emphasizing program evaluation over program development. Program evaluation certainly has important implications for continuing program improvement—a form of program development. However, it is necessary to study the process of putting a program into practice *before* its eventual effects can be assessed. Program development has been left more to social work, community development, and program management, but this scene is changing as evaluation researchers become more concerned with program planning.

DEVELOPMENT OF HUMAN SERVICE PROGRAMS

What Are Human Service Programs?

In the twentieth century, the provision of human services to people in need has become a major activity. Government departments and private agencies have taken over many of the supportive activities that were once performed by family, tribe, clan, or community. In the developed countries, government spending on human service programs constitutes a large proportion of the national budget. Such major investments in social programming demand a competent effort to develop viable programs and to evaluate their effectiveness (Attkisson, Hargreaves, Horowitz & Sorensen, 1978; Rossi, Freeman & Wright, 1979; Tripodi, Fellin & Epstein, 1971).

Human service programs are planned activities that provide comprehensive, integrated help to people who need assistance in matters of health, mental health,

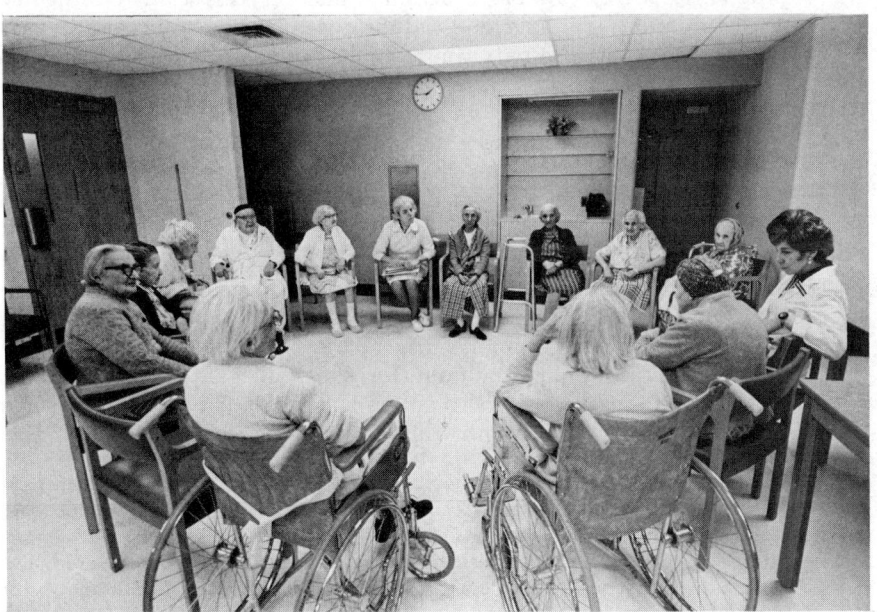

In the twentieth century, government departments and private agencies have taken over many of the supportive activities—such as care of the elderly—that were once performed by family, tribe, clan, or community. (© *Sepp Seitz/Woodfin Camp & Associates*)

education, social welfare, and criminal justice—in fact, in all aspects of the social and physical environment that affect people's lives. Hospitals, community mental health centers, schools, universities, social services departments, prisons, and halfway houses are all engaging in activities that would be considered human service programs. The overall goal of such programs is to improve the quality of people's lives by resolving their difficulties (many of which are interconnected) through individual growth and adjustment, through social change, or through a combination of both (Attkisson & Broskowski, 1978). This is a tall order to fill, so much so that the present human service system is often deemed inefficient and fragmented. There are too many agencies, too many programs, too many significant gaps in service, and too many barriers to accessibility. Program evaluation should therefore be seen as part of a development process that promotes program accountability to citizens, clients, and funders, and that provides a linkage mechanism for the integration of human services.

Human service programs vary on several dimensions (Tripodi et al., 1971). A large program may cover a state or an entire nation (for example, the Community Action Program of the War on Poverty); a small one may provide services to only one town or city (such as a teen drop-in center organized by a local youth club). Thus, federal, state, or provincial programs may involve many separate projects or program implementations at the local level in different geographic locations. Programs may be government supported and managed or may be private and voluntary, operating with or without government assistance. Because the duration of programs is highly variable, program evaluation is especially worthwhile in identifying programs that have outlived their usefulness. The complexity and breadth of program goals also vary considerably. Some programs in compensatory education, such as Head Start, seek a number of challenging goals for both the individual child and the family. On the other hand, a criminal justice program that diverts juvenile delinquents from the court system may only seek to reduce the economic costs of trial and sentencing. Equally diverse are the organizational components of different programs—such as staff size, staff makeup, and management structure. A small employment counseling program, for example, might have only three counselors—all trained in social work—who make program decisions by consensus. A large government unit providing employment counseling might have fifteen staff from differing educational backgrounds—social work, business management, personnel, psychology—organized into a hierarchical structure with a director, assistant director, supervisors, and counselors.

Regardless of this variety, all social programs have similar problems to solve in order to provide their services and achieve their goals (Tripodi et al., 1971):

- All must demonstrate or assume an initial need for their existence. For example, an employment counseling program would point to unemployment due to inadequate placing of individuals in jobs as its reason to exist.
- All must secure the financial, technological, and human resources required; and they must effectively allocate these resources to their operations. The developers of an employment counseling program must convince government funders to allocate dollars to the program, must arrange for suitable offices and equipment, and must hire staff who are trained to provide counseling.

- All must make adequate contact with their clientele and effectively supply their service. The employment counselors must make their service known and have unemployed persons seeking the counseling service.
- All must maintain an operating budget, report to interested parties, and justify their decisions to appropriate authorities. The employment counseling program must report to government funders on the operation of the program so that continued support is forthcoming.

In order to approach these generic problems of program functioning, human service programs tend to go through identifiable stages of development.

Stages of Program Development

Program development can be seen as a variant of the general problem-solving sequence discussed in Chapter 4, and many of the same principles and requirements apply. The problem or need must be defined and diagnosed adequately before we move to developing alternative solutions or activities to remedy the problem. The chosen alternative should be implemented on a trial basis and monitored closely so that improvements can be made where necessary. In addition, all the social or interactive requirements of problem solving can be applied to program development: that is, people experiencing the problem should be involved in problem definition; and people who take part in choosing the solution will have a much greater commitment to the activities than those who do not participate. It is unfortunate that the complex and difficult task of program development has not received the attention it deserves in the professional literature. Rather than assume that programs will somehow automatically change, scientist/practitioners must become concerned with developing models and theories about this crucial area of practice (Hasenfeld, 1979).

Program development is a sequential process that moves through the three interrelated stages of program initiation, program contact, and program implementation (Hage & Aiken, 1970; Tripodi et al., 1971). In *program initiation*, the first stage, the basic ideas and goals for a program are articulated and translated into a concrete plan of action; and all the necessary human, financial, and physical resources are acquired. During *program contact*, the second stage, the program staff make connections with the clientele or target population. During *program implementation*, the third stage, the staff delivers its services, moving to attain the ultimate goals of the program. At each stage, the program staff emphasizes particular activities and seeks to achieve certain objectives. This is because each stage builds on the previous one, and the requirements of each stage must be met in order for program development to proceed successfully. But since the stages overlap somewhat, a program might be simultaneously concerned with the requirements of two or even three stages. In practice, program development is a recycling process in which, over time, the major emphases correspond to the three stages.

In addition, program evaluation enters in to give a complete overview of the process of social programming. This overview, presented in Figure 13.1, shows the major activities within each stage of program development and evaluation and indicates the cyclical nature of human service programs.

Program initiation often begins informally in the minds and discussions of decision makers and/or potential clientele who perceive a need for service in a particular area. The need for the program may be based solely on such collective impressions, but often some type of more objective assessment of needs is required. This is where the research skills of the applied social psychologist can be put to good use. Interviews may be held with community leaders or service providers in a related area to see if they perceive a need based on their contact with potential users of the program. For example, in the development of a program to divert juvenile delinquents from the court system, probation officers can give their impressions of the need for and usefulness of such a program. Survey research has often been used for need assessment. For instance, in developing a recreational program for disadvantaged children, a survey of low-income families can give planners a sense of what areas of programming would be most appealing. Sometimes, when needs are documented by available social indicators, the program planners can simply refer to such statistics to support their proposals. The need for many of the programs that were part of the War on Poverty was obviously based on existing measures of income level, educational attainment, employment, and similar indicators.

The documentation of need involves another important element of program initiation: identification of the potential clientele or target population—the people to whom the program services are directed. Potential users are often specified by some combination of demographic factors: age, sex, occupation, residence, in-

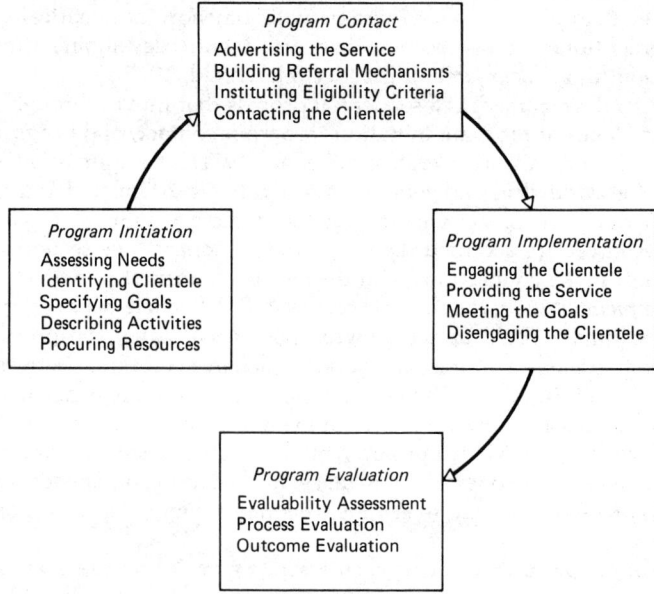

Figure 13.1   Overview of Program Development and Evaluation.

come level, and so on. For example, a youth employment program might see its target population as unemployed young males between 16 and 20 who have not completed high school and live in an impoverished area of the city. The flip side of this element is that programs may often set eligibility criteria: services are made available only to those individuals who exhibit certain characteristics or fall into certain classes. Welfare programs, for example, devote considerable effort to the question of who qualifies for assistance and who does not.

Along with assessing needs and identifying recipients, program initiation requires the specification of program goals or objectives and the description of program activities designed to meet those goals. The program should be clear about what it wishes to accomplish and how it will know when it has done so. Often, the articulation of goals is one of the most difficult areas of program development and evaluation. Goal statements may be vague or too general or incomplete or unmeasurable or inadequate in some way that hampers proper program implementation and functioning. Sometimes, goals are confused with activities or services, since these are in a way subgoals that must be met for the overall goals to be achieved. For example, a program developed to provide counseling for families with a mentally retarded child might come to see its goals as simply providing the service. But in so doing, it may fail to ask the more important question of what effects the counseling actually has on family relations. It is therefore important to spell out the activities of the program staff and to see these as stepping stones toward the actual changes that constitute the program goals.

To complete the program-initiation stage, planners must procure all the physical, technological, and human resources required to operate the program. This is an obvious requirement, but the important point is that resource selection and development must be compatible with program activities and objectives. The physical location and environment should be conducive to providing the designated service. The development of storefront clinics is a good example of finding an innovative way to reach alienated youth, urban poor, and other less traditional target populations. Staff must be selected, trained, and integrated to form an effective working unit. The techniques of skill training, small-group facilitation, and team building discussed in earlier chapters are very useful for staff development. The organizational structure, policies, and procedures must be set in place to coordinate and support the provision of service. All these factors help determine the ultimate viability and effectiveness of the program.

Program contact brings the staff into interaction with the potential clientele so that services may be provided during program implementation. Clients may be contacted through mass media advertising, word-of-mouth campaigns, contacts with service personnel in related programs, and so on. When new programs are developed within an existing service organization or government department, referrals automatically flow from other parts of the organization. If, for example, a mental health clinic starts up an assertiveness training program for shy and withdrawn adults, referrals of appropriate clients will begin to flow in from social workers, psychiatrists, family counselors, and others working within the clinic. If a program is planned in collaboration with representatives of potential beneficiaries, these opinion leaders often bring forward clients from their various constituencies. If the youth employment program is developed in conjunction with a community board, these representatives will use word-of-mouth to encourage young people to give the service a try. Any of these approaches include the screening of both potential and ineligible clients.

I was once involved in developing a program that failed at the stage of program contact (Fisher, 1977). The program was designed as an after-hours crisis-line service for students living in university apartments; its goal was to reduce the incidence and severity of mental health problems among the students. Since this was a pilot program, our main concern was to develop a service and see if it was utilized. Through interviews with mental health workers on campus, we assessed the need for our program, then built a broad base of support among people in the student government and the residence administration. We procured the necessary physical resources and selected a team of volunteer peer counselors who were then trained by psychiatrists and psychologists in the knowledge and skills of interpersonal communication and crisis intervention. The service was advertised in the campus newspaper, through flyers and posters in the residence, and by a word-of-mouth campaign by the volunteers. However, during the 4-month trial period, the service was used only twice. For whatever reasons, the potential clients were reluctant to use the service, and the program was terminated. In this case, the stage of program contact was the acid test for both program development and evaluation.

During *program implementation*, the final stage of program development, the staff fully engages the clientele and provides the activities, services, or treatments that are logically expected to result in the intended outcomes or goals of the program. The success of this stage depends on both the relevance of the service and its utility. This includes the effectiveness of its particular technology, whether it is directed toward alcoholism, counseling, preventive health care, job placement, or whatever. If the activities are properly implemented—and it is very important to document this—then we expect to see the intended changes in the client system. Effective alcoholism counseling, for example, should lead to a significant decrease in alcohol abuse in some proportion of the clientele. If compensatory preschool education is provided to some children, we expect them to perform better in school than comparable children who do not participate in the program.

A final element of program implementation is the disengagement of the clientele. Most programs do not keep the same recipients forever, but are expected to "graduate" their clientele once the program goals have been reached. This may involve either termination (such as the ending of successful family counseling) or an integration of the clientele into another institution (such as a job training program that finds positions for its graduates). But when are clients ready for disengagement? This is a difficult question in many human service programs, especially mental health services where it is hard to judge when someone is "better enough." Program managers are always in the difficult position of having to allot resources in such a way that the services will help enough of their clients enough of the time.

Program evaluation logically follows program development; yet many of the activities of program evaluation may relate back to any of the three stages shown in Figure 13.1. Looking at program initiation, program evaluation might ask whether the needs were accurately assessed before the program was implemented, or whether the staff members were adequately trained to provide the intended services. As for program contact, evaluation research could assess the effectiveness of the ongoing publicizing of the service, the identity of the clientele contacted, or the adequacy of the referral mechanisms. In evaluating program implementation, two major questions emerge. Are the activities or services being implemented as described in the program initiation stage? If the activities are being carried out as planned, are the program goals being met?

Evaluators make distinctions among the types of evaluation brought into play. *Process evaluation* describes and documents ongoing activities. *Outcome evaluation* assesses the attainment of the program's goals. *Evaluability assessment*, a useful prerequisite to both types of evaluation, asks whether the program can be usefully appraised. Have the activities been implemented in the appropriate manner and environment so that we can logically expect the desired goals to be achieved? If the answer to this question is yes, then it is both reasonable and useful to subject the program to an evaluation, particularly an outcome evaluation.

Obviously the processes of program development and program evaluation are inextricably linked in complex and subtle ways (see Perkins, 1977). Comprehending these connections is one of the most challenging aspects of understanding why some programs succeed while others fail. Some of the difficulties of program development inherent in the rural sector of the War on Poverty are highlighted in Box 13.1.

Small-Group Methods for Program Development

Program development is a form of human problem solving. It involves a variety of individuals with different ideas and needs coming together to define a problem, develop alternate solutions, and implement the best one. Ideally, program development involves not just government or agency planners but also potential recipients, skilled resource people, and administrators who hold the purse strings. Program development therefore poses the challenge of requiring a coordinated problem-solving effort from diverse participants. Furthermore, a great deal of program development occurs in small groups—that is, committees, task forces, and other program groups charged with the jobs of assessing needs, developing program objectives and activities, securing funding, selecting staff, and so on. Thus, the dealing with small-group processes are highly relevant to the activities of program development.

A Program Planning Model (PPM). One example of a group-process model for problem identification and program planning has been developed by Delbecq and Van de Ven (1971) from their experience with the Community Action Agency of the Office of Economic Opportunity. This Program Planning Model (PPM) is a systematic sequence of small-group, problem-solving activities consisting of five phases: problem exploration, knowledge exploration, priority development, program development, and program evaluation. In terms of the phases of program development described previously, PPM is primarily concerned with program

Box 13.1   FOCUS ON RESEARCH
Lessons in Program Development from the Rural War on Poverty

A major thrust of the War on Poverty was the establishment of the President's National Advisory Commission on Rural Poverty, which was charged with the task of wiping out poverty in rural America. Programs were developed to create jobs, to provide employment training, and to establish rural cooperatives. However, extensive evaluation reports indicated that these programs had little impact on rural poverty. What went wrong? Sociologist Sally Bould of the University of Delaware provides a sobering analysis of the errors in program development that reduced ultimate effectiveness.

Bould examined the evaluation reports on three sets of programs: (1) Community Development Corporations (CDC) to create jobs for unemployed poor people, (2) Concentrated Employment Programs (CEP) to provide job training to the unemployed poor, and (3) rural cooperatives to organize poor farmers in collective marketing and purchasing activities. In developing all these programs, the planners made a fundamental error—they stressed the economics of poverty rather than the politics of poverty and they assumed that local communities would welcome programs for economic development. They ignored the possibilities that poverty serves positive functions for the nonpoor and that economic changes would be strongly resisted by the status quo (see Chapter 11).

The CDC programs *were* successful in obtaining jobs. However, most were low-paying, unskilled positions that raised few people above the poverty line. Programs tended to be staffed and controlled by higher status individuals—leading citizens—and the net effect was to provide a low-wage labor pool to perform the community's menial work. Similarly, CEP in effect trained workers for low-paying work—program dropouts generally found higher-paying jobs than program graduates. An apparent conspiracy among local businesses was against upgrading the poor and creating economic development since this would mean having to pay higher wages. Rural cooperatives met direct local resistance, with political lobbying going right up to the federal level. For example, in Alabama, white county officials appeared threatened at the prospect of poor black farmers organizing themselves and gaining more economic and political power. In most cases, resistance, intimidation, and harassment led to cuts and delays in funding and the imposition of program modifications which reduced overall effectiveness.

Bould concludes that the CDC and CEP programs should have been redesigned to alter the assumptions that jobs would reduce poverty and that high wage industries would be welcomed by local residents once a trained labor force was available. In addition, findings of evaluation reports should have led to program changes to overcome resistances. In either case, social researchers should get more involved in program development and implementation to help increase program effectiveness.

Source: Bould, S. Rural poverty and economic development: Lessons from the War on Poverty. *The Journal of Applied Behavioral Science*, 1977, *13*, 471–488.

initiation, where most of the planning activities occur. The goal is to institute the problem-solving process in typical program-planning situations. At this stage, a variety of fragmented interest groups with different backgrounds, values, and expertise must be coordinated and integrated.

Phase 1 of PPM, *problem exploration*, brings together a cross section of potential clients with personnel from the programming agency. This emphasizes client needs as the starting point for program development and legitimates later program proposals as having come partly from the clients themselves. A detailed outline for a Phase 2 meeting is given in Table 13.1.

The introduction to the Phase 1 meeting expresses the agency's interest in the client's problems and emphasizes the importance at this stage of focusing on problems rather than solutions. (There is a common tendency in problem solving of wanting to move quickly to solutions before the problem is understood.)

Next, Delbecq and Van de Ven use the Nominal Group Technique (NGT) to elicit individual perceptions of important problems. At the meeting, participants are divided into small groups, and each group member is instructed to make his or her own problem list; this is done without discussion. Then, in a round-robin procedure, individual ideas are listed on a large flip chart, with each member contributing one idea each time around the group. This facilitates full participation and generates many ideas, avoiding the common pitfalls of domination by a vocal minority, a discussion stuck on a single issue, or the premature evaluation of ideas. Discussion of each item on the chart is useful for clarification and elaboration, but items are not condensed or removed. Evaluation enters in by having all members vote for the five highest priority items on the list. The voting gives equal power to all members: the poverty-stricken welfare recipient has as many votes as the agency supervisor with three college degrees. These votes are tabulated in a

Table 13.1   AGENDA FOR PHASE I OF THE PROGRAM PLANNING MODEL

I. *Selection of Client or Consumer Sample* (divided according to age, geography, technical application, or other appropriate categories)

II. *Meeting with Clients or Consumer Groups to Explore Problem Dimensions*
  A. Introduction (10 minutes)
    1. Welcome
    2. Expression of interest of organization(s) in clients' problems
    3. Indication that focus is on problems, not solutions
    4. Explanation of "personal" vs. "organizational" problems
  B. Directions for small-group participation
    1. Assign clients to small groups of six to nine
    2. Instruct them in nominal group format
      a. Listing "personal" problem dimensions on 5-by-7-inch cards (15 minutes)
      b. Listing "organizational" problem dimensions on 5-by-7-inch cards (15 minutes)
    3. Provide flip chart and recorder for round-robin sharing of individually noted items
      a. Items from individual cards (first organizational, then personal)
      b. New items suggested by process
  C. Fifteen-minute break
  D. Interacting group discussion of each item on flip chart in serial fashion for clarification, elaboration, and/or defense, but not for collapsing or condensing items
  E. Nominal group voting on 3-by-5-inch cards for top five priority items on both "personal" and "organizational" lists
  F. General session—discussion of tabulated votes from each small group
  G. Explanation of PPM and election of representatives) for Phase II

Source: Delbecq & Van de Ven (1971).

general session, leading to the final product of Phase 1: a priority listing of problems. At this point, the remaining stages of PPM are explained, and representatives of Phase 1 are elected to participate in Phase 2 to maintain continuity of involvement.

Knowledge exploration in Phase 2 draws on programming specialists from the sponsoring agency and from external organizations (such as universities and institutes). The introduction focuses on the priority problems listed by the clients in Phase 1, and asks the specialists to respond to these as "idea people" rather than as representatives of programs or organizations. Once again, the participants are assigned to small groups, and the NGT is used to develop a listing of the *critical components* that must be included in any solution to the identified problems. In addition, each specialist develops a list of existing and new resources that would be required to develop an appropriate program. These techniques make it less likely that the specialists will slip into the role of defending existing programs or policies with which they may be associated. NGT also equalizes participation among various levels of specialists. For example, in health planning, medical doctors usually speak while nurses listen. For optimal solutions, such differences in participation need to be overcome. The techniques also increase the chance that innovative combinations of old and new ideas and resources might emerge.

After a round-robin sharing of ideas, each small group engages in discussion to produce a package of resources and solution components for each problem. Each group then reports to the general session, and a master list of ideas is compiled. As in Phase 1, participants then vote for those solution components and resources considered to be absolutely essential for an effective program to solve high-priority problems. Phase 2 thus calls attention to the essential components of program development and provides a legitimate endorsement of specialists for these. A program in juvenile diversion, for example, has a greater chance of receiving funding if it has the approval of criminologists, social workers, psychologists, and so on. Representatives from Phase 2 are then elected to continue with the PPM process.

Phase 3 involves *priority development*, the most crucial stage of PPM. It brings together the representatives of Phases 1 and 2 with the key administrators and resource controllers who have the power to make life-or-death decisions on program proposals. Phase 3 seeks to get reactions from these key people while program components are flexible enough to be modified to gain acceptance. (When program proposals come to administrators in an inflexible form, or when apparently unchangeable aspects threaten existing programs or systems, the proposal is usually rejected.) By implementing Phase 3, program sponsors can respond to administrators' criticisms and plan further program details accordingly. The Phase 3 meeting brings out any reservations and qualifications that key persons may have about ideas offerd in Phases 1 and 2. It also uses small-group discussion to specify the changes needed to ensure a full endorsement of the program proposal. If, for example, the chief of police has reservations about implementing a juvenile diversion program, such reservations should be addressed now rather than at the time of final decision making on the program proposal. Through negotiation, the essential concerns of all three groups— clients, specialists, and administrators—can be incorporated into the program proposal. The desired outcome is a "green light" for final program development.

Phase 4, involving *program development*, is similar to the program initiation stage. This time, however, program sponsors are in a position to draw on the results of Phases 1, 2, and 3 to develop a program that represents input from all concerned groups, including the sponsoring agency. Using this input, technical specialists and supervisory personnel from the sponsoring agency develop a final, specific, and detailed program proposal. In doing so, they must remain sensitive to the critical elements developed in prior phases. In this way, a program is developed that is responsive to the needs of potential clientele, is realistic in terms of suggested solutions and necessary resources, and reflects the limitations imposed by resource controllers and administrators.

The final phase of the PPM sequence is *program evaluation*—specifically, an evaluation of the final proposal. Representatives from Phases 1, 2, and 3 are brought together for a final session in which the program sponsors present the detailed proposal. Each important element of the proposal is related to the input from the previous stages. The final plan of action is linked to priority problems, solution components, and resource elements, and administrative and specialist concerns. Criticisms result either in modifications or a commitment to evaluate any aspect of the program that might prove to be a weakness. Thus, Phase 5 involves all interested groups to see if their concerns have been met, and to rekindle support and develop commitment to the program proposal. Because of its orderly sequence, Delbecq and Van de Ven maintain that PPM provides a group-process model that highlights crucial issues and provides a guideline for developing innovative programs.

Other Small-Group Methods. Delbecq, Van de Ven, and Gustafson (1975) present a general application of small-group techniques to program planning. They develop the rationale and requirements of the Nominal Group Technique (NGT) used in PPM and the Delphi Technique (described herein) as ways of increasing the rationality, creativity, and participation in problem-solving meetings associated with program planning. Both the NGT and the Delphi Technique are used in situations where individual ideas need to be tapped and pooled in a constructive fashion. As used in PPM, NGT involves the silent generation of ideas, round-robin recording, clarification, and elaboration, and rank-ordering of ideas through priority voting. NGT is thus a noninteractive group method that overcomes some of the disadvantages of interacting groups—such as conformity pressures or coalition formation. NGT is useful for generating citizen involvement and for improving communication and collaboration among people from diverse professional and nonprofessional backgrounds. In combination with interactive methods (see Chapter 7), noninteractive methods can provide a useful ingredient of program development activities.

The Delphi Technique, originally used to forecast technological developments, takes its name from the Delphic Oracle of ancient Greece, who was purported to foretell the future. Like NGT, the Delphi Technique restricts group interaction to heighten concentration and creativity free from premature evaluation or social pressure. The method involves the use of a sequence of mailed questionnaires to collect information on a particular topic, interspersed with the feedback of information derived from earlier responses. With Delphi, the planning group does not need to meet face-to-face, but develops consensus through repeated measures and reactions that are shared with all members. As with NGT, a priority listing of ideas is the final outcome. Delphi is useful when participants are in different locations. It requires less time from participants than NGT, but it does take more personnel time to construct, distribute, and tally the questionnaires. However, since Delphi does not allow for group discussion it is not useful for resolving strong disagreements that often develop in program planning. These techniques can thus be added to small-group methods that involve greater interaction (such as brainstorming) to give the program planner a broader choice of methods.

EVALUATION OF HUMAN SERVICE PROGRAMS

The initial emphasis in evaluation research was to assess the impact that a social policy or program had on the problem or condition that required alleviation. This emphasis was largely motivated by a concern about getting adequate value for money spent and was spurred by skepticism about social programs resulting from reports of ineffectiveness (Rutman, 1977). However, evaluation research is now also seen as a useful input for the policy making and planning that precedes the actual implementation of services. As such it deals with the effects of programs, the activities designed to produce the effects, and the linkages between activities and effects. For example, in evaluating a school counseling program to increase academic achievement, we are interested not only in any changes in course grades, but also in the counseling procedures that are expected to lead to improved performance. Thus, in a broader sense, *evaluation research* is defined as a set of social research activities that occurs during the planning, design, development, and implementation of human service programs (Rossi et al., 1979).

The purpose of program evaluation depends on the perspective we take of it, such as these three identified by Chelimsky (1978):

- From an *accountability perspective*, the purpose of evaluation is to make the best possible use of funds by holding program managers accountable for the worth of their programs.
- From a *knowledge perspective*, the purpose of evaluation is to establish new knowledge about social problems and the effectiveness of policies and programs designed to alleviate them.
- From a *management perspective*, evaluation is seen as a management tool for assessing and improving the operational efficiency of the program.

Because these different perspectives ask different research questions and involve different purposes and priorities, they may conflict as evaluations are planned and executed. All evaluations contribute to decision making about social programs and policies. Within this context, Anderson and Ball (1978) see six different purposes that are served by program evaluation:

- to contribute to decisions about program initiation by ascertaining the needs, testing the ideas, and assessing the adequacy of available resources
- to contribute to decisions about program continuation by assessing effects to determine if the program is still needed

- to contribute to decisions about program modification by examining the adequacy of the program content and activities
- to obtain supportive evidence that demonstrates the need for or effectiveness of a given program
- to obtain critical evidence that demonstrates the lack of need for or ineffectiveness of a given program
- to contribute to the understanding of basic psychological or social processes by studying these as a secondary element of the evaluation

Program evaluation thus involves a complex variety of research objectives that may be interspersed throughout the entire sequence of program development, implementation, and termination. But it is equally complex in its social and political aspects. Because evaluation involves many different actors—clients, managers, funders, evaluators, citizens—it is no surprise that people take very different perspectives of it and see very different purposes for it. We must try to unravel this complexity by looking at both technical and social components. We have to ask whether all programs can be evaluated, and we must ask about the relationship of the evaluator to the program managers, funders, and clients within the social and political context of the evaluation. We must examine the types and methods of evaluation and the importance of design and measurement. And finally we must look at future trends in this intriguing area of interdisciplinary research, an area in which applied social psychologists play a central role.

Can All Programs Be Evaluated?

In September 1971, the Minnesota Restitution Center began a community-based residential corrections program for adult male offenders (Hudson, 1977). The program diverted offenders to the center four months after their admission to the regular prison system, facilitating the negotiation of a restitution agreement between the offender and his victim. The offender lived at the center under a parole order and, with supervision, was expected to complete a restitution schedule. Restitution involved work designed to make up for losses caused by the criminal offense. Persons convicted of property crimes, such as theft, were randomly assigned to the center. Most offenders assigned had a long list of prior convictions and imprisonments and were considered poor risks for rehabilitation.

Hudson enumerates a number of problems that made it almost impossible to evaluate this program or to expect that it would have any positive effect. To begin with, restitution was a feeble sort of intervention. On the average, it amounted to only a few hundred dollars—a minor concern to an offender with a long criminal history. Most restitution agreements also seemed inconsequential to members of the parole board, and they refused to release program residents from parole once restitution was completed, as was specified in the original program design. Thus, the program staff had to continue parole supervision of discharged residents in the community, and it became difficult if not impossible to describe and measure what these supervisory activities actually involved. In addition, since many residents were drug addicts, group counseling sessions were initiated to deal with the underlying psychological difficulties. All this made it virtually impossible to separate the effects of the restitution agreement from the effects of the continuing parole supervision and the group counseling.

To complicate matters even more, intervention emphases changed over time to reflect changed perceptions of offender needs. In short, it was not possible to accurately describe or measure a common treatment provided to all residents, and it was not clear how any results could be replicated or generalized to other programs. Thus, the rigor of using an experimental, control group design was wasted because the independent variable could not be defined or described adequately.

These problems were serious enough for the restitution program, but there were more. The program goal of reducing *recidivism*—a vague concept that here meant parole violation and return to prison—was difficult to assess because authorities may have departed from their normal way of dealing with parole violations of program participants. In sum, it was not clear what factors were affecting the program goals in what way. Hudson concludes that numerous practical problems can arise from a lack of congruence between the purpose of an evaluation and the developmental life of the program that is being evaluated.

Preconditions of Program Evaluation. The basic difficulty of the Minnesota Residential Center's program is that it failed to meet any of the preconditions or requirements for evaluation. Rutman (1977) sees three major preconditions of an evaluable program: (1) a clearly articulated program, (2) clearly specified goals and/or effects, and (3) a rationale or logical relationship linking the program activities to the goals and/or effects. These preconditions help us to understand why some programs can be usefully evaluated while others cannot. Unfortunately, it is too often *after* the evaluation attempt that researchers realize the impossibility of their task: that the program was simply not evaluable. The solution obviously lies in greater sensitivity to the necessary preconditions and their relationship to program development. Through collaboration with program planners and managers, evaluation researchers can help describe activities, specify goals, and illuminate causal relationships.

Many human service programs carry imprecise labels. "Mental health center," "juvenile diversion program," "community action program," and the like are labels that include a diversity of approaches and activities with no common meaning. Unless there is an accurate and coherent definition of the program, it is not possible to attribute the program effects to a clearly recognized and measurable intervention. In the terminology of experimentation, extraneous variables act in concert with the independent variable to determine outcomes on the dependent variable. Therefore, we cannot attribute changes in the dependent variable (the program effects) to the manipulation of the independent variable (the program activities). Of course, even a clear program definition does not guarantee proper implementation. But if the program is articulated in measurable terms, then we can collect information on how well it has been implemented. By articulating and monitoring a program's operation, we make it possible to attribute the program outcomes to the planned interventions rather than to some confounding element of the treatment program.

Rutman's second precondition concerns clearly specified goals and/or effects. Unfortunately, it is common to find programs with goals that are vague or that are contradictory or unrelated to program activities. Sometimes goals at the local program level are different from those specified at the national level. For example, one large-scale federal program for assistance to upgrade small-farm operations showed a variety of objectives at the local level (Edwards, Orden & Buccola, 1980). Some projects emphasized farm management practices, others marketing procedures, and others improvement in production. Different groups may also have different goals for the same program. In employment training, clients may be looking for short-term support, while programmers want long-term change in work behavior. Goals must be clearly specified in measurable terms if they are to serve as the criteria for judging program effectiveness. This assures us that the crucial outcome variables have been identified and included in the evaluation. The identification must include formally stated goals as well as informal goals or unintended effects. In the extreme, "goal-free evaluation" looks for *actual* program effects regardless of formally specified goals (Scriven, 1972). For example, the stated goal of a juvenile diversion program might be to reduce future criminal activity of the individual offender; its informal goal might be to increase the offender's sense of social responsibility. An unintended *positive* effect might be improved family relations; an unintended *negative* effect might be increased delinquency due to decreased deterrence.

Rossi et al. (1979) point out that goal setting requires either assumptions or knowledge about two fundamental aspects of the social situation: societal values and existing conditions. Our sense of existing values determines our goals; our sense of existing conditions determines how much room there is for improvement. If we value that children should have equal educational opportunity regardless of race, and research indicates that this equal opportunity does not exist, then something needs to be done. Thus, programs set goals to reduce the gap between the quality of life people value and the quality of life *experienced* by the target population. Existing conditions must be assessed accurately and comprehensively, and clear goal statements are essential for a meaningful evaluation.

The third precondition for evaluation is a linking rationale that explains why the program activities are expected to produce the anticipated effects. If this relationship cannot be described, there is no logical basis for evaluating the program. We need to ask these questions: Is any program activity directed toward the program goals? If so, is the activity appropriate and adequate to generate changes? In the case of the restitution program, for example, the small amount of restitution would probably have little or no effect on recidivism. Furthermore, we can't assume that the attainment of immediate or modest goals will result in the reaching of ultimate or significant goals. A crisis counseling program designed to help suicidal patients might reduce anxiety in the aftermath of an attempted suicide, but might do nothing to prevent future attempts.

Rossi and his colleagues use the term *causal hypothesis* to indicate the anticipated theoretical relationship between processes or characteristics and the condition that is the object of the program. The hypothesis must be stated in ways that render the variables measurable. Then an *intervention hypothesis* is developed, specifying the relationship between what is actually done in the program and the condition to be changed. Finally, the linkage between the program activities and the specific outcomes must be studied in the actual situation. This is a costly and time-consuming procedure involving multiple measures. However, only when these relationships are fully specified is it possible to comprehensively evaluate the program.

Evaluability Assessment. How can we determine if the preconditions for evaluating a program have been met? As noted earlier, a methodology known as *evaluability assessment* answers this and related questions by assessing to what degree a program can be usefully evaluated (Rutman, 1980; Wholey, 1977, 1979). Wholey points out that evaluability assessment answers two questions: Is program performance likely to be adequate? Is evaluation likely to be useful in improving program performance? Strictly speaking, any program can be evaluated. For example, the Minnesota Restitution Center program was "evaluated" even though it met none of the preconditions. The issue is whether the evaluation will have meaning and utility. Evaluability assessment helps assure us that it will.

In a nutshell, evaluability assessment

> . . . tests the extent to which managers and policy-makers have defined measureable program objectives and defined specific uses for information on program performance; documents ongoing program activities including resource and information flows; assesses the plausibility of program objectives and the feasibility of measuring progress toward program objectives; and identifies opportunities to change program activities, objectives, and uses of information in ways likely to improve program performance. (Wholey, 1979, p. 13)

To accomplish this, the evaluator gathers information from program documents and program personnel, analyzes this information conceptually to study the various preconditions, and presents this analysis back to the program managers.

In practice, evaluability assessment has grown rapidly in complexity and scope. Different evaluators use different terms and variations of the same process, and the number of basic steps continue to expand. In 1977, Wholey listed five steps in an evaluability assessment. His 1979 work describes eight steps:

1. Define the program by determining what activities are involved.
2. Collect information on the program from documentation (such as legislation and grant applications), and through interviews with program managers and policymakers. This step documents the intended program activities, program objectives, and the causal assumptions linking the activities to the objectives.
3. Develop a concise *logic model* of the program that illustrates the information collected in Step 2. This includes resources required for the activities, as well as any potential side effects beyond the intended objectives.
4. Analyze the extent to which the activities and objectives can be measured. This includes developing a *measurement model* that includes only those activities and objectives for which adequate measures have been developed.
5. Collect information on program reality from program documents (such as work plans and annual reports) and from observations of program operations.
6. Clarify which program objectives are measurable and plausible—that is, which ones are likely to result from the activities underway.
7. Develop an *evaluable model* that shows only plausible and measurable objectives and the activities in operation that are likely to lead to these objectives. This model captures the portion of the program that can be usefully evaluated.

8. Present the results of the conceptual analysis, including the models and options, to program management. These show how program activities, objectives, and data collection could be changed to improve program performance and evaluability.

Evaluability assessment can be a crucial initial phase in program evaluation in which program managers collaborate with evaluation researchers to improve the clarity, performance, and evaluability of human service programs. Along with performance monitoring and evaluation of program results, evaluability assessment provides an essential link in the developing technology of program evaluation. An example of how this works in mental health programming is presented in Box 13.2.

Types of Program Evaluation

In our earlier look at the cycle of program development and evaluation (see Figure 13.1), we saw that evaluators made distinctions between two basic types of program evaluation. *Process evaluation* consists of research activities that describe and monitor program services and effects for the purpose of improving program performance. *Outcome evaluation* consists of research activities that document the effectiveness and efficiency of the program in attaining its specified objectives.

Scriven (1967), one of the first to distinguish between types of program evaluation, was concerned with evaluating school curricula. He saw that *formative evaluation* produces information useful to programmers in the formation or development of the curriculum or program. On the other hand, *summative evaluation* assesses the effectiveness of the program once it has been developed. This distinction has broadened over the years to reflect a concern with program operations or processes versus an emphasis on program outcomes or achievements. Of course, both types of evaluation can provide information to improve program functioning, and both are required to produce a comprehensive program evaluation (Rutman, 1977; Rossi et al., 1979).

Process Evaluation. Rutman (1977) refers to process evaluation as *formative research*, pointing out its importance in further assessing the evaluability of a program beyond an initial assessment. This purpose ties in with the need of program managers or policymakers who want the findings of evaluation research to contribute to program development and management. Thus, formative research helps to determine evaluability by monitoring the actual operation of the program once the preconditions have been met and the program is under way.

As for program activities or services, formative research verifies the presence of the activities and describes how they are actually implemented. Is the crisis counseling service providing the type of counseling that was intended? Is the juvenile diversion program using the eligibility criteria in the ways that were planned? These are the type of questions that must be answered by process evaluation.

Rossi (1978) sees three important questions that must be asked about program activities. First, is the treatment effective as determined by a theoretical model and as studied under the most favorable conditions? This question requires highly valid small-scale pilot studies that emphasize the causal linkage between treatment and effect. For example, the children's television program, *Sesame Street*, was successfully tested with small groups of children under careful observation before it was run on the full network.

The second question is whether the treatment can be effectively delivered

Box 13.2   FOCUS ON RESEARCH
Evaluability Assessment in the Mental Health Field

Evaluability assessment uses reviews of program documents, interviews with staff, and observations of activities to gauge the degree to which a program is evaluable. Joseph Wholey of the Urban Institute of Washington, D.C., presents a number of examples of how institute staff have assisted federal programs through this procedure.

An evaluability assessment was conducted in the National Institute of Mental Health on the functioning of the Community Mental Health Center (CMHC) program. This assessment used descriptions of the program and interviews with CMHC division managers to develop a picture of program objectives, activities, and measures of performance.

The CMHC program provides federal grants for constructing, staffing, and running hundreds of centers with the goals of providing psychiatric care in the community, of keeping people out of large psychiatric hospitals, and of assisting people returning to the community from mental institutions.

The evaluability assessment identified six outcome objectives of the CMHC program. However, five of these had not been defined in measurable terms. For example, one objective was to reduce the inappropriate use of state psychiatric hospitals, but there was no measure of what constituted "inappropriate use." Similarly, the objective of increasing services to special target groups was not measurable since these services had not been defined. Only one objective—to produce economically visible CMHCs—had an agreed-upon measure: that the center would get funding from other identified sources if the federal grants were terminated.

In the same vein, forty-seven process objectives were identified, only one of which had a measuring instrument: a format for site visits to determine if centers were operating in accordance with the federal guidelines. Most objectives such as "promote improved planning" or "improve the quality of technical assistance" had not been defined in measurable terms. As a result, only two evaluations could be suggested. One would test whether CMHCs would be financially viable without federal grants. The other would test whether CMHCs were operating in ways that met federal guidelines.

The most important outcome of evaluability assessment is to identify gaps in information. By constructing measures for other objectives, the CMHC program could move toward developing a more evaluable program.

Source: Wholey, J. S. *Evaluation: Promise and performance.* Washington, D.C.: The Urban Institute, 1979.

within the context of a general service delivery system. Sometimes, programs that work well in a small pilot study run by specially trained and highly dedicated personnel do not transfer well to more complex, less committed settings—a problem of external validity or generalizability. Effective alcoholism treatment programs may fail on the wider community level, for example, because police might prefer to arrest people for drunkenness rather than escort them to treatment centers.

The third and final question is whether the treatment is being delivered as intended when implemented on a large scale—at the federal level, for instance. This requires ongoing program-monitoring systems that measure and assess treatment delivery. This requires not only quantitative measures—such as number of clients seen or number of referrals accepted—but also qualitative assessments of the service—such as respect given to the clients. You can imagine that it is much easier and less expensive to count numbers than it is to measure quality—one of the major difficulties of process evaluation. Project Head Start, one of the War on Poverty programs, supported local communities in setting up preschool learning experiences for disadvantaged children. Because of differing sponsoring agencies, activities, and so, there was so much variation across projects that it hardly made sense to evaluate the program as a whole.

Ongoing programs must also be monitored to determine if the delivery of service is consistent with the specifications of program design and is reaching the intended clientele (Rossi et al., 1979). Experience tells us that program failure is often due to faulty or nonimplementation of activities rather than to the inherent ineffectiveness of the intervention (Rossi & Wright, 1977). For example, a birth control clinic set up to provide contraceptive services to black ghetto residents on Chicago's South Side was so swamped with student clientele from the nearby university that it made few efforts to reach the original target population (Rossi, 1977).

Rossi et al. (1979) recommend three ways to see if the program is reaching the appropriate target population: through records kept by the program, through surveys of participants, and by using community surveys. Almost all programs keep records; if they are reliable and up-to-date, we can ascertain if the clients who are using the services are indeed the people for whom the program was planned. Unfortunately, records are often inadequate for evaluation purposes and may even be distorted to make the program look good. In one program providing academic advising to college students, for example, there were more advisees reported to have received service than there were students (Rossi, 1977).

When records are inadequate, or too large to monitor easily, surveys of program participants are a workable alternative. Surveys can collect the information on client characteristics to see if their identity matches program intentions. For example, a program designed to provide health services to new mothers and their infants could survey a sample of patients to see if they represented both lower- and middle-income groups, as intended by the program design.

Finally, community surveys can be used when an entire community rather than a particular group is the target of a program. For example, Rossi cites the evaluation of *Feeling Good*, a television program designed to increase preventive health care in areas such as nutrition and exercise. The evaluation required a number of national surveys conducted while the program was televised. The data indicated that the program was not reaching the prime target population of low-income families.

We can turn to various social research methods to answer the question of whether the implemented program is consistent with its initial design. Rossi et al. (1979) identify four major sources and a number of techniques for monitoring program activities. These include direct observation of activities; the analysis of service records; eliciting information from program staff through reports, ratings, interviews, or questionnaires; and collecting data from clients or others through interviews or questionnaires.

Direct observation of program operations is the clearest route to monitoring activities, but the observer must be unobtrusive and not interfere with or modify staff or client behavior. (The method of participant observation and the methods for coding observational data discussed in Chapter 3 are relevant here.) The use of direct observation, however, can have its problems. This was the case in the Kansas City Preventive Patrol Experiment, in which observers rode in patrol cars with police officers. Even before the experiment could begin, the observers had to overcome the officers' reservations about interference with their duties. Then some observers soon became biased toward the police point of view and wanted to withhold any observations they thought might reflect negatively on the officers. Once these and other difficulties were overcome, the observational method provided valuable information about the experiment.

The use of records can also help draw a clear picture of how program activities are being carried out. Program staff use data forms to record what services were given to clients and what were the outcomes of treatment. This information can then be used to automatically monitor both the process and the outcomes of service provision often through the use of sophisticated computer information systems (see Ciarlo, 1977; Miller & Miller, 1977; Weinstein, 1975). However, records are not as simple as they seem. Record forms must be well designed and staff must be trained and motivated to record information accurately and fully. It is far more efficient to collect information on a few items in a reliable manner than to use a comprehensive and detailed record system that program staff resent as a burdensome nuisance.

Program staff themselves are an important source of information about implementation. As in evaluability assessment, interviews with staff can provide guidance on whether and in what ways intended services are being provided. The use of diaries or written logs is a good way to gain narrative accounts of how staff members spend their time in providing service to clients. For example, social workers helping runaway adolescents on the street could provide a useful description of their unique and varied activities simply by writing down their daily experiences.

Similarly, the program clients or recipients—the final source of monitoring data—can be approached through interviews or questionnaires. This approach yields a picture of the services as they were received and perceived by the clients—a personal point of view that may differ in important ways from the perceptions of program staff. It is important to ascertain if program services have not just been received but have been understood and used in the manner that was intended. For example, a family planning program is more concerned with the actual use of birth control devices than it is with their initial delivery. It is only responses from service recipients that can answer such questions.

Process evaluation can also give us useful initial information about the effects of a program and the causal linkages between activities and effects. Rutman (1977) suggests that formative research attempts to *identify* the intended effects and discover the side effects of a program, whereas outcome evaluation determines the degree to which the effects were actually produced. Rather than accepting the stated program goals as given, formative research can use observation and interviews with staff and clients to determine both the general and specific effects of program activities. Monitoring the ongoing implementation of the program also answers the question of whether program activities are directed at the identified needs in ways that should logically bring about the intended effects.

The sources of data on program implementation serve three major purposes (Rossi et al., 1979). First, they can generate a description of the program in operation. Second, they can be used to compare the implementation of the same program at different sites, looking for similarities and differences. Third, they can assess the degree of conformity between program design and program implementation. If there are clear divergences, then program modifications and further formative evaluation are required. If the implementation follows nicely from the design, we are in a position to move toward an outcome evaluation of the program.

Outcome Evaluation. Outcome evaluation assesses the effectiveness and efficiency of program activities in reaching the specified goals. In other words, what are the effects of the program? And how economically efficient is the program in producing these effects? These two aspects of outcome evaluation are often treated as separated components. For example, Rossi et al. (1979) refer to the former as impact assessment, and to the latter as cost-benefit or cost-effectiveness studies. (For the sake of simplicity, and since both are concerned with program objectives, let us include both under outcome evaluation. Later in this chapter, we will consider cost-effectiveness analysis as a specific method of program evaluation.)

Outcomes or objectives are what most people think of when they discuss program evaluation. This makes sense since the most important question we can ask of human service programs is whether they are having the effects they were designed and funded to bring about. Hargreaves and Attkisson (1978) point out the crucial issues in evaluating program outcomes: first, to determine if a program is worth its cost; second, to increase the benefits received for the expenditures. To accomplish this, they suggest these three general procedures:

- monitoring program quality, using ratings of clients, assessments of client satisfaction, and additional measures such as interviews of clients' relatives

- demonstrating program effectiveness in indirect ways—for example, by using existing research findings from similar programs, or by comparing client change to a set of human service norms
- designing specific outcome studies to aid decisions about continuing a new service, or about assigning clients to the most beneficial service

Naturally, these different approaches and methods can vary a great deal in how systematically and rigorously they evaluate program outcomes. In fact, the major issue in outcome evaluation is how to apply the methods of social science to best assess the causal linkages between program activities and effects. In discussing impact assessment (What are the effects of the program?), Rossi et al. (1979) state:

> Impact assessment is directed at establishing, with as much certainty as possible, whether or not an intervention is producing its intended effects. In order to do so, it is necessary to measure as rigorously as possible the outcome of social interventions and to purify these results by removing the influence of forces other than the intervention being evaluated.
>
> The outcomes of social programs are assessed by comparing information about participants and nonparticipants, before and after an intervention, or other less powerful research designs. But the essential considerations involve the systematic rejection of alternative, competing explanations for the observed outcomes other than the intervention. The measurement of the outcome must be carried out by means of valid and reliable indicators. (p. 159)

Thus, we must distinguish between more rigorous methods of outcome evaluation and less rigorous ones. Rigorous methods include experimental and quasi-experimental designs. Less rigorous approaches include assessments by program administrators or experts, client ratings, and data from record systems, and are based on limited or less relevant data. They are also less effective in ruling out the contaminating influences of variables other than the program intervention. Any program outcome can be affected by variables other than the program activities. A preschool education program may produce increased scholastic ability since it happened to select more motivated children. A counseling program for disabled adults may produce positive effects simply because it gets them out of the house twice a week. Approximate methods are therefore recommended only when more rigorous approaches cannot be applied due to a lack of time or resources (Rossi et al., 1979). This general approach to outcome evaluation, which I strongly support, makes clear the crucial role of design and measurement in program evaluation—the topic of the next section.

Importance of Design and Measurement

The crucial task of sorting fact from fancy in evaluating program outcomes requires all the technical expertise that evaluation researchers can muster. We must bring all the concepts and skills of social research to bear (see Chapter 3). We must measure variables accurately and reliably, and we must measure what we intended to measure—that is, with validity. We must construct research designs that maximize our ability to attribute any program effects to the program activities themselves, rather than to some extraneous variable. Quite a challenge! And one that confronts program evaluators every time they take on a new job.

The trends of the late 1960s and early 1970s, however, told a different story. Less rigorous methods were widely accepted, and experimental designs were criticized. But a movement toward rigorous methodology, stressing the importance, necessity, and advantages of design and measurement in evaluation research, had been given high priority by social psychologists from Northwestern University. Since the early days of evaluation research, Donald Campbell, Thomas Cook, Robert Boruch, and their colleagues have stressed the feasibility and power of experimental methods for controlling extraneous variables (Boruch & Rindskopf, 1977; Campbell & Stanley, 1966; Cook & Campbell, 1976, 1979; Cook, Cook & Mark, 1977). As a result of these efforts, the field in the late 1970s and early 1980s appears to have generally acknowledged the importance of design and measurement and is actively seeking ways of improving evaluations on these dimensions (for example, Datta & Perloff, 1979). The ultimate question, of course, is how we can use rigorous, quantitative methods of assessment in conjunction with less rigorous, qualitative procedures so that we gain the most comprehensive and useful picture of the development, implementation, and effects of human service programs.

Reliability and Validity of Measures. Reliability and validity have been discussed in Chapter 3, but what concerns us here is the significance of these characteristics of measures in evaluation research. But for reasons such as the cost of developing good measures and the ease of using available indicators, evaluation researchers often show less concern with these qualities than would be tolerated in basic research. This is unfortunate since the validity of the entire evaluation enterprise rests in good part upon the quality of the measures that are used.

Reliability refers to the consistency and stability of measurement. A reliable measure always produces the same results, that is, shows internal consistency among its items, and yields similar results when administered to the same respondents on different occasions. You can foresee the problem if the outcomes of a program were assessed by an unreliable measure. The pre- and post-measures could show differences that might be attributed to the program activities when in fact they were due to a lack of reliability. Or actual program effects could be masked or diluted by the random fluctuations of an unreliable measure.

To counteract such difficulties, evaluators can follow certain guidelines (Rutman, 1977). We should use existing measures of demonstrated realiability whenever possible. If this is not feasible, we must assess the reliability of new measures or of new uses of data, such as information drawn from record systems. In administering measures, we should take precautions to reduce some of the sources of measurement error, such as respondent fatigue and mistakes in tabulation. In these ways, we can increase the probability of securing reliable estimates of program effects.

Validity of measurement is more difficult to achieve than reliability, since it is a more complex and elusive quality. A valid measure is one that measures what it is designed to measure, and there are various means to assess this. We must have valid measures of outcomes if we are to conclude that the program produced the effects that it was intended to produce. If the measure is invalid, our conclusions will be wrong. Various types of validity have been defined, and all are relevant to evaluation research. In designing a program evalution, the first choice is to use measures of demonstrated validity. If this is not possible, it's a good idea to use multiple measures of outcome and see if they agree. For example, a program designed to reduce heart attack might look at changes in diet and exercise as perceived by both the target persons and close relatives or co-workers. In this way, each measure can validate the other. The costs and implications of evaluation research demand the best in measurement expertise that the evaluator can bring to bear.

Question of Design. Evaluating the outcome of a human service program is identical to studying the causal relationship between the independent and dependent variables in a controlled experiment. In both cases, we are concerned with making causal inferences about the effect that one set of conditions and manipulations has on some specified outcomes. Thus, we are interested in using experimental designs that can most effectively rule out the effects of extraneous variables on the outcomes. Put another way, we must rule out threats to internal validity that might be taken as plausible explanations for program effects, replacing the program intervention itself. Internal validity (see Chapter 3) refers to the degree of confidence we have that the experimental treatment or program activity actually led to the observed outcomes. Cook and Campbell (1976, 1979) include these major threats to internal validity:

- *History.* The observed effect may be due to any event other than the program activity that takes place between the pretest and the posttest.
- *Maturation.* The observed effect may be due to the respondents growing older, wiser, more experienced, and so on, between the pretest and the posttest.
- *Instrumentation.* The effect may result from a change in the measuring instrument at pretest and posttest.
- *Selection.* The effect may be due to initial differences between the people in the treatment group and those in the control group.
- *Statistical regression.* This occurs when participants are assigned to treatments (that is, groups) on the basis of pretest scores on an unreliable measure (which all measures are to some degree). Because of unreliability and the tendency of scores to regress toward the mean, respondents who scored higher on the pretest will score lower on the posttest and respondents who scored low on the pretest will tend to score higher on the posttest. Such changes, resulting in group differences, are due to a statistical artifact rather than to the treatment.
- *Compensatory rivalry.* When the control group receives a less desirable treatment and the treatment conditions are made public (as frequently they must be for ethical reasons such as informed consent), the members of the control group may be motivated by competition to compensate for their disadvantage. This increased motivation—especially in the case of intact groups such as departments or work teams—can override the effect of the experimental treatment and result in the program showing no effects—that is, no differences between treatment and control groups.

These and other threats to internal validity can influence the clarity with which we can attribute program outcomes to program activities. *The different experimental designs vary in the number of threats they can rule out.* The only design that can render all the threats implausible is the control group experiment with randomized assignment of participants to groups—the "true experiment." All other quasi-experimental or nonexperimental designs are vulnerable to varying amounts of threat to their internal validity. For ease of discussion, quasi-experimental designs can be grouped into nonequivalent control group designs and interrupted time-series designs (Cook & Campbell, 1979).

The randomized or true experiment is the optimum approach to program evaluation, because it achieves comparability of composition between the experimental or treatment group and the control or no-treatment group. The key to comparability is the random assignment to the groups of participants from the same population. Thus, only chance determines who is in the treatment group and who is in the control group. Since the participants are randomly selected from the same population, the groups are usually equivalent on all important variables (such as age, experience, motivation, and so on). Hence, if this equivalence is maintained throughout the program—that is, if all participants are treated similarly and react similarly except with respect to the independent variable (the program activities)—then any differences between the groups at the end of the program can be attributed to the program activities. Threats to internal validity, such as history, maturation, and selection, are adequately controlled and rendered implausible as influences on the outcomes. The randomized experiment is therefore the most powerful design for evaluating social programs. Box 13.3 presents a large-scale example of using the true experimental design to evaluate the controversial policy of the negative income tax.

However, the randomized control group design does not necessarily rule out all threats to internal validity (Cook & Campbell, 1979). In fact, it is particularly vulnerable to some of them, such as compensatory rivalry. Therefore we must guard against such effects and carefully monitor their occurrence while the evaluation is going on. You can see that random assignment guarantees only the initial comparability of the groups at the beginning of the evaluation. It does not guarantee that comparability will be maintained over the course of the evaluation right up to the posttest. Other variables, such as different rates of attrition between the treatment and control groups, will occur, and we may have to make statistical adjustments to compensate for these. Random assignment is only one part of experimental design; by itself, it is no guarantee that other aspects of the evaluation will be carried out effectively.

Different variations of true experiments are often necessary to rule out particular threats to internal validity. This is usually accomplished by adding more treatment and/or control groups in order to assess the potential effect of some extraneous variable. For example, we might be concerned that the pretest measure is affecting the posttest results of the experimental and control groups in different ways. In that case, we could add additional experimental and control groups, skipping a pretest measure for both but assessing both at the posttest. Thus, the effects of testing—that is, of the instrumentation interacting with the treatment—would be controlled.

Box 13.3 FOCUS ON RESEARCH
The Negative Income Tax Experiments

The War on Poverty consisted of three major initiatives: public employment, community action, and income maintenance. The last of these components was largely operationalized by the negative income tax or guaranteed income. This provided the unique opportunity to conduct large-scale social experiments on the effects of a guaranteed income. Opponents of this proposal argued that it would eliminate the incentive to work, while supporters saw it as a potential avenue for reforming the welfare system and for dispelling the belief that the able-bodied poor would quit working if provided a guaranteed income.

In 1967, the Office of Economic Opportunity awarded a grant to the Institute for Research on Poverty of the University of Wisconsin and to Mathematica Inc., a private research firm, for the purpose of conducting the first major social experiment on the negative income tax. Robert Haveman and Harold Watts of the Institute have provided a description of the implementation and results of this mammoth undertaking, which covered almost 7 years' work and cost $8 million.

A total of 1,357 poor families containing an able-bodied male were selected in three metropolitan areas of New Jersey and one in neighboring Pennsylvania. A little more than half of these families were randomly assigned to a number of different guaranteed income conditions in the experimental group, while the remainder were assigned to a control group. Families in the experimental conditions received a guaranteed level of income (calculated as a percentage of the poverty line), but these payments were reduced by a fixed percentage for each dollar of other income received. Each family was observed for 3 years, filled out an income report every 4 weeks, and was interviewed every 3 months as well as 3 months after the experiment ended.

The results? For husbands, there was no reduction in labor-force participation as a result of the experimental payments. For wives, who were mostly part-time workers, there was a slight reduction in employment for white families, but not for black or Spanish-speaking families. In general, the results indicated that a national income maintenance program would not reduce the labor supply. Where did families spend their increased income? Mostly on buying or renting better homes with some increased expenditures for food and clothing—hardly the type of behavior one could attribute to an irresponsible "welfare bum."

Source: Haveman, R. H. & Watts, H. W. Social experimentation as policy research: A review of negative income tax experiments. In G. V. Glass (Ed.), *Evaluation studies review annual* (Vol. 1). Beverly Hills: Sage, 1976.

Nonequivalent control-group designs construct a control group by some procedure other than random assignment. In the most common approach, known as *matching,* we would select control participants on the basis of characteristics that are similar to those of the experimental participants who receive the program intervention. For example, families from the same socioeconomic background and neighborhood might serve as controls for a program in which experimental families receive preventive health care services from a community nurse. It is especially important that matched control groups be equivalent to the treatment groups on variables that are suspected to affect the outcomes of the program. Unfortunately, we cannot guarantee that the groups are initially equivalent on unmatched variables that might affect the comparability of groups during the program or at the posttest.

Another common method of constructing control groups is to use statistical methods, particularly analysis of covariance, that render the scores of nonequivalent control groups and treatment groups comparable at the pretest. We can then look at posttest differences as evidence of program effect. However, these designs are vulnerable to a number of threats to internal validity, particularly that of statistical regression. In other words, if our measures are unreliable or open to error, we cannot use statistical procedures to equate nonequivalent control groups. It is impossible to know to what degree program outcomes are due to either statistical artifacts or to the actual intervention. A classic example of such problems occurred with the initial evaluations of Head Start (see Box 13.4).

Interrupted time-series designs involve an extension of the before-and-after method in which participants serve as their own controls. That is, we compare posttest and pretest scores to see if the program has had an effect. With only one pretest and posttest measure, any change may be influenced by a number of threats to validity—the threats of history, maturation, and instrumentation are good examples—in addition to the intervention itself. The time-series design attempts to rule out the plausibility of these factors by taking a large number of repeated measures over time. This establishes a stable baseline of multiple observations before the intervention is introduced. If the treatment has impact, we expect an "interruption" to occur and the observations from that point on to be different in some predictable way. Then we would introduce a series of measures following the interruption to assess the permanence of the effect as well as its immediacy (that is, is the effect immediate or delayed?). Various designs are available for testing these different qualities of the effect. Interrupted time-series designs are especially useful for gauging the effects of sudden interventions.

Time-series designs are relatively weak approaches to judging program impact since several threats to internal validity remain plausible. Also, many treatments cannot be implemented rapidly to produce a sharp interruption that would show the clearest effect. Furthermore, many effects occur with unpredictable time delays, and many available data series do not yield the number of multiple observations that should be included. Finally, there are problems with the archival data that is often used for time-series analysis: data may be missing; there may have been periodic changes in coding procedures; and there are archivists who are reluctant to release their data for analysis. As a result, time-series designs are best used when they are the only appropriate or feasible approach to evaluating a program. But we can also combine them with stronger designs (such as multiple observations of both treatment and control groups) to further enhance our power to separate the impact of the program from the effects of other confounding factors.

We would have to conclude that the randomized experiment is the strongest approach available for assessing program effects. However, its critics—including

Box 13.4   FOCUS ON RESEARCH
The Controversy over Head Start

Head Start began in 1965 as a compensatory education program to prepare disadvantaged preschool children to function effectively in the education system. The program received enthusiastic support from all quarters, and in 1968 an outcome evaluation was undertaken to assess the impact on cognitive and affective development. Scores on standardized tests and other measures from a random sample of Head Start children (now in grades 1, 2, and 3) were compared with scores obtained from a matched sample of children who had not attended the program. The results were disappointing. Out of over 1,300 comparisons, only sixty-two significantly favored the Head Start children.

However, the evaluation study was criticized for several reasons. It was argued that the benefits of the program had been wiped out by the subsequent school experiences of the children. On technical grounds, the study was criticized as not being a true experiment since children were not randomly assigned to Head Start or to a control condition. Selection biases could be positive (for example, creaming off the children most likely to succeed in the program) or negative (for example, trying to reach the most disadvantaged). In either case, the treatment group would be likely to differ from a comparison group matched on the variables of age, sex, ethnicity, and so on. Furthermore, the threat to internal validity of regression toward the mean would lead the analysis to underestimate the true impact of the program.

To bring some clarity to this controversy, Burt Barnow and Glen Cain of the Institute for Research on Poverty at the University of Wisconsin reanalyzed the original Head Start data in a more refined manner. They first controlled statistically for differences between the groups on additional variables that might relate to selection procedures and to initial ability. Next, they analyzed the results separately for different groups of children.

The results, while generally pessimistic, were more encouraging than those of the original study. No positive effects were found for children in the second and third grades. For grade one, black children showed the most positive effects of the program—equivalent to gains in IQ ranging from 4 to 10 points. White children showed few positive gains, except for those from mother-headed families. The researchers conclude that, when possible, a randomized experiment is the only design that would permit an unbiased estimate of the effects of Head Start.

Source: Barnow, B. S. & Cain, G. G. A reanalysis of the effect of Head Start on cognitive development: Methodology and empirical findings. *The Journal of Human Resources*, 1977, *12*, 177–197.

program managers, policymakers, and evaluation researchers—have alleged that experiments are impractical, are difficult or impossible to implement, are costly in terms of time and money, and are unethical in cases where control participants may be denied program services. Rossi et al. (1979) contend that randomized experiments constitute a small proportion of total evaluations being carried out and identify a number of instances in which a randomized design is impossible. For example, random selection and assignment cannot be undertaken when a policy or program is legally available to all those eligible, or when a program has been operating for some time and the evaluation cannot randomly assign participants to different conditions. Randomized experiments can be used when a new program is available and cannot serve all who might be interested. In this situation, random selection may be the only equitable way of providing the service to some and not others.

The criticisms against true experiments have been countered by the Northwestern group and others, most notably Robert Boruch. He defends the true experiment by documenting the existence and utility of the approach (Boruch, 1976; Boruch, McSweeney & Soderstrom, 1978). Randomized experiments are feasible and have been implemented with success in every major area of human service programming, particularly in the case of new programs. Even though some of these finished as quasi-experiments due to attrition of participants, random selection is still superior to other forms of assignment. True experiments are not always more costly than other designs; but when they are, the benefits of rigorous evaluation are worth it. Quasi-experimental designs that include statistical adjustments simply do not have the same power to yield unbiased estimates of program effects. Randomized experiments should be used as the standard against which other designs for assessing impact are judged through competing analyses of program data (Boruch & Rindskopf, 1977). On the question of ethics, there are design options that would not withhold services from potential participants. For example, treatment for control-group members can be delayed while the intervention is being tested. This is even more feasible since services often cannot be provided to all potential recipients at once. Boruch also raises the point that failure to evaluate programs rigorously is unethical since programmers might continue to offer unbeneficial, if not totally useless, services.

Although the feasibility and desirability of true experiments have been substantiated, their limitations have not been ignored. Cook and Campbell (1979) outline both the helpful conditions and the major obstacles to conducting true experiments in field settings. The task of evaluation is to assess the needs and constraints of each situation and to design the most appropriate evaluation.

An emphasis on true experiments and rigorous measurement is justified, but a readiness to use less rigorous methods, alone or in combination with quantitative methods, will often yield useful and comprehensive evaluations. Qualitative methods such as participant observation and case-study analysis can yield valuable information about program activities and outcomes. As evaluators, we should not be debating which approach is superior, rather we should be looking for ways of combining qualitative and quantitative methods into a more powerful whole (see Cook & Reichardt, 1979).

Methods of Program Evaluation

The field of evaluation research is varied, complex, and expanding at a rapid pace. It is characterized by a variety of research techniques, at least two basic types of program evaluation, a number of major approaches, and a long list of specific methods to ask particular questions at different points along the program-development continuum. There is little agreement on how to characterize or order all these elements. Nonetheless, it is useful to indicate some of the major approaches and to illustrate some of the specific methods that have been developed.

Evaluators have not settled on any single way to describe the complexity of their work. However, there appears to be a trend to relate the research activities to particular stages of program development and implementation. For example, Rossi et al. (1979) use a rough grouping of activities according to types of evaluation, divided into research for program planning and development, monitoring evaluation, impact evaluation, and cost-effectiveness. Similarly, Posavac and Carey (1980) see four common types of evaluation—of need, of process, of outcome, and of efficiency. In the next section, I have moved along the same lines, suggesting that a given method of program evaluation can relate primarily to a given stage in program development. We will look at *need assessment,* which is useful in program initiation; *goal attainment scaling,* which is helpful during program implementation to study both the process and outcomes of a program; and *cost-effectiveness analysis,* which relates the utility of program outputs to the cost of program inputs. These illustrations will demonstrate in a more concrete way the variety and complexity of this important area of theory, research, and practice.

Need Assessment. Social programs are developed to address social problems. Obviously, we should then study and document the existence of the social problem before developing the program. *Need assessment*—a crucial first step in program development—is a systematic verification of the existence, prevalence, location, and importance of a social problem as it is expressed in needs for service (Rossi et al., 1979; Siegel, Attkisson & Carson, 1978). We must first document that the need exists, going beyond the sometimes overzealous claims of service professionals or client representatives. Then we must describe in detail the needs that do exist so that program planning can be tailored to meet them adequately. While the stated goals of a program usually define the needs and the target population, we need a more precise estimate of the size, location, and distribution of the potential clientele. For example, if a youth recreation program is developed to reduce delinquency and vandalism, we need to know to what age range the services are directed, what educational and socioeconomic levels are involved, the geographic distribution of target individuals, and many more details before we can proceed to initiate and implement the program.

A number of methods have been developed for carrying out need assessment. Siegel et al. (1978) group these into social indicator analysis, survey methods, and community group approaches. The *social indicator approach* uses available information such as census and public health data. Analysis then integrates this information in new ways, giving a concise picture of existing needs and potential clientele. For example, a program being developed for low-income housing could rely on government data about housing characteristics in relation to income level and geographic location.

The *survey approach* assesses existing services and resources in an area of need as well as gaps in service. Potential demands for service can be identified by surveying both service agencies and community residents, asking them how they perceive their unmet needs. If, for instance, we were planning a program to provide mental health services for the aged, we could include an interview survey of a representative sample of the elderly. This would tell us about their perceptions of the types of emotional problems they experience and the avenues of help that are or are not available to deal with these problems. Rossi et al. (1979) point out that the sample survey provides the most direct and accurate data on target problems and populations.

The third strategy for need assessment, the *community group approach*, uses different methods to draw on both individual and group perceptions of need. Informal interviews with key informants—that is, community leaders or experts with first-hand knowledge of the problem—can provide useful impressions of needs and target populations. A group method known as the *community forum* brings together interested members of the community to share their opinions about existing problems. This is similar to some methods of community develop-ment (see Chapter 10). The forum is good for gathering a wide range of impres-sions quickly and for generating participation in program planning, but the sessions require careful planning and implementation to ensure productivity. The Nominal Group Technique and the Delphi Technique discussed earlier are also examples of the community-group approach to need assessment and program planning.

The important principle of need assessment is to use different methods with their advantages and disadvantages offsetting one another—to gain a wider picture. Through a convergent analysis of existing and new information, we can then develop an integrated assessment of the scope and character of needs and potential clientele, which is essential to successful program development and evaluation.

Goal Attainment Scaling. Programs always involve goals, even when such goals are implicit or vague. Mental health programming can be particularly susceptible to general goals such as improving mental well-being, reducing dysfunctional approaches, or enhancing life satisfaction. To assess progress toward such goals, mental health programs often use measurement devices, such as psychological tests, to provide comprehensive measures of mental and emotional functioning. But in using the same general measures for all clients, the approach ignores the wide diversity of individual characteristics and problems that clients bring to the program. Thus, some clients may be evaluated on variables that are irrelevant to their particular circumstances.

For these and other reasons, Thomas Kiresuk and his co-workers at the Hennepin County Medical Health Center in Minneapolis developed the method of goal attainment scaling (Kiresuk & Sherman, 1968). *Goal attainment scaling* (GAS) asserts that mental health services can best be described by using individu-alized and diverse goals developed for each particular client; GAS provides a systematic procedure for doing just that. The specification of individual goals is completed at the time of first contact between the client and the program, and later follow-up determines to what degree the goals have been achieved. GAS therefore provides a system for routinely describing in concrete terms the actual goals undertaken by program staff. The method can also be used to compare groups of clients who receive treatment with those who do not—the case, for example, in a delayed-treatment, control-group design.

The procedure of goal selection and scaling usually involves a program staff person setting the goals after an initial interview with the client. However, as the method has developed, both the client and the client's therapist may be involved directly in the goal-setting process. In any case, the goal selector must decide on a realistic set of mental health goals for the client. Then, for each goal that is specified, a scale is developed consisting of a series of possible treatment outcomes ranging from the least favorable (-2) to the most favorable ($+2$). The scale points should have precise and objective descriptions so that an independent judge could determine whether the client is above or below that point. This is particularly important for follow-up, when a program staff person not involved in treatment will make an assessment of goal attainment.

A sample set of client goals developed by GAS is shown in Table 13.2. The goals show the variety of areas that may be used. It is also possible to specify different weights for each goal, reflecting their relative importance.

Program activities are begun after goal selection. Then, after a predetermined interval, the client's case is referred to follow-up staff who contact the client and review progress toward the goals. The client's position on each of the scales is determined, and a composite GAS score is calculated from the differences between the follow-up level and the zero-point of expected level of treatment success. The standardized composite GAS score can be used to determine whether groups of patients randomly assigned to different treatments show different levels of success in attaining their individual goals. This procedure allows individual uniqueness to be taken into account at the same time that programs are evaluated for their general impact.

The adoption of GAS has proliferated rapidly. Kiresuk and Lund (1975) broadened the method by including process measurement as well as outcome evaluation, and by suggesting the inclusion of process indicators (such as number of visits) in the GAS follow-up guide. Through the publication and educational activities of the Program Evaluation Resources Center at Minneapolis, many mental health programs have adopted GAS. It has been used successfully to deal with a broad range of mental health problems, from anxiety and depression to alcoholism and marital discord, and has been applied in such diverse areas as crisis intervention, drug treatment, and court services. GAS is possibly the most popular evaluation technique currently used in the field of human services.

As we have seen so often, however, popularity is balanced by criticism—in this instance, that the quality of Kiresuk and Sherman's (1968) original method has not been retained and extended. Critical reviews of GAS have also indicated other problems. Even though there are initial indications of the reliability and validity of GAS (Brintnall & Garwick, 1976), Calsyn and Davidson (1978) point out that the reliability and, moreover, the validity of goal attainment scales have not been shown to be as high as the more general measures that GAS was designed to replace. The growing use of client and therapist ratings, replacing the ratings of independent goal selectors and follow-up judges, has introduced possible biases into the method, thus raising questions about the accuracy of results. In addition, the original suggestion of using GAS in conjunction with random assignment to

Table 13.2   AN EXAMPLE GOAL ATTAINMENT SCALE

	Goals			
Outcome Value	Fear of Sex Involvement	Dependency on Mother	Decision making	Social Functioning
Most unfavorable treatment outcome thought likely (−2)	Avoidant No dating No sex	Lives at home Does nothing without mother's approval	No new decisions made, still weighing same alternatives (job, vocation)	Institutionalized prison or hospital
Less than expected success with treatment (−1)			Complains of being unable to make up mind	On probation Further arrests
Expected level of treatment success (0)	Dating Petting	Chooses own friends, activities without checking with mother	Makes up mind on vocation, other major items	On probation No further arrests for peeping
More than expected success with treatment (1)	Some satisfactory intercourse	Returns to school		No contact with police, states peeping no longer a problem
Best anticipated treatment success (2)	Regular dating Regular satisfactory intercourse Marriage	Establishes own way of life Chooses when to consult mother		

Source: Kiresuk & Sherman (1968).

treatment groups has been followed in only a small proportion of the studies using the method for evaluation purposes. This is particularly problematic since GAS does not assign initial scores that can be used to adjust for differences between nonequivalent groups. Some users of GAS are now assigning an initial rating on the scales, and assessing outcomes in terms of pre- versus post-differences. Even with this procedure, however, the lack of random assignment allows individual goal-setting to result in nonequivalent groups and, therefore, in ambiguous results.

Cytrynbaum, Ginath, Birdwell, and Brandt (1979) present a more comprehensive and even more critical review of GAS. By critically evaluating the more than two hundred published studies on GAS, these authors selected forty-one studies of acceptable enough research quality to be included in their review. Even in these studies, they found that only a small proportion (five out of forty-one) had followed all the original requirements of GAS for independent goal selection and follow-up and for random assignment. The authors raise serious questions about the reliability and validity of GAS and point out numerous deficiencies in its use. However, in line with Calsyn and Davidson (1978), they note that the involvement of clients and therapists in goal-setting has been shown to increase the effectiveness of counseling (see LaFerriere & Calsyn, 1978). Thus, GAS appears to have a therapeutic value in its own right and as such should be included along with other more reliable and valid general measures in the evaluation of mental health programs. However the popularity of the method as an evaluation tool does not appear to be justified, partly because adoptions of GAS have largely failed to adhere to the requirements of the original model.

Cost-Effectiveness Analysis. Process evaluation and outcome evaluation are designed to tell us whether a social program has been implemented as intended and whether it is producing the impact that is desired. However, knowing the operation and impact of a program tells us little about the efficiency of the program, particularly in comparison with other programs or policies that are directed toward achieving the same social objective. To choose between alternative programs, we need to know something about the costs that are incurred to produce the related outcomes. This means that program evaluators must be equally concerned with cost-effectiveness analysis (Levin, 1975; Posavac & Carey, 1980; Rossi et al., 1979). *Cost-effectiveness analysis* is not a new form of program evaluation, but rather is a method that brings cost considerations into standard evaluation designs so that we can make a more comprehensive evaluation of the program.

Cost-effectiveness analysis is a form of the more general method of *cost-benefit analysis* (Andrieu, 1977; Levin, 1975). Cost-benefit analysis compares the costs and benefits of a program by using the same scale (typically the monetary value) to show net differences—that is, a *cost/benefit ratio*. This type of analysis was initially developed to assess government investment projects such as water resource development and public transportation; it has only recently been applied to social programs.

The major problem in applying cost-benefit analysis to human service programs lies in the difficulty (sometimes, the impossiblity) of translating their benefits into monetary terms that give their market value. How do we estimate the dollar value of increasing a child's self-esteem, or preventing a divorce, or saving a human life? Not only is it difficult to track down all the future benefits of such outcomes, but it is a sticky question of philosophical values to place dollar figures on these kinds of benefits. One rather sobering analysis of attempts to apply cost-benefit analysis to social programming is presented by Noble (1977). Based on directives from the United States federal government, many programs providing rehabilitation services for physically and mentally handicapped persons attempted to institute a cost-benefit approach in their evaluations. However, due to insufficient cost data, difficulties in forecasting future benefits, and problems in meeting the assumptions of the method, cost-benefit analysis was not seen as a viable way to evaluate programs and set priorities (Noble, 1977). Until the method is improved, we may have to depend on the traditional political process to make decisions about such programs. Nonetheless, since some evaluations have included worthwhile estimates of social benefits in relation to program costs, researchers have recommended a continuing consideration of how to measure human service benefits (Johnson, 1977; Rossi et al., 1979; Sussna, 1977).

Because it is difficult to apply cost-benefit analysis to social programs, the method of cost-effectiveness analysis seems to be more appropriate for their evaluation. In this approach, the effectiveness of a program is expressed by relating its psychological or social outcomes to its financial costs or material resources. For example, if a juvenile diversion program is just as successful as conviction and confinement in reducing delinquency but costs much less per individual, policymakers would have a clear basis for deciding which type of program should get more funds.

In applying cost-effectiveness analysis, it is appropriate to make a broad definition of costs. Estimates must include not only the obvious direct costs—such as personnel, facilities, and materials—but also indirect costs such as the "opportunity cost" of foregone alternatives that were sacrificed for program participation. In calculating the cost of a college education, for instance, you include not only tuition, room and board, and materials, but also the salary dollars that have been lost by not taking a full-time job for four years. When an adequate accounting of costs is feasible, cost-effectiveness analysis adds the element of efficiency to the art of program evaluation. Because economic factors are invariably important, and economic efficiency an essential concern, we must regard cost-effectiveness analysis as a fundamental component of comprehensive evaluation (Rossi et al., 1979).

Social and Political Context of Program Evaluation

The evaluation of social programs is a technical challenge that demands excellent research skills. Questions of design and problems of measurement plague the evaluation enterprise from start to finish. In particular, human service research in community settings involves forces that work against good evaluation (Cowen, 1978). It is difficult to get unbiased data and to set up the ideal research design.

Programs often change over time, and it is difficult to find appropriate control groups. Since it is therefore unlikely that program evaluation will mirror the rigor of laboratory research, the evaluator may have to reach conclusions by using converging findings from studies that are less than ideal.

The technical demands of program evaluation are great, but they are intertwined with an even more important fact of life in this area of research: the social and political context. Evaluation research does not occur in a vacuum. It goes on in a highly charged environment in which different individuals and groups may have very different values and needs, and very different viewpoints about the rationale, objective, and utility of program evaluation. Thus, evaluation is part of a political process in which influence is brought to bear, and decisions are made about the ways that resources are allocated to people.

In a review of the relationship between sociopolitical factors and evaluation research, Wilderman (1979) states:

> A major difficulty in assessing the effectiveness of the community social program is not so much a lack of evaluation research technology as it is the fact that evaluation takes place in the sociopolitical structure of a complex, human-service organization. The "sociopolitical structure" is defined here as all of the tangible and intangible rules, values, needs, implicit and explicit goals of the organization, and of the individuals involved in the organization, as well as the organization's relationship with the world around it. In this context, the evaluation process may conflict with the social values and political arrangements that sustain the program. It is now well known that such is often the case. (pp. 93–94)

Evaluation is therefore a social-psychological process that is part and parcel of political decision making. Whether the results of program evaluation are actually used for program improvement, or whether they actually affect decisions about the program's continuation, will depend on a variety of sociopolitical factors. These factors can influence the introduction, the execution, and the utilization of evaluation research in community settings (Wilderman, 1979).

The introduction of evaluation is often met with a variety of resistances by program staff. These include, for example, the agency's emphasis on service rather than research, a lack of payoffs from research for the agency, ideological or value differences between researchers and service providers, and bureaucratic restraints on doing research (Mannarino & Durlak, 1980). Our experience tells us that outcome evaluation is as likely to produce negative results as positive results—and negative results can have serious implications for program continuance. It is therefore not surprising that program staff often react with fear, anxiety, and even hostility to evaluation projects. These individuals are usually committed to the rationale and objectives of their program and can hardly be expected to heartily welcome a procedure that might demonstrate that they are misguided or ineffective.

Consequently, evaluation researchers have developed suggestions for reducing staff resistance. Wilderman (1979) speaks of the importance of fully explaining the process of evaluation to program staff to reduce the fear of the unknown. The use of formative research or process evaluation directed toward program improvement is more appropriate in early phases of evaluation and is likely to be less threatening to program staff. An emphasis on evaluating the rationale of the treatment rather than the behavior of persons will also reduce resistance. Rossi et al. (1979) also consider ways of reducing conflicts of interest between the various parties to the evaluation—including not just evaluators and program staff, but other groups such as clients, the evaluation sponsors, policymakers, and administrators of competing programs. All parties should share an understanding of the overall design and the goals to be evaluated.

Rossi and McLaughlin (1979) have developed useful methods for establishing the objectives of the evaluation through systematic interactions of evaluators and program administrators. It is not clear whether external, independent evaluators are more effective than those who work inside the organization as part of the program staff. Because each type of relationship appears to have its advantages and disadvantages (see Meyers, 1975), we do not yet know how this element of the sociopolitical structure affects the evaluation process. There is no question, however, that the type of relationship between evaluator and program does influence the degree of resistance to evaluation.

As for the actual implementation of evaluation, the social context harbors a number of inhibiting factors (Wilderman, 1979). Although experimental designs are the most appropriate means of assessing program impact, the social context is often unstable. Changes can occur in the treatment approach (a staff member may resign), or in the agency procedures (new eligibility criteria may appear), or in other aspects that pose serious threats to the validity of the results. It is sometimes difficult to get the program to remain stable long enough to allow for an experimental evaluation.

Programs change internally, but tend to resist externally imposed changes. Groups, organizations, communities, and other social systems generally resist change (see Chapters 9 through 11), and the implementation of evaluation is no exception. Box 13.5 presents an example of how sociopolitical factors hampered the evaluation of diversion programs in a criminal justice system.

Successful evaluation requires the development of a relationship between evaluators and program staff that allows and encourages each side to accept change and use it to its advantage. The evaluator and programmer must develop trust, openness, and understanding through effective communication and collaborative problem solving. When this type of consulting relationship is established, the evaluation can be designed and implemented to satisfy the needs of both sides, and issues of resistance will not sabotage the evaluation.

The political aspect of evaluation flows in large measure from the fact that many evaluations are required by law or funding requirements and that the results may affect the future of the program. Evaluation research is thus embroiled in political decision making about what services will be provided to what target population in what manner. Outcome evaluation in particular may be considered either a nuisance that interferes with program evaluation operation or a threat to the very existence of the program (Wilderman, 1979). In the former case, it is not unlikely that programs deemed ineffective by evaluation will be continued for political reasons, such as satisfying the demands of a target group for recognition or serving the values of a particular position. Conversely, programs that are

Box 13.5   FOCUS ON RESEARCH
The Political Context of Evaluating Diversion Programs

Diversion programs are receiving a great deal of attention in the criminal justice system. Apprehended offenders are given the option of making restitution for their crime or providing community service rather than going through the courts. Diversion is expected to be a less expensive alternative and may reduce the level of recidivism—the proportion of offenders who commit further crime.

Program evaluation could provide much useful information about diversion programs. Unfortunately, this yield may be restricted by political forces. Michael Agopian of the University of Southern California draws on his experience in evaluating adult diversion programs throughout California to provide a description of the political context of such programs. The term "political" refers to the aims, policies, or principles of the administrators of government services providing the programs.

First, politics—that is, the inclinations of the administrators—affects the way that diversion is implemented. Narrow definitions restrict diversion to pretrial interventions, whereas broad definitions refer to any attempt to reduce the offender's contact with the criminal justice system. Thus, for example, in one program, individuals who received citations were placed on diversion with no court appearance. In another program, offenders were booked and appeared in court three times—for arraignment, to request diversion, and to grant a continuance to allow diversion.

Second, political considerations affect the goals of the evaluation. Often administrators fear negative results that would threaten program funding and are often skeptical of the validity of research studies. The evaluator should strive to compile data within a comprehensive description of the program rather than just providing a superficial list of statistics. In one study, evaluation was limited to reviews of client records every three months. Programmers quickly saw the shallowness of the effort but said nothing since they did not want to jeopardize program funding.

Third, politics can severely limit the gathering of data. Researchers should apply methods that adequately capture program characteristics and should involve administrators and staff in planning the evaluation. In one study of several projects under one program, the evaluators planned the research only with the program director and a steering committee. They then arrived at the local projects armed with a letter of approval from the director. Project staff resisted the evaluation—they were concerned about a loss of staff time and about interference with project activities. Data collection was limited, and a full program evaluation became impossible.

Agopian concludes that a lack of attention to these three crucial areas of political influence can clearly undermine the entire evaluation effort.

Source: Agopian, M. W. Politics of evaluating diversion programs. *Evaluation Quarterly*, 1979, *3*, 81–88.

demonstrated to be effective may nonetheless be discontinued for political reasons, as the early budget cuts of the Reagan administration amply illustrate. The fact is that evaluators comprise only one interest group among many that are concerned with social programs.

Political factors are most apparent when the times comes to decide how evaluation results will be used—decidedly a mixed picture (Rossi et al., 1979; Wilderman, 1979). Some evaluators maintain that results, to be properly used, must be consistent with prevailing values and beliefs; otherwise results are ignored. Many factors that affect utilization are the same ones that act against the introduction of evaluation: aspects of the organization, the participants, communication channels, and the research itself (Cohen, 1977). At the same time, examples of effective utilization are beginning to emerge. For example, Windle and Volkman's (1973) survey of community mental health centers found that the majority had made program changes as a result of evaluation. The important questions seems to be which factors and procedures make utilization more likely and which do not.

The question of utilization raises the more basic issue of the role of evaluation research in decision making (Guttentag, 1977; Rossi et al., 1979). The political decision making process requires the blending of the positions of many interested parties, and the results of evaluation usually constitute only one element of a given position. (Evaluators should not be surprised if their results are apparently ignored or resisted.) Guttentag (1977) maintains that the evaluator should be only one voice—and not the dominating one—in deciding what information should be collected and how it should be used in decision making. The diverse groups involved in evaluation should not be seen as disruptive sources of resistance to proper evaluation, but as legitimate agents in making decisions about what services to adopt, change, or discontinue. Thus, Guttentag (1977) calls for a new paradigm, or way of doing evaluation research, that takes into account the multiple objectives of different groups and sees decision making as the central process in which evaluation results may play a part. One recent approach, Patton's (1978) *utilization-focused evaluation*, emphasizes the utilization of results right from the initiation of the evaluation. This model provides a framework in which the individuals involved (evaluators, programmers, and so on) can develop, right from the start, an evaluation design with a built-in utilization component. The goal of this and similar approaches is clear: that the results of evaluation research should play an active role and serve a useful purpose in the decision-making processes that seriously influence the life of human service programs.

Future Trends in Program Evaluation

Evaluation research has become one of the most active areas of applied social science. Models of evaluation are being created at a rapid pace without the order of a widely accepted paradigm or way of doing things (Glass & Ellett, 1980). But what can we predict about the future of program evaluation in the 1980s and beyond? Will the rapid proliferation of methods and applications continue at an unprecedented pace toward chaos and disintegration? Or will the bubble burst as program funders, staff, and clients fail to see the utility in all this activity? It is likely that we will see neither extreme. Rather, we can expect the field to remain strong because of the needs it serves and the steady progress that comes from experience. The basic reasons for evaluation research will not go away. In return for money spent, grant-giving agencies and tax-paying citizens will continue to want value from human service programs. Even in the current wave of budget restraints, government funders still require evaluations. Program staff and clients will continue to look for ways to develop and improve programs, seeking the most effective ways to resolve social problems. And evaluation researchers from both universities and research corporations (for example, Abt, 1980) will continue to look for the challenges and the rewards that the field has to offer.

The field will not remain static. We can already spot the development of discernible trends—part real, part hunch, part hope—that will help shape the identity of evaluation research in future years. First, we can expect to see a growing emphasis on the full range of program evaluation rather than on just outcome evaluation. Evaluability assessment, program monitoring, and process evaluation will grow in importance so that the effort put into impact assessments and cost-effectiveness is not wasted. Process evaluation in particular will receive greater attention than it did in the 1970s (Freeman, 1977). There will also be a greater emphasis on program development as a prerequisite to viable programs and useful evaluations. This implies that applied social psychologists, with greater opportunities to serve as program development consultants, will have to give more attention to practice skills (see Chapter 4). Program development and program evaluation together offer an exciting arena for the blending of theory, research, and practice directed toward improving human welfare.

Second, the importance of rigorous design and measurement will continue to be stressed in program evaluation. Many ways of improving evaluations will be explored (such as Datta & Perloff, 1979). Thus, we must carefully examine the assumptions of both the experimental methods and evaluation research in general and continue to look for common ground (see Mitroff & Bonoma, 1978).

Third, the issue of utilization must be successfully resolved if evaluation research is to remain viable. Why should people pay money for evaluations that have no effect on program efficiency? It is possible that management-oriented approaches (such as Wholey, 1979) or decision-theoretic approaches (such as Guttentag, 1977) or utilization-focused evaluation (such as Patton, 1978) will grow in popularity since they specifically look for ways of increasing utilization. More emphasis will be placed on translating evaluation results into public policy (for example, Rich, 1979). These approaches will require greater collaboration between programmers, evaluators, and others in a manner that is consistent with the humanistic value base of applied social psychology.

Fourth, we can expect to see more analysis and assessment of existing evaluation studies. This will occur in two ways. One way, the method of *secondary analysis*, uses data already collected, reanalyzing it to see if similar or different results are obtained (see Boruch, 1978). The existing data might be from a previous evaluation project (such as Head Start), or it might exist in government archives or data banks (see Roos, Nicol, Johnson & Roos, 1979). The second way, *metaevaluation*, involves an evaluation of existing evaluation studies to improve the quality of work that is being done (for example, Cook & Gruder, 1978; Zucker, 1977). Although metaevaluation can involve secondary analysis, its more important functions are to develop standards for good evaluation research and examine ways in which existing studies have attempted to reach these standards. A more detailed scrutiny of completed evaluation studies should increase the quality of future evaluations.

Fifth, the training of program evaluators should receive consistent attention in the decade ahead, assuming that the demand for evaluation remains high. In the 1970s, there was an extremely short supply of sophisticated evaluation researchers (Freeman, 1977). The response to this need has been dramatic, with the development of graduate training programs occurring in numerous universities across the whole field of social science. The training of evaluators and the evaluation of their competencies has thus become a major activity that will continue through the 1980s (Anderson & Ball, 1978). The theory, research, and practice demands of evaluation will continue to challenge academia to develop effective training programs and will raise issues about how best to train evaluators (Schulberg & Perloff, 1979).

Finally, I hope that the interdisciplinary quality of evaluation research remains strong even while its connections to social psychology are maintained and strengthened. Many disciplines and subdisciplines want to become involved. They should be encouraged to do so, but without any sacrifice in either the quality of training of evaluators or the execution of projects. At the same time, the utility of the psychological perspective and the potential roles for psychologists in evaluation research is clear (for example, Wortman, 1975), and the continuing similarity between psychological research and evaluation is evident (for example, Fine & Saxe, 1978).

Furthermore the linkage between social psychology and program evaluation remains immutable. Not only are the research and practice skills of applied social psychology essential to good evaluation research, but we may be able to find ways to apply and test social-psychological theories through our involvement in program development and evaluation (Bickman, 1979a). Bonoma (1976) and Mitroff and Bonoma (1978) have argued that social psychology and social evaluation are not different endeavors involving different problems. In fact, the two areas are remarkably similar in their assumptions, difficulties, and methods. The greater complexity of field settings, including the social and political context, simply challenges evaluation researchers to apply their general theories and research methods of human interaction to the evaluation of human service programs. This, in fact, is the greatest challenge facing program evaluation in the years ahead: to continue the development of evaluation competency to the point where all the interest groups involved in human service are satisfied that the job has been well done. Applied social psychology has enormous potential to contribute significantly to this most important endeavor.

Summary

Evaluation research is the application of social research methods to assess the effects of a social program or policy.

Program development and program evaluation are complex and difficult, but important, elements of human service programming. Human service programs are planned activities designed to provide assistance to people in the areas of health, mental health, education, social welfare, and criminal justice. All such programs have the goal of improving the quality of people's lives through individual and/or social change. All human service programs tend to go through similar stages of development.

Program development is a problem-solving process involving three stages: (1) program initiation in which the goals are translated into a concrete plan of action and in which the necessary human, financial, and physical resources are acquired; (2) program contact in which the staff actively engage the clientele; and (3) program implementation in which the staff deliver the services in the direction of attaining the program goals.

The Program Planning Model (PPM) is an example of one means of systematic program development using small-group methods. PPM involves five phases: (1) problem exploration involving potential clients, (2) knowledge exploration involving specialists, (3) priority development involving resource controllers and administrators, (4) program development of a detailed proposal, and (5) program evaluation of the proposal before implementation.

Program evaluation serves the overall purpose of contributing to decision making about the initiation, modification, or termination of social programs or policies. Evaluation serves a number of purposes and can take three different perspectives including the accountability, knowledge, and management perspectives.

Not all programs can be usefully evaluated. Preconditions for evaluation include clearly articulated program activities, clearly specified goals, and a logical relationship linking activities to the goals. Evaluability assessment determines to what degree a program is evaluable—that is, can be evaluated in a useful manner.

The two major types of program evaluation are: (1) process evaluation, which describes program activities and effects for the purpose of program improvement, and (2) outcome evaluation, which documents the effectiveness and efficiency of the program in attaining its goals.

Good research design and reliable, valid measurement are essential to program evaluation. The true experiment with randomized assignment of clients to different groups is the most powerful means for studying the causal relationship between program activities and program effects. Alternatively, quasi-experimental designs may be used, but require sensitivity to the confounding effects of the various threats to internal validity.

Illustrative methods of program evaluation include need assessment, goal attainment scaling (GAS), and cost-effectiveness analysis.

Evaluation research takes place in a complex and highly charged social and political context in which a variety of groups have different interests and needs and often see the objectives of program evaluation very differently. Numerous sociopolitical factors affect the introduction, execution, and utilization of evaluation research. A collaborative approach that takes all interest groups into account and emphasizes utilization from the start will likely be most successful.

Further Readings

Anderson, S. B. & Ball, S. *The profession and practice of program evaluation.* San Francisco: Jossey-Bass, 1978.

Posavac, E. J. & Carey, R. G. *Program evaluation: Methods and case studies.* Englewood Cliffs, N.J.: Prentice-Hall, 1980.

Rossi, P. H., Freeman, H. E. & Wright, S. R. *Evaluation: A systematic approach.* Beverly Hills: Sage, 1979.

Rutman, L. (Ed.). *Evaluation research methods: A basic guide.* Beverly Hills: Sage, 1977.

Wholey, J. S. *Evaluation: Promise and performance.* Washington, D.C.: The Urban Institute, 1979.

CHAPTER OUTLINE

UNDERSTANDING SOCIAL CONFLICT
Agression and Violence in Human Social Conflict
Levels of Violence across Different Societies
Functions of Social Conflict
Sources and Escalation of Conflict
A Typology of Conflict
Escalation of Conflict
Levels of Conflict: Similarities and Differences
Interpersonal Conflict
Conflict in Groups
Conflict in Organizations
Studying Conflict through Experimental Games

METHODS OF CONFLICT RESOLUTION
Prosocial Behavior
Approaches to Managing Conflict
Win-Lose
Lose-Lose
Win-Win
Two-Dimensional Model of Conflict Management
Third-Party Consultation
A Model
Implementing and Evaluating the Model

SUMMARY

FURTHER READINGS

FOURTEEN

The Resolution of Social Conflict

UNDERSTANDING SOCIAL CONFLICT

Every night when I pick up the evening paper or turn on the television news, the horrendous cost of human conflict stares me in the face. I see a little Laotian refugee boy, his crying face a picture of anguish and pain while his older brother tries to comfort him. I see a young Cambodian mother carrying her dead child, his body shriveled by starvation. The mother's face portrays shock, sorrow, and resignation. The Laotian boy and the mother and child are all the tragic victims of a conflict they do not understand and of a cruelty that none of us should accept. Their condition is repeated around the world, wherever decision makers in power choose violence as a means to their own ends.

The story does not end in Laos or Cambodia. It continues right around the corner. I see a man lying on the street, most of his head blown away in a gunfight with members of the Ku Klux Klan and the American Nazi Party. The victim was one of several demonstrators at an anti-Klan rally in North Carolina who, in chanting "Death to the Klan," found death themselves. I hear the latest figures on murders resulting from family conflict, and I think of the survivors, especially the children, whose lives have been shattered by a last-ditch resort to violence.

These incidents illustrate only the most vicious and dramatic costs of destructive human conflict. Every day, human beings in every walk of life suffer the pain of dysfunctional attempts to resolve differences among themselves. We have come a long way since the days of the cave dwellers. We have developed social mechanisms and legal institutions to handle conflict more peacefully and productively. And yet we have a long way to go. The costs of conflict are immense on any scale, by any measure. We can do better.

At the same time, we must recognize that conflict can be an important source of social change and movement toward social justice. Revolutions free people from oppression while sanctioning violence. Conflicting group interests are at the core of our democratic, pluralistic North American society. The issue of independence versus dependence and control must be faced in families and other social organizations, so that individuals have freedom along with responsibility.

**"Every cave owner has the right
to own a hand club."**

There is no simple answer to the question of whether conflict is good or bad. It simply *is*. It is a central fact of human existence and a core process of human relations. Therefore, the first task of social psychologists who study conflict is simply to describe it, to provide observations, theories, and research studies that help us better understand what conflict is all about. However, going beyond this purely descriptive approach, many social psychologists also want to become prescriptive or normative—that is, to say what is actually good or bad about conflict. They pose the basic question about conflict: Is it handled destructively or productively? This suggests that conflict can be managed and resolved in ways that are nonviolent and mutually acceptable to all involved people whose needs should be met.

This tells us that we can reduce the tragic costs of destructive conflict even while we realize the creative benefits of social change—a tall order that will never be filled in all situations. But almost everyone agrees that we can do better than we are doing now. We can find more productive ways to resolve conflict if we understand the sources and processes of conflict, and if, in managing conflict, we develop solutions that reduce the costs while maintaining the benefits.

Social psychologists grapple with difficult issues of social conflict. Is violent conflict an inherent element of human nature, rooted in irrational animallike urges of aggression? Can destructive violence be controlled when people's needs are severely frustrated? Is social conflict a necessary and functional element of social progress, an element for which we must pay the price? How can we best study human conflict to increase our understanding and our options? How can we use this knowledge to develop and prescribe more productive ways to resolve social conflict? These major questions indicate some of the complexity of the puzzling phenomenon of conflict that unfolds through numerous processes at several levels of analysis. The study of conflict resolution is imperative if we are in any way concerned about human satisfaction and humanity's survival.

Aggression and Violence in Human Social Conflict

Conflict is usually defined as a social situation in which incompatible goals and activities occur between two or more parties (individuals or groups) who hold antagonistic feelings toward each other and attempt to control each other. It involves the perceptions, feelings, and behaviors of antagonists who are in some form of dispute. *Aggression*, on the other hand, is behavior intended to inflict harm or injury on another person or object. A simpler notion than conflict, aggression occurs in a conflict situation when one party to the dispute intends to inflict injury on the other in order to reach desired goals. This definition of instrumental aggression is sometimes distinguished from expressive aggression, which merely seems to ventilate hostility without reaching any particular goals. The methods of social psychology have added much to our understanding of this important human phenomenon (Baron, 1977; Zillman, 1979).

The most active debate about human aggression is whether it is innate or learned. Freud saw aggression as a biologically based instinct that required expression in one form or another. In this way, human aggression is similar to aggressive behavior found in most forms of life: an unconscious instinctive drive that will be expressed regardless of environmental circumstances. This point of view is also shared by biologists and ethologists (scientists who study animal behavior) such as Lorenz (1966, 1981) who see humans expressing the same innate aggressive drive found in other species in animals.

According to some ethologists, aggressive behavior is elicited by certain environmental cues, called *releasers*, that trigger the expression of aggressive energy. Although the aggressive instinct cannot be suppressed, it can be channeled in less violent directions. For example, two street gangs could release their aggression by playing tackle football rather than going at each other with switch-blade knives and motorcycle chains. Lorenz and others also point out that the human species is the only one that has not acquired any natural inhibitors of aggressive behavior. In contrast with other animals, there appears to be no limit to the human capacity to inflict pain and destruction, regardless of the response of the victims. Lower animals have more ritualized patterns of aggression that often limit the extent of injury that is inflicted. For example, in some species of ducks, a female engaged in a quarrel with another mating couple will run toward the other female with head lowered in fighting readiness only to retreat and stand behind her own drake. These expressions of aggression may lead one couple to withdraw before real violence ensues. Even the vicious timber wolf backs off when his beaten foe bares his neck. Not human beings. During the holocaust of World War II, Jews were still annihilated long after they were rendered powerless.

But ethologists also see the positive functions of aggression: for instance the survival and selective breeding of the fittest and the protection of family and territory. Whether these arguments hold for human beings is questionable. Lorenz's analysis has been questioned both within and outside his field (for example, Nelson, 1974). What is clear, however, is that humans have the emotional, mental, and physical capacity to engage in a great deal of aggressive behavior.

Psychologists have added to our understanding of aggression through the development of the *frustration-aggression hypothesis* (Dollard, Doob, Miller, Mowrer & Sears, 1939). This statement says that the existence of frustration leads to some form of aggression, and that the occurrence of aggressive behavior always presupposes the existence of frustration. *Frustration* is defined as the interference with or blocking of goal-directed activities. The child who cannot reach the cookie jar experiences frustration the same as the statesman whose resolution fails at the United Nations. The actual *amount* of aggression is proportional to the strength of the behavior and to the degree of frustration; the *form* of aggression is determined by inhibitors in the environment. This hypothesis, originally stated in rather absolute terms, has been modified over the years: conditions other than frustration may lead to aggression; and frustration may

Investigators have found that spectators become more hostile after attending an aggressive event such as a hockey game. *(Jim Anderson/Woodfin Camp & Associates)*

lead to responses other than aggression (see Berkowitz, 1969b). For example, a frustrated person may withdraw in apathy, or regress to an earlier form of behavior, or persevere in some meaningless, repetitive behavior.

More recent approaches to learning theory, particularly that of observational learning (see Chapter 2), have added to our understanding of aggressive behavior. Bandura (1973) sees aggression as a learned behavior acquired mainly through the process of modeling. That is, children acquire very detailed and sophisticated patterns of aggressive behavior by observing the adult role models around them. Through the processes of acquisition and disinhibition, children come to express the level and form of violence that appear appropriate to their society. Disinhibition effects can at times be dramatic, such as when viewing aggressive sports leads to spectator violence (Arms, Russell & Sandilands, 1979). Fan rowdyism and fighting following soccer matches reached the point in one contest in Guatemala where supporters of the losing team attacked winning fans with machetes, killing five people. Arms et al. (1979) replicated an earlier field study showing that fans at the annual Army-Navy football game scored higher on a hostility scale following the contest. In a more controlled design, these investigators found increased spectator hostility following aggressive events (such as hockey, wrestling) but not following nonaggressive competition (swimming). The belief that spectator sports provide a safety valve to drain off fan hostility appears to be unfounded.

Frustration has come to be seen as only one source of general arousal; the situation must be perceived as appropriate for aggressive behavior in order for it to occur (Berkowitz, 1969b). According to Bandura (1973), reinforcement is important in affecting the probability that aggressive behavior will be expressed, but reinforcement is not necessary for the acquisition of such behavior. Others contend that in some situations, reinforcement is sufficient for learning aggressive behavior. It appears that we do learn some aggressive behavior through modeling and express aggression when we perceive the appropriate cues and rewards in the environment.

What are the implications of these different theories of aggression for the understanding of human conflict? In a review of biological approaches to the study of conflict (including those of ethology and comparative psychology), Nelson (1974) points out that these approaches have limited themselves to the study of aggression per se—but a single element in the complex character of social conflict. Biological approaches must be complemented by psychological and sociological theories in order to contribute to our understanding. Otherwise, they are at best severely restricted and at worst highly misleading. Much of their evidence on aggression, coming from the study of lower animals, simply cannot be extrapolated to human beings. There is, for example, no counterpart to human warfare among the other animals. Even at the human level, the applicability of biological theories varies considerably with the type of aggression being considered. Some cases of individual violence, such as child beating, may relate in part to biological factors; but socially organized violence, such as war, probably has no causes in biological factors. War does not result from the cumulative outpouring of individual aggression, as we saw in Chapter 12, but from the planned and coordinated use of coercive power and violence to reach certain goals that have not been achieved by peaceful means. The importance of biological factors lies in the fact that human beings have great destructive capacity and that they are subject to emotional and perceptual limitations that lead more easily to the escalation of conflict than to its resolution.

Even though biological theories of aggression have limited utility in understanding social conflict, their social and political implications can be significant. Nelson (1975) points out that the scientific debate over innate aggression involves basic assumptions about human nature and policy recommendations about how people should be treated. All our social and political structures are based on our fundamental premises of human nature, which we use in turn to justify the structures we impose. If we believe that human beings are innately aggressive, we are more likely to develop social structures that coerce and control people; we are more likely to think of official violence (such as police action or war) as legitimate and necessary; we are more likely to believe that aggression will be reduced by changing individuals rather than the social and political systems in which they live. We will believe that violent criminal acts stem from individual expressions of aggression; we will not see them as responses to a frustrating social situation or to a lack of reward within the legitimate society. The biological approach leads us to make person-blame attributions in which individuals, usually the victims, are held responsible. We will accept this rather than admit that social and cultural changes are necessary to reduce inequity, racism, crime, and other societal problems. We will believe that existing social, political, and economic arrangements are justified, thus perpetuating an ideology of control over individuals. Biological explanations are appealing because of their simplicity, and because they allow citizens who are not at odds with the system to relieve themselves of any responsibility for the human destructiveness of individual or collective violence.

Because of these serious implications, Nelson (1975) contends that a number of safeguards should be instituted to minimize the potential abuse of biological theories of conflict. These include the need for interdisciplinary research, a caution against combining preliminary ideas with broad policy recommendations, and a concerted effort to enlighten the public about the complexity of the issues involved. In these ways, we may come to see violence not as a problem in its own right but as a symptom of much more serious underlying problems in society itself. If we could create a world of justice, dignity, equal opportunity, and equitably distributed resources, the resulting reduction in human aggression would provide the acid test for the biological theories of human conflict.

The frustration-aggression approach to the study of conflict has also been criticized for its limitations and implications. Most research on frustration and aggression has been carried out in the social pscyhology laboratory, permitting a systematic study of the important conditions that affect the strength and form of aggressive behavior. In typical experiments, subjects are initially frustrated through interference with some goal-directed activity, or they may witness models of aggressive behavior. Subjects are then given an opportunity to engage in some form of aggressive behavior, such as administering shock to another person. In most cases the aggression is reactive or retaliatory in response to frustration or attack and is in line with appropriate cues in the situation.

But Tedeschi, Gaes, and Rivera (1977) say that this research fails to take account of the more common forms of aggressive behavior that are *initiated* by a transgressor. Retaliatory aggression is justified by the norm of reciprocity—"an eye for an eye"—and by the norm of self-defense, both of which are culturally sanctioned in many societies. These norms do not justify the more serious cases where violence is initiated to obtain desired outcomes—stealing a person's money, say, or taking over a country's resources. These critics suggest that a reconceptualization of harmful behavior, using the concept of coercive power, would clearly distinguish retaliatory actions from actions that are initiated by the transgressor. Furthermore, in our attempts to understand violent behavior, an emphasis on the use of coercive power would shift attention from biological causes and pent-up frustrations to social-psychological processes such as reciprocity, conflict, and power.

Coercive power is a means of gaining compliance through force or threat of force to injure or destroy the other party. (This is similar to the concept of deterrence discussed in Chapter 12.) It is often used when other means of influence such as persuasion or rewards have not worked or are not expected to work. Defensive coercion parallels retaliatory aggression and should not be confused with offensive coercion or instrumental aggression. The causes and conditions of these two types of violent behavior may be very different, and studies of defensive coercion may tell us little about offensive coercion. To predict and prevent violent behavior, we must particularly understand the social norms operating in the situation, along with other factors. By taking a broader social-psychological perspective, the frustration-aggression hypothesis can become part of a comprehensive and more valid treatment of destructive human behavior.

Social learning theory in conjuction with a social-psychological analysis may allow us to understand and reduce the level of personal violence in contemporary society. Just as children learn aggressive behavior by watching the models presented by parents and television programs, people can learn nonaggressive methods of solving conflicts through observation (Bandura, 1973). There is evidence, for example, that white aggression toward blacks can be reduced by modeling and that this effect may generalize to help increase interracial harmony (Donnerstein, Mueller & Wilson, 1979). The level of violence portrayed in the media can be reduced through public pressure and government legislation. The socialization of children needs to be changed so children learn problem-solving skills as an alternative to aggression as a means of getting what you want. Eron (1980) suggests that boys—who are generally the more aggressive of the sexes—be socialized more like girls to help develop socially positive, cooperative, and sensitive qualities. Unfortunately, much violence is condoned through the norms of reciprocity and self-defense, even to the point of using violence to prevent potential violence before it occurs. Some of the policemen who waded into crowds of protesting students at the 1968 Democratic Party Convention in Chicago probably saw the swinging of their billy clubs as a means of preventing an outbreak of violence.

We must also recognize that norms of equality and equity may simply not fit into the lives of the poor and disadvantaged. Many of these people, experiencing deprivation (compared to the standards of the middle-class majority) and perceiving inequity for themselves, may feel justified in using illegitimate and violent means to restore equity (Tedeschi et al., 1977). This is especially likely when they have observed models who have successfully redressed a similar grievance, such as what happened in the ghetto riots of the 1960s. Destruction and looting by some served a modeling function for the participation of numerous others. We can hardly understand aggressive behavior if we look only at the individual or interpersonal levels of analysis. We must also examine the societal conditions and the social norms that, under certain conditions, cause frustration and support violence. Certainly individual motives, perceptions, and characteristics play a part in aggressive behavior, but we must examine the system as a whole if we wish to find peaceful means of resolving social conflicts.

Levels of Violence across Different Societies. How to assess the level of violence in different societies is a most complex question. But the very fact that aggressive behavior at all levels of analysis varies considerably from country to country indicates the significant role of social, cultural, and political factors in determining the level of violence. A comprehensive attempt to measure the degree and breadth of violence in different nations is presented by Gurr and Bishop (1976), who assessed eighty-six countries on eight different facets of violence. These ranged from individual aggression (such as assassination) to transnational violence (war), and included physical violence (protest) as well as structural violence (discrimination). Events during the 1950s and 1960s were studied to assess the extent of violence, and an overall violence rating was also calculated. Countries ranking high on violence included the Republic of South Vietnam, Zaire, and South Africa; countries at the low end included the Republic of Ireland, Costa Rica, and Switzerland. Although the Soviet Union and the United States ranked very close together (twenty-third and twenty-fourth, respectively, out of eighty-six countries), social protest was more widespread in America and the long-term impact of war was greater on Russia. This analysis again shows the many faces of human violence beyond the level of individual aggression.

Another way to understand the social conditions of violence is to study societies that do not engage in violence and to look for common characteristics in their social struture. Anthropologists have long presented reports of how various cultures differ in the level and forms of aggression that they tolerate. For example, David Fabbro (1978), a peace researcher interested in illuminating the social preconditions of peace, studied seven different peaceful societies. They included the Semai of Malaya, the Sirions of Eastern Bolivia, the Kung Bushmen of the Kalahari Desert, the Mbuti pygmies of Africa, the Copper Eskimo of Canada, the Hutterites of North America, and the Islanders of Tristan da Cunha in the South Pacific. Fabbro examined their social aspects, incuding decision-making processes, methods of social control, and strategies for resolving conflict. In general, these peaceful societies are small communities with an egalitarian social structure that lacks a formal pattern of social stratification and places no limits on the number of people who can exercise authority or occupy positions of prestige. These societies do tend to readily share material rewards and wealth through reciprocity and equitable distribution. Although sexism (a form of structural violence) exists in all these groups, Fabbro suggests the possibility of a society having social justice without recourse to physical violence. It thus appears possible to control the biological capacity for aggression and to reduce the level of

The gentle Tasaday of the Philippines are one of the few societies in the world that do not engage in violence. *(John Nancel/Panamin)*

frustration within a society so that people may live in peace. Human nature depends for its expression on the social context over which human beings have control. The implications for peaceful societies and a peaceful world are obvious.

Functions of Social Conflict

Most social psychologists who study conflict are motivated by the humanistic value base that says that enforcing decisions on people through coercion and violence is unacceptable. Equally unacceptable are the incredible costs of dysfunctional conflict in terms of human suffering and death. At the same time, however, the use of coercive power is sometimes necessary to reach the humanistic goals of equality, justice, and dignity for all people. Hence, the debate over the positive functions of conflict bears similarity to the question of when the power-coercive approach to social change is to be used in place of the empirical-rational or normative re-educative strategies (see Chapter 11).

Do we see societies as based mainly on value consensus, where competing interest groups vie within a common social and political framework to get their share of resources? Such a view regards conflict as dysfunctional and disruptive and looks to the control and rehabilitation of individuals to resolve social issues. Or do we see society as split between the powerful and the powerless, with the latter being held in an oppressed and disadvantaged position through force and the threat of violence? Such a view regards social conflict as necessary for productive social change. Our decision to side either with the structural-functionalist theorists, such as Parsons (1960), or with the conflict theorists, such as Marx or Dahrendorf (1959, 1967), makes a great difference in how much we are willing to bear the costs of social conflict in order to reap its potential benefits. We must therefore examine both the goals and the means of conflict in order to judge its acceptability within a humanistic framework.

Conflict may also serve additional functions for groups and societies beyond its role of social change toward equality. The foremost proponent of the positive functions of conflict is Lewis Coser (1956, 1967), an American sociologist who has developed a number of propositions about the utility of social conflict based on the earlier work of the German sociologist Georg Simmel (1955).

Coser (1956) saw a decreasing interest in the value of social conflict and a clear tendency to regard conflict as an unfortunate disruption in social systems. Coser adopts Simmel's argument that conflict is an essential ingredient of group functioning, that groups require discord in order to develop and survive. To support this view, a number of propositions are developed; some of these are stated here in simplified form:

- Differences and antagonisms within a group can create a system of social divisions that reciprocally support each other. For example, the Hindu caste system in India rests on a hierarchy of separate yet complementary divisions whose mutual repulsion creates a balance and maintains the entire system.
- The expression of conflict serves as a safety valve that allows the hostile member to air his or her grievances in a useful manner, rather than suffer calmly until a desperate reaction ends the relationship. Thus, a group that suppresses all forms of hostility is taking a chance on long-term survival.

- Conflict between groups increases the internal cohesion within the groups. In times of war, for example, a country often shows a great concerted effort to forget domestic squabbles and pull together toward victory over the enemy.
- Conflict between two parties is often necessary to gauge the actual strength of each other and subsequently enter into a balance of power that prevents continuing struggle. This apparent paradox indicates that some degree of conflict is necessary to reduce conflict to a long-term, acceptable minimum. For example, the Cold War between the United States and the Soviet Union has established a power balance that prevents the outbreak of a "hot war."
- Conflict creates coalitions among allies that otherwise might not exist. Social relationships, with their many rewards, often come about because groups of nations band together in reaction to a common and more powerful enemy. Competing entrepreneurs may form a business association to further their common interests. Countries that form military alliances may go on to establish mutually beneficial trade pacts.

Following from these propositions, Coser (1956) concludes that conflict serves positive as well as negative functions, and that a restricted view one way or the other is not justified. He also notes that conflict tends to be dysfunctional for a social structure that is rigid and unresponsive to conflict. Such a structure oppresses dissent and permits hostilities to accumulate toward a major cleavage in the system. Systems that handle conflict openly and productively can maximize the benefits while reducing the costs.

In a further work, Coser (1967) continues this line of reasoning by arguing that neither consensus theories nor conflict theories give the most basic or complete picture of society; both are required in the larger attempt to understand and account for social structures and processes. Coser extends his earlier treatment to cover new areas such as the social functions of violence. While we may view this approach as asking us to look on the bright side of the often destructive phenomenon of social conflict, it does lead to a more balanced analysis than a simplistic "conflict-is-evil" view of the world. However, we must remember that the theories on which Coser's position is based came from the early twentieth century, when the negative outcomes of conflict were serious but could not realistically lead to the demise of the human race, as is now possible through the use of nuclear weapons.

Certain of Coser's propositions have received support from subsequent social-psychological research. Dion (1979) reviews a variety of experiments showing that intergroup conflict does increase ingroup cohesion in both field and laboratory situations. Although there are a number of explanations for this relationship, the existence of threat from an outgroup may be the key in inducing the ethnocentric reaction (see Chapter 8) of heightened ingroup cohesion and loyalty (Holmes & Grant, 1979).

Bonoma and Milburn (1977) also suggest that social psychologists have tended to ignore the benefits of conflict in their research and theorizing. The primary emphasis in the 1950s and 1960s was to examine ways that conflict could be resolved in nonviolent and mutually satisfactory ways. While there is much merit in this quest, the assumptions ignore the potentially integrative functions of conflict. Therefore, Bonoma and Milburn recommend that we study the conditions under which conflict is functional and in what situations violence is socially facilitative. Working within these wider perspectives, social psychologists are in a better position to continue their studies of conflict in ways that are relevant to the challenges of the coming decade.

Sources and Escalation of Conflict

Each of the social sciences is concerned with conflict, and each takes its own approach and makes its own contribution to this important study (McNeil, 1965). These different approaches also emphasize different causes or sources of conflict. In discussing the psychology of human conflict, Stagner (1965) explores the individual processes of perception, cognition, and personality functioning that are particularly important in understanding destructive conflict. The social psychology of human conflict, according to Katz and Withey (1965), must deal with psychological factors that are relevant to understanding those characteristics and actions of the social structure that are important in hostile or cooperative relations with other systems.

Within the many definitions of conflict, incompatible goals and activities are often a main element. Morton Deutsch (1973), a student of Kurt Lewin and specialist in the study of conflict, suggests that conflict exists whenever incompatible activities occur within a person, a group, or a nation (that is, intrapersonal, intragroup, and intranational conflict); or between persons, groups, or nations (that is, interpersonal, intergroup, or international conflict). An incompatible activity is one that prevents, obstructs, interferes, injures, or in some way makes another activity less likely or less effective. Thus two children who fight over the use of a tricycle are in the same conflict as two corporate directors who jockey for position at a board meeting.

Deutsch also points out that we must distinguish between conflict and competition. Competition can produce conflict, as we saw in Sherif's Robbers Cave experiments (Chapter 8), but not all instances of conflict reflect competition. In competition, each party strives for the same prize; the goal of each is to achieve that end and reduce the probability of the other party achieving it instead. Thus, in conflict derived from competition, incompatible activities derive from incompatible goals. But conflict can also occur where there are no incompatible goals. Two parties may value the same goal, but disagree over how to get there. For example, both parents may want to stop their teenager from hanging around with undesirable friends, but may experience conflict about the most effective way to do so. Thus, conflict can be an element of cooperation as well as competition.

Competition also differs from conflict in one other important way. As Katz and Kahn (1978) point out, competition involves no direct action of one party to interfere with the ongoing activities of the other. Conflict comes with interference. For example, track and field events in sports are competitive; each runner or pole vaulter attempts to do his or her best, competing alongside other contestants. Hockey and football, on the other hand, are conflictual; each team defends its own goal, interferes with the goal-directed activity of the other team, and initiates offensive actions against its opponent. This point, however, illuminates a further distinction between competition and conflict. Competition, whether conflictual or parallel, occurs within a set of agreed-upon rules; behavior *outside* of the rules is punished in ways that detract from attaining the goal. Pure conflict is a case of "no holds barred." All is fair in the interpersonal conflict of love or the international conflict of war: incompatible activities may be reciprocated and escalated to destructive levels. It is with this type of interaction that social psychologists are most concerned.

Deutsch and others make a fundamental distinction between destructive and constructive conflicts. A conflict has destructive consequences when the participants are dissatisfied with the outcomes and have a sense of loss. Constructive conflict involves productive consequences: all participants are satisfied with their outcomes and feel they have gained as a result of the conflict. And there are intermediate cases, in which some participants are satisfied while others are not. In most real-life situations, it is possible to judge the destructiveness or constructiveness of conflicts. For example, a quarrel between spouses that clears up misunderstandings and leads to greater intimacy is very different from one that produces bitterness and estrangement.

Social scientists have also tried to define the basic properties of social conflict. In a classic review, Mack and Snyder (1957) present basic properties and suggested propositions drawn from the social science literature. In a similar vein, Stagner (1967) develops basic dimensions on which conflicts may vary: these include duration, intensity, degree of regulation, and difference in power between the parties. A later review by Fink (1968) illustrates the variety of definitions and propositions today. Fink defines conflict as a social process in which the parties are linked by at least one form of antagonistic psychological relation (incompatible goals, emotional hostility) and by one form of antagonistic interaction (violent struggle, indirect interference).

If it is hard to agree on a basic definition of conflict, you can imagine the difficulty of agreeing on the major sources and types of conflict. The reviews by Mack and Snyder (1957) and Fink (1968) bring into contrast many competing typologies of social conflict. First, there is the question of whether conflict arises from some objective difference in the real world, or whether it exists only in the perceptions of those involved. This distinction has been referred to as *realistic-versus-unrealistic conflict*. If, in imagining that someone else wants something you want, you begin to influence their behavior in other directions, then you may be creating a conflict that never existed. Similarly, national decision makers may perceive their country's interests as threatened when in fact that was never the intention of the other party.

Unrealistic conflict is thus a result of misperception, miscommunication, and other processes that create conflict where no basic incompatibilities exist. In contrast, *realistic conflict* stems from objective differences among the parties that trigger actions intended to control the other party and create antagonistic feelings toward the other.

Realistic conflict often grows to incorporate some of the elements of unrealistic conflict. That is, initial differences threaten each party and lead to misperception, miscommunication, prejudice, stereotyping, and so on; these in turn escalate the interaction into a mixture of realistic and unrealistic conflict. The reverse mechanism is also possible but less probable. That is, parties engaged in unrealistic conflict might well generate real differences among themselves as a means of justifying and escalating the conflict. Since most conflicts are a mixture of basic incompatibilities and irrational factors, this social process becomes even more complex and difficult to understand and resolve.

A Typology of Conflict. One of the simplest and most useful typologies of social conflict is offered by Katz (1965). It distinguishes three main types of conflict: *economic conflict,* due to competing motives to obtain scarce resources; *power conflict,* in which each party wishes to maximize the amount of influence it has; and *value conflict,* involving incompatibility in ideology, religion, or way of life.

Economic disputes are the clearest form of realistic conflict: each party wants its share of a scarce resource or space. Each party wants to get the most that it can, often with no perceived limits, and directs its behavior to maximizing its gain at the cost of the other party. Union-management conflict, for example, has as one of its common issues the incompatible demands of each party for slicing up the "economic pie," a pastry that is only so big. At the same time, the demands on the pie, along with related tensions, being unrealistic to most outside observers, may define a resource scarcity that need not exist. Thus, even economic conflict is intertwined with the irrational social-psychological processes of conflict.

Many of the crucial conflicts in the world today, such as that between rich and poor nations, revolve around the issue of how best to distribute economic wealth. But a strictly human relations approach to this issue—that is, one that sees the roots of conflict in miscommunication, or a lack of common goals—is doomed to failure. Economic conflict will not be resolved by improving communication, but by difficult and detailed negotiations among the parties.

Power conflict is essentially a struggle for dominance in social relations, whether it is within a marriage or between nations. Both parties work to maximize their impact, and it is impossible for one party to be stronger without the other being weaker—at least in terms of direct influence over each other. This type of conflict usually ends in a victory for one party and a defeat for the other, or in a standoff that involves a continuing state of tension. This state of tension is a very uncomfortable source of stress, especially in interpersonal relations dominated by power conflict. The crucial issue is not resource scarcity or differences in basic values, but simply a question of control and related matters such as pride, recognition, and future material rewards that power may bring.

Value conflict involves incompatible principles and practices that people believe in—their ideology, their religion, their political system, their culture. Sometimes, opposing values can be compromised or accommodated, but often they cannot (Mack & Snyder, 1957). It is possible that a basic value of one party (free speech, for instance) requires the denial of a basic value of the other (the acceptance of official ideology in a totalitarian society). Religious conflict may be characterized not just by a clash in basic principles of faith but by a commitment to convert those of other faiths. International conflict—the East-West schism, for one—often has a strong value or ideological basis: each side asserts the ultimate superiority and rightness of its political-economic system. Since value conflicts lie at the very heart of a people's identity, they are extremely difficult to resolve. Because they have few negotiable items, we must seek more creative, problem-solving approaches, either to integrate opposing values or to find superordinate values that allow for peaceful coexistence of incompatible systems.

Most conflicts do not have a single source or represent a pure type. Most conflicts involve a mixture of realistic economic, power, or value differences as well as an unrealistic ingredient of misperception and miscommunication. A conflict may begin from one source but broaden to include other elements. A union-management dispute, for example, often escalates from economic differences into a power struggle; then, saving face and winning take priority over the actual monetary settlement. Since attempts to control are a basic ingredient of all conflict, power automatically enters in to some degree.

Escalation of Conflict. The mixture of sources tends to escalate conflict. Unless it is handled constructively at an early stage, conflict has a definite predisposition to escalate, to become more intense and hostile, to proliferate more issues, and to involve stronger and more destructive attempts to control. A social-psychological analysis of conflict suggests a number of good reasons for escalation (Bonoma, 1975). First, we assume, as learning theory does, that humans behave in ways calculated to maximize their goals and minimize their losses. The behavior of each party in conflict imposes constraints on the potential satisfactions of the other; therefore, each party employs social-influence strategies in an attempt to control the other's behavior.

Escalation is defined as the "controlled and specified application of sanctions in a fashion of increasing magnitude over time." *De-escalation* involves the same process with a "decreasing magnitude over time" (Bonoma, 1975, p. 37). Defining escalation as a social-influence process allows social psychologists to study it in a variety of ways—particularly by using experimental games and simulations that may shed light on escalation in real-world conflicts (see the following section).

As we have seen in intergroup and international relations, escalation feeds on fear and defensiveness. Deterrence typically leads to an arms race that typically erupts into armed hostility. Threat designed to deter leads to counterthreat, and each go-round involves higher stakes. Selective and distorted perception justifies a competitive, cautious approach rather than a trusting, cooperative one. The self-fulfilling prophecy comes into play. Each party attributes negative intentions to the other and takes precautionary measures against the other. However, when the other party perceives this as an attempt to control, and responds with a counteraction, each party becomes more adamant in its belief that the other is unreasonable and must change. Such a "locking-in" greatly increases the probability that violent means of coercion will be used to terminate the conflict.

Useful analyses of the escalation of international conflict are offered by political scientists Quincy Wright (1965) and J. David Singer (1970). Wright sees conflict as comprising four stages: (1) the awareness of incompatibilities, (2) rising tensions, (3) pressures short of force to resolve the incompatibilities, and (4) the use of force to dictate a solution. Wright developed a formula involving the major motivations related to escalation and analyzed forty-five different conflicts beginning with World War I. The factors that promoted escalation toward armed hostility or all-out war included perceptions that vital national interests were involved, a relative equality of forces, and the belief by each party that it could increase its own strength through arms production or the formation of alliances. In contrast, factors promoting de-escalation included inequality of forces or equality but great capacity for destruction (there is some evidence for deterrence in this case), high costs of potential conflict in relation to the nation's economy, and a strong world opinion demanding de-escalation. Singer (1970) focuses on basic self-aggravating mechanisms that tend to escalate international conflict (see Box 14.1).

Box 14.1   FOCUS ON THEORY
Escalation in International Conflict

International conflict appears to have a built-in tendency toward escalation, toward more extreme rhetoric, toward costly rivalries, and often toward tragic wars that might have been prevented. How does this spiraling cycle rise to higher and higher levels of antagonism and violence? J. David Singer, a political scientist with postdoctoral training in social psychology, has provided a simple feedback model of escalation in international conflict.

One basic characteristic of most nations is that the same people—the national political elite—are the major actors in both domestic and international politics. Therefore, they must respond to demands from two different systems—demands that are often incompatible and that often exacerbate international conflict. When a dispute occurs, the usual response of the government is to stand firm on its original demands—this is usually applauded by other politicians and the public alike. The other option of initiating and/or reciprocating moves of a conciliatory nature is usually challenged by the political opposition which questions the competence, courage, or patriotism of the government leaders.

However, this typical, hard-line approach to international conflict is only the beginning of the escalation process. Singer identifies four major, self-aggravating mechanisms in the feedback process.

First, the *government in power* and *the political opposition*—whether in a democracy or not—interact in ways that inhibit de-escalation. The initial hard line is often made firmer to ward off opposition attacks on the government. Stronger rhetoric is used to impress both the other country and one's own public of the government's firm determination. However, the adversary's government refuses to be intimidated—it has to look strong in the eyes of *its* opposition and public, too—and is spurred to higher levels of rhetoric in defense of justice, national honor, and so on. Second, *psychological and military mobilization* occurs. A weaker country is especially likely to begin conscripting more soldiers and acquiring more arms. However, the other country responds in kind, thus raising the conflict to new levels of hostility and potential violence. Third, *amplification via the media* supports the government position and fosters and legitimizes further escalation of the conflict. Finally, a *redistribution of political power occurs* in which the military-industrial-labor-academic complex gains more members and influence as preparedness for war becomes a national priority. At this point, the two countries are locked into a mutually destructive course of interaction.

Source: Singer, J. D. Escalation and control in international conflict: A simple feedback model. *General Systems*, 1970, *15*, 163–173.

Levels of Conflict: Similarities and Differences

Conflict occurs at all levels of human social functioning. The high school senior can't decide whether to apply to college or learn a skilled trade. Two roommates spend more time fighting over who will do the dishes than it takes to do them. A work group or an entire organization can be divided over the issue of high-priority goals and appropriate strategies to reach them. And so on. Every human situation has potential for conflict. How well we understand and deal with it determines a great deal of the satisfaction and productivity of our lives.

Personal or intrapersonal conflict exists within one individual's experience. Incompatibility between one's competing motives, attitudes, thoughts, or feelings can create considerable tension, suffering, and psychopathology. Many personality theories include intrapersonal conflict as an important ingredient. We can see decisional conflict—opposing tendencies within the individual that interfere with decision making—in the actions of leaders involved in intergroup or international conflict (Janis, 1959). For example, the attempted but futile appeasement of Hitler just prior to the outbreak of World War II is often attributed to the indecision of other European leaders, particularly the British prime minister, Neville Chamberlain. However, too many differences exist between individual and collective decision making for us to automatically draw any analogies between the two (Singer & Ray, 1966). Intrapersonal conflict is appropriate to the study of personality; social conflict from the interpersonal to the international levels is the appropriate focus for applied social psychology.

Interpersonal Conflict. Interpersonal conflict exists when two people in a relationship have incompatible needs, goals, or ways of relating to others. Antagonistic feelings and attempts to control the behavior of the other person also ensue. Strong differences in major personal motives can be a source of interpersonal conflict. If one marriage partner is motivated by need achievement, but the other is motivated by affiliation, we can expect differences to surface. The first person may wish to spend evenings and weekends working or doing something constructive around the house, while the second is more motivated to hold parties and engage in other social activities.

Conflict can also result from both parties being high on the same motive, particularly need power. The phrase "personality conflict" is often used to refer to a relationship in which both parties have a high need for power and both want to be dominant in the relationship—a clear impossibility. This usually leads to a competitive power struggle in which one party wins and the other loses—usually withdrawing in the process—or to a stalemate in which a continuing state of tension exists.

Interpersonal conflict can also result from scarcity, especially in relationships where resources are limited. Marital conflict may stem from differing priorities of how to divide up less money than will meet all the apparent needs. Breakdown in communication can be a basic source of interpersonal conflict, but ineffective communication and problem solving are more likely to be sources of escalation once a conflict has started.

In his treatment of interpersonal conflicts, Filley (1975) points out that many destructive conflicts occur in which each party is intent upon defeating, harming, or driving away the opponent. The atmosphere is one of stress, anger, and fear in which the parties will use whatever means are necessary to bring about the defeat of the adversary. The emotional intensity in interpersonal conflict is invariably high since the parties are directly involved as individuals, and there is a strong tendency to personalize the conflict. Susan does not say, for example, that Bob does not listen well to her interests and does not help with household chores. Rather, she says, "Bob is a self-centered, inconsiderate creep!" The conflict is seen as *his* personal problem and not a behavioral difficulty in *their* relationship.

There are also limitations to the regulation or institutionalization of interpersonal conflict. Disputes between friends or workers or marriage partners may escalate to the point of no return before they are acknowledged by the surrounding social system. When some form of dispute resolution is finally imposed on the parties, it is often in reaction to personal violence, or in response to one party's request to end the relationship—a divorce or a transfer to another job. The mechanisms for dealing with interpersonal conflict in a preventive or remedial manner are sadly lacking in most social systems.

Filley (1975) defines conflict as a process that takes place between two or more parties and involves six steps or phases. Figure 14.1 presents a model incorporating these six steps.

A conflict begins with identifiable *antecedent conditions* or sources. Within groups or organizations, ambiguous role definitions and unclear boundaries of responsibilities are common sources of interpersonal conflict, that is, role conflict (see Chapter 2). The new sales manager may begin imposing new sales quotas on sales staff without realizing that the former manager set these jointly with each

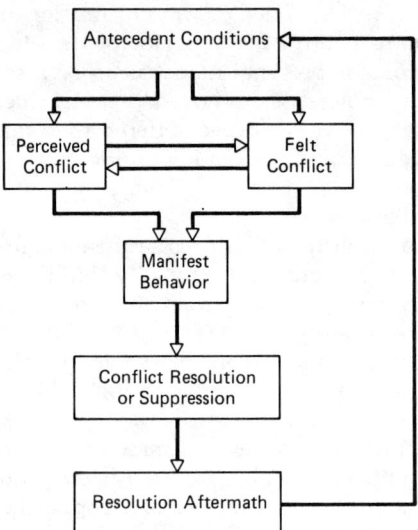

Figure 14.1   Process of Interpersonal Conflict.
Source: Filley (1975).

subordinate. The sales staff may react with hostility and reduced motivation, but say nothing. Conflict over scarce resources and communication barriers are also important antecedent conditions. John, a freshman, and his father may disagree on how much money John needs to attend college. The father expects John to spend nothing on recreation and other leisure activities. John says he has to enjoy life a little in order to succeed; he cannot work every hour of the day. The father may be so concerned about John "making it" that he doesn't listen to his son's concerns. John finally drops out of college, and his father is furious.

One source that might often be overlooked is the degree of association between the parties, that is, the extent of informal relations and the degree of participation in decision making. Contrary to some expectations, the closer the association, the greater the likelihood of conflict since parties are relating on many more dimensions and issues. Participative decision making thus requires skills in interpersonal conflict resolution.

Antecedent conditions may or may not lead to a sense of *perceived conflict*. We are likely to perceive real sources of conflict, but we may also perceive conflict when no antecedent conditions exist, that is, unrealistic conflict. The manager, feeling threatened by a talented subordinate, may perceive a conflict over decision-making power—when in fact the subordinate has no intention of taking over the manager's responsibilities. Perceived conflict may lead to *felt conflict*. Here the issue is personalized; that is, the whole being of one or both parties is threatened, and there are strong feelings of hostility, fear, and mistrust.

Perceptions and feelings lead to *manifest behavior* that may be destructive or constructive. Conscious attempts to interfere with the other party through aggression, competition, or debate are common destructive behaviors in interpersonal conflict. Less common are conscious attempts at cooperation and problem solving

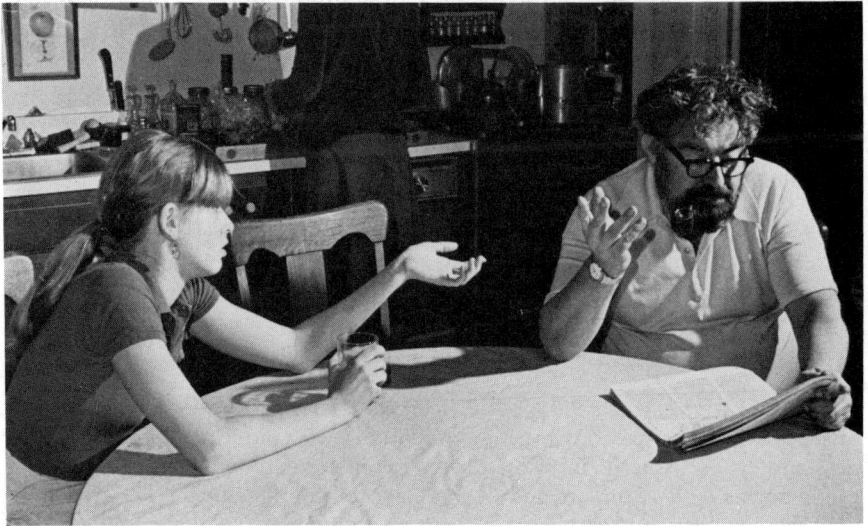

Parent-child conflict is common; in fact, the closer the association between two parties, the more likely they are to conflict. (© *1981 Laimute E. Druskis*)

directed toward mutual goal attainment. Behavior blends into the termination of the conflict either through *conflict resolution* or *suppression*. Resolution involves agreement among all parties. Conflict suppression is the result of the defeat of one party, or the imposition of a settlement by a powerful outsider, often the boss of two subordinates in organizational settings. In either case, the *resolution aftermath* leaves a legacy that will affect future relations between the parties. Defeat usually leaves the loser with antagonistic feelings that set the stage for future conflict. A mutually acceptable resolution brings the parties closer together by increasing trust and cooperation, resulting in a greater commitment to the agreement and the relationship. The resolution aftermath thus cycles back into the antecedent conditions, setting the stage for further conflict and conflict resolution as the interpersonal relationship continues to develop.

Our social-psychological understanding of interpersonal conflict is being extended by the work of Harold Kelley and his students at UCLA. A series of studies have looked at both sources and processes of conflict in young heterosexual couples, either married or cohabiting (Kelley, 1977, 1979). Conflict arises not only from typical difficulties (such as failure to give attention, problems in division and fulfillment of responsibility), but also from *differences in handling conflict itself* (such as inadequate communication, nagging, hostility). Part of these differences relate to sex roles: females are more likely to criticize their partner as inconsiderate and insensitive; males typically reject their partner's emotionality and call for a logical approach. In sum, males tend to be conflict avoiders, while females are frustated by this avoidance.

A special source of conflict lies in the different attributions that partners make of each other's behavior. Undesirable behavior is typically explained by the complaining partner in terms of personal characteristics of their spouses ("You are irresponsible," "You don't care about me"). In contrast, the actor's causal explanations attempt to justify or excuse the behavior ("I did it for you" or "My friends made me do it"). The problem is that the aggrieved partner generalizes from the behavior to personal traits or attitudes, whereas the actor locates the behavior in a certain context and sees it as a special case. Interpersonal conflict thus illustrates the general differences between actors and observers in making causal attributions (see Chapter 2).

Models such as Filley's and Kelley's can help us understand what goes on in interpersonal conflict, whether we are a participant or an observer. By analyzing our own and others' behavior, we can come to see how conflict is often mismanaged at high cost in both human and material terms. We are then in a more informed position to undertake alternate behaviors that are more in accord with the values of dignity and decency in interpersonal relations.

Conflict in Groups. Much of our social life is characterized by conflict, either open or suppressed. Groups bring together individuals with differing opinions, priorities, and styles. Role definitions, power relations, communication structures, group norms, and so on, are not always clear to group members. Differences in how these various structural elements of the group are perceived and reacted to can lead to conflict between individuals and between subgroups or coalitions.

How a group approaches its general functioning can influence how well it will handle conflict within the group. Walton (1976) has distinguished between the strategies of conflict and collaboration in group settings. The conflict or competitive approach (A) can be differentiated from the cooperative or collaborative approach (B) on the basis of a number of behaviors within the group:

Approach A: Conflict
1. Behavior is directed toward own goals
2. Secrecy
3. Misrepresents own needs
4. Unpredictable, surprise behavior
5. Threats, bluffs, and so forth

Approach B: Collaboration
1. Behavior is directed toward common goals
2. Openness
3. Accurate representation of own needs
4. Predictable, appropriate behavior
5. No threats, bluffs, and so forth

Approach A is the way group members tend to behave in a situation they assume to be *distributive*. That is, there are only so many rewards available to be distributed among members; what one person gains, another must lose. A poker game is a good example of a distributive social situation. In Approach B, members perceive the group as an *integrative* social situation: that is, that members are integrating their skills and resources toward a common task. This happens when several people work on a jigsaw puzzle. (Recall Elliott Aronson's jigsaw method of learning in racially mixed groups of schoolchildren—an effective way to foster true integration. See Chapter 11.)

Walton (1976) relates the two approaches to the experience of sensitivity training in small groups (see Chapter 7). Early in the life of the group, most members adopt Approach A. Then members make the rational discovery that only by taking Approach B will they satisfy their needs for recognition and influence. They make the emotional adjustment away from a strong personal need to prove themselves, moving toward a genuine concern for the whole group.

To apply these shifts in behavior to everyday group situations, the trick is to determine which situation is logically distributive and which is integrative. Many situations are a mixture of the two: there are both individual and common goals; there is both competition and cooperation. However, by taking Approach A, we often induce conflict where none need exist. You know people who approach every discussion as a debate, and every meeting as an opportunity to prove their superiority. Conflict is often the result. However, if we look for the integrative aspects of a situation and take a mixed approach of A and B, chances are better that we will identify conflict, resolve it productively, and meet the common goals of the group.

Situations are partly what we make them. However, if there is real conflict in goals and a clearly distributive reward structure, then an emphasis on Approach A is appropriate. The abilities to accurately diagnose situations and respond in a flexible manner are two of the keys to handling group conflict effectively. A classic research study by Guetzkow and Gyr (1954) on the conditions and behaviors associated with effective conflict resolution in decision-making groups is presented in Box 14.2.

Box 14.2   FOCUS ON RESEARCH
Conflict Resolution in Decision-Making Groups

Conflict in small decision-making groups often leads to frustration and disappointment. Yet conflict may hold the seeds of creative solutions if differing opinions can be synthesized toward common goals. What conditions determine whether groups move through conflict to consensus or end their deliberations in disagreement? A classic field study by Harold Guetzkow and John Gyr completed at the University of Michigan addressed this fundamental question.

These investigators observed group meetings (five to twenty persons each) involving a total of 700 people from a variety of business and government organizations. The meetings involved ongoing groups of representatives from different departments that were dealing with important policy and staff decisions. Before the meeting, the researchers interviewed the chairperson to obtain background information. Then a team of three specialists observed the meeting itself: one coded every communication on the problem-solving function it served (such as proposing a solution); the second noted behaviors that expressed self-oriented needs (such as dominating the group); and the third made global observations of group functioning. Group members' reactions to the meeting were elicited by a postmeeting questionnaire and by a personal interview a day or so later.

Two types of conflict were assessed: *substantive conflict* relating to the group's task, and *affective conflict* deriving from the emotional aspects of interpersonal relations. Consensus was measured by the amount of difference between each member's final opinions and the decision the group reached. Little difference indicated high consensus and vice versa.

As expected, groups high in either type of conflict reached consensus less than groups low in conflict. More importantly, the results identified conditions under which both types of conflict *did* lead to consensus and satisfaction: the absence of strong self-oriented needs, a positive emotional atmosphere, an orderly discussion of topics, and the ability of members to understand each other. Some conditions related only to substantive conflict ending in consensus (for example, high use of factual information, good give-and-take, and warm, supportive relations). These conditions did not help resolve affective conflict. That task required reducing the forces that were hindering the achievement of consensus. This was accomplished through such behaviors as members withdrawing from the discussion and the postponement of dealing with controversial items.

In short, good communication and problem solving aided the resolution of substantive conflict, but affective conflict was moved toward consensus by reducing the involvement of members with the task and with each other. Formal devices, such as the use of parliamentary procedure, were of little help in achieving consensus in the face of intense conflict.

Source: Guetzkow, H. & Gyr, J. An analysis of conflict in decision-making groups. *Human Relations*, 1954, 7, 367–382.

Conflict in Organizations. Organizations are social systems that are as susceptible to conflict as groups. The main difference is that, within the context of the organization, intergroup differences are added to interpersonal disputes. Every aspect of organizational life that creates order and coordination must overcome other tendencies; this creates the potential for conflict (Kahn & Boulding, 1964; Katz & Kahn, 1978; Thomas, 1976). See Chapter 9. For example, rewards are necessary inducements for organizational performance, but there is no consensus on how rewards should be allocated. Authority reduces conflict by requiring submission to organizational norms and goals, but its effect is never perfect. And so on.

Much of the conflict in organizations is intergroup conflict—that is, between subunits or departments with differing goals and approaches (Walton, Dutton & Cafferty, 1969). Pondy (1967) identifies three types of conflict among organizational subunits: bargaining conflict among interest groups in competition for scarce resources (labor-management, for instance); bureaucratic conflict between parties to a superior-subordinate relationship (supervisor-worker); and systems conflict among parties to a lateral working relationship (production and sales department). In all cases, Pondy sees conflict as a sequence of episodes or interactions, each of which goes through a series of stages: from latency to feeling to perception to manifestation to aftermath. (Note the similarity between this process model of conflict and Filley's model for interpersonal conflict.)

Some common hypotheses about the causes and consequences of organizational conflict were tested in Smith's (1966) comparative study of six different organizations. The *communication hypothesis* states that barriers to effective communication between echelons in large organizations are a source of conflict since they hamper decision making and coordination. The *conflict-of-interest hypothesis* sees differences among competing subgroups as a major determinant of disputes. The *consensus hypothesis* interprets organizational conflict as stemming from a lack of shared perceptions, attitudes, and values among members of the different echelons.

Smith found partial support for each of these general hypotheses, thus indicating the complexity of organizational conflict. But the study also found that conflict did not necessarily have negative consequences on the organization's performance. What made the difference were the techniques of leadership and control used to manage the conflict. This finding supports the approach of organization development (see Chapter 9) that attempts to manage conflict in ways that are conducive to organizational improvement and growth. The idea is that if people can learn to handle conflict productively, they can handle anything.

Conflicts at the intergroup and international levels of analysis (see Chapters 8 and 12) have their unique characteristics, but many of the social-psychological processes are similar to those identified by general principles of conflict behavior. Escalation of conflict, for example, is similar at all levels of analysis. Nonetheless, since the complexity and overall impact of destructive conflict increases as we move up the scale of social systems, we must try to understand the unique properties of each level of conflict.

Studying Conflict through Experimental Games

Consider the following situation. As a student in an undergraduate psychology course, you have volunteered to participate as a research subject in a laboratory experiment. You arrive at the designated place at the designated time. You are informed by a personable research assistant that your task will involve interacting with another person in a particular manner. You are seated in an isolated cubicle with a simple array of buttons and lights in front of you. You may choose to push either a red button or a blue button; your partner has the same choice. You will choose without knowing your partner's choice; the same holds true for your partner.

When you have both made your choices, one of the lights will come on. That light will indicate the combination of choices made by both of you. Each combination results in different outcomes or payoffs for each of you. The possibilities are given to you in the form of a payoff matrix, like the one shown in Figure 14.2. The first number in each cell is Person One's payoff; the second number is Person Two's payoff. Payoffs may be in the form of pennies, tokens, or points with no tangible value.

You are instructed to continue the interaction over a given number of trials. It immediately becomes apparent to you that (1) you have some difficult decisions to make, and (2) that how your partner in the interaction behaves can profoundly affect your rewards. (We will get back to your dilemma in a moment.)

This scenario is one example of an *experimental game*—a laboratory task used to study how people behave in an interdependent situation in which each individual makes decisions affecting the welfare of all participants. "Welfare" is related to numerical outcomes chosen beforehand by the experimenter (Pruitt & Kimmel, 1977). Social-psychological research on experimental games has been very active for the past twenty-five years, producing over 1,000 studies. Interest in games was supported by the development of theories of social exchange (see Chapter 2) that emphasize the importance of rewards and penalties, controlled by others, in influencing behavior. Game theory from mathematics and economics is partly concerned with developing models of rational choices in which people are dependent on one another for their outcomes. (A general discussion of the utility of game theory for studying social conflict is presented by Rapoport, 1965.) Experimental games thus provided the social psychologist with a precise method for studying how people react in interdependent situations in which the outcomes of different behaviors are clearly specified. (Other person and situation variables can also be studied in relation to game behavior.)

Experimental games include negotiation games, coalition games, locomotion games, and matrix games (Pruitt & Kimmell, 1977). The majority of research has been done on matrix games, the most popular one being the Prisoner's Dilemma

Figure 14.2   Payoff Matrix for an Experimental Game.

Game (PDG). The PDG was developed out of a hypothetical situation in which two armed-robbery suspects are given two choices by the district attorney (Luce & Raiffa, 1957). The suspects are isolated from each other and asked to squeal on the other. The first to turn state's evidence will not be charged, but his partner will be convicted. If neither confesses, the D.A. will try for their joint conviction on a lesser charge. If both confess, they will be tried, but the D.A. will ask for leniency.

The possible outcomes in this situation are similar to those represented in Figure 14.2—actually a PDG payoff matrix. Each person must make a choice in ignorance of the other's choice; each has the option of competing with or cooperating with his partner. If one chooses to compete with his partner by turning state's evidence, and the partner does not, he wins big ($+10$) while the partner loses big (-10) (Cells B or C). However, if the partner also competes, both incur small losses (-5, -5) of a minor charge (Cell A).

In the laboratory situation (back to your dilemma), blue and red buttons replace the cooperative and competitive choices of the prisoner's dilemma, but the basic rationale is the same. By competing (red) while your partner cooperates (blue), you can maximize your own gain ($+10$) at your partner's expense (-10). If you both choose to compete (red), you will both incur small losses (-5, -5). If you both cooperate, you will both make small gains ($+5$, $+5$).

The PDG is thus a *mixed-motive game* wherein each party is partly motivated to compete and partly motivated to cooperate. However, the behavioral choices and strategies of cooperation or competition over the long term are actually related to at least three different underlying motives (McClintock, 1972). A player who is motivated toward "joint gain"—that is, maximizing both players' rewards—will tend to cooperate. A motive of "own gain" will lead the player to ignore the needs of the partner while attempting to maximize his or her own rewards. This motive would be more likely to lead to a competitive strategy. Finally a motive of "relative gain" will lead the player to ignore absolute reward, seeking only to come out better than the partner—even if "better" means a small loss. Because the PDG represents the very common social situation of mixed motives, it has readily lent itself to the study of conditions that lead people to cooperate and/or to compete.

A certain amount of theory regarding conflict, particularly the processes of cooperation and competition, has been tested using the paradigm of experimental games (for example, Deutsch, 1973; Deutsch & Krauss, 1960). A number of reviews of the major findings of games research have been prepared (such as Patchen, 1970; Wrightsman, O'Connor & Baker, 1972). Without going into detail, we will look generally at the consistent results before we look critically at this area of research.

The major question in games research centers around knowing which of the variables tends to influence cooperative behavior or competitive behavior. The norm of reciprocity (see Chapter 2) has been tested under different conditions. By controlling the responses of one partner—a pseudo-player, in effect—the experimenter can present either a cooperative or a competitive strategy, or any combination of the two, and observe the effects on the real subject's responses over a series of trials. When the real player's choices are reciprocated, on a trial-by-trial basis, there is a general trend toward cooperative behavior since this maximizes outcomes in the long run. However the norm of reciprocity appears stronger with competition than with cooperation. Players who initially cooperate, but who are taken advantage of, very quickly shift to a mutually competitive stance in which both players experience relatively minor losses. When a fixed or constant proportion of responses is cooperative or competitive, the real player tends to go with a competitive strategy. The tendency to cooperate is also greater if the players are friends or are perceived as friendly, as opposed to being strangers or perceived as being hostile. One recent study suggests that to be effective in the PDG requires cooperating as long as the other player does, being somewhat forgiving of competitive moves, and being optimistic about the other's responsiveness (Axelrod, 1980).

Communication has pronounced effects on the PDG. When players are allowed to communicate verbally or nonverbally, they tend to cooperate much more readily. In fact, full communication of intentions and effects virtually destroys the game paradigm since players can reach agreement on how to maximize their joint outcomes through cooperative behavior. In the controlled situation, however, the competitive strategy tends to predominate, although it can be affected by other variables. These may include the personal characteristics of the players, although traditional personality traits have shown little or mixed relations to PDG behavior. The one exception is a relationship between need achievement and cooperation: apparently those who strongly wish to maximize their gains are attracted to interacting cooperatively with others in an attempt to do so.

The utility of games research has long been a controversial question. Proponents of experimental games point out the distinct advantages of their paradigm for studying social conflicts. Many of these advantages reflect the general utility of laboratory experimentation for studying human social behavior (see Chapter 3). In games research, a small number of selected variables can be carefully controlled and precisely measured by the experimenter in a situation having potentially high internal validity. This means that hypotheses about variables related to competitive and cooperative responses can be tested in a well-controlled manner. In addition to these advantages, the games serve certain functions (Schlenker & Bonoma, 1978):

- Games serve as an analogy of actual conflict situations by representing the essential aspects of such situations.
- Games serve as a learning device to suggest new ways of thinking about conflict phenomena.
- Games are useful to study how rational and irrational processes affect conflict behavior.
- Games are a method for testing theoretically relevant hypotheses about conflict.

Critics of games research have centered on the question of external validity—that is, the generalizability of results to other situations and settings at different times—especially the differences between experimental games and real-life situations (Pruitt, 1967). Game participants are rewarded with trivial or imaginary rewards, are not allowed to communicate, are not able to try out a decision and then reverse it, and are not influenced by social norms on the appropriateness of cooperation. Since every one of these factors is the opposite or very different in real life, how can we generalize the results of gaming to the real world?

Pruitt and Kimmel (1977) present a more recent review that covers twenty years of gaming research; again the question of external validity is raised. Not only are researchers unwilling or unable to generalize their results to the real world, but games research simply does not represent the complexity of background conditions and interactions among variables that occur in real life. The review also points out two other major deficiencies in games research: a lack of theory and an overreliance on a single method. Hypotheses are usually based on hunches rather than derived from theory, and research results have not been interrelated or cumulated toward theory-building. Reviews of studies simply classify results on the basis of the superficial characteristics on which variables were manipulated and studied in relation to cooperative or competitive responses. The field is method-bound: researchers seize on games as a way of studying behavior and on variables that are easy to manipulate; they put less emphasis on what they are going to study. Such tendencies detract from building and testing valid theories of social conflict.

Schlenker and Bonoma (1978) defend games research by countering a number of major criticisms. They acknowledge that researchers are prone to follow Kaplan's law of the instrument: "Give a small boy a hammer, and he will find that everything in sight needs pounding" (1964, p. 28). However, many gaming studies focus only on the method in order to test the paradigm's characteristics and limitations. Pennies and points may have little motivational meaning, but studies using rewards of higher values have not produced more consistent results. It is true that games restrict the freedom of participants and do not allow changing values to operate. As such, they are an analogue of the structural properties of conflict, but not of its complex processes. Thus, games are a method for testing propositions about conflict; they are not meant to be simulations or models of conflict. The question of external validity, therefore, should be leveled at our theories of conflict—not at the experimental game. Games should only be used to discover new possibilities and to test theoretically derived hypotheses with a clear understanding of their functions and limitations.

This analysis attempts to move the focus of criticism away from games research to the wider process of the scientific study of conflict. But we should be careful not to downplay the deficiencies of games research. The basic paradigm *does* lack external validity, and this restricts the utility of results whether they are used for theory-building or theory-testing. Theories are only as valid as the results on which they are based, and it is clear that the findings from games research will contribute much less to theories of social conflict than was initially envisaged by some.

Games *do* attempt to represent both the structure and process of conflict situations, but in such a superficial and highly restricted manner that they certainly cannot be considered as simulations or models of conflict. Therefore, we must become increasingly aware of the proper place of games research in the study of conflict. As the restricted utility of experimental games becomes more apparent, it is doubtful that the next twenty years will see another 1,000 studies. We are more likely to see an increasing reliance on the more complex social simulations that are now gaining in popularity (see Klimoski, 1978; Wesner, 1977). We can only hope that the use of simulations will yield adequate experimental control while giving us a reasonable representation of the structure and process of real-world conflict.

METHODS OF CONFLICT RESOLUTION

The social sciences have contributed much to the study of conflict (for example, McNeil, 1965; Smith, 1971). We have paid attention to important recurring themes and made significant progress in understanding conflict (Deutsch, 1977, 1980). We have continued to contemplate future directions (Boulding, 1978). We have accumulated an impressive amount of theory and research. But the humanistic value base of applied social psychology demands more.

Understanding is only the first step of a socially concerned scientist/practitioner. The second step is action: action through providing consultation to others on how to resolve conflict constructively; action through direct involvement in conflict-resolution activities. The tripartite demand for theory, research, and practice in applied social psychology will be met only through a concerted effort to apply our knowledge and our skills in ways that reduce human suffering through actual intervention—both indirect and direct in human affairs. The worldwide problem of destructive social conflict remains as one of the most important and demanding areas for such involvement.

Prosocial Behavior

Until now we have emphasized aggression, violence, and destructive social conflict. But we know full well that there is a positive side to human social behavior. There is a caring, sharing, helping, and cooperating side that often goes unnoticed. A great deal of human accomplishment comes from the productive and cumulative behavior of "nonconflict" (Boulding, 1977). The roots of caring, sharing, and helping run deep in our socialization process, supported by strong social norms of altruism (Mussen & Eisenberg-Berg, 1977). This does not mean that such behavior will always be forthcoming in apparently appropriate situations. It does mean that we have as great a tendency toward prosocial behavior as we do toward antisocial acts. Social psychology has recently shown an increased interest in *prosocial behavior*—activities that have positive social consequences for others (Wispé, 1977, 1978).

Many behaviors are considered prosocial: giving to charity, doing someone a favor, cooperating toward a common goal, helping someone in distress, and so on. Such behaviors reflect the motive of *altruism* or unselfish concern for the welfare of other people. We study prosocial behavior to illuminate the situational conditions and personal characteristics that relate to the likelihood of engaging in altruistic acts. One such incident, now almost legendary, has stimulated our study of helping behavior, particularly intervention in emergencies.

At 3 A.M. on a morning in 1964, in the borough of Queens in New York City, Kitty Genovese was returning home from work when she was attacked by a knife-wielding assailant. For more than half an hour, she fought off the attacker, all the time screaming for help. Her screams awakened many of her neighbors, and twice the assailant was frightened away by lights and noises. But no one intervened.

Thirty-eight people witnessed this vicious atack, but only one called the police—
after Kitty Genovese was dead (Rosenthal, 1964).

The media talked about apathy, alienation, and the dehumanizing effects of
urban living. They asked in outrage how so many people could watch, without
anyone trying to help. Two New York City social psychologists, Bibb Latané and
John Darley, turned the question around to say that maybe no one helped *because*
so many watched (Wheeler, 1970). This unique interpretation led to a series of
experiments on bystander intervention in emergencies, and to numerous investigations of the conditions affecting helping behavior (Latané & Darley, 1976;
Wheeler, Deci, Reis & Zuckerman, 1978).

Latané and Darley (1968) first conducted a number of experiments that
indeed indicated that people were less likely to intervene in an emergency when
other bystanders were present. In one experiment, subjects were seated in a small
room completing a questionnaire when smoke began to puff into the room
through a wall vent. Subjects working alone were much more likely to leave the
room to report the smoke than subjects who were working in groups of threes. In
a similar experiment, subjects were seated in separate cubicles connected by
intercoms for the ostensible purpose of discussing life and learning in the urban
environment. The first person to speak was a confederate of the experimenters.
After mentioning early that he was prone to epileptic seizures, the confederate
became increasingly loud and incoherent, and began stammering, calling for help,
choking, and falling silent. Again, subjects in groups were much less likely to help
than those who were alone. These early studies have been followed by many
laboratory and field experiments that have replicated and generalized the initial
results in a number of directions.

Wheeler et al. (1978) present a model of the bystander-intervention process,
summarizing much of the research on helping behavior in emergencies. The
model, presented in Table 14.1, indicates four major stages leading to an intervention, as well as the factors involved in decision making at each stage. Keep in mind
that many of the same variables operate in other forms of prosocial behavior—
such as doing someone a favor or donating to a charity. Latané and Darley (1976)
add this point: the helper must decide what form of assistance he or she can give
and how to implement the chosen form of assistance.

What helps determine whether a situation is perceived as an emergency? First
of all, clear distress cues are essential. Let me give an illustration. In New York
City, my wife and I were walking to a meeting of the annual convention of the
American Psychological Association. Along the way, we encountered a woman
who appeared disoriented, staring blankly and swaying slightly from side to side.
She did not appear to be in any danger, but also did not seem to be completely all
right. In terms of the model, the distress cues were ambiguous. Was she physically
ill, mentally confused, drunk, stoned, or just behaving in her usual albeit abnormal fashion? A couple of men were loading a truck near the woman, and two other
pedestrians had just walked by her. These bystanders appeared to be interpreting
the situation as a nonemergency. This might have been due to a cultural norm to
appear calm and cool, which misleads bystanders into a state of shared ignorance
in which no one really knows if there is an emergency. The behavior of other
bystanders partly influenced me not to intervene. We walked on by as well, partly

Table 14.1   MODEL OF BYSTANDER INTERVENTION

Stages Leading to Intervention	*Determinants of Decisions Made at Each Stage*
I. Perceiving an emergency	1. Degree of ambiguity of the distress cues
	2. Reactions of other bystanders to the incident
	3. Likelihood of escape from the distress cues
II. Assuming responsibility for the victim's fate	1. Number of other bystanders present at the emergency
	2. Acquaintance between the victim and the bystander
III. Wanting to help the victim	1. Characteristics of the bystander
	2. Cost of helping
	3. Modeling effects
IV. Having the ability to help the victim	

Source: Wheeler et al. (1978).

because it was easy to escape. If she had fallen down in front of us, it would have been much more difficult to interpret the situation as a nonemergency and to keep on going.

It was relatively easy for me not to assume responsibility for the woman's fate (Stage II). *Diffusion of responsibility* occurred for me, and I expect it had occurred for other passersby (see Chapter 7). In this process, each individual in the group denies responsibility and expects someone else to exercise it. The Kitty Genovese murder and the experiment by Latané and Darley (1968), which simulated an epileptic seizure, appear to involve diffusion of responsibility, because the on-lookers were *unable to see each other* and therefore could not pick up cues indicating calmness or a nonemergency interpretation. Wheeler et al. (1978) note that diffusion of responsibility appears to be less when the bystanders are friends or when some of the bystanders are unable to help and thereby share responsibility. Concurrently, a bystander who is acquainted with the victim is more likely to help, presumably because he or she is more likely to see the emergency as real, to feel responsible, and to fear the potential repercussions of not helping. If, in my dilemma, I had known the woman on the sidewalk and therefore had known if she was behaving differently than usual, I would have immediately stopped to see if she needed assistance.

Another possible reason for not assuming responsibility has been described as the *just-world hypothesis* (Lerner, 1970), which states that in general the world is fair and equitable and victims are simply getting what they deserve, and are therefore undeserving of aid. If bystanders take this view and have any basis for perceiving the victim as unworthy or guilty, we would expect them to withhold aid. The characteristics of the victim become important in affecting the attributions made and the degree to which a bystander assumes responsibility.

The third stage of wanting to help the victim again depends on multiple conditions. Personal characteristics of the bystander, the cost of helping, and modeling by other bystanders all play a role. The norms of prosocial behavior are internalized and adhered to differently by different people. Thus, measures of personal and social responsibility, moral development, and so on have been found to be related to the tendency to help in emergency situations (see Staub, 1974). In addition, the existence of temporary emotional states such as guilt or empathy have been shown to increase helping behavior. However, helping can be costly in both psychological and physical terms, and studies of donating to charities, as well as helping individual victims, show that high costs reduce prosocial behavior. In the Kitty Genovese situation, some would-be helpers may have feared for their own lives. In my case, I was in a hurry and did not want to miss the meeting. In addition, other bystanders appeared unconcerned. The process of modeling can have facilitative, disinhibitory, or inhibitory effects on help giving (see Chapter 2). Helpful or generous behavior at the stage of giving help appears to increase both the probability and the magnitude of the bystanders' response.

Finally, the bystander must decide whether he or she has the ability to help the victim. Competence based on knowledge or training has been found to increase helping behavior in situations which demand particular interventions. Bystanders who have less competence in a given area tend to withhold assistance. As I walked by the woman on the sidewalk, I was in doubt about how to intervene, not knowing in an unfamiliar environment how to get whatever assistance she might require. I must admit the dissonance-reducing thought also crossed my mind that the situation was a social-psychological experiment, and I was not predisposed to being a participant. Now I'll never know about that, but I'll also never know if the person actually needed assistance.

The four stages outlined by Wheeler et al. (1978) are part of a single process which is ongoing and complex, as my dilemma illustrates. The decisions are not made in any strictly logical and sequential order with total rationality and objectivity (Latané & Darley, 1976). The same factors may operate at more than one stage to determine the final outcome.

Thus, the research which began with Darley and Latané's question, along with other studies of prosocial behavior, shows that human beings are capable of truly altruistic and genuinely cooperative behavior. The important question is how to maximize these types of behaviors in difficult situations, particularly in social conflicts. That question is the topic of the next section.

Approaches to Managing Conflict

Since people can be both humanely prosocial and destructively antisocial, it follows that social conflict may be approached in different ways. Regardless of the source of conflict, the level of conflict, or the intensity of conflict, differing approaches can be taken to deal with the existing incompatibilities and unrealities of the situation. Each of these approaches makes its own assumptions about people and about conflict. Each has its particular set of attitudes and behavior that are appropriate to conflict management. Each has its characteristic outcomes in terms of destructiveness or creativity.

If conflict is handled openly and creatively, the antagonists can often find new and mutually satisfactory solutions. At times this will involve a redistribution of resources, or the creation of new resources, thus serving the goals of social justice and equity while adhering to the norm of nonviolence. This sounds appealing, but it is not a simple or easy process. In fact resolving conflict effectively is often the hardest work of all in human relations.

Win-Lose. Effective conflict resolution means changing either a *win-lose* approach or a *lose-lose* approach into a *win-win* approach (Blake, Shepard & Mouton, 1964; Filley, 1975). The *win-lose approach* is very common. We learn the behaviors of destructive conflict early in life, arguing with our parents, fighting with our siblings, competing with no holds barred on the school playground. Dominance, competition, aggression, and defense permeate many of our social relationships during our formative years. The win-lose approach assumes that conflict among people is inevitable, but that agreement is impossible (Blake et al., 1964). Therefore the appropriate behavior is to defeat the adversary to reach your goal. We also make the assumption that what one party gains, the other loses. This "fixed-pie" assumption may be accurate when we talk about economic or territorial resources, but it tends to generalize to *all* elements of the conflict. As a result creative solutions *that might increase the size of the pie* are never even imagined, let alone considered!

The underlying goal of win-lose conflict is to force the other side to capitulate. Sometimes this is done through socially acceptable means: we may invoke the legitimate authority of the leader or try to win a majority vote. Sometimes victory is pursued through covert manipulation, threat, or innuendo—whatever works is acceptable. The typical ethnocentric attitudes of destructive intergroup conflict tend to accompany win-lose conflict. *We* are right, superior, more deserving, and so on. *They* are wrong, inferior, and undeserving. These simplistic attitudes and destructive behaviors escalate the conflict toward its typical outcome: one party is the righteous victor; the other is the vanquished foe who submits or withdraws in shame (but who prepares very carefully for the next round). In the long run, no one wins and everybody loses. Some of the dynamics of win-lose conflict, studied in a laboratory simulation, are presented in Box 14.3.

Lose-Lose. The *lose-lose approach* to conflict is so named because neither side really accomplishes what it wants (Filley, 1975). It assumes that half a loaf is better than none and that avoidance of conflict is preferable to open confrontation. It also assumes that although there is conflict, some agreement is possible (Blake et al., 1964). Thus, the lose-lose approach is exemplified by smoothing over the conflict or by reaching the simplest of compromises. In neither case is the creative potential of productive conflict resolution explored or realized. In extreme cases, where no agreement seems possible, the common reactions are withdrawal and isolation. The use of rules and the appeal to third-party arbitration are mechanisms designed for lose-lose outcomes. Parties are more willing to follow a lose-lose approach when the stakes are relatively low. Splitting the difference gains each party something and costs less than the win-lose approach, at least for the loser. For both parties, the lose-lose approach is less risky than the potential of a

Box 14.3   FOCUS ON RESEARCH
Win-Lose Conflict in a Laboratory Simulation

Intense conflict has a number of negative effects on the perceptions, behavior, and evaluations of the parties involved. Social psychologists Rhonda Love, Richard Rozelle, and Daniel Druckman used a simulation of negotiations in an interreligious council to systematically study the effects of conflicts of interest.

Participants were asked to play the role of a representative of one of two real-world religious groups who were providing services to prisons. Participants were briefed on the groups' interests and history of interaction, the position of their group and the opponents' group, the programs preferred by each group, the role of the representatives as negotiators and the agenda for the negotiating session. High conflict of interest was induced by a history of noncooperation between the groups as shown by few instances of combining resources to provide programs in the prisons. The groups also differed in their ideological positions—one was concerned with maintaining the status quo through programs such as the spiritual enlightenment of prisoners, whereas the other stressed social change through programs that would serve as alternatives to prisons.

Participants represented the group whose ideology was similar to their own as measured by a pre-questionnaire. Participants negotiated in dyads with an individual of the same sex who held an opposing ideological position. The dyad was instructed to negotiate a decision about which prison programs were to receive financial support from the two groups. A post-questionnaire measured participants' perception of the conflict and their opponent—and their impressions of the negotiating session.

Conflict of interest clearly affected participants' perceptions and evaluations. In the high conflict-of-interest condition, participants perceived the conflict as a win-lose competition, were less willing to compromise, and saw compromise as defeat. They saw the negotiating session as more hostile, futile, and emotional and expressed less satisfaction with the outcomes.

Perceptions of the conflict also affected outcomes. More funds were allocated by negotiators who initially saw the negotiations as problem solving rather than competition, who did not see compromise as defeat, and who did not need to come out favorably in the negotiations. The more funds allocated, the more participants saw their opponent as fair, compromising, and cooperative.

The researchers conclude that a strong relationship exists between actual outcomes of conflict resolution and the perceptions of the conflict situation. High conflict-of-interest produces perceptions that hinder the process and outcomes of negotiation and moves the relationship between the parties in the win-lose direction.

Source: Love, R. L., Rozelle, R. M. & Druckman, D. *Conflict resolution through bargaining and negotiation in interreligious councils.* Paper presented at the Annual Convention of the American Psychological Association, San Francisco, September 1977.

win-lose outcome, and less costly in terms of energy invested than a win-win approach.

The win-lose and lose-lose approaches have some interesting characteristics in common (Filley, 1975). There is a clear "we-they" distinction between the parties, and each sees the issue only from its own point of view. The emphasis is on a quick solution rather than on the motives, goals, or values that will be furthered by the solution. Conflict tends to be personalized, and the parties usually focus on the immediate disagreement, not the relationship. (A relationship orientation would focus on the long-term effect of the differences, and on the manner in which they are resolved.) Thus, win-lose and lose-lose approaches tend *not* to increase the parties' effectiveness in dealing with conflict nor to improve their wider relationship.

Win-Win. In contrast to these strategies, the *win-win approach* is a conscious, systematic attempt to maximize the gains of both parties through collaborative problem solving. The conflict is seen as a mutual problem to be solved rather than as a war to be won or a battle to be avoided. This approach focuses on the needs and constraints of both parties rather than upon strategies designed to conquer or cut losses. By jointly making decisions and solving problems, the parties work toward solutions that are not unacceptable to either. Full problem definition and analysis, and the development of alternatives precede the setting of priorities and the selection of a mutually agreeable solution.

The term *conflict resolution* is best reserved for the reaching of outcomes that are mutually satisfactory and that receive a long-term commitment from both parties. In contrast, the other approaches to conflict management lead to conflict termination, in which partly unacceptable decisions are enforced or accepted in the short term.

The win-win approach focuses on building the quality of the wider relationship among the parties. Appropriate behaviors include open and direct communication and the use of the problem-solving stages. Attitudes of respect and trust are more appropriate than hostility and suspicion. This approach assumes that creative solutions are possible, given the full range of resources existing in the relationship. The win-win approach requires a very high degree of patience and skill in human relations.

These general descriptions of conflict-management approaches, all eminently sensible, are based on a considerable amount of experience in group and organizational settings, and are supported by research. However, the amount of research done on the *effectiveness* of these approaches is unfortunately rather limited. What research we do have has broken down the major approaches into five more specific strategies, following the lead of Blake and Mouton (1964):

- *withdrawing*—avoiding conflict by retreating or remaining silent (a lose-lose strategy)
- *smoothing*—playing down differences, emphasizing commonalities, and avoiding discussion of contentious issues (a lose-lose strategy)
- *compromising*—a simple splitting of the difference through negotiation (a lose-lose strategy)
- *forcing*—an antagonistic, competitive approach that pushes for an all-or-nothing solution (a win-lose strategy)
- *confrontation and problem-solving*—exchanging views openly, and working through the differences to a mutually acceptable and optimal solution (a win-win strategy)

Most investigations have examined these strategies in the context of superior-subordinate (interpersonal) conflict in organizational settings. Blake et al. (1964) have also examined the varied usefulness of the approaches in both experimental and organizational situations of intergroup conflict (see Chapters 8 and 9). All of these applications are generally supportive of the win-win approach.

In a study of six different organizations, Lawrence and Lorsch (1967) looked at the strategies of smoothing, forcing, and confrontation in relation to overall organizational performance. In the two highest-performing organizations, confrontation was used more than in the remaining four organizations. In the two intermediate organizations, confrontation was used more than in the lowest two. Overall, the absence of forcing and smoothing was related to organizational effectiveness. At the level of the work group, Hill (1977) found that the managers of high-productivity project teams in a large oil company reacted very differently to interpersonal conflict than managers of low-performing teams. They were willing to listen and absorb the aggression of their subordinates, they encouarged openness and emotional expression, and they were aware of the productive utility of conflict. In short, they took a confronting, win-win approach to conflict resolution.

Burke (1970) examined all five strategies in relation to other organizational variables in the areas of job performance and satisfaction. One study asked managers to tell about the typical strategies that they and their supervisors used to resolve conflict in their relationship. Confrontation turned out to the most frequently used method. The type of strategy was then related to the manager's perception of how constructively conflict was dealt with, and of the effectiveness of job planning and evaluation involving both parties. Confrontation and smoothing were positively related to the constructive use of conflict; forcing and withdrawal were negatively related to the same measure. In terms of job planning and evaluation, confrontation was positively related to all measures: the subordinate's participation, the supervisor's helpfulness, and the openness of communication. Forcing, on the other hand, related negatively to these measures. These results indicate that the approach of confrontation and problem solving is one aspect of a more effective interpersonal supervisory relationship.

In a second study, Burke (1970) asked a different group of managers to describe times when they felt particularly good and particularly bad about the way an interpersonal conflict was handled. Their descriptions were then coded into one of the five strategies of conflict resolution. Again confrontation was the most common method (59 percent), followed by forcing (25 percent), and compromise (11 percent). Confrontation was also the most frequently used strategy in cases of effective resolution. Forcing, followed by withdrawal, were the most prominent strategies in cases of ineffective resolution. (In almost all cases where forcing was thought to be effective, the description was provided by the winner of a win-lose conflict!) In Burke's (1970) third study, examining the attitudes underlying confrontation, he found that a supervisor's encouragement and acceptance of disagreement were associated with higher job satisfaction.

We would have to conclude that the attitudes and behaviors of the problem-solving strategy have positive effects on the quality of the supervisory relationship and on the level of satisfaction experienced by the parties. In interpersonal relations especially, it is important to consider all of the implications of the different strategies of conflict management.

A final important note on methods of managing conflict is to consider the effectiveness of a pacifist or nonviolent strategy. As a method of social change, nonviolence is exemplified by the efforts of Mahatma Gandhi toward the independence of India from Britain and of Martin Luther King toward equality for black Americans. These efforts represent a power-coercive strategy of change (see Chapter 11) and a win-lose approach to conflict which, because of its nondestructiveness, paradoxically has the potential of moving the relationship toward greater respect and cooperation.

Some time ago, Janis and Katz (1959) pointed out that social scientists had not given much attention to positive forces and ethical principles in society that might reduce intergroup hostility. They drew on Naess' (1958) systematic statement of Gandhian ethics to develop examples of independent variables that might produce humanitarian ends. For example, refraining from any form of verbal or overt violence and making visible sacrifices for one's cause are central strategies of pacifism. Janis and Katz (1959) also listed dependent variables for assessing the effectiveness of the independent variables, for example, a reduction in violence and a favorable attitude change among the rival group toward the nonviolent group. Hypotheses linking the actions to the effects could be tested with a combination of social-scientific methods.

Unfortunately, only a limited amount of research has been done on pacifist strategies in conflict resolution and what has been done yields mixed results (Reychler, 1979). In experimental games, pacifist players tend to be exploited by their competitive partners. However, Reychler did find that the pacifist strategy was more effective when certain conditions were present: the human distance between opponents is small; the intentions of the pacifist are well known; the opponent must justify his or her behavior afterwards; and a third party is observing the interaction. These are similar to some of the conditions under which nonviolence has been successful in the real world.

Two-Dimensional Model of Conflict Management

Imagine that you are a first-year law student in a prestigious Ivy League school. You are assigned to a study team with five other students. The team's task is to determine the information to be covered, decide on what topics should be given most priority, assign team members to cover particular topics in detail, and use the discussion sessions well so that everyone gets the best possible grades. These are not easy decisions for the team to make, and you soon observe that conflict arises over questions like "Who wants to do what?" and "What topics should we emphasize?"

Having majored in social psychology, you become quite sensitive to the differing ways in which group members approach situations involving conflict. Greg, the outgoing, energetic holder of a hockey scholarship, always pushes to get his way. He talks loud and fast and criticizes alternate proposals. In response to this, mild-mannered Charlie always gives in. He says things like, "Sure Greg, sure. Whatever you think." However, Jan, the captain of the first-year debating team, does not go along that easily. She confronts Greg on the disadvantages of his proposals, presents her own ideas and feelings clearly, and emphasizes that the team must work together effectively so that everyone does well. Charlene is less confronting than Jan, but does offer compromise proposals whenever there is a difference of opinion. Meanwhile, Randy never says a word. He sits back from the table and when asked his opinion says something like, "Oh no, you guys decide. I don't mind." Often, when there is a session with a lot of disagreement, Randy leaves early. Nonetheless, the study team struggles on, and everyone passes the first-term exams.

In times past, social psychologists have taken a rather simplistic view of conflict in situations such as this hypothetical study team. They would attempt to describe everyone's behavior in terms of a single dimension: *competitiveness versus cooperativeness*. Thus, for example, Greg would be seen as highly competitive and Charlie as highly cooperative, and Charlene (the compromiser) as midway in between. But what about Jan or Randy? Jan seems to be both competing and cooperating; Randy is neither. How could their behavior be explained on that single dimension? It cannot, and that's why a more complex model of conflict behavior is required.

The unidimensional definition of conflict has been challenged in recent years by a number of researchers, most notably Kenneth Thomas and his colleagues (Ruble & Thomas, 1976; Thomas, 1976). Following the lead of Blake and Mouton (1964), Thomas (1976) sees that two separate dimensions are important in conflict behavior. One, relating to the party's desire to satisfy his or her own concerns, is *assertiveness*. The second, reflecting the party's desire to satisfy the other's concerns, is *cooperativeness*. By placing these two dimensions at right angles to each other (indicating their independence from each other), we are able to construct a *two-dimensional model of conflict behavior* (see Figure 14.3).

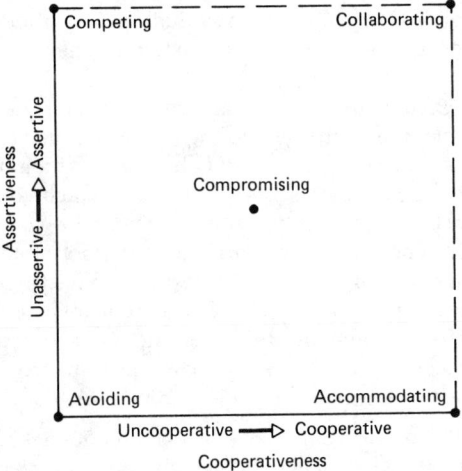

Figure 14.3 Two-Dimensional Model of Conflict Management.
Source: Thomas & Kilmann (1976).

Different combinations of the two basic dimensions of assertiveness and cooperativeness yield the five strategies of conflict management we discussed earlier. These *conflict-handling modes* (Thomas, 1976) include:

- *competing* (or *forcing*), which is highly assertive but uncooperative, in which one party pursues his or her own interests at the other's expense (Greg's style in the study team)
- *avoiding* (or *withdrawal*), which is low on both assertiveness and cooperativeness, and induces a lack of interest in pursuing the concerns of either oneself or the other party (Randy)
- *accommodating* (or *smoothing*), which is high on cooperativeness but low on assertiveness, in which one party sacrifices his or her own interests in order to satisfy the other party (Charlie)
- *compromising*, which is intermediate on both dimensions, and involves finding an expedient, acceptable solution (Charlene)
- *collaborating* (or *confronting* or *problem solving*), in which there is high concern for the interests of both oneself and the other party (Jan)

The two-dimensional model offers a more realistic picture of social conflict, especially since it identifies the high assertive, high cooperative mode of collaborating as an effective strategy for resolving conflict. In the study team, Jan knows that she can be accepting and confronting at the same time. She does not assume that in conflict one must either compete to win *or* cooperate and lose. She works to do both, thus meeting her own goals and those of other members simultaneously.

Research has supported the validity of the two-dimensional model. Ruble and Thomas (1976) found that the two major dimensions of assertiveness and cooperativeness were related to the two general factors of activity and evaluation which people use to assign meaning to much of our social behavior (as shown by research on the Semantic Differential—see Chapter 3). They also found that the collaborating mode is perceived as high in both activity and evaluation whereas competing is high on activity but low on evaluation. The model thus predicts how people perceive the various modes in relation to the general factors of activity and evaluation.

In a more practical vein, Thomas and his colleagues have developed a self-report measure of the five conflict-handling modes—called the *MODE* (Management of Differences Exercise) *Instrument* (Thomas & Kilmann, 1974; Kilmann & Thomas, 1977). This measure presents situations in which your (the respondent's) wishes differ from those of another person, and asks you to chose how you usually respond. The choices are presented in pairs, each statement representing a particular mode, and you are asked to choose one. This forced-choice technique was followed in developing the MODE Instrument to reduce social desirability responding that affects some of the other measures of conflict management strategies (see Chapter 3). Here are some example items from the MODE Instrument with the underlying mode shown in parentheses:

1. (a) I try to find a compromise solution. (compromising)
   (b) I attempt to deal with all of his and my concerns. (collaborating)
2. (a) I try to avoid creating unpleasantness for myself. (avoiding)
   (b) I try to win my position. (competing)

3. (a) I attempt to get all concerns and issues immediately out into the open.
(collaborating)
   (b) I might try to soothe the other's feelings and preserve our relationship.
(accommodating)

After completing all questions, you score your own instrument by adding up the number of choices you gave for each mode. You then use the two-dimensional model to interpret your score. Thomas and Kilmann (1974) stress that there are no right or wrong answers—all five modes are useful in some situations. Few people are charateried as having only a single, rigid style of dealing with conflict (as in our hypothetical study team). Most of us are capable of moving from mode to mode as appropriate. There are times when it is best to avoid, to compete, to compromise, and to accommodate. However, when conditions are right, it is the collaborating mode that will bring the most accomplishment and satisfaction to *both* parties.

The MODE Instrument is a reliable and valid measure for assessing individual approaches to managing conflict (Kilmann & Thomas, 1977). A number of studies have related mode scores to other measures of personality in ways that support the validity of the instrument. Introverted individuals tend to score higher on avoidance while persons who emphasize expressing feeling rather than thinking score higher on accommodating (Kilmann & Thomas, 1975). Persons strong on achievement tend to use the collaborating mode, whereas high aggression relates to competing. Finally, Kilmann and Thomas (1977) report a positive relationship between compromising and Machiavellianism scores (see Chapter 6), which indicate a tendency to get the best deal regardless of principles. Personality characteristics and motives thus relate in meaningful ways to the manner in which people deal with conflict.

The two-dimensional model thus helps us understand conflict behavior more clearly. But what are the practical implications? How can we put the model into practice?

First, let's consider how we put the two dimensions of cooperativeness and assertiveness into action. Cooperativeness means showing a genuine concern for the other person's outcomes. If you are genuinely concerned—and if this is reflected in your basic attitude toward the other party—you can use the appropriate communication skills and core interpersonal skills (see Chapter 6) to demonstrate cooperativeness. Paraphrasing and perception-checking, or empathizing with the other person's thought and feelings, can go a long way to show that you understand his or her point of view and respect that person's concerns. The other person is then much more predisposed to take a cooperative stance toward *your* concerns.

The dimension of assertiveness is expressed in the way you describe your own feelings or genuineness, describe your own and the other party's behavior, and use concreteness to improve the accuracy of communication. The more advanced interpersonal skills of immediacy (sharing mutual perceptions of each other and your relationship) and confrontation (pointing out discrepancies in the other's behavior) are also essential to assertiveness.

Finally, sensitivity to the problem-solving sequence (see Chapter 4) is necessary if you want to put the collaborative strategy into practice. All of these awarenesses and behaviors must be blended into a systematic process of interpersonal or intergroup conflict resolution for maximum effectiveness.

Resolving interpersonal conflict is one of the most complex and difficult tasks I know. It usually involves issues that people really care about and strong feelings that are difficult to express clearly and cleanly. When we are angry, for example, we often make accusations, call names, or give ultimatums. These behaviors may only make the situation worse. That is why it is so important to follow a systematic sequence of problem solving to confront conflict.

Let's imagine that you are a student representative on a university committee that oversees the running of the student center on campus. The other student rep, Sheila, is an old acquaintance, but not a close friend. This is the first time you have ever worked on a committee together and you are initially enthusiastic about this. However, almost every time you begin to talk at committee meetings, Sheila interrupts with her own ideas and then takes the discussion away from your area of concern. You are initially surprised, and then angry about her consistent interjections. You find yourself at an impasse. What do you do? Stop contributing to the meetings? Interrupt Sheila and get the focus back on your concerns? Before jumping to solutions, you have to decide whether it is appropriate and worthwhile to confront the conflict openly. Do the potential benefits outweigh the possible risks? Is your relationship with Sheila worth the effort? If you do decide to talk directly with Sheila, the following steps are crucial elements of the problem-solving process:

1. *Contracting.* Approach Sheila about the problem and reach an agreement to sit down and talk about it. You should state the problem with genuineness and clear behavior description rather than being vague and accusing. For example, "Sheila, I've been interrupted several times by you in the committee meetings and I'm becoming angry about it," rather than "I need to talk with you about your inconsiderate behavior in the committee meetings." You should also agree upon a mutually agreeable time and place to meet, free from interruptions, to discuss the issue.

2. *Problem Definition and Diagnosis.* Both you and Sheila can use the interpersonal skills to gain a clear understanding of the conflict as you both see it. Paraphrasing and perception-checking are very useful here. You may be in for some surprises: Sheila says, "I'm surprised I interrupted you that much, and I am sorry about it. But did you realize that a number of times you were changing the topic under discussion, and I was attempting to bring it back on track. I was afraid the faculty and administrators would see us as not being able to stick to an agenda."

3. *Problem Solution.* Given adequate diagnosis, you and Sheila develop some alternative behaviors to resolve the difficulty. You agree to watch the agenda more closely. Sheila agrees not to interrupt you, but to directly bring the discussion back to the agenda if necessary when you are finished.

4. *Closure.* Both you and Sheila reaffirm your understanding of the behaviors that will contribute to the solution, and you agree to evaluate the outcomes following a trial implementation. It's also a good idea to share your perceptions and feelings about resolving the conflict since the experience can help establish a more open and trusting relationship. In the next committee meeting, you stay on topic more and Sheila interrupts less. You are both very pleased with your new found effectiveness.

Productively resolving interpersonal conflict such as in this example can and does happen if people put a lot of patience and skill into their relationships. Usually, the more intimate the relationship, the more difficult to resolve conflict because the issues are more important and the feelings stronger. Detailed strategies for skill usage and problem solving in marriages and other close relationships have been developed by George Bach and his colleagues (Bach & Wyden, 1968; Bach & Goldberg, 1974). Similar guidelines for resolving parent-child and parent-teenager conflict are offered by Haim Ginott (1965, 1969). See Box 14.4 for an example of resolving roommate conflicts in a college setting.

Box 14.4   FOCUS ON PRACTICE AND RESEARCH
Resolving Interpersonal Conflict Between College Roommates

In college residence halls, conflict often arises between roommates due to the obnoxious behavior of one roommate as experienced by the other. For example, one roommate may be typing a paper at 2 A.M., thus preventing the other from getting any sleep. The annoyed individual attempts to change the obnoxious behavior, for example, by using sarcasm ("Boy, you're sure a high achiever!"), or by refusing to lend typing paper, or even by moving out. Such responses are usually unproductive. Grant Miller and Stephen Zoradi of the California Polytechnic State University applied and evaluated a more productive, seven-step problem-solving approach for resolving such conflicts.

- First, the residence hall adviser achieves *problem recognition* by setting up a meeting to discuss the conflict with the two roommates. For example, one student, Jan, came to her adviser in tears about her roommate Liz's cigarette smoking, to which Jan was allergic. The adviser discussed the problem with Liz, established some trust, and arranged a time for all three to meet.
- Second, the adviser achieves *problem definition* by listening to the stories of both roommates. Jan maintained she could not live in a room filled with cigarette smoke.
- Third, each roommate must give a *commitment* to solve the problem by negotiating an agreement or contract. Even though Jan and Liz felt hostile toward each other, they agreed to try this approach.
- Fourth, the adviser helps the roommates *highlight pleasing and displeasing behaviors* that can then be negotiated to satisfy the needs of both. Jan disliked Liz's smoking in the room, her insistence that the window be left closed, and her watching television while Jan was studying. Liz appreciated Jan's help with her homework.
- The fifth step of *negotiation* involves trading behaviors until a mutually satisfactory solution is achieved. Liz agreed to smoke in the hall or lounge if Jan would keep the window closed until 11 P.M. and study in the library three evenings a week so Liz could watch television.
- The sixth step of *contracting* requires the listing of the specific behavioral commitments signed by the two roommates.
- Seventh, *follow-up* is provided by negotiating new contracts weekly as provided, a process from which the adviser withdraws as soon as possible. Jan and Liz established a more open, trusting relationship, and after one week a contract was no longer required.

Miller and Zoradi evaluated their approach by training advisers in one residence hall and consulting with them on a weekly basis. A similar residence hall served as a control. Halfway through the academic year, the trained advisers had reported forty-one conflicts and had used the procedure twenty-four times. The control hall advisers reported only eighteen conflicts, probably because they were less sensitive to conflict than the trained advisers. More importantly, there were ninety-seven roommate changes in the control hall and only forty-eight in the trained hall. It is likely that the conflict resolution program was a major factor in this dramatic reduction.

Source: Miller, G. D. & Zoradi, S. D. Roommate conflict resolution. *Journal of College Student Personnel*, 1977, May, 228–230.

Third-Party Consultation

All of the material in this chapter constitutes useful knowledge and guidance for people who wish to handle social conflict more effectively. But there is one more step that applied social psychologists can take; we can use our knowledge and our skills to intervene directly in situations of social conflict. In doing so, we can study the processes and outcomes of conflict while we help the people involved deal with their differences more effectively.

My prime reason for becoming an applied social psychologist was to help find ways to reduce the destructiveness of both intergroup and international conflict. After studying the ethnocentric attitudes that typically attend intergroup conflict, my first interest in entering doctoral study at the University of Michigan was to search for ways to increase the effectiveness of international negotiation. However, my adviser at the time, Daniel Katz, brought to my attention a pioneering manuscript by Richard Walton on resolving interpersonal conflicts between business executives (Walton, 1969). (See Box 14.5).

I soon related to Walton's ideas the work of Robert Blake and his colleagues on intergroup conflict in industry (see Chapter 9), and that of John Burton on controlled communication in international relations (see Chapter 12). What struck me most were the similarities in these different approaches: the involvement of a social-science consultant as an impartial third party working to help the antagonists resolve their differences more effectively. Based on this realization, I became involved in the development, application, and evaluation of a general model of third-party consultation.

It is important to distinguish this type of work from other forms of third-party intervention such as arbitration and mediation. *Arbitration* involves a third-party judgment that is arrived at by considering the merits of the opposing cases and then imposing a settlement. *Mediation* involves a skilled third party who attempts to help the clients reach a compromise on specific issues that are amenable to negotiation. *Third-party consultation* seeks exploration and creative problem solving with regard to the basic relationship and the emotional issues of the conflict. There is no interest in imposing or facilitating the negotiation of specific issues, although consultation is designed to de-escalate the conflict so that

Box 14.5   FOCUS ON PRACTICE
Third-Party Consultation

Interpersonal conflict is a fact of social life in all organizations. Disagreements over substantive issues, such as organizational policy, as well as interpersonal antagonisms, typically arise between interdependent individuals. Richard Walton of Harvard University's Graduate School of Business was the first scholar/practitioner to propose a systematic model through which an outside third party could facilitate the resolution of intense interpersonal conflicts in organizational settings. Equipped with knowledge of organizational behavior and the skills of a sensitivity trainer, Walton performed the third-party role in a number of conflicts and developed a model based on his experience.

Bill and Lloyd were both program directors in a large government agency. Bill was responsible for the development of a new information sharing system for the organization, but had to rely on Lloyd's unit to supply much of the professional talent for the project. At a large meeting of staffs from both units and other departments, Lloyd expressed some misgivings about the project which were quite disconcerting to Bill. Bill wanted to build a better working relationship with Lloyd and requested the third-party consultant to meet with them. Lloyd agreed to discuss his concerns about the project and to try to improve his relationship with Bill.

At the confrontation meeting, Lloyd charged that his staff were involved only as technicians and advisers rather than as planners and designers of the project and that he had little say in how they were used. Bill responded to these concerns. At this point, the third party intervened to summarize and move the confrontation to the interpersonal level, for example, to Lloyd's dislike of Bill's loose leadership style and Bill's insensitivity to Lloyd's need for recognition. Discussion of these interpersonal issues facilitated by the third party helped Bill and Lloyd understand each other better and establish a dialogue on the issues between them. Several months later, the project was operating well, and Lloyd and Bill had developed a high regard for each other.

Walton sees the key to successful conflict resolution as direct confrontation wherein the parties engage each other and discuss the issues between them. The third party facilitates productive confrontation through a number of strategic functions—synchronizing confrontation efforts, pacing the phases of the dialogue through differentiation and integration, promoting openness, enhancing communication, and maintaining a productive level of tension. To enact this demanding role, a number of attributes are required including professional expertise and neutrality regarding outcomes. When conditions are appropriate, a third party can serve an important if not essential role in resolving interpersonal conflict.

Source: Walton, R. L. *Interpersonal peacemaking: Confrontations and third party consultation.* Reading, Mass.: Addison-Wesley, 1969.

meaningful and rational negotiation can take place. In the process, consultation hopes to shift the parties from a win-lose or lose-lose approach to a win-win orientation in terms of both attitudes and behaviors.

A Model. My initial model of third-party consultation (Fisher, 1972) was based mainly on the approaches of Walton (1969), Blake et al. (1964), and Burton (1969). The work of Leonard Doob on intergroup and international conflict resolution and of Virginia Satir on family therapy also influenced my thinking. The model was an attempt to simply describe the essential elements of third-party consultation so we could better understand this type of intervention. A revision of the initial model (Fisher, 1976b) is given in Figure 14.4.

Each of the circles represents a major component of the method; the only major addition to the initial 1972 model is the helping-relationship component. First, we must consider who is appropriate and able to serve as a third-party consultant. My view is that the *third-party identity* should be that of an impartial, skilled social scientist/practitioner. The consultant should not be biased toward one side or the other in the conflict and should behave in a fair and unbiased manner in order to maintain impartiality.

Skill at intervening is based on both knowledge and training in human relations in general and on conflict resolution in particular. The knowledge required is the knowledge that social science has accumulated on the sources, variations, processes, and outcomes of social conflict. The skills come from training experiences in interpersonal relations, small-group facilitation, and or-

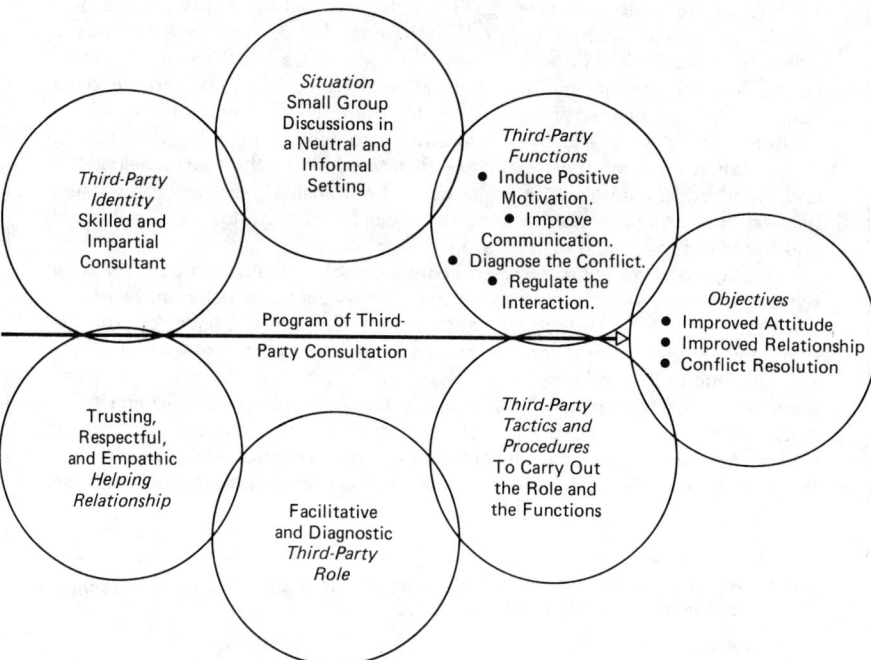

Figure 14.4   Model of Third-Party Consultation.
Source: Fisher (1976).

ganizational and community consulting (see Chapter 4). The knowledge and skills are necessary for the third party to facilitate productive confrontation between the parties—that is, to encourage them to discuss the conflict as they see it and feel it, and to look for collaborative mechanisms that will resolve it peacefully.

This identity lays the basis for an effective *helping relationship* with each of the parties, involving trust, respect, and understanding. This helping relationship, built on the humanistic value base, is similar to that which must be established to do effective counseling, teaching, or consulting (see Chapter 6).

The *situation* describes the essential physical and social arrangements of the method. Usually, the consultant arranges a series of informal small-group discussions that focus directly on the nature of the conflict. The setting or meeting place should be on neutral ground and have an atmosphere of informality to encourage openness and innovation.

The *third-party role* refers to the pattern of behavior that is appropriate to the method. It is basically facilitative and diagnostic; that is, the consultant works to help the parties analyze and understand their relationship and the conflict between them. The consultant must also be nonevaluative and noncoercive so that the parties will express themselves and make their decisions openly and freely. The consultant is nondirective over solutions or outcome, but does control the process of the discussions.

The core strategies of the method are expressed in the *third-party functions.* These include:

- inducing mutual positive motivation for collaborative problem solving
- improving both the openness and accuracy of communication through the use of interpersonal and group skills
- diagnosing the conflict by applying social science concepts and theories
- regulating the interaction by confronting and limiting destructive behavior, and by moving the discussions through the phases of problem solving

The functions are put into practice through the *third-party tactics and procedures.* Tactics are specific behaviors such as paraphrasing or confronting; procedures are more complex exercises such as the development and exchange of intergroup images. If the functions, tactics, and procedures are operationalized effectively, the consultant will be successful in establishing the related conditions of problem-solving motivation, open and accurate communication, diagnostic orientation, and regulated interaction—all of which are essential to productive confrontation.

There is then some chance of reaching the *objectives* of third-party consultation. These include:

- improved attitudes in which the parties come to see each other more realistically and feel less antagonistic toward each other
- an improved relationship, involving a shift from a destructive, competitive win-lose approach to a trusting, collaborative win-win orientation
- true resolution of the conflict, involving solutions that are freely agreed upon and mutually satisfactory, and a commitment to work on future differences before they escalate into an intense conflict

One further objective specified in the initial model is the study of conflict. In other words, third-party consultation provides an excellent opportunity for social scientists to get out in the real world and study ongoing conflicts in a detailed and intensive manner. If we can come to understand conflict as it unfolds before our eyes, we have the chance of gaining insights that are not available through any other method. Third-party consultation thus has the potential of serving both the needs of social science and the needs of humanity.

Implementing and Evaluating the Model. After developing the initial model of third-party consultation, I intended to implement the method in a variety of conflicts and to evaluate its effectiveness for guiding practice and for producing the specified objectives. It was necessary that initial application involve pilot research on low-intensity conflicts, so that I did not run the ethical and practical risk of intervening ineffectively in highly charged crises.

To evaluate the model well, I needed a combination of research methods and a variety of evaluations in order to focus on different aspects of the consultation process. Case study observations had to be complemented by quantitative measures such as rating scales, questionnaires, and interviews in order to understand both the process and the outcomes of third-party consultation. Brief illustrations of the model as it has been implemented and evaluated follow.

After graduating from Michigan, I went to the University of Guelph and became involved in community development activities. Along with a colleague, James White, I served as a third-party consultant to help resolve conflicts among different community groups. These applications resulted in some successes and some failures and were described using the case study method (Fisher & White, 1976a). During the same period, I continued my own training in interpersonal and small-group skills to further develop my ability to enact the third-party role.

One of the conflicts involved an insidious division between public housing tenants and private homeowners living in a suburban neighborhood (Fisher & White, 1976b). Five streets in the area were physically split down the middle—the drab and uniform public housing units on one side, the attractive and varied private dwellings on the other. This division was paralleled by a social-psychological schism that exhibited many of the common characteristics of destructive intergroup conflict: stereotyping, discrimination, hostility, ineffective communication, and a lack of motivation to improve the relationship. Many private homeowners saw the public housing tenants as lazy "welfare bums" who contributed little to the commuity and whose housing units reduced property values in the neighborhood. Public housing families were seen as "problem families" whose lack of motivation and morals were a source of such social problems as delinquency and crime. From the other side, many tenants saw homeowners as "cold, conceited snobs" whose main concern was their property values and their sense of self-importance. While there was some overt hostility and discrimination, mainly among the children, the two groups tended to live in segregation with little interaction or hope of improvement. A number of worthwhile community projects, such as the acquisition of a neighborhood recreation center, had not only been thwarted by the conflict but had become issues through which the conflict had escalated.

James White and I organized a pilot program of third-party consultation that brought members of the two groups together to discuss their perceptions of each other and the neighborhood and to speculate about what an ideal relationship would be. We hoped that some positive attitude change would result in the areas of increased complexity, favorableness, and orientations toward the conflict. Consequently, we first interviewed all potential participants and assigned them to a discussion group or a nondiscussion control group. Following the problem-solving discussions, which consisted of four meetings of 3 hours each, all discussion and control group members were again interviewed. The interviews were intensive, structured sessions that used open questions to assess the respondent's perceptions of the neighborhood, the intergroup relationship, the other group, the ideal relationship, and the future of the neighborhood.

To transform the interview responses into a quantitative measure of attitudes, we used content analysis. Based on earlier consultation work involving high school students and teachers (Fisher, 1976a), we developed rating scales and coding categories to measure the complexity, positiveness, and behavioral orientations of each person's attitudes (Fisher, 1977b). This yielded a reliable numerical measure from the rich information provided in the interview. Analysis of the results showed significant differences in attitude change between the discussion group and the control group in the areas of complexity and positiveness, but not in orientations to improve the relationship. Participants' reactions to the program of consultation were quite positive, and a number of people from both sides became more involved in community development activities.

These outcomes pleased us both as socially concerned practitioners and as social scientists since we had demonstrated that the method was effective in reaching the outcome of improved attitudes. But the *process* of third-party consultation deserves further study to see how the role, the functions, and the tactics are actually put into action in establishing the problem-solving atmosphere.

I was able to study the process of a third-party consultation in a workshop that focused on a difficult arena of international relations: the India-Pakistan conflict. A small group of Indian and Pakistani nationals living in Canada took part in a pilot program of third-party consultation that was organized with the help of William Feader, the international student adviser at the University of Saskatchewan (Fisher, 1980a). We held a series of discussions about the present relationship between the countries, the national images of one's own group and the other group, the ideal relationship, and the major issues and potential solutions to the conflict. Case study analysis and postinterviews indicated that the model was successfully instituted and that the workshop had beneficial effects on the attitudes of the participants. At the same time, a number of difficult issues were not resolved, including the status of the territory of Kashmir, an independent state at the time India and Pakistan were formed, and a state still claimed by both countries.

In order to study the process of the workshop, all sessions were tape-recorded and subjected to content analysis using Bales' Interaction Process Analysis (see Chapter 3). In addition, the behavior of the consultants was coded using a set of categories based on the functions and tactics described in the model. The

Interaction Process Analysis indicated that the workshop sessions were very similar to other types of small-group, problem-solving discussions.

The analysis of third-party functions and tactics made sense in terms of the model (see Table 14.2). Inducing problem-solving motivation was the most prominent function, especially at the beginning of the workshop where it was essential. Improving communication was important throughout and peaked during the middle sessions. Diagnosing the conflict became more important toward the end of the workshop when problem-solving motivation and communication were more established. Regulating the interaction, used more at the beginning, decreased throughout as participants adjusted to the norms and atmo-

Table 14.2   PROCESS OF THIRD-PARTY CONSULTATION IN TERMS OF FUNCTIONS AND TACTICS

Function and Tactic	Observed Percentage of Total Acts				
	Meeting 1	Meeting 2	Meeting 3	Meeting 4	All Meetings
1. *Inducing positive motivation*					
a. Encouraging problem solving	5.7	6.7	3.6	1.1	4.5
b. Supporting participants	40.3	19.2	37.8	28.6	30.8
c. Maintaining optimum tension	2.2	3.0	1.0	8.2	3.5
d. Balancing situational power	1.5	3.7	1.3	.0	1.8
Total	49.7	32.6	43.7	37.9	40.6
2. *Improving communication*					
a. Eliciting information	9.5	16.6	12.0	6.0	11.4
b. Paraphrasing, empathizing	3.2	1.0	3.3	.5	2.0
c. Translating, clarifying	8.5	18.6	23.0	14.2	16.2
d. Summarizing	2.7	3.4	6.5	1.9	3.6
Total	23.9	39.6	44.8	22.6	33.2
3. *Diagnosing the conflict*					
a. Injecting information	5.5	11.5	4.6	34.9	13.6
b. Processing and feedback	.2	.4	.3	.8	.4
c. Stimulating self-diagnosis	2.5	1.8	1.8	.5	1.7
Total	8.2	13.7	6.7	36.2	15.7
4. *Regulating the interaction*					
a. Pacing the phases	4.5	1.6	1.0	.0	1.8
b. Initiating-monitoring agenda	12.7	8.9	2.8	3.3	7.1
c. Controlling disruptive interaction	1.0	3.6	1.0	.0	1.6
Total	18.2	14.1	4.8	3.3	10.5

Source: Fisher (1980a).

sphere of the workshop. These initial results appear to support the validity of the model for guiding and capturing the essential features of third-party consultation.

In my opinion, the potential utility of third-party consultation for resolving social conflict has been adequately demonstrated. However, a great deal remains to be done. Recently, I reviewed a wide range of intergroup interventions in community, organizational, and international settings that can be subsumed under the model (Fisher, 1981a). While the work is truly promising, most of the evaluation is based on pilot studies using case study analysis. Although there has been a wide variety of applications, the theoretical base is limited mainly to a general description of the method, with a few guidelines for the would-be practitioner. Few applications have been assessed with quantitative measures within well-controlled research designs. Thus, it would be premature to conclude that the method is effective for resolving intergroup conflict. Most pilot work involves participants who are members of the groups in conflict but not representatives or decision makers. Thus, attitudes may improve among participants but this does not improve the wider relationship between the parties.

Future research must become more concerned with how to transfer the effects of consultation to real-world conflicts. We must also show greater concern for the training of third-party consultants (Fisher, 1976b). Given the potential of third-party consultation for increasing our awareness and ability to deal with dysfunctional conflict, we should proceed with all possible haste. The existence and costs of destructive social conflict will not go away by themselves.

Summary

The costs of destructive human conflict are tragically apparent, but conflict is also an important source of useful social change. Conflict involves incompatible goals and activities between individuals or groups who hold antagonistic feelings toward each other and attempt to control each other.

Aggression—one element of social conflict—refers to behavior that is intended to inflict harm or injury. Some social scientists believe that aggression is an innate instinct or drive, others see it as a response to frustration, while others perceive it primarily as a learned behavior.

Definitions of conflict emphasize incompatibility and attempt to distinguish conflict from related social processes, particularly competition. Common types of conflict include economic, power, and value conflict. Most conflicts do not have a single source and most are prone to escalation where stronger attempts to influence are mixed with increasing misperception and hostility.

Interpersonal conflict is often the result of incompatible motives, styles or goals and can be seen as moving through six stages. Conflict in groups arises from numerous sources, and the general approach (conflictual or collaborative) that groups take to social relations (based on perceptions of the situation as distributive or integrative) will strongly influence how much conflict occurs and how it is handled. Much of the conflict in organizations is between competing interest groups and sources are generally found in problems of communication, conflicts of interest, and a lack of consensus on perceptions and values.

The humanistic value base calls for the involvement of applied social psychologists as scientist/practitioners in conflict resolution—applying knowledge and skills through consultation in order to find constructive means for resolving social conflict.

Human beings have at least as much potential for caring, sharing, and cooperating as they do for aggression, competing, and destroying. Prosocial behaviors are activities that have positive social consequences for others. Bystander intervention in emergencies has received much attention in an attempt to delineate the conditions that affect helping behavior. Research on the stages of perceiving an emergency, assuming responsibility, wanting to help, and having the ability to help show that a number of factors in each stage determines whether help is given.

Approaches to managing conflict differ in assumptions about people and about conflict, characteristic attitudes and behaviors, and typical outcomes. The win-lose approach assumes conflict is inevitable, but agreement is impossible. The lose-lose approach assumes avoidance of conflict is preferably to open confrontation and half a loaf is better than none. The win-win approach is a conscious and systematic attempt to maximize the gains of both parties through collaborative problem solving.

The two-dimensional model of conflict states that assertiveness (to satisfy own concerns) and cooperativeness (to satisfy other's concerns) are both necessary to understand people's approach and behavior toward conflict. The model yields five conflict-handling modes, which are similar to the strategies defined under the major approaches. The MODE Instrument has enabled the study of the relationship between conflict-handling modes and personality characteristics. We need to use the interpersonal communication skills and the problem-solving sequence to operationalize both assertiveness and cooperativeness in order to resolve conflict constructively.

Based on our knowledge of conflict and our skills in human relations, applied social psychologists have the oportunity to intervene directly in situations of destructive social conflict. The method of third-party consultation centers on the facilitative and diagnostic actions of an impartial social-science consultant who helps the antagonists understand and resolve their differences. The major components of the model include the identity, role, functions, and tactics of the third party, the helping relationship, the situation, and the objectives.

Further Readings

Baron, R. A. *Human aggression.* New York: Plenum, 1977.

Coser, L. A. *Continuities in social conflict.* Glencoe, Ill.: Free Press, 1967.

Deutsch, M. *The resolution of conflict: Constructive and destructive processes.* New Haven: Yale University Press, 1973.

Filley, C. *Interpersonal conflict resolution.* Glenview, Ill.: Scott, Foresman, 1975.

McNeil, E. B. (Ed.). *The nature of human conflict.* Englewood Cliffs, N.J.: Prentice-Hall, 1965.

Walton, R. E. *Interpersonal peacemaking: Confrontations and third party consultation.* Reading, Mass.: Addison-Wesley, 1969.

CHAPTER OUTLINE

FIFTEEN

Contemporary Areas of Application: Education, Environment, and Law

It is 1970. A member of the Black Panthers (a militant black civil rights group) is charged with the murder of a white police officer in Toledo, Ohio. The evidence is mainly circumstantial. The defense attorneys are concerned about the prospect of getting a fair trial by jury. They arrange to have two well-known social psychologists testify during the jury selection process. The social psychologists produce research results and testify that in their opinion it is doubtful that an unbiased jury could be selected from the juror list of predominantly white, older, nonprofessional people. Survey findings are used to indicate that older, less educated, white male jurors would likely be biased against a young black militant and would tend to favor the death penalty. On this basis, the judge allows the defense attorneys to ask the potential jurors detailed questions about their opinions and attitudes. A jury of ten whites and two blacks is chosen. They are unable to reach a verdict.

In New York City, an apartment building is constructed over a multilane highway. The traffic noise is conspicuous on the lower floors. Three social-environmental psychologists become concerned about the effects of the noise on the children who live in the building. First, they measure the noise levels and find them to be significantly higher on the lower floors. Next, they assess the hearing and reading performance of the children. Compared to children living on the higher floors, those living on the lower floors show deficiencies on both measures. These results support a growing concern about the negative effects of environmental stress on human development and behavior.

Two organizational psychologists implement a program of organization development in seven schools. Teams of teachers and principals participate in training workshops that focus on human relations and problem-solving skills. Follow-up consultation, intensive training, and coordinating meetings are provided. Compared to untrained teachers in control schools, teachers from the seven schools subsequently report greater participation in discussion and decision making and more direct handling of conflict. Furthermore, new teachers entering these schools after one year show a similar level of acquisition and use of the human relations skills. In addition, teachers who participate in the program show increased agreement on the educational goals of their school.

Each of these situations shows the involvement of social psychologists in important areas of social concern: the fair dispensation of justice, the effects of environmental stress, the quality of education. Each represents an attempt to apply in some combination the theory, research, and practice skills that are developing within applied social psychology. Each represents a growing area of endeavor that will continue to expand as social psychology moves through the 1980s.

However, it would be inaccurate and unfair to imply that the involvement of psychologists in social problems is limited to the current work of applied social psychologists. In one of the first comprehensive statements of applied psychology's contributions to social problems, Anastasi (1964) identified a number of fields of applied psychology—including clinical, counseling, personnel, engineering, and consumer psychology—and the contributions that psychologists were making to law, education, and medicine. Many of these joint efforts, integrating the work of professionals from many different specialties, go back many years, in some cases to the early 1900s. In each case, Anastasi maintains that the most distinctive contribution that psychologists can make is in the application of their research methods, rather than through theoretical understanding or practice expertise.

This brings us to the important similarities between applied psychology and applied social psychology. Both involve psychologists in real-world settings, working on problems of concern to society. Both require the application of research expertise, a distinctive asset, directed toward interdisciplinary efforts. Theory and practice are not ignored, but ideally are integrated with research into a powerful combination of understanding and action.

Applied psychology, however, focuses almost entirely on the individual, applied social psychology is concerned with all levels of analysis, with particular emphasis on the group, the program unit, the organization, and the community. (It would therefore be appropriate to speak of "applied individual psychology" as contrasted to applied social psychology.) In addition, applied social psychology, with its two contributing disciplines of psychology and sociology, is inherently interdisciplinary; applied psychology is an extension of psychology into interdisciplinary settings. Thus, we can identify applied social psychology as a distinctive, relatively new and emerging expansion and application of social-psychological theory, research, and practice. The individual level is important, but not central; the challenge is to integrate theory, research, and practice at levels of analysis that are relevant to the problem being addressed.

SOCIAL PSYCHOLOGY OF EDUCATION

Just think of the large part of our lives that we spend in school. From age six (or earlier) to age eighteen (or later), we spend the largest portion of our waking hours in educational settings—in playschools, elementary schools, secondary schools, colleges, and universities. Many of us are well into adulthood (I was 28) before we leave the school setting to fully embark on our careers and our lives.

During all this time in educational settings, we are involved in many important processes and outcomes. True, we are learning facts, but we are also being socialized in the predominant values and roles of our culture. We are interacting with some of the most significant individuals we will ever meet—our teachers. We establish interpersonal relationships with others, and we become members of many influential peer groups. We are also learning to be members of an organization that has many counterparts in our later lives. In short, our experience in school is a dynamic, complex process with important outcomes that shape our future in a variety of subtle and pervasive ways.

Because of the importance of social interaction in schools, you might expect that social psychologists would have long shown an intense interest in educational settings. Not so. Early social psychology barely dealt with the relationship between social psychology and education, at least in any systematic fashion (Getzels, 1969). In the first handbook of social psychology (Lindzey, 1954), there was no chapter on education, and the index of over 1,000 items contained only three references to education. The few early studies that did look at social variables in education settings emphasized instruction or teaching and evaluation of student performance (Lindgren, 1978).

Over the last twenty years, however, the picture has changed. The late 1940s showed an interest in social-psychological variables. By the 1970s, this trend had clearly developed, emphasizing social processes and structures in educational settings. Social psychologists were ready to contribute to the understanding and improvement of educational institutions. In the second handbook of social psychology, Getzel's (1969) chapter developed an orderly framework for a social psychology of education, derived a number of basic issues, and reviewed empirical work relating to these issues. Getzels' fundamental point is that the social psychology of education should deal with behavior in the educational setting *conceived as a social system*—a system that provides the context for interpersonal and group behavior.

From age six (or earlier) to age eighteen (or later), we spend most of our waking hours in school. (© *Michael Heron 1981/Woodfin Camp & Associates*)

In a more recent text, Bar-Tal and Saxe (1978) lament the relatively few applications of social psychology to education compared with the contributions of learning theory or developmental psychology. These authors distinguish between social psychology *for* education and social psychology *of* education. (This distinction is similar to the one I made in Chapter 1—the difference between "applying social psychology" and "applied social psychology.") Social psychology *for* education merely uses basic social-psychological principles—derived largely through laboratory research on college students—to explain problems in educational settings. While this may acquaint educators with social-psychological thinking, it lacks the validity and relevance to educational issues. In contrast, the social psychology *of* education takes a problem focus by emphasizing social-psychological issues that concern the social functioning of individuals and groups in educational systems. For example, teachers can understand conformity pressures enforcing social norms by reading about experimental studies in the laboratory. It is quite a different matter to grasp how student norms actually develop in the classroom and how students influence one another toward conformity. Thus, the problems arise from and are studied in educational settings using the conceptual and methodological tools of social psychology. This in turn can be useful for social psychology since unique educational problems can challenge the discipline to develop new theories and methods that may have general utility and relevance.

Most approaches to the social psychology of education try to apply general principles while covering studies that focus on specific problems in educational settings (such as Backman & Secord, 1968; Guskin & Guskin, 1970; Johnson, 1970). These approaches thus fall within *educational psychology*, a broader field concerned with the relationship between the entire field of psychology and the processes and outcomes of education (Lindgren, 1962; 1978). Along similar lines, the social psychology of education is related to *educational sociology*, a subdiscipline that emphasizes social interaction, socialization, and the place of the school in the larger commuity and in society (Brookover, 1955; Brookover & Erickson, 1975).

One of the easier ways to comprehend the social psychology of education is to use the levels-of-analysis approach. A great deal of work in educational psychology has focused on the individual level of analysis, looking at individual student or teacher characteristics and behavior in relation to educational outcomes.

There has also been considerable interest in matching students to teaching styles or educational environments most conducive to their learning. The subfield of *instructional psychology* (Glaser, 1978; McKeachie, 1974; Wittrock & Lumsdaine, 1977) has evolved to address this question of maximizing the teaching-learning process. This focus blends into the interpersonal level of analysis (the first truly social-psychological level), emphasizing the relationship between the student and the teacher, including their role expectations and the quality of their social interaction.

The group is an essential level of analysis in the social psychology of education. The dynamics of group functioning, including the aspect of leadership, greatly influence what happens in classrooms. Similarly, intergroup relations are played out in ways that have profound impact on educational settings. Furthermore, since schools are organizations, a focus on the organizational level of analysis helps us better understand schools and develop strategies for useful educational change. Finally, because the school is embedded in the larger community and in society, we must not lose sight of these larger systems if we wish to understand the educational process.

This brief invocation of the levels of analysis indicates the complexity and challenge of the social psychology of education. Although in the limited space we have here we cannot do justice to the range and the depth of this relatively well-developed area of applied social psychology, we can look at illustrations of theory, research, and practice that will give us its flavor. It is especially worthwhile to examine applications and interventions that can improve the quality of educational outcomes for students and teachers—and, consequently, for all of us.

Understanding the Educational Process

Let us look at one theory and one research technique particularly helpful in illuminating the educational process. The theory of interest is role theory, as discussed in Chapter 2; the research method is that of interaction analysis, described in Chapter 3.

Role Theory. The power of role theory lies in its capacity to explain the behavior of different personalities by emphasizing how actions derive from the expectations and obligations of a social position (Guskin & Guskin, 1970). Thus role theory has excellent applicability to educational settings because of the limited number of central roles in such settings: namely the teacher, the student, and the administrator.

The role of the teacher consists of the pattern of behavior that matches the role expectations of administrators, other teachers, students, parents, and of course the teacher's own beliefs (Guskin & Guskin, 1970). Differences in role expectations can lead to role conflict for teachers—a topic of special interest in the social psychology of education.

Parents tend to emphasize the disciplinary aspect of the teacher's role. Students expect teachers to spend less time in supervision and more time in individual activities such as marking exams and talking to other teachers. Administrators, almost all of whom have been teachers, tend to see the role much as teachers themselves do. Thus, teachers are generally supported by the legitimate authorities in the educational system. The differing expectations between students and teachers do not strongly influence teacher behavior because students have relatively little power to affect the teacher's role. Thus, role conflict that might lead to tension and overt hostility between such highly interdependent role partners is not directly addressed; it is suppressed by the higher power and stronger sanctions that teachers and administrators hold over students. The kinds of issues that this power imbalance gives rise to are illustrated in Box 15.1.

As for the student role in educational settings, the teacher's expectations are especially important. The teacher holds legitimate authority and controls the rewards and punishments made available by the organization. Teacher expectations can greatly affect the performance of individual students or groups of students. For instance, the self-fulfilling prophecy (see Chapter 2), has been well documented in educational settings through the pioneering work of Rosenthal and Jacobson (1968). They found that elementary school students who were randomly identified to teachers as "late bloomers" actually gained in intellectual performance over the school year. Teachers also came to see these children as more interesting, more appealing, and better adjusted—in short, they liked them, and

Box 15.1 FOCUS ON RESEARCH AND PRACTICE
Issues in the Teacher-Student Relationship

The role relationship between teachers and students typically involves a number of concerns from both points of view. As part of my doctoral study at the University of Michigan, I completed a group discussion project that focused on high school students' perceptions and concerns. The discussions were facilitated using the method of third-party consultation (see Chapter 14) in which I served as an impartial consultant to help the parties analyze and deal with problems in their relationship.

The discussions were held in two large, white suburban high schools. Four discussion groups were formed in each school, each consisting of four students and three teachers. The groups met over a 4-week period to discuss the following topics: (1) general perceptions of the teacher-student relationship, (2) the main problems in the relationship, (3) perceptions of an ideal relationship, and (4) ideas for improving the relationship. Most of the meetings were involving and effective, with an open dialogue occurring between students and teachers.

The major issues perceived by the students were:

1. *Control of daily behavior:* Students saw their behavior as overly controlled by rigid and arbitrary rules, for example, on attendance and tardiness. They saw teachers partly as a police force, not just as professionals helping them to learn.
2. *Outmoded and formal instruction:* Students disliked strict and archaic ways of teaching that emphasized straight facts without flexibility or a genuine exchange of information between students and teachers.
3. *Lack of respect:* Students perceived a lack of respect for themselves as individuals, with teachers being unresponsive to their needs and using hurtful sarcasm and embarrassment as means of control. A lack of trust and some stereotyping of students also interfered with mutual respect.
4. *Lack of social status:* Students resented their lack of privileges and saw many teachers as condescending toward students. They wanted more contact on an equal and informal basis.
5. *Lack of change:* No matter what the problem, students held little hope for constructive change. Some felt trapped in school by the necessity of a diploma, and most saw teachers, school administrators, and society as caring little about adolescents and their problems.

Teachers responded to student issues with their own perceptions, and the two sides increased their understanding of the other's role and their mutual concerns. Two groups met with school administrators to discuss problems. Based on the meetings, I included a number of suggestions for improving the teacher-student relationship in the final report to the schools.

Source: Fisher, R. J. A discussion project on high school adolescents' perceptions of the relationship between students and teachers. *Adolescence*, 1976, *11*, 88–95.

most likely behaved in ways that showed this to the children. Although questions have been raised about the adequacy of the original research, further studies suggest that expectancy effects do operate in a variety of teaching and learning situations through the mechanism of teachers' behavior. In a comprehensive review, Cooper (1979) suggests that teachers tend to give more criticism to low-expectation students in order to control their interaction with them. In contrast, high-expectation students receive both praise and criticism in ways that improve their performance. The conclusion that teacher expectations can sustain inadequate student performance becomes particularly problematic when teachers have differing role expectations for entire groups of students that may negatively affect their performance in school. Especially with students from disadvantaged minority groups, such as blacks or native Indians, the concern is that prejudice and stereotyping may combine with role expectations to lock students into inferior performance. In the words of black psychologist Kenneth Clark, "Children who are treated as if they are uneducable almost invariably become uneducable" (1965, p. 128). The value of role theory in understanding the educational process is that it views such expectations and behavior as changeable, and therefore invites changes that can optimize the outcomes of teaching and learning. For example, Brophy and Good (1974), in their studies of teacher-student relationships, found that feedback to teachers on their behavior enabled them to significantly increase their contact with low-participation students.

Another advantage of role theory is that it encourages a focus on actual teacher and student behavior in the classroom. The central question becomes "How are roles enacted and how does this affect the process of education?" The most useful research method for answering this question derives from the systematic observation approach known as Interaction Process Analysis (see Chapter 3). Researchers have adopted and extended this approach to develop coding schemes for observing and categorizing the verbal and nonverbal behavior of teachers and students.

Interaction Analysis. Flanders' (1970) method of interaction analysis—one of the better-known and tested techniques—focuses mainly on the teacher's verbal behavior that directly or indirectly attempts to influence students' behavior. The rationale is to select a small number of elements of verbal communication that can help analyze teacher behavior, improve instruction, train future teachers, and predict educational outcomes. The basic ten-category system initially developed by Flanders and his co-workers is shown in Table 15.1. This system has been modified and expanded for different research purposes, but still captures the essence of the method. Teacher initiatives, or direct attempts to influence, consist of behaviors such as lecturing, criticizing, justifying authority, and giving directions. Indirect attempts to influence consist of teacher responses to students' communication—accepting ideas or feelings, and giving praise or encouragement. These two sets of categories show some similarity to the autocratic-versus-democratic styles of leadership, and also to the directive-versus-nondirective or client-centered approach to helping relationships.

Flanders (1970) is negative about general teacher behavior. Teachers tend to talk more than all the pupils combined, tend to ignore students' ideas, and generally control both the structure and the process of classroom interaction. Students initiate very little and tend to ask for clarification rather than make

Table 15.1   FLANDERS'S INTERACTION ANALYSIS CATEGORIES

Teacher Talk	Response	1. *Accepts feeling.* Accepts and clarifies an attitude or the feeling tone of a pupil in a nonthreatening manner. Feelings may be positive or negative. Predicting and recalling feelings are included.
		2. *Praises or encourages.* Praises or encourages pupil action or behavior. Jokes that release tension, but not at the expense of another individual; nodding head, or saying "Um hm?" or "go on" are included.
		3. *Accepts or uses ideas of pupils.* Clarifying, building, or developing ideas suggested by a pupil. Teacher extensions of pupil ideas are included but as the teacher brings more of his or her own ideas into play, shift to category five.
		4. *Asks questions.* Asking a question about content or procedure, based on teacher ideas, with the intent that a pupil will answer.
	Initiation	5. *Lecturing.* Giving facts or opinions about content or procedures; expressing *his or her own* ideas, giving *his or her own* explanation, or citing an authority other than a pupil.
		6. *Giving directions.* Directions, commands, or orders to which a pupil is expected to comply.
		7. *Criticizing or justifying authority.* Statements intended to change pupil behavior from nonacceptable to acceptable pattern; bawling someone out; stating why the teacher is doing what he or she is doing; extreme self-reference.
Pupil Talk	Response	8. *Pupil-talk—response.* Talk by pupils in response to teacher. Teacher initiates the contact or solicits pupil statement or structures the situation. Freedom to express own ideas is limited.
	Initiation	9. *Pupil-talk—initiation.* Talk by pupils which they initiate. Expressing own ideas; initiating a new topic; freedom to develop opinions and a line of thought, like asking thoughtful questions; going beyond the existing structure.
Silence		10. *Silence or confusion.* Pauses, short periods of silence, and periods of confusion in which communication cannot be understood by the observer.

Source: Flanders (1970).

thought-provoking inquiries. Most teachers, however, say they want to be more attentive to students' ideas and initiatives; when this does occur, students achieve more and have more positive attitudes toward school.

Flanders concludes that most students experience chains of events in the classroom that are inconsistent with society's educational aspirations. In other words, a democratic society expects its members to take initiative and exercise responsibility; yet most student behavior in the classroom is passive and powerless. Flanders considers it a tragedy that social science has had to document such problems as lack of student involvement and has had to develop ways of improving teaching practices that are being ignored by the educational system. He is optimistic, however, in his conclusions: by actually studying what goes on in classrooms, teachers can enter into self-development programs that can change teaching behavior toward more effective classroom instruction. For this to happen, teachers and teachers-in-training must explore different patterns of interaction and discover for themselves which are most effective.

But how does a teacher go about making changes in his or her classroom behavior? Not easily, to begin with; any change or possibility of lessening control in the classroom is likely to be threatening. However, Flanders suggests a self-development program that uses interaction analysis to study and change teacher behavior. Teachers or teachers-in-training work in pairs or partnerships within a small cooperative study team of four to eight teachers. Classroom interaction is conceived as having both cognitive and affective components; both require attention in developing effective teacher behavior.

Working together, the partners move through five steps of a mutual development program. First, each teacher must clearly specify the pattern of student behavior that he or she would like to see in the classroom. Often such behaviors will revolve around involvement, motivation, participation, inquiry, responsibility, and so on. Second, each partner helps the other identify patterns of teacher behavior that theory and research indicate would lead to the desired student behavior. For example, to encourage greater student participation in discussions, teachers might use more open questions, paraphrase what students are saying, and support the expression of student opinions, rather than ignore or criticize what students say.

Third, the teachers practice the required behavior in simulated social-skill training, and their behavior is recorded and coded using interaction process analysis. Feedback and discussion adds to earlier skill training to help each teacher develop their desired pattern of behavior. Next, after the development of a design for testing the effectiveness of the behavior, actual classroom behavior is recorded and analyzed. Assuming the program is successful, teacher behavior would be observed to lead to the desired student behavior pattern. If not, it would be back to the drawing board to make modifications or develop a new set of behaviors and hypotheses to be tested.

This type of program combines the power of experience-based learning with the systematic technology of interaction analysis. Such procedures could be used in colleges of education or in in-service training programs for working teachers. The appeal of such programs lies in their power to help reduce the gaps between intentions, actions, and outcomes that are experienced by many dedicated, yet frustrated, teachers in today's school system.

Improving the Outcome of Education

Too often there are significant deficiencies in teacher-student interaction—deficiencies that restrict student initiative and achievement. Harsh indictments of the educational system have come from numerous critics, including some who are experienced teachers. John Holt, for example, has decried the manner in which traditional teaching practices inhibit true learning. In *How Children Fail*, Holt (1964) describes how the schools take even bright children and destroy their capacity for learning and intellectual growth. Teachers essentially make children afraid of not pleasing others, of making mistakes and, most of all, of failing. This strips the children of their curiosity, their initiative, their ability to experience and to grow. The fear of failure is used to control children, to maintain the upper hand in the disciplinary power struggle that characterizes many classrooms.

For these and other reasons, educational critics such as Holt (1976) and Illich (1970) have questioned the need for the present school system and have suggested alternative ways to provide true learning experiences for our children. The basic issue underlying these criticisms and alternatives is the need for educational change. The harsher the criticism, the more radical is the recommended change.

In a similar vein, the role of applied social psychology is to help document the existing reality, including its deficiencies, and to suggest a range of possible methods to improve the educational experience for both student and teacher. Although applications of theory and practice are possible at all levels of analysis, let us focus here on but three: the interpersonal relationship between teacher and student, the use of small group methods in teaching, and the application of organization development to educational systems. Even this brief sampling will illustrate the potential that applied social psychology has for useful educational change.

Interpersonal Relations. In the teacher-student relationship, seen as a *helping* relationship, teaching neither directs nor instructs, but stimulates initiative and facilitates learning. This distinction is made clear in Carl Rogers' *Freedom to Learn* (1969), his statement of a student-centered approach to teaching and learning. At the core of the climate of freedom essential for true learning are the basic qualities of an effective helping relationship (see Chapter 6). A teacher who presents himself or herself as a real and genuine person, not as a role, tends to elicit a more genuine and active involvement by his or her students in the educational process. A teacher who accepts, trusts, and prizes students in a nonpossessive manner, unlocks a capacity for growth and learning that may otherwise go undetected. A teacher who actively understands the thoughts and feelings of students—in essence, their point of view—draws them into a climate of self-initiated learning where motivation and accomplishment flourish.

Rogers uses numerous examples from teachers' experiences to show how the basic qualities of genuineness, nonpossessive warmth, and empathic understanding have improved educational outcomes from the primary grades to university classes. Similarly, research studies by Carkhuff and his associates (such as Aspy, 1969) indicate that a teachers' qualities of genuineness, respect, and empathy in the classroom are positively related to student achievement. The implications for teacher training and development are abundantly clear. For example, Thomas Gordon (1974) has adapted the interpersonal skills of active listening and collaborative problem solving into a systematic program of *Teacher Effectiveness Training*. By increasing their interpersonal effectiveness, teachers can experience greater accomplishment and satisfaction for themselves and their students. The student-centered approach to teaching has merit. However, the contingency model of leadership (see Chapter 7) alerts us to the possibility that different classroom situations may require different teaching styles to maximize learning. Some situations may require a more controlling approach, for example, when student motivation is low and the task is simple, while other situations will be compatible with the democratic, student-centered style.

Small-Group Processes. Most learning situations involve a small group of people—a teacher and twenty or thirty students in a classroom. It therefore seems natural and appropriate to ask how the principles and practices of small-group dynamics (see Chapter 7) can be applied to education—a question with a relatively long and rich history within applied social psychology and related fields. As knowledge has developed about small-group processes—such as communication, decision making, norms, and leadership—this conceptual understanding has been useful in analyzing classroom behavior and suggesting more effective teaching methods (see Miles, 1959; Schmuck & Schmuck, 1975). The growth of human relations training fostered the development of numerous methods and techniques for experiential learning that have also been applied in educational settings (for example, Gorman, 1969; Miles, 1969; Stanford, 1977). These developments have been congruent with the principles of experiential learning fostered in the field of adult education (see Knowles, 1970, 1975), and with the personal and emotional involvement that characterizes the approach of affective education (Lyon, 1971; Thayer, 1976). In short, all these approaches attempt to involve the student as an active, experiencing, participating, whole person in a supportive and creative group-learning situation.

The first step in adapting group methods to teaching is to acknowledge that the class is indeed a group of people with shared expectations, norms, and goals; it is not a collection of separate teacher-student relationships. Schmuck and Schmuck (1975) analyze classroom behavior in terms of group process, then develop the implications and possible actions for the teacher. On the topic of norms, for example, they point out that student peer-group norms on appropriate behavior will frequently be in opposition to the goals of teachers and school administrators. Through group discussion methods, the class can gain control over its own learning culture and change norms through the collaborative effort of the teacher and students. Among their illustrations of this point, the authors describe a high school class that developed norms of active participation and shared responsibility by planning and executing a research study on available career choices in the community. Involvements of this sort channel student interest and initiative within the context of a team effort. Thus, the steps of recognition, analysis, and developing implications must be followed by action.

What are the barriers to collaborative learning that abound in many classrooms? What forces work against the formation of an effective learning group? Stanford (1977) provides some illuminating answers to these questions, as well as some solutions:

> A classroom full of people is not necessarily a group. The individuals may have no sense of group identity. If they are not comfortable with one another, they hesitate to contribute much for fear of ridicule or embarrassment. Usually they compete with one another fiercely. When they can be induced to cooperate, their efforts are frequently ineffective because they lack the skills necessary for working together cooperatively.
>
> To become a group this classroom of individuals must undergo certain changes. It must, in effect, mature. Sometimes a class develops into a group with a minimum of intervention from the teacher. Sometimes this evolution takes place smoothly and effortlessly; almost magically a class becomes an effective working unit.
>
> But most classes never develop into groups. Nothing happens to push them toward maturity. They remain a collection of individuals, lacking the attitudes and the skills needed to work together effectively. As a result, class discussions rarely get off the ground, and group projects fail disastrously. Students resist group tasks. No one feels very good about spending time together each day. (p. 3)

To overcome such difficulties, Stanford has developed and adapted a variety of human relations exercises into a systematic technology for group development in the classroom. This developmental model of group process includes the stages of orientation, establishing norms, coping with conflict, productivity, and termination. For each stage, Stanford provides a theoretical description, suggestions for helpful teacher behavior, and a set of structured exercises that help facilitate the continuous development of the classroom group. His approach was developed from his own experience as a teacher, by using it with some classes and not others, and by studying the results achieved by other teachers using the methods. The result is a detailed strategy that can be easily adapted to many teaching situations.

Let's take a look at just one example from Stanford's program: developing a norm for shared responsibility in the group. Establishing group norms follows the initial stage of orientation: students share their expectations, get acquainted with one another, and begin building trust through helpful teacher behavior and a series of structured exercises. To develop responsibility, the group must have opportunities to learn the necessary skills and to practice directing its own activities. The teacher must train the group and allow for the exercise of reasonable independence. The teacher does not relinquish all control, but is very active in planning and implementing classroom activities.

Helpful teacher behaviors include:

- shifting from teacher-centered to group-centered activities
- arranging seats in a circle
- involving students in setting learning goals
- serving as an observer and resource rather than as leader
- grading the group as a whole

One example of structured exercises that foster group responsibility is the *mystery games.* These cooperative tasks, requiring the participation of all members, are similar to Elliot Aronson's jigsaw method of teaching (see Chapter 11). The mystery games are adapted to different subject areas—such as literature, math, or chemistry—by developing problems whose content is specific to these areas. Regardless of subject area, the general procedure remains the same.

First, clues are developed that are essential to solving the mystery. After the class reviews useful behaviors for working together as a group, they are seated in a circle. All clues are handed around so that each student has at least one. The teacher instructs the group to arrive at the answer to the mystery together, but does not allow clues to be passed around. If the activity is to be graded, this is done in relation to how fast the group solves the mystery. The teacher observes how the group works and, once the task is completed, conducts the follow-up discussion of group process, focusing on group communication and cooperation. This allows the students to analyze their own behavior and to develop principles about what behaviors help group problem solving. These learnings can then be compared with other classroom activities. Thus the *content* of learning is combined with the *process* of learning in ways that increase students' motivation and ability to work together as a productive unit.

The important conclusion is that the power of group process to facilitate learning is readily available to those teachers and students who are willing to take the risk and acquire the necessary skills. An educational system based on group learning would go a long way to reduce or eliminate the deficiencies that many critics have identified. Students and teachers would collaborate in a meaningful and exciting enterprise toward learning goals that were shared and valued by all.

Organization Development in Schools. The practice of organization development (see Chapter 9) has also been applied to educational institutions with beneficial results. At the forefront of this research is the work of Richard Schmuck, Philip Runkel, and their associates at the Center for Educational Policy and Management at the University of Oregon. In an overview of organization development in schools, Schmuck and Miles (1971) provide a comprehensive collection of strategies for improving educational outcomes. These include the improvement of classroom group processes and problem-solving procedures, the use of survey data feedback, the use of change agent teams, and the facilitation of student advocacy. The scope of this work is illustrated by the OD Cube (see Figure 15.1), which categorizes interventions according to the diagnosed problem, the focus of attention (level of analysis), and the mode of the intervention.

Schmuck and Runkel have also produced two handbooks of organization development in schools (Schmuck, Runkel, Saturin, Martell & Derr, 1972; Schmuck, Runkel, Arends & Arends, 1977). These handbooks present a detailed picture of how a variety of training and consultation activities (see Chapter 4) can be adapted to educational settings. Included are methods for clarifying communication, establishing goals, managing conflict, improving meetings, solving problems, and making decisions. The authors also consider the underlying organizational theory and the design and evaluation of interventions. One exam-

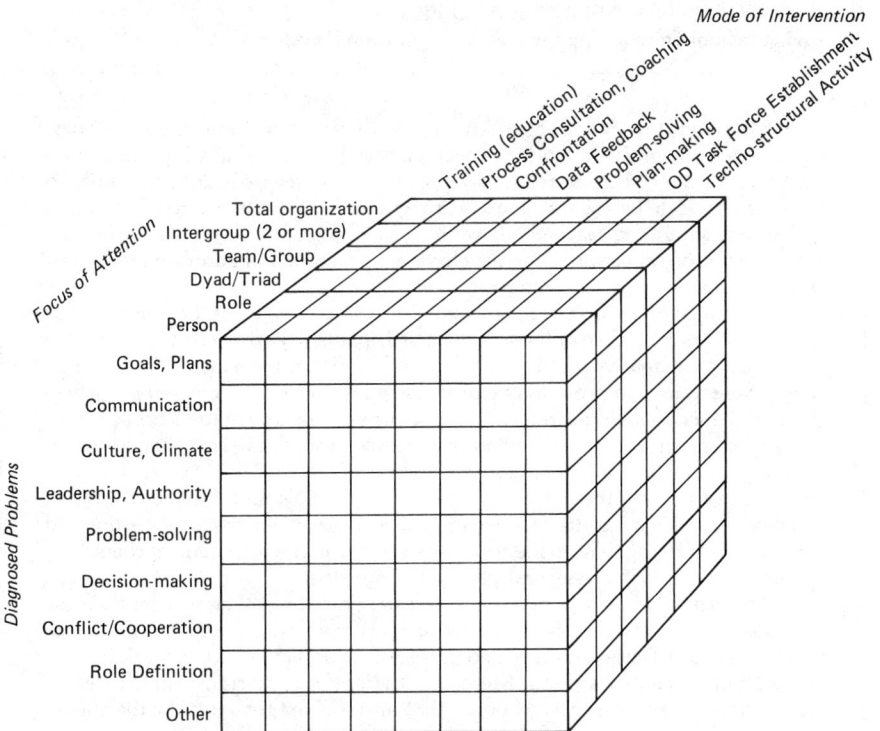

Figure 15.1   The OD Cube for Classifying OD Interventions.
Source: Schmuck & Miles (1971).

ple of planned organizational change in an educational setting is presented in Box 15.2.

Again, as with small group processes, the organizational theory and technology required for educational change are readily available, but little used. Because the resistances to change in education are great, a careful and systematic approach to planning and implementing change is essential for maximum effectiveness (Zaltman, Florio & Sikorski, 1977).

Alternate forms of schools can help point the way to greater student involvement in education. The classic model is provided by A. S. Neill (1960) in developing a free school called Summerhill in England. At Summerhill, traditional authority was abolished and children participated actively in deciding what they wanted to learn and how they wanted to learn it. The goals of personal development and interest in life were pursued through respect for the child and the acquisition of freedom with responsibility. The 1960s saw the establishment of many alternate schools in North America, often supported by the existing educational system. In analyzing two of these experiences, Swidler (1979) points to the

Box 15.2   FOCUS ON RESEARCH AND PRACTICE
Improving School Functioning through Organization Development

Organizational theory and research suggest that participation in setting goals should assist members in working together effectively, especially if participation involves the use of human relations skills. But how well does this idea apply to schools that can be seen as loosely integrated organizations, requiring little collaboration among teachers? Psychologists Christopher Keys and Jean Bartunek report on an organization development program that addressed this question in seven Chicago elementary schools.

Training workshops were provided for teams consisting of the principal and seven teachers from each of the schools. Participants were trained in communication skills, participative problem solving, and conflict management. Then participants were trained to provide similar training sessions to the remaining teachers back in the schools. In the following academic year, faculty in the schools met to identify common goals that would form the basis for educational change. Questionnaires from all teachers and interviews with two teachers from each school were used to assess the extent of agreement on goals and the use of human relations skills. Similar data were gathered from seven control schools that did not receive training. The same measures were also given to new teachers who joined the schools in the second year of the program.

The experimental schools showed greater gains in goal agreement than the control schools. Teachers in the trained schools reported greater participation in discussions and decision making and more use of conflict management skills than teachers in the control schools. Moreover, these effects transferred to new teachers entering the experimental schools—they also showed greater use of the human relations skills.

Keys and Bartunek conclude that OD training can increase the effectiveness of member participation in problem solving and decision making. The intervention was successful even though the entire faculty of the schools did not receive direct training from external consultants; the diffusion of the effects to other teachers demonstrates the possibility of ongoing organizational improvement. Because teachers do work independently, involvement and supportive relationships may be required to counteract isolation.

Source: Keys, C. B. & Bartunek, J. Organization development in schools: Goal agreement, process skills, and diffusion of change. *Journal of Applied Behavioral Science,* 1979, *15,* 61–78.

crucial necessity of replacing the absence of traditional authority with some participative form of social control and coordination to enhance initiative and productivity. At the same time, it is clear that society wants a continuing emphasis on basic skills in language arts, mathematics, and so on. The crucial question is how to maintain the quality of teaching basic skills while simultaneously involving students as responsible social beings in the process of their own education. It is on this question that the social psychology of education can contribute significantly to the improvement of existing educational systems.

ENVIRONMENTAL PSYCHOLOGY

Human beings have created some of the most beautiful and some of the most horrendous environments imaginable. The aesthetic beauty of the Taj Mahal or the gardens of Versailles are testimonies to our ability to create attractive and peaceful settings in harmony with nature. But on this same planet, many of our large urban centers have so deteriorated that we must question the rationality of living in them.

Air, water, and noise pollution have already reached levels that are physically and psychologically damaging. The smog in Tokyo has at times been so thick that police officers have had to carry oxygen masks to assist pedestrians with respiratory ailments—people who simply couldn't breathe the foul air. In Cleveland, Ohio, the Cuyahoga River is so polluted with industrial wastes that it has actually caught fire. In response to urbanization, hundreds of thousands of city dwellers annually trek to wilderness areas and parks to regain contact with nature. But even here many bring their urban attitudes with them, leaving the scene littered, vandalized, and polluted.

Human beings have created some of the most beautiful environments imaginable—and some of the ugliest. Many large urban centers are so deteriorated that the rationality of living in them is questionable. *(Charles Harbutt © 1970/Archive Pictures Inc.)*

On a day-to-day basis, the noise, crowding, and sense of alienation within large cities around the world are contributing to health and mental health problems that could be prevented by more livable environments. We are becoming more aware of and more concerned about these crucial environmental issues, sometimes to the point of actually doing something about them in Tokyo, in Cleveland, and around the world. But we have a long, long way to go.

From the point of view of an applied social psychologist, *environmental issues are social issues.* They are problems that concern a significant number of people. They are problems that involve situations and behaviors that can be studied, understood, and changed using the methods of social science. For the past two decades, social scientists and practitioners have focused more and more on how environments affect people and on how people affect environments. This is the growing interdisciplinary area of activity called environmental psychology.

There is no agreed-upon definition of environmental psychology, but a general understanding of the field is now emerging. Bell, Fisher, and Loomis (1978) define *environmental psychology* as "the study of the interrelationship between behavior and the built and natural environment" (p. 6). Such a definition would have been difficult to formulate in the 1960s, when the field was just beginning to take shape. Of course the specific effects of the environment on human behavior had been studied since the early days of psychology. Perception studies looked at environmental stimuli such as light and noise. Learning theory described the effects of environmental events that affected behavior through the principle of reinforcement. Early industrial psychologists who espoused machine theory studied the influence of environmental conditions—such as the effect of light and spatial arrangement on the performance of workers.

Kurt Lewin urged social psychologists to study both elements in the formula $B = f(P, E)$, that is, behavior is a function of the Person and the Environment. In his early theorizing, E represented the *psychological* environment of the individual, represented by the life space of cognitive and motivational determinants of behavior. However, as Lewin moved from being a personality psychologist to a full-fledged social psychologist, he broadened his conception of the life space to include other individuals, groups, and social institutions (Cartwright, 1978). The environment *(E)* thus became the full *subjective* environment as perceived by the person—a basic element of the phenomenological approach. Lewin and his followers were less concerned with the physical or objective environment. Nonetheless, Lewin's call to include environmental factors went largely unheeded until the 1960s, when a new approach to the study of environment and behavior began to emerge (Altman, 1976; Bell et al., 1978; Stokols, 1978).

The only follower of Lewin to study the physical environment in relation to behavior was Roger Barker, whose methods of naturalistic observation and ecological psychology were described in Chapter 3. Barker and his colleagues have provided detailed descriptions of different behavior settings and the activities of people in these settings (see Barker, 1968). Although Barker's work was long ignored by mainstream social psychology, his contributions have been warmly received in the new subdiscipline of environmental psychology and have been extended through applications in a number of areas (Wicker, 1979).

Other researchers of the 1960s also began sensitizing social scientists to the importance of the physical environment. Robert Sommer (1969) demonstrated the influence of furniture arrangements and other aspects of the physical environment on social interaction; he also showed how people arrange the physical environment to manage social contacts. Edward Hall (1966) studied the hidden dimension of personal space, showing how interpersonal distance between people is related to the intimacy of their relationship, the norms of their culture, and other social variables.

By the early 1970s, these various interests had come together under the umbrella of environmental psychology, and the field expanded at an amazing pace (Stokols, 1978). Professional associations were created or revitalized— including the Division of Population and Environmental Psychology of the APA—and a number of new journals and other publications joined the field. Following the lead of Harold Proshansky at the City University of New York, many universities established graduate programs in environmental psychology or other areas of human-environment study. Thus environmental psychology matured to take a strong role as part of an interdisciplinary effort that involves such related specialties as human geography, urban sociology, architecture, and natural resources management.

Within the general study of human-environment interaction, environmental psychology places a unique emphasis on basic psychological processes and on the individual and group levels of analysis (Stokols, 1978). Along with that emphasis, there are orientations and characteristics that distinguish environmental psychology from psychology proper and from the social psychology of the 1950s and 1960s (Altman, 1976; Bell et al., 1978; Stokols, 1978).

These distinguishing characteristics include:

- *A systems approach* that studies behavior-environment relationships as a unit in which there is mutual and reciprocal influence. This ecological perspective, in other words, sees the person and the setting as a social unit that must be studied in ongoing interaction in order to understand complex cause-and-effect relationships. In this approach it would be inappropriate to take a strictly analytical stance that studies causal relationships that are unidirectional and limited to one level of analysis.
- *A problem orientation* that sees the solution of pressing environmental issues as a legitimate task. Basic theoretical research is to be fused with applied research to produce useful knowledge and develop practical solutions—essentially the goal of action research (see Chapter 3). Environmental issues are social issues.
- *An interdisciplinary emphasis* that involves a variety of research methods and a broad conceptual base. Theories from many disciplines are required to understand and predict human-environment interaction at all levels of analysis.
- *A social-psychological perspective* that emphasizes how social relationships and social interaction are mutually related to the physical environment. There are many common interests and methods between environmental psychology and social psychology and there could be much cross-fertilization if the first three characteristics are followed.

The relationship between environmental psychology and social psychology has been a debatable issue in recent years. Two leaders in this controversy are Irwin Altman and Harold Proshansky; both are social psychologists who have helped establish the new field of environmental psychology. Altman (1976) is optimistic about the benefits that the two areas have to offer each other. The theories and research methods of social psychology can help focus and guide the array of unconnected research areas that are developing in environmental psychology. Rigorous research methods, particularly experimentation, can improve the quality of environmental research.

In response, contemporary social psychology has much to gain from environmental psychology. Theories that are developed and refined in insulated laboratory settings need to have their generalizability tested in field settings. The over-reliance on the laboratory method might give way to a broader use of various methods as social psychologists become more concerned with environmental issues relevant to social well-being. These pressures might influence social psychology to move toward the study of *intact* social units, replacing its emphasis on the dissection of social behavior into independent processes that are studied in isolation, often never to be put back together again. In short, environmental psychology challenges experimental social psychology to examine its most basic assumptions and its approaches to the generation of knowledge.

Proshansky (1976) is much more pessimistic about any reciprocal contributions between the two fields. Given the predominance of the simplistic laboratory-experimental model, social psychology has produced theories of doubtful external validity. Environmental psychology will have to develop its own theories, using its own methods in a problem-oriented manner that does not reduce complex forms of human behavior to basic psychological processes. Social psychology has not fulfilled its promise of understanding social behavior or of helping to solve social problems, because the laboratory-experimental model fails to incorporate the complexity and integrity of person-environment interaction. Even when the social psychologist ventures into the real world, the experimental model goes along. Therefore, environmental psychology must of necessity turn its back on the last three decades of social psychology.

Many of these concerns about social psychology are identical to the issues we discussed in Chapter 1. Mainstream social psychology is in difficulty on a number of fronts: it lacks relevance, for instance, and relies too heavily on the laboratory method. Many of the new directions these researchers suggest for environmental psychology strongly parallel the fundamental characteristics of applied social psychology—including a systems orientation and the use of a wide variety of research methods.

Environmental psychology may well find a strong ally in applied social psychology if both fields avoid the past pitfalls of social psychology and faithfully follow constructive guidelines (see Epstein, 1976; Krupat, 1977). However, the proof is in the pudding. We must look into the major areas of research in environmental psychology to gain some idea of how well the basic orientations are being followed.

According to Stokols (1978), environmental psychology has not yet developed into a comprehensive, coherent field of endeavor; rather, it is comprised of a number of semi-independent research domains. The interrelationships between these domains are just beginning to be studied, and some common themes are starting to emerge. To understand what is going on, we need to explore the three major areas of environmental research: first, the perceptions and attitudes that individuals hold toward the environment, and the effects these variables may have on behavior; second, human spatial behavior; and third, environmental effects on behavior, including those of environmental stressors and residential design. Finally we must question how environments can be designed, changed, or preserved to improve the human-environment fit in our quest for a better quality of life.

Environmental Perceptions and Attitudes

The environment is what we perceive it to be. How we see the world determines how we respond to it. Studies of enviromental perception emphasize how different people perceive the same environment in different ways and how, as a result, they vary in their attitudes and behavior toward the environment. Drop a farm boy from Kansas into New York City, and he will be awe-stricken by the canyon streets and the never-ending skyline. He may also be more sensitive to the noise, the crowds, and the air pollution. He may very well develop an unfavorable attitude and engage in escape behavior the first chance he gets! Drop a New York girl onto a wilderness campsite, and she may be fear-stricken by the miles of emptiness and the absence of familiar comforts. She may notice the awesome silence—a void in which the cry of a bird becomes an exaggerated scream. She may evaluate the situation very negatively and catch the next canoe home!

These two individuals are perceiving and reacting to their environments out of very different experiences, backgrounds, values, and preferences. Although our responses to different settings stem largely from experience with the environment (Bell et al., 1978), we cannot predict environmental perception and attitudes solely on the basis of experience. Many farm boys love the varied, fast-paced stimuli of large cities; many city girls long for the beauty and tranquility of the wilderness.

Perception and attitudes are determined by many factors other than experience, including individual personality characteristics, that are too numerous to detail here. In fact, Stokols (1978) points out that research on human comprehension of the environment has become one of the most active areas in environmental psychology during the 1970s. This research can be broken down into *environmental cognition*—the perceptual, cognitive, and affective processes by which we come to know our environment (see Bell et al., 1978), and *cognitive mapping*—the process of acquiring and using mental maps that give the locations and characteristics of phenomena in our environment (see Lynch, 1960; Milgram, 1976).

To illustrate the process of environmental perception and how it can be studied, we should look at a recent piece of work on perceptions of the energy crisis—a matter of much current interest and concern—and at the role of attitudes in environmental cognition and their relationship to behavior.

Environmental concern about the pollution and deterioration of the environment has been widespread for years. Researchers have developed measures of environmental concern (see Maloney & Ward, 1973; Smythe & Brook, 1980; Weigel & Weigel, 1978), and related those to other salient variables such as political ideology (see Buttel & Flynn, 1978). However, the recent energy crisis and the resulting economic concerns worldwide now conflict with environmental concerns. It costs more to have clean energy: some sources of energy, such as coal or nuclear power, involve existing or potential costs to the environment, as well as very real risks to the people who live in it.

To study perceptions of the energy crisis, Hummel, Levitt, and Loomis (1978) developed a survey to systematically assess people's perceptions about energy and related environmental problems. They were particularly interested in who gets blamed for the energy crisis, and how citizens react to the necessary trade-offs between environmental concern and economic lifestyle. Two identical surveys were conducted in a small Colorado city—one, at a time of acute energy crisis (a gasoline shortage); the second, some months later when it was apparent that energy problems would be a chronic or continuing issue. Mailed questionnaires, covering a number of items, were used to elicit respondents' perceptions of blame for the energy problem, motives for energy-conserving behavior, and the perceived immediate and future effects of the energy problem. These variables were used to predict respondents' support for voluntary or mandatory actions to help both energy and environmental problems, as well as preferences for different trade-offs between environmental protection and energy needs. For example, people were asked if they would prefer cleaner air at the expense of greater energy consumption *or* financial cost.

The study found that respondents in the first sample (the acute crisis) were more likely to blame the oil companies for the energy crisis; those in the second sample (the chronic problem) placed more responsibility on the individual consumer, and were more supportive of mandatory controls and actions that would ease the energy crisis but damage the environment. Both groups showed the greatest preference for voluntary actions rather than mandatory controls or actions that would hurt the environment. In terms of relationships among variables, blaming the individual consumer was related to support for most actions that would protect the environment. Blaming environmentalists for creating the energy crisis (presumably through protection measures) was related to a lack of support for environmental safeguards.

Hummel et al. (1978) conclude that perceptions of the cause of the energy crisis may be very important in determining a person's behavioral intentions about energy and environmental issues. In addition, if government wants support for more costly energy and, at the same time, for environmental protection, it may need to persuade the public that the individual consumer, rather than environmentalists or the oil companies, are to blame for the chronic energy crisis. These results and implications suggest that attribution theory can play a useful role in analyzing the public's perceptions of blame and the resulting effects on environmental attitude and behavior.

The study of environmental attitudes is similar to the study of environmental perceptions: both look at people's internal representations of the environment (Stokols, 1978). However, the study of attitudes shifts the emphasis to evaluative reactions and their effect on behavior. Research on environmental attitudes has recently concentrated on two major issues: attitudes regarding environmental problems such as pollution, and the degree of consistency between attitudes and behavior in areas such as energy conservation.

On the first issue, a considerable amount of work has gone into the development of measures of environmental quality (Bell et al., 1978). Indices have been developed to measure respondents' attitudes toward many specific aspects of the environment—scenic resources, pollution, residential quality, recreational facilities, and so on. These measures are useful for comparing attitudes toward different environments and for assessing the impact of environmental intervention or change on residents' attitudes. Environmental attitudes, like other attitudes, are primarily formed through learning and can be measured and changed through the usual procedures.

The question of congruence between attitudes and behavior toward environmental issues is as problematic and complex as the same question applied to any other domain (see Chapter 2). For example, there appears to be a general discrepancy between environmental concern on the one hand and, on the other hand, a lack of willingness to curb consumption of resources (Stokols, 1978). (We do want to have our cake and eat it too!) This discrepancy may be due to insufficient knowledge about environmental problems, or to mistaken beliefs that governments or someone else have a magic solution to energy shortages. While conservation behavior may increase at times of acute shortages, long-term actions do not seem to reflect knowledge of environmental limitations or beliefs in the need for conservation (Bell et al., 1978; O'Riordan, 1976). Again, we must still take into account other factors such as social norms and related attitudes, and the power of behavior to affect future attitudes. Social psychologists can play important roles in conducting research and influencing public policy toward a conserving rather than a consuming society (Oskamp, 1981).

In any event, policy makers are faced with a perplexing situation. For example, recent studies (at the University of Michigan's Institute for Social Research) found that most Americans have positive attitudes toward fuel economy, but that this concern has no discernible effect on their use of the automobile (Hill & Hill, 1979). Judging from a national sample, respondents who believed that gasoline consumption must be decreased were no more likely to restrict their driving habits than respondents who were unconcerned. The major variable that affected driving behavior was the cost of gasoline! The conclusion is that government measures to reduce fuel consumption will work only if they are accompanied by higher prices at the pump. The general implication is that changes in environmental behavior may require direct reinforcement *plus* attempts to change attitudes. An example of how social scientists can help assess the impact of environmental conservation campaigns appears in Box 15.3.

Human Spatial Behavior

You are sitting at a table in the library. Someone comes in and sits less than a foot away from you. How do you feel?

You are drying yourself off in a locker room after a shower. A nude person comes up and stands very close to you. How do you react?

Or, assuming you are male, do you think your behavior would be affected if you were standing at a urinal in a men's room and another male came in and stood at the urinal next to you?

At the library, you would probably leave sooner than you had intended. Or you might turn away, or engage in other behaviors designed to block off the other person. In the locker room, you would probably dress in a hurry, then leave as fast

Box 15.3   FOCUS ON RESEARCH
Changing Attitudes and Behavior toward Water Conservation

The Goleta County Water District provides water for a 33,000-acre area of Santa Barbara, California. Due to rapid urbanization during the late 1960s and early 1970s, the demand for water began to exceed the supply. In late 1972, the board instituted a conservation campaign to reduce water consumption. This led to an intense local debate over the effectiveness of the campaign. Judith Maki, Donnie Hoffman, and Richard Berk of the University of California at Santa Barbara carried out a detailed time-series analysis in order to provide more valid information on the conservation campaign's utility.

Annual water sales did show a decrease following the onset of the conservation campaign. However, this dip might have been due to other factors such as weather, especially rainfall. To gain a more accurate estimate of the effects of the campaign, the investigators related several variables to sales on a month-by-month basis over a 10-year period using the correlational technique of multiple regression (see Chapter 3). The conservation campaign included several strategies: a moratorium on new hookups, a rebate program for conservative consumers, conservation messages on water bills, laws against wasting water, and the distribution of water conservation kits to reduce home usage. Other variables included in the analysis were rainfall, the season of the year, and population growth.

The results indicated that the conservation campaign did have a significant effect in decreasing water sales. Population growth and seasonal variations were also related to sales. In real terms, the campaign resulted in a saving of 177 acre-feet or 58 million gallons of water every month. This saving was equivalent to an average 15 percent reduction in consumption for the 3 years following the onset of the campaign.

The researchers conclude that the conservation campaign substantially decreased consumers' demands for water in Goleta County. However, since the analysis looked at the total effect of the campaign, no conclusions could be drawn about the relative effectiveness of its component strategies (the moratorium, laws, education, and so forth). This more detailed information would be especially useful for future policy making. However, the research certainly added relevant information to the debate about the overall usefulness of the campaign.

Source: Maki, J. E., Hoffman, D. M. & Berk, R. A. A time series analysis of the impact of a water conservation campaign. *Evaluation Quarterly,* 1978, 2, 107–118.

as you could. In the men's room, you would probably begin urinating later, then leave more quickly than you would if you were alone. Such are the findings of a few of the field experiments in which confederates have intruded upon the personal space of unsuspecting subjects to observe their reactions. In the case of the urinal experiment, for example, an experimenter sat in an adjacent toilet stall and used a periscope and two stopwatches to record the onset and duration of urination.

These types of experiments generally relate the characteristics of the subjects (sex or race, for example), the invader (such as status), the situation (similarity among actors, for instance, or the form of interaction) to two elements: personal space, or interaction distance between people, and the individual's reactions to invasions of personal space. Through experiments of this sort, environmental researchers have generated a considerable amount of information about this element of human spatial behavior.

Proshansky (1976), however, is concerned about moving experimental methods from the laboratory to the field in ways that simply replicate many of the deficiencies of experimental social psychology. For example, in the hundreds of studies of personal space, each one typically looks at the simple relationsihp between two or three variables rather than at the complex flow of person-environment interaction.

Many of these studies also bring up such ethical concerns as invasion of privacy, manipulation, and deception—all without informed consent. Thus, the trade-off between protecting the welfare of the subject and the need for social scientific knowledge becomes paramount (see Chapter 3). Experimental environmental researchers are well aware of these concerns, and have made ethical judgments that the benefits of doing the research outweigh the costs. I'm not so sure that this is true in all cases. Some of these interventions I find offensive, and their results trivial—and my reactions are often "of course," and "so what." For example, I question whether environmental researchers have nothing better to do than observe people urinating under different conditions of social influence. However, once we have identified this concern, we should acknowledge a more positive side: that through a combination of methods, environmental researchers are accumulating valid findings and building useful theories of human spatial behavior.

The study of human spatial behavior is called *proxemics*—an examination of the ways in which people use physical space to regulate social interaction (Stokols, 1978). Proxemics is concerned with four basic phenomena:

- *personal space*—the maintenance of an invisible boundary around oneself;
- *territoriality*—the ownership and defense of physical areas;
- *crowding*—the experience of spatial and social interference by others;
- *privacy*—the control of access to oneself.

The concept of personal space was actively initiated by the anthropologist Edward Hall, *The Hidden Dimension* (1966), and by social psychologist Robert Sommer in *Personal Space: The Behavioral Basis of Design* (1969). The term *personal space* refers to the invisible zone, or "bubble" around each individual into which most others should not trespass. The purpose of personal space is to protect us from the threat and anxiety of too much intimacy or stimulation, and also to facilitate interpersonal interaction in socially approved ways. Personal space thus serves both a protective and a communicative function (Bell et al., 1978).

The appropriate personal space we maintain in a given situation varies in relation to numerous other variables. Hall (1966) identifies four different ranges of personal space or spatial zones: intimate, personal, social, and public.

- The *intimate zone* involves an interpersonal distance from 0–1.5 feet, and is appropriate for intimate relationships and behaviors—making love, for example, or comforting a close friend.

The *intimate zone* is an interpersonal zone of 0 to 1.5 feet. It is appropriate for intimate relationships and behaviors such as touching. (© *Richard KALVAR magnum*)

- The *personal zone* (1.5–4.0 feet) is appropriate for interaction among friends and acquaintances. It relies more on verbal communication; the intimate zone involves more touching.
- The *social spatial zone* (4–12 feet) is appropriate for impersonal contacts in business or similar settings.
- The *public distance zone* (12–25 feet) involves very formal contact between an individual—such as an actor or politician—and the public, usually in the form of an audience.

Each of these zones has its own degree of intensity and awareness of sensory inputs: the intimate is very high; the public, very low. Each zone is appropriate for particular relationships, activities, and settings, and not for others, as decreed by the social norms of one's society.

As an anthropologist, Hall also emphasized the importance of cultural differences in the use of personal space, as well as in other aspects of proxemics. For example, Northern Europeans generally prefer to interact at a greater personal distance than Southern Europeans—a source of difficulties when people from different cultures get together. A French person may be puzzled as the English person keeps backing away during their conversation. The English person is offended and concludes that all French people are pushy, whereas, the French person ruminates over the aloofness of the English. Thus the use of personal space is partly a cultural characteristic that we gain through our society's socialization process. A mutual awareness of resulting cultural differences can help prevent misunderstanding and misattribution. The cultural antecedents of personal space, as well as Hall's general theory of spatial zones, have received substantial support from further research in human spatial behavior (Stokols, 1978).

The field experiments that introduced this section involve invasions or violations of appropriate personal space in different social settings. Hall (1966) indicated that deviation from appropriate interpersonal distance would usually elicit negative feelings and negative inferences about the other person. Following the lead of Sommer (1969) and his co-workers, researchers have conducted numerous studies of the effects of invading someone's personal space. The results are predictable. Subjects are threatened, offended, and so on, and attempt to cope with the unexpected situation by flight or defensive behaviors. The potential utility of this work is that, in verifying the existence and range of different spatial zones, the results could be used to design more appropriate, more compatible environments.

Another line of research has investigated personal, relationship, and situation variables that relate to the interpersonal distance that is chosen by the people themselves. Similarity between people (for instance, the same age, status, or race) generally leads to closer interpersonal distances. Variables such as degree of acquaintance, physical attractiveness, and pleasantness of interaction have also been examined. In general the results are compatible with the findings on interpersonal attraction: similarity increases attraction and consequently reduces personal distance (see Byrne, Ervin & Lamberth, 1970).

Territorial behavior is commonly observed throughout the animal kingdom, serving important survival functions relating to food gathering, mating, and childrearing. *Human territoriality* generally refers to the exclusive ownership, use, and defense of areas and objects by persons and groups (Altman, 1975; Bell et al., 1978). In contrast to personal space, territory is visible, has a definite geographic location, centers around the home, and regulates *who* will interact rather than *how* they will interact (Sommer, 1969). Territoriality among animals appears to be biologically determined; human territoriality appears to be learned. Humans mark out their "turf," control interaction within it, and in some cases violently defend their rights of ownership.

The next time you are in different social settings, you might try to observe some common elements of territorial behavior. The sweater draped over the vacant chair in the library is a marker of temporary ownership. The same table gets used by the same friendship group in the residence cafeteria. After a small class has met for a few times, you usually know who sits where. The fence that cuts through a grassy lawn clearly indicates whose yard is whose.

Altman (1975) has identified three different types of territory among humans:

- *Primary territory*, such as one's home or office, is a physical location over which the owner has complete control and personlizes in a relatively permanent manner. Offices often have pictures of the family, favorite sayings on wall plaques or elsewhere, and diplomas, awards or other signs of merit that have been received by the individual occupant.
- *Secondary territory*, such as a classroom or playground, is a location that legitimate users may partially personalize and partially regulate while they are occupying it. For example, I teach a class in interpersonal communication: each time the class meets we rearrange the chairs into small groupings for discussions and other exercises.
- *Public territories*, such as train stations or beaches, are areas where control is difficult to assert and ownership is transient and tenuous. If you temporarily leave your bench in the bus station without leaving a marker, chances are it will be occupied when you return. If it's really busy, it might be occupied anyway, marker or not.

Hence, the different types of territory are placed on a continuum from the high to low personalization, ownership, and control.

What are the functions of human territoriality? Territories serve mainly social and organizational functions by identifying roles such as owning, hosting, and visiting, and by defining socially appropriate behavior. Territories support individual and group identity ("our place"), allow us to regulate our degree of interaction and arousal, and create consistency and stability in our lives. For these reasons, research on human territoriality has placed more emphasis on its social-organizational functions than on its biological or physical functions (Stokols, 1978).

Crowding—the third element of spatial behavior—is the negative *subjective* experience we have when a relatively large number of individuals occupy a given spatial area. Thus crowding is a phenomenological concept that has to be distinguished from actual physical density. What is crowding to some people is not crowding to others. When we get that feeling of crowding, we usually get a sense of spatial or social interference from others and want to reduce our contact with them (Stokols, 1978). (In the next section, we will look at high density as a common source of stress in the environment and at its damaging effects.)

Privacy—the final aspect of human spatial behavior we will consider here—concerns the control we exert over others to regulate interpersonal interaction, enhance our autonomy, and minimize our vulnerability to outside influences (Margulis, 1977). In short, we are using the physical environment to limit social contact to whatever level we so desire. One aspect of recent systematic studies on the nature of privacy relates privacy to other social-psychological concepts such as social power, personal control, roles, and norms. (A recent special issue of the *Journal of Social Issues* was devoted to these differing conceptions and their interdisciplinary applications; Margulis, 1977).

Irwin Altman (1975) has developed an *integrative model of proxemic behavior* that relates privacy to personal space, territoriality, and crowding. For Altman, the essence of privacy is the selective control of access to oneself. We open and close ourselves to others by controlling social interaction with others in an attempt to achieve an optimum level of contact. Too much interaction, creating the experience of crowding, is also unsatisfactory. Thus crowding is essentially a lack of privacy—a situation in which the desired level of privacy is greater than the achieved level.

How do we regulate the amount of privacy we experience? Altman identifies the four mechanisms of verbal behavior, nonverbal behavior, environmental mechanisms, and social norms. Personal space and territoriality enter into the model as environmental or boundary mechanisms that we use to control access to ourselves. This permits us to maintain our preferred balance between desired and achieved levels of privacy. By allowing others to enter certain zones of our personal space, or by attempting to move into others' personal space, we open up access to ourselves and reduce privacy. Conversely, by marking, restricting, or closing off our turf, we increase privacy.

All human spatial behavior can be conceived of as an interdependent system designed to use the physical environment to achieve optimal privacy. You can see the similarities between Altman's theory of privacy and his theory of social penetration (see Chapter 6). Both are concerned with interaction mechanisms and with the degree to which we interact with and let ourselves be known to other people. At the same time the model of privacy extends the earlier work on social penetration in a number of important directions (Margulis, 1977), particularly as it interrelates the concept of self with social behavior and with environmental processes. As such it serves as a useful general theory of both social interaction and human spatial behavior.

Environmental Effects on Behavior

Environmental psychology stresses the interaction between the person and the environment. We create the built environment and we modify the natural environment, and all the while these environments are influencing our behavior in return. Environmental effects on behavior fall into three major categories (Stokols, 1978): the effects of environmental stressors, the influence of built environments, and the human response to the natural environment.

Environmental Stressors: Noise and Spatial Density. Can you imagine building a high-rise apartment over a freeway? Of course you can if you live in a large urban center where land is scarce and the limits of rational planning are exceeded every day. Wouldn't it be rather noisy on the lower floors? Would it ever! In the introduction to this chapter, we touched on this very problem, and how the study conducted by three social-environmental psychologists (Cohen, Glass & Singer, 1973) indicated the damaging effects of the noise on the educational development of children living on the lower floors of that building. And these children are not the only victims. Throughout the industrialized world, noise and other stressors negatively affect our physical and mental health (Bell et al., 1978).

Stress has become a popular concept, used to explain the negative effects of a wide range of environmental conditions. Baum, Singer, and Baum (1981) regard stress as "a process in which environmental events or forces, called stressors, threaten an organism's existence and well-being and the organism responds to this threat" (p. 4). They conceive of the stress process as similar to that of attitude change through persuasive communication: there is a source (the stressor), the transmission of the message (is the stressor perceived and understood as threatening?), and the audience (the recipient of stressful transmission whose characteristics determine vulnerability to stress). The environment is a source of numerous stressors—for purpose of illustration we will look at just two: noise and spatial density.

One person's music is often another person's noise. In other words, *noise* is essentially sound that is unwanted, and therefore distracting and irritating. *How annoying and damaging noise can be is determined by its volume, its predictability, and the amount of control the listener has over it.* Noise that is loud, unpredictable, and uncontrollable usually generates greater stress on individuals (Glass & Singer, 1972). The negative effects caused by extreme, long-term exposure to noise include hearing loss, elevated blood pressure, increased frequency of physical illness, and higher incidence of mental health problems. However, many of these results are based on correlational field studies in which extraneous variables, including other environmental stressors, were not adequately controlled (Bell et al., 1978).

Laboratory studies on the effect of noise on task performance have also shown mixed results. However, knowledge of the characteristics of disruptive noise (that it is loud, unpredictable, and uncontrollable) generally helps predict the amount of interference with task performance. Uncontrollable noise has also been shown to have damaging effects on social behaviors such as interpersonal attraction, aggression, helping, and frustration tolerance (Bell et al., 1978; Stokols, 1978). Experimental studies have thus helped sort out some of the conditions under which this important environmental stressor has negative consequences for human beings.

The negative physical and social consequences of high spatial density have been well-demonstrated through laboratory and field studies involving various species of animals. A classic study by Calhoun (1962) illustrated the effects of crowding on laboratory mice and stimulated a great deal of research in this area. Beginning with four healthy male and female mice, Calhoun started a colony in a laboratory enclosure designed as a comfortable environment for forty-eight mice. Ample food and water were provided, and the mice multiplied and engaged in normal behavior patterns. Dominant males accumulated a harem and defended their territory. Females built nests and raised their young. However, at a critical point of overpopulation, social disintegration began. The young were prematurely pushed out of the nest to fend for themselves. Infant mortality was over 80 percent in some of the colonies. Some dominant males were able to continue their roles, but many males became either passive and inactive or hyperactive, homosexual, and cannibalistic. Some females also became inactive, giving up their sexual and maternal functions. In certain areas of the enclosure, called "behavioral sinks," extremely high density detroyed almost all aspects of normal social functioning.

Research following Calhoun's study has continued to document the destructive effects of crowding on a variety of species. However we must be cautious in generalizing these results to human beings, whose behavior is much more determined by learning and culture (Bell et al., 1978). Animal studies are useful in generating hypotheses about interventions and effects that would be unethical to carry out with human subjects.

With humans the distinction between high physical density and the subjective experience of crowding becomes much more important. Not all high-density situations lead to the unpleasant and potentially damaging experience of crowding. Rock concerts, football games, and open markets are settings to which people willingly flock for the excitement, stimulation, and other rewards that are provided. When we deal with human participants, therefore, we must study their subjective reactions to high density even as we look at physiological and behavioral effects. To study this form of environmental stress, environmental psychology uses both laboratory experimentation and field methods (Bell et al., 1978)—with results that generally give cause for concern (Stokols, 1978).

High density usually leads to anxiety and other negative emotional reactions. High density also leads to physiological arousal—as measured by indices such as blood pressure, skin conductance, and heart rate—establishing a limited degree of relationship between high density and physical illness.

High density also affects social behavior. Crowding has been found to relate to reduced interpersonal attraction, increased withdrawal, diminished helping behavior, and increased aggression. The effects on aggression have been somewhat inconsistent, particularly in studies involving children. An interesting field study that provides a clear test of this relationship appears in Box 15.4.

The generally harmful effects of crowding have been observed in a number of real-world environments, particularly in prisons (see Megargee, 1977; Paulus, Cox, McCain & Chandler, 1975). Given these predominantly negative findings, we can predict that the consequences of crowding and the need for improved environmental design will continue as a major thrust in environmental psychology (see Aiello & Baum, 1979; Gurkaynak & LeCompte, 1979). At the same time, we need more intensive case studies of groups, such as families, who sometimes live under conditions of high density and yet cope successfully (Epstein, 1981).

If you add the environmental stressors of noise and crowding to air pollution and other forms of environmental contamination, you reach the inevitable question of whether it pays to live in cities these days! But the greater population of industrialized countries *does* live in cities. No wonder then that this crucial issue demands the attention of environmental researchers.

Social psychologist Stanley Milgram (1970) was one of the first to investigate the experience of urban life. While the varied, stimulating environment of the city is one of its great appeals, Milgram contends that this high amount of stimulation leads to overload. People simply cannot process all the input, and so they develop a variety of coping mechanisms. People allocate less time to each input (for instance, they greet others brusquely). They disregard low-priority inputs (ignoring someone, for example). They put up barriers (unlisted telephone numbers and the like). And they reduce the intensity of inputs (such as being very superficial). The outcome of these adaptations is a new set of social norms that reflect impersonal anonymity, uncaring noninvolvement, superficial role behavior, and a decreased sense of social responsibility.

Box 15.4   FOCUS ON RESEARCH
Spatial Density and Aggression among Children

Studies with animals suggest the amount of environmental space influences aggressive behavior. It has been assumed that this relationship holds for humans as well. However, the few studies completed with humans have yielded equivocal and conflicting results. Harvey Ginsburg and his colleagues in the Department of Psychology at Southwest Texas State University set out to provide a clear test of the relationship between spatial density and aggression in humans.

The researchers unobtrusively videotaped the playground behavior of elementary school boys on two different sized play areas—the larger one being about seven times the area of the smaller one. The same boys played on the two different playgrounds on alternate days during the observation period. In all, eight episodes of playground behavior covering 40 minutes each were videotaped for each of three grade levels (third to the fifth). The videotapes were then subjected to a content analysis to determine the amount of aggressive behavior. Five specific types of aggressive behavior were noted: hitting, jumping upon, pushing, pulling, and kicking.

Significantly more aggressive behavior occurred on the smaller playground. Of 120 samples of interaction, 63 on the smaller area involved fighting, whereas only 29 on the larger area involved aggression. The fights on the small playground usually involved more than two children and were of briefer duration than those on the larger playground. No differences related to grade level were found.

The results thus indicate that crowding increases aggression, at least in an unstructured playground situation involving male school children. On a positive note, the duration of aggressive behavior on the smaller playground was often reduced by other children coming to the aid of the child under attack. In the small area, it appeared that benefactors could more easily perceive and more quickly respond to instances of aggression.

The researchers recommend the use of naturalistic observation to study the effects of population density on human behavior. They also suggest that playground design should insure adequate spacing among children to reduce aggressive behavior.

Source: Ginsburg, H. J., Pollman, V. A., Wauson, M. S. & Hope, M. L. Variation of aggressive interaction among male elementary school children as a function of changes in spatial density. *Environmental Psychology and Nonverbal Behavior,* 1977, 2(2), 67–75.

Milgram points to studies on bystander intervention in emergencies as one example of the norms of indifference (see Chapter 14). For another example, four of Milgram's students knocked on doors in Manhattan and in several small towns outside New York City. At each place they asked if they could use the telephone to call a nearby friend whose address they had misplaced. Residents of small towns were two to five times more likely to accede to this request. But 75 percent of the Manhattan residents shouted through the door rather than open it—a clear demonstration of the perceived dangers of living in the higher crime area of the city. In contrast, 75 percent of the small town residents opened the door and let the caller in. Milgram concludes that the concept of overload helps explain many of the differences between city behavior and town behavior.

There are other explanations of the impersonal and destructive behavior in cities (Bell et al., 1978). It may be that specific stresses such as noise and crowding rather than general overload lead to anxiety, aggression, and other stress reactions (see, Glass & Singer, 1972).

It is clear that those of us who live in the large city may be paying a price for doing so. We reduce our affiliation with strangers. We decrease our prosocial behavior. Sometimes our task performance suffers. But, at the same time, the advantages of city life remain: excitement, variety, challenge, and so on. In short the city dweller, in freely choosing his or her living environment, must always identify and accept the mixture of costs and benefits of that preferred environment.

Effects of Environmental Design. The impact of residential design on interpersonal relations was first demonstrated in the classic study of married-student housing by Festinger, Schachter, and Back (1950). This research found that friendships formed more readily among neighbors living in closer proximity (see Chapter 7). Environmental researchers have subsequently studied the impact of interior design on a number of personal and social variables (Stokols, 1978).

Baum and Valins (1977) compared a traditional corridor design student residence with suite-style dormitories. The two designs were identical in terms of space per person, but the corridor design required thirty-four students to share the same lounge and bathrooms. In the suite design, the same facilities were shared by only four or six people. Thus the corridor design led to a much greater frequency of social contact. These residents complained of crowding and forced interaction, behaved in a less sociable manner, and formed fewer friendships on their floor. In independent laboratory observations, corridor dorm residents also showed reduced social contact and decreased performance on cooperative tasks. Baum and Valins conclude that these students had undergone a social learning process that reduced their positive orientations toward others. Other studies have indicated important relationships between physical design of university residences and students evaluations of social climate (see Moos, 1978).

The design of the high-rise apartment has consistently been associated with psychological distress and a reduction in prosocial behavior. Typical symptoms include alienation, withdrawal, delinquency, and decreased altruism. One study found reduced perceptions of trust and lower rates of helping behavior in university high-rise residences, as compared to medium-sized and small dormitories (Bickman, Teger, Gabriele, McLaughlin, Berger & Sunaday, 1973). However, the most glaring tragedies in residential design have occurred in high-rise public housing projects developed in many cities during the 1950s and 1960s. Through urban renewal projects, thousands of lower-income families were moved from existing social communities into massive complexes of high-rise towers. The result was almost invariably disastrous. Social isolation, a lack of social responsibility, and unbelievably high crime rates turned many of these projects into nightmares (see Newman, 1972; Yancey, 1972). Most explanations center around aspects of the design that elicited such reactions and behavior (Bell et al., 1978). There were few spaces that promoted positive social interactions, or that led to a sense of ownership or territoriality on the part of residents. But there were many hidden, crime-prone areas such as stairwells and hallways where vandalism and other illegal behavior could go on virtually unnoticed. The lessons learned from these architectural blunders have been costly, most of all to the residents who endured the consequences of poor environmental design.

Designing, Changing, and Preserving Environments

Theory and research on environmental effects on behavior have given us enough information to design environments that reduce negative consequences while promoting constructive behavior. *Environmental design* refers to the systematic process of adjusting the built environment to meet human needs more effectively (Bell et al., 1978). Such research has been applied to schools, hospitals, offices, prisons, museums, and homes (see Krasner, 1978).

The design process begins with an awareness of needs and of alternative arrangements that might serve these needs. For example, should university residences be built in a dormitory style or apartment style to provide for both personal and educational needs? Specific behavioral standards are required to test the success or failure of the different design alternatives. How can the effect of design on social interaction and study habits of students in residences be measured? This form of evaluation research identifies and then assesses the effects of the alternative that is implemented. Do students in apartment-style residences perform academically as well or worse than students in traditional dorms? The end result should be the design of a more habitable environment that fits the needs and behaviors of people who live in it.

Recently, the concepts and methods of ecological psychology developed by Roger Barker and his associates have been applied to environmental design (Stokols, 1978; Wicker, 1979). The basic unit of analysis—*the behavior setting*—is composed of a recurring pattern of activity in the same time and space boundaries (a basketball game, for instance). The concept of *manning* has led to the study of the consequences of undermanning or overmanning—that is, having fewer or more than the number of people required to maintain a behavior setting at an optimum level. (Ever try to play basketball with twenty-seven people on each team?) After the behavior setting has been carefully analyzed, changes can be instituted to improve the setting's functioning and the outcomes for occupants. For example, one study involved the installation of a queuing device for lineups at crowded bus stops in order to reduce overmanning and stress and to make the boarding process safer and more equitable. In these ways, environmental psychologists can play an important role in enhancing the fit between people and their environments.

Many environments, however, do *not* need changing. This is particularly the case with natural environments that need protection and preservation rather than modification. Unfortunately, there has been relatively little research on the human response to the natural environment (Stokols, 1978). The greatest challenge appears to be how to change human attitudes and behaviors toward a more respectful and conserving approach to our natural surroundings. Various strategies of environmental education have been developed to inform people about the scope of the problem and to present alternatives to alleviate environmental problems such as pollution and energy waste (Bell et al., 1978). While such programs effectively increase environmental awareness, the link between education and behavior remains weak. The important goal at present is to identify aspects of the program and the participants that relate to success versus failure, and to design future programs with these elements in mind. The direct use of reinforcement in relation to environmental behavior may be a more effective strategy for preserving environments than attitude-change programs. In addition the use of environmental "prompts" (such as antilittering signs) have been found to be moderately effective. By combining such strategies, government departments, industry, and environmental protection groups may possibly have some impact before it is too late.

SOCIAL PSYCHOLOGY AND THE LAW

Crime is a growing social issue in contemporary North American society. A recent report of the United States Bureau of Justice Statistics (1980) shows that *30 percent of U.S. households are touched by crime each year.* Common crimes include personal larceny (such as purse snatching), household larceny, burglary, crime of violence (rape, assault), and motor vehicle theft. With the generally rising crime rate, more and more people are worried about their safety and are concerned about the costs of crime to individuals and to society. There is also increasing attention being devoted to white-collar crime—fraud and embezzlement—which work through the misuse of trust and which perpetrate considerable economic and moral damage on society (Stotland, 1977; Geis & Stotland, 1980). We are giving more attention to compensation for the victims of crime. We are more and more frustrated by the difficulties of changing individual behavior and social conditions that contribute to criminal activity. The costs of the criminal justice system are reaching staggering proportions. It now costs the American taxpayer approximately $10,000 to keep one inmate in prison for one year—and there are nearly a half million persons incarcerated (National Institute of Justice, 1980). Furthermore, imprisonment is more likely to elicit rather then prevent further criminal behavior.

These widespread concerns tag crime as a social issue of considerable importance. While there is no clearly identified social movement calling for reform in the criminal justice system, there are many calls for change. Essentially people want protection and restitution at the same time they want cost effectiveness—a tall order in combating a major social issue.

Crime is made more difficult to deal with because it is linked to racism, poverty, and other fundamental social issues (see Chapter 11). In North America, crime rates are higher among the poor and the disadvantaged, particularly among racial minority groups such as blacks and Indians. The disproportionate representation of the disadvantaged permeates every aspect of the criminal justice system. Minority group members are more likely to be the perpetrators as well as the victims of crime. If investigated, they are more likely to be arrested and charged. If tried, they are more likely to be convicted. If sentenced, they are more likely to be imprisoned (Stark, 1975).

What is happening here? What allows such apparent bias to exist in a system designed to dispense justice in a fair and equitable manner? Prejudice and discrimination are certainly involved. But the bias certainly represents the wider inequity and injustice within society at large. The criminal justice system, like education or health care, is a human social system. As such it is a system composed of social structures and processes that are social-psychological in nature. Individuals are interacting and influencing each other, and are being affected by the norms, expectations, and other elements of the social environment.

If we wish to understand the criminal justice system, we must begin asking social-psychological questions about each part of the process. We must ask questions about arrest, about conviction, about imprisonment, and about rehabilitation or the lack of it. We must ask how social perception and attitudes affect behavior (what happens when a police officer makes an arrest?). We must ask how group forces influence decision making (how does a jury reach a guilty verdict?). And we must ask how public assumptions and concerns affect government decision making (how, for example, do we decide to build more prisons?).

We clearly need a social psychology of the criminal justice system, a linkage between social psychology and the law—more specifically, the criminal law. Only then can we begin to understand crime and our response to it as a social-psychological process, as well as a legal matter. Out of social psychology's contributions to an understanding of the criminal justice system, we can hope to achieve the goal of greater fairness and humaneness for all those touched by it.

Psychology and the law are no strangers. Their initial connections date back to the beginning of the century (Tapp, 1976). Even then we were interested in how the processes of perception affect eyewitness testimony. We wanted to know how individual personality characteristics related to criminal behavior. Then other disciplines—such as psychiatry, anthropology, and sociology—contributed major empirical studies on the law. This work has been coupled with the development of criminology as an interdisciplinary behavioral science that draws on biology, psychology, and sociology (Jeffery, 1978).

However, according to Tapp (1976), the relationship between psychology and the law generally reflected little progress. Only since the late 1960s has there been a consistent and useful exchange between psychologists and lawyers. Much of this exchange has involved social psychologists. This growing relationship between law and psychology is indicated by interdiscipliinary conferences and publications, by new societies and training programs, and by integrative textbooks and reviews (such as Saks & Hastie, 1978; Tapp & Levine, 1977; Toch, 1979; Thibaut & Walker, 1975).

Tapp (1976) identifies three key themes or areas that are at the interface of psychology and the law: (1) the process of legal socialization that takes place in the community and society at large, (2) the judicial process that involves the courts, and (3) the criminal justice process that deals with convicted offenders in prisons and elsewhere.

Legal socialization involves the acquisition of legal attitudes and behaviors and the development of individual standards for making legal judgments about what is right and wrong. It also involves learning to use the legal system for solving problems encountered in society (Tapp, 1971). Theories and studies of moral development have been especially useful in understanding the relation between the behavior of the individual and the laws of society.

The *judicial process* covers jury selection and decisions, eyewitness identification and testimony, and the overall functioning of the adversary system followed by the courts. To this we should add the initial contact of the individual with the system: investigation, arrest, police interrogation, and plea bargaining between legal defenders and prosecutors.

The *criminal justice process* involves the field of corrections—the prisons, and the training and related programs designed to constrain and rehabilitate the offender in accordance with society's norms of acceptable behavior.

Clinical, developmental, and social psychologists have contributed to a greater understanding of each of these major areas, with social psychologists showing a particular interest in individual attitudes, interpersonal influences and group processes.

In our examination of the total criminal justice system, we should single out one concept that may be especially useful for social-psychological analysis (Shaver, Gilbert & Williams, 1975). *Discretion* is the power of public officials to act according to their individual judgment and conscience within the rules and principles of the law. The purpose of discretion is to make justice flexible and individualized so that the unique circumstances of each case are considered. However, the exercise of discretion is affected by numerous social-psychological factors, including attitudes, attributions, values, roles, interpersonal attraction, and group norms.

Why does an officer arrest someone? What leads the prosecutor to proceed with a charge? How does the jury weigh the evidence? Why does a prison warden use solitary confinement as a punishment? Each of these questions involves the exercise of discretion—an exercise that (according to many legal scholars) is inadequately controlled at all levels of the criminal justice system. Shaver et al. (1975) suggest that the principle of discretion might establish the role of social psychologists in the law. Such a role would involve a description and analysis of the system, emphasizing factors that affect discretion as well as evaluations and interventions that would improve accuracy and equity in the dispensing of justice.

In our examination of some of the existing and potential contributions of social psychology to the functioning of the criminal justice system, we will see that at each step in the system social psychology has something to offer toward the pursuit of justice.

Arrest, Interrogation, and Prosecution

The police are the bridge between the criminal justice system and the average citizen—a function complicated by the need to enforce the law while maintaining good relations with the public. To explore the police role still further, social psychologists have focused on a number of concerns, even devoting a special issue of the *Journal of Social Issues* to the police (Stotland, 1975).

One concern centers around the observation that police officers and their families tend to live separately from the rest of the community. In a sense they have become an in-group, with their own interests, concerns, attitudes, and values. Studies of the predominant values held by police have indeed shown some striking and consistent differences between police officers and citizens. Rokeach, Miller, and Snyder (1971) found that police tend to value a sense of accomplishment and an exciting life more than other community members. They give less priority to equality and a world of beauty. Compared to the average citizen, police value the behaviors of self-control and obedience over cheerfulness, helpfulness, and forgiveness.

These findings have been replicated and extended by Griffith and Cafferty (1977), generally reinforcing a picture of the police holding more conservative values and attitudes than the general public. At the same time, many values such as freedom, happiness, self-respect, and true friendship showed no difference between police and citizens, and most values were ranked in similar orders of priority. Griffith and Cafferty conclude that programs designed to improve police-community relations should begin by looking at these areas of value consensus, and then examine critical differences on values such as equality. Such efforts, aimed at greater mutual understanding and respect, would improve relations between the police and the public and make a difficult job more effective.

In the sequential steps of the criminal justice system, the police are the first with an opportunity to exercise discretion (Shaver et al., 1975). This discretion lies in their decision to arrest or not to arrest, a choice that may be influenced by social-psychological variables as well as legal factors (see Black, 1971; La Fave, 1965). The police officer has an opinion about the law in question; he or she notes the suspect's attitude of respect or disrespect—simple examples of social attitudes and interaction that affect the arrest decision. Once a suspect is apprehended, he or she is interrogated—a second opportunity for the continued exercise of discretion. The police may resort to social-psychological tactics to gain a confession (see Zimbardo, 1969). The interrogator may attempt to establish a friendly and understanding but false relationship with the suspect—"a Dutch uncle." The interrogator can then manipulate the suspect using social approval as a reinforcer. Ingratiation techniques such as flattery and nonverbal techniques such as a pat on the shoulder place further subtle demands on the suspect to cooperate. According to Shaver et al. (1975), the choice of interrogation technique depends as much on social-psychological factors as it does on established procedure or regulations (Shaver et al., 1975).

An admission of guilt is a central factor in the procedure of *plea bargaining*—yet another opportunity for the exercise of discretion. The prosecuting attorney (at his or her discretion) negotiates a reduction of the charge against the defendant in exchange for a guilty plea and a waiver of the right to trial. Plea bargaining has become the rule rather than the exception in the criminal justice system, with over 90 percent of the felony convictions in the United States obtained this way.

Negotiation is a social-psychological process (see Chapter 12), drawing the attention of social psychologists to its role in plea bargaining. Gregory, Mowen, and Linder (1978) designed a controlled laboratory procedure to study plea bargaining, and to examine the effect of variables that are important in legal decisions. University students engaged in a role play in which they were asked to imagine that they had been arrested for armed robbery. They listened to a recording of their defense attorney's summary of the evidence and were given details of the charges against them and the punishment they would receive if convicted. They were then offered a plea bargain to plead guilty to the lesser

In deciding whether to make an arrest, the police are the first within the criminal justice system to exercise *discretion*—the power of public officials to act according to their individual judgment and conscience within the rules and principles of the law. *(Eugene Richards/Magnum Photos, Inc.)*

charge of second-degree burglary and to take a 3-month jail sentence. The results appear in Table 15.2. Subjects who were told that they were innocent were much less likely to accept the plea bargain than those who were told that they were guilty. Subjects faced with a higher number of charges (armed robbery, grand theft with a dangerous weapon, assault with a deadly weapon, and first-degree burglary) were more likely to plead guilty than those charged only with armed robbery. In addition, the prospect of a more severe punishment (10–15 years in prison versus 1–2 years) induced a higher frequency of guilty pleas.

These results suggest that the practice of overcharging effectively draws guilty pleas from guilty defendants. But overcharging and threat of penalties

Table 15.2   PERCENTAGE OF DEFENDANTS ACCEPTING A PLEA BARGAIN IN RELATION TO NUMBER OF CHARGES AND SEVERITY OF PUNISHMENT

	Innocent Defendants				Guilty Defendants			
	High Charge		Low Charge		High Charge		Low Charge	
Severity	%	n	%	n	%	n	%	n
High	33	18	12	17	100	19	82	17
Low	11	18	13	15	83	23	63	16

Source: Gregory, Mowen & Linder (1978).

might also induce some innocent defendants to plead guilty to a crime they never committed. As Shaver et al. (1975) point out, these discretionary practices by prosecuting attorneys virtually demand further research by social psychologists.

Social Psychology in Court: The Judicial Process

Both legal professionals and social scientists who study the law are concerned with two issues: the attainment of justice for individuals, and the role of law in achieving a just social order (Tapp, 1976). In this balance between justice and law and order, judicial process plays the central role in the dispensation of justice through the functioning of the courts. The concern of social psychologists with the judicial process is shown, for example, in a recent comprehensive review entitled *Social Psychology in Court* (Saks & Hastie, 1978). These authors examine the characteristics and behaviors of judges; jury selection, composition and decision making; the behavior of lawyers and defendants; and the presentation of evidence including eyewitness testimony.

The role of the eyewitness in the judicial process is often quite central if not dramatic. The identification of the suspect, or alternately, the provision of an alibi, can be crucial elements in decisions to convict or acquit the defendant. But psychologists have their own perspective of this issue. Long interested in eyewitness accuracy, they have found reason to question this sort of evidence as unreliable (Buckhout, 1974; Yarmey, 1979). However, as Tapp (1976) notes, eyewitness evidence continues to be deemed reliable, and research results have had little impact on reducing the unwarranted reliance on this element of the judicial process.

It may be time for some rethinking and redirecting. Wells (1978) offers a more charitable and more complex view of eyewitness research and its applications to the criminal justice system. Wells believes that eliminating eyewitness testimony from the judicial process is neither desirable nor feasible. Then he distinguishes between two types of eyewitness research, each looking at its own distinct type of variables. The first examines variables that affect eyewitness accuracy, but are not under the control of the criminal justice system. This type includes characteristics of the crime (its seriousness, for example), the defendant (race, age, and so on), and the witness (for example, how he or she perceives things). This research tells us the eye is not a camera, but it does not yield results that tell us how to increase the accuracy of eyewitness testimony. We cannot, for example, change a defendant's race or the seriousness of the crime already committed.

The second type of eyewitness research has much more potential. It focuses on system variables such as the method of questioning eyewitnesses, the use of mug shots, and the structure of the suspect lineup. In identifying how inaccuracies and deficiencies creep into eyewitness testimony, the results can be used to improve the practices that are involved. Thus system-variable research by social psychologists can provide tested alternatives for the criminal justice system without attempting to eliminate eyewitness testimony.

Moving toward the arena of practice, Wells and his colleagues have examined the effects of expert advice on jurors' judgments of eyewitness accuracy (Wells, Lindsay & Tousignant, 1980). Recent research on eyewitness testimony shows that jurors appear overwilling to believe in the accuracy of eyewitness testimony and many rely too heavily on the confidence of the eyewitness in evaluating the accuracy of the testimony. Subjects who were potential jurors were shown a videotape of an eyewitness who had identified the perpetrator of a staged crime. The conditions of the crime varied so that eyewitnesses either had poor, moderate, or good witnessing conditions. Before the eyewitness videotape was shown, expert advice was given to one half of the subjects via a videotaped courtroom examination of a psychologist being questioned by a defense attorney on eyewitness memory. The main points of the advice were that eyewitness confidence shows little relationship to accuracy. The advice took. Subjects who viewed the expert testimony were less likely to believe that eyewitnesses had made accurate identifications, especially in the poor and moderate witnesssing conditions. Expert advice also greatly reduced the jurors' reliance on eyewitness confidence as an indicator of accuracy. In short, social psychologists have developed some promising guidelines for increasing the effective use of eyewitness testimony in the judicial process.

As mentioned previously, the role of social psychologists in the judicial process does at times go beyond research to actual involvement in court procedddings. In Toledo, Ohio, in the early morning of September 18, 1970, a police officer was shot and killed while sitting in his squad car a half block away from the headquarters of the local chapter of the Black Panthers. Minutes later, a known member of the Black Panthers was arrested; he was later charged with murder. The defense counsel asked social psychologists Milton Rokeach and Neil Vidmar to testify in order to challenge the assumption that a reasonably unbiased jury could be selected. The existing juror list tended to exclude both young people and blacks.

Rokeach and Vidmar (1973) presented both national survey data on attitudes and values of the American population and studies about attitudes toward capital punishment. They demonstrated that older, less educated, white male jurors would be biased against the defendant (a young black with a militant philosophy), and would tend to favor the death penalty. Their testimony had an effect on jury selection in that defense attorneys were allowed to question prospective jurors about their specific opinions and attitudes. In the subsequent trial, the jury— composed of ten whites and two blacks—was unable to reach a verdict.

In similar ways, social scientists have aided defense attorneys in selecting juries in a number of highly publicized trials of activists, including the Harrisburg Seven, Dennis Banks of the American Indian Movement, and Angela Davis (Wrightsman, 1978). The current box score indicates that in a total of nine such situations, the defense has won seven cases (Berk, 1976).

In legal terms, one part of the jury selection process is known as the *voir dire*, roughly translated as "to speak the truth" or "to see what he or she says" (Suggs & Sales, 1978). It refers to the process whereby prospective jurors may be rejected by the judge and the attorneys. Jurors may be removed because they do not meet some statutory requirement for jury service (residency, for example), or because the attorneys demonstrate that the juror is too biased or prejudiced to render a fair and impartial verdict. Lawyers have long attempted to develop valid generalizations about what type of jurors are best for their case, but there is little scientific support for these assumptions. For example, it has been suggested that jurors of Jewish, Irish, or southern European descent are more favorable toward defendants than jurors of British or Northern European ancestry. Moreover, what little data there are indicate that lawyers spend most of their time in voir dire attempting to win jurors over to their side through indoctrination and ingratiation (Blunk & Sales, 1977).

Adding to the experience of legal professionals, social scientists have developed systematic procedures for jury selection. These include demographic rating systems to predict juror attitudes, background investigations of individual jurors, and in-court observations of prospective jurors (Suggs & Sales, 1978). Other characteristics, including authoritarianism and legal development (related to moral development), have also been suggested for selecting more impartial and fair juries. Whether these techniques should be used, however, is an ethical controversy that has been hotly debated (Tapp, 1976; Wrightman, 1978). Are social psychologists helping to produce an unbiased jury, or simply one biased toward the side that is paying their fee? If that is so, it has been said that their hands are no less stained than those of attorneys who attempt to select a favorable jury. Suggs and Sales suggest that in any event the social science approach is no more or less effective than the legal approach; consequently, the conduct of the voir dire process still remains more of an art than a science. Nevertheless, it does appear to be an essential safeguard in the administration of justice (Tapp, 1976).

Jury selection is important, but it is only the beginning of that most dramatic and often controversial element of the judicial process—the jury trial. Trial by jury of one's peers was developed in the British system of common law and transplanted to North America in colonial times. In their study of the law, social psychologists have concentrated on the jury trial by analyzing court records and recollections of participants, and by developing laboratory methods to partly simulate trial proceedings. When you realize that *less than 5 percent* of all crimes ever come to trial, so much attention seems surprising. However, trial by jury not only deals with the most dramatic and controversial crimes, but also seems to be a test of society's commitment to a just legal order (Tapp, 1976).

Nonetheless, the legal and social science communities have been rather critical of the jury system. In his 1978 Presidential Address to the Society for the Psychological Study of Social Issues, Lawrence Wrightsman puts the "American trial jury on trial," and reviews research by social psychologists that has questioned many of the assumptions on which the jury system is based. The functioning of the Canadian jury system, similarly derived from the British model, has also been scrutinized by social psychologists (such as Doob, 1976).

Wrightsman (1978) examines the judicial assumption that jurors are able to separate evidence from nonevidence—specifically the opening statements of attorneys and evidence that is ruled inadmissible. Opening statements are not to be regarded as evidence, but studies indicate that they do influence perceptions of guilt or innocence and provide a framework into which evidence is assimilated. The question of inadmissible evidence is even more controversial. What happens when a jury has been ordered to disregard some information because the judge sustains an attorney's objection to it? Not only are they unable to do so, but in fact there may be a boomerang or reactance effect that gives even greater impact to the piece of inadmissible evidence.

It has also been repeatedly demonstrated that a host of other irrelevant or "extra-evidential" factors influence jury decisions. The defendant's age or race or sex or physical attractiveness can influence the severity of verdicts rendered by juries. Or the outcome may be affected by the order of presentation of evidence or by an attorney's personal style. These findings clearly question the assumption that juries operate in a rational, objective, and fair manner, uninfluenced by irrelevant factors.

Still other assumptions are questioned by social science evidence. The concept of reasonable doubt is difficult to define, and judges vary in how they convey appropriate instructions to juries. Even our limited research questions whether the meaning of reasonable doubt is actually understood by all jurors. We must also question the ability of jurors to retain all or most of the trial information when they move into the deliberation process. And it is very doubtful that jury deliberations are objective and free from conformity pressures, giving each juror a chance to voice his or her honest opinion and verdict. Studies and recounts of jury deliberations indicate that supposedly irrelevant factors, such as a juror's status or sex, influence his or her power, and that the deliberations may proceed in an irrational and unpredictable manner. If these results and observations are generalizable, we might conclude that it is a good thing that only 3–5 percent of crimes are tried by juries!

Based on his review, Wrightsman (1978) offers suggestions for possible reforms in the jury procedure. The use of videotape might effectively help juries remember all information from the trial. Videotape replay can also delete inadmissible evidence. Judge's instructions could be more standardized, particularly on difficult concepts such as reasonable doubt. The jury deliberation process certainly needs reform, but there is so little direct information on what actually goes on that it is premature to make suggestions.

The use of social-psychological findings for the reform of legal procedures is hampered by more than just inadequate information; there are at least two other major considerations. The first is that judges and attorneys understandably prefer to make decisions based on their experience and judgment rather than on social science findings; at times, too, they have misinterpreted such findings when they *were* used. Second, there are some major limitations in social-psychological research on judicial process that reduce the generalizability and utility of the results.

An illustration of the first problem is Wrightsman's (1978) discussion of two recent jury reforms in the United States: the use of six-person juries, and the change to a nonunanimous decision rule. These reforms were based on research evidence, but the legal system's conception of acceptable empirical evidence falls far short of what social scientists find acceptable. The so-called research on jury size consisted of a small number of uncontrolled observational studies and on expressions of opinion. The decision to drop the requirement for a unanimous verdict was partly based on a misinterpretation of small-group research on conformity! Social scientists are now conducting research to determine the effects of these reforms on both the deliberation process and the outcomes of jury trials. Whether these results will be used more effectively will depend on whether social scientists and legal professionals can establish a more effective collaborative relationship in the years ahead.

As noted, the second reason for lack of utilization of social-psychological research has to do with limitations in the research itself. Denied access to jury deliberation by law, researchers have had to rely on recollections or simulations to study the decision-making process. Unfortunately, many of these studies are not true simulations of legal events, but involve mock jurors (usually college students) responding individually to tape recordings or written booklets that present the trial information. The individual role play of plea bargaining by Gregory et al. (1978), discussed earlier, is an example of this type of simulation. The problem with this approach is that it omits the crucial aspects of small-group interaction in which social psychologists have developed considerable expertise (see Chapter 7). While laboratory "simulations" make it easy to manipulate variables such as the defendant's race or physical attractiveness, they do not involve the subject as a participant in a truly mock jury trial and deliberation. Consequently, it is not surprising that when greater reality is injected into simulated jury studies, different results may be obtained (Wilson & Donnerstein, 1977). It is also likely that the individual deliberations used in most simulations produce different results than group deliberations (see McGuire & Bermant, 1977).

Jury research has generally produced disorderly studies that lack systematic theory and are deficient in their external validity or generalizability (Davis, Bray & Holt, 1976; Tapp, 1976). A number of these limitations, as well as some general concerns, were expressed by Jane Louin Tapp in her 1979 Presidential Address to the Society for the Psychological Study of Social Issues (see Box 15.5). If we expect the legal system to use social-psychological findings, we must do a much better job of producing relevant and valid results, and of convincing legal professionals that we have something valuable to offer. If this occurs, we can expect to see a continuing and growing use of social science research as legal evidence (Loftus & Monahan, 1980; Tanke & Tanke, 1979).

Deterrence, Imprisonment, and Alternatives

The criminal justice system, like world politics (see Chapter 12), bases much of its functioning on the concept of deterrence. Deterrence assumes that criminal behavior can be controlled by the threat of punishment. Hence, crimes of varying severity are punished with sentences of corresponding severity—the fear of punishment being thought to constrain the criminal behavior of would-be offenders. The purse snatcher gets one year; the murderer gets life imprisonment.

Theory and research on social learning (see Chapter 2) indeed tell us that negative reinforcement, punishment, or even lack of positive reinforcement, can sometimes be effective in suppressing an unwanted behavior. Moreover, the work

Box 15.5   FOCUS ON RESEARCH
Contributions of Psychology to the Law

The 1970s brought an unprecedented involvement of psychologists in the study of the legal system. This furthered the development of an exciting field of interdisciplinary activity with diffuse and sprawling boundaries. One of the leaders of this movement, Jane Louin Tapp, took stock of the developments in her 1979 Presidential Address to the Society for the Psychological Study of Social Issues.

The interface of psychology and the law can be expressed in three major areas: legal socialization, the judicial process, and the criminal justice process. An impressive outpouring of publications in all these areas demonstrates the heightened activity in theory, research, and policy making. Yet questions have been raised about the appropriate roles for psychologists studying the law. Tapp identifies four themes that limit the contributions of psychology.

First, there has developed an "overcriminalization of psychology," an overemphasis on things criminal—the criminal personality, eyewitness testimony. This ignores the fact that the law is a *complex social institution* and that it involves broader *social issues*—crime, social control. For example, studies of the judicial process have emphasized the criminal courts with little attention given to civil proceedings.

Second, the drama of the courtroom has seduced psychologists to spend a disproportionate amount of their time studying the jury trial. This apparent equating of the jury process with the entire judicial process misrepresents reality. The majority of disputes are resolved through adjudication and increased study of negotiation processes is in order.

Third, psychologists have relied too much on laboratory simulations of doubtful external validity for studying judicial processes. College students serving as "mock jurors," under conditions very different from the real thing, actually show the mockery of jury research. Researchers should work more closely with legal professionals to select questions and formulate designs that guarantee relevance.

Fourth, psychologists—while recognizing the limitations of psychology—should not see the law as the source of all wisdom on morality or legality. All social systems (churches, unions, universities) are in some sense legal, and psychologists should not look to any particular institution to define normative behavior and societal rules of conduct.

In sum, psychologists have overemphsized individual factors at the expense of social variables and research technology at the expense of theory and values. In the 1980s, Tapp recommends devising better theories and broader methods to study people in real-world legal settings. Only then will psychology make useful policy contributions to help people use the law more effectively.

Source: Tapp, J. L. Psychological and policy perspectives on the law: Reflections on a decade. *Journal of Social Issues*, 1980, *36*(2), 165–192.

on vicarious learning indicates that an observer will refrain from behavior for which a model has been punished. However, rather than affecting what is truly learned, reinforcement (positive or negative) or punishment is more likely to affect the *expression* of a behavior. If a person has learned the behavior and if the prospect of punishment seems remote, the behavior may in fact be undertaken to reach the goals the person wants. For example, the heroin addict needs a fix, and stealing and fencing someone's stereo is the way to get it—with limited risk of getting caught. Deterrence has little effect in this case.

The deterrence model also assumes that the potential offender is aware of the punishments and makes a rational choice about committing a crime or not. But most people are *not* aware of the specific punishments for a criminal act. A great deal of criminal behavior also appears to be irrational or spontaneous; it is rarely a carefully planned excursion that weighs its potential benefits and consequences.

Although the deterrence model suffers from a number of these general weaknesses (Jeffery, 1978; Meier, 1979), it is the cornerstone of the classic approach to criminology and is the model most accepted by legal and political decision makers. Ignoring the importance of personal or environmental factors, deterrence strategy invokes the use of punishment against those who voluntarily violate the law. While there may be some empirical and moral bases for deterrence, the classical approach to criminology has failed. More people are in jails than ever before, and most return following their release. In contrast to deterrence, Jeffery (1978) proposes a new model of criminology that would shift the emphasis from punishment to prevention and give more attention to the physical environment in which crime occurs. Unfortunately, the current sociopolitical trends indicate that there will be more punishment, more prisons, and less prevention and rehabilitation. Jeffery concludes that government has failed to learn from its past failures.

Short of the gas chamber or electric chair, imprisonment is seen as the ultimate deterrent to criminal behavior. The purpose of imprisonment or confinement is not simply punishment or retribution; it also includes protection of society from dangerous offenders and rehabilitation of the offender. Retribution and constraint are obviously achieved, but rehabilitation is generally a myth. Most studies of recidivism (conviction and return to prison following release) indicate that the majority of offenders, often more than 75 percent, commit further crimes. What happens in prisons to account for this?

First, of course, there may be a failure to rehabilitate a person whose social and physical environment produced an effective process of criminal socialization. On top of that, a continuing socialization occurs in prison that supports criminal activity and teaches increasingly sophisticated criminal techniques to the young offender. The power of the inmate group and of prison's informal social system to affect prisoner behavior has repeatedly been demonstrated by sociological studies of offender populations (such as Street, 1970; Sykes & Messinger, 1960). This deviant socialization is supported by the social-psychological processes of prison interaction—a scenario that is dramatically illustrated in the prison simulation by Phillip Zimbardo and his colleagues (see Chapter 8). Prisoners are segregated, depersonalized, and dehumanized. All aspects of life are routinized and controlled by others. Prison officials and guards have a great deal of discretion in the treatment of prisoners, and yet very little is known about how this discretionary power is used (Shaver et al., 1975). Obviously, we need much more research and practice if we are to understand why prisons fail at rehabilitation, and to determine if improvements can be made (see Adams, 1977; Holt, 1976).

Box 15.6   FOCUS ON RESEARCH
An Evaluation of Preventive Policing

The general public, their elected officials, and the police themselves believe that the presence of police officers on patrol severely inhibits criminal activity. Thus, one common response to spiraling crime rates is to increase the number of police "on the street." However, beginning in the 1960s, criminologists and others began to question the relationship between police patrol and crime. In 1972, George Kelling and his colleagues undertook a comprehensive and rigorous field experiment to evaluate the effectivenesas of routine preventive patrol. The impetus for this study came from within the Kansas City Police Department and a research grant was provided by the Police Foundation.

Under the research agreement, the police department committed itself to a 1-year experiment, provided that crime did not reach unacceptable levels. In the design, fifteen Kansas City police beats were randomly divided into three groups: (1) reactive beats in which routine preventive patrol was eliminated and in which officers responded only to calls for service, (2) control beats in which patrol was maintained at its usual level of one car per beat, and (3) proactive beats in which patrol was intensified to two or three times the usual level—partly by using cars from reactive beats.

A variety of survey questionnaires, interviews, observations, and police department data were used to assess the effects of the experiment. The results were strongly at variance with the traditional claims regarding the benefits of preventive policing. The different levels of patrol had no effect on burglaries, auto thefts, robberies, or vandalism—crimes considered to be deterred by preventive policing. There were no consistent differences across experimental conditions in rates of reporting crime or in citizen attitudes toward the police. Citizen fear of crime and citizen satisfaction with police did not vary with the different rates of patrol. The findings therefore point to a large discrepancy between what the public wants the police to do and what they can and should do.

However, the researchers point out that the findings do not show that the police are not important in solving crime, nor do they automatically justify reductions in the level of policing. In all experimental conditions, police were still available, and it would be inappropriate to suggest that total police withdrawal from an area is part of the answer to crime.

Source: Kelling, G. L., Pate, T., Dieckman, D. & Brown, C. E. The Kansas City preventive patrol experiment: A summary report. In G. V. Glass (Ed.), *Evaluation studies review annual* (Vol. 1). Beverly Hills: Sage, 1976.

To improve the criminal justice system, we must also consider new ways of dealing with crime prevention and treatment of the offender. In the development and evaluation of alternate strategies and programs, social psychologists have decisive roles to play as applied researchers, program development consultants, and program evaluators (see Chapter 13). Research can be executed and organized in ways that will contribute to improvements in policies related to criminal justice (see Waller, 1979). New methods of prevention can be successfully evaluated using rigorous methods of social research (see Box 15.6).

Alternatives to incarceration are being developed, and these also require careful evaluation. A program of juvenile diversion, for example, diverts young offenders from the judicial process of the courts and may require them to make restitution to the victim or the community (see Bohnstedt, 1978). Another example is the alternative of work-release programs for convicted offenders who would otherwise be imprisoned (see Waldo & Chiricos, 1977).

As these developments occur, we will continue to confront public and scientific debate over the effectiveness of deterrence versus rehabilitation. Rather than take a black/white stance on one side or the other, social scientists and practitioners can advocate an incremental approach to policy making and recommend the strengthening of effective rehabilitative efforts (Spiro, 1978). This will require a detailed understanding of the criminal justice system as a complex and multipurpose organization (Newman, 1979). If applied social psychologists are willing to grapple with this complexity and controversy, there is no question that our contributions—through theory, research, and practice—can significantly improve our criminal justice system.

Summary

Education is a social experience of much importance in our lives. However, social psychology initially showed little interest in education. Now the field is actively applying social-psychological concepts, and more importantly, studying the social functioning of the educational system at all levels of analysis.

Role theory has been useful for understanding the attitudes and behavior of students, teachers, and administrators in educational settings. Teachers' expectations of student performance may result in self-fulfilling prophecies which have considerable impact. Interaction Process Analysis demonstrates that teachers take a very active role in classroom communication while students tend to remain passive.

Applied social psychology can contribute to constructive educational change at the interpersonal group, and organizational levels. A student-centered approach to teaching sees the student-teacher relationship as a helping relationship in which the qualities of genuineness, respect, and empathic understanding are crucial to student satisfaction and achievement. The knowledge and skills of group processes can be translated into structured exercises to enhance teaching and learning. Organization development in educational settings shows a variety of training and consultation activities with beneficial outcomes.

Environmental psychology is an interdisciplinary field that studies the interrelationship between human behavior and the built and natural environment. It is distinguished by a systems approach emphasizing the reciprocal influence of behavior and environment, a problem orientation, an interdisciplinary emphasis, and a social-psychological perspective.

Research on the congruence between environmental attitudes and behavior has typically shown a lack of consistency. Direct reinforcement may be the crucial variable affecting environmental behavior.

The study of human spatial behavior or proxemics looks at the way people use physical space as a means for regulating social interaction. Altman's model of proxemic behavior integrates the four concepts of personal space, territoriality, crowding, and privacy.

Environmental effects on behavior include the impact of environmental stressors, the influence of built environments, and the human response to the natural environment. Noise and high density, if of sufficient intensity, can produce unpleasant consequences for humans. Large urban centers combine a number of environmental stressors and also involve stimulus overload leading to psychological and social costs. Environmental design has been shown to affect both personal and social variables.

The relationship between psychology and the law has a long but limited history. Aspects of arrest, interrogation, and prosecution have been studied. Attitudes and social interaction may affect decisions made during arrest and interrogation. Plea bargaining appears to be affected by the offender's sense of guilt or innocence, the number of charges, and the severity of the predicted punishment.

Research on the judicial process has focused on eyewitness testimony, jury selection, and jury decision making. The unreliability of eyewitness identification has led to a suggestion that researchers concentrate on system variables that can be changed to improve eyewitness testimony. Social psychologists have assisted in jury selection through a variety of methods, the effectiveness of which remain to be satisfactorily documented.

Deterrence is the cornerstone of the criminal justice system but appears to have severe limitations. Applied social psychologists can make significant contributions to the development and evaluation of alternative programs for preventing crime and for rehabilitating offenders.

Further Readings

Altman, I. *The environment and social behavior.* Monterey, Calif.: Brooks-Cole, 1975.

Bar-Tal, D. & Saxe, L. *Social psychology of education: Theory and research.* Washington, D.C.: Hemisphere, 1978.

Bell, P. A., Fisher, J. D. & Loomis, R. *Environmental psychology.* Philadelphia: W. B. Saunders, 1978.

Guskin, A. E. & Guskin, S. L. *A social psychology of education.* Reading, Mass.: Addison-Wesley, 1970.

Saks, M. J. & Hastie, R. *Social psychology in court.* Florence, Kentucky: Van Nostrand Reinhold, 1978.

CHAPTER OUTLINE

SIXTEEN

Emerging Areas of Application and the Future

We have come a long way in this book, and the journey has been demanding and at times complicated. It is not easy to say how all the pieces of our experience fit together, or whether indeed they should. We have started with a picture and a vision. The picture sees contemporary social psychology in a time of flux—some say of crisis. Strong criticisms have been made of the overreliance on the laboratory method and the trivial nature of much theoretical and empirical work. Yet, we have seen that social psychologists share with other social scientists a range of theories, research methods, and practice skills that have much potential for understanding human social behavior and for improving human welfare. Motivated by the humanistic value base, we have traveled through several levels of analysis and areas of application wherein social psychologists are making significant contributions to understanding and action. Thus, we have pursued a vision that sees applied social psychologists involved in the meaningful and humane activities of helping to alleviate social problems of considerable variety, complexity, and intransigence.

We now stand on the crest of a hill. Behind us stretch the accomplishments and achievements in numerous areas of application—from groups to organizations to the institutions of education and criminal justice to society and the world at large. Each of these areas is continuing its development as a vital component of a concerned and compassionate applied social psychology. But just ahead of us we see new activities and new opportunities barely on the threshold of realization. Beyond that, we dimly sense the future potential of applied social psychology. We see the need for the further clarification of the identity, role, and responsibilities of applied social psychologists. We see the need for new training programs to incorporate the knowledge and skills we have acquired, so that we may send our progeny boldly into the challenge of the future. And we see the need to clarify and continue our relationship with the broader field of social psychology and its parent disciplines of psychology and sociology. There is much to be done. But the potential benefits to social psychology and to society make the effort and the risk worthwhile.

In this chapter, I would first like to look at three emerging areas of application in applied social psychology: health care, consumer behavior, and public policy, all of which typify the rapid developments taking place today. Then we will look to the future of applied social psychology as a coherent and identifiable arena of activity, and as a creative compromise between traditional and radical social psychology.

EMERGING AREAS OF APPLICATION

Social Psychology and Health Care

The pursuit of health as a prerequisite to a happy and productive life is not only part of the American Dream but is an objective pursued by all people. That good health is one of the most cherished values of the American people is borne out by

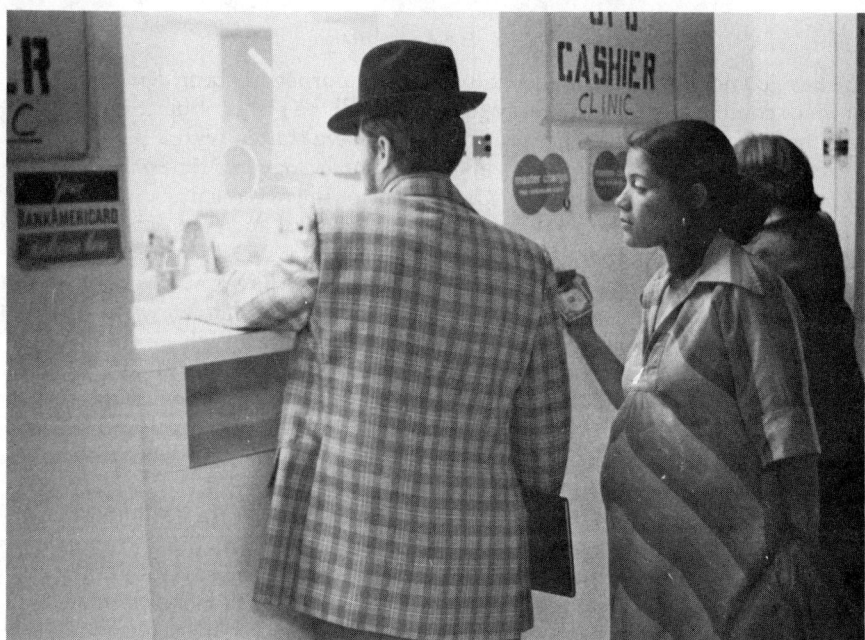

Americans spend over $100 billion a year on health care, thus making it the largest single area of human service. *(Martha Rudenstein)*

the fact that in 1977 alone over $100 billion was devoted to health care, making it the largest single area of human service (Taylor, 1978). This growth pattern is recreated throughout the industrialized world, opening up vast numbers of challenging and demanding opportunities for the involvement of social psychologists in health care systems.

The involvement of psychologists in the field of medicine is certainly not an overnight phenomenon. In 1911, the American Psychological Association (APA) recommended the introduction of psychology courses into the medical school curriculum. In the years that followed, psychologists have been deeply involved in medical research and training (Nathan, Lubin, Matarazzo & Persely, 1979)—an involvement that has increased dramatically since World War II. By the 1970s, medical psychology had developed as an identified subdiscipline of psychology, with more and more psychologists performing a variety of roles in health care settings (Asken, 1979). This mushrooming activity led to the creation of a new APA Division of Health Care Psychology in 1978, to the creation of new journals such as *Behavioral Medicine*, and to the publication of special issues of psychology journals focusing on health care—including *Professional Psychology* (Budman & Wertlieb, 1979), the *Journal of Social Issues*, (Friedman & DiMatteo, 1979), and the *Journal of Applied Behavioral Science* (Weisbord & Goodstein, 1978).

Given this rapid proliferation of involvement and ideas, it is not surprising that the diversity and complexity of medical psychology almost defies definition. To encompass this diversity, Asken (1979) defined *medical psychology* as "the study of psychological factors related to any and all aspects of physical health, illness and its treatment at the individual, group and systems level" (p. 67)—a study that involves research, application, intervention, and teaching.

To further clarify the field, Asken identifies four major areas of medical psychology:

- *psychosomatics*, which studies how psychological stress results in physical illness
- *somatopsychology*, which investigates the effects of physical changes on psychological functioning
- *behavioral medicine*, which is concerned with the psychological reactions of patients to physical illness and treatment, and the effect of these reactions on recovery
- *health care studies*, which look at health care systems from a macro-perspective rather than at an individual level, and ask questions about overall utilization and effectiveness

Asken proposes that the continuing coordination of these diverse areas will further the goals of preventing illness and providing the most complete and efficient care to those who suffer from physical illness.

How can social psychologists contribute in unique and useful ways to the rapidly expanding field of medical psychology? The answer to that question constitutes the theme of this section. Just as clinical and social psychology have fused into community psychology directed toward the enhancement of mental well-being, these two subdisciplines can collaborate to make major cooperative contributions to health care psychology, directed toward greater physical well-being for all people.

Taylor (1978) presents a compelling case for developing the role of social psychologists in medicine and medical practice. Until now, social psychologists have made only modest contributions, when in fact they have much to say that is relevant and useful. However, we must distinguish between a social psychology *of* medicine and a social psychology *in* medicine. The former refers to studying health care from an academic base; the latter involves the social psychologist as a member of interdisciplinary medical teams, helping to train health care professionals and conducting research in medical settings. (To some degree, this distinction again parallels the more general one between *applying social psychology* and *applied social psychology.*)

Taylor also points out that social psychology brings a unique focus to the study of health care: the integration of the individual with the social structure through the study of situational variables that affect behavior. Other disciplines tend to concentrate on only one part of the picture. Psychiatry and clinical psychology emphasize personality dispositions and individual interventions in the development and treatment of physical illness. Sociology (of which medical sociology is an important branch) analyzes the social struture of delivery systems, partly in relation to the larger society.

The involvement of social psychology in health care is also facilitated by some enormous changes that have taken place in medicine in the last few decades. Taylor sees a clear shift in health care delivery from the treatment of acute infectious disease to the management of chronic disease and the prevention of illness. For example, medical practice is now less concerned with the treatment of smallpox or polio and more concerned with the patient's adjustment to terminal cancer or with the effect of lifestyle on heart disease. Governments—the major funders of health care—are also recommending a shift from traditional treatment to prevention. In 1975, the Canadian government completed a position paper that clearly indicated that environmental and life-style factors were the major contributors to illness and premature death (Lalonde, 1975). The major contributors to

Environmental and life-style factors, such as driving habits, are major contributors to illness and premature death. *(Ad Council/U.S. Department of Transportation)*

early death were car accidents, followed by heart disease, other accidents, and respiratory disease including lung cancer—all largely attributable to "living dangerously" in terms of driving habits, eating habits, and the use of alcohol and tobacco. Similarly, most illness was attributable to self-imposed risks in the areas of drug usage (particularly alcohol), poor diet, and a lack of adequate exercise. Consequently, the report recommends a clear strategy of health promotion—to influence and assist individuals and organizations to adopt healthier lifestyles. This new approach, now being adopted throughout the world, involves a host of social-psychological questions in areas such as social influence and attitude and behavior change.

Patients have also become more informed and alert consumers and must take more responsibility for the management of their own illness and life-style. Increasing specialization, group practice, and prepaid service plans have altered the traditionally close interpersonal relationship between doctor and patient. As a result there may be increasing feelings of dissatisfaction among patients, a sense of depersonalization, and an inclination to ignore medical advice. All these changes involve social-psychological processes.

The rationale for the involvement of social psychologists in medicine and medical practice is compelling. But where in the sequence of health care can unique contributions be made? *At every point in the process.* More specifically, Taylor (1978) proposes that social psychology can make valuable contributions to problems in five related areas: in the *etiology,* or causation, of physical illness; in the prevention of illness; in the management of chronic disease, particularly in self-management by the patient; in the treatment of illness, including the control of reactions to both the illness and the medical treatment; and in the delivery of health care services.

Etiology and Prevention of Illness. How we choose to live in Western industrialized society contributes significantly to the onset and severity of illness, especially such serious chronic illnesses as heart disease and cancer. In relating life-style variables to physical health, psychologists (including social psychologists) have found that heart disease, for example, may stem from stress and how we cope with it, from the use of tobacco, from the foods we eat, and from the amount of exercise we get (see Glass, 1977). Stress, in fact, has been isolated as a major cause of both mental and physical illness.

If we know that many people are living dangerously, that their life-style behavior is increasing the probability of illness, what can we do about it? The answer lies in prevention. Social psychologists can contribute to preventive programs involving life-style interventions that encourage people to eat better, stop smoking, reduce alcohol use, get fit, and so on (see Evans, 1980). Along with this element of behavioral medicine, we must also develop a *preventive psychology* (Taylor, 1978). This would involve training individuals in effective ways of dealing with stress, designing effective support groups for people who are ill, and designing organizational environments to reduce stress on the job and elsewhere. All these endeavors presuppose that we understand the functioning of self-destructive life-styles before we attempt to intervene. Again, social psychology holds promise—in this case, through its theories. For example, alcoholism, a physical and social problem of immense proportions, can be partly understood using social-psychological theories (Sadava, 1979). In particular, attribution theory suggests that causal explanations of alcoholism help determine how alcoholics are treated—by their family, by people trying to help them, and by themselves. All indications point to the making of internal (or victim-blame) attributions that mediate feelings of dislike and tendencies of rejection toward the alcoholic (McHugh, Beckman & Frieze, 1979).

Social psychologists might profitably draw on the knowledge of prevention developed in community psychology (see Chapter 10). Wertlieb (1979) discusses how the concepts of primary, secondary, and tertiary prevention used in public health and preventive mental health can be adapted to health care psychology. This approach assumes a new model of physical illness that sees the causes of illness in social, psychological, and biological factors.

Primary prevention would try to reduce the overall incidence of illness by reducing life stress and promoting competent and healthy living.

Secondary prevention would require early intervention following the onset of stress or illness, in an attempt to reduce its physical and psychosocial effects. For example, we can provide psychological support to couples who are facing the stress of separation or divorce. By helping them deal with stress, we would hope to reduce the incidence of any resulting physical illness.

Tertiary prevention would attempt to help the sick deal more effectively with their illness and the resulting stress. This is the purpose, for example, of support programs to help terminally ill patients and their families cope with the fear and anxiety of dying.

Despite the distinctions among these different types of prevention, any intervention might serve in any of the preventive modes. Relaxation training—to name but one kind of intervention—could be taught to school children as a general stress reducer (primary prevention); or could be used to help people with a high risk of heart disease (secondary prevention); or could help rehabilitate victims of heart attack, and prevent further illness (tertiary prevention). We must be aware of the various types of prevention if we are to involve ourselves effectively in health care.

An excellent example of the involvement of social psychologists in prevention is provided by the work of Richard Evans and his colleagues at the University of Houston. In one study, they developed and tested an educational program to deter the onset of cigarette smoking among seventh-graders (Evans, Rozelle, Mittlemark, Hansen, Bane & Havis, 1978). Although the children knew that it was a dangerous habit, they were still starting to smoke. The researchers identified peer pressure, parents who smoke, mass media influence, and relatively low concern about long-term effects on health as reasons why the students were smoking.

To help the children respond to these influences, a videotape program was created to teach them to recognize peer, parent, and media pressures, and to develop specific techniques for resisting these pressures. For example, a videotape on media influences and advertising techniques described and analyzed the use of subtle appeals to smoke, based on implied sexual attractiveness and social popularity. Students were also shown a demonstration of the immediate physiological effects of smoking, using an analysis of the nicotine content in saliva specimens.

The effect of the program was evaluated by assigning almost 400 nonsmoking seventh-grade students to four different conditions: (1) the full treatment group in which students were exposed to the complete nonsmoking program including feedback and testing, (2) the feedback condition in which students received reports on the number of students in the study who had begun to smoke, (3) a testing only condition in which students were exposed to the pretest and three posttests, and (4) the control group which received only the pretest and one posttest. Thus, all students except the control group were tested on their smoking behavior on three occasions during the study—at 1 week, 5 weeks, and 10 weeks following the pretest.

The results of the study showed a significantly lower onset of smoking in the three experimental groups as compared to the control group (18.3 percent versus 9.6 percent). The full treatment group did not differ from the feedback or testing only groups. The researchers suggest this was due to the strong effect of the demonstration on the immediate effects of smoking which was shown to all the experimental groups.

Evans et al. (1978) concluded that their investigation "serves as a demonstration of how social psychologists working with biomedical researchers and school systems can develop, implement, and evaluate an intervention strategy to deal with a crucial public health problem" (p. 134). I can only agree with this belief and with its implications for our extended future role in the prevention of physical illness.

Management and Treatment of Illness. Modern medicine has reduced the incidence of acute infectious disease and prolonged the lives and reduced the suffering of those with chronic illnesses. With the emphasis on chronic disease has come a growing awareness of the importance of managing illness, particularly self-management by the patients. Only the individual can change his or her eating habits, exercise regimen, and ways of dealing with stress or coping with illness. In accordance with this shifting focus in health care, Taylor (1978) sees three issues that could profitably be addressed by social psychologists:

- the importance of the doctor-patient relationship in educating and motivating patients to engage in successful self-management of their illness
- increased consumer behavior among long-term patients, who often demand more information about and more involvement in their own care
- understanding the psychological reactions to chronic illness in ways that will help patients and their families cope with the stress that is involved

Friedman and DiMatteo (1970) stress the fundamental importance of the interpersonal relationship in health care. They see medical practice moving to a more holistic orientation in which interpersonal factors play an integral role in the healing process, along with any technical or physical intervention that is undertaken. The ultimate success of surgery, for example, does not depend simply on the skill of the surgeon and the sophistication of the equipment, but on the patient's psychological state as it is affected by the interpersonal relations surrounding the intervention. In short, based on accumulating evidence, ignoring interpersonal factors is in fact a scientific error.

Friedman and DiMatteo suggest that the relation between interpersonal processes and health care is expressed in three major themes. The first theme sees health care as a process of social influence: an independent, powerful expert attempts to change the attitudes and behaviors of a dependent, ignorant, lower-status patient. This process has important affective, cognitive, and behavioral aspects that are evident in the nonverbal and verbal communication between doctor and patient. The most important behavioral element—referred to as patient compliance or cooperation—is whether or not the patient follows the practitioner's prescriptions. To understand and predict patient cooperation, we would have to look at various social-psychological concepts. For example, Rodin and Janis (1979), analyzing practitioner powers to influence patients, offer a conceptual framework and a number of relationship-building techniques for promoting more healthful behavior on the part of the patient. Referent power (based on liking, acceptance, and admiration) is likely the strongest source of influence the practitioner has on the patient. Yet it appears to be used less than power based on reward, coercion, or expertise. To get patients to internalize and adhere to treatment recommendations, practitioners could stress similarities between themselves and their patients (thus increasing interpersonal attraction) and could convey a benevolent attitude of providing help out of genuine caring. Studies suggest that even a limited use of interpersonal skills, such as respect and genuineness, increase the number of successful cases in treatment. Improving patient care also requires the study of how health care administrators and medical practitioners *themselves* influence the provision of services by other patient-care personnel (Raven & Haley, 1980). For example, quite a bit is known about how to prevent infections among hospitalized patients, but a large part of the problem is motivating health care workers to follow the prescribed procedures to reduce the incidence of such infections.

The second theme is concerned with the patient being treated as an object—a powerless recipient of highly technical, assembly line medical care in which treatment is given to *cases* rather than planned with *people*. There are many good reasons to take the humanistic approach—to treat patients as active, responsible participants who can contribute to their own medical care. Studies indicate that patients who are viewed and respected as individuals are more likely to cooperate and be satisfied with their treatment and are less likely to show negative psychological reactions such as helplessness or depression.

The first two themes both relate to the third theme: seeing the patient as a consumer. Health care is a significant political issue in which consumers are no longer satisfied with a highly technical "fixing" of acute illness, or with a system that closes its doors to the poor and the disadvantaged. Giving increased responsibility and control to patients regarding their treatment may increase their involvement and satisfaction, but may be hotly contested by health care practitioners who demand total control in what can be life-and-death situations. Nonetheless, the approach of patient-as-consumer raises the possibility of actively matching the best treatment to the particular individual in ways that benefit both the patient and the practitioner. We will need complex research designs to discover the most appropriate treatments for different combinations of patients and settings.

A final aspect of management and treatment has to do with understanding patients' reactions to long-term illness (Taylor, 1978). Social psychologists can help study how patients feel about their illness and its causes and how they interpret changes in their condition. Attribution theory, among others, can be especially useful in understanding these processes. For example, Rodin (1978), describing how the attribution process affects the patient's psychological state and behavior, points out how errors in attribution could have significant consequences on these factors. Patients who engage in self-blame for their illness may be less likely to promptly seek the medical attention they require. During treatment social psychology can also help understand and control patients' reactions. For example, the difficult task of managing pain is one that is affected by the attributions and control behaviors of the patient. Thus the control of symptoms and reactions to treatment is another crucial area to which the social psychologist can make a strong contribution.

Delivery of Health Care Services. Health care is a major service industry composed of a massive bureaucracy of poorly organized and coordinated services (Taylor, 1978). There appear to be several reasons for this (Katz & Kahn, 1978; Weisbord & Goodstein, 1978):

- Delivery systems tend to be organized for the convenience of the staff rather than the patients and are often provided in a highly technical, impersonal manner.
- Medical organizations such as hospitals have no single line of authority since power is split three ways among the administrators, the medical staff, and the board of trustees, thus creating considerable strain and conflict.
- Coordination of medical services is hampered by a lack of interdependence among subsystems as compared to business organizations.
- Medical systems often have abstract goals and there is little research on how goals influence practice.

These difficulties in functioning have been suggested by research on medical systems, particularly Georgopoulos' (1975) review of over 1,000 pieces of organizational research in hospitals. However, Weisbord and Goodstein (1978) suggest that the existing knowledge base is still inadequate for facilitating organizational change in medical systems. Furthermore, comprehensive organization development efforts designed to improve the quality of service have met with resistance from health care practitioners, especially when they require integration of different professionals. Nonetheless, examples of useful research and practice interventions are beginning to appear (see Box 16.1).

Benefits for Social Psychology. What are the advantages for the social psychologist in the world of health care? Taylor (1978) reminds us that the medical arena is an intriguing real-world setting in which to test the validity and generalizability of theories developed in laboratory settings. The sources of its personal satisfaction only begin with the gratitude of patients, and with the sense of accomplishment that comes from influencing the way that services are delivered. For the discipline of social psychology, the potential rewards include new courses, new training programs, new jobs, and the accumulation of scientific knowledge. There are, of course, liabilities and difficult issues to be dealt with, but these are more than balanced by the vast opportunities to make a difference in this corner of the world in need.

Box 16.1   FOCUS ON RESEARCH
Using Action Research to Improve Patient Satisfaction

As health care services become more technical and bureaucratic, personalized care becomes more difficult. This may be part of the cause of growing patient dissatisfaction—a problem about which health care organizations are increasingly concerned. Reuben Harris of the School of Management at the Massachusetts Institute of Technology directed an innovative action research project to improve patient satisfaction with medical services provided by the United States Navy.

Previous research indicated that patient satisfaction with Navy health care facilities was lower than with private civilian care. The Navy took immediate action to empasize patient satisfaction in staff training programs. In addition, an action research project was developed to provide direct information on patient satisfaction at the treatment level. Harris assumed that the Navy health care staff had positive attitudes toward patients and could treat them respectfully, but what they lacked was knowledge about patients' needs, expectations, and levels of satisfaction.

A pilot project was developed in eight different Navy health care clinics. The research staff met with clinic personnel to gain commitment and to agree on the patient satisfaction information to be collected. Questionnaires tapping patient reactions following treatment were developed and administered in each clinic on a 3-month trial basis. Approximately 100 patients per week were randomly selected in each clinic to complete the questionnaire. Results were tabulated by the research staff and fed back to the clinics on a regular basis.

The effect of the project on patient satisfaction depended a great deal on the level of involvement of clinic staff. When staff were highly involved in the development of the questionnaire and set up formal mechanisms for feedback of results (such as at staff meetings), patient satisfaction increased the most. In clinics with low staff input (such as, a few key physicians selected the questionnaire items) and no systematic feedback (such as, clinic chief tells staff informally), gains in patient satisfaction were also positive, but moderate. In contrast, patient satisfaction *decreased* in clinics with little staff involvement and feedback.

Harris concludes that staff who were actively involved in the project and had ready access to results reacted in ways that enhanced patient satisfaction. These staff also saw the feedback as valuable for their work. Most of the clinics planned to use the questionnaires on a regular basis to monitor patient satisfaction. Such a step would likely go a long way in reversing the current trend toward depersonalization in health care.

Source: Harris, R. T. Improving patient satisfaction through action research. *Journal of Applied Behavioral Science,* 1978, *1,* 382-399.

Social Psychology and the Consumer

I am now living in what I call my "age of acquisition." That is the period from young adulthood through middle age when many of us acquire the material possessions offered by our industrialized, affluent, consuming society. Assuming we've got a decent job, we acquire a home, a car or two, furniture, appliances, and all the other paraphernalia that complement modern living—not to mention some camping equipment or a recreational vehicle as a means of getting away from it all once we've got it. In many ways, modern society is a society of the consumer; never before have so many had so much to spend on acquiring goods and services. In fact, the acquisition and disposition of material goods and the provision and use of services entail a great deal of the human social behavior in contemporary North America. These interactions of buying, selling, and trading clearly involve psychological and social-psychological processes. No wonder then that we have developed a subdiscipline called consumer psychology.

Consumer psychology began in the first decade of this century with studies of advertising and selling conducted with the objective of promoting effective communication from the manufacturer to the consumer (Anastasi, 1964). Soon communication from the consumer to the seller was being examined in order to prepare more effective advertising. Consumer surveys were first conducted to identify attractive features of products, and later to incorporate consumer preferences in the actual design of products. Advertising psychology, which produces studies of emotional, motivational, perceptual, and cognitive factors in advertising, involves many of the theories and methods of general psychology in attempts to increase the effectiveness of advertising. Advertising psychology became incorporated into the broader field of consumer psychology, and in 1960 the Division of Consumer Psychology was formed within the American Psychological Association.

Consumer psychology, as it is defined today, is "that branch of psychology which seeks, through the utilization of distinctively psychological concepts and methods, to understand the dynamics underlying and determining consumer behavior, including the factors that influence such behavior" (Jacoby, 1975, p. 980).

In turn, *consumer behavior* involves the acquisition, consumption, and disposition of goods and services by individuals, families, and organizations—in short, a behavior that includes *all* the interaction between the person and his or her acquisition. Consumer behavior therefore involves complex overlays of decision making and choosing that take place in the social context of everyday life (Jacoby, 1975).

Since consumer behavior is largely social behavior, we can understand why recent developments in consumer psychology have tended to rely more and more on social-psychological concepts and methods. In his article entitled "Consumer Psychology as a Social Psychological Sphere of Action," Jacob Jacoby (1975) maintains that until the 1970s consumer psychology was regarded as a variant of industrial psychology, and fewer ideas were borrowed from social psychology than from other areas such as perception and learning. But the late 1960s and early 1970s witnessed an information explosion in consumer psychology (Jacoby, 1976a). As part of this development, the overwhelming majority of studies published in the consumer psychology literature had become clearly social-psychological in nature (Jacoby, 1975). They consistently examined variables such as attitudes, role expectations and behavior, decision making, group influence, attribution processes, interpersonal communication, and persuasive communication. Consumer psychology thus grew apart from industrial psychology, becoming more like organizational psychology (see Chapter 9) in that both fields drew their basic concepts and methods from social psychology (Jacoby, 1976b).

Why should social psychologists show more interest in consumer behavior? Let's look at some of Jacoby's (1975) answers to this question.

- The application of ideas and methods from social psychology will provide richer meaning and fill significant gaps in our knowledge. For example, research on persuasive communication has ignored the personality characteristics of the sender while concentrating on the receiver. To fully apply this body of knowledge to consumer behavior, this omission must be corrected.
- The external validity of theories can be tested in consumer settings. For example, similarity leads to interpersonal attraction between seller and buyer just as it does in laboratory studies with college students.
- Research on consumer behavior in natural settings will help increase the meaningfulness and relevance of social psychology as compared to the artificiality and triviality of much laboratory research.
- Consumer psychology will produce socially useful research in the tradition of Kurt Lewin while providing exciting career opportunities for social psychologists.

In line with these potential benefits, consumer psychology is now developing as a sophisticated field of endeavor seeking to explain rather than simply describe behavior. From a subdiscipline of psychology serving the needs of business, it has grown to a socially conscious interdisciplinary effort, as concerned with protecting the welfare of the consumer as it is with selling a product (Jacoby, 1976a). The increasing use of social-psychological concepts and methods has been an integral part of this development. Let's look at a few illustrations.

Consumer Attitudes, Behavior, and Decision Making. "No other single psychological construct has permeated consumer research as has the construct of attitude." With that unequivocal statement, Jacoby (1976a, p. 337) opens his review of how attitude and its related concepts have been applied to the study of consumer behavior.

Why is the concept of attitude so appealing and so prevalent in consumer research? Because attitude is a general predisposition to respond positively or negatively toward an object (see Chapter 2). If advertising can produce a positive attitude toward a product, that product will sell. Since the bottom line in consumer research is buying behavior, it is possible to organize most of the work in the field around the process of buying (see Woodside, Sheth & Bennett, 1977). For this reason we are interested not only in the *concept* of attitude but in the *process* of attitude change as well—especially the role of persuasive communication in advertising (Jacoby, 1976a).

Over the past decade consumer research, like social psychology proper, passed through a flirtation with cognitive dissonance, then moved toward a greater interest in attribution theory (see Chapter 2). It remains to be seen, however, whether attribution theory as developed primarily in laboratory settings will prove to be useful for understanding consumer behavior. Box 16.2 provides one example of the promise and pitfalls of attribution theory and research in the real world of buying behavior.

Box 16.2   FOCUS ON THEORY AND RESEARCH
Attribution Theory and Consumer Research

Interpersonal influence is regarded as a major determinant of consumer behavior. Other people help determine what we buy and when we buy it. Most explanations for this focus on the characteristics and norms of social groups as the important variables affecting consumer choice. However, social psychologist Bobby Calder of Northwestern Univerity and Robert Burnkrant, a professor of marketing at the University of California at Berkeley, suggest a more general approach is needed. This approach would specify in psychological terms how the consumer as an actor is influenced by others. Attribution theory might form the basis of such an approach.

In buying and using products, the consumer is a social actor, observed by others who make attributions about the consumer's personal dispositions. These judgments help determine how the observer behaves toward the consumer and thus influences the consumer. In addition, if the consumer is sensitive to the attributions of others, he or she will behave in ways that are designed to create desirable attributions. The young male consumer, for example, may think that if he buys an expensive three-piece suit, women will see him as handsome, intelligent, and attractive.

To begin studying the effect of attribution processes on consumer behavior, Calder and Burnkrant chose to look at how an observer infers personal dispositions from a consumer's behavior. Attribution theory would predict that an observer is more likely to make a personal attribution when there are no plausible, external explanations for the behavior. Specifically, if a consumer chose a less well-known and less socially desirable brand, an observer would be more likely to make an internal attribution ("She chose it because she's particular"). In addition, the greater the choice available to the consumer (and therefore the more distinctive the choice), the more likely for the observer to make an internal attribution.

To test these propositions, Calder and Burnkrant designed an experiment in which home economics students were asked to play the role of observers while reading scenarios of a consumer's behavior. The situations varied on whether the consumer chose a well-known cosmetic product (Revlon) versus a private-label brand (Walgreen's), and on whether the consumer had high choice (four dissimilar brands) versus low choice (two similar brands). Internal attributions were assessed by looking at the extremeness and confidence of observers' ratings of the consumer on bipolar adjective scales reflecting personality traits such as introvert/extrovert, submissive/dominating, and so on.

Contrary to predictions, the highly desirable brand choice led to stronger rather than weaker internal attributions, the consumer being seen as a socially popular person. The effect of degree of choice on attributions was not consistent, but depended on the type of product and its usage. Existing attribution theory thus appears inadequate to explain judgments of consumers' behavior, possibly because it fails to consider the perceived significance of the choice for the consumer.

Source: Calder, B. J. & Burnkrant, R. E. Interpersonal influence on consumer behavior: An attribution theory approach. *Journal of Consumer Research*, 1977, 4 (June), 29–38.

Consumer research has also paid close attention to models of attitude structure and functioning, particularly those of Rosenberg (1960) and Fishbein (1967). These models have been used to predict both the consumer's preferences for certain products and the consumer's actual choice behavior at the time of acquisition (Jacoby, 1976a). The Fishbein model in particular has stirred up controversy about how the model should be applied and how well it actually predicts consumer behavior (Lutz & Bettman, 1977).

Fishbein's initial model of attitude proposed that a person's attitude toward an object is a summation of his or her beliefs about the object multiplied by the evaluations of those beliefs: Attitude = Sum of Beliefs × Evaluations. In other words, we have more favorable feelings toward an object if we hold a greater number of positive beliefs about that object. Fishbein later extended his model to take into account the effect of social norms upon intention and behavior (Fishbein & Ajzen, 1975).

One illustrative study used the initial Fishbein model to see how previous behavior and present attitude affect the current choice behavior of male beer drinkers (Beardon & Woodside, 1977). The respondents were members of a representative sample of consumers—a statewide consumer panel established by a large university. Respondents were asked which of four brands of beer—Pabst, Schlitz, Old Milwaukee, and Budweiser—they most preferred and most often consumed. They were also asked how much they had actually consumed during the last week. Attitudes toward the different brands were measured by a seven-point scale of liking. Measures of previous attitudes and previous behavior were available from a similar survey completed several months earlier with the same panel.

To operationalize the Fishbein model, beliefs and evaluations were collected on several different product attributes. For example, a respondent could indicate his belief as to what degree Budweiser was "for young people." Subjects then provided their evaluation of each attribute on a seven-point scale of agreement, rating, for example, how much they preferred "a lively beer."

The best predictor of current choice of beer was previous choice behavior. Current attitude had a significant but less powerful effect. The combined attitude score based on beliefs and evaluations did not relate to choice, thus disconfirming the utility of the Fishbein model in this instance. However, further analysis showed that different attributes were important in forming attitudes toward different brands. This type of information is useful for marketers to understand consumer attitudes toward their product and for developing promotional strategies to influence choice behavior. For example, if the attribute "a lively beer" was important in forming attitudes toward Old Milwaukee, then this attribute could be incorporated into subsequent advertising. Beardon and Woodside's results also support the position that consumer behavior is comparatively stable and predictable; it is not quite so random and spontaneous as suggested by some researchers (for example, Bass, 1974). We can expect that consumer research will continue its exploration of the concept of attitude and models of attitude structure to examine the nature of buying behavior.

The involvement of social psychologists in consumer research also raises a very important question of values, well-illustrated in the preceding example.

Should we assist marketers in selling products, such as beer and other alcoholic beverages, that can be part of destructive lifestyles that create significant physical and social problems, such as alcoholism? On the one hand, the humanistic value base says that individuals are free to choose their style of life; on the other, social psychologists may be accused of helping to surreptitiously influence individuals against their better interests. Few studies in consumer research have addressed such questions. A laudable exception is the work of Bourgeois and Barnes (1979) who studied the relationship between advertising and alcohol consumption. Their general conclusion was that advertising affects choice of product rather than absolute level of consumption. It appears that societal factors primarily beyond anyone's control, such as income level and degree of urbanization, are more related to increasing alcohol consumption than controllable factors such as price or advertising regulations. Nonetheless, the value dilemma posed by consumer research is worthy of continuing attention.

The question of congruence between consumer attitudes and consumer behavior leads directly into the decision-making process that results in choosing and buying a particular product. This is invariably regarded as a dynamic process that moves from awareness of need to general interest in products, then from search and evaluation to acquisition, and finally to post-purchase behavior. In their study of this decision-making process, consumer researchers have concentrated on pre-acquisition processes, particularly on available information sources and the nature of the search, and on acquisition itself, with an emphasis on how information is processed and what criteria are used in making the decision to buy.

Before acquisition the consumer has both internal and external sources of information. The internal sources of information are in the person's memory and have been studied very little. In contrast, the external sources of information—advertising, salespersons, packaging, and so on—have been studied in great depth, aimed at increasing their effectiveness to influence the consumer's decision. This decision is also affected by word-of-mouth communication and the preferences of opinion leaders. Compared with the amount of external information that is available, however, the amount of information that is actually sought is relatively limited (Jacoby, 1976a). In general—based on studies of the amount of search and the many determinants of search (see Newman, 1977)—findings show that consumers will search more before making a choice when the purchase is an important one in terms of price or style or some other reasons. However, in some cases the small amount of searching is surprising. For example, almost half of new car buyers consider only one make and shop at only one dealer!

Consumer decision making appears to follow a general rule similar to that of organizational decision making—that of "satisficing" or choosing the first satisfactory solution that appears (see Chapter 9). Consumers follow a purchase strategy that satisfies rather than optimizes meeting their needs. This is congruent with the idea that consumers prefer to process only the minimal amount of information needed to make a satisfactory decision. For example, to go on and on trying on a hundred pair of shoes before buying one simply seems ineffective and not worth the effort. What seems to count the most in making acquisition decisions relates mainly to the qualities of the product (such as warranty), but other factors—driving time, for one—can be important. Information processing and decision making will therefore remain a complex field of active investigation in consumer research (Chestnut & Jacoby, 1977).

The major contribution to consumer research may not be confined to theoretical input or research results alone. It may come about through increasing the methodological rigor and sophistication with which consumer research is done. Jacoby (1976a) points to several serious problems that plague consumer research. Many investigators seem to be unaware of the vital necessity of establishing the reliability, validity, and sensitivity of measures before using them to test causal hypotheses. Central constructs such as brand loyalty, opinion leadership, and consumer attitudes lack adequate and consistent measures that have been properly developed and evaluated. Dependent variables are often assessed in simplistic terms, and studies seldom examine more than one dependent variable at a time. There is also very little replication of results or programmatic research to corroborate and further develop research findings.

Jacoby estimates that 85 percent of published research prior to 1968 was of poor quality and questionable worth. However, even at the time of his review, the picture was improving: in 1975 he estimated that only 50 percent of published articles were based on unacceptable research. Whether the increasing involvement of social psychologists is partly responsible for improving the quality of consumer research is difficult to say. However, since one strength of social psychology lies in methodological expertise, it is likely that increased quality of research may be the major outcome of our involvement in studying consumer behavior.

Social Psychology and Consumer Economics. Economics is a social science that studies and develops lawful relationships among major economic variables such as prices, savings, interest rates, unemployment, investment, and so on. Psychology, including social psychology, studies the behavior of people in terms of individual variables such as motives or attitudes, and social variables such as group pressure. These two disciplines have been brought closer together through the work of George Katona and his colleagues at the University of Michigan's Institute for Social Research (Katona, 1975, 1979). Katona contends that we must account for the human factor in economic affairs if we wish to truly understand economic functioning at the societal or macro level. We must study the attitudes and behaviors of consumers, businessmen, and policy makers at the individual or micro level, and relate these to macro economic variables such as inflation, savings, or the Gross National Product (the GNP is the total value of goods and services produced in one year). Crucial questions focus on what kinds of behavior occur and what kinds of decisions are made about buying, selling, investing, and so on, by different groups of people under different conditions. The answers to these questions form the knowledge base of the new cross-discipline of *economic psychology* or *psychological economics*.

For over thirty years, Katona and his associates have been using the survey method to study consumer attitudes, expectations, and interactions, as well as objective variables such as income and expenditures. To yield a standard Index of Consumer Sentiment, these researchers have combined a number of questions such as "Do you think that a year from now you'll be better off financially or worse off, or just about the same as now?" Representative national samples of consumers respond on a regular basis to provide an ongoing measure of consumer sentiment—in sum, a reliable and valid national measure of consumers' willingness to buy. The performance of the measure, now published monthly, has been studied extensively, and the Index has been adopted for use in several other countries, including Canada and Australia. The survey method has thus provided the avenue for assessing the micro variables of consumer attitudes and expectations.

Research based on measures such as the Index of Consumer Sentiment has shown the importance of micro data in understanding and predicting consumer behavior at the national level (Katona, 1974). Economists traditionally viewed the consumer sector as a simple and unimportant transmitter of income. That is, consumers simply spent whatever income they received from the business and government sectors. It is now clear that consumer expenditures depend not only on the ability to buy (income), but also on the confidence or willingness to buy (attitude), and that consumer purchases are discretionary, fluctuating to a much greater extent than income. Growing affluence in North America has provided much of the population with a degree of choice—to buy, to save, to invest—that they have never had before. Thus, through its focus on consumer attitudes and expectations, micro data effectively supplements macro data on the GNP and its parts by providing advance indications of consumer spending. Since psychological economics examines social-psychological variables, and traditional economics does not, it is natural that their analyses and predictions will differ from one another (Katona, 1974; 1975). The traditional approach, relying solely on macro variables, assumes that individuals will behave rationally or mechanistically, and that individual variations will not affect the larger economic picture. General principles are stated, such as "consumer expenditures are a function of income," or "inflation is the result of purchasing power exceeding available supplies." Individual, subjective variables are usually ignored, even when the general principles fail to predict economic events.

In contrast, psychological economics assumes that a change in one variable (income, for example) may lead to *different* responses (expenditures, for instance), depending on other circumstances, including subjective factors such as expectations. If a person expects hard times ahead, he or she would likely save rather than spend any excess income. To validate this point, Katona analyzes a number of significant economic problems over time to show the gain in understanding that is provided by the psychological approach to economics.

One problem Katona considers is that of inflation—the continuous spiraling of prices that has plagued the world's economy for more than a decade. Traditional economics makes two assumptions about inflation: (1) when incomes grow faster than the quantity of available goods, demand exceeds supply and prices rise; and (2) when people expect prices to go up they will stock up on goods, thereby further increasing demand and fueling inflation. However, Katona points out that most people resent inflation and see an inflationary period as a comparatively *bad* time to buy. In addition, survey results show that expectations of price increases actually *reduce* discretionary expenditures. People believe they will need that money for future purchases of essential goods and services. This means that saving, not spending, increases during inflationary periods.

Katona's analysis, supported by over thirty years of data gathering, reveals only two exceptions to the general results—and both can be explained by further analysis of consumer's psychological reactions. These events were the military defeat in Korea in 1950, and the fear of food shortages in 1973. Both led to panic buying that increased spending at a time of high inflation. A further exception occurred during 1978-1979, when a high degree of consumer pessimism led to advance buying in fear of further price increases. Double-digit inflation thus has disastrous effects on consumer expectations by fueling speculation and reducing productivity (Katona, 1980). These exceptions aside, the overall response to creeping inflation has been consistent: the people remain cautious; the people postpone buying.

In studies of the relation between price trends and attitudes, Katona (1975, 1979) compared scores on the Index of Consumer Sentiment to periods of inflation and recession. His findings were consistent: when inflation accelerated, the index turned down, indicating consumer pessimism and a decline in expenditures. When inflation subsided, the Index improved. In fact, through the deterioration of consumer attitudes, it was possible to *predict* the recessions of 1957, 1969, and 1971! In each case, the recession set in about six to nine months after a downturn in the Index (see Figure 16.1—a striking illustration of how consumers' attitudes can reliably predict discretionary expenditures and future economic trends).

Katona (1979) points out that predictions made about individual consumer behavior are much less reliable—any one consumer may or may not behave in accordance with his or her attitudes and expectations. This conclusion has also been borne out at the family level. Morgan (1977) and his colleagues, studying 5,000 American families longitudinally for over ten years, found that attitudes show little relation to economic well-being, and that over a period of time many diverse changes take place in economic status. However, when the attitudes of a representative national sample are totaled up, it is quite possible to predict macro economic trends. This is because the optimism or pessimism of the aggregate changes gradually, canceling out many factors that affect individuals (such as

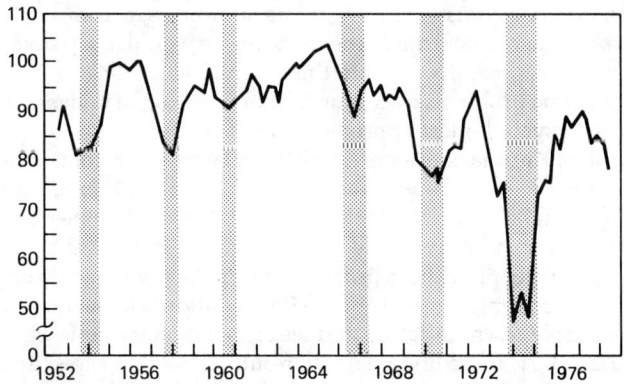

Figure 16.1   Index of Consumer Sentiment in Relation to Economic Recessions (Shaded Portions).
Source: Katona (1979).

mood). Katona suggests that a "macropsychology" should be developed to study these regularities in mass behavior and their underlying psychological determinants.

Regardless of the future of a macropsychology, the work of George Katona amply illustrates the importance of social-psychological factors in the field of consumer economics. In conjunction with theory and research on consumer behavior and decision making, the survey approach to consumer attitudes further exemplifies the role and value of social-psychological contributions to the interdisciplinary field of consumer psychology.

Social Psychology and Public Policy

We have seen that one of the major roles of the applied social psychologist is that of the applied scientist (Chapter 1). We have considered the methods of research used to operationalize this role (Chapter 3). In our discussion about social issues and social change (Chapter 11), we saw that research could be used to document the existence and the effects of injustice, and that these results could be a stimulus for social change. And we saw the science and art of program development and evaluation (Chapter 13) as a major example of how the research skills of the applied social psychologist can be directed toward the amelioration of social problems. All of these endeavors have one theme in common: their potential effect on public policy.

The effects of governments on society are largely translated through *public policy*—that is, the laws, regulations, and guidelines developed by government to regulate social interaction and to meet the physical and social needs of citizens. Although the study of public policy has usually been the domain of the political scientist and the economist, it has become of increasing concern to the social psychologist as well. The source of this concern is the growing role of government in the development and provision of human service programs—in education, health, criminal justice, and the like. Because it is virtually impossible to involve oneself in human service programs without being affected by the policies underlying these programs, we must concern ourselves with how policy decisions are made by legislators and administrators, and with how social scientists can affect these decisions. It is only by bringing humanistic values and valid research results to bear on the policy-making process that we can hope to work toward the development of public policies that are both effective and equitable.

Social Psychology and Society. The involvement of social scientists in public policy raises difficult questions. What is the ideal relationship between social science and society at large? What are the roles and mechanisms by which social scientists can become involved in the policy-making process? What are the ways in which social research can contribute to public policy? How can psychologists become involved in political activities in ways that further the objectives of their discipline?

The turmoil and ferment of the late 1960s and early 1970s raised even more (and more specific) questions: Should scientists be held responsible for the destructive use of their theory and technology—be it through weapons of war or strategies of behavior change? How should the conflicts between the roles of scientist and citizen be resolved? Throughout this book, I have argued for the direct involvement of social scientists as concerned citizens in the amelioration of social problems. Not all my colleagues agree, and the issue remains controversial.

In an eloquent address entitled "The Sound of the Wind That's Blowing," psychologist William Bevan (1976) of Duke University focused on the interface between the scientific community and the public at large. The "wind that's blowing" is the challenge to innovation and involvement that social problems bring to social scientists. Will we stand up and face the wind and confront the future? Or will we lay low in our safe areas of specialization and watch the world go by?

Bevan contends that science is not an ethically neutral enterprise. Like all human endeavors, it involves value judgments. Like all human endeavors, it must be accountable to society at large. Physical science and technology have helped create human problems. We face environmental pollution. We face the threat of nuclear war. Development has outstripped our social machinery to deal rationally with its effects. What we need, however, is not less science and technology. We need the effective development and use of social science to move social policy in more humane directions.

This use of science for the common good requres a much better understanding, by both scientists and the public, of science as a social institution and of the roles that scientists should play in society. Scientists must be accountable to the public, and mechanisms for this public accountability must be developed. Scientists should be encouraged to take on roles beyond that of laboratory researcher—roles such as legislative staff officer, public interpreter of science, and analyst of large social systems. The world of public affairs is vastly different from the world of the laboratory, but we cannot risk ignoring our responsibility to improve the quality of life for the larger society. We must stand up and face that wind of social challenge!

How can we become more involved in the formation of public policy? The answer is—"not easily." According to Michael Paquin (1977), the understanding and improvement of the human condition is partly a political task that psychologists have largely ignored. Even though there are many calls for a more relevant and involved psychology (see Chapter 1), less than 5 percent of the psychologists in the United States and Canada are directly involved in the formation of public policy. Despite their knowledge and understanding of human social behavior, psychologists rarely function as legislative advisors or policy makers. Why this unwillingness or inability to become involved?

Paquin suggests that a conservative, value-free self-image by many psychologists places the emphasis of the discipline on developing basic knowledge rather than on its application. There are other limitations—a lack of liaison between psychologists and government decision makers, for instance, and problems in developing the necessary interdisciplinary collaboration. Furthermore, psychologists must be willing to become more than researchers who simply evaluate policies and programs developed by others. According to Paquin:

. . . the psychologist must be more than a technician or a data analyst. Effective social change demands such political activity as value and goal specification, for example, in terms of survival value; policy formulation and design, based on empirically substantiated theories of behavior; program execution and project administration, following principles of optimal behavior change; and assessment and evaluation, using the methodological and research skills that psychologists traditionally possess. (1977, p. 353)

These sentiments are partly echoed in the thoughts of Marshall Segal of Syracuse University, who has completed a major work on political psychology— that is, the application of psychology to public policy analysis (Segall, 1976). Psychologists already know a great deal about human behavior in areas such as intellectual capacities, intergroup relations, and violence. To apply the part of their knowledge that bears on social issues, psychologists can follow several approaches to political psychology. Segall outlines three such models:

- the psychologist as *expert witness*, wherein psychological knowledge is simply offered to policy makers for application
- the psychologist as *policy evaluator*, in which research expertise is used to help policy makers determine the effectiveness of social programs
- the psychologist as *social engineer*, in which techniques for controlling human behavior are applied

This last approach is the most controversial since it involves ethical issues about individual freedom, personal dignity, and informed consent. (You will recall my criticism of Varela's approach of social technology—see Chapter 4— because it violates the humanistic value base of applied social psychology.) Most of the existing work that Segall sees as political psychology involves the first two models—that is, the application of theories and research methods. On this basis psychology already has available many of the resources required to take a stronger role in the formulation, execution, and evaluation of public policy.

To bring about the greater involvement of psychologists in public policy, Paquin suggests fundamental changes in graduate training, the resocialization and sensitization of psychologists to the needs of public policy making and their potential roles in it, and the creation of new institutional mechanisms, such as public policy research institutes. These directions are reinforced by Bevan (1980) in calling for constructive political and social action on the part of social scientists. In addition to political lobbying to improve the relationship between government and science there are a myriad other potentially useful activities—workshops on the public policy process, special seminars on legislative issues, and dialogue with legislators on policy developments. Involvement is essential to a respectful and useful relationship between scientists and government.

Social Research and Policy Formation. The use of research results for the guidance of government decision making reached a high point in the mid-1960s, suffered serious setbacks due to the failures of the War on Poverty, then rose again in the mid-1970s (Weiss, 1977). Now, as we move through the 1980s, we face the challenge of dealing with this most complex process. We must sort out the issues that affect research utilization and develop approaches for effective utilization, even while we realize that social science does not have a corner on truth. Weiss contends that social scientists can affect public policy, but must expect continuing difficulties in improving utilization.

Moving along these same lines, Frank and Smith (1976) develop three different normative or prescriptive models for the most effective involvement of social scientists in policy making:

- *the post-hoc model:* This approach limits the participation of social scientists to research only after a policy has been formulated and implemented. They take the role of evaluators who measure the results of policies and programs, and only these results, rather than broader social science knowledge, can be used in future policy formulation.
- *the limited or social experimentation model:* In this approach, pioneered by Donald Campbell (see Chapters 3 and 13), the social scientist's role is to systematically test alternative policies within controlled social settings. The social scientist collaborates with the policy maker to form policy alternatives into testable conditions within a rigorous research design. The results then bear directly on decisions about policy implementation.
- *the inclusive model:* This model defines a larger number of roles for social scientists at all stages of the policy process. These include assessing problems, setting goals, generating and testing alternatives, and implementing and evaluating the policy. (All of the activities of program development and evaluation covered in Chapter 13 are included here.)

The major problem with all these models is their assumption that there is a definite demand for social science knowledge and research. This is often *not* the case. Demand is often latent and unrecognized, and is not expressed as a felt need by policy makers. For a felt need to occur, the policy maker must first perceive a lack of information, then expect that research will produce information that will be useful in the policy making process. This shift depends largely on the degree of consensus or agreement that exists about the desired ends, and about the policy means to achieve those ends. The degree of consensus on means and ends will in turn influence the most appropriate research model that should be used.

Figure 16.2 depicts the different conditions of agreement and disagreement about means and ends in relation to the models of policy research. In the case of agreement on both means and ends, decision making is often regularized in laws

		Ends of Policy	
		Agreement	Disagreement
Measures of Policy	Agreement	Post-hoc	Post-hoc
	Disagreement	Social Experimentation	Inclusive

Figure 16.2   Consensus on Policy and Models of Policy Research.

or in bureaucratic procedures that describe policies and related programs. Decision makers are quite clear on their objectives and on the activities required to meet these objectives. For example, it is accepted by almost everyone that a certain amount of general education is valuable; therefore we have laws, which are seldom questioned, to keep children in school up to a specified age. There is no need to formulate competing policies or to evaluate alternate programs. The most appropriate research model is a post-hoc evaluation to see if the policy is attaining its objectives; this element is often built into legislation or regulations.

In the case where there is agreement on means but disagreement on ends, the post-hoc model is also appropriate. For example, different policy makers may agree that giving foreign aid is a worthwhile activity. One, however, may believe it is a moral responsibility to reduce inequity; another may want to ensure political stability in friendly developing countries. Each wishes to support the program, but for differing reasons, and each is interested in a post-hoc evaluation to see if the program is reaching their goals.

The social experimentation model is most appropriate where there is agreement on ends, but disagreement on means. Such a situation requires information on the effectiveness of alternative programs or activities. Each proponent of a particular program hopes to gain support for his or her alternative and will therefore support program evaluation. For example, most policy makers agree on the goal of providing housing to low-income families. But there are different ways to do this, including the provision of public housing, interest subsidies to help with the purchase of a home, and outright housing allowances. Social scientists can help frame these alternatives into testable variables within the design of a social experiment.

The work of George Fairweather and his colleagues at Michigan State University is an excellent example of using experimental methods for social policy research (Fairweather & Tornatzky, 1977). Over a 20-year period, these scientist/practitioners have developed and evaluated an alternate model for the treatment of chronic mental patients—the community lodge (see Chapter 10). Social experimentation was used at each stage of development to test the effectiveness of the innovative program in relation to existing alternatives. Once the innovation was fully developed, various approaches of disseminating it on a wide scale to other mental hospitals were evaluated. Principles of successful adoption were derived from the first dissemination attempt and were then tested for effectiveness on hospitals that had failed to adopt the lodge program. This systematic approach to social experimentation demonstrates the combination of ingenuity and rigor which social scientists can bring to policy making.

When there is disagreement on both ends and means, the felt need for information is often very high. Policy makers disagree on where they want to go and how to get there, and welcome any research that may help light the way. A good example is the issue of desegregation and busing in the United States public school system. There is disagreement over the desirability of desegregation. And there is disagreement over the use of busing to achieve desegregation. Social science research has been used to support arguments on all sides, and the need for inclusive research is clear. Goals need to be clarified, and the effects of alternate strategies need to be evaluated. Whether such research increases the rationality of policy making in such a highly charged, value-laden arena is also a crucial question. Nonetheless, the felt need for information certainly exists.

Let's look at one example of the involvement of social scientists in public policy research. In 1967, the government of Great Britain enacted one of the most successful countermeasures against drinking and driving—the roadside breath test. A research evaluation showed a 45 percent reduction in serious accidents on weekend nights and this was interpreted as due to an increase in the perceived likelihood of arrest in the public mind. This interpretation was never tested. In 1976, the Canadian government enacted similar legislation in an attempt to reduce the tragic toll of traffic accidents—there is greater loss of potential years of life from traffic accidents than from heart disease, and at least half of fatal accidents involve alcohol abuse.

Social psychologist Barry Bragg and his colleagues with the Road and Motor Vehicle Traffic Safety Branch of the Canadian government were requested to complete an evaluation of the enactment of the law and of a public education campaign designed to increase awareness about the law. This research followed the post-hoc model presented by Frank and Smith (1976).

The first challenge was to develop a reliable and valid measure of the perceived probability of arrest under the new law. Next, a laboratory study of the public education materials evaluated the effect of three television commercials and four newspaper ads on the perceived probability of arrest. A television commercial showing a cemetery and a newspaper ad showing a hospital scene proved to be the most effective (Bragg & Cousins, 1977). However, the advertising agency conducting the campaign wanted to use two television commercials and two newspaper ads, thus creating the opportunity for a field study to further assess the impact of the various ads.

The purpose of the research now shifted to assessing the impact of the new law and finding out if the media campaign would increase that impact. Fortunately, the law was not proclaimed in all the provinces of Canada at the same time, and the campaign was delayed in some locations. This allowed the researchers to assess three different conditions in a field experiment (Cousins, 1980). In two test cities, the law was instituted and the campaign was initiated at the same time. In one control city, the law was proclaimed, but the campaign was delayed; and in a second control city neither the law nor the campaign was instituted. In the test cities, both awareness of the law and perceived probability of arrest increased significantly while there were no changes in the control cities. Also, the same ads that had been demonstrated effective in the laboratory study also had the most impact in the field. The message for policy makers is to complement the implementation of new policies with a public education campaign and an evaluation of effectiveness using the methods of social science research.

Frank and Smith (1976) thus emphasize that only certain models of policy research are appropriate under certain conditions. Social scientists must be sensitive to these conditions to plan and execute research that will be utilized in policy formulation. However three further questions still remain: Is social science research actually being used in policy making? If so, in what ways? And how can utilization be increased?

In their review and prescription on the use of social science knowledge in policy formation, Hennigan, Flay, and Cook (1980) admit that many commentators are pessimistic about utilization. However they review several studies that attempted to determine the actual usage by decision makers (for example, Caplan, 1977; Patton, 1978). The results? Policy makers report using social science knowledge on an ongoing basis, but not in a direct manner. That is, social science knowledge and perspectives help to define problems and formulate policy alternatives in indirect ways, rather than particular studies being used for specific program decisions. Theories and research results provided background understanding and complement subjective impressions rather than giving specific guides to decision making. For example, community development programs may be partly guided by a knowledge of what constitutes good interpersonal relations and effective group decision making and by an understanding of the strategies of social change.

Why is utilization limited? Hennigan et al. (1980) summarize the many reasons put forward by social scientists: Social problems are complex and intractable. Policy makers are under political pressures and time limits to make decisions. Research methods are inadequate to yield practical results. And there are limited incentives to conduct applied research.

But there may be a much more serious reason. Social scientists and policy makers live in very different worlds. They have different values, languages, and rewards. There is a wide gap of mistrust and misunderstanding that severely limits utilization (see Caplan, 1977). The public policy system looks for simple yes-no answers that are compatible with the adversary approach to political decision making. Decision makers say "gimme the facts" and "what's the bottom line," while social scientists talk about limitations of results and contradictory findings. Hennigan et al. (1980) discuss a number of examples of government policy that illustrate the struggle between the information demands of policy makers and the complex quest for truth that is followed by social scientists. To cite one case, Box 16.3 describes how social science knowledge was incorporated into the United States federal government's approach to the regulation of violence on television.

How can we effectively improve the utilization of social science knowledge? Hennigan et al. (1980) suggest strategies for producing clear, credible, and concise policy-relevant research reports that would more likely provide useful theoretical and empirical input to decision making. They also pick up on two suggestions for specific mechanisms that might increase the likelihood that valid information would actually be used. One is the concept of a "science court," in which impartial scientist-judges would hear arguments from two advocates, each presenting social science knowledge in support of one side of the decision. Testimony and cross-examination would attempt to discuss what is scientifically known about the issue and policy in question. The judge would prepare a report listing what is known, presenting a consensus that could be used in further policy deliberations.

The second suggestion is to establish permanent standing committees of experts in given policy areas. These committees would conduct hearings, issue reports, and be available for consultation with legislators, government officials, and other decision makers.

These mechanisms would be added to already existing arrangements that

Box 16.3   FOCUS ON RESEARCH AND PRACTICE
Utilization of Social Science Research in the Regulation of Television Violence

The policy makers say, "Give me the facts," and the researchers reply, "We're not sure if there are many things called facts, and when there are, we don't know what they mean for action." In this fashion, social psychologists Karen Hennigan, Brian Flay, and Thomas Cook point out a significant gap between the policy community and the social research community: The former demands certainty, the latter argues that truth is elusive. The problems that this fundamental schism creates are well illustrated by the role that social science knowledge played in policy decisions reducing violence on television.

The long-standing fear that violence on television would lead to violence in society reached a peak in the mid-1960s. Senator Pastore of the Senate Subcommittee on Communications, who was a supporter of the television networks, called for a report from the surgeon general that would not be hedged by "ifs and buts." The first step was to assemble a panel of experts to review past research, commission new research, and present a comprehensive report. A list of potential members was submitted to the networks for approval, presumably to guarantee the credibility of the final report in the eyes of the television industry. Two of the networks rejected the inclusion of a number of academic researchers whose studies had suggested that television viewing caused violence. At the same time, network representatives and academics who had consulted for the networks were included. Presumably they were not prejudiced in their views, as the academic scholars were.

The panel commissioned a variety of the laboratory and field studies only one of which looked at causal relationships in a longitudinal and naturalistic manner. In reaction to the results, the panel split into three camps: one said little; one, supporting the television industry, argued the evidence was inconclusive, being based on artificial laboratory experiments or correlational field studies that did not show causation; and one, composed mainly of academics, pointed out that all the different studies led to the same conclusion—viewing television violence leads to aggressive behavior in children.

The panel finally compromised on a unanimous report stressing the limitations of the research, but concluding that prolonged viewing of violence can cause aggressive behavior in some children. News reports of the findings stressed the qualifications and created more confusion than clarity. However, at subsequent Senate hearings in 1972, the surgeon general testified that television violence causes violence. The network representatives grudgingly agreed with this conclusion, and the level of violence in television programs was subsequently reduced. Even with a considerable gap between policy makers and researchers, the surgeon general's report had played a crucial role in this beneficial outcome.

Source: Hennigan, K. M., Flay, B. R. & Cook, T. D. "Give me the facts": Some suggestions for using social science knowledge in national policy-making. In R. F. Kidd & M. J. Saks (Eds.), *Advances in applied social psychology* (Vol. 1). Hillsdale, N.J.: Erlbaum, 1968.

require researchers to disseminate their findings and that establish review panels to fund research and advise policy makers. Hennigan et al. suggest that there is a great need to experiment with different institutional models designed to make higher-quality social science input relevant to government decision making.

Was this behavior induced by viewing violence on television? (© *John Garrett 1978/ Woodfin Camp & Associates*)

In the coming years we can look forward to the exploration of a number of mechanisms for increasing the involvement of psychologists in policy formulation. Charles Kiesler (1980), a well-known social psychologist who served as Executive Officer of the American Psychological Association, has offered several suggestions for increasing the contribution that psychology and other behavioral sciences can make to public policy. In addition to more problem-oriented research, he suggests better communication about specific problem areas and about research that is being carried out. Psychologists also need better methods and structures to develop "crystallized advice" that would capture the existing consensus of knowledge relevant to a social problem. Keisler suggests an Institute for Applied Social Psychology to serve as a "think tank" for crystallizing knowledge and increasing its usability.

In recent years professional associations have become far more active in policy areas. The *APA Monitor*, the official newsletter of the American Psychological Association, regularly carries articles on legislative and policy matters. In 1974, the Association for the Advancement of Psychology (AAP) was founded to provide a direct voice for psychologists in government hearings and legislative committees dealing with policy issues. The AAP now includes over 5,000 members and spends one quarter of a million dollars annually on lobbying and education activities on behalf of psychologists. The Canadian Psychological Association has recently formed an Applied Division, which comprises a number of interest groups, most of whom are partly concerned with public policy. And a new interdisciplinary journal, *Knowledge: Creation, Diffusion, Utilization*, will concentrate on the processes by which social science knowledge is developed and brought to bear on public policy.

All of these developments indicate the active potential that social psychology has to offer society. According to Charles Kiesler:

> The field of psychology is at a critical decision point regarding what it will be in the future, how useful it will be, and how much it gives back to the broader society that has supported it. There are significant problems in sharpening psychology's utility in social policy, but there are significant benefits as well, both for the field and for society. (1980, p. 66)

TRAINING AND DEVELOPMENT: THE FUTURE

Current Development

In Chapter 1, I defined applied social psychology as social-psychological research and practice in real-world settings, directed toward the understanding of human social behavior and the solution of social problems. I stressed the rationale that all human problems involve a social component, and that the most serious social problems—prejudice, war, and poverty, to name but three—are primarily social in nature. I also stressed the importance of blending theory, research, and practice at all levels of analysis, and the need for an interaction perspective.

Between the two covers of this book, I have tried to include and illustrate the theories, research methods, and practice skills that I believe should constitute a viable and useful applied approach to social psychology. This has not been a simple task. At each level of analysis, it is not easy to ascertain which theoretical concepts or research results might prove the most illuminating in understanding social behavior, or might be most useful in alleviating social problems. For each topic we've looked at, it is not always known how theory, research, and practice blend together in ways that increase our understanding and our ability to act. Within each area of application, there is some degree of fragmentation into separate research domains, and it is not always clear how these combine—or if in fact they do. On a wider scale, it is not a simple matter to know which topics should constitute part of an applied approach to social psychology. If we cover applications in the areas of education and health care, what about religion and political behavior? These difficult questions relate to the basic definition of applied social psychology on which there is only limited agreement at present.

Motivated by the humanistic value base, I have presented you with my vision of an applied approach to social psychology. The picture is as fragmented and complex as it is exciting and challenging. However, I believe that there are common themes running throughout the areas we have covered. These central themes constitute the identity of applied social psychology—a socially concerned field that seeks to understand human social behavior as a complex, multidetermined, primarily rational process, and that seeks to ameliorate social problems through the application of theories, research methods, and practice skills.

I recently articulated these themes as necessary touchstones for applied social psychology (Fisher, 1980b) (see Table 16.1). Touchstones were used in times gone by to test the purity of pieces of gold and silver. The precious metal was rubbed across the black touchstone, and the streak that was left was judged for its purity. We need some touchstones to judge our aspirations and activities, to see if they represent the pure gold and silver of applied social psychology. You have seen these touchstones used throughout this book as standards to assess current work and as guideposts to orientate future directions.

Where is the current development of applied social psychology in relation to the seven touchstones? There is cause for both optimism and pessimism. On some dimensions, such as research in social problem areas (crime, for example, or environmental issues), the field is developing rapidly. On other dimensions, such as the development of practice skills (in program development, conflict resolution, and so on), the gains remain limited. However, the forces for change in social psychology that I spelled out in Chapter 1 will continue to have impact on the discipline. The calls for relevance, the decline in academic positions, the rechanneling of funds to applied research—all will continue to influence social psychologists in applied directions.

These influences are resulting in a shift toward applied work in social psychology. We have seen many examples of social psychologists moving to new areas of research in consumer behavior, health care, criminal justice, environmental psychology, and so on. As they do, they find that knowledge and expertise in more traditional applied areas such as group processes and organizational psychology are essential to their success.

Throughout this book, we have noted the introduction of new journals such

---

Table 16.1   SEVEN TOUCHSTONES OF APPLIED SOCIAL PSYCHOLOGY

1. A central focus on fundamental social problems at all levels of analysis.
2. The continuous integration of theory, research, and practice.
3. The development of middle-range theories stressing the reciprocal interaction of the person and the environment.
4. The application of a variety of complementary research methods.
5. The expansion of practice expertise partly through interdisciplinary collaboration.
6. The adherence to a clearly articulated humanistic value base and a professional code of ethics.
7. A commitment to continuous professional development and role versatility.

Source: Fisher (1980b).

as *Group & Organization Studies, Evaluation Review, Environment and Behavior,* and the creation of new societies and associations concerned with applied issues. Recently, we have witnessed the creation of two new series of yearly volumes intended to define and integrate the field of applied social psychology as it develops during the next decade and beyond. These are the *Applied Social Psychology Annual* (Bickman, 1980) and the *Advances in Applied Social Psychology* (Kidd & Saks, 1980). By bringing together various viewpoints on applied social psychology and by illustrating ongoing applications, these volumes will perform an essential role in the development of the field.

The short and recent history of applied social psychology shows some interesting trends (Bickman, 1980; Shippee, 1979). After the Lewinian tradition of integrating theory, research, and practice had been lost to mainstream social psychology for almost three decades (from the late 1940s to the late 1970s), a renewed interest sprang up. Many social psychologists began turning their attention to social problems. However, much of this initial response consisted of field research studies conducted to test theoretical propositions developed in the laboratory. This research was essentially basic research directed toward increased understanding of human behavior; as such, it was no more helpful in dealing with social problems than was the related laboratory research (Bickman, 1980). According to Shippee (1979), these studies represent a "pseudo-relevant" social psychology in which traditional laboratory methods and basic and/or irrelevant questions were forced into field settings.

The future development of applied social psychology raises again the question of basic versus applied research, and the issue of the appropriate roles of theory and practice. The pernicious schism between basic and applied research, and the lack of integration among theory, research, and practice, continue to plague the field. Bickman (1980) points out that after Lewin's death, experimental social psychology flourished in academic settings; at the same time, social psychologists who were concerned about social problems moved into the human relations movement.

As a further division in the discipline, Daniel Katz (1978) has identified a "second social psychology" that, in contrast to experimental social psychology, has joined hands with the other social sciences to study practical problems in the real world. This second expression of social psychology has remained active since World War II and has relied upon survey research methods, case studies, and field experiments in areas such as organizational psychology, political behavior, and consumer economics (see Box 16.4). I have attempted to incorporate much of this work into the current definition of applied social psychology.

These different forms of social psychology have essentially split the field into three parts: theory and basic research (theoretical-experimental social psychology), applied research (the "second social psychology"), and social practice (the human relations movement). How can we get it all back together? How can we increase our relevance and effectiveness in dealing with social problems? That is the true challenge for the future of social psychology.

Figure 16.3 represents the existing and potential relationships between theory, research, and practice within social psychology (Fisher, 1981b). It shows the distinction and yet the relationship between theoretical-experimental social

Box 16.4   FOCUS ON THEORY, RESEARCH, AND PRACTICE
The Second Social Psychology

The mainstream of social psychology has for the past three decades emphasized theories at the individual level of analysis and the methods of laboratory experimentation. It has virtually ignored the arena of practice. In contrast, social psychologists interested in field studies have joined hands with the other social sciences to understand the real social world—thus creating the "second social psychology." From his fifty years of productive experience in social psychology, Daniel Katz of the University of Michigan provides a historical overview and a contemporary statement on the second social psychology.

The second social psychology contributes to the study of sociological, political, and economic issues. While it gathers data at the level of the individual, it develops concepts and theories at the system levels of analysis—the group, the organization, the nation. It uses case studies, field experiments, and especially surveys to understand how social reality affects human behavior. The development of the second social psychology was fostered by the creation of the Society for the Psychological Study of Social Issues during the Depression and by the collaboration between psychologists and sociologists in field studies of practical problems during World War II.

Today, the second social psychology finds expression in at least three forms. Psychological economics as exemplified by the work of George Katona has shown the importance of psychological variables in economic matters. Individual attitudes, expectations, and decision-making processes must be assessed in order to understand the relationships between economic variables such as income and consumption. The study of political behavior has been extended by social-psychological theories and methods. Survey research has been used to study voting behavior, confidence in the political system, the strength of political parties, and other important issues. The study of organizational behavior has been extended beyond the individual emphasis of industrial psychology. Survey research, the study of work groups, and the consideration of system-level variables has culminated in the current expressions of organization psychology and organization development.

Thus, the second social psychology has and will continue to make significant contributions to the understanding of human social behavior. What is required for further development, however, is an integrated set of concepts for the cumulation of general knowledge. The systems theory approach may provide the key for even further understanding of role systems and social structures as both the effects and causes of social behavior.

Source: Katz, D. Social psychology in relation to the social sciences: The second social psychology. *American Behavioral Scientist*, 1978, 21, 779–792.

psychology and applied social psychology. It follows the potential connections between theory, research, and practice initially spelled out in Chapter 1.

You have seen many examples of how these connections have been made in various spheres of applied social psychology. More importantly, you have now been exposed to a number of major areas of research and practice, including

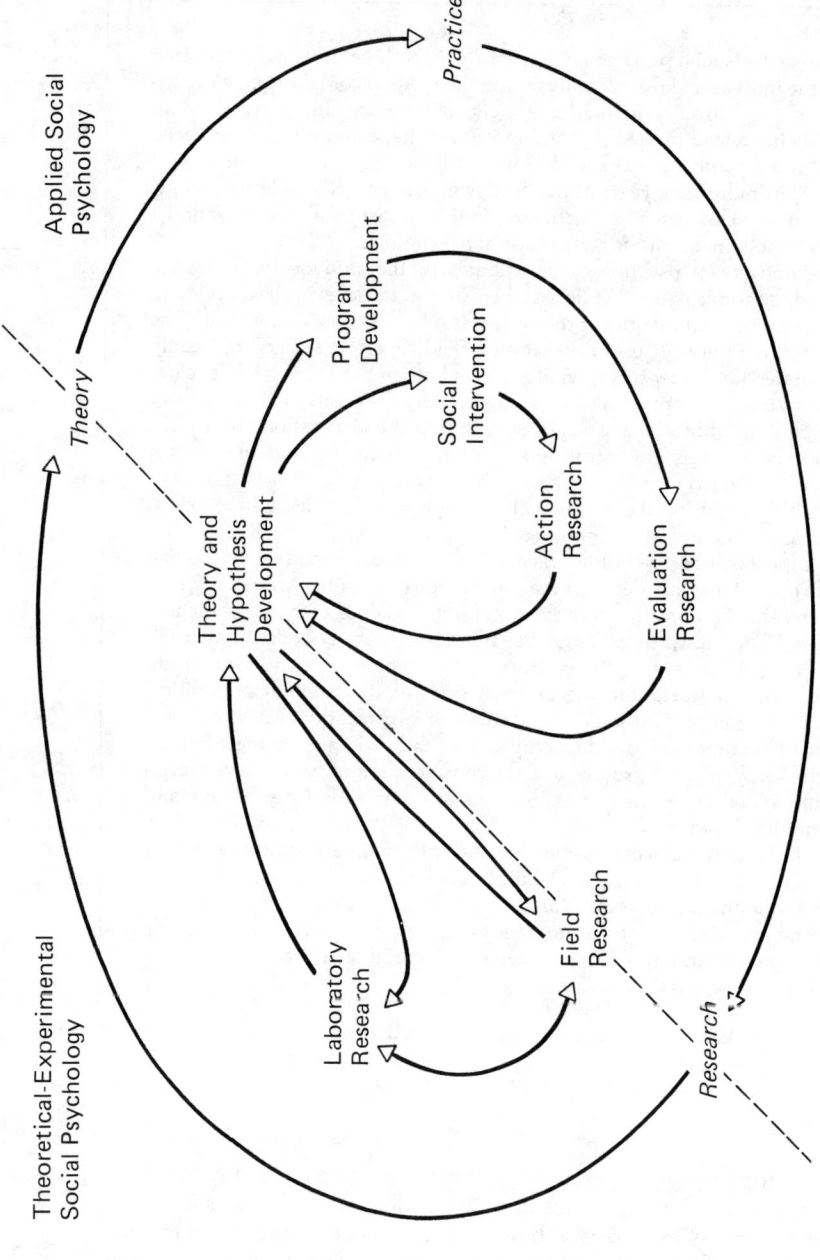

Figure 16.3   Theory, Research and Practice in Social Psychology.
Source: Fisher (1981b). Copyright 1981, Canadian Psychological Association.
Reprinted by permission.

evaluation research, program development, organization development, and the methods of social change.

A number of commentaries in the field have supported the connections depicted in Figure 16.3. Triandis (1978) maintains that basic research is the lifeblood of social psychology—a necessary component for discovering important theoretical relationships that generalize to a wide range of populations and settings. Theories can be tested in both laboratory and field situations to validate their generalizability. Working with valid theories, social psychologists can then help develop social programs designed to alleviate social problems. Finally, we can use our research skills to provide evaluations of social programs.

Similar comments on the integration between theory and evaluation research have been made by Bickman (1979, 1980) and Saks (1978b). Theory should be used (and thus tested) in the development of social programs. Evaluation research then provides feedback on both the validity of the theory and the effectiveness of the program. Cialdini (1980) proposes a "full-cycle social psychology" that begins with natural observation of important social phenomena. Hypotheses are derived from these observations and tested in the well-controlled environment of the social psychology laboratory. The results are then verified or invalidated through field studies, including more natural observation. Theory development and testing can thus come full circle to provide more valid knowledge that will be more directly applicable to the solution of social problems. The growing application of attribution theory to understand social problems—drug abuse, crime, marital conflict—is a good example of this approach (Frieze, Bar-Tal & Carroll, 1979).

To increase the utilization of social-psychological knowledge, a number of commentators suggest moving beyond program and policy development to other social interventions. Such interventions could include many of the practice strategies outlined in this book, including process consultation, community development, and social advocacy. Saxe and Fine (1980) speak of reorienting social psychology toward application, particularly through the use of social experimentation. Psychologists can serve as design consultants who assist policy makers in operationalizing policies into programs within well-designed evaluations. A broader framework is provided by Mayo and LaFrance (1980) in developing their model of an "applicable social psychology" that includes the central elements of: (1) improving the quality of life, (2) knowledge building through theory and research, and (3) utilization and intervention activities. By linking the elements in a cycle that may flow in either direction, the model provides a flexible integration of theory, research, and practice.

Shippee (1979) makes an even stronger case for the role of social psychologists in practice activities through the approach of experimental social innovation. Following the model proposed by Fairweather and his colleagues (Fairweather, 1967; Fairweather & Tornatzky, 1977), Shippee calls for research activities that are motivated and oriented solely for the solution of pressing social problems. This requires involvement in the design, implementation, evaluation, and dissemination of socially beneficial innovations. Oftentimes, this process feeds back to the development, extension, or revision of social-psychological theory at various levels of analysis. The powerful linkages between theory, research, and practice as shown in Figure 16.3 are thus optimized by the social innovation model.

In Chapter 1, I decried the lack of practice involvement by social psychologists (except those attracted to the human relations movement), and throughout this book I have stressed the importance of practice for an applied approach to social psychology. Recently Dorwin Cartwright has provided a very valuable statement on the relationship between theory and practice as envisaged by Kurt Lewin and as operationalized in contemporary social psychology. From his close association with Lewin and his ideas, Cartwright underscores Lewin's essential point that the theorist and practitioner share common interests and interdependent tasks: *it is the special obligation of the theorist to provide theory that is useful for solving social problems.* Useful theory is that which deals with the concrete determinants of behavior within the contemporary life space of the individual, including the effects of groups, institutions, and wider social systems. In contrast, most social-psychological theory of today (for example, dissonance or attribution) deals primarily with cognitive processes within the individual. While these theories help us understand how individuals acquire and process information, they give insufficient attention to other important influences on behavior—such as groups, organizations, social power, and the distribution of economic resources.

In short, "social psychology has in recent years . . . become increasingly less social, and as a result we do not have the kind of theory that can be used in the construction of programs of social action that are intended to solve some of our most serious social problems" (Cartwright, 1978, p. 175). What is required for the creation of useful theory is the development of concepts and methods that describe the social environment as it affects and is affected by individual behavior. By expanding the interaction equation $B = f(P,E)$, social psychologists may yet achieve the Lewinian vision of creating valid theory that informs the practice of improving human welfare.

Training Programs

The definition and development of applied social psychology clearly imply a new kind of professional training to meet the challenges of the coming decades. The academic job market is limited, and social psychologists trained in theoretical-experimental areas will continue to compete for a very small number of college positions. Graduate training programs in the United States award close to 200 Ph.D.'s in social psychology per year. But departments of psychology need only 25 percent of these graduates; the others must find work in other university departments or in nonacadmic settings. With this realization in mind, some departments are adding applied courses and initiating contacts with nonacademic settings to increase the job prospects for their graduates. Unfortunately, these changes are limited because too few academic departments of psychology recognize the clear imbalance between the number of Ph.D.'s granted and the number of academic positions available (Levy, 1979).

Traditional graduate training in social psychology emphasizes theoretical knowledge, primarily at the individual level, and research skills, most notably laboratory experimentation. The Ph.D. graduate is thus prepared to carry out experimental studies of fairly specific theoretical questions of interest mainly to other academic social psychologists. The results of this endeavor, which I have termed theoretical-experimental social psychology, are reported in traditional journals (for example, *The Journal of Personality and Social Psychology*) and in most undergraduate textbooks.

The definition and development of applied social psychology requires a much broader identity for the contemporary professional. Theoretical knowledge must expand beyond the individual level of analysis. Research skills must be developed well beyond those required for laboratory experimentation. Practice expertise must be developed to support work on social problems in real-world settings.

A truly applied approach to social psychology will only come about through significant changes in traditional programs or the development of new training programs. These training programs will maintain the theoretical perspective and research orientation of traditional social psychology, but will expand the research and practice base in new and integrative directions. The socialization of students must be drastically changed to create graduates who can work skillfully and comfortably in applied settings. The character and quality of our discipline in the year 2,000 will be determined by what we do now.

When we speak of training in social psychology, we are speaking mainly of graduate training at the masters or doctoral level. This is because involvement in the design, implementation, and coordination of applied or academic projects requires graduate training. The master's degree usually requires one to two years and includes the thesis as a major research project. The doctorate usually requires two additional years and includes the dissertation. Individuals with undergraduate degrees who have had courses in social-psychological theory and research methods also have an important role to play. They will continue to serve as assistants in research or practice interventions in roles such as interviewers, observers, coders, and so on. Some universities are also offering undergraduate programs in human service work that require an applied orientation. Therefore, a broader and more applied approach to training social psychology at the undergraduate level will help prepare graduates to fulfill a variety of important roles.

Common Core of Training. How can we train social psychologists to enact the research and practice roles described in Chapter 1—applied researcher, program evaluator, trainer, and consultant. How can we develop training programs that follow the touchstones or main themes of applied social psychology? We can discern at least three core experiences that applied training programs should involve (Fisher, 1981b):

1. Integration of theory, research, and practice. Most applied training programs seek to train graduates who can follow the theory-research-practice cycle, that is, who are scientist-practitioners. Deutsch (1975) presents valuable suggestions for training "problem-oriented social psychologists." Familiarity with social-psychological knowledge, and the ability to formulate and modify theories, provide a strong base for the development of research and practice skills. Furthermore, the applied social psychologist must give more attention to the social skills necessary for effective interaction with others. According to Deutsch:

Although the social skills involved in conducting basic social psychological research are not trivial, they are minor compared to those necessary
for effective applied work. . . . These (include) such entry skills as tact,
social poise and persuasiveness—all of which are necessary to initiate
and establish working relations with people whose status, intellectual
background, social and cultural values, and interests may be quite
different from those of the social scientist. They also include the skills
involved in creating a sense of trust, respect and clarity of roles in the
working relationship that is established. (1975, p. 264)

In addition to these general social skills, the applied social psychologist must
acquire to some degree the practice skills of training and consultation to work
effectively with groups and organizations.

2. Real-world involvement. Applied training programs require actual immersion
in field settings through course projects, practicums, and/or internships (see
Severy, 1979). Practicums and internships involve a part-time or full-time
placement in a field setting over a period of months in which the student is
treated similarly to a regular employee of the organization. We learn applied
work by doing it, and there can be no substitute for experience. But experience
alone is not enough. We must analyze and evaluate our experience to give it
meaning and to transform it into a part of our training process. This is
accomplished through supervision and consultation with program faculty and
setting personnel. A further aspect of internships is the potential interdisciplinary contact that is often provided by social research or service organizations. Although the student maintains his or her identity as a social
psychologist, the opportunity to work with other professionals is an invalu-
able learning and socialization experience. The student learns the importance
of working as a team member in which individuals contribute different
knowledge and skills to collaborative efforts.

3. Apprenticeship model. In some manner applied training should involve students working as apprentices with program faculty and agency personnel.
Even while students are able to model the important research and practice
skills of applied work, they are being socialized as professional social psychologists rather than as academics. When they graduate they will be able to
move more easily from the academic environment to field settings, and will
not experience an identity crisis—or a competency gap—in undertaking applied work. At the same time, one of the most important aspects of academic
training is maintained: the ability to do independent work. The thesis and
dissertation requirements of training programs will continue to demand the
initiative, creativity, and perseverance necessary to complete a major individual research project. In this way, the applied social psychologist remains a
social scientist, but one who can also operate effectively as a researcher/
practitioner toward the alleviation of social problems.

Example Training Programs. How can we reorientate or develop training programs that include the core experiences outlined above? How can we graduate
professional social psychologists in the scientist/practitioner mold? There are
many answers to these questions, but three different approaches can be identified
at the present time (Fisher, 1981b). Let's take a quick look at these approaches as
illustrated by three existing training programs in applied social psychology.

First, new applied courses and field experiences can be added to existing
traditional programs in social psychology. The Department of Psychology at the

Box 16.5   FOCUS ON PRACTICE
Training Applied Social Psychologists

How can the core experiences for training applied social psychologists be put into practice at the program level? The development of the Applied Social Psychology Program at the University of Saskatchewan provides one example of integrating theory, research, and practice through continuous real-world involvement following the apprenticeship model.

Incoming students, who already possess a 4-year degree in psychology, are immediately placed in a one-day-a-week practicum arranged by the student, a faculty supervisor, and a field supervisor. The student takes on the role of research assistant, using skills acquired in his or her undergraduate training, and applying new skills that he or she acquires through courses in statistics, psychometric theory, social research methods, and program evaluation. Practice skills are acquired through human relations training workshops in interpersonal communication and small group processes. Following the 8-month academic year, the student spends a full-time, 4-month summer internship in the field setting.

The second year of study also involves a practicum placement while course work shifts toward substantive areas of applied social psychology such as group processes, organizational psychology and development, and community psychology. Students also elect courses in other areas such as medical sociology, counseling, personnel management, and industrial relations. The completion of a master's thesis often coincides with practicum interests and adds the element of individual scholarship to the apprenticeship model.

The practicum, internship, and thesis activities of students have covered the full range of applied research on human service provision, with an emphasis on program development and program evaluation. Students have worked mainly in the areas of health, mental health, and criminal justice in a variety of community agencies and government departments. Example projects include a need assessment for an aftercare program for recovered alcoholics, an evaluability assessment of a counseling program, a process evaluation of a parent training program, the evaluation of a juvenile diversion program, and the development of a prediction device for criminal recidivism.

Graduates of the master's program have found challenging positions as research officers, program evaluators, and personnel officers. Some have continued on to the doctoral program, now in the pilot stage, which emphasizes the utilization of research in the formation of public policy and the development of consultation skills. The experience to date confirms the necessity of continuous, interdisciplinary teamwork in field settings for the training of applied social psychologists.

Source: Fisher, R. J. Training in applied social psychology: Rationale and core experiences. *Canadian Psychology,* 1981, *22,* 250–259.

State University of New York at Buffalo offers such a combination and choice of academic and applied training (Bunker, 1979). Background in social-psychological theories and research methods is followed by specialization and application to social problems. Three new applied minors have been added in measurement, program evaluation, and group and organizational consulting. In addition to applied courses, each minor includes the completion of two research or consultation projects completed in field settings. Students may prepare for either an academic or applied career. A survey of graduates indicates that the program provides a valuable basis for applied work (Garvin, Aidala & Rice, 1980).

Second, some training programs have made a major shift in their emphasis from theoretical-experimental to applied social psychology. One example is the Applied Social Psychology Program at Loyola University of Chicago which over a few years changed its orientation significantly toward applied work (Posavac, 1979). In addition to basic theory and methodology courses, there is a one semester, fulltime research internship. The goals of the program are to train applied social psychologists who can diagnose organizational problems, conduct problem-orientated research, and propose constructive changes. Students unanimously regard the internship as an excellent learning experience.

The third approach is to develop a new applied training program by combining existing elements of graduate training in psychology with new applied courses, field placements, and skill training. This approach approximates the development of the Applied Social Psychology Program at the University of Saskatchewan which I have been coordinating for several years (Fisher, 1981b). The design of this program flowed from the definition and touchstones of applied social psychology in a way that attempts to fully operationalize the core elements of training (see Box 16.5).

Approaching the Future

My one burning desire in writing this book has been to provide a vision of a social psychology that can contribute to improving human welfare. I see social psychology as part of the solution to the many problems that beset humanity. Social psychologists share an immense opportunity to collaborate with others in striving toward a more humane, equitable, and peaceful world. However, there are many deficiencies in contemporary social psychology, particularly in theoretical-experimental social psychology, that limit our ability to aid human progress (see Chapter 1).

In view of this dilemma and of the crisis it places us in, it seems appropriate to close this book with a presentation of three alternative views of the future of social psychology, and to indicate how each is related to the role of our discipline either as part of the solution to humanity's problems, or as part of the problem—or both.

Business-as-Usual Approach. One view within contemporary social psychology is that there is little need for change. Social psychology has developed within the tradition of modern science to study how individuals affect each other—and has been doing a pretty good job of just that. This was the business-as-usual stance represented in William McGuire's 1979 APA address, "Toward Social Psychology's Second Century." McGuire (1979), a theoretical-experimental social psychologist, linked the development of social psychology to the respected traditions of science and philosophy. He described the evolution of "ways of knowing," and listed numerous methods of generating hypotheses about social behavior. He provided a categorization of social-psychological theories that gave a wide overview and synthesis of the development and current state of the field. He then made some predictions about the future of social psychology in terms of both the process and the products of the discipline—for instance, more work on attitude research, more emphasis on theory development as opposed to testing, and so on.

In McGuire's impressive overview of social psychology, the relationship of the discipline to society at large was virtually ignored—as though the slow evolution of social psychology was divorced from the world around it, as though social psychology in the tradition of ancient philosophy was free to invest society's resources in studying whatever topic caught its fancy. McGuire did note, however, that social psychologists do choose topics for study partly in response to current social problems. But in doing so, the social psychologist typically gets more involved in the process of the research, whereas society is more interested (and often disappointed) in the product or knowledge that is generated.

Most of McGuire's suggestions for change were directed toward improving the functioning of theoretical-experimental social psychology as represented in the left half of Figure 16.3. A number of his ideas are similar to Cialdini's (1980) call for "full-cycle" social psychology. Thus, the business-as-usual approach is more concerned with generating basic knowledge about social behavior and with examining and reorienting the philosophy of science to improve the generation of knowledge. Within this approach, there is only a hint that in the long term this knowledge may be usefully applied toward improving human welfare.

From the perspective of the humanistic value base, I must conclude that the business-as-usual approach is more a part of the problem than of the solution. Without greater accountability to society, and without a collaborative approach to studying social issues, there is little likelihood that theoretical-experimental social psychology will contribute directly to human welfare. It is, of course, possible that the evolutionary development and diffusion of social-psychological knowledge will eventually contribute to a more enlightened and humane world.

Dialectical Social Psychology. A second view within contemporary social psychology calls for radical change. This orientation is represented by the critics of theoretical-experimental social psychology who call for the direct involvement of social psychologists as advocates for social change, and who call for the development of "dialectical social psychology" (such as Rappoport, 1977).

This approach, based on Marxist philosophy, sees the opposing forces of conflict (mainly among economic classes) as the main dynamic of society (see Chapter 11). According to Smith (1977), a Marxist social psychology "would be critically concerned with the ideological aspect of social psychological theories . . . would emphasize the primacy of economic classes, and stress conflict rather than consensus . . . (and) would favor a role for social psychology in criticism of the existing social order and in the service of transformation to a more just society" (p. 719).

Dialectical social psychology does not appear to be as all-encompassing as would a fully Marxist social psychology, but it would certainly share the same philosophical base. In Rappoport's (1977) view, it would be characterized by the study of individuals and groups as historical entities who experience contradictions and conflicts within themselves and in relation to their circumstances. The experience and history of individuals in relation to society and the role of conflict are therefore central elements of dialectical social psychology. Thus, more emphasis would be given to the conflict and the interaction between the person and the social system as the major vehicles of social change.

In this light, the dialectical perspective would not see science as the value-free accumulation of facts, but as a value-loaded process that is influenced by social concerns, historical circumstances, political motives, and the class background of social scientists (Cvetkovich, 1977). With regard to the relationship between social psychology and society, the dialectical approach sees contemporary social psychology as supporting the status quo or, even more extremely, as an agent by which the powerful classes maintain control over the economically and politically disadvantaged. It is these more radical accusations of social psychology that will lead many in the field to reject the dialectical approach.

However, the dialectical perspective offers a serious alternative and some useful propositions to contemporary social psychology (Smith, 1977). We need a more critical appraisal of our history, but we should not become dogmatic in our criticism. The historical, developmental, and interactive elements of dialectical social psychology are particularly appealing. In short, social psychology needs to be developmental and historical to be adequately scientific. Nonetheless, the chances of dialectical social psychology significantly affecting the wider discipline appear quite limited at best (Gergen, 1977).

The Middle Road. An applied approach to social psychology walks the middle road between business-as-usual and radical change. It calls for the increased integration of basic and applied research, but in the service of social change and not simply knowledge production. It accepts the scientific tradition of social psychology, but also sees the need for a much more collaborative and responsive relationship with all segments of society. It sees conflict as a stimulus for social change. It sees democratic consensus as a vehicle for societal improvement. Applied social psychology would thus seek to minimize its contribution to the problems and to maximize its role in solutions directed toward a better world.

Applied social psychology can become part of the solution by following the seven touchstones I outlined earlier. To some degree, it shares a humanistic value base with both theoretical-experimental social psychology and dialectical social psychology. It seeks to integrate theory, research, and practice toward both immediate and long-term benefits for humanity. Moving in these directions, and supported by caring, courage, and skill, this approach hopefully represents the wave of the future.

Social Psychology and the Future. The world is an enigma of complex and frustrating contradictions:

- Individuals seek love and support in close interpersonal relationships, but often reap aggression and estrangement.
- Groups set laudable goals to accomplish, but often dissolve in disharmony and disappointment.

- Organizations attempt to motivate members toward productivity, but often produce alienation, stress, and apathy.
- People of goodwill seek to combat racism and sexism, but these spectres of prejudice and discrimination lumber on.
- Urban communities deteriorate into noxious and mistrustful jungles in which the fittest (including those without compassion or conscience) survive—some only to be imprisoned in another jungle behind bars.
- Governments spend millions combatting poverty, but the have-nots do not gain on the haves.
- Governments in turn cut millions from social programs in the false hope that the economic system will somehow produce magic solutions to social problems.
- Technology whirls into the future like a tornado that grips and spews out human beings and their environment in a wide swath of unforseen physical and social consequences.
- World leaders speak of wanting peace while harboring weapons of horrendous and unconscionable destructive violence.

In this perplexing world it is hard to know what *can* be changed and *how* to change it. The difficult question of values also asks what *should* be changed? However, to recede into apathy or into support for the status quo is not acceptable to the humanistic value base of applied social psychology. We can and must search for ways of improving human welfare at every level of analysis and in every situation that we encounter.

We have come through a varied history in the relationship between the social sciences and social action (McGrath, 1980). The 1940s and early 1950s was a time of great pessimism about social problems and yet of unbridled optimism, as exemplified by Kurt Lewin, about social science's ability to help solve these problems. The key was to get policy makers to listen. Then came a decade of rising doubts. Had we over-sold the potential of social science? Did we really have new and powerful ideas and strategies to offer, now that policy makers were listening? The mid-1960s to mid-1970s brought bitter disillusionment. We realized that social science could be used for good *or* evil, and that all social scientists were not necessarily on the side of good. The criticism of social psychology as an irrelevant and sterile enterprise peaked during this period.

Now moving into the future we must forge a more mature and balanced relationship between social science and social change. We do have an effective technology of social science (McGrath, 1980). We are more aware of the complex and contradictory value dilemmas underlying social issues. We see there are no simple, once-and-for-all solutions that are accepted by everyone. Social change is not easy, but we can do the best we can with what we have—the theories, research methods, and practice skills of social psychology and other disciplines.

Social psychology *can* have impact on social problems in the many ways described in this book. By helping to change groups, organizations, and communities, applied social psychologists can improve human social functioning. By confronting injustice and inequality in a rational and yet compassionate manner, applied social psychology offers fresh hope for the amelioration of social issues. But social scientist/practitioners working alone will accomplish little. Individuals at large need to become more informed and socially conscious citizens acquiring new insights about social relations. Collaborative efforts on the part of all members of society—government leaders, policy makers, educators, human service personnnel, and individual citizens—are required for successful social change. In this evolutionary effort, the role of individuals such as yourself should not be underestimated.

Each of us can gain knowledge about social behavior and try out new ways of relating more effectively to others. Each of us can look for ways to better the human condition. My hope is that an applied approach to social psychology offers ideas and behaviors that you can use to improve your social life—as an individual and as a citizen of the world. This book opens the door part way on a vision of a more humane future based on democratic consensus rather than on apathetic denial or autocratic dogmatism. Change in the human condition will not come easily, and maybe not in time for our survival. But change can come by building on the foundation of the humanistic value base and the scientific method in concert with others. Change can come by using the ideas and developing the skills offered by social psychology and related disciplines. As a member of your family, your organizations, your community, your society and the world, you can help improve human satisfaction and productivity. The future is yours. Use it well.

Summary

The current development of applied social psychology evidences uncertainty about the definition and scope of the field. Nonetheless, seven central themes of applied social psychology are expressed as touchstones that stress the integration of theory, research, and practice at all levels of analysis directed toward the amelioration of social problems. The shift toward applied work in social psychology is readily apparent in areas such as criminal justice, health care, and environmental psychology, and is signaled by new publications and associations. The ideal arrangement is to strengthen the linkages between theoretical-experimental social psychology and applied social psychology within the encompassing cycle of theory, research and practice.

The development of applied social psychology has clear implications for graduate training. The common core of training in applied social psychology includes the integration of theory, research, and practice, significant real world involvement through internships, and the apprenticeship model of education. A shift toward applied training is happening, and this involves modifications to existing programs, changes in the basic emphasis of existing programs, and the creation of new programs.

The final question remains: What is the future of social psychology? Will we continue with the "business-as-usual" approach of theoretical-experimental social psychology and thus be seen as part of the problem that resists social change by tacitly supporting the status quo? Will we shift to the radical approach of dialectical social psychology, thus attempting to provide immediate solutions to social problems, but potentially alienating the majority of society in the process?

Or will we follow the middle road of an applied approach to social psychology that places our discipline strongly in the service of constructive social change? The future demands the constructive involvement of each individual in order to improve the human condition.

Further Readings

Bickman, L. (Ed.). *Applied social psychology annual* (Vol. 1). Beverly Hills: Sage, 1980.

Fairweather, G. W. & Tornatzky, L. G. *Experimental methods for social policy research.* New York: Pergamon, 1977.

Katona, G. *Psychological economics.* New York: Elsevier, 1975.

Kidd, R. F. & Saks, M. J. (Eds.). *Advances in applied social psychology* (Vol. 1). Hillsdale, N.J.: Erlbaum, 1980.

Weiss, C. H. (Ed.). *Using social research in public policy making.* Lexington, Mass.: Lexington, 1977.

Woodside, A. G., Sheth, J. N. & Bennett, P. D. *Consumer and industrial buying behavior.* New York: Elsevier North Holland, 1977.

Acknowledgments (continued from page iv)

Figure 1.1 from *Consultation*, by Robert Blake and Jane Syrgley Mouton. Reading, Mass: Addison Wesley Publishing Company, 1976, p. 7. Reprinted by permission. **Table 5.1** adapted from R. B. Cattell, *The Scientific Analysis of Personality*, 1966, Aldine Publishing Co., Hawthorne, N.Y. Reprinted by permission of the author. **Figure 5.2** adapted from Figure 1, Four types of variability in social behavior. M. Argyle and B. R. Little. Do personality traits apply to social behavior? *Journal for the Theory of Social Behaviour*, 1972, 2, 1–35. Reprinted by permission of Basil Blackwell Publisher Ltd., Oxford, England. **Box 6.1** adapted from Table 1, Proportion of similar attitudes and attitudinal discrepancy as a function of sociometric choice. W. Griffitt and R. Veitch. Pre-acquaintance attitude similarity and attraction revisited. *Sociometry*, 1974, 37(2), 163–173. Copyright © 1974 by the American Sociological Association. Reprinted by permission of the publisher and author. **Figure 6.2** reproduced, with permission, from the *Annual Review of Psychology*, Volume 29. © 1978 by Annual Reviews Inc. **Figure 6.4** written by John Wallen, Northwest Regional Educational Laboratory, Portland, Oregon, 1973. **Figure 6.5** adapted from *Group Processes: An Introduction to Group Dynamics*, by Joseph Luft. By permission of Mayfield Publishing Company. Copyright © 1963, 1970 by Joseph Luft. Adaptation from D. W. Johnson, *Contemporary Social Psychology*, 1973, p. 56, reprinted by permission of Harper & Row. **Table 6.3** adapted from *Helping and Human Relations*, Volume 1, by Robert R. Carkhuff, Copyright © 1969 by Holt, Rinehart and Winston. Reproduced by permission of the publisher and author. **Box 6.5** adapted from A. C. Bohart et al., Effects of paraprofessional training on one aspect of generalized interpersonal effectiveness. *American Journal of Community Psychology*, 1976, Volume 4. Reprinted by permission of Plenum Publishing Corporation and the author. **Figure 7.1** adapted from M. E. Shaw, Communication Networks in L. Berkowitz (Ed.), *Advances in Experimental Social Psychology*, Volume 1, 1964. Reprinted by permission of Academic Press and the author. **Table 7.1** adapted from R. T. Golembiewski and A. Blumberg (Eds.), *Sensitivity Training and the Laboratory Approach*, Third Edition, 1977, pp. 85–87. Reproduced by permission of the publisher, F. E. Peacock Publishers, Inc., Itasca, Illinois. **Box 7.3** adapted from Figure 1, Group productivity as a function of group structure and members' psychological motivation. J. P. Wilson, J. Aranoff, and L. A. Messé. Social structure, member motivation and group productivity. *Journal of Personality and Social Psychology*, 1975, 32, 1097. Copyright 1975 by the American Psychological Association. Reprinted by permission of the publisher and author. **Figure 8.1** adapted from G. W. Allport, Prejudice: A problem in psychological and social causation. *Journal of Social Issues*, 1950, Supplement Series, No. 4. Reprinted by permission of Plenum Publishing Corporation. **Table 8.2** adapted from *Ethnocentrism: Theories of Conflict, Ethnic Attitudes and Group Behavior*, R. A. Levine and D. T. Campbell, 1972, adapted with permission of John Wiley & Sons. Adaptation from Table 5.1, Facets of Ethnocentrism, in W. G. Austin and S. Worchel (Eds.), *The Social Psychology of Intergroup Relations*, 1979, p. 73, Brooks/Cole Publishing Company, Monterey, CA. Copyright 1979 by Wadsworth Inc. Reprinted by permission of Brooks/Cole Publishing Co., Monterey, CA. **Figure 8.2** adapted from Figure 6.2 from *Group Dynamics: Key to Decision Making*, by Robert Blake and Jane Syrgley Mouton. Houston: Gulf Publishing Company, Copyright © 1974, p. 71. Reprinted by permission. **Cartoon, p. 324,** by Ben Wicks. Reprinted with permission of Toronto Star Syndicate. **Table 9.1** adapted from Edgar H. Schein, *Organizational Psychology*, © 1980, p. 86. Reprinted by permission of Prentice-Hall, Inc., Englewood Cliffs, N.J. **Figure 9.1** adapted from Figure 7.1, A theoretical model of factors involved in the taking of organizational roles. D. Katz and R. L. Kahn. *The Social Psychology of Organizations* (2nd ed.), 1978. John Wiley & Sons, N.Y. **Box 9.3** adapted from A. S. Tannenbaum, *Hierarchy in Organizations*, 1974, Jossey-Bass Inc., San Francisco. **Figure 9.2** reproduced by special permission from *The Journal of Applied Behavioral Science*, "A Systems Approach to Organization Development," by Michael Beer and Edgar F. Huse, Volume 8, Number 1, p. 84, copyright 1972, NTL Institute. **Figure 9.3** adapted from *New Patterns of Management* by Rensis Likert. Copyright © 1961. Used with the permission of McGraw-Hill Book Company. **Figure 9.4** reprinted from Blake, Robert R., and Jane S. Mouton. *The New Managerial Grid.* Houston: Gulf Publishing Company. Copyright © 1964, 1978, p. 11. Reprinted by permission. **Figure 10.1** adapted from B. S. Dohrenwend, Social stress and community psychology. *American Journal of Community Psychology*, 1978, Volume 6. Reprinted by permission of Plenum Publishing and the author. **Table 10.1** reprinted from J. Rothman, Three models of community organization practice, in National Conference on Social Welfare, *Social Work Practice 1968*, Revised, 1978, by permission of Columbia University Press. **Figure 11.1** adapted from T. F. Pettigrew, Racially separate or together, *Journal of Social Issues*, 1969, Volume 25. Reprinted with permission of the author and the Society for the Psychological Study of Social Issues. **Table 11.3** adapted from Table 1, Modified format of quality of life scale. D. Kedenburg. Quality of life scale: A preliminary analysis. *Professional Psychology*, 1980, 11, 599–605. Copyright 1980 by the American Psychological Association. Reprinted by permission of the publisher. **Table 12.1** adapted from U. Bronfenbrenner, The mirror image in Soviet-American relations: A social-psychologist's report. *Journal of Social Issues*, 1961, Volume 17, Reprinted with permission of Plenum Publishing Corporation and the author. **Figure 12.1** reprinted with permission from the *International Journal of Intercultural Relations*, Volume 4, A. Haque and E. D. Lawson, The mirror image phenomenon in the context of the Arab-Israeli conflict. Copyright 1980, Pergamon Press, Ltd. **Table 12.2** reprinted from "War, Peace, and Integrative Complexity," by P. Suedfeld et al. in the *Journal of Conflict Resolution*, Vol. 21 (March, 1977), with permission of the publisher, Sage Publications, Beverly Hills/London. **Figure 12.2** reprinted from "War, Peace, and Integrative Complexity," by P. Suedfeld et al. in the *Journal of Conflict Resolution*, Vol. 21 (June, 1977), pp. 427–441, with permission of the publisher, Sage Publications, Beverly Hills/London. **Figure 12.3** adapted from *International Behavior: A Social-Psychological Analysis*, edited by Herbert D. Kelman. Copyright © 1965 by Holt, Rinehart and Winston, Inc. Reproduced by permission of Holt, Rinehart and Winston. **Table 13.1** reproduced by special permission from *The Journal of Applied Behavioral Science*, "A group process model for problem identification and program planning," Volume 7, Number 4, p. 473, copyright 1971, NTI Institute. **Table 13.2** reprinted from Goal Attainment Scaling by T. J. Kiresuk and R. E. Sherman, *Community Mental Health Journal*, Volume 4, published by Human Sciences Press, 72 Fifth Avenue, New York, N.Y. © 1968. **Cartoon, p. 566,** by Ben Wicks. Reprinted by permission of Canada Wide Features Services Limited (Toronto). **Figure 14.1** adapted from Interpersonal Conflict Resolution by Allan C. Filley. Copyright © 1975 Scott, Foresman and Company. Reprinted by permission. **Table 14.1** adapted from Table 6.1, A model of the intervention process, L. Wheeler et al., *Interpersonal Influence* (2nd. ed.), 1978, Allyn & Bacon, Inc., Boston, Mass. **Figure 14.3** adapted from Figure 4, Five conflict-handling orientations. K. Thomas, Chapter 21, Conflict and Conflict Management. In M. D. Dunnette (Ed.), *Handbook of Industrial and Organizational Psychology*, 1976, Rand McNally College Publishing Co. Reprinted by permission of the author. **Figure 14.4** adapted from Figure 1, A model of third-party consultation. R. J. Fisher. Third-Party Consultation: A Skill for Professional Psychologists in Community Practice. *Professional Psychology*, 1976, 7, 344–351. Copyright © 1976 by the American Psychological Association. Reprinted by permission of the publisher and author. **Table 14.2** reprinted from R. J. Fisher, A third-party consultation workshop on the Indo-Pakistan conflict, *Journal of Social Psychology*, 1980, 112, p. 202, by permission of The Journal Press, Provincetown, Mass. **Table 15.1** adapted

Glossary

acquisition: learning that occurs when an observer sees a model engage in novel responses and as a result can repeat these responses at a later time. (Bandura)

action research: a basic type of applied research, created by Kurt Lewin, in which the applied scientist collaborates with a group or organization that is experiencing difficulty, collecting data relevant to a social problem which is interpreted and transformed into appropriate action that is then evaluated by collecting further data.

advocate: social psychologist or other professional who uses his or her expertise to press for social change, usually in collaboration with a specific group or institution that is working to change some aspect of society.

affiliative conflict theory: theory stipulating that eye contact is related to our need to affiliate with others, and that approach and avoidance tendencies produce an equilibrium between proximity, eye contact, and other elements of intimacy. (Argyle & Dean, 1965)

aggression: behavior intended to inflict harm or injury on another person or object.

altruism: unselfish concern for the welfare of other people.

androgyny: the possession of approximately equal portions of feminine and masculine characteristics. (Bem, 1975)

applying social psychology: attempts to explain real-world social behavior by using theories developed mainly from laboratory research.

arbitration: involves a third-party judgment that is arrived at by considering the merits of the opposing cases and then imposing a settlement.

assimilation: supports the absorption of racial minorities, racially and/or culturally, into the dominant majority; the opposite of pluralism.

attitude: an individual's tendency to evaluate and respond to social objects in a consistently favorable or unfavorable way.

attribution theory: theory about how we infer the causation of others' behavior, especially in relation to internal versus external factors.

balance theory: consistency theory stating that we are motivated to maintain a "balanced" state of consistent relationships in our perceptions and knowledge of other people and social objects. (Heider, 1958)

before-and-after design: experimental design in which a group of subjects receives the treatment of an independent variable and is assessed on a dependent variable measure both before and after treatment; also called *pretest-posttest design*.

behavior setting: the basic unit of analysis, in Barker's ecological psychology, that is composed of a recurring pattern of activity in the same time and space boundaries.

bureaucratic model: Max Weber's (1947) ideal type of production organization in which goals are accomplished in the most efficient and just manner.

chain network: communication pattern in which members may only communicate with the person adjacent to them. (Shaw, 1954)

circle network: communication network with virtually free communication among all members. (Shaw, 1954)

classic drive theory: theory that a limited number of primary drives (such as hunger, thirst, sex, and pain avoidance) lead to states of internal excitation that, in turn, lead to behavior designed to satisfy the drive and reduce the tension.

coercive power: a means of gaining compliance through force or threat of force to injure or destroy the other party.

cognitive consistency theories: theories which state that each of us has a tendency to look for consistency among our beliefs, and that we are motivated to maintain consistency in our thoughts, feelings, and behavior.

cognitive dissonance theory: theory of cognitive consistency which states that a person experiences unpleasant dissonance whenever any two cognitive elements are incongruent and that the person is motivated to reduce this dissonance.

community developer: one who organizes community members to work toward the solution of common problems that restrict the quality of their lives.

community development: area of practice concerned with organizing community members to work toward the solution of common problems that restrict the quality of their lives.

community forum: a group method which brings together interested members of the community to share their opinions about existing problems.

community group approach: strategy for need assessment that uses different methods, such as informal interviews with key informants, to draw on both individual and group perceptions of need.

community lodge: a social system located in the community that provides the small-group support needed by discharged psychiatric patients. (Fairweather, Sanders, Cressler & Maynard, 1969; Fairweather, Sanders & Tornatzky, 1974)

community psychology: a subfield of psychology concerned with the contribution of social and environmental factors to mental illness and mental health and with the prevention of mental illness and the promotion of mental health through social environmental interventions.

companionate love: "the affection we feel for those with whom our lives are deeply intertwined." (Bersheid & Walster, 1978)

conflict: social situation in which incompatible goals and activities occur between two or more parties (individuals or groups) who hold antagonistic feelings toward each other and attempt to control each other.

conflict (or alienation) approach: a theory of society which argues that fundamental tensions or built-in contradictions exist between classes or people—essentially between the powerful and the powerless—and these problems can be resolved only through radical changes in society.

conflict-handling modes: a set of five strategies of conflict management (avoiding, accommodating, compromising, competing, collaborating) that is a combination of assertiveness and cooperativeness. (Thomas, 1976)

conflict-of-interest hypothesis: hypothesis that sees real differences among competing subgroups as the major determinant of disputes.

conflict resolution: the settlement of a dispute through the reaching of outcomes that are mutually satisfactory and that receive a long-term commitment from both parties.

conflict theory: theory that views community and society as an arena in which various groups compete to attain maximum gain for themselves.

confrontation meeting: a one-day intensive assessment of the "state of the organization," it is essentially a problem-solving session involving all management personnel, or in the case of a small organization, possibly all of its members. (Beckhard, 1967)

consensus: the degree to which others act in the same way in the same situation as the person being observed. (Kelley, 1967, 1973)

construct validity: degree to which an instrument adequately measures a theoretically important variable or construct.

consulcube: Blake and Mouton's (1976) general model of consultation which classifies interventions by type, by focus, and by unit or target of change.

consultant: role in which the social psychologist serves as an expert on social process and social theory, helping groups, organizations, or communities that are experiencing difficulties.

consultation: help-giving process in which the consultant uses his or her expertise to facilitate the problem solving of the client system.

consumer behavior: the acquisition, consumption, and disposition of goods and services by individuals, families, and organizations.

consumer psychology: "that branch of psychology which seeks, through the utilization of distinctively psychological concepts and methods, to understand the dynamics of underlying and determining consumer behavior, including the factors that influence such behavior" (Jacoby, 1975).

content analysis: the coding or categorizing of written or spoken information into a set of smaller descriptive categories.

content validity: the adequacy or representativeness with which a measuring instrument samples a domain of content.

contingency model of leadership: model which emphasizes that the success of a particular leadership style is contingent upon characteristics of the group situation. (Fielder, 1967)

correlation analysis: statistical technique used for estimating the degree of relationship between variables.

correlation coefficient: a statistic that describes the direction and extent to which two measures are related.

correlational research: research that studies whether certain variables are related to one another.

cost-benefit analysis: method of program evaluation that compares costs and benefits by using the same scale (typically the monetary value) to show net differences.

cost-effectiveness analysis: method of program evaluation that relates the utility of program outputs to the cost of program inputs.

criminal justice process: involves the field of corrections—the prisons, and the training and related programs designed to constrain and rehabilitate the offender in accordance with society's norms of acceptable behavior.

cross-lagged panel correlations: statistical technique that measures two variables at more than one time and then computes the cross-lagged correlation between the variables.

debriefing: a researcher's full explanation of the research, given to the subjects at the *conclusion* of a study.

deduction: reasoning that moves from the general to the particular, from a theory to a particular hypothesis.

de-escalation: in conflict, the controlled and specified application of sanctions in a fashion of decreasing magnitude over time. (Bonoma, 1975)

deindividuation: a state of affairs in which individuals in a group do not behave as individual persons but become submerged and experience loss of personal identity. (Festinger, Pepitone & Newcomb, 1952)

demand characteristics: implicit and explicit perceptual cues that communicate what is expected in the experimental setting. (Orne, 1962)

democratic pluralism: ideology proposing that diverse racial and cultural groups can live together harmoniously and can share the fruits of their integrated labor.

dependent variable: the condition in an experimental design that may be shown to be dependent on the condition that is manipulated (the independent variable).

descriptive research: research that documents the existing social reality by describing characteristics and their frequency of occurrence.

determinism: view which holds that social behavior is determined or caused by a variety of factors that are open to empirical investigation.

deterrence: involves the threat to use force as a response in order to prevent the use of force by an adversary. (Morgan, 1977)

diffusion of responsibility: a decrease in the sense of individual responsibility for decisions or actions that are taken in a group setting.

discrepancy theory: theory in which a person's perceived outcome is compared with the outcomes the person wants or believes he or she should receive.

discretion: the power of public officials to act according to their individual judgment and conscience within the rules and principles of the law.

discrimination: overt behavior restricting an individual's rights or access on the basis of membership in a particular group.

discrimination training: training in which the trainee must acquire the sensitivity to pick out which skills are being used and at what level of effectiveness.

economic conflict: conflict whose source lies in competing motives to obtain scarce resources.

educational psychology: area of psychology concerned with the relationship between the entire field of psychology and the processes and outcomes of education. (Lindgren, 1962, 1978)

educational sociology: subdiscipline of sociology which emphasizes social interaction, socialization, and the place of the school in the larger community and in society.

ego: that element of personality which is the conscious, rational mediator that attempts to satisfy id impulses within the constraints of the environment and social reality. (Freud, 1962)

empirical-rational strategy: strategy which assumes that people are rational and will act in their own best interests when they are given information that justifies change. (Bennis, 1976)

empirical theory: theory based on observation that describes a relationship that can be verified by the scientific method. (Lewin, 1951)

empiricism: philosophical approach which maintains that knowledge is acquired through observation and experience, that is, by way of the senses.

encounter group: an experiential group emphasizing emotional expressivity, personal growth, and the deepening of interpersonal relations.

encounter group casualty: a person who becomes more distressed or pathological following an encounter-group experience.

environmental cognition: the perceptual, cognitive, and affective processes by which one comes to know the environment.

environmental design: the systematic process of adjusting the built environment to meet human needs more effectively.

environmental psychology: "the study of the interrelationship between behavior and the built and natural environment" (Bell, Fisher, & Loomis, 1978).

equity theory: theory that equity exists in an interpersonal relationship when each person's ratio of rewards to costs is approximately equal.

escalation: "controlled and specific application of sanctions in a fashion of increasing magnitude over time" (Bonoma, 1975).

ethnic group: a collection of people having a common racial or national background, a common culture and language, or a combination of these characteristics. (Harding, Proshansky, Kutner & Chein, 1969)

ethnocentrism: provincialism or cultural narrowness wherein the individual is "ethnically centered"—that is, rigidly accepting those who are culturally alike, and just as rigidly rejecting those who are different. (Sumner, 1906)

evaluability assessment: evaluation of whether a human service program can be usefully evaluated.

evaluation research: a type of applied research involving the use of social-science research methods to evaluate the process and results of a social policy or program.

experiential learning: learning through direct participation.

experimental game: a laboratory task used to study how people behave in an interdependent situation in which each individual makes decisions affecting the welfare of all participants.

experimental research: a type of research that tests causal linkages among variables. The experimenter manipulates the independent variable, controls extraneous conditions, and assesses the effect on a dependent variable.

experimenter bias: the unintentional influence of the expectations and characteristics of the experimenter on the results.

external reward: in an organization, a motivational pattern involving pay, promotion, fringe benefits, or social approval. (Katz & Kahn, 1978)

external validity: the degree to which results can be validly generalized from one setting to another.

extinction: the decrease in the expression of a behavior following the withdrawal of positive reinforcement.

extraneous variable: variable existing in an experimental situation that is not being tested, but which may affect the dependent variable if not controlled.

factor analysis: advanced statistical procedure based on correlation and used to study the relationships among a large number of variables.

feedback: a complex skill used in human relations training that combines behavior description and description of feelings.

field experiment: experiment in which the researcher intervenes in a real-world setting by introducing or manipulating the independent variable and assessing the resulting effects on the dependent variable.

field theory: theory that the behavior of the individual *(B)* is a function *(b)* of the life space, which includes both person *(P)* and environmental *(E)* forces. (Lewin, 1951)

forced-choice technique: in personality or attitude scale construction, a technique in which the respondent must choose between two items of different content that are equivalent in judged social desirability, thus eliminating social desirability responding as a factor in the choice.

formal organization: a social system designed to coordinate the specialized activities of a large number of people toward the efficient achievement of a stated objective.

formative evaluation: type of program evaluation that is useful to programmers in the formation or development of a curriculum or program. (Scriven, 1967)

Friendship Relations Survey: self-report questionnaire used to test one's general approach to others in terms of self-disclosure and feedback. (Johnson, 1972)

frustration: interference with or blocking of goal-directed activities.

frustration-aggression hypothesis: hypothesis that the existence of frustration leads to some form of aggression, and that the occurrence of aggressive behavior always presupposes the existence of frustration.

general systems theory: theory which seeks laws and concepts that apply at all levels of scientific analysis from a single cell to an entire society.

goal attainment scaling (GAS): system for routinely describing in concrete terms the actual goals undertaken by program staff in relation to each individual in the program. (Kiresuk & Sherman, 1968)

Grid Organization Development: comprehensive program of organizational intervention, developed by Blake and Mouton (1969), that consists of several phases of development over a 3-to-5-year period, using several research and practice methods that focus on increasingly complex levels of analysis.

group development theories: theories of how groups develop, including the sequential phase, recurring phase, and changing leadership models.

group dynamics: area of study focusing on the social forces or pressures that affect the behavior of the individual in a small group.

group functioning: processes occurring at the level of a total group, including how decisions are made and to what effect, how cohesion develops, how norms are developed and enforced, how conflict is dealt with, etc.

group norm: standard of behavior that is prescribed and enforced by the group through the use of rewards and sanctions.

groupthink: process by which a cohesive and insulated group fosters concurrence-seeking to the point that it overrides the realistic appraisal of alternate courses of action. (Janis, 1972)

halo effect: phenomenon in which one's general impression of a person leads one to evaluate most of his or her other qualities in a similar manner.

Hawthorne effect: phenomenon in which experimental manipulation has unintended consequences, such as increased motivation, simply due to the attention given to the subjects.

hindering functions: individual needs for recognition, acceptance, and security whose strong expression interferes with group functioning.

horizontal communication: in an organization, communication among peers or members at the same hierarchical level to coordinate their activities.

humanism: philosophy which contends that the basis for moral values should be found in human experience and human needs. (Kurtz, 1960, 1971)

humanistic psychology: field of psychology concerned with the full development of individual potential. (Bugental, 1967, 1971)

human relations approach: in organizations, an approach that stresses the individuality and emotionality of the members and the importance of social interaction.

human relations trainer: individual who designs and facilitates experiential learning situations in which participants learn to deal with social problems in personal and organizational environments.

human resource development: highly systematic form of human relations training involving both discrimination and communication training of the core interpersonal skills. (Carkhuff, 1969)

human service programs: planned activities that provide comprehensive, integrated help to people who need assistance in matters of health, mental health, education, social welfare, and criminal justice, and all aspects of the social and physical environment that affect people's lives.

human territoriality: concept of the exclusive ownership, use, and defense of areas and objects by persons and groups. (Altman, 1975; Bell et al., 1978)

hypothesis: statement describing the relationship between two or more variables.

id: the unconscious mind's storehouse of powerful innate instincts, which seeks immediate gratification in accordance with the pleasure principle of tension reduction. (Freud, 1962)

image: the organized representation of a social object, particularly national groups, in a person's cognitive system. (Kelman, 1965)

impression formation: the perceptual and cognitive process by which we come to form our general image of another person.

incremental exchange theory: theory that interpersonal relationships develop over time as individuals exchange social rewards of increasing value.

independent variable: in experimental research, a variable or condition that is manipulated.

individual theories: personality theories which look for the causes of behavior within the dynamics of the individual.

induction: reasoning that moves from the particular to the general, and that forms theories based on a number of individual occurrences.

informed consent: in social research, the ethical principle which specifies that people have a right to know about their participation in any activity and have a right to free choice regarding participation.

ingratiation: an individual's covert behaviors that are designed to illicitly influence another person concerning the individual's personality qualities in a positive direction. (Jones, 1964)

inhibition: phenomenon that occurs when an observer who sees a model being punished for certain behaviors shows fewer imitative responses than would be shown if the model were not punished.

instructional psychology: branch of psychology emphasizing the relationship between student and teacher, including their role expectations and the quality of their social interaction.

interactional approach: theory of leadership stipulating that the qualities and skills of the individual combine with the demands of the situation to determine the emergence and effectiveness of his or her leadership.

Interaction Process Analysis: technique for the systematic observation and coding of behavior in small groups. (Bales, 1950)

interaction psychology: field of psychology which considers the complex interplay of persons and situations in determining behavior.

intergroup conflict: situation in which groups perceive themselves as having incompatible goals and engage in antagonistic actions in order to control each other.

internalized motivation: motivational pattern involving the intrinsic job satisfaction experienced by a worker and the internalization of the organization's goals as part of the worker's value system. (Katz & Kahn, 1978)

internal validity: the degree to which the results of an experiment are accurate within the conditions of the experiment.

interpersonal communication: transmission of a message from one person to another with the intention of having an effect.

interpersonal gap: "degree of congruence between one person's intentions and the effect produced in the other" (Wallen, 1973).

interrole conflict: conflict that exists when a person holds two or more positions that require contradictory role enactment.

interrupted-time-series design: experimental method which involves measuring the dependent variable at a number of points over time in order to gauge the effect of a change or intervention.

interview: as a research method, "a two-person conversation, initiated by the interviewer for the specific purpose of obtaining research-relevant information, and focused by him or her on contents specified by research objectives of systematic description, prediction, or explanation" (Cannell & Kahn, 1968).

intrarole conflict: conflict in which two or more partners or groups hold different role expectations.

judicial process: process that includes jury selection and decisions, eyewitness identification and testimony, and the overall functioning of the adversary system followed by the courts.

just-world hypothesis: hypothesis stating that the world is fair and equitable and that victims are simply getting what they deserve and are therefore undeserving of aid. (Lerner, 1970)

kibbutz: agricultural cooperative in Israel that provides a democratic alternative to the predominantly bureaucratic structure of most profit-making and public service organizations.

laboratory game: type of simulation in which the participant is given a role in a situation designed and controlled by the experimenter.

leadership functions: behaviors that are essential if a group is to perform in an effective and satisfying manner.

learned helplessness: state that results when events are uncontrollable, when the outcome of events is independent of the voluntary responses the person makes. (Seligman, 1975)

legal socialization: acquisition, behaviors, and development of individual standards for making legal adjustments about what is right and wrong.

level of significance: very low probability that the results of a study are due to chance alone and are therefore attributed to the variables under study.

locality development: a form of community organization that stresses direct citizen participation in bringing about community change. (Rothman, 1978)

logical positivism: a way of knowing which stipulates that meaningful knowledge is developed and verified through observation and experiment.

loneliness: social deficiency that exists to the extent that one's network of relationships is smaller or less satisfying than one desires.

lose-lose approach: approach to conflict in which both sides accomplish only part of what they want.

Machiavellianism: a strategy of control and manipulation for self-gain that is based on the contention that people are basically evil and corrupt and should be manipulated for personal and political gain. (Christie & Geis, 1970)

machine approach: approach to understanding organizations that likens them to machines, emphasizing their impersonal rationality and legalistic procedures.

maintenance functions: functional leadership roles designed to build a supportive climate of communication and to productively resolve conflicts within a group.

manning: having the number of people required to maintain a behavior setting at an optimum level.

Maslow's hierarchy of needs: set of basic human needs organized into a hierarchy in which the needs at the lower end of the hierarchy must be satisfied before a person can move up to the next level of needs. (Maslow, 1943, 1970)

mediation: attempt by a skilled third party to help a client reach a compromise on specific issues that are amenable to negotiation.

medical psychology: "the study of psychological factors related to any and all aspects of physical health, illness and its treatment at the individual, group and systems level" (Asken, 1979).

membership group: group in which an individual is an active participant.

mere desegregation: the common situation of interracial contact: although institutions are biracial, there is little cross-racial acceptance.

metaevaluation: an evaluation of existing evaluation research to improve the quality of work that is being done.

minority group: usually an ethnic group whose distinguishing characteristic is not necessarily that it is a minority in numbers, but that it is in a minority position in terms of power, status, and wealth. (Simpson & Yinger, 1972)

mirror image: a phenomenon in international relations in which each national group holds similar positive self-images and similar negative images of the other.

mixed-motive game: laboratory game that studies the mixture of cooperation and competitive behavior in negotiation and conflict resolution.

model of facet satisfaction: approach to understanding job satisfaction that considers all facets or aspects of a job that lead to satisfaction. (Lawler, 1973)

multiple correlation: a method for correlating a number of prediction variables with one outcome variable; multiple regression.

natural experiment: experiment in which an investigator studies the effects of a change in a real-world independent variable and on an appropriate dependent variable.

need assessment: systematic verification of the existence, prevalence, location, and importance of a social problem as it is expressed in needs for service.

negative correlation: a relationship in which increases in one variable are shown to be associated with decreases in another.

negative reinforcement: condition or event whose withdrawal increases the probability that the preceding behavior will be repeated.

negotiation: process through which two parties interact to develop agreements that guide and regulate their future behavior.

neo-conservative approach: a revitalization of classic conservatism which maintains that in a world of scarce resources, some of us are destined to be among the elite, others to remain poor.

nonequivalent control-group design: design in which a control group is constructed by a procedure other than random assignment, such as by matching on relevant characteristics.

nonprofessional: an individual who is recruited to provide mental health services without having completed customary training in one of the helping professions.

normative-reeducative strategy: strategy for planned change which assumes that people are rational and that social norms and the individual's commitment to them are very powerful determinants of behavior. (Bennis et al., 1976) objective empiricism: the use of refined experience to generate knowledge about the world.

observation: the selecting, recording, and encoding of both the behaviors and the characteristics of settings for the empirical aims of description or theory development. (Weick, 1968)

observational learning: learning that occurs vicariously by watching a model and without behavior or reinforcement at the time of learning.

open systems theory: approach to organizations which includes the interrelationships among different levels of analysis—and that begins at the level of the social system rather than of the individual.

operant conditioning: procedure in which an organism's response is immediately reinforced; thus, the response is learned, and the effect of reinforcement is seen as the later cause of the behavior, rather than any internal motive or need.

operationism: a principle that states that only propositions based on operations that are public and repeatable are admissible as scientific evidence. (Stevens, 1963)

organizational consultant: role of a social psychologist who serves as an expert on social process and social theory, helping organizations that are experiencing difficulties.

organizational control: the ability to influence organizational decisions.

organizational socialization: social learning process by which organizational members acquire knowledge, attitudes, and behaviors necessary for successful participation in the social system of the organization.

organization development: a collection of practice and research interventions designed to improve organizational effectiveness and the satisfaction and productivity of members.

outcome evaluation: a type of program evaluation which consists of research activities that document the effectiveness and efficiency of a program in attaining its specified objectives.

outgroup: ethnic, racial, or religious group that we see as different from our own.

paralanguage: aspect of verbal communication that considers how something is said rather than what is said.

partial correlation: technique which estimates the degree of relationship between two variables while a third related variable is held constant.

partial inclusion: characteristic of organizational roles in which the organization, in fulfilling functional roles, wants to include only a segment or part of a person rather than the whole person. (Allport, 1933)

partial individual approach: the selective application of psychological principles to increase the overall understanding of international relations.

participant observation: an observational method in which the observer describes a social situation in which he or she is actively involved.

perceived conflict: conflict that is perceived whether or not it actually exists.

perceptual distortion: the tendency to see what one wants to see and to distort whatever comes through the senses in order for this to happen.

perceptual selectivity: a basic process of social perception by which one brings order to the social and physical world by filtering out certain elements and focusing on others.

personality: the individual's unique set of enduring dispositions that are related to his or her behavior.

personal space: the invisible zone or "bubble" around each individual into which most others should not trespass.

person-blame causal attribution bias: bias which blames the individual or victim rather than the social environment for existing problems.

person-role conflict: strain or inconsistency between individual characteristics, such as values and beliefs, and the role behavior expected of the individual.

phenomenology: a philosophical approach which maintains that we develop a picture of the world through our senses, and that our subjective experience is the reality out of which we operate.

planned change: change that "self-consciously and experimentally employs social knowledge to help solve the problems of men and societies" (Bennis et al., 1976).

planned renegotiation: bargaining technique that provides for ongoing changes in role expectations. (Sherwood & Glidewell, 1972)

plea bargaining: situation in which a prosecuting attorney negotiates a reduction of a charge against a defendant in exchange for a guilty plea and waiver of the right to trial.

positive reinforcement: condition or event whose presence increases the probability that a preceding behavior will be repeated.

power-coercive strategy: strategy which assumes that people change when they are forced to change through the application of social influence. (Bennis et al., 1976)

power conflict: conflict in which each party wishes to maximize the amount of influence it has.

predictive validity: the ability of a measure to estimate a subsequent behavior such as job performance.

prejudice: simplistic, hostile attitude toward a group of people and the individuals in that group.

primacy effect: principle that the first side presented in a two-sided argument has the most impact.

primary group: group with which an individual has frequent face-to-face contact on an intimate basis, such as the family.

primary prevention: type of prevention aimed at reducing the overall incidence of mental illness. (Caplan, 1964)

problem solving: systematic sequence of steps through which solutions to difficulties are developed, implemented, and evaluated.

process consultation: "a set of activities of the consultant which help the client to perceive, understand and act upon process events which occur in the client's environment" (Schein, 1969).

process consultation and intervention approach: approach to organization development that focuses on the human-process aspects of an organization rather than on its physical technology or social structure.

process evaluation: a type of program evaluation which consists of activities that describe and monitor program services and effects in order to improve program performance.

program consultation: the provision, by a consultant, of diagnosis, information, and guidance relative to the planning, implementation, administration, and evaluation of a human service program.

program contact: second stage in program development in which the program staff makes connections with clientele or target population.

program developer: professional practitioner concerned with the most effective methods of developing or improving social programs.

program evaluation: the application of research methods to assess the functioning and impact of a human service program.

program implementation: third stage of progam development in which the staff delivers its services, moving to attain the ultimate goals of the program.

program initiation: first stage in program development in which the basic ideas and goals for a program are articulated and translated into a concrete plan of action, and all the necessary human, financial, and physical resources are acquired.

prosocial behavior: activity that has positive social consequences for others.

proxemics: study of human spatial behavior examining ways in which people use physical space to regulate social interaction; a communicator's physical distance from and relative position to a person perceiving the message.

psychoanalysis: the original psychodynamic approach to personality pioneered by Sigmund Freud.

psychodynamics: approach to studying personality that emphasizes underlying forces or motives, often of an unconscious nature.

psychological reactance: theory which states that if an individual's freedom of choice is eliminated, he or she will attempt to restore it.

psychology: scientific study of the principles of individual behavior.

psychotherapy: psychological treatment of mental, emotional, and nervous disorders.

punishment: aversive condition or event that decreases the frequency or strength of a preceding behavior.

quasi-experimental design: research study in which the experimenter has partial rather than full experimental control over the variables and setting.

race: group of people with distinctive physical characteristics that are genetically transmitted.

racism: combination of prejudice and discrimination based on the belief that race is the primary determinant of human capabilities and that racial differences produce an inherent superiority of one race over others.

rating scale: self-report measure in which the respondent directly rates the amount of a variable, basing the rating on personal judgment.

realistic conflict: conflict stemming from objective differences among two parties that trigger actions intended to control each other and that create antagonistic feelings toward each other.

realistic group conflict theory: theory which states that real or objective conflicts of interests between groups cause conflict. (Campbell, 1965)

recency effect: principle that the second side presented in a two-sided argument has the most impact.

reciprocity: law of social behavior stating that in social interactions we usually get what we give.

reference group: a group of similar others to which an individual refers his or her behavior, attitudes, or other characteristics for purpose of social comparison. (Hyman, 1942, 1960; Merton & Kitt, 1950)

regression: process by which high random variations tend to regress back toward the average on subsequent measures.

releaser: environmental cue which triggers the expression of aggressive behavior.

reliability: consistency and stability of measurement.

representative sample: sample of a population under study from which the results obtained can be generalized to the entire population.

research consultation: involves the provision of knowledge and guidance relevant to the execution of a social research project.

response facilitation: in observational learning, the elicitation of existing responses.

response set: tendency of people to respond in a certain way regardless of the content of the item.

reverse discrimination: treatment of minority group members that is better than the treatment accorded to majority group members. (Dutton, 1976)

risky-shift phenomenon: tendency for individuals in groups to make riskier decisions than they would make acting alone.

role: pattern of behavior appropriate to a person's position in life.

role analysis technique: technique which clarifies roles in new organizations or in situations where role ambiguity exists. (Dayal & Thomas, 1968)

role conflict: conflict due to differing role expectations by members of a role set.

role expectation: belief about appropriate behaviors, obligations, rights and privileges that are assigned to a role position.

role negotiation: process of bargaining in which role partners explicitly state what behaviors they want from each other and what behaviors they are prepared to change to get what they want. (Harrison, 1972)

role partner: a person who plays a complementary role within a role set.

role position: the category or grouping of people who exhibit common attributes and behavior and who are subject to similar sanctions from others.

role set: the collection of interdependent roles within a social system.

role socialization: learning what is appropriate behavior for any given position.

role strain: *see* role conflict.

romantic love: passionate love; a state of intense physiological arousal and intense absorption with another person, leading to a sense of complete fulfillment. (Walster & Walster, 1978)

rule enforcement: motivational pattern in which members accept role prescriptions and organizational directives because they come from legitimate sources of authority and carry legal sanctions. (Katz & Kahn, 1978)

sampling: the process by which the sample of respondents to be included in a study are selected.

scapegoat theory of prejudice: theory which states that the blocking of goals leads to anger that is displaced onto minority groups.

scientific management: management technique that aims to find the most effective ways of integrating people with machines for maximum production. (Taylor, 1923)

scientific method: sequence of steps that scientists follow to create and verify knowledge about the world.

secondary analysis: method of evaluation in which data that have already been collected are reanalyzed to see if similar or different results are obtained.

secondary group: group consisting of a larger, more impersonal collection of individuals, in which there is a lower level of interaction and intimacy than in primary groups; for example, professional organizations and community service clubs.

secondary prevention: designed to limit the duration and severity of problems that have become visible and could lead to serious disorders. (Caplan, 1964)

self-actualization: becoming "everything that one is capable of becoming" (Maslow, 1970).

self-disclosure: communicating information about oneself to someone else.

self-fulfilling prophecy: a phenomenon in which one person's expectations influence another person's behavior in the expected directions, thus confirming the original expectations.

self-perception theory: theory that people simply observe their behavior and the conditions in which it occurs, and then infer their attitudes from their behavior.

self-report measure: a measuring technique in which the respondent gives written replies to questions provided by the researcher.

sensitivity training: a type of experiential learning in which participants can increase their self-awareness, their interpersonal effectiveness, and their understanding of group processes.

sex typing: phenomenon whereby children acquire sex role behavior appropriate to their gender.

simulation: intentional imitation of the essential processes and outcomes of a real (social) situation, carried out in order to better understand the underlying mechanisms of that situation. (Abelson, 1968)

social action model: model which assumes that a disadvantaged segment of a community needs to be organized and mobilized to gain more power and resources in accord with the principles of democracy and social justice. (Rothman, 1978)

social advocacy: role in which a social psychologist acts as participant activist, joining forces with disadvantaged people to increase their power and improve their standard of living.

social change: modification or alteration in the social structure of a society—that is, in the basic arrangements of living as expressed in the society's shared values, norms, roles, and so on.

social comparison theory: principle that we approach others to gain self-evaluation. (Festinger, 1954)

social desirability: tendency for respondents to agree with statements that they believe will present them in a socially desirable light, and to reject statements that will not.

social-emotional leader: leader who works to keep a group together by supporting members and by smoothing over conflict.

social impact assessment: the use of research methods to measure the effects of technological or physical change on social life.

social indicator: standardized measure that can be used on a regular basis to yield a concrete picture of society's well-being. (Bauer, 1966)

social indicator approach: need-assessment approach that analyzes available information, such as census and public health data, to give a picture of existing needs and potential clientele.

social issue: harmful condition that affects a significant proportion of society and is perceived by a significant number of people as requiring redress by society.

socialization: complex learning process by which we acquire the knowledge, skills, and attitudes necessary for successful participation in society.

social learning: learning that involves other people.

social movement: a concerned group of citizens who carry out activities to effect social change by removing harmful conditions in society.

social penetration: model that sees mutual self-disclosure as the basic process that determines how interpersonal relationships develop and decay over time.

social perception: perception which exists when other people are involved, directly or indirectly, in the process of experiencing the world.

social-psychological approach: attempt to explain the processes of social interaction that make up international behavior.

social psychology: the scientific study of how the behavior of an individual is influenced by and in turn influences the actions of others in the social environment.

social technology: application of social-psychological knowledge to the solution of social problems. (Varela, 1971)

social theory of personality: personality theory that focuses on differences among situations rather than individuals. (Bavelas, 1978)

sociogram: diagram on which the results of a sociometric test are plotted.

sociology: study of social systems—families, organizations, and societies—and of complex social processes, such as social change and socialization of children.

sociometric technique: self-report method for describing interpersonal relations, especially interpersonal liking.

sociometry: measurement of interpersonal preferences. (Moreno, 1934)

sociotechnical/structural approach: approach to organizational development that seeks to change either the social structure of an organization and/or its physical technology and arrangements of work activities.

stereotype: a simplistic set of beliefs held by an individual regarding the attributes of another group.

stratified random sampling: method of drawing a sample in which respondents are randomly selected from certain categories (age, occupation, and so on) in numbers proportionate to the size of those categories in the total population.

statistic: single number whose size represents the strength of the effect that has occurred.

subjective empiricism: the combining of one's raw experience of sensing the world with reasoning, in order to draw conclusions about the world.

substantive conflict: in a small decision-making group, conflict relating to the group's task.

summated ratings: a method of attitude scaling that presents a combination of favorable and unfavorable statements in order to determine the favorability of a respondent's attitude to an object in question. (Rensis Likert, 1932)

summative evaluation: type of program evaluation that assesses the impact of a program. (Scriven, 1967)

super-ego: the element of personality that internalizes society's moral standards and the individual's conscience, representing judgments of "good" and "bad." (Freud, 1962)

superordinate goal: common goal that can only be achieved by inter-group cooperation. (Sherif, 1966)

support system: "an enduring pattern of continuous or intermittent ties that play a significant part in maintaining the psychological and physical integrity of the individual over time" (Caplan, 1974).

survey approach: an approach to need assessment that assesses existing services and resources in an area of need as well as gaps in service.

survey feedback approach: approach to organization development that collects questionnaire data to diagnose organizational problems to which interventions are then directed.

survey method: method of data collection in applied social research involving the collection of data by questionnaires or interviews from a sample of respondents.

symbolic interactionism: a general approach to social psychology that emphasizes social interaction as the shaper of the self and society.

systems approach: approach to organization development that views the organization as a whole in relation to its environment.

systems theory: theory which stresses the integrated wholeness of the social system through the coordination of interdependent, specialized subsystems.

task functions: functional leadership roles required to facilitate and coordinate group effort in the selection, definition, and solution of a task confronting a group.

task leader: within a group, a leader who tends to give opinions and ask for suggestions, and who pushes to get the job done, sometimes offending other members.

Tavistock group: a type of experiential learning group that focuses on group processes and interprets all individual behavior as an expression of group forces.

team building: activities designed to enhance the effective operation of work teams by analyzing concerns, developing group skills, improving coordination, setting goals, and building stronger relationships.

tertiary prevention: approach aimed at reducing the degree of impairment once emotional disorder has occurred, and at improving the person's capacity to cope with future problems.

third-party consultation: a method for the resolution of conflict in which a skilled and knowledgeable consultant helps the antagonists understand and deal directly with the conflict.

third-party functions: core strategies of third-party consultation.

third-party procedure: in third-party consultation, an exercise that is more complex than a tactic, such as the development and exchange of intergroup images.

third-party role: pattern of behavior appropriate to the method of third-party consultation.

third-party tactic: a specific behavior in third-party consultation, such as paraphrasing or confronting.

Thorndike's Law of Effect: theory that behavior which has a satisfying effect on an organism will tend to be repeated, whereas behavior that has an unpleasant effect will tend not to be repeated.

total individual approach: approach to international relations that uses the characteristics of individuals to explain interactions among nations.

trait: enduring characteristic, quality, or predisposition to respond in a consistent manner.

true integration: humanistic goal that all races can have a sense of autonomy and independence while living in a racially interdependent world of institutional integration and cross-racial friendship.

ultimate attribution error: cognitive error that occurs when a prejudiced observer (who is a member of an ingroup) sees a member of an outgroup engage in undesirable behavior and attributes it to personal causes believed to be innate in members of the outgroup. (Pettigrew, 1979)

unrealistic conflict: conflict resulting from miscommunication, and other processes that create conflict where no basic incompatibilities exist.

validity: degree to which an instrument adequately measures a theoretically important variable or construct.

value conflict: conflict involving incompatibility in ideology, religion, or way of life.

vertical communication: communication in an organization that is up or down between levels of the hierarchy.

voir dire: (French "to speak the truth" or "to see what he or she says") one part of the jury-selection process whereby prospective jurors may be rejected because they do not meet some statutory requirement for jury service, or because the attorneys demonstrate that the juror is too biased or prejudiced to render a fair and impartial verdict.

wheel network: communication network in which only the central person is allowed to communicate with the other members of a group. (Shaw, 1954)

win-lose approach: a competitive approach to managing conflict which assumes that agreement is impossible.

win-win approach: a collaborative approach to managing conflict, involving a conscious, systematic attempt to maximize the gains of both parties through joint problem solving.

References

Abelson, R. P. Simulation of social behavior. In G. Lindzey & E. Aronson (Eds.), *The handbook of social psychology* (2nd ed.) (Vol. 2). Reading, Mass.: Addison-Wesley, 1968.

Abramson, L. Y., Seligman, M. E. P. & Teasdale, J. D. Learned helplessness in humans: Critique and reformulation. *Journal of Abnormal Psychology*, 1978, *87*, 49–74.

Abt, C. C. Social science in the contract research firm. In R. F. Kidd & M. J. Saks (Eds.), *Advances in applied social psychology* (Vol. 1). Hillsdale, N.J.: Erlbaum, 1980.

Adair, J. G. *The human subject: The social psychology of the psychological experiment*. Boston: Little Brown, 1973.

Adams, J. S. Inequity in social exchange. In L. Berkowitz (Ed.), *Advances in experimental social psychology* (Vol. 2). New York: Academic Press, 1965.

Adams, J. D. (Ed.). *Theory and method in organization development: An evolutionary process*. Arlington, Va.: NTL Institute, 1974.

Adams, S. Evaluating correctional treatments: Toward a new perspective. *Criminal Justice and Behavior*, 1977, *4*, 323–339.

Adorno, T. W., Frenkel-Brunswik, E., Levinson, D. J. & Sanford, R. N. *The authoritarian personality*. New York: Harper & Row, 1950.

Agnew, N. & Pyke, S. *The science game: An introduction to research in the behavioral sciences* (2nd ed.). Englewood Cliffs, N.J.: Prentice-Hall, 1978.

Agopian, M. W. Politics of evaluating diversion programs. *Evaluation Quarterly*, 1979, *3*, 81–88.

Agurén, S., Hansson, R. & Karlsson, K. G. *The impact of new design on work organization*. Stockholm: The Rationalization Council SAF-LO, 1976.

Aiello, J. R. & Baum, A. (Eds.). *Residential crowding and design*. New York: Plenum, 1979.

Alderfer, C. P. An empirical test of a new theory of human needs. *Organizational Behavior and Human Performance*, 1969, *4*, 142–175.

Alderfer, C. P. Organization development. *Annual Review of Psychology*, 1977a, *28*, 197–223.

Alderfer, C. P. Improving organizational communication through long-term intergroup intervention. *The Journal of Applied Behavior Science*, 1977b, *13*, 193–210.

Alderfer, C. P. The methodology of organizational diagnosis. *Professional Psychology*, 1980, *11*, 459–468.

Alevy, D. I., Bunker, B., Doob, L. W., Foltz, W. J., French, N., Klein, E. B. & Miller, J. C. Rationale, research, and role relations in the Stirling Workshop. *Journal of Conflict Resolution*, 1974, *18*, 276–284.

Alger, C. F. Personal contact in intergovernmental organizations. In H. C. Kelman (Ed.), *International behavior: A social-psychological analysis*, New York: Holt, Rinehart & Winston, 1965.

Alinsky, S. *Reveille for Radicals*. Chicago: University of Chicago Press, 1946.

Alinsky, S. *Rules for radicals*. New York: Random House, 1971.

Allen, V. L. (Ed.). *Psychological factors in poverty*. Chicago: Markham, 1970.

Allen, R. F., Pilnick, S. & Silverzweig, S. Conflict resolution team building for police and ghetto residents. *Journal of Criminal Law, Criminology, and Police Science*, 1969, *60*, 251–255.

Allport, F. H. *Institutional behavior*. Chapel Hill: University of North Carolina Press, 1933.

Allport, G. W. *The nature of prejudice*. Cambridge, Mass.: Addison-Wesley, 1954.

Allport, G. W. *Pattern and growth in personality*. New York: Holt, Rinehart & Winston, 1961.

Allport, G. W. Traits revisited. *American Psychologist*, 1966, *21*, 1–10.

Allport, G. W. The historical background of modern social psychology. In G. Lindzey & E. Aronson (Eds.), *The handbook of social psychology* (2nd ed.) (Vol. 1). Reading, Mass.: Addison-Wesley, 1968.

Allport, G. W. & Postman, L. J. The basic psychology of rumor. *Transactions of the New York Academy of Sciences*, Series II, 1945, *8*, 61–81.

Altman, I. A. *The environment and social behavior*. Monterey, Calif.: Brooks-Cole, 1975.

Altman, I. A. Environmental psychology and social psychology. *Personality and Social Psychology Bulletin*, 1976, *2*, 96–113.

Altman, I. A. & Haythorn, W. W. Interpersonal exchange in isolation. *Sociometry*, 1965, *28*, 411–426.

Altman, I. A. & Taylor, D. A. *Social penetration: The development of interpersonal relationships*. New York: Holt, Rinehart & Winston, 1973.

Altmann, H. A. & Black, D. B. Enhancing student self-concept with communication skill training. *Small Group Behavior*, 1978, *9*, 80–91.

Altrocchi, J. Mental health consulation. In S. E. Golann & C. Eisdorfer (Eds.), *Handbook of community mental health*. Englewood Cliffs, N.J.: Prentice-Hall, 1972.

Amir, Y. Contact hypothesis in ethnic relations. *Psychological Bulletin*, 1969, *71*, 319–342.

Amir, Y. The role of intergroup contact in change of prejudice and ethnic relations. In P. A. Katz (Ed.), *Towards the elimination of racism*. New York: Pergamon, 1976.

Anand, R. P. The development of a universal international law. In A. Lepawsky, E. H. Beuhring & H. D. Lasswell (Eds.), *The search for world order*. New York: Appleton-Century-Crofts, 1971.

Anastasi, A. *Fields of applied psychology*. New York: McGraw-Hill, 1964.

Anderson, N. H. Averaging versus adding as a stimulus-combination rule in impression formation. *Journal of Experimental Psychology*, 1965, *70*, 394–400.

Anderson, N. H. Application of a linear-serial model to a personality-impression task using serial presentation. *Journal of Personality and Social Psychology*, 1968, *10*, 354–362.

Anderson, D. A. The family growth group: Guidelines for an emerging means of strengthening families. *Family Coordinator*, 1974, *23*, 7–13.

Anderson, S. B. & Ball, S. *The profession and practice of program evaluation*. San Francisco: Jossey-Bass, 1978.

Andrews, F. M. & Withey, S. B. *Social indicators of well being*. New York: Plenum, 1976.

Andrieu, M. Benefit cost evaluation. In L. Rutman (Ed.), *Evaluation research methods: A basic guide*, Beverly Hills, Calif.: Sage, 1977.

Argyle, M. & Dean, J. Eye-contact, distance, and affiliation. *Sociometry*, 1965, *28*, 289–304.

Argyle, M. & Little, B. R. Do personality traits apply to social behavior? *Journal for the*

Theory of Social Behavior, 1972, 2, 1-35.

Argyris, C. *Interpersonal competence and organizational effectiveness*. Homewood, Ill.: Irwin-Dorsey, 1962.

Argyris, C. *Integrating the individual and the organization*. New York: Wiley, 1964.

Argyris, C. The incompleteness of social-psychological theory: Examples from small group, cognitive consistency, and attribution research. *American Psychologist*, 1969, 24, 893-908.

Argyris, C. *Intervention theory and method: A behavioral science view*. Reading, Mass.: Addison-Wesley, 1970.

Argyris, C. Dangers in applying results from experimental social psychology. *American Psychologist*, 1975, 30, 469-485.

Argyris, C. Leadership, learning and changing the status quo. *Organizational Dynamics*, 1976, 4, 29-43.

Arms, R. L., Russell, G. W. & Sandilands, M. L. Effects on the hostility of spectators of viewing aggressive sports. *Social Psychology Quarterly*, 1979, 42, 275-279.

Aronson, E., Blaney, N., Sikes, J., Stephan, C. & Snapp, M. Bussing and racial tension: The jig-saw route to learning and liking. *Psychology Today*, 1975, 8, 43-50.

Aronson, E. & Carlsmith, J. M. Experimentation in social psychology. In G. Lindzey & E. Aronson (Eds.), *The handbook of social psychology* (2nd ed.) (Vol. 2). Reading, Mass.: Addison-Wesley, 1968.

Aronson, E. & Mills, J. Effect of severity of initiation on liking for a group. *Journal of Abnormal and Social Psychology*. 1959, 59, 177-181.

Aronson, E., Stephan, C., Sikes, J., Blaney, N. & Snapp, M. *The jigsaw classroom*. Beverly Hills, Calif.: Sage, 1978.

Asante, M. K., Newmark, E. & Blake, C. A. *Handbook of intercultural communication*. Beverly Hills, Calif.: Sage, 1979.

Asch, S. E. Forming impressions of personality. *Journal of Abnormal and Social Psychology*, 1946, 41, 258-290.

Asch, S. E. Studies of independence and conformity: I. A minority of one against a unanimous majority. *Psychological Monographs*, 1956, 70, No. 416.

Ashmore, R. D. The today and likely tomorrow of American race relations. *Journal of Social Issues*, 1976, 32(2), 1-8.

Asken, M. J. Medical psychology: Toward definition, clarification, and organization. *Professional Psychology*, 1979, 10, 66-73.

Aspy, D. N. The effect of teacher-offered conditions of empathy, congruence and positive regard upon student achievement. *Florida Journal of Educational Research*, 1969, 11, 39-48.

Aspy, D. N. Empathy: Let's get on with it. *Counseling Psychologist*, 1975, 5, 10-14.

Astin, A. W. *The college environment*. Washington, D.C.: American Council on Education, 1968.

Atkinson, R. C. Reflections on psychology's past and concerns about its future. *American Psychologist*, 1977, 32, 205-210.

Attkisson, C. C. & Broskowski, A. Evaluation and the emerging human service concept. In C. C. Attkisson, W. A. Hargreaves, M. J. Horowitz & J. E. Sorensen (Eds.), *Evaluation of human service programs*. New York: Academic Press, 1978.

Attkisson, C. C., Hargreaves, W. A., Horowitz, M. J. & Sorensen, J. E. (Eds.). *Evaluation of human service programs*. New York: Academic Press, 1978.

Austin, W. G. & Worchel, S. (Eds.). *The social psychology of intergroup relations*. Monterey, Calif.: Brooks/Cole, 1979.

Axelrod, R. Effective choice in the Prisoner's Dilemma. *Journal of Conflict Resolution*, 1980, 24, 3-26.

Babbie, E. *Survey research methods.* Belmont, Calif.: Wadsworth, 1973.

Bach, G. R. & Goldberg, H. *Creative aggression: The art of assertive living.* New York: Avon, 1974.

Bach, G. R. & Wyden, P. *The intimate enemy: How to fight fair in love and marriage.* New York: Avon, 1968.

Backman, C. W. & Secord, P. F. *A social psychological view of education.* New York: Harcourt, Brace & World, 1968.

Bagozzi, R. P. & Burnkrant, R. E. Attitude organization and the attitude-behavior relationship. *Journal of Personality and Social Psychology,* 1979, *37,* 913–929.

Bakeman, R. & Dabbs, J. M. Social interaction observed: Some approaches to the analysis of behavior streams. *Personality and Social Psychology Bulletin,* 1976, *2,* 335–345.

Bales, R. F. A set of categories for the analysis of small group interaction. *American Sociological Review,* 1950a, *15,* 257–263.

Bales, R. F. *Interaction process analysis: A method for the study of small groups.* Reading, Mass.: Addison-Wesley, 1950 (b).

Bales, R. F. *Personality and interpersonal behavior.* New York: Holt, Rinehart & Winston, 1970.

Bales, R. F. & Slater, P. E. Role differentiation in small decision making groups. In T. Parsons (Ed.), *Family socialization and interaction process.* New York: Free Press, 1955.

Bales, R. F. & Strodtbeck, F. L. Phases in group problem solving. *Journal of Abnormal and Social Psychology,* 1951, *46,* 485–495.

Ball, S. & Bogatz, G. A. *The first year of Sesame Street: An evaluation.* Princeton, N.J.: Educational Testing Service, 1971.

Bandura, A. Vicarious processes: A case of no-trial learning. In L. Berkowitz (Ed.), *Advances in experimental social psychology* (Vol. 2). New York: Academic Press, 1965.

Bandura, A. *Aggression: A social-learning analysis.* New York: Holt, Rinehart & Winston, 1973.

Bandura, A. *Social learning theory.* Englewood Cliffs, N.J.: Prentice-Hall, 1977.

Bar-Tal, D. & Saxe, L. *Social psychology of education: Theory and research.* Washington, D.C.: Hemisphere, 1978.

Barber, W. H. & Nord, W. Transactions between consultants and clients: A taxonomy. *Group and Organization Studies,* 1977, *2,* 198–215.

Bard, M. *Training police as specialists in family crisis intervention.* Washington, D.C.: National Institute of Law Enforcement and Criminal Justice, 1970.

Bard, M. & Berkowitz, B. Training police as specialists in family crisis intervention. A community psychology action program. *Community Mental Health Journal,* 1967, *3,* 315–317.

Barker, R. G. *The stream of behavior.* New York: Appleton-Century-Crofts, 1963.

Barker, R. G. *Ecological psychology: Concepts and methods for studying the environment of human behavior.* Stanford, Calif.: Stanford University Press, 1968.

Barker, R. G. & Schoggen, P. *Qualities of community life.* San Francisco: Jossey-Bass, 1973.

Barker, R. G. & Wright, H. F. *One boy's day: A specimen record of behavior.* New York: Harper, 1951.

Barker, R. G. & Wright, H. F. *Midwest and its children: The psychological ecology of an American town.* Evanston, Ill.: Row, Peterson, 1954.

Barnaby, F. World armament and disarmament. *Bulletin of the Atomic Scientists,* 1976, *32*(June), 25–32.

Barnow, B. S. & Cain, G. G. A reanalysis of the effect of Head Start on cognitive development: Methodology and empirical findings. *The Journal of Human Resources*, 1977, *12*, 177–197.

Baron, R. A. *Human aggression*. New York: Plenum, 1977.

Barry, H., Bacon, M. K. & Child, I. L. A cross-cultural survey of some sex differences in socialization. *Journal of Abnormal and Social Psychology*, 1957, *55*, 327–332.

Bass, F. M. The theory of stochastic preference and brand switching. *Journal of Marketing Research*, 1974, *11*, 1–20.

Bates, F. L. & Bacon, L. The community as a social system. *Social Forces*, 1972, *50*, 371–379.

Bauer, R. A. *Social indicators*. Cambridge: MIT Press, 1966.

Baum, A., Singer, J. E. & Baum, C. S. Stress and the environment. *Journal of Social Issues*, 1981, *37*(1), 4–35.

Baum, A. & Valins, S. *Architecture and social behavior: Psychological studies in social density*. Hillsdale, N.J.: Erlbaum, 1977.

Baumrind, D. Principles of ethical conduct in the treatment of subjects: Reactions to the draft report of the committee on ethical standards in psychological research. *American Psychologist*, 1971, *26*, 887–896.

Baumrind, D. Reaction to the May 1972 draft report of the Ad Hoc Committee on Ethical Standards in Psychological Research. *American Psychologist*, 1972, *27*, 1083–1086.

Bavelas, A. Communication patterns in task-oriented groups. *Journal of the Acoustical Society of America*, 1950, *22*, 725–730.

Bavelas, J. B. *Personality: Current theory and research*. Monterey, Calif.: Brooks/Cole, 1978.

Beardon, W. O. & Woodside, A. G. The effects of attitudes and previous behavior on consumer choice. *Journal of Social Psychology*, 1977, *103*, 129–137.

Bebout, J. & Gordon, B. The value of encounter. In L. Solomon & B. Berzon (Eds.), *New perspectives on encounter groups*. San Francisco: Jossey-Bass, 1972.

Beckhard, R. Organization development in large systems. In K. D. Benne, L. P. Bradford, J. R. Gibb & R. O. Lippitt (Eds.), *The laboratory method of changing and learning: Theory and application*. Palo Alto, Calif.: Science and Behavior Books, 1975.

Beckhard, R. The confrontation meeting. *Harvard Business Review*, March-April 1967, *45*, 149–155.

Bednar, R. L. & Kaul, T. J. Experiential group research: Current perspectives. In S. L. Garfield & A. Bergin (Eds.), *Handbook of psychotherapy and behavior change*. New York: Wiley, 1978.

Bednar, R. L. & Kaul, T. J. Experiential group research: What never happened! *Journal of Applied Behavioral Science*, 1979, *15*, 311–319.

Beer, F. A. World order and world futures. *Journal of Conflict Resolution*, 1979, *23*, 174–192.

Beer, M. The technology of organization development. In M. D. Dunnette (Ed.), *Handbook of industrial and organizational psychology*, Chicago: Rand McNally, 1976.

Beer, M. & Huse, E. F. A systems approach to organization behavior. *Journal of Applied Behavioral Science*, 1972, *8*, 79–101.

Bell, P. A., Fisher, J. D. & Loomis, R. *Environmental psychology*. Philadelphia: W. B. Saunders, 1978.

Bell, R. L., Cleveland, S. E., Hanson, P. G. & O'Connell, W. E. Small group dialogue and discussion: An approach to police-community relationships. *Journal of Criminal Law, Criminology, and Police Science*, 1969, *60*, 242–246.

Bem, D. J. Self perception: An alternative interpretation of cognitive dissonance phenomena. *Psychological Review*, 1967, 74, 183–200.

Bem, D. J. *Beliefs, attitudes, and human affairs*. Monterey, Calif.: Brooks/Cole, 1970.

Bem, D. J. Self-perception theory. In L. Berkowitz (Ed.), *Advances in experimental social psychology* (Vol. 6). New York: Academic Press, 1972.

Bem, D. J. & Allen, A. On predicting some of the people some of the time: The search for cross-situational consistencies in behavior. *Psychological Review*, 1974, *81*, 506–520.

Bem, D. J. & Lord, C. G. Template matching: A proposal for probing the ecological validity of experimental settings in social psychology. *Journal of Personality and Social Psychology*, 1979, 37, 833–846.

Bem, S. L. Sex role adaptability: One consequence of psychological androgyny. *Journal of Personality and Social Psychology*, 1975, *31*, 634–643.

Benne, K. D., Bennis, W. G. & Chin, R. Planned change in America. In W. G. Bennis, K. D. Benne, R. Chin & K. E. Corey (Eds.), *The planning of change* (3rd ed.). New York: Holt, Rinehart & Winston, 1976.

Benne, K. D., Bradford, L. D., Gibb, J. R. & Lippitt, R. O. *The laboratory method of changing and learning: Theory and application*. Palo Alto, Calif.: Science and Behavior Books, 1975.

Benne, K. D. & Sheats, P. Functional roles of group members. *Journal of Social Issues*, 1948, 4(2), 41–49.

Bennet, C. C., Anderson, L. S., Cooper, S., Hossol, L., Klein, D. C. & Rosenblum, G. (Eds.). *Community psychology: A report of the Boston conference on the education of psychologists for community mental health*. Boston, Mass.: Boston University Press, 1966.

Bennis, W. G. *Changing organizations*. New York: McGraw-Hill, 1966.

Bennis, W. G. The change agents. In R. T. Golembiewski & A. Blumberg (Eds.), *Sensitivity training and the laboratory approach: Readings about concepts and applications* (2nd ed.). Itasca, Ill.: Peacock, 1973.

Bennis, W. G., Benne, K. D., Chin, R. & Corey, K. E. (Eds.). *The planning of change* (3rd ed.). New York: Holt, Rinehart & Winston, 1976.

Bennis, W. G. & Shepard, H. A. A theory of group development. *Human Relations*, 1956, *9*, 415–457.

Berelson, B. *Content analysis in communication research*. New York: Free Press, 1952.

Berk, R. A. Social science and jury selection: A case study of a civil suit. In G. Bermant, C. Nemeth & N. Vidmar (Eds.), *Psychology and the law: Research frontiers*. Lexington, Mass.: Lexington, 1976.

Berkowitz, L. Social motivation. In G. Lindzey & E. Aronson (Eds.), *Handbook of social psychology* (2nd ed.) (Vol. 3). Reading, Mass.: Addison-Wesley, 1969a.

Berkowitz, L. *Roots of aggression: A re-examination of the frustration-aggression hypothesis*. New York: Atherton, 1969b.

Berlo, D. K. *The process of communication*. New York: Holt, Rinehart & Winston, 1960.

Berne, E. *Games people play*. New York: Grove Press, 1964.

Bernhardson, C. S. & Fisher, R. J. Perceptions of social desirability and endorsement with a forced-choice technique. *Multivariate Behavioral Research*, 1971, *6*, 63–73.

Berry, J. W. Social psychology: Comparative societal and universal. *Canadian Psychological Review*, 1978, *19*, 93–104.

Berry, J. W., Kalin, R. & Taylor, D. M. *Multiculturalism and Ethnic Attitudes in Canada*. Ottawa: Minister of State for Multiculturalism, 1977.

Berscheid, E. & Walster, E. Physical attractiveness. In L. Berkowitz (Ed.), *Advances in experimental social psychology* (Vol. 7). New York: Academic Press, 1974.

Berscheid, E. & Walster, E. *Interpersonal attraction* (2nd ed.). Reading, Mass.: Addison-Wesley, 1978.

Bertcher, H. J. *Group participation techniques for leaders and members.* Beverly Hills, Calif.: Sage, 1979.

Bettelheim, B. & Janowitz, M. *Social change and prejudice.* New York: The Free Press of Glencoe, 1964.

Bevan, W. The sound of the wind that's blowing. *American Psychologist,* 1976, *31,* 481–491.

Bevan, W. Getting into bed with a lion. *American Psychologist,* 1980, *35,* 779–789.

Bhatt, R. V., Pachauri, S., Pathak, N. D. & Chauhan, L. Female sterilization in small camp settings in rural India. *Studies in Family Planning,* 1978, *9,* 39–43.

Biberman, G. Trainer behavior in a T-group setting. A survey of current practices. *Small Group Behavior,* 1979, *10,* 501–522.

Bickman, L. Observational methods. In C. Selltiz, L. S. Wrightsman & S. W. Cook (Eds.), *Research methods in social relations* (3rd ed.). New York: Holt, Rinehart & Winston, 1976.

Bickman, L. Program evaluation and social psychology: Toward the achievement of relevancy. *Personality and Social Psychology Bulletin,* 1979, *5,* 483–490.

Bickman, L. (Ed.). *Applied social psychology annual* (Vol. 1). Beverly Hills, Calif.: Sage, 1980.

Bickman, L., Teger, A., Gabriele, T., McLaughlin, C., Berger, M. & Sunaday, E. Dormitory density and helping behavior. *Environment and Behavior,* 1973, *5,* 465–490.

Biddle, B. J. & Thomas, E. J. (Eds.). *Role theory: Concepts and research.* New York: Wiley, 1966.

Biddle, W. W. & Biddle, L. J. *The community development process. The rediscovery of local initiative.* New York: Holt, Rinehart & Winston, 1965.

Bierman, R. Dimensions of interpersonal facilitation in psychotherapy and child development. *Psychological Bulletin,* 1969, *72,* 338–352.

Bierman, R., Davison, B., Finkelman, L., Leonidas, J., Lumley, C. & Simister, S. *Toward meeting fundamental human needs: Preventive effects of the Human Service Community.* Final report to Department of National Health and Welfare, March, 1976.

Bierman, R. & Lumley, C. Toward the humanizing community. *Ontario Psychologist,* 1973, *5*(5), 10–19.

Bindman, A. J. Mental health consultation: Theory and practice. *Journal of Consulting Psychology,* 1959, *23,* 473–482.

Bion, W. R. *Experiences in groups.* New York: Basic Books, 1961.

Black, D. The social organization of arrest. *Stanford Law Review,* 1971, *23,* 1087–1111.

Blake, R. R. & Mouton, J. S. Union-management relations: From conflict to collaboration. *Personnel,* 1961a, *38,* November/December, 38–51.

Blake, R. R. & Mouton, J. S. *Group dynamics: Key to decision-making.* Houston, Texas: Gulf, 1961b.

Blake, R. R. & Mouton, J. S. *The new managerial grid.* Houston, Texas: Gulf, 1978.

Blake, R. R. & Mouton, J. S. *Building a dynamic corporation through grid organization development.* Reading, Mass.: Addison-Wesley, 1969.

Blake, R. R. & Mouton, J. S. Change by design, not by default. In J. S. Jun & W. B. Storm (Eds.), *Tomorrow's organizations: Challenges and strategies.* Glenview, Ill.: Scott Foresman, 1973.

Blake, R. R. & Mouton, J. S. *Consultation.* Reading, Mass.: Addison-Wesley, 1976.

Blake, R. R. & Mouton, J. S. Toward a general theory of consultation. *Personnel and Guidance Journal,* 1978, *57,* 328–330.

Blake, R. R., Mouton, J. S., Barnes, L. B. & Greiner, L. E. Breakthrough in organization development. *Harvard Business Review*, November-December 1964, *42*, 133–155.

Blake, R. R., Mouton, J. S. & Sloma, R. L. The union-management intergroup laboratory. *Journal of Applied Behavioral Science*, 1965, *1*, 25–57.

Blake, R. R., Shepard, H. A. & Mouton, J. S. *Managing intergroup conflict in industry*. Houston, Texas: Gulf, 1964.

Blakely, E. J. (Ed.). *Community development research: concepts, issues and strategies*. New York: Human Sciences Press, 1979.

Blanton, J. & Alley, S. Clinical and nonclinical aspects of program development consultation. *Professional Psychology*, 1978, *9*, 315–321.

Blau, P. M. *Exchange and power in social life*. New York: Wiley, 1964.

Blau, P. M. Interaction, IV: Social exchange. In D. L. Sills (Ed.), *International encyclopedia of the social sciences* (Vol. 7). New York: MacMillan-Free Press, 1968.

Block, J. Some reasons for the apparent inconsistency of personality. *Psychology Bulletin*, 1968, *70*, 210–212.

Bloom, B. L. Strategies for the prevention of mental disorders. In G. Rosenblum (Ed.), *Issues in community psychology and preventive mental health*, New York: Behavioral Publications, 1971.

Bloom, B. L. The domain of community psychology. *American Journal of Community Psychology*, 1973, *1*, 8–11.

Bloom, B. L. Midstream and middream. *American Journal of Community Psychology*, 1978, *6*, 205–217.

Bloom, B. L. Prevention of mental disorders: Recent advances in theory. *Community Mental Health Journal*, 1979, *15*, 179–191.

Bloom, B. L. Social and community interventions. *Annual Review of Psychology*, 1980, *31*, 111–142.

Bloom, B. L. & Parad, H. J. The psychologist in the community mental health center. *American Journal of Community Psychology*, 1978, *6*, 371–379

Blumberg, A. & Golembiewski, R. T. *Learning and change in groups*. Markham, Ont.: Penguin, 1976.

Blumer, H. Social problems as collective behavior. *Social Problems*, 1971, *18*, 298–306.

Blunk, R. A. & Sales, B. D. Persuasion during the voir dire. In B. D. Sales (Ed.), *Psychology in the legal process*. New York: Spectrum, 1977.

Bochner, S., Lin, A. & McLeod, B. M. Cross-cultural contact and the development of an international perspective. *Journal of Social Psychology*, 1979, *107*, 29–41.

Boehringer, G. H., Zeruolis, V., Bayley, J. & Boehringer, K. Stirling: The destructive application of group techniques to a conflict. *Journal of Conflict Resolution*, 1974, *18*, 257–275.

Bohart, A. C., Hewitt, B., Heilmann, A. & Threlkeld, D. Effects of paraprofessional training on one aspect of generalized interpersonal effectiveness. *American Journal of Community Psychology*, 1976, *4*, 309–312.

Bohnstedt, M. Answers to three questions about juvenile diversion. *Journal of Research in Crime and Delinquency*, 1978, *15*, 109–123.

Bonoma, T. V. *Conflict: Escalation and deescalation*. Beverly Hills, Calif.: Sage, 1975.

Bonoma, T. V. Social psychology and social evaluation. *Representative Research in Social Psychology*, 1976, *7*, 147–159.

Bonoma, T. V. & Milburn, T. W. Social conflict: Another look. *Journal of Social Issues*, 1977, *33*(1), 1–8.

Boruch, R. F. On common contentions about randomized field experiments, In G. V. Glass (Ed.), *Evaluation studies review annual* (Vol. 1), Beverly Hills: Sage, 1976.

Boruch, R. F. (Ed.). *Secondary analysis*. San Francisco, Calif.: Jossey-Bass, 1978.

Boruch, R. F., McSweeney, A. J. & Soderstrom, E. J. Randomized field experiments for program planning, development, and evaluation: An illustrative bibliography. *Evaluation Quarterly*, 1978, *2*, 655–695.

Boruch, R. F. & Rindskopf, D. On randomized experiments, approximation to experiments, and data analysis. In L. Rutman (Ed.), *Evaluation research methods: A basic guide*, Beverly Hills, Calif.: Sage, 1977.

Bould, S. Rural poverty and economic development: Lessons from the War on Poverty. *Journal of Applied Behavioral Science*, 1977, *13*, 471–488.

Boulding, K. E. The power of nonconflict. *Journal of Social Issues*, 1977, *33*(1), 22–33.

Boulding, K. E. Future directions in conflict and peace studies. *Journal of Conflict Resolution*, 1978, *22*, 342–354.

Bourgeois, J. C. & Barnes, J. G. Does advertising increase alcohol consumption? *Journal of Advertising Research*, 1979, *19*, 19–29.

Bowers, D. G. OD techniques and their results in 23 organizations: The Michigan ICL study. *Journal of Applied Behavioral Science*, 1973, *9*, 21–43.

Bowers, D. G. Organizational development: Promises, performances, possibilities. *Organizational Dynamics*, 1976, *4*, 50–62.

Bowers, D. G. & Franklin, J. L. *Survey-guided development I: Data based organizational change*. Ann Arbor: Organizational Development Research Program, Institute for Social Research, University of Michigan, 1976.

Bowers, D. G., Franklin, J. L. & Pecorella, P. A. Matching problems, precursors and interventions in OD: A system approach. *Journal of Applied Behavioral Science*, 1975, *11*, 391–409.

Bowers, K. S. Situationism in psychology: An analysis and a critique. *Psychological Review*, 1973, *80*, 307–336.

Boyte, H. C. *The backyard revolution: Understanding the new citizen movement*. Philadelphia, Penn.: Temple University Press, 1981.

Bradburn, N. *The structure of psychological well-being*. Chicago: Aldine, 1969.

Bradburn, N. M. & Sudman, S. *Improving interview method and questionnaire design*. San Francisco: Jossey-Bass, 1979.

Bradford, L. P. The teaching-learning transaction. *Adult Education*, 1958.

Bradford, L. P. (Ed.). *Group development*. Washington, D.C.: National Training Laboratories and National Education Association, 1961.

Bradford, L. P. Biography of an institution. *Journal of Applied Behavioral Science*, 1967, *2*, 127–143.

Bradford, L. P. The laboratory method: A historical perspective. *Group and Organization Studies*, 1976a, *1*, 415–429.

Bradford, L. P. *Making meetings work: A guide for leaders and group members*. La Jolla, Calif.: University Associates, 1976b.

Bradford, L. P. (Ed.). *Group development* (2nd ed.). La Jolla, Calif.: University Associates, 1978.

Bradley, P. H. Power, status, and upward communications in small decision-making groups. *Communication Monographs*, 1978, *45*, 33–43.

Bragg, B. W. E. & Cousins, L. S. *Changing the subjective probability of arrest for impaired driving*. Paper presented at the Seventh International Conference on Alcohol, Drugs and Traffic Safety, Melbourne, Australia, January, 1977.

Brehm, J. W. Postdecision changes in the desirability of alternatives. *Journal of Abnormal and Social Psychology*, 1956, *52*, 384–389.

Brehm, J. W. *A theory of psychological reactance*. New York: Academic Press, 1966.

Brehm, J. W. Responses to loss of freedom: A theory of psychological reactance. In

J. W. Thibaut, J. T. Spence & R. C. Carson (Eds.), *Contemporary topics in social psychology*. Morristown, N.J.: General Learning Press, 1976.

Brehm, J. W. & Cohen, A. R. Choice and chance relative deprivations as determinants of cognitive dissonance. *Journal of Abnormal and Social Psychology*, 1959, *58*, 383–387.

Brehm, J. W. & Cohen, A. R. *Explorations in cognitive dissonance*. New York: Wiley, 1962.

Brewer, M. The role of enthnocentrism in intergroup conflict. In W. G. Austin & S. Worchel (Eds.), *The social psychology of intergroup relations*. Monterey, Calif.: Brooks/Cole, 1979.

Brill, H. *Why organizers fail: The story of a rent strike*. Berkeley: University of California Press, 1971.

Brintnall, J. & Garwick, G. (Eds.). *Applications of goal attainment scaling*. Minneapolis, Minn.: Program Evaluation Resource Center, 1976.

Brislin, R. W. Structured approaches to dealing with prejudice and intercultural misunderstanding. *International Journal of Group Tensions*, 1978, *8*, 33–48.

Brislin, R. W. *Cross-cultural encounters: Face-to-face interaction*. Elmsford, N.Y.: Pergamon, 1981.

Brislin, R. W. & Pederson, P. *Cross-cultural orientation programs*. New York: Gardner, Wiley & Halstead, 1976.

Broadfoot, B. *Years of sorrow, years of shame*. Toronto: Doubleday Canada, 1977.

Bronfenbrenner, U. The mirror image in Soviet-American relations: A social psychologist's report. *Journal of Social Issues*, 1961, *17*(3), 45–56.

Brookover, W. B. *A sociology of education*. New York: American Book Company, 1955.

Brookover, W. B. & Erickson, E. L. *Sociology of education*. Georgetown, Ont.: Irwin-Dorsey, 1975.

Brophy, J. E. & Good, T. L. *Teacher-student relationships: Causes and consequences*. New York: Holt, Rinehart & Winston, 1974.

Broverman, I. K., Vogel, S. R., Broverman, D. M. Clarkson, F. E. & Rosenkrantz, P. S. Sex-role stereotypes: A current appraisal. *Journal of Social Issues*, 1972, *28*(2), 59–78.

Brown B. R. Face-saving following experimentally induced embarrassment. *Journal of Experimental Social Psychology*, 1970, *6*, 255–271.

Brown, J. F. *Psychology and the social order*. New York: McGraw-Hill, 1936.

Brown, L. D. Can "haves" and "have-nots" cooperate? Two efforts to bridge a social gap. *Journal of Applied Behavioral Science*, 1977, *13*, 211–224.

Brown, R. *Social psychology*. New York: The Free Press, 1965.

Bruner, J. & Taguiri, R. The perception of people. In G. Lindzey (Ed.), *Handbook of social psychology* (Vol. 2). Reading, Mass.: Addison-Wesley, 1954.

Buchanan, P. C. Crucial issues in organizational development. In G. Watson (Ed.), *Change in school systems*, Washington: National Educational Association, 1967.

Buckhout, R. Eyewitness testimony. *Scientific American*, 1974, *231*, (December), 23–31.

Budman, S. H. & Wertlieb, D. Psychologists in health settings: An introduction. *Professional Psychology*, 1979, *10*, 339–401.

Bugental, J. F. T. (Ed.). *Challenges of humanistic psychology*. New York: McGraw-Hill, 1967.

Bugental, J. F. T. The humanistic ethic—The individual in psychotherapy as a societal change agent. *Journal of Humanistic Psychology*, 1971, *10*, 11–26.

Bunker, B. B. *Applied social psychology at SUNY at Buffalo*. Paper presented at the annual meeting of the American Psychological Association, New York, September, 1979.

Bureau of Justice Statistics. *The prevalence of crime*. Washington, D.C.: Author, 1980.

Burke, R. J. Methods of resolving superior-subordinate conflict. The constructive use of subordinate differences and disagreements. *Organizational Behavior and Human Performance*, 1970, *5*, 393–411.

Burke, W. W. (Ed.). *Contemporary organization development: Conceptual orientation and interventions*. Arlington, Va.: NTL Institute, 1972.

Burke, W. W. Managing conflict between groups. In J. D. Adams (Ed.), *Theory and method in organization development: An evolutionary process*, Arlington, Va.: NTL Institute, 1974.

Burke, W. W. (Ed.). *Current issues and strategies in organization development*. New York: Human Sciences Press, 1977.

Burke, W. W. (Ed.). *The cutting edge: Current theory and practice in organization development*. La Jolla, Calif.: University Associates, 1978.

Burns, R. Peace education: Between research and action. *Peace Research*, 1980, *12*, 131–140.

Burt, R. S. (Ed.). *Applied network analysis: An overview*. Beverly Hills, Calif.: Sage, 1978.

Burton, J. W. *Conflict and communication: The use of controlled communication in international relations*. London: MacMillian, 1969.

Bush, M. & Gordon, A. C. People and bureaucracies: Introduction. *Journal of Social Issues*, 1978, *34*(4), 1–5.

Buss, A. R. The emerging field of the sociology of psychological knowledge. *American Psychologist*, 1975, *30*, 988–1002.

Buss, A. R. The trait-situation controversy and the concept of interaction. *Personality and Social Psychology Bulletin*, 1977, *3*, 196–201.

Buttel, F. H. & Flinn, W. L. The politics of environmental concern: The impact of party identification and political ideology on environmental attitudes. *Environment and Behavior*, 1978, *10*, 17–36.

Buys, C. J. Humans would do better without groups. *Personality and Social Psychology Bulletin*, 1978, *4*, 123–125.

Byrne, D. *The attraction paradigm*. New York: Academic Press, 1971.

Byrne, D. & Clore, G. L. A reinforcement model of evaluative responses. *Personality: An International Journal*, 1970, *1*, 103–128.

Byrne, D., Ervin, C. R. & Lamberth, J. Continuity between the experimental study of attraction and "real life" computer dating. *Journal of Personality and Social Psychology*, 1970, *16*, 157–165.

Calder, B. J. & Burnkrant, R. E. Interpersonal influence on consumer behavior: An attribution theory approach. *Journal of Consumer Research*, 1977, *4*, 86–88.

Calder, B. J. & Ross, M. Attitudes: Theories and issues. In J. W. Thibaut, J. T. Spence & R. C. Carson (Eds.), *Contemporary topics in social psychology*. Morristown, N.J.: General Learning Press, 1976.

Calhoun, J. B. Population density and social pathology. *Science*, 1962, *206*, 139–148.

Calsyn, R. J. & Davidson, W. S. Do we really want a program evaluation strategy based solely on individualized goals? A critique of goal attainment scaling. *Community Mental Health Journal*, 1978, *14*, 300–308.

Campbell, A., Converse, P. E. & Rodgers, W. L. *The quality of American life*. New York: Russell Sage Foundation, 1976.

Campbell, A. & Katona, G. The sample survey: A technique for social science research.

In L. Festinger & D. Katz (Eds.), *Research methods in the behavioral sciences*. New York: Holt, Rinehart & Winston, 1953.

Campbell, D. T. Ethnocentrism and other altruistic motives. In D. Levine (Ed.), *Nebraska symposium on motivation* (Vol. 13). Lincoln: University of Nebraska Press, 1965.

Campbell, D. T. Reforms as experiments. *American Psychologist*, 1969, *24*, 409–429.

Campbell, D. T. The social scientist as methodological servant of the experimenting society. *Policy Studies Journal*, 1973, *2*, 72–75.

Campbell, D. T. & McCandless, B. R. Ethnocentrism, xenophobia and personality. *Human Relations*, 1955, *4*, 185–192.

Campbell, D. T. & Ross, H. L. The Connecticut crackdown on speeding: Time-series data in quasi-experimental analysis. *Law and Society Review*, 1968, *3*, 33–53.

Campbell, D. T. & Stanley, J. C. *Experimental and quasi-experimental designs for research*. Chicago: Rand McNally, 1966.

Campbell, J. P. & Dunnette, M. D. Effectiveness of T-group experiences in managerial training and development. *Psychological Bulletin*, 1968, *70*, 73–104.

Cannell, C. F. & Kahn, R. L. Interviewing. In G. Lindzey & E. Aronson (Eds.), *The handbook of social psychology* (2nd ed.) (Vol. 2). Reading, Mass.: Addison-Wesley, 1968.

Caplan, G. *Principles of preventive psychiatry*. New York: Basic Books, 1964.

Caplan, G. *The theory and practice of mental health consultation*. New York: Basic Books, 1970.

Caplan, G. *Support systems and community mental health*. New York: Behavioral Publications, 1974.

Caplan, N. A minimal set of conditions necessary for the utilization of social science knowledge in policy formulation at the national level. In C. H. Weiss (Ed.), *Using social research in public policy making*. Lexington, Mass.: Lexington, 1977, 183–197.

Caplan, N. & Nelson, S. D. On being useful: The nature and consequences of psychological research on social problems. *American Psychologist*, 1973, *28*, 199–212.

Carkhuff, R. R. The differential functioning of lay and professional helpers. *Journal of Counseling Psychology*, 1968, *15*, 117–126.

Carkhuff, R. R. *Helping and human relations* (Vols. I and II). New York: Holt, Rinehart & Winston, 1969.

Carkhuff, R. R. The development of systematic human resource development models. *Counselling Psychologist*, 1972a, *3*, 4–10.

Carkhuff, R. R. Rejoinder: What's it all about anyway? Some reflections on helping and human resource development models. *Counselling Psychologist*, 1972b, *3*, 79–87.

Carkhuff, R. R. & Banks, G. Training as a preferred mode of facilitating relations between races and generations. *Journal of Counseling Psychology*, 1970, *17*, 413–418.

Carkhuff, R. R. & Berenson, B. G. *Beyond counseling and therapy* (2nd ed.). New York: Holt, Rinehart & Winston, 1977.

Carkhuff, R. R. & Bierman, R. Training as a preferred mode of treatment of parents of emotionally disturbed children. *Journal of Counseling Psychology*, 1970, *17*, 157–161.

Carkhuff, R. R. & Griffin, A. H. The selection and training of human relations specialists. *Journal of Counseling Psychology*, 1970, *17*, 443–450.

Carlson, R. Where is the person in personality research? *Psychological Bulletin*, 1971, *75*, 203–219.

Carroll, J. B. *The study of language*. Cambridge, Mass.: Harvard University Press, 1955.

Carson, R. C. *Interaction concepts of personality*. Chicago: Aldine, 1969.

Cartwright, D. Social psychology in the United States during the Second World War.

Human Relations, 1948, *1,* 333–352.

Cartwright, D. Achieving change in people. Some applications of group dynamics theory. *Human Relations,* 1951, *4,* 381–392.

Cartwright, D. Risk-taking by individuals and groups. An assessment of research involving choice dilemmas. *Journal of Personality and Social Psychology,* 1971, *20,* 361–378.

Cartwright, D. Determinants of scientific progress: The case of research on the risky shift. *American Psychologist,* 1973, *28,* 222–231.

Cartwright, D. Theory and practice. *Journal of Social Issues,* 1978, *34*(4), 168–180.

Cartwright, D. Contemporary social psychology in historical perspective. *Social Psychology Quarterly,* 1979, *42,* 82–93.

Cartwright, D. & Zander, A. (Eds.). *Group dynamics. Research and theory* (3rd ed.). New York: Harper & Row, 1968.

Carver, C. S., Glass, D. C. & Katz, I. Favorable evaluations of blacks and the handicapped: Positive prejudice, unconscious denial or social desirability? *Journal of Applied Social Psychology,* 1978, *8,* 97–106.

Cattell, R. B. *Personality: A systematic theoretical and factual study.* New York: McGraw-Hill, 1950.

Cattell, R. B. *The scientific analysis of personality,* Chicago: Aldine, 1966.

Cattell, R. B. & Kline, P. *The scientific analysis of personality and motivation.* New York: Academic Press, 1977.

Chaikin, A. L. & Derlega, V. J. Self-disclosure. In J. W. Thibaut, J. T. Spence & R. C. Carson (Eds.), *Contemporary topics in social psychology.* Morristown, N.J.: General Learning Press, 1976.

Chein, I., Cook, S. & Harding, J. The field of action research. *American Psychologist,* 1948, *3,* 43–50.

Chelimsky, E. Differing perspectives of evaluation. In C. C. Rentz & R. R. Rentz (Eds.), *Evaluating federally sponsored programs.* San Francisco: Jossey-Bass, 1978.

Chelune, G. J. (Ed.). Self-disclosure: origins, patterns, and implications of openness in interpersonal relations. San Francisco, Calif.: Jossey-Bass, 1979.

Chesler, M. A. Ethnocentrism and attitudes toward the physically disabled. *Journal of Personality and Social Psychology,* 1965, *2,* 877–882.

Chestnut, R. W. & Jacoby, J. Consumer information processing: Emerging theory and findings. In A. G. Woodside, J. N. Sheth & P. O. Bennett (Eds.), *Consumer and industrial buying behavior.* New York: Elsevier North-Holland, 1977.

Chin, R. & Benne, K. D. General strategies for effecting change in human systems. In findings. In A. G. Woodside, J. N. Sheth & P. O. Bennett (Eds.), *Consumer and industrial buying behavior.* New York: Elsevier North-Holland, 1977, 119–133.

Chin, R. & Benne, K. D. General strategies for effecting change in human systems. In W. G. Bennis, K. D. Benne, R. Chin & K. E. Corey (Eds). *The planning of change* (3rd ed.). New York: Holt, Rinehart & Winston, 1976.

Christie, R. & Geis, F. L. (Eds.). *Studies in Machiavellianism,* New York: Academic Press, 1970.

Cialdini, R. B. Full-cycle social psychology. In L. Bickman (Ed.), *Applied social psychology annual* (Vol. 1). Beverly Hills, Calif.: Sage, 1980.

Cialdini, R. B. & Insko, C. A. Attitudinal verbal reinforcement as a function of informational consistency: A further test of two factor theory. *Journal of Personality and Social Psychology,* 1969, *12,* 342–350.

Ciarlo, J. A. Monitoring and analysis of mental health program outcome data. In M. Guttentag (Ed.), *Evaluation studies review annual* (Vol. 2). Beverly Hills, Calif.: Sage, 1977.

Clark, G. & Sohn, L. B. *World peace through world law* (3rd ed.). Cambridge, Mass.:

Harvard University Press, 1965.

Clark, K. B. *Dark ghetto: Dilemmas of social power.* New York: Harper & Row, 1965.

Clark, K. B. Empathy: A neglected topic in psychological research. *American Psychologist*, 1980, *35*, 187–190.

Clark, K. B. & Hopkins, J. *A relevant war against poverty.* New York: Harper & Row, 1968.

Cleveland, S. E. Psychological intervention in a community crisis. In H. E. Adams and W. K. Boardman (Eds.), *Advances in experimental clinical psychology.* New York: Pergamon, 1971.

Clore, G. L., Bray, R. M., Itkin, S. M. & Murphy, P. Interracial attitudes and behavior at a summer camp. *Journal of Personality and Social Psychology*, 1978, *36*, 107–116.

Coan, R. W. Toward a psychological interpretation of psychology. *Journal of the History of the Behavioral Sciences*, 1973, *9*, 313–327.

Cobbs, P. M. Ethnotherapy in groups. In L. Solomon & B. Berzon (Eds.), *New perspectives on encounter groups.* San Francisco: Jossey-Bass, 1972.

Coch, L. & French, J. R. P. Overcoming resistance to change. *Human Relations*, 1948, *4*, 512–533.

Coelho, G. V. *Changing images of America: A study of Indian students' perceptions.* New York: Free Press, 1958.

Cohen, A. R. Upward communication in experimentally created hierarchies. *Human Relations*, 1958, *11*, 41–53.

Cohen, A. R. An experiment on small rewards for discrepant compliance and attitude change. In J. W. Brehm & A. R. Cohen (Eds.), *Explorations in cognitive dissonance.* New York: Wiley, 1962.

Cohen, L. H. Factors affecting the utilization of mental health evaluation research findings. *Professional Psychology*, 1977, *8*, 526–534.

Cohen, S., Glass, D. C. & Singer, J. E. Apartment noise, auditory discrimination and reading ability in children. *Journal of Experimental Social Psychology*, 1973, *9*, 407–422.

Cohen, S. P., Kelman, H. C., Miller, F. D. & Smith, B. L. Evolving intergroup techniques for conflict resolution: An Israeli-Palestinian pilot workshop. *Journal of Social Issues*, 1977, *33*(1), 165–189.

Collier, J. United States Indian administration as a laboratory of ethnic relations. *Social Relations*, 1977, *12*, 265–303.

Condran, J. G. Changes in white attitudes towards blacks: 1963-1979. *Public Opinion Quarterly*, 1979, 463–476.

Conger, D. S. (Ed.). *Readings in life skills.* Prince Albert, Sask.: Saskatchewan New Start and Training Research and Development Station, Department of Manpower and Immigration, 1973.

Conway, J. B. *Biases in cognitive-affective processing across interpersonal styles and interpersonal stress.* Unpublished manuscript, The University of Saskatchewan, 1980.

Cook, S. W. Desegregation: A psychological analysis. *American Psychologist*, 1957, *12*, 1–13.

Cook, S. W. A preliminary study of attitude change. In M. Wertheimer (Ed.), *Confrontation: Psychology and the problems of today.* Glenview, Ill.: Scott, Foresman, 1970.

Cook, S. W. Social science and school desegregation: Did we mislead the Supreme Court? *Personality and Social Psychology Bulletin*, 1979, *5*, 420–437.

Cook, S. W. Ethical implications. In L. H. Kidder (Ed.), *Selltiz, Wrightsman and Cook's research methods in social relations* (4th ed.). New York: Holt, Rinehart & Winston, 1981.

Cook, T. D., Appleton, H., Conner, R. F., Shaffer, A., Tomkin, G. & Weber, S. J. "Ses-

ame Street" revisited. New York: Russell Sage Foundation, 1975.

Cook, T. D. & Campbell, D. T. The design and conduct of quasi-experiments and true experiments in field settings. In M. D. Dunnette (Ed.), *Handbook of industrial and organizational psychology*, Chicago: Rand McNally, 1976.

Cook, T. D. & Campbell, D. T. *Quasi-experimentation: Design and analysis for field settings*. Chicago: Rand McNally, 1979.

Cook, T. D., Cook, F. L. & Mark, M. M. Randomized and quasi-experimental designs in evaluation research. In L. Rutman (Ed.), *Evaluation research methods: A basic guide*, Beverly Hills, Calif.: Sage, 1977.

Cook, T. D. & Gruder, C. L. Metaevaluation research. *Evaluation Quarterly*, 1978, *2*, 5–51.

Cook, T. D. & Reichardt, C. S. *Qualitative and quantitative methods in evaluation research*. Beverly Hills, Calif.: Sage, 1979.

Cooper, C. L. How psychologically dangerous are T-groups and encounter groups? *Human Relations*, 1975, *28*, 249–260.

Cooper, C. L. Adverse and growthful effects of experiential learning groups. The role of the trainer, participant, and group characteristics. *Human Relations*, 1977, *30*, 1103–1129.

Cooper, H. M. Pygmalion grows up: a model for teacher expectation, communication and performance influence. *Review of Educational Research*, 1979, *49*, 389–410.

Corey, S. M. *Action research to improve school practice*. New York: Teachers College, Columbia University, 1953.

Coser, L. A. *The functions of social conflict*. Glencoe, Ill.: Free Press, 1956.

Coser, L. A. *Continuities in the study of social conflict*. New York: Free Press, 1967.

Costello, C. G. A critical review of Seligman's laboratory experiments on learned helplessness and depression in humans. *Journal of Abnormal Psychology*, 1978, *87*, 21–31.

Cousins, L. S. The effects of public education on subjective probability of arrest for impaired driving: A field study. *Accident Analysis and Prevention*, 1980, *12*, 131–141.

Cowen, E. L. Social and community interventions. *Annual Review of Psychology*, 1973, *24*, 423–472.

Cowen, E. L. Baby-steps toward primary prevention. *American Journal of Community Psychology*, 1977a, *5*, 1–22.

Cowen, E. L. Psychologists and primary prevention: Blowing the cover story. *American Journal of Community Psychology*, 1977b, *5*, 481–489.

Cowen, E. L. Some problems in community program evaluation research. *Journal of Consulting and Clinical Psychology*, 1978, *46*, 792–805.

Cowen, E. L., Davidson, E. R. & Gesten, E. L. Program dissemination and the modification of delivery practices in school mental health. *Professional Psychology*, 1980, *11*, 36–47.

Cowen, E. L., Gesten, E. L., Boike, M., Norton, P., Wilson, A. B. & DeStefano, M. A. Hairdressers as caregivers. I. A descriptive profile of interpersonal help-giving involvements. *American Journal of Community Psychology*, 1979, *7*, 633–648.

Cowen, E. L., Gesten, E. L. & Wilson, A. B. The Primary Mental Health Project (PMHP): Evaluation of current program effectiveness. *American Journal of Community Psychology*, 1979, *7*, 293–303.

Cowen, E. L., Izzo, L. D., Miles, H., Telschow, E. F., Trost, M. A. & Zax, M. A preventive mental health program in the school setting: Description and evaluation. *Journal of Psychology*, 1963, *56*, 307–356.

Cowen, E. L., Lorion, R. P. & Dorr, D. Research in the community cauldron: A case history. *Canadian Psychologist*, 1974, *15*, 313–325.

Cowen, E. L., Trost, M. A., Lorion, R. P., Dorr, D., Isso, L. D. & Isaacson, R. V. *New ways in school mental health: Early detection and prevention of school maladaption.* New York: Human Sciences Press, 1975.

Cox, F. M., Erlich, J. L., Rothman, J. & Tropman, J. E. (Eds.). *Strategies of community organizations* (3rd ed.). Itasca, Ill.: Peacock, 1979.

Cox, K. K. Changes in sterotyping of Negroes and Whites in magazine advertisements. *Public Opinion Quarterly,* 1969, *33,* 603–606.

Cozby, P. C. Self-disclosure: A literature review. *Psychological Bulletin,* 1973, *79,* 73–91.

Crano, W. D. & Brewer, M. B. *Principles of research in social psychology.* New York: McGraw-Hill, 1973.

Cronbach, L. J. Response sets and test validity. *Educational and Psychological Measurement,* 1946, *6,* 475–494.

Cronbach, L. J. The two disciplines of scientific psychology. *American Psychologist,* 1957, *12,* 671–684.

Cronbach, L. J. Beyond the two disciplines of scientific psychology. *American Psychologist,* 1975, *30,* 116–127.

Crow, W. J. A study of strategic doctrines using the Inter-Nation Simulation. *Journal of Conflict Resolution,* 1963, *7,* 580–598.

Crutchfield, R. S. Conformity and character. *American Psychologist,* 1955, *10,* 191–198.

Cutter, H. S. G., Boyatzis, R. E. & Clancy, D. D. The effectiveness of power motivation training in rehabilitating alcoholics. *Journal of Studies on Alcohol,* 1977, *38,* 131–141.

Cvetkovich, G. Dialectical perspectives on empirical research. *Personality and Social Psychology Bulletin,* 1977, *3,* 688–696.

Cytrynbaum, S., Ginath, Y., Birdwell, J. & Brandt, L. Goal attainment scaling: A critical review. *Evaluation Quarterly,* 1979, *3,* 5–40.

Dahrendorf, R. *Class and class conflict in industrial society.* Stanford: Stanford University Press, 1959.

Dahrendorf, R. *Conflict after class: New perspectives on the theory of social and political conflict.* London: Longmans, Green, 1967.

Danziger, K. *Nonverbal communication.* New York: Pergamon, 1976.

Datta, L. E. & Perloff, R. (Eds.). *Improving evaluations.* Beverly Hills, Calif.: Sage, 1979.

D'Augelli, A. R., Danish, S. J. & Brock, G. W. Untrained paraprofessionals' verbal helping behavior: Description and implications for training. *American Journal of Community Psychology,* 1976, *4,* 275–282.

Davis, J. H., Bray, R. M. & Holt, R. W. The empirical study of social decision processes in juries. In J. L. Tapp & F. J. Levine (Eds.), *Law, justice and the individual in society.* New York: Holt, Rinehart & Winston, 1976.

Davis, L. N. & McCallon, E. *Planning, conducting and evaluating workshops.* Austin, Texas: Learning Concepts, 1974.

Davis, T. R. V. & Specht, P. S. Citizen participation in community mental-health programs: A study in intergroup conflict and cooperation. *Group and Organization Studies,* 1978, *3,* 456–466.

Dayal, I. & Thomas, J. M. Operation KPE: Developing a new organization. *Journal of Applied Behavioral Science,* 1968, *4,* 473–506.

Dean, J. P. & Rosen, A. *A manual of intergroup relations.* Chicago: University of Chicago Press, 1955.

Dearborn, D. C. & Simon, H. A. Selective perception: A note on the departmental identification of executives. *Sociometry,* 1958, *21,* 140–144.

Deaux, K. *The behavior of women and men.* Belmont, Calif.: Brooks/Cole, 1976.

Dedring, J. *Recent advances in peace and conflict research: A critical survey.* Beverly Hills, Calif.: Sage, 1976.

Delbecq, A. L., Van de Ven, A. H. & Gustafson, G. H. *Group techniques for program planning: A guide to nominal group and Delphi processes.* Glenview, Ill.: Scott, Foresman, 1975.

Delbecq, A. L. & Van de Ven, A. H. A group process model for problem identification and program planning. *Journal of Applied Behavioral Science,* 1971, *7,* 466–492.

Depue, R. A. & Monroe, S. M. Learned helplessness in the perspective of the depressive disorders: Conceptual and definitional issues. *Journal of Abnormal Psychology,* 1978, *87,* 3–20.

de Sola Pool, I. Effects of cross-national contact on national and international images. In H. C. Kelman (Ed.), *International behavior: a social-psychological analysis,* New York: Holt, Rinehart & Winston, 1965.

Deutsch, M. Field theory in social psychology. In G. Lindzey & E. Aronson (Eds.), *Handbook of social psychology* (2nd ed.) (Vol. 1). Reading, Mass.: Addison-Wesley, 1968.

Deutsch, M. Socially-relevant science: Reflections on some studies of interpersonal conflict. *American Psychologist,* 1969, *24,* 1076–1092.

Deutsch, M. *The resolution of conflict: Constructive and destructive processes.* New Haven: Yale University Press, 1973.

Deutsch, M. Graduate training of the problem-oriented social psychologist. In M. Deutsch & H. A. Hornstein (Eds.), *Applying social psychology: Implications for research, practice and training.* Hillsdale, N.J.: Erlbaum, 1975.

Deutsch, M. Recurrent themes in the study of social conflict. *Journal of Social Issues,* 1977, *33*(1), 222–225.

Deutsch, M. Fifty years of conflict. In L. Festinger (Ed.), *Four decades of social psychology,* Oxford, England: Oxford University Press, 1980.

Deutsch, M. & Horsnstein, H. *Applying social psychology: Implications for research, practice and training.* Hillsdale, N.J.: Erlbaum, 1975.

Deutsch, M. & Krauss, R. M. The effect of threat on interpersonal bargaining. *Journal of Personality and Social Psychology,* 1960, *61,* 181–189.

DeVries, D. L., Edwards, K. J. & Slavin, R. E. Biracial learning teams and race relations in the classroom: Four field experiments using Teams-Games-Tournament. *Journal of Educational Psychology,* 1978, *78,* 356–362.

Diamond, M. J. & Lobitz, W. C. When familiarity breeds respect: The effects of an experimental depolarization program on police and student attitudes toward each other. *Journal of Social Issues,* 1973, *29*(4), 95–109.

Dimock, H. G. How to observe your group. Part II, *Leadership and group development.* Montreal, Quebec: Concordia University, 1970.

Dimock, H. G. The use of system-improvement research in developing a change strategy for human services organizations. *Group and Organization Studies,* 1978, *3,* 365–375.

Dion, K. L. Intergroup conflict and intergroup cohesiveness. In W. G. Austin & S. Worchel (Eds.), *The social psychology of intergroup relations.* Monterey, Calif.: Brooks/Cole, 1979.

Dohrenwend, B. P. & Dohrenwend, B. S. Social and cultural influences in psychopathology. *Annual Review of Psychology,* 1974, *25,* 417–452.

Dohrenwend, B. S. Social stress and community psychology. *American Journal of Community Psychology,* 1978, *6,* 1–14.

Dollard, J., Doob, L., Miiler, N., Mowrer, O. & Sears, R. *Frustration and aggression* New Haven: Yale University Press, 1939.

Donleavy, M. R. & Pugh, C. A. Multi-ethnic collaboration to combat racism in educational settings. *Journal of Applied Behavioral Science*, 1977, *13*, 360–372.

Donley, R. E. & Winter, D. G. Measuring the motives of public officials at a distance: An exploratory study of American presidents. *Behavioral Science*, 1970, *15*, 227–236.

Donnerstein, E., Mueller, C. & Wilson, D. W. The effects of models and choice in promoting positive behaviors. *Journal of Social Psychology*, 1979, *109*, 49–57.

Doob, A. N. Evidence, procedure, and psychological research. In G. Bermant, C. Nemeth & N. Vidmar (Eds.), *Psychology and the law: Research frontiers*. Lexington, Mass.: Lexington, 1976.

Doob, L. W. (Ed.). *Resolving conflict in Africa: The Fermeda workshop*. New Haven, Conn.: Yale University Press, 1970.

Doob, L. W. A Cyprus workshop: An exercise in intervention methodology. *Journal of Social Psychology*, 1974, *94*, 161–178.

Doob, L. W. Unofficial intervention in destructive social conflicts. In R. W. Brislin (Ed.), *Cross-cultural perspectives on learning*, New York: Wiley, 1975.

Doob, L. W. & Foltz, W. J. The Belfast Workshop: An application of group techniques to a destructive conflict. *Journal of Conflict Resolution*, 1973, *17*, 489–512.

Doob, L. W. & Foltz, W. J. The impact of a workshop upon grassroots leaders in Belfast. *Journal of Conflict Resolution*, 1974, *18*, 237–256.

Doob, L. W., Foltz, W. J. & Stevens, R. B. The Fermeda workshop: A different approach to border conflicts in Eastern Africa. *Journal of Psychology*, 1969, *73*, 249–266.

Dow, R. Experiential learning. In R. Eiben & A. Milliren (Eds.), *Educational change: A humanistic approach*. La Jolla, Calif.: University Associates, 1976.

Doyle, M. & Straus, D. *How to make meetings work: The new interaction method*. New York: Wyden Books, 1976.

Druckman, D. *Human factors in international negotiations: Social-psychological aspects of international conflict*. Beverly Hills, Calif.: Sage, 1973.

Druckman, D. (Ed.). *Negotiations: Social-psychological perspectives*. Beverly Hills, Calif.: Sage, 1977.

Druckman, D. & Mahoney, R. Processes and consequences of international negotiations. *Journal of Social Issues*, 1977, *33*(1), 60–87.

Duncan, B. L. Differential social perception and attribution of intergroup violence: Testing the lower limits of stereotyping of blacks. *Journal of Personality and Social Psychology*. 1976, *34*, 590–598.

Dunn, W. N. & Swierczek, F. W. Planned organizational change: Toward grounded theory. *Journal of Applied Behavioral Science*, 1977, *13*, 135–157.

Durlak, J. A. Comparative effectiveness of paraprofessional and professional helpers. *Psychological Bulletin*, 1979, *86*, 80–92.

Dutton, D. G. Tokenism, reverse discrimination, and egalitarianism in interracial behavior. *Journal of Social Issues*, 1976, *32*(2), 93–108.

Dyer, W. G. *Modern theory and method in group training*. New York: Van Nostrand Reinhold, 1972.

Dyer, W. G. *Insight to impact: Strategies for interpersonal and organizational change*. Provo, Utah: Brigham Young University Press, 1976.

Dyer, W. G. *Team building: Issues and alternatives*. Reading, Mass.: Addison-Wesley, 1977.

Eagley, A. H. Sex differences in influenceability. *Psychological Bulletin*, 1978, *85*, 86–116.

Eagley, A. H. & Himmelfarb, S. Attitudes and opinions. *Annual Review of Psychology*, 1978, *29*, 517–554.

Eckhardt, W. United Nations voting as an alternative to war. *Peace Research*, 1980, *12*,

159-163.

Ecklein, J. L. & Lauffer, A. A. Alinsky starts a FIGHT. In *Community organizers and social planners*. New York: Wiley, 1972.

Edwards, A. L. The relationship between the judged desirability of a trait and the probability that the trait will be endorsed. *Journal of Applied Psychology*, 1953, *37*, 90-93.

Edwards, A. L. *Techniques of attitude scale construction*. New York: Appleton-Century-Crofts, 1957 (a).

Edwards, A. L. *The social desirability variable in personality assessment and research*. New York: Dryden Press, 1957 (b).

Edwards, J. D. Improving employment opportunities and the public image of social psychologists. *American Psychologist*, 1975, *30*, 784-785.

Edwards, P. K., Orden, D. & Buccola, S. T. Evaluating the impact of federal human service programs with locally differentiated constituencies. *Journal of Applied Behavioral Science*, 1980, *16*, 13-28.

Egan, G. *Encounter: Group processes for interpersonal growth*. Belmont, Calif.: Brooks/Cole, 1970.

Egan, G. *The skilled helper: A model for systematic helping and interpersonal relating*. Monterey, Calif.: Brooks/Cole, 1975a.

Egan, G. *Exercises in helping skills*. Monterey, Calif.: Brooks/Cole, 1975b.

Egan, G. *Interpersonal living: A skills/contract approach to human-relations training in groups*. Monterey Calif.: Brooks/Cole, 1976.

Ehrlich, H. J. Instrument error and the study of prejudice. *Social Forces*, 1964, *43*, 197-206.

Ehrlich, H. J. Attitudes, behavior and the intervening variables. *American Sociologist*, 1969, *4*, 29-34.

Ehrlich, H. J. *The social psychology of prejudice*. New York: Wiley, 1973.

Eisner, M. S. Ethical problems in social psychological experimentation in the laboratory. *Canadian Psychological Review*, 1977, *18*, 233-241.

Elkins, S. M. *Slavery: A problem in American institutional and intellectual life* (2nd ed.). Chicago: University of Chicago Press, 1968.

Elms, A. C. The crisis of confidence in social psychology. *American Psychologist*, 1975, *30*, 967-976.

Emery, F. E. & Thorsrud, E. *Form and content of industrial democracy*. London: Tavistock, 1969.

Emery, F. E. & Thorsrud, E. *Democracy at work* (Vol. 2). Leiden, The Netherlands: Martinus Nijhoff, 1976.

Emery, F. E. & Trist, E. L. *Management science models and techniques* (Vol. 2). London: Pergamon, 1960.

Endler, N. S. The person versus the situation—a pseudo issue? A response to Alker. *Journal of Personality*, 1973, *41*, 287-303.

Endler, N. S. The case for person-situation interactions. *Canadian Psychological Review*, 1975, *16*, 12-21.

Endler, N. S. Grand illusions: Traits or interactions. *Canadian Psychological Review*, 1976, *17*, 174-181.

Endler, N. S. & Magnusson, D. Toward an interactional psychology of personality. *Psychological Bulletin*, 1976, *83*, 956-974.

Epstein, Y. M. Comment on environmental psychology and social psychology. *Personality and Social Psychology Bulletin*, 1976, *2*, 346-349.

Epstein, Y. M. Crowding stress and human behavior. *Journal of Social Issues*, 1981, *37*(1), 126-144.

Erikson, E. H. *Childhood and society* (2nd ed.). New York: Norton, 1963.

Erikson, E. H. *Identity, youth and crisis*. New York: Norton, 1968.

Eron, L. D. Prescription for reduction of aggression. *American Psychologist*, 1980, *35*, 244-252.

Etzioni, A. *The hard way to peace*. New York: Collier, 1962.

Etzioni, A. The Kennedy experiment. *The Western Political Quarterly*, 1967, *20*, 361-380.

Etzioni, A. Social psychological aspects of international relations. In G. Lindzey & E. Aronson (Eds.), *Handbook of social psychology* (2nd ed.) (Vol. 5). Reading, Mass.: Addison-Wesley, 1969.

Etzioni, A. *Social problems*. Englewood Cliffs, N.J.: Prentice-Hall 1976.

Evans, R. I. Behavioral medicine: a new applied challenge to social psychologists. In L. Bickman (Ed.), *Applied social psychology annual* (Vol. 1). Beverly Hills, Calif.: Sage, 1980.

Evans, R. I., Rozelle, R. M., Mittelmark, M. B., Hansen, W. B., Bane, A. L. & Haws, J. Deterring the onset of smoking in children: Knowledge of immediate physiological effects and coping with peer pressure, media pressure, and parent modeling. *Journal of Applied Social Psychology*, 1978, *8*, 126-135.

Eysenck, H. J. *The scientific study of personality*. London: Routledge and Paul, 1952.

Eysenck, H. J. *The dynamics of anxiety and hysteria*. London: Routledge and Paul, 1957.

Eysenck, H. J. & Eysenck, S. B. G. *Personality structure and measurement*. San Diego, Calif.: Knapp, 1969.

Fabbro, D. Peaceful societies: An introduction. *Journal of Peace Research*, 1978, *15*, 67-83.

Fairweather, G. W. *Methods for experimental social innovation*. New York: Wiley, 1967.

Fairweather, G. W. A process of innovation and dissemination experimentation. In L. Rutman (Ed.), *Evaluation research methods: A basic guide*. Beverly Hills, Calif.: Sage, 1977.

Fairweather, G. W., Sanders, D. H., Cressler, D. L. & Maynard, H. *Community life for the mentally ill: An alternative to institutional care*. Chicago: Aldine, 1969.

Fairweather, G. W., Sanders, D. H. & Tornatzky, L. G. *Creating change in mental health organizations*. New York: Pergamon Press, 1974.

Fairweather, G. W. & Tornatzky, L. G. *Experimental methods for social policy research*. New York: Pergamon, 1977.

Feinberg, S. F. Some questions about ethics and responsibilities in sensitivity training. In R. T. Golembiewski & A. Blumberg (Eds.), *Sensitivity training and the laboratory approach: Readings about concepts and applications* (3rd ed.). Itasca, Ill.: Peacock, 1977.

Fessler, D. R. *Facilitating community change: A basic guide*. La Jolla, Calif.: University Associates, 1976.

Festinger, L. Informal social communication. *Psychological Review*, 1950, *57*, 271-282.

Festinger, L. A theory of social comparison processes. *Human Relations*, 1954, *7*, 117-140.

Festinger, L. *A theory of cognitive dissonance*. Evanston, Illinois: Row, Peterson, 1957.

Festinger, L. & Carlsmith, J. M. Cognitive consequences of forced compliance. *Journal of Abnormal and Social Psychology*, 1959, *58*, 203-210.

Festinger, L., Pepitone, A. & Newcomb, T. Some consequences of deindividuation in a group. *Journal of Abnormal and Social Psychology*, 1952, *47*, 382-389.

Festinger, L., Schachter, S. & Back, K. W. *Social pressure in informal groups*. New York: Harper, 1950.

Fiedler, F. E. *A theory of leadership effectiveness*. New York: McGraw-Hill, 1967.

Fiedler, F. E., Chemers, M. M. & Mahar, L. *Improving leadership effectiveness: The leader match concept* (rev. ed.). New York: Wiley, 1977.

Fiedler, F. E. & Mahar, L. The effectiveness of contingency model training: A review of the validation of leader match. *Personnel Psychology*, 1979, *32*, 45–62.

Filley, A. C. *Interpersonal conflict resolution*. Glenview, Ill.: Scott, Foresman, 1975.

Finch, F. E. Collaborative leadership in work settings. *Journal of Applied Behavioral Science*, 1977, *13*, 292–302.

Fine, M. & Saxe, L. *Evaluation research and psychology: Toward synthesis*. Paper presented at the annual meeting of the American Psychological Association, Toronto, Canada, August, 1978.

Finison, L. J. Unemployment, politics and the history of organized psychology. *American Psychologist*, 1976, *31*, 741–755.

Fink, C. F. Some conceptual difficulties in the theory of social conflict. *Journal of Conflict Resolution*, 1968, *12*, 412–460.

Finsterbusch, K. *Understanding Social Impacts*. Beverly Hills, Calif.: Sage, 1980.

Finsterbusch, K. & Wolf, C. P. (Eds.). *Methodology of social impact assessment*. Stroudsburg, Penn.: Dowder, Hutchinson & Ross, 1977.

Firestone, I. J. Reconciling verbal and nonverbal models of dyadic communication. *Environmental Psychology and Nonverbal Behavior*, 1977, *2*, 30–44.

Fishbein, M. Attitude and the prediction of behavior. In M. Fishbein (Ed.), *Readings in attitude theory and measurement*. New York: Wiley, 1967.

Fishbein, M. & Ajzen, I. *Belief, attitude, intention, and behavior*. Reading, Mass.: Addison-Wesley, 1975.

Fisher, R. J. Third party consultation: A method for the study and resolution of conflict. *Journal of Conflict Resolution*, 1972, *16*, 67–94.

Fisher, R. J. A discussion project of high school adolescents' perceptions of the relationship between students and teachers. *Adolescence*, 1976a, *11*, 87–95.

Fisher, R. J. Third party consultation: A skill for professional psychologists in community practice. *Professional Psychology*, 1976b, *7*, 344–351.

Fisher, R. J. *Training and consultation in the university community*. Paper presented at the annual meeting of the Canadian Psychological Association, Vancouver, June 1977a.

Fisher, R. J. Toward the more comprehensive measurement of the intergroup attitudes: An interview and rating scale procedure. *Canadian Journal of Behavioural Science*, 1977b, *9*, 283–294.

Fisher, R. J. Applied social psychology: A partial response to Sarason's suggested divorce. *Canadian Psychological Review*, 1977c, *18*, 346–352.

Fisher, R. J. A third-party consultation workshop on the India-Pakistan conflict. *Journal of Social Psychology*, 1980a, *112*, 191–206.

Fisher, R. J. Touchstones for applied social psychology. In R. F. Kidd & M. J. Saks (Eds.), *Advances in applied social psychology* (Vol. 1). Hillsdale, N.J.: Erlbaum, 1980b.

Fisher, R. J. *Studies of third party consultation as a method of intergroup conflict resolution*. Unpublished manuscript, University of Saskatchewan, 1981a.

Fisher, R. J. Training in applied social psychology: Rationale and core experiences. *Canadian Psychology*, 1981b, *22*, 250–259.

Fisher, R. J. & Andrews, J. J. The impact of self-selection and reference group identification in a university living-learning center. *Social Behavior and Personality*, 1976, *4*, 209–218.

Fisher, R. J. & White, J. H. Intergroup conflicts resolved by outside consultants. *Journal of the Community Development Society*, 1976a, *7*, 88–98.

Fisher, R. J. & White, J. H. Reducing tensions between neighbourhood housing groups:

A pilot study in third party consultation. *International Journal of Group Tensions,* 1976b, *6,* 41–52.

Fiske, D. W. The limits of the conventional science of personality. *Journal of Personality,* 1974, *42,* 1–11.

Flanders, N. A. *Analyzing teaching behavior.* Reading, Mass.: Addison-Wesley, 1970.

Follett, M. *Creative experience.* New York: Longmans, Green, 1924.

Fouraker, L. & Siegel, S. *Bargaining behavior.* New York: McGraw-Hill, 1963.

Frank, J. D. Breaking the thought barrier: Psychological challenge of the nuclear age. *Psychiatry,* 1960, *23,* 245–266.

Frank, J. E. & Smith, R. A. Social scientists in the policy process. *Journal of Applied Behavioral Science,* 1976, *12,* 104–117.

Franke, R. H. & Kaul, J. D. The Hawthorne experiments: First statistical interpretation. *American Sociological Review,* 1978, *43,* 623–643.

Franklin, J. L. Characteristics of successful and unsuccessful organization development. *Journal of Applied Behavioral Science,* 1976, *12,* 471–492.

Freedman, J. L. & Fraser, S. C. Compliance without pressure: The foot-in-the-door technique. *Journal of Personality and Social Psychology,* 1966, *4,* 195–202.

Freeman, H. E. The present status of evaluation research. In M. Guttentag (Ed.), *Evaluation Studies Review Annual* (Vol. 2). Beverly Hills, Calif.: Sage, 1977.

French, W. L. & Bell, C. H. *Organization development: Behavioral science interventions for organization improvement* (2nd ed.). Englewood Cliffs, N.J.: Prentice-Hall, 1978.

Freud, S. *An outline of psychoanalysis.* J. Strachey translation (1940). New York: Norton, 1949.

Freud, S. *The ego and the id.* J. Riviere Translation (1923). J. Strachey revision. New York: Norton, 1962.

Friedan, B. *The feminine mystique.* New York: Norton, 1963.

Friedlander, F. The facilitation of change in organizations. *Professional Psychology,* 1980, *11,* 520–530.

Friedlander, F. & Brown, L. D. Organization development. *Annual Review of Psychology,* 1974, *25,* 313–342.

Friedman, H. S. & DiMatteo, M. R. Health care as an interpersonal process. *Journal of Social Issues,* 1979, *35*(1), 1–11.

Frieze, I. H., Bar-Tal, D. & Carroll, J. S. (Eds.). *New approaches to social problems.* San Francisco: Jossey-Bass, 1979.

Fromkin, H. L. & Sherwood, J. J. Intergroup and minority relations: An experiential handbook. La Jolla, Calif.: University Associates, 1976.

Frost, C. F., Wakely, J. H. & Ruh, R. A. *The Scanlon Plan for organizational development: Identity, participation and equity.* Lansing: Michigan State University Press, 1974.

Galtung, J. Peace thinking. In A. Lepawsky, E. H. Beuhrig & H. D. Lasswell (Eds.), *The search for world order.* New York: Appleton-Century-Crofts, 1971.

Gans, H. J. The positive functions of poverty. *American Journal of Sociology,* 1972, *78,* 275–289.

Gardner, G. Workers participation: A critical evaluation of Coch and French. *Human Relations,* 1977, *30,* 1071–1078.

Garvin, C. D. & Cox, F. M. A history of community organizing since the Civil War with special reference to oppressed communities. In F. M. Cox, J. L. Erlich, J. Rothman & J. E. Tropman (Eds.), *Strategies of community organization* (3rd ed.). Itasca, Ill.: Peacock, 1979.

Garvin, D., Aidala, L. & Rice, R. Nonacademic social psychologists: A telephone survey of SUNY/AB graduates. *Society for the Advancement of Social Psychology*

Newsletter, 1980, *6*,(2), 7–8.

Gazda, G. M. *Human relations development: A manual for educators.* Boston: Allyn and Bacon, 1973.

Geis, G. & Stotland, E. *White-collar crime: Theory and research.* Beverly Hills, Calif.: Sage, 1980.

Genthner, R. W. & Falkenberg, V. Changes in personal responsibility as a function of interpersonal skills training. *Small Group Behavior*, 1977, *8*, 533–539.

Georgopoulos, B. S. *Hospital organization research: Review and source book.* Philadelphia: W. B. Saunders, 1975.

Gerard, H. & Miller, N. *School desegregation.* New York: Plenum Press, 1975.

Gergen, K. J. Social psychology as history. *Journal of Personality and Social Psychology*, 1973, *26*, 309–320.

Gergen, K. J. Social psychology, science and history. *Personality and Social Psychology Bulletin*, 1976, *2*, 373–383.

Gergen, K. J. On taking dialectics seriously. *Personality and Social Psychology Bulletin*, 1977, *3*, 714–718.

Gergen, K. J. Toward generative theory. *Journal of Personality and Social Psychology*, 1978a, *36*, 1344–1360.

Gergen, K. J. Experimentation in social psychology: A reappraisal. *European Journal of Social Psychology*, 1978b, *8*, 507–527.

Getzels, J. W. A social psychology of education. In G. Lindzey & E. Aronson (Eds.), *The handbook of social psychology* (2nd ed.) (Vol. 5). Reading, Mass.: Addison-Wesley, 1969, 459–537.

Gibb, J. R. Defensive communication. *Journal of Communication*, 1961, *11*, 141–148.

Gibb, J. R. Is help helpful? *Forum*, 1964a, February, 25–27.

Gibb, J. R. Climate for trust formation. In L. P. Bradford, J. R. Gibb & K. D. Benne (Eds.), *T-group theory and the laboratory method.* New York: Wiley, 1964b.

Gibb, J. R. The effects of human relations training. In A. E. Bergin & S. L. Garfield (Eds.), *Handbook of psychotherapy and behavior change.* New York: Wiley, 1971.

Gibb, J. R. The training group. In K. D. Benne, L. P. Bradford, J. R. Gibb & R. O. Lippitt (Eds.), *The laboratory method of changing and learning: Theory and application.* Palo Alto, Calif.: Science and Behavior Books, 1975.

Giffin, K. & Patton, B. *Fundamentals of interpersonal communication* (2nd ed.). New York: Harper & Row, 1976.

Gilbert, G. M. Stereotype change and persistence among college students. *Journal of Abnormal and Social Psychology*, 1951, *46*, 245–254.

Ginott, H. G. *Between parent and child.* New York: Avon, 1965.

Ginott, H. G. *Between parent and teenager.* New York: Avon, 1969.

Ginsburg, H. J., Pollman, V. A., Wauson, M. S. & Hope, M. L. Variation of aggressive interaction among male elementary school children as a function of changes in spatial density. *Environmental Psychology and Nonverbal Behavior*, 1977, *2*, 67–75.

Gladstein, G. A. Is empathy important in counselling? *Personnel and Guidance Journal*, 1970, *48*, 823–827.

Gladstein, G. A. Empathy and counselling outcome: An empirical and conceptual review. *The Counselling Psychologist*, 1977, *6*, 70–79.

Glaser, E. M. & Taylor, S. H. Factors influencing the success of applied research. *American Psychologist*, 1973, *23*, 140–146.

Glaser, R. (Ed.). *Advances in instructional psychology* (Vol. 1). Hillsdale, N.J.: Erlbaum, 1978.

Glass, D. C. *Behavior patterns, stress, and coronary disease.* Hillsdale, N.J.: Erlbaum, 1977.

Glass, D. C. & Singer, J. E. *Urban stress.* New York: Academic Press, 1972.

Glass, G. V. & Ellett, F. S., Jr. Evaluation research. *Annual Review of Psychology*, 1980, *31*, 211–228.

Glidewell, J. C. A social psychology of mental health. In S. E. Golann & C. Eisdorfer (Eds.), *Handbook of community mental health*. Englewood Cliffs, N.J.: Prentice-Hall, 1972.

Glock, C. Y. (Ed.). *Survey research in the social sciences*. New York: Russell Sage Foundation, 1967.

Goffman, E. On face-work: An analysis of the ritual elements in social interaction. *Psychiatry*, 1955, *18*, 213–231.

Goffman, E. *The presentation of self in everyday life*. Garden City, N.Y.: Doubleday Anchor, 1959.

Goffman, E. *Asylums: Essays on the social situation of mental patients and other inmates*. Garden City, N.Y.: Anchor Books, 1961.

Goffman, E. *Interaction ritual: Essays on face-to-face behavior*. Garden City, N.Y.: Doubleday, 1967.

Golann, S. E. & Eisdorfer, C. Mental health and the community: The development of issues. In S. E. Golann & C. Eisdorfer (Eds.), *Handbook of community mental health*. Englewood Cliffs, N.J.: Prentice-Hall, 1972.

Golding, S. L. Flies in the ointment: Methodological problems in the analysis of the percentage of variance due to persons and situations. *Psychological Bulletin*, 1975, *82*, 278–288.

Goldstein, I. L. Training in work organizations. *Annual Review of Psychology*, 1980, *31*, 229–272.

Golembiewski, R. T. Organizational development in public agencies: Perspectives on theory and practice. *Public Administration Review*, 1969, *29*, 367–378.

Golembiewski, R. T. Enriching marriages through the laboratory approach: Tentative step toward the "open couple." In R. T. Golembiewski & A. Blumberg (Eds.), *Sensitivity training and the laboratory approach: Readings about concepts and applications* (2nd ed.). Itasca, Ill.: Peacock, 1973.

Golembiewski, R. T., Billingsley, K. & Yeager, S. Measuring change and persistence in human affairs: Types of change generated by OD designs. *Journal of Applied Behavioral Science*, 1976, *12*, 133–157.

Golembiewski, R. T. & Blumberg, A. *Sensitivity training and the laboratory approach: Readings about concepts and applications* (3rd ed.). Itasca, Ill.: Peacock, 1977.

Goodman, L. A. Causal analysis of data from panel studies and other kinds of surveys. *American Journal of Sociology*, 1973, *78*, 1135–1191.

Goodstein, L. D. *Consulting with human service systems*. Reading, Mass.: Addison-Wesley, 1978.

Goodstein, L. D. & Reinecker, V. M. Factors affecting self-disclosure: A review of the literature. *Progress in experimental personality research*, 1974, *7*, 49–77.

Goodstein, L. D. & Sandler, I. Using psychology to promote human welfare: A conceptual analysis of the role of community psychology. *American Psychologist*, 1978, *33*, 882–892.

Gorden, R. L. *Interviewing: Strategy, techniques and tactics* (3rd ed.). Homewood, Ill.: Dorsey, 1980.

Gordon, T. *Parent effectiveness training: The tested new way to raise responsible children*. New York: Wyden, 1970.

Gordon, T. *Teacher effectiveness training*. New York: David McKay, 1974.

Gorman, A. H. *Teachers and learners: The interactive process of education*. Boston: Allyn and Bacon, 1969.

Gortmaker, S. L. Poverty and infant mortality in the United States. *American Sociological Review*, 1979, *44*, 280–297.

Goslin, D. A. (Ed.). *Handbook of socialization theory and research.* Chicago: Rand-McNally, 1969.

Gottlieb, A. Social psychology as history or science: An addendum. *Personality and Social Psychology Bulletin,* 1977, *3,* 206–210.

Gottlieb, B. H. Re-examining the preventive potential of mental health consultation. *Canada's Mental Health,* 1974, *22,* 4–6.

Gottlieb, B. H. Lay influences on the utilization and provision of health services: A review. *Canadian Psychological Review,* 1976, *17,* 126–136.

Gottlieb, B. H. & Shroter, C. Collaboration and resource exchange between professionals and natural support systems. *Professional Psychology,* 1978, *9,* 614–622.

Gouldner, A. W. *Patterns of industrial bureaucracy.* New York: Free Press, 1954.

Graen, G. Role-making processes in organizations. In M. D. Dunnette (Ed.), *Handbook of industrial and organizational psychology,* Chicago: Rand McNally, 1976.

Granberg, D. GRIT in the final quarter: Reversing the arms race through unilateral initiatives. *Bulletin of Peace Proposals,* 1978, *9,* 210–221.

Greenberg, M. A concept of community. *Social Work,* 1974, *19,* 64–72.

Greenspoon, T. The reinforcing effect of two spoken sounds on the frequency of two responses. *American Journal of Psychology,* 1955, *62,* 409–416.

Gregory, W. L., Mowen, J. C. & Linder, D. E. Social psychology and plea bargaining: Applications, methodology and theory. *Journal of Personality and Social Psychology,* 1978, *36,* 1521–1530.

Greiner, L. E. Patterns of organization change. *Harvard Business Review,* 1967, May-June, 119–130.

Griffith, R. W. & Cafferty, T. P. Police and citizen value systems: Some cross-sectional comparisons. *Journal of Applied Social Psychology,* 1977, *7,* 191–204.

Griffiths, F. & Polanyi, J. C. (Eds.). *The dangers of nuclear war.* Toronto, Ont.: University of Toronto Press, 1979.

Griffitt, W. & Veitch, R. Preacquaintance attitude similarity and attraction revisited: Ten days in a fall-out shelter. *Sociometry,* 1974, *37,* 163–173.

Guerney, B. G. (Ed.). *Relationship enhancement.* San Francisco: Jossey-Bass, 1977b.

Guerney, L. A description and evaluation as a skill training program for foster parents. *American Journal of Community Psychology,* 1977a, *5,* 361–371.

Guetzkow, H. & Gyr, J. An analysis of conflict in decision-making groups. *Human Relations,* 1954, *7,* 367–382.

Guilford, J. P. *Psychometric methods* (2nd ed.). New York: McGraw-Hill, 1954.

Guildord, J. P. & Fruchter, B. *Fundamental statistics in psychology and education* (6th ed.). New York: McGraw-Hill, 1978.

Gurkaynak, M. R. & LeCompte, W. A. (Eds.). *Human consequences of crowding.* New York: Plenum, 1979.

Gurr, T. R. & Bishop, V. F. Violent nations, and others. *Journal of Conflict Resolution,* 1976, *20,* 79–110.

Guskin, A. E. & Guskin, S. L. *A social psychology of education.* Reading, Mass.: Addison-Wesley, 1970.

Guttentag, M. Evaluation and society. *Personality and Social Psychology Bulletin,* 1977, *3,* 31–40.

Haan, N., Smith, M. B. & Block, J. Moral reasoning of young adults: Political-social behavior, family background and personality correlates. *Journal of Personality and Social Psychology,* 1968, *10,* 183–201.

Hage, J. *Communication and organizational control: Cybernetics in health and welfare settings.* New York: Wiley, 1974.

Hage, J. & Aiken, M. *Social change in complex organizations.* New York: Random House, 1970.

Hagen, R. L. & Kahn, A. Discrimination against competent women. *Journal of Applied Social Psychology*, 1975, *5*, 362–376.

Halkides, G. *An experimental study of four conditions necessary for therapeutic change.* Unpublished Doctoral Dissertation, University of Chicago, 1958.

Hall, C. S. & Lindzey, G. *Theories of personality* (3rd ed.). New York: Wiley, 1978.

Hall, E. *The hidden dimension.* Garden City, N.Y.: Doubleday, 1966.

Hall, J. & Williams, M. S. Group dynamics training and improved decision making. *Journal of Applied Behavioral Science*, 1970, *6*, 39–68.

Hamilton, D. L. A cognitive-attributional analysis of stereotyping. In L. Berkowitz (Ed.), *Advances in experimental social psychology* (Vol. 12). New York: Academic Press, 1979.

Hammer, M. R., Gudykunst, W. B. & Wiseman, R. L. Dimensions of intercultural effectiveness: An exploratory study. *International Journal of Intercultural Relations*, 1978, *2*, 382–393.

Hammock, T. & Brehm, J. W. The attractiveness of choice alternatives when freedom to choose is eliminated by a social agent. *Journal of Personality*, 1966, *34*, 546–554.

Haney, C., Banks, W. C. & Zimbardo, P. G. Interpersonal dynamics in a simulated prison. *International Journal of Criminology and Penology*, 1973, *1*, 69–97.

Haque, A. Mirror image hypothesis in the context of the Indo-Pakistan conflict. *Pakistan Journal of Psychology*, 1973, *6*, 13–22.

Haque, A. & Lawson, E. D. The mirror image phenomenon in the context of the Arab-Israeli conflict. *International Journal of Intercultural Relations*, 1980, *4*, 107–116.

Harding, J., Proshansky, H., Kutner, B. & Chein, I. Prejudice and ethnic relations. In G. Lindzey & E. Aronson (Eds.), *The handbook of social psychology* (2nd ed.) (Vol. 5). Reading, Mass.: Addison-Wesley, 1969.

Hare, H. P. & Bales, R. F. Setting position and small group interaction. *Sociometry*, 1963, *4*, 480–486.

Hare, P. *Handbook of small group research* (2nd ed.). New York: Free Press, 1976.

Hargreaves, W. A. & Attkisson, C. C. Evaluating program outcomes. In C. C. Attkisson, W. A. Hargreaves, M. J. Horowitz & J. E. Sorensen (Eds.), *Evaluation of human service program.* New York: Academic Press, 1978.

Harper, R. G., Wiens, A. N. & Matarazzo, J. D. *Nonverbal communication: The state of the art.* New York: Wiley-Interscience, 1978.

Harris, R. T. Improving patient satisfaction through action research. *Journal of Applied Behavioral Science*, 1978, *14*, 382–399.

Harris, T. A. *I'm OK—You're OK.* New York: Avon, 1967.

Harrison, A. A., Hwalek, M., Raney, D. F. & Fritz, J. G. Cues to deception in an interview situation. *Social Psychology*, 1978, *41*, 156–161.

Harrison, R. When power conflicts trigger team spirit. *European Business*, 1972, Spring, 27–65.

Hartley, D., Roback, H. B. & Abramowitz, S. I. Deterioration effects in encounter groups. *American Psychologist*, 1976, *31*, 247–255.

Hartley, E. L. *Problems in prejudice.* New York: King's Crown Press, 1946.

Hasenfeld, Y. & English, R. A. *Human service organizations.* Ann Arbor: University of Michigan Press, 1974.

Hasenfeld, Y. Program development. In F. M. Cox, J. L. Erlich, J. Rothman & J. E. Tropman (Eds.), *Strategies of community organization* (3rd ed.). Itasca, Ill.: Peacock, 1979.

Havelock, R. G. *Planning for innovation through dissemination and utilization of knowledge.* Ann Arbor, Mich.: Institute for Social Research, 1969.

Haveman, R. H. (Ed.). *Decade of federal antipoverty programs: Achievements, failures and lessons.* New York: Academic Press, 1977.

Haveman, R. H. & Watts, H. W. Social experimentation as policy research: A review of negative income tax experiments. In G. V. Glass (Ed.), *Evaluation studies review annual* (Vol. 1), Beverly Hills, Calif.: Sage, 1976.

Heider, F. *The psychology of interpersonal relations.* New York: Wiley, 1958.

Heller, J. & Monahan, J. *Psychology and community change.* Homewood, Ill.: Dorsey, 1977.

Helmreich, R. Applied social psychology: The unfulfilled promise. *Personality and Social Psychology Bulletin,* 1975, *1,* 548–560.

Helmreich, R. L., Spence, J. T. & Holahan, C. K. Psychological androgyny and sex role flexibility: A test of two hypothesis. *Journal of Personality and Social Psychology,* 1979, *37,* 1631–1644.

Helson, R. & Mitchell, V. Personality. *Annual Review of Psychology,* 1978, *29,* 555–586.

Hennig, M. & Jardim, A. *The managerial woman.* Garden City, N.Y.: Anchor Press/Doubleday, 1977.

Hennigan, K. M., Flay, B. R. & Cook, T. D. "Give me the facts": Some suggestions for using social science knowledge in national policy-making. In R. F. Kidd & M. J. Saks (Eds.), *Advances in applied social psychology* (Vol. 1) Hillsdale, N.J.: Erlbaum, 1980.

Henry, F. *Forgotten Canadians: The Blacks of Nova Scotia.* Don Mills, Ont.: Longman Canada, 1973.

Henshel, A. *Sex structure.* Don Mills, Ont.: Longman Canada, 1973.

Herbert, W. The "deinstitutionalization" business: Frontiers and back alleys. *APA Monitor,* September/October 1978, *9,* 20–23.

Herzberg, F. *Work and the nature of man.* Cleveland, Ohio: World, 1966.

Hill, D. H. & Hill, M. S. Consumer attitudes and perceptions and automobile fuel economy standards. *Economic Outlook, U.S.A.,* 1979, *6,* 39–47.

Hill, R. E. Managing interpersonal conflicts in project teams. *Sloan Management Review,* 1977, *18,* 45–61.

Himsl, R. (Ed.). *The life skills coaching manual.* Prince Albert, Sask.: Saskatchewan Newstart, 1972.

Hinkle, S. & Schopler, J. Ethnocentrism in the evaluation of group products. In W. G. Austin & S. Worchel (Eds.), *The social psychology of intergroup relations.* Monterey, Calif.: Brooks/Cole, 1979.

Holland, T. P. The community: Organism or arena. *Social Work,* 1974, *19,* 73–80.

Hollingshead, B. B. & Redlich, F. C. *Social class and mental illness: A community study.* New York: Wiley, 1958.

Holmes, J. G. & Grant, P. Ethnocentric reactions to social threat. In L. H. Strickland (Ed.), *Social psychology: East-west perspectives,* Oxford, England: Pergamon, 1979.

Holsti, O. R. Content analysis. In G. Lindzey & E. Aronson (Eds.), *The handbook of social psychology* (2nd ed.) (Vol. 2). Reading, Mass.: Addison-Wesley, 1968.

Holsti, O. R. *Crisis, escalation, war.* Montreal: McGill-Queens University Press, 1972.

Holsti, O. R., Brody, R. A. & North, R. C. The management of international crisis: Affect and action in American-Soviet relations. *Journal of Peace Research,* 1964, *3-4,* 170–190.

Holt, J. *How children fail.* New York: Pitman, 1964.

Holt, J. *Instead of education.* New York: Dell, 1976.

Homans, G. C. Social behavior as exchange. *The American Journal of Sociology,* 1958, *63,* 597–606.

Homans, G. C. *Social behavior: Its elementary forms* (rev. ed.). New York: Harcourt, Brace, Jovanovich, 1974.

Hornstein, H. A. Social psychology as social intervention. In M. Deutsch & H. A.

Hornstein (Eds.), *Applying social psychology: Implications for research, practice, and training.* Hillsdale, N.J.: Erlbaum, 1975.

Hovland, C. I. Reconciling conflicting results derived from experimental and survey studies of attitude change. *American Psychologist,* 1959, *14,* 8–17.

Hovland, C. I., Janis, I. & Kelley, H. H. *Communication and persuasion.* New Haven, Conn.: Yale University Press, 1953.

Hovland, C. I., Lumsdaine, A. A. & Sheffield, F. D. *Experiments on mass communication.* Princeton: Princeton University Press, 1949.

Howard, J. J. & Williams, J. R. Internal-external control and black militancy. *Journal of Social Issues,* 1970, *26*(1), 75–92.

Hudson, J. Problems of measurement in criminal justice. In L. Rutman (Ed.), *Evaluation research methods: A basic guide,* Beverly Hills, Calif.: Sage, 1977.

Huesmann, L. R. & Levinger, G. Incremental exchange theory: A formal model for progression in dyadic social interaction. In L. Berkowitz & E. Walster (Eds.), *Advances in experimental social psychology* (Vol. 9). New York: Academic Press, 1976.

Hummel, C. F., Levitt, L. & Loomis, R. J. Perceptions of the energy crisis: Who is blamed and how do citizens react to environment-lifestyle trade-offs? *Environment and Behavior,* 1978, *10,* 37–88.

Hunt, D. E. The B-P-E paradigm for theory, research and practice. *Canadian Psychological Review,* 1975, *16,* 185–197.

Hunt, D. E. & Sullivan, E. V. *Between psychology and education.* Hinsdale, Ill.: Dryden, 1974.

Huston, T. L. & Levinger, G. Interpersonal attraction and relationships. *Annual Review of Psychology,* 1978, *29,* 115–156.

Hyman, H. H. The psychology of status. *Archives of Psychology,* 1942, No. 269.

Hyman, H. H. *Survey design and analysis.* New York: Free Press, 1955.

Hyman, H. H. Reflections on reference groups. *Public Opinion Quarterly,* 1960, *24,* 383–396.

Iklé, F. C. *How nations negotiate.* New York: Harper, 1964.

Illich, I. *Deschooling society.* New York: Harper & Row, 1970.

Insko, C. A. *Theories of attitude change.* New York: Appleton-Century-Crofts, 1967.

Insko, C. A. & Wilson, M. Interpersonal attraction as a function of social interaction. *Journal of Personality and Social Psychology,* 1977, *35,* 908–911.

Iscoe, I. Community psychology and the competent community. *American Psychologist,* 1974, *29,* 607–613.

ISR Newsletter. Americans enjoy participating in surveys, ISR study shows. Ann Arbor, Mich.: Institute for Social Research, 1978, *6*(1), 7.

Jackson, E. *Meeting of minds.* New York: McGraw-Hill, 1952.

Jacoby, J. Consumer psychology as a social psychological sphere of action. *American Psychologist,* 1975, *30,* 977–987.

Jacoby, J. Consumer psychology: An octennium. *Annual Review of Psychology,* 1976a, *27,* 331–358.

Jacoby, J. Consumer and industrial psychology: Prospects for theory corroboration and mutual contribution. In M. D. Dunnette (Ed.), *The handbook of industrial and organizational psychology.* Chicago: Rand McNally, 1976b.

Jahoda, G. A cross-cultural perspective on experimental social psychology. *Personality and Social Psychology Bulletin,* 1979, *5,* 142–148.

James, D. *Poverty, politics and change.* Englewood Cliffs, N.J.: Prentice-Hall, Inc., 1972.

Janis, I. L. Decisional conflicts: A theoretical analysis. *Journal of Conflict Resolution,* 1959, *3,* 6–27.

Janis, I. L. *Victims of groupthink.* Boston: Houghton Mifflin, 1972.

Janis, I. L. & Katz, D. The reduction of intergroup hostility: Research problems and hypotheses. *Journal of Conflict Resolution*, 1959, *3*, 85–100.

Jeffery, C. R. Criminology as an interdisciplinary behavioral science. *Criminology*, 1978, *16*, 149–169.

Jervis, R. *Perception and misperception in international policies.* Princeton: Princeton University Press, 1976.

Johnson, D. W. *Social psychology of education.* New York: Holt, Rinehart & Winston, 1970.

Johnson, D. W. *Reaching out: Interpersonal effectiveness and self-actualization.* Englewood Cliffs, N.J.: Prentice-Hall, 1972.

Johnson, D. W. *Contemporary social psychology.* New York: Lippincott, 1973.

Johnson, W. G. *A model for the economic evaluation of mental health care.* Paper presented at the annual meeting of the American Psychological Association, San Francisco, August, 1977.

Johnston, S. D. Dynamics of confrontation: The Arab-Israeli conflict. *Social Science*, 1977, *52*, 195–205.

Jones, E. E. *Ingratiation.* New York: Appleton-Century-Crofts, 1964.

Jones, E. E. & Davis, K. E. From Acts to dispositions: The attribution process in person perception. In L. Berkowitz (Ed.), *Advances in experimental social psychology* (Vol. 2). New York: Academic Press, 1965.

Jones, E. E. & Nisbett, R. E. The actor and the observer: Divergent perceptions of the causes of behavior. In E. E. Jones, D. E. Kanouse, H. H. Kelley, R. E. Nisbett, S. Valins & B. Weiner, *Attribution: Perceiving the causes of behavior.* Morristown, N.J.: General Learning Press, 1972.

Jones, E. E. & Sigall, H. The bogus pipeline: A new paradigm for measuring affect and attraction. *Psychological Bulletin*, 1971, *76*, 349–364.

Jourard, S. M. Healthy personality and self-disclosure. *Mental Hygiene*, 1959, *43*, 499–507.

Jourard, S. M. *The transparent self.* Princeton, N.J.: Van Nostrand, 1964.

Jourard, S. M. *Disclosing man to himself.* Princeton, N.J.: Van Nostrand, 1968.

Jourard, S. M. *The transparent self* (2nd ed.). New York: Van Nostrand, 1971.

Kahle, L. R. & Berman, J. J. Attitudes cause behaviors: A cross-lagged panel analysis. *Journal of Personality and Social Personality*, 1979, *37*, 315–321.

Kahn, R. L. In search of the Hawthorne effect. In E. L. Cass & F. G. Zimmer (Eds.), *Man and work in society.* New York: Van Nostrand Reinhold, 1975.

Kahn, R. L. & Boulding, E. (Eds.). *Power and conflict in organizations.* New York: Basic Books, 1964.

Kahn, R. L., Wolfe, D. M., Quinn, R. P., Snoek, J. D. & Rosenthal, R. A. *Organizational stress: Studies in role conflict and ambiguity.* New York: Wiley, 1964.

Kandel, D. B. Similarity in real-life adolescent friendship pairs. *Journal of Personality and Social Psychology*, 1978, *36*, 306–312.

Kanter, R. M. *Men and women of the corporation.* New York: Basic Books, 1977.

Kaplan, A. *The conduct of inquiry.* San Francisco: Chandler, 1964.

Kaplan, R. E. The conspicuous absence of evidence that process consultation enhances task performance. *Journal of Applied Behavioral Science*, 1979, *15*, 346–360.

Karlins, M., Coffman, T. L. & Walters, G. On the fading of social stereotypes: Studies on three generations of college students. *Journal of Personality and Social Psychology*, 1969, *13*, 1–16.

Karlsruher, A. E. The non-professional as a psychotherapeutic agent: A review of the empirical evidence pertaining to his effectiveness. *American Journal of Community Psychology*, 1974, *2*, 61–77.

Karlsruher, A. E. The influence of supervision and facilitative conditions on the psychotherapeutic effectiveness of nonprofessional and professional therapists. *American Journal of Community Psychology*, 1976, *4*, 145–154.

Katona, G. Psychology and consumer economics. *Journal of Consumer Research*, 1974, *1*, 1–8.

Katona, G. *Psychological economics*. New York: Elsevier, 1975.

Katona, G. Toward a macropsychology. *American Psychologist*, 1979, *34*, 118–126.

Katona, G. *Essays on behavioral economics*. Ann Arbor, Mich.: Institute for Social Research, 1980.

Katz, D. Studies in social psychology in World War II. *Psychological Bulletin*, 1951, *48*, 512–519.

Katz, D. The functional approach to the study of attitudes. *Public Opinion Quarterly*, 1960, *24*, 163–204.

Katz, D. Nationalism and strategies of international conflict resolution. In H. C. Kelman (Ed.), *International behavior: A social-psychological analysis*, New York: Holt, Rinehart & Winston, 1965.

Katz, D. Factors affecting social change: A social-psychological interpretation. *Journal of Social Issues*, 1974, *30*,(3), 159–180.

Katz, D. Social psychology in relation to the social sciences: The second social psychology. *American Behavioral Scientist*, 1978, *21*, 779–792.

Katz, D. & Braly, K. Racial stereotypes in one hundred college students. *Journal of Abnormal and Social Psychology*, 1933, *28*, 280–290.

Katz, D. & Golomb, N. Integration, effectiveness and adaptation in social systems: A comparative analysis of Kibbutzim communities. *Administration and Society*, 1974, *6*, 283–315.

Katz, D. & Kahn, R. L. Leadership practices in relation to productivity. In D. Cartwright & A. Zander (Eds.), *Group dynamics*. Evanston, Ill.: Row, Peterson, 1953.

Katz, D. & Kahn, R. L. *The social psychology of organizations*. New York: Wiley, 1966.

Katz, D. & Kahn, R. L. *The social psychology of organizations* (2nd ed.). New York: Wiley, 1978.

Katz, D. & Stotland, E. A preliminary statement to a theory of attitude structure and change. In S. Koch (Ed.), *Psychology: A study of a science* (Vol. 3). New York: McGraw-Hill, 1959.

Katz, D. & Withey, S. The social psychology of human conflict. In E. B. McNeil (Ed.), *The nature of human conflict*, Englewood Cliffs, N.J.: Prentice-Hall, 1965.

Keller, R. T. A longitudinal assessment of a managerial grid seminar training program. *Group and Organization Studies*, 1978, *3*, 343–355.

Kelley, H. H. Two functions of reference groups. In G. E. Swanson, T. M. Newcomb & E. L. Hartley (Eds.), *Readings in social psychology*. New York: Holt, Rinehart & Winston, 1952.

Kelley, H. H. Attribution theory in social psychology. In D. Levine (Ed.), *Nebraska symposium on motivation* (Vol. 15). Lincoln: University of Nebraska Press, 1967.

Kelley, H. H. *Attribution in social interaction*. Morristown, N.J.: General Learning Press, 1971.

Kelley, H. H. *Causal schemata and the attribution process*. Morristown, N.J.: General Learning Press, 1972.

Kelley, H. H. The processes of causal attribution. *American Psychologist*, 1973, *28*, 107–128.

Kelley, H. H. *Interpersonal conflict*. Paper presented at the annual meeting of the Canadian Psychological Association, Vancouver, June, 1977.

Kelley, H. H. *Personal relationships: Their structures and processes*. Hillsdale, N.J.: Erlbaum, 1979.

Kelley, H. H. & Michela, J. L. Attribution theory and research. *Annual Review of Psychology*, 1980, *31*, 457–501.

Kelley, H. H. & Thibaut, J. W. Group problem solving. In G. Lindzey & E. Aronson (Eds.), *Handbook of social psychology* (2nd ed.) (Vol. 4). Reading, Mass.: Addison-Wesley, 1969.

Kelley, V. R., Kelley, P. L., Gauron, E. F. & Rawlings, E. I. Training helpers in rural mental health delivery. *Social Work*, 1977, *22*, 229–232.

Kelling, G. L., Pate, T., Dieckman, D. & Brown, C. E. The Kansas City preventive patrol experiment: A summary report. In G. V. Glass (Ed.), *Evaluation studies review annual* (Vol. 1). Beverly Hills, Calif.: Sage, 1976, 605–657.

Kelly, J. G. Ecological constraints on mental health services. *American Psychologist*, 1966, *21*, 535–539.

Kelly, J. G. Toward an ecological conception of prevention interventions. In J. Carter (Ed.), *Research contributions from psychology to community mental health*, New York: Behavioral Publications, 1968.

Kelly, J. G. The quest for valid preventive interventions. In C. D. Spielberger (Ed.), *Current topics in clinical and community psychology* (Vol. 2), New York: Academic Press, 1970.

Kelly, J. G., Snowden, L. R. & Munoz, R. F. Social and community intervention methods. *Annual Review of Psychology*, 1977, *28*, 323–361.

Kelman, H. C. (Ed.). *International behavior: A social-psychological analysis*. New York: Holt, Rinehart & Winston, 1965.

Kelman, H. C. Human use of human subjects: The problem of deception in social psychological experiments. *Psychological Bulletin*, 1967, *67*, 1–11.

Kelman, H. C. *A time to speak*. San Francisco: Jossey-Bass, 1969.

Kelman, H. C. The problem-solving workshop in conflict resolution. In R. L. Merritt (Ed.), *Communication in international politics*, Urbana: University of Illinois Press, 1972.

Kelman, H. C. & Cohen, S. P. The problem-solving workshop: A social-psychological contribution to the resolution of international conflict. *Journal of Peace Research*, 1976, *13*, 79–90.

Kelman, H. C. & Cohen, S. P. Reduction of international conflict: An interactional approach. In W. G. Austin & S. Worchel (Eds.), *The social psychology of intergroup relations*. Monterey, Calif.: Brooks/Cole, 1979.

Kelman, H. C. & Ezekiel, R. *Cross-cultural encounters*. San Francisco: Jossey-Bass, 1970.

Kelman, H. C. & Warwick, D. P. Bridging micro and macro approaches to social change: A social-psychological perspective. In G. Zaltman (Ed.), *Processes and phenomena of social change*, New York: Wiley, 1973.

Kenny, D. A. Cross-lagged panel correlation: A test for spuriousness. *Psychological Bulletin*, 1975, *82*, 887–903.

Kenny, D. A. *Correlation and causality*. New York: Wiley, 1979.

Kessler, M. & Albee, G. W. Primary prevention. *Annual Review of Psychology*, 1975, *26*, 557–591.

Keys, C. & Bartunek, J. M. Organization development in schools: Goal agreement, process skills and diffusion of change. *Journal of Applied Behavioral Science*, 1979, *15*, 61–78.

Kidd, R. F. & Saks, M. J. (Eds.). *Advances in applied social psychology* (Vol. 1). Hillsdale, N.J.: Erlbaum, 1980.

Kidder, L. H. *Selltiz, Wrightsman and Cook's research methods in social relations* (4th ed.). New York: Holt, Rinehart & Winston, 1981.

Kiesler, C. A. Psychology and public policy. In L. Bickman (Ed.), *Applied social psy-*

chology annual (Vol. 1). Beverly Hills, Calif.: Sage, 1980.

Kiesler, S. B. Research funding for psychology. *American Psychologist*, 1977, *32*, 23–32.

Kilmann, R. H. & Thomas, K. W. Interpersonal conflict-handling behavior as reflections of Jungian personality dimensions. *Psychological Reports*, 1975, *37*, 971–980.

Kilmann, R. H. & Thomas, K. W. Developing a forced choice measure of conflict-handling behavior: The "MODE" instrument. *Educational and Psychological Measurement*, 1977, *37*, 309–325.

Kinder, D. R. & Weiss, J. A. In lieu of rationality: Psychological perspectives on foreign-policy decision-making. *Journal of Conflict Resolution*, 1978, *22*, 707–736.

King, A. S. Expectation effects in organizational change. *Administrative Sciences Quarterly*, 1974, *19*, 221–230.

King, L. M. Social and cultural influences on psychopathology. *Annual Review of Psychology*, 1978, *29*, 405–433.

Kiresuk, T. J. & Lund, S. H. Process and outcome measurement using goal attainment scaling. In J. Zuomen & C. R. Wurster (Eds.), *Program evaluation: Alcohol, drug abuse, and mental health services*. Lexington, Mass.: Heath, 1975.

Kiresuk, T. J. & Sherman, R. E. Goal attainment scaling: A general method of evaluating comprehensive community mental health programs. *Community Mental Health Journal*, 1968, *4*, 443–453.

Klein, D. C. Sensitivity training and community development. In E. H. Schein & W. G. Bennis (Eds.), *Personal and organizational change through group methods*. New York: Wiley, 1965.

Klein, D. C. *Community dynamics and mental health*. New York: Wiley, 1968.

Klein, E. G., Thomas, C. S. & Bellis, E. When warring groups meet: The use of a group approach in police–Black community relations. *Social Psychiatry*, 1971, *6*, 93–99.

Klein, L. *New forms of work organization*. Cambridge: Cambridge University Press, 1976.

Klimoski, R. J. Simulation methodologies in experimental research on negotiations by representatives. *Journal of Conflict Resolution*, 1978, *22*, 61–78.

Klineberg, O. *The human dimension in international relations*. New York: Holt, Rinehart & Winston, 1964.

Knowles, M. S. *The modern practice of adult education: Andragogy versus pedagogy*. New York: Association Press, 1970.

Knowles, M. S. *Self-directed learning: A guide for learners and teachers*. New York: Association Press, 1975.

Knox, R. E. & Inkster, J. A. Post-decision dissonance at post time. *Journal of Personality and Social Psychology*, 1968, *4*, 319–323.

Koch, S. Epilogue. In S. Koch (Ed.), *Psychology: A study of a science* (Vol. 3). New York: McGraw-Hill, 1959.

Kolb, D. A., Rubin, I. M. & McIntyre, J. M. *Organizational behavior: An experiential approach* (2nd ed.). Englewood Cliffs, N.J.: Prentice-Hall, 1974.

Krasner, L. (Ed.). *Environmental design and human behavior: A psychology of the individual in society*. Elmsford, N.Y.: Pergamon, 1978.

Krech, D. & Cartwright, D. On SPSSI's first twenty years. *American Psychologist*, 1956, *11*, 470–473.

Krech, D., Crutchfield, R. S. & Ballachey, E. L. *Individual in society: A textbook of social psychology*. New York: McGraw-Hill, 1962.

Krupat, E. Environmental and social psychology: How different must they be? *Personality and Social Psychology Bulletin*, 1977, *3*, 51–53.

Kurtz, P. Editorial: A definition of humanism. *Humanist*, 1968, *28*, 1.

Kurtz, P. Editorial: The moral revolution: Toward a critical radicalism. *Humanist*, 1971, *31*, 4-6.

La Fave, W. R. *Arrest: The decision to take a suspect into custody.* Boston: Little, Brown, 1965.

LaFerriere, L. & Calsyn, R. Goal attainment scaling: An effective treatment technique in short term therapy. *American Journal of Community Psychology*, 1978, *6*, 271-282.

LaFrance, M. Observational and archival data. In L. H. Kidder (Ed.), *Selltiz, Wrightsman and Cook's research methods in social relations* (4th ed.). New York: Holt, Rinehart & Winston, 1981.

Lakin, M. Some ethical issues in sensitivity training. *American Psychologist*, 1969, *24*, 923-928.

Lakin, M. *Interpersonal encounter: Theory and practice in sensitivity training.* New York: McGraw-Hill, 1972.

Lakin, M., Lomranz, J. & Lieberman, M. A. *Arab & Jew in Israel: A case study in a human relations approach to conflict.* Washington, D.C.: NTL Institute for Applied Behavioral Science, 1969.

Lall, A. *Modern international negotiation.* New York: Columbia University Press, 1966.

Lalonde, M. *A new perspective on the health of Canadians.* Ottawa: Information Canada, 1975.

Lamb, D. H. & LaFave, F. The use of para-professionals in university mental health settings: A national survey. *American Journal of Community Psychology*, 1977, *5*, 321-326.

Lambert, M. J. & DeJulio, S. S. Outcome research in Carkhuff's human resource development training programs: Where is the donut? *Counseling Psychologist*, 1977, *4*, 79-86.

Lambert, M. J. DeJulio, S. S. & Stein, D. M. Therapist interpersonal skills: Process, outcome, methodological considerations, and recommendations for future research. *Psychological Bulletin*, 1978, *85*, 467-489.

Latané, B. & Darley, J. M. Group inhibition of bystander intervention in emergencies. *Journal of Personality and Social Psychology*, 1968, *10*, 215-221.

Latané, B. & Darley, J. M. Help in a crisis: Bystander response to an emergency. In J. W. Thibaut, J. T. Spence & R. C. Carson (Eds.), *Contemporary topics in social psychology*. Morristown, N.J.: General Learning Press, 1976.

Lauer, R. H. & Handel, W. H. *Social psychology: The theory and application of symbolic interactionism.* Boston: Houghton Mifflin, 1977.

Lawler, E. E. *Motivation in work organizations.* Monterey, Calif.: Brooks/Cole, 1973.

Lawrence, P. R. & Lorsch, J. W. Differentiation and integration in complex organizations. *Administrative Science Quarterly*, 1967, *12*, 1-47.

Lazerwitz, B. Sampling theory and procedures. In H. M. Blalock & A. B. Blalock (Eds.), *Methodology in social research*. New York: McGraw-Hill, 1968.

Leary, T. *Interpersonal diagnosis of personality—A functional theory and methodology for personality evaluation.* New York: Ronald Press, 1957.

Leavitt, H. J. Some effects of certain communication patterns on group performance. *Journal of Abnormal and Social Psychology*, 1951, *46*, 38-50.

Lehmann, S. Community and psychology and community psychology. *American Psychologist*, 1971, *26*, 554-560.

Leighton, A. H. Poverty and social change. *Scientific American*, 1965, *212*(5), 21-27.

Leng, R. J. & Wheeler, H. G. Influence strategies, success, and war. *Journal of Conflict Resolution*, 1979, *23*, 655-684.

Lenski, G. Marxist experiments in destratification: An appraisal. *Social Forces*, 1978, *57*, 364–383.

Lepawsky, A., Buehrig, E. H. & Lasswell, H. D. (Eds.). *The search for world order.* New York: Appleton-Century-Crofts, 1971.

Lerner, M. J. The desire for justice and reactions to victims. In J. McCauley & L. Berkowitz (Eds.), *Altruism and helping behavior: Social psychological studies of some antecedents and consequences.* New York: Academic Press, 1970.

Lesieur, F. G. & Puckett, E. S. The Scanlon Plan has proved itself. *Harvard Business Review*, 1969 September–October, *47*, 109–118.

Levi W. On the causes of war and peace. *Journal of Conflict Resolution*, 1960, *4*, 411–420.

Levin, H. M. Cost-effectiveness analysis in evaluation research. In M. Guttentag & E. L. Streuning (Eds.), *Handbook of evaluation research* (Vol. 2). Beverly Hills, Calif.: Sage, 1975.

Levine, H. Psychologist to the powerless. In F. F. Korten, S. W. Cook & J. I. Lacey (Eds.), *Psychology and the problems of society.* Washington, D.C.: American Psychological Association, 1970.

Levine, M. & Levine, A. *A social history of the helping services.* New York: Appleton-Century-Crofts, 1970.

Levine, R. A. & Campbell, D. T. *Ethnocentrism: Theories of Conflict, ethnic attitudes and group behavior.* New York: Wiley, 1972.

Levinger, G. *Models of close relationships: Some new directions.* Paper presented at the annual meeting of the American Psychological Association, Toronto, Ontario, August, 1978.

Levinger, G. & Moles, O. C. (Eds.). *Divorce and separation: Context, causes and consequences.* New York: Basic Books, 1979.

Levinger, G. & Snoek, D. J. *Attraction in relationship: A new look at interpersonal attraction.* Morristown, N.J.: General Learning Press, 1972.

Levinson, D. J. The intergroup relations workshop: Its psychological aims and effects. *Journal of Psychology*, 1954, *38*, 103–126.

Levinson, D. J. & Schermerhorn, R. A. Emotional-attitudinal effects of an intergroup relations workshop on its members. *Journal of Psychology*, 1951, *31*, 243–256.

Levitt, T. *The third sector: New tactics of a responsive society.* New York: Amacom Press, 1973.

Levy, L. H. Self-help groups: Types and psychological processes. *Journal of Applied Behavioral Science*, 1976, *12*, 310–322.

Levy, L. H. Self-help groups viewed by mental health professionals: A survey and comments. *American Journal of Community Psychology*, 1978, *6*, 305–314.

Levy, S. G. The employment environment for social psychologists. In P. J. Woods (Ed.), *Career opportunities for psychologists: Expanding and emerging areas.* Washington, D.C.: American Psychological Association, 1976.

Levy, S. G. Graduate training and prospects in social psychology. *Personality and Social Psychology Bulletin*, 1979, *5*, 504–506.

Lewin, K. Group decision and social change. In T. M. Newcomb & E. L. Hartley (Eds.), *Readings in Social Psychology.* New York: Holt, Rinehart & Winston, 1947.

Lewin, K. *Resolving social conflicts.* New York: Harper, 1948.

Lewin, K. *Field theory in social science.* New York: Harper, 1951.

Lewin, K., Lippitt, R. & White, R. K. Patterns of aggressive behavior in experimentally created "social climates". *Journal of Social Psychology*, 1939, *10*, 271–299.

Lewin, M. A. Kurt Lewin's view of social psychology: The crisis of 1977 and the crisis of 1927. *Personality and Social Psychology Bulletin*, 1977, *3*, 159–172.

Lieberman, M. A. Change induction in small groups. *Annual Review of Psychology*, 1976, *27*, 217–250.

Lieberman, M. A. & Glidewell, J. C. Overview: Special issue on the helping process. *American Journal of Community Psychology*, 1978, *6*, 405–412.

Lieberman, M. A., Yalom, I. D. & Miles, M. *Encounter groups: First facts*. New York: Basic Books, 1973.

Lieberman, S. The effects of changes in roles on the attitudes of role occupants. *Human Relations*, 1956, *2*, 385–402.

Likert, R. A technique for the measurement of attitudes. *Archives of Psychology*, 1932, No. 140.

Likert, R. *New patterns of management*. New York: McGraw-Hill, 1961.

Likert, R. *The human organization*. New York: McGraw-Hill, 1967.

Likert, R. & Likert, J. G. *New ways of managing conflict*. New York: McGraw-Hill, 1976.

Lindgren, H. C. *Educational psychology in the classroom* (2nd ed.). New York: Wiley, 1962.

Lindgren, H. C. Trends in social psychology research in education. In D. Bar-Tal & L. Saxe (Eds.), *Social psychology of education: Theory and research*. Washington, D.C.: Hemisphere, 1978.

Lindholm, R. *Job reform in Sweden*. Stockholm: Swedish Employer's Confederation, 1975.

Lindskold, S. Managing conflict through announced conciliatory initiatives backed with retaliatory capacity. In W. G. Austin & S. Worchel (Eds.), *The social psychology of intergroup relations*. Monterey, Calif.: Brooks/Cole, 1979.

Lindskold, S. & Collins, M. G. Inducing co-operation by groups and individuals: Applying Osgood's GRIT strategy. *Journal of Conflict Resolution*, 1978, *22*, 679–690.

Lindzey, G. (Ed.). *Handbook of social psychology*. Cambridge, Mass.: Addison-Wesley, 1954.

Lippitt, G. *Organization renewal: Achieving viability in a changing world*. New York: Appleton-Century-Crofts, 1969.

Lippitt, G. Developing professional skills and expertise. *Training and Development Journal*, 1979, May, 66–70.

Lippitt, G. & Lippitt, R. *The consulting process in action*. La Jolla, Calif.: University Associates, 1978.

Lippitt, G. & This, L. E. Leaders for laboratory training: Selected guidelines for group trainers utilizing the laboratory method. *Training and Development Journal*, 1967, *21*, 2–13.

Lippitt, R. *Training in community relations*. New York: Harper & Brothers, 1949.

Lippitt, R. & Bradford, L. Building a democratic work group. *Personnel*, 1945, *22*(3), 1–12.

Lippitt, R., Watson, J. & Westley, B. *The dynamics of planned change*. New York: Harcourt Brace Jovanovich, 1958.

Lipsett, P. D. & Steinbruner, M. An experiment in police-community relations: A small group approach. *Community Mental Health Journal*, 1969, *5*, 172–179.

Littrell, D. W. *The theory and practice of community development: A guide for practitioners*. Columbia: University of Missouri Extension Division, 1973.

Littrell, W. B. Bureaucracies in the eighties: Editor's introduction. *Journal of Applied Behavioral Science*, 1980, *16*, 263–277.

Lockhart, C. *The efficacy of threats in international interaction strategies*. Beverly Hills, Calif.: Sage, 1973.

Loftus, E. & Monahan, J. Trial by data: Psychological research as legal evidence. *Amer-*

ican Psychologist, 1980, *35*, 270–283.

Lomranz, J., Lakin, M. & Schiffman, H. Variants of sensitivity training and encounter: Diversity and fragmentation? *Journal of Applied Behavioral Science*, 1972, *8*, 399–420.

Lorenz, K. *On aggression*. London: Methuen, 1966.

Lorenz, K. *The foundations of ethology*. New York: Springer-Verlag, 1981.

Love, R. L., Rozelle, R. M. & Druckman, D. *Conflict resolution through bargaining and negotiation in interreligious counsels*. Paper presented at the annual meeting of the American Psychological Association, San Francisco, 1977.

Lowe, R. H. A survey of social psychological methods, techniques, and designs: A response to Helmreich. *Personality and Social Psychology Bulletin*, 1976, *2*, 116–118.

Lubin, B. & Eddy, W. G. The laboratory training model: Rationale, method and some thoughts for the future. *International Journal of Group Psychotherapy*, 1970, *20*, 305–339.

Luce, R. D. & Raiffa, H. *Games and decisions*. New York: Wiley, 1957.

Luchins, A. S. Primacy-recency in impression formation. In C. I. Hovland (Ed.), *The order of persuasion*. New Haven, Conn.: Yale University Press, 1957.

Luft, J. *Group processes: An introduction to group dynamics* (2nd ed.). Palo Alto, Calif.: Mayfield Publishing, 1970.

Luke, R. & Benne, K. D. Ethical issues and dilemmas in laboratory practice. In K. D. Benne, L. P. Bradford, J. R. Gibb & R. O. Lippitt (Eds.), *The laboratory method of changing and learning: Theory and application*. Palo Alto: Science and Behavior Books, 1975.

Lundgren, D. C. & Knight, D. J. Sequential stages of development in sensitivity training groups. *Journal of Applied Behavioral Science*, 1978, *14*, 204–222.

Lupfer, M., Kay, J. & Burnette, S. A. The influence of picketing on the purchase of toy guns. *Journal of Social Psychology*, 1969, *77*, 197–200.

Lutz, R. J. & Bettman, J. R. Multiattribute models in marketing: A bicentennial review. In A. G. Woodside, J. N. Sheth & P. D. Bennett (Eds.), *Consumer and industrial buying behavior*. New York: Elsevier North-Holland, 1977.

Lynch, K. *The image of the city*. Cambridge, Mass.: The Technology Press, 1960.

Lyon, H. C. *Learning to feel—Feeling to learn*. Columbus, Ohio: C. E. Merrill, 1971.

Maccoby, E. E. (Ed.). *The development of sex differences*. Stanford, Calif.: Stanford University Press, 1966.

Maccoby, E. E. & Jacklin, C. N. *The psychology of sex differences*. Stanford, Calif.: Stanford University Press, 1974.

Mack, R. W. & Snyder, R. C. The analysis of social conflict—Toward an overview and synthesis. *Journal of Conflict Resolution*, 1957, *1*, 212–248.

MacLennan, B. W., Quinn, R. D. & Schroeder, D. The scope of community mental health consultation. In F. V. Mannino, B. W. MacLennan & M. F. Shore (Eds.), *The practice of mental health consultation*. Adelphi, Md.: National Institute of Mental Health, 1975.

Magnusson, D. & Endler, N. S. (Eds.). *Personality at the crossroads: Current issues in interactional psychology*. Hillsdale, N.J.: Erlbaum, 1976.

Maier, N. R. F. *Problem-solving discussions and conferences*. New York: McGraw-Hill, 1963.

Maier, N. R. F. Assets and liabilities in group problem solving: The need for an integrative function. *Psychological Review*, 1967, *74*, 239–249.

Maier, N. R. F. *Problem solving and creativity in individuals and groups*. Belmont, Calif.: Brooks/Cole, 1970.

Maki, J. E., Hoffman, D. M. & Berk, R. A. A time series analysis of the impact of a water conservation campaign. *Evaluation Quarterly*, 1978, *2*, 107–118.

Maloney, M. P. & Ward, M. P. Ecology: Let's hear from the people: An objective scale for the measurement of ecological attitudes and knowledge. *American Psychologist*, 1973, *28*, 583–586.

Manes, A. L. & Melnyk, P. Televised models of female achievement. *Journal of Applied Social Psychology*, 1974, *4*, 365–374.

Mann, F. C. Studying and creating change: A means to understanding social organizations. *Research in Industrial Human Relations*. Industrial Relations Research Association, 1957, *17*, 146–167.

Mann, L. & Taylor, K. F. Queue counting: The effect of motives upon estimates of the number of people waiting in lines. *Journal of Personality and Social Psychology*, 1969, *12*, 95–103.

Mannarino, A. P. & Durlak, J. A. Implementation and evaluation of service programs in community settings. *Professional Psychology*, 1980, *11*, 220–227.

Mannino, F. V., MacLennan, B. W. & Shore, M. F. *The practice of mental health consultation*. Adelphi, Maryland: National Institute of Mental Health, 1975.

Mannino, F. V. & Shore, M. F. The effects of consultation: A review of empirical studies. *American Journal of Community Psychology*, 1975, *3*, 1–21.

March, J. G. & Simon, H. A. *Organizations*. New York: Wiley, 1958.

Margulis, S. T. Conceptions of privacy: Current status and next steps. *Journal of Social Issues*, 1977, *33*(3), 5–21.

Mark, M. M., Cook, T. D. & Diamond, S. S. Fourteen years of social psychology: A growing commitment to field experimentation. *Personality and Social Psychology Bulletin*, 1976, *2*, 154–157.

Markus, G. B. *Analyzing panel data*. Beverly Hills, Calif.: Sage. 1980.

Marris, P. & Rein, M. *Dilemmas of social reform* (2nd ed.). Chicago: Aldine, 1973.

Marrow, A. J. *The practical theorist: The life and work of Kurt Lewin*. New York: Basic Books, 1969.

Marrow, A. J., Bowers, D. G. & Seashore, S. E. *Management by participation*. New York: Harper & Row, 1967.

Marx, M. H. The general nature of theory construction. In M. H. Marx (Ed.), *Theories in contemporary psychology*. New York: MacMillan, 1963.

Maslach, C. The social psychologist as agent of change. In M. Deutsch & H. A. Hornstein (Eds.), *Applying social psychology: Implications for research, practice, and training*. Hillsdale, N.J.: Erlbaum, 1975.

Maslow, A. H. A theory of human motivation. *Psychological Review*, 1943, *50*, 370–396.

Maslow, A. H. *Toward a psychology of being* (2nd ed.). New York: Van Nostrand, 1968.

Maslow, A. H. *Motivation and personality* (2nd ed.). New York: Harper & Row, 1970.

Mastenbroek, W. F. G. Negotiating: A conceptual model. *Group and Organization Studies*, 1980, *5*, 324–339.

Mathes, E. W. & Edwards, L. L. An empirical test of Maslow's theory of motivation. *Journal of Humanistic Psychology*, 1978, *18*(1), 75–77.

Matlin, M. W. & Stang, D. J. *The Pollyanna Principle: Selectivity in language, memory and thought*. New York: Schenkman, 1978.

Mayo, C. & LaFrance, M. Toward an applicable social psychology. In R. F. Kidd & M. J. Saks (Eds.), *Advances in applied social psychology* (Vol. 1). Hillsdale, N.J.: Erlbaum, 1980.

McArthur, C. C. Comment on "effectiveness of counselors and counselor aides". *Journal of Counseling Psychology*, 1970, *17*, 335–336.

McArthur, L. Z. & Resko, B. G. The portrayal of men and women in American television commercials. *Journal of Social Psychology*, 1975, *97*, 209–220.

McClelland, D. C. *The achieving society.* Princeton, N.J.: Van Nostrand, 1961.

McClelland, D. C. N. achievement and entrepreneurship: A longitudinal study. *Journal of Personality and Social Psychology,* 1965a, *1,* 389–393.

McClelland, D. C. Toward a theory of motive acquisition. *American Psychologist,* 1965b, *20,* 321–333.

McClelland, D. C. *Power: The inner experience.* New York: Irvington, 1975.

McClelland, D. C. The impact of power motivation training on alcoholics. *Journal of Studies on Alcohol,* 1977, *38,* 142–144.

McClelland, D. C. Managing motivation to expand human freedom. *American Psychologist,* 1978, *33,* 201–210.

McClelland, D. C., Atkinson, J. W. Clark, R. A. & Lowell, E. L. (Eds.). *The achievement motive.* New York: Appleton-Century-Crofts, 1953.

McClelland, D. C. & Burnham, D. H. Power is the great motivator. *Harvard Business Review,* 1976, *54,* 100–110.

McClelland, D. C., Rhinesmith, S. & Kristensen, R. The effects of power training on community action agencies. *Journal of Applied Behavioral Science,* 1975, *11,* 92–115.

McClelland, D. C. & Winter, D. G. *Motivating economic achievement.* New York: Free Press, 1971.

McClintock, C. G. Game behavior and social motivation in interpersonal settings. In C. G. McClintock (Ed.), *Experimental social psychology,* New York: Holt, Rinehart & Winston, 1972.

McCrosky, J. C. *An introduction to rhetorical communication.* Englewood Cliffs, N.J.: Prentice-Hall, 1968.

McCrosky, J. C., Larson, C. E. & Knapp, M. L. *Introduction to interpersonal communication.* Englewood Cliffs, N.J.: Prentice-Hall, 1971.

McDougall, W. *Introduction to social psychology.* London: Methuen, 1908.

McGrath, J. E. Social science, social action and the Journal of Social Issues. *Journal of Social Issues,* 1980, *36*(4), 109–124.

McGrath, J. E. & Altman, I. *Small group research: a synthesis and critique of the field.* New York: Holt, Rinehart & Winston, 1966.

McGregor, D. *The human side of enterprise.* New York: McGraw-Hill, 1960.

McGuire, M. V. & Bermant, G. Individual and group decisions in response to a mock trial: A methodological note. *Journal of Applied Social Psychology,* 1977, *7,* 220–226.

McGuire, W. J. Some impending reorientations in social psychology: Some thoughts provoked by Kenneth Ring. *Journal of Experimental Social Psychology,* 1967, *3,* 124–139.

McGuire, W. J. The nature of attitudes and attitude change. In G. Lindzey & E. Aronson (Eds.), *The handbook of social psychology* (2nd ed.) (Vol. 3). Reading, Mass.: Addison-Wesley, 1969b.

McGuire, W. J. Theory-oriented research in natural settings: The best of both worlds for social psychology. In M. Sherif & C. W. Sherif (Eds.), *Interdisciplinary relationships in the social sciences.* Chicago: Aldine, 1969a.

McGuire, W. J. The Yin and Yang of progress in social psychology. Seven Koan. *Journal of Personality and Social Psychology,* 1973, *26,* 446–456.

McGuire, W. J. *Toward social psychology's second century.* Paper presented at the annual meeting of the American Psychological Association, New York, September, 1979.

McHugh, M., Beckman, L. & Frieze, I. H. Analyzing alcoholism. In I. H. Freize, D. Bar-Tal & J. S. Carroll (Eds.), *New approaches to social problems.* San Francisco: Jossey-Bass, 1979.

McKeachie, W. J. The psychology department and society. *American Psychologist*, 1972, *27*, 643–646.

McKeachie, W. J. Instructional psychology. *Annual Review of Psychology*, 1974, *25*, 161–194.

McNeil, E. B. (Ed.). *The nature of human conflict*. Englewood Cliffs, N.J.: Prentice-Hall, 1965.

Mead, G. H. *Mind, self, and society*. Chicago: University of Chicago Press, 1934.

Mears, P. Structuring communication in a working group. *Journal of Communication*, 1974, *24*, 71–79.

Megargee, E. I. The association of population density, reduced space, and uncomfortable temperatures with misconduct in a prison community. *American Journal of Community Psychology*, 1977, *5*, 289–298.

Mehrebian, A. Inference of attitudes from the positive orientation and distance of a communicator. *Journal of Consulting and Clinical Psychology*, 1968, *32*, 296–308.

Mehrebian, A. *Nonverbal communication*. Chicago, Ill.: Aldine-Atherton, 1972.

Meier, R. E. Correlates of deterrence: Problems of theory and method. *Journal of Criminal Justice*, 1979, *7*, 11–20.

Mendlowitz, S. H. (Ed.). *On the creation of a just world order*. New York: Free Press, 1975.

Merton, R. K. *Social theory and social structure* (rev. ed.). New York: Free Press, 1957.

Merton, R. K. & Kitt, S. Contributions to the theory of reference group behavior. In R. K. Merton & P. F. Lazarsfeld (Eds.), *Continuities in social research: Studies in the scope and method of the American soldier*. Glencoe, Ill.: Free Press, 1950.

Meyers, W. R. The politics of evaluation research: The peace corps. *Journal of Applied Behavioral Science*, 1975, *11*, 261–280.

Milburn, T. W. The nature of threat. *The Journal of Social Issues*, 1977, *33*(1), 126–139.

Miles, M. B. *Learning to work in groups: A program guide for educational leaders*. New York: Bureau of Publications, Teachers College, Columbia University, 1959.

Miles, M. B. The T group and the classroom. In L. P. Bradford, J. R. Gibb & K. D. Benne (Eds.), *T-group theory and the laboratory method*. New York: Wiley, 1969.

Milgram, S. Behavioral study of obedience. *Journal and Abnormal and Social Psychology*, 1963, *67*, 371–378.

Milgram, S. Some conditions of obedience and disobedience to authority. In I. D. Steiner & M. Fishbein (Eds.), *Current studies in social psychology*. New York: Holt, Rinehart & Winston, 1965.

Milgram, S. The small-world problem. *Psychology Today*, 1967, *1*(1), 61–67.

Milgram, S. The experience of living in cities. *Science*, 1970, *167*, 1461–1468.

Milgram, S. Psychological maps of Paris. In H. M. Proshansky, W. H. Ittelson & L. Rivlin (Eds.), *Environmental psychology* (2nd ed.). New York: Holt, Rinehart & Winston, 1976.

Milgram, S. & Toch, H. Collective behavior: Crowds and social movements. In G. Lindzey & E. Aronson (Eds.), *The handbook of social psychology* (2nd ed.) (Vol. 4). Reading, Mass.: Addison-Wesley, 1969.

Mill, C. R. Feedback: The art of giving and receiving help. In C. R. Mill & L. C. Porter (Eds.), *Reading book for human relations training*. Arlington, Virginia: NTL Institute for Applied Behavioral Science, 1976.

Miller, G. A. Psychology as a means of promoting human welfare. *American Psychologist*, 1969, *24*, 1063–1075.

Miller, G. D. & Zoradi, S. D. Roommate conflict resolution. *Journal of College Student Personnel*, 1977, *2*, 228–230.

Miller, G. H. & Miller, B. Information systems for evaluation and feedback in mental health organizations. In L. Rutman (Ed.), *Evaluation research methods: A basic guide*, Beverly Hills, Calif.: Sage, 1977.

Miller, J. G. Toward a general theory for the behavioral sciences. *American Psychologist*, 1955, *10*, 513–531.

Miller, J. G. *Living systems*. New York: McGraw-Hill, 1978.

Miller, N. E. & Bugelski, R. The influence of frustration imposed by the in-group on attitudes expressed toward outgroups. *Journal of Psychology*, 1948, *25*, 437–442.

Mills, J. & Mintz, P. M. Effect of unexplained arousal on affiliation. *Journal of Personality and Social Psychology*, 1972, *24*, 11–13.

Miner, F. C., Jr. A comparative analysis of three diverse group decision making approaches. *Academy of Management Journal*, 1979, *22*, 81–91.

Mirvis, P. H. & Berg, D. N. (Eds.). *Failures in organizational development and change.* New York: Wiley-Interscience, 1977.

Mischel, W. A social learning view of sex differences in behavior. In E. E. Maccoby (Ed.). *The development of sex differences.* Stanford, Calif.: Stanford University Press, 1966.

Mischel, W. *Personality and assessment.* New York: Wiley, 1968.

Mischel, W. Toward a cognitive social learning reconceptualization of personality. *Psychological Review*, 1973, *80*, 252–283.

Mischel, H. Sex bias in the evaluation of professional achievements. *Journal of Educational Psychology*, 1974, *66*, 157–166.

Mischel, W. *Introduction to personality* (2nd ed.). New York: Holt, Rinehart & Winston, 1976.

Mischel, W. *Looking for personality.* Paper presented at the annual meeting of the American Psychological Association, New York, September, 1979.

Misler, A. L. Personal contact in international exchanges. In H. C. Kelman (Ed.), *International behavior: A social-psychological analysis*, New York: Holt, Rinehart & Winston, 1965.

Mitroff, I. & Bonoma, T. V. Psychological assumptions, experimentation and real world problems. *Evaluation Quarterly*, 1978, *2*, 235–260.

Miyamoto, S. F. The forced evacuation of the Japanese minority during World War II. *Journal of Social Issues*, 1973, *29*(2), 11–31.

Moos, R. H. Conceptualizations of human environments. *American Psychologist*, 1973, *28*, 652–665.

Moos, R. H. *The social climate scales: An overview.* Palo Alto: Consulting Psychologists Press, 1974.

Moos, R. H. *The human context: Environmental determinants of behavior.* New York: Wiley-Interscience, 1976.

Moos, R. H. Social environments of university student living groups: Architectural and organizational correlates. *Environment and Behavior*, 1978, *10*, 109–125.

Moos, R. H. & Insel, P. M. (Eds.). *Issues in social ecology.* Palo Alto, Calif.: National Press Books, 1974.

Moreno, J. L. *Who shall survive?* Washington, D.C.: Nervous and Mental Disease Publishing Company, 1934.

Moreno, J. L. *Sociometry, experimental method and the science of society.* Beacon, N.Y.: Beacon House, 1951.

Moreno, J. L. (Ed.). *The sociometry reader.* Glencoe, Ill.: Free Press, 1960.

Morgan, J. N. *Five thousand American families—Patterns of economic progress* (Vols. 1 to 5). Ann Arbor, Mich.: Institute for Social Research, 1974 to 1977.

Morgan, P. M. *Deterrence: A conceptual analysis.* Beverly Hills, Calif.: Sage, 1977.

Morris, W. C. & Sashkin, M. *Organization behavior in action: Skill building experiences.* St. Paul, Minn.: West, 1976.

Morse, N. & Reimer, E. The experimental change of a major organizational variable. *Journal of Abnormal and Social Psychology*, 1956, *52*, 120–129.

Moscovici, S. Society and theory in social psychology. In J. Israel & H. Tajfel (Eds.), *The context of social psychology: A critical assessment*. London: Academic Press, 1972.

Moscovici, S. & Zavalloni, M. The group as a polarizer of attitudes. *Journal of Personality and Social Psychology*, 1969, *12*, 125–135.

Moynihan, D. P. *Maximum feasible misunderstanding*. New York: Free Press, 1969.

Murphy, K. C. & Strong, S. R. Some effects of similarity self-disclosure. *Journal of Counseling Psychology*, 1972, *19*, 121–124.

Murray, H. A. *Explorations in personality*. New York: Oxford University Press, 1938.

Murrell, S. A. *Community psychology and social systems*. New York: Behavioral Publications, 1973.

Mussen, P. H. Early sex-role development. In D. A. Goslin (Ed.), *Handbook of socialization theory and research*. Chicago: Rand-McNally, 1969.

Mussen, P. & Eisenberg-Berg, N. *Roots of caring, sharing and helping: The development of prosocial behavior in children*. San Francisco: W. H. Freeman, 1977.

Myers, D. G. Discussion-induced attitude polarization. *Human Relations*, 1975, *28*, 699–714.

Myers, D. G. & Kaplan, M. F. Group-induced polarization in simulated juries. *Personality and Social Psychology Bulletin*, 1976, *2*, 63–66.

Myers, D. G. & Lamm, H. The polarizing effect of group discussion. *American Scientist*, 1975, *63*, 297–303.

Nadler, D. A. *Feedback and organization development: Using data-based methods*. Reading, Mass.: Addison-Wesley, 1977.

Nadler, D. A. & Pecorella, P. A. Differential effects of multiple interventions in an organization. *Journal of Applied Behavior Science*, 1975, *11*, 348–366.

Nadler, L. & Nadler, Z. *The conference book*. Houston, Texas: Gulf, 1977.

Naess, A. A systematization of Gandhian ethics of conflict resolution. *Journal of Conflict Resolution*, 1958, *2*, 140–155.

Napier, R. W. & Gershenfeld, M. K. *Groups: Theory and experience*. Boston: Houghton Mifflin, 1973.

Naper, R. W. & Gershenfeld, M. K. *Groups: Theory and experience* (2nd ed.). Boston: Houghton Mifflin, 1981.

Naroll, R., Bullough, V. L. & Naroll, F. *Military deterrence in history: A pilot cross-historical survey*. Albany: State University of New York Press, 1974.

Nathan, R. G., Lubin, B., Matarazzo, J. D. & Persely, G. W. Psychologists in Schools of Medicine: 1955, 1964, and 1977. *American Psychologist*, 1979, *34*, 622–627.

National Institute of Justice. *American prisons and jails. Volume III. Conditions and costs of confinement*. Washington, D.C.: Author, 1980.

Neill, A. S. *Summerhill: A radical approach to child rearing*. New York: Hart, 1960.

Nelson, C. E. & Kannenberg, P. H. Social psychology in crisis: A study of the references in the *Handbook of Social Psychology* (2nd ed.). *Personality and Social Psychology Bulletin*, 1976, *2*, 14–21.

Nelson, S. D. Nature/nurture revisited I: A review of the biological basis of conflict. *Journal of Conflict Resolution*, 1974, *18*, 285–335.

Nelson, S. D. Nature/nuture revisited II: Social, political and technological implications of biological approaches to human conflict. *Journal of Conflict Resolution*, 1975, *19*, 734–761.

New York Times Service. *Outdated security concept*. James Reston, June 1979.

Newcomb, T. M. *Personality and social change*. New York: Holt, Rinehart & Winston, 1943.

Newcomb, T. M. The prediction of interpersonal attraction. *American Psychologist,* 1956, *11,* 575–586.

Newcomb, T. M. *The acquaintance process.* New York: Holt, Rinehart & Winston, 1961.

Newcomb, T. M. The acquaintance process: Looking mainly backward. *Journal of Personality and Social Psychology,* 1978, *36,* 1075–1083.

Newcomb, T. M. Reciprocity of interpersonal attraction: A nonconfirmation of a plausible hypothesis. *Social Psychology Quarterly,* 1979, *42,* 299–306.

Newman, D. J. Issues of organization, process and reform. *American Behavioral Scientist,* 1979, *22,* 733–757.

Newman, G. *The punishment response.* Philadelphia, Penn.: Lippincott, 1978.

Newman, J. W. Consumer external search: Amount and determinants. In A. G. Woodside, J. N. Sheth & P. D. Bennett (Eds.), *Consumer and Industrial buying behavior.* New York: Elsevier North-Holland, 1977.

Newman, O. *Defensible space: People and design in the violent city.* New York: Macmillan, 1972.

Nisbett, R. E. & Wilson, T. D. The halo effect: Evidence for the unconscious alteration of judgments. *Journal of Personality and Social Psychology,* 1977, *35,* 250–256.

Noble, J. H. The limits of cost-benefit analysis as a guide to priority-setting in rehabilitation. *Evaluation Quarterly,* 1977, *1,* 347–380.

Nord, W. R. & Durand, D. E. What's wrong with the human resources approach to management? *Organizational Dynamics,* 1978, *6,* 13–25.

Norman, W. T. "To see oursels as ithers see us": Relations among self-perceptions, peer-perceptions and expected peer-perceptions of personality attributes. *Multivariate Behavioral Research,* 1969, *4,* 417–443.

North, R. C., Holsti, O. R., Zaninovich, M. G. & Zinnes, D. A. *Content analysis: A handbook with applications for the study of international crises.* Evanston, Ill.: Northwestern University Press, 1963.

NTL Institute, *1981 programs.* Arlington, Virginia: Author, 1981.

Nunnally, J. C. *Psychometric theory* (2nd ed.). New York: McGraw-Hill, 1978.

O'Connell, B. *Effective leadership in voluntary organizations: How to make the greatest use of citizen service and influence.* New York: Association Press, 1976.

O'Leary, V. E. Some attitudinal barriers to occupational aspirations in women. *Psychological Bulletin,* 1974, *81,* 809–826.

Oliver, L. Women in aprons: The female stereotype in children's readers. *Elementary School Journal,* 1974, *74,* 253–259.

O'Reilly, C. A. & Roberts, K. H. Task group structure, communication, and effectiveness in three organizations. *Journal of Applied Psychology,* 1977, *62,* 674–681.

O'Riordan, T. Attitudes, behavior and environmental policy issues. In I. Altman & J. F. Wohlwill (Eds.), *Human behavior and environment: Advances in theory and research* (Vol. 1). New York: Plenum, 1976.

Orne, M. T. On the social psychology of the psychological experiment: With particular reference to demand characteristics and their implications. *American Psychologist,* 1962, *17,* 776–783.

Osgood, C. E. (Ed.). Psycholinguistics: A survey of theory and research problems. *Journal of Abnormal and Social Psychology,* 1954, *49,* Supplement.

Osgood, C. E. *An alternative to war or surrender.* Urbana: University of Illinois Press, 1962.

Oskamp, S. Attitudes towards U. S. and Russian actions: A double standard. *Psychological Reports,* 1965, *16,* 43–46.

Oskamp, S. *Attitudes and opinions.* Englewood Cliffs, N.J.: Prentice-Hall, 1977.

Oskamp, S. *Psychology's role in the conserving society.* Presidential address to Division

34 at the annual meeting of the American Psychological Association, Los Angeles, August, 1981.

Packard, V. *The hidden persuaders.* New York: McKay, 1957.

Packard, V. *The people shapers.* Boston: Little, Brown and Company, 1977.

Paquin, M. J. The role of psychology in government and the policy formation process. *Professional Psychology,* 1977, *8,* 349–360.

Pargament, K. I., Habib, M. & Antibi, D. Community participation in mental health. *Social Casework,* 1978, *59,* 597–604.

Parsons, T. *Structure and process in modern societies.* New York: Free Press, 1960.

Patchen, M. Models of cooperation and conflict: A critical review. *Journal of Conflict Resolution,* 1970, *14,* 389–407.

Patten, T. H. & Dorey, L. E. Long-range results of a team building OD effort. *Public Personnel Management,* 1977, January-February, 31–50.

Patten, T. H. & Fraser, K. L. Using organizational rewards system as an OD lever: Case study of data-based intervention. *Journal of Applied Behavioral Science,* 1975, *11,* 457–474.

Patterson, C. H. *Relationship counselling and psychotherapy.* New York: Harper & Row, 1974.

Patton, M. Q. *Utilization-focused evaluation.* Beverly Hills, Calif.: Sage, 1978.

Paulus, P., Cox, V., McCain, G. & Chandler, J. Some effects of crowding in a prison evnvironment. *Journal of Applied Social Psychology,* 1975, *5,* 86–91.

Pelligrini, R. J., Hicks, R. A., Myers-Winter, S. & Antal, B. G. Physical attractiveness and self-disclosure in mixed-sex dyads. *Psychological Record,* 1978, *28,* 509–516.

Pelz, E. B. Some factors in "group decision." In E. E. Maccoby, T. M. Newcomb & E. L. Hartley (Eds.), *Readings in social psychology* (3rd ed.). New York: Holt, Rinehart & Winston, 1958.

Peplau, L. A. & Perlman, D. Blueprint for a social psychological theory of loneliness. In M. Cook & G. Wilson (Eds.), *Love and attraction: An international conference.* New York: Pergamon Press, 1979.

Peplau, L., Russell, D. & Heim, M. The experience of loneliness. In I. H. Freize, D. Bar-Tal & J. S. Carroll (Eds.), *New approaches to social problems: Applications for attribution theory.* San Francisco, Calif.: Jossey-Bass, 1979.

Perkins, D. N. T. Evaluating social interventions: A conceptual schema. *Evaluation Quarterly,* 1977, *1,* 639–656.

Perlman, D. & Peplau, L. A. Toward a social psychology of loneliness. In R. Gilmour & S. Duck (Eds.), *Personal relationships in disorder.* Vol. 3 in *Personal relationships.* New York: Academic Press, 1981.

Perlman, R. & Gurin, A. *Community organization and social planning.* New York: Wiley, and the Council for Social Work Education, 1972.

Perloff, R. & Perloff, E. Evaluation of psychological service delivery programs: The state of the art. *Professional Psychology,* 1977, *8,* 379–388.

Perrow, C. *Complex organizations.* Glenview, Ill.: Scott, Foresman, 1972.

Perry, R. W., Gillespie, D. F. & Parker, H. A. *Social movements and the local community.* Beverly Hills, Calif.: Sage, 1976.

Pettigrew, T. F. *Racially separate or together?.* New York: McGraw-Hill, 1971.

Pettigrew, T. F. The ultimate attribution error: Extending Allport's cognitive analysis of prejudice. *Personality and Social Psychology Bulletin,* 1979, *5,* 461–476.

Pfeiffer, J. W. & Jones, J. E. (Eds.). *A handbook of structured experiences for human relations training* (Vols. 1–8). La Jolla, Calif.: University Associates, 1980.

Phares, E. J. & Lamiell, J. T. Personality. *Annual Review of Psychology,* 1977, *28,* 113–140.

Pilisuk, M. & Hayden, T. Is there a military industrial complex which prevents peace?

Consensus and countervailing power in pluralistic systems. *Journal of Social Issues*, 1965, *21*(3), 67–117.

Pilisuk, M. & Skolnick, P. Inducing trust: A test of the Osgood proposal. *Journal of Personality and Social Psychology*, 1968, *8*, 121–133.

Plotnick, R. & Skidmore, F. *Progress against poverty: A review of the 1964–1974 decade*. New York: Academic Press, 1975.

Pondy, L. R. Organizational conflict: Concepts and models. *Administrative Science Quarterly*, 1967, *12*, 296–320.

Porras, J. I. The comparative impact of different OD techniques and intervention intensities. *Journal of Applied Behavioral Science*, 1979, *15*, 156–178.

Porter, E. H. *Therapeutic counseling*. Boston: Houghton Mifflin, 1950.

Posavac, E. J. Applied social psychology at Loyola University of Chicago. Paper presented at the annual meeting of the American Psychological Association, New York, September, 1979.

Posavac, E. J. & Carey, R. G. *Program evaluation: Methods and case studies*. Englewood Cliffs, N.J.: Prentice-Hall, 1980.

Poser, E. G. The effect of therapists' training on group therapeutic outcome. *Journal of Consulting Psychology*, 1966, *30*, 283–289.

President's Commission on Mental Health. *Report to the President*. Washington, D.C.: U.S. Government Printing Office, 1978.

Price, R. H. The taxonomic classification of behaviors and situations and the problem of behavior-environment congruence. *Human Relations*, 1974, *27*, 567–585.

Price, R. H. & Cherniss, C. Training for a new profession: Research as social action. *Professional Psychology*, 1977, *8*. 222–231.

Proshansky, H. M. Comment on environmental and social psychology. *Personality and Social Psychology Bulletin*, 1976, *2*, 359–363.

Prothro, E. T. Ethnocentrism and anti-Negro attitudes in the deep south. *Journal of Abnormal and Social Psychology*, 1952, *47*, 105–108.

Pruitt, D. G. Definition of the situation as a determinant of international action. In H. C. Kelman (Ed.), *International behavior: A social-psychological analysis*, New York: Holt, Rinehart & Winston, 1965.

Pruitt, D. G. Reward structure and cooperation: The decomposed Prisoner's Dilemma game. *Journal of Personality and Social Psychology*, 1967, *7*, 21–27.

Pruitt, D. G. Choice shifts in group discussion: An introductory review. *Journal of Personality and Social Psychology*, 1971, *20*, 339–360.

Pruitt, D. G. & Kimmel, M. J. Twenty years of experimental gaming: Critique, synthesis and suggestions for the future. *Annual Review of Psychology*, 1977, *28*, 363–392.

Pyke, S. W. & Neely, C. A. Training and evaluation of communication skills. *Canadian Counsellor*, 1975, *9*, 20–30.

Quey, R. L. Functions and dynamics of work groups. *American Psychologist*, 1971, *26*, 1077–1082.

Rabbie, J. M. & Bekkers, F. Threatened leadership and intergroup competition. *European Journal of Social Psychology*, 1978, *8*, 9–20.

Rand, N. E. Organization development: A new modality for community mental health. *American Journal of Community Psychology*, 1978, *6*, 157–170.

Rapoport, A. Game theory and human conflict. In E. B. McNeil (Ed.), *The nature of human conflict*, Englewood Cliffs, N.J.: Prentice-Hall, 1965.

Rappaport, J. *Community psychology: Values, research and action*. New York: Holt, Rinehart & Winston, 1977.

Rappoport, L. Symposium: Toward a dialectical social psychology: Introduction. *Personality and Social Psychology Bulletin*, 1977, *3*, 678–680.

Raven, B. H. & Haley, R. W. Social influence in a medical context. In L. Bickman (Ed.),

Applied social psychology annual (Vol. 1). Beverly Hills, Calif.: Sage, 1980.

Reich, M. Who benefits from racism? The distribution among whites of gains and losses from racial inequality. *Journal of Human Resources*, 1978, *13*, 524–544.

Repucci, N. D. & Sarason, S. B. Public policy and human service institutions. *American Journal of Community Psychology*, 1979, 7, 521–542.

Resnick, J. H. & Schwartz, T. Ethical standards as an independent variable in psychological research. *American Psychologist*, 1973, *28*, 134–139.

Reychler, L. The effectiveness of a pacifist strategy in conflict resolution: An experimental study. *Journal of Conflict Resolution*, 1979, *23*, 228–260.

Rich, R. F. *Translating evaluation into policy.* Beverly Hills, Calif.: Sage, 1979.

Richardson, S. A., Dohrenwend, B. S. & Klein, D. *Interviewing: Its forms and functions.* New York: Basic Books, 1965.

Riger, S. & Galligan, P. Women in management: An exploration of competing paradigms. *American Psychologist*, 1980, *35*, 902–910.

Ring, K. Experimental social psychology: Some sober questions about frivolous values. *Journal of Experimental Social Psychology*, 1967, *3*, 113–123.

Robinson, J. A. & Snyder, R. C. Decision-making in international politics. In H. C. Kelman (Ed.), *International behavior: A social-psychological analysis*, New York: Holt, Rinehart & Winston, 1965.

Robinson, J. P. & Shaver, P. R. *Measures of social psychological attitudes.* Ann Arbor, Mich.: Institute for Social Research, 1969.

Rodin, J. Somatopsychics and attribution. *Personality and Social Psychology Bulletin*, 1978, *4*, 531–540.

Rodin, J. & Janis, I. The social power of health-care practitioners as agents of change. *Journal of Social Issues*, 1979, *35*(1), 60–81.

Roethlisberger, F. J. & Dickson, W. J. *Management and the worker.* Cambridge, Mass.: Harvard University Press, 1939.

Rogers, C. R. *Client-centered therapy: Its current practice, implications, and theory.* Boston: Houghton Mifflin, 1951.

Rogers, C. R. A theory of therapy, personality and interpersonal relationships as developed in the client-centered framework. In S. Koch (Ed.), *Psychology: A study of a science. Vol. 3. Formulations of the person and the social context.* New York: McGraw-Hill, 1959.

Rogers, C. R. *On becoming a person: A therapist's view of psychotherapy.* Boston: Houghton Mifflin, 1961.

Rogers, C. R. (Ed.). *The therapeutic relationship and its impact.* Madison: The University of Wisconsin Press, 1967.

Rogers, C. R. *Freedom to learn.* Columbus, Ohio: C. E. Merrill, 1969.

Rogers, C. R. *Carl Rogers on encounter groups.* New York: Harper & Row, 1970.

Rogers, C. R. *Becoming partners: Marriage and its alternatives.* New York: Dell, 1972.

Rogers, C. R. Interpersonal relationships: U.S.A. 2000. In J. S. Jun & W. B. Storm (Eds.), *Tomorrow's organizations: Challenges and strategies.* Glenview, Ill.: Scott, Foresman, 1973.

Rogers, C. R. *Carl Rogers on personal power.* New York: Delacorte Press, 1977.

Rogers, C. R. & Dymond, R. F. (Eds.). *Psychotherapy and personality change.* Chicago: University of Chicago Press, 1954.

Rokeach, M. *The open and closed mind.* New York: Basic Books, 1960.

Rokeach, M., Miller, M. G. & Snyder, J. A. The value gap between police and policed. *Journal of Social Issues*, 1971, *27*(2), 155–177.

Rokeach, M. & Vidmar, N. Testimony concerning possible jury bias in a Black Panther murder trial. *Journal of Applied Social Psychology*, 1973, *3*, 19–29.

Roos, L. L., Nicol, J. P., Johnson, C. F. & Roos, N. P. Using administrative data banks for research and evaluation: A case study. *Evaluation Quarterly*, 1979, *3*, 236–255.

Rorer, L. G. The great response style myth. *Psychological Bulletin*, 1965, *63*, 129–156.

Rose, A. Anti-Semitism's root in city-hatred. *Commentary*, 1948, *6*, 374–378.

Rosen, B. & Jerdee, T. H. Sex stereotyping in the executive suite. *Harvard Business Review*, 1974 March-April, *52*, 45–58.

Rosenbaum, M. Some comments on the use of untrained therapists. *Journal of Consulting Psychology*, 1966, *30*, 292–294.

Rosenberg, M. J. A structural theory of attitude dynamics. *Public Opinion Quarterly*, 1960, *24*, 319–340.

Rosenhan, D. L. On being sane in insane places. *Science*, 1973, *179*, 250–258.

Rosenthal, A. M. *Thirty-eight witnesses*. New York: McGraw-Hill, 1964.

Rosenthal, R. On the social psychology of the psychological experiment: The experimenter's hypothesis as unintended determinant of experimental results. *American Scientist*, 1963, *51*, 268–283.

Rosenthal, R. *Experimenter effects in behavioral research*. New York: Appleton-Century-Crofts, 1966.

Rosenthal, R. & Jacobson, L. *Pygmalian in the classroom*. New York: Holt, Rinehart & Winston, 1968.

Rosenthal, R. & Rosnow, R. L. (Eds.). *Artifact in behavioral research*. New York: Academic Press, 1969.

Rosenthal, R. & Rosnow, R. L. *The volunteer subject*. New York: Wiley, 1975.

Ross, E. A. *Social psychology*. New York: MacMillan, 1908.

Rossell, C. White flight: Pros and cons. *Social Policy*, 1978, *9*, 46–51.

Ross, H. L. & Campbell, D. T. The Connecticut speed crackdown: A study of the effects of legal change. In H. L. Ross (Ed.), *Perspectives on the social order: Readings in sociology* (2nd ed.). New York: McGraw-Hill, 1968.

Rossi, P. H. Issues in the evaluation of human services delivery. *Evaluation Quarterly*, 1978, *2*, 573–599.

Rossi, P. H., Freeman, H. E. & Wright, S. R. *Evaluation: A systematic approach*. Beverly Hills, Calif.: Sage, 1979.

Rossi, P. H. & McLaughlin, D. H. Establishing evaluation objectives. *Evaluation Quarterly*, 1979, *3*, 331–346.

Rossi, P. H. & Wright, S. R. Evaluation research: An assessment of theory, practice and politics. *Evaluation Quarterly*, 1977, *1*, 5–51.

Rossi, P. H., Wright, J. D. & Wright, S. R. The theory and practice of applied social research. *Evaluation Quarterly*, 1978, *2*, 171–191.

Ross, M. G. *Community organization: Theory and practice* (rev. ed.). New York: Harper Brothers, 1967.

Rothman, J. *Planning and organizing for social change: Action principles from social science research*. New York: Columbia University Press, 1974.

Rothman, J. Three models of community organization practice. In National Conference on Social Welfare, *Social work practice* (rev. ed.). New York: Columbia University Press, 1978.

Rothman, J. Introduction. Part One, Overview. In F. M. Cox, J. L. Erlich, J. Rothman & J. E. Tropman (Eds.), *Strategies of community organization* (3rd ed.). Itasca, Ill.: Peacock, 1979.

Rothman, J., Erlich, J. L. & Teresa, J. G. *Promoting innovation and change in organizations and communities*. New York: Wiley, 1976.

Rotter, J. B. Generalized expectancies for internal versus external control of reinforcement. *Psychological Monographs*, 1966, *80* (whole No. 609).

Rotter, J. B. Some problems and misconceptions related to the construct of internal versus external control of reinforcement. *Journal of Consulting and Clinical Psychology,* 1975, *43,* 56–57.

Rowan, J. Encounter group research: No joy? *Journal of Humanistic Psychology,* 1975, *15,* 19–28.

Rubin, Z. Measurement of romantic love. *Journal of Personality and Social Psychology,* 1970, *16,* 265–273.

Rubin, Z. *Liking and loving: An invitation to social psychology.* New York: Holt, Rinehart & Winston, 1973.

Rubin, J. Z. & Brown, B. *The social psychology of bargaining and negotiation.* New York: Academic Press, 1975.

Ruble, T. L. & Thomas, K. W. Support for a two-dimensional model of conflict behavior. *Organizational Behavior and Human Performance,* 1976, *16,* 143–155.

Russ, S. W. Group consultation: Key variables that affect change. *Professional Psychology,* 1978, *9,* 145–152.

Russell, D., Peplau, L. A. & Cutrona, C. E. The revised UCLA Loneliness Scale: Concurrent and discriminant validity evidence. *Journal of Personality and Social Psychology,* 1980, *39,* 472–480.

Rutman, L. (Ed.). *Evaluation research methods: A basic guide.* Beverly Hills, Calif.: Sage, 1977.

Rutman, L. *Planning useful evaluations through evaluability assessment.* Beverly Hills, Calif.: Sage, 1980.

Ryan, W. *Blaming the victim.* New York: Pantheon, 1971.

Rychlak, J. F. The similarity, compatibility, or incompatibility of needs in interpersonal selection. *Journal of Personality and Social Psychology,* 1965, *2,* 334–340.

Sadava, S. W. *Alcoholism and professional practice: Some social psychological perspectives.* Unpublished manuscript, Brock University, 1979.

Saha, S. K. Contingency theories of leadership: A study. *Human Relations,* 1979, *32,* 313–322.

Saks, M. J. Social psychological contributions to a legislative subcommittee on organ and tissue transplants. *American Psychologist,* 1978a, *33,* 680–690.

Saks, M. J. *High-impact applied social psychology.* Paper presented at the annual meeting of the American Psychological Association, Toronto, Ontario, August, 1978b.

Saks, M. J. & Hastie, R. *Social psychology in court.* Florence, Kentucky: Van Nostrand Reinhold, 1978.

Salancik, J. R. Liberation or poverty? An indirect assessment of the impact of future events on society. *Journal of Applied Social Psychology,* 1975, *5,* 173–185.

Salazar, J. M. & Marin, G. National stereotypes as a function of conflict and territorial proximity: A test of the mirror image hypothesis. *Journal of Social Psychology,* 1977, *101,* 13–19.

Saltman, J. Implementing open housing laws through social action. *Journal of Applied Behavioral Science,* 1975, *11,* 39–61.

Sanford, A. C., Hunt, G. T. & Bracey, H. J. *Communication behavior in organizations.* Columbus, Ohio: C. E. Merrill, 1976.

Sanford, N. Whatever happened to action research? *Journal of Social Issues,* 1970, *26* (4), 3–23.

Sanford, N. Is the concept of prevention necessary or useful? In S. E. Golann & C. Eisdorfer (Eds.), *Handbook of community mental health.* Englewood Cliffs, N.J.: Prentice-Hall, 1972.

Sarason, S. B. *The psychological sense of community: Prospects for a community psychology.* San Francisco, Calif.: Jossey-Bass, 1974.

Sarason, S. B. Community psychology, networks and Mr. Everyman. *American Psy-*

chologist, 1976, *31*, 317–328.

Sarason, S. B. The nature of problem solving in social action. *American Psychologist*, 1978a, *33*, 370–380.

Sarason, S. B. An unsuccessful war on poverty?. *American Psychologist*, 1978b, *33*, 831–839.

Sarata, B. P. V. & Jeppesen, J. C. Job design and staff satisfaction in human service settings. *American Journal of Community Psychology*, 1977, *5*, 229–236.

Sarbin, T. R. & Allen, V. L. Increasing participation in a natural group setting: A preliminary report. *Psychological Record*, 1968a, *18*, 1–7.

Sarbin, T. R. & Allen, V. L. Role theory. In G. Lindzey & E. Aronson (Eds.), *The handbook of social psychology* (2nd ed.) (Vol. 1). Reading, Mass.: Addison-Wesley, 1968b.

Sashkin, M., Morris, W. C. & Horst, L. A comparison of social and organizational change models: Information flow and data use processes. *Psychological Review*, 1973, *80*, 510–526.

Sawyer, J. & Guetzkow, H. Bargaining and negotiation in international relations. In H. C. Kelman (Ed.), *International behavior: A social-psychological analysis*, New York: Holt, Rinehart & Winston, 1965.

Saxe, L. & Fine, M. Reorienting social psychology toward application: A methodological analysis. In L. Bickman (Ed.), *Applied social psychology annual* (Vol. 1). Beverly Hills, Calif.: Sage, 1980.

Schachter, S. *The psychology of affiliation*. Stanford, Calif.: Stanford University Press, 1959.

Schein, E. H. *Process consultation: Its role in organization development*. Reading, Mass.: Addison-Wesley, 1969.

Schein, E. H. The role of the consultant: Content expert or process facilitator? *Personnel and Guidance Journal*, 1978, *57*, 339–343.

Schein, E. H. *Organizational psychology* (3rd ed.). Englewood Cliffs, N.J.: Prentice-Hall, 1980.

Schein, E. H. & Bennis, W. G. (Eds.). *Personal and organizational change through group methods: The laboratory approach*. New York: Wiley, 1965.

Schellenberg, J. A. *Masters of social psychology: Freud, Mead, Lewin, and Skinner*. New York: Oxford University Press, 1978.

Schindler-Rainman, E. Community development through laboratory methods. In K. D. Benne, L. P. Bradford, J. R. Gibb & R. O. Lippitt (Eds.), *The laboratory method of changing and learning: Theory and application*. Palo Alto, Calif.: Science and Behavior Books, 1975.

Schindler-Rainman, E. & Lippitt, R. *Team training for community change: Concepts, goals, strategies & skills*. Riverside, Calif.: University of California Extension, 1972.

Schindler-Rainman, E., Lippitt, R. & Cole, J. *Taking your meetings out of the doldrums*. La Jolla, Calif.: University Associates, 1975.

Schlenker, B. R. Social psychology and science. *Journal of Personality and Social Psychology*, 1974, *29*, 1–15.

Schlenker, B. R. Social psychology and science: Another look. *Personality and Social Psychology Bulletin*, 1976, *2*, 418–420.

Schlenker, B. R. & Bonoma, T. V. Fun and games: The validity of games for the study of conflict. *The Journal of Conflict Resolution*, 1978, *22*, 7–38.

Schlenker, B. R. & Miller, R. S. Group cohesiveness as a determinant of egocentric perceptions in cooperative groups. *Human Relations*, 1977, *30*, 1030–1055.

Schmuck, R. A. & Miles, M. B. *Organization development in schools*. La Jolla, Calif.: University Associates, 1971.

Schmuck, R. A., Runkel, P. J., Arends, J. H. & Arends, R. I. *Second handbook of or-*

ganization development in the schools. Palo Alto, Calif.: Mayfield, 1977.

Schmuck, R. A., Runkel, P. J., Saturin, S. L., Martell, R. T. & Derr, C. B. *Handbook of organization development in schools.* New York: National Press, 1972.

Schmuck, R. A. & Schmuck, P. A. *Group processes in the classroom* (2nd ed.). Dubuque, Iowa: Wm. C. Brown, 1975.

Schnare, A. B. *The persistence of racial segregation in housing.* Washington, D.C.: The Urban Institute, 1978.

Schulberg, C. & Perloff, R. Academia and the training of human service delivery program evaluators. *American Psychologist, 1979, 34,* 247–254.

Schultz, B. Characteristics of emergent leaders of continuing problem-solving groups. *Journal of Psychology, 1974, 88,* 167–173.

Schultz, B. Predicting emergent leaders: An exploratory study of salience of communicative functions. *Small Group Behavior, 1978, 9,* 109–114.

Schutz, W. C. *FIRO: A three-dimensional theory of interpersonal behavior.* New York: Rinehart, 1958.

Schutz, W. C. *Joy: Expanding human awareness.* New York: Grove Press, 1967.

Schutz, W. C. *Here comes everybody.* New York: Harper & Row, 1971.

Schutz, W. C. Not encounter and certainly not facts. *Journal of Humanistic Psychology, 1975, 15*(2), 7–18.

Scott, W. A. Psychological and social correlates of international images. In H. C. Kelman (Ed.), *International Behavior: A social-psychological analysis.* New York: Holt, Rinehart & Winston, 1965.

Scott, W. A. Attitude measurement. In G. Lindzey & E. Aronson (Eds.), *The handbook of social psychology* (2nd ed.) (Vol. 2). Reading, Mass.: Addison-Wesley, 1968.

Scriven, M. The methodology of evaluation. In R. W. Tyler, R. M. Gagne & M. Scriven (Eds.), *Perspectives of curriculum evaluation.* Chicago: Rand McNally, 1967.

Scriven, M. Pros and cons about goal-free evaluation. *Evaluation Comment, 1972, 3,* 1–7.

Seashore, C. What is sensitivity training? In C. R. Mill & L. C. Porter (Eds.), *Reading book for human relations training.* Arlington, Va.: NTL Institute for Applied Behavioral Science, 1976.

Seashore, S. E. & Bowers, D. G. The durability of organizational change. *American Psychologist, 1970, 25,* 227–233.

Secord, P. F. Social psychology in search of a paradigm. *Personality and Social Psychology Bulletin, 1977, 3,* 41–50.

Secord, P. F. & Backman, C. W. *Social psychology* (2nd ed.) New York: McGraw-Hill, 1974.

Seeman, M. Alienation and social learning in a reformatory. *American Journal of Sociology, 1963, 69,* 270–284.

Segall, M. H. *Human behavior and public policy: A political psychology.* New York: Pergamon, 1976.

Seligman, M. P. *Helplessness: On depression, development and death.* San Francisco: Freeman, 1975.

Selltiz, C., Wrightsman, L. S. & Cook, S. W. (Eds.). *Research methods in social relations* (3rd ed.). New York: Holt, Rinehart & Winston, 1976.

Severy, L. J. Graduate research training internships in social psychology. *Personality and Social Psychology Bulletin, 1979, 5,* 507–510.

Shaffer, J. B. P. & Galinsky, M. D. *Models of group therapy and sensitivity training.* Englewood Cliffs, N.J.: Prentice-Hall, 1974.

Shambaugh, P. W. The development of the small group. *Human Relations, 1978, 31,* 283–295.

Shannon, C. E. & Weaver, W. *The mathematical theory of communication.* Urbana:

University of Illinois Press, 1949.

Shaver, K. G., Gilbert, M. A. & William, M. C. Social psychology, criminal justice and the principle of discretion: A selective review. *Personality and Social Psychology Bulletin*, 1975, *1*, 471–484.

Shaw, M. E. Some effects of problem complexity upon problem solution efficiency in different communication nets. *Journal of Experimental Psychology*, 1954, *48*, 211–217.

Shaw, M. E. Communications networks. In L. Berkowitz (Ed.), *Advances in experimental social psychology* (Vol. 1). New York: Academic Press, 1964.

Shaw, M. E. *Group dynamics: The psychology of small group behavior* (3rd ed.). New York: McGraw-Hill, 1981.

Shaw, M. E. & Costanzo, P. R. *Theories of social psychology.* New York: McGraw-Hill, 1970.

Shaw, M. E. & Wright, J. M. *Scales for the measurement of attitudes.* New York: McGraw-Hill, 1967.

Shepard, H. A. *An action research program for organization improvement.* Ann Arbor, Mich.: The Foundation for Research on Human Behavior, 1960.

Sherif, M. A study of some social factors in perception. *Archives of Psychology*, 1935, No. 187.

Sherif, M. *The psychology of group norms.* New York: Harper & Row, 1936.

Sherif, M. *In common predicament: Social psychology of intergroup conflict and cooperation.* Boston: Houghton Mifflin, 1966.

Sherif, M. On the relevance of social psychology. *American Psychologist*, 1970, *25*, 144–156.

Sherif, M. Crisis in social psychology: Some remarks toward breaking through the crisis. *Personality and Social Psychology Bulletin*, 1977, *3*, 368–382.

Sherif, M., Harvey, O. J., White, B. J., Hood, W. R. & Sherif, C. W. *Intergroup conflict and cooperation: The Robbers Cave experiment.* Norman: University of Oklahoma Book Exchange, 1961.

Sherif, M. & Sherif, C. W. *Groups in harmony and tension.* New York: Harper, 1953.

Sherwood, J. J. & Glidewell, J. C. Planned renegotiation: A norm-setting OD intervention. In W. W. Burke (Ed.), *Contemporary organization development: Conceptual orientations and interventions.* Arlington, VA: NTL, 1972.

Shippee, G. Experimental social innovation as an alternative to a pseudo-relevant social psychology. *Personality and Social Psychology Bulletin*, 1979, *5*, 491–498.

Shostrum, E. L. An inventory for the measurement of self-actualization. *Educational and Psychological Measurement*, 1964, *24*, 207–218.

Shostrum, E. L. Group therapy: Let the buyer beware. *Psychology Today*, 1969, *2*(12), 37–40.

Shostrom, E. L. *Manual for the personal orientation inventory.* San Diego, Calif.: Educational and Industrial Testing Service, 1974.

Shuey, A. M., King, N. & Griffith, B. Stereotyping of Negroes and Whites: An analysis of magazine pictures. *Public Opinion Quarterly*, 1953, *17*, 281–287.

Shulman, L. A study of practice skills. *Social Work*, 1978, *23*, 274–280.

Siegel, J. M. Mental health volunteers as change agents. *American Journal of Community psychology*, 1973, *1*, 138–158.

Siegel, L. M., Attkisson, C. C. & Carson, L. G. Need identification and program planning in the community context. In C. C. Attkisson, W. A. Hargreaves, M. J. Horowitz & J. E. Sorenson (Eds.), *Evaluation of human service programs.* New York: Academic Press, 1978.

Silverman, I. Crisis in social psychology: The relevance of relevance. *American Psychologist*, 1971, *26*, 583–584.

Silverman, I. Nonreactive methods and the law. *American Psychologist*, 1975, *38*, 764–769.

Silverman, I. Why social psychology fails. *Canadian Psychological Review*, 1977a, *18*, 353–358.

Silverman, I. *The human subject in the psychological laboratory.* New York: Pergamon, 1977b.

Simmel, G. *Conflict and the web of group affiliations.* New York: Free Press, 1955.

Simmons, J. J. A study of leadership styles in task-oriented committees. *Journal of Applied Behavioral Science*, 1972, *8*, 241–247.

Simmons, R. S. & Ashraf, A. Implementing family planning in a ministry of health: Organizational barriers at the state and district levels. *Studies in Family Planning*, 1978, *19*, 22–34.

Simpson, G. E. & Yinger, M. J. *Racial and cultural minorities: An analysis of prejudice and discrimination* (4th ed.). New York: Harper & Row, 1972.

Singer, B. O. Violence, protest, and war in television news: The U.S. and Canada compared. *Public Opinion Quarterly*, 1970–71, *34*, 611–616.

Singer, J. D. Threat-perception and the armament-tension dilemma. *Journal of Conflict Resolution*, 1958, *2*, 90–105.

Singer, J. D. Soviet and American foreign policy attitudes: A content analysis of elite articulations. *Journal of Conflict Resolution*, 1964, *8*, 424–485.

Singer, J. D. Man and world politics: The psycho-cultural interface. *Journal of Social Issues*, 1968, *24*(3), 127–156.

Singer, J. D. Escalation and control in international conflict: A simple feedback model. *General Systems*, 1970, *15*, 163–173.

Singer, J. D. & Ray, P. Decision-making in conflict: From inter-personal to inter-national relations. *Bulletin of the Menninger Clinic*, 1966, *5*(5), 300–312.

Siroka, R. W., Siroka, E. K. & Schloss, G. A. (Eds.). *Sensitivity training and group encounter: An introduction.* New York: Grosset & Dunlap, 1971.

Skinner, B. F. *The behavior of organisms.* New York: Appleton-Century-Crofts, 1938.

Skinner, B. F. *Science and human behavior.* New York: MacMillan, 1953.

Slavin, R. E. & Madden, N. C. *School practices that improve race relations: A reanalysis.* Paper presented at the annual meeting of the American Psychological Association, Toronto, Canada, August, 1978.

Smelser, N. J. *Theory of collective behavior.* New York: Free Press, 1962.

Smith, C. G. A comparative analysis of some conditions and consequences of intra-organizational conflict. *Administrative Sciences Quarterly*, 1966, *10*, 504–529.

Smith, C. G. (Ed.). *Conflict resolution: Contributions of the behavioral sciences.* Notre Dame, Ind.: University of Notre Dame Press, 1971.

Smith, M. B. Is experimental social psychology advancing? *Journal of Experimental Social Psychology*, 1972, *8*, 86–96.

Smith, M. B. Is psychology relevant to new priorities? *American Psychologist*, 1973, *28*, 463–471.

Smith, M. B. *Humanizing social psychology.* San Francisco: Jossey-Bass, 1974.

Smith, M. B. A dialectical social psychology? Comments on a symposium. *Personality and Social Psychology Bulletin*, 1977, *3*, 719–724.

Smith, M. B., Bruner, J. S. & White, R. W. *Opinions and personality.* New York: Wiley, 1956.

Smith, P. B. Controlled studies of the outcome of sensitivity training. *Psychological Bulletin*, 1975, *82*, 597–622.

Smith, P. B. The T-group trainer—Group facilitator or prisoner of circumstance? *Journal of Applied Behavioral Science*, 1980, *16*, 63–78.

Smythe, P. C. & Brook, R. C. Environmental concerns and actions: A social-psychological investigation. *Canadian Journal of Behavioral Science*, 1980, *12*, 175–186.

Snyder, M., Berscheid, E. & Tanke, E. D. Social perception and interpersonal behavior: On the self-fulfilling nature of social stereotypes. *Journal of Personality and Social Psychology*, 1977, *35*, 656–666.

Sobey, F. *The nonprofessional revolution in mental health.* New York: Columbia University Press, 1970.

Sommer, R. *Personal space: The behavioral basis of design.* Englewood Cliffs, N.J.: Prentice-Hall, 1969.

Spaull, H. *The co-operative movement in the world today.* London: Barrie and Rockliff, 1965.

Spergel, I. A. (Ed.). *Community organization: Studies in constraint.* Beverly Hills, Calif.: Sage, 1972.

Spiro, B. E. The future course of corrections. *Social Work*, 1978, *23*, 315–320.

Spivak, G. & Shure, M. B. *Social adjustment of young children: A cognitive approach to solving real-life problems.* San Francisco: Jossey-Bass, 1974.

Srole, L. Measurement and classification in socio-psychiatric epidemiology: Midtown Manhattan study (1954) and Midtown Manhattan restudy (1974). *Journal of Health and Social Behavior*, 1976, *17*, 347–364.

Srole, L., Langner, T. S., Michael, S. T., Opler, M. K. & Rennie, T. A. C. *Mental health in the metropolis: The Midtown Manhattan study* (Vol. 1). New York: McGraw-Hill, 1962.

St. John, N. H. *School desegregation: Outcomes for children.* New York: Wiley, 1975.

Stagner, R. The psychology of human conflict. In E. B. McNeil (Ed.), *The nature of human conflict.* Englewood Cliffs, N.J.: Prentice-Hall, 1965.

Stagner, R. (Ed.). *The dimensions of human conflict.* Detroit: Wayne State University Press, 1967.

Stanford, G. Human relations training in the classroom. *Human Relations Training News*, 1970, *14*, 1–3, 8.

Stanford, G. *Developing effective classroom groups: A practical guide for teachers.* New York: Hart, 1977.

Starbuck, E. D. *The psychology of religion.* London: Scott, 1899.

Stark, R. *Social problems.* New York: Random House, 1975.

Statistics Canada. *Perspectives Canada II: A compendium of social statistics 1977.* Ottawa: Minister of Supply and Services, 1977.

Staub, E. Helping a distressed person: Social, personality, and stimulus determinants. In L. Berkowitz (Ed.), *Advances in experimental social psychology* (Vol. 7), New York: Academic Press, 1974.

Steiner, B. H. On controlling the Soviet-American nuclear arms competition. *Armed Forces and Society*, 1978, *5*, 53–71.

Steiner, I. D. Whatever happened to the group in social psychology? *Journal of Experimental Social Psychology*, 1974, *10*, 94–108.

Steinkalk, E. & Taft, R. The effect of a planned intercultural experience on the attitudes and behavior of participants. *International Journal of Intercultural Relations*, 1979, *3*, 187–197.

Stening, B. W. Problems in cross-cultural contact: A literature review. *International Journal of Intercultural Relations*, 1979, *3*, 269–314.

Stephan, W. G. School desegregation: An evaluation of predictions made in Brown vs. Board of Education. *Psychological Bulletin*, 1978, *85*, 217–238.

Stephan, W. G. & Rosenfield, D. Effects of desegregation on racial attitudes. *Journal of Personality and Social Psychology*, 1978, *36*, 795–804.

Stevens, S. S. Operationism and logical positivism. In M. G. Marx (Ed.), *Theories in contemporary psychology.* New York: MacMillan, 1963.

Stewart, C. J. & Cash, W. B. *Interviewing: Principles and practices* (2nd ed.). Dubuque, Iowa: Wm. C. Brown, 1978.

Stockholm International Peace Research Institute. *World armaments and disarmament.* Stockholm, Sweden: Author, 1978.

Stockton, R. Reviews and bibliographies of experiential small group research: Survey and perspective. *Small Group Behavior,* 1978, *9,* 435–447.

Stogdill, R. M. *Handbook of leadership: A survey of theory and research.* New York: Free Press, 1974.

Stogdill, R. M. & Coons, A. E. *Leader behavior: Its description and measurement.* Columbus: Ohio State University, Bureau of Business Research, 1957.

Stokols, D. Environmental psychology. *Annual Review of Psychology,* 1978, *29,* 253–296.

Stotland, E. (Ed.). Police and community. *Journal of Social Issues,* 1975, *31*(1). Whole Issue.

Stotland, E. White collar criminals. *Journal of Social Issues,* 1977, *33*(4), 179–196.

Stouffer, S. A., Guttman, L., Suchman, E. A., Lazarsfeld, P. F., Star, S. A. & Clausen, J. A. *Measurement and prediction.* Princeton: Princeton University Press, 1950.

Stouffer, S. A., Lumsdaine, A. A., Lumsdaine, M. H., Williams, R. M., Smith, M. B., Janis, I. L., Star, S. A. & Cottrell, L. S. *The American soldier: Combat and its aftermath.* Princeton: Princeton University Press, 1949a.

Stouffer, S. A., Suchman, E. A., DeVinney, L. S., Star, S. A. & Williams, R. M. *The American soldier: Adjustment during army life.* Princeton: Princeton University Press, 1949b.

Street, D. The inmate group in custodial and treatment settings. In D. Gruskey & G. A. Miller (Eds.), *The sociology of organization.* New York: Free Press, 1970.

Streufert, S. & Suedfeld, P. Simulation as a research method: A problem in communication. *Journal of Applied Social Psychology,* 1977, *7,* 281–285.

Strickland, L. H., Aboud, F. E. & Gergen, K. J. *Social psychology in transition.* New York: Plenum Press, 1976.

Suchman, E. *Evaluation research.* New York: Russell Sage Foundation, 1967.

Suedfeld, P. Review of J. A. Varela's *Psychological solutions to social problems. Behavior Therapy,* 1973, *4,* 301.

Suedfeld, P. & Tetlock, P. Integrative complexity of communications in international crises. *Journal of Conflict Resolution,* 1977, *21,* 169–184.

Suedfeld, P., Tetlock, R. E. & Raminez, C. War, peace and integrative complexity: UN speeches on the Middle East problem, 1947–1976. *Journal of Conflict Resolution,* 1977, *21,* 427–441.

Suessmuth, P. *Ideas for training managers and supervisors.* Toronto: University Associates of Canada, 1978.

Suggs, D. & Sales, B. D. The art and science of conducting the voir dire. *Professional Psychology,* 1978, *9,* 367–388.

Sullivan, H. S. *The interpersonal theory of psychiatry.* New York: Norton, 1953.

Sullivan, P. L. & Adelson, J. Ethnocentrism and misanthropy. *Journal of Abnormal and Social Psychology,* 1954, *49,* 246–250.

Suls, J. M. & Miller, R. L. (Eds.). *Social comparison processes: Theoretical and empirical perspectives.* Washington: Hemisphere, 1977.

Summers, D. A. Quality of life. In M. Wertheimer & L. Rappaport (Eds.), *Psychology and the problems of today.* Glenview, Ill.: Scott, Foresman, 1978.

Sumner, W G. *Folkways.* Boston: Ginn & Co., 1906.

Sussna, E. Measuring mental health program benefits: Efficiency or justice? *Profes-*

sional Psychology, 1977, *8*, 435–441.

Swensen, C. H. *Introduction to interpersonal relations.* Glenview, Ill.: Scott, Foresman, 1973.

Swidler, A. *Organization without authority: Dilemmas of social control in free schools.* Cambridge, Mass.: Harvard University Press, 1979.

Sykes, G. M. & Messinger, S. L. The inmate social system. In R. A. Cloward et al. (Eds.), *Theoretical studies in the social organization of the prison.* New York: Social Science Research Council, 1960.

Szasz, T. S. *The manufacture of madness: A comparative study of the inquisition and the mental health movement.* New York: Harper & Row, 1970.

Szasz, T. S. *The myth of mental illness: Foundations of a theory of personal conduct* (rev. ed.). New York: Harper & Row, 1974.

Tajfel, H. Experiments in intergroup discrimination. *Scientific American,* 1970, *223*(5), 96–102.

Tajfel, H. Individuals and groups in social psychology. *British Journal of Social and Clinical Psychology,* 1979, *18*, 183–190.

Tajfel, H. & Turner, J. An integrative theory of intergroup conflict. In W. G. Austin & S. Worchel (Eds.), *The social psychology of intergroup relations.* Monterey, Calif.: Brooks/Cole, 1979.

Tanke, E. D. & Tanke, T. J. Getting off a slippery slope: Social science in the judicial process. *American Psychologist,* 1979, *34*, 1130–1138.

Tannenbaum, A. S. *Control in organizations.* New York: McGraw-Hill, 1968.

Tannenbaum, A. S. *Hierarchy in organizations.* San Francisco: Jossey-Bass, 1974.

Tannenbaum, A. S. *Social psychology of the work organization.* Belmont, Calif.: Brooks/Cole, 1976.

Tannenbaum, R., Weschler, I. R. & Massarik, F. *Leadership and organization.* New York: McGraw-Hill, 1961.

Tapp, J. L. (Ed.). Socialization, the law, and society. *Journal of Social Issues,* 1971, *27*(2), Whole Issue.

Tapp, J. L. Psychology and the law: An overture. *Annual Review of Psychology,* 1976, *27*, 359–404.

Tapp, J. L. Psychological and policy perspectives on the law: Reflections on a decade. *Journal of Social Issues,* 1980, *36*(2), 165–192.

Tapp, J. L. & Levine, F. (Eds.). *Law, justice and the individual in society: Psychological and legal issues.* New York: Holt, Rinehart & Winston, 1977.

Taylor, D. M. & Jaggi, V. Ethnocentrism and causal attribution in a South Indian context. *Journal of Cross-Cultural Psychology,* 1974, *5*, 162–171.

Taylor, D. M. & Simard, L. M. *Socially desirable and undesirable consequences of ethnic stereotyping in intergroup relations.* Paper presented at the annual meeting of the Canadian Psychological Association, Ottawa, June, 1978.

Taylor, F. W. *The principles of scientific management.* New York: Harper, 1923.

Taylor, J. & Bowers, D. *The survey of organizations: A machine-scored standardized questionnaire instrument.* Ann Arbor, Mich.: Institute for Social Research, 1972.

Taylor, S. E. A developing role for social psychology in medicine and medical practice. *Personality and Social Psychology Bulletin,* 1978, *4*, 515–523.

Tedeschi, J. T., Gaes, G. G. & Rivera, A. N. Aggression and the use of coercive power. *Journal of Social Issues,* 1977, *33*(1), 101–125.

Terborg, J. R. Women in management: A research review. *Journal of Applied Psychology,* 1977, *62*, 647–664.

Terhune, K. W. Nationalistic aspiration, loyalty and internationalism. *Journal of Peace Research,* 1965, *2*, 277–287.

Tetlock, P. E. Identifying victims of groupthink from public statements of decision makers. *Journal of Personality and Social Psychology,* 1979, *37,* 1314–1324.

Thayer, L. (Ed.). *Affective education: Strategies for experiential learning.* La Jolla, Calif.: University Associates, 1976.

Thibaut, J. W. & Kelley, H. H. *The social psychology of groups.* New York: Wiley, 1959.

Thibaut, J. W. & Walker, L. *Procedural justice: A psychological analysis.* Hillsdale, N.J.: Erlbaum, 1975.

Thomas, K. W. Conflict and conflict managment. In M. Dunnette (Ed.), *Handbook of Industrial and organizational psychology,* Chicago: Rand-McNally, 1976.

Thomas, K. W. & Kilmann, R. H. *The Thomas-Kilmann Conflict MODE Instrument.* Tuxedo Park, N.Y.: Xicom, 1974.

Thorndike, E. L. *Animal intelligence.* New York: Macmillan, 1911.

Thurstone, L. L. & Chave, E. J. *The measurement of attitude.* Chicago: University of Chicago Press, 1929.

Toch, H. *The social psychology of social movements.* New York: Bobbs-Merrill, 1965.

Toch, H. (Ed.). *Psychology of crime and criminal justice.* New York: Holt, Rinehart & Winston, 1979.

Triandis, H. C. *Attitude and attitude change.* New York: Wiley, 1971.

Triandis, H. C. Social psychology and cultural analysis. *Journal for the Theory of Social Behavior,* 1975, *5,* 81–106.

Triandis, H. C. Cross-cultural social and personality psychology. *Personality and Social Psychology Bulletin,* 1977, *3,* 143–158.

Triandis, H. C. Basic research in the context of applied research on personality and social psychology. *Personality and Social Psychology Bulletin,* 1978, *4,* 383–387.

Triandis, H. C. (Ed.). *Handbook of cross-cultural psychology* (Vols. 1–6). Boston: Allyn and Bacon, 1979.

Triandis, H. C. & Vassiliou, V. Frequency of contact and stereotyping. *Journal of Personality and Social Psychology,* 1967, *7,* 316–328.

Triplett, N. The dynamogenic factors in pacemacing and competition. *American Journal of Psychology,* 1897, *9,* 507–533.

Tripodi, T., Fellin, P. & Epstein, I. *Social program evaluation.* Itasca, Ill.: Peacock, 1971.

Trower, P., Bryant, B., Argyle, M. & Marzillier, J. *Social skills and mental health.* Pittsburgh, Pa.: University of Pittsburgh Press, 1978.

Truax, C. B. & Carkhuff, R. R. *Toward effective counseling and psychotherapy: Training and practice.* Chicago: Aldine, 1967.

Truax, C. B. & Lister, J. L. Effectiveness of counselors and counselor aides. *Journal of Counseling Psychology,* 1970, *17,* 331–334.

Truax, C. B. & Mitchell, K. J. Research on certain therapist interpersonal skills in relation to process and outcome. In A. E. Bergin & S. L. Garfield (Eds.), *Handbook of psychotherapy and behavior change.* New York: Wiley, 1971.

Tuckman, B. W. Developmental sequence in small groups. *Psychological Bulletin,* 1965, *63,* 384–399.

Turner, R. K. The theme of contemporary social movements. *British Journal of Sociology,* 1969, *20,* 390–405.

Turner, C. F. & Krauss, E. Fallible indicators of the subjective state of the nation. *American Psychologist,* 1978, *33,* 456–470.

Tyler, L. E. Design for a hopeful psychology. *American Psychologist,* 1973, *28,* 1021–1029.

Underwood, W. Roles that facilitate and inhibit group development. In R. T. Golembiewski & A. Blumberg (Eds.), *Sensitivity training and the laboratory approach: Readings about concepts and applications* (3rd. ed.). Itasca, Ill.: Peacock, 1977.

Van Dyke, V. Violations of human rights as threats to peace. In A. Lepawsky, E. H. Buehrig & H. D. Lasswell (Eds.), *The search for world order.* New York: Appleton-Century-Crofts, 1971.

Van Maanen, J. Breaking in: Socialization to work. In R. Dubin (Ed.), *Handbook of work, organization, and society,* Chicago: Rand McNally, 1976.

Van Maanen, J. People processing: Strategies of organizational socialization. *Organizational Dynamics,* 1978, Summer, 19–36.

Vance, E. T. Social disability. *American Psychologist,* 1963, *28,* 498–511.

Varela, J. A. *Psychological solutions to social problems: An introduction to social technology.* New York: Academic Press, 1971.

Varela, J. A. Can social psychology be applied? In M. Deutsch & H. A. Hornstein (Eds.), *Applying social psychology: Implications for research, practice, and training.* Hillsdale, N.J.: Erlbaum, 1975.

Varela, J. A. Social technology. *American Psychologist,* 1977, *32,* 914–923.

Vayda, A. M. & Perlmutter, F. D. Primary prevention in community mental health centers: A survey of current activity. *Community Mental Health Journal,* 1977, *13,* 343–351.

Vinokur-Kaplan, D. To have—or not to have—another child: Family planning attitudes, intentions, and behavior. *Journal of Applied Social Psychology,* 1978, *8,* 29–46.

Vitales, M. S. *Motivation and morale in industry.* London: Staples Press, 1954.

Von Bertalanffy, L. General system theory. *General Systems,* 1956, *1,* 1–10.

Vroom, V. Industrial social psychology. In G. Lindzey & E. Aronson (Ed.), *Handbook of social psychology* (2nd ed.) (Vol. 5), Reading, Mass.: Addison-Wesley, 1969.

Wagenfeld, M. O. The primary prevention of mental illness: A sociological perspective. *Journal of Health and Social Behavior,* 1972, *13,* 195–203.

Waldo, G. P. & Chiricos, T. G. Work release and recidivism: An empirical evaluation of a social policy. *Evaluation Quarterly,* 1977, *1,* 87–107.

Wall, T. D. & Lischeron, J. A. *Worker participation: A critique of the literature and some fresh evidence.* London, England: McGraw-Hill, 1977.

Wallace, M. D. Arms race and escalation: Some new evidence. *Journal of Conflict Resolution,* 1979, *23,* 3–16.

Wallach, M. A., Kogan, N. & Bem, D. J. Group influence on individual risk taking. *Journal of Abnormal and Social Psychology,* 1962, *65,* 75–86.

Wallach, M. A., Kogan, N. & Bem, D. J. Diffusion of responsibility and level of risk taking in groups. *Journal of Abnormal and Social Psychology,* 1964, *68,* 263–274.

Wallen, J. L. Developing effective interpersonal communication. In R. W. Pace, B. D. Peterson & T. R. Radcliffe (Eds.), *Communicating interpersonally.* Columbus, Ohio: C. E. Merrill, 1973.

Wallenstein, P. Disarmament and development: A scheme for action. *Bulletin of Peace Proposals,* 1978, *9,* 11–13.

Waller, I. Organizing research to improve criminal justice policy. A perspective from Canada. *Journal of Research in Crime and Delinquency,* 1979 (July), 196–217.

Walster, E., Berscheid, E. & Walster, G. W. New directions in equity research. *Journal of Personality and Social Psychology,* 1973, *25,* 151–176.

Walster, E. & Walster, G. W. *Love.* Reading, Mass.: Addison-Wesley, 1978.

Walster, E., Walster, G. W. & Berscheid, E. *Equity: Theory and research.* Boston: Allyn and Bacon, 1978.

Walton, R. E. *Interpersonal peacemaking: Confrontations and third party consultation.* Reading, Mass.: Addison-Wesley, 1969.

Walton, R. E. A problem-solving workshop on border conflicts in Eastern Africa. *Journal of Applied Behavioral Science,* 1970, *6,* 453–459.

Walton, R. E. How to choose between strategies of conflict and collaboration. In C. R. Mill & L. C. Porter (Eds.), *Reading book for human relations training.* Arlington, Va.: NTL Institute for Applied Behavioral Science, 1976.

Walton, R. E., Dutton, J. M. & Cafferty, T. P. Organizational context and interdepartmental conflict. *Administrative Sciences Quarterly,* 1969, *14,* 522–542.

Walton, R. E. & Schlesinger, L. A. Do supervisors thrive in participative work systems? *Organizational Dynamics,* 1979, Winter, 25–38.

Warwick, D. P. Social scientists ought to stop lying. *Psychology Today,* 1975, *8,* 38–40.

Webb, E. J., Campbell, D. T., Schwartz, R. D. & Sechrest, L. *Unobtrusive measures: Nonreactive research in the social sciences.* Chicago: Rand-McNally, 1966.

Weber, M. *The theory of social and economic organization* (A. M. Henderson & T. Parsons translation). New York: Free Press, 1947.

Wechsler, H., Solomon, L. & Kramer, B. M. (Eds.). *Social psychology and mental health.* New York: Holt, Rinehart & Winston, 1970.

Wagner, D. M. & Vallacher, R. R. *Implicit psychology: An introduction to social cognition.* New York: Oxford University Press, 1977.

Weick, K. E. Systematic observational methods. In G. Lindzey & E. Aronson (Eds.), *The handbook of social psychology* (2nd ed.) (Vol. 2). Reading, Mass.: Addison-Wesley, 1968.

Weick, K. E. Social psychology in an era of social change. *American Psychologist,* 1969, *24,* 990–998.

Weigel, R. & Weigel, J. Environmental concerns: The development of a measure. *Environment and Behavior,* 1978, *10,* 3–15.

Weigel, R. H., Wiser, P. L. & Cook, S. W. The impact of cooperative learning experiences on cross-ethnic relations and attitudes. *Journal of Social Issues,* 1975, *31*(1), 219–244.

Weiner, B. *Achievement motivation and attribution theory.* Morristown, N.J.: General Learning Press, 1974.

Weinstein, A. S. Evaluation through medical records and related information systems. In E. L. Struening & M. Guttentag (Eds.), *Handbook of evaluation research* (Vol. 1). Beverly Hills, Calif.: Sage, 1975.

Weisbord, M. R. & Goodstein, L. D. Towards healthier medical systems: Can we learn from experience? *Journal of Applied Behavioral Science,* 1978, *14,* 263–264.

Weiss, C. H. *Evaluation research: Methods for assessing program effectiveness.* Englewood Cliffs, N.J.: Prentice-Hall, 1972.

Weiss, C. H. (Ed.). *Using social research in public policy making.* Lexington, Mass.: Lexington, 1977.

Weitzman, L. J., Eifler, D., Hokada, E. & Ross, C. Sex-role socialization in picture books for preschool children. *American Journal of Sociology,* 1972, 77, 1125–1149.

Wells, G. L. Applied eyewitness-testimony research: System variables and estimator variables. *Journal of Personality and Social Psychology,* 1978, *36,* 1546–1557.

Wells, G. L., Lindsay, R. C. L. & Tousignant, J. P. Effects of expert psychological advice on human performance in judging the validity of eyewitness testimony. *Law and Human Behavior,* 1980, *4,* 275–285.

Wertlieb, D. A preventive health paradigm for health care psychologists. *Professional Psychology,* 1979, *10,* 548–557.

Wesner, R. W. About the new gamed social simulations. *International Journal of Group Tensions,* 1977, *7,* 109–121.

Wheeler, L. *Interpersonal influence.* Boston: Allyn and Bacon, 1970.

Wheeler, L., Deci, E. L., Reis, H. T. & Zuckerman, M. *Interpersonal influence* (2nd ed.). Boston: Allyn and Bacon, 1978.

White, J. K. The Scanlon Plan: Causes and correlates of success. *Academy of Manage-*

ment Practice, 1979, *22,* 292–312.

White, R. K. Images in the context of international conflict: Soviet perceptions of the U.S. and U.S.S.R. In H. C. Kelman (Ed.), *International behavior: A social-psychological analysis.* New York: Holt, Rinehart & Winston, 1965.

White, R. K. Misperception and the Vietnam War. *Journal of Social Issues,* 1966, *22*(3), 1–164.

White, R. K. *Nobody wanted war: Misperception in Vietnam and other wars.* Garden City: Doubleday, 1970.

White, R. K. Misperception in the Arab-Israeli conflict. *Journal of Social Issues,* 1977, *33*(1), 190–221.

Wholey, J. S. Evaluability assessment. In L. Rutman (Ed.), *Evaluation research methods: A basic guide,* Beverly Hills, Calif.: Sage, 1977.

Wholey, J. S. *Evaluation: Promise and performance.* Washington, D. C.: The Urban Institute, 1979.

Whyte, W. F. Corner boys: A study of clique behavior. *The American Journal of Sociology,* 1941, *46,* 647–664.

Whyte, W. F. & Hamilton, E. L. *Action research for management.* Homewood, Ill.: Irwin-Dorsey Press, 1964.

Wicker, A. W. An application of the multitrait-multimethod logic to the reliability of observational records. *Personality and Social Psychology Bulletin,* 1975, *1,* 575–579.

Wicker, A. W. Ecological psychology: Some recent and prospective developments. *American Psychologist,* 1979, *34,* 755–765.

Wicklund, R. A. & Brehm, J. W. *Perspectives on cognitive dissonance.* Hillsdale, N.J.: Erlbaum, 1976.

Wiggins, J. A psychological taxonomy of trait-descriptive terms: The interpersonal domain. *Journal of Personality and Social Psychology,* 1979, *37,* 395–412.

Wilder, D. A. Reduction of intergroup discrimination through individuation of the outgroup. *Journal of Personality and Social Psychology,* 1978, *36,* 1361–1374.

Wilderman, R. Evaluation research and the sociopolitical structure: A review. *American Journal of Community Psychology,* 1979, *7,* 93–106.

Willerman, B. & Swanson, L. Group prestige in voluntary organizations. *Human Relations,* 1953, *6,* 57–77.

Williams, R. M., Jr. *Strangers next door: Ethnic relations in American communities.* Englewood Cliffs, N.J.: Prentice Hall, 1964.

Wilson, D. W. & Donnerstein, E. Legal and ethical aspects of nonreactive social psychological research: An excursion into the public mind. *American Psychologist,* 1976, *31,* 765–773.

Wilson, D. W. & Donnerstein, E. Guilty or not guilty? A look at the "simulated" jury paradigm. *Journal of Applied Social Psychology,* 1977, *7,* 175–190.

Wilson, J. P., Aronoff, J. & Messé, L. A. Social structure, member motivation and group productivity. *Journal of Personality and Social Psychology,* 1976, *32,* 1094–1098.

Winch, R. F. *Mate selection: A study of complementary needs.* New York: Harper & Row, 1958.

Windle, C. & Volkman, E. Evaluation in the centers program. *Evaluation,* 1973, *1,* 69–70.

Wirtenburg, T. J. & Nakamura, C. Y. Education: Barrier or boon to changing occupation roles of women? *Journal of Social Issues,* 1976, *32*(3), 165–180.

Wishner, J. Reanalysis of "impressions of personality." *Psychological Review,* 1960, *67,* 96–112.

Wispé, L. (Ed.). *The psychology of sympathy and altruism.* Cambridge, Mass.: Harvard University Press, 1977.

Wispé, L. (Ed.). *Altruism, sympathy and helping.* New York: Academic Press, 1978.

Wittig, M. A. & Peterson, M. A. (Eds.). *Sex-related differences in cognitive functioning: Developmental issues.* New York: Academic Press, 1979.

Wittrock, M. C. & Lumsdaine, A. A. Instructional psychology. *Annual Review of Psychology*, 1977, *28*, 417–459.

Woods, P. J. (Ed.). *Career opportunities for psychologists: Expanding and emerging areas.* Washington, D.C.: American Psychological Association, 1976.

Woodside, A. G., Sheth, J. N. & Bennett, P. D. *Consumer and industrial buying behavior.* New York: Elsevier North Holland, 1977.

Worchel, S. Cooperation and the reduction of intergroup conflict: Some determining factors. In W. G. Austin & S. Worchel (Eds.), *The social psychology of intergroup relations.* Monterey, Calif.: Brooks/Cole, 1979.

Wortman, P. M. Evaluation research: A psychological perspective. *American Psychologist*, 1975, *30*, 562–575.

Wright, Q. Escalation of international conflicts. *Journal of Conflict Resolution*, 1965, *9*, 434–449.

Wrightman, L. S. The American trial jury on trial: Empirical evidence and procedural modifications. *Journal of Social Issues*, 1978, *34*(4), 137–164.

Wrightsman, L. S., O'Connor, J. & Baker, N. J. (Eds.). *Cooperation and competition: Readings on mixed-motive games.* Monterey, Calif.: Brooks/Cole, 1972.

Wulf, C. (Ed.). *Handbook on peace education.* Frankfurt, Germany: International Peace Research Association, 1974.

Yancey, W. L. Architecture, interaction, and social control: The case of a large scale housing project. In J. F. Wohlwill & D. H. Carson (Eds.), *Environment and the social sciences: Perspectives and applications.* Washington, D.C.: American Psychological Association, 1972.

Yarmey, A. D. *The psychology of eyewitness testimony.* New York: Free Press, 1979.

Y.M.C.A. *Training volunteer leaders.* New York: National Board of Young Men's Christian Associations, 1974.

Zajonc, R. B. Attitudinal effects of mere exposure. *Journal of Personality and Social Psychology*, 1968, *9*, Monograph Supplement, 1–29.

Zajonc, R. B. Feeling and thinking: Preferences need no inferences. *American Psychologist*, 1980, *35*, 151–177.

Zaltman, G., Florio, D. H. & Sikorski, L. *Dynamic educational change: Models, strategies, tactics and management.* New York: Free Press, 1977.

Zander, A. The study of group behavior during four decades. *Journal of Applied Behavioral Science*, 1979, *15*, 272–282.

Zartman, I. W. Introduction: Special issue on negotiation. *Journal of Conflict Resolution*, 1977, *21*, 563–564.

Zax, M. & Specter, G. A. *An introduction to community psychology.* New York: Wiley, 1974.

Zellman, G. L. The role of structural factors in limiting women's institutional participation. *Journal of Social Issues*, 1976, *32*(3), 33–46.

Zillman, D. *Hostility and aggression.* Hillsdale, N.J.: Erlbaum 1979.

Zimbardo, P. G. The psychology of police confessions. In *Readings in psychology today.* Del Mar, Calif.: CRM, 1969.

Zimbardo, R. G. The human choice: Individuation, reason, and order versus deindividuation, impulse, and chaos. In W. J. Arnold & D. Levine (Eds.), *Nebraska symposium on motivation, 1969.* Lincoln: University of Nebraska Press, 1970.

Zimbardo, P. G. *Shyness: What it is, what to do about it.* Reading, Mass.: Addison-Wesley, 1977.

Zimbardo, P. & Ebbesen, E. B. *Influencing attitudes and changing behavior.* Reading, Mass.: Addison-Wesley, 1969.

Zimbardo, P. G., Haney, C., Banks, W. C. & Jaffe, D. A Pirandellian prison: The mind is a formidable jailer. *New York Times Magazine,* April 8, 1973, 38–60.

Zucker, L. G. The state of the art. Evaluating evaluation research: Standards for judging research quality. *Sociological Practice, 1977, 2,* 107–124.

Zuckerman, M., DeFrank, R. S., Hall, J. A., Larrance, D. T. & Rosenthal, R. Facial and vocal cues of deception and honesty. *Journal of Experimental Social Psychology, 1979, 15,* 378–396.

Subject Index

Author Index